EDITION **2**

Accounting
and Control

Cost
Management

Don R. Hansen
Oklahoma State University

Maryanne M. Mowen
Oklahoma State University

SOUTH-WESTERN College Publishing

An International Thomson Publishing Company

Accounting Team Director: Mary H. Draper
Sponsoring Editor: David L. Shaut
Developmental Editor: Mignon D. Worman
Production Editor: Peggy A. Williams
Production Services: Litten Editing and Production with GTS Graphics
Cover and Interior Designer: Joseph M. Devine
Photo Editor: Jennifer Mayhall
Marketing Manager: Steven W. Hazelwood
Cover Photos:
© 1996 PhotoDisc
© Steven Peters/Tony Stone Images
© Bruce Ayres/Tony Stone Images

ISBN: 0-538-86445-1

1 2 3 4 5 6 7 8 9 VH 3 2 1 0 9 8 7 6

Printed in the United States of America

I(T)P
International Thomson Publishing
South-Western College Publishing is an ITP Company. The ITP trademark is used under license.

Material from the Uniform CPA Examination, Questions and Unofficial Answers, Copyright © 1972, 1975, 1976, 1977, 1980, 1981, 1984, 1985 by the American Institute of Certified Public Accountants, Inc., is reprinted with permission.

Materials from the Certificate in Management Accounting Examinations, Copyright 1981, 1982, 1983, 1984, 1985, 1989, 1990, 1991, 1992, 1993 by the Institute of Management Accountants are reprinted and/or adapted with permission.

Library of Congress Cataloging-in-Publication Data
Hansen, Don R.
    Cost management : accounting and control / Don R. Hansen, Maryanne
  M. Mowen. — 2nd ed.
      p. cm.
    Includes index.
    ISBN 0-538-86445-1
    1. Cost accounting. 2. Activity-based accounting. 3. Managerial
  accounting. I. Mowen, Maryanne M. II. Title.
  HF5686.C8H239 1996
  658. 15'52—dc20
                                                                    96-7314
                                                                      CIP

To Our Parents:
 Lindell and Leola Wise and
 John L. Myers and Marjorie H. Myers

Preface

*C*ost Management, second edition, continues to capture the dynamics of cost management in today's organization. The changes in the business environment over the past twenty years continue to profoundly affect cost accounting and cost management. An increased emphasis on providing value to customers, total quality management, time as a competitive element, advances in information and manufacturing technology, globalization of markets, service industry growth, and morality management are just a few examples of these changes. All these changes are driven by the need to create and sustain a competitive advantage. For many firms, the information required to create and sustain a competitive advantage no longer can be derived from traditional cost management information systems. As a result, firms operating in the contemporary environment demand more sophisticated information to support the requirements of this new environment. Typically, the contemporary cost management system is more detailed and more accurate than a traditional cost management system and, thus, more costly to operate. The emergence of contemporary systems therefore suggests that in many cases, the benefits of the more sophisticated system outweigh its costs. On the other hand, the continued existence of and reliance on traditional systems suggest the opposite for other firms.

The coexistence of traditional and contemporary cost management systems also implies a need to study both. Studying both systems provides both flexibility and depth of understanding. Thus, in creating a text on cost management, we decided that a *systems approach* provided a convenient and logical framework. Using a systems framework allows us to make a clear distinction between the traditional and contemporary approaches and in a way that would make it easy for students to grasp. It also avoids any artificial "integration" of the two systems. Integration is achieved by developing a common terminology—a terminology that allows us to define each system and discuss how they differ. We then discuss the traditional and contemporary approaches to costing and control in separate chapters. We believe this separation minimizes confusion and allows students to appreciate the differences that exist between contemporary and traditional approaches. It also permits an emphasis on either the traditional or contemporary approaches, depending on preferences. However, we did not follow the same pattern for the chapters on decision making. For these chapters, we felt that it would be more useful for students to see how the decision changes as the information set changes. For example, how does a make-or-buy decision change as we move from a unit-based traditional cost management system to the richer, activity-based cost management system?

AUDIENCE

This text is written primarily for students at the undergraduate level. The text presents a thorough treatment of traditional and contemporary approaches to cost management, accounting, and control, and can be used for a one- or two-semester course. The text also has sufficient depth for graduate-level courses.

KEY FEATURES

We feel that the text offers a number of distinctive and appealing features—features that should make it much easier to teach students about the emerging themes in today's business world. One of our objectives was to reduce the time and resources expended by instructors so that students can be exposed to contemporary topics and practices. To give you a clear picture of the text's innovative approach, we have provided a detailed description of its key features.

Systems Framework

The text's organization follows a *systems framework.* Chapters 1 through 3 introduce the basic concepts and tools associated with cost management information systems (p. 31). Chapters 4 through 9 are concerned with product costing systems. This section addresses the first major objective of a cost management information system: providing information for costing out services, products, and other objects of interest to management. The section is subdivided into traditional and contemporary approaches. Providing information for decision making is also a major objective of a cost management information system. Chapters 10 through 15 deal with traditional and contemporary decision-making approaches. The third major objective of a cost management system is that of planning and control. Chapters 16 through 22 deal with these topics. This section is also subdivided into traditional and contemporary topics.

Contemporary Topics

The emerging themes of cost management are covered in depth and are integrated throughout the text. Integration, however, means more than simply adding a few pages within chapters that primarily focus on traditional cost management. It means that we have provided a framework for treating both traditional and contemporary topics and have used a common terminology that links the two approaches. It also means recognizing that the contemporary and traditional approaches are different enough that separate and comprehensive treatments are often called for. The nature and extent of the coverage of contemporary topics is described below. As this summary reveals, there is sufficient coverage of contemporary topics to provide a course that strongly emphasizes contemporary themes.

Historical Perspective Chapter 1 provides a brief history of cost accounting. The historical perspective allows students to see why traditional cost management systems work well in some settings but no longer work for other settings. The forces that are changing cost management practices are described. The changing role of the management accountant is also described, with particular emphasis on why the need to develop a cross-functional expertise is so critical in today's environment. We think that this chapter is innovative in its thrust and offers more substance than is typically found in an introductory chapter. The chapter sets the tone for the entire text.

Providing Value to Customers The provision of value to customers is illustrated by the _value chain_, which is first introduced in Chapter 1 and defined and illustrated more completely in Chapter 2. Chapter 9 provides a detailed discussion of value-chain analysis. Value-chain analysis means that managers must understand and exploit internal and external linkages so that a sustainable competitive advantage can be achieved. Examples are provided that illustrate how value-chain analysis works. The examples show how the value-chain concepts can be operationalized—something which has not been clearly described by other treatments (pp. 360–365). Thus, we feel that the operational examples are a significant feature of the text.

Accounting and Cost Management Systems In Chapter 2, the accounting information system and its different subsystems are defined. Distinctions are made between the financial accounting and cost management information systems (they serve different purposes). The cost management information system is broken down into the cost accounting information system and the operational control system. The differences between traditional and contemporary cost management systems are defined and illustrated (pp. 58–59). The criteria for choosing a contemporary system over a traditional system are also discussed.

In Chapter 2, three methods of cost assignment are delineated: direct tracing, driver tracing, and allocation. Activity, resource, and cost drivers are also defined. Once the general cost assignment model is established, the model is used to help students understand the differences between traditional and contemporary cost management systems. A clear understanding of how the two systems differ is fundamental to the organizational structure that the text follows (p. 59).

Activity-Based Costing and Management Much has been written on the uses and applications of ABC. This text presents a comprehensive approach to activity-based costing and management.

The _activity-based product costing model_ is introduced in Chapter 2 and described in detail in Chapter 8. In Chapter 8, the advantages of ABC over unit-based costing are related (pp. 303–304). Chapter 8 also describes how activities are identified and classified so that homogeneous cost pools can be formed. Activity attributes and activity inventories are described. How costs are assigned to activities using resource drivers is illustrated. We feel that the ABC coverage is richer than most.

To fully understand how an ABC system works, students must also understand the data needed to support the system. Thus, we show (in Chapter 8) how the general ledger system must be unbundled to provide activity information. We also define and illustrate an _ABC relational data base_. This helps the student understand the very practical requirements of an ABC system and is a unique feature of this text (pp. 324–328).

Activity costs change as activity output changes. Variable, fixed, and mixed activity cost behavior is first defined in Chapter 2. Later, in Chapter 3, methods of breaking out fixed and variable activity costs are described. The chapter on cost behavior analysis is more general than usual chapters that treat the subject. Traditional treatment usually focuses on cost as a function of production volume.

We break away from this pattern and focus on cost as a function of changes in activity output with changes in production activity as a special case.

The *activity resource usage model* is used to define activity cost behavior (in terms of when resources are acquired) and is defined and discussed in Chapter 3. This resource usage model plays an important role in numerous contemporary applications. It is used in value-chain analysis (Chapter 9), tactical decision and relevant costing analysis (Chapter 11), and in activity-based responsibility accounting (Chapter 20). The extensive applications of the activity resource usage model represent a unique feature of the text.

Just-in-Time Effects JIT manufacturing and purchasing are defined and their cost management practices are discussed in Chapters 9, 13, and 20. JIT is compared and contrasted with traditional manufacturing practices. The effects on cost trace-ability, inventory management, product costing, responsibility accounting, and so on are carefully delineated (pp. 372–380, 557–565).

Life Cycle Cost Management In Chapter 9, we define and contrast three different life cycle viewpoints: production life cycle, marketing life cycle, and the consumable life cycle. We then show how these concepts can be used for strategic planning and analysis. In later chapters, we show how life cycle concepts are useful for pricing and profitability analysis (Chapters 14 and 15). Finally, life cycle budgeting is discussed in the chapter on contemporary responsibility accounting (Chapter 20). The breadth, depth, and numerous examples illustrating life cycle cost applications allow the student to see as never before the power and scope of this methodology (pp. 878–879).

Responsibility and Process Value Analysis The new responsibility accounting focuses on controlling and managing processes. The mechanism for doing this is called process value analysis. *Process value analysis* is defined and thoroughly discussed in Chapter 20. Numerous examples are given to facilitate understanding. Value-added and nonvalue-added cost reports are described (pp. 864–875).

In Chapter 20, we compare and contrast the traditional responsibility accounting system with the contemporary system. This allows students to understand the essential conceptual differences between the two approaches. It also reveals the limitations of traditional approaches to control in the new manufacturing environment (pp. 860–863).

Costs of Quality: Measurement and Control Often textual treatments simply define quality costs and present cost of quality reports. In Chapter 21, we go beyond this simple presentation and discuss cost of quality performance reporting. We also describe quality activities in terms of their value-added content. Finally, we introduce and describe ISO 9000, an important quality assurance and reporting system that many firms must now follow (pp. 921–926).

Productivity: Measurement and Control The new manufacturing environment demands new approaches to performance measurement. Productivity is one of these approaches, yet it is either not treated or is superficially discussed in most cost and management accounting texts. In Chapter 22, we offer a thorough treatment of the topic, including some new material on how to measure activity and process productivity (pp. 960–968).

Strategic Cost Management A detailed introduction to strategic cost management is provided in Chapter 8. Understanding strategic cost analysis is a vital part of the new manufacturing accounting. We feel that we have provided a more extensive introduction to this topic than anything currently available.

Theory of Constraints In Chapter 13, we provide a thorough introduction to the theory of constraints (TOC). TOC is described using a linear programming framework. This framework not only facilitates the description of TOC but it also provides a setting where students can see the value of linear programming. In fact, our treatment of linear programming is motivated by the need to develop the underlying concepts so that TOC can be presented and discussed.

Service Sector Focus

The significance of the service sector is recognized in this text through the extensive application of cost management principles to services. The text explains that services are not simply less complicated manufacturing settings, but instead have their own characteristics. These characteristics require modification of cost management accounting principles. Sections addressing services appear in a number of chapters, including product costing, pricing, and quality and productivity measurement (pp. 127–131, 233, 312–314, 966).

Professional Ethics

Strong professional ethics are part of the personal foundation every accountant must have. We are convinced that students are interested in ethical dimensions of business and can be taught areas in which ethical conflicts can occur. Chapter 1 introduces the role of ethics; the ethical standards developed by the Institute of Management Accountants are reprinted there. To reinforce coverage of ethics, every chapter includes an ethics case for discussion. In addition, many chapters include sections on ethics. For example, Chapter 14, on pricing and revenue analysis, introduces the student to research on community standards of fairness and ethical dimensions of pricing. Chapter 19, on international issues, explores the dilemmas of differing ethical systems throughout the world.

Behavioral Issues

Ethical behavior is just one aspect of human behavior that is affected by cost management systems. The systems used for planning, control, and decision making can affect the way in which people act. Insights from behavioral decision theory are presented in appropriate sections of the text. For example, a simplified approach to prospect theory is presented in Chapter 15 to motivate a discussion of attitudes toward profit and loss. Chapter 16, on budgeting, includes a section on the behavioral impact of budgets. We believe that an integration of behavioral issues with accounting issues leads to a more complete understanding of the role of the accountant today.

Real World Examples

Our years of experience in teaching cost and management accounting have convinced us that students like and understand real world applications of accounting concepts. These real world examples make the abstract accounting ideas concrete and provide meaning and color. Besides, they're interesting and fun.

Therefore, real world examples are integrated throughout every chapter. The company index at the end of the text will help you locate these examples (pp. 369, 636, 639–640, 681–682, 924).

Outstanding Pedagogy

We think of this text as a tool that can help students learn cost accounting and cost management concepts. Of paramount importance is text readability. We have written a very readable text and added numerous examples, real world applications, and illustrations of important cost accounting and cost management concepts. Specific "student-friendly" features of the pedagogy include the following.

Two photo essays designed to pictorially illustrate cost management concepts are included. The first photo essay, following Chapter 7, depicts cost concepts from firms using a traditional approach. The second photo essay, following Chapter 15, depicts cost concepts from firms using contemporary approaches. The inclusion of both photo essays supports our contention that both the traditional and contemporary approaches have their place in firms today (pp. 296–299, 670–673).

All chapters (except Chapter 1) include at least one review problem and solution. These problems demonstrate the computational aspects of chapter materials and reinforce the students' understanding of chapter concepts before they undertake end-of-chapter materials (pp. 329–332).

All chapters include comprehensive end-of-chapter materials. These are divided into "Questions for Writing and Discussion" and "Exercises and Problems." The questions for writing and discussion emphasize communication skill development. Exercises and problems to support every learning objective are included, and the relevant topics and learning objectives are noted in the text margins. The exercises and problems are graduated in difficulty from easy to challenging. CMA exam problems are included to enable the student to practice relevant problem material. Every chapter includes at least one ethics case.

An innovative supplement to this text is the continuing systems problem, which revolves around the Open Road, Inc., bicycle company. The Open Road, Inc., problems enable students to apply chapter concepts to a database problem using either Excel or Lotus 1-2-3®.[1]

Lotus and Excel Template problems are identified in the end-of-chapter materials with appropriate icons.[2] These problems are designed to help students use computer tools to solve cost accounting problems.

A glossary of key terms is included at the end of the text. Key terms are also listed in the end-of-chapter material and identify the text pages to refer to for fuller explanation.

Whenever possible, graphical exhibits are provided to illustrate concepts. In our experience, some students need to "see" the concept, so we have attempted to portray key concepts to enhance understanding. Of course, many numerical examples are also provided (pp. 244, 249).

At the end of each of the four parts, a comprehensive problem is provided for those instructors who prefer to explore chapter concepts in a more integrated manner (pp. 665–669). Questions at the end of each comprehensive problem enable the instructor to pick and choose the chapters to be emphasized in the case.

1. Lotus and 1-2-3 are registered trademarks of the Lotus Development Corporation. Excel is a registered trademark of the Microsoft Corporation. Any reference to Lotus, 1-2-3, or Excel refers to this footnote.
2. Lotus and Excel template problems carry the following icon.

COMPREHENSIVE ANCILLARIES PACKAGE

Instructor's Manual, Prepared by Jay S. Holmen, University of Wisconsin. The instructor's manual contains a complete set of lecture notes for each chapter, a listing of all exercises and problems with estimated difficulty and time required for solution, problem statements and instructions for Open Road Inc., and a transition guide for other widely used cost management accounting texts. The manual also includes the section "Cooperative Learning Techniques," written by Philip G. Cottell Jr., Miami University, and Barbara J. Millis, University of Maryland. This section details techniques for integrating cooperative learning into the cost accounting course. Strategies, carefully linked to the learning objectives of this text, are offered to help incorporate teaching and learning approaches recommended by the AECC.

Solutions Manual. This supplement contains the solutions for all end-of-chapter material. Solutions have been independently verified to ensure their accuracy and reliability.

Solutions Transparencies. The transparencies include solutions to end-of-chapter exercises, problems, and comprehensive cases.

Test Bank, Prepared by Marvin L. Bouillon, Iowa State University. A test bank of multiple choice questions and examination problems accompanied by solutions is available in both printed and microcomputer (MicroExam 4.0) versions. The Test Bank is designed to save time in preparing and grading periodic and final examinations.

Study Guide, Prepared by Jay S. Holmen. The study guide provides a detailed review of each chapter and allows students to check their understanding of the material through review questions and exercises. Specifically, students are provided with a Chapter Review, Review Questions and Exercises, and a "Can You?" Checklist that helps students test their knowledge of key concepts in the chapter.

Open Road, Inc., Database Problems, Prepared by Marvin L. Bouillon. The continuing database problems expose students to the problems of data selection and acquisition found in the business world. In addition, they give students the opportunity to apply concepts from the chapter. The database is provided in Lotus 1-2-3 and Excel and is free to adopters of this text. Instructions for using the database and solutions to all the problems are included in the instructor's and solutions manuals.

Spreadsheet Applications. Select end-of-chapter exercises and problems may be solved using Lotus 1-2-3 and Excel template diskettes. Exercises and problems are identified with an icon in the margin. The diskettes, which also provide a Lotus 1-2-3 tutorial, are provided free of charge to instructors at educational institutions who adopt this text.

PowerPoint Slides, Prepared by Ted Compton, Ohio University. Selected transparencies of key concepts and exhibits from the text are available in PowerPoint®[3] presentation software. These slides provide a comprehensive outline of each chapter.

---

3. PowerPoint is a registered trademark by Microsoft Corporation. Any reference to PowerPoint refers to this footnote.

Video Supplements. Three videos are available with the text. In a light, but highly demonstrative video entitled GE Lighting Systems, GE employees, in a mock setting, test the effectiveness of the newer manufacturing concepts of JIT, total production maintenance, and total quality control against traditional manufacturing methods and compare the results. A second video, Activity-Based Costing: The Next Generation, presents a joint teleconference from the Public Broadcasting System and Robert Morris College in which three partners from Big Six firms discuss their experiences in implementing ABC systems for clients. The third video is a series of segments featuring interviews with management accountants from various companies and footage of their operations. Included are segments that show the new manufacturing environment and how such concepts as JIT and ABC are applied in real situations.

Cases in Cost Management: A Strategic Emphasis, Written by John K. Shank, Dartmouth College. This set of cases is offered for those instructors who want to augment their cost management accounting course with richer, longer "fun" problems. Each case includes specific numerical questions to challenge and help develop the students' calculation skills with cost management accounting techniques. Each case also includes broader discussion questions to sharpen the controversial aspects of the calculations and to emphasize the cost management and managerial issues behind the numbers. Accompanying the book is an instructor's manual, which contains comprehensive teaching commentaries for each of the cases.

Readings and Issues in Cost Management, Edited by James Reeve, University of Tennessee. This text is designed to expose students to the concepts and information they need to become responsive and flexible managers. Articles in the text cover topics such as TQM, employee empowerment, reengineering, continuous improvement, and short-cycle management.

ACKNOWLEDGMENTS

Many people have helped us to write this text. Survey respondents and focus group participants helped in developing a strong framework. Insightful and often extensive comments from reviewers were instrumental in developing a comprehensive and readable book. We appreciate the efforts of each of them.

Adnan M. Abdeen
California State University—Los Angeles

Al Chen
North Carolina State University

Philip G. Cottell Jr.
Miami University

James M. Emig
Villanova University

Steven A. Fisher
California State University—Long Beach

Robert Giacoletti
Eastern Kentucky University

Donald W. Gribbon
Southern Illinois University at Carbondale

Mahendra Gupta
Washington University

Robert Hansen
Western Kentucky University

Jan R. Heier
Auburn University at Montgomery

Jay S. Holmen
University of Wisconsin—Eau Claire

David E. Keys
Northern Illinois University

Leslie Kren
University of Wisconsin, Milwaukee

Joseph Lambert
University of New Orleans

Douglas Poe
University of Kentucky

Anthony Presutti
Miami University

Roderick B. Posey
University of Southern Mississippi

Jack M. Ruhl
Louisiana State University

John H. Salter
University of Central Florida

Douglas Sharp
Wichita State University

Dan Swenson
University of Idaho

Lakshmi U. Tatikonda
University of Wisconsin—Oshkosh

Les Turner
Northern Kentucky University

Catherine A. Usoff
Bentley College

Philip Vorherr
University of Dayton

Timothy D. West
Iowa State University

Special thanks are due to our verifier. Marvin Bouillon of Iowa State University error-checked the text and solutions manual. His efforts helped us produce a higher quality book.

We are also grateful to Marvin Bouillon for revising the Open Road, Inc., materials. His contribution greatly enhanced the systems structure of the text and has given us new insights into the ways in which the cost management information system supports management decision making, planning, and control.

To the many students at Oklahoma State University who have reacted to the material in *Cost Management: Accounting and Control*, we owe special thanks. Students represent our true constituency. The common sense and good humor of our student reviewers has resulted in a clearer, more readable text.

We also want to express our gratitude to the Institute of Management Accountants for its permission to use adapted problems from past CMA examinations. It has also given us permission to reprint the ethical standards of conduct for management accountants. We are also grateful to the American Institute of Certified Public Accountants for allowing us to adapt selected questions from past CPA examinations.

Finally, we wish to acknowledge the exceptional efforts of our team at South-Western College Publishing. Mary Draper, team leader, consistently provided outstanding support. Her organizational and creative skills made this book a reality. Mignon Worman, developmental editor, kept us on schedule. Peggy Williams, production editor, and Malvine Litten of Litten Editing and Production took manuscript and transformed it into a text suited for the 21st century. Joe Devine, cover and internal designer, and Jennifer Mayhall, photo editor, helped us transform abstract accounting concepts into state-of-the-art graphics, chapter openers, and photo essays. Mark Hubble, Steve Hazelwood, Dave Shaut, and Elizabeth Bowers took us from start to finish; their support and creative efforts are much appreciated.

Don R. Hansen and Maryanne M. Mowen

About the Authors

Dr. Don R. Hansen is Professor of Accounting at Oklahoma State University. He received his Ph.D. from the University of Arizona in 1977. He has an undergraduate degree in mathematics from Brigham Young University. His research interests include productivity measurement, activity-based costing, and mathematical modeling. He has published articles in both accounting and engineering journals including *The Accounting Review, The Journal of Management Accounting Research, Accounting Horizons,* and *IIE Transactions.* He has served on the editorial board of *The Accounting Review* and is currently serving as an associate editor of the *Journal of Accounting Education.* His outside interests include playing basketball, watching sports, and studying Spanish and Portuguese.

Dr. Maryanne M. Mowen is Associate Professor of Accounting at Oklahoma State University. She received her Ph.D. from Arizona State University in 1979. Dr. Mowen brings an interdisciplinary perspective to teaching and writing in cost and management accounting, with degrees in history and economics. In addition, she does scholarly research in behavioral decision theory. Dr. Mowen has consulted for a variety of companies; among them are IBM, Clarke Industries, Phelps Dodge, Energy Education, and the Arizona State Department of Education. Dr. Mowen's interests outside the classroom include reading, playing golf, traveling, and working crossword puzzles.

Brief Contents

Contents

PART 1
FUNDAMENTAL COST MANAGEMENT CONCEPTS

PART 2

COST ACCOUNTING SYSTEMS

Traditional Cost Accounting

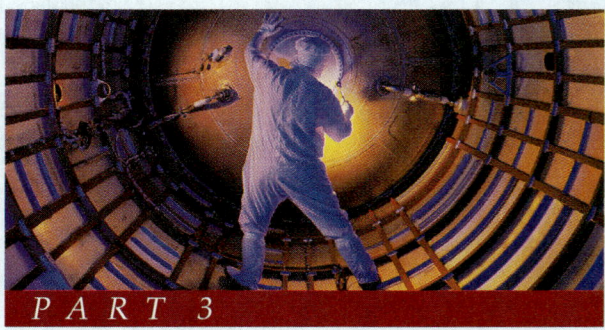

P A R T 3

DECISION MAKING: TRADITIONAL AND CONTEMPORARY APPROACHES

PART 4

COST PLANNING AND CONTROL
SYSTEMS

Traditional Control Systems

Chapter 1

Introduction to Cost Accounting and Cost Management

Anita Roddick, owner of The Body Shop, stands outside one of her stores. The Body Shop is a company which includes both manufacturing and retail service. As a result, its cost management needs are more extensive than those of a retail store or a manufacturing plant alone. Adhering to environmentally sound and socially responsible business practices are very important to The Body Shop. To illustrate its commitment, the company publishes a green book to track environmental performance.

LEARNING OBJECTIVES

After studying this chapter, you should be able to:

1. Explain the similarities and differences among financial, management, and cost accounting.
2. Describe the evolution of accounting.
3. Identify and discuss the emerging themes in cost accounting.
4. Discuss the importance of the accounting system for internal and external reporting.
5. Explain the need for cross-functional expertise in today's cost accountant.
6. Describe the role of cost accountants in an organization.
7. Explain the importance of ethical behavior for managers and accountants.
8. Identify the three forms of certification available to internal accountants.

Traditionally, cost accounting focused on determining the cost of inventory and of goods produced. Costs were classified into functional categories, and the determination of manufacturing costs consumed much effort. While it is still important to know the cost of goods produced, today's accountant must provide even more information. Companies like the Body Shop, pictured at the beginning of this chapter, need accurate cost information to integrate production and retail services. Their production methods and types of products change rapidly. The emphasis on quality and productivity requires new measures of control. The flattening of the hierarchical pyramid and the empowerment of lower levels of management require operationally relevant information to support broad-based decision making from all employees. The company accountant is taking on a new role, one with broader implications and less narrow definition. It is in this way that cost accounting is evolving into cost management.

FINANCIAL, MANAGEMENT, AND COST ACCOUNTING

Objective 1
Explain the similarities and differences among financial, management, and cost accounting.

financial accounting

management accounting

cost accounting

The accounting information system within an organization has two major subsystems: a financial accounting system and a management accounting system. The principal distinction between the two systems is the targeted user. **Financial accounting** is devoted to providing information for external users; these users include investors, government agencies, banks, and so on. Because the information needs of this group of external users are so diverse, the financial accounting system is designed in accordance with clearly defined accounting rules and formats, or Generally Accepted Accounting Principles (GAAP). **Management accounting** produces information for internal users. Specifically, management accounting identifies, collects, measures, classifies, and reports information that is useful to managers in planning, controlling, and decision making. Because the internal information needs of each company differ, and because managers control the internal accountants, no one set of rules and formats is necessary. Each company may develop its own internal accounting system.

Cost accounting is a hybrid of financial and management accounting. It provides information on a company's costs and may be used for both external and internal purposes. When cost accounting is used for financial accounting, it measures the costs of production and sales in accordance with GAAP. When used for internal purposes, cost accounting information provides the basis for planning, controlling, and decision making.

It should be emphasized that the cost accounting information system, the management accounting information system, and the financial accounting information system are part of the total accounting information system. Unfortunately, all too often the content of the cost and management accounting systems is driven by the needs of the financial accounting system. The reports of both management and financial accounting are frequently derived from the same data base, which was originally established to support the reporting requirements of financial accounting. Many organizations need to expand this data base, or to create additional data bases, in order to satisfy more fully the needs of the internal users. For example, a firm's profitability is of interest to investors, but managers need to know the profitability of individual products. The accounting system should be designed to provide both total profits and profits for individual products. The key point here is flexibility—the accounting system should be able to supply different data for different purposes. The cost accountant must be able to develop an accounting system that can bridge the needs of both internal and external users.

cost management

Today we speak of cost management. This change in terminology is not merely cosmetic. **Cost management** requires a deeper understanding of the cost structure of the firm. Managers must be able to determine the long-run and short-run costs of activities and processes as well as the costs of goods and services. The costs of activities and processes do not appear on the financial statements. These are costs used for planning, controlling, and decision making. For example, Chrysler's accountants used activity-based costing to determine the best number of wiring harnesses to use in its minivans. Wiring harnesses yoke together bundles of wires like the ones you can find under the dashboard of your car. The design team wanted to use nine harnesses; assembly wanted one. Other departments had different ideas. When activity-based costing was used to cost the activities associated with the wiring harnesses throughout the production of the minivan, it became clear that the optimal number was two.[1] Two decades ago, accounting would not have become involved at the planning stage. It would have costed the harnesses after they were installed in the minivans.

THE EVOLUTION OF ACCOUNTING

Objective 2
Describe the evolution of accounting.

The history of accounting systems extends back 10,000 years. Early civilizations developed accounting systems as trade developed. More sophisticated accounting systems were demanded as trade grew and transactions became more complex.

Early Accounting Systems

Accounting has its roots far back in human history. Exhibit 1-1 depicts a number of the accounting tools used through the ages. The earliest tools, created 5,000 to 10,000 years ago, include stones with red dots and dried mud packets with cuneiform writing on the outside. Anthropologists believe that the first attempts at writing were for the purpose of keeping track of assets and that the inspiration for cuneiform was the Sumerian need for accounting techniques. The stones were tokens used by prehistoric farmers to count and keep track of goods. Certain shapes, such as cones, spheres, and pyramids, took on specific meanings. For example, a cylinder might have stood for one animal, two cylinders stood for two animals, and so on. Sumerians began to store these tokens in hollow clay balls, labeling the outside of the balls with symbols to specify the owner and the number and kinds of products involved. Soon clay tablets marked with cuneiform writing replaced the clay balls.[2]

By the fifteenth century, trade was extensive, and owners of goods required a more sophisticated system to keep track of numerous economic exchanges. Fra Lucas Pacioli, the Italian monk who is credited with the invention of double-entry bookkeeping, lived and wrote in a time which required the recording of commercial transactions. His *Summa de Arithmetica, Geometria, Proportioni et Proportionalita*, published in Venice in 1494, is the first accounting textbook. The

---

1.   Terence P. Pare, "A New Tool for Managing Costs," *Fortune*, June 14, 1993, pp. 124–129.
2.   Bruce Bower, "The Write Stuff," *Science News*, Vol. 143, March 6, 1993, pp. 152–154.

Exhibit 1-1
Classic Accounting Tools

Though generally associated with the Chinese, the abacus first appeared in Babylon around 1700 B.C. (left)

Around A.D. 1300, the Incas of ancient Peru recorded information on quipus—*knots on various colored strings attached to a main string. In 1527, when the Spanish invaders visited the Inca's court, they slaughtered the* quipu *accountants, mistaking them for priests because the* quipus *resembled the rosaries of Catholic priests. Due in part to the loss of this ancient database, the Inca empire soon collapsed. (right)*

increased accuracy and organization of the double-entry bookkeeping system was an important step forward in the development of accounting systems.

The Industrial Revolution increased the need for the development of a financial accounting system. Manufacturing shifted from home production to power-driven factories. These large manufacturing firms required monetary investment from a number of individuals and banks. This extensive outside investment, and the development of the corporate form of business, meant that owners and managers were different individuals. Consistent financial statements and independent auditing assumed greater importance in communicating financial information to external parties. Cost accounting developed in an environment characterized by increased mechanization and standardization. These characteristics help us to understand the functional basis of manufacturing cost classification.

Accounting in the Twentieth Century

Most of the product-costing and internal accounting procedures used in the twentieth century were developed between 1880 and 1925.[3] Interestingly, many of the early developments (until about 1914) concerned managerial product costing—tracing a firm's profitability to individual products and using this information for strategic decision making. By 1925, however, most of this emphasis had been abandoned in favor of inventory costing—assigning manufacturing costs to products so that the cost of inventories could be reported to external users of a firm's financial statements.

---

3.   The historical information in this section is taken from the following source: H. Thomas Johnson and Robert Kaplan, *Relevance Lost: The Rise and Fall of Management Accounting,* Harvard Business School Press, Boston, 1987.

Exhibit 1-1
Concluded

Shown here is a more recent model of the first commercially successful calculating machine, patented by William Seward Burroughs in 1892. (left)

The electronic calculator, shown right, was originally priced at $100 in 1971. Today, faster, smaller, and more versatile models are available for less than $5.00.

Financial reporting became the driving force for the design of cost accounting systems. Managers and firms were willing to accept aggregated average cost information about individual products. Apparently, more detailed and accurate cost information about individual products was not needed. As long as a company had relatively homogeneous products that consumed resources at about the same rate, the average cost information supplied by a financially driven cost system was good enough. Furthermore, for some firms, even as product diversity increased, the need to have more accurate cost information was offset by the high cost of the processing required to provide the information. For many firms, the cost of a more detailed cost system apparently exceeded its benefits.

Some effort to improve the managerial usefulness of conventional cost systems took place in the 1950s and 1960s. Efforts to improve the system, however, essentially centered on making the financial accounting information more useful to internal users rather than producing an entirely new set of information and procedures apart from the external reporting system.

The product-costing methods and the management accounting practices that have been developed and used over the past several decades were suitable for a particular type of decision environment and for a particular type of manufacturing technology. The decades following World War II were characterized by rapid economic growth. Strong productivity and demand for goods lulled companies into a false sense of security in their accounting systems. Product and inventory costs generated by accountants fulfilled the need for GAAP-constructed financial statements. As long as overall profits were high, companies felt no pressing need for individual product line profit information. Economic recessions of the 1980s and 1990s along with skyrocketing international competition, however, shaved profit margins and gave accurate product costing and enhanced cost control crucial roles in management decision making.

EMERGING THEMES IN COST ACCOUNTING

Objective 3
Identify and discuss
the emerging themes
in cost accounting.

Today's economic environment has required a restructuring of cost accounting and cost management. In recent years, worldwide competitive pressures have changed the nature of our economy and have caused many U.S. manufacturers to change dramatically the way in which they operate their businesses. These changes are creating a new environment for cost accounting for a significant number of organizations. As the environment changes, the traditional accounting system may not yield sufficient useful information. For many firms, the benefits of a more detailed, accurate cost system may now exceed its costs. Thus, advanced cost management accounting systems are emerging. The major trends that are bringing about these changes are

- Customer orientation
- Total quality management
- Time as a competitive element
- Advances in information technology
- Advances in the manufacturing environment
- Service industry growth
- Global competition

A brief discussion of these themes is needed to understand their impact on cost and management accounting.

Customer Orientation

value chain

Firms are concentrating on the delivery of value to the customer. Accountants and managers refer to the **value chain** as the set of activities required to design, develop, produce, market and deliver products and services to customers. As a result, a key question to be asked about any process or activity is whether or not it is important to the customer. The advanced cost management system must track information relating to a wide variety of activities important to customers. For example, customers now count the delivery of the product or service as part of the product. Companies must compete not only in technological and manufacturing terms but also in terms of the speed of delivery and response. Firms like Federal Express have exploited this desire by locating and developing a market the U.S. Post Office could not serve. Today, many customers believe that delivery delayed is delivery denied. The accounting system must measure new indicators of customer satisfaction to track quality and productivity.

It is important to note that companies have internal customers as well. The staff functions of a company exist to serve the line functions. For example, the accounting department creates cost reports for production managers. Accounting departments that are "customer driven" assess the value of the reports to be sure that they report significant information in a timely and readable fashion. Reports that do not measure up are dropped.

Customer focus is at the heart of the cost management system. Thus, the concept of the value chain is integrated throughout the text and applied to both internal and external customers.

Total Quality Management

Continual improvement and elimination of waste are the two foundation principles that govern a state of manufacturing excellence. Manufacturing excellence is the key to survival in today's world-class competitive environment. Producing products that actually perform according to specifications and with little waste

total quality
management

are the twin objectives of world-class firms. A philosophy of **total quality management**, in which managers strive to create an environment that will enable workers to manufacture perfect (zero-defects) products, is replacing the acceptable quality attitudes of the past.

The service industries are also dedicated to quality improvement. Service firms present special problems because quality may differ from employee to employee. As a result, service firms are emphasizing consistency through the development of systems to support employee efforts. For example, USAA, a financial services company specializing in insurance for current and former military officers, invested heavily in information technology in the mid-1980s. Incoming documents (e.g., policy applications, checks, appraisals) are scanned electronically and stored on optical disks. When a customer calls USAA to see if a policy application for a new house has been received, a service representative can check the customer's file on the computer and answer the question immediately. This is contrasted with the old system, which required USAA reps to search a warehouse or other reps' desks for the relevant files—a process that could take up to two weeks.[4] Considered a worldwide leader in rapid customer response, USAA conducts tours of its San Antonio facilities each month for other companies interested in benchmarking the technology for their own businesses. Quality cost measurement and reporting are key features of the contemporary cost management system for both manufacturing and service industries.

Time as a Competitive Element

Time is a crucial element in all phases of the value chain.[5] World-class firms reduce time to market by compressing design, implementation and production cycles. These firms deliver products or services quickly by eliminating nonvalue-added time, time of no value to the customer (e.g., the time a product spends on the loading dock). Interestingly, *decreasing* nonvalue-added time appears to go hand-in-hand with *increasing* quality. The USAA example given in the previous section demonstrates the improvement in service quality that resulted from the insightful management of time. The overall objective, of course, is to increase customer responsiveness.

What about the relationship between time and product life cycles? The rate of technological innovation has increased for many industries, and the life of a particular product can be quite short. Managers must be able to respond quickly and decisively to changing market conditions. Information to allow them to accomplish this must be available. For example, Hewlett-Packard has found that it is better to be 50 percent over budget in new product development than to be six months late. This correlation between cost and time is a part of the cost management system.

Advances in Information Technology

Two significant advances relate to information technology. One is intimately connected with computer-integrated manufacturing. With automated manufacturing, computers are used to monitor and control operations. Because a computer is being used, a considerable amount of useful information can be collected and

---

4.   Myron Magnet, "Who's Winning the Information Revolution," *Fortune*, November 30, 1992, pp. 110–117.

5.   An excellent analysis of time as a competitive element is contained in the following source: A. Faye Borthick and Harold P. Roth, "Accounting for Time: Reengineering Business Processes To Improve Responsiveness," *Journal of Cost Management*, Fall 1993, pp. 4–14.

reported to managers about what is happening on the floor almost as it happens. It is now possible to track products continuously as they move through the factory and to report (on a real-time basis) such things as units produced, material used, scrap, and product cost. The outcome is an operational information system that fully integrates manufacturing with marketing and accounting data.

Automation increases both the quantity and the timeliness of information. For managers to exploit the value of the more complex information system fully, they must have access to the data of the system—they must be able to extract and analyze the data from the information system quickly and efficiently. This, in turn, implies that the tools for analysis must be powerful.

The second major advance supplies the required tools: the availability of personal computers (PCs), spreadsheet software, and graphics packages. The PC serves as a communications link to the company's information system, and spreadsheet and graphics programs supply managers with the analytical capability to use that information. PCs and software aids are available to managers in all types of organizations. PCs and user-friendly software packages allow managers to do much of their own analysis and to decrease their dependence on a centralized information system department. If a PC also acts as a terminal and is connected to an organization's data base, managers can access information more quickly and prepare many of their own reports. The ability to enhance managerial product costing is now available. Cost accountants have the flexibility to respond to the managerial need for more complex product costing. In addition, the vast computing capability now available makes it possible for accountants to generate individualized reports on an as-needed basis. Many firms have found that the increased responsiveness of the contemporary cost management system has allowed them to realize significant cost savings by eliminating the huge volume of internally generated monthly financial reports.

Advances in the Manufacturing Environment

The impact of improved technology on manufacturing is dramatic and is having a correspondingly dramatic effect on cost and management accounting. Product-costing systems, control systems, allocation, inventory management, cost structure, capital budgeting, variable costing, and many other accounting practices are being affected because of the changing environment. The study of these changes and of their effects on cost accounting practices is crucial for prospective managers and accountants.

Activity-Based Costing Peter Drucker, internationally respected management guru, points out the growing importance of activity-based costing in accounting for a firm's customer responsiveness.

Traditional cost accounting in manufacturing does not record the cost of nonproducing, such as the cost of faulty quality, or of a machine being out of order, or of needed parts not being on hand. Yet these unrecorded and uncontrolled costs in some plants run as high as the costs that traditional accounting does record. By contrast, a new method of cost accounting developed in the past 10 years—called "activity-based" accounting—records all costs. And it relates them, as traditional cost accounting cannot, to value added. Within the next 10 years it should be in general use, and then we will have operational control in manufacturing.[6]

---

6.   Peter F. Drucker, "We Need to Measure, Not Count," *The Wall Street Journal*, April 13, 1993, p. A14.

Activity-based costing not only "records all costs" but it does so by taking a fresh perspective on cost. The costs of underlying activities and processes are analyzed and recorded in order to ferret out nonvalue-added activities, and to enhance the efficiency of value-added activities.

Computer-Integrated Manufacturing Automation of the manufacturing environment allows firms to reduce inventory, increase productive capacity, improve quality and service, decrease processing time, and increase output. In other words, automation can produce a competitive advantage for a firm. The implementation of automated manufacturing typically follows JIT and is a response to the increased needs for quality and shorter response times. As more firms automate, competitive pressures will force other firms to do likewise. For many manufacturing firms, automation may be equivalent to survival.[7]

There are three possible levels of automation: the stand-alone piece of equipment, the cell, and the completely integrated factory. However, before firms attempt any level of automation, they should first do all they can to produce a more focused, simplified manufacturing process. Experience has indicated that about 80 percent of the benefits of going to a completely integrated factory can be achieved simply by implementing JIT manufacturing.[8]

If automation is justified, it may mean installation of a *computer-integrated manufacturing (CIM) system*. CIM implies the following capabilities: (1) the products are designed through the use of a *computer-assisted design (CAD) system*; (2) a *computer-assisted engineering (CAE) system* is used to test the design; (3) the product is manufactured using a *computer-assisted manufacturing (CAM) system* (CAMs use computer-controlled machines and robots); and (4) an information system connects the various automated components.

A particular type of CAM is the flexible manufacturing system. Flexible manufacturing systems are capable of producing a family of products from start to finish using robots and other automated equipment under the control of a mainframe computer. This ability to produce a variety of products with the same set of equipment is clearly advantageous.

just-in-time (JIT) manufacturing

Just-In-Time Manufacturing A demand-pull system, **Just-In-Time (JIT) manufacturing** strives to produce a product only when it is needed and only in the quantities demanded by customers. Demand pulls products through the manufacturing process. Each operation produces only what is necessary to satisfy the demand of the succeeding operation. No production takes place until a signal from a succeeding process indicates the need to produce. Parts and materials arrive just in time to be used in production.

JIT manufacturing typically reduces inventories to much lower levels than found in conventional systems, increases the emphasis on quality control, and produces fundamental changes in the way production is organized and carried out. Basically, JIT manufacturing focuses on continual improvement by reducing inventory costs and dealing with other economic problems. Reducing inventories frees up capital that can be used for more productive investments. Increasing quality enhances the competitive ability of the firm. Finally, changing from a traditional manufacturing setup to JIT manufacturing allows the firm to focus more

---

7.   For a detailed discussion of the need to automate, see Howell and Soucy, "The New Manufacturing Environment: Major Trends for Management Accounting," *Management Accounting*, July 1987, pp. 21–27.
8.   Steven M. Hronec, "The Effects of Manufacturing Productivity on Cost Accounting and Management Reporting," *Cost Accounting for the 90s*, pp. 117–125.

on quality and productivity and, at the same time, allows a more accurate assessment of what it costs to produce products.

Growth of the Service Industry

As the traditional smokestack industries have declined in importance, the service sector of the economy has increased in importance. The service sector comprises approximately three-quarters of the United States economy and employment. Many services are exported; these accounted for a $59 billion trade *surplus* in 1992. Experts predict that this sector will continue to expand in size and importance as service productivity grows. Deregulation of many services (e.g., airlines and telecommunications) has increased competition in the service industry. Many service organizations are scrambling to survive. The increased competition has made managers in this industry more conscious of the need to use accounting information for planning, controlling, and decision making. With its demand for better information and productivity, the service sector will increase its demand for management accounting information.

The central issue of the service-sector trend is the need for an increased awareness of cost accounting's usefulness. The objective of increasing awareness can be achieved to a large extent by illustrating the applicability of cost management concepts to service-based settings. Additionally, the unique characteristics of service firms require us to extend and adapt cost management to their particular circumstances.

Global Competition

Vastly improved transportation and communications have led to a global market for many manufacturing and service firms. Several decades ago, firms neither knew nor cared what similar firms in Japan, France, Germany, and Singapore were making. These foreign firms were not competitors, since the markets were separated by geographical distance. Both large and small firms are affected by the opportunities offered by global competition. For example, tiny Vitro Technology, Ltd., a maker of specialty glass tubing, solved a problem of bloated inventory by selling to overseas customers.[9] At the other end of the size scale, Procter & Gamble, Coca Cola, and Mars, Inc., are developing sizable markets in China. Now automobiles made in Japan can be in the United States in two weeks. Investment bankers and management consultants can communicate with foreign offices instantly. Improved transportation and communication have upped the ante for all firms, and they are now held to a higher standard of quality and productivity. Again, accounting information is required to control costs, improve productivity, and assess profitability.

A SYSTEMS APPROACH

Objective 4
Discuss the importance of the accounting system for internal and external reporting.

The accounting system can be viewed as an approach to record transactions that are of interest to us. The system developed ranges from simple to complex, depending on the underlying processes it describes. For example, the financial system of a typical college student is quite simple. It may consist of a checkbook and a wallet. Cash on hand may be counted when necessary to see if a purchase is possible. Similarly, from time to time the checkbook is balanced to see if the bank's view is similar to the checkbook holder's view. There probably is not

9.   Tim Smart and Katheryn Hayes, "Look Who's Showing Small Fry the Ropes," Business Week/Enterprise, E6–8.

much paperwork and no need for a journal and chart of accounts. One individual is responsible for purchases and payments. However, as the entity grows, say as a small business with several employees, the simple system does not work. One person cannot keep track of all the detail; several people may be responsible for payments and purchases as well as sales. Certain standardized techniques are required.

The systems approach for the modern company is a data-based, relationship accounting approach. What does that mean? We can examine that question by looking first at the traditional accounting system. Exhibit 1-2 shows the traditional accounting system as a funnel. We begin by making transactions and accumulating their supporting documents. These documents have a wealth of data. For example, a purchase order may show the type, amount, and cost of the materials to be purchased as well as the date and the individual who requested them. This purchase is entered into the journal, and only the date, account name, and dollar amount are retained. In other words, much potentially useful information is eliminated. The amounts in the journal are aggregated in the general ledger. Still more information is lost at this stage. Finally, the ledger amounts are summarized in financial reports—and still more information is deleted. On the other hand, the data-based, or relationship, accounting system preserves information. The rectangle represents the new accounting system. All information pertinent to a transaction is entered into the accounting system, which takes the form of a data base. Now, various users of information can extract what they need from the data base and create custom accounting reports. Information is not lost. It is still available for other users with different needs. For example, if a salesperson writes up an order, data on the customer name and address, product ordered, quantity, price, and date to be delivered are entered into the data base. The marketing manager may use information on the price and quantity ordered to determine the sales commission. The production manager may need information on product type, quantity, and delivery date to schedule production. Of course, the moving force behind this shift from an external report-based accounting system

Exhibit 1-2
Traditional Accounting System Versus Data-Based Relationship Accounting System

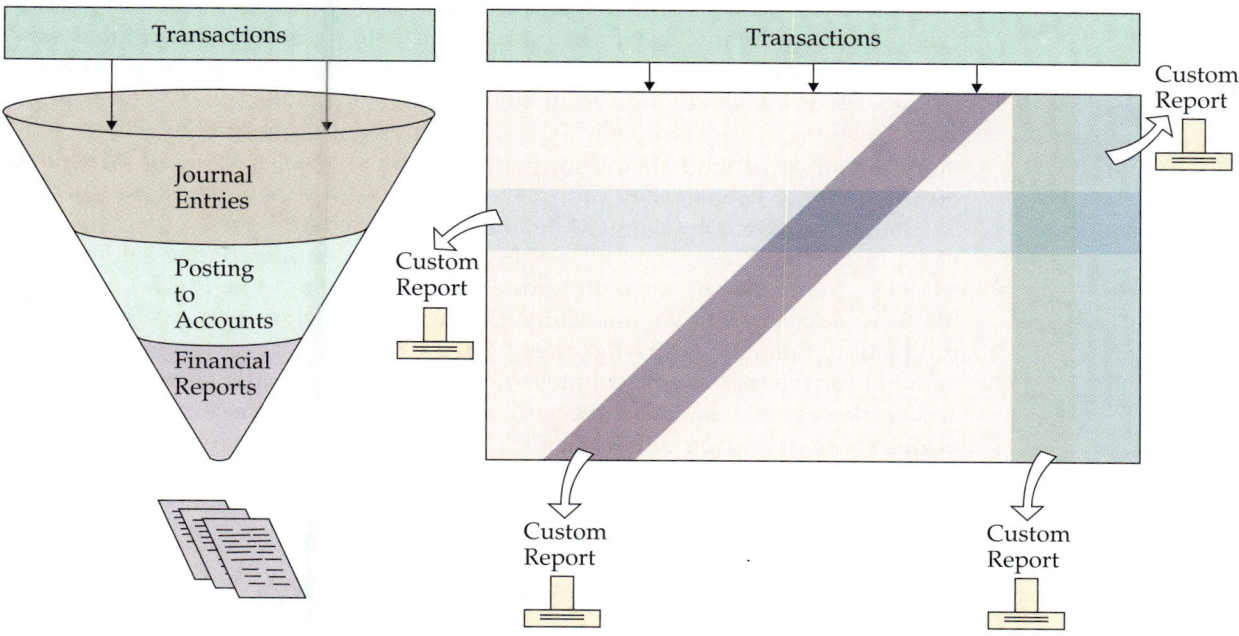

to a relationship-based accounting system is the widespread availability of technology. Powerful personal computers and networked systems make the accounting system available to a wide variety of users within the company. This has forced a shift in perspective. Accountants must consider their impact on internal decision makers when setting up a system and formulating supporting documents. This text takes a systems approach to cost management. We emphasize the use of accounting data—both financial and nonfinancial—by managers for internal and external decision making.

COST MANAGEMENT—A CROSS-FUNCTIONAL PERSPECTIVE

Objective 5
Explain the need for cross-functional expertise in today's cost accountant.

Today's management accountant must understand many functions of the business, from manufacturing to marketing to distribution to customer service. This need is particularly important when the company is involved in international trade. We see this, for example, in the varying definitions of product cost. The company's internal accountants have moved beyond the traditional manufacturing cost approach to a more inclusive approach. This newer approach to product costing may take into account initial design and engineering costs, as well as manufacturing costs, and the costs of distribution, sales and service. An individual well-schooled in the various definitions of cost, who understands the shifting definitions of cost from the short run to the long run, can be invaluable in determining what information is relevant in decision making.

Individuals with the ability to think cross-functionally can shift perspectives, expanding their understanding of the problems and their solutions. For example, where did the Japanese automakers get their idea of JIT production? In a 1956 trip to the United States, Taiichi Ohno (the creator of Toyota's JIT production system) toured the American automakers and also American supermarkets. The impressive array of goods, and constant turnover, led to Ohno's understanding of the way that grocery customers "pulled" product through the stores. That understanding led to Toyota's attempt to "pull" parts through production precisely when and where needed.[10]

Why try to relate cost management to marketing, management, and finance? Can't cost accountants just measure manufacturing costs in a traditional way? No. When we take a systems approach to the company, we see that these disciplines are interrelated; a decision affecting one affects the others. For example, many manufacturing companies engage in frequent trade loading, the practice of encouraging (often by offering huge discounts) wholesalers and retailers to buy more product than they can quickly resell. As a result, inventories become bloated, and the wholesalers and retailers stop purchasing for a time. This looks like a marketing problem, but it is not—at least not entirely. When selling stops, so does production. As a result, trade-loading companies like Procter and Gamble, Bristol-Myers Squibb, and Duracell found themselves with wild swings in production. Sometimes the factories were producing around the clock to meet demand for the (heavily discounted) product; other times the factories were idle and workers were laid off. In effect, the sales were costing the companies millions of dollars of added production cost.[11] A cross-functional systems approach lets us see the forest, not just one or two of the trees.

---

10.   Jeremy Main, "How to Steal the Best Ideas Around," *Fortune*, October 19, 1992, pp. 102–106.
11.   Patricia Sellers, "The Dumbest Marketing Ploy," *Fortune*, October 5, 1992, pp. 88–94.

The Need for Flexibility

There is no one cost management system. Costs important to one firm may be irrelevant to another. Similarly, costs that are important in one context to a firm are unimportant in other contexts. For example, a member of the board of directors for Stillwater's Mission of Hope, a nonprofit shelter for the homeless asked his accountant how to value the building used as the shelter. In other words, what did it cost? The accountant's answer was: "Why do you want to know? If you need to know the value for insurance purposes—to determine how much insurance to buy—then perhaps replacement cost would be the answer. If you are trying to set a price to sell the building (and build another one elsewhere), then market value of the real estate would be the answer. If you need the cost for the balance sheet, then historical cost may work." The point is that we need different costs for different purposes. The intelligent cost accountant does not just churn out an answer but instead probes to find the reason for the question in order to suggest an appropriate answer. A good cost management system facilitates the answer to such questions.

An understanding of the structure of the business environment in which the company operates is an important input in designing a cost management system. A primary distinction is made between manufacturing and service firms. However, there is considerable overlap between the two. Some manufacturing firms emphasize service to customers. Some service firms emphasize the quality of their "product." Retailing is another classification, and its needs would require still another system.

Behavioral Impact of Cost Information

Cost accounting is not neutral; it does not stand in the background, merely reflecting what has happened in an unbiased way. Instead, the cost accounting information system also shapes business. By keeping track of certain information, the owners of the business are saying that these things are important. By ignoring other information, the implication is that they are not important. There is an old joke that an accountant is someone who knows the cost of everything and the value of nothing. Naturally, we don't believe that. In fact, today's accountant is expert at valuing things. This text includes material on methods of costing and achieving quality, of differentiating between value-added and nonvalue-added activities, and of measuring and accounting for productivity. Thus, it is crucial that owners, managers, and accountants be aware of what signals are being sent out by the accounting information system.

THE ROLE OF TODAY'S COST AND MANAGEMENT ACCOUNTANT

Objective 6
Describe the role of cost accountants in an organization.

Today's business press writes about world-class firms. These are firms that are at the cutting edge of customer support. They know their market and their product. They strive continually to improve product design, manufacture, and delivery. These companies can compete with the best of the best in a global environment. Accountants, too, can be termed world-class. Those who merit this designation are intelligent and well-prepared. They not only have the education and training to accumulate and provide financial information but stay up to date in the field and in business. In addition, world-class accountants must be familiar with the customs and financial accounting rules of the countries in which the firm operates. Because of its importance, one chapter is devoted to the discussion of cost management in an international setting.

Line and Staff Positions

The role of cost and management accountants in an organization is one of support. They assist those individuals who are responsible for carrying out an organization's basic objectives. Positions that have direct responsibility for the basic objectives of an organization are referred to as **line positions**. In general, individuals in line positions produce and sell their company's product or service. Positions that are supportive in nature and have only indirect responsibility for an organization's basic objectives are called **staff positions**.

For example, assume that the basic mission of an organization is to produce and sell laser printers. The vice presidents of manufacturing and marketing, the factory manager, and assemblers are all line positions. The vice presidents of finance and human resources, the cost accountant, and the purchasing manager are all staff positions.

The partial organization chart shown in Exhibit 1-3 illustrates the organizational positions for production and finance. Because one of the basic objectives of the organization is to produce, those directly involved in production hold line positions. Although management accountants such as controllers and cost accounting managers may exercise considerable influence in the organization, they have no authority over the managers in the production area. The managers in line positions are the ones who set policy and make the decisions that impact production. However, by supplying and interpreting accounting information, accountants can have significant input into policies and decisions.

The Controller The **controller**, the chief accounting officer, supervises all accounting departments. Because of the critical role that management accounting plays in the operation of an organization, the controller is often viewed as a member of the top-management team and encouraged to participate in planning, controlling, and decision-making activities. As the chief accounting officer, the controller has responsibility for both internal and external accounting requirements. This charge may include direct responsibility for internal auditing, cost accounting, financial accounting (including SEC reports and financial statements), systems accounting (including analysis, design, and internal controls), and taxes. The duties and organization of the controller's office vary from firm to firm. For example, in some companies, the internal audit department may report directly to the financial vice president; similarly, the systems department may report directly to the financial vice president or even to another staff vice president. A possible organization of a controller's office is also shown in Exhibit 1-3.

The Treasurer The **treasurer** is responsible for the finance function. Specifically, the treasurer raises capital and manages cash and investments. The treasurer may also be in charge of credit and collections and insurance. As shown in Exhibit 1-3, the treasurer reports to the financial vice president.

Information for Planning, Controlling, and Decision Making

The cost and management accountant is responsible for generating financial information required by the firm for internal and external reporting. Thus, this individual is responsible for collecting, processing, and reporting information that will help managers in their planning, controlling, and decision-making activities.

Exhibit 1-3
Partial Organization Chart, Manufacturing Company

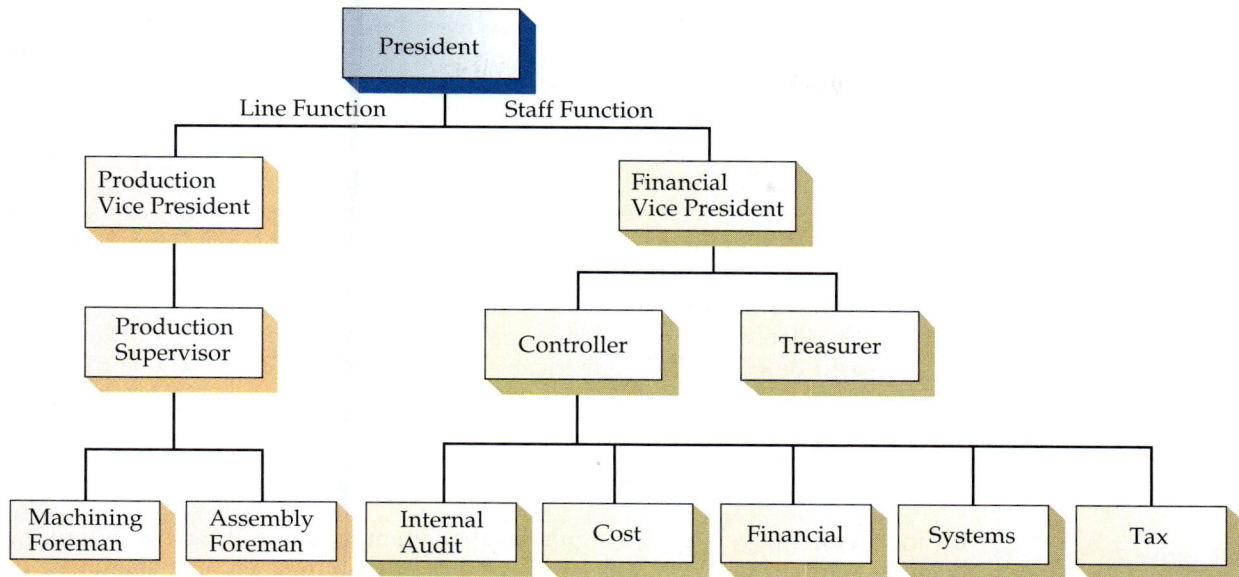

Planning The detailed formulation of action to achieve a particular end is the management activity called **planning**. Planning therefore requires setting objectives and identifying methods to achieve those objectives. For example, a firm may have the objective of increasing its short-term and long-term profitability by improving the overall quality of its products. By improving product quality, the firm should be able to reduce scrap and rework, decrease the number of customer complaints and warranty work, reduce the resources currently assigned to inspection, and so on, thus increasing profitability. But how is this to be accomplished? The plan developed may include working with suppliers to improve the quality of incoming raw materials, establishing quality control circles, and studying defects to ascertain their cause.

planning

Controlling The monitoring of a plan's implementation and taking corrective action as needed is referred to as **controlling**. Control is usually achieved with the use of feedback. **Feedback** is information that can be used to evaluate or correct the steps being taken to implement a plan. Based on the feedback, a manager may decide to let the implementation continue as is, take corrective action of some type to put the actions back in harmony with the original plan, or do some midstream replanning.

controlling
feedback

Feedback is a critical facet of the control function. It is here that accounting once again plays a vital role. Accounting reports that provide feedback by comparing planned data with actual data are called **performance reports**. These performance reports can have a dramatic impact on managerial planning. For example, American Airlines implemented a massive growth plan in the latter half of the 1980s. Though initially profitable, by 1990 losses began to occur. In the first three years of the 1990s, American incurred losses of $1.2 billion. The growth plan has been scrapped; the airline is now retrenching.[12]

performance reports

12. Stephen D. Solomon, "The Bully of the Skies Cries Uncle," *The New York Times Magazine*, September 5, 1993, pp. 12–15, 29, 34, 37–38.

decision making

Decision Making The process of choosing among competing alternatives is **decision making**. This pervasive managerial function is intertwined with planning and control. A manager cannot plan without making decisions. Managers must choose among competing objectives and methods to carry out the chosen objectives. Only one of numerous competing plans can be chosen. Similar comments can be made concerning the control function.

Decisions can be improved if information about the alternatives is gathered and made available to managers. One of the major roles of the accounting information system is to supply information that facilitates decision making. American Airlines exercises cost control in all areas of airline operation. For example, the decision to eliminate olives from passengers' salads saved the company $80,000 per year.[13] While this amount is not large in the context of the company's overall revenues and costs, over time these decisions add up. Of course, the managers must balance the cost savings against the value to passengers of the good or service to be eliminated. American's passengers probably never noticed the change.

ACCOUNTING AND ETHICAL CONDUCT

Objective 7

Explain the importance of ethical behavior for managers and accountants.

Business ethics have received a great deal of attention lately. People wonder how business ethics differ from any other kind of ethics. They ask if it should be or even can be taught in business courses. Traditionally, the economic performance of the firm has been the overriding concern. Yet, managers and management accountants should not become so focused on profits that they develop a belief that the *only* goal of business is maximizing the firm's net worth. The objective of profit maximization should be constrained by the requirement that profits be achieved through legal and ethical means. While this has always been an implicit assumption of the cost and management accounting methodology, the assumption should be made explicit. To help achieve this objective, many of the problems in this book force explicit consideration of ethical issues.

Ethical Behavior

ethical behavior

Ethical behavior involves choosing actions that are "right," "proper," and "just." People often differ in their views of the meaning of these ethical terms, and certainly the ethical climate seems to vary in different countries around the world. However, a common principle underlying all ethical systems can be expressed by the belief that each member of a group bears some responsibility for the well-being of other members. Willingness to sacrifice one's self-interest for the well-being of the group is the heart of ethical action.[14]

This notion of sacrificing one's self-interest for the well-being of others produces some core values—values that describe what is meant by right and wrong in more concrete terms. James W. Brackner, writing for the Ethics Column in *Management Accounting*, made the following observation:[15]

---

13. Ibid., p. 29.
14. For a detailed discussion of ethical behavior, see LaRue Tone Hosmer, *The Ethics of Management*, Irwin, Homewood, Illinois, 1987.
15. James W. Brackner, "Consensus Values Should Be Taught," *Management Accounting*, August 1992, p. 19. For a more complete discussion of the 10 core values, see also M. Josephson, "Teaching Ethical Decision Making and Principled Reasoning," *Ethics Easier Said Than Done*, The Josephson Institute, Los Angeles, Winter 1988, pp. 29–30.

For moral or ethical education to have meaning, there must be agreement on the values that are considered "right." Ten of these values are identified and described by Michael Josephson in, "Teaching Ethical Decision Making and Principled Reasoning." The study of history, philosophy, and religion reveals a strong consensus as to certain universal and timeless values essential to the ethical life.

These ten core values yield a series of principles *that delineate right and wrong in general terms. Therefore, they provide a guide to behavior....*

The ten core values referred to in the quotation are listed below.

1. Honesty
2. Integrity
3. Promise keeping
4. Fidelity
5. Fairness
6. Caring for others
7. Respect for others
8. Responsible citizenship
9. Pursuit of excellence
10. Accountability

Although it may seem contradictory, sacrificing one's self-interest for the collective good may not only be right and bring a sense of individual worth but may also be good business sense. Companies with a strong code of ethics can create strong customer and employee loyalty. While liars and cheats may win on occasion, their victories are often short-term. Companies in business for the long term find that it pays to treat all of their constituents honestly and fairly.

Standards of Ethical Conduct for Management Accountants

Organizations commonly establish standards of conduct for their managers and employees. Professional associations also establish ethical standards. For example, the Institute of Management Accountants has established ethical standards for management accountants. On June 1, 1983, the Management Accounting Practices Committee of the IMA issued a statement outlining standards of ethical conduct for management accountants.[16] In this statement, management accountants are told that "they shall not commit acts contrary to these standards nor shall they condone the commission of such acts by others in their organizations." The standards and the recommended resolution of ethical conflicts are presented in Exhibit 1-4.

To illustrate an application of the code, suppose a manager's bonus is linked to reported profits, with the bonus increasing as profits increase. Thus, the manager has an incentive to find ways to increase profits, including unethical approaches. For example, a manager could increase profits by delaying promotions of deserving employees or by using cheaper parts to produce a product. In either case, if the motive is simply to increase the bonus, the behavior could be labeled as unethical. Neither action is in the best interest of the company or its employees. Yet where should the blame be assigned? After all, the reward system

---

16. *Statement on Management Accounting No. 1C,* "Standards of Ethical Conduct for Management Accountants," Institute of Management Accountants, Montvale, N.J., 1983. The Standards of Ethical Conduct are reprinted with permission from the Institute of Management Accountants.

Exhibit 1-4
Standards of Ethical Conduct for Management Accountants

I. Competence

Management accountants have a responsibility to:
1. Maintain an appropriate level of professional competence by ongoing development of their knowledge and skills.
2. Perform their professional duties in accordance with relevant laws, regulations, and technical standards.
3. Prepare complete and clear reports and recommendations after appropriate analyses of relevant and reliable information.

II. Confidentiality

Management accountants have a responsibility to:
1. Refrain from disclosing confidential information acquired in the course of their work except when authorized, unless legally obligated to do so.
2. Inform subordinates as appropriate regarding the confidentiality of information acquired in the course of their work and monitor their activities to ensure the maintenance of that confidentiality.
3. Refrain from using or appearing to use confidential information acquired in the course of their work for unethical or illegal advantage either personally or through a third party.

III. Integrity

Management accountants have a responsibility to:
1. Avoid actual or apparent conflicts of interest and advise all appropriate parties of any potential conflict.
2. Refrain from engaging in any activity that would prejudice their abilities to carry out their duties ethically.
3. Refuse any gift, favor, or hospitality that would influence their actions.
4. Refrain from either actively or passively subverting the attainment of the organization's legitimate and ethical objectives.
5. Recognize and communicate professional limitations or other constraints that would preclude responsible judgment or successful performance of an activity.
6. Communicate unfavorable as well as favorable information and professional judgments or opinions.
7. Refrain from engaging in or supporting any activity that would discredit the profession.

IV. Objectivity

Management accountants have a responsibility to:
1. Communicate information fairly and objectively.
2. Disclose fully all relevant information that could reasonably be expected to influence an intended user's understanding of the reports, comments, and recommendations presented.

Resolution of Ethical Conflict

In applying the standards of ethical conduct, management accountants may encounter problems in identifying unethical behavior or in resolving ethical conflict. When faced with significant ethical issues, management accountants should follow the established policies of the organization bearing on the resolution of such conflict. If these policies do not resolve the ethical conflict, management accountants should consider the following courses of action:

Exhibit 1-4
Concluded

1. Discuss such problems with the immediate supervisor except when it appears that the superior is involved, in which case the problem should be presented initially to the next higher management level. If satisfactory resolution cannot be achieved when the problem is initially presented, submit the issues to the next higher management level.
2. If the immediate superior is the chief executive officer, or equivalent, the acceptable reviewing authority may be a group such as the audit committee, executive committee, board of directors, board of trustees, or owners. Contact with levels above the immediate superior should be initiated only with the superior's knowledge, assuming the superior is not involved.
3. Clarify relevant concepts by confidential discussion with an objective advisor to obtain an understanding of possible courses of action.
4. If the ethical conflict still exists after exhausting all levels of internal review, the management accountant may have no other recourse on significant matters than to resign from the organization and to submit an informative memorandum to an appropriate representative of the organization.
5. Except where legally prescribed, communication of such problems to authorities or individuals not employed or engaged by the organization is not considered appropriate.

strongly encourages the manager to increase profits. Is the reward system at fault or is it the manager who chooses to increase profits? Or both?

In reality, both probably are at fault. It is important to design the evaluation and reward system so that incentives to pursue undesirable behavior are minimized. Yet designing a perfect reward system is not a realistic expectation. Managers also have an obligation to avoid abusing the system. Standard III-3 of the code makes this clear: Management accountants should "refuse any gift, favor, or hospitality that would influence their actions." Manipulating income to increase a bonus can be interpreted as a violation of this standard. Basically, the prospect of an increased bonus (e.g., a favor) should not influence a manager to engage in unethical actions.

Ethical Conduct

Ethical dilemmas for the internal accountant frequently center on the need to impart "bad news." How does the accountant adhere to the Standards of Conduct for Management Accountants? In a poignant article in *Accounting Horizons*, Roger M. Boisjoly, a former engineer with Morton Thiokol, describes his decision to recommend against the launch of the ill-fated *Challenger*.[17] Mr. Boisjoly states that "the most powerful lesson learned from practicing ethical conduct during [his] 27-year engineering career in the aerospace industry is that we, as individuals, become the resultant sum of each ethical confrontational event as experienced from the beginning of our careers." He describes three choices for those responding to ethical dilemmas: exit, voice, and loyalty.[18] Exit is practiced by those who leave the company or department to avoid an ethical confrontation. Voice is practiced by those who vocally stand up for ethical principles. Loyalty

17.   Roger M. Boisjoly, "Personal Integrity and Accountability," *Accounting Horizons*, March 1993, pp. 59–69. While Mr. Boisjoly is an engineer, his thoughts on personal ethics apply equally well to other professionals.
18.   Ibid., These options are taken from Albert O. Hirschman, *Exit, Voice, & Loyalty: Responses to Decline in Firms, Organizations, and States*, Harvard University Press, *1970.*

is practiced by those who protect their own interests and career at the expense of others.

In clear terms, the code of conduct encourages accountants not only to act ethically themselves but also to *voice* their ethical concerns to the appropriate parties.

CERTIFICATION

Objective 8
Identify the three forms of certification available to internal accountants.

Currently, three different forms of certification are available to internal accountants: a Certificate in Management Accounting (CMA), a Certificate in Public Accounting (CPA), and a Certificate in Internal Auditing (CIA). Each certification offers particular advantages to a cost or management accountant. In each case, an applicant must meet specific educational and experience requirements and pass a qualifying examination to become certified. Thus, all three certifications offer evidence that the holder has achieved a minimum level of professional competence. Furthermore, all three certifications require the holder to engage in continuing professional education in order to maintain certification. Because certification reveals a commitment to professional competency, most organizations encourage their management accountants to be certified.

The CMA

Certified Management Accountant (CMA)

In 1974, the Institute of Management Accountants (IMA) developed the *Certificate in Management Accounting*. This certificate was designed to meet the specific needs of management accountants. A **Certified Management Accountant (CMA)** has passed a rigorous qualifying examination, has met an experience require-ment, and participates in continuing education.

One of the key requirements for obtaining the CMA is passing a qualifying examination. Four areas are emphasized: (1) economics, finance, and manage-ment; (2) financial accounting and reporting; (3) management reporting, analysis, and behavioral issues; and (4) decision analysis and information systems. The parts to the examination reflect the needs of management accounting and under-score the earlier observation that management accounting has more of an inter-disciplinary flavor than other areas of accounting.

One of the main purposes of the CMA was to establish management account-ing as a recognized, professional discipline, separate from the profession of pub-lic accounting. Since its inception, the CMA program has been very successful. Many firms now sponsor and pay for classes that prepare their management accountants for the qualifying examination, as well as provide other financial incentives to encourage acquisition of the CMA.

The CPA

Certified Public Accountants (CPAs)

The Certificate in Public Accounting is the oldest certification in accounting. Unlike the CMA, the purpose of the Certificate in Public Accounting is to provide minimal professional qualification for external auditors. The responsibility of external auditors is to provide assurance concerning the reliability of a firm's financial statements. Only **Certified Public Accountants (CPAs)** are permitted (by law) to serve as external auditors. CPAs must pass a national examination and be licensed by the state in which they practice. Although the Certificate in Public Accounting does not have a management accounting orientation, it is held by many management accountants.

The CIA

Another certification available to internal accountants is the Certificate in Internal Auditing (CIA). The forces that led to the creation of this certification in 1974 are similar to those that resulted in the CMA. An important part of the company's control environment, internal auditors evaluate and appraise various activities within the company. While internal auditors are independent of the departments being audited, they do report to the top management of the company. Since internal auditing differs from both external auditing and management accounting, many internal auditors felt a need for a specialized certification. The **Certified Internal Auditor (CIA)** has passed a comprehensive examination designed to ensure technical competence and has two years' experience.

Certified Internal Auditor (CIA)

SUMMARY

Managers use accounting information to identify problems, solve problems, and evaluate performance. Essentially, accounting information helps managers carry out their roles of planning, controlling, and decision making. Planning is the detailed formulation of action to achieve a particular end. Controlling is the monitoring of a plan's implementation. Decision making is choosing among competing alternatives.

Management accounting differs from financial accounting primarily in its targeted users. Management accounting information is intended for internal users, whereas financial accounting information is directed towards external users. Management accounting is not bound by the externally imposed rules of financial reporting. It provides more detail than financial accounting, and it tends to be broader and multidisciplinary.

Management accountants are responsible for identifying, collecting, measuring, analyzing, preparing, interpreting, and communicating information used by management to achieve the basic objectives of the organization. Management accountants need to be sensitive to the information needs of managers. Management accountants serve as staff members of the organization and are responsible for providing information; they are usually intimately involved in the management process as valued members of the management team.

Changes in the manufacturing environment brought about by customer focus, total quality management, time as a competitive factor, the advanced manufacturing environment, and global competition are having a significant effect on the management accounting environment. Many traditional management accounting practices will be altered because of the revolution taking place among many manufacturing firms. Deregulation and growth in the service sector of our economy are also increasing the demand for management accounting practices.

Management accounting aids managers in their efforts to improve the economic performance of the firm. Unfortunately, some managers have overemphasized the economic dimension and have engaged in unethical and illegal actions. Many of these actions have relied on the management accounting system to bring about and even support that unethical behavior. To emphasize the importance of the ever-present constraint of ethical behavior on profit-maximizing behavior, this text presents ethical issues in many of the problems appearing at the end of each chapter.

There are three certifications available: the CMA, the CPA, and the CIA. The CMA is a certification designed especially for management accountants. The prestige of the CMA has increased significantly over the years and is now well-regarded by the industrial world. The CPA is primarily intended for those practicing public accounting; however, this certification is highly regarded and is held by many management accountants. The CIA serves internal auditors and is also well-regarded.

KEY TERMS

Certified Internal Auditor
(CIA) *21*
Certified Public
Accountant (CPA) *20*
Certified Management
Accountant (CMA) *20*
Controller *14*

Controlling *15*
Cost accounting *2*
Cost management *3*
Decision making *16*
Ethical behavior *16*
Feedback *15*
Financial accounting *2*

Just-in-time (JIT)
manufacturing *9*
Line position *14*
Management accounting
2
Performance reports *15*

Planning *15*
Staff position *14*
Total quality management
7
Treasurer *14*
Value chain *6*

QUESTIONS FOR WRITING AND DISCUSSION

1. What is cost management, and how does it differ from cost accounting?
2. Describe the connection among planning, controlling, and feedback.
3. What role do performance reports play with respect to the control function?
4. How do management accounting and financial accounting differ?
5. What is the difference between a staff position and a line position?
6. The controller should be a member of the top management staff. Do you agree or disagree? Explain.
7. Explain the role of financial reporting in the development of management accounting. Is external reporting the only reason firms choose to use inventory costs for product costing? Explain.
8. Identify and discuss the emerging themes that are affecting the way cost accounting is practiced.
9. How has expanded global competition affected businesses' need for accounting information?
10. PCs significantly increase a manager's capabilities to process and use accounting information. Do you agree? Explain.

11. What is a flexible manufacturing system?
12. What is the role of the controller in an organization? Describe some of the activities over which he or she has control.
13. What is ethical behavior? Is it possible to teach ethical behavior in a management accounting course?
14. Firms with higher ethical standards will experience a higher level of economic performance than firms with lower or poor ethical standards. Do you agree? Why or why not?
15. Review the code of ethical conduct for management accountants. Do you believe that the code will have an effect on the ethical behavior of management accountants? Explain.
16. Identify the three forms of accounting certification. Which form of certification do you believe is best for a management accountant? Why?
17. What are the four parts to the CMA examination? What do they indicate about management accounting versus financial accounting?

EXERCISES AND PROBLEMS

**1-1
Financial and
Management
Accounting**

LO 1

Susan Draper is a senior majoring in early childhood development. She wants to open a child care center upon graduation and realizes that she needs some solid business training in addition to her coursework in caring for young children. Susan has decided to take at least one accounting course but cannot decide between financial or management accounting. She needs some information on the advantages each course offers.

REQUIRED: Prepare a letter advising Susan of the differences and similarities of financial and management accounting. Describe the advantages each might offer the director of a child care center.

**1-2
Accounting
History**

LO 2

In the 1400s Europeans valued the gold, gems, drugs, and spices that came from the Orient. However, these goods were very costly, since they could only be transported to Europe via long overland caravans. Portuguese sailors tried to reach the Orient by sea—around Africa. Christopher Columbus felt that a shorter, easier route lay to the west. He offered Queen Isabella of Spain a business proposition: financing for three completely outfitted ships, honors, titles and a percentage of the trade in exchange for opening up a direct route to the Indies and establishing a city devoted to trade. King John II of Portugal had previously turned down his offer, but Queen Isabella accepted. On August 3, 1492, the Nina, Pinta, and Santa Maria set sail from Palos, Spain.

REQUIRED: Suppose that a communication device had existed in 1492 that permitted Isabella to talk with Columbus for 15 minutes once each month during the eight-month voyage. What types of information would she have wanted to obtain regarding the success of the enterprise? Write down a list of the questions she might have asked. Classify each question as a financial or cost management type of question. Do the questions change as the months go on or not? (Hint: A little reading up on Columbus in an encyclopedia will make the role playing in this problem easier.)

1-3
Customer
Orientation
LO 3

A number of mail-order computer and software companies have set up customer service telephone lines. Some are toll-free, some are not. A customer can wait on hold anywhere from 3 seconds to 20 minutes.

REQUIRED: Evaluate all of the costs that these companies might consider when setting up the customer service lines. (Hint: Should you also consider costs to the customer?)
DIRECT and INDIRECT COSTS

1-4
Ethical Behavior
LO 4, 5, 7

Consider the following scenario:

Manager: "If I can increase my revenues by $75,000 during this last quarter, my division will show a profit 10 percent above the planned level, and I will receive a $10,000 bonus. However, given the projections for the fourth quarter, it does not look promising. I really need that $10,000. I know one way I can qualify. All I have to do is strong-arm my three most aggressive salespeople to book orders from customers who are leaning toward our product. We can always cancel them after the first of the year."

REQUIRED: What is the right choice for the manager to make? Why did the ethical dilemma arise? Is there any way to redesign the accounting reporting system to discourage the type of behavior the manager was contemplating?

1-5
Behavioral Impact
of Cost
Information
LO 5

Mark Munson, the plant manager, was grumbling about the new quality cost system the plant controller wanted to put into place. "If we start trying to track every bit of spoiled material, we'll never get any work done. Everybody knows when they ruin something. Why bother to keep track? This is a waste of time and I won't allow it!"

REQUIRED:

1. Why do you suppose that the controller wants a written record of spoiled material? If "everybody knows" what the spoilage rate is, what benefits can come of keeping a written record?
2. Now take Mark Munson's position. In what way(s) could he be correct?

1-6
Managerial Uses
of Accounting
Information
LO 6

Each of the following scenarios requires the use of accounting information to carry out one or more of the following managerial activities: planning, controlling (including performance evaluation), or decision making. Identify the managerial activity or activities applicable for each scenario, and indicate the role of accounting information in the activity.

A. *Manager*: "A supplier approached me recently and offered to sell our company vacuum hoses for $20 each. We currently manufacture our own hoses. I need to know what costs we will avoid if we buy the vacuum hoses."
B. *Manager*: "This report indicates that we have spent 20 percent more on materials than originally planned. An investigation into the cause has revealed the problem. We were using a lower-quality material than expected and the waste has been higher than normal. By switching to the quality level originally specified, we can cut the excess cost to 10 percent."

C. *Manager*: "Our salespeople indicate that they expect to sell 15 percent more units than last year. I want a projection of the effect this increase in sales will have on profits. I also want to know our expected cash receipts and cash expenditures on a month-by-month basis. I have a feeling that some short-term borrowing may be necessary."

D. *Manager*: "Given the intensity of competition, we need to do something about increasing the efficiency of our manufacturing process. Currently, we are considering the implementation of two different automated manufacturing systems. I need to know the future cash flows associated with each system."

E. *Manager*: "At the last board meeting, we established an objective of earning a 25 percent return on sales. I need to know how many units of our product we need to sell to meet this objective. Once I have the estimated sales in units, we then need to outline a promotional campaign that will take us where we want to be. However, in order to compute the targeted sales in units, I need to know the expected unit price and a lot of cost information."

F. *Manager*: "Perhaps the Harrison Medical Clinic should not offer a full range of medical services. Some services seem to be having a difficult time showing any kind of profit. I am particularly concerned about the mental health service. It has not shown a profit since the clinic opened. I want to know what costs can be avoided if I drop the service. I also want some assessment of the impact on the other services we offer. Some of our patients may choose this clinic because we offer a full range of services."

1-7
Role of
Management
Accountants
LO 6

Management accountants are actively involved in the process of managing the entity. This process includes making strategic, tactical, and operating decisions while helping to coordinate the efforts of the entire organization. To fulfill these objectives, the management accountant accepts certain responsibilities that can be identified as (1) planning, (2) controlling, (3) evaluating performance, (4) ensuring accountability of resources, and (5) external reporting.

REQUIRED: Describe each of these responsibilities of the management accountant and identify examples of practices and techniques.

(CMA adapted)

1-8
Line Versus Staff
LO 6

The job responsibilities of three employees of Barney Manufacturing are described below.

Tyranna Davis, cost accounting manager, is responsible for measuring and collecting costs associated with the manufacture of the purple stuffed dinosaur product line. She is also responsible for preparing periodic reports comparing actual costs with planned costs. These reports are provided to the production line managers and the plant manager. Tyranna helps explain and interpret the reports.

Steg Swenson, production manager, is responsible for the manufacture of the purple stuffed dinosaurs. He supervises the line workers, helps develop the production schedule, and is responsible for seeing that production quotas are met. He is also held accountable for controlling manufacturing costs.

Rex Anders, marketing manager, is responsible for selling and delivering the product to retail toy stores. He supervises the development of marketing materials and ad campaigns and oversees the salesforce. He also supervises the delivery truck drivers. He is accountable for controlling all marketing related costs.

REQUIRED: Identify Tyranna, Steg, and Rex as line or staff and explain your reasons.

1-9
Ethical Issues
LO 7

Assess and comment on each of the following statements that have appeared in newspaper editorials:

1. Business students come from all segments of society. If they have not been taught ethics by their families and by their elementary and secondary schools, there is little effect a business school can have.

2. Sacrificing self-interest for the collective good won't happen unless a majority of Americans also accept this premise.

3. Competent executives manage people and resources for the good of society. Monetary benefits and titles are simply the by-products of doing a good job.
4. Unethical firms and individuals, like high rollers in Las Vegas, are eventually wiped out financially.

1-10
Ethical Issues
LO 7

The Alert Company is a closely held investment service group that has been very successful over the past five years, consistently providing most members of the top management group with 50 percent bonuses. In addition, both the chief financial officer and the chief executive officer have received 100 percent bonuses. Alert expects this trend to continue.

Recently, the top management group of Alert, which holds 35 percent of the outstanding shares of common stock, has learned that a major corporation is interested in acquiring Alert. Alert's management is concerned that this corporation may make an attractive offer to the other shareholders and that management would be unable to prevent the takeover. If the acquisition occurs, this executive group is uncertain about continued employment in the new corporate structure. As a consequence, the management group is considering changes to several accounting policies and practices that, although not in accordance with generally accepted accounting principles, would make the company a less attractive acquisition. Management has told Roger Deerling, Alert's controller, to implement some of these changes. Deerling has also been informed that Alert's management does not intend to disclose these changes immediately to anyone outside the immediate top management group.

REQUIRED: Using the code of ethics for management accountants, evaluate the changes that Roger's management is considering and discuss the specific steps that he should take to resolve the situation.

(CMA adapted)

1-11
Ethical Behavior
LO 7

Webson Manufacturing Company produces component parts for the airline industry and has recently undergone a major computer system conversion. Michael Darwin, the controller, has established a trouble-shooting team to alleviate accounting problems that have occurred since the conversion. Michael has chosen Maureen Hughes, assistant controller, to head the team that will include Bob Randolph, cost accountant; Cynthia Wells, financial analyst; Marjorie Park, general accounting supervisor; and George Crandall, financial accountant.

The team has been meeting weekly for the last month. Maureen insists on being part of all the team conversations in order to gather information, to make the final decision on any ideas or actions that the team develops, and to prepare a weekly report for Michael. She has also used this team as a forum to discuss issues and disputes about him and other members of Webson's top management team. At last week's meeting, Maureen told the team that she thought a competitor might purchase the common stock of Webson, because she had overheard Michael talking about this on the telephone. As a result, most of Webson's employees now informally discuss the sale of Webson's common stock and how it will affect their jobs.

REQUIRED: Is Maureen Hughes' discussion with the team about the prospective sale of Webson unethical? Discuss, citing specific standards from the code of ethical conduct to support your position.

(CMA adapted)

1-12
Ethical
Responsibilities
LO 7

JLA Electronics is a U.S.-based, high-tech company that manufactures and distributes computer and telecommunications equipment. JLA has developed a hand-held, light-weight fax system, Porto-Fax, that will allow the user total freedom in receiving and transmitting information. Marketing research studies indicate that the potential market for this item is large, and immediate action in test marketing the product is recommended.

Despite the fact that JLA has excess capacity at its current manufacturing facility, the company has decided to build a new manufacturing plant to accommodate the Porto-Fax and is in the process of deciding where to locate the plant. The current unionized employees believe this move is being made to eliminate union involvement in the Porto-Fax manufacturing process. The management team that was formed to oversee the site selection process has already received bids from several locales, both domestic and foreign, offering a wide range of incentives to encourage the company to select particular sites.

Some of the incentives are personal in nature, such as housing at reduced cost for the selection team, reduced property taxes, open accounts at certain restaurants, and free tickets to local sporting events. Other incentives offered affect corporate profitability and include reduced tax rates, low-interest or no-interest loans, outright grants, and low-cost property. The marketing research team has reported that product price will have a major effect on the sale of Porto-Fax and recommends that the selection team pick a site that minimizes costs.

REQUIRED:

1. What is meant by the term *corporate social responsibility*?
2. Should JLA Electronics consider its social responsibility when making the final decision regarding the site selection?
3. Describe the ethical responsibilities of the individuals on the site selection team.
4. Discuss the responsibilities that the union at the current manufacturing facility may have in this situation.

(CMA adapted)

1-13
Ethics
LO 7

The external auditors for Heart Health Procedures (HHP) are currently performing the annual audit of HHP's financial statements. As part of the audit, the external auditors have prepared a representation letter to be signed by HHP's Chief Executive Office (CEO) and Chief Financial Officer (CFO). The letter provides, among other items, a representation that appropriate provisions have been made for

Reductions of any excess or obsolete inventories to net realizable values, and
Losses from any purchase commitments for inventory quantities in excess of requirements or at prices in excess of market.

HHP began operations by developing a unique balloon process to open obstructed arteries to the heart. In the last several years, HHP's market share has grown significantly because its major competitor was forced by the Food and Drug Administration (FDA) to cease its balloon operations. HHP purchased the balloon's primary and most expensive component from a sole supplier. Two years ago, HHP entered into a five-year contract with this supplier at the then current price, with inflation escalators built into each of the five years. The long-term contract was deemed necessary to ensure adequate supplies and discourage new competition. However, during the past year, HHP's major competitor developed a technically superior product, which utilizes an innovative, less costly component. This new product was recently approved by the FDA and has been introduced to the medical community, receiving high acceptance. It is expected that HHP's market share, which has already seen softness, will experience a large decline and that the primary component used in the HHP balloon will decrease in price as a result of the competitor's use of its recently developed superior, cheaper component. The new component has been licensed by the major competitor to several outside sources of supply to maintain available quantity and price competitiveness. At this time, HHP is investigating the purchase of this new component.

HHP's officers are on a bonus plan that is tied to overall corporate profits. Jim Honig, vice president of manufacturing, is responsible for both manufacturing and warehousing. During the course of the audit, he advised the CEO and CFO that he was not aware of any obsolete inventory nor any inventory or purchase commitments where current or expected prices were significantly below acquisition or commitment prices. Honig took this position even though Marian Nevins, assistant controller, had apprised him of both the existing excess inventory attributable to the declining market share and the significant loss associated with the remaining years of the five-year purchase commitment.

Nevins has brought this situation to the attention of her superior, the controller, who also participates in the bonus plan and reports directly to the CFO. Nevins works closely with the external audit staff and subsequently ascertained that the external audit manager was unaware of the inventory and purchase commitment problems. Nevins is concerned about the situation and is not sure how to handle the matter.

REQUIRED:

1. Assuming that the controller did not apprise the CEO and CFO of the situation, explain the ethical considerations of the controller's apparent lack of action by discussing specific standards of "Standards of Ethical Conduct for Management Accountants."
2. Assuming Marian Nevins believes the controller has acted unethically and not apprised the CEO and CFO of his findings, describe the steps that she should take to resolve the situation. Refer to the "Standards of Ethical Conduct for Management Accountants" in your answer.
3. Describe actions that HHP can take to improve the ethical situation within the company.

(CMA adapted)

1-14
Research
Assignment
LO 8

Describe the CMA, CPA, and CIA. What are the relative advantages of each for the internal accountant? (You may want to write to the Institute of Management Accountants, your state Board of Accountancy, and the Institute of Internal Auditors for more information on the CMA, CPA, and CIA, respectively.)

1-15
Research
Assignment
LO 8

The Body Shop has been considered an ethical model for business. For example, it does not test products on animals and is known for paying first-world wages in third-world countries. Yet recently, the Body Shop has been criticized for engaging in unethical practices (e.g., making false advertising claims). Do some library research on the Body Shop. Do you believe that the Body Shop is an ethical or unethical business? Write a 3–5 page position paper stating your views. Be sure to support your views by referring to the articles you read.

Part 1
Fundamental Cost Management Concepts

Chapter 2
Basic Cost Management Concepts

GM's Saturn Corporation created a new type of car and a new management style. Employees at the Spring Hill, Tennessee, plant have more decision-making authority than their counterparts at other GM plants. In addition, the advanced manufacturing structure of the factory means that a fresh perspective must be taken regarding costs.

LEARNING OBJECTIVES

After studying this chapter, you should be able to:

1. Describe a cost management information system, its objectives and major subsystems, and indicate how it relates to other operating and information systems.
2. Explain the cost assignment process.
3. Define tangible and intangible products, and explain why there are different product cost definitions.
4. Prepare income statements for manufacturing and service organizations.
5. Describe the relationship between activity drivers and cost behavior.
6. Explain the differences between traditional and contemporary cost management systems.

The study of cost accounting and cost management requires an understanding of fundamental cost concepts and terms and the associated information systems that produce them. Some basic framework must be developed so that we can make sense of the variety of topics that appear in the field of cost accounting and cost management. A systems perspective provides a useful framework for achieving this objective. But what is an *information system?* Are there different systems for different purposes? Similarly, what is meant by *cost?* Are there different costs for different purposes? This chapter addresses these basic questions and provides a foundation needed for the study of the rest of the text. In providing this foundation, we make no attempt to be exhaustive in our coverage of different systems and different costs. Other system and cost concepts are discussed in later chapters. However, a thorough understanding of the concepts presented in this chapter is essential for success with later chapters.

A SYSTEMS FRAMEWORK

Objective 1

Describe a cost management information system, its objectives and major subsystems, and indicate how it relates to other operating and information systems.

system

A **system** is a set of interrelated parts that performs one or more processes to accomplish specific objectives. To illustrate, consider an air conditioning system for a home. This system has a number of interrelated parts such as the compressor, the fan, the thermostat, and duct work. The most obvious process is the cooling of air. Another process is delivery of the cooled air. The primary objective of the system is to provide a comfortable, cool environment for the rooms of the house. Notice that each part of the system is critical for achievement of the overall objective. For example, if the duct system is missing, there would be no ability to cool even if the other parts were present and functional.

But how does a system work? The operational heart of a system is its processes. Essentially, a system receives inputs that are transformed by processes into outputs that satisfy the system's objectives. Consider the cooling process. This process requires inputs such as warm air, freon, and electricity. The inputs are transformed into cooled air, an output of the cooling process. The output of the process, cooled air, is obviously critical to achieving the overall objective of the system. The cooled air and energy become inputs to the delivery process. This process transforms the inputs so that a portion of the total cooled air is delivered to each room of the house (the output is delivered air). In this way, all rooms are cooled to the desired temperature, thereby achieving the system's objective. The operational model for the air conditioning system is shown in Exhibit 2-1.

Accounting Information Systems

Accounting information systems are described by the same general pattern: (1) interrelated parts, (2) processes, and (3) objectives. The interrelated parts consist of such things as order entry and sales, billing accounts receivable and cash receipts, inventory, general ledger, and cost accounting. Each of these interrelated parts is itself a system and is therefore referred to as a *subsystem* of the accounting information system. Processes include such things as collecting, recording, sum-

Exhibit 2-1
Operational Model of the Air Conditioning System

marizing, and managing data. Some processes may also be formal decision models—models that use inputs and provide recommended decisions as the information output. The overall objective of an accounting information system is to provide output information to users. Thus, an **accounting information system** is a system consisting of interrelated manual and computer parts, using processes such as collecting, recording, summarizing, analyzing (using decision models), and managing data to provide output information to users.

accounting
information system

Operationally, an accounting information system uses processes to transform inputs into outputs that satisfy the overall objectives of the system. Thus, the operational model for an accounting information system also follows the same pattern as that described for systems in general. There are, however, two distinguishing characteristics. First, inputs for an accounting information system are usually economic events. Second, the operational model of an accounting information system has one important additional feature: *the user of information*. The output of the information system produces user actions. In some cases, the output may serve as the *basis* for action. This is particularly true for tactical and strategic decisions but less true for day-to-day decisions. In other cases, the output may serve to *confirm* that the actions taken had the intended effects.[1] Another possible user action is *feedback*, which becomes an input for subsequent operational system performance. The operational model for an accounting information system is illustrated in Exhibit 2-2. Examples of the inputs, processes, and outputs are provided in the exhibit. (The list is not intended to be exhaustive.) Notice that personal communication is listed as an information output. Often users may not wish to wait for formal output and can obtain needed information on a more timely basis by communicating with information providers (e.g., accountants).

Up to this point, the focus has been on the accounting information system. In reality, our study will focus primarily on a major subsystem of the accounting information system. The accounting information system can be divided into two major subsystems: (1) the *financial accounting information system* and (2) the *cost management information system*. Of the two systems, we will emphasize the second, although it should be noted that the two systems need not be independent.[2] Ideally, the two systems should be integrated and have linked data bases. Output of each of the two systems can be used as input for the other system.

financial accounting
information system

Financial Accounting Information System The **financial accounting information system** is an accounting information subsystem that is primarily concerned with producing outputs for external users and uses well-specified economic events as inputs and processes that meet certain rules and conventions. For financial accounting, the nature of the inputs and the rules and conventions governing processes are defined by the Securities Exchange Commission (SEC) and the

---

1.   This role of information output is described in William J. Bruns, Jr., and Sharon M. McKinnon, "Information and Managers: A Field Study," *Journal of Management Accounting Research*, Volume 5, Fall 1993, pp. 86–108. The paper reports a field study undertaken to assess how managers use accounting information. The authors also point out that formal information output does not seem to be used for day-to-day decisions. Managers often use interpersonal relationships to acquire information for daily use. Apparently, accessing information by the use of informal channels can provide more timely information than the formal information system.

2.   Much of the material from this point on in this section relies on information found in the following three articles: Robert S. Kaplan, "The Four-Stage Model of Cost Systems Design," *Management Accounting*, February 1990, pp. 22–26; Steven C. Schnoebelen, "Integrating an Advanced Cost Management System Into Operating Systems (Part 1)," *Journal of Cost Management*, Winter 1993, pp. 50–54; Steven C. Schnoebelen, "Integrating an Advanced Cost Management System Into Operating Systems (Part 2)," *Journal of Cost Management*, Spring 1993, pp. 60–67.

Exhibit 2-2

Operational Model of an Accounting Information System

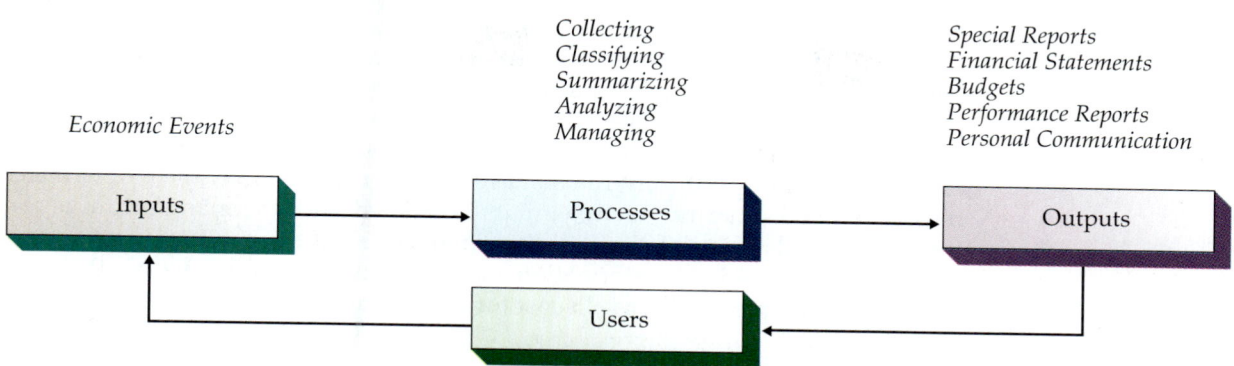

Financial Accounting Standards Board (FASB). The overall objective is the preparation of external reports (financial statements) for investors, creditors, government agencies, and other outside users. This information is used for such things as investment decisions, stewardship evaluation, monitoring activity, and regulatory measures.

The Cost Management Information System The **cost management information system** is an accounting information subsystem that is primarily concerned with producing outputs for internal users using inputs and processes needed to satisfy management objectives. Notice that the cost management information system is not bound by any formal criteria that define inputs and processes. Instead, the criteria that govern the inputs and processes are set internally based on management objectives. The cost management information system has three broad objectives:[3]

1. To provide information for costing out services, products, and other objects of interest to management.
2. To provide information for decision making.
3. To provide information for planning and control.

The information requirements for satisfying the first objective depend on the nature of the object being costed and why management wants to know the cost. For example, product costs that satisfy the FASB rules are needed to value inventories (for balance sheet presentation) and prepare income statements (cost of sales is needed). In this case, the cost of materials, labor, and other manufacturing inputs are needed. In other cases, managers may want to know all costs that are associated with a product, for purposes of tactical and strategic profitability analysis. If so, then additional cost information may be needed concerning activities such as product design, development, marketing, and distribution. Cost information also is a basic input for planning and control. It should help managers decide what should be done, why it should be done, how it should be done,

(left margin) cost management information system

---

3. These three broad objectives serve as the basis for the organization of the topics presented in this text. First, we introduce the basic concepts for cost management systems. The next section of the text, made up of Chapters 4–9, focuses primarily on the first objective, product costing. The third section of the text, Chapters 10–15, focuses primarily on the second objective (decision making), and the fourth section, Chapters 16–22, on the third objective (planning and control). It should also be pointed out that the decision-making objective is also present in the product costing and control sections. The distinction for the third section is the discussion of specific decision-making models that rely on accounting information as input.

and how well it is done. For example, information about the *expected* revenues and costs for a new product may affect how the product is designed and marketed. At this stage, the expected revenues and costs may cover the entire life of the new product. Thus, projected costs of design, development, testing, production, marketing, distribution, and servicing would be essential information. Finally, cost information is a critical input for many managerial decisions. For example, a manager deciding whether to continue making a component internally or to buy it from an external supplier needs relevant, timely, and accurate cost information. Specifically, the manager would need to know the cost of materials, labor, and other productive inputs associated with the manufacture of the component and which of these costs would vanish if the product is no longer produced. Also needed is information concerning the cost of purchasing the component, including any increase in cost for internal activities such as receiving and storing goods.

Relationship to Other Operational Systems and Functions

The cost information produced by the cost management information system must be useful and beneficial to the organization as a whole. Thus, a high-quality cost management system should have an organizationwide perspective. Managers in many different areas of a business make decisions and evaluations that require cost information. For example, an engineering manager must make strategic decisions concerning product design. Different designs produce different costs (costs of production, marketing, and servicing can vary widely depending on the design). Having reliable and accurate cost information about different designs is clearly critical for sound decision making. To provide this cost information, the cost management system must not only interact with the design and development system but also with the production, marketing, and customer service systems. Cost information for tactical decision making is also important. For example, a sales manager needs reliable and accurate cost information when faced with a decision concerning an order that may be sold for less than the normal selling price. Such a sale may only be feasible if the production system is reporting idle capacity. In this case, a sound decision mandates interaction among the cost management system, the marketing and distribution system, and the production system. These two examples illustrate that the cost management system should have an organizationwide perspective and that it must be properly integrated with the nonfinancial functions and systems within an organization. In the past, little effort was made to integrate the cost management system with other operational systems. However, the current competitive environment dictates that companies pay much greater attention to cost management in all functional areas. Exhibit 2-3 illustrates the expected interactive relationships.

Exhibit 2-3 implies that the cost management system receives information from all operational systems and also supplies information to these systems. To the extent possible, the cost management system should be integrated with the organization's operational systems. Integration reduces redundant storage and use of data, improves the timeliness of information, and increases the efficiency of producing reliable and accurate information.

An integrated cost management system, as portrayed in Exhibit 2-3, suggests a need for management to emphasize cost management for the entire *value chain*. The **value chain** is the set of activities required to design, develop, produce, mar-

value chain

Exhibit 2-3
*An Integrated Cost
Management System*

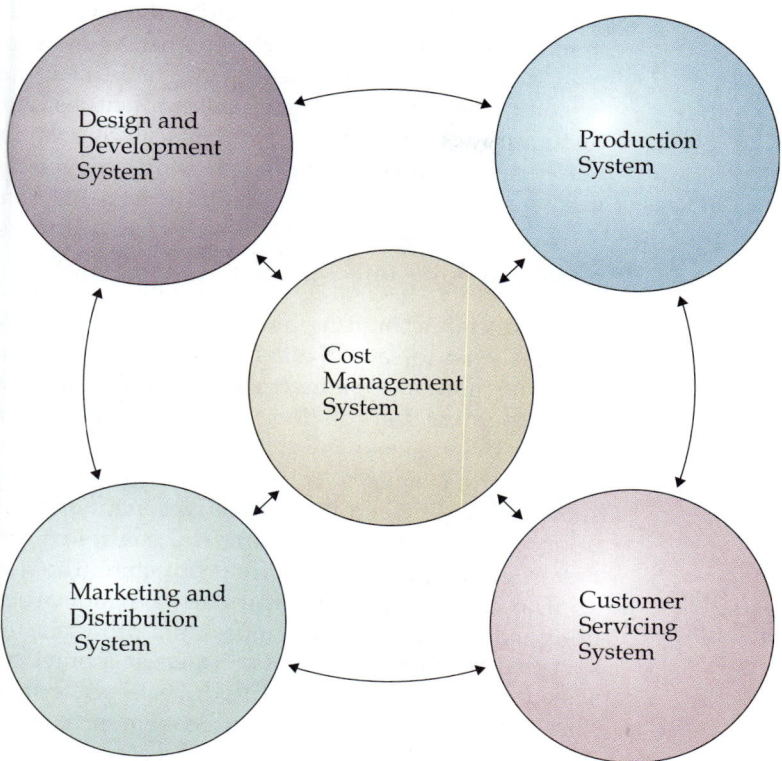

ket, distribute, and service a product (the product can be a service). The value chain is illustrated in Exhibit 2-4.

Value-chain costing assigns costs to the set of activities that define the value chain. Reporting the cost of value-chain activities is an important output of cost management systems. One possible application is product costing. Assigning the costs of different value-chain activities to products creates different product cost definitions. For example, the traditional product cost definition (mandated for valuing inventories and determining cost of sales for external reporting) assigns only the cost of production activities to products. The costs of all other value-chain activities are expensed in the period in which they are incurred. More will be said about product cost definitions later on. For now, you need to understand

Exhibit 2-4
*Value-Chain Activities
for a Product or Service*

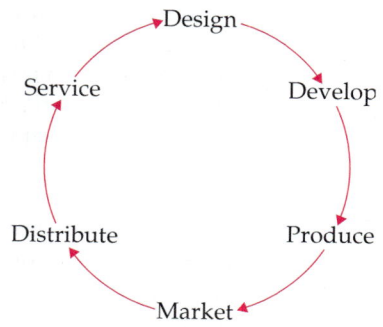

that the way we view the value chain can affect the design of the cost management information system. There must be an explicit recognition that the cost management system should be designed to support the cost management needs of nonfinancial functions such as product design, engineering, purchasing, production, marketing, sales, customer service, and distribution. These broad design objectives may demand much more from the cost management system than information output that simply satisfies external reporting requirements.

Different Systems for Different Purposes

The financial accounting and cost management systems illustrate that different systems exist to satisfy different purposes. (Can you identify the different purposes of the two systems?) As indicated, these two systems are subsystems of the accounting information system. The cost management information system also has two major subsystems: the *cost accounting information system* and the *operational control information system*. The objectives of these two subsystems correspond to the first and third objectives mentioned earlier for the cost management information system (the costing and control objectives). The output of these two cost systems satisfies the second objective (the decision-making objective).

cost accounting
information system

  The **cost accounting information system** is a cost management subsystem designed to assign costs to individual products and services and other objects as specified by management. For external financial reporting, the cost accounting system must assign costs to products to value inventories and determine cost of sales. Furthermore, these assignments must conform to the rules and conventions set by the SEC and FASB. These rules and conventions do not require that all costs assigned to individual products be causally related to the demands of individual products. Thus, using financial accounting principles to define product costs may lead to under- and overstatements of individual product costs. For reporting inventory values and cost of sales, this may not matter. Inventory values and cost of sales are reported in the aggregate, and the under- and overstatements may wash out to the extent that the values reported on the financial statements are reasonably accurate.

  However, at the individual product level, distorted product costs can cause managers to make significant decision errors. For example, a manager might erroneously de-emphasize and overprice a product that is, in reality, highly profitable. For decision making, accurate product costs are needed. If possible, the cost accounting system should produce product costs that simultaneously are accurate and satisfy financial reporting conventions. If not, then the cost system must produce two sets of product costs: one that satisfies financial reporting criteria and one that satisfies management decision-making needs.

operational control
information system

  The **operational control information system** is a cost management subsystem designed to provide accurate and timely feedback concerning the performance of managers and others relative to their planning and control of activities. Operational control is concerned with what activities should be performed and assessing how well they are performed. It focuses on identifying opportunities for improvement and helping to find ways to improve. A good operational control information system provides information that helps managers engage in a program of continuous improvement of all aspects of their business.

  Product cost information plays a role in this process but by itself is not sufficient. The information needed for planning and control is broader and encompasses the entire value chain. For example, every profit-making manufacturing and service organization exists to serve customers. Thus, one objective of an operational control system is to improve the value received by customers. Products and services should be produced that fit specific customer needs (observe how this affects the design and development system in the value chain). Quality, affordable prices, and low post-purchase costs for operating and maintaining the product are also important customer wants. A second, related objective is to improve profits by providing this value. Well-designed, quality products that are affordable can be offered only if they also provide an acceptable return to the owners of the company. Cost information concerning quality, different product designs, and post-purchase customer needs is vital for managerial planning and control.[4]

COST ASSIGNMENT: DIRECT TRACING, DRIVER TRACING, AND ALLOCATION

Objective 2
Explain the cost assignment process.

To study cost accounting and operational control systems, it is necessary to understand the meaning of cost and to become familiar with the cost terminology associated with the two systems. One also must understand the process used to assign costs. Cost assignment is one of the key processes of the cost accounting system. Improving the cost assignment process has been one of the major developments in the cost management field in recent years. Before discussing the cost assignment process, we first need to define what we mean by cost.

cost

Cost is the cash or cash equivalent value sacrificed for goods and services that are expected to bring a current or future benefit to the organization. We say *cash equivalent* because noncash assets can be exchanged for the desired goods or services. For example, it may be possible to exchange equipment for materials used in production.

Costs are incurred to produce future benefits. In a profit-making firm, future benefits usually mean revenues. As costs are used up in the production of revenues, they are said to expire. Expired costs are called **expenses**. In each period, expenses are deducted from revenues in the income statement to determine the period's profit. A **loss** is a cost that expires without producing any revenue benefit. For example, the cost of uninsured inventory destroyed by a flood would be classified as a loss on the income statement. Many costs do not expire in a given period. These unexpired costs are classified as **assets** and appear on the balance sheet. Computers and factory buildings are examples of assets lasting more than one period. Note that the main difference between a cost being classified as an expense or an asset is timing. This distinction is important and will be referred to in the development of other cost concepts later in the text.

expenses

loss

assets

Cost Objects

Management accounting systems are structured to measure and assign costs to entities, called *cost objects*. A **cost object** is any item, such as products, customers, departments, projects, activities, and so on, for which costs are measured and

cost object

4.   The two objectives—improving customer value and improving profits by providing this value—are discussed in more detail in the following article: Peter B. B. Turney, "Activity-Based Management," *Management Accounting*, January 1992, pp. 20–25.

assigned. For example, if we want to determine what it costs to produce a bicycle, then the cost object is the bicycle. If we want to determine the cost of operating a maintenance department within a plant, then the cost object is the maintenance department. If the objective is to determine the cost of developing a new toy, then the cost object is the new toy development project. As a final example, activities should be mentioned. An **activity** is a basic unit of work performed within an organization. An activity can also be defined as an aggregation of actions within an organization useful to managers for purposes of planning, controlling, and decision making. In recent years, activities have emerged as important cost objects. Activities play a prominent role in assigning costs to other cost objects and are essential elements of a contemporary management accounting system. Examples of activities include setting up equipment for production, moving materials and goods, purchasing parts, billing customers, paying bills, maintaining equipment, expediting orders, designing products, and inspecting products. Notice that an activity is described by an action verb (e.g. paying and designing) and an object (e.g., bills and products) that receives the action. Notice also that the action verb and object reveal very specific goals.

activity [margin note]

Accuracy of Assignments

Assigning costs *accurately* to cost objects is crucial. Our notion of accuracy is not evaluated based on knowledge of some underlying "true" cost. Rather it is a relative concept and has to do with the reasonableness and logic of the cost assignment methods that are being used. The objective is to measure and assign as accurately as possible the cost of the resources consumed by a cost object. Some cost assignment methods are clearly more accurate than others. For example, suppose you want to determine the cost of lunch for Elaine Day, a student that frequents Hideaway, an off-campus pizza parlor. One cost assignment approach is to count the number of customers Hideaway has between 12:00 P.M. and 1:00 P.M. and then divide the total receipts earned by Hideaway during this period. Suppose that this comes out as $4.50 per lunch-time customer. Thus, based on this approach we would conclude that Elaine spends $4.50 per day for lunch. Another approach is to go with Elaine and observe how much she spends. Suppose that she has a slice of pizza and a medium drink each day, costing $2.50. It is not difficult to see which cost assignment is more accurate. The $4.50 cost assignment is distorted by the consumption patterns of other customers (cost objects). As it turns out, most lunch-time clients order the luncheon special for $4.99 (a mini-pizza, salad, and medium drink). Distorted cost assignments can produce erroneous decisions and bad evaluations. For example, if a plant manager is trying to decide whether to continue producing power internally or to buy it from a local utility company, then an accurate assessment of how much it is costing to produce the power is fundamental to the analysis. An overstatement of the cost of power production could suggest to the manager that the internal power department should be shut down in favor of external purchase, whereas a more accurate cost assignment might suggest the opposite. It is easy to see that bad cost assignments can prove to be costly.

Traceability The relationship of costs to cost objects can be exploited to help increase the accuracy of cost assignments. Costs are directly or indirectly associated with cost objects. **Indirect costs** are costs that cannot be easily and accurately traced to a cost object. **Direct costs** are those costs that can be easily and

indirect costs [margin note]
direct costs [margin note]

accurately traced to a cost object.[5] Easily traced means that the costs can be assigned in an economically feasible way, and accurately traced means that the costs are assigned using a *causal relationship*. Thus, **traceability** is simply the ability to assign a cost directly to a cost object in an economically feasible way by means of a causal relationship. The more costs that can be traced to the object, the greater the accuracy of the cost assignments. Establishing traceability is a key element in building accurate cost assignments. One additional point needs to be emphasized. Cost management systems typically deal with many cost objects. Thus, it is possible for a particular cost item to be classified as both a direct cost and an indirect cost. It all depends on *which* cost object is the point of reference. For example, if the plant is the cost object, then the cost of heating and cooling the plant is a direct cost; however, if the cost object is products produced in the plant, then this utility cost is an indirect cost.

Methods of Tracing Traceability means that costs can be assigned easily and accurately, whereas **tracing** is the actual assignment of costs to a cost object using an *observable* measure of the resources consumed by the cost object. Tracing costs to cost objects can occur in one of two ways: (1) *direct tracing* and (2) *driver tracing*. **Direct tracing** is the process of identifying and assigning costs to a cost object that are specifically or physically associated with the cost object. Identifying costs that are specifically associated with a cost object is most often accomplished by *physical observation*. For example, assume that the power department is the cost object. The salary of the power department's supervisor and fuel used to produce power are examples of costs that can be specifically identified (by physical observation) with the cost object (the power department). As a second example, consider the materials and labor used to make a product. Both are physically observable, and therefore, the costs of materials and labor can be directly charged to a product. Ideally, all costs should be charged to cost objects using direct tracing. Unfortunately, it is often not possible to physically observe the exact amount of resources being consumed by a cost object. The next best approach is to use cause-and-effect reasoning to identify factors—called *drivers*—that can be observed and which measure a cost object's resource consumption. **Drivers** are factors that *cause* changes in resource usage, activity usage, costs, and revenues. **Driver tracing** is the use of *drivers* to assign costs to cost objects. Although less precise than direct tracing, if the cause-and-effect relationship is sound, then a high degree of accuracy can be expected.

Driver tracing uses two types of drivers for tracing costs to cost objects: *resource drivers* and *activity drivers*. **Resource drivers** measure the demands placed on resources by activities and are used to assign the cost of resources to activities. Consider the activity "maintaining equipment." This activity consumes resources such as parts, equipment, tools, labor, and energy (power to run the equipment and tools). Some of these resources, such as equipment, tools, and materials are directly traceable to the activity. Other resources such as power and labor may not be directly traceable. Physically observing how much power is used would require a meter to measure the power consumption of the maintenance equipment. Metering may not be practical. Thus, a resource driver such as "machine

Margin terms: traceability · tracing · direct tracing · drivers · driver tracing · resource drivers

5.   This definition of direct costs is based on the glossary of terms prepared by Computer Aided Manufacturing-International, Inc. (CAM-I). See Norm Raffish and Peter B. B. Turney, "Glossary of Activity-Based Management," *Journal of Cost Management*, Fall 1991, pp. 53–63. Other terms defined in this chapter and in the text also follow the CAM-I glossary.

hours" could be used to assign the cost of power. For example, if the power cost per machine hour is $0.50 and the activity, maintaining equipment, uses 20,000 machine hours, then $10,000 of the power cost ($0.50 × 20,000) would be assigned to the activity. The total cost of the activity is the sum of the directly traceable resource costs and the resource driver-assigned costs. Once the total cost of maintaining equipment is determined, then the cost of this activity can be assigned to objects that consume the activity by using *activity drivers*. **Activity drivers** measure the demands placed on activities by cost objects and are used to assign the cost of activities to cost objects. For example, the activity driver, number of maintenance hours worked, might be used to assign the cost of the activity, maintaining equipment, to the cost object, production departments. Thus, if the cost of providing the activity, maintaining equipment, is $20 per maintenance hour and a production department (say grinding) uses 2,000 maintenance hours, then $40,000 of the activity's cost ($20 × 2,000 maintenance hours) would be assigned to grinding. A list of sample activities and their potential activity drivers is provided in Exhibit 2-5.

The driver tracing model just described is summarized in Exhibit 2-6. The driver tracing model is the heart of a cost-assignment approach known as *activity-based costing*. **Activity-based costing** assigns costs to cost objects by first tracing costs to activities and then tracing costs to cost objects. The computational procedures for tracing costs to activities and other cost objects are described in detail in later chapters. At this point, the important thing to understand is that it is possible to assign costs to cost objects through the use of direct tracing, resource drivers, and activity drivers.

activity drivers

activity-based costing

Exhibit 2-5
Sample of Activities with Potential Activity Drivers

ACTIVITY	POTENTIAL ACTIVITY DRIVER
Setting up equipment	Number of setups
Moving materials	Number of moves
Ordering materials	Number of purchase orders placed
Drilling holes	Number of machine hours
Redesigning products	Number of engineering orders
Paying bills	Number of invoices
Inspecting finished goods	Number of batches produced
Maintaining equipment	Number of maintenance hours
Providing power	Number of kilowatt hours
Packing goods	Number of boxes
Scheduling production	Number of different products

Exhibit 2-6
Assignment of Costs Using Driver Tracing

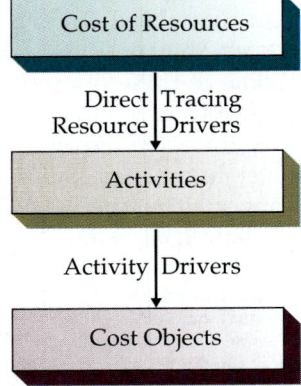

allocation

Assigning Indirect Costs Indirect costs cannot be traced to cost objects. This means that no causal relationship exists between the cost and the cost object or that tracing is not economically feasible. Assignment of indirect costs to cost objects is called **allocation**. Since no causal relationship exists, allocating indirect costs is based on *convenience* or some *assumed* linkage. For example, consider the cost of heating and lighting a plant that manufactures five products. Suppose that this utility cost is to be assigned to the five products. Clearly, it is difficult to see any causal relationship. A convenient way to allocate this cost is simply to assign it in proportion to the direct labor hours used by each product. Arbitrarily allocating indirect costs to cost objects reduces the overall accuracy of the cost assignments. Accordingly, the best costing policy may be that of assigning only traceable direct costs to cost objects. However, it must be admitted that allocations of indirect costs may serve other purposes besides accuracy. For example, allocating indirect costs to products (a cost object) may be required to satisfy external reporting conventions. Nonetheless, most managerial uses of cost assignments are better served by accuracy. At the very least, direct and indirect cost assignments should be reported separately.

Cost Assignment Summarized The foregoing discussion reveals three methods of assigning costs to cost objects: direct tracing, driver tracing, and allocation. These methods are illustrated in Exhibit 2-7. Of the three methods, direct tracing is the most precise, since it relies on physically observable causal relationships. Direct tracing is followed by driver tracing in terms of cost assignment accuracy. Driver tracing relies on causal factors called drivers to assign costs to cost objects. The precision of driver tracing depends on the quality of the causal relationship described by the driver. Identifying drivers and assessing the quality of the causal relationship is much more costly than either direct tracing or allocation. In fact, one advantage of allocation is its simplicity and low cost of implementation. However, allocation is the least accurate cost assignment method, and its use should be minimized (avoided where possible). In many cases, the benefits of increased accuracy by driver tracing outweigh its additional measurement cost. This cost-benefit issue is discussed more fully later in the chapter. What it really entails is choosing among competing cost management systems.

Exhibit 2-7
Cost Assignment Methods

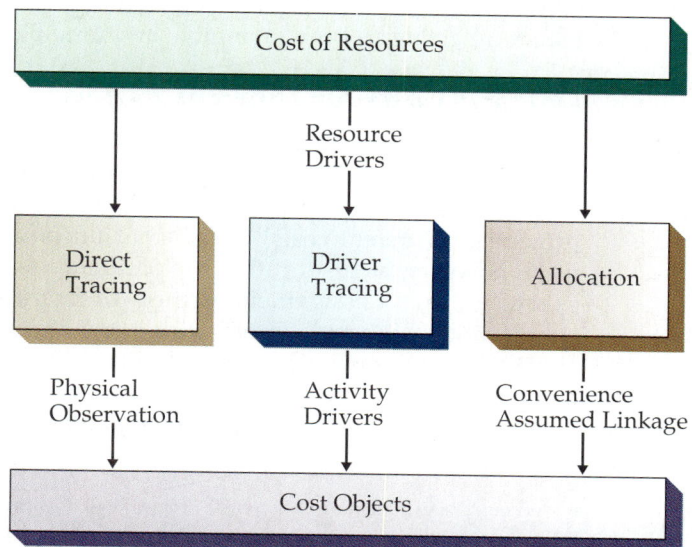

PRODUCT AND SERVICE COSTS

Objective 3
Define tangible and intangible products, and explain why there are different product cost definitions.

tangible products
services

The output of organizations represents one of the most important cost objects. There are two types of output: tangible products and services. **Tangible products** are goods produced by converting raw materials through the use of labor and capital inputs such as plant, land, and machinery. Televisions, hamburgers, automobiles, computers, clothes, and furniture are examples of tangible products. **Services** are tasks or activities performed for a customer or an activity performed by a customer using an organization's products or facilities. Services are also produced using materials, labor, and capital inputs. Insurance coverage, medical care, dental care, funeral care, and accounting are examples of service activities performed for customers. Car rental, video rental, and skiing are examples of services where the customer uses an organization's products or facilities.

Services differ from tangible products on three important dimensions: intangibility, perishability, and inseparability. Intangibility means that buyers of services cannot see, feel, hear, or taste a service before it is bought. Thus, services are *intangible products*. Perishability means that services cannot be stored (there are a few unusual cases where tangible goods cannot be stored). Finally, inseparability means that producers of services and buyers of services must usually be in direct contact for an exchange to take place. In effect, services are often inseparable from their producers. For example, an eye examination requires both the patient and the optometrist to be present. However, producers of tangible products need not have direct contact with the buyers of their goods. For example, buyers of automobiles never need to have contact with the engineers and assembly line workers that produce automobiles.

Organizations that produce tangible products are called *manufacturing* organizations. Those that produce intangible products are called *service* organizations. Managers of organizations that produce goods or services need to know how much individual products cost for a number of reasons, including profitability analysis and strategic decisions concerning product design, pricing, and product mix. For example, Fleming Co., an Oklahoma City based food distributor, notes that separating the cost of products from the cost of servicing the retail customer is a key part of its flexible marketing plan.[6] Individual product cost can refer to either a tangible or an intangible product. Thus, when we discuss product costs, we are referring to both intangible and tangible products.

Different Costs for Different Purposes

product cost

Product cost is a cost assignment that satisfies a well-specified managerial objective. Thus, what product cost means depends on the managerial objective being served. The product cost definition illustrates a fundamental cost management principle: "Different costs for different purposes." This principle should not be used, however, as justification for proliferation of product costing methods. For example, the cost assignment method for financial reporting could rely primarily on allocations, whereas direct tracing and driver tracing could be relied on primarily for providing accurate individual product cost assignments needed for managerial planning and decision making. However, as long as the costs assigned fit the FASB's definition of product cost, the cost assignment *method*

---

6.   Glen A Beres, "Fleming CEO Details Progress in Retooling," *Supermarket News,* September 18, 1995, pp. 6 and 62.

used for financial reporting can be identical to that used to satisfy other managerial product costing objectives. Using more product costing methods than necessary can be confusing (especially to nonfinancial managers) and could undermine the credibility of the cost management information system.[7]

Product cost definitions can differ according to the objective being served. Exhibit 2-8 provides three examples of product cost definitions and some of the objectives they satisfy. For pricing decisions, product mix decisions, and strategic profitability analysis, all traceable costs need to be assigned to the product and include the costs of the major value-chain activities: research and development, production, marketing, and customer service. For strategic product design decisions and tactical profitability analysis, production, marketing, and customer service costs (including customer post-purchase costs) are needed. For external financial reporting, FASB rules and conventions mandate that only production costs be used in calculating product costs. Other objectives may use other product cost definitions (beyond those in Exhibit 2-8).

Product Costs and External Financial Reporting

One of the central objectives of a cost management system is the calculation of product costs for external financial reporting. For product costing purposes, externally imposed conventions dictate that costs be classified in terms of the special purposes, or functions, they serve. Costs are subdivided into two major functional categories: production and nonproduction. **Production costs** are those costs associated with the manufacture of goods or the provision of services. **Nonproduction costs** are those costs associated with the functions of selling and administration. For tangible goods, production and nonproduction costs are often referred to as *manufacturing costs* and *nonmanufacturing costs*, respectively. Production costs can be further classified as *direct materials*, *direct labor*, and *overhead*.

production costs
nonproduction costs

Exhibit 2-8
Examples of Product Cost Definitions

Product Cost Definition	Value-Chain Product Costs	Operating Product Costs	Traditional Product Costs
	Research and Development		
	Production	Production	Production
	Marketing	Marketing	
	Customer Service	Customer Service	
Managerial Objectives Served	Pricing Decisions Product Mix Decisions Strategic Profitability Analysis	Strategic Design Decisions Tactical Profitability Analysis	External Financial Reporting

7.   For further discussion of this point, see Steven C. Schnoebelen, "Integrating an Advanced Cost Management System Into Operating Systems."

Only these three cost elements can be assigned to products for external financial reporting.

direct materials

Direct Materials **Direct materials** are those materials traceable to the good or service being produced. The cost of these materials can be directly charged to products because physical observation can be used to measure the quantity consumed by each product. Materials that become part of a tangible product or those that are used in providing a service are usually classified as direct materials. For example, steel in an automobile, wood in furniture, alcohol in cologne, denim in jeans, braces for correcting teeth, surgical gauze and anesthesia for an operation, a casket for a funeral service, and food on an airline are all direct materials.

direct labor

Direct Labor **Direct labor** is labor that is traceable to the goods or services being produced. As with direct materials, physical observation can be used to measure the quantity of labor used to produce a product or service. Those employees who convert raw materials into a product or who provide a service to customers are classified as direct labor. Workers on an assembly line at Chrysler, a chef in a restaurant, a surgical nurse attending an open-heart operation, and a pilot for Delta Airlines are examples of direct laborers.

overhead

Overhead All production costs other than direct materials and direct labor are lumped into one category called **overhead**. In a manufacturing firm, overhead is also known as *factory burden* or *manufacturing overhead*. The overhead cost category contains a wide variety of items. Many inputs other than direct labor and direct materials are needed to produce products. Examples include depreciation on buildings and equipment, maintenance, supplies, supervision, material handling, power, property taxes, landscaping of factory grounds, and plant security.

supplies

Supplies are generally those materials necessary for production but that do not become part of the finished product or are not used in providing a service. Dishwasher detergent in a fast-food restaurant and oil for production equipment are examples of supplies.

Direct materials that form an insignificant part of the final product are usually lumped into the overhead category as a special kind of indirect material. This is justified on the basis of cost and convenience. The cost of the tracing is greater than the benefit of increased accuracy. The glue used in furniture or toys is an example.

The cost of overtime for direct laborers is usually assigned to overhead as well. The rationale is that typically no particular production run can be identified as the cause of the overtime. Accordingly, overtime cost is common to all production runs and is therefore an indirect manufacturing cost. Note that *only* the overtime cost itself is treated this way. If workers are paid an $8 regular rate and a $4 overtime premium, then only the $4 overtime premium is assigned to overhead. The $8 regular rate is still regarded as a direct labor cost. In certain cases, however, overtime is associated with a particular production run, for example, a special order taken when production is at 100 percent capacity. In these special cases, it is appropriate to treat overtime premiums as a direct labor cost.

Selling and Administrative Costs There are two categories of nonmanufacturing costs: selling costs and administrative costs. For external financial reporting, sell-

noninventoriable
(period) costs

ing and administrative costs are *noninventoriable* or *period* costs. **Noninventoriable (period) costs** are expensed in the period in which they are incurred. Thus, none of these costs can be assigned to products or appear as part of the reported values of inventories on the balance sheet. In a manufacturing organization, the level of these costs can be significant (often greater than 25 percent of sales revenue), and controlling them may bring greater cost savings than the same control exercised in the area of production costs. For example, since 1992 General Motors has cut its $3.8 billion annual health care bill by 8 percent.[8] Procter & Gamble, on the other hand, spends enormous amounts on advertising in order to develop and dominate the market for shampoo and detergent in China. P&G buys more air time each month than even the most media conscious Chinese companies spend in a year. Couple that with the cost of free samples and thousands of Chinese who distribute them and we see that marketing expense in China is a significant portion of P&G's budget.[9] For service organizations, the relative importance of selling and administrative costs depends on the nature of the service being produced. Physicians and dentists, for example, do very little marketing and thus have very low selling costs. An airline, on the other hand, may incur substantial marketing costs.

marketing (selling)
costs

Those costs necessary to market and distribute a product or service are **marketing** or **selling costs**. They are often referred to as *order-getting* and *order-filling* costs. Examples of selling costs include the following: salaries and commissions of sales personnel, advertising, warehousing, shipping, and customer service. The first two items are examples of order-getting costs; the last three are order-filling costs.

administrative costs

All costs associated with the general administration of the organization that cannot be reasonably assigned to either marketing or production are **administrative costs**. General administration has the responsibility of ensuring that the various activities of the organization are properly integrated so that the overall mission of the firm is realized. The president of the firm, for example, is concerned with the efficiency of *both* marketing and production as they carry out their respective roles. Proper integration of these two functions is essential to maximize the overall profits of a firm. Examples, then, of administrative costs are top-executive salaries, legal fees, printing the annual report, general accounting, and research and development.

Prime and Conversion Costs   The manufacturing and nonmanufacturing classifications give rise to some related cost concepts. The functional delineation between nonmanufacturing and manufacturing costs is essentially the basis for the concepts of noninventoriable costs and inventoriable costs—at least for purposes of external reporting. Combinations of different production costs also produce the concepts of conversion costs and prime costs.

prime cost
conversion cost

Prime cost is the sum of direct materials cost and direct labor cost. **Conversion cost** is the sum of direct labor cost and overhead cost. For a manufacturing firm, conversion cost can be interpreted as the cost of converting raw materials into a final product.

8.   Alex Taylor III, GM: "Some Gain, Much Pain," *Fortune*, May 29, 1995, pp. 78–84.
9.   Joseph Kahn, "P&G Viewed China as a National Market and Is Conquering It," *Wall Street Journal*, September 12, 1995, pp. A1 and A6.

EXTERNAL FINANCIAL STATEMENTS

Objective 4
Prepare income statements for manufacturing and service organizations.

The functional classification is the cost classification required for external reporting. In preparing an income statement, production costs and selling and administrative costs are segregated. They are segregated because production costs are viewed as product costs and selling and administrative costs are viewed as belonging to the period. Thus, production costs attached to the products sold are recognized as an expense (cost of sales) on the income statement. Production costs attached to products that are not sold are reported as inventory on the balance sheet. Selling and administrative expenses are viewed as costs of the period and must be deducted each and every period as expenses. None of these costs would appear on the balance sheet.

Income Statement: Manufacturing Firm

The income statement based on a functional classification for a manufacturing firm is displayed in Exhibit 2-9. This income statement follows the traditional format taught in an introductory financial accounting course. Income computed by following a functional classification is frequently referred to as **absorption-costing income** or **full-costing income** because *all* manufacturing costs are fully assigned to the product.

absorption-costing (full-costing) income

Under the absorption-costing approach, expenses are segregated according to function and then deducted from revenues to arrive at income before taxes. As can be seen in Exhibit 2-9, there are two major functional categories of expense: cost of goods sold and operating expenses. These categories correspond, respectively, to a firm's manufacturing and nonmanufacturing expenses. **Cost of goods sold** is the cost of direct materials, direct labor, and overhead attached to the units sold. To compute the cost of goods sold, it is first necessary to determine the cost of goods manufactured.

cost of goods sold

Cost of Goods Manufactured The **cost of goods manufactured** represents the total cost of goods completed during the current period. The only costs assigned to goods completed are the manufacturing costs of direct materials, direct labor,

cost of goods manufactured

Exhibit 2-9

	Manufacturing Organization Income Statement For the Year Ended December 31, 1998		
Sales			$2,000,000
Cost of goods sold:			
Beginning finished goods inventory		$ 250,000	
Add: Cost of goods manufactured		1,200,000	
Goods available for sale		$1,450,000	
Less: Ending finished goods inventory		(150,000)	1,300,000
Gross margin			$ 700,000
Less: Operating expenses			
Selling expenses		$ 300,000	
Administrative expenses		150,000	(450,000)
Income before taxes			$ 250,000

and overhead. The details of this cost assignment are given in a supporting schedule, called the *statement of cost of goods manufactured*. An example of this supporting schedule for the income statement in Exhibit 2-9 is shown in Exhibit 2-10.

Notice in Exhibit 2-10 that the total manufacturing costs added during the period are added to the manufacturing costs found in beginning work in process, yielding total manufacturing costs to account for. The costs found in ending work in process are then deducted from total manufacturing costs to arrive at the cost of goods manufactured. If the cost of goods manufactured is for a single product, then the average unit cost can be computed by dividing the cost of goods manufactured by the units produced. For example, assume that the statement in Exhibit 2-10 was prepared for the production of bottles of perfume and that 240,000 bottles were completed during the period. The average unit cost is $5 per bottle ($1,200,000/240,000).

work in process   **Work in process** consists of all partially completed units found in production at a given point in time. Beginning work in process consists of the partially completed units on hand at the beginning of a period. Ending work in process consists of those on hand at the period's end. In the statement of cost of goods manufactured, the cost of these partially completed units is reported as the cost of beginning work in process and the cost of ending work in process. The cost of beginning work in process represents the manufacturing costs carried over from the prior period; the cost of ending work in process represents the manufacturing costs that will be carried over to the next period. In both cases, additional manufacturing costs must be incurred to complete the units in work in process.

Exhibit 2-10

Statement of Cost of Goods Manufactured
For the Year Ended December 31, 1998

Direct materials:		
Beginning inventory	$200,000	
Add: Purchases	450,000	
Materials available	$650,000	
Less: Ending inventory	(50,000)	
Direct materials used		$ 600,000
Direct labor		350,000
Manufacturing overhead:		
Indirect labor	$122,500	
Depreciation	177,500	
Rent	50,000	
Utilities	37,500	
Property taxes	12,500	
Maintenance	50,000	450,000
Total manufacturing costs added		$1,400,000
Add: Beginning work in process		200,000
Total manufacturing costs		$1,600,000
Less: Ending work in process		(400,000)
Cost of goods manufactured		$1,200,000

Income Statement: Service Organization

An income statement for a service firm is shown in Exhibit 2-11. In a service organization, the cost of services sold is computed differently from the cost of goods sold in a manufacturing firm. Unlike a manufacturing firm, the service firm has no finished goods inventories—it is not possible to store services. Thus, in a direct comparison with manufacturing firms, cost of services sold would always correspond to cost of goods manufactured. Furthermore, as Exhibit 2-11 reveals, the cost of services sold during a period (equivalent to cost of goods manufactured) can be computed following the same format shown in Exhibit 2-9. Exhibit 2-11 reveals that it is possible to have work in process for services. For example, an architect may have drawings in process and an orthodontist may have numerous patients in various stages of process for braces.

ACTIVITY DRIVERS AND COST BEHAVIOR

Objective 5
Describe the relationship between activity drivers and cost behavior.

Although preparing cost information for external financial reporting is important, cost information for other product costing objectives and for operational control is also vital. Understanding cost behavior is fundamental to satisfying these additional objectives. In particular, understanding the behavior of activity costs is critical. Knowing how activity costs behave facilitates product costing assignments and provides important input for such activities as budgeting and make or buy decisions. To understand cost behavior, some additional activity terminology is needed.

Cost Behavior Concepts

activity inputs

Every activity has inputs and outputs. **Activity inputs** are the resources consumed by an activity in producing its output. Activity inputs are the factors that

Exhibit 2-11

Service Organization Income Statement For the Year Ended December 31, 1998			
Sales			$325,000
Less:			
Cost of services sold:			
Beginning work in process		$ 10,000	
Service costs added:			
Direct materials	$ 50,000		
Direct labor	90,000		
Overhead	115,000		
		255,000	
Total		$265,000	
Less: Ending work in process		15,000	250,000
Gross margin			$ 75,000
Less: Operating expenses			
Selling expenses		$ 4,000	
Administrative expenses		17,500	21,500
Income before taxes			$ 53,500

activity output

activity output
measure

cost behavior

enable the activity to be performed and can be classified into four categories: materials, energy, labor, and capital. Activities transform the inputs to produce an *output*. **Activity output** is the result or product of an activity. For example, if the activity is moving materials, the inputs would be such things as crates (materials), fuel (energy), a forklift operator (labor), and a forklift (capital). The output would be material movement. An **activity output measure** provides an assessment of the number of times the activity is performed. It is the quantifiable measure of the output. For example, number of moves is a possible output measure of moving materials. The output measure effectively is a measure of the demands placed on an activity and therefore corresponds to an activity driver. **Cost behavior** describes how the costs of activity inputs change with respect to changes in activity output. Exhibit 2-12 illustrates the relationship between inputs, activities, activity output, and cost behavior. Thus, to assess cost behavior, the activity must be defined, its outputs and inputs must be identified and measured, and the effect on the cost of inputs as activity output changes must be calculated. Perhaps the most difficult task in assessing cost behavior is identifying good activity output measures.

Identification of activity output measures is simplified by classifying activities into one of four general categories: (1) unit-level, (2) batch-level, (3) product-level, and (4) facility-level.[10] Classifying activities into these general categories is useful because the costs of activities associated with the different levels respond to different *types* of activity drivers. The definition of the activities belonging to each general category clearly illustrates this feature. **Unit-level activities** are those that are performed each time a unit is produced. Grinding, polishing, and assembly are examples of unit-level activities. Output measures for unit-level activities, referred to as **unit-level drivers**, include such possibilities as units of product, direct labor hours, and machine hours. **Batch-level activities** are those that are performed each time a batch of goods is produced. The costs of batch-level activities vary with the number of batches but are fixed with respect to the number of units in each batch. Setups, inspections, production scheduling, and material han-

unit-level activities

unit-level drivers
batch-level activities

Exhibit 2-12
*Activity Cost
Behavior Model*

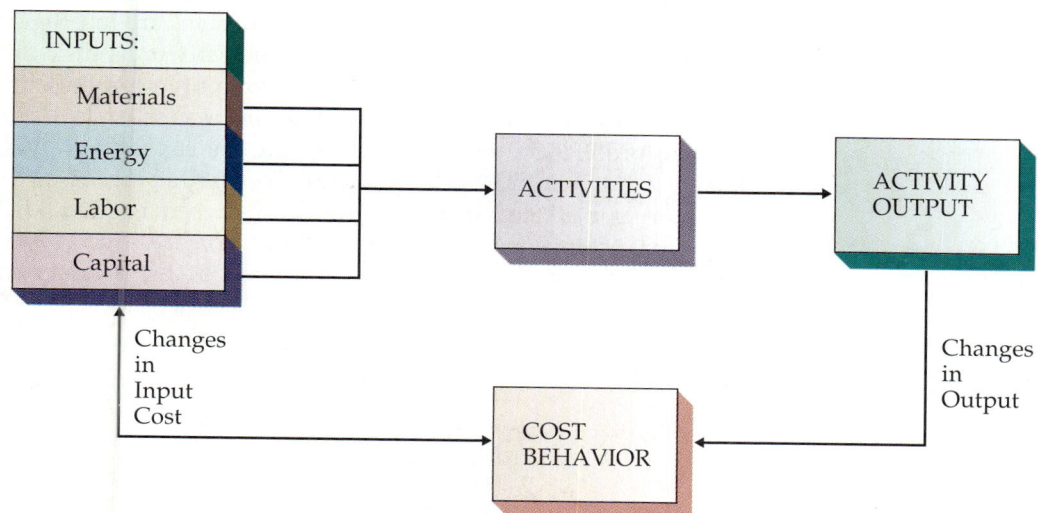

---

10.   This classification and the associated definitions are taken from Robin Cooper, "Cost Classification in Unit-Based and Activity-Based Manufacturing Cost Systems," *Journal of Cost Management*, Fall 1990, pp. 4–14.

dling are examples of batch-level activities. Output measures for batch-level activities are called **batch-level drivers**. Possible batch-level drivers are number of batches, inspection hours, number of production orders, and number of moves. **Product-level (sustaining) activities** are those that are performed as needed to support the various products produced by a company. These activities consume inputs that develop products or allow products to be produced and sold. These activities and their costs tend to increase as the number of different products increases. Engineering changes, developing product-testing procedures, marketing products, engineering processes, and expediting goods are examples of product-level activities. Activity output measures for product-level activities are **product-level drivers** and include number of change orders, number of products, number of processes, and number of expediting orders. **Facility-level activities** are those that sustain a factory's general manufacturing processes. Providing facilities, maintaining grounds, and providing plant security are examples. Useful output measures are difficult to define for this category of activities but might include such things as plant size (square feet), acres of ground maintained, and number of security personnel.

Look again at the photograph at the beginning of this chapter. It shows workers at the Saturn plant in Tennessee. Saturn is GM's experiment in a new way to build and market automobiles. Workers have interdisciplinary skills and are expected to be able to do many tasks. As you look at this photo, identify any unit-level, batch-level, product-level and facility-level activities you see, or can imagine.

Knowing the behavior of activity costs can be very useful information—information that can help in budgeting, supporting continuous improvement efforts, tactical decision making, and product costing. Generally, cost behavior can be described as fixed, variable, or mixed.

Fixed Costs

fixed costs

Fixed costs are costs that *in total* are constant within the relevant range as the level of the activity driver varies. To illustrate fixed cost behavior, consider a plant that produces personal computers. One of the departments of the plant is responsible for inserting 3½-inch disk drives. Two drives are inserted in each computer passing through the department. Define the activity as disk drive insertion and let the activity driver be the number of computers processed. The department operates two production lines. Each line can process up to 10,000 computers per year. The production workers of each line are supervised by a production-line manager who is paid $24,000 per year. For production up to 10,000 units, only one supervisor is needed; for production between 10,001 and 20,000 units, two supervisors are needed. The cost of supervision for several levels of production is given below for the plant (which is owned by Days Computers).

Days Computers

Supervision	Computers Processed	Unit Cost
$24,000	4,000	$6.00
24,000	8,000	3.00
24,000	10,000	2.40
48,000	12,000	4.00
48,000	16,000	3.00
48,000	20,000	2.40

The first step in assessing cost behavior is defining an appropriate activity driver. In this case, the activity driver is the number of computers processed. The relevant range second step is defining what is meant by **relevant range**, the range over which the assumed fixed cost relationship is valid for the normal operations of a firm. Assume that the relevant range is 12,000 to 20,000 computers processed. Notice that the *total* cost of supervision remains constant within this range as more computers are processed. Days Computers pays $48,000 for supervision regardless of whether it processes 12,000, 16,000, or 20,000 computers.

Pay particular attention to the words *in total* in the definition of fixed costs. While the total cost of supervision remains unchanged as more computers are processed, the unit cost changes as the level of the activity driver changes. As the example in the table shows, within the relevant range, the unit cost of supervision decreases from $4 to $2.40. Because of the behavior of per-unit fixed costs, it is easy to get the impression that fixed costs are affected by changes in the level of the activity driver, when in reality they are not. Unit fixed costs can often be misleading and may adversely affect some decisions. It is often safer to work with total fixed costs.

We can gain additional insight into the nature of fixed costs by portraying them graphically. The graph representing fixed cost behavior is given in Exhibit 2-13. As can be seen, for the relevant range, fixed cost behavior is described by a horizontal line. Notice that at 12,000 computers processed, supervision cost is $48,000; at 16,000 computers processed, supervision is also $48,000. This line visually demonstrates that cost remains unchanged as the level of the activity driver varies. For the relevant range, total fixed costs can be represented by the following simple linear equation:

$$F = \text{Total fixed costs}$$

In our example for Days Computers, supervision cost amounted to $48,000 for any level of output between 10,001 and 20,000 computers processed. Thus, supervision is a fixed cost, and the fixed cost equation in this case is F = $48,000. Strictly speaking, this equation assumes that the fixed costs are $48,000 for all levels (as if the line extends to the vertical axis as indicated by the dashed portion

Exhibit 2-13
Fixed Cost Behavior

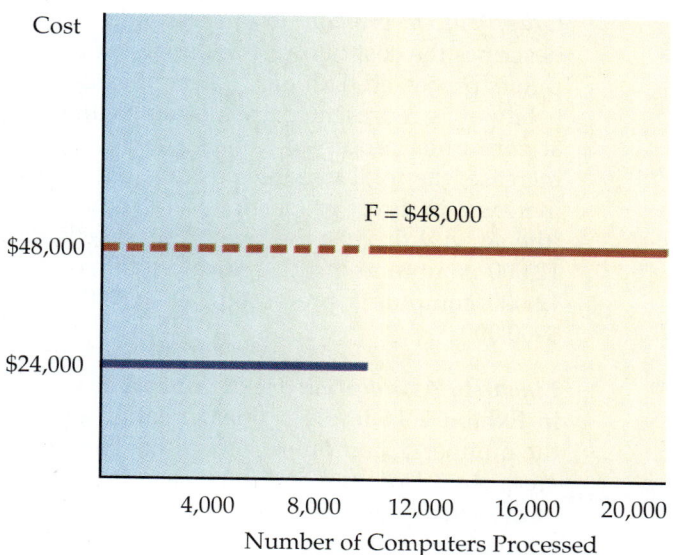

in Exhibit 2-13). Although this assumption is not true, it is harmless if the operating decisions are confined to the relevant range.

Variable Costs

variable costs

Variable costs are defined as costs that in total vary in direct proportion to changes in an activity driver. To illustrate, let's expand the Days Computers example to include the cost of disk drives. As with supervision, the activity is disk drive insertion and the activity driver is number of computers processed. Each computer requires two 3½-inch disk drives costing $30 each. Thus, the cost of disk drives per computer is $60 (2 × $30). The cost of disk drives for various levels of activity is given below:

Days Computers

Cost of Disk Drives	Number of Computers Processed	Unit Cost
$ 240,000	4,000	$60
480,000	8,000	60
720,000	12,000	60
960,000	16,000	60
1,200,000	20,000	60

As more computers are produced, the total cost of disk drives increases in direct proportion. For example, as production doubles from 8,000 to 16,000 units, the *total* cost of disk drives doubles from $480,000 to $960,000. Notice also that the unit cost of direct materials is constant.

Variable costs can also be represented by a linear equation. Here total variable costs depend on the level of activity driver. This relationship can be described by the equation below:

$$Y_v = VX$$

where Y_v = Total variable costs

V = Variable cost per unit

X = Number of units of activity driver

Graphical Description In our example for Days Computers, the relationship that describes the cost of direct material is $Y_v = \$60X$, where X = the number of computers processed. Exhibit 2-14 graphically illustrates a variable cost. Variable cost behavior is represented by a straight line coming out of the origin. Notice that at zero units processed, total variable cost is zero. However, as units produced increase, the total variable cost also increases. Here it can be seen that total cost increases in direct proportion to increases in the number of computers processed (the activity driver); the rate of increase is measured by the slope of the line. At 12,000 computers processed, the total cost of disk drives is $720,000 (or $60 × 12,000 computers processed); at 16,000 computers processed, the total cost is $960,000.

Linearity Assumption The definition of variable costs given above and the graph in Exhibit 2-14 imply a linear relationship between the cost of disk drives and the number of computers processed. How reasonable is the assumption that costs are linear? Do costs really increase in direct proportion to increases in the level of the activity driver? If not, then how well does this assumed linear cost function approximate the underlying cost function?

Economists usually assume that variable costs increase at a decreasing rate up to a certain volume, at which point they increase at an increasing rate. This type of *nonlinear behavior* is displayed in Exhibit 2-15. Here variable costs increase as the number of units increases, but not in direct proportion.

What if the nonlinear view more accurately portrays reality? What do we do then? One possibility is to determine the actual cost function—but every activity could have a different cost function, and this approach could be very time-consuming and expensive (if it can even be done). It is much simpler to assume a linear relationship.

If the linear relationship is assumed, then the main concern is how well this assumption approximates the underlying cost function. Exhibit 2-16 gives us some idea of the consequences of assuming a linear cost function. As with fixed costs, we can define the *relevant range* as the range of activity for which the

Exhibit 2-14
Variable Cost Behavior

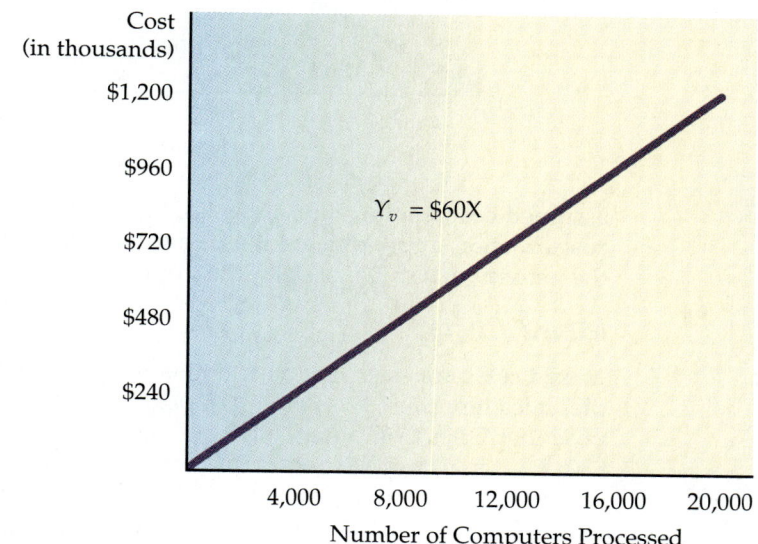

$Y_v = \$60X$

Exhibit 2-15
Nonlinearity of Variable Costs

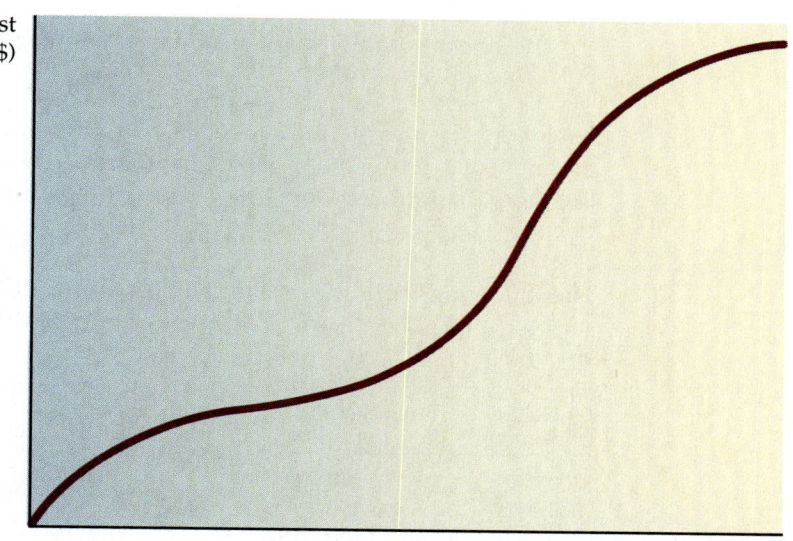

Units of Activity Driver

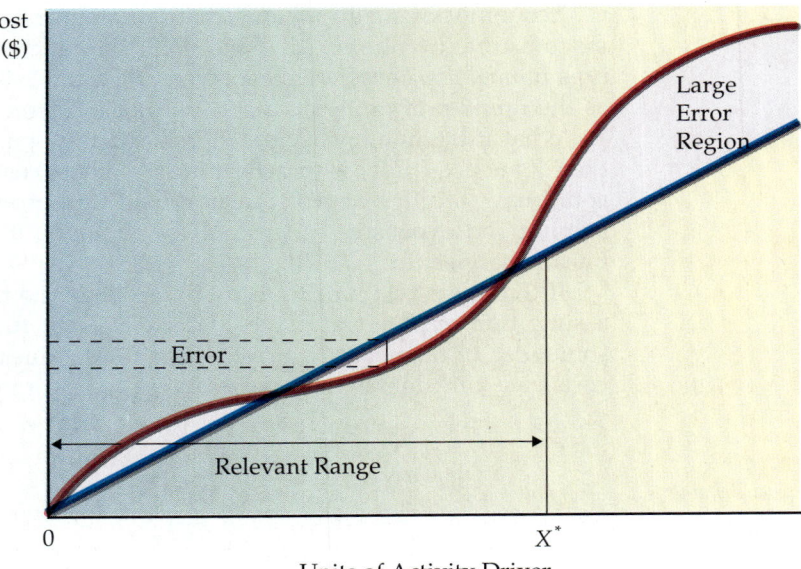

assumed cost relationships are valid. Here validity refers to how closely the linear cost function approximates the underlying cost function. Note that for units of the activity driver beyond X^*, the approximation appears to break down.

Mixed Costs

mixed costs

Mixed costs are costs that have both a fixed and a variable component. For example, sales representatives are often paid a salary plus a commission on sales. Suppose that Days Computers has ten sales representatives, each earning a salary of $30,000 per year plus a commission of $50 per computer sold. The activity is selling, and the activity driver is units sold. If 10,000 computers are sold, then the total selling cost (associated with the sales representatives) is $800,000—the sum of the fixed salary cost of $300,000 (10 × $30,000) and the variable cost of $500,000 ($50 × 10,000).

The linear equation for a mixed cost is given by

$$Y = \text{Fixed cost} + \text{Total variable cost}$$
$$Y = F + VX$$
$$\text{where } Y = \text{Total cost}$$

For Days Computers, the selling cost is represented by the following equation:

$$Y = \$300,000 + \$50X$$

The following table shows the selling cost for different levels of sales activity:

		Days Computers		
Fixed Cost of Selling	*Variable Cost of Selling*	*Total Cost*	*Computers Sold*	*Selling Cost Per Unit*
$300,000	$ 200,000	$ 500,000	4,000	$125.00
300,000	400,000	700,000	8,000	87.50
300,000	600,000	900,000	12,000	75.00
300,000	800,000	1,100,000	16,000	68.75
300,000	1,000,000	1,300,000	20,000	65.00

The graph for our mixed cost example is given in Exhibit 2-17 (the graph assumes that the relevant range is 0 to 20,000 units). Mixed costs are represented by a line that intercepts the vertical axis (at $300,000 for this example). The intercept corresponds to the fixed cost component, and the slope of the line gives the variable cost per unit of activity driver (slope is $50 for the example portrayed).

TRADITIONAL AND CONTEMPORARY COST MANAGEMENT SYSTEMS

Objective 6

Explain the differences between traditional and contemporary cost management systems.

Cost management systems can be broadly classified as *traditional* and *contemporary*.[11] Both traditional and contemporary approaches are found in practice. Traditional cost management systems currently are more widely used than contemporary systems. The use of contemporary cost management systems is increasing, however, particularly among organizations faced with increased product diversity, more product complexity, shorter product life cycles, increased quality requirements, and intense competitive pressures. These organizations often adopt a just-in-time manufacturing approach and implement advanced manufacturing technology (discussed in detail in Chapter 9). For firms operating in this advanced manufacturing environment, a traditional cost management system may not work well. More relevant and timely cost information is needed for these organizations to build a sustainable long-term competitive advantage. Organizations must improve the value received by their customers while increasing their profits at the same time. Better assessment of cost behavior, increased accuracy in product costing, and striving for continuous cost improvement are all critical for the advanced manufacturing environment.

Traditional Cost Management Systems: A Brief Overview

Recall that cost management systems are made up of two subsystems: the cost accounting system and the operational control system. Thus, when discussing

Exhibit 2-17
Mixed Cost Behavior

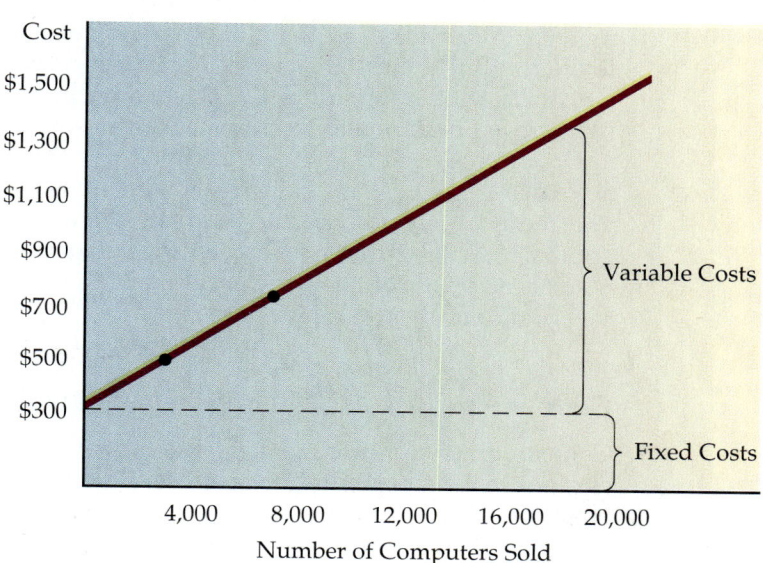

Number of Computers Sold

11.   The first two major parts of this text correspond to the cost accounting and operational control subsystems of the cost management system. Each of these parts, in turn, is subdivided based on traditional and contemporary design features. The features of traditional and contemporary cost management systems are so different that an attempt to integrate the two approaches would seem contrived and would likely be confusing.

cost management systems, it is logical and convenient to discuss each subsystem separately. Of course, what is true for a subsystem is true for the overall cost management system.

Traditional Cost Accounting Traditional cost accounting systems assume that all costs can be classified as fixed or variable with respect to changes in the *units* or *volume* of product produced. Thus, units of product or other drivers highly correlated with units produced, such as direct labor hours and machine hours, are the only drivers *assumed* to be of importance. These unit- or volume-based drivers are used to assign production costs to products. A cost accounting system that uses only unit-based activity drivers to assign costs to cost objects is called a **traditional cost system**. Since unit-based activity drivers usually are not the only drivers that explain causal relationships, much of the product cost assignment activity must be classified as allocation (recall that allocation is cost assignment based on *assumed* linkages or convenience). We can say, therefore, that traditional cost accounting systems tend to be allocation-intensive.

    The product costing objective of a traditional cost accounting system is typically satisfied by assigning production costs to inventories and cost of goods sold for purposes of financial reporting. More comprehensive product cost definitions, such as the value-chain and operating cost definitions illustrated in Exhibit 2-8, are not available for management use. However, traditional cost accounting systems often furnish useful variants of the traditional product cost definition. For example, prime costs and variable manufacturing costs per unit may be reported (variable manufacturing costs are direct materials, direct labor, and variable overhead, where variable behavior is defined with respect to a unit-based activity driver).

traditional cost system

traditional operation control system

Traditional Cost Control A **traditional operation control system** assigns costs to organizational units and then holds the organizational unit manager responsible for controlling the assigned costs. Performance is measured by comparing actual outcomes with standard or budgeted outcomes. The emphasis is on financial measures of performance (nonfinancial measures are usually ignored). Managers are rewarded based on their ability to control costs. Thus, the traditional approach traces costs to individuals who are responsible for incurrence of costs. The reward system is used to motivate these individuals to manage costs. The approach assumes that maximizing the performance of the overall organization is achieved by maximizing the performance of individual organizational subunits (referred to as responsibility centers).

Contemporary Cost Management Systems: A Brief Overview

Contemporary cost management systems have evolved in response to significant changes in the competitive business environment faced by both service and manufacturing firms. The overall objective of a contemporary cost management system is to improve the quality, content, relevance, and timing of cost information.[12] Generally, more managerial objectives can be met with a contemporary system than with a traditional system.

---

12.   Steven C. Schnoebelen, "Integrating an Advanced Cost Management System Into Operating Systems."

contemporary cost accounting system

activity-based cost system

activity-based management

Contemporary Cost Accounting A **contemporary cost accounting system** emphasizes tracing over allocation. The role of driver tracing is significantly expanded by identifying drivers unrelated to the volume of product produced (called *non-unit-based activity drivers*). The use of both unit and nonunit-based activity drivers increases the accuracy of cost assignments and the overall quality and relevance of cost information. A cost accounting system that uses both unit and nonunit-based activity drivers to assign costs to cost objects is called an **activity-based cost system**. For example, consider the activity "moving raw materials and partially finished goods from one point to another within a factory." The number of moves required for a product is a much better measure of the product's demand for the material handling activity than the number of units produced. In fact, the number of units produced may have nothing to do whatsoever with measuring products' demands for material handling. (A batch of 10 units of one product could require as much material handling activity as a batch of 100 units of another product.) Thus, we can say that a contemporary cost accounting system tends to be tracing-intensive.

Product costing in a contemporary system tends to be flexible. The contemporary cost management system is capable of producing cost information for a variety of managerial objectives, including the financial reporting objective. More comprehensive product costing definitions are emphasized for better planning, control, and decision making. Thus, the maxim of "different costs for different purposes" takes on real meaning.

Contemporary Cost Control The contemporary operational control subsystem also differs significantly from that of a traditional system. The emphasis of the traditional cost management accounting system is on managing costs. The emerging consensus, however, is that management of activities—not costs—is the key to successful control in the advanced manufacturing environment. Thus, *activity-based management* is the heart and soul of a contemporary operational control system. **Activity-based management** focuses on the management of activities with the objective of improving the value received by the customer and the profit received by providing this value. It includes driver analysis, activity analysis, and performance evaluation and draws on activity-based costing as a major source of information (see Exhibit 2-18).[13] Notice from Exhibit 2-18 that the vertical dimension emphasizes tracing costs to cost objects—by tracing the cost of resources to activities and then to the cost objects. This is the activity-based costing dimension (referred to as the *cost view*) and serves as important input to the control dimension, which is called the *process view*. The process view is concerned with identifying factors that cause an activity's cost (explains why costs are incurred), assessing what work is done (identifies activities), and evaluating the work performed and the results achieved (how well the activity is performed). Thus, a contemporary control system requires detailed information on activities.

This new approach focuses on accountability for activities rather than costs and emphasizes the maximization of systemwide performance instead of individual performance. Activities cut across functional and departmental lines, are systemwide in focus, and require a global approach to control. Essentially, this form of control admits that maximizing the efficiency of individual subunits does

13.   This definition of activity-based management and the illustrative model in Exhibit 2-18 are based on the following source: Norm Raffish and Peter B. B. Turney, "Glossary of Activity-Based Management," *Journal of Cost Management*, Fall 1991, pp. 53–63. Other terms throughout the text relating to activity-based management are also drawn from this source.

Exhibit 2-18
Activity-Based Management Model

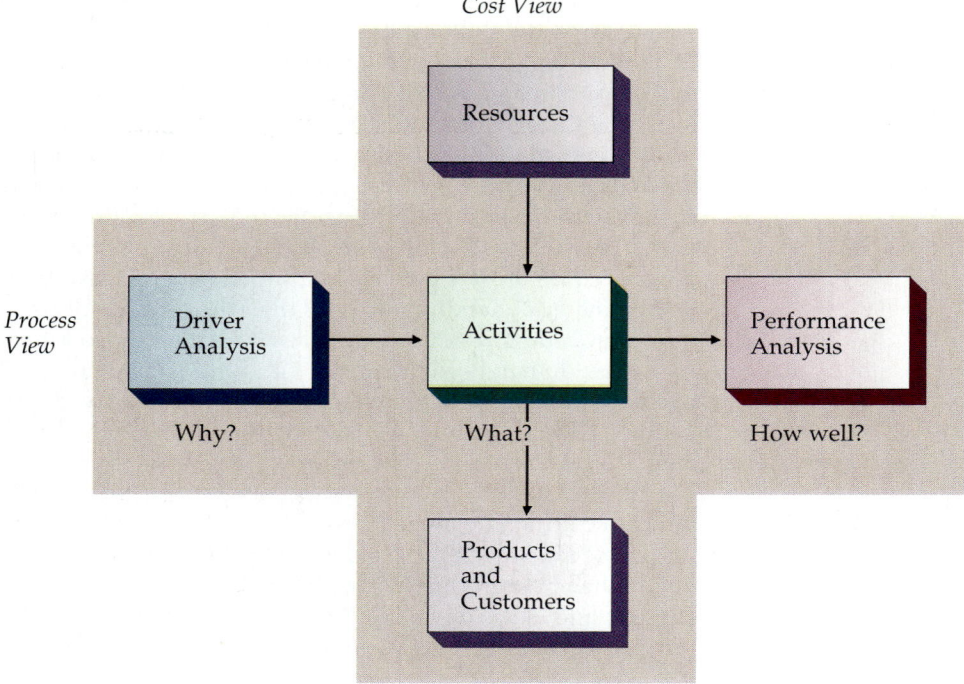

Cost View

Resources

Process View

Driver Analysis → Activities → Performance Analysis

Why?   What?   How well?

Products and Customers

not necessarily lead to maximum efficiency for the system as a whole. Another significant difference also should be mentioned. In the contemporary operational control information system, both financial and nonfinancial measures of performance are important. Exhibit 2-19 compares the characteristics of the traditional and contemporary cost management systems.

Choice of a Cost Management System

A contemporary cost management system offers significant benefits, including the following: greater product-costing accuracy, improved decision making, enhanced strategic planning, and better ability to manage activities. These benefits, however, are not obtained without costs. A contemporary cost management system is more complex, and it requires a significant increase in measurement activity—and measurement can be costly.

In deciding whether to implement a contemporary cost management system, a manager must assess the tradeoff between the cost of measurement and the cost of errors.[14] **Measurement costs** are the costs associated with the measurements required by the cost management system. **Error costs** are the costs associated with making poor decisions based on inaccurate product costs or, more generally, bad cost information. An **optimal cost management system** is the one that minimizes the sum of measurement costs and error costs. Note, however, that the two costs conflict. More complex cost management systems produce lower error costs but have higher measurement costs (consider, for example, the number of activities that must be identified and analyzed, along with the num-

measurement costs
error costs

optimal cost
   management system

14.   The discussion of these issues is based on the following article: Robin Cooper, "The Rise of Activity-Based Costing—Part Two: When Do I Need an Activity-Based Cost System?" pp. 41–48.

Exhibit 2-19
Comparison of Traditional and Contemporary Cost Management Systems

Traditional	Contemporary
1. Unit-based drivers	1. Unit and nonunit-based drivers
2. Allocation-intensive	2. Tracing-intensive
3. Narrow and rigid product costing	3. Broad, flexible product costing
4. Focus on managing costs	4. Focus on managing activities
5. Sparse activity information	5. Detailed activity information
6. Maximization of individual unit performance	6. Systemwide performance maximization
7. Uses financial measures of performance	7. Uses both financial and nonfinancial measures of performance

ber of drivers that must be used to assign costs to products). The tradeoff between error and measurement costs is illustrated in Exhibit 2-20. The message is clear. For some organizations, the optimal cost system may not be a contemporary cost management system even though it is a more accurate system. Depending on the tradeoffs, the optimal cost management system may very well be a simpler, traditional, unit-based system. This could explain, in part, why most firms still maintain a traditional system.

There are some changes, however, that are taking place in the manufacturing environment that are increasing the attractiveness of more complex and accurate cost management systems. New information technology, for example, is decreasing the cost of measurement. Computerized production planning systems and more powerful, less expensive computers make it easier to collect data and perform calculations. As measurement costs decrease, the measurement cost curve in Exhibit 2-20 shifts downward and to the right, causing the total cost curve to shift to the right. The optimal cost management system is now one that allows more accuracy.

The cost of errors has also changed for many organizations. As the degree and nature of competition changes, the cost of errors can increase. For example,

Exhibit 2-20
The Optimal Cost Management System

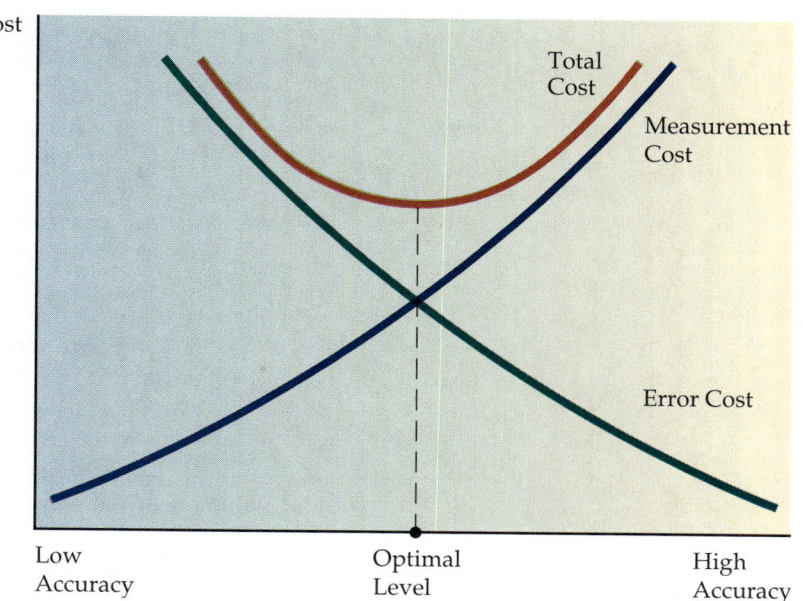

increased competition may lead a firm to drop what *appear* to be unprofitable products. If the nature of the competition changes, error costs can increase as well. For example, if single-product-focused competitors emerge, then their pricing and marketing strategies will be based on more accurate cost information (because all costs are known to belong to the single product). Because of better cost information, the more focused firms may gain market share at the expense of multiple-product producers (whose cost systems may be allocating rather than tracing costs to individual products). Other factors such as deregulation and JIT manufacturing (which leads to a more focused production environment) can also increase the cost of errors. As the cost of errors increases, the error-cost curve of Exhibit 2-20 shifts upward and to the right, causing the total cost curve to shift to the right. Thus, a more accurate cost system will become optimal.

Another cost which is increasing for firms is the cost of unethical conduct. For example, Metropolitan Life Insurance Company paid over $20 million in fines and must refund more than $50 million to policyholders because some of its agents illegally sold policies as retirement plans.[15] A contemporary system which tracks policy sales by type, age of policyholder, agent, and objective the policyholder hoped to achieve could give an early warning signal of problems. A key point is that companies are expected to exercise control over their operations. If there is room for ethical misconduct, the company must develop the means to identify and correct abuses.

As the cost of measurement decreases and the cost of errors increases, the existing cost management system is no longer optimal. Exhibit 2-21 illustrates how changing error and measurement costs can make an existing cost management system obsolete. As the exhibit illustrates, a more accurate cost management system is mandated because of changes in error and measurement costs.

Exhibit 2-21
Shifting Costs: Justification for a More Contemporary Cost System

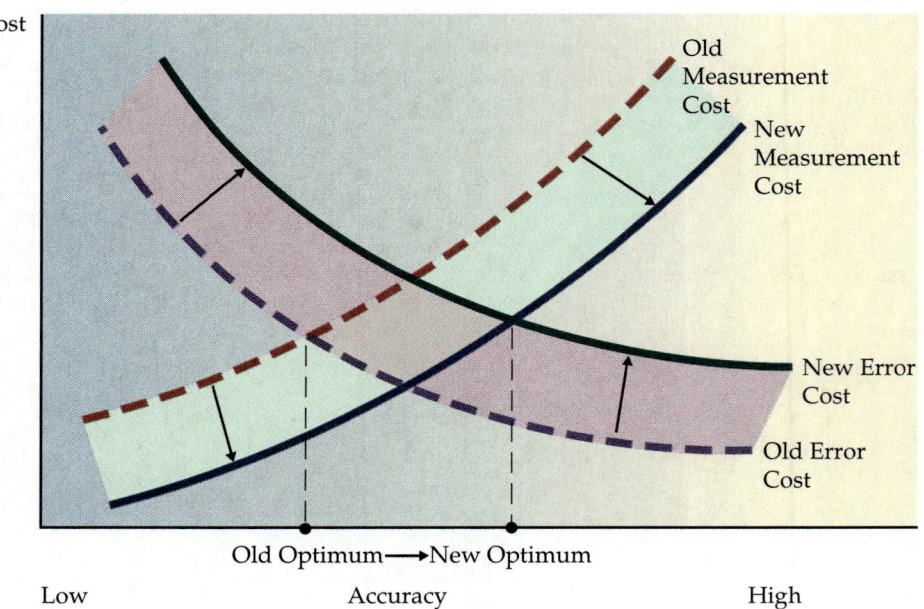

15.   Chris Roush, "Fields of Green—And Disaster Areas," *Business Week*, January 9, 1995, p. 94.

Firms, then, should consider implementing a contemporary cost management system if they have experienced a decrease in measurement costs and an increase in error costs.

Although the majority of firms still use a traditional cost management system, the use of activity-based costing and activity-based management is spreading and the interest in the contemporary cost management systems is high. Firms like the following have adopted activity-based costing and management systems.[16]

- Hughes Aircraft
- Caterpillar
- Xerox
- National Semiconductor
- Tektronix
- Dayton Extruded Plastics
- Armistead Insurance
- Zytec

Furthermore, this is only a very small listing of firms that are using more contemporary systems.

16.   See: Peter B. B, Turney, "Activity-Based Management," *Management Accounting,* January 1992, pp. 20–25; Jack Hedicke and David Feil, "Hughes Aircraft," *Management Accounting,* February 1991, pp. 29–33; and Lou F. Jones, "Product Costing at Caterpillar," *Management Accounting,* February 1991, pp. 34–42.

SUMMARY

A systems framework affords a logical basis for the study of cost management. The cost management system is a subsystem of the accounting information system and must be designed to satisfy costing, controlling, and decision-making objectives. The costing and controlling objectives serve to define two major subsystems: the cost accounting system and the operational control system.

A major feature of the operational model of the cost accounting system is the cost assignment process. The major objective of the cost accounting system is the assignment of costs to cost objects. This assignment process is achieved by three subprocesses: direct tracing, driver tracing, and allocation. Allocation is the least accurate and the least desirable approach, and generally, a cost accounting system should be designed to minimize allocations. Understanding the assignment process is fundamental to understanding cost management systems. In this chapter, all you need to do is grasp the broad, conceptual framework for cost assignment. Subsequent chapters will explore the mechanics of cost assignment in greater detail.

Product and service costs were also introduced. Several product cost definitions were provided. The product cost definition for external financial reporting is of particular importance and was discussed in detail. The format for external income statements was presented and discussed for both manufacturing and service firms. Given the increasing magnitude of the service sector, you should pay particular attention to what services are and how they differ from tangible products. Cost management for service organizations will receive more emphasis in this text than is traditionally available.

Cost behavior is also fundamental to cost accounting and control. Activity drivers are factors that cause changes in activity costs. Activity drivers can therefore be used to explain and describe cost behavior. Cost behavior is explained at the activity level and comes in three types: fixed, variable, and mixed. Be sure that you understand the definitions of each. The chapters on traditional and contemporary control rely heavily on cost behavior concepts.

Finally, we discussed the difference between traditional and contemporary cost management systems. Exhibit 2-19 lists some of the major differences between the two systems and should be studied carefully. Again, the objective is simply to provide a broad, conceptual understanding of the differences. An in-depth, detailed understanding of the differences will come only after studying the chapters that focus on the different types of systems.

REVIEW PROBLEMS AND SOLUTIONS

I.
Services, Cost Behavior, and Income Statement

Serenity Funeral Home offers a full range of services. Based on past experience, Serenity uses the following formula to describe its total overhead costs: $Y = \$100,000 + \$250X$, where Y = total overhead costs and X = number of funerals. Overhead costs are assigned by dividing the total overhead by the number of funerals. For a given funeral, the cost of direct materials ranges from $750 to $5,000 depending on the family's selection of a coffin. The average is $2,000. Direct labor averages $500 per funeral. During 1997, Serenity conducted 1,000 funerals. The average price charged for each funeral is $3,500. Serenity incurs selling and administrative costs each year totaling $100,000. (The ratio of administrative costs to selling costs is 3:1.)

REQUIRED:

1. Does Serenity sell a tangible or intangible product? Explain.
2. Does Serenity use a traditional or contemporary cost accounting system? Explain. Do you think this is a good choice? Explain.
3. What is the total expected overhead cost by Serenity for the year?
4. What is the total expected fixed overhead cost for the year?
5. What is the total expected variable overhead cost for the year?
6. What is the overhead cost per funeral for the year?
7. Calculate the unit product cost for the year.
8. Prepare an income statement for Serenity.

Solution

1. Funerals are intangible products. They are services and cannot be stored and are connected to the consumer (inseparability).
2. The use of a unit-based driver (number of funerals) to assign overhead costs (and apparently direct materials and direct labor) suggests a traditional system. A traditional system probably will work quite well for a local funeral home business. There is very little product diversity, selling and administrative expenses represent a small portion of total costs, and there are virtually no preproduction costs (research and development costs are absent). Thus, product cost is essentially defined by production costs. Furthermore, the absence of a great variety of products coupled with the fact that overhead costs represent a small percentage of product costs makes driver tracing much less important (direct materials and direct labor can be assigned using direct tracing).
3. $Y = 100,000 + 250(1,000)$
   $Y = 100,000 + 250,000$
   $Y = \$350,000$
4. $100,000
5. $250,000
6. $350,000/1,000 = \$350$
7. Unit product cost:

Direct materials	$2,000
Direct labor	500
Overhead	350
	$2,850

8.

Serenity Funeral Home
Income Statement
For the Year Ended December 31, 1997

Sales		$ 3,500,000
Cost of services sold:		
Direct materials	$2,000,000	
Direct labor	500,000	
Overhead	350,000	(2,850,000)
Gross margin		$ 650,000
Less: Operating expenses		
Selling expenses	$ 25,000	
Administrative expenses	75,000	(100,000)
Income before taxes		$ 550,000

II.
Traditional Versus Contemporary Cost Management Systems

Jazon Manufacturing produces two different models of cameras. One model has an automatic focus, whereas the other requires the user to determine the focus. The two products are produced in batches. Each time a batch is produced, the equipment must be configured (set up) for the specifications of the camera model being produced. The manual-focus camera requires more parts than the automatic-focus model. The manual-focus model is also more labor-intensive, requiring much more assembly time but less machine time. Although the manual model is more labor-intensive, the machine configuration required for this product is more complex, causing the manual model to consume more of the setup activity resources than the automatic camera. Many, but not all, of the parts for the two cameras are purchased from external suppliers. Because it has more parts, the manual model makes more demands on the purchasing and receiving activities than does the automatic camera. Jazon currently assigns only manufacturing costs to the two products. Overhead costs are collected in one plantwide pool and are assigned to the two products in proportion to the direct labor hours used by each product. All other costs are viewed as period costs.

Jazon budgets costs for all departments within the plant—both support departments like maintenance and purchasing, as well as production departments like machining and assembly. Departmental managers are evaluated and rewarded on their ability to control costs. Individual managerial performance is assessed by comparing actual costs with budgeted costs.

REQUIRED:

1. Is Jazon using a traditional or contemporary cost management system? Explain.
2. Assume that you want to design a more accurate cost accounting system. What changes would you need to make? Be specific. Explain why the changes you make will improve the accuracy of cost assignments.
3. What changes would need to be made to implement a contemporary operational control system? Explain why you believe the changes will offer improved control.

Solution

1. Given the description provided, we can conclude that Jazon uses a traditional cost management system. First, evidence exists that product costs are only determined by production costs. Apparently, the financial accounting system is driving the type of product cost information being produced. Second, only direct labor hours, a unit-based driver, are used to assign overhead costs. Since many overhead costs are likely to be caused by nonunit drivers, this also suggests a strong reliance on allocation for cost assignment. Third, the company attempts to control costs by encouraging departmental managers to meet budgeted levels of expenditures. The focus is on departmental performance rather than systemwide performance. Further, departmental performance is measured only by financial instruments.

2. Product costing accuracy can be improved by placing more emphasis on tracing and less on allocation. There is enough information provided to reveal that the two products make quite different demands on certain activities. Setup, receiving, and purchasing resources are clearly consumed differently by the two products. Furthermore, it is doubtful that direct labor hours would have anything to do with the two products' patterns of resource consumption for these three activities. Thus, using activity drivers that better reflect the differential resource consumption would improve the cost assignments. Jazon would need to assign costs to the activities using direct tracing and resource drivers and then assign the cost of the activities to the two products using activity drivers. Jazon also should consider the possibility of computing different— more managerially relevant—product costs such as value-chain costs and operational costs.

3. Jazon would need to change its control focus from managing costs to managing activities. This also would entail a shift in emphasis from departmental performance maximization to systemwide performance maximization. To bring about this change, Jazon will need to provide detailed information concerning activities. Since activities cause costs, managing activities is a more logical approach to controlling costs.

KEY TERMS

Absorption-costing (full-costing) income 46
Accounting information system 32
Activity 38
Activity drivers 40
Activity inputs 48
Activity output 49
Activity output measure 49
Activity-based cost system 57
Activity-based costing 40
Activity-based management 57
Administrative costs 45
Allocation 41
Assets 37
Batch-level activities 49
Batch-level drivers 50
Contemporary cost accounting system 57

Conversion cost 45
Cost 37
Cost accounting information system 36
Cost behavior 49
Cost management information system 33
Cost object 37
Cost of goods manufactured 46
Cost of goods sold 46
Direct costs 38
Direct labor 44
Direct materials 44
Direct tracing 39
Drivers 39
Driver tracing 39
Error costs 58
Expenses 37
Facility-level activities 50

Financial accounting information system 32
Fixed costs 50
Indirect costs 38
Loss 37
Marketing (selling) costs 45
Measurement costs 58
Mixed costs 54
Noninventoriable (period) costs 45
Nonproduction costs 43
Operational control information system 36
Optimal cost management system 58
Overhead 44
Prime cost 45
Product cost 42
Production costs 43

Product-level drivers 50
Product-level (sustaining) activities 50
Relevant range 51
Resource drivers 39
Service 42
Supplies 44
System 31
Tangible products 42
Traceability 39
Tracing 39
Traditional cost system 56
Traditional operation control system 56
Unit-level activities 49
Unit-level drivers 49
Value chain 34
Variable costs 52
Work in process 47

QUESTIONS FOR WRITING AND DISCUSSION

1. What is a system?
2. What is an accounting information system?
3. What is the difference between a financial accounting information system and a cost management information system?
4. What are the objectives of a cost management information system?
5. What is the value chain?
6. Why should the cost management system be integrated with the operational systems of the value chain?
7. Define and explain the two major subsystems of the cost management system.
8. What is a cost object? Give some examples.
9. What is an activity? Give some examples of activities within a manufacturing firm.
10. What is a direct cost? An indirect cost?
11. What does traceability mean? Tracing?
12. Explain the difference between direct tracing and driver tracing.
13. What is allocation?
14. What are drivers? Resource drivers? Activity Drivers? Give an example of a resource driver and an example of an activity driver.
15. Explain how driver tracing works.
16. What is a tangible product?
17. What is a service?
18. Explain how services differ from tangible products.
19. Give three examples of product cost definitions. Why do we need different product cost definitions?
20. Identify the three cost elements that determine the cost of making a product (for external reporting).
21. How do the income statements of a manufacturing firm and a service firm differ?
22. Explain why knowledge of cost behavior is useful information for a manager to have.
23. What are activity inputs? Activity outputs?
24. What role does the relevant range play in the definition of a fixed cost? A variable cost?
25. On a per-unit basis, fixed costs are variable and variable costs are fixed. Do you agree? Explain your reasoning.
26. Describe some of the major differences between a traditional cost management system and a contemporary cost management system.
27. When would a company choose a contemporary management cost system over a traditional system? What forces are moving firms to implement contemporary management cost systems?

EXERCISES AND PROBLEMS

2-1
Systems Concepts
LO 1

In general, systems are described by the following pattern: (1) interrelated parts, (2) processes, and (3) objectives. Operational models of systems also identify inputs and outputs. Consider the following list of items associated with an automotive system.

a. Engine
b. Fuel
c. Drive train
d. Oxygen
e. Safe, reliable transportation
f. Electrical system
g. Combustion
h. Energy
i. Movement

REQUIRED:

1. Classify the items into one of the following categories:
   a. Interrelated parts
   b. Processes
   c. Objectives
   d. Inputs
   e. Outputs

2. Draw an operational model for the automotive system.
3. Discuss how a cost management information system is similar to an automotive system. What are two major differences between the two systems? Use an operational model for the cost management information system to help illustrate your answer.

2-2
Cost Accounting Information System
LO 1

The items below are associated with a *cost accounting information system.*

a. Usage of direct materials
b. Assigning direct materials cost to each product
c. Direct labor cost incurrence
d. Depreciation on production equipment
e. Cost accounting personnel
f. Submitting a bid using product cost plus 25%
g. Power cost incurrence
h. Material handling cost incurrence
i. Computer
j. Assignment of direct labor costs to products
k. To cost out products
l. Deciding to continue making a part rather than buying it
m. Printer
n. Report that details individual product costs
o. Assignment of overhead costs to individual products

REQUIRED:

1. Classify the items into one of the following categories:
   a. Interrelated parts
   b. Processes
   c. Objectives
   d. Inputs
   e. Outputs
   f. User actions
2. Draw an operational model diagram that illustrates the cost accounting system—with the items used as examples for each component of the model.
3. Based on your operational model, identify which product cost definition is being used: value-chain, operating, or traditional.

2-3
Cost Assignment Methods
LO 2

Grant Company uses manufacturing cells to produce its products. One manufacturing cell produces alternators for automobiles. Suppose that the alternator manufacturing cell is the cost object. Assume that all or a portion of the following costs must be assigned to the cell.

a. Salary of cell supervisor *direct tracing*
b. Power to heat and cool the plant in which the cell is located *allocation*
c. Materials used to produce the alternators *direct tracing*
d. Maintenance for the cell's equipment (provided by the maintenance department) *driver tracing*
e. Labor used to produce alternators *direct tracing*
f. Cafeteria that services the plant's employees *driver tracing*
g. Depreciation on the plant *allocation*
h. Depreciation on equipment used to produce the alternators *direct tracing*
i. Ordering costs for materials used in production *driver tracing*
j. Engineering support (provided by the engineering department) *driver tracing*
k. Cost of maintaining plant and grounds *allocation*
l. Cost of plant's personnel office *driver tracing*
m. Property tax on plant and land *allocation*

cost driver - hours
cost driver - # of employees
cost driver - # of orders
cost driver - # of hours
cost driver - # of people hired

REQUIRED: Identify which cost assignment method would likely be used to assign the costs of each activity to the alternator manufacturing cell: direct tracing, driver tracing, or allocation. When driver tracing is selected, identify a potential activity driver that could be used for the tracing.

**2-4
Product Cost
Definitions**

LO 3

Three possible product cost definitions were introduced: (1) value-chain, (2) operating, and (3) traditional. Identify which of the three product cost definitions best fits the following situations (justify your choice):

a. Setting the price for a new product.
b. Valuation of finished goods inventories for external reporting.
c. Choosing among different products in order to maintain a product mix that will provide the company with a long-term sustainable competitive advantage.
d. Choosing among competing product designs.
e. Calculating cost of goods sold for external reporting.
f. Deciding whether or not to increase the price of an existing product.
g. Deciding whether to accept or to reject a special order, where the price offered is lower than the normal selling price.
h. Determining which of several potential new products should be developed, produced, and sold.

**2-5
Cost of Goods
Manufactured and
Sold**

LO 5

Thompson Company manufactures desk lamps. At the beginning of September, the following information was supplied by its accountant:

Raw materials inventory	$18,500
Work in process inventory	12,000
Finished goods inventory	10,200

During September, direct labor cost was $40,500, raw materials purchases were $80,000, and the total overhead cost was $105,750. The inventories at the end of September were:

Raw materials inventory	$16,800
Work in process inventory	23,500
Finished goods inventory	9,100

REQUIRED:

1. Prepare a cost of goods manufactured statement for September.
2. Prepare a cost of goods sold statement for September.

**2-6
Preparation of
Income Statement:
Manufacturing
Firm**

LO 4

Danan, Inc., manufactures a stuffed rabbit called Puggsy. Last year 50,000 rabbits were made and sold for $20 each. The actual unit cost for the stuffed rabbit is given below.

Direct materials	$ 2.00
Direct labor	3.00
Variable overhead	2.50
Fixed overhead	4.00
Total unit cost	$11.50

The only selling expenses were a commission of $2 per unit sold and advertising totaling $100,000. Administrative expenses, all fixed, equaled $50,000. There were no beginning and ending finished goods inventories.

REQUIRED: Prepare an absorption-costing income statement.

2-7
Cost of Goods Manufactured and Sold
LO 4

Morgon Company, a manufacturing firm, has supplied the following information from its accounting records for 1998:

Direct labor cost	$12,500
Purchases of raw materials	7,500
Supplies used	675
Factory insurance	350
Commissions paid	2,000
Factory supervision	1,225
Advertising	782
Material handling	2,745
Work in process inventory, Dec. 31, 1997	12,500
Work in process inventory, Dec. 31, 1998	14,250
Materials inventory, Dec. 31, 1997	3,475
Materials inventory, Dec. 31, 1998	2,000
Finished goods inventory, Dec. 31, 1997	5,685
Finished goods inventory, Dec. 31, 1998	3,250

REQUIRED:

1. Prepare a cost of goods manufactured statement.
2. Prepare a cost of goods sold statement.

2-8
Income Statement; Cost Concepts; Service Company
LO 3, 4

Bill Johnson owns and operates three Frazer Speedo outlets in Wichita, Kansas. Frazer Speedo is an oil and lubrication service outlet—one of many franchise outlets popular throughout the Midwest. The Frazer Speedo outlets also change transmission and power steering fluids. In May, purchases of materials equaled $80,000, the beginning inventory of material was $47,300, and the ending inventory of material was $15,250. Payments to direct labor during the month totaled $63,000. Overhead incurred was $110,000. The Wichita outlet also spent $5,000 on advertising during the month. A franchise fee of $2,000 per outlet is paid every month. Revenues for May were $400,000.

REQUIRED:

1. What was the cost of materials used for oil and lubrication services during May?
2. What was prime cost for May?
3. What was conversion cost for May?
4. What was total service cost for May?
5. Prepare an income statement for May.

2-9
Cost Behavior
LO 5

Morrison Company manufactures calculators. Based on past experience, Morrison has found that its total maintenance costs can be represented by the following formula: Maintenance cost = $100,000 + $2X, where X = Number of calculators. During 1998, Morrison produced 200,000 calculators. Actual maintenance costs for 1998 were as expected.

REQUIRED:

1. What is the activity and the activity driver for the activity?
2. What is the total maintenance cost incurred by Morrison in 1998?

3. What is the total fixed maintenance cost incurred by Morrison in 1998?
4. What is the total variable maintenance cost incurred by Morrison in 1998?
5. What is the maintenance cost per unit produced?
6. What is the fixed maintenance cost per unit?
7. What is the variable maintenance cost per unit?
8. Recalculate requirements 5, 6, and 7 for the following levels of production: (a) 100,000 units and (b) 400,000 units. Explain this outcome.

2-10
Activity
Classification
LO 5

Classify the following activities as unit-level, batch-level, product-level, or facility-level. Also identify a potential activity driver (output measure) for each activity.

a. Setting up equipment
b. Processing checks in a bank
c. Unloading shipments—raw materials
d. Desalinizing water (water treatment facility)
e. Shipping goods
f. Ordering supplies
g. Reworking products
h. Administering parts
i. Moving materials
j. Testing for blood type prior to an operation
k. Providing plant-wide security
l. Processing insurance claims
m. Providing space for production
n. Special product testing
o. Providing heating and air conditioning for the plant
p. Expediting batches of goods
q. Product support engineering

2-11
Cost Classification
LO 5

Classify the costs of activity inputs below as variable, fixed, or mixed. Identify the activity and the associated activity driver that allows you to define the cost behavior. For example, assume that the resource input is "cloth in a shirt." The activity would be "sewing shirts," the behavior "variable," and the driver "units produced." Prepare your answer in the following format:

Activity	Cost Behavior	Activity Driver
Sewing shirts	Variable	Units produced

a. Power to operate a drill
b. Engine in a lawn mower
c. Advertising
d. Sales commissions
e. Fuel for a forklift
f. Depreciation on a warehouse
g. Depreciation on a forklift used to move partially completed goods
h. X-ray film used in a radiology department of a hospital
i. Rental car provided for a client
j. Amalgam used by a dentist
k. Salaries, equipment, and materials used for setting up production equipment
l. Forms used to file insurance claims
m. Equipment, labor, and parts used to repair and maintain production equipment
n. Printing and postage for advertising circulars
o. Salaries, forms, and postage associated with purchasing

2-12
Cost Behavior;
Classification and
Graphing
LO 5

Smith Concrete Company owns ten ready-mix trucks. Each truck can deliver (on average) 10,000 cubic yards of concrete per year (considering the truck's capacity, weather, and distance to each job). One driver per truck is needed. The labor cost of each driver is $25,000 per year. Depreciation on each truck averages $20,000. Raw materials (cement, gravel, and so on) cost about $25 per cubic yard of cement.

REQUIRED:

1. Prepare a graph for each of three costs: truck drivers' wages, truck depreciation, and raw materials. Use the vertical axis for cost and the horizontal axis for cubic yards of cement. Assume that concrete sales range from 0 to 100,000 cubic yards.
2. Assume that the normal operating range for the company is 80,000 to 90,000 cubic yards per year. How would you classify each of the three types of cost?

2-13
Unit-Based
Activity Drivers
LO 5

A traditional cost accounting system relies on unit-based activity drivers to assign costs to cost objects. These drivers explain changes in cost attributable to changes in units produced. A unit-based driver measures usage of activity each and every time a unit is produced. Identify which of the following activity drivers explain changes in cost attributable to changes in the number of units produced. Classify the remaining drivers as batch-level, product-level, or facility-level.

a. Number of setups
b. Direct labor hours
c. Number of purchase orders
d. Kilowatt hours (machine-intensive production setting)
e. Machine hours
f. Number of material moves
g. Direct labor dollars
h. Direct material dollars
i. Number of inspection hours
j. Number of rework hours (rework hours are labor hours used to correct a defective or faulty product)

2-14
Cost Information
and Decision
Making; Unit and
Nonunit-Based
Drivers;
Contemporary
Versus Traditional
Systems
LO 5, 6

Wright Plastic Products is a small company that specialized in the production of plastic dinner plates until several years ago. Although profits for the company had been good, they have been declining in recent years because of increased competition. Many competitors offered a full range of plastic products, and management felt that this created a competitive disadvantage. The output of the plants owned by the company was exclusively devoted to plastic dinner plates. Three years ago, a decision to add additional product lines was made. Management determined that existing idle capacity in each plant could easily be adapted to produce other plastic products. Each plant would produce one additional product line. For example, the Atlanta plant would add a line of plastic cups. Moreover, the variable cost of producing a package of cups (one dozen) was virtually identical to that of a package of plastic plates. (Variable costs referred to here are those that change in total as the units produced change and include direct materials, direct labor, and unit-based variable overhead such as power and other machine costs.) Since the fixed expenses would not change, the new product was forecast to increase profits significantly (for the Atlanta plant).

Two years after the addition of the new product line, the profits of the Atlanta plant (as well as other plants) had not improved—in fact, they had actually dropped. Upon investigation, the president of the company discovered that profits had not increased as expected because the so-called fixed cost pool had increased dramatically. The president interviewed the manager of each support department at the Atlanta plant. Typical responses from four of those managers are given below.

Material Handling: The additional batches caused by the cups increased the demand for material handling. We had to add one fork lift and hire additional material-handling labor.

Inspection: Inspecting cups is more complicated than plastic plates. We only inspect a sample drawn from every batch, but you need to understand that the number of batches has increased with this new product line. We had to hire more inspection labor.

Purchasing: The new line increased the number of purchase orders. We had to use more resources to handle this increased volume.

Accounting: There were more transactions to process than before. We had to increase our staff.

REQUIRED:

1. Explain why the results of adding the new product line were not accurately projected.
2. Could this problem have been avoided with a contemporary cost management system? If so, would you recommend that the company adopt a contemporary system? Explain and discuss the differences between a contemporary cost management system and a traditional cost management system.

2-15
Systems Concepts;
Traditional Versus
Contemporary Cost
Accounting
Systems
LO 1, 6

The items below are associated with a *traditional cost accounting information system,* a *contemporary cost accounting information system,* or both (that is, some elements are common to the two systems).

a. Usage of direct materials
b. Direct materials cost assigned to products using direct tracing
c. Direct labor cost incurrence
d. Direct labor cost assigned to products using direct tracing
e. Setup cost incurrence
f. Setup cost assigned using number of setups as the activity driver
g. Setup cost assigned using direct labor hours as the activity driver
h. Cost accounting personnel
i. Submitting a bid using product cost plus 25%
j. Purchasing cost incurrence
k. Purchasing cost assigned to products using direct labor hours as the activity driver
l. Purchasing cost assigned to products using number of orders as the activity driver
m. Material handling cost incurrence
n. Material handling cost assigned using the number of moves as the activity driver
o. Material handling cost assigned using direct labor hours as the activity driver
p. Computer
q. To cost out products
r. Deciding to continue making a part rather than buy it
s. Printer
t. Customer service costs incurred
u. Customer service costs assigned to products using number of complaints as the activity driver
v. Report that details individual product costs
w. Commission costs
x. Commission costs assigned to products using units sold as the activity driver
y. Plant depreciation
z. Plant depreciation assigned to products using direct labor hours

REQUIRED:

1. For each cost system, classify the items into one of the following categories:
   a. Interrelated parts
   b. Processes
   c. Objectives
   d. Inputs
   e. Outputs
   f. User actions

Explain the choices that differ between the two systems. Which system will provide the best support for the user actions? Explain.

2. Draw an operational model diagram that illustrates each cost accounting system—with the items that belong to the system used as examples for each component of the model.

3. Based on the operational models, comment on the relative costs and benefits of the two systems. Which system should be chosen?

2-16
Contemporary
Versus Traditional
Operational
Control Systems
LO 1, 6

The actions listed below are associated with either a *contemporary operational control system* or a *traditional operational control system.*

a. Budgeted costs for the maintenance department are compared with the actual costs of the maintenance department.
b. The maintenance department manager receives a bonus for "beating" budget.
c. The costs of resources are traced to activities and then to products.
d. The purchasing department is set up as a responsibility center.
e. Activities are identified and listed.
f. Activities are categorized as adding value or not adding value to the organization.
g. A standard for a product's material usage cost is set and compared against the product's actual material usage cost.
h. The cost of performing an activity is tracked over time.
i. The distance between moves is identified as the cause of material-handling cost.
j. A purchasing agent is rewarded for buying parts below the standard price set by the company.
k. The cost of the material-handling activity is reduced dramatically by redesigning the plant layout.
l. An investigation is undertaken to find out why the actual labor cost for the production of 1,000 units is greater than the labor standard allowed.
m. The percentage of defective units is calculated and tracked over time.
n. Engineering has been given the charge to find a way to reduce setup time by 75%.
o. The manager of the receiving department lays off two receiving clerks so that the fourth-quarter budget can be met.

REQUIRED: Classify the above actions as belonging to either a contemporary operational control system or a traditional control system. Explain why you classified each action as a contemporary or traditional control feature.

2-17
Income Statement;
Cost of Goods
Manufactured
LO 3, 4

Hannibal Company produced 2,000 leather saddles during 1998. These saddles sell for $350 each. Hannibal had 250 saddles in finished goods inventory at the beginning of the year. At the end of the year, there were 350 saddles in finished goods inventory. Hannibal's accounting records provide the following information:

Purchases of raw materials	$160,000
Raw materials inventory, January 1, 1998	23,400
Raw materials inventory, December 31, 1998	33,400
Direct labor	100,000
Indirect labor	20,000
Rent, factory building	21,000
Depreciation, factory equipment	30,000
Utilities, factory	5,978
Salary, sales supervisor	55,000
Commissions, salespersons	38,000
General administration	61,000

Work in process inventory, January 1, 1998	$ 6,520
Work in process inventory, December 31, 1998	7,498
Finished goods inventory, January 1, 1998	40,000
Finished goods inventory, December 31, 1998	57,050

REQUIRED:

1. Prepare a cost of goods manufactured statement.
2. Compute the cost of producing one unit of product in 1998.
3. Prepare an income statement on an absorption-costing basis.

2-18
Cost of Goods Manufactured; Cost Identification; Solving for Unknowns
LO 2, 4

Golding Company creates, produces, and markets video games. Most of the games involve some sort of brain teaser. Harold Nonscents, the owner of Golding, is convinced that his employees must have strong analytical and problem-solving skills. Before any employee is hired, a puzzle of some sort must be successfully solved. The puzzle always relates to the employee's area of expertise. You are applying for a job as an entry-level accountant. The controller of the firm wishes to test your knowledge of basic cost terms and concepts and, at the same time, evaluate your analytical skills. The controller has gathered information (presented below) for one of Golding's plants (for 1998). The plant produces three different video games. The video games consume identical amounts of resources, and so each costs the same to produce. A study revealed that direct labor dollars is the best cost driver for overhead costs. No nonunit drivers were important causal factors. Direct materials and direct labor vary in direct proportion to the units produced.

a. Overhead cost formula: $Y = \$20,000 + 0.25X$, where X = Direct labor dollars.
b. Per-unit variable manufacturing cost (Direct materials + Direct labor + Variable overhead) is $20.
c. Total current variable manufacturing costs equal 200 percent of current conversion cost.
d. Units produced (of all types) were 10,000.
e. Beginning work in process is one-half the cost of ending work in process.
f. There are no beginning or ending inventories for raw materials or finished goods.
g. Cost of goods sold is $190,000.

REQUIRED: Prepare a statement of cost of goods manufactured for 1998.

2-19
Income Statement; Cost of Services Provided; Service Attributes
LO 3, 4

Kreative Company is a tax services firm. The firm is located in Chicago and employs 10 professionals and 5 staff. The firm does tax work for small businesses and well-to-do individuals. The following data are provided for the year ended July 31, 1998:

Returns processed	2,000
Returns in process, August 1, 1997	$60,000
Returns in process, July 31, 1998	$100,000
Cost of services sold	$890,000
Beginning direct materials inventory	$20,000
Purchases, direct materials	$40,000
Direct labor	$800,000
Overhead	$100,000
Administrative	$50,000
Selling	$60,000

REQUIRED:

1. Prepare a statement of cost of services sold.
2. Refer to the statement prepared in Requirement 1. What is the dominant cost? Will this always be true of service organizations? If not, provide an example of an exception.

3. Assuming that the average fee for processing a return is $700, prepare an income statement for Kreative Company.
4. Discuss three differences between services and tangible products. How do these differences affect the computations in Requirement 1?

2-20
Cost of Goods Manufactured; Income Statement
LO 3, 4

Lamson Company produces circuit boards that are used by manufacturers of microcomputers. For 1998, Lamson reported the following:

Work in process inventory, January 1	$ 12,500
Work in process inventory, December 31	12,500
Finished goods inventory, January 1 (24,000 units)	120,000
Finished goods inventory, December 31 (12,000 units)	60,000
Raw materials inventory, January 1	20,000
Raw materials inventory, December 31	30,000
Direct materials used	70,000
Direct labor	100,000
Plant depreciation	15,000
Salary, production supervisor	30,000
Indirect labor	20,000
Utilities, factory	6,000
Sales commissions	8,000
Salary, sales supervisor	20,000
Depreciation, factory equipment	5,000
Administrative costs	12,000
Supplies	4,000

Lamson produced 50,000 units during 1998 and sold 62,000 units at $12 per unit.

REQUIRED:

1. Prepare a statement of cost of goods manufactured. Calculate the full manufacturing cost per unit produced.
2. Prepare an absorption-costing income statement.

2-21
Cost Behavior; Contemporary Versus Traditional Cost Systems; Multiple Drivers
LO 2, 5, 6

Oliphant, Inc., produces electronic circuit boards. One plant, located in White Plains, New York, produces a circuit board used in VCRs (this is the only product produced by the plant). A manufacturing cost formula based on direct labor hours for this product is given below.

Total manufacturing costs = $300,000 + $15X (where X is direct labor hours)

The plant is producing 10,000 units per year but has the capacity to produce 15,000. Market conditions will likely not permit any expansion of production for the VCR circuit board. The company, however, is exploring the possibility of adding a new product: a circuit board for small television sets. Existing equipment can be adapted to produce the product (the two boards would be produced in batches, allowing the equipment to be set up for each type of board). Engineers estimate that the same direct labor hours will be used per unit. Given this information, the controller argues that the same variable cost per direct labor hour will be incurred. The controller also notes that the fixed costs will remain at $300,000—after all, these costs should not change as production activity increases. Thus, the manufacturing cost formula will not change for the two-product setting.

Before making a final decision on the new product, a consultant was hired to assess the impact of the new product on the costs of the firm. The consultant identified three major activities in the firm that would be affected by the new product: purchasing, engineering, and setting up equipment. The costs of purchasing and engineering were currently viewed as fixed costs. However, the consultant noted that the costs actually varied in response to nonunit activity drivers—and that the demand for these activities (as measured by the drivers) would increase with the addition of a new product. She also noted that moving from a single product to a multiple-product setting would add a new overhead activity: the need to reconfigure the equipment so that the products can be produced in batches. Based on further analysis, the remaining manufacturing costs were lumped together, since the consultant believed that their cost behavior could be explained by direct labor hours, a unit-based activity driver. The consultant then assigned costs (by tracing) to the three nonunit-driven overhead activities. Finally, the following cost formulas were developed using four different activity drivers:

Purchasing cost = $40,000 + $30X_1$, where X_1 = Number of purchase orders
Engineering cost = $50,000 + $100X_2$, where X_2 = Number of engineering orders
Setup costs = $15,000 + $1,000X_3$, where X_3 = Number of setups
Remaining overhead cost = $100,000 + $15X_4$, where X_4 = Direct labor hours

The consultant also provided the following estimates of activity demands for each product:

	VCR Board	Television Board
Units of product	10,000	5,000
Direct labor hours	20,000	10,000
Purchase orders	2,000	2,000
Engineering orders	500	1,000
Setups	10	10

REQUIRED:

1. Calculate the total cost of producing the VCR circuit boards without the new product. Do you think this cost is accurate? Explain.
2. Using only the original direct-labor-hour cost formula, calculate the total cost of producing both products.
3. Using the cost formulas developed by the consultant, calculate the total cost of producing both products. Explain why the two numbers differ. Which approach do you think provides the more accurate prediction and why?
4. Using only the variable cost portion of the original unit-based cost formula, calculate the variable cost per unit for each product. Now calculate the cost per unit using the variable elements from each of the consultant's formulas. Which method produces the most accurate cost assignments? Explain.
5. Explain the role that direct tracing, resource drivers, and activity drivers may have played in the consulting engagement.

2-22
Cost Classification;
Income Statement;
Unit-Based Cost
Behavior; Service
Organization
LO 2, 3, 4, 5

Gateway Construction Company is a family-operated business, founded in 1950 by Samuel Gateway. In the beginning, the company consisted of Gateway and three employees laying gas, water, and sewage pipelines as subcontractors. Currently, the company employs 25 to 30 people and is directed by Jack Gateway, Samuel's son. The main line of business continues to be laying pipeline.

Most of Gateway's work comes from contracts with city and state agencies. All of the company's work is located in the state of Nebraska. The company's sales volume averages $3.0 million, and profits vary between 0 and 10 percent of sales.

Sales and profits have been somewhat below average for the past three years due to a recession and intense competition. Because of this competition, Jack Gateway is constantly reviewing the prices that other companies bid for jobs. When a bid is lost, he makes every attempt to analyze the reasons for the differences between his bid and that of his competitors. He uses this information to increase the competitiveness of future bids.

Jack has become convinced that Gateway's current accounting system is deficient. Currently, all expenses are simply deducted from revenues to arrive at net income. No effort is made to distinguish among the costs of laying pipe, obtaining contracts, and administering the company. Yet all bids are based on the costs of laying pipe.

Jack also knows that knowledge of cost behavior is important. He is certain that the company could offer more competitive bids if he knew which costs were variable and which were fixed. For example, Gateway often has idle equipment (the company needs more equipment than is often necessary so that it can bid on larger projects). If Gateway could bid enough to cover its variable costs and use the idle equipment, equipment operators could be more productively utilized and have more job stability. In fact, if the bid covered more than variable costs, profits would increase as well, since the fixed costs remain unchanged for increased activity.

With these thoughts in mind, Jack began a careful review of the income statement for the previous year (shown below). First, he noted that jobs were priced on the basis of equipment hours, with an average price of $165 per equipment hour. However, when it came to classifying costs and identifying their behavior, he decided that he needed some help. One thing that really puzzled him was how to classify his own salary of $114,000. About half of his time was spent in bidding and securing contracts, and the other half was spent in general administrative matters.

Gateway Construction Company
Income Statement
For the Year Ended December 31, 1998

Sales (18,200 equipment hours at $165)		$3,003,000
Less: Expenses		
Utilities	$ 24,000	
Wages of machine operators	218,000	
Rent (office building)	24,000	
CPA fees	20,000	
Other direct labor	265,700	
Administrative salaries	114,000	
Supervisor salaries	70,000	
Pipe	1,401,340	
Tires and fuel	418,600	
Depreciation, equipment	198,000	
Salaries of mechanics	50,000	
Advertising	15,000	
Total expenses		2,818,640
Net income		$ 184,360

REQUIRED:

1. Classify the costs shown in the income statement as: (1) costs of laying pipe (production costs); (2) costs of securing contracts (selling costs); and (3) costs of general administration. For production costs, identify direct materials, direct labor, and overhead costs. The company never has significant work in process (most jobs are started and completed within a day).

2. Using the functional classification developed in requirement 1, prepare an absorption-costing income statement. What is the average cost per equipment hour for laying pipe?
3. Assume that the only significant activity driver is equipment hours. Also assume that costs are either strictly fixed or strictly variable. Classify the costs as fixed or variable. Build a cost formula that describes Gateway's cost structure.
4. Suppose that Jack has idle equipment and wants to prepare a bid for a prospective job. He is confident that a bid of $140 will win the job. Describe how knowledge of cost behavior (see Requirement 3) can help him with the bidding decision.

2-23
Cost Information and Ethical Behavior; Service Organization

LO 2

Joann Wilson, manager and owner of an architectural company in Atlanta, Georgia, had arranged a meeting with Kit Applegate, the chief accountant of a large, local competitor. Joann and Kit were first cousins and had grown up together in a small town in western Georgia.

Kit was a competent, successful accountant but currently was experiencing some personal financial difficulties. The problems were created by some medical bills caused by his son's serious illness, leaving Kit with a $20,000 debt to pay off—just at the time that his oldest daughter was scheduled to enter college.

Joann, on the other hand, was struggling to establish a successful architectural business. She had recently acquired the rights to open a branch office of a large regional architectural firm headquartered in Orlando, Florida. During her first two years, she had managed to build a small, profitable practice. However, the chance to gain a significant foothold in the Atlanta architectural market hinged on the success of winning a bid to do the architectural work for Georgia's new state office building. The meeting Joann had scheduled with Kit concerned the bid she planned to submit.

"Kit, I'm at a critical point in my business venture. If I can win the bid for the state's architectural dollars, I'll be set. Winning the bid will bring $600,000 to $700,000 of revenues into the firm. On top of that, I estimate that the publicity will bring another $200,000 to $300,000 of new business."

"I understand," replied Kit. "My boss is anxious to win that business as well. It would mean a huge increase in profits for my firm. It's a competitive business, though. As new as you are, I doubt that you'll have much chance of winning."

"You may be wrong. You're forgetting two very important considerations. First, I have the backing of all the resources and talent of a regional firm. Second, I have some political connections. Last year, I was heavily involved in the governor's campaign. I was the co-chair for fund raising. He was impressed with my work and would like me to have this business. I am confident that the proposals I submit will be very competitive. My only concern is to submit a bid that beats your firm. If I come in with a lower bid and with good proposals, the governor can see to it that I get the work."

"Sounds promising. If you do win, however, there will be a lot of upset people. After all, they are going to claim that the business should have been given to local architects, not to some out-of-state firm. Given the size of your office, you'll have to get support from Orlando. You could take a lot of heat."

"True. But I am the owner of the branch office. That fact alone should blunt most of the criticism. Who can argue that I'm not a local? Listen, with your help, I think I can win this bid. Furthermore, if I do win it, you can reap some direct benefits. With that kind of business, I can afford to hire an accountant, and I'll make it worthwhile for you to transfer jobs. I can offer you an up-front bonus of $20,000. That's been authorized by Orlando. They really want a strong branch in Atlanta. On top of that, I'll increase your annual salary by 20 percent. That should solve most of your financial difficulties. After all, we have been close from childhood—and as you know, a family needs to help each other. Right?

"Joann, my wife would be ecstatic if I were able to improve our financial position as quickly as this opportunity affords. I certainly hope that you win the bid. What kind of help can I provide?"

"Simple. To win, all I have to do is beat the bid of your firm. Before I submit my bid, I would like you to review it. With the financial skills you have, it should be easy for you to spot any excessive costs that I may have included. Or perhaps I included the wrong kind of costs. By cutting excessive costs and eliminating costs that may not be directly related to the project, my bid should be competitive enough to meet or beat your firm's bid."

"Joann, this sounds good, but what would people think if you won the bid and I then went to work for your firm? Wouldn't they be suspicious? After all, most think my firm has the best chance of getting the job. If they ever found out that I reviewed your work, I would be in big trouble. And it wouldn't take much for the press to find out we're related."

"Well, you have a point. We need to be very careful. I think I can arrange a bigger bonus. Perhaps working for me isn't such a good idea. With my connections, however, I think I can arrange for a lucrative state job—perhaps somewhere in the state audit agency."

REQUIRED:

1. What would you do if you were Kit? Fully explain the reasons for your choice.
2. What is the likely outcome if Kit agrees to review the bid? What concerns did Kit express? Should these concerns be a factor in the decision? Essentially, should Kit be more interested in Joann's modified proposal (more bonus and a government job)? Should the likelihood of "getting caught" have any bearing on Kit's decision?
3. Apply the code of ethics for management accountants (see Chapter 1) to the proposal given Kit. What standards would be violated if Kit agrees to review the bid? Assume that Kit is a member of the IMA and holds a CMA.

Chapter 3
Activity Cost Behavior

Starbucks started out as a coffee house in Seattle and expanded rapidly throughout the Pacific and the Mountain West. The cost behavior of Starbucks' many activities is a crucial input in a variety of management decisions—from where to expand next, to the number of flavors offered, to the types of complementary merchandise offered in their stores. The people in the photograph are taste-testing flavors in Starbucks' lab. What activities do you see? How would you classify them?

LEARNING OBJECTIVES

After studying this chapter, you should be able to:

1. Define and describe cost behavior, and explain the role of the resource usage model in understanding cost behavior.
2. Separate mixed costs into their fixed and variable components using the high-low method, the scatterplot method, and the method of least squares.
3. Evaluate the reliability of a cost formula.
4. Explain how multiple regression can be used to assess cost behavior.
5. Discuss the use of managerial judgment in determining cost behavior.

Costs can display variable, fixed, or mixed behavior. Knowing how costs change as activity output changes is an essential part of planning, controlling, and decision making. For example, budgeting, deciding to keep or drop a product line, and evaluating the performance of a segment all benefit from knowledge of cost behavior. In fact, not knowing and understanding cost behavior can lead to poor—even disastrous—decisions. This chapter discusses cost behavior in depth so that a proper foundation is laid for its use in studying other cost management topics. A variable-costing system, for example, requires that all costs be classified as fixed or variable. But can all costs realistically be classified into one of these two categories? What are the assumptions and limitations associated with classifying costs in this way? Furthermore, just how good are our definitions of variable and fixed costs? Finally, what procedures can we use to break out the fixed and variable components of mixed costs? How do we assess the reliability of these procedures?

COST BEHAVIOR AND THE RESOURCE USAGE MODEL

Objective 1
Define and describe cost behavior, and explain the role of the resource usage model in understanding cost behavior.
cost behavior

Cost behavior is the general term for describing whether a cost is fixed or variable in relation to changes in the levels of activity output. A cost that remains the same in total as activity output increases or decreases is a fixed cost. A variable cost is one that increases in total with an increase in activity output and decreases in total with a decrease in activity output. In economics, it is usually *assumed* that fixed and variable costs are known. Management accountants must deal with the requirements to assess fixed and variable costs. Practical assessment of cost behavior requires consideration of time horizon, resource usage, and activity output measurement. Knowing these concepts helps us understand the difficulties and problems associated with assessing cost behavior.

Time Horizon

long run
short run

Determining whether a cost is fixed or variable depends on the time horizon. According to economics, in the **long run**, all costs are variable; in the **short run**, at least one cost is fixed. But how long is the short run? Different costs have different length short runs. Direct materials, for example, are relatively easy to adjust. Starbucks Coffee, shown in the picture at the beginning of this chapter, may treat coffee beans (a direct material) as strictly variable, even though for the next few hours the amount already on hand is fixed. The lease of space for their coffee shop in Cherry Creek, however, is more difficult to adjust; it may run for one or more years. Thus, this cost is typically seen as fixed. The length of the short-run period depends to some extent on management judgment and the purpose for which cost behavior is being estimated. For example, submitting a bid on a one-time, special order may span only a month—long enough to create a bid and produce the order. Other types of decisions, such as product discontinuance or product mix decisions, will affect a much longer period of time. In this case, the costs that must be considered are long-run variable costs, including product design, product development, market development, and market penetration. Short-run costs often do not adequately reflect all the costs necessary to design, produce, market, distribute, and support a product. Recently, there have been some new insights that help shed light on the nature of long-run and short-run cost behavior.[1] These insights relate to activities and the resources needed to enable an activity to be performed.

Activities, Resource Usage, and Cost Behavior

activity capacity

Activity capacity is simply the ability to perform activities. To perform an activity, capacity must be acquired. How much capacity is needed depends on the level of performance required for each activity. Usually we can assume that the activity capacity needed corresponds to the level where the activity is performed efficiently. This efficient level of activity performance is called **practical capacity**. *Resources* are needed to enable activities to be performed. **Resources** are simply economic elements that are consumed in performing activities. **Resource spending** is the cost of *acquiring* capacity to perform an activity. **Resource usage** is the *amount* of activity capacity used in producing an activity's output. Thus, resource usage is equivalent to activity output. If all of the activity capacity acquired is not used, then we have **unused capacity**, which is the difference between the acquired capacity and the actual activity output. The relationship between resource spending and resource usage can be used to define variable and fixed cost behavior. To see how, we need to understand how resources are supplied.

practical capacity
resources
resource spending
resource usage

unused capacity

Resources are supplied in one of two ways: (1) as used (and needed) and (2) in advance of usage. **Resources supplied as used and needed** are those that are acquired from outside sources, where the terms of acquisition do not require any long-term commitment for any given amount of the resource. Thus, the organization is free to buy only the quantity of resource needed. As a result, the quantity of the resource supplied equals the quantity demanded. There is no unused activity capacity for this category of resources (resource usage = resources supplied). **Resources supplied in advance of usage** are those acquired by the use of either an explicit or implicit contract to obtain a given quantity of resource, regardless of whether the quantity of the resource available is fully used or not. Resources supplied in advance may exceed the demand for their usage; thus, unused capacity is possible.

resources supplied as
used and needed

resources supplied in
advance of usage

Resources Supplied As Needed and Cost Behavior Since the cost of the resources supplied as needed equals the cost of resources used, the total cost of the resource increases as demand for the resource increases. Thus, we generally can treat the cost of resources supplied as needed as a variable cost. For example, in a just-in-time manufacturing environment, materials are acquired and used as needed. Using units produced as the activity output measure or activity driver, it is clear that as the units produced increase, the usage (and cost) of raw materials would increase proportionately. Similarly, power is acquired and used as needed. Using kilowatt hours as the activity output measure (activity driver), as the demand for power increases, the cost of power increases. Note that in both examples, resource supply and usage is measured by an activity output measure (activity driver).

Resources Supplied in Advance and Cost Behavior Many resources are acquired before the actual demands for the resource are realized. There are two examples of this category of resource acquisition. First, organizations acquire many *multi-*

---

1.   The concepts presented in the remainder of this section are based on the following two articles: Alfred M. King, "The Current Status of Activity-Based Costing: An Interview with Robin Cooper and Robert S. Kaplan," *Management Accounting,* September 1991, pp. 22–26; Robin Cooper and Robert S. Kaplan, "Activity-Based Systems: Measuring the Costs of Resource Usage," *Accounting Horizons,* September 1992, pp. 1–13.

period service capacities by paying cash up front or by entering into an explicit contract that requires periodic cash payments. Buying or leasing buildings and equipment are examples of this form of advance resource acquisition. The annual expense associated with the multiperiod category is independent of actual usage of the resource; thus, these expenses can be defined as fixed expenses. They essentially correspond to **committed fixed expenses**—costs incurred that provide long-term activity capacity.

committed fixed
expenses

A second and more important example concerns organizations that acquire resources in advance through implicit contracts—usually with their employees. These implicit contracts require an ethical focus, since they imply that the organization will maintain employment levels even though there may be temporary downturns in the quantity of activity used. One way companies manage the difficulties associated with maintaining this fixed level of expense is by using contingent, or temporary, workers when needed. Companies state that the key reason for the use of contingent workers is flexibility—in meeting demand fluctuations, in controlling downsizing, and in buffering core workers against job loss.[2]

discretionary fixed
expenses

Resource spending for this category essentially corresponds to **discretionary fixed expenses**—costs incurred for the acquisition of short-term activity capacity. Hiring three sustaining engineers for $150,000 who can supply the capacity of processing 7,500 change orders is an example of implicit contracting (change orders is the driver used to measure resource capacity and usage).[3] Certainly, none of the three engineers would expect to be laid off if only 5,000 change orders were actually processed—unless, of course, the downturn in demand is viewed as being permanent.

Implications for Control and Decision Making The activity-based resource usage model just described can improve both managerial control and decision making. Operational control information systems encourage managers to pay more attention to controlling resource usage and spending. For example, a well-designed operational system would allow managers to assess the changes in resource demands that will occur from new product mix decisions. Adding new, customized products may increase the demand for various overhead activities; if sufficient unused activity capacity does not exist, then resource spending must increase. Similarly, if activity management brings about excess activity capacity (by finding ways to reduce resource usage), managers must carefully consider what is to be done with the excess capacity. Eliminating the excess capacity may decrease resource spending and thus improve overall profits. Alternatively, using the excess capacity to increase output could increase revenues without a corresponding increase in resource spending. How resource usage and spending are affected by managing activities is more fully explored in Chapter 20.

The activity-based resource usage model also allows managers to calculate the changes in resource supply and demand resulting from implementing such decisions as make or buy, accept or reject special orders, and keep or drop product lines. Additionally, the model increases the power of a number of traditional management accounting decision-making models. The impact on decision making is explored in the decision-making chapters found in Part 3 (Chapters 10–15). Most of the decision-making models in those chapters depend heavily on knowledge of cost behavior.

2.   "Contingent Employment On The Rise," *Deloitte and Touche Review,* September 4, 1995, pp. 1–2.
3.   Often, in response to customer feedback and competitive pressures, products and processes need to be redesigned or modified. An engineering change order is the document that initiates this process.

Measures of Activity Output

Variable costs move in total with changes in activity output. Fixed costs, however, remain unchanged as activity output changes. Thus, describing cost behavior requires measurement of activity output. From Chapter 2, we know that activity output is measured by activity drivers. Therefore, in order to understand the behavior of costs we must first determine the underlying activities and the associated drivers that measure activity capacity and output. The need to understand this cost-activity relationship leads us to the determination of an appropriate measure of activity output, or activity driver. For example, material handling output may be measured by number of moves, shipping goods output by the units sold, and laundering hospital bedding output by pounds of laundry. The choice of driver is tailored not only to the particular firm but also to the particular activity or cost being measured.

activity output (usage)   Activity drivers explain changes in activity costs by measuring changes in **activity output (usage).** There are two general categories of activity drivers: unit-level drivers and nonunit-level drivers. Unit-level drivers explain changes in cost as units produced change. Pounds of direct materials, kilowatt hours used to run production machinery, and direct labor hours are examples of unit-based activity drivers. Nonunit-level drivers explain changes in cost as factors other than units change. There are three nonunit-level categories: batch-level, product-level, and facility-level. Batch-level costs tend to vary as the number of batches changes. Product-level costs tend to change as the number of different products increases. Facility-level costs tend to stay constant and can be viewed as globally fixed costs—at least for the short run. Examples of nonunit-based activity output measures include setups, work orders, engineering change orders, inspection hours, and material moves.

In a traditional cost management system, cost behavior is assumed to be described by unit-based drivers only. In a contemporary cost management system, both unit- and nonunit-based drivers are used. Thus, the contemporary system tends to produce a much richer view of cost behavior than traditional systems. There is also a need, however, to identify cost behavior patterns for a much broader set of activities.

We now take a closer look at variable and fixed activity costs. If the cost-behavior pattern of an activity is strictly variable or fixed, then that cost can be assigned to the appropriate category. For mixed cost settings, we must break out their variable and fixed components so that each component can be assigned to the correct category. From Chapter 2, we know that a linear cost function with fixed and variable components may not exactly correspond to how costs actually behave. The underlying cost function may actually be nonlinear. What we hope is that classifying cost behavior as either fixed or variable (or mixed) approximates reality well enough to be useful. To illustrate, it is useful to consider the use of fixed and variable cost categories when cost behavior follows a step function.

Step-Cost Behavior

In our discussion of cost behavior, we have assumed that the cost function (be it linear or nonlinear) is continuous. In reality, some cost functions may be discontinuous, as shown in Exhibit 3-1. This type of cost function is known as a *step function.* A **step-cost function** has the property of displaying a constant level of cost for a range of activity output and then jumping to a higher level of cost at some point, where it remains for a similar range of activity. In Exhibit 3-1, the

step-cost function

Exhibit 3-1
Step-Cost Function

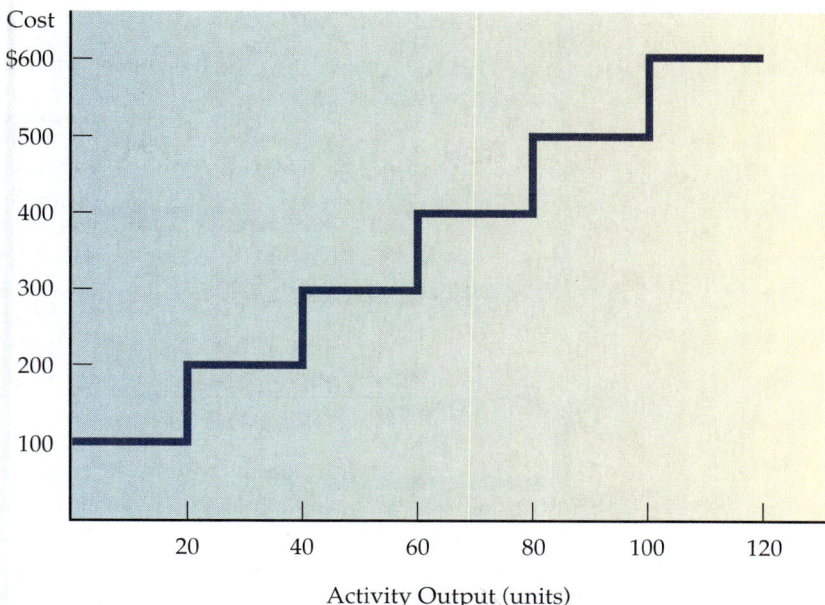

cost is $100 as long as activity output is between 0 and 20 units. If the volume is between 20 and 40 units, the cost jumps to $200.

Step-Variable Costs Items that display a step-cost behavior must be purchased in chunks. The width of the step defines the range of activity output for which a quantity of the resource must be acquired. The width of the step in Exhibit 3-1 is 20 units of activity. If the width of the step is narrow, as in Exhibit 3-1, the cost of the resource changes in response to fairly small changes in resource usage (as measured by activity output). Costs that follow a step-cost behavior with narrow **step-variable costs** steps are defined as **step-variable costs**. If the width of the step is narrow, we usually approximate step-variable costs with a strictly-variable cost assumption.

Step-Fixed Costs In reality, many so-called fixed costs probably are best described by a step-cost function. Many resources acquired in advance of usage—particularly those that involve implicit contracting—follow a step-cost function. Suppose, for example, that a company hires three sustaining engineers—engineers who are responsible for redesigning existing products to meet customer requirements. By hiring the engineers, the company has acquired the ability to perform an activity: engineering redesign. The salaries paid the engineers represent the cost of acquiring the engineering redesign capacity, and the number of engineering changes that can be *efficiently* processed by the three engineers is a quantitative measure of that capacity. The number of change orders processed, on the other hand, is a measure of the actual usage. Assume the engineers are each paid an annual salary of $50,000 and that each engineer can process 2,500 engineering change orders per year. The company has acquired the capacity to process 7,500 (3 × 2,500) change orders per year at a total cost of $150,000 (3 × $50,000). The nature of the resource requires that the capacity be acquired in chunks (one engineer hired at a time). The cost function for this example is displayed in Exhibit 3-2. Notice that the width of the steps is 2,500 units—a much wider step than the cost function displayed in Exhibit 3-1. Costs that follow a step-cost behavior **step-fixed costs** with wide steps are defined as **step-fixed costs**.

Exhibit 3-2
Step-Fixed Costs

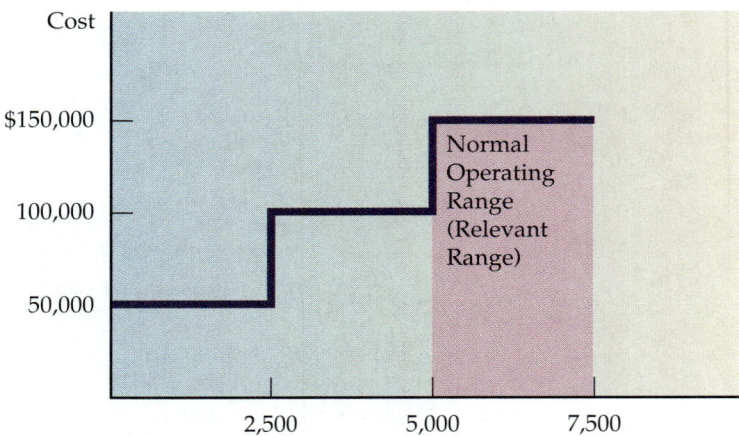

Activity Output: Number of Engineering Change Orders

In terms of treatment, step-fixed costs are assigned to the fixed cost category. Most step-fixed costs are fixed over the normal operating range of a firm. If that range is 5,000 to 7,500 change orders (as shown in Exhibit 3-2), then the firm will spend $150,000 on engineering resources. This is equivalent to spending $20 per change order ($150,000/7,500). The average unit cost, obtained by dividing the resource expenditure by the activity's practical capacity, is the **activity rate**. The activity rate is used to calculate the cost of resource usage and of unused activity.

For example, during the year, the company may not actually process 7,500 orders—that is, all of the available order-processing capacity may not be used. Resource usage is the number of change orders *actually* processed. Assume that 6,000 change orders were processed during the year. The **cost of resource usage** is the activity rate × the actual activity output: $20 × 6,000 = $120,000. Further, the **cost of unused activity** is the activity rate × the unused activity: $20 × 1,500 = $30,000. Note that the cost of unused capacity occurs because the resource (engineering redesign) must be acquired in lumpy (whole) amounts. Even if the company had anticipated the need for only 6,000 change orders, it would have been difficult to hire the equivalent of 2.4 engineers (6,000/2,500).

The example illustrates that when resources are acquired in advance, there may be a difference between the *resources supplied* and the *resources used (demanded)* to perform activities. This can only occur for activity costs that display a fixed cost behavior (resources acquired in advance of usage). Typically, the traditional cost management system provides information only about the cost of the resources supplied. A contemporary cost management system, on the other hand, tells us how much of the activity is used and the cost of its usage. Furthermore, the relationship between resources supplied and resources used is expressed by either of the following two equations:

$$\text{Activity availability} = \text{Activity output} + \text{Unused capacity} \qquad (3.1)$$

$$\text{Cost of activity supplied} = \text{Cost of activity used} + \text{Cost of unused activity} \qquad (3.2)$$

Equation 3.1 expresses the relationship between supply and demand in physical units, while Equation 3.2 expresses it in financial terms.

Margin terms: activity rate / cost of resource usage / cost of unused activity

For the engineering order example, the relationships appear as follows:

Physical units (Equation 3.1):

$$\text{Available orders} = \text{Orders used} + \text{Orders unused}$$
$$7,500 \text{ orders} = 6,000 \text{ orders} + 1,500 \text{ orders}$$

Financial terms (Equation 3.2):

$$\text{Cost of orders supplied} = \text{Cost of orders used} + \text{Cost of unused orders}$$
$$\$150,000 = \$120,000 + \$30,000$$

Activities and Mixed Cost Behavior

Since it is possible that activities may have resources associated with them that are acquired in advance and resources that are acquired as needed, activity costs can display a mixed cost behavior. Assume that a plant has its own power department. The plant has acquired long-term capacity for supplying power by investing in building and equipment (resources acquired in advance). The plant also acquires fuel to produce power as needed (resources acquired as needed). The cost of building and equipment is independent of the kilowatt hours produced, but the cost of fuel increases as the demand for kilowatt hours increases. The activity of supplying power has both a fixed cost component and a variable cost component, using kilowatt hours as the activity output measure.

As the power plant example reveals, mixed costs have a fixed and a variable component. Now let's consider a more specific example. Assume that a firm leases a photocopier. The lease agreement calls for a lease payment of $3,000 paid at the beginning of each year. The firm is responsible for paying for the operating costs, which average $0.02 per copy and cover the cost of toner, paper, and maintenance. The copier is leased for five years and has the capability of producing 600,000 copies. Thus, the $3,000 represents the cost of resources acquired in advance of usage, and the $0.02 represents the cost of acquiring resources as needed and used. The cost behavior for the copying activity is expressed by the following equation:

$$Y = \$3,000 + \$0.02X$$
$$\text{where } Y = \text{Total cost per year}$$
$$X = \text{The number of copies per year}$$

The fixed charge of $3,000 makes the copying capacity available, but use of that capacity also produces a cost. In fact, for every copy produced, the company must pay an additional $0.02. The more copies made, the more the company must pay. If 100,000 copies are made during the year, then the total cost is $5,000 [$3,000 + ($0.02 × 100,000)]. If 150,000 copies are produced, total cost is $6,000 [$3,000 + ($0.02 × 150,000)]. Total cost increases as the activity increases, but regardless of how many copies are made, the company must pay at least $3,000. Exhibit 3-3 displays the mixed cost relationship. Notice that at zero units of activity output, there is some cost. As activity output increases, total cost increases.

What the Accounting Records Reveal Sometimes it is easy to identify the variable and fixed components of a mixed cost, as in the photocopier example. Many times, however, the only information available is the total cost of an activity and a measure of activity output (the variables Y and X). For example, the accounting system will usually record both the total cost of the maintenance activity for a given period and the number of maintenance hours provided during that period.

Exhibit 3-3
Mixed Cost

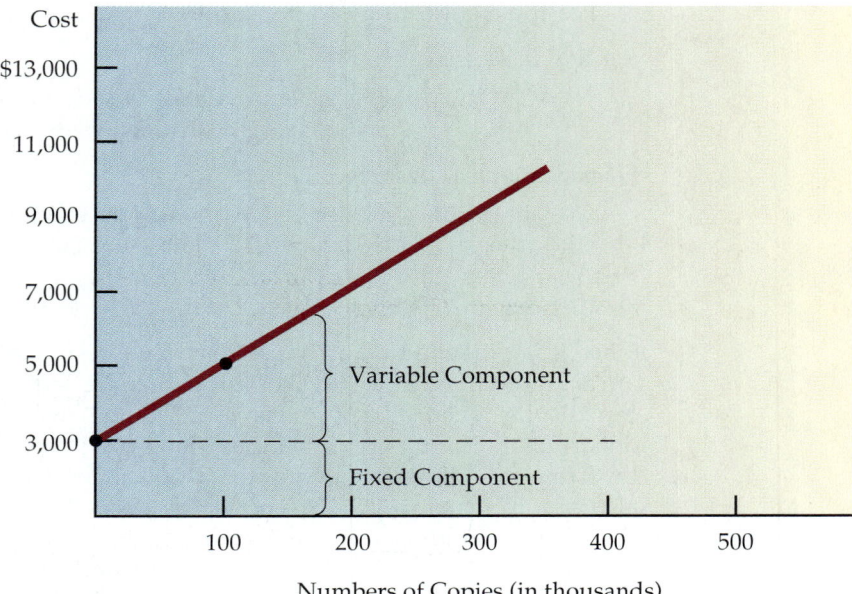

Numbers of Copies (in thousands)

How much of the total maintenance cost represents a fixed charge and how much represents a variable charge is not revealed by the accounting records. (In fact, the accounting records may not even reveal the breakdown of costs in the photocopier example.) Often, the total cost is simply recorded with no attempt to segregate the fixed and variable costs.

Need for Cost Separation Since accounting records typically reveal only the total cost and the associated activity output of a mixed cost item, it is necessary to separate the total cost into its fixed and variable components. Only through a formal effort to separate costs can all costs be classified into the appropriate cost behavior categories.

   If mixed costs are a very small percentage of total costs, however, formal cost separation may be more trouble than it's worth. In this case, mixed costs could be assigned to either the fixed- or variable-cost category without much concern for the classification error or its effect on decision making. Alternatively, the total mixed cost could be arbitrarily divided between the two cost categories. This option is seldom available though. Mixed costs for many firms are large enough to warrant separation. Given the need for separating costs, how is it done?

METHODS FOR SEPARATING MIXED COSTS INTO FIXED AND VARIABLE COMPONENTS

Objective 2
Separate mixed costs into their fixed and variable components using the high-low method, the scatterplot method, and the method of least squares.

There are three widely used methods of separating a mixed cost into its fixed and variable components: the high-low method, the scatterplot method, and the method of least squares. Each method requires us to make the simplifying assumption of a linear cost relationship. Therefore, before we examine each of these methods more closely, let's review the expression of cost as an equation for a straight line.

$$Y = F + VX$$

where Y = Total activity cost (the dependent variable)
  F = Fixed cost component (the intercept parameter)
  V = Variable cost per unit of activity (the slope parameter)
  X = Measure of activity output (the independent variable)

dependent variable

independent variable

intercept parameter

slope parameter

The **dependent variable** is a variable whose value depends on the value of another variable. In the above equation, total activity cost is the dependent variable; it is the cost we are trying to predict. The **independent variable** is a variable that measures activity output and explains changes in the activity cost. It is an activity driver. The choice of an independent variable is related to its economic plausibility. That is, the manager will attempt to find an independent variable that causes or is closely associated with the dependent variable. The **intercept parameter** corresponds to fixed activity cost. Graphically, the intercept parameter is the point at which the mixed cost line intercepts the cost (vertical) axis. The **slope parameter** corresponds to the variable cost per unit of activity. Graphically, this represents the slope of the mixed cost line.

Since the accounting records reveal only X and Y, those values must be used to estimate the parameters F and V. With estimates of F and V, the fixed and variable components can be estimated, and the behavior of the mixed cost can be predicted as activity output changes. Three methods will be described for estimating F and V. These methods are the high-low method, the scatterplot method, and the method of least squares.

The same data will be used with each method so that comparisons among them can be made. The data have been accumulated for a material-handling activity. The plant manager believes that the number of material moves is a good activity driver for the activity. Assume that the accounting records of Anderson Company disclose the following material-handling costs and number of material moves for the past ten months:

Month	Material-Handling Cost	Number of Moves
January	$2,000	100
February	2,500	125
March	2,500	175
April	3,000	200
May	7,500	500
June	4,500	300
July	4,000	250
August	5,000	400
September	6,500	475
October	6,000	425

The High-Low Method

From basic geometry, we know that two points are needed to determine a line. Once we know two points on a line, then its equation can be determined. Recall that F, the fixed cost component, is the intercept of the total cost line, and that V, the variable cost per unit, is the slope of the line. Given two points, the slope and the intercept can be determined. The **high-low method** preselects the two points that will be used to compute the parameters F and V. Specifically, the

high-low method

method uses the high and low points. The high point is defined as the point with the highest activity level. The low point is defined as the point with the lowest activity level.

Letting (X_1, Y_1) be one point, say the low point, and (X_2, Y_2) be the second point, the high point, the equations for determining the slope and intercept are, respectively:

$$V = \text{Change in cost/Change in activity}$$
$$= (Y_2 - Y_1)/(X_2 - X_1)$$

and

$$F = \text{Total mixed cost} - \text{Variable cost}$$
$$= Y_2 - VX_2$$

or

$$F = Y_1 - VX_1$$

Notice that the fixed cost component is computed using the total cost at either (X_1, Y_1) or (X_2, Y_2).

For Anderson, the high point is $7,500 material-handling cost when 500 moves were made, or (500, $7,500). The low point is $2,000 of material-handling cost when 100 moves were made, or (100, $2,000). Once the high and low points are defined, the values of F and V can be computed.

$$V = (Y_2 - Y_1)/(X_2 - X_1)$$
$$= (\$7,500 - \$2,000)/(500 - 100)$$
$$= \$5,500/400$$
$$= \$13.75$$
$$F = Y_2 - VX_2$$
$$= \$7,500 - (\$13.75 \times 500)$$
$$= \$625$$

The cost formula using the high-low method is

$$Y = \$625 + \$13.75X$$

If the number of moves for November is expected to be 350, this cost formula will predict a total cost of $5,437.50, with fixed costs of $625 and variable costs of $4,812.50.

The high-low method has the advantage of objectivity. That is, any two people using the high-low method on a particular data set will arrive at the same answer. In addition, the high-low method allows a manager to get a quick fix on a cost relationship using only two data points. For example, a manager may have only two months of data. Sometimes this will be enough to get a crude approximation of the cost relationship.

The high-low method is usually not as good as the other methods. Why? First, the high and low points often can be what are known as outliers. They may represent atypical cost-activity relationships. If so, the cost formula computed using these two points will not represent what usually takes place. The **scatterplot method** can help a manager avoid this trap by selecting two points that appear to be representative of the general cost-activity pattern. Second, even if these points are not outliers, other pairs of points may clearly be more representative. Again, the scatterplot method allows the choice of the more representative points.

scatterplot method

Scatterplot Method

scattergraph

The first step in applying the scatterplot method is to plot the data points so that the relationship between material-handling costs and activity output can be seen. This plot is referred to as a **scattergraph** and is shown in Exhibit 3-4. The vertical axis is total activity cost, and the horizontal axis is activity output (material handling cost and number of moves, respectively, for the example). Inspecting Exhibit 3-4 gives us increased confidence that the assumption of a linear relationship between material-handling costs and number of moves is reasonable for the indicated range of activity. Thus, one purpose of a scattergraph is to assess the validity of the assumed linear relationship. Additionally, inspecting the scattergraph may reveal several points that do not seem to fit the general pattern of behavior. Upon investigation, it may be discovered that these points (the outliers) were due to some irregular occurrences. This knowledge can provide justification for their elimination and perhaps lead to a better estimate of the underlying cost function.

A scattergraph can help provide insight concerning the relationship between cost and activity output. In fact, a scattergraph allows one to visually fit a line to the points on the scattergraph. In doing so, the line should be chosen that appears to fit the points the best. In making that choice, a manager or cost analyst is free to use past experience with the behavior of the cost item. Experience may provide a good intuitive sense of how material-handling costs behave; the scattergraph then becomes a useful tool to quantify this intuition. Fitting a line to the points in this way is how the scatterplot method works. Keep in mind that the scattergraph and the other statistical aids are tools that can help managers improve their judgment. Using the tools does not restrict the manager from using judgment to alter any of the estimates produced by formal methods.

Examine Exhibit 3-4 carefully. Based only on the information contained in the graph, how would you fit a line to the points in it? Suppose that you decide that a line passing through points 1 and 6 provides the best fit. If so, how could this

Exhibit 3-4
Scattergraph for Anderson Company

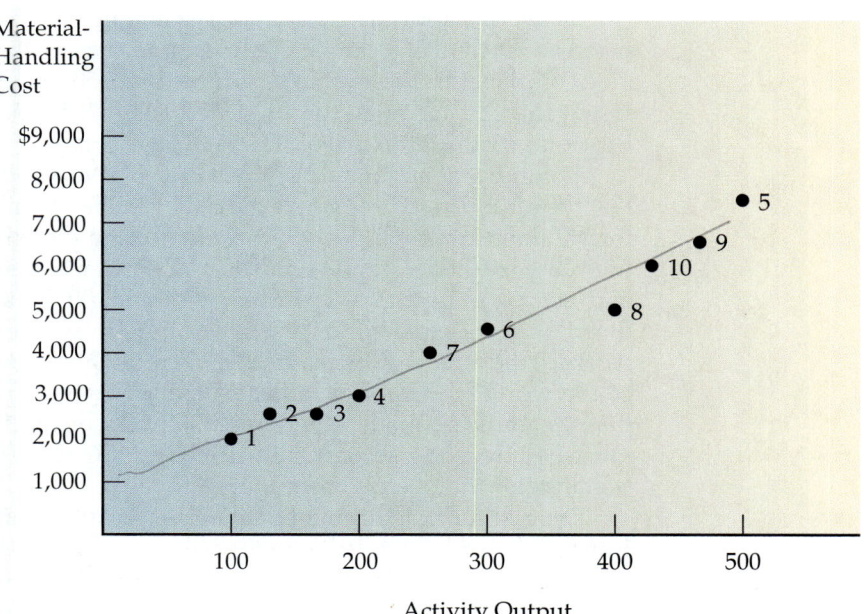

decision be used to compute the parameters F and V so that the fixed and variable cost components can be estimated?

Assuming your choice of the best-fitting line is the one passing through points 1 and 6, the variable cost per unit can be computed in the following way. First, let point 1 be designated by $X_1 = 100$, $Y_1 = \$2,000$ and point 6 by $X_2 = 300$, $Y_2 = \$4,500$. [This designation is arbitrary—it really doesn't matter which point is designated (X_1, Y_1) and which one is designated (X_2, Y_2).] Next, use these two points to compute the slope:

$$V = (Y_2 - Y_1)/(X_2 - X_1)$$
$$= (\$4,500 - \$2,000)/(300 - 100)$$
$$= \$2,500/200$$
$$= \$12.50$$

Thus, the variable cost per material move is $12.50. Given the variable cost per unit, the final step is to compute the fixed-cost component using (X_2, Y_2) in the intercept equation:

$$F = Y_2 - VX_2$$
$$= \$4,500 - \$12.50(300)$$
$$= \$750$$

Of course, the fixed cost component can also be computed using (X_1, Y_1), which produces the same result.

$$F = Y_1 - VX_1$$
$$= \$2,000 - \$12.50(100)$$
$$= \$750$$

cost formula

The fixed and variable components of material-handling cost have now been identified. The **cost formula** for the material-handling activity can be expressed as:

$$Y = \$750 + \$12.50X$$

Using this formula, the total cost of material handling for activity output between 100 and 500 can be predicted and then broken down into fixed and variable components. For example, assume that 350 moves are planned for December. Using the cost formula, the predicted cost is $5,125 [$750 + ($12.50 × 350)]. Of this total cost, $750 is fixed and $4,375 is variable.

A significant advantage of the scatterplot method is that it affords a cost analyst the opportunity to inspect the data visually. Exhibit 3-5 illustrates cost behavior situations that are not appropriate for the straightforward application of the high-low method. Graph A shows a nonlinear relationship between activity cost and activity output. An example of this might be a volume discount given on direct materials or evidence of learning by workers (e.g., as more hours are worked, the total cost increases at a decreasing rate due to the increased efficiency of the workers). Graph B indicates that there is an upward shift in cost if more than X_1 units are made—perhaps this could mean that an additional supervisor must be hired or a second shift run. Graph C shows outliers that are not representative of the overall cost relationship.

The cost formula for material handling was obtained by fitting a line to points 1 and 6 in Exhibit 3-4. Judgment was used to select the line. Whereas one person may decide, by inspection, that the best-fitting line is the one that passes through points 1 and 6, others, using their own judgment, may decide that the line should pass through points 2 and 4—or points 1 and 5.

Exhibit 3-5
Cost Behavior Patterns

Graph A – Nonlinear Relationship

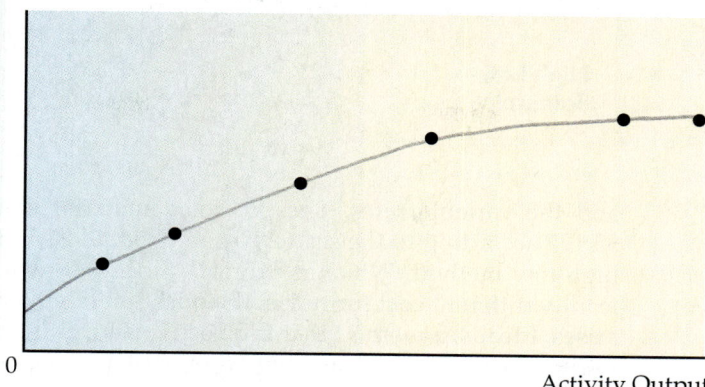

Graph B – Upward Shift in Cost Relationship

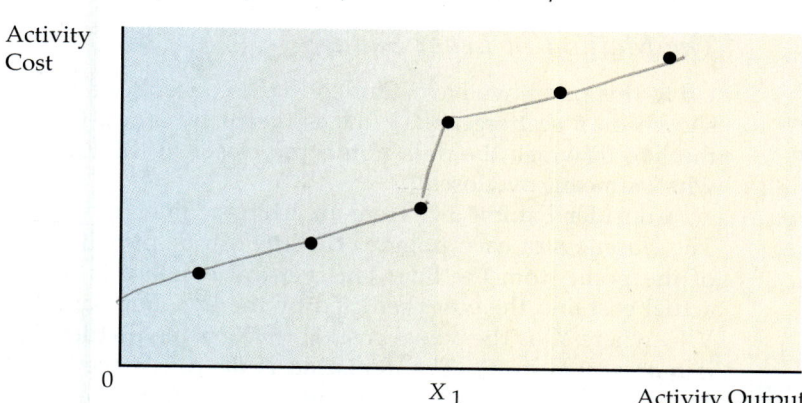

Graph C – Presence of Outliers

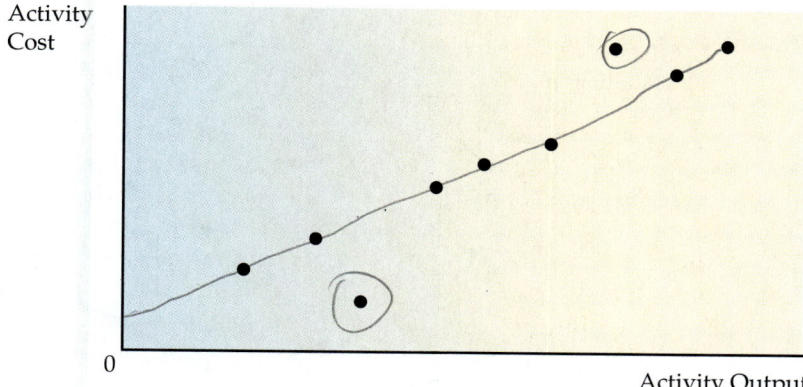

The scatterplot method suffers from the lack of any objective criterion for choosing the best-fitting line. The quality of the cost formula depends on the quality of the subjective judgment of the analyst. The high-low method removes the subjectivity in the choice of the line. Regardless of who uses the method, the same line will result.

Exhibit 3-6 compares the results of the scatterplot method with those of the high-low method. There is a large difference between the fixed cost components

	Fixed Cost	Variable Rate	Material-Handling Cost for 350 Moves
High-Low	$625	$13.75	$5,438
Scatterplot	750	12.50	5,125

and the variable rates. The predicted material handling cost for 350 moves is $5,125 according to the scatterplot method and $5,438 (rounded) according to the high-low method. Which is "right?" Since the two methods can produce significantly different cost formulas, the question of which method is the best naturally arises. Ideally, a method that is objective and, at the same time, produces the best-fitting line is needed. The method of least squares defines *best-fitting* and is objective in the sense that using the method for a given set of data will produce the same cost formula.

The Method of Least Squares

Up to this point, we have alluded to the concept of a line that best fits the points shown on a scattergraph. What is meant by a best-fitting line? Intuitively, it is the line in which the data points are closer to the line than any other line. But what is meant by closer?

Consider Exhibit 3-7. Here an arbitrary line $(Y = F + VX)$ has been drawn. The closeness of each point to the line can be measured by the vertical distance of the point from the line. This vertical distance is the difference between the actual cost and the cost predicted by the line. For point 8, this is $E_8 = Y_8 - F + VX_8$, where Y_8 is the actual cost, $F + VX_8$ is the predicted cost, and the deviation is represented by E_8. The **deviation** is the difference between the predicted and actual cost, which is shown by the distance from the point to the line.

deviation

The vertical distance measures the closeness of a single point to the line, but what is needed is a measure of closeness of *all* points to the line. One possibility

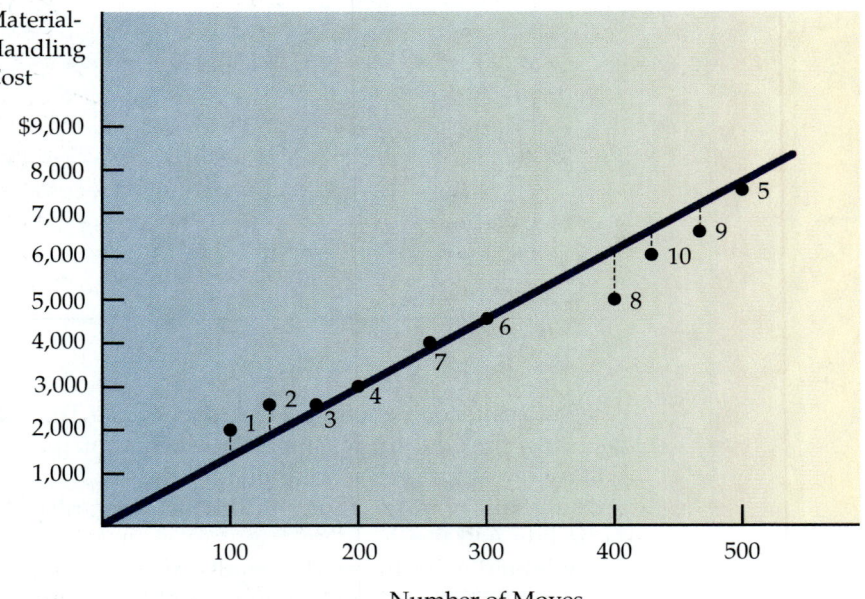

Number of Moves

is to add all the single measures to obtain an overall measure. However, since the single measures can have positive or negative signs, this overall measure may not be very meaningful. For example, the sum of small positive deviations could result in an overall measure greater in magnitude than the sum of large positive deviations and large negative deviations because of the canceling effect of positive and negative numbers. To correct for this problem, we could first square each single measure of closeness and then sum these squared deviations as the overall measure of closeness. Squaring the deviations avoids the cancellation problem caused by a mix of positive and negative numbers.

To illustrate this concept, a measure of closeness will be calculated for the cost formula produced by the scatterplot method.

Actual Cost	Predicted Cost[a]	Deviation[b]	Deviation Squared
$2,000	$2,000	$ —	—
2,500	2,313	187	34,969
2,500	2,938	−438	191,844
3,000	3,250	−250	62,500
7,500	7,000	500	250,000
4,500	4,500	—	—
4,000	3,875	125	15,625
5,000	5,750	−750	562,500
6,500	6,688	−188	35,344
6,000	6,063	−63	3,969
Total measure of closeness			1,156,751

[a] Predicted cost = $750 + $12.50X, where X is the actual measure of activity output associated with the actual activity cost and cost is rounded to nearest dollar.
[b] Deviation = Actual cost − Predicted cost.

Since the measure of closeness is the sum of the squared deviations of the points from the line, the smaller the measure, the better the line fits the points. For example, the scatterplot method line has a closeness measure of 1,156,751. A similar calculation produces a closeness measure of 2,429,313 for the high-low line. Thus, the scatterplot line fits the points better than the high-low line. This outcome supports the earlier claim that the use of judgment in the scatterplot method is superior to the high-low method.

In principle, comparing closeness measures can produce a ranking of all lines from best to worst. The line that fits the points better than any other line is called the **best-fitting line**. It is the line with the smallest (least) sum of squared deviations. The **method of least squares** identifies the best-fitting line. We rely on statistical theory to obtain the formulas that produce the best-fitting line. These formulas are given below.

best-fitting line
method of least squares

$$V = [\Sigma XY - \Sigma X \Sigma Y/n]/[\Sigma X^2 - (\Sigma X)^2/n] \qquad (3.3)$$

$$F = \Sigma Y/n - v(\Sigma X/n) \qquad (3.4)$$

Manual Computation In order to compute V and F, five inputs are needed: n, ΣX, ΣY, ΣXY, and ΣX^2. The first input, n, is the easiest to obtain—simply count the number of data points in the data set. For the Anderson Company example, there are ten data points. The other four inputs are computed as follows:

ΣX	ΣY	ΣXY	ΣX^2
100	$ 2,000	$ 200,000	10,000
125	2,500	312,500	15,625
175	2,500	437,500	30,625
200	3,000	600,000	40,000
500	7,500	3,750,000	250,000
300	4,500	1,350,000	90,000
250	4,000	1,000,000	62,500
400	5,000	2,000,000	160,000
475	6,500	3,087,500	225,625
425	6,000	2,550,000	180,625
2,950	$43,500	$15,287,500	1,065,000

Substituting the above summations (Σ) into Equations 3.3 and 3.4, we obtain:

$$V = [15{,}287{,}500 - (2{,}950 \times 43{,}500)/10]/[1{,}065{,}000 - (2{,}950)^2/10]$$
$$= 2{,}455{,}000/194{,}750$$
$$= \$12.61$$

and

$$F = \$43{,}500/10 - \$12.61(2{,}950/10)$$
$$= \$630$$

Thus, the cost formula for the method of least squares can be expressed as follows:

$$Y = \$630 + \$12.61X$$

Since this cost formula is the best-fitting line, it should produce better predictions of material-handling costs. For 350 moves, the material-handling cost predicted by the least-squares line is $5,044 [$630 + $12.61(350)], with a fixed component of $630 plus a variable component of $4,414. Using this prediction as a standard, the scatterplot line most closely approximates the least-squares line.

Computer Computation Computing the formula manually is tedious, even with only ten data points. As the number of data points increases, manual computation becomes impractical. Fortunately, spreadsheet packages such as Lotus® 1-2-3, Quattro® Pro, and Microsoft® Excel have regression routines that will perform the computations. All that the user needs to do is input the data points. A computer printout for the Anderson example is provided in Exhibit 3-8 (any differences in the estimates of the coefficients are caused by rounding error in the manual computation). The computer printout supplies more than the estimates of the coefficients.

RELIABILITY OF COST FORMULAS

Objective 3
Evaluate the reliability of a cost equation.

The computer output in Exhibit 3-8 provides information that can be used to assess how reliable the estimated cost formula is. This is a feature not provided by either the scatterplot or high-low methods. The printout in Exhibit 3-8 will serve as the point of reference for discussing three statistical assessments concerning the cost formula's reliability: *hypothesis test of cost parameters, goodness*

Exhibit 3-8
Computer Printout:
Anderson Example

Parameter	Estimate	t for H_0 Parameter $= 0$	$Pr > t$	Standard Error of Parameter
Intercept	631.25	2.326	0.045	271.394
Number of moves	12.61	15.156	0.000	0.832

R Square (R^2) 0.97
Standard Error (S_e) 367
Observations 10

hypothesis test of cost parameters
goodness of fit

confidence intervals

of fit, and *confidence intervals.* The **hypothesis test of cost parameters** indicates whether the parameters are different from zero. For our setting, **goodness of fit** measures the degree of association between cost and activity output. This measure is important because the method of least squares identifies the best-fitting line, but it does not reveal how good the fit is. The best-fitting line may not be a good-fitting line. It may perform miserably when it comes to predicting costs. **Confidence intervals** provide a range of values for the actual cost with a pre-specified degree of confidence. Confidence intervals allow managers to predict a range of values instead of a single prediction. Of course, if the degree of association is perfect, then the confidence interval will consist of a single point and the actual cost will always coincide with the predicted cost. Thus, goodness of fit and confidence intervals are related and provide cost analysts some idea of how reliable the resulting cost equation is.

Hypothesis Test of Parameters

Refer once again to Exhibit 3-8. The last three columns of the table present some statistical data concerning the fixed cost and variable cost parameters (F and V_1). The third column presents t statistics for each of these parameters. These t statistics are used to test the hypothesis that the parameters are different from zero. The fourth column presents the level of significance achieved. The fixed cost parameter, F, is significant at the .045 level. The variable cost parameter is significant at the .000 level (1.03×10^{-7} is the actual level computed). Thus, the number of moves appears to be a highly significant explanatory variable—a driver for material-handling costs. Furthermore, the presence of fixed material-handling costs is also reasonably ensured. The fifth column presents the standard error for each *parameter.* This value is used to compute the t statistic in column 3. This is done by dividing the coefficient in column 2 by the corresponding standard error.

Goodness-of-Fit Measures

Initially, we assume that a single activity driver (activity output variable) explains changes (variability) in activity cost. Our experience with the Anderson Company example suggests that number of moves can explain changes in material-handling costs. The scattergraph shown in Exhibit 3-4 confirms this belief because it reveals that material-handling cost and activity output (as measured by number of moves) seem to move together. It is quite likely that a significant percentage of the total variability in cost is explained by our activity output variable. We can determine statistically just how much variability is explained by looking at the coefficient of determination. The percentage of variability in the dependent variable explained by an independent variable (in this case, a measure of activity

coefficient of determination

output) is called the **coefficient of determination**. This percentage is a goodness-of-fit measure. The higher the percentage of cost variability explained, the better the fit. Since the coefficient is the *percentage* of variability explained, it always has a value between 0 and 1.00. In the printout in Exhibit 3-8, the coefficient of determination is labeled R Square (R^2). The value given is 0.97, which means that 97% of the variability in material-handling cost is explained by the number of moves. This result tells us that the least-squares line is a good-fitting line.

There is no cut-off point for a good versus a bad coefficient of determination. Clearly, the closer R^2 is to 1.00, the better. However, is 89 percent good enough? How about 73 percent? Or even 46 percent? The answer is that it depends. If your cost equation yields a coefficient of determination of 75 percent, you know that your independent variable explains three-fourths of the variability in cost. You also know that some other factor or combination of factors explains the remaining one-fourth. Depending on your tolerance for error, you may want to improve the equation by trying different independent variables (for example, material-handling hours worked rather than number of moves) or by trying multiple regression (which is explained in a succeeding section of this chapter).

Manual Computation The coefficient of determination (R^2) is computed by the following formula:

$$R^2 = V[\Sigma XY - \Sigma X \Sigma Y/n]/[\Sigma Y^2 - (\Sigma Y)^2/n] \qquad (3.5)$$

where V = the slope computed using the method of least squares

To compute the coefficient of determination (R^2) for the material-handling cost example, the required inputs are V, n, ΣX, ΣXY, ΣY, and ΣY^2. In our prior computation of V, the same inputs were required except for ΣY^2. The computation of ΣY^2 is as follows:

ΣY^2
$ 4,000,000
6,250,000
6,250,000
9,000,000
56,250,000
20,250,000
16,000,000
25,000,000
42,250,000
36,000,000
$221,250,000

Using the above inputs, the coefficient of determination can be calculated.

$$R^2 = 12.61[15,287,500 - (2,950 \times 43,500)/10]/[221,250,000 - (43,500)^2/10]$$
$$= 12.61(2,455,000)/32,025,000$$
$$= 0.97$$

This result tells us that the least-squares line is a good-fitting line.

coefficient of correlation

Coefficient of Correlation An alternative measure of goodness of fit is the **coefficient of correlation**, which is the square root of the coefficient of determination. Since square roots can be negative, the value of the coefficient of correlation can range between −1 and +1. If the coefficient of correlation is positive, then the two variables (in this example, cost and activity) move together in the *same direction* and positive correlation exists. Perfect positive correlation would yield a value of 1.00 for the coefficient of correlation. If, on the other hand, the coefficient of correlation is negative, then the two variables move in a predictable fashion but in *opposite directions*. Perfect negative correlation would yield a coefficient of correlation of −1.00. A coefficient-of-correlation value close to zero indicates no correlation. That is, knowledge of the movement of one variable gives us no clue as to the movement of the other variable. Exhibit 3-9 illustrates the concept of correlation.

For the Anderson Company example, the coefficient of correlation (r) is computed as follows:

$$r = \sqrt{0.97}$$
$$= 0.98$$

The square root is positive because the correlation between X and Y is positive. In other words, as activity output (number of moves) increases, the material-handling cost increases. This positive correlation is reflected by a positive value for V. If cost decreases as activity output increases, then the coefficient of correlation (and the value of V) is negative. The sign of V reveals the sign of the coefficient of correlation. The very high positive correlation between material-handling cost and number of moves indicates that the number of moves represents a good choice for an activity driver.

Exhibit 3-9
Correlation Illustrated

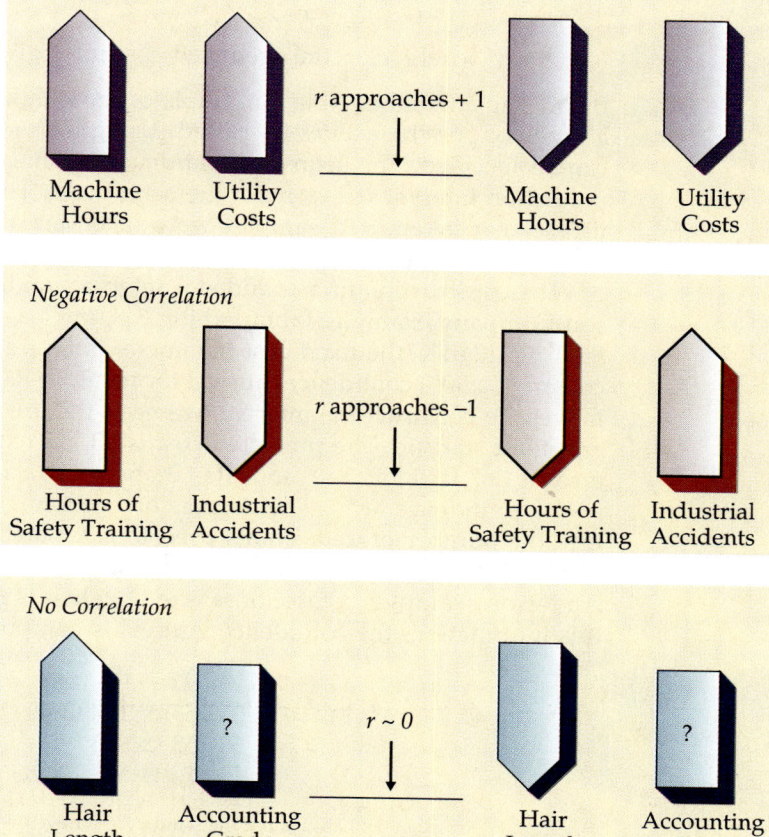

Confidence Intervals

The least-squares cost equation can be used to predict cost for different levels of activity output. For example, if the number of moves is 200, then the material-handling cost predicted by the least-squares equation is $3,153 ($631.25 + $12.61(200) and rounded to the nearest dollar). Usually we can expect the predicted value to be different from the actual cost. There are two reasons. First, in building the cost equation, only one activity driver (independent variable) has been used. It is possible that the cost equation has omitted other important factors—other activity output that affect cost (the dependent variable). These omitted factors are assumed to randomly affect the cost variable. The consequence of omission is to produce a distribution of cost values for every value of X (the measure of activity output appearing in the cost equation). This distribution is assumed to be normal. Second, the cost equation is based on estimated values using a sample of observed outcomes. Errors in estimating the slope, V, and the intercept, F, of the cost equation can also cause a discrepancy between the actual cost and the predicted cost.

The dispersion caused by these two effects can be measured, and the resulting measure can be used to help build a confidence interval around a predicted cost. If the number of data points is large enough, the measure of dispersion can be approximated by the standard error, S_e. For example, in Exhibit 3-8, the standard error is $367.[4]

Given S_e, a confidence interval for the predicted value of Y can be constructed by using a t statistic for the desired level of confidence:

$$Y_f \pm tS_e$$

where Y_f = the predicted cost for a given level of activity

By adding and subtracting a multiple of the standard error to the predicted cost, a range of possible values is created. Using the t statistic, a degree of confidence can be specified. The degree of confidence is a measure of the likelihood that the prediction interval will contain the actual cost. Thus, a 95% confidence interval means that if repeated samples were taken and 100 confidence intervals were constructed, we would expect 95 of the 100 to contain the actual cost.

The construction of a confidence interval can be illustrated using the Anderson Company example. From Exhibit 3-8, the least-squares cost equation is Y = $631 + $12.61X (the fixed cost parameter is rounded to the nearest dollar). Let's construct a 90% confidence interval for material-handling cost given that X = 200 moves. To construct the interval, we need the predicted cost, the standard error, and the t statistic. The predicted cost is $3,153 (computed earlier), the standard error is 367 (Exhibit 3-8), and the t statistic is 1.86 for 8 degrees of freedom and a 90% confidence level. The degrees of freedom are calculated by n − p, where n = the number of data points used to calculate the cost formula and p = the number of parameters in the cost equation (ten and two, respectively, for the Anderson example). A table of selected t values is provided in Exhibit 3-10. Using this information, the confidence interval is computed below:

$$Y_f \pm tS_e$$
$$\$3,153 \pm 1.86(367)$$
$$\$3,153 \pm 683$$
$$\$2,470 \leq Y \leq \$3,836$$

---

4.   For simplicity, we will always use the standard error even when the sample size is small.

Exhibit 3-10
Table of Selected Values:
t Distribution*

Degrees of Freedom	90%	95%	99%
1	6.314	12.708	63.657
2	2.920	4.303	9.925
3	2.353	3.182	5.841
4	2.132	2.776	4.604
5	2.015	2.571	4.032
6	1.943	2.447	3.707
7	1.895	2.365	3.499
8	1.860	2.306	3.355
9	1.833	2.262	3.250
10	1.812	2.228	3.169
11	1.796	2.201	3.106
12	1.782	2.179	3.055
13	1.771	2.160	3.055
14	1.761	2.145	3.012
15	1.753	2.131	2.947
16	1.746	2.120	2.921
17	1.740	2.110	2.898
18	1.734	2.101	2.878
19	1.729	2.093	2.861
20	1.725	2.086	2.845
30	1.697	2.042	2.750
∞	1.645	1.960	2.576

*Values are based on the assumption that two-tails are important—as they would be with confidence intervals and hypothesis tests of regression coefficients. For values above 30, simply use the last row.

Thus, we can say with 90% confidence that the actual cost, Y, associated with 200 moves will be between $2,470 and $3,836. This outcome produces a very large range of possible values. This outcome reveals very quickly that the cost equation is not as useful for prediction as it might first appear based only on the coefficient of determination. The width of the interval diminishes the attractiveness of the cost equation. However, the width of this interval often can be reduced by using a larger sample (more data points) to calculate the cost equation. With a larger sample, the standard error may decrease and the t statistic will decrease. If a company has a limited history for the activity being evaluated (sample size must be small), it may have to rely more on the detection of association than cost prediction. Finding a strong statistical association between an activity cost and an activity driver, however, can provide evidence to a manager about the correctness of the driver selection—an important issue when searching for causal factors to assign costs to cost objects.

MULTIPLE REGRESSION

Objective 4
Explain how multiple regression can be used to assess cost behavior.

In the Anderson Company example, 97 percent of the variability in material-handling cost was explained by changes in activity output (number of moves). Suppose that only 55 percent of the variability could be explained by this variable. In this case, a search should be made for additional explanatory variables. For example, total distance moved might be useful—particularly if the plant layout is such that significant time is consumed moving parts and products from one location to another.

In the case of two explanatory variables (activity drivers), the linear equation is expanded to include the additional variable:

$$Y = F + V_1X_1 + V_2X_2$$

$$\text{where } X_1 = \text{number of moves}$$
$$X_2 = \text{the total distance}$$

With three variables (Y, X_1, X_2), a minimum of three points is needed to compute the parameters F, V_1, and V_2. Seeing the points becomes difficult because they must be plotted in three dimensions. Using the scatterplot method or the high-low method is not practical.

However, the extension of the method of least squares is straightforward. It is relatively simple to develop a set of equations that provides values for F, V_1, and V_2 that yields the best-fitting equation. Whenever least squares is used to fit an equation involving two or more explanatory variables, the method is called **multiple regression**. The computational complexity of multiple regression, which increases significantly, is facilitated by the computer. In fact, any practical application of multiple regression requires use of a computer.

Let's return to the Anderson Company example. There is no real need to try to improve on the results of material-handling cost estimation by choosing additional activity drivers. The independent variable (number of moves) explains about 97 percent of the variability in material-handling cost. Assume that Anderson decides to use regression analysis to explain what drives setup costs. Suppose that the cost analysts for Anderson Company have tried several different activity drivers to explain the variability in setup cost. The best single driver was setup hours, which explained 55% of the total cost variability. After further investigation, the cost analysts have decided that number of parts—a measure of product complexity—might be an additional driver of setup costs. The more complex products require the use of different tools and more skilled labor than the less complex products, thus increasing setup costs (or so argued the production managers). Using 150 different setups as a data source, a multiple regression was run using setup hours and the number of parts. A computer printout for the regression is shown in Exhibit 3-11.

The computer printout conveys some very interesting and useful information. The cost equation is defined by the first two columns. The parameter column identifies the individual cost components. The intercept is the fixed activity cost, and the two activity drivers are setup hours and number of parts. The estimate column identifies the estimated fixed cost and the variable cost per unit for each activity driver. Thus, the cost equation can be written as follows:

$$Y = \$2{,}000 + \$50X_1 + \$200X_2$$

As with the cost equation involving a single activity driver, the above equation can be used to predict activity cost. For example, suppose that a setup is expected to take 20 hours and produce a product that has five parts. The predicted setup cost is as follows:

$$Y = \$2{,}000 + \$50(20) + \$200(5)$$
$$= \$4{,}000$$

Notice in Exhibit 3-11 that the coefficient of determination is 93%—a significant improvement in explanatory power is achieved by adding the product complexity variable (only 55% of the variability in setup cost was explained by a single driver equation). For multiple regression, R^2 is usually referred to as the

multiple regression

Exhibit 3-11
Partial Printout for Multiple Regression: Setup Cost Equation

Parameter	Estimate	t for H_0 Parameter = 0	Pr > t	Standard Error of Parameter
Intercept	2,000	1.96	.025	1,020.000
Setup hours	50	81.96	.0001	0.610
Number of parts	200	9.50	.0001	21.053

Multiple R Square (R^2) 0.93
Standard Error (S_e) 60
Observations 150

multiple coefficient of determination. Notice also that the standard error of estimate, S_e, is available in a multiple regression setting. As indicated earlier, the standard error of estimate can be used to build confidence intervals around cost predictions. To illustrate, consider the 95% confidence interval for the predicted setup cost when X_1 = 20 hours and X_2 = 5 parts (t = 1.96 for 95% confidence and 147 degrees of freedom):[5]

$$\$4,000 - 1.96(\$60) \leq Y \leq \$4,000 + 1.96(\$60)$$
$$\$3,882 \leq Y \leq \$4,118$$

Refer once again to Exhibit 3-11. Columns 3–5 of the table present some statistical data concerning the three parameters (F, V_1, and V_2). The third column presents t statistics for each of these parameters. These t statistics are used to test the hypothesis that the parameters are different from zero. The fourth column presents the level of significance achieved. The fixed cost parameter, F, is significant at the .025 level. The other two parameters are significant at the .0001 level. Thus, we can have some confidence that the two drivers are useful and that the setup activity has associated with it a fixed cost component. This example illustrates very clearly that multiple regression can be a useful tool for identifying the behavior of activity costs.

MANAGERIAL JUDGMENT

Objective 5

Discuss the use of managerial judgment in determining cost behavior.

Managerial judgment is critically important in determining cost behavior and is by far the most widely used method in practice.[6] Many managers simply use their experience and past observation of cost relationships to determine fixed and variable costs. This method, however, may take a number of forms. Some managers simply assign particular activity costs to the fixed category and others to the variable category. They ignore the possibility of mixed costs. Thus, a chemical firm may regard materials and utilities as strictly variable, with respect to pounds of chemical produced, and all other costs as fixed. Even labor, the textbook example of a unit-based variable cost, may be fixed for this firm. The appeal of this method is simplicity. Before opting for this course, management would do well to make sure that each cost is predominantly fixed or variable

5.   Degrees of freedom is computed as n − p, where p is the number of parameters being estimated. For this example, there are 150 data points and 3 parameters. The three parameters are F, V_1, and V_2. These t statistics come from Exhibit 3-10.
6.   Maryanne M. Mowen, *Accounting for Costs as Fixed and Variable* (Montvale, N.J.: National Association of Accountants, 1986), pp. 19–20. This practice of using managerial judgment to assign costs to cost behavior categories has continued to be practiced on the more advanced cost accounting systems.

and that the decisions being made are not highly sensitive to errors in classifying costs as fixed or variable. To illustrate the use of judgment in assessing cost behavior, consider Elgin Sweeper Company, a leading manufacturer of motorized street sweepers. Using production volume as the measure of activity output, Elgin revised its chart of accounts to organize costs into fixed and variable components. Elgin's accountants used their knowledge of the company to assign expenses to either a fixed or variable category, using a decision rule that categorized an expense as fixed if it were fixed 75 percent of the time and as variable if it were variable 75 percent of the time.[7]

Management may instead identify mixed costs and divide these costs into fixed and variable components by deciding just what the fixed and variable parts are—that is, using experience to say that a certain amount of a cost is fixed and that therefore the rest must be variable. Our photocopier example with the fixed cost of $3,000 per year and the variable rate of $0.02 per copy falls into this category. Then the variable component can be computed using one or more cost/volume data points. This has the advantage of accounting for mixed costs but is subject to a similar type of error as the strict fixed/variable dichotomy. That is, management may be wrong in its assessment.

Finally, management may use experience and judgment to refine statistical estimation results. Perhaps the experienced manager might "eyeball" the data and throw out several points as being highly unusual or might revise results of estimation to take account of projected changes in cost structure or technology. For example, Tecnol Medical Products, Inc. radically changed its method of manufacturing medical face masks. Traditionally, face-mask production was very labor intensive, requiring hand stitching. Tecnol developed its own highly automated equipment and became the industry's low cost supplier—besting both Johnson & Johnson and 3M. Tecnol's rapid expansion into new product lines and European markets means that historical data on costs and revenues are, for the most part, irrelevant.[8] Tecnol's management must look forward, not back, to predict the impact of changes on profit. Statistical techniques are highly accurate in depicting the past, but they cannot foresee the future, which of course is what management really wants.

The advantage of using managerial judgment to separate fixed and variable costs is its simplicity. In situations in which the manager has a deep understanding of the firm and its cost patterns, this method can give good results. However, if the manager does not have good judgment, errors will occur. Therefore, it is important to consider the experience of the manager, the potential for error, and the effect that error could have on related decisions.

7.   John P. Callan, Wesley N. Tredup, Randy S. Wissinger, "Elgin Sweeper Company's Journey Toward Cost Management," *Management Accounting*, July 1991, pp. 24–27.
8.   Stephanie Anderson Forest, "Who's Afraid of J&J and 3M?" *Business Week*, December 5, 1994, pp. 66 and 68.

SUMMARY

Cost behavior is the way in which a cost changes in relation to changes in activity output. The time horizon is important in determining cost behavior because costs can change from fixed to variable depending on whether the decision takes place over the short run or the long run. Variable costs are those which change in total as activity usage changes. Usually we assume that variable costs increase in direct proportion to increases in activity output. Fixed costs are those which do not change in total as activity output changes. Mixed costs have both a variable and a fixed component. The resource usage model adds additional understanding of cost behavior.

Resources acquired in advance of usage are categorized as committed fixed and discretionary fixed expenses. Resources acquired as used and needed are variable expenses. Some costs—especially discretionary fixed costs—tend to follow a step-cost function. These resources are acquired in lumpy amounts. If the width of the step is sufficiently large, then the costs are viewed as fixed; otherwise they are approximated by a variable cost function.

There are three formal methods of decomposing mixed costs: the high-low method, the scatterplot method, and the method of least squares. In the high-low method, the two points chosen from the scattergraph are the high and the low points with respect to activity level. These two points are then used to compute the intercept and the slope on the line on which they lie. The high-low method is objective and easy. However, if either the high or low point is not representative of the true cost relationship, the relationship will be misestimated.

The scatterplot method involves inspecting a scattergraph (a plot showing total mixed cost at various activity levels) and selecting two points that seem best to represent the relationship between cost and activity. Since two points determine a line, the two selected points can be used to determine the intercept and the slope of the line on which they lie. The intercept gives an estimate of the fixed-cost component and the slope an estimate of the variable cost per unit of activity. The scatterplot method is a good way to identify nonlinearity, the presence of outliers, and the presence of a shift in the cost relationship. Its disadvantage is that it is subjective.

The method of least squares uses all of the data points (except outliers) on the scattergraph and produces a line that best fits all of the points. The line is best fitting in the sense that it is closest to all the points as measured by the sum of the squared deviations of the points from the line. The method of least squares produces the line that best fits the data points and is therefore recommended over the high-low and scatterplot methods.

The least-squares method has the advantage of offering methods to assess the reliability of cost equations. The coefficient of determination allows an analyst to compute the amount of cost variability explained by a particular activity driver. The standard error of estimate can be used to build a prediction interval for cost. If the interval is too wide, it may suggest that the equation is not very useful for prediction, even if the driver explains a high percentage of the cost variability. The least-squares method can also be used to build a cost equation using more than one activity output. Equations built using multiple regression can also be evaluated for their reliability.

Managerial judgment can be used alone or in conjunction with the high-low, scatterplot, or least-squares methods. Managers use their experience and knowledge of cost and activity-level relationships to identify outliers, understand structural shifts, and adjust parameters due to anticipated changing conditions.

REVIEW PROBLEMS AND SOLUTIONS

I.
Resource Usage and Cost Behavior

Thompson Manufacturing Company has three salaried clerks to process purchase orders. Each clerk is paid a salary of $28,000 and is capable of processing 5,000 purchase orders per year (working efficiently). In addition to the salaries, Thompson spends $7,500 per year for forms, postage, etc. Thompson assumes 15,000 purchase orders will be processed. During the year, 12,500 orders were processed.

REQUIRED:

1. Calculate the activity rate for the purchase order activity. Break the activity into fixed and variable components.
2. Compute the total activity availability and break this into activity output and unused activity.
3. Calculate the total cost of resource supplied and break this into activity output and unused activity.

Solution

1.

$$\text{Activity rate} = [(3 \times \$28,000) + \$7,500]) / 15,000$$
$$= \$6.10 / \text{order}$$
$$\text{Fixed rate} = \$84,000 / 15,000$$
$$= \$5.60 / \text{order}$$
$$\text{Variable rate} = \$7,500 / 15,000$$
$$= \$0.50 / \text{order}$$

2. $$\text{Activity availability} = \text{Activity output} + \text{Unused capacity}$$
$$15{,}000 \text{ orders} = 12{,}500 \text{ orders} + 2{,}500 \text{ orders}$$
3. $$\text{Cost of activity supplied} = \text{Cost of activity used} + \text{Cost of unused activity}$$
$$\$84{,}000 + (\$0.50 \times 12{,}500) = (\$6.10 \times 12{,}500) + (\$5.60 \times 2{,}500)$$
$$\$90{,}250 = \$76{,}250 + \$14{,}000$$

II. High-Low Method and Method of Least Squares

Linda Jones, accountant for Golding, Inc., has decided to estimate the fixed and variable components associated with the company's repair activity. She has collected the following data for the past six months:

Repair Hours	Total Repair Costs
10	$ 800
20	1,100
15	900
12	900
18	1,050
25	1,250

REQUIRED:

1. Estimate the fixed and variable components for the repair costs using the high-low method. Using the cost formula, predict the total cost of repair if 14 hours are used.
2. Estimate the fixed and variable components using the method of least squares. Using the cost formula, predict the total cost of repairs if 14 hours are used.
3. For the method of least squares, compute the coefficient of determination and the coefficient of correlation.

Solution

1. The estimate of fixed and variable costs using the high-low method, where Y = total cost and X = number of hours, is as follows:

$$V = (Y_2 - Y_1)/(X_2 - X_1)$$
$$= (\$1{,}250 - \$800)/(25 - 10)$$
$$= \$450/15$$
$$= \$30 \text{ per hour}$$
$$F = Y_2 - VX_2$$
$$= \$1{,}250 - \$30(25)$$
$$= \$500$$
$$Y = \$500 + \$30X$$
$$= \$500 + \$30(14)$$
$$= \$920$$

2. The calculation using the method of least squares is as follows:

ΣX	ΣY	ΣXY	ΣX^2
10	$ 800	$ 8,000	100
20	1,100	22,000	400
15	900	13,500	225
12	900	10,800	144
18	1,050	18,900	324
25	1,250	31,250	625
100	$6,000	$104,450	1,818

$$V = [\Sigma XY - \Sigma X\Sigma Y/n]/[\Sigma X^2 - (\Sigma X)^2/n]$$
$$= [104,450 - (100 \times 6,000/6)]/[1,818 - (100 \times 100/6)]$$
$$= \$4,450/151.33$$
$$= \$29.41 \text{ per hour}$$
$$F = \Sigma Y/n - V\Sigma X/n$$
$$= \$6,000/6 - \$29.41(100/6)$$
$$= \$509.83$$
$$Y = 509.83 + 29.41X$$
$$= 509.83 + 29.41(14)$$
$$= \$921.57$$

3. The computation of the coefficient of determination (R^2) and the correlation coefficient (r) is as follows:

ΣY^2
$ 640,000
1,210,000
810,000
810,000
1,102,500
1,562,500
$6,135,000

$$R^2 = [V(\Sigma XY - \Sigma X\Sigma Y/n]/[\Sigma Y^2 - (\Sigma Y)^2/n]$$
$$= 29.41(4,450)/(6,135,000 - 6,000,000)$$
$$= 0.969$$
$$r = \sqrt{0.969}$$
$$= 0.985$$

KEY TERMS

Activity capacity 82
Activity rate 86
Activity output (usage) 84
Best-fitting line 95
Coefficient of correlation 98
Coefficient of determination 98
Committed fixed expenses 83
Confidence interval 97
Cost behavior 81

Cost formula 92
Cost of resource usage 86
Cost of unused activity 86
Dependent variable 89
Deviation 94
Discretionary fixed expenses 83
Goodness of fit 97
High-low method 89
Hypothesis test of cost parameters 97

Independent variable 89
Intercept parameter 89
Long run 81
Method of least squares 95
Multiple regression 102
Practical capacity 82
Resource spending 82
Resources 82
Resources supplied as used and needed 82

Resources supplied in advance of usage 82
Resource usage 82
Scattergraph 91
Scatterplot method 90
Short run 81
Slope parameter 89
Step-cost function 84
Step-fixed cost 85
Step-variable cost 85
Unused capacity 82

QUESTIONS FOR WRITING AND DISCUSSION

1. Why is knowledge of cost behavior important for managerial decision making? Give an example to illustrate your answer.
2. How does the length of the time horizon affect the classification of cost as fixed or variable? What is the meaning of short run? Long run?
3. Explain the difference between resource spending and resource usage.

4. What is the relationship between resources supplied as needed and cost behavior?

5. What is the relationship between resources supplied in advance of usage and cost behavior?

6. Explain the difference between committed and discretionary fixed costs. Give examples of each.

7. Describe the difference between a variable cost and a step-variable cost. When is it reasonable to treat step-variable costs as if they were variable costs?

8. What is the difference between a step-fixed cost and a step-variable cost?

9. What is an activity rate?

10. Why do mixed costs pose a problem when it comes to classifying costs into fixed and variable categories?

11. Why is a scattergraph a good first step in decomposing mixed costs into their fixed and variable components?

12. Describe how the scatterplot method breaks out the fixed and variable costs from a mixed cost. Now describe how the high-low method works. How do the two methods differ?

13. What are the advantages of the scatterplot method over the high-low method? The high-low method over the scatterplot method?

14. Describe the method of least squares. Why is this method better than either the high-low method or the scatterplot method?

15. What is meant by the best-fitting line?

16. Is the best-fitting line necessarily a good-fitting line? Explain.

17. Describe what is meant by goodness of fit. Explain the meaning of the coefficient of determination.

18. What is the difference between the coefficient of determination and the coefficient of correlation? Which of the two measures of goodness of fit do you prefer? Why?

19. What is the purpose of a confidence interval?

20. When is multiple regression required to explain cost behavior?

21. Some firms assign mixed costs to either the fixed or variable cost categories without using any formal methodology to separate them. Explain how this practice can be defended.

EXERCISES AND PROBLEMS

3-1
Resource Usage Model and Cost Behavior
LO 1

For the activities and their associated resources listed below, identify the following: (1) a cost driver, (2) resources acquired as needed, (3) long-term resources acquired in advance of usage, and (4) short-term resources acquired in advance of usage. Also, label each resource as one of the following with respect to the cost driver: (a) variable, (b) committed fixed, and (c) discretionary fixed.

Activity	Resource Description
Maintenance	Equipment, labor, parts
Inspection	Test equipment, inspectors (each inspector can inspect five batches per day), units inspected (process requires destructive sampling*)
Packing	Materials, labor (each packer places five units in a box), conveyor belt
Payable processing	Clerks, materials, equipment and facility
Assembly	Conveyor belt, supervision (one supervisor for every three assembly lines), direct labor, materials

*Destructive sampling occurs whenever it is necessary to destroy a unit as inspection occurs.

3-2
Resource Supply and Usage; Activity Rates; Service Organization
LO 1

Alva Community Hospital has five laboratory technicians responsible for doing a series of standard blood tests. Each technician is paid a salary of $30,000 and is capable of processing 4,000 tests per year. The lab facility represents a recent addition to the hospital and cost $300,000. It is expected to last 20 years. Equipment used for the testing cost $10,000 and has a life expectancy of five years. Both facility and equipment are depreciated on a straight-line basis. In addition to the salaries, facility, and equipment, Alva expects to spend $200,000 for chemicals, forms, power, and other supplies (assuming 20,000 tests are processed). During the year, 16,000 blood tests were run.

REQUIRED:

1. Classify the resources associated with the blood-testing activity into one of the follow-ing: (1) long-term resources supplied in advance, (2) short-term resources supplied in advance, or (3) resources supplied as needed.
2. Calculate the activity rate for the blood-testing activity. Break the activity rate into fixed and variable components.
3. Compute the total activity availability, and break this into activity output and unused activity.
4. Calculate the total cost of resources supplied, and break this into the cost of activity used and the cost of unused activity.

3-3
Step Costs;
Relevant Range
LO 1

Harker, Inc., produces large industrial machinery. Harker has a machining department and a group of direct laborers called machinists. Each machinist is paid $24,000 and can machine up to 250 units per year. Harker also hires supervisors to develop machine spec-ification plans and to oversee production within the machining department. Given the planning and supervisory work, a supervisor can oversee at most three machinists. Har-ker's accounting and production history reveals the following relationships between units produced and the costs of materials handling and supervision (measured on an annual basis):

Units Produced	Direct Labor	Supervision
0–250	$ 24,000	$ 40,000
251–500	48,000	40,000
501–750	72,000	40,000
751–1,000	96,000	80,000
1,001–1,250	120,000	80,000
1,251–1,500	144,000	80,000
1,501–1,750	168,000	120,000
1,751–2,000	192,000	120,000

REQUIRED:

1. Prepare two graphs, one that illustrates the relationship between direct labor cost and units produced and one that illustrates the relationship between the cost of supervision and units produced. Let cost be the vertical axis and units produced the horizontal axis.
2. How would you classify each cost? Why?
3. Suppose that the normal range of activity is between 1,251 and 1,500 units and that the exact number of machinists are currently hired to support this level of activity. Further suppose that production for the next year is expected to increase by an additional 500 units. By how much will the cost of direct labor increase (and how will this increase be realized)? Cost of supervision?

3-4
Cost Behavior;
Classification and
Graphing
LO 1

PLW Concrete Company owns ten ready-mix trucks. Each truck can deliver (on average) 10,000 cubic yards of concrete per year (considering the truck's capacity, weather, and dis-tance to each job). One driver per truck is needed. The labor cost of each driver is $25,000 per year. Depreciation on each truck averages $20,000. Raw materials (cement, gravel, and so on) cost about $25 per cubic yard of concrete.

REQUIRED:

1. Prepare a graph for each of three costs: truck drivers' wages, truck depreciation, and raw materials. Use the vertical axis for cost and the horizontal axis for concrete sold per year. Assume concrete sales can range from 0 to 100,000 cubic yards.

2. How would you classify each of the three types of cost? Why? Assume that the normal operating range for the company is 80,000 to 90,000 cubic yards. Does this change your cost classification? Why?

3-5
Scatterplot Method; Service Setting
LO 2

Betty Yeager has been operating a dental practice for the past five years. As part of her practice, she provides a dental hygiene service. She has found that her costs for this service increase with patient load. Costs for this service over the past eight months are as follows:

Month	Patients Served	Total Cost	XY	X²	Y²
May	320	$2,000	640,000	100,400	4,000,000
June	480	2,500	1,200,000		
July	600	3,000			
August	200	1,900			
September	720	4,500			
October	560	2,900			
November	630	3,400			
December	300	2,200			

(handwritten totals) 3,810   22,400   11,636,000   2,051,700   7,920,

REQUIRED:

1. Prepare a scattergraph based on the above data. Use cost for the vertical axis and number of patients for the horizontal. Based on an examination of the scattergraph, does there appear to be a linear relationship between the cost of dental hygiene services and number of patients served?
2. Upon examining the scattergraph, suppose that a cost analyst decides that the points (560, 2,900) and (300, 2,200) best describe the relationship between costs and activity. Determine the equation of this line. What points would you have chosen? What is the equation of your line?
3. Assume that 450 patients are expected to receive dental hygiene services in January. Using the equation you found in Requirement 2 (based on the analyst's selection), what is the predicted cost of dental hygiene services for that month?

3-6
High-Low Method
LO 2

Refer to the data in **3-5**. (*Note:* Either do **3-5** before **3-6** or exclude Requirement 3.)

REQUIRED:

1. Compute the cost formula for dental hygiene services using the high-low method.
2. Calculate the predicted cost of dental hygiene services for January for 450 patients using the formula found in Requirement 1.
3. Which cost formula—the one you computed using the scatterplot method or the one using the high-low method—do you think is the best? Explain.

3-7
Method of Least Squares
LO 2, 3

Refer to the data in **3-5**.

REQUIRED:

1. Compute the cost formula for dental hygiene services using the method of least squares.
2. Using the formula computed in Requirement 1, what is the predicted cost of dental hygiene services for January for 450 patients?
3. Compute the coefficient of determination. What does this measure tell you about the cost formula computed in Requirement 1?

3-8
High-Low Method;
Cost Formulas

LO 2

During the past year, the high and low levels of resource usage occurred in April and October (for three different resources). The three resources are associated with the machining activity. Machine hours is the activity driver. The total costs of the three resources and the activity output, as measured by machine hours, for the two different levels are presented below:

Resource	Machine Hours	Total Cost
Machine depreciation		
Low	10,000	$130,000
High	25,000	130,000
Power		
Low	10,000	13,000
High	25,000	32,500
Drilling labor		
Low	10,000	22,000
High	25,000	37,000

REQUIRED:

1. Determine the cost behavior of each activity input (resource). Use the high-low method to assess the fixed and variable components.
2. Using your knowledge of cost behavior, predict the cost of each item for an activity output level of 15,000 machine hours.
3. Construct a cost formula that can be used to predict the total cost of the three resources combined. Using this formula, predict the total machining cost if activity output is 18,000 machine hours. In general, when can cost formulas be combined to form a single cost formula?

3-9
Method of Least
Squares;
Evaluation of Cost
Equation

LO 2, 3

The method of least squares was used to develop a cost equation to predict the cost of purchasing. Eighty data points were used for the regression. The following computer output was received:

Intercept	$30,500
Slope	10
Coeffficient of correlation	0.85
Standard error	$1,500

The activity driver used was number of purchase orders.

REQUIRED:

1. What is the cost formula?
2. Using the cost formula, predict the cost of purchasing if 10,000 orders are processed. Now prepare a 95% confidence interval for this prediction.
3. What percentage of the variability in purchasing cost is explained by number of purchase orders? Do you think the equation will predict well? Why or why not?

3-10
Multiple
Regression

LO 4

Materhorn, Inc., a manufacturer of VCRs, is interested in determining the cost of its warranty repair activity. Two activity drivers have been identified that are believed to be important in explaining the cost of this activity: (1) the number of defective products produced and (2) the hours of inspection. To see if the belief is valid, the company's cost analysts gathered 100 weeks of data and ran a multiple regression analysis. The following printout was obtained:

Parameter	Estimate	t for H_o Parameter = 0	Pr > t	Standard Error of Parameter
Intercept	2,000	80.00	.0001	25.000
Number of defects	60	2.58	.0050	23.256
Inspection hours	−10	−1.96	.0250	5.103

$R^2 = 0.88$
$S_e = 150$
Observations 100

REQUIRED:

1. Write out the cost equation for Materhorn's warranty repair activity.
2. If Materhorn expects to have 100 defects per week and to spend 150 hours on inspection, what are the anticipated warranty repair costs?
3. Calculate a 99% confidence interval for the prediction made in Requirement 2.
4. Is number of defects positively or negatively correlated with warranty repair costs? Are inspection hours positively or negatively correlated with quality control costs?
5. What does R^2 mean in this equation? Overall, what is your evaluation of the cost equation that was developed for the warrant repair activity?

3-11
Cost Behavior Patterns
LO 1

The following graphs represent cost behavior patterns that might occur in a company's cost structure. The vertical axis represents total cost and the horizontal axis represents activity output.

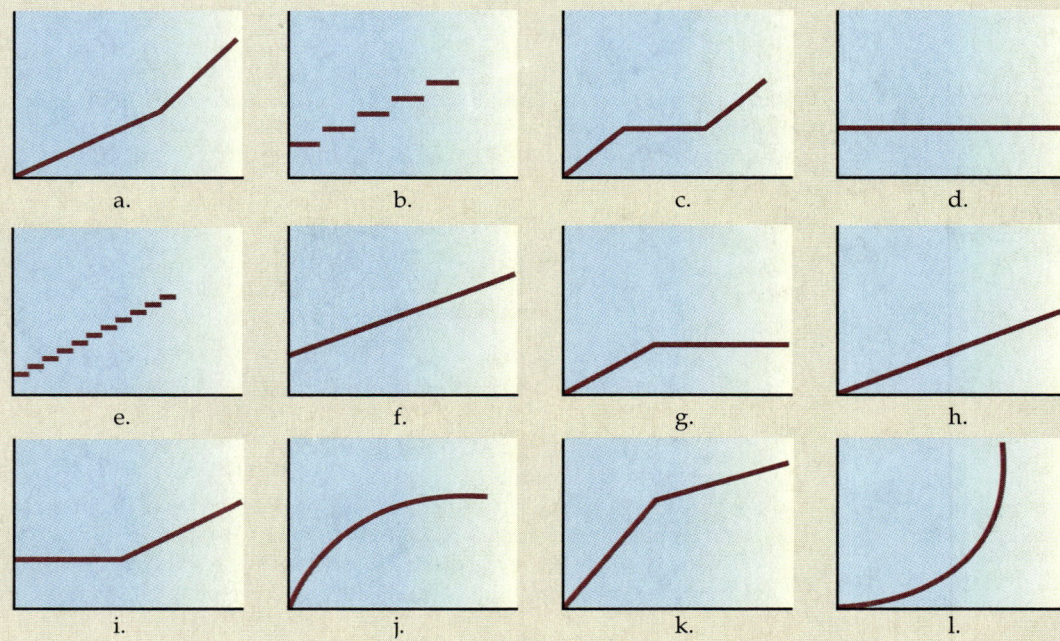

REQUIRED: For each of the following situations, choose the graph from the group on the previous page that best illustrates the cost pattern involved. Also, for each situation, identify the driver that measures activity output.

1. The cost of power when a fixed fee of $500 per month is charged plus an additional charge of $0.12 per kilowatt hour used.
2. Commissions paid to sales representatives. Commissions are paid at the rate of 5 percent of sales made up to total annual sales of $500,000, and 7 percent of sales above $500,000.
3. A part purchased from an outside supplier costs $12 per part for the first 3,000 parts and $10 per part for all parts purchased in excess of 3,000 units.
4. The cost of surgical gloves, which are purchased in increments of 100 units (gloves come in boxes of 100 pairs).
5. The cost of tuition at a local college that charges $250 per credit hour up to fifteen credit hours. Hours taken in excess of fifteen are free.
6. The cost of tuition at another college that charges $4,500 per semester for any course load ranging from twelve to sixteen credit hours. Students taking fewer than twelve credit hours are charged $375 per credit hour. Students taking more than sixteen credit hours are charged $4,500 plus $300 per credit hour in excess of sixteen.
7. A beauty shop's purchase of soaking solution to remove artificial nails. Each jar of solution can soak off approximately fifty nails before losing effectiveness.
8. Purchase of diagnostics equipment by a company for inspection of incoming orders.
9. Use of disposable gowns by patients in a hospital.
10. Cost of labor at a local fast-food restaurant. Three employees are always on duty during working hours; more employees can be called in during periods of heavy demand to work on an "as-needed" basis.
11. A manufacturer found that maintenance cost of its heavy machinery was tied to the age of the equipment. Experience indicated that maintenance cost increased at an increasing rate as the equipment aged.

3-12

Cost Behavior; Resource Usage Model

LO 1

Rolertyme Company manufactures roller skates. With the exception of the rollers, all parts of the skates are produced internally. Neeta Booth, president of Rolertyme, has decided to make the rollers instead of buying them from external suppliers. The company needs 100,000 sets per year (currently it pays $1.90 per set of rollers).

The rollers can be produced using an available area within the plant. Equipment, however, for production of the rollers would need to be leased ($30,000 per year lease payment). Additionally, it would cost $0.50 per machine hour for power, oil, and other operating expenses. The equipment will provide 60,000 machine hours per year. Direct material costs will average $0.75 per set of four, and direct labor will average $0.25 per set. Since only one type of roller would be produced, there would be no additional demands made on the setup activity. Other overhead activities (besides machining and setups), however, would be affected. The company's cost management system provides the following information about the current status of the overhead activities that would be affected (the supply and demand figures do not include the effect of roller production on these activities). The lumpy quantity indicates how much capacity must be purchased should any expansion of activity supply be needed. The purchase price is the cost of acquiring the capacity represented by the lumpy quantity. This price also represents the cost of current spending on existing activity supply (for each block of activity).

Activity Price	Cost Driver	Supply	Usage	Lumpy Quantity	Purchase
Purchasing	Orders	25,000	23,000	5,000	$25,000
Inspection	Hours	10,000	9,000	2,000	30,000
Material handling	Moves	4,500	4,300	500	15,000

The demands that *production* of rollers would place on the overhead activities follow:

Activity	Resource Demands
Machining	50,000 machine hours
Purchasing	2,000 purchase orders (associated with raw materials used to make the rollers)
Inspection	750 inspection hours
Material handling	500 moves

Producing the rollers also means that the purchase of outside rollers will cease. By not purchasing the rollers, purchase orders (associated with the outside acquisition of rollers) will drop by 5,000. Similarly, the moves for the handling of incoming orders will decrease by 200. The company has not inspected the rollers purchased from outside suppliers.

REQUIRED:

1. Classify all resources associated with the production of rollers as resources acquired as needed and resources acquired in advance of usage. For resources acquired in advance of usage, label them as short- or long-term commitments. How should we describe the cost behavior of these short- and long-term resource commitments? Explain.
2. Calculate the total annual resource spending (for all activities except for setups) that the company will incur *after* production of the rollers begins. Break this cost into fixed and variable activity costs. In calculating these figures, assume that the company will spend no more than necessary. What is the effect on resource spending caused by production of the rollers?
3. Refer to Requirement 2. For each activity, break the cost of activity supplied into the cost of activity output and the cost of unused activity.
4. Prepare a graph for the cost function associated with each of the following two activities: (a) machining and (b) purchasing.

3-13
Cost Behavior;
High-Low Method;
Pricing Decision
LO 1, 2

Monson Medical Clinic offers a number of specialized medical services, one of which is cancer care. Because of the reputation the clinic's physicians (oncologists) have developed over the years, demand for these services is strong. As a result, Monson recently added a 100-bed cancer wing to the clinic. The cost of the cancer facility is depreciated on a straight-line basis. All equipment within the facility is leased.

Since the clinic had no experience with in-patient cancer services, it decided to operate the cancer care center for two months before determining how much to charge per patient day on an ongoing basis. As a temporary measure, the clinic adopted a patient-day charge of $100, an amount equal to the charges made by a hospital specializing in cancer care in a nearby city.

This initial per-day charge was quoted to patients entering the cancer care center during the first two months with assurances that if the actual operating costs of the new center justified it, the charge could be less. In no case would the charges be more. A temporary policy of billing after sixty days was adopted so that any adjustments could be made.

The cancer care center opened on January 1. During January, the center had 2,100 patient days of activity. During February, the activity was 2,250 patient days. Costs for these two levels of activity output are as follows:

	2,100 Patient Days	2,250 Patient Days
Salaries, nurses	$ 6,000	$ 6,000
Aides	1,200	1,200
Laboratory	110,000	117,500
Pharmacy	31,000	32,500
Depreciation	11,800	11,800
Laundry	16,800	18,000
Administration	12,000	12,000
Lease (equipment)	30,000	30,000

REQUIRED:

1. Classify each cost as fixed, variable, or mixed, using patient days as the activity driver.
2. Use the high-low method to separate the mixed costs into fixed and variable.
3. Karl Johnson, the administrator of the cancer center, has estimated that the center will average 2,000 patient days per month. If the center is to be operated as a nonprofit organization, how much will it need to charge per patient day? How much of this charge is variable? How much is fixed?
4. Suppose the cancer center averages 2,500 patient days per month. How much would need to be charged per patient day for the center to cover its costs? Explain why the charge per patient day decreased as the activity output increased.

3-14
High-Low Method; Method of Least Squares; Correlation; Confidence Interval
LO 2, 3, 5

Farnsworth Company has gathered data on its overhead activities and associated costs for the past ten months. Tracy Heppler, a member of the controller's department, has convinced management that overhead costs can be better estimated and controlled if the fixed and variable components of each overhead activity are known. Tracy has identified 150 different activities and has grouped activities into sets based on her belief that they share a common activity driver. (This classification process has reduced the number of cost formulas needed from 150 to 25.) For example, she has decided that unloading incoming goods, counting goods, and inspecting goods can be grouped together as a more general receiving activity. This is based on her belief that the costs of the three related activities are all driven by the same activity driver, number of purchase orders. To confirm her activity classification and activity driver assignment, she has gathered data for each set of activities. Ten months of data have been gathered for the receiving activity and are presented below:

Month	Receiving Orders	Receiving Cost
1	1,000	$18,000
2	700	15,000
3	1,500	28,000
4	1,200	17,000
5	1,300	25,000
6	1,100	21,000
7	1,600	29,000
8	1,400	24,000
9	1,700	27,000
10	900	16,000

REQUIRED:

1. Prepare a scattergraph, plotting the receiving costs against the number of receiving orders. Use the vertical axis for costs and the horizontal for hours.
2. Select two points that make the best fit, and compute a cost formula for receiving costs.
3. Using the high-low method, prepare a cost formula for the receiving activity.
4. Using the method of least squares, prepare a cost formula for the receiving activity. What is the coefficient of determination?
5. Prepare a 95% confidence interval for receiving cost when 1,200 purchase orders are expected. Assume $S_e = 2{,}176$.

3-15
Cost Formulas; Single and Multiple Activity Drivers; Coefficient of Correlation
LO 1, 3, 4

Kimball Company has developed the following cost formulas:

Material usage: $Y_m = \$80X$; $r = 0.95$
Labor usage (direct): $Y_l = \$20X$; $r = 0.96$
Overhead activity: $Y_o = \$350{,}000 + \$100X$; $r = 0.75$
Selling activity: $Y_s = \$50{,}000 + \$10X$; $r = 0.93$

where X = direct labor hours

The company has a policy of producing on demand and keeps very little, if any, finished goods inventory (thus, units produced = units sold).

The president of Kimball Company has recently implemented a policy that any special orders will be accepted if they cover the costs that the orders cause. This policy was implemented because Kimball's industry is in a recession and the company is producing well below capacity (and expects to continue doing so for the coming year). The president is willing to accept orders that at least cover their variable costs so that the company can keep its employees and avoid layoffs. Also, any orders above variable costs will increase overall profitability of the company.

REQUIRED:

1. Compute the total unit variable cost. Suppose that Kimball has an opportunity to accept an order for 20,000 units at $220 per unit. Each unit uses one direct labor hour for production. Should Kimball accept the order? (The order would not displace any of Kimball's regular orders.)
2. Explain the significance of the coefficient-of-correlation measures for the cost formulas. Did these measures have a bearing on your answer in Requirement 1? Should they have a bearing? Why?
3. Suppose that a multiple regression equation is developed for overhead costs: $Y = $100,000 + $100X_1 + $5,000X_2 + $300X_3$, where X_1 = direct labor hours, X_2 = number of setups, and X_3 = engineering hours. The correlation coefficient for the equation is 0.94. Assume that the order of 20,000 units requires 12 setups and 600 engineering hours. Given this new information, should the company accept the special order referred to in Requirement 1? Is there any other information about cost behavior that you would like to have? Explain.

3-16
Scattergraph;
High-Low Method;
Method of Least
Squares
LO 2

The management of Fernelius Company has decided to develop cost formulas for its major overhead activities. Fernelius uses a highly automated manufacturing process, and power usage is considered a major activity. Power costs are a significant manufacturing cost. Cost analysts have decided that power costs are mixed; thus, they must be broken into their fixed and variable elements so that the cost behavior of the power usage activity can be properly described. Machine hours have been selected as the activity driver for power costs. The following data for the past eight quarters have been collected:

Quarter	Machine Hours	Power Cost
1	20,000	$26,000
2	25,000	38,000
3	30,000	42,500
4	22,000	37,000
5	21,000	34,000
6	18,000	29,000
7	24,000	36,000
8	28,000	40,000

REQUIRED:

1. Prepare a scattergraph by plotting power costs against machine hours. Fit a line to the data set; select two points and determine the cost formula for power.
2. Using the high and low points, compute a power cost formula.
3. Use the method of least squares to compute a power cost formula. Also compute the coefficient of determination.
4. Compute the expected cost for 23,000 machine hours using each of the three formulas. Which cost formula would you recommend? Explain.

3-17
Method of Least Squares
LO 1, 2, 3

Dotter Company is developing a cost formula for its packing activity. Past experience has convinced management that packing costs and the number of customer orders are highly correlated. Data for the past twenty months have been gathered, and the following expressions have been computed:

$$\Sigma X = 40{,}000; \ \Sigma XY = \$1{,}200{,}000{,}000; \ \Sigma X^2 = 120{,}000{,}000; \ \Sigma Y = \$500{,}000$$

REQUIRED:

1. Using the method of least squares, determine the packing cost formula.
2. Suppose that $\Sigma Y^2 = 13{,}600{,}000{,}000$. Is the management of Dotter Company justified in assuming that packing costs and customer orders are highly correlated?
3. Predict the total packing cost for 2,000 customer orders. How much of this total cost is a fixed activity cost? How much is variable? Now suppose that the fixed activity cost provides an activity capacity for processing 2,500 orders. What is the cost of the unused activity for a level of 2,000 orders?
4. Suppose that $S_e = \$800$. Prepare a 99% confidence interval for the total packing cost predicted for 2,000 customer orders.

3-18
High-Low Method; Scatterplot
LO 2, 5

Weber Valley Regional Hospital has collected data on all of its activities for the past seven months. Data for cardiac nursing care follow:

	Cost	Hours of Nursing Care
September 1997	$69,500	1,700
October 1997	64,250	1,550
November 1997	52,000	1,200
December 1997	66,000	1,600
January 1998	83,000	1,800
February 1998	66,550	1,330
March 1998	79,500	1,700

REQUIRED:

1. Using the high-low method, calculate the variable rate per hour and the fixed cost for the nursing care activity.
2. Prepare a scatterplot for the nursing care activity using the above data. (*Hint:* Use one symbol, perhaps an "x," for observations occurring in 1997 and another symbol for observations occurring in 1998.)
3. Upon looking into the events that happened at the end of 1997, you find that the cardiology ward bought a cardiac-monitoring machine for the nursing station. A decision was also made to add a new supervisory position for the evening shift. Monthly depreciation on the monitor and the salary of the new supervisor totals $10,000. Now, using the scatterplot from Requirement 2, calculate the fixed cost and variable rate applicable to October 1997 and the fixed cost and variable rate applicable to March 1998. Discuss your findings. Which cost formula should be used to budget the cost of the cardiac nursing care activity for the remainder of 1998?

3-19
Comparison of Regression Equations (computer required)
LO 1, 2, 5

Loving Toys Company is attempting to determine cost behavior of its overhead activities for its Kansas City plant. One of the major activities is the setup activity. Two possible activity drivers have been mentioned: setup hours and number of setups. The plant controller has accumulated the following data for the setup activity:

Month	Setup Costs	Setup Hours	Number of Setups
February	$ 7,700	2,000	70
March	7,650	2,100	50
April	10,052	3,000	50

continued

Month	Setup Costs	Setup Hours	Number of Setups
May	$ 9,400	2,700	60
June	9,584	3,000	20
July	8,480	2,500	40
August	8,550	2,400	60
September	9,735	2,900	50
October	10,500	3,000	90

REQUIRED:

1. Estimate a regression equation with setup hours as the activity driver and only independent variable. If the Kansas City plant forecasts 2,600 setup hours for the next month, what will be the budgeted setup cost?
2. Estimate a regression equation with number of setups as the activity driver and only independent variable. If the Kansas City plant forecasts 80 setups for the next month, what will be the budgeted setup cost?
3. Which of the two regression equations do you think does a better job of predicting setup costs? Explain.
4. Using a regression program (e.g., Lotus or Excel), determine the cost equation using both activity drivers. What are the budgeted setup costs for 2,600 setup hours and 80 setups?

3-20
Multiple
Regression;
Reliability of Cost
Formula (computer
required)
LO 2, 4

Randy Harris, controller, has been given the charge to implement an advanced cost management system. As part of this process, he needs to identify activity drivers for the activities of the firm. During the past four months, Randy has spent considerable effort identifying activities, their associated costs, and possible drivers for the activities' costs. Initially, Randy made his selections based on his own judgment using his experience and input from employees who perform the activities. Later, he used regression analysis to confirm his judgment. Randy prefers to use one driver per activity, provided that an R^2 of at least 80% can be produced. Otherwise, multiple drivers will be used, based on evidence provided by multiple regression analysis. For example, the activity of inspecting finished goods produced an R^2 of less than 80% for any single activity driver. Randy believes, however, that a satisfactory cost formula can be developed using two activity drivers: number of batches and inspection hours. Data collected for a 15-month period are given below:

Inspection Cost	Hours of Inspection	Number of Batches
$17,689	100	10
18,350	120	20
13,125	60	15
28,000	320	30
30,560	240	25
31,755	200	40
40,750	280	35
29,500	230	22
47,570	350	50
36,740	270	45
43,500	350	38
26,780	200	18
28,500	140	28
17,000	160	14

REQUIRED:

1. Calculate the cost formula for inspection costs using the two drivers, inspection hours and number of batches. Are both activity drivers useful? What does the R^2 indicate about the formula?

2. Using the formula developed in Requirement 1, calculate the inspection cost when 300 inspection hours are used and 30 batches are produced. Prepare a 90% confidence interval for this prediction.

**3-21
Simple and
Multiple
Regression,
Evaluating
Reliability of
Equation**
LO 2, 3, 4

The Lockit Company manufactures door knobs for residential homes and apartments. Lockit is considering the use of simple (single-driver) and multiple regression analysis to forecast annual sales because previous forecasts have been inaccurate. The sales forecast will be used to initiate the budgeting process and to identify better the underlying process that generates sales.

Larry Husky, the controller of Lockit, has considered many possible independent variables and equations to predict sales and has narrowed his choices to four equations. Husky used annual observations from 20 prior years to estimate each of the four equations.

Following is a definition of the variables used in the four equations and a statistical summary of these equations:

S_t = Forecasted sales in dollars for Lockit in period t.

S_{t-1} = Actual sales in dollars for Lockit in period t − 1.

G_t = Forecasted United States gross domestic product in period t.

G_{t-1} = Actual United States gross domestic product in period t − 1.

N_{t-1} = Lockit's net income in period t − 1.

Statistical Summary of Four Equations

Equation	Dependent Variable	Independent Variable(s)	Intercept	Independent Variable (Rate)	Standard Error	R Square	t–Value
1	S_t	S_{t-1}	$ 500,000	$ 1.10	$500,000	0.94	5.50
2	S_t	G_t	$1,000,000	$ .00001	$510,000	0.90	10.00
3	S_t	G_{t-1}	$ 900,000	$ .000012	$520,000	0.81	5.00
4	S_t		$ 600,000		$490,000	0.96	
		N_{t-1}		$10.00			4.00
		G_t		$ .000002			1.50
		G_{t-1}		$ .000003			3.00

REQUIRED:

1. Write equations 2 and 4 in the form Y = a + bx.
2. If actual sales are $1,500,000 in 1995, what would be the forecasted sales for Lockit in 1996?
3. Explain why Larry Husky might prefer equation 3 to equation 2.
4. Explain the advantages and disadvantages of using equation 4 to forecast sales.

(CMA adapted)

**3-22
Suspicious
Acquisition of
Data; Ethical
Issues**
LO 5

Bill Lewis, manager of the Thomas Electronics Division, called a meeting with his controller, Brindon Peterson, CMA, and his marketing manager, Patty Fritz. The following is a transcript of the conversation that took place during the meeting.

Bill: Brindon, the variable costing system that you developed has proved to be a big plus for our division. Our success in winning bids has increased, and as a result, our revenues have increased by 25 percent. However, if we intend to meet this year's profit targets, we are going to need something extra—am I not right, Patty?

Patty: Absolutely. While we have been able to win more bids, we still are losing too many, particularly to our major competitor, Kilborn Electronics. If I knew more about their bidding strategy, I imagine we could be more successful competing with them.

Bill: Would knowing their variable costs help?

Patty: Certainly. It would give me their minimum price. With that knowledge, I'm sure we could find a way to beat them on several jobs, particularly for those jobs where we are at least as efficient. It would also help us identify where we are not cost competitive. With this information, we might be able to find ways to increase our efficiency.

Bill: Well, I have good news. I have some data here in these handouts that reveal bids that Kilborn made on several jobs. I have also been able to obtain the direct labor hours worked for many of these jobs. But that's not all. I have monthly totals for manufacturing costs and direct labor hours for all jobs for the past ten months. Brindon, with this information, can you estimate what the variable manufacturing cost per hour is? If you can, we can compute the variable costs for each job and the markup that Kilborn is using.

Brindon: Yes, an analysis of the data you're requesting is possible. I have a question, though, before I do this. How did you manage to acquire these data? I can't imagine that Kilborn would willingly release this information.

Bill: What does it matter how the data were acquired? The fact is, we have them, and we have an opportunity to gain a tremendous competitive advantage. With that advantage, we can meet our profit targets, and we will all end the year with a big bonus.

After the meeting, in a conversation with Patty, Brindon learned that Bill was dating Jackie Wilson, a cost accountant (and CMA) who happened to work for Kilborn. Patty speculated that Jackie might be the source of the Kilborn data. Upon learning this, Brindon expressed some strong reservations to Patty about analyzing the data.

REQUIRED:

1. Assume that Bill did acquire the data from Jackie Wilson. Comment on Jackie's behavior. Which standards of ethical conduct did she violate (see Chapter 1)?
2. Were Brindon's instincts correct—should he have felt some reservations about analyzing the data? Would it be ethical to analyze the data? Do any of the IMA standards of ethical conduct apply (see Chapter 1)? What would you do if you were Brindon? Explain.

Macphon Bell Corporation (MBC) operates in the telecommunication business. MBC has two divisions: a phone division and a cable service division. The phone division manufactures telephones in a large plant in Ohio. The product lines run from relatively inexpensive touch-tone wall and desk phones to expensive, high-quality cellular phones. MBC also operates a cable TV service in the Ohio area. The cable service offers three products: (1) a basic package, which includes 25 channels, (2) a basic package plus one movie channel, and (3) a basic package plus two movie channels.

The cable service division of the company reported the following activity for March:

	Basic	Basic Plus One	Basic Plus Two
Sales (units)	300,000	150,000	50,000
Price per unit	$20	$30	$35
Unit costs:			
Directly attributable	5	6	7
Driver traced	2	4	6
Allocated	10	14	15

The unit costs are divided as follows: 70% production and 30% marketing and customer service. Direct labor hours is the only driver used for tracing. Typically, the division uses only production costs to define unit costs. The above unit product cost information was provided at the request of the marketing manager and was the result of a special study.

Kent Bunker, the president of MBC, is reasonably satisfied with the performance of the cable division. March's performance is fairly typical of what has been happening over the past two years. The phone division, however, is another matter. Its overall profit performance has been declining. Two years ago, profit before taxes was about 25% of sales. March's dismal performance was also typical for what had been happening this year and was expected to continue—unless some action by management was taken to reverse the trend. During March, the phone division reported the following results:

Inventories:	
Raw materials, March 1	$ 10,000
Raw materials, March 31	20,000
Work in process, March 1	130,000
Work in process, March 31	40,000
Finished goods, March 1	480,000
Finished goods, March 31	380,000
Costs:	
Direct labor	$100,000
Plant and equipment depreciation	60,000
Materials handling	80,000
Inspections	60,000
Scheduling	36,000
Power	24,000
Plant supervision	8,000

continued

Manufacturing engineering	$ 20,000
Sales commissions	120,000
Salary, sales supervisor	6,000
Supplies	2,000
Warranty work	15,000
Rework	30,000

During March, the phone division purchased raw materials totaling $290,000. There are no significant inventories of supplies (beginning or ending). Supplies are accounted for separately from raw materials. MBC's phone division had sales totaling $1,100,000 for March.

Based on March's results, Kent decided to meet with three of the phone division's managers: Susan Dixon, divisional manager, Kirk Wimberly, divisional controller, and Larry Hartley, sales manager. A transcript of their recorded conversation is given below:

Kent: March's profit performance is down once again, and I think we need to see if we can identify the problem and correct it—before it's too late. Susan, what's your assessment of the situation?

Susan: Foreign competition is eating us alive. They are coming in with lower priced phones with the same or higher quality than our own. I've talked with several of the retailers that carry our lines and they say the same. They are convinced that we can sell more if we lower our prices.

Larry: They're right. If we could lower our prices by 10%-15%, I think that we'd regain most of our lost market share. But we also need to make sure that the quality of our products meets that of our competitors. As you know, we are spending a lot of money each month on rework and warranties. That worries me. I'd like to see that warranty cost cut by 70%-80%. If we could do that, then customer satisfaction with our products would increase, and I bet that we'd not only regain market share but we'd increase it.

Kirk: Lowering prices without lowering per-unit costs will not help us increase our profitability. I think we need to improve our cost accounting system. I am not confident that we really know how much each of our product lines is costing us. It may be that we are overpricing some of our units because we are overcosting them. And we may be underpricing other units.

Larry: This sounds promising—especially if the overcosting is for some of our high-volume lines. A price decrease for these products would make the biggest difference—and if we knew they were overcosted, then we could offer immediate price reductions.

Kent: Kirk, I need more explanation. We have been using the same cost accounting system for the last ten years. Why would it be a problem?

Kirk: I think that our manufacturing environment has changed. Over the years, we have added a lot of different product lines. Some of these products make very different demands on our manufacturing overhead resources. We trace—or attempt to trace—overhead costs to the different products using direct labor cost, a unit-based activity driver. We may be doing more allocation than tracing. If so, then we probably don't have a very good idea of what our product costs are. Also, as you know, with the way computer technology has changed over time, it is easier and cheaper to collect and use detailed information—information that will allow us to assign costs more accurately.

Kent: This may be something we should explore. Kirk, what do you suggest? What do we need to do?

Kirk: If we want more accurate product costs and if we really want to get in the cost reduction business, then we need to understand how costs behave. In particular, we need to understand activity cost behavior. Knowing what activities we perform, why we perform them, and how well we perform them will help us identify areas for improvement. We also need to know how the different products consume activity resources. What this boils down to is the need to use an activity-based management system. But before we jump into this, we need some idea of whether nonunit-based drivers add anything. Activity-based management is not an inexpensive undertaking. So I suggest that we do a preliminary study to see if direct labor hours are adequate for tracing. If not, then maybe some nonunit-drivers might be needed. In fact, if you would like, I can gather some data that will provide evidence of the usefulness of the activity-based approach.

Kent: What do you think Susan? It's your division.

Susan: What Kirk has said sounds promising. I think he should pursue it and quickly. I also think that we need to look at improving our quality. It sounds like we have a problem there. If quality could be improved, then our costs will drop. I'll talk to our quality people. Kirk, in the meantime, find out for us if moving to an activity-based system is the way to go. How much time do you need?

Kirk: I have already been gathering data. I could probably have a report within two weeks.

Within a two-week period, Kirk sent the following memo to Susan Dixon:

MEMO

TO: Susan Dixon
FROM: Kirk Wimberly
SUBJECT: Preliminary Analysis

Based on my initial analysis, I am confident that an ABC system will offer significant improvement. I regressed total monthly overhead cost on monthly labor cost using the following 15 months of data:

Overhead	Direct Labor Cost
$360,000	$100,000
300,000	100,000
350,000	90,000
400,000	100,000
320,000	90,000
380,000	100,000
300,000	90,000
280,000	90,000
340,000	95,000
410,000	100,000
375,000	100,000
360,000	85,000
340,000	85,000
330,000	90,000
300,000	80,000

The results were revealing. Although direct labor cost appeared to be a driver of overhead cost, it really didn't explain a lot of the variation. I then searched for other drivers—particularly nonunit drivers—that might offer more insight into overhead cost behavior. Every time a batch is produced, material movement occurs regardless of the size of the batch. The number of moves seemed like a more logical driver. I was only able to gather 10 months of data. (Our information system doesn't provide the number of moves, so I had to build the data set by interviewing production personnel.) This information is provided below:

Material-Handling Cost	Number of Moves
$80,000	1,500
60,000	1,000
70,000	1,250
72,000	1,300
65,000	1,100
85,000	1,700
67,000	1,200
73,500	1,350
83,000	1,400
84,000	1,700

The regression results were impressive. There is no question in my mind that number of moves is a good driver of materials-handling costs. Using the number of moves to assign materials-handling costs to products would likely be better than the cost assignment using direct labor cost. Furthermore, since smaller batches use the same number of moves as do large batches, we have some evidence that we may be overcosting our high-volume products.

I looked at one more overhead activity: inspecting products. We have 15 inspectors who are paid an average of $4,000 per month. Each inspector offers about 160 hours of inspection capacity per month. However, it appears that they only actually work about 80% of those hours. The drop in demand we have experienced explains this idle time. I see no evidence of variable cost behavior here. I'm not exactly sure how to treat inspection cost, but I think that it is more related to inspection hours than to direct labor cost. Some of the other overhead activities seem to be nonunit-level as well—enough, in fact, to be concerned about how we assign costs.

REQUIRED:

1. Compute two different unit costs for each of the cable service division's products. What managerial objectives are being served by these unit cost computations?
2. Three different cost categories are provided by the cable service division: direct tracing, driver tracing, and allocation. Discuss the meaning of each. Based on how costs are assigned, do you think that the Cable division is using a traditional or contemporary cost accounting system? What other differences exist between traditional and contemporary cost accounting systems?
3. Discuss the differences between the cable service division's products and the phone division's products.
4. Prepare an income statement for the cable service division for March.
5. Prepare an income statement for the phone division for March. Include a supporting cost of goods manufactured statement.
6. The phone division has been using the same cost accounting system for over ten years. Explain why its cost accounting system may be outmoded. What factors determine when a new cost accounting system is warranted?
7. Using the method of least squares, calculate two cost formulas: one for overhead using direct labor cost as the driver and one for materials-handling cost using number of moves as the driver. Comment on Kirk Wimberly's observations concerning the outcomes.
8. How would you describe the cost behavior of the inspection activity? Assume that the quality control manager implements a program that reduces the number of defective units by 50%. Because of the improved quality, the demand for inspection hours will also drop by 50%. What is the potential monthly reduction in inspection costs? How did knowledge of inspection's cost behavior help?

Part 2
Cost Accounting Systems

Chapter 4

Product and Service Costing: Overhead Application and Job-Order System

Levittown, the original housing development created on Long Island, NY, just after World War II, provided only a few different models of houses. Times have changed, and today's home builders know that consumers want a wide variety of flexible designs and unique features to suit their particular lifestyles. The costing for these houses must account for their uniqueness by using job order costing.

LEARNING OBJECTIVES

After studying this chapter, you should be able to:

1. Differentiate the cost accounting systems of service and manufacturing firms and of unique and standardized products.
2. Discuss the interrelationship of cost accumulation, cost measurement, and cost assignment.
3. Compute a predetermined overhead rate, and use the rate to assign overhead to production.
4. Explain the difference between job-order and process costing, and identify the source documents used in job-order costing.
5. Describe the cost flows associated with job-order costing, and prepare the journal entries.
6. Explain why multiple overhead rates may be preferred to a single, plant-wide rate.

Now that we have an understanding of basic cost terminology, we need to look more closely at the system that the firm sets up to account for costs. In other words, we need to determine how we accumulate costs and associate them with different cost objects. In a traditional cost accounting setting, the cost object is the unit of product or service. In this chapter, we will focus on traditional accounting systems.

CHARACTERISTICS OF THE PRODUCTION PROCESS

Objective 1
Differentiate the cost accounting systems of service and manufacturing firms and of unique and standardized products.

In general, a firm sets up a cost management system that mirrors the production process. A cost management system modeled after the production process allows managers to better monitor the economic performance of the firm. A production process may yield a tangible product or a service. Those products or services may be similar in nature or unique. These characteristics of the production process determine the best approach for developing a cost management system.

Manufacturing Firms Versus Service Firms

Manufacturing involves putting together materials, labor, and overhead to produce a new product. The good produced is tangible and can be inventoried and transported from the plant to the customer. A service is characterized by its intangible nature. It is not separable from the customer and cannot be inventoried. Traditional cost accounting has emphasized manufacturing and virtually ignored services. Now, more than ever, that approach will not do. Our economy has grown increasingly service-oriented. Managers must be able to track the costs of services rendered just as precisely as they must track the costs of goods manufactured. In fact, the controller for a company may find it necessary to cost both goods and services as managers take an internal customer approach.

The range of manufacturing and service firms can be represented by a continuum as shown in Exhibit 4-1. The pure service is shown at the left. The pure service involves no raw materials and no tangible item for the customer. There are few pure services. Perhaps an example would be bungee jumping. In the middle of the continuum and still very much a service is a beauty salon, which uses raw materials on customers when performing the service, e.g., hair spray and mousse. At the other end of the continuum is the manufactured product. Examples include automobiles, cereal, cosmetics, and drugs. Even these, however, often have a service component. For example, a prescription drug must be prescribed by a physician and dispensed by a licensed pharmacist. Automobile dealers stress the continuing service associated with their cars. And how would we categorize food services? Does Taco Bell provide a product or a service? There are elements of both.

intangibility
inseparability
heterogeneity

perishability

Four areas in which services differ from products are: intangibility, inseparability, heterogeneity, and perishability. **Intangibility** refers to the nonphysical nature of services as opposed to products. **Inseparability** means that production and consumption are inseparable for services. **Heterogeneity** refers to the greater chances for variation in the performance of services than in the production of products. **Perishability** means that services cannot be inventoried but must be consumed when performed. These differences affect the types of information needed for planning, control, and decision making in the production of services. Exhibit 4-2 illustrates the features associated with the production of services and their interface with the cost management system.

128

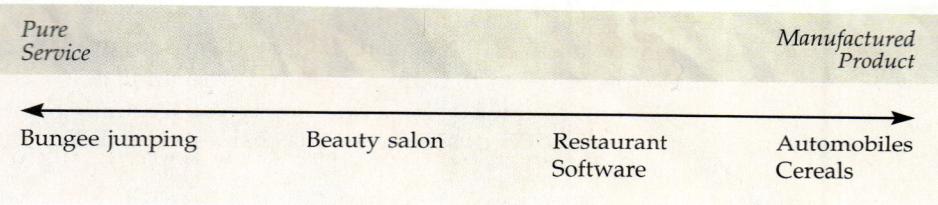

Exhibit 4-1
Continuum of Services and Manufactured Products

Pure Service			Manufactured Product
Bungee jumping	Beauty salon	Restaurant Software	Automobiles Cereals

Exhibit 4-2
Features of Service Firms and Their Interface with the Cost Management System

Feature	Relationship to Business	Impact on Cost Management System
Intangibility	Services cannot be stored.	There are no inventory accounts.
	Services cannot be protected through patents.	There is a strong ethical code.
	Services cannot readily be displayed or communicated.	
	Prices are difficult to set.	Costs must be related to entire organization.
Inseparability	Consumer is involved in production.	Costs are accounted for by customer type.
	Other consumers are involved in production.	
	Centralized mass production of services is difficult.	System must be generated to encourage consistent quality.
Heterogeneity	Standardization and quality control are difficult.	A strong systems approach is needed.
		Productivity measurement is ongoing.
		TQM is critical.
Perishability	Service benefits expire quickly.	There are no inventories.
	Service may be repeated often for one customer.	There needs to be a standardized system to handle repeat customers.

First two columns adapted from Valarie Zeithaml, A. Parasuraman, and Leonard L. Berry, "Problems and Strategies in Services Marketing," *Journal of Marketing*, 49, Spring 1985, pp. 34–46.

Intangibility of services leads to a major difference in the accounting for services as opposed to products. A service company cannot inventory the service and therefore has minimal to moderate inventories of supplies. A manufacturing company has inventories of raw materials, supplies, work in process, and finished goods. Because of the significance and complexity of inventories in manufacturing, we will spend more time on manufacturing companies in accounting for the cost of inventories.

Another important difference between service and manufacturing companies is heterogeneity of labor. Service firms are keenly aware of the importance of human resources; the service is provided by people. A key assumption of microeconomics is the homogeneity of labor. That is, one direct laborer is assumed to be identical to another. This assumption is the basis of labor standards in standard costing. Service companies know that one worker is *not* identical to another.

For example, Walt Disney World hires "backstage employees" and "on-stage employees." The backstage employees may do maintenance, sew costumes, and work in personnel (called "central casting"), but they do not work with the paying public (called guests). On-stage employees, hired both for their particular skills and their ability to interact well with people, do work directly with the guests. A further aspect of labor heterogeneity is that a worker is not the same from one day to the next. Workers can be affected by the job undertaken, the mix of other individuals with whom they work, their education and experience, and personal factors such as home life. These factors make the provision of a consistent level of service difficult. The measurement of productivity and quality in a service company must be ongoing and sensitive to these factors.

Inseparability means that differences in customers affect the service firm more than the manufacturing firm. When Proctor-Silex sells a toaster, the mood and personal qualities of the customer are irrelevant. When Sloan-Kettering Memorial Hospital sells a service to a customer, however, the disposition of the customer may affect the amount of service required as well as the quality of the service rendered. Inseparability also means that customers evaluate services differently from products. As a result, service companies may need to spend more money on some resources and less on others than would be necessary in a manufacturing plant. For example, consumers may use price and physical facilities as the major cues to service quality. Service firms, then, tend to incur higher costs for attractive places of business than do manufacturing firms. One of the initial impressions you may get of a manufacturing plant is how large, noisy, and dingy it is. Floors are concrete; the ceiling is typically unfinished. In short, it is not a pretty sight. However, as long as a high-quality product is made, the consumer does not care. How different that is from the service environment. Banks, doctors' offices, and restaurants are pleasant places, tastefully decorated, and filled with plants. This is cost effective to the extent that customers are drawn to such an environment to conduct business. In addition, the environment may allow the service firm to charge a higher price—signaling its higher quality.

Perishability of services is very similar to intangibility. For example, there are no work in process or finished goods inventories of services. However, there is a subtle distinction between intangibility and perishability that merits discussion. A service is perishable if the effects are short-term. Not all services fall into this category. Plastic surgery is not perishable, but haircuts are. The impact on cost management is that perishable services require systems to easily handle repeat customers. The repetitive nature of the service also leads us to the use of standardized processes and costing. Examples are financial services (e.g., check clearing by banks), janitorial services, and beauty and barber shops.

Customers may perceive greater risk when buying services than when buying products. Ethics are important here. The internal accountant who is responsible for gathering data on service quality must accurately report the good news as well as the bad. A customer who has been stung once by misleading advertising or failure to deliver the promised performance will be loathe to try that firm again. A manufacturer can offer a warranty or product replacement. But the service firm must consider the customer's wasted time. Therefore, the service firm must be especially careful not to promise more than can or will be delivered. Consider the example of Lexus which discovered a defect shortly after introducing the car into the United States. Lexus dealers contacted each buyer personally and arranged for loaner cars while the defect was fixed. In the case of buyers who lived far from a dealership, Lexus brought the repair people to the buyers.

Contrast this experience with that undergone by many GM buyers who must go through several layers of automotive hierarchy in order to get a defect repaired. Clearly, Lexus understood the value of the customers' time in arranging the service.

Service companies are particularly interested in planning and control techniques that apply to their special types of firms. Productivity measurement and quality control are very important. Pricing may involve different considerations for the service firm.

The important point is that service and manufacturing companies may have different needs for accounting data and techniques. It is important for the accountant to be aware of relevant differences in order to provide appropriate support. It is critical that the accountant be cross-functionally trained. Take McDonald's for example. Is this a manufacturing or service entity? In the kitchen, McDonald's runs a production line. The product is rigidly consistent. Each hamburger contains the same amount of meat, mustard, ketchup, and pickles. The buns are identical. The burgers are cooked the prescribed amount of time to the right temperature. They are wrapped in a methodic manner and join other burgers in the warming bin. Standard cost accounting techniques work well for this phase, and McDonald's uses them. At the counter, however, the company becomes a service organization. Customers want their orders taken and filled quickly and correctly. In addition, they want a smile and maybe some help finding certain items on the menu. Clean restrooms are critical. McDonald's emphasizes nonfinancial measures of performance for service areas: counter customers are to be served within 60 seconds; drive-through customers are to be served within 90 seconds; restrooms are to be checked and cleaned at least once an hour.

Unique Versus Standardized Products and Services

A second way of characterizing products and services is according to the degree of uniqueness. If a firm produces unique products, in small batches, and if those products incur different costs, then the firm must keep track of the costs of each product or batch. This is referred to as a job-order costing system, the focus of this chapter. At the other extreme, the company may make many identical units of the same product. Since the units are the same, then the costs of each unit are also the same. Accounting for the costs of the identical units is relatively easy and is referred to as a process-costing system, examined in a later chapter.

It is important to note that the uniqueness of the products (or units) for cost accounting purposes relates to unique costs. Look, for example, at the picture at the beginning of this chapter. Drees Construction builds houses in the Midwest. While the houses are based on several standard models, buyers can customize their houses by selecting different types of brick, tile, carpet, and so on. However, these selections are taken from a set menu of choices. Therefore, while one house is painted white while its neighbor is green, the cost is the same. However, if different selections have different costs, then those costs must be accounted for separately. Thus, if one Drees home buyer selects a whirlpool tub while another selects a standard model, the different cost of the two tubs must be tracked to the correct house. As one builder said, "All we can do is offer choices and keep close track of our costs."[1] Therefore, a production process that appears to produce similar products may incur different costs for each product. In this type of situation, the firm should track costs using a job-order costing system.

---

1.   June Fletcher, "New Developments: Same Frames, One-of-a-Kind Frills," *Wall Street Journal*, September 8, 1995, pp. B1 and B8.

Both service firms and manufacturing firms use the job-order costing approach. Custom-cabinet makers and home builders manufacture unique products, which must be accounted for using a job-costing approach. Dental and medical services also use job-order costing. The costs associated with a simple filling clearly differ from those associated with a root canal. Printing, automotive repair, and appliance repair are also services using job-order costing.

Firms in process industries mass-produce large quantities of similar, or homogeneous, products. Each product is essentially indistinguishable from its companion product. Examples of process manufacturers include food, cement, petroleum, and chemical firms. The important point here is that the cost of one product is identical to the cost of another. Therefore, service firms can also use a process-costing approach. Discount stockbrokers, for example, incur much the same cost to execute a customer order for one stock as for another; check-clearing departments of banks incur a uniform cost to clear a check, no matter the size of the check or to whom it is written.

Interestingly, companies are gravitating toward job-order costing because of the increased variety of products. Improved technology is making customization possible. An excellent example is Israel's Indigo, Ltd., new Omnium One-Shot Color printing system which makes it possible to print cans, bottles, labels, etc., in smaller lots than ever before. The Omnium machine could be used to print soft drink cans customized for weekend tailgate parties ("Ride 'em, Cowboys!"), or to print coordinated kitchen curtains and tiles.[2] Thus, a combination of customer demand for specialized products, flexible manufacturing, and improved information technology has led world-class manufacturers to approximate a job-order environment.

SETTING UP THE COST ACCOUNTING SYSTEM

Objective 2
Discuss the interrelationship of cost accumulation, cost measurement, and cost assignment.

cost accumulation
cost measurement
cost assignment

Given the characteristics of the firm's production process, it is time to set up the system to be used in generating appropriate cost information. A good cost accounting information system is flexible and reliable. It provides information for a variety of purposes and can be used to answer a variety of questions. In general, the system is used to satisfy the needs for cost accumulation, cost measurement, and cost assignment. **Cost accumulation** is the recognition and recording of costs. **Cost measurement** involves determining the dollar amounts of direct materials, direct labor, and overhead used in production. **Cost assignment** is the association of production costs with the units produced. Exhibit 4-3 illustrates the relationship of cost accumulation, cost measurement, and cost assignment.

Cost Accumulation

source document

Cost accumulation refers to the recognition and recording of costs. The cost accountant needs to develop source documents, which keep track of costs as they occur. A **source document** describes a transaction. Data from these source documents can then be recorded in a data base. The recording of data in a data base allows accountants and managers the flexibility to analyze subsets of the data as needed to aid in management decision making. The cost accountant can also use

2. Peter Coy and Neal Sandler, "A Package for Every Person," *Business Week,* February 6, 1995, p. 44.

Exhibit 4-3
Relationship of Cost Ac-
cumulation, Cost Mea-
surement, and Cost
Assignment

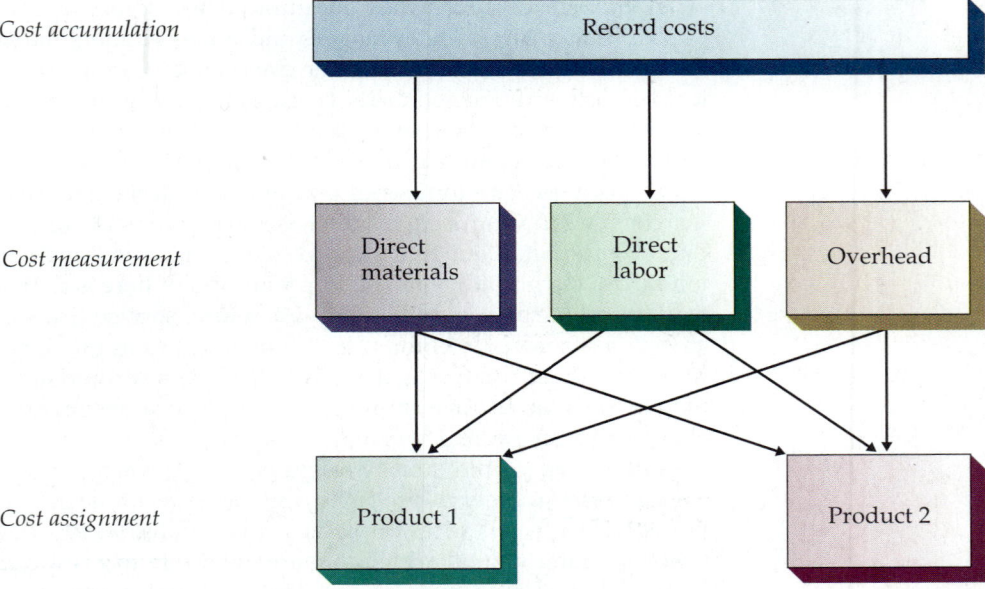

the data base to see that the relevant costs are recorded in the general ledger and posted to appropriate accounts for purposes of external financial reporting.

Well-designed source documents can supply information in a flexible way. In other words, the information can be used for multiple purposes. For example, the sales receipt written up by a clerk when a customer buys merchandise lists the date, the items purchased, the quantities, the prices, sales tax paid, and the total received. Just this one source document can be used in determining sales revenue for the month, the sales by product, the tax owed to the state, and cash received or accounts receivable. Similarly, employees fill in labor time tickets, telling which job was worked on, on what date, and for how long. Data from the labor time ticket can be used in determining direct labor cost used in production, the amount to pay the worker, the degree of productivity improvement achieved over time, and the amount to budget for labor for an upcoming job.

Cost Measurement

Accumulating costs simply means that they are recorded for use. We must then classify or organize these costs in a meaningful way and then associate these costs with the units produced. Cost measurement refers to classifying the costs; it consists of determining the dollar amounts of direct materials, direct labor, and overhead used in production. The dollar amounts may be the actual amounts expended for the manufacturing inputs or they may be estimated amounts. Often bills for overhead items arrive after the unit cost must be calculated; therefore, estimated amounts are used to ensure timeliness of cost information or to control costs.

There are two commonly used ways to *measure* the costs associated with production: actual costing and normal costing. Actual costing requires the firm to use the actual cost of all resources used in production to determine unit cost. While intuitively reasonable, this method has drawbacks, as we shall see. The second method, normal costing, requires the firm to apply actual costs of direct materials and direct labor to units produced. However, overhead is applied based on a predetermined estimate. Normal costing is more widely used in practice and will be further discussed in this chapter.

actual cost system

Actual Costing An **actual cost system** uses actual costs for direct materials, direct labor, and overhead to determine unit cost. In practice, strict actual cost systems are rarely used because they cannot provide accurate unit cost information on a timely basis. Interestingly, per-unit computation of the direct materials and direct labor costs is not the source of the difficulty. Direct materials and direct labor have a definite, identifiable relationship with units produced. The main problem with using actual costs for calculation of unit cost is with manufacturing overhead. Overhead items do not have the direct relationship that direct materials and direct labor do. For example, how much of a security guard's salary should be assigned to a unit of product? Because overhead items are indirectly related to the units produced, per-unit overhead costs must be calculated by averaging. Averaging requires totaling manufacturing overhead costs for a given period and then dividing this total by the number of units produced.

If the time period chosen is relatively short (say, a month), so that cost information can be produced in a timely manner, averaging can yield per-unit overhead costs that fluctuate dramatically from month to month. This occurs for two major reasons. First, many overhead costs are not incurred uniformly throughout the year. Thus, they can differ significantly from one period to the next. Second, per-unit overhead costs fluctuate dramatically because of nonuniform production levels.

To illustrate, consider the following example. Assume a company produces rock stops for cellos. A rock stop is a rubber disk with an indentation in the center. The cellist places the cello pin in the indentation to prevent the cello from scooting around the floor while it is being played. Each rock stop requires two ounces of rubber and six minutes of direct labor. For the technology used, this input-output relationship is reasonably stable. Thus, the quantity of raw materials and the direct labor used for each rock stop are essentially the same regardless of how many rock stops are produced or when they are produced. The unit cost of these two inputs can be accurately computed.

If the cost of rubber is $0.30 per ounce and the price of labor is $8 per hour, then the cost of rubber per rock stop is $0.60 ($0.30 × 2 ounces), and the cost of direct labor per rock stop is $0.80 ($8 × 0.10 hours). The actual prime cost per rock stop, then, is $1.40 ($0.60 + $0.80). If the prices of materials and labor are reasonably stable, then the $1.40 per-unit prime cost is the same regardless of how many rock stops are made or when they are produced during the year.

If actual overhead costs for the manufacturer were $20,000 in April and 40,000 rock stops were produced, then the per-unit overhead cost is $20,000/40,000, or $0.50 per rock stop. Unfortunately, this averaging approach has some severe limitations, as shown in the following figures:

	April	*June*	*August*
Actual overhead	$20,000	$40,000	$40,000
Actual units produced	40,000	40,000	160,000
Per-unit overhead*	$0.50	$1.00	$0.25

*Actual overhead/Actual production

Notice that the overhead cost per unit is different for each of the three months. April and June have the same production but different monthly overhead costs. The difference in overhead cost could be attributable to higher utility costs due to increased cooling requirements in the month of June. Thus, the rock stops produced in June have a higher per-unit overhead cost ($1.00 rather than $0.50) just because they happened to be produced when cooling was required. The difference in the per-unit overhead cost is because overhead costs were incurred nonuniformly.

Nonuniform production is the second reason for variability in per-unit overhead costs, as June and August figures show. Both months have the same total monthly overhead costs but different output levels. August' output may be much larger because of anticipation of back-to-school sales. Whatever the reason, the higher output in August creates a lower per-unit overhead cost ($0.25 compared to June's $1.00).

Notice that the varying per-unit overhead costs do not signal differences in value or even in the underlying cost structure. A rock stop produced in April is identical to one produced in June or August. The higher utility costs in June may equal June utility costs of the previous year. The problem of fluctuating per-unit overhead costs can be avoided if the firm waits until the end of the year to assign the overhead costs. For example, if April, June, and August were the only months of operation for the rock stop manufacturer, then the total overhead costs for the year are $100,000 ($20,000 + $40,000 + $40,000), and the total production is 240,000 rock stops (40,000 + 40,000 + 160,000). The per-unit overhead cost is $100,000/240,000, or $0.417. By waiting until the end of the year, the firm eliminates the problems of nonuniform overhead cost incurrence and nonuniform production. The result is the same overhead cost per unit for every unit produced.

Unfortunately, waiting until the end of the year to compute an overhead rate is unacceptable. A company needs unit cost information throughout the year. This information is needed on a timely basis both for interim financial statements and to help managers make decisions such as pricing. Most decisions requiring unit cost information simply cannot wait until the end of the year. Managers must react to day-to-day conditions in the marketplace in order to maintain a sound competitive position.

Normal Costing A possible solution to the problems associated with actual costing is to approximate the end-of-the-year actual overhead rate at the *beginning* of the year and then use the predetermined rate throughout the year to obtain the needed unit cost information. The end-of-the-year actual rate can be approximated by estimating the overhead costs for the coming year and dividing these estimated costs by expected production. Suppose that the rock stop manufacturer had estimated on January 1 that overhead costs for the year would be $90,000 and that expected production is 225,000 units. Using this estimated data, the predetermined overhead rate would be $0.40 ($90,000/225,000).

normal costing systems

Cost systems that measure overhead costs on a predetermined basis and use actual costs for direct materials and direct labor are called **normal costing systems**. The principal difficulty with normal costing is that the predetermined rate is likely to differ from the actual rate. Either actual overhead costs differ from the estimated costs or the actual level of production differs from the expected level, or both.

If the measurement error is small, however, the product cost resulting from normal costing will not differ significantly from the actual product cost determined after the fact. In the example above, the predetermined rate was $0.40, and the end-of-the-year actual rate was $0.417. Most would agree that this is not a significant difference.

Virtually all firms assign overhead to production on a predetermined basis. This fact seems to suggest that most firms successfully approximate the end-of-the-year overhead rate. Thus, the measurement problems associated with the use of actual overhead costs are solved by the use of estimated overhead costs. A job-order cost system that uses actual costs for materials and labor and estimated costs for overhead is called a *normal job-order cost system*.

Cost Assignment

Once costs have been accumulated and measured, they are assigned to units of product manufactured or units of service delivered. Unit costs are important for a wide variety of purposes. For example, bidding is a common requirement in the markets for custom homes and industrial buildings. It is virtually impossible to submit a meaningful bid without knowing the costs associated with the units to be produced. Product cost information is vital in a number of other areas as well. Decisions concerning product design and introduction of new products are affected by expected unit costs. Decisions to make or buy a product, to accept or reject a special order, or to keep or drop a product line require unit cost information.

In its simplest form, computing the unit manufacturing or service cost is easy. The unit cost is the total product cost associated with the units produced divided by the number of units produced. For example, if a toy company manufactures 100,000 tricycles and the total cost of materials, labor, and overhead for these tricycles is $1,500,000, then the cost per tricycle is $15 ($1,500,000/100,000). Although the concept is simple, the practical reality of the computation is more complex and breaks down when there are products that differ from one another or when the company needs to know the cost of the product before all of the actual costs associated with its production are known.

Importance of Unit Costs to Manufacturing Firms Unit cost is a critical piece of information for a manufacturer. Unit costs are essential for valuing inventory, determining income, and making a number of important decisions.

Disclosing the cost of inventories and determining income are financial reporting requirements that a firm faces at the end of each period. In order to report the cost of its inventories, a firm must know the number of units on hand and the unit cost. The cost of goods sold, used to determine income, also requires knowledge of the units sold and their unit cost.

Whether or not the unit cost information should include all manufacturing costs depends on the purpose for which the information is going to be used. For financial reporting, full or absorption unit cost information is required. If a firm is operating below its production capacity, however, variable cost information may be much more useful in a decision to accept or reject a special order. Simply put, unit cost information needed for external reporting may not supply the information necessary for a number of internal decisions, especially those decisions that are short-run in nature. Different costs are needed for different purposes.

It should be pointed out that full cost information is useful as an input for a number of important internal decisions as well as for financial reporting. In the long run, for any product to be viable, its price must cover its full cost. Decisions to introduce a new product, to continue a current product, and to analyze long-run prices are examples of important internal decisions that rely on full unit cost information.

Importance of Unit Costs to Nonmanufacturing Firms Service and nonprofit firms also require unit cost information. Conceptually, the way we accumulate and assign costs is the same whether or not the firm is a manufacturing firm. The service firm must first identify the service "unit" being provided. In an auto repair shop, the service unit would be the work performed on an individual customer's car. Because each car is different in terms of the work required (an oil change versus a transmission overhaul, for example), the costs must be assigned individually to each job. A hospital would accumulate costs by patient, patient day, and type of procedure (e.g., x-ray, complete blood count test). A governmental agency must also identify the service provided. For example, city government might provide household trash pickup and calculate the cost by truck run or by pickup per house.

Service firms use cost data in much the same way that manufacturing firms do. They use costs to determine profitability, the feasibility of introducing new services, and so on. However, because service firms do not produce physical products, they do not need to value work in process and finished goods inventories. Of course, they may have supplies, and the inventory of supplies is simply valued at historical cost.

Nonprofit firms must track costs to be sure that they provide their services in a cost-efficient way. Governmental agencies have a fiduciary responsibility to taxpayers to use funds wisely. This requires accurate accounting for costs.

Production of Unit Cost Information To produce unit cost information, both cost measurement and cost assignment are required. We have already considered two types of cost measurement systems, actual costing and normal costing. We have seen that normal costing is preferred because it provides information on a more timely basis. Shortly, we will address the cost assignment method of job-order costing. First, however, it is necessary to take a closer look at determining overhead costs per unit.

OVERHEAD APPLICATION: A NORMAL COSTING VIEW

Objective 3
Compute a predetermined overhead rate, and use the rate to assign overhead to production.

predetermined
  overhead rate

In normal cost systems, overhead is assigned to production through the use of a predetermined overhead rate.

Predetermined Overhead Rates

The basic difference between actual costing and normal costing is the use of a predetermined overhead rate. A **predetermined overhead rate** is calculated using the following formula:

Overhead rate = Budgeted annual overhead/Budgeted annual activity level

Budgeted overhead is simply the firm's best estimate of the amount of overhead (utilities, indirect labor, depreciation, etc.) to be incurred in the coming year. The estimate is often based on last year's figures, adjusted for anticipated changes in the coming year. The budgetary accountants of a firm are responsible for developing these estimates. The second input requires that the value for the activity level be specified. Activity level is sometimes referred to as the *denominator activity level*, since it appears in the denominator of the computation. This second input has two steps: first, identify a measure of production activity to serve as the activity driver; second, predict the level of this activity.

Notice that the formula for the predetermined overhead rate included budgeted amounts in *both* the numerator and the denominator. This is because the predetermined overhead rate is calculated in advance, usually at the beginning of the year. It is impossible to use actual overhead or actual activity level for the year, because on January 1, we do not know what actual levels will be. Therefore, only estimated or budgeted amounts are used in calculating the predetermined overhead rate.

Choosing the Activity Base

There are many different measures of production activity. In assigning overhead costs, it is important to select an activity base that is correlated with overhead consumption. This will ensure that individual products receive an accurate assignment of overhead costs. While there are many choices available, five commonly used activity drivers are:

1. Units produced
2. Direct labor hours
3. Direct labor dollars
4. Machine hours
5. Direct materials

The most obvious measure of production activity is output. If there is only one product, then overhead costs are clearly incurred to produce that product. In a single-product setting, the overhead costs of the period are directly traceable to the period's output. Clearly, for this case, units produced satisfies the cause-and-effect criterion. Most firms, however, produce more than one product. Since different products typically consume different amounts of overhead, this assignment method is inaccurate. At Kraft, for example, one plant produces salad dressing, ketchup, and marshmallow creme—each in a range of sizes from personal application packs to 32-ounce jars. In a multiple-product setting like this, overhead costs are common to more than one product, and different products may consume overhead at different rates.

Suppose a company produces components for aircraft engines. One type of component has a very simple round housing (the outer covering for the engine). Another type of component has a more elaborately turned and carved housing. Both types of housing require the use of a lathe (a machine in which a piece of material is held and turned while being shaped by a tool); therefore, both types should share the cost of using this machine. Suppose that the cost of operating the lathe is $80,000 and that 10,000 units of each type of housing are produced. Using units produced, the overhead cost assigned to each product would be $4 ($80,000/20,000). But one product may spend sixty minutes on the lathe, the other only fifteen. Since one product spends four times as much time on the lathe as the other, many would argue that it should receive more of the machine's cost. Using the units-produced method has not given a very accurate, meaningful, or fair assignment of overhead costs. How, then, should overhead be assigned?

Some believe that the assignment of overhead is essentially arbitrary. There is no single approach to assigning overhead that will satisfy all parties concerned. It could be argued that overhead should be assigned on an ability-to-bear basis with overhead assigned in proportion to revenues generated. Using this criterion, if the product spending less time on the lathe generates more revenues than the other product, then more overhead would be allocated to it than to the other product.

The position taken in this text is that the assignment of overhead costs should follow, as nearly as possible, a cause-and-effect relationship. Efforts should be made to identify those factors that cause the consumption of overhead. Once identified, these causal factors, or *activity drivers*, should be used to assign overhead to products. It seems reasonable to argue that for products using the lathe, machine hours reflect differential machine time and consequently the consumption of machine cost. Units produced does not necessarily reflect machine time or consumption of the machine cost; therefore, it can be argued that machine hours is a better activity driver and should be used to assign this overhead cost.

In the aircraft engine housing example shown in Exhibit 4-4, the simple housing uses fifteen minutes of machine time, and the complicated housing uses one hour. The total machine hours consumed by the two products is 12,500 (2,500 + 10,000). The overhead cost assigned per machine hour (MHr) is $80,000/12,500, or $6.40 per MHr. Using this rate, the per-unit overhead assigned to the simple housing is $1.60 (0.25 machine hours × $6.40), and the per-unit overhead assigned to the complicated housing is $6.40 (1 machine hour × $6.40).

As the example illustrates, activity measures other than units of product are needed when a firm has multiple products. The last four measures listed earlier (direct labor hours, direct labor dollars, machine hours, and direct materials) are all useful for multiple-product settings. Some may be more useful than others, depending on how well they correlate with the actual overhead consumption. As we will discuss later, it may even be appropriate to use multiple rates.

Choosing the Activity Level

Now that we have determined which measure of activity to use, we still need to predict the level of activity usage that applies to the coming year. Although any reasonable level of activity could be chosen, the two leading candidates are expected actual activity and normal activity. **Expected activity level** is simply the

expected activity level

Exhibit 4-4
Data on Engine Housing

Cost of operating lathe		$20,000
Total units produced		20,000
Total machine hours used		12,500

	Simple	Complicated
Number of housings	10,000	10,000
Time on lathe	0.25 MHr	1 MHr
Operating cost assigned using units produced	$4.00	$4.00
Operating cost assigned using machine time	$1.60	$6.40

normal activity level

production level the firm expects to attain for the coming year. **Normal activity level** is the average activity usage that a firm experiences in the long term (normal volume is computed over more than one year).

For example, assume that Paulos Manufacturing expects to produce 18,000 units next year and has budgeted overhead for the year at $216,000. Over the past four years, Paulos Manufacturing produced the following number of units:

1995	22,000
1996	17,000
1997	21,000
1998	20,000

If expected actual capacity is used, Paulos Manufacturing will apply overhead using a predetermined rate of $12 ($216,000/18,000). However, if normal capacity is used, then the denominator of the equation for predetermined overhead is the average of the past four years of activity, or 20,000 units [(22,000 + 17,000 + 21,000 + 20,000)/4]. Then the predetermined overhead rate to be used for the coming year is $10.80 ($216,000/20,000).

Which choice is better? Of the two, normal activity has the advantage of using the same activity level year after year. As a result, it produces less fluctuation from year to year in the assignment of per-unit overhead cost. Of course, if activity stays fairly stable, then the normal capacity level is roughly equal to the expected actual capacity level.

Other activity levels used for computing predetermined overhead rates are those corresponding to the theoretical and practical levels. **Theoretical activity level** is the absolute maximum production activity of a manufacturing firm. It is the output that can be realized if everything operates perfectly. **Practical activity level** is the maximum output that can be realized if everything operates efficiently. Efficient operation allows for some imperfections such as normal breakdowns, some shortages, workers operating at less than peak capability. Normal and expected actual activities tend to reflect consumer demand, while theoretical and practical activities reflect a firm's production capabilities. Exhibit 4-5 illustrates these four measures of activity.

theoretical activity
level

practical activity level

Given budgeted overhead, an activity driver, and an activity level, a predetermined overhead rate can be computed and applied to production. Understanding exactly how overhead is applied is critical to understanding normal costing.

The Basic Concept of Overhead Application

Predetermined overhead rates are used to apply overhead costs to production as the actual production activity unfolds. The total overhead assigned to actual production at any point in time is called **applied overhead**. Applied overhead is computed using the following formula:

applied overhead

Applied overhead = Overhead rate × Actual production activity

The activity driver used to determine the predetermined overhead rate must be the same as the measure of *actual* production activity. That is, if the predetermined overhead rate is calculated on the basis of budgeted direct labor hours, overhead must be applied on the basis of actual direct labor hours. Overhead can be applied daily, weekly, monthly, or as the need requires.

Exhibit 4-5
Measures of Activity Level

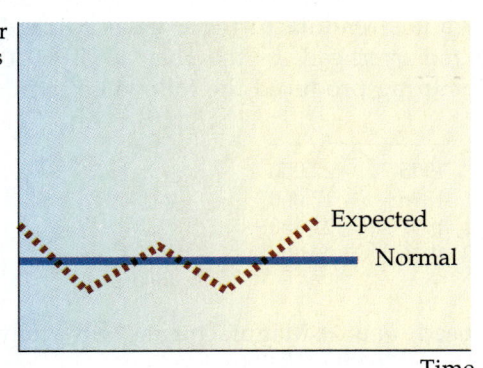

Consumer Demand-
Oriented Measures of
Activity Level

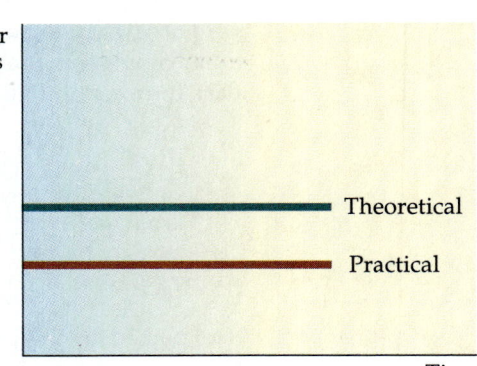

Productive Capability
Measures of Activity Level

In attempting to understand the concept of applied overhead, there are two points that should be emphasized.

1. Applied overhead is the basis for computing per-unit overhead cost.
2. Applied overhead is rarely equal to a period's actual overhead.

These points are best illustrated with an example. Suncalc, Inc., produces two unique, solar-powered products: a pocket calculator and a currency translator used to convert foreign currency exchange rates into dollars and vice versa. The company has the following estimated and actual data for 1996:

Budgeted overhead	$360,000
Normal activity (in direct labor hours)	120,000
Actual activity (in direct labor hours)	100,000
Actual overhead	$320,000

Now assume that the firm bases its predetermined overhead rate on normal activity measured in direct labor hours (*DLH*). Thus, for 1996:

$$\text{Predetermined overhead rate} = \text{Budgeted overhead/Normal activity}$$
$$= \$360,000/120,000 \text{ direct labor hours}$$
$$= \$3 \text{ per } DLH$$

Using the overhead rate, applied overhead for 1996 is:

$$\text{Applied overhead} = \text{Overhead rate} \times \text{Actual activity usage}$$
$$= \$3 \text{ per } DLH \times 100,000 \ DLH$$
$$= \$300,000$$

Per-Unit Overhead Cost In a normal cost system, the predetermined overhead rate is the basis for per-unit overhead cost calculation. For example, assume that 40 percent of the actual direct labor hours worked were used to produce 80,000 units of the pocket calculator, and the remaining 60 percent of direct labor time was used to produce 90,000 units of the currency translator. Since the predeter-

100,000 × 40% [handwritten]

mined overhead rate is $3 per *DLH*, the pocket calculator would be assigned a total of $120,000 of overhead ($3 × 40,000), and the currency translator would be assigned $180,000 ($3 × 60,000). The per-unit overhead cost of the pocket calculator is $120,000/80,000, or $1.50, and for the currency translator, $180,000/90,000, or $2.

100,000 × 60% [handwritten]

	Pocket Calculator	Currency Translator
Units produced	80,000	90,000
Direct labor hours	40,000	60,000
Overhead applied to production ($3 × *DLH*)	$120,000	$180,000
Overhead per unit	$1.50	$2.00

Underapplied and Overapplied Overhead Notice that the amount of overhead applied to production ($300,000) differs from the actual overhead ($320,000). Since the predetermined overhead rate is based on estimated data, applied overhead will rarely equal actual overhead. Since only $300,000 was applied in our example, the firm has *underapplied* overhead by $20,000. If applied overhead had been $330,000, too much overhead would have been applied to production. The firm would have *overapplied* overhead by $10,000. We call the difference between actual overhead and applied overhead an **overhead variance**. If the difference is positive (i.e., if actual overhead is greater than applied overhead), then the variance is called **underapplied overhead**. If the difference is negative (i.e., if applied overhead is greater than actual overhead), then the variance is called **overapplied overhead**.

Overhead variances occur because it is impossible to estimate perfectly future overhead costs and production activity. Their presence is virtually inevitable. A problem arises if the overhead variances are not corrected. In essence, the firm has traded off costing accuracy for convenience by applying overhead throughout the year. At year end, however, costs reported on the financial statements must be actual—*not* estimated amounts. Accordingly, at the end of a reporting period, procedures must exist to dispose of any overhead variance.

overhead variance

underapplied overhead

overapplied overhead

Disposition of Overhead Variances

From an actual costing perspective, the overhead variance represents an error in assigning overhead costs to production. At the end of the reporting period, something must be done with the overhead variance. Usually, the variance is disposed of in one of two ways.

1. All overhead variance is allocated to cost of goods sold.
2. The overhead variance is allocated among work in process, finished goods, and cost of goods sold.

Assigned to Cost of Goods Sold The most common practice is simply to assign the entire overhead variance to cost of goods sold. This practice is justified on the basis of materiality, the same principle used to justify expensing the entire cost of a pencil sharpener in the period acquired rather than allocating (through depreciation) its cost over the life of the sharpener. Since the overhead variance is usually relatively small, the method of disposition is not a critical matter, because all production costs should appear in cost of goods sold eventually.

Additionally, if the balances in work in process and finished goods are stable from one period to the next, the entire period's production cost ends up in cost of goods sold and the overhead variance belongs there.

Thus, the overhead variance is added to the cost of goods sold if underapplied and subtracted from cost of goods sold if overapplied. For example, assume that Suncalc has an ending balance in its cost of goods sold account equal to $500,000. The underapplied variance of $20,000 would be added to produce a new, adjusted balance of $520,000. (This makes sense—applied overhead was $300,000, while actual was $320,000. Thus, production costs were *under*stated by $20,000, and cost of goods sold must be increased to correct the problem.) If the variance had been overapplied, it would have been subtracted from cost of goods sold to produce a new balance of $480,000.

Allocation to Production Accounts If the overhead variance is material, it should be allocated to the period's production. Conceptually, the overhead costs of a period belong to the production of the period. Overhead costs for a period should be associated with goods started but not completed (work in process), goods finished but not sold (finished goods), and goods finished and sold (cost of goods sold). Because a period's overhead costs flow through these three different accounts, the overhead variance should be allocated to these accounts as well.

The recommended way to achieve this allocation is to prorate the overhead variance based on the ending *applied overhead balances* in each account. Although other ending balances could be used to allocate the variance (e.g., total manufacturing costs), the applied overhead balance best reflects the additional overhead that should be assigned to each account. Using applied overhead captures the original cause-and-effect relationships used to assign overhead. Using another balance, such as total manufacturing costs, may result in an unfair assignment of the additional overhead. For example, two products identical on all dimensions except for the cost of raw material inputs should receive the same overhead assignment. Yet, if total manufacturing costs were used to allocate an overhead variance, then the product with the more expensive materials would receive a higher overhead assignment.

To illustrate the disposition of the overhead variance using the recommended approach, assume that Suncalc's accounts had the following applied overhead balances for the end of 1996:

Work in Process	$ 60,000
Finished Goods	90,000
Cost of Goods Sold	150,000
Total dollar balance	$300,000

Given the above data, the percentage allocation of any overhead variance to the three accounts in 1996 is

Work in Process	20%	(60,000/300,000)
Finished Goods	30%	(90,000/300,000)
Cost of Goods Sold	50%	(150,000/300,000)

Recall that in 1996, Suncalc had an overhead variance that was $20,000 underapplied. Thus, Work in Process would receive 20 percent of $20,000 ($4,000), Finished Goods would receive 30 percent of $20,000 ($6,000), and Cost of Goods Sold would receive 50 percent of $20,000 ($10,000). Since underapplied means that too little overhead was assigned, these individual prorated amounts would be *added* to the ending account balances. Adding these amounts produces the following new adjusted balances of the three accounts:

	Unadjusted Balance	Prorated Underapplied Overhead	Adjusted Balance
Work in Process	$ 60,000	$ 4,000	$ 64,000
Finished Goods	90,000	6,000	96,000
Cost of Goods Sold	150,000	10,000	160,000

Of course, if too much overhead was assigned to production, overapplied amounts would have been *subtracted* from the account balances.

We now have an understanding of how manufacturing costs are measured in a normal cost system. Considerable emphasis has been placed on describing how overhead costs are treated, because this is the key to normal costing. Before we seriously examine any method for assigning costs, we first should know how these costs are to be measured. The way costs are measured affects the procedures followed in either job-order costing or process costing.

THE JOB-ORDER COSTING SYSTEM: GENERAL DESCRIPTION

Objective 4

Explain the difference between job-order and process costing, and identify the source documents used in job-order costing.

As we have seen, manufacturing and service firms can be divided into two major industrial types based on the uniqueness of their product. The degree of product or service heterogeneity affects the way in which we track costs. As a result, two different cost assignment systems have been developed: job-order costing and process costing. Job-order costing systems will be described in this chapter.

Overview of the Job-Order Costing System

Firms operating in job-order industries produce a wide variety of products or jobs that are usually quite distinct from each other. Customized or built-to-order products fit into this category, as do services that vary from customer to customer. Examples of job-order processes include printing, construction, furniture making, automobile repair, and beautician services. In manufacturing, a job may be a single unit such as a house, or it may be a batch of units such as eight tables. Job-order systems may be used to produce goods for inventory that are subsequently sold in the general market. Often, however, a job is associated with a particular customer order. The key feature of job-order costing is that the cost of one job differs from that of another job and must be kept track of separately.

job-order costing system

For job-order production systems, costs are accumulated by *job*. This approach to assigning costs is called a **job-order costing system**. In a job-order firm, collecting costs by job provides vital information for management. Once a job is completed, the unit cost can be obtained by dividing the total manufacturing costs by the number of units produced. For example, if the production costs for printing 100 wedding announcements total $300, then the unit cost for this job is $3. Given the unit cost information, the manager of the printing firm can determine whether the prevailing market price provides a reasonable profit margin. If not, then this may signal to the manager that the costs are out of line with other printing firms, and action can be taken to reduce costs. Alternatively, other types of jobs for which the firm can earn a reasonable profit margin might be emphasized. In fact, the profit contributions of different printing jobs offered by the firm can be computed, and this information can then be used to select the most profitable mix of printing services to offer.

In illustrating job-order costing, we will assume a normal cost measurement approach. The actual costs of direct materials and direct labor are assigned to jobs along with a predetermined overhead rate. *How* these costs are actually assigned to the various jobs, however, is the central issue. In order to assign these costs, we must identify each job and the direct materials and direct labor associated with it. Additionally, some mechanism must exist to allocate overhead costs to each job.

job-order cost sheet

The document that identifies each job and accumulates its manufacturing costs is the **job-order cost sheet**. An example is shown in Exhibit 4-6. The cost accounting department creates such a cost sheet upon receipt of a production order. Orders are written up in response to a specific customer order or in conjunction with a production plan derived from a sales forecast. Each job-order cost sheet has a job-order number that identifies the new job.

work-in-process file

In a manual accounting system, the job-order cost sheet is a document. In today's world, however, most accounting systems are automated. The cost sheet usually corresponds to a record in a work-in-process master file. The collection of all job cost sheets defines a **work-in-process file**. In a manual system, the file would be located in a filing cabinet, whereas in an automated system, it is stored electronically on magnetic tape or disk. In either system, the file of job-order cost sheets serves as a subsidiary work-in-process ledger.

Both manual and automated systems require the same kind of data in order to accumulate costs and track the progress of a job. A job cost system must have the capability to identify the quantity of direct materials, direct labor, and overhead consumed by each job. In other words, documentation and procedures are needed to associate the manufacturing inputs used by a job with the job itself. This need is satisfied through the use of materials requisitions for direct material, time tickets for direct labor, and predetermined rates for overhead.

Materials Requisitions

materials requisition form

The cost of direct materials is assigned to a job by the use of a source document known as a **materials requisition form**, illustrated in Exhibit 4-7. Notice that the form asks for the description, quantity, and unit cost of the direct materials issued and, most importantly, for the number of the job. Using this form, the cost accounting department can enter the total cost of direct materials directly onto the job-order cost sheet. If the accounting system is automated, the data are entered directly at a computer terminal, using the materials requisitions forms as source documents. A program then enters the cost of direct materials onto the record for each job.

In addition to providing essential information for assigning direct materials costs to jobs, the materials requisition form may also have other data items such as requisition number, date, and signature. These data items are useful for maintaining proper control over a firm's inventory of direct materials. The signature, for example, transfers responsibility for the materials from the storage area to the person receiving the materials, usually a production supervisor.

Exhibit 4-6
The Job-Order Cost Sheet

For	Benson Company		Job Number	16
Item Description	Valves		Date Ordered	April 2, 1998
Quantity Completed	100		Date Completed	April 24, 1998
			Date Shipped	April 25, 1998

Materials		Direct Labor				Overhead		
Requisition Number	Amount	Ticket Number	Hours	Rate	Amount	Hours	Rate	Amount
12	$300	68	8	$6	$ 48	8	10	$ 80
18	450	72	10	7	70	10	10	100
	$750				$118			$180

Cost Summary

Direct materials	$750
Direct labor	$118
Overhead	$180
Total cost	$1,048
Unit cost	$10.48

Exhibit 4-7
Materials Requisition Form

Date	April 8, 1998		Materials Requisition Number 678
Department	Grinding		
Job Number	62		

Description	Quantity	Cost/Unit	Total Cost
Casing	100	$3	$300

Authorized Signature   *Jim Lawson*

No attempt is made to trace the cost of other materials, such as supplies, lubricants, and so on, to a particular job. You will recall that these indirect materials are assigned to jobs through the predetermined overhead rate.

Job Time Tickets

time ticket

Direct labor also must be associated with each particular job. The means by which direct labor costs are assigned to individual jobs is the source document known as a **time ticket** (see Exhibit 4-8). When an employee works on a particular job, she fills out a time ticket that identifies her name, wage rate, hours worked, and job number. These time tickets are collected daily and transferred to the cost accounting department, where the information is used to post the cost of direct labor to individual jobs. Again, in an automated system, posting involves entering the data onto the computer.

Time tickets are used only for direct laborers. Since indirect labor is common to all jobs, these costs belong to overhead and are allocated using the predetermined overhead rate.

Overhead Application

Jobs are assigned overhead costs with the predetermined overhead rate. Typically, direct labor hours is the measure used to calculate overhead. For example, assume a firm has estimated overhead costs for the coming year of $900,000 and expected activity is 90,000 direct labor hours. The predetermined rate is $900,000/ 90,000 direct labor hours = $10 per direct labor hour.

Since the number of direct labor hours charged to a job is known from time tickets, the assignment of overhead costs to jobs is simple once the predetermined rate has been computed. For instance, Exhibit 4-8 reveals that Ann Wilson worked a total of eight hours on Job 16. From this time ticket, overhead totaling $80 ($10 × 8 hours) would be assigned to Job 16.

What if overhead is assigned to jobs based on something other than direct labor hours? Then that other driver must be accounted for as well. That is, the actual amount used of the other driver (for example, machine hours) must be collected and posted to the job cost sheets. A source document that will track the machine hours used by each job must be created. A machine time ticket could easily accommodate this need.

Exhibit 4-8
Job Time Ticket

					Job Time Ticket Number 68
Employee Number		45			
Name		Ann Wilson			
Date		April 12, 1998			
Start Time	Stop Time	Total Time	Hourly Rate	Amount	Job Number
8:00	10:00	2	$6	$12	16
10:00	11:00	1	6	6	17
11:00	12:00	1	6	6	16
1:00	6:00	5	6	30	16

Approved by _Jim Lawson_
Department Supervisor

Unit Cost Calculation

Once a job is completed, its total manufacturing cost is computed by first totaling the costs of direct materials, direct labor, and overhead, and then summing these individual totals. The grand total is divided by the number of units produced to obtain the unit cost. (Exhibit 4-6 illustrates these computations).

All completed job-order cost sheets of a firm can serve as a subsidiary ledger for the finished goods inventory. In a manual accounting system, the completed sheets would be transferred from the work-in-process files to the finished goods inventory file. In an automated accounting system, an updating run would delete the finished job from the work-in-process master file and add this record to the finished goods master file. In either case, adding the totals of all completed job-order cost sheets gives the cost of finished goods inventory at any point in time. As finished goods are sold and shipped, the cost records would be pulled (or deleted) from the finished goods inventory file. These records then form the basis for calculating a period's cost of goods sold.

JOB-ORDER COSTING: SPECIFIC COST FLOW DESCRIPTION

Objective 5
Describe the cost flows associated with job-order costing, and prepare the journal entries.

Recall that cost flow is how we account for costs from the point at which they are incurred to the point at which they are recognized as an expense on the income statement. Of principal interest in a job-order system is the flow of manufacturing costs. Accordingly, we begin with a description of exactly how we account for the three manufacturing cost elements (direct materials, direct labor, and overhead).

A simplified job shop environment is used as the framework for this description. All Signs Company, recently formed by Bob Fredericks, produces a wide variety of customized signs. Bob leased a small building and bought the necessary production equipment. For the first month of operation (January), Bob has finalized two orders: one for twenty street signs for a new housing development and a second for ten laser-carved wooden signs for a golf course. Both orders must be delivered January 31 and will be sold for manufacturing cost plus 50 percent. Bob expects to average two orders per month for the first year of operation.

Bob created two job-order cost sheets and assigned a number to each job. Job 101 is the street signs, and Job 102 the golf course signs.

Accounting for Materials

Since the company is beginning business, it has no beginning inventories. To produce the thirty signs in January and have a supply of materials on hand at the beginning of February, Bob purchases, on account, $2,500 of raw materials. This purchase is recorded as follows:

1. Raw Materials   2,500
      Accounts Payable   2,500

Raw Materials is an inventory account. It also is the controlling account for all raw materials. When materials are purchased, the cost of these materials "flows" into the raw materials account.

From January 2 to January 19, the production supervisor used three requisition forms to remove $1,000 of raw materials from the storeroom. From January 20 to January 31, two additional requisition forms for $500 of raw materials were used. The first three forms revealed that the raw materials were used for Job 101;

the last two requisitions were for Job 102. Thus, for January, the cost sheet for Job 101 would have a total of $1,000 in direct materials posted, and the cost sheet for Job 102 would have a total of $500 in direct materials posted. In addition, the following entry would be made:

2. Work in Process   1,500
    Raw Materials   1,500

This second entry captures the notion of raw materials flowing from the storeroom to work in process. All such flows are summarized in the Work in Process account as well as being posted individually to the respective jobs. Work in Process is a controlling account, and the job cost sheets are the subsidiary accounts. Exhibit 4-9 summarizes the raw materials cost flows. Notice that the source document that drives the materials cost flows is the materials requisition form.

Accounting for Direct Labor Cost

Since two jobs were in progress during January, time tickets filled out by direct laborers must be sorted by each job. Once the sorting is completed, the hours worked and the wage rate of each employee are used to assign the direct labor cost to each job. For Job 101, the time tickets showed 120 hours at an average wage rate of $5 per hour, for a total direct labor cost of $600. For Job 102, the total was $250, based on 50 hours at an average hourly wage of $5. In addition to the postings to each job's cost sheet, the following summary entry would be made:

3. Work in Process   850
    Wages Payable   850

The summary of the labor cost flows is given in Exhibit 4-10. Notice that the direct labor costs assigned to the two jobs exactly equal the total assigned to Work in Process. Note also that the time tickets filled out by the individual laborers are the source of information for posting the labor cost flows. Remember that the labor cost flows reflect only direct labor cost. Indirect labor is assigned as part of overhead.

Exhibit 4-9
Summary of Raw Materials Cost Flows

Subsidiary Accounts (Cost Sheets)

Job 101 Materials	
Req. No.	Amount
1	$ 300
2	200
3	500
	$1,000

Job 102 Materials	
Req. No.	Amount
4	$ 250
5	250
	$ 500

Source Documents: Materials Requisition Forms

Exhibit 4-10
Summary of Direct Labor Cost Flows

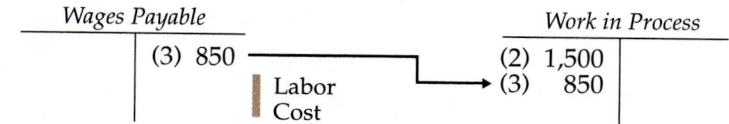

Wages Payable		Work in Process	
(3) 850 —		(2) 1,500	
	Labor Cost	(3) 850	

WIP Subsidiary Accounts (Cost Sheets)

Job 101
Labor

Ticket	Hours	Rate	Amount
1	30	5	$ 150
2	40	5	200
3	50	5	250
	120		$ 600

Job 102
Labor

Ticket	Hours	Rate	Amount
4	25	5	$ 125
5	25	5	125
	50		$ 250

Source Documents: Time Tickets

Accounting for Overhead

Under a normal costing approach, actual overhead costs are *never* assigned to jobs. Overhead is applied to each individual job using a predetermined overhead rate. Even with this system, however, actual overhead costs incurred must be accounted for. Thus, we will first describe how to account for applied overhead and then discuss accounting for actual overhead.

Accounting for Overhead Application Assume that Bob has estimated overhead costs for the year at $9,600. Additionally, since he expects business to increase throughout the year as he becomes established, he estimates 4,800 total direct labor hours. Accordingly, the predetermined overhead rate is as follows:

Overhead rate = $9,600/4,800 = $2 per direct labor hour

Overhead costs flow into Work in Process via the predetermined rate. Since direct labor hours are used to load overhead into production, the time tickets serve as the source documents for assigning overhead to individual jobs and to the controlling work in process account.

For Job 101, with a total of 120 hours worked, the amount of overhead cost posted is $240 ($2 × 120). For Job 102, the overhead cost is $100 ($2 × 50). A summary entry reflects a total of $340 (i.e., all overhead applied to jobs worked on in January) in applied overhead.

4. Work in Process	340	
Overhead Control		340

applied

The credit balance in the overhead control account equals the total applied overhead at a given point in time. In normal costing, only applied overhead ever enters the work in process account.

Accounting for Actual Overhead Costs To illustrate how actual overhead costs are recorded, assume that All Signs incurred the following indirect costs for January:

Lease payment	$200
Utilities	50
Equipment depreciation	100
Indirect labor	65
Total overhead costs	$415

As indicated earlier, actual overhead costs never enter the work in process account. The usual procedure is to record actual overhead costs on the debit side of the overhead control account. For example, the actual overhead costs would be recorded as follows:

5. Overhead Control	415	
Lease Payable		200
Utilities Payable		50
Accumulated Depreciation–Equipment		100
Wages Payable		65

Thus, the debit balance in Overhead Control gives the total actual overhead costs at a given point in time. Since actual overhead costs are on the debit side of this account and applied overhead costs are on the credit side, the balance in Overhead Control is the overhead variance at a given point in time. For All Signs Company at the end of January, the actual overhead of $415 and applied overhead of $340 produce underapplied overhead of $75 ($415 – $340).

The flow of overhead costs is summarized in Exhibit 4-11. To apply overhead to work in process, a company needs information from the time tickets and a predetermined overhead rate based on direct labor hours.

Exhibit 4-11
Summary of Overhead Cost Flows

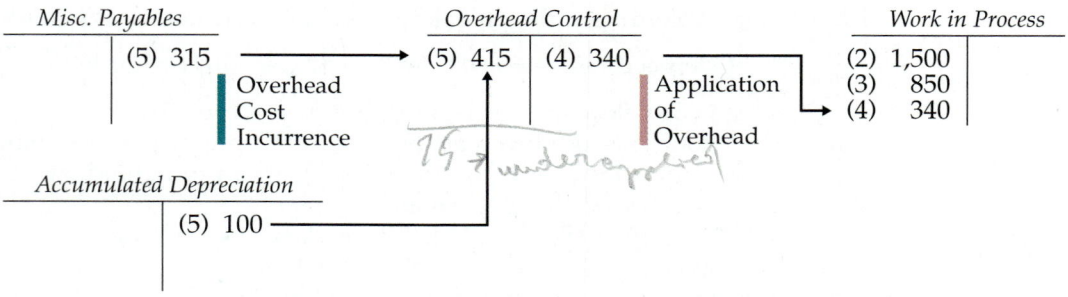

Job 101 Applied Overhead		
Hours	Rate	Amount
120	$2	$240

Job 102 Applied Overhead		
Hours	Rate	Amount
50	$2	$100

Source Documents: Time Ticket
Other Source: Predetermined Rate

Accounting for Finished Goods

We have already seen what takes place when a job is completed. The columns for direct materials, direct labor, and applied overhead are totaled. These totals are then transferred to another section of the cost sheet where they are summed to yield the manufacturing cost of the job. This job cost sheet is then transferred to a finished goods file. Simultaneously, the costs of the completed job are transferred from the Work in Process account to the Finished Goods account.

For example, assume that Job 101 was completed in January with the completed cost sheet shown in Exhibit 4-12. Since Job 101 is completed, the total manufacturing costs of $1,840 must be transferred from the Work in Process account to the Finished Goods account. This transfer is described by the following entry.

6. Finished Goods   1,840
      Work in Process   1,840

A summary of the cost flows occurring when a job is finished is shown in Exhibit 4-13.

Exhibit 4-12
Completed Job-Order Cost Sheet

For ___Housing Development___   Job Order Number ___101___
Item Description ___Street Signs___   Date Ordered ___Jan. 1, 1998___
Quantity Completed ___20___   Date Started ___Jan. 2, 1998___
Date Finished ___Jan. 15, 1998___

Materials		Direct Labor				Applied Overhead		
Requisition Number	Amount	Ticket Number	Hours	Rate	Amount	Hours	Rate	Amount
1	$ 300	1	30	$5	$150	30	$2	$ 60
2	200	2	40	5	200	40	2	80
3	500	3	50	5	250	50	2	100
	$1,000				$600			$240

Cost Summary

Direct materials ___$1,000___
Direct labor ___$600___
Overhead ___$240___
Total cost ___$1,840___
Unit cost ___$92___

Exhibit 4-13
Summary of Finished Goods Cost Flow

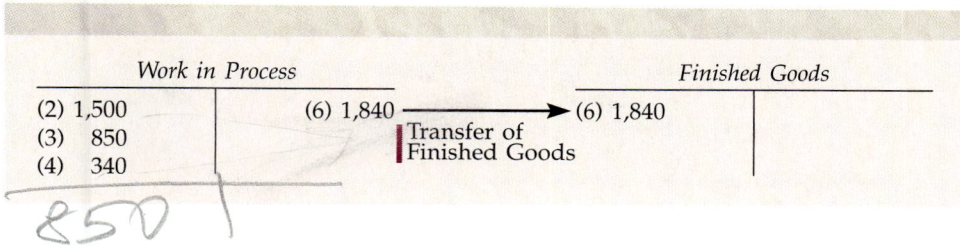

Work in Process		Finished Goods	
(2) 1,500	(6) 1,840 ───────▶	(6) 1,840	
(3) 850	Transfer of		
(4) 340	Finished Goods		

850

Completion of goods in a manufacturing process represents an important step in the flow of manufacturing costs. Because of the importance of this stage in a manufacturing operation, a schedule of the cost of goods manufactured is prepared periodically to summarize the cost flows of all production activity. This report is an important input for a firm's income statement and can be used to evaluate a firm's manufacturing effort. The statement of cost of goods manufactured was first introduced in Chapter 2. However, in a normal cost system, the report is somewhat different from the actual cost report presented in that chapter.

The statement of the cost of goods manufactured presented in Exhibit 4-14 summarizes the production activity of All Signs Company for January. The key difference between this report and the one appearing in Chapter 2 is the use of applied overhead to arrive at the cost of goods manufactured. Finished goods inventories are carried at normal cost rather than the actual cost.

Notice that ending work in process is $850. Where did we obtain this figure? Of the two jobs, Job 101 was finished and transferred to finished goods at a cost of $1,840. This amount is credited to Work in Process, leaving an ending balance of $850. Alternatively, we can add up the amounts debited to Work in Process for all remaining unfinished jobs. Job 102 is the only job still in process. The manufacturing costs assigned thus far are direct materials, $500; direct labor, $250; and overhead applied, $100. The total of these costs gives the cost of ending work in process.

Exhibit 4-14

All Signs Company
Statement of Cost of Goods Manufactured
For the Month Ended January 31, 1998

Direct materials:		
Beginning raw materials inventory	$ 0	
Add: Purchases of raw materials	2,500	
Total raw materials available	$2,500	
Less: Ending raw materials	1,000	
Raw materials used		$1,500
Direct labor		850
Manufacturing overhead:		
Lease	$ 200	
Utilities	50	
Depreciation	100	
Indirect labor	65	
	$ 415	
Less: Underapplied overhead	(75)	
Overhead applied		340
Current manufacturing costs		$2,690
Add: Beginning work in process		0
Less: Ending work in process		$ (850)
Cost of goods manufactured		$1,840

Accounting for Cost of Goods Sold

In a job-order firm, units can be produced for a particular customer or they can be produced with the expectation of selling the units as market conditions warrant. When the job is shipped to the customer, the cost of the finished job becomes the cost of the goods sold. When Job 101 is shipped, the following entries would be made (recall that the selling price is 150 percent of manufacturing cost).

7a. Cost of Goods Sold	1,840	
Finished Goods		1,840
7b. Accounts Receivable	2,760	
Sales Revenue		2,760

In addition to these entries, a schedule of cost of goods sold usually is prepared at the end of each reporting period (e.g., monthly and quarterly). Exhibit 4-15 presents such a schedule for All Signs Company for January. Typically, the overhead variance is not material and is therefore closed to the cost of goods sold account. Cost of goods sold *before* adjustment for an overhead variance is called **normal cost of goods sold**. After adjustment for the period's overhead variance takes place, the result is called the **adjusted cost of goods sold**. It is this latter figure that appears as an expense on the income statement.

normal cost of goods sold

adjusted cost of goods sold

However, closing the overhead variance to the Cost of Goods Sold account is not done until the end of the year. Variances are expected each month because of nonuniform production and nonuniform actual overhead costs. As the year unfolds, these monthly variances should, by and large, offset each other so that the year-end variance is small. Nonetheless, to illustrate how the year-end overhead variance would be treated, we will close out the overhead variance experienced by All Signs Company in January.

Closing the underapplied overhead to cost of goods sold requires the following entry:

8. Cost of Goods Sold	75	
Overhead Control		75

Notice that debiting Cost of Goods Sold is equivalent to adding the underapplied amount to the normal cost of goods sold figure. If the overhead variance had been overapplied, then the entry would reverse and Cost of Goods Sold would be credited.

Exhibit 4-15

All Signs Company Statement of Cost of Goods Sold For the Month Ended January 31, 1998	
Beginning finished goods inventory	$ 0
Cost of goods manufactured	1,840
Goods available for sale	$1,840
Less: Ending finished goods inventory	(0)
Normal cost of goods sold	$1,840
Add: Underapplied overhead	75
Adjusted cost of goods sold	$1,915

If Job 101 had not been ordered by a customer but had been produced with the expectation that the signs could be sold to various other developers, then all twenty units may not be sold at the same time. Assume that on January 31, fifteen signs were sold. In this case, the cost of goods sold figure is the unit cost times the number of units sold ($92 × 15, or $1,380). The unit cost figure is found on the cost sheet in Exhibit 4-12.

Closing out the overhead variance of Cost of Goods Sold completes the description of manufacturing cost flows. To facilitate a review of these important concepts, Exhibit 4-16 shows a complete summary of the manufacturing cost flows for All Signs Company. Notice that these entries summarize information from the underlying job-order cost sheets. Although the description in this exhibit is specific to the example, the pattern of cost flows shown would be found in any manufacturing firm that uses a normal job-order cost system.

Manufacturing cost flows, however, are not the only cost flows experienced by a firm. Nonmanufacturing costs are also incurred. A description of how we account for these costs follows.

Accounting for Nonmanufacturing Costs

Recall that costs associated with selling and general administrative activities are classified as nonmanufacturing costs. These costs are period costs and are *never* assigned to the product in a traditional cost system. They are not part of the manufacturing cost flows. They do not belong to the overhead category and are treated as a totally separate category.

Exhibit 4-16
All Signs Company Summary of Manufacturing Cost Flows

Raw Materials				Wages Payable			Overhead Control		
(1)	2,500	(2)	1,500		(3)	850	(5)	415	(4)	340
									(8)	75

Work in Process				Finished Goods				Cost of Goods Sold	
(2)	1,500	(6)	1,840	(6)	1,840	(7a)	1,840	(7a)	1,840
(3)	850					(8)	75	(8)	75
(4)	340								

(1) Purchase of raw materials	$2,500	
(2) Issue of raw materials	1,500	
(3) Incurrence of direct labor cost	850	
(4) Application of overhead	340	
(5) Incurrence of actual overhead cost	415	
(6) Transfer of Job 101 to finished goods	1,840	
(7a) Cost of goods sold of Job 101	1,840	
(8) Closing out underapplied overhead	75	

To illustrate how these costs are accounted for, assume All Signs Company had the following additional transactions in January:

Advertising circulars *payable*	$ 75	
Sales commission *wages*	125	
Office salaries	500	
Depreciation, office equipment *office*	50	

The following compound entry could be used to record the above costs:

Selling Expense Control	200	
Administrative Expense Control	550	
Accounts Payable		75
Wages Payable		625
Accumulated Depreciation—Office Equipment		50

Controlling accounts accumulate all of the selling and administrative expenses for a period. At the end of the period, all of these costs flow to the period's income statement. An income statement for All Signs Company is shown in Exhibit 4-17.

With the description of the accounting procedures for selling and administrative expenses completed, the basic essentials of a normal job-order costing system are also complete. This description has assumed that a single plantwide overhead rate was being used.

SINGLE VERSUS MULTIPLE OVERHEAD RATES

Objective 6
Explain why multiple overhead rates may be preferred to a single, plantwide rate.

Using a single rate based on direct labor hours to assign overhead to jobs may result in unfair cost assignments (unfair in the sense that too much or too little overhead is assigned to a job). This can occur if direct labor hours do not correlate well with the consumption of overhead resources.

Exhibit 4-17

All Signs Company
Income Statement
For the Month Ended January 31, 1998

Sales		$2,760
Less: Cost of goods sold		(1,915)
Gross margin		$ 845
Less: Selling and administrative expenses		
Selling expense	$200	
Administrative expense	550	(750)
Net income		$ 95

To illustrate, consider a company with two departments, one that is labor-intensive (Department A) and the other machine-intensive (Department B). The expected annual overhead costs and the expected annual usage of direct labor hours and machine hours for each department are shown in Exhibit 4-18.

Currently the company uses a plantwide overhead rate based on direct labor hours. Thus, the overhead rate used for product costing is $12 per direct labor hour ($240,000/20,000).

Now consider two recently completed jobs, Job 23 and Job 24. Exhibit 4-19 provides production-related data concerning each job. The data reveal that Job 23 spent all of its time in Department A, while Job 24 spent all of its time in Department B. Using the plantwide overhead rate, Job 23 would receive a $6,000 overhead assignment ($12 × 500 direct labor hours) and Job 24 would receive a $12 overhead assignment ($12 × 1 direct labor hour). Thus, the total manufacturing cost of Job 23 is $11,000 ($5,000 + $6,000), yielding a unit cost of $11. The total manufacturing cost of Job 24 is $5,012 ($5,000 + $12), yielding a unit cost of $5.012. Clearly, something is wrong. Using a plantwide rate, Job 23 received 500 times the overhead cost assignment than Job 24 received. Yet, as Exhibit 4-18 shows, Job 24 was produced in a department that is responsible for producing 75 percent of the plant's total overhead. Imagine the difficulties that this type of costing distortion can cause for a company. Some products would be overcosted while others would be undercosted, and the result could be incorrect pricing decisions that adversely affect the firm's competitive position.

The distortion in product costs is caused by the assumption that direct labor hours properly reflect the overhead consumed by the individual jobs. One driver for the firm as a whole does not seem to work. This type of problem can be

Exhibit 4-18
Departmental Overhead Costs and Activity

	Department A	Department B	Total
Overhead costs	$60,000	$180,000	$240,000
Direct labor hours	15,000	5,000	20,000
Machine hours	5,000	15,000	20,000

Exhibit 4-19
Production Data for Jobs 23 and 24

Job 23			
	Department A	Department B	Total
Prime costs	$5,000	$0	$5,000
Direct labor hours	500	0	500
Machine hours	1	0	1
Units produced	1,000	0	1,000

Job 24			
	Department A	Department B	Total
Prime costs	$0	$5,000	$5,000
Direct labor hours	0	1	1
Machine hours	0	500	500
Units produced	0	1,000	1,000

resolved by using multiple overhead rates, where each rate uses a different activity driver. For this example, a satisfactory solution might be to develop an overhead rate for each department. In the case of the machine-intensive Department B, the rate could be based on machine hours instead of direct labor hours. It seems reasonable to believe that machine hours relate better to machine-related overhead than direct labor hours do and that direct labor hours would be a good driver for a labor-intensive department. If so, then more accurate product costing can be achieved by computing two departmental rates instead of one plantwide rate. Therefore, in this example, we are making two improvements: using departmental overhead rates and basing the rates on different drivers.

Using data from Exhibit 4-18, the overhead rate for Department A is $4 per direct labor hour ($60,000/15,000), and the overhead rate for Department B is $12 per machine hour ($180,000/15,000). Using these rates, Job 23 would be assigned $2,000 of overhead ($4 × 500 direct labor hours) and Job 24 $6,000 of overhead ($12 × 500 machine hours). Job 24 now receives three times as much overhead cost as Job 23, which seems more sensible, since Department B incurs three times as much overhead cost as does Department A.

	Department A	Department B
Overhead cost	$60,000	$180,000
Cost driver	15,000 DLH	15,000 MHr
Department overhead rate	$4/DLH	$12/MHr
Overhead applied to Job #23	$2,000	—
Overhead applied to Job #24	—	$6,000

Moving to departmental rates may be considered a step toward activity-based costing, especially in the example used above where different activity drivers were chosen based on the types of overhead incurred in each department. While departmental rates may provide sufficient product-costing accuracy for some firms, even more attention to how overhead is assigned may be necessary for other firms. This chapter has focused on activity drivers that are correlated with production volume (e.g., direct labor hours and machine hours). Greater product-costing accuracy may be possible through the use of nonvolume-related activity drivers. However, this discussion is left to a later chapter.

SUMMARY

In this chapter, we have examined the cost accounting system and its relationship to the production process. Two characteristics of the production process were shown to have an impact on cost accounting. These characteristics are the tangible product versus service nature of the firm and the degree of uniqueness of the product or service.

The cost accounting system is set up to serve the company's needs for cost accumulation, cost measurement, and cost assignment. In general, normal costing is preferred to actual costing in determining unit production costs. In normal costing, actual prime costs are assigned to units, but overhead is applied based on a predetermined rate.

Job-order costing is used for both manufacturing and service firms that produce unique or heterogeneous products. Cost is accounted for by individual job using a subsidiary account called the job-order cost sheet.

Sometimes a single overhead rate may not adequately capture the cause-and-effect relationship between overhead cost and production. In such cases, multiple overhead rates may be required.

APPENDIX: ACCOUNTING FOR SPOILAGE IN A TRADITIONAL JOB ORDER SYSTEM

Throughout this chapter, we have assumed that the units produced are good units. In that case, all manufacturing costs are associated with good units and flow into cost of goods sold. However, on occasion mistakes are made; defective units are produced and are either thrown away or reworked and sold. How do we account for those costs?

Traditional job-order costing makes a distinction between normal and abnormal spoilage. To understand this distinction, let's look at an example. Petris, Inc. manufactures cabinets on a job-order basis. Job 98-12 calls for 100 units with the following costs.

Direct materials	$2,000
Direct labor (100 hours)	$1,000

Overhead is applied at the rate of 150 percent of direct labor cost. At the end of the job, 100 units are produced. However, three of the cabinets required rework due to improper installation of shelving. The rework involved six extra direct labor hours and an additional $50 of material. How is the rework accounted for? It depends on the reason for the defective work.

If the defective work was a consequence of the demanding nature of this particular job, then rework is assigned to the job as follows.

Direct materials	$2,050
Direct labor	1,060
Overhead	1,590
Total job cost	$4,700
Unit job cost	$47

On the other hand, suppose that the defective work was a consequence of assigning new, untrained labor to the job. Defects are expected in that case, and the rework is not assigned to the job but to overhead control. The costs are assigned as follows.

Job 98-12		_Debited to Overhead Control_	
Direct materials	$2,000	Direct materials	$ 50
Direct labor	1,000	Direct labor	60
Overhead	1,500	Overhead	90
Total job cost	$4,500	Total	$200
Unit job cost	$45		

The cost of spoiled units that cannot be reworked are similarly charged to the job if caused by the demands of the job, and to overhead control if not.

REVIEW PROBLEM AND SOLUTION

Bostian Company uses a normal job-order costing system. It processes most jobs through two departments. Selected budgeted and actual data for the past year follow. Data for one of several jobs completed during the year also follow.

	Department A	Department B
Budgeted overhead	$100,000	$500,000
Actual overhead	110,000	520,000
Expected activity (direct labor hours)	50,000	10,000
Expected machine hours	10,000	50,000
Actual direct labor hours	51,000	9,000
Actual machine hours	10,500	52,000

	Job 10
Direct materials	$20,000
Direct labor cost:	
Department A (5,000 hrs. @ $6)	$30,000
Department B (1,000 hrs. @ $6)	$6,000
Machine hours used:	
Department A	100
Department B	1,200
Units produced	10,000

Bostian Company uses a plantwide predetermined overhead rate to assign overhead (OH) to jobs. Direct labor hours (DLH) is used to compute the predetermined overhead rate.

REQUIRED:

1. Compute the predetermined overhead rate.
2. Using the predetermined rate, compute the per-unit manufacturing cost for Job 10.
3. Compute the overhead variance for the year, and label it as over- or underapplied. Assuming that the variance is immaterial, provide the journal entry that will dispose of the variance at the end of the year.
4. Recalculate the per-unit manufacturing cost for Job 10 using departmental overhead rates. Use direct labor hours for Department A and machine hours for Department B. Does this approach provide a more accurate unit cost? Explain.

Solution

1. Predetermined overhead rate = $600,000/60,000 = $10 per DLH. Add the budgeted overhead for the two departments and divide by the total expected direct labor hours ($DLH = 50,000 + 10,000$).

2.

Direct materials	$ 20,000
Direct labor	36,000
Overhead ($10 × 6,000 DLH)	60,000
Total manufacturing cost	$116,000
Unit cost ($116,000/10,000)	$11.60

3. Applied overhead = Overhead rate × Total actual direct labor hours
   = $10 × (51,000 + 9,000)
   = $600,000

   Overhead variance = Total actual OH − Applied OH
   = $630,000 − $600,000
   = $30,000 underapplied

Cost of Goods Sold	30,000	
Overhead Control		30,000

4. Predetermined rate for Department A: $100,000/50,000 = $2 per DLH. Predetermined rate for Department B: $500,000/50,000 = $10 per machine hour.

Direct materials	$20,000
Direct labor	36,000
Overhead:	
Department A: $2 × 5,000	10,000
Department B: $10 × 1,200	12,000
Total manufacturing costs	$78,000
Unit cost ($78,000/10,000)	$7.80

Overhead assignment using departmental rates is more accurate because there is a higher correlation with the overhead assigned and the overhead consumed. Notice that Job 10 spends most of its time in Department A, the least overhead-intensive of the two departments. Departmental rates reflect this differential time and consumption better than plantwide rates do.

KEY TERMS

Actual cost system 133
Adjusted cost of goods sold 153
Applied overhead 139
Cost accumulation 131
Cost assignment 131
Cost measurement 131
Expected activity level 138
Heterogeneity 127

Inseparability 127
Intangibility 127
Job-order cost sheet 144
Job-order costing system 143
Materials requisition form 144
Normal activity level 139

Normal cost of goods sold 153
Normal costing system 134
Overapplied overhead 141
Overhead variance 141
Perishability 127
Practical activity level 139

Predetermined overhead rate 136
Source document 131
Theoretical activity level 139
Time ticket 146
Underapplied overhead 141
Work-in-process file 144

QUESTIONS FOR WRITING AND DISCUSSION

1. What is cost measurement? Cost accumulation? What is the difference between the two?
2. Explain why an actual overhead rate is rarely used for product costing.
3. Explain the differences between job-order costing and process costing.
4. What are some differences between a manual job-order cost system and an automated job-order cost system?
5. What is an overhead variance? Explain the difference between an underapplied and an overapplied overhead variance.
6. How are overhead variances disposed of at the end of the year? Which method of disposal is most common? Why?
7. What is the role of materials requisition forms in a job-order cost system? Time tickets? Predetermined overhead rates?
8. Explain why multiple overhead rates are often preferred to a plantwide overhead rate.
9. Explain the role of activity drivers in assigning overhead costs to products.

10. Define the following terms: *expected actual activity, normal activity, practical activity,* and *theoretical activity*.
11. Why would some prefer normal activity to expected actual activity to compute a predetermined overhead rate?
12. When computing a predetermined overhead rate, why are units of output not commonly used as a measure of production activity?
13. Explain how overhead is assigned to production when a predetermined overhead rate is used.
14. What is the difference between applied overhead and budgeted overhead? Will they ever be the same? If so, explain how. What is the difference between applied overhead and actual overhead? Will these two ever be the same? If so, when?
15. Wilson Company has a predetermined overhead-rate of $5 per direct labor hour. The job-order cost sheet for Job 145 shows 1,000 direct labor hours costing $10,000 and materials requisitions totaling $7,500. Job 145 had 500 units completed and transferred to finished goods. What is the cost per unit for Job 145?
16. Why are the accounting requirements for job-order costing more demanding than those for process costing?
17. Explain the difference between normal cost of goods sold and adjusted cost of goods sold.

EXERCISES AND PROBLEMS

4-1

Classifying Firms as Either Manufacturing or Service

LO 1

Classify the following types of firms as either manufacturing or service. Explain the reasons for your choice in terms of the four features of service firms (heterogeneity, inseparability, intangibility, and perishability).

a. Bicycle production
b. Pharmaceuticals
c. Income tax preparation
d. Application of artificial nails
e. Glue production
f. Child care

4-2

Characteristics of Production Process, Cost Measurement

LO 1, 2

Lee Frazer and Company makes hand-tooled leather saddles for western pleasure riding. The saddles are made to customer specification and vary according to the type of materials used and the degree of hand tooling required. Lee Frazer and Company estimated the following for the year:

Number of saddles	1,000
Number of direct labor hours	15,000
Direct material cost	$175,000
Direct labor cost	$180,000
Overhead cost	$90,000

During the year the following actual amounts were experienced:

Number of saddles produced	1,100
Number of direct labor hours	16,775
Direct materials used	$185,000
Direct labor incurred	$201,300
Overhead	$98,000

REQUIRED:

1. Should Lee Frazer and Company use process costing or job-order costing? Explain.
2. If Lee Frazer and Company uses a normal costing system and overhead is applied on the basis of direct labor hours, what is the cost of a saddle that takes $165 of direct materials and 18 direct labor hours?
3. Explain why Lee Frazer and Company would have difficulty using an actual costing system.

4-3
Overhead Application and Over- or Underapplied Overhead
LO 3

Refer to the data in **4-2** above.

REQUIRED:

1. At the end of the year, how much overhead has been applied to production?
2. Is overhead over- or underapplied and by how much?
3. Assuming that any overhead variance is closed to cost of goods sold, will the cost of goods sold increase or decrease?

4-4
Characteristics of Production Process, Cost Measurement
LO 1, 2

Lee Frazer, owner of Lee Frazer and Company of 4-2 above, noticed that a large number of orders were from dude ranches and pony clubs. These orders required a fairly standardized saddle with little decorative tooling. Lee organized a new enterprise called SaddleUp that would produce the standard model saddle. In its first three months in business, SaddleUp experienced the following:

	March	*April*	*May*
Number of saddles produced	100	110	120
Direct materials used	$10,000	$11,000	$12,000
Direct labor incurred	$9,000	$9,900	$10,800
Overhead	$8,000	$2,200	$2,280

REQUIRED:

1. Should SaddleUp use process costing or job-order costing? Explain.
2. If SaddleUp uses an actual costing system, what is the cost of a single saddle produced in March? In April? In May?
3. Now assume that SaddleUp uses a normal costing system. Estimated overhead for the year is $30,000, and estimated production is 1,200 saddles. What is the predetermined overhead rate per saddle? What is the cost of a single saddle produced in March? In April? In May?

4-5
Predetermined Overhead Rate; Application of Overhead; Variances; Journal Entries
LO 3

Harris Company uses a normal job-order cost system. Budgeted overhead for the coming year is $600,000. Expected actual activity is 200,000 direct labor hours. During the year, Harris worked a total of 190,000 direct labor hours and actual overhead totaled $562,000.

REQUIRED:

1. Compute the predetermined overhead rate for Harris Company.
2. How much overhead will the company assign to the work in process account? Prepare the journal entry that corresponds to this assignment.
3. Compute the overhead variance and label the variance as under- or overapplied overhead. Assuming the variance is not material, write the journal entry that disposes of the variance at the end of the year.

4-6
Predetermined
Overhead Rate;
Applied Overhead;
Unit Cost

LO 3

Bethel Industries costs products using a normal costing system. The following data are available for last year:

Budgeted:	
Overhead	$675,000
Machine hours	25,000
Direct labor hours	75,000
Actual:	
Overhead	$681,000
Machine hours	25,050
Direct labor hours	75,700
Prime cost	$957,000
Number of units	400,000

Overhead is applied on the basis of direct labor hours.

REQUIRED:

1. What is the predetermined overhead rate? →
2. What is the applied overhead for last year? →
3. Was overhead over- or underapplied, and by how much? →
4. What is the normal cost per unit produced? → 4.1

[handwritten: 675,000 ÷ 75,000 = 9]
[handwritten: 75,700 × 9 = 681,300]
[handwritten: 300 over applied]

4-7
Predetermined
Overhead Rate;
Applied Overhead;
Unit Cost

LO 3

Using the information from **4-6** above, suppose Bethel Industries applied overhead to production on the basis of machine hours instead of direct labor hours.

REQUIRED:

1. What is the predetermined overhead rate?
2. What is the applied overhead for last year?
3. Is overhead over- or underapplied, and by how much?
4. What is the normal cost per unit produced?
5. How can Bethel decide whether to use direct labor hours or machine hours as the basis for applying factory overhead?

4-8
Predetermined
Overhead Rate;
Application of
Overhead

LO 3

Alpha Company and Beta Inc. both use predetermined overhead rates to apply factory overhead to production. Alpha's is based on direct labor hours and Beta's is based on materials cost. Budgeted production and cost data for Alpha and Beta are as follows:

	Alpha	Beta
Manufacturing overhead	$240,000	$300,000
Units	10,000	20,000
Direct labor hours	6,000	7,500
Material cost	$150,000	$400,000

At the end of the year, Alpha Company had incurred overhead of $221,000 and had produced 9,800 units using 6,100 direct labor hours and materials costing $147,000. Beta Inc. had incurred overhead of $316,500 and had produced 20,500 units using 7,550 direct labor hours and materials costing $411,000.

REQUIRED:

1. Compute the predetermined overhead rates for Alpha and Beta.
2. Was overhead over- or underapplied for each company, and by how much?

4-9
Journal Entries;
T-Accounts

LO 5

Kaycee, Inc., manufactures brown paper grocery bags. During the month of May, the following occurred:

a. Materials were purchased on account for $23,175.
b. Materials totaling $19,000 were requisitioned for use in production.
c. Direct labor payroll for the month was $17,850 with an average wage of $8.50 per hour.
d. Actual overhead of $15,500 was incurred and paid.
e. Factory overhead is charged to production at the rate of $7 per direct labor hour.
f. Completed units costing $36,085 were transferred to finished goods.
g. Bags costing $30,000 were sold on account for $36,000.

Beginning balances as of May 1 were:

Materials	$ 5,170
WIP	11,200
Finished Goods	2,630

REQUIRED:

1. Prepare the journal entries for the above events.
2. Calculate the ending balances of:
   a. Materials
   b. WIP
   c. Overhead Control
   d. Finished Goods

4-10
Predetermined
Overhead Rate;
Overhead
Variances; Journal
Entries

LO 3

Rayburn Company uses a predetermined overhead rate to assign overhead to jobs. Because Rayburn's production is machine-dominated, overhead is applied on the basis of machine hours. The expected overhead for the year was $2.5 million, and the practical level of activity is 50,000 machine hours.

During the year, Rayburn used 48,000 machine hours and incurred actual overhead costs of $2 million. Rayburn also had the following balances of applied overhead in its accounts:

Work in Process	$ 460,000
Cost of Goods Sold	1,440,000
Finished Goods	500,000

REQUIRED:

1. Compute a predetermined overhead rate for Rayburn.
2. Compute the overhead variance, and label it as under- or overapplied.
3. Assuming the overhead variance is immaterial, prepare the journal entry to dispose of the variance at the end of the year.
4. Assuming the overhead variance is material, prepare journal entries that appropriately dispose of the overhead variance at the end of the year.

4-11
Journal Entries;
T-Accounts

LO 5

Porter Company uses job-order costing. During January, the following data were reported:

a. Materials purchased: direct materials, $82,000; indirect materials, $10,500.
b. Materials issued: direct materials, $72,500; indirect materials, $7,000.
c. Labor cost incurred: direct labor, $52,000; indirect labor, $15,750.
d. Other manufacturing costs incurred (all payables), $49,000.

e. Overhead is applied on the basis of 125 percent of direct labor cost.

f. Work finished and transferred to finished goods cost $160,000.

g. Finished goods costing $140,000 were sold on account for 150 percent of cost.

h. Any over- or underapplied overhead is closed to COGS.

REQUIRED:

1. Prepare journal entries to record these transactions.

2. Prepare a T-account for Manufacturing Overhead. Post all relevant information to this account. What is the ending balance in this account?

3. Prepare a T-account for Work in Process. Assume a beginning balance of $10,000 and post all relevant information to this account. Did you assign any actual overhead costs to Work in Process? Why or why not?

4-12
Applied Overhead;
Cost of Goods
Manufactured
LO 3

Hamblin Products, Inc., provided the following data for the year:

Labor:	
Direct labor cost (25,000 hours)	$175,000
Indirect labor	35,000
Materials:	
Direct materials:	
Inventory, Jan. 1, 1996	25,000
Purchases on account	200,000
Issued to production	190,000
Indirect materials (issued)	10,000
Other factory overhead costs:	
Depreciation	55,000
Maintenance	25,000
Miscellaneous	15,500
Work in process:	
Beginning inventory	110,000
Ending inventory	80,250

The company uses a predetermined overhead rate based on direct labor hours. The rate for the year was $5.20 per direct labor hour.

REQUIRED:

1. Compute the applied overhead for the year. Is the overhead over- or underapplied? By how much?

2. Prepare a statement of cost of goods manufactured. Did you use actual or applied overhead when you prepared the statement of cost of goods manufactured? Explain.

4-13
Departmental
Overhead Rates
LO 6

Bryan Company uses a normal job-order cost system. Currently, a plantwide overhead rate is used, based on machine hours. Sam Perkins, the plant manager, has heard that departmental overhead rates can offer significantly better cost assignments than can a plantwide rate. Bryan has the following data for its two departments for the coming year:

	Department A	Department B
Overhead costs (expected)	$50,000	$22,000
Normal activity (machine hours)	10,000	8,000

REQUIRED:

1. Compute a predetermined overhead rate for the plant as a whole based on machine hours.
2. Compute predetermined overhead rates for each department using machine hours.
3. Job 15 used 20 machine hours from Department A and 50 machine hours from Department B. Job 22 used 50 machine hours from Department A and 20 from Department B. Compute the overhead cost assigned to each job using the plantwide rate computed in Question 1. Repeat the computation using the departmental rates found in Requirement 2. Which of the two approaches gives the fairest assignment? Why?
4. Repeat Requirement 3 assuming the expected overhead cost for Department B is $40,000. Now, would you recommend departmental rates over a plantwide rate?

4-14
Unit Cost; Ending Work in Process; Journal Entries

LO 4, 5

During October, Tyson Company worked on two jobs. Data relating to these two jobs follow:

	Job 68	Job 69
Units in each order	120	200
Units sold	120	—
Materials requisitioned	$744	$640
Direct labor hours	360	400
Direct labor cost	$1,980	$2,480

Overhead is assigned on the basis of direct labor hours at a rate of $3.75. During October, Job 68 was completed and transferred to finished goods. Job 69 was the only unfinished job at the end of the month.

REQUIRED:

1. Calculate the per-unit cost of Job 68.
2. Compute the ending balance in the work in process account.
3. Prepare the journal entries reflecting the completion and sale of Job 68. The selling price is 140 percent of cost.

4-15
Predetermined Overhead Rates; T-Accounts; Cost Flows

LO 3, 4, 5

Golding Company applies overhead based on direct labor cost. During the first quarter, the following activity took place in each of the accounts listed below:

Work in Process				Finished Goods		
Bal.	20,000	230,000	Bal.	40,000		200,000
DL	80,000			230,000		
OH	120,000					
DM	40,000					
Bal.	30,000		Bal.	70,000		

Overhead			Cost of Goods Sold	
	128,500	120,000	200,000	
Bal.	8,500			

Job 32 was the only job in process at the end of the first quarter. A total of 1,000 direct labor hours at $10 per hour were charged to Job 32.

REQUIRED:

1. Assuming that overhead is applied on the basis of direct labor cost, what was the overhead rate used during the first quarter?
2. What was the applied overhead for the first quarter? The actual overhead? The under- or overapplied overhead?
3. What was the cost of the goods manufactured for the quarter?
4. Assume that the overhead variance is closed to Cost of Goods Sold. Prepare the journal entry to close out the overhead account. What is the adjusted balance in Cost of Goods Sold?
5. For Job 32, identify the costs incurred for direct labor, direct materials, and overhead.

**4-16
Predetermined
Overhead Rates;
Overhead
Variances; Unit
Costs**

LO 3, 4

Sanderson Company uses a predetermined overhead rate to apply overhead. Overhead is applied on the basis of direct labor hours in Department 1 and on the basis of machine hours in Department 2. At the beginning of the year, the following estimates are provided:

	Department 1	Department 2
Direct labor hours	100,000	20,000
Machine hours	10,000	30,000
Direct labor cost	$750,000	$160,000
Overhead cost	$250,000	$162,000

Actual results reported for all jobs during the year are as follows:

	Department 1	Department 2
Direct labor hours	98,000	21,000
Machine hours	11,000	32,000
Direct labor cost	$748,000	$168,000
Overhead cost	$247,500	$175,000

The accounting records of the company show the following data for Job 689:

	Department 1	Department 2
Direct labor hours	125	50
Machine hours	10	205
Direct materials cost	$1,580	$2,650
Direct labor cost	$937	$400

REQUIRED:

1. Compute the predetermined overhead rate for each department.
2. Compute the applied overhead for all jobs during the year. What is the under- or overapplied overhead for each department? For the firm?
3. Prepare the journal entry that disposes of the overhead variance, assuming it is not material in amount.
4. Compute the total cost of Job 689. If there are 50 units in Job 689, what is the unit cost?

4-17
Job Cost Sheets;
Journal Entries;
Inventories

LO 4, 5

On July 1, Jason Company had the following balances in its inventory accounts:

Raw Materials	$12,000
Work in Process	8,000
Finished Goods	20,000

Work in process is made up of two jobs with the following costs:

	Job 17	Job 18
Raw materials	$2,000	$1,410
Direct labor	1,500	1,200
Applied overhead	1,050	840

During July, Jason experienced the transactions listed below:

a. Materials purchased on account, $15,000.
b. Materials requisitioned: Job 17, $12,500; Job 18, $11,200.
c. Job tickets were collected and summarized: Job 17, 250 hours at $10 per hour; Job 18, 275 hours at $11 per hour.
d. Overhead is applied on the basis of direct labor cost.
e. Actual overhead was $4,000.
f. Job 18 was completed and transferred to the finished goods warehouse.
g. Job 18 was shipped, and the customer was billed for 160 percent of the cost.

REQUIRED:

1. Prepare job cost sheets for Jobs 17 and 18. Post the beginning inventory data, and then update the cost sheets for the July activity.
2. Prepare journal entries for the July transactions.
3. Prepare a schedule of inventories on July 31.

4-18
Journal Entries;
T-Accounts; Cost
of Goods
Manufactured and
Sold

LO 3, 4, 5

During February, the following transactions were completed and reported by Bixby Products, Inc.:

a. Raw materials purchased on account, $43,500.
b. Materials issued to production to fill job-order requisitions, $35,000; supplies, $12,200.
c. Payroll for the month: direct labor, $60,000; indirect labor, $20,000; administrative, $18,000; sales, $9,000.
d. Depreciation on factory plant and equipment, $8,500.
e. Property tax accrued during the month, $450 (on factory).
f. Insurance expired with a credit to the prepaid account, $6,200.
g. Factory utilities, $6,200.
h. Advertising, $5,000.
i. Depreciation on office equipment, $1,500; on sales vehicles, $650.
j. Legal fees for preparation of lease agreements, $750.
k. Overhead is charged to production at a rate of $6 per DLH. Records show 8,000 direct labor hours were worked during the month.
l. Cost of jobs completed during the month, $135,000.

The company also reported the following beginning balances in its inventory accounts:

Beg. Balances

Raw Materials	$ 5,000
Work in Process	30,000
Finished Goods	60,000

REQUIRED:

1. Prepare journal entries to record the transactions occurring in February.
2. Prepare T-accounts for Raw Materials, Overhead, Work in Process, and Finished Goods. Post all relevant entries to these accounts.
3. Prepare a statement of cost of goods manufactured.
4. If the overhead variance is all allocated to Cost of Goods Sold, by how much will Cost of Goods Sold decrease or increase?

4-19
Journal Entries; T-Accounts; Disposition of Overhead; Income Statement
LO 3, 4, 5

At the beginning of the year, Polson Manufacturing Company had the following balances in its inventory accounts:

Raw Materials	$70,000
Work in Process	20,000
Finished Goods	45,000

Polson applies overhead on the basis of 150 percent of direct labor cost. During the year, Polson experienced transactions as described below.

a. Direct materials purchased, $280,000.
b. Direct materials issued, $300,000.
c. Indirect materials issued, $82,000.
d. Labor costs:

Direct labor	$110,000
Indirect labor	60,000
Selling and administrative	70,000

e. Factory insurance expired, $5,000.
f. Advertising costs, $30,000.
g. Factory rent, $24,000.
h. Depreciation on office equipment, $10,000.
i. Miscellaneous factory costs, $7,850.
j. Utilities (70 percent factory, 30 percent office), $10,000.
k. Overhead was applied to production.
l. Sales totaled $983,000.

Ending balances in the inventory accounts were

	Total
Raw Materials	$50,000
Work in Process	30,000
Finished Goods	20,000

REQUIRED:

1. Prepare journal entries for the above transactions.
2. Post the journal entries relating to manufacturing costs to the appropriate T-accounts.
3. Compute the under- or overapplied overhead variance. Give the journal entry that disposes of the variance by closing it out to Cost of Goods Sold. Give the journal entry required to close out the variance if it is prorated among the appropriate accounts.
4. Prepare an income statement assuming that the variance is closed to Cost of Goods Sold. Prepare another income statement based on prorating the variance. What is the difference in income figures? Would you judge the difference to be significant?

4-20
Predetermined Overhead Rate; Departmental Overhead Rates; Job Cost
LO 3, 6

Anselmo's Kwik Print provides a variety of photocopying and printing services. On June 5, Anselmo invested in some computer-aided photography equipment that enables customers to reproduce a picture or illustration, input it digitally into the computer, enter text into the computer, and then print out a four-color professional quality brochure. Prior to the purchase of this equipment, Kwik Print's overhead averaged $35,000 per year. After the installation of the new equipment, the total overhead increased to $85,000 per year. Kwik Print has always costed jobs on the basis of actual materials and labor plus overhead assigned using a predetermined overhead rate based on direct labor hours. Budgeted direct labor hours for the year are 5,000, and the wage rate is $6 per hour.

REQUIRED:

1. What was the predetermined overhead rate prior to the purchase of the new equipment?
2. What was the predetermined overhead rate after the new equipment was purchased?
3. Suppose Jim Hargrove brought in several items he wanted photocopied. The job required 100 sheets of paper at $.015 each and 12 minutes of direct labor time. What was the cost of Jim's job on May 20? On June 20?
4. Suppose that Anselmo decides to calculate two overhead rates, one for the photocopying area based on direct labor hours as before, and one for the computer-aided printing area based on machine time. Estimated overhead applicable to the computer-aided printing area is $50,000, and forecasted usage of the machines is 2,000 hours. What are the two overhead rates? Which overhead rate system is better—one rate or two?

4-21
Multiple Overhead Rates
LO 6

Chesbro, Inc., manufactures customized pressure washers. The washers pass through two departments: fabrication and painting. Chesbro uses a normal costing system. Estimated overhead and direct labor hours for the year are as follows:

	Fabrication	Painting
Estimated overhead	$20,000	$36,250
Estimated direct labor hours	10,000	5,000

Job 416 required $57 of direct materials and $45 direct labor (3 hours in Fabrication and 1 hour in Painting).

REQUIRED:

1. Compute the predetermined overhead rate, based on direct labor hours, for the plant as a whole. What is the total cost of Job 416 using this rate?
2. Compute predetermined overhead rates, based on direct labor hours, for each department. What is the total cost of Job 416 using these rates?
3. Should Chesbro use one plantwide overhead rate or use departmental overhead rates? Explain.

4-22
Multiple Overhead Rates
LO 6

Jurgens Tailoring is a costume company located in Manhattan. Jurgens designs and creates costumes for theatrical presentations. Additionally, Jurgens alters and repairs costumes. Jurgens has three departments: design, machine sewing, and beading. The design department overhead consists of computers and software for computer-assisted design. The machine-sewing department overhead consists of thread, sewing machines, and small tools (e.g., scissors and seam rippers). The beading department has very little overhead, just thread and some glue. Of course, all departments are assigned a share of utilities, rent, and so on. Information on estimated overhead and direct labor hours for the year by department are as follows:

	Estimated Overhead	Estimated Direct Labor Hours
Design Department	$55,000	2,000
Sewing Department	42,000	7,000
Beading Department	3,000	1,000

The Hoboken Ballet has just contracted with Jurgens for twenty new tutus for the Nutcracker Ballet. Hoboken has decided to stick with tried and true patterns, which Jurgens already has in stock, but to splurge on fancier materials and beading. As a result, no Design Department services are needed. Direct materials for the job will cost $6,000. The job will take 160 hours of Sewing Department time at $8 per direct labor hour and 400 hours of Beading Department time at $12.50 per direct labor hour.

REQUIRED:

1. Calculate a single overhead rate for Jurgens. What is the total cost of the Hoboken job using this rate?
2. Calculate departmental overhead rates for each department based on direct labor hours. What is the total cost of the Hoboken job using these rates?
3. Assuming that Jurgens charges customers cost plus 25%, why might it be in Jurgens' best interests to use a departmental overhead rate?

4-23
Characteristics of the Production Process
LO 1

Refer to the data in **4-22** above. Is Jurgens a manufacturing firm or a service firm? Explain.

4-24
Job-Order Costing: Housing Construction
LO 4, 5

Sutton Construction, Inc., is a privately held, family-founded corporation that builds single- and multiple-unit housing. Most projects Sutton Construction undertakes involve the construction of multiple units. Sutton Construction has adopted a job-order cost system for determining the cost of each unit. The costing system is fully computerized. Each project's costs are divided into the following five categories:

1. *General conditions*, including construction site utilities, project insurance permits and licenses, architect's fees, decorating, field office salaries, and cleanup costs.
2. *Hard costs*, such as subcontractors, direct materials, and direct labor.
3. *Finance costs*, including title and recording fees, inspection fees, and taxes and discounts on mortgages.
4. *Land costs*, which refer to the purchase price of the construction site.
5. *Marketing costs*, such as advertising, sales commissions, and appraisal fees.

Recently, Sutton Construction purchased land for the purpose of developing twenty new single-family houses. The cost of the land was $250,000. Lot sizes vary from 1/4 to 1/2 acre. The twenty lots occupy a total of eight acres.

General condition costs for the project totaled $120,000. This $120,000 is common to all twenty units that were constructed on the building site.

Job 3, the third house built in the project, occupied a 1/4-acre lot and had the following hard costs:

Materials	$ 8,000
Direct labor	6,000
Subcontractor	14,000

For Job 3, finance costs totaled $4,765 and marketing costs $800. General condition costs are allocated on the basis of units produced. Each unit's selling price is determined by adding 40 percent to the total of all costs.

REQUIRED:

1. Identify all production costs that are directly traceable to Job 3. Are all remaining production costs equivalent to overhead found in a manufacturing firm? Are there nonproduction costs that are directly traceable to the housing unit? Which ones?
2. Develop a job-order cost sheet for Job 3. What is the cost of building this house? Did you include finance and marketing costs in computing the unit cost? Why or why not? How did you determine the cost of land for Job 3?
3. Which of the five cost categories corresponds to overhead? Do you agree with the way in which this cost is allocated to individual housing units? Can you suggest a different allocation method?
4. Calculate the selling price of Job 3. Calculate the profit made on the sale of this unit.

**4-25
Plantwide
Overhead Rate
Versus
Departmental
Rates; Effects on
Pricing Decisions**

LO 6

Cherise Ortega, marketing manager for Romer Company, was puzzled by the outcome of two recent bids. The company's policy was to bid 150 percent of the full manufacturing cost. One job (labeled Job 97-28) had been turned down by a prospective customer, who had indicated that the proposed price was $3 per unit higher than the winning bid. A second job (Job 97-35) had been accepted by a customer, who was amazed that Romer could offer such favorable terms. This customer revealed that Romer's price was $43 per unit lower than the next lowest bid.

Cherise has been informed that the company was more than competitive in terms of cost control. Accordingly, she began to suspect that the problem was related to cost assignment procedures. Upon investigating, Cherise was told that the company uses a plantwide overhead rate based on direct labor hours. The rate is computed at the beginning of the year using budgeted data. Selected budgeted data are given below.

	Department A	Department B	Total
Overhead	$500,000	$2,000,000	$2,500,000
Direct labor hours	200,000	50,000	250,000
Machine hours	20,000	120,000	140,000

Cherise also discovered that the overhead costs in Department B were higher than those in Department A because B has more equipment, higher maintenance, higher power consumption, higher depreciation, and higher setup costs. In addition to the general procedures for assigning overhead costs, Cherise was supplied with the following specific manufacturing data on Job 97-28 and Job 97-35:

Job 97-28

	Department A	Department B	Total
Direct labor hours	5,000	1,000	6,000
Machine hours	200	500	700
Prime costs	$100,000	$20,000	$120,000
Units produced	14,400	14,400	14,400

Job 97-35

	Department A	Department B	Total
Direct labor hours	400	600	1,000
Machine hours	200	3,000	3,200
Prime costs	$10,000	$40,000	$50,000
Units produced	1,500	1,500	1,500

REQUIRED:

1. Using a plantwide overhead rate based on direct labor hours, develop the bid prices for Job 97-28 and Job 97-35 (express the bid prices on a per-unit basis).
2. Using departmental overhead rates (use direct labor hours for Department A and machine hours for Department B), develop per-unit bid prices for Job 97-28 and Job 97-35.
3. Compute the difference in gross profit that would have been earned had the company used departmental rates in its bids instead of the plantwide rate.
4. Explain why the use of departmental rates in this case provides a more accurate product cost.

4-26

Case on Selection of Overhead Rates; Ethical Issues

LO 2, 3

Abby Greene, CMA and controller of the Parts Division of Gunderson, Inc., was meeting with Bart Adams, manager of the division. The topic of discussion was the assignment of overhead costs to jobs and their impact on the division's pricing decisions. Their conversation is presented below.

Abby: Bart, as you know, about 25 percent of our business is based on government contracts, with the other 75 percent based on jobs from private sources won through bidding. During the last several years, our private business has declined. We have been losing more bids than usual. After some careful investigation, I have concluded that we are overpricing some jobs because of improper assignment of overhead costs. Some jobs are also being underpriced. Unfortunately, the jobs being overpriced are coming from our higher-volume, labor-intensive products, and so we are losing business.

Bart: I think I understand. Jobs associated with our high-volume products are being assigned more overhead than they should be receiving. When we then add our standard 40 percent markup, we end up with a higher price than our competitors, who assign costs more accurately.

Abby: Exactly. We have two producing departments, one labor-intensive and the other machine-intensive. The labor-intensive department generates much less overhead than does the machine-intensive department. Furthermore, virtually all of our high-volume jobs are labor-intensive. We have been using a plantwide rate based on direct labor hours to assign overhead to all jobs. As a result, the high-volume, labor-intensive jobs receive a greater share of the machine-intensive department's overhead than they deserve. This problem can be greatly alleviated by switching to departmental overhead rates. For example, an average high-volume job would be assigned $100,000 of overhead using a plantwide rate and only $70,000 using departmental rates. The change would lower our bidding price on high-volume jobs by an average of $42,000 per job. By increasing the accuracy of our product costing, we can make better pricing decisions and win back much of our private-sector business.

Bart: Sounds good. When can you implement the change in overhead rates?

Abby: It won't take long. I can have the new system working within four to six weeks—certainly by the start of the new fiscal year.

Bart: Hold it. I just thought of a possible complication. As I recall, most of our government contract work is done in the labor-intensive department. This new overhead assignment scheme will push down the cost on the government jobs and we will lose revenues. They pay us full cost plus our standard markup. This business is not threatened by our current costing procedures, but we can't switch our rates for only the private business. Government auditors would question the lack of consistency in our costing procedures.

Abby: You do have a point. I thought of this issue also. According to my estimates, we will gain more revenues from the private sector than we will lose from our government contracts. Besides, the costs of our government jobs are distorted; in effect, we are overcharging the government.

Bart: They don't know that and never will unless we switch our overhead assignment procedures. I think I have the solution. Officially, let's keep our plantwide overhead rate. All of the official records will reflect this overhead costing approach for both our private and government business. Unofficially, I want you to develop a separate set of books that can be used to generate the information we need to prepare competitive bids for our private-sector business.

REQUIRED:

1. Do you believe that the solution proposed by Bart Adams is ethical? Explain.
2. Suppose that Abby Greene decides that Adams's solution is not right. In your opinion, is Greene supported in this view by the IMA standards of ethical conduct?
3. Suppose that, despite Greene's objections, Adams insists strongly on implementing the action. What should Abby Greene do?

4-27
Case on Job-Order Costing: Dental Practice
LO 4, 5

Dr. Sherry Bird is employed by Dental Associates. Dental Associates recently installed a computerized job costing system to help monitor the cost of its services. Each patient is treated as a job and assigned a job number when he or she checks in with the receptionist. The receptionist-bookkeeper notes the time the patient enters the treatment area and when the patient leaves the area. The difference between the entry and exit times is the patient hours used and is the direct labor time assigned to the dental assistant (a dental assistant is constantly with the patient). Fifty percent of the patient hours is the direct labor time assigned to the dentist (the dentist typically splits her time between two patients).

The chart filled out by the dental assistant provides additional data that is entered into the computer. For example, the chart contains service codes that identify the nature of the treatment, such as whether the patient received a crown, a filling, or a root canal. The chart not only identifies the type of service but its level as well. For example, if a patient receives a filling, the dental assistant indicates (by a service-level code) whether the filling was one, two, three, or four surfaces. The service and service-level codes are used to determine the rate to be charged to the patient. The costs of providing different services and their levels also vary.

Costs assignable to a patient consist of materials, labor, and overhead. The types of materials used—and the quantity—are identified by the assistant and entered into the computer by the bookkeeper. Material prices are kept on file and accessed to provide the necessary cost information. Overhead is applied on the basis of patient hours. The rate used by Dental Associates is $20 per patient hour. Direct labor cost is also computed using patient hours and the wage rates of the direct laborers. Dr. Bird is paid an average of $36 per hour for her services. Dental assistants are paid an average of $6 per hour. Given the treatment time, the software program calculates and assigns the labor cost for the dentist and her assistant; overhead cost is also assigned using the treatment time and the overhead rate.

The overhead rate does not include a charge for any X rays. The X ray Department is separate from dental services; X rays are billed and costed separately. The cost of an X ray is $3.50 per film; the patient is charged $5 per film. If cleaning services are required, cleaning labor costs $9 per patient hour.

Glen Johnson, a patient (Job 267), spent thirty minutes in the treatment area and had a two-surface filling. He received two Novocain shots and used three ampules of amalgam. The cost of the shots was $1. The cost of the amalgam was $3. Other direct materials used are insignificant in amount and are included in the overhead rate. The rate charged to the patient for a two-surface filling is $45. One X ray was taken.

REQUIRED:

1. Prepare a job-cost sheet for Glen Johnson. What is the cost for providing a two-surface filling? What is the gross profit earned? Is the X ray a direct cost of the service? Why are the X rays costed separately from the overhead cost assignment?
2. Suppose that the patient time and associated patient charges are given for the following fillings:

	1 Surface	2 Surface	3 Surface	4 Surface
Time	20 minutes	30 minutes	40 minutes	50 minutes
Charge	$35	$45	$55	$65

Compute the cost for each filling and the gross profit for each type of filling. Assume that the cost of Novocain is $1 for all fillings. Ampules of amalgam start at two and increase by one for each additional surface. Assume also that only one X-ray film is needed for all four cases. Does the increase in billing rate appear to be fair to the patient? Is it fair to the dental corporation?

4-28
Case on Job-Order Costing and Pricing Decisions
LO 4, 5

Nutratask, Inc., is a pharmaceutical manufacturer of amino-acid-chelated minerals and vitamin supplements. The company was founded in 1974 and is capable of performing all manufacturing functions, including packaging and laboratory functions. Currently, the company markets its products in the United States, Canada, Australia, Japan, and Belgium.

Mineral chelation enhances the mineral's availability to the body, making the mineral a more effective supplement. Most of the chelates supplied by Nutratask are in powder form, but the company has the capability to make tablets or capsules.

The production of all chelates follows a similar pattern. Upon receiving an order, the company's chemist prepares a load sheet (a bill of materials that specifies the product, the theoretical yield, and the quantities of raw materials that should be used). Once the load sheet is received by production, the materials are requisitioned and sent to the blending room. The chemicals and minerals are added in the order specified and blended together for two to eight hours, depending on the product. After blending, the mix is put on long trays and sent to the drying room, where it is allowed to dry until the moisture content is 7 to 9 percent. Drying time for most products is from one to three days.

After the product is dry, several small samples are taken and sent to a laboratory to be checked for bacterial level and to see whether the product meets customer specifications. If the product is not fit for human consumption or if it fails to meet customer specifications, additional materials are added under the direction of the chemist to bring the product up to standard. Once the product passes inspection, it is ground into a powder of different meshes (particle sizes) according to customer specifications. The powder is then placed in heavy cardboard drums and shipped to the customer (or, if requested, put in tablet or capsule form and then shipped).

Since each order is customized to meet the special needs of its customers, Nutratask uses a job-order costing system. Recently, Nutratask received a request for a 300-kilogram order of potassium aspartate. The customer offered to pay $8.80/kg. Upon receiving the

Part 2   Cost Accounting Systems

request and the customer's specifications. Lanny Smith, the marketing manager, requested a load sheet from the company's chemist. The load sheet prepared showed the following material requirements:

Material	Amount Required
Aspartic acid	195.00 kg
Citric acid	15.00 kg
K_2CO_3 (50%)	121.50 kg
Rice	30.00 kg

The theoretical yield is 300 kg.

Lanny also reviewed past jobs that were similar to the requested order and discovered that the expected direct labor time was 16 hours. The production workers at Nutratask earn an average of $6.50 per hour plus $6 per hour for taxes, insurance, and additional benefits.

Purchasing sent Smith a list of prices for the materials needed for the job.

Material	Price/kg
Aspartic acid	$5.75
Citric acid	2.02
K_2CO_3	4.64
Rice	0.43

Overhead is applied using a companywide rate based on direct labor costs. The rate for the current period is 110 percent of direct labor costs.

Whenever a customer requests a bid, Nutratask usually estimates the manufacturing costs of the job and then adds a markup of 30 percent. This markup varies depending on the competition and general economic conditions. Currently, the industry is thriving, and Nutratask is operating at capacity.

REQUIRED:

1. Prepare a job-order cost sheet for the proposed job. What is the expected per-unit cost? Should Nutratask accept the price offered by the prospective customer? Why or why not?
2. Suppose Nutratask and the prospective customer agree on a price of cost plus 30 percent. What is the gross margin that Nutratask expects to earn on the job?
3. Suppose that the actual costs of producing 300 kg of potassium aspartate were as follows:

Direct materials:	
Aspartic acid	$1,170
Citric acid	30
K_2CO_3	577
Rice	13
Total materials cost	$1,790.00
Direct labor	225.00
Overhead	247.50

What is the actual per-unit cost? The bid price is based on expected costs. How much did Nutratask gain (or lose) because of the actual costs differing from the expected costs? Suggest some possible reasons why the actual costs differed from the projected costs.

4. Assume that the customer had agreed to pay *actual* manufacturing costs plus 30 percent. Suppose the actual costs are as described in Question 3 with one addition: an underapplied overhead variance is allocated to Cost of Goods Sold and spread across all jobs sold in proportion to their total cost (unadjusted cost of goods sold). Assume that the underapplied overhead cost added to the job in question is $30. Upon seeing the addition of the underapplied overhead in the itemized bill, the customer calls and complains about having to pay for Nutratask's inefficient use of overhead costs. If you were assigned to deal with this customer, what kind of response would you prepare? How would you explain and justify the addition of the underapplied overhead cost to the customer's bill?

4-29
Predetermined
Overhead Rates;
Overhead
Variances; Unit
Costs

LO 3, 6

Palace Lighting Fixtures, Inc., uses a predetermined overhead rate to apply overhead. Overhead is applied on the basis of direct labor hours in Department 1 and on the basis of machine hours in Department 2. At the beginning of the year, the following estimates are provided:

	Department 1	Department 2
Direct labor hours	100,000	20,000
Machine hours	10,000	35,000
Direct labor cost	$900,000	$190,000
Overhead cost	$300,000	$196,000

Actual results reported for all jobs during the year are as follows:

	Department 1	Department 2
Direct labor hours	98,000	21,000
Machine hours	11,000	36,000
Direct labor cost	$882,400	$168,000
Overhead cost	$301,000	$200,600

The accounting records of the company show the following data for Job 689:

	Department 1	Department 2
Direct labor hours	125	50
Machine hours	10	205
Direct materials cost	$1,610	$3,000
Direct labor cost	$1,125	$400

REQUIRED:

1. Compute the predetermined overhead rate for each department.
2. Compute the applied overhead for all jobs during the year. What is the under- or overapplied overhead for each department? For the firm?
3. Prepare the journal entry that disposes of the overhead variance, assuming it is not material in amount.
4. Compute the total cost of Job 689. If there are fifty units in Job 689, what is the unit cost?

4-30
APPENDIX: Cost
of Spoiled Units

Garvey Company is a specialty print shop. Usually, printing jobs are priced at standard cost plus 50 percent. Job 94-301 involved printing 500 wedding invitations with the following standard costs:

Direct materials	$200
Direct labor	20
Overhead	30
Total	$250

Normally, the invitations would be taken from the machine, the top one inspected for correct wording, spelling, and quality of print, and all of the invitations wrapped in plastic and stored on shelves designated for completed jobs. In this case, however, the technician decided to go to lunch before inspecting and wrapping the job. He stacked the unwrapped invitations beside the printing press and left. One hour later, he returned and found the invitations had fallen on the floor and been stepped on. It turned out that about 100 invitations were ruined and had to be discarded. An additional 100 invitations were then printed to complete the job.

REQUIRED:

1. Calculate the cost of the spoiled invitations. How should the spoilage cost be accounted for?
2. What is the price of job 94-301?
3. Suppose that another job, 94-442, also required 500 wedding invitations. The standard costs are identical to those of job 94-301. However, job 94-442 required an unusual color of ink which could only be obtained in a formula which was difficult to use. Garvey printers know from experience that getting this ink color to print correctly requires trial and error. In the case of job 94-442, the first 100 invitations had to be discarded due to inconsistencies in the color of ink. What is the cost of the spoilage and how would it be treated?
4. What is the price of job 94-442?

4-31
APPENDIX: Cost
of Reworked Units

Jackson's Sporting Goods Store sells a variety of sporting goods and clothing. In a back room, Jackson's has set up heat-transfer equipment to personalize T-shirts for little league teams. Typically, each team has the name of the individual player put on the back of the T-shirt. Last week, Taffy Barnhart, coach of the Stingers, brought in a list of names for her team. Her team consisted of 12 players with the following names: Freda, Cara, Katie, Tara, Heather, Sarah, Kim, Jennifer, Mary Beth, Elizabeth, Kyle, and Wendy. Taffy was quoted a price of $.50 per letter.

Chip Russell, Jackson's newest employee, was assigned to Taffy's job. He selected the appropriate letters, arranged the letters in each name carefully on a shirt, and heat-pressed them on. When Taffy returned, she was appalled to see that the names were on the front of the shirts. Jim Jackson, owner of the sporting goods store, assured Taffy that the letters could easily be removed by applying more heat and lifting them off. This process ruins the old letters, so new letters must then be placed correctly on the shirt backs. He promised to correct the job immediately and have it ready in an hour and a half.

Costs for heat-transferring are as follows:

Letters (each)	$0.15
Direct labor (per hour)	8.00
Overhead (per direct labor hour)	4.00

Taffy's job originally took one hour of direct labor time. The removal process goes more quickly and should take only 15 minutes.

REQUIRED:

1. What was the original cost of Taffy's job?
2. What is the cost of rework on Taffy's job? How should the rework cost be treated?
3. How much did Jim Jackson charge Taffy?

**4-32
Research
Assignment**
LO 1, 2, 4

Interview an accountant who works for a service organization that uses job-order costing. For a small firm, you may need to talk to an owner/manager. Examples are a funeral home, insurance firm, repair shop, medical clinic, and dental clinic. Write a paper that describes the job-order cost system used by the firm. Some of the questions that the paper should address are:

a. What service or services does the firm offer?
b. What document or procedure do you use to collect the costs of the services performed for each customer?
c. How do you assign the cost of direct labor to each job?
d. How do you assign overhead to individual jobs?
e. How do you assign the cost of direct materials to each job?
f. How do you determine what to charge each customer?
g. How do you account for a completed job?

As you write the paper, state how the service firm you investigated adapted the job-order accounting procedures described in this chapter to its particular circumstances. Were the differences justified? If so, explain why. Also, offer any suggestions you might have for improving the approach that you observed.

Chapter 5
Product and Service Costing: A Process Systems Approach

With speedy PowerPC chips and an elegant operating system that served as the benchmark for Windows 95, Apple Computer, Inc., hopes to double the market share of Macs and Mac-clones by the end of the century. To do that, the manufacturing process of Apple and its licensees must proceed smoothly. Apple believes that the increased volume will enable them to cut prices and remain profitable.

LEARNING OBJECTIVES

After studying this chapter, you should be able to:

1. Describe the basic characteristics of process costing, including cost flows, journal entries, and the cost of production report.
2. Describe process costing for settings without work in process inventories.
3. Define *equivalent units*, and explain their role in process costing.
4. Prepare a departmental production report using the FIFO method.
5. Prepare a departmental production report using the weighted average method.
6. Prepare a departmental production report with transferred-in goods and changes in output measures.
7. Describe the basic features of operation costing.

Methods of production affect the design of product costing systems. Services and products can be produced using either a job approach or a process approach, depending on the nature of the products and services. Job and process production methods differ significantly. These differences produce different system designs. This simply emphasizes the fact that cost accounting systems should be structured to meet the demands of the underlying operations. In this chapter, we explore *process costing systems*. The principal objective of a process costing system is product costing; thus, the cost object is a product. Apple Computer, for example, is interested in the cost of each computer. We will restrict our definition of product cost to the traditional view; specifically, our only concern is how manufacturing costs are assigned to products. Furthermore, we also confine our study to traditional cost accounting systems. Thus, only unit-based activity drivers are used to assign production costs to products. In later chapters (Chapters 8 and 9), we extend our study of both job and process costing systems to include alternative product cost definitions and contemporary cost accounting systems.

PROCESS COSTING SYSTEMS: BASIC OPERATIONAL AND COST CONCEPTS

Objective 1

Describe the basic characteristics of process costing, including cost flows, journal entries, and the cost of production report.

process

To understand a process costing system, it is necessary to understand the underlying operational system. An operational process system is characterized by a large number of homogeneous products passing through a series of *processes*, where each process is responsible for one or more operations that bring a product one step closer to completion. Thus, a **process** is a series of activities (operations) that are linked to perform a specific objective. For example, a manufacturer of a multiple vitamin and mineral product has three processes: picking, encapsulating, and bottling. Consider the picking process. The picking process consists of three linked activities: selecting, measuring, and mixing. Direct laborers *select* the appropriate herbs, vitamins, minerals, and inert materials (typically some binder such as cornstarch) for the product to be manufactured. Then, the materials are *measured* and *combined* in a mixer to blend them thoroughly in the prescribed proportions.

In each process, materials, labor, and overhead inputs may be needed (typically in equal doses). Upon completion of a particular process, the partially completed goods are transferred to another process. For example, when the mix prepared by the picking department is finished, the resulting mixture is sent to the encapsulating process. The encapsulating process consists of four linked activities: loading, filling, matching, and sealing. Initially, the vitamin, mineral, and herb blend is loaded into a machine that fills one-half of a gelatin capsule. The filled half is matched to another half of the capsule and a safety seal is applied. The final process is bottling. It also has four linked activities: loading, counting, capping, and packing. Filled capsules are transferred to this department, loaded into a hopper, and automatically counted into bottles. Filled bottles are mechanically capped, and direct labor then manually packs the correct number of bottles into boxes which are transferred to the warehouse. Exhibit 5-1 summarizes the operational process system for the vitamin and mineral manufacturer.

Cost Flows

The cost flows for a process cost system are basically similar to those of a job-order costing system. There are two key differences. First, a job-order cost system accumulates production costs by job and a process cost system accumulates pro-

Exhibit 5-1
An Operational Process System

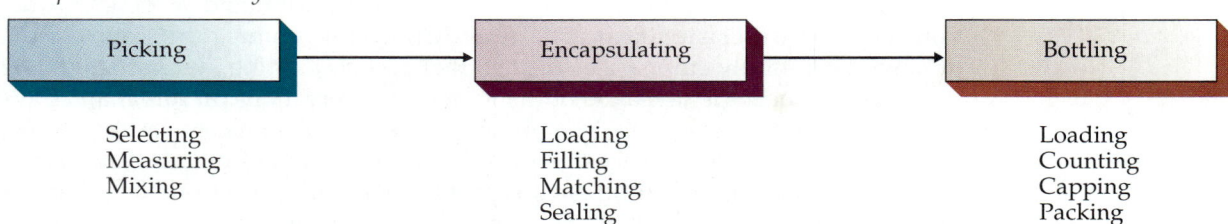

Picking	Encapsulating	Bottling
Selecting	Loading	Loading
Measuring	Filling	Counting
Mixing	Matching	Capping
	Sealing	Packing

duction costs by process. Second, for manufacturing firms, the job-order cost system uses a single work in process account, while the process cost system has a work in process account for every process. Exhibit 5-2 illustrates the first key difference: the different approaches to cost accumulation. Notice that job systems assign manufacturing costs to jobs (which act as subsidiary work in process accounts) and transfer these costs directly to the finished goods account when the job is completed. When units are finished for a process, manufacturing costs are transferred from one process department's account to the next. The last process transfers the costs to Finished Goods. Exhibit 5-3 highlights the cost flow differences involving work in process accounts.

Exhibit 5-3 not only illustrates the use of multiple Work in Process accounts, but it also reveals some important concepts concerning the nature of process costing. Consider, for example, the journal entries for the Encapsulating Department.

1. Work in Process—Encapsulating	600	
Work in Process—Picking		600
To transfer goods to encapsulating.		
2. Work in Process—Encapsulating	400	
Materials		100
Payroll		125
Overhead Control		175
To record additional manufacturing costs.		
3. Work in Process—Bottling	800	
Work in Process—Encapsulating		800
To transfer finished goods to bottling.		

When goods are completed in one process, they are transferred with their costs to the subsequent process. For example, Picking transferred $600 of their costs to Encapsulating and Encapsulating (after further processing) transferred $800 of costs to Bottling. The costs transferred from a prior process to a subsequent process are referred to as **transferred-in costs**. These transferred-in costs are (from the viewpoint of the process receiving them) a type of raw material cost. This is true because the subsequent process receives a partially completed unit that must be subjected to additional manufacturing activity, which includes more direct labor, more overhead, and, in some cases, additional raw materials. For example, the second journal entry for the Encapsulating Department reveals that $400 of additional manufacturing costs were added after receiving the transferred-in good from Picking. Thus, while Picking sees the mineral and vitamin powder as a combination of raw materials, labor and overhead costs, Encapsulating sees only the powder—a raw material costing $600.

transferred-in costs

Exhibit 5-2
Comparison of Cost Accumulation Methods

Job-Order Costing

Manufacturing Costs

Direct materials
Direct labor
Applied overhead

| Job 205 | Job 206 | Job 207 |

| Finished goods | Finished goods | Finished goods |

Process Costing

Manufacturing Costs

Direct materials
Direct labor
Applied overhead

Picking → Encapsulating → Bottling

Finished goods

    Although a process costing system has more Work in Process accounts than
a job-order system, it is a simpler and less expensive system to operate. In a process cost system, there are no individual jobs and no job-order cost sheets. There
is no need to track materials to individual jobs. Materials are tracked to processes,
but there are many fewer processes than jobs. Further, there is no need to use
time tickets for assigning costs to processes. Since laborers typically work their
entire shift within a particular process, no detailed tracking of labor is needed.
In fact, in many firms, labor costs are such a small percentage of total process
costs that they are simply combined with overhead costs, creating a conversion
cost category.

Exhibit 5-3
Comparison Using
Work in Process
Accounts

Job-Order Costing

Work in Process				Finished Goods	
DM	20,000	30,000 ⟶		30,000	
DL	10,000				
OH	15,000				

The transfer reflects completion of a job (or jobs) costing $30,000.

Process Costing

Work in Process Picking				Work in Process Encapsulating			Work in Process Bottling			Finished Goods	
DM	350	600	⟶	600	800	⟶	800	1,200	⟶	1,200	
DL	100			DM	100		DM	200			
OH	200			DL	125		DL	75			
				OH	175		OH	325			
EI	50			EI	200		EI	200			

Note: DM = Direct Materials; DL = Direct Labor; OH = Applied Overhead; and EI = Ending Inventory.

The Production Report

production report

In process costing, costs are accumulated by department for a period of time. The **production report** is the document that summarizes the manufacturing activity that takes place in a process department for a given period of time. The production report also serves as a source document for transferring costs from the work in process account of a prior department to the work in process account of a subsequent department. In the department that handles the final stage of processing, it serves as a source document for transferring costs from the work in process account to the finished goods account.

A production report provides information about the physical units processed in a department and also about the manufacturing costs associated with them. Thus, a production report is divided into a unit information section and a cost information section. The unit information section has two major subdivisions: (1) units to account for and (2) units accounted for. Similarly, the cost information section has two major subdivisions: (1) costs to account for and (2) costs accounted for. In summary, a production report traces the flow of units through a department, identifies the costs charged to the department, shows the computation of unit costs, and reveals the disposition of the department's costs for the reporting period.

Unit Costs

A key input to the cost of production report is unit costs. In principle, calculating unit costs in a process system is very simple. First, measure the manufacturing costs for a process department for a given period of time. Second, measure the output of the process department for the same period of time. Finally, the unit cost for a process is computed by dividing the costs of the period by the output of the period. With the exception of the final process, the unit cost calculated is for a *partially completed unit*. The unit cost for the final process is the cost of the fully completed product. Exhibit 5-4 summarizes the basic features of a process costing system.

While the basic features seem relatively simple, the actual details of process costing are somewhat more complicated. A major source of difficulty is concerned with how costs and output of the period are defined when calculating the unit cost of each process. The presence of significant work in process inventories complicates the cost and output definitions needed for the unit cost calculation. For example, partially finished units in beginning work in process carry with them work and costs associated with a prior period. Yet these units must be finished this period and they will also have current period costs and work associated with them. A fundamental question is how to deal with the prior period costs and work. Another important and related complicating factor is nonuniform application of production costs, i.e., units half completed may not have half of each input needed. Much of our discussion of process costing will deal with the approaches taken to deal with these complicating factors.

PROCESS COSTING WITH NO WORK IN PROCESS INVENTORIES

Objective 2
Describe process costing for settings without work in process inventories.

Perhaps the best starting point is to begin with a discussion of process costing in settings where there are no work in process inventories. Seeing how process costing works without work in process inventories makes it easier to understand the procedures that are needed to deal with work in process inventories. Study of the no inventory setting is also justified because there are many firms that operate in such a setting.

Service Organizations

Any service that is basically homogeneous and repetitively produced can take advantage of a process costing approach. Check processing in a bank, cleaning teeth by a hygienist, air travel between Dallas and New York City, sorting mail by zip code, and laundering and pressing shirts are examples of homogeneous services that are repetitively produced. Although many services consist of a single process, there are examples where the service requires a sequence of processes. Air travel between Dallas and New York City, for example, involves the following sequence of services: reservation, ticketing, baggage checking and seat confirmation, flight, and baggage delivery and pickup. Although services cannot

Exhibit 5-4
Basic Features of Process Costing

1. Homogeneous units pass through a series of similar processes.
2. Each unit in each process receives a similar dose of manufacturing costs.
3. Manufacturing costs are accumulated by a process for a given period of time.
4. There is a Work in Process account for each process.
5. Manufacturing cost flows and the associated journal entries are generally similar to job-order costing.
6. The departmental production report is the key document for tracking manufacturing activity and costs.
7. Unit costs are computed by dividing the departmental costs of the period by the output of the period.

be stored, it is possible for firms engaged in service production to have work in process inventories. For example, a batch of tax returns can be partially completed at the end of a period. However, many services are provided in a way so that there are no work in process inventories. Teeth cleaning, funerals, surgical operations, sonograms, and carpet cleaning are a few examples where work in process inventories would be virtually nonexistent.

To illustrate how services without work in process inventories are costed using a process approach, consider the teeth cleaning process offered by most dentists. This is a single process usually carried out in a room dedicated to the service, with a hygienist (direct labor), materials, and equipment. In this case, the service is labor and overhead intensive. The direct materials used in the process are a small percentage of the total service cost. The production costs and the number of cleanings (patients served) for the month of March are given below:

Direct materials	$ 200
Hygienist salary	2,500
Overhead	1,800
Total production cost	$4,500
Number of cleanings	300

Given the above data, the unit cost of the service can be computed:

$$\text{Unit cost} = \text{Costs of the period/Output of the period}$$
$$= \$4,500/300 \text{ cleanings}$$
$$= \$15 \text{ per cleaning}$$

process costing principle

The calculation reveals the **process costing principle:** *To calculate the period's unit cost, divide the costs of the period by the output of the period.* Theoretically, the current period unit cost should use only costs and output that belong to the period. This principle is a theoretical concept and applies in settings that are more complicated.

JIT Manufacturing Firms

Many firms have adopted a just-in-time (JIT) manufacturing approach.[1] The overall thrust of JIT manufacturing is supplying a product that is needed, when it is needed, and in the quantity that is needed. JIT manufacturing emphasizes continuous improvement and the elimination of waste. Since carrying unnecessary inventory is viewed as wasteful, JIT firms strive to minimize inventories. *Successful* implementation of JIT policies tends to reduce work in process inventories to insignificant levels. Furthermore, the way manufacturing is carried out in a JIT firm usually is structured so that process costing can be used to determine product costs. Essentially, work cells are created that produce a product or subassembly from start to finish.

Costs are collected by cell for a period of time and output for the cell is measured for the same period. Unit costs are computed by dividing the costs of the period by output of the period (following the process costing principle). The com-

---

1.   JIT manufacturing and the implications for cost accounting and control are discussed in detail in Chapter 9.

putation is identical to that illustrated by the service organization example. Why? Because there is no ambiguity concerning what costs belong to the period and how output is measured. One of the objectives of JIT manufacturing is simplification. Keep this in mind as you study the process costing requirements of manufacturing firms that carry work in process inventories. The difference between the two settings is impressive and illustrates one of the significant benefits of JIT.

PROCESS COSTING WITH ENDING WORK IN PROCESS INVENTORIES

Objective 3

Define *equivalent units*, and explain their role in process costing.

The unit cost is needed both to compute the cost of goods transferred out of a process department and to value ending work in process. Work in process inventories affect the unit cost computation by affecting the way output of the period is measured. For example, consider a medical laboratory (a service organization) that serves a metropolitan area and several outlying communities. The laboratory has several departments, one of which specializes in PSA tests for urologists. Urologists in the region send blood samples to the laboratory. The PSA department runs the test and inputs the resulting data into the computer so that a statistical analysis of the PSA level can be conducted. The PSA levels are also tracked over time for patients who follow a regimen of annual examinations. Printouts are sent to urologists so that they can be placed in the patient's record. During the month of January, 20,000 tests were run and analyzed, and printouts were sent to the referring urologists. These "units" were finished and transferred out by mailing the results of the tests to the urologists. Because of the holiday season, the PSA department rarely has any work in process at the beginning of January. However, at the end of January, there were units (blood samples) that were worked on but not finished, producing an ending work in process inventory. By definition, ending work in process is not complete. Thus, a unit completed and transferred out during the period is not identical (or equivalent) to one in ending work in process inventory, and the cost attached to the two units should not be the same. In computing the unit cost, the output of the period must be defined. A major problem of process costing is making this definition.

Equivalent Units as Output Measures

To illustrate the output problem created by work in process inventories, assume that the PSA Department had the following data for January (output is measured in number of tests):

Units, beginning work in process	—
Units started	24,000
Units completed	20,000
Units, ending work in process (25% complete)	4,000
Total production costs	$168,000

What is the output in January for this department? 20,000 units? 24,000 units? If we say 20,000 units, we ignore the effort expended on the units in ending work in process. Furthermore, the production costs incurred in January belong to both the units completed and to the partially completed units in ending work in process. On the other hand, if we say 24,000 units, we ignore the fact that the 4,000 units in ending work in process are only partially completed. Somehow output must be measured so that it reflects the effort expended on both completed and partially completed units.

The solution is to calculate equivalent units of output. **Equivalent units of output** are the complete units that could have been produced given the total amount of productive effort expended for the period under consideration. Determining equivalent units of output for transferred-out units is easy; a unit would not be transferred out unless it were complete. Thus, every transferred-out unit is an equivalent unit. Units remaining in ending work in process inventory, however, are not complete. Thus, someone in production must "eyeball" ending work in process to estimate its degree of completion. In the example, the 4,000 units in ending work in process are 25 percent complete with respect to all production costs; this is equivalent to 1,000 fully completed units (4,000 × 25%). Therefore, the equivalent units for January would be the 20,000 completed units plus 1,000 equivalent units in ending work in process, a total of 21,000 units of output.

Cost of Production Report Illustrated

Recall that the cost of production report has a unit information section and a cost information section. The unit information section is concerned with output measurement, and the cost information section is concerned with unit cost computation and cost assignment and reconciliation. The unit information section has two major subdivisions: (1) units to account for and (2) units accounted for. Similarly, the cost information section has two major subdivisions: (1) costs to account for and (2) costs accounted for. A cost of production report for the PSA Department example is illustrated in Exhibit 5-5.

Reviewing some of the computations in Exhibit 5-5 illustrates some important points. Knowing the output for a period (equivalent work completed of 21,000 units) and the production costs for the department for that period ($168,000 in this example), we can calculate a unit cost, which in this case is $8/unit ($168,000/21,000). The unit cost is used to assign a cost of $160,000 ($8 × 20,000) to the 20,000 units transferred out and a cost of $8,000 ($8 × 1,000) to the 4,000 units in ending work in process. This unit cost is $8 per *equivalent* unit. Thus, when valuing ending work in process, the $8 unit cost is multiplied by the equivalent units, not the actual number of physical units in process.

There are five steps that must be followed in preparing a cost of production report:

1. Analysis of the flow of physical units
2. Calculation of equivalent units
3. Computation of unit cost
4. Valuation of inventories (goods transferred out and ending work in process)
5. Cost reconciliation

Knowing the physical units in beginning and ending work in process, their stage of completion, and the units completed and transferred out (Step 1) provides essential information for the computation of equivalent units (Step 2). This computation, in turn, is a prerequisite to computing unit cost (Step 3). Unit cost information and information from the equivalent unit schedule are both needed to value goods transferred out and goods in ending work in process (Step 4). Finally, the costs in beginning work in process and the costs incurred during the current period should equal the total costs assigned to goods transferred out and

Exhibit 5-5
PSA Department
Production Report for
January

Unit Information		
Units to account for:		
Units in beginning work in process	0	
Units started	24,000	
Total units to account for	24,000	

	Physical Flow	Equivalent Units
Units accounted for:		
Units completed	20,000	20,000
Units in ending work in process		
(25% complete)	4,000	1,000
Units accounted for	24,000	
Work completed		21,000

Cost Information		
Costs to account for:		
Beginning work in process	$ 0	
Incurred during the period	168,000	
Total costs to account for	$168,000	
Divide by equivalent units	÷21,000	
Cost per equivalent unit	$ 8	
Costs accounted for:		
Goods transferred out ($8 × 20,000)	$160,000	
Ending work in process ($8 × 1,000)	8,000	
Total costs accounted for	$168,000	

cost reconciliation

to goods in ending work in process (Step 5). Step 5 (**cost reconciliation**), of course, is simply a check on the accuracy of the report itself.

Nonuniform Application of Productive Inputs

Up to this point, we have assumed that work in process being 25 percent complete meant that 25 percent of materials, labor, and overhead needed to complete the process have been used and that another 75 percent are needed to finish the units. In other words, we have assumed that the productive inputs are applied uniformly as the manufacturing process unfolds.

Assuming uniform application of conversion costs (direct labor and overhead) is not unreasonable. Direct labor input is usually needed throughout the process, and overhead is normally assigned on the basis of direct labor hours. Direct materials, on the other hand, are not as likely to be applied uniformly. In many instances, materials are added at either the beginning or the end of the process.

For example, consider the PSA Department in our example. It is more likely that materials (e.g., special chemicals) would be added at the beginning of the process rather than uniformly throughout the process. If so, then ending work in process that is 25% complete with respect to conversion inputs would be 100% complete with respect to material inputs.

Different percentage completion figures for productive inputs at the same stage of completion pose a problem for the calculation of equivalent units. Fortunately, the solution is relatively simple. Equivalent unit calculations are done for each category of input. Thus, there are equivalent units calculated for *each* category of materials and for conversion cost. For the PSA Department, if materials are added at the beginning of the process, equivalent units of work for each category would be calculated as follows:

	Materials	*Conversion Costs*
Units completed	20,000	20,000
Units, ending work in process:		
4,000 × 100% materials	4,000	
4,000 × 25% conversion		1,000
Equivalent units of output	24,000	21,000

Of course, having separate categories of equivalent units requires that the costs of each category be measured separately. Unit costs are then calculated for each input category, and the total unit cost is the sum of individual category unit costs. For example, the following cost breakdown would produce the indicated unit costs:

	Materials	*Conversion*	*Total*
Total cost	$126,000	$42,000	$168,000
Equivalent units	24,000	21,000	—
Unit cost	$5.25	$2.00	7.25

Beginning Work in Process Inventories

The PSA process example only showed the effect of ending work in process inventories on output measurement. The presence of beginning work in process inventories also complicates output measurement. Since many firms have partially completed units in process at the beginning of a period, there is a clear need to address the issue. The work done on these partially completed units represents prior-period work, and the costs assigned to them are prior-period costs. In computing a *current period* unit cost for a department, two approaches have evolved for dealing with the prior-period output and prior-period costs found in beginning work in process: the *first-in, first-out (FIFO) costing method* and the *weighted average method*. Both methods follow the same five steps described for preparing a cost of production report. However, the two methods usually only produce the same result for Step 1. The two methods are best illustrated by example. The FIFO method is discussed first, followed by a discussion of the weighted average method.

FIFO COSTING METHOD

Objective 4
Prepare a departmental production report using the FIFO method.

FIFO costing method

The process costing principle requires that the costs of the period be divided by the output of the period. Thus, theoretically, only *current* period costs and *current* period output should be used to compute *current* period unit costs. The FIFO method attempts to follow this theoretical guideline. Under the **FIFO costing method**, the equivalent units and manufacturing costs in beginning work in process are *excluded* from the current-period unit cost calculation. Thus, FIFO recognizes that the work and costs carried over from the prior period legitimately belong to that period.

Since FIFO excludes prior-period work and costs, we need to create two categories of completed units. FIFO assumes that units in beginning work in process are completed first, before any new units are started. Thus, one category of completed units is that of beginning work in process units. The second category is for those units started *and* completed during the current period.

These two categories of completed units are needed in the FIFO method so that each category can be costed correctly. For the units started and completed, the unit cost is obtained by dividing total current manufacturing costs by the current-period equivalent output. However, for the beginning work in process units, the total associated manufacturing costs are the sum of the prior-period costs plus the costs incurred in the current period to finish the units. Thus, the unit cost is this total cost divided by the units in beginning work in process.

To illustrate the FIFO method, consider Estrella Company, a company that mass produces a widely used pain medication. This company uses three processes: mixing, tableting, and packaging. In mixing, the various ingredients are measured, sifted, and blended together. The tableting department receives a powdered mixture from mixing, adds a binding agent, and then presses the mixture into capsule-shaped tablets, and coats each tablet to make swallowing easier. Packaging is responsible for placing eight tablets in small metal boxes. October's cost and production data for the Mixing Department are given in Exhibit 5-6. All materials are added at the beginning of the mixing process. Output is measured in ounces. Given the October data for Estrella, the five steps of the FIFO method can be illustrated.

Exhibit 5-6
Estrella Company Mixing Department Production and Cost Data: October

Production:	
Units in process, October 1, 70% complete*	10,000
Units completed and transferred out	60,000
Units in process, October 30, 40% complete*	20,000
Costs:	
Work in process, October 1:	
Materials	$ 1,000
Conversion costs	350
Total	$ 1,350
Current costs:	
Materials	$12,600
Conversion costs	3,050
Total	$15,650

*With respect to conversion costs, materials are 100% complete because they are added at the beginning of the process.

Step 1: Physical Flow Analysis

The purpose of Step 1 is to trace the physical units of production. Physical units are *not* equivalent units; they are units that may be in any stage of completion. The data reveal that there are 80,000 physical units (ounces) to account for. In this example, 10,000 units are from beginning inventory. Another 70,000 units were started in October. Finally, 20,000 units remain in ending inventory, 40 percent complete. The analysis of physical flow of units is usually accomplished by preparing a **physical flow schedule** similar to the one shown in Exhibit 5-7.

physical flow
schedule

To construct the schedule from the information given in the example, two calculations are needed. First, units started and completed in this period are obtained by subtracting the units in beginning work in process from the total units completed. Next, the units started are obtained by adding the units started and completed to the units in ending work in process. Notice that the "total units to account for" must equal the "total units accounted for." The physical flow schedule in Exhibit 5-7 is important because it contains the information needed to calculate equivalent units (Step 2).

Step 2: Calculation of Equivalent Units

Exhibit 5-8 illustrates the calculation of equivalent units under the FIFO method. Notice that the equivalent units in beginning work in process—work done in the prior period—are not counted as part of the total equivalent work (work means either adding materials or conversion activity). Only the equivalent work to be completed this period is counted. The equivalent work to be completed for the units from the prior period is computed by multiplying the number of units in beginning work in process by the percentage of work remaining. Since in this example the materials are added at the beginning of the process, no additional materials are needed. However, the units are only 70% complete with respect to conversion activity. Thus, 30% additional conversion activity is needed, which converts to 3,000 additional equivalent units of work (30% × 10,000).

Step 3: Computation of Unit Cost

The computation of the unit cost relies only on current costs and current output. The calculation is shown below:

$$
\begin{aligned}
\text{Unit materials cost} &= \$12{,}600/70{,}000 \\
&= \$0.18 \\
\text{Unit conversion cost} &= \$3{,}050/61{,}000 \\
&= \$0.05 \\
\text{Unit cost} &= \text{Unit materials cost} + \text{Unit conversion cost} \\
&= \$0.18 + \$0.05 \\
&= \$0.23 \text{ per ounce}
\end{aligned}
$$

Step 4: Valuation of Inventories

The FIFO unit costs are used to value output that is related to the *current period*. There are three categories of current period output: equivalent units in ending work in process, units started and completed, and the equivalent units of work necessary to *finish* the units in beginning work in process.

Exhibit 5-7
Physical Flow Schedule:
Mixing Department

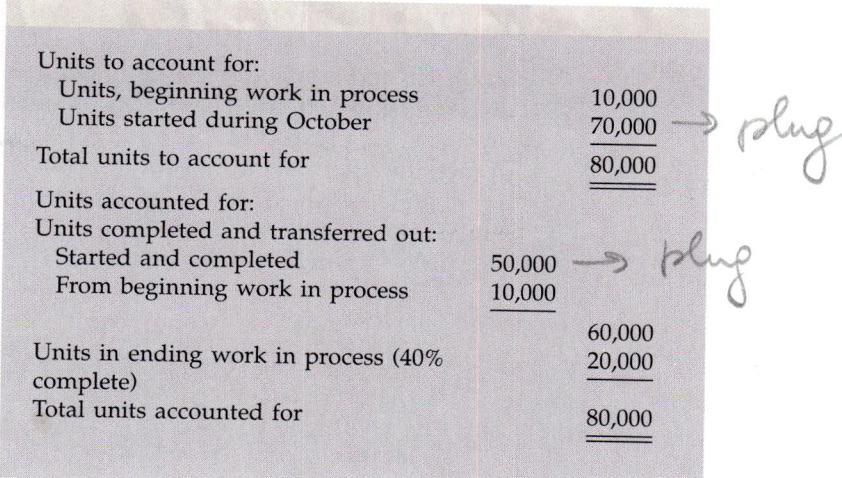

Units to account for:	
Units, beginning work in process	10,000
Units started during October	70,000 → plug
Total units to account for	80,000
Units accounted for:	
Units completed and transferred out:	
Started and completed	50,000 → plug
From beginning work in process	10,000
	60,000
Units in ending work in process (40% complete)	20,000
Total units accounted for	80,000

Since all equivalent units in ending work in process are current-period units (see Exhibit 5-8), the cost of ending work in process is computed as follows:

Materials (0.18 × 20,000) → 100%	$3,600
Conversion costs (0.05 × 8,000) → 40%	400
Total	$4,000

When it comes to valuing goods transferred out, two categories of completed units must be considered: those that were started and completed and those that were completed from beginning work in process. Of the 60,000 completed units, 50,000 are units started and completed in the current period and 10,000 are units completed from beginning work in process (see Exhibit 5-7). The 50,000 units that were started and completed in the current period represent current output and are valued at $0.23 per unit. For these units, the use of the current-period unit cost is entirely appropriate. However, the cost of the 10,000 beginning work in process units that were transferred out is another matter. These units started the period with $1,350 of manufacturing costs already incurred (cost taken from Exhibit 5-6), 10,000 equivalent units of materials already added, and 7,000 equiv-

Exhibit 5-8
Equivalent Units of Pro-
duction: FIFO Method

	Materials	Conversion
Units started and completed	50,000	50,000
Add: Units, beginning work in process × fraction to complete:		
10,000 × 0%	—	
10,000 × 30%		3,000
Add: Units, ending work in process × percentage complete:		
20,000 × 100%	20,000	—
20,000 × 40%	—	8,000
Equivalent units of output	70,000	61,000

alent units of conversion activity already completed. To these beginning costs, additional costs were needed to finish the units. As we saw in Step 2, the effort expended to complete these units required an additional 3,000 equivalent units of conversion activity. These 3,000 equivalent units of conversion activity were produced this period at a cost of $0.05 per equivalent unit. Thus, the total cost of finishing the units in beginning work in process is $150 ($0.05 × 3,000). Adding this $150 to the $1,350 in cost carried over from the prior period gives a total manufacturing cost for these units of $1,500. The total cost of goods transferred out can be summarized as follows:

Units started and completed ($0.23 × 50,000)		$11,500
Units, beginning work in process:		
Prior period costs	$1,350	
Costs to finish ($0.05 × 3,000)	150	1,500
Total		$13,000

Step 5: Cost Reconciliation

Manufacturing costs are reconciled as follows:

Costs to account for:		
Beginning work in process		$ 1,350
Incurred during the period:		
Materials	$12,600	
Conversion cost	3,050	15,650
Total		$17,000
Costs accounted for:		
Goods transferred out:		
Units, beginning work in process		$ 1,500
Units started and completed		11,500
Goods in ending work in process		4,000
Total		$17,000

The cost of production report for the FIFO method is given in Exhibit 5-9.

Journal Entries

The journal entries associated with the Mixing Department's activities for October are given below and at the top of the next page:

1. Work in Process—Mixing   12,600
       Materials   12,600
     To record requisitions of materials for October.

2. Work in Process—Mixing   3,050
       Conversion Cost Control   3,050
     To record the application of overhead and incurrence of direct labor.

3. Work in Process—Tableting   13,000

       Work in Process—Mixing   13,000

To record the transfer of cost of goods completed from Mixing to Tableting.

Exhibit 5-9

Estrella Company
Mixing Department
Production Report for October
(FIFO Method)

Unit Information

		Units accounted for:	
Units to account for:			
Units, beginning work in process	10,000	Units completed	60,000
Units started	70,000	Units, EWIP	20,000
Total units to account for	80,000	Total units accounted for	80,000

	Materials	Conversion
Units started and completed	50,000	50,000
Units, beginning work in process	—	3,000
Units, ending work in process	20,000	8,000
Equivalent units of output	70,000	61,000

Cost Information

Costs to account for:

	Materials	Conversion Cost	Total
Beginning work in process	$ 1,000	$ 350	$ 1,350
Incurred during the period	12,600	3,050	15,650
Total costs to account for	$13,600	$3,400	$17,000
Cost per equivalent unit:			
Current costs	$12,600	$ 3,050	
Divided by equivalent units	÷70,000	÷61,000	
Equivalent cost per unit	$ 0.18	$ 0.05	$ 0.23

Costs accounted for:

Units transferred out:

Units, beginning work in process

	Materials	Conversion Cost	Total
From prior period	$ 1,350		
From current period ($0.05 × 3,000)	150		
Units started and completed ($0.23 × 50,000)	11,500		$13,000
Ending work in process:			
Materials (20,000 × $0.18)	$ 3,600		
Conversion (8,000 × $0.05)	400	4,000	
Total costs accounted for			$17,000

WEIGHTED AVERAGE COSTING METHOD

Objective 5

Prepare a departmental production report using the weighted average method.

weighted average costing method

Excluding prior period work and costs creates some bookkeeping and computational complexity that can be avoided if certain conditions are satisfied. Specifically, if the costs of production remain very stable from one period to the next, then it may be possible to use the weighted average method. This method does not track prior period output and costs separately from current period output and costs. The **weighted average costing method** picks up beginning inventory costs and the accompanying equivalent output and treats them as if they belong to the current period. Prior-period output and manufacturing costs found in beginning work in process are merged with the current-period output and manufacturing costs.

The merging of beginning inventory output and current period output is accomplished by the way in which equivalent units are calculated. Under the weighted average method, equivalent units of output are computed by adding units completed to equivalent units in ending work in process. The equivalent units in beginning work in process are included in the computation. Thus, these units are counted as part of the current period's equivalent units of output.

The weighted average method merges prior-period costs with current-period costs by simply adding the manufacturing costs in beginning work in process to the manufacturing costs incurred during the current period. The total cost is treated as if it were the current period's total manufacturing cost.

The illustration of the weighted average method is based on the same Estrella Company data found in Exhibit 5-6. Using the same data highlights the differences between the two methods. The five steps to cost out production are given below.

Step 1: Physical Flow Analysis

The purpose of Step 1 is to trace the physical units of production. This is accomplished by preparing a physical flow schedule. This schedule, shown in Exhibit 5-10, is identical for both methods.

Exhibit 5-10
Physical Flow Schedule: Mixing Department

Units to account for:	
Units, beginning work in process	10,000
Units started during October	70,000
Total units to account for	80,000
Units accounted for:	
Units completed and transferred out:	
Started and completed	50,000
From beginning work in process	10,000
	60,000
Units in ending work in process (40% complete)	20,000
Total units accounted for	80,000

Step 2: Calculation of Equivalent Units

Given the information in the physical flow schedule, the weighted average equivalent units for October can be calculated. This calculation is shown in Exhibit 5-11.

Notice that October's output is measured as 80,000 units for materials and 68,000 units for conversion activity. The 10,000 equivalent units of materials (10,000 × 100%) found in beginning work in process are included in the 60,000 units completed. Similarly, the 7,000 equivalent units of conversion (70% × 10,000) found in beginning work in process are also included in the 60,000 units completed for the conversion category.[2] Thus, beginning inventory units are treated as if they were started and completed during the current period.

Step 3: Computation of Unit Cost

In addition to the period's equivalent units, the period's direct materials cost and conversion costs are needed to compute a unit cost. The weighted average method merges current manufacturing costs and the manufacturing costs associated with the units in beginning work in process. Thus, the total direct materials cost for October is defined as $13,600 ($1,000 + $12,600) and the total conversion cost is defined as $3,400 ($350 + $3,050).

When different categories of equivalent units exist, a unit cost for each category must be computed. The cost per completed unit is the sum of these individual unit costs. The computations for the example are as follows:

$$\text{Unit materials cost} = (\$1,000 + \$12,600)/80,000$$
prior costs are included
$$= \$0.17$$
$$\text{Unit conversion cost} = (\$350 + \$3,050)/68,000$$
$$= \$0.05$$
$$\text{Total unit cost} = \text{Unit materials cost} + \text{Unit conversion cost}$$
$$= \$0.17 + \$0.05$$
$$= \$0.22 \text{ per completed unit}$$

Step 4: Valuation of Inventories

Valuation of goods transferred out (Step 4) is accomplished by multiplying the unit cost by the goods completed.

Exhibit 5-11
Equivalent Units of Production: Weighted Average Method

	Materials	Conversion
Units completed	60,000	60,000
Add: Units, ending work in process × percentage complete:		
20,000 × 100%	20,000	—
20,000 × 40%	—	8,000
Equivalent units of output	80,000	68,000

2.   You should note that if we subtract the 10,000 equivalent units of material from the 80,000 units computed by weighted average we arrive at the 70,000 units computed by FIFO; similarly, if we subtract out the 7,000 equivalent units from the 68,000 conversion equivalent units computed by weighted average, we obtain the 61,000 units computed by FIFO. This illustrates the point that weighted average counts prior period output in the measurement of output for the current period.

$$\text{Cost of goods transferred out} = \$0.22 \times 60,000$$
$$= \$13,200$$

Costing out ending work in process is done by obtaining the cost of each manufacturing input and then adding these individual input costs. For the example, this requires adding the cost of the materials in ending work in process to the conversion costs in ending work in process.

The cost of materials is the unit material cost multiplied by the material equivalent units in ending work in process. Similarly, the conversion cost in ending work in process is the unit conversion cost times the conversion equivalent units. Thus, the cost of ending work in process is as follows:

Materials: $0.17 \times 20,000$	$3,400
Conversion: $0.05 \times 8,000$	400
Total cost	$3,800

Step 5: Cost Reconciliation

The total manufacturing costs are accounted for as follows:

Costs to account for:	
Beginning work in process	$ 1,350
Incurred during the period	15,650
Total	$17,000
Costs accounted for:	
Goods transferred out	$13,200
Ending work in process	3,800
Total	$17,000

Production Report

Steps 1 through 5 provide all of the information needed to prepare a production report for the Mixing Department for October. This report is given in Exhibit 5-12. The journal entries for the weighted average method follow the same pattern shown for the FIFO method. Thus, there is no reason to repeat the entries.

FIFO Compared With Weighted Average

FIFO and the weighted average methods differ on two key dimensions: (1) how output is computed, and (2) what costs to use for calculating the period's unit cost. The unit cost computation for the Mixing Department is shown below:

	FIFO		Weighted Average	
	Materials	*Conversion Costs*	*Materials*	*Conversion Costs*
Costs	$12,600	$ 3,050	$13,600	$ 3,400
Output	70,000	61,000	80,000	68,000
Unit cost	$0.18	$0.05	$0.17	$0.05

Exhibit 5-12

Estrella Company
Mixing Department
Production Report for October
(Weighted Average Method)

Unit Information

Units to account for:		Units accounted for:	
Units, beginning work in process	10,000	Units completed	60,000
Units started	70,000	Units EWIP	20,000
Total units to account for	80,000	Total units accounted for	80,000

	Equivalent Units	
	Materials	Conversion Cost
Units completed	60,000	60,000
Units in ending work in process	20,000	8,000
Total equivalent units	80,000	68,000

Cost Information

Costs to account for:

	Materials	Conversion Cost	Total
Beginning work in process	$ 1,000	$ 350	$ 1,350
Incurred during the period	12,600	3,050	15,650
Total costs to account for	$13,600	$ 3,400	$17,000
Divided by equivalent units	÷80,000	÷68,000	
Cost per equivalent unit	$ 0.17	$ 0.05	$ 0.22

Costs accounted for:

	Materials	Conversion Cost	Total
Goods transferred out (60,000 × $0.22)			$13,200
Ending work in process:			
Materials (20,000 × $0.17)	$ 3,400		
Conversion (8,000 × $0.05)	400		3,800
Total costs accounted for			$17,000

The two methods use different total costs and different measures of output. The FIFO method is the more theoretically appealing because it divides the cost of the period by the output of the period. The weighted average method, however, merges costs in beginning work in process with current period costs and merges the output found in beginning work in process with current period output. This creates the possibility for errors—particularly if the weighted average method is used for settings where input costs are changing significantly from one period to the next.

In the Mixing Department example, the FIFO unit cost and the weighted average unit cost for conversion costs are the same; evidently, the cost of this input remained the same for the two periods being considered. The unit materials cost for FIFO, however, is $0.18 versus $0.17 for the weighted average method.

Apparently, the cost of materials has increased, and merging the lower materials cost of the prior period with that of the current period creates a weighted average materials cost that underestimates the current period materials cost. The resulting difference in the cost of a fully completed unit is only $0.01 ($0.23 − $0.22). On the surface this seems harmless.

The difference in the costs reported under each method for goods transferred out and the ending work in process inventories is only $200 (see Exhibits 5-9 and 5-12). This is less than a 2% difference for goods transferred out and only about a 5% difference for ending work in process. The $0.01 unit cost difference does not appear to be material. Yet, if the final product is considered, even a $0.01 difference may be significant. Recall that Estrella passes the powder from the mixing department to the tableting department, where the powder is converted to caplets. Next, the caplets are sent to the Packaging Department where eight tablets are placed in small metal boxes. The output of the mixing department is measured in ounces. Suppose that 4 ounces of powder convert to eight tablets. The difference in the cost of the final product would be understated by $0.04— not $0.01. Using this unit cost information may produce erroneous decisions such as under- or overpricing. Furthermore, if the other two departments also use weighted average, the costs in those departments could also be understated. The cumulative effect could produce a significant distortion in cost for the final product—magnifying the effect.

A second disadvantage of weighted average costing should also be mentioned. The weighted average method also combines the performance of the current period with that of a prior period. Often it is desirable to exercise control by comparing the actual costs of the current period with the budgeted or standard costs for the period. The weighted average method makes this comparison suspect because the performance of the current period is not independent of the prior period.

The major benefit of the weighted average method is simplicity. By treating units in beginning work in process as belonging to the current period, all equivalent units belong to the same time period when it comes to calculating unit costs. As a consequence, the requirements for computing unit cost are greatly simplified. Yet, as has been mentioned, accuracy and performance measurement are impaired. The FIFO method overcomes both of these disadvantages. It should be mentioned, however, that both methods are widely used. Perhaps we can conclude that there are many settings in which the distortions caused by the weighted average method are not serious enough to be of concern.

TREATMENT OF TRANSFERRED-IN GOODS

Objective 6

Prepare a departmental production report with transferred-in goods and with changes in output measures.

In process manufacturing, some departments invariably receive partially completed goods from prior departments. For example, under FIFO, the transfer of goods from Mixing to Tableting is valued at $13,000. These transferred-in goods are a type of raw material for the subsequent process—materials that are added at the beginning of the subsequent process. The usual approach is to treat transferred-in goods as a separate material category when calculating equivalent units. Thus, we now have three categories of manufacturing inputs: transferred-in materials, materials added, and conversion costs. For the Estrella Company example, Tableting receives transferred-in materials, a powdered mixture, from

Mixing, adds a binder and coating (direct materials), and uses labor and overhead to convert the powder into tablets.

In dealing with transferred-in goods, three important points should be remembered. First, the cost of this material is the cost of the goods transferred out computed in the prior department. Second, the units started in the subsequent department correspond to the units transferred out from the prior department, assuming that there is a one-to-one relationship between the output measures of both departments. Third, the units of the transferring department may be measured differently than the units of the receiving department. If this is the case, then the goods transferred in must be converted to the units of measure used by the second department.

To illustrate how process costing works for a department that receives transferred-in work, we will use the Tableting Department of the Estrella Company. The Tableting Department receives a powder from Mixing, adds a binder, presses the powder into caplet shapes, and then coats the tablets. The units of the Mixing Department are measured in ounces, and the units of the Tableting Department are measured in tablets. To convert ounces to tablets, we need to know the relationship between ounces and tablets. The binding agent is added at the beginning of the process and increases the ounces of material by 10%. Every ounce of this new mix then converts to four tablets. Thus, to convert the transferred-in material to the new output measure, we must multiply by 1.1 and multiply by four, or equivalently, we must multiply the transferred-in units by 4.4.

Now let's consider the month of October for Estrella Company and focus our attention on the Tableting Department. We will assume that Estrella Company uses the weighted average method. October's cost and production data for the Tableting Department are given in Exhibit 5-13. Notice that the transferred-in cost for October is the Mixing Department's transferred-out cost (Exhibit 5-12 shows that the Mixing Department transferred out 60,000 ounces of powder, costing $13,200). Also notice that output for the Tableting Department is measured in tablets. Given the data in Exhibit 5-13, the five steps of process costing can be illustrated for the Tableting Department.

Step 1: Physical Flow Schedule

In constructing a physical flow schedule for the Tableting Department, its dependence on the Mixing Department must be considered:

Units to account for:	
Units, beginning work in process	16,000
Units transferred in during October	264,000* ← plug
Total units to account for	280,000
Units accounted for:	
Units completed and transferred out:	
Started and completed	234,000 ← plug
From beginning work in process	16,000
	250,000
Units in ending work in process	30,000
Total units accounted for	280,000

*60,000 × 4.4 (converts transferred-in units from ounces to tablets)

Exhibit 5-13

Estrella Company Tableting Department Production and Cost Data: October

Production:		
Units in process, October 1, 80% complete[a]	16,000	(tablets)
Units completed and transferred out	250,000	
Units in process, October 30, 30% complete[a]	30,000	
Costs:		
Work in process, October 1:		
Transferred-in cost	$ 800	
Materials (binding agent)[b]	300	
Conversion costs	180	
Total	$1,280	
Current costs:		
Transferred-in costs	$13,200	
Materials (binding agent)[b]	2,500	
Conversion costs	5,000	
Total	$20,700	

[a] With respect to conversion costs, materials are 100% complete because they are added at the beginning of the process.

[b] The cost of tablet coating materials is insignificant and therefore added to the conversion cost category.

Step 2: Calculation of Equivalent Units

The calculation of equivalent units is shown in Exhibit 5-14. Notice that the transferred-in goods from Mixing are treated as materials added at the beginning of the process. Transferred-in materials are always 100% complete, since they are added at the beginning of the process.

Step 3: Computation of Unit Costs

The unit cost is computed by calculating the unit cost for each input category:

$$\text{Unit transferred-in cost} = (\$800 + \$13,200)/280,000$$
$$= \$0.05$$
$$\text{Unit materials cost} = (\$300 + \$2,500)/280,000$$
$$= \$0.01$$
$$\text{Unit conversion cost} = (\$180 + \$5,000)/259,000$$
$$= \$0.02$$
$$\text{Total unit cost} = \$0.05 + \$0.01 + \$0.02$$
$$= \$0.08$$

Step 4: Valuation of Inventories

The cost of goods transferred out is simply the unit cost multiplied by the goods completed:

$$\text{Cost of goods transferred out} = \$0.08 \times 250,000$$
$$= \$20,000$$

Costing out ending work in process is done by computing the cost of each input and then adding to obtain the total:

Exhibit 5-14
Equivalent Units of Production: Weighted Average Method

	Transferred-in Materials	Materials Added	Conversion Costs
Units completed	250,000	250,000	250,000
Add: Units, ending work in process × percentage complete:			
30,000 × 100%	30,000		
30,000 × 100%	—	30,000	
30,000 × 30%	—	—	9,000
Equivalent units of output	280,000	280,000	259,000

Transferred in: $0.05 × 30,000	$1,500
Materials added: $0.01 × 30,000	300
Conversion costs: $0.02 × 9,000	180
Total	$1,980

The cost of production report, including Step 5 (which was skipped), is shown in Exhibit 5-15.

The only additional complication introduced in the analysis for a subsequent department is the presence of the transferred-in category. As has just been shown, dealing with this category is similar to handling any other category. However, it must be remembered that the current cost of this special type of raw material is the cost of the units transferred in from the prior process and that the units transferred in are the units started (adjusted for any differences in output measurement).

OPERATION COSTING

Objective 7
Describe the basic features of operation costing.

batch production processes

Not all manufacturing firms have a pure job production environment or a pure process production environment. Some manufacturing firms have characteristics of both job and process environments. Firms in these *hybrid* settings often use *batch production processes*. **Batch production processes** produce batches of different products which are identical in many ways but differ in others. In particular, many firms produce products that make virtually the same demands on conversion inputs but different demands on material inputs. Thus, the conversion activities are similar or identical, but the materials used are significantly different. For example, the conversion activities required to produce cans of pie filling are essentially identical for apple or cherry pie filling, but the cost of the materials can differ significantly. Similarly, the conversion activities for women's skirts may be identical, but the cost of materials can differ dramatically, depending on the nature of the fabric used (wool versus polyester, for example). Clothes, textiles, shoes, and food industries are examples where batch production may take place. For these firms, a costing system known as operation costing is often adopted.

Exhibit 5-15

Estrella Company
Tableting Department
Production Report for October
(Weighted Average Method)

Unit Information

Units to account for:		Units accounted for:	
Units, beginning work in process	16,000	Units completed	250,000
Units started	264,000	Units, EWIP	30,000
Total units to account for	280,000	Total units accounted for	280,000

	Equivalent Units		
	Transferred In	*Materials*	*Conversion Cost*
Units completed	250,000	250,000	250,000
Units in ending work in process	30,000	30,000	9,000
Total equivalent units	280,000	280,000	259,000

Cost Information

Costs to account for:	*Transferred in*	*Materials*	*Conversion Cost*	*Total*
Beginning work in process	$ 800	$ 300	$ 180	$ 1,280
Incurred during the period	13,200	2,500	5,000	20,700
Total costs to account for	$ 14,000	$ 2,800	$ 5,180	$21,980
Divide by equivalent units	÷280,000	÷280,000	÷259,000	
Cost per equivalent unit	$ 0.05	$ 0.01	$ 0.02	$ 0.08

Costs accounted for:			
Goods transferred out (250,000 × $0.08)			$ 20,000
Ending work in process:			
Transferred in ($0.05 × 30,000)		$ 1,500	
Materials (30,000 × $0.01)		300	
Conversion (9,000 × $0.02)		180	1,980
Total costs accounted for			$ 21,980

Basics of Operation Costing

operation costing

Operation costing is a blend of job and process costing procedures applied to batches of homogeneous products. This costing system uses *job-order procedures* to assign materials costs to batches and *process procedures* to assign conversion costs. A hybrid costing approach is used because each batch uses different doses of materials but makes the same demands on the conversion resources of individual processes (usually called operations). Although different batches may pass through different operations, the demands for conversion activities for the *same* process do not differ among batches.

Work orders are used to collect production costs for each batch. Work orders also are used to initiate production. Using work orders to initiate and track costs to each batch is a job-costing characteristic. However, since individual products of different batches consume the same conversion resources as they pass through the same operation, then each product (regardless of batch membership) can be treated as a single homogeneous unit. This last trait is a process-costing characteristic and can be exploited to simplify the assignment of conversion costs.

Materials requisition forms are used to identify the materials, quantity and prices, and work order number. Using the materials requisition form as the source document, the cost of materials is posted to the work order sheet. Conversion costs are collected by *process* and assigned to products using a *predetermined conversion rate* (identical in concept to predetermined overhead rates). Conversion costs are budgeted for each department and a single conversion rate is computed for each department (process) using a unit-based activity driver such as direct labor hours or machine hours. For example, assume that the budgeted conversion costs for a sewing operation are $100,000 (consisting of items such as direct labor, depreciation, supplies, and power) and the practical capacity of the operation is 10,000 machine hours. The conversion rate is computed as follows:

$$\text{Conversion rate} = \$100,000/10,000 \text{ machine hours}$$
$$= \$10 \text{ per machine hour}$$

Now consider two batches of shoes that pass through the sewing operation: one batch consists of 50 pairs of men's leather boots and the second batch consists of 50 pairs of women's leather sandals. First, it should be clear that the batches have different material requirements and so the cost of materials should be tracked separately (job-costing feature). Second, it should also be obvious that the sewing activity is the same for each in the sense that one hour of sewing time should consume the same resources regardless of whether the product is boots or sandals (the process-costing feature). If the batch of boots takes 25 machine hours, the batch will be assigned $250 of conversion costs ($10 × 25 hours). If the batch of sandals takes 12 machine hours, it will be assigned $120 of conversion costs ($10 × 12). Again, even though the products consume the same resources per machine hour, the batches can differ in total amount of resources consumed in an operation. So it is necessary to use a work order for each batch to collect costs.

Exhibit 5-16 illustrates the physical flow and cost flow features of operation costing. The illustration is for two batches and three processes. Panel A illustrates the physical flows and Panel B shows the cost flows. The letters *a* and *f* represent the assignment of materials cost to the two batches. This example assumes that all materials are issued at the very beginning. Thus, materials cost would be assigned to the work in process account for the beginning process for each batch. The example also illustrates that batches do not have to participate in every process. Batch A uses Processes 2 and 3, while Batch B uses Processes 1 and 2. The letters immediately following the process represent the application of conversion costs to the respective batches.

Operation Costing Example

To illustrate operation costing, let's return to the vitamin and mineral example discussed at the beginning of the chapter. However, instead of producing only one multivitamin mineral product, let's assume that the company produces a variety of vitamin and mineral products. Thus, in addition to the multivitamin

Exhibit 5-16
Basic Features of Operation Costing
Panel A: Physical Flows

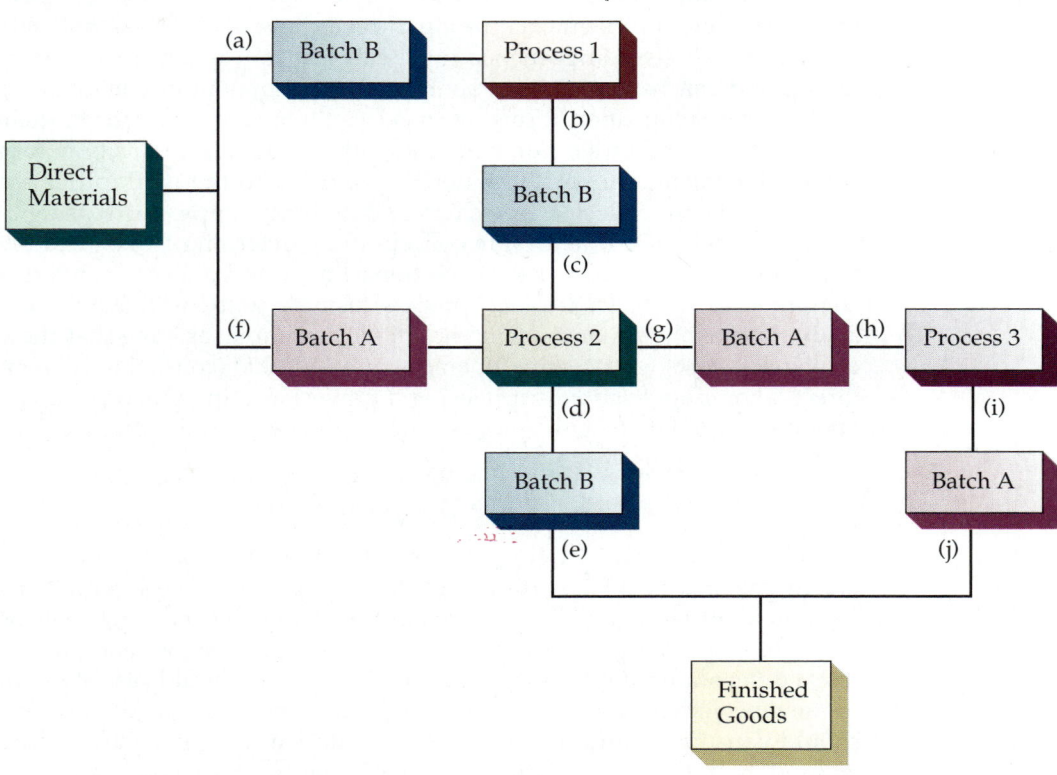

Panel B: Cost Flows (shown by letter in Panel A and in dollars below)

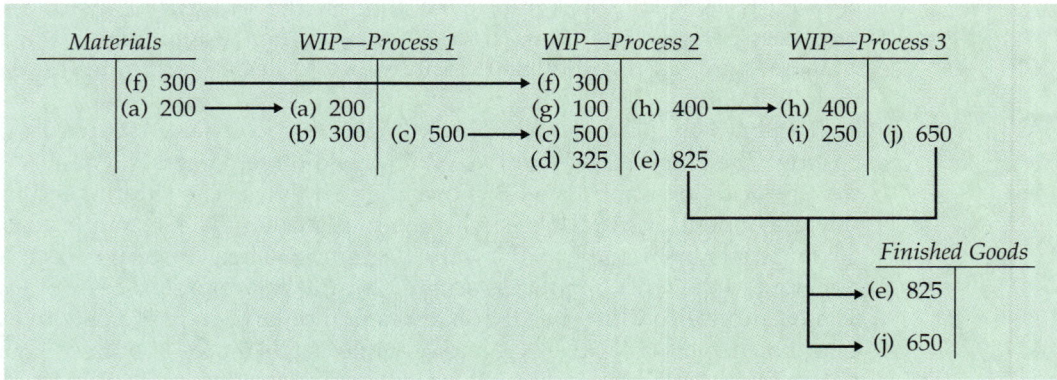

and mineral product, the company also produces single vitamin and mineral products, e.g., bottles of vitamin C, E, calcium, etc. Assume that the company also produces different strengths of vitamins (for example, 200 mg and 1,000 mg doses of vitamin C). The company also uses different sizes of bottles (for example, 60 and 120 capsules). There are four operations: picking, encapsulating, tableting, and bottling. Consider the following two work orders:

	Work Order 100	Work Order 101
Direct materials	Ascorbic acid	Vitamin E
	Capsules	Vitamin C
	Bottle (100 capsules)	Vitamin B-1
	Cap and labels	Vitamin B-2
		Vitamin B-4
		Vitamin B-12
		Biotin
		Zinc
		Bottle (60 tablets)
		Cap and labels
Operations	Picking	Picking
	Encapsulating	Tableting
	Bottling	Bottling
Number in batch	5,000 bottles	10,000 bottles

Notice how the work order specifies the direct materials needed, the operation required, and the size of the batch. Assume the following costs are collected by work order:

	Work Order 100	Work Order 101
Direct materials	$4,000	$15,000
Conversion costs:		
Picking	1,000	3,000
Encapsulating	3,000	—
Tableting	—	4,000
Bottling	1,500	2,000
Total production costs	$9,500	$24,000

The journal entries associated with Work Order 100 are illustrated below. The first entry assumes that all materials needed for the batch are requisitioned at the start. Another possibility is to requisition the materials needed for the batch in each process as the batch enters that process.

1. Work in Process—Picking	4,000	
Materials		4,000
2. Work in Process—Picking	1,000	
Conversion Costs Applied		1,000
3. Work in Process—Encapsulating	5,000	
Work in Process—Picking		5,000
4. Work in Process—Encapsulating	3,000	
Conversion Costs Applied		3,000
5. Work in Process—Bottling	8,000	
Work in Process—Encapsulating		8,000
6. Work in Process—Bottling	1,500	
Conversion Costs Applied		1,500
7. Finished Goods	9,500	
Work in Process—Bottling		9,500

The journal entries for the other work order are not shown but would follow a similar pattern.

SUMMARY

This chapter has presented the basic framework for a process costing system. The cost flows, journal entries, and the cost of production report have been described. Additionally, we have shown that process costing can be used in service organizations and JIT manufacturing firms. These two settings often have no significant work in process inventories and, therefore, present the simplest and most straightforward applications of the approach.

The use of process costing is complicated by the presence of work in process inventories. When work in process inventories are present, equivalent units must be used to measure output. Also, with beginning work in process inventories, we must decide what to do with prior period work and prior period costs. Two approaches were described for dealing with beginning work in process inventories: the FIFO approach and the weighted average approach. The FIFO approach is theoretically appealing because it follows the process costing principle: a period's unit cost is computed by dividing the costs of the period by the output of the period. To accomplish this, prior period work and costs must be excluded. This work and its costs must be tracked separately, creating some complexity in the approach. The weighted average approach is less complicated but poses some problems when control and accuracy issues are important.

The chapter also illustrates how to apply process costing to a multiple department setting. The effect of transferred-in goods and possible changes in the way output is measured were explored. Finally, we introduced a hybrid costing approach called operation costing. This approach is useful for manufacturing settings where batches of homogeneous products are produced.

APPENDIX: SPOILED UNITS

When spoilage takes place in a process costing situation, its effects ripple through the cost of production report. Let's take Payson Company as an example. Payson Company produces a product that passes through two departments: Mixing and Cooking. In the Mixing Department, all materials are added at the beginning of the process. All other manufacturing inputs are added uniformly. The following information pertains to the Mixing Department for February:

a. Beginning work in process (BWIP), February 1: 100,000 pounds, 40 percent complete with respect to conversion costs. The costs assigned to this work are as follows:

Materials	$20,000
Labor	10,000
Overhead	30,000

b. Ending work in process (EWIP), February 28: 50,000 pounds, 60 percent complete with respect to conversion costs.
c. Units completed and transferred out: 360,000 pounds. The following costs were added during the month:

Materials	$211,000
Labor	100,000
Overhead	270,000

d. All units are inspected at the 80 percent point of completion, and any spoiled units identified are discarded. During February, 10,000 pounds were spoiled.

We can look at the five steps of the cost of production report. First, we must create a physical flow schedule.

Units to account for:	
Units, beginning work in process	100,000
Units started	320,000
Total units to account for	420,000
Units accounted for:	
Units transferred out	360,000
Units spoiled	10,000
Units, ending work in process	50,000
Total units accounted for	420,000

The second step is the creation of a schedule of equivalent units.

	Materials	Conversion
Units completed	360,000	360,000
Units spoiled × Fraction complete:		
Materials (10,000 × 100%)	10,000	
Conversion (10,000 × 80%)		8,000
Units in ending work in process × Fraction complete:		
Materials (50,000 × 100%)	50,000	
Conversion (50,000 × 60%)	—	30,000
Equivalent units of output	420,000	398,000

The cost per equivalent unit is as follows:

DM unit cost = ($20,000 + $211,000)/420,000 = $0.55
CC unit cost = ($40,000 + $370,000)/398,000 = $1.03
Total unit cost = $1.58 per equivalent unit

Now we must calculate the cost of goods transferred out and cost of ending work in process. If the spoilage is normal (expected), the cost of spoiled units is added to the cost of the good units. In this case, the inspection occurred at the 80 percent point of completion. Therefore, none of the spoiled units are from ending work in process (as these units are only 60 percent complete and have not yet been inspected). Thus, all spoilage cost is assigned to the good units transferred out.

Cost of goods transferred out:	
Good units $1.58 × 360,000	$568,800
Spoiled units ($0.55 × 10,000) + ($1.03 × 8,000)	13,740
	$582,540
Cost of ending work in process = ($0.55 × 50,000) + ($1.03 × 30,000)	$58,400

Costs are reconciled as follows:

Costs to account for:	
Beginning work in process	$ 60,000
Costs added	581,000
Total costs to account for	$641,000
Costs accounted for:	
Goods transferred out	$582,540
Ending work in process	58,400
Total costs accounted for	$640,940*

*$60 difference is due to rounding error.

Suppose that the spoilage was abnormal. Then the spoilage cost is assigned to a spoilage loss account. The costs are accounted for as follows.

Cost of good units transferred out = $1.58 \times 360,000 =	$568,800
Spoiled units = ($0.55 \times 10,000) + ($1.03 \times 8,000) =	13,740
Cost of ending work in process = ($0.55 \times 50,000) + ($1.03 \times 30,000) =	$58,400

Costs are reconciled as follows:

Costs to account for:	
Beginning work in process	$ 60,000
Costs added	581,000
Total costs to account for	$641,000
Costs accounted for:	
Goods transferred out	$568,800
Loss from abnormal spoilage	13,740
Ending work in process	58,400
Total costs accounted for	$640,940*

*$60 difference is due to rounding error.

Notice the difference between the treatment of normal and abnormal spoilage. When spoilage is assumed to be normal, it is not tracked separately but is embedded in the total cost of good units. As a result, no one knows precisely how much spoilage adds to total manufacturing costs and whether or not an effort should be made to reduce it. The treatment of spoilage as abnormal is more in keeping with an emphasis on total quality management where there is no tolerance allowed for waste. At least the product cost of spoiled goods is tracked in a separate account. Of course, a factory engaged in total quality management would not stop at classifying spoilage as abnormal, but would also identify the activities that are associated with these spoiled goods, in an effort to discover the root causes of poor quality.

REVIEW PROBLEM AND SOLUTION

Payson Company produces a product that passes through two departments: Mixing and Cooking. Both departments use the weighted average method. In the Mixing Department, all materials are added at the beginning of the process. All other manufacturing inputs are added uniformly. The following information pertains to the Mixing Department for February:

a. Beginning work in process (BWIP), February 1: 100,000 pounds, 100 percent complete with respect to materials and 40 percent complete with respect to conversion costs. The costs assigned to this work are as follows:

Materials	$20,000
Labor	10,000
Overhead	30,000

b. Ending work in process (EWIP), February 28: 50,000 pounds, 100 percent complete with respect to materials and 60 percent complete with respect to conversion costs.
c. Units completed and transferred out: 370,000 pounds. The following costs were added during the month:

Materials	$211,000
Labor	100,000
Overhead	270,000

REQUIRED:

1. Prepare a physical flow schedule.
2. Prepare a schedule of equivalent units.
3. Compute the cost per equivalent unit.
4. Compute the cost of goods transferred out and the cost of ending work in process.
5. Prepare a cost reconciliation.

Solution   1. Physical flow schedule:

Units to account for:	
Units, BWIP	100,000
Units started	320,000	← plug
Total units to account for	420,000
Units accounted for:	
Units completed and transferred out:	
Started and completed	270,000	← plug
From BWIP	100,000
	370,000
Units, EWIP	50,000
Total units accounted for	420,000

2. Schedule of equivalent units:

	Materials	*Conversion*
Units completed	370,000	370,000
Units, EWIP × Fraction complete:		
Materials (50,000 × 100%)	50,000	—
Conversion (50,000 × 60%)	—	30,000
Equivalent units of output	420,000	400,000

3. Cost per equivalent unit:

$$\text{DM unit cost} = (\$20,000 + \$211,000)/420,000 = \$0.550$$
$$\text{CC unit cost} = (\$40,000 + \$370,000)/400,000 = \$1.025$$
$$\text{Total unit cost} = \$1.575 \text{ per equivalent unit}$$

4. Cost of goods transferred out and cost of ending work in process:

$$\text{Cost of goods transferred out} = \$1.575 \times 370,000$$
$$= \$582,750$$
$$\text{Cost of EWIP} = (\$0.55 \times 50,000) + (\$1.025 \times 30,000)$$
$$= \$58,250$$

5. Cost reconciliation:

Costs to account for:	
BWIP	$ 60,000	20 + 10 + 30
Costs added	581,000	211 + 100 + 270
Total to account for	$641,000
Costs accounted for:	
Goods transferred out	$582,750
EWIP	58,250
Total costs accounted for	$641,000

KEY TERMS

Batch production
  processes 203
Cost reconciliation 189
Equivalent units of
  output 188

FIFO costing method 191
Operation costing 204
Physical flow schedule
  192

Process 181
Process costing principle
  186
Production report 184

Transferred-in cost 182
Weighted average costing
  method 196
Work orders 205

QUESTIONS FOR WRITING AND DISCUSSION

1. What is a process? Provide an example that illustrates the definition.
2. Describe the differences between process costing and job-order costing.
3. What journal entry would be made as goods are transferred out from one department to another department? From the final department to the warehouse?
4. What are the similarities and differences in the manufacturing cost flows for job-order firms and process firms?
5. What are transferred-in costs?
6. Explain why transferred-in costs are a special type of raw material for the receiving department.
7. What is a production report? What purpose does this report serve?
8. Can process costing be used for a service organization? Explain.
9. Explain how process costing can be used for JIT manufacturing firms.
10. What are equivalent units? Why are they needed in a process cost system?
11. How is the equivalent unit calculation affected when materials are added at the beginning or end of the process rather than uniformly throughout the process?
12. Describe the five steps in accounting for the manufacturing activity of a processing department, and indicate how they interrelate.
13. Under the weighted average method, how are prior-period costs and output treated? How are they treated under the FIFO method?
14. Under what conditions will the weighted average and FIFO methods give essentially the same results?
15. In assigning costs to goods transferred out, how do the weighted average and FIFO methods differ?
16. What are the disadvantages of the weighted average method? Advantages?
17. How are transferred-in costs treated in the calculation of equivalent units?
18. What is operation costing? When is it used?
19. What is the role of work orders in operation costing?

EXERCISES AND PROBLEMS

**5-1
Journal Entries**
LO 1

Naranja Company has three process departments: Molding, Assembly, and Finishing. At the beginning of the year (January 1), there were no work in process or finished goods inventories. The following data are made available for the month of January:

Department	Manufacturing Costs Added*	Ending Work in Process
Molding	$120,000	$30,000
Assembly	110,000	25,000
Finishing	100,000	5,000

*Includes only the direct materials, direct labor, and the overhead used to process the partially finished good received from the prior department. The transferred-in cost is not included.

REQUIRED:

1. Prepare journal entries that show the transfer of costs from one department to the next (including the entry to transfer the costs of the final department).
2. Prepare T-accounts for the entries made in Requirement 1. Use arrows to show the flow of costs.

5-2
Process Costing,
Service
Organization

LO 2

A local post office sorts letters by zip code. During the ~~month~~ ... letters were sorted. The cost of sorting includes the following:

Direct labor	$5,000
Overhead	2,000
Total	$7,000

REQUIRED:

1. Explain why process costing is appropriate for the sorting operation.
2. Calculate the cost per letter for the sorting operation.
3. There are no direct materials used for the sorting operation. Is the absence of direct materials typical of services? If not, provide examples of services that use direct materials.

5-3
JIT Manufacturing
and Process
Costing

LO 2

Ireland Company uses JIT manufacturing. There are several manufacturing cells set up within one of its factories. One of the cells makes space heaters. The cost of production for the month of March is given below:

Cell labor	$ 20,000
Direct materials	50,000
Overhead	40,000
Total	$110,000

During March, 10,000 space heaters were produced and sold.

REQUIRED:

1. Explain why process costing can be used for computing the cost of production for the space heaters.
2. Calculate the cost per unit for a space heater.

5-4
Physical Flow;
Equivalent Units;
Unit Costs, No
Beginning WIP
Inventory

LO 3

Sitemay, Inc., produces a standard frame for nonprescription reading glasses. The frames are produced in two departments: Molding and Assembly. The data for the Molding Department are as follows:

Beginning work in process	—
Units started	92,500
Raw materials cost	$92,500
Direct labor cost	$9,150
Overhead applied	$13,725
Units, ending work in process (100% materials; 80% conversion)	5,000

REQUIRED:

1. Prepare a physical flow schedule.
2. Calculate equivalent units of production for:
   a. Raw materials
   b. Conversion

3. Calculate unit costs for:
   a. Raw materials
   b. Conversion
   c. Total manufacturing
4. Provide the following information:
   a. The total cost of units transferred out.
   b. The journal entry for transferring costs from Molding to Assembly.
   c. The cost assigned to units in ending inventory.

5-5
Production Report;
No Beginning
Inventory
LO 1, 3

Wantler Company manufactures a household detergent. The Mixing Department, the first process department, mixes the chemicals required for the detergent. The following data are for 1998:

Work in process, 1/1/98	—
Gallons started	75,000
Gallons transferred out	63,000
Raw materials cost	$75,000
Direct labor cost	$148,800
Overhead applied	$223,200

Materials are added at the beginning of the process. Ending inventory is 95 percent complete with respect to labor and overhead.

REQUIRED: Prepare a production report for the Mixing Department in 1998.

5-6
Weighted Average
Method; FIFO;
Physical Flow;
Equivalent Units
LO 3, 4, 5

Feranga Company manufactures a product that passes through two processes. The following information was obtained for the first department for June:

1. All materials are added at the beginning of the process.
2. Beginning work in process had 6,000 units, 30 percent complete with respect to conversion costs.
3. Ending work in process had 4,400 units, 25 percent complete with respect to conversion costs.
4. Started in process, 10,000 units.

REQUIRED:

1. Prepare a physical flow schedule.
2. Compute equivalent units using the weighted average method.
3. Compute equivalent units using the FIFO method.

5-7
FIFO Method;
Valuation of
Goods Out and
Ending Work in
Process
LO 4

Enders Company uses FIFO to account for the costs of production. For the first processing department, the following equivalent unit schedule has been prepared:

	Materials	Conversion Cost
Units started and completed	22,000	22,000
Units, beginning work in process:		
10,000 × 0%	—	—
10,000 × 40%	—	4,000
Units, ending work in process:		
8,000 × 100%	8,000	—
8,000 × 75%	—	6,000
Equivalent units of output	30,000	32,000

The cost per equivalent unit for the period was as follows:

Materials	$1.50
Conversion cost	2.50
Total	$4.00

The cost of beginning work in process was materials, $10,000; conversion costs, $20,000.

REQUIRED:

1. Determine the cost of ending work in process and the cost of goods transferred out.
2. Prepare a physical flow schedule.

5-8
Equivalent Units—
Weighted Average
Method
LO 5

The following are data for four independent process-costing departments. Inputs are added continuously.

	A	B	C	D
Beginning inventory	3,200	1,500	—	27,000
Percent completion	33	40	—	75
Units started	19,200	20,000	48,000	33,000
Ending inventory	4,000	—	9,000	8,000
Percent completion	25	—	30	20

REQUIRED: Compute the equivalent units of production for each of the above departments using the weighted average method.

5-9
Equivalent Units;
FIFO Method
LO 4

Using the data from **5-8,** compute the equivalent units of production for each of the four departments using the FIFO method.

5-10
Weighted Average
Method; Unit Cost;
Valuation of
Goods Out and
Ending Work in
Process
LO 5

Watson Products, Inc., produces plastic cases used for video cameras. The product passes through three departments. For May, the following equivalent unit schedule was prepared for the first department:

	Materials	Conversion Cost
Units completed	5,000	5,000
Units, ending work in process × Fraction complete:		
6,000 × 100%	6,000	—
6,000 × 50%	—	3,000
Equivalent units of output	11,000	8,000

Costs assigned to beginning work in process: materials, $30,000; conversion, $5,000. Manufacturing costs incurred during May: materials, $25,000; conversion, $65,000. Watson uses the weighted average method.

REQUIRED:

1. Compute the unit cost for May.
2. Determine the cost of ending work in process and the cost of goods transferred out.

5-11
FIFO Method; Unit Cost; Valuation of Goods Out and Ending Work in Process

LO 4

White Company produces men's shorts and uses FIFO to account for its manufacturing costs. The product White makes passes through two processes: Cutting and Sewing. During April, White's controller prepared the following equivalent unit schedule for the Cutting Department:

	Materials	*Conversion Cost*
Units started and completed	8,000	8,000
Units, beginning work in process:		
2,000 × 0%	—	—
2,000 × 50%	—	1,000
Units, ending work in process:		
4,000 × 100%	4,000	—
4,000 × 25%	—	1,000
Equivalent units of output	12,000	10,000

Costs in beginning work in process were materials, $2,000; conversion costs, $8,000. Manufacturing costs incurred during April were materials, $24,000; conversion costs, $32,000.

REQUIRED:

1. Prepare a physical flow schedule for April.
2. Compute the cost per equivalent unit for April.
3. Determine the cost of ending work in process and the cost of goods transferred out.
4. Prepare the journal entry that transfers the costs from Cutting to Sewing.

5-12
Weighted Average Method; Equivalent Units, Unit Cost; Multiple Departments

LO 5, 6

Manford Company has a product that passes through two processes: Mixing and Cooking. During October, the Mixing Department transferred 10,000 units to the Cooking Department. The cost of the units transferred into the second department was $20,000. Materials are added uniformly in the second process. Units are measured the same way in both departments.

The second department (cooking) had the following physical flow schedule for October:

Units to account for:		
Units, beginning work in process	2,000	(40% complete)
Units started	12,000	
Total units to account for	14,000	
Units accounted for:		
Units, ending work in process	4,000	(50% complete)
Units completed	10,000	
Units accounted for	14,000	

Costs in beginning work in process for the Cooking Department were materials, $2,500; conversion costs, $3,000; transferred in, $4,000. Costs added during the month: materials, $16,000; conversion costs, $25,000; transferred in, $20,000.

REQUIRED:

1. Assuming the use of the weighted average method, prepare a schedule of equivalent units.
2. Compute the unit cost for the month.

5-13
FIFO Method;
Equivalent Units;
Unit Cost; Mul-
tiple Departments
LO 4, 6

Using the same data found in **5-12**, assume the company uses the FIFO method.

REQUIRED: Prepare a schedule of equivalent units and compute the unit cost for the month of October.

5-14
Journal Entries;
Cost of Ending
Inventories
LO 1, 3

Baxter Company has two processing departments: Assembly and Finishing. A predetermined overhead rate of $10 per DLH is used to assign overhead to production. The company experienced the following operating activity for April:

a. Raw materials issued to Assembly, $24,000.
b. Direct labor cost: Assembly, 500 hours at $9.20 per hour; Finishing, 400 hours at $8 per hour.
c. Overhead applied to production.
d. Goods transferred to Finishing, $32,500.
e. Goods transferred to finished goods warehouse, $20,500.
f. Actual overhead incurred, $10,000.

REQUIRED:

1. Prepare the required journal entries for the above transactions.
2. Assuming Assembly and Finishing have no beginning work in process inventories, determine the cost of each department's ending work in process inventories.

5-15
Weighted Average
Method; Physical
Flow; Equivalent
Units; Unit Costs;
Cost Assignment
LO 3, 5

Novel Mask, Inc., manufactures plastic water guns. Each gun's left and right frames are produced in the Molding Department. The left and right halves are then transferred to the Assembly Department where the trigger mechanism is inserted and the halves are glued together. (The left and right halves together define the unit of output for the Molding Department.) In June, the Molding Department reported the following data:

a. In Molding, all materials are added at the beginning of the process.
b. Beginning work in process consisted of 3,000 units, 20 percent complete with respect to direct labor and overhead. Cost in beginning inventory included direct materials, $450; and conversion costs, $138.
c. Costs added to production during the month were direct materials, $950; and conversion costs, $2,174.50.
d. At the end of the month, 9,000 units were transferred out to Finishing. Then 1,000 units remained in ending work in process, 25 percent complete.

REQUIRED:

1. Prepare a physical flow schedule.
2. Calculate equivalent units of production for direct materials and conversion cost.
3. Compute unit cost.
4. Calculate the cost of goods transferred to Finishing at the end of the month. Calculate the cost of ending inventory.
5. Prepare the journal entry that transfers the goods from Molding to Assembly.

5-16
FIFO Method;
Physical Flow;
Equivalent Units;
Unit Costs; Cost
Assignment
LO 3, 4

Refer to the data in **5-15**. Assume that the FIFO method is used.

REQUIRED:

1. Prepare a physical flow schedule.
2. Calculate equivalent units of production for direct materials and conversion cost.
3. Compute unit cost.
4. Calculate the cost of goods transferred to Finishing at the end of the month. Calculate the cost of ending inventory.

5-17
Operation Costing: Bread Manufacturing
LO 7

Tasty Bread makes and supplies bread throughout the state of Kansas. There are three types of bread produced: loaves, rolls, and buns. Seven operations describe the production process.

a. Mixing: Flour, milk, yeast, salt, butter, and so on are mixed in a large vat.
b. Shaping: A conveyor belt transfers the dough to a machine that weighs it and shapes it into loaves, rolls or buns, depending on the type being produced.
c. Rising: The individually shaped dough is allowed to sit and rise.
d. Baking: The dough is moved to a 100-foot-long funnel oven. (The dough enters the oven on racks and spends twenty minutes moving slowly through the oven.)
e. Cooling: The bread is removed from the oven and allowed to cool.
f. Slicing: For loaves and buns (hamburger and hot dog), the bread is sliced.
g. Packaging: The bread is wrapped (packaged).

Tasty produces its products in batches. The size of the batch depends on the individual orders that must be filled (orders come from retail grocers throughout the state). Usually, as soon as one batch is mixed, a second batch begins the mixing operation.

REQUIRED:

1. Identify the conditions that must be present for operation costing to be used in this setting. If these conditions are not met, explain how process costing would be used. If process costing is used, would you recommend the use of weighted average or FIFO? Explain.
2. Assume that operation costing is the best approach for this bread manufacturer. Describe in detail how you would use operation costing. Use a batch of dinner rolls (consisting of 1,000 packages of 12 rolls) and a batch of whole wheat loaves (consisting of 5,000, 24-oz. sliced loaves) as examples.

5-18
Operation Costing: Unit Costs and Journal Entries
LO 7

Jacson Company produces two brands of a popular pain medication: regular strength and extra strength. Regular strength is produced in tablet form and extra strength is produced in capsule form. The work orders for two batches of the products are shown below, along with some associated cost information:

	Work Order 121	Work Order 122
Direct materials (actual costs)	$ 9,000	$15,000
Applied conversion costs:		
Mixing	?	?
Tableting	5,000	—
Encapsulating	—	6,000
Bottling	2,000	3,000
Batch size (bottles of 100 units)	12,000	12,000

In the Mixing Department, conversion costs are applied on the basis of direct labor hours. Budgeted conversion costs for the department for the year were $60,000 for labor and $190,000 for overhead. Budgeted direct labor hours were 5,000. It takes one minute to mix the ingredients needed for a 100-unit bottle (for either product).

REQUIRED:

1. What are the conversion costs applied in the Mixing Department for each batch?
2. Calculate the cost per bottle for the regular and extra strength pain medication.
3. Prepare the journal entries that record the costs of the 12,000 regular strength batch as it moves through the various operations.

5-19

Weighted Average Method; Single Department Analysis; Uniform Costs

LO 5

Patterson Company produces a product that passes through two processes: Molding and Assembly. All manufacturing costs are added uniformly for both processes. The following information was obtained for the Assembly Department for October 1996:

a. Work in process, October 1, had 5,000 units (40 percent completed) and the following costs:

Direct materials	$4,000
Direct labor	6,000
Overhead	2,000

b. During the month of October, 10,000 units were completed and transferred to the Finishing Department, and the following costs were added to production:

Direct materials	$12,000
Direct labor	18,000
Overhead	6,000

c. On October 31, there were 2,500 partially completed units in process. These units were 80 percent complete.

REQUIRED: Prepare a cost of production report for the Assembly Department for October using the weighted average method of costing. The report should disclose the physical flow of units, equivalent units, and unit costs and should track the disposition of manufacturing costs.

5-20

FIFO Method; Single Department Analysis; One Cost Category

LO 4

Refer to the data in **5-19**.

REQUIRED: Prepare a cost of production report for the Assembly Department for October using the FIFO method of costing.

5-21

Weighted Average Method; Three Cost Categories

LO 5

Loadmear Chemicals produces an agricultural pesticide that passes through three processes: blending, drying, and bagging. The weighted average method is used to account for the costs of production. Two chemicals, X and Y, are added at the beginning of the blending process and allowed to cook for six to seven hours. After blending, the resulting product is sent to the Drying Department, where it is dried under heat lamps for twenty-four hours. After drying, the granulated product is sent to bagging, where 25-pound bags of the product are produced. The following information relates to the blending process for the month of May.

a. Work in process, May 1, 20,000 pounds, 60 percent complete with respect to conversion costs. Costs associated with partially completed units:

Material X	$1,000
Material Y	5,000
Direct labor	500
Overhead	1,500

b. Work in process, May 31, 30,000 pounds, 70 percent complete with respect to conversion costs.

c. Units completed and transferred out: 500,000 pounds. Costs added during the month:

Material X	$ 25,500
Material Y	127,500
Direct labor	12,750
Overhead	38,250

REQUIRED:

1. Prepare the following: (a) a physical flow schedule and (b) an equivalent unit schedule with cost categories for Material X, Material Y, and conversion cost.
2. Calculate the unit cost for each cost category.
3. Compute the cost of ending work in process and the cost of goods transferred out.
4. Prepare a cost reconciliation.

5-22
Service Organization with Work in Process Inventories; Multiple Departments; FIFO Method; Unit Cost
LO 3, 4, 6

Granger Credit Corporation is a wholly owned susidiary of a large manufacturer of computers. Granger is in the business of financing computers, software, and other services that the parent corporation sells. Granger has two departments that are involved in financing services: the credit department and the business practices department. The credit department receives requests for financing from field sales representatives, records customer information on a preprinted form, and then enters the information into the computer system to check the creditworthiness of the customer (other actions may be taken if the customer is not in the data base). Once creditworthiness information is known, a printout is produced with this information plus other customer specific information. The completed form is transferred to the business practices department.

The business practices department modifies the standard loan covenant as needed (in response to customer request or customer risk profile). When this activity is completed, the loan is priced. This is done by keying information from the partially processed form into a personal computer spreadsheet program. The program provides a recommended interest rate for the loan. Finally, a form specifying the loan terms is attached to the transferred-in document. A copy of the loan-term form is sent to the sales representative and serves as the quote letter.

The following cost and service activity data for the business practices department are provided for the month of May:

Transferred-in applications	2,800
Applications in process, May 1, 40% complete*	500
Applications in process, May 31, 25% complete*	800

*All materials and supplies are used at the end of the process.

Costs:

	Transferred in	Materials	Conversion Costs
Beginning work in process	$ 4,500	—	$ 2,800
Costs added	28,000	$1,250	37,500

REQUIRED:

1. How would you define the output of the business practices department?
2. Using the FIFO method, prepare the following for the business practices department:

    a. A physical flow schedule
    b. An equivalent units schedule
    c. Calculation of unit costs
    d. Cost of ending work in process and cost of units transferred out
    e. A cost reconciliation

5-23
**Weighted Average/
FIFO Method; Cost
of Production
Report**
LO 4, 5

Wallace, Inc., produces a product that goes through three departments: Machining, Assembly, and Polishing. Materials are added at the beginning of the machining operation; labor and overhead are added uniformly throughout the process. The Machining Department had work in process at the beginning and end of 1998 as follows:

| | Percentage of Completion | |
	Materials	Conversion Costs
January 1, 1998, 2,500 units	100	60
December 31, 1998, 4,000 units	100	50

The company completed 42,500 units during the year and incurred the following manufacturing costs:

Direct materials	$158,000
Direct labor	98,750
Overhead	79,000

The inventory at the beginning of the year was carried at the following costs:

Direct materials	$9,750
Direct labor	6,125
Overhead	4,950

REQUIRED:

1. Prepare a cost of production report using the weighted average method.
2. Prepare a cost of production report using the FIFO method.

5-24
**Weighted Average
Method;
Transferred-in
Goods**
LO 5

Lemmons Company manufactures a product that passes through three departments: Mixing, Cooking, and Bottling. In the Cooking Department, materials are added at the end of the process. Conversion costs are incurred uniformly throughout the process. During the month of December, the Cooking Department received 30,000 units from the Mixing Department. The transferred-in cost of the 30,000 units was $69,900.
    Costs added by Cooking during December included the following:

Direct materials	$35,200
Direct labor	56,000
Overhead	25,600

On December 1, the Cooking Department had 5,000 units in inventory that were 30 percent complete with respect to conversion costs. On December 31, 6,000 units were in inventory, one-third complete with respect to conversion costs. The costs associated with the 5,000 units in beginning inventory were as follows:

Transferred in	$11,650
Direct labor	8,750
Overhead	4,000

REQUIRED: Prepare a cost of production report using the weighted average method. Use the five steps outlined in the chapter to produce the information required by the report.

5-25
FIFO Method;
Multiple
Department
Analysis;
Transferred-in
Goods
LO 4, 6

Jenny, Inc., produces a drink extract that passes through three processes: mixing, blending, and bottling. During the second quarter, the Blending Department received 20,000 gallons of liquid from the Cooking Department (transferred in at $9,600). Upon receiving the liquid, the Blending Department adds sugar and stirs the mixture for twenty minutes. The product is then passed on to the Bottling Department.

There were 4,000 gallons in process at the beginning of the quarter, 75 percent complete with respect to conversion costs. The costs attached to the beginning inventory were as follows:

Transferred in	$1,900
Powder	268
Conversion costs	600

Costs added by the Blending Department during the second quarter were:

Powder	$1,400
Conversion costs	3,040

There were 3,500 gallons in ending inventory, 20 percent complete with respect to conversion costs.

REQUIRED: Prepare a cost of production report using the FIFO method. Follow the five steps outlined in the chapter in preparing the report.

5-26
Weighted Average
Method; Trans-
ferred-in Goods
LO 5, 6

Refer to **5-25**.

REQUIRED: Prepare a cost of production report for the Blending Department using the weighted average method.

5-27
Weighted Average
Method; Journal
Entries
LO 1, 5

Muskoge Company uses a process costing system. The company manufactures a product that is processed in two departments: Molding and Assembly. In the Molding Department, materials are added at the beginning of the process; in the Assembly Department, additional materials are added at the end of the process. In both departments, conversion costs are incurred uniformly throughout the process. As work is completed, it is transferred out. The following summarizes the production activity and costs for February:

	Molding	Assembly
Beginning inventories:		
Physical units	10,000	8,000
Costs:		
Transferred in	—	$45,200
Direct materials	$22,000	—
Conversion costs	$13,800	$16,800

continued

prior period
costs

	Molding	Assembly
Current production:		
Units started	25,000	?
Units transferred out	30,000	35,000
Costs:		
Transferred in	—	?
Direct materials	$56,250	$39,550
Conversion costs	$103,500	$136,500
Percentage completion:		
Beginning inventory	40	50
Ending inventory	80	50

REQUIRED:

1. Using the weighted average method, prepare the following for the Molding Department:
   a. A physical flow schedule
   b. An equivalent units calculation
   c. Calculation of unit costs
   d. Cost of ending work in process and cost of goods transferred out
   e. A cost reconciliation
2. Prepare journal entries that show the flow of manufacturing costs for the Molding Department.
3. Repeat Requirements 1 and 2 for the Assembly Department.

5-28
FIFO Method; Two-Department Analysis
LO 4, 6

Refer to the data in **5-27**.

REQUIRED: Repeat the requirements in **5-27** using the FIFO method.

5-29
Weighted Average Method; Two-Department Analysis; Change in Output Measure
LO 5, 6

Healthway uses a process costing system to compute the unit costs of the minerals that it produces. It has three departments: Picking, Encapsulating, and Bottling. In Picking, the ingredients for the minerals are measured, sifted, and blended together. The mix is transferred out in gallon containers. The Encapsulating Department takes the powdered mix and places it in capsules. One gallon of powdered mix converts into 1,600 capsules. After the capsules are filled and polished, they are transferred to bottling where they are placed in bottles, which are then affixed with a safety seal and a lid and labeled. Each bottle receives fifty capsules.

During July, the following results are available for the first two departments (materials are added at the beginning in both departments):

	Picking	Encapsulating
Beginning inventories:		
Physical units	5 gallons	4,000
Costs:		
Materials	$120	$32
Labor	$128	$20
Overhead	$?	$?
Transferred in	$—	$140
Current production:		
Transferred out	125 gallons	198,000
Ending inventory	6 gallons	6,000

continued

	Picking	Encapsulating
Costs:		
Materials	$3,144	$1,584
Transferred in	$—	$?
Labor	$4,096	$1,944
Overhead	$?	$?
Percentage of completion:		
Beginning inventory	40	50
Ending inventory	50	40

Overhead in both departments is applied as a percentage of direct labor costs. In the Picking Department, overhead is 200 percent of direct labor. In the Encapsulating Department, the overhead rate is 150 percent of direct labor.

REQUIRED:

1. Prepare a cost of production report for the Picking Department using the weighted average method. Follow the five steps outlined in the chapter.
2. Prepare a cost of production report for the Encapsulating Department. Follow the five steps outlined in the chapter.

5-30
FIFO Method;
Two-Department
Analysis
LO 4, 6

Refer to the data in **5-29.**

REQUIRED: Prepare a cost of production report for each department using the FIFO method.

5-31
Case on Process
Costing; Operation
Costing; Impact
on Resource
Allocation
Decision
LO 3, 5, 7

Golding Manufacturing, a division of Farnsworth Sporting, Inc., produces two different models of bows and eight models of knives. The bow-manufacturing process involves the production of two major subassemblies: the limbs and the handle. The limbs pass through four sequential processes before reaching final assembly: lay-up, molding, fabricating, and finishing. In the Lay-up Department, limbs are created by laminating layers of wood. In Molding, the limbs are heat treated, under pressure, to form a strong resilient limb. In the Fabricating Department, any protruding glue or other processing residue is removed. Finally, in Finishing, the limbs are cleaned with acetone, dried, and sprayed with the final finishes.

The handles pass through two processes before reaching final assembly: pattern and finishing. In the Pattern Department, blocks of wood are fed into a machine that is set to shape the handles. Different patterns are possible, depending on the machine's setting. After coming out of the machine, the handles are cleaned and smoothed. They then pass to the Finishing Department where they are sprayed with the final finishes. In Final Assembly, the limbs and handles are assembled into different models using purchased parts such as pulley assemblies, weight adjustment bolts, side plates, and string.

Golding, since its inception, has been using process costing to assign product costs. A predetermined overhead rate is used based on direct labor dollars (80 percent of direct labor dollars). Recently, Golding has hired a new controller, Karen Jenkins. After reviewing the product costing procedures, Karen requested a meeting with the divisional manager, Aaron Suhr. The following is a transcript of their conversation:

Karen: Aaron, I have some concerns about our cost accounting system. We make two different models of bows and are treating them as if they were the same product. Now I know that the only real difference between the models is the handle. The processing of the handles is the same, but the handles differ significantly in the amount and quality of wood used. Our current costing does not reflect this difference in material input.
Aaron: Your predecessor is responsible. He believed that tracking the difference in material cost wasn't worth the effort. He simply didn't believe that it would make much difference in the unit cost of either model.

Karen: Well, he may have been right, but I have my doubts. If there is a significant difference, it could affect our views of which model is the more important to the company. The additional bookkeeping isn't very stringent. All we have to worry about is the Pattern Department. The other departments fit what I view as a process costing pattern.

Aaron: Why don't you look into it? If there is a significant difference, go ahead and adjust the costing system.

After the meeting, Karen decided to collect cost data on the two models: the Deluxe model and the Econo model. She decided to track the costs for one week. At the end of the week, she had collected the following data from the Pattern Department:

a. There were a total of 2,500 bows completed: 1,000 Deluxe models and 1,500 Econo models.

b. There was no beginning work in process; however, there were 300 units in ending work in process: 200 Deluxe and 100 Econo models. Both models were 80 percent complete with respect to conversion costs and 100 percent complete with respect to materials.

c. The Pattern Department experienced the following costs:

Direct materials	$114,000
Direct labor	45,667

d. On an experimental basis, the requisition forms for materials were modified to identify the dollar value of the materials used by the Econo and Deluxe models:

Econo model	$30,000
Deluxe model	84,000

REQUIRED:

1. Compute the unit cost for the handles produced by the Pattern Department assuming that process costing is totally appropriate.
2. Compute the unit cost of each handle using the separate cost information provided on materials.
3. Compare the unit costs computed in Requirements 1 and 2. Is Karen justified in her belief that a pure process costing relationship is not appropriate? Describe the costing system that you would recommend.
4. In the past, the marketing manager has requested more money for advertising the Econo line. Aaron has repeatedly refused to grant any increase in this product's advertising budget because its per-unit profit (selling price less manufacturing cost) is so low. Given the results in Requirements 1 through 3, was Aaron justified in his position?

5-32
Case on
Equivalent Units;
Valuation of Work
in Process
Inventories; FIFO
Versus Weighted
Average
LO 1, 3, 4, 5, 6

AKL Foundry manufactures metal components for different kinds of equipment used by the aerospace, commercial aircraft, medical equipment, and electronic industries. The company uses investment casting to produce the required components. Investment casting consists of creating, in wax, a replica of the final product and pouring a hard shell around it. After removing the wax, molten metal is poured into the resulting cavity. What remains after the shell is broken is the desired metal object ready to be put to its designated use.

Metal components pass through eight processes: gating, creating shell, foundry work, cut off, grinding, finishing, welding, and strengthening. Gating creates the wax mold and clusters the wax pattern around a sprue (a hole through which the molten metal will be poured through the gates into the mold in the foundry process), which is joined and supported by gates (flow channels) to form a tree of patterns. In the shell process, the wax molds are alternately dipped in a ceramic slurry and a fluidized bed of progressively coarser refractory grain until a sufficiently thick shell (or mold) completely encases the wax pattern. After drying, the mold is sent to the foundry process. Here the wax is melted out of the mold and the shell is fired, strengthened, and brought to the proper temperature. Molten metal is then poured into the dewaxed shell. Finally, the ceramic shell is removed and the finished product is sent to the cut-off process, where the parts are separated from the tree by the use of a band saw. The parts are then sent to grinding, where the gates that allowed the molten metal to flow into the ceramic cavities are ground off using large abrasive grinders. In finishing, rough edges caused by the grinders are removed by small hand-held pneumatic tools. Parts that are flawed at this point are sent to welding for corrective treatment. The last process, heat, treats the parts to bring them to the desired strength.

In 1998, the two partners who owned AKL Foundry decided to split up and divide the business. In dissolving their business relationship, they were faced with the problem of dividing the business assets equitably. Since the company had two plants—one in Arizona and one in New Mexico—a suggestion was made to split the business on the basis of geographic location—one partner would assume ownership of the plant in New Mexico and the other would assume ownership of the plant in Arizona. However, this arrangement had one major complication: the work in process inventory located in the Arizona plant.

The Arizona facilities had been in operation for more than a decade and were full of work in process. The New Mexico facility had been operational for only two years and had much smaller work in process inventories. The partner located in New Mexico argued that to disregard the unequal value of the work in process inventories would be grossly unfair.

Unfortunately, during the entire business history of AKL Foundry, work in process inventories had never been assigned any value. In computing the cost of goods sold each year, the company had followed the policy of adding depreciation to the out-of-pocket costs of direct labor, direct materials, and overhead. Accruals for the company are nearly nonexistent, and there are hardly ever any ending inventories of raw materials.

During 1998, the Arizona plant had sales of $2,028,670. The cost of goods sold is itemized as follows:

Direct materials	$378,000
Direct labor	530,300
Overhead	643,518

Upon request, the owners of AKL provided the following supplementary information (percentages are cumulative):

	Costs Used by Each Process as a Percentage of Total Cost	
	Materials	Total Labor Cost
Cost gating	23%	35%
Creating shell	70	50
Foundry work	100	70
Cut off	100	72
Grinding	100	80
Finishing	100	90
Welding	100	93
Strengthening	100	100

The Gating Department had 10,000 units in beginning work in process, 60 percent complete. Assume that all materials are added at the beginning of each process. During the year, 50,000 units were completed and transferred out. The ending inventory had 11,000 unfinished units, 60 percent complete.

REQUIRED:

1. The partners of AKL want a reasonable estimate of the cost of work in process inventories. Using the Gating Department's inventory as an example, prepare an estimate of the cost of the ending work in process. What assumptions did you make? Did you use FIFO or weighted average? Why?
2. Assume that the creating shell process has 8,000 units in beginning work in process, 20 percent complete. During the year, 50,000 units were completed and transferred out (all 50,000 units were sold; no other units were sold). The ending work in process inventory had 8,000 units, 30 percent complete. Compute the value of the Creating Shell Department's ending work in process. What additional assumptions had to be made?

5-33

Cost of Production Report; Ethical Behavior

LO 3

Consider the following conversation between Gary Means, manager of a division that produces industrial machinery, and his controller, Donna Simpson, a CMA and CPA:

Gary: Donna, we have a real problem. Our operating cash is too low, and we are in desperate need of a loan. As you know, our financial position is marginal, and we need to show as much income as possible—and our assets need bolstering as well.

Donna: I understand the problem, but I don't see what can be done at this point. This is the last week of the fiscal year, and it looks like we'll report income just slightly above break-even.

Gary: I know all this. What we need is some creative accounting. I have an idea that might help us, and I wanted to see if you would go along with it. We have 200 partially finished machines in process, about 20 percent complete. That compares with the 1,000 units that we completed and sold during the year. When you computed the per-unit cost, you used 1,040 equivalent units, giving us a manufacturing cost of $1,500 per unit. That per-unit cost gives us cost of goods sold equal to $1.5 million and ending work in process worth $60,000. The presence of the work in process gives us a chance to improve our financial position. If we report the units in work in process as 80 percent complete, this will increase our equivalent units to 1,160. This, in turn, will decrease our unit cost to about $1,345 and cost of goods sold to $1.345 million. The value of our work in process will increase to $215,200. With those financial stats, the loan would be a cinch.

Donna: Gary, I don't know. What you're suggesting is risky. It wouldn't take much auditing skill to catch this one.

Gary: You don't have to worry about that. The auditors won't be here for at least six to eight more weeks. By that time, we can have those partially completed units completed and sold. I can bury the labor cost by having some of our more loyal workers work overtime for some bonuses. The overtime will never be reported. And, as you know, bonuses come out of the corporate budget and are assigned to overhead—next year's overhead. Donna, this will work. If we look good and get the loan to boot, corporate headquarters will treat us well. If we don't do this, we could lose our jobs.

REQUIRED:

1. Should Donna agree to Gary's proposal? Why or why not? To assist in deciding, review the standards of ethical conduct for management accountants described in Chapter 1. Do any apply?
2. Assume that Donna refuses to cooperate and that Gary accepts this decision and drops the matter. Does Donna have any obligation to report the divisional manager's behavior to a superior? Explain.
3. Assume that Donna refuses to cooperate; however, Gary insists that the changes be made. Now what should Donna do? What would you do?
4. Suppose that Donna is sixty-three and that the prospects for employment elsewhere are bleak. Assume again that Gary insists that the changes should be made. Donna also

knows that Gary's superior, the owner of the company, is his father-in-law. Under these circumstances, would your recommendations for Donna differ? If you were Donna, what would you do?

5-34
APPENDIX:
Spoiled Units in
Process Costing

Armour Company produces a product in three departments. The weighted average method is used in all three departments. The following information pertains to the second department for the month of May.

a. There was no beginning work in process.

b. Ending work in process, May 31: 25,000 pounds, 80 percent complete with respect to conversion costs.

c. Units completed and transferred out: 165,000 pounds. The following costs were added during the month:

Materials	$380,000
Conversion	925,000

d. Materials are added at the beginning of the process, and units are lost evenly throughout the process.

REQUIRED:

1. Calculate equivalent units of production for materials and conversion cost.
2. Calculate unit direct materials cost and unit conversion cost.
3. What is the total cost of units transferred out? What is the cost of ending work in process inventory?

5-35
APPENDIX:
Abnormal Spoiled
Units in Process
Costing

Refer to **5-34**. Suppose that instead of losing units evenly throughout the process, an inspection takes place at the end of the process and 10,000 spoiled units are discovered at that time. All spoilage is considered abnormal.

REQUIRED:

1. Calculate equivalent units of production for materials and conversion cost.
2. Calculate unit direct materials cost and unit conversion cost.
3. What is the total cost of units transferred out, the cost of ending inventory, and the cost of spoiled units?
4. Give the journal entry to account for the cost of the spoiled units.

5-36
APPENDIX:
Normal Spoilage
in Process Costing

Refer to **5-34**. Suppose that instead of losing units evenly throughout the process, an inspection takes place at the end of the process and 10,000 spoiled units (all normal spoilage) are discovered at that time.

REQUIRED:

1. Calculate equivalent units of production for materials and conversion cost.
2. Calculate unit direct materials cost and unit conversion cost.
3. What is the total cost of units transferred out and the cost of ending inventory? How is the cost of spoilage treated?

Chapter 6
Support Department Cost Allocation

It looks like a Beetle, but VW designers call it the Concept 1. Meant to recall people's fond memories of the old VW bug, yet to provide modern technology, the Concept 1 was designed to be simple and easy to update. The result is that manufacturing becomes easier and uses less of the expensive support department service from engineering.

LEARNING OBJECTIVES

After studying this chapter, you should be able to:

1. Describe the difference between support departments and producing departments.
2. Explain five reasons why support costs may be assigned to producing departments.
3. Calculate charging rates, and distinguish between single and dual charging rates.
4. Allocate support center costs to producing departments using the direct method, the sequential method, and the reciprocal method.
5. Calculate departmental overhead rates.

The complexity of many modern firms leads the accountant to allocate costs of support departments to a variety of cost objectives, such as divisions, departments, and individual product lines. Allocation is simply a means of dividing a pool of costs and assigning those costs to various subunits. It is important to realize that allocation does not affect the total cost. Total cost is neither reduced nor increased by allocation. However, the amounts of cost assigned to the subunits can be affected by the allocation procedure chosen. Because cost allocation can affect bid prices, the profitability of individual products, and the behavior of managers, it is an important topic.

AN OVERVIEW OF COST ALLOCATION

Objective 1
Describe the difference between support departments and producing departments.

common costs

producing departments

support departments

Mutually beneficial costs, which occur when the same resource is used in the output of two or more services or products, are **common costs**. While these common costs may pertain to periods of time, individual responsibilities, sales territories, and classes of customers, this chapter will concentrate on the costs common to departments and to products. For example, the wages paid to security guards at a factory are a common cost of all of the different products manufactured there. The benefits of security are applicable to each product, yet the assignment of security cost to the individual products is an arbitrary process. In other words, while it is clear that the products (or services) require the common resource and that the resource cost should be assigned to these cost objects, it is often not clear how best to go about assigning the cost. Usually common cost assignment is made through a series of consistent allocation procedures.

Types of Departments

The first step in cost allocation is to determine just what the cost objects are. Usually they are departments. There are two categories of departments: producing departments and support departments. **Producing departments** are directly responsible for creating the products or services sold to customers. In a large public accounting firm, examples of producing departments are Auditing, Tax, and Management Advisory Services (Computer Systems Services). In a manufacturing setting such as Volkswagen (whose newly redesigned Beetle is shown at the beginning of this chapter), producing departments are those that work directly on the products being manufactured (e.g., Assembly, Painting). **Support departments** provide essential services for producing departments. These departments are indirectly connected with an organization's services or products. At VW, those departments might include Engineering, Maintenance, Personnel, and Building and Grounds.

Once the producing and support departments have been identified, the overhead costs incurred by each department can be determined. Note that this involves tracing costs to the departments, not allocating costs, because the costs are directly associated with the individual department. The factory cafeteria, for example, would have food costs, wages of cooks and servers, depreciation on dishwashers and stoves, and supplies (e.g., napkins and plastic forks). Overhead directly associated with a producing department such as Assembly in a furniture-making plant would include utilities (if measured in that department), supervisory salaries, and depreciation on equipment used in that department. Overhead that cannot be easily assigned to a producing or support department is assigned to a catchall department such as General Factory. General Factory might include depreciation on the factory building, rental of a Santa Claus suit for the factory Christmas party, the cost of restriping the parking lot, the plant manager's salary, and telephone service. In this way, all costs are assigned to a department.

Exhibit 6-1 shows how a manufacturing firm and a service firm can be divided into producing and support departments. The manufacturing plant, which makes furniture, may be departmentalized into two producing departments (Assembly and Finishing) and four support departments (Materials Storeroom, Cafeteria, Maintenance, and General Factory). The service firm, a bank, might be departmentalized into three producing departments (auto loans, commercial lending, and personal banking) and three support departments (data processing, drive through, and bank administration). Overhead costs are traced to each department. Note that each factory or service company overhead cost must be assigned to one, and only one, department.

Once the company has been departmentalized and all overhead costs have been traced to the individual departments, support department costs are

Exhibit 6-1
Examples of Departmentalization for a Manufacturing Firm and a Service Firm

Manufacturing Firm: Furniture Maker

Producing Departments	*Support Departments*

Assembly:
  Supervisors' salaries
  Small tools
  Indirect materials
  Depreciation on machinery
Finishing:
  Sandpaper
  Depreciation on sanders and buffers
	Materials storeroom:
	  Clerk's salary
	  Depreciation on forklift
	Cafeteria:
	  Food
	  Cooks' salaries
	  Depreciation on stoves
	Maintenance:
	  Janitors' salaries
	  Cleaning supplies
	  Machine oil and lubricants
	General factory:
	  Depreciation on building
	  Security
	  Utilities

Service Firm: Bank

Producing Departments	*Support Departments*

Auto loans:
  Loan processors' salaries
  Forms and supplies
Commercial lending
  Lending officers' salaries
  Depreciation on office equipment
  Bankruptcy prediction software
Personal banking:
  Supplies and postage for statements
	Drive through:
	  Tellers' salaries
	  Depreciation on equipment
	Data processing:
	  Personnel salaries
	  Software
	  Depreciation on hardware
	Bank administration:
	  Salary of CEO
	  Receptionist's salary
	  Telephone costs
	  Depreciation on bank and vault

assigned to producing departments and overhead rates are developed to cost products. Although support departments do not work directly on the products or services that are sold, the costs of providing these support services are part of the total product cost and must be assigned to the products. This assignment of costs consists of a two-stage allocation: (1) allocation of support department costs to producing departments and (2) assignment of these allocated costs to individual products. The second-stage allocation, achieved through the use of departmental overhead rates, is necessary because there are multiple products being worked on in each producing department. If there were only one product within a producing department, all the support costs allocated to that department would belong to that product. Recall that a predetermined overhead rate is computed by taking total estimated overhead for a department and dividing it by an estimate of an appropriate base. Now we see that a producing department's overhead consists of two parts: overhead directly associated with a producing department and overhead allocated to the producing department from the support departments. A support department cannot have an overhead rate that assigns overhead costs to units produced, because it does not make a salable product. That is, products do not pass through support departments. The nature of support departments is to service producing departments, not the products that pass through the producing departments. For example, maintenance personnel repair and maintain the equipment in the Assembly Department, not the furniture that is assembled in that department. Exhibit 6-2 summarizes the steps involved.

Types of Allocation Bases

causal factors

In effect, producing departments *cause* support activities; therefore, the costs of support departments are also caused by the activities of the producing departments. **Causal factors** are variables or activities within a producing department that provoke the incurrence of support costs. In choosing a basis for allocating support department costs, every effort should be made to identify appropriate causal factors (activity drivers). Using causal factors results in product costs being more accurate; furthermore, if the causal factors are known, managers are more able to control the consumption of services.

To illustrate the types of activity drivers that can be used, consider the following three support departments: Power, Personnel, and Materials Handling. For Power costs, a logical allocation base is kilowatt hours, which can be measured by separate meters for each department. If separate meters do not exist, perhaps machine hours used by each department would provide a good proxy, or way to approximate power usage. For Personnel costs, both the number of producing department employees and the labor turnover (e.g., number of new

Exhibit 6-2

Steps in Allocating Support Department Costs to Producing Departments

1. Departmentalize the firm.
2. Classify each department as a support department or a producing department.
3. Trace all overhead costs in the firm to a support or producing department.
4. Allocate support department costs to the producing departments.
5. Calculate predetermined overhead rates for producing departments.
6. Allocate overhead costs to the units of individual product through the predetermined overhead rates.

hires) are possible activity drivers. For Materials Handling, the number of material moves, the hours of material handling used, and the quantity of material moved are all possible activity drivers. Exhibit 6-3 lists some possible activity drivers that can be used to allocate support department costs. When competing activity drivers exist, managers need to assess which provides the most convincing relationship.

While the use of a causal factor to allocate common cost is the best, sometimes an easily measured causal factor cannot be found. In that case, the accountant looks for a good proxy. For example, the common cost of plant depreciation may be allocated to producing departments on the basis of square footage. Though square footage does not cause depreciation, it can be argued that the number of square feet a department occupies is a good proxy for the services provided to it by the factory building. The choice of a good proxy to guide allocation is dependent upon the company's objectives for allocation.

OBJECTIVES OF ALLOCATION

Objective 2

Explain five reasons why support costs may be assigned to producing departments.

A number of important objectives are associated with the allocation of support department costs to producing departments and ultimately to specific products. The following major objectives have been identified by the IMA:[1]

1. To obtain a mutually agreeable price.
2. To compute product-line profitability.
3. To predict the economic effects of planning and control.
4. To value inventory.
5. To motivate managers.

Competitive pricing requires an understanding of costs. Only by knowing the costs of each service or product can the firm create meaningful bids. If costs are not accurately allocated, some costs could be overstated, resulting in bids that

Exhibit 6-3

Examples of Possible Activity Drivers for Support Departments

Accounting:
   Number of transactions
Cafeteria:
   Number of employees
Data processing:
   Number of lines entered
   Number of hours of service
Engineering:
   Number of change orders
   Number of hours
Maintenance:
   Machine hours
   Maintenance hours
Materials storeroom:
   Number of material moves
   Pounds of material moved
   Number of different parts

Payroll:
   Number of employees
Personnel:
   Number of employees
   Number of firings or layoffs
   Number of new hires
   Direct labor cost
Power:
   Kilowatt hours
   Machine hours
Purchasing:
   Number of orders
   Cost of orders
Shipping:
   Number of orders

---

1.   *Statements of Management Accounting (Statement 4B),* "Allocation of Service and Administrative Costs" (Montvale, NJ: NAA, 1985). The NAA is now known as the Institute of Management Accountants (IMA).

are too high and a loss of potential business. Alternatively, if the costs are understated, bids could be too low, producing losses on these products.

Good estimates of individual product costs also allow a manager to assess the profitability of individual products and services. Multiproduct companies need to be sure that all products are profitable and that the overall profitability of the firm is not disguising the poor performance of individual products. This meets the profitability objective identified by the IMA.

By assessing the profitability of various support services, a manager may evaluate the mix of support services offered by the firm. From this evaluation, it may be decided to drop some support services, reallocate resources from one to another, reprice certain support services, or exercise greater cost control in some areas. These steps would meet the IMA's planning and control objective. The validity of any evaluation, however, depends to a great extent on the accuracy of the cost assignments made to individual products.

For a service organization such as a hospital, the IMA objective of inventory valuation is not relevant. For manufacturing organizations, however, this objective must be given special attention. Rules of financial reporting (GAAP) require that direct manufacturing costs and all indirect manufacturing costs be assigned to the products produced. The procedure of allocating support department costs to producing departments and then reassigning those costs to products going through the producing departments is in keeping with this requirement. Inventories and cost of goods sold must include direct materials, direct labor, and all manufacturing overhead.

Allocations also can be used to motivate managers. If the costs of support departments are not allocated to producing departments, managers may tend to overconsume these services. Consumption of a support service may continue until the marginal benefit of the service equals zero. In reality, the marginal cost of a service is of course greater than zero. By allocating the costs and holding managers of producing departments responsible for the economic performance of their units, the organization ensures that managers will use a support service until the marginal benefit of the service equals its marginal cost. Thus, allocation of support department costs helps each producing department select the correct level of support service consumption.

There are other behavioral benefits. Allocation of support department costs to producing departments encourages managers of those departments to monitor the performance of support departments. Since the costs of the support departments affect the economic performance of their own departments, those managers have an incentive to control these costs through means other than simple usage of the support service. For instance, the managers can compare the internal costs of the support service with the costs of acquiring it externally. If a support department is not as cost effective as an outside source, perhaps the company should not continue to supply the service internally. For example, many university libraries are moving toward the use of outside contractors for photocopying services. They have found that these contractors are more cost efficient and provide a higher level of service to library users than did the previous method of using professional librarians to make change, keep the copy machines supplied with paper, fix paper jams, etc. This possibility of comparison should result in a more efficient internal support department. Monitoring by managers of producing departments will also encourage managers of support departments to be more sensitive to the needs of the producing departments.

Clearly, then, there are good reasons for allocating support department costs. The validity of these reasons depends, however, on the accuracy and fairness of the cost assignments made. Although it may not be possible to identify a single method of allocation that simultaneously satisfies all of these objectives, several guidelines have been developed to assist in determining the best allocation method. These are: cause and effect, benefits received, fairness, and ability to bear. Another guideline to be used in conjunction with any of the others is cost-benefit. That is, the method used must provide sufficient benefits to justify any effort involved.

Cause and effect requires the determination of causal factors to guide allocation. For example, the corporate legal department may track the number of hours spent on legal work for the various divisions (e.g., handling patent applications, lawsuits, etc.). The number of hours worked by lawyers and paralegals has a clear cause-and-effect relationship with the overall cost of the legal department and may be used to allocate the cost of the corporate legal department to the various company divisions.

The benefits-received guideline associates the cost with perceived benefits. Research and development (R&D) costs may be allocated on the basis of the sales of each division. The idea would be that not all R&D efforts pay off and that while the successful efforts may happen to benefit one division in one year, all divisions have a stake in corporate R&D and will at some point have increased sales because of it.

Fairness or equity is a guideline often mentioned in government contracting. In the case of cost allocation methods, fairness usually means that the government contract should be costed in a method similar to nongovernmental contracts. For example, an airplane engine manufacturer may allocate a portion of corporate legal department costs to the government contract if these costs are usually allocated to private contracts.

Ability to bear is the least desirable guideline. It tends to "penalize" the most profitable division by allocating to it the largest proportion of a support department cost—no matter whether the profitable division receives any services from the allocated department or not. As a result, no motivational benefits of allocation are realized.

In determining how to allocate support department costs, the guideline of cost-benefit must be considered. In other words, the costs of implementing a particular allocation scheme must be compared to the benefits to be derived. As a result, companies try to use easily measured and understood bases for allocation.

ALLOCATING ONE DEPARTMENT'S COSTS TO ANOTHER DEPARTMENT

Objective 3
Calculate charging rates, and distinguish between single and dual charging rates.

Frequently the costs of a support department are allocated to another department through the use of a charging rate. In this case, we focus on the allocation of one department's costs to other departments. For example, a company's data-processing department may serve various other departments. The cost of operating the data-processing department is then allocated to the user departments. While this seems simple and straightforward, a number of considerations go into determining an appropriate charging rate. The two major factors are (1) the choice of a single or a dual charging rate and (2) the use of budgeted versus actual support department costs.

A Single Charging Rate

Some companies prefer to develop a single charging rate. Suppose, for example, that Hamish and Barton, a large regional public accounting firm, develops an in-house photocopying department to serve its three producing departments (Audit, Tax, and Management Advisory Systems, or MAS). The costs of the photocopying department include fixed costs of $26,190 per year (salaries and machine rental) and variable costs of $.023 per page copied (paper and toner). Estimated usage (in pages) by the three producing departments is as follows:

Audit Department	94,500
Tax Department	67,500
MAS Department	108,000
Total	270,000

If a single charging rate is used, the fixed costs of $26,190 will be combined with estimated variable costs of $6,210 (270,000 × $.023). Total costs of $32,400 are divided by the estimated 270,000 pages to be copied to yield a rate of $0.12 per page.

The amount charged to the producing departments is solely a function of the number of pages copied. Suppose that the actual usage for Audit is 92,000 pages, 65,000 pages for Tax, and 115,000 pages for MAS. The total photocopying department charges would be as shown.

	Number of Pages	×	*Charge Per Page*	*Total Charges*
Audit	92,000		$0.12	$11,040
Tax	65,000		0.12	7,800
MAS	115,000		0.12	13,800
Total	272,000			$32,640

Notice that the use of a single rate treats the fixed cost as if it were variable. In fact, to the producing departments, photocopying is strictly variable. Did the photocopying department need $32,640 to copy 272,000 pages? No, it needed only $32,446 [$26,190 + (272,000 × $.023)]. The extra amount charged is due to the treatment of a fixed cost in a variable manner.[2]

Dual Charging Rates

While the use of a single rate is simple, it ignores the differential impact of changes in usage on costs. The variable costs of a support department increase as the level of service increases. For example, the costs of paper and toner for the Photocopying Department increase as the number of pages copied increases. Fixed costs, on the other hand, do not vary with the level of service. For example, the rental payment for photocopying machines does not change as the number

---

2.   Note that the Photocopying Department would have charged out less than the cost needed if the number of pages copied had been less than the budgeted number of pages. You might calculate the total cost charged for a total of 268,000 pages ($0.12 × 268,000 = $32,160) and compare it with the cost incurred of $32,354 [$26,190 + (268,000 × $.023)].

of pages increases or decreases. We can avoid the treatment of fixed costs as variable by developing two rates: one for fixed costs and one for variable costs. The development of dual charging rates (which are used as the basis for pricing) is particularly important in companies such as public utilities.

Developing a Fixed Rate Fixed service costs can be considered capacity costs; they are incurred to provide the capacity necessary to deliver the service units required by the producing departments. When the support department was established, its delivery capability was designed to serve the long-term needs of the producing departments. Since the original support needs caused the creation of the support service capacity, it seems reasonable to allocate fixed costs based on those needs.

Either the normal or peak activity of the producing departments provides a reasonable measure of original support service needs. Normal capacity is the average capacity achieved over more than one fiscal period. If service is required uniformly over the time period, normal capacity is a good measure of activity. Peak capacity allows for variation in the need for the support department, and the size of the department is structured to allow for maximum need. In our example, the Tax Department may need much more photocopying during the first four months of the year, and its usage may be based on that need. The choice of normal or peak capacity in allocating budgeted fixed service costs depends on the needs of the individual firm. Budgeted fixed costs are allocated in this way regardless of whether the purpose is product costing or performance evaluation.

The allocation of fixed costs follows a three-step procedure.

1. *Determination of budgeted fixed support service costs.* The fixed support service costs that should be incurred for a period need to be identified.
2. *Computation of the allocation ratio.* Using the practical or normal capacity of each producing department, it is necessary to compute an allocation ratio. The allocation ratio simply gives a producing department's share or percentage of the total capacity of all producing departments.

Allocation ratio = Producing department capacity/Total capacity

3. *Allocation.* The fixed support service costs are then allocated in proportion to each producing department's original support service needs.

Allocation = Allocation ratio × Budgeted fixed support service costs

Let's assume that the three departments in our example originally decided that they would need an amount equal to the budgeted number given before:

	Number of Copies	Percent
Audit	94,500	35
Tax	67,500	25
MAS	108,000	40
	270,000	100

The fixed costs allocated, then, are the relevant percentages for each department multiplied by the support department's fixed costs.

Developing a Variable Rate The variable rate depends on the costs that change as the activity driver changes. In the Photocopying Department, the activity driver is the number of pages copied. As the number of pages increases, more paper and toner are used. Since these average $.023 per page, the variable rate is $.023. This variable rate is used in conjunction with the fixed amount allocated to determine total charges. In our example, the Audit Department would be allocated 35 percent of fixed cost plus $.023 per page copied. The Tax Department would be allocated 25 percent of fixed cost plus $.023 per page copied. MAS would be allocated 40 percent of fixed cost plus $.023 per page copied. Let's see how photocopying costs are allocated under the dual rate method.

	Number of Copies	Fixed Amount	Variable Amount	Total Charge
Audit	92,000	$ 9,167	$2,116	$11,283
Tax	65,000	6,548	1,495	8,043
MAS	115,000	10,476	2,645	13,121
Total	272,000	$26,191	$6,256	$32,447

Under the dual charging rates, the fixed photocopying rates are charged to the departments in accordance with their original capacity needs. Especially in a case like this one, in which fixed costs are such a high proportion of total costs, the additional effort needed to develop the dual rates may be worthwhile. Additionally, the dual rate method has the benefit of sending the correct signal regarding increased usage of the support department. Suppose that the Tax Department wants to have several research articles on changes in the tax law copied for clients. Should this be done "in house" by the Photocopying Department or sent to a private photocopying firm that charges $.06 per page? Under the single rate method, the in-house cost charged would be too high because it wrongly assumes that fixed cost will increase as pages copied increase. However, under the dual rate method, the additional cost would be only $.023 per page, which correctly approximates the additional cost of the job.

Budgeted Versus Actual Usage

The second factor to be considered in charging costs from a single service department to other departments is whether actual usage or budgeted usage should be the basis for allocating costs. In truth, this factor only has an impact on allocated costs when fixed costs are involved. As a result, we need to consider it in the case of a single charging rate (which combines fixed with variable costs to generate a rate) and of the fixed portion of the dual charging rate.

When we allocate support department costs to the producing departments, should we allocate actual or budgeted costs? The answer is budgeted costs. There are two basic reasons for allocating support department costs. One is to cost units produced. In this case, the budgeted support department costs are allocated to producing departments as a preliminary step in forming the overhead rate. Recall that the overhead rate is calculated at the beginning of the period, when actual costs are not known. Thus, budgeted costs must be used. The second usage of allocated support department costs is for performance evaluation. In this case too, budgeted support department costs are allocated to producing departments.

Managers of support and producing departments usually are held accountable for the performance of their units. Their ability to control costs is an important factor in their performance evaluation. This ability is usually measured by comparing actual costs with planned or budgeted costs. If actual costs exceed budgeted costs, the department may be operating inefficiently, with the difference between the two costs serving as the measure of that inefficiency. Similarly, if actual costs are less than budgeted costs, the unit may be operating efficiently.

A general principle of performance evaluation is that managers should not be held responsible for costs or activities over which they have no control. Since managers of producing departments have significant input regarding the level of support service consumed, they should be held responsible for their share of support service costs. This statement, however, has an important qualification: A department's evaluation should not be affected by the degree of efficiency achieved by another department.

This qualifying statement has an important implication for the allocation of support department costs. *Actual* costs of a support department should not be allocated to producing departments, because they include efficiencies or inefficiencies achieved by the support department. Managers of producing departments have no control over the degree of efficiency achieved by a support department manager. By allocating *budgeted* costs instead of actual costs, no inefficiencies or efficiencies are transferred from one department to another.

Whether budgeted usage or actual usage is used depends on the purpose of the allocation. For *product costing*, the allocation is done at the beginning of the year on the basis of budgeted usage so that a predetermined overhead rate can be computed. If the purpose is *performance evaluation*, however, the allocation is done at the end of the period and is based on actual usage. The use of cost information for performance evaluation is covered in more detail in the chapter on standard costing.

Let's return to our photocopying example. Recall that annual budgeted fixed costs were $26,190 and the budgeted variable cost per page was $.023. The three producing departments, Audit, Tax, and MAS, estimated usage at 94,500 copies, 67,500 copies, and 108,000 copies, respectively. Given these data, the costs allocated to each department at the *beginning* of the year are shown in Exhibit 6-4.

Exhibit 6-4
Use of Budgeted Data for Product Costing: Comparison of Single and Dual Rate Methods

Single Rate Method:

	Number of Copies	×	Total Rate	=	Allocated Cost
Audit	94,500		$.12		$11,340
Tax	67,500		.12		8,100
MAS	108,000		.12		12,960
Total					$32,400

Dual Rate Method:

	(Number of Copies	×	Variable Rate)	+	Fixed Allocation	=	Allocated Cost
Audit	94,500		$.023		$ 9,167		$11,340
Tax	67,500		.023		6,548		8,100
MAS	108,000		.023		10,476		12,960
Total							$32,400

Note that the single rate method produces the same allocation as does the dual rate method when budgeted figures are used. This is because budgeted fixed cost is just absorbed by the number of budgeted pages.

When the allocation is done for the purpose of budgeting the producing departments' costs, then, of course, the budgeted support department costs are used. The photocopying costs allocated to each department would be added to other producing department costs, including those directly traceable to each department plus other support department allocations, to compute each department's anticipated spending. In a manufacturing plant, the allocation of budgeted support department costs to the producing departments would precede the calculation of the predetermined overhead rate.

During the year, each producing department would also be responsible for actual charges incurred based on the actual number of pages copied. Going back to the actual usage assumed previously, a second allocation is now made to measure the actual performance of each department against its budget. The actual photocopying costs allocated to each department for performance evaluation purposes are shown in Exhibit 6-5.

Fixed Versus Variable Bases: A Note of Caution

Using normal or practical capacity to allocate fixed support service costs provides a *fixed* base. As long as the capacities of the producing departments remain at the level originally anticipated, there is no reason to change the allocation ratios. Thus, each year the Audit Department receives 35 percent of the budgeted fixed photocopying costs, the Tax Department 25 percent, and the MAS Department 40 percent, no matter what their actual usage is. If the capacities of the departments change, the ratios should be recalculated.

In practice, some companies choose to allocate fixed costs in proportion to actual usage or expected actual usage. Since usage may vary from year to year, allocation of fixed costs would then use a variable base. Variable bases, however,

---

Exhibit 6-5
Use of Actual Data for Performance Evaluation Purposes: Comparison of Single and Dual Rate Methods

Single Rate Method:

	Number of Copies	×	Total Rate	=	Allocated Cost
Audit	92,000		$.12		$11,040
Tax	65,000		.12		7,800
MAS	115,000		.12		13,800
Total					$32,640

Dual Rate Method:

	(Number of Copies	×	Variable Rate)	+	Fixed Allocation	=	Allocated Cost
Audit	92,000		$.023		$ 9,167		$11,283
Tax	65,000		.023		6,548		8,043
MAS	115,000		.023		10,476		13,121
Total							$32,447

have a significant drawback: they allow the actions of one department to affect the amount of cost allocated to another department.

To see how this is so, let's return to Hamish and Barton's Photocopying Department and assume that fixed costs are allocated on the basis of anticipated usage for the coming year. The Audit and Tax Departments budget the same number of copies as before. However, the MAS Department anticipates much less activity due to a regional recession, which will cut down the number of new clients served; the anticipated number of photocopies for this department falls to 68,000. The adjusted fixed cost allocation ratios and allocated fixed cost based on the newly budgeted usage are as follows.

	Number of Copies	Percent	Allocated Fixed Cost
Audit	94,500	41.1	$10,764
Tax	67,500	29.3	7,674
MAS	68,000	29.6	7,752
Total	230,000	100.0	$26,190

Notice that both the Audit and Tax Departments' allocation of fixed costs increased even though the fixed costs of the Photocopying Department remained unchanged. This increase is caused by a decrease in the MAS Department's use of photocopying. In effect, the Audit and Tax Departments are being penalized because of MAS's decision to reduce the number of pages copied. Imagine the feelings of the first two managers when they realize that their copying charges have increased due to the increase in allocated fixed costs! The penalty occurs because a variable base is used to allocate fixed support service costs; it can be avoided by using a fixed base.

CHOOSING A SUPPORT DEPARTMENT COST ALLOCATION METHOD

Objective 4

Allocate support center costs to producing departments using the direct method, the sequential method, and the reciprocal method.

So far, we have considered cost allocation from a single support department to several producing departments. We used the direct method of support department cost allocation, in which support department costs are allocated only to producing departments. This was appropriate in the earlier example because no other support departments existed. This would also be appropriate when there is no possibility of interaction among support departments. Many companies do have multiple support departments, and they frequently interact. For example, in a factory, Personnel and Cafeteria serve each other and other support departments as well as the producing departments.

Ignoring these interactions and allocating support costs directly to producing departments may produce unfair and inaccurate cost assignments. For example, Power, although a support department, may use 30 percent of the services of the Maintenance Department. The maintenance costs caused by the Power Department belong to the Power Department. By not assigning these costs to the Power Department, its costs are understated. In effect, some of the costs caused by Power are "hidden" in the Maintenance Department because maintenance costs would be lower if the Power Department did not exist. As a result, a producing department that is a heavy user of power and an average or below-average user of maintenance may then receive, under the direct method, a cost allocation that is understated.

In determining which support department cost allocation method to use, companies must determine the extent of support department interaction. In addition, they must weigh the costs and benefits associated with the three methods. In the next three sections, the direct, sequential, and reciprocal methods are described and illustrated.

Direct Method of Allocation

When companies allocate support department costs only to the producing departments, they are using the **direct method** of allocation. The direct method is the simplest and most straightforward way to allocate support department costs. Variable service costs are allocated directly to producing departments in proportion to each department's usage of the service. Fixed costs are also allocated directly to the producing department, but in proportion to the producing department's normal or practical capacity.

Exhibit 6-6 illustrates the lack of support department reciprocity on cost allocation in using the direct method. In Exhibit 6-6, we see that by using the direct

Exhibit 6-6
Allocation of Support Department Costs to Producing Department Using the Direct Method

Suppose there are two support departments, Power and Maintenance, and two producing departments, Grinding and Assembly, each with a "bucket" of directly traceable overhead cost.

Objective: Distribute all Power and Maintenance costs to Grinding and Assembly using the direct method.

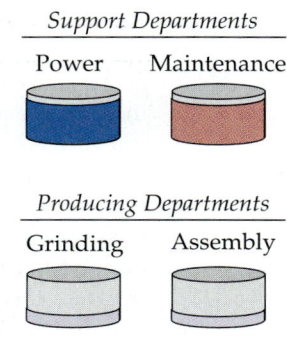

Direct Method— Allocate Power and Maintenance costs only to Grinding and Assembly.

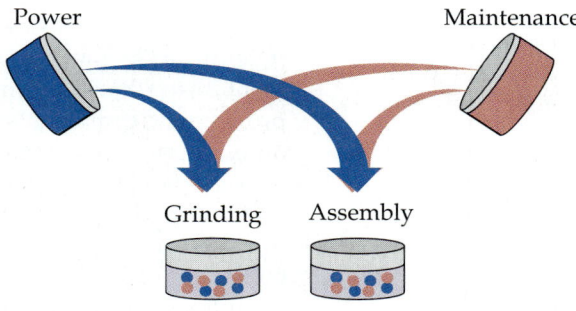

After allocation— Zero cost in Power and Maintenance, all overhead cost in Grinding and Assembly.

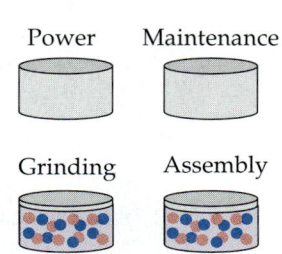

method, support department cost is allocated to producing departments only. No cost from one support department is allocated to another support department. Thus, no support department interaction is recognized.

To illustrate the direct method, consider the data in Exhibit 6-7. The data show the budgeted activity and budgeted costs of two support departments and two producing departments. (Note that the same data are used to illustrate the sequential method; for the time being, ignore the allocation ratios at the bottom of Exhibit 6-7 that correspond to the sequential method.) Assume that the causal factor for power costs is kilowatt hours and the causal factor for maintenance costs is maintenance hours. These causal factors are used as the bases for allocation. In the direct method, only the kilowatt hours and the maintenance hours in the producing departments are used to compute the allocation ratios. The direct allocations based on the data given in Exhibit 6-7 are shown in Exhibit 6-8. (To simplify the illustration, no distinction is made between fixed and variable costs.)

Sequential Method of Allocation

sequential (or step) method

The **sequential (or step) method** of allocation recognizes that interactions among the support departments occur. However, the sequential method does not fully recognize support department interaction. Cost allocations are performed in step-

Exhibit 6-7
Data for Illustrating Allocation Methods

	Support Departments		Producing Departments	
	Power	Maintenance	Grinding	Assembly
Direct costs*	$250,000	$160,000	$100,000	$60,000
Normal activity:				
Kilowatt hours	—	200,000	600,000	200,000
Maintenance hours	1,000	—	4,500	4,500
Allocation ratios				
Direct method:				
Kilowatt hours	—	—	0.75	0.25
Maintenance hours	—	—	0.50	0.50
Sequential method:				
Kilowatt hours	—	0.20	0.60	0.20
Maintenance hours	—	—	0.50	0.50

*For a producing department, direct costs refer only to overhead costs that are directly traceable to the department.

Exhibit 6-8
Direct Allocation Illustrated

	Support Departments		Producing Departments	
	Power	Maintenance	Grinding	Assembly
Direct costs	$250,000	$160,000	$100,000	$ 60,000
Power[a]	(250,000)	—	187,500	62,500
Maintenance[b]	—	(160,000)	80,000	80,000
	$ 0	$ 0	$367,500	$202,500

[a] Allocation of power based on ratios from Exhibit 6-7: 0.75 × $250,000; 0.25 × $250,000.
[b] Allocation of maintenance based on ratios from Exhibit 6-7: 0.50 × $160,000; 0.50 × $160,000.

down fashion, following a predetermined ranking procedure. Usually, the sequence is defined by ranking the support departments in order of the amount of service rendered, from the greatest to the least. Degree of support service is usually measured by the direct costs of each support department; the department with the highest cost is seen as rendering the greatest service.

Exhibit 6-9 illustrates the sequential method. First, the support departments are ranked, usually in accordance with direct costs; here Power is first, then Maintenance. Then, Power costs are allocated to Maintenance and the two producing departments. Then the costs of Maintenance are allocated only to producing departments.

The costs of the support department rendering the greatest support service are allocated first. They are distributed to all support departments below it in the sequence and to all producing departments. Then the costs of the support department next in sequence are similarly allocated, and so on. In the sequential method, once a support department's costs are allocated, it never receives a subsequent allocation from another support department. In other words, costs of a support department are never allocated to support departments *above* it in the sequence. Also note that the costs allocated from a support department are its direct costs *plus* any costs it receives in allocations from other support departments. The direct costs of a department are those that are directly traceable to the department.

To illustrate the sequential method, consider the data provided in Exhibit 6-7. Using cost as a measure of service, the support department rendering more service is Power. Thus, its costs will be allocated first, followed by those for Maintenance. The allocation ratios shown in Exhibit 6-7 will be used to execute the allocation. Note that the allocation ratios for the Maintenance Department ignore the usage by the Power Department, since its costs cannot be allocated to a support department above it in the allocation sequence.

The allocations obtained with the sequential method are shown in Exhibit 6-10. Notice that $50,000 of the Power Department's costs are allocated to the Maintenance Department. This reflects the fact that the Maintenance Department uses 20 percent of the Power Department's output. As a result, the cost of operating the Maintenance Department increases from $160,000 to $210,000. Also notice that when the costs of the Maintenance Department are allocated, no costs are allocated back to the Power Department, even though it uses 1,000 hours of the output of the Maintenance Department.

The sequential method may be more accurate than the direct method because it recognizes some interactions among the support departments. It does not recognize all interactions, however; no maintenance costs were assigned to the Power Department even though it used 10 percent of the Maintenance Department's output. The reciprocal method corrects this deficiency.

Reciprocal Method of Allocation

reciprocal method

The **reciprocal method** of allocation recognizes all interactions of support departments. Under the reciprocal method, the usage of one support department by another is used to determine the total cost of each support department, where the total cost reflects interactions among the support departments, and then the new total of support department costs is allocated to the producing departments. This method fully accounts for support department interaction.

Exhibit 6-9

Allocation of Support Department Costs to Producing Departments Using the Sequential Method

Suppose there are two support departments, Power and Maintenance, and two producing departments, Grinding and Assembly, each with a "bucket" of directly traceable overhead cost.

Objective: Distribute all Power and Maintenance costs to Grinding and Assembly using the Sequential Method.

Support Departments

Power   Maintenance

Producing Departments

Grinding   Assembly

Step 1: Rank support departments—
#1 Power, #2 Maintenance.

Step 2: Distribute Power to Maintenance, Grinding, and Assembly.

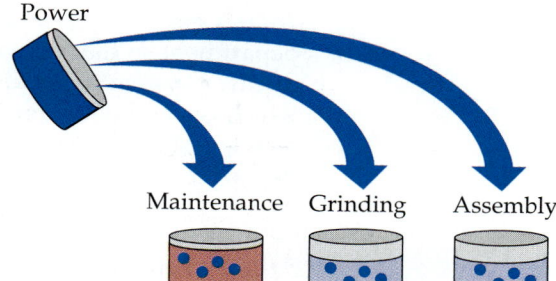

Then, distribute Maintenance to Grinding and Assembly.

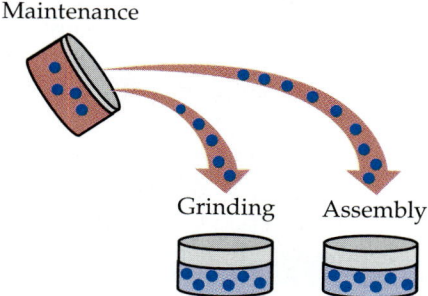

After allocation—
Zero cost in Power and Maintenance, all overhead cost in Grinding and Assembly.

Power   Maintenance

Grinding   Assembly

Exhibit 6-10
Sequential Allocation
Illustrated

	Support Departments		Producing Departments	
	Power	Maintenance	Grinding	Assembly
Direct costs	$250,000	$160,000	$100,000	$ 60,000
Power[a]	(250,000)	50,000	150,000	50,000
Maintenance[b]	—	(210,000)	105,000	105,000
	$	$ 0	$355,000	$215,000

[a] Allocation of power based on ratios from Exhibit 6-7: 0.20 × $250,000; 0.60 × $250,000; 0.20 × $250,000.
[b] Allocation of maintenance costs based on ratios from Exhibit 6-7: 0.50 × $210,000; 0.50 × $210,000.

Total Cost of Service Departments To determine the total cost of a support department so that this total cost reflects interactions with other support departments, a system of simultaneous linear equations must be solved. Each equation, which is a cost equation for a support department, is the sum of the department's direct costs plus the proportion of service received from each other support department.

$$\text{Total cost} = \text{Direct costs} + \text{Allocated costs}$$

The method is best described using an example. The same data used to illustrate the direct and sequential methods will be used to illustrate the reciprocal method in Exhibit 6-11. The allocation ratios needed for the simultaneous equations are interpreted as follows: Maintenance receives 20 percent of Power's output, and Power receives 10 percent of Maintenance's output.

Exhibit 6-11
Data for Illustrating
Reciprocal Method

	Support Departments		Producing Departments	
	Power	Maintenance	Grinding	Assembly
Direct costs*				
Fixed	$200,000	$100,000	$ 80,000	$ 50,000
Variable	50,000	60,000	20,000	10,000
Total	$250,000	$160,000	$100,000	$ 60,000
Normal activity:				
Kilowatt hours	—	200,000	600,000	200,000
Maintenance hours	1,000	—	4,500	4,500

	Proportion of Output Used by			
	Power	Maintenance	Grinding	Assembly
Allocation ratios:				
Power	—	0.20	0.60	0.20
Maintenance	0.10	—	0.45	0.45

*For a producing department, direct costs are defined as overhead costs that are directly traceable to the department.

Now let P equal the total cost of the Power Department and M equal the total cost of the Maintenance Department. As indicated above, the total cost of a support department is the sum of its direct costs plus the proportion of service received from other support departments. Using the data and allocation ratios from Exhibit 6-11, the cost equation for each support department can be expressed as follows:

$$P = \text{Direct costs} + \text{Share of Maintenance's cost} \qquad (6.1)$$
$$= \$250,000 + 0.1M \text{ (Maintenance's cost equation)}$$
$$M = \text{Direct costs} + \text{Share of Power's costs} \qquad (6.2)$$
$$= \$160,000 + 0.2P \text{ (Power's cost equation)}$$

The direct-cost components of each equation are taken from Exhibit 6-11, as are the allocation ratios.

The Power cost equation (Equation 6.1) and the Maintenance cost equation (Equation 6.2) can be solved simultaneously to yield the total cost for each support department. Substituting Equation 6.1 into Equation 6.2 gives the following:

$$M = \$160,000 + 0.2(\$250,000 + 0.1M)$$
$$M = \$160,000 + \$50,000 + 0.02M$$
$$0.98M = \$210,000$$
$$M = \$214,286$$

Substituting this value for M into Equation 6.1 yields the total cost for Power:

$$P = \$250,000 + 0.1(\$214,286)$$
$$= \$250,000 + \$21,429$$
$$= \$271,429$$

After the equations are solved, the total costs of each support department are known. These total costs, unlike the direct or sequential methods, reflect all interactions between support departments.

Allocation to Producing Departments Once the total costs of each support department are known, the allocations to the producing departments can be made. These allocations, based on the proportion of output used by each producing department, are shown in Exhibit 6-12. Notice that the total costs allo-

Exhibit 6-12
Reciprocal Allocation Illustrated

		Allocated to	
	Total Cost	Grinding[a]	Assembly[b]
Power	$271,429	$162,857	$ 54,286
Maintenance	214,286	96,429	96,429
Total		$259,286	$150,715

[a] Power: 0.60 × $271,429; Maintenance: 0.45 × $214,286
[b] Power: 0.20 × $271,429; Maintenance: 0.45 × $214,286

cated to the producing departments equal $410,000, the total direct costs of the two support departments ($250,000 + $160,000).

Comparison of the Three Methods

Exhibit 6-13 gives the cost allocations from the Power and Maintenance Departments to the Grinding and Assembly Departments using the three support department cost allocation methods. How different are the results? Does it really matter which method is used? Depending on the degree of interaction of the support departments, the three allocation methods can give radically different results. In this particular example, the direct method allocated $12,500 more to the Grinding Department (and $12,500 less to the Assembly Department). Surely the manager of the Assembly Department would prefer the direct method and the manager of the Grinding Department would prefer the sequential method. Because allocation methods do affect the cost responsibilities of managers, it is important for the accountant to understand the consequences of the different methods and to have good reasons for the eventual choice.

It is important to keep a cost-benefit perspective in choosing an allocation method. The accountant must weigh the advantages of better allocation against the increased cost using a more theoretically preferred method, such as the reciprocal method. For example, about twenty years ago, the controller for the IBM Poughkeepsie plant decided that the reciprocal method of cost allocation would do a better job of allocating support department costs. He identified over 700 support departments and solved the system of equations using a computer. Computationally, he had no problems. However, the producing department managers did not understand the reciprocal method. They were sure that extra cost was being allocated to their departments, but they just were not sure how. After months of meetings with the line managers, the controller threw in the towel and returned to the sequential method—which everyone did understand.

Another factor to be considered in allocating support department cost is the rapid change in technology. Many firms currently find that support department cost allocation is useful for them. However, the move toward activity-based costing and just-in-time manufacturing can virtually eliminate the need for support department cost allocation. In the case of the JIT factory with manufacturing cells, much of the service (e.g., maintenance, materials handling, and setups) is performed by cell workers. Allocation is not necessary.

Exhibit 6-13
Comparison of Support Department Cost Allocations Using the Direct, Sequential, and Reciprocal Methods

	Direct Method		Sequential Method		Reciprocal Method	
	Grinding	*Assembly*	*Grinding*	*Assembly*	*Grinding*	*Assembly*
Direct costs	$100,000	$ 60,000	$100,000	$ 60,000	$100,000	$ 60,000
Allocated from Power	187,500	62,500	150,000	50,000	162,857	54,286
Allocated from Maint.	80,000	80,000	105,000	105,000	96,429	96,429
Total cost	$367,500	$202,500	$355,000	$215,000	$359,286	$210,715

DEPARTMENTAL OVERHEAD RATES AND PRODUCT COSTING

Objective 5
Calculate
departmental
overhead rates.

Upon allocating all support service costs to producing departments, an overhead rate can be computed for each department. This rate is computed by adding the allocated service costs to the overhead costs that are directly traceable to the producing department and dividing this total by some measure of activity, such as direct labor hours or machine hours.

For example, from Exhibit 6-10, the total overhead costs for the Grinding Department after allocation of support service costs are $355,000. Assume that machine hours are the base for assigning overhead costs to products passing through the Grinding Department and that the normal level of activity is 71,000 machine hours. The overhead rate for the Grinding Department is computed as follows:

$$\text{Overhead rate} = \$355,000/71,000 \text{ machine hours}$$
$$= \$5 \text{ per machine hour}$$

Similarly, assume that the Assembly Department uses direct labor hours to assign its overhead. With a normal level of activity of 107,500 direct labor hours, the overhead rate for the Assembly Department is as follows:

$$\text{Overhead rate} = \$215,000/107,500 \text{ direct labor hours}$$
$$= \$2 \text{ per direct labor hour}$$

Using these rates, the product's unit cost can be determined. To illustrate, suppose a product requires two machine hours of grinding per unit produced and one hour of assembly. The overhead cost assigned to one unit of this product would be $12 [(2 × $5) + (1 × $2)]. If the same product uses $15 of materials and $6 of labor (totalled from Grinding and Assembly), then its unit cost is $33 ($12 + $15 + $6).

One might wonder, however, just how accurate this $33 cost is. Is this really what it costs to produce the product in question? Since materials and labor are directly traceable to products, the accuracy of product costs depends largely on the accuracy of the assignment of overhead costs. This in turn depends on the degree of correlation between the factors used to allocate support service costs to departments and the factors used to allocate the department's overhead costs to the products. For example, if power costs are highly correlated with kilowatt hours and machine hours are highly correlated with a product's consumption of the Grinding Department's overhead costs, then we can have some confidence that the $5 overhead rate accurately assigns costs to individual products. However, if the allocation of support service costs to the Grinding Department or the use of machine hours is faulty—or both—then product costs will be distorted. The same reasoning can be applied to the Assembly Department. To ensure accurate product costs, great care should be used in identifying and using causal factors for both stages of overhead assignment. More will be said about this in a later chapter.

SUMMARY

Producing departments create the products or services that the firm is in business to manufacture and sell. Support departments serve producing departments but do not themselves create a salable product. Because support departments exist to support a variety of producing departments, the costs of the support departments are common to all producing departments and must be allocated to them to satisfy a number of important objectives. These objectives include inventory valuation, product-line profitability, pricing, and planning and control. Allocation can also be used to encourage favorable managerial behavior.

When the costs of one support department are allocated to other departments, a charging rate must be developed. A single rate combines variable and fixed costs of the support department to generate a charging rate. A dual rate separates the fixed and variable costs. Fixed support department costs are allocated on the basis of original capacity, and a variable rate is developed on the basis of budgeted usage.

Budgeted costs, not actual costs, should be allocated so that the efficiencies or inefficiencies of the support departments themselves are not passed on to the producing departments. Because the causal factors can differ for fixed and variable costs, these types of cost should be allocated separately.

Three methods can be used to allocate support service costs to producing departments: the direct method, the sequential method, and the reciprocal method. They differ in the degree of support department interaction considered. By considering support department interactions, more accurate product costing is achieved. The result can be improved planning, control, and decision making. Two methods of allocation recognize interactions among support departments: the *sequential (or step) method* and the *reciprocal method*. These methods allocate support service costs among some (or all) interacting support departments before allocating costs to the producing departments.

Departmental overhead rates are calculated by adding direct departmental overhead costs to those costs allocated from the support departments and dividing the sum by the budgeted departmental base.

REVIEW PROBLEM AND SOLUTION

Antioch Manufacturing produces machine parts on a job-order basis. Most business is obtained through bidding. Most firms competing with Antioch bid full cost plus a 20 percent markup. Recently, with the expectation of gaining more sales, Antioch reduced its markup from 25 percent to 20 percent. The company operates two support departments and two producing departments. The budgeted costs and the normal activity levels for each department are given below.

	Support Departments		Producing Departments	
	A	B	C	D
Overhead costs	$100,000	$200,000	$100,000	$50,000
Number of employees	8	7	30	30
Maintenance hours	2,000	200	6,400	1,600
Machine hours	—	—	10,000	1,000
Labor hours	—	—	1,000	10,000

The direct costs of Department A are allocated on the basis of employees, those of Department B on the basis of maintenance hours. Departmental overhead rates are used to assign costs to products. Department C uses machine hours, and Department D uses labor hours.

The firm is preparing to bid on a job (Job K) that requires three machine hours per unit produced in Department C and no time in Department D. The expected prime costs per unit are $67.

REQUIRED:

1. Allocate the support service costs to the producing departments using the direct method.
2. What will be the bid for Job K if the direct method of allocation is used?
3. Allocate the service costs to the producing departments using the sequential method.
4. What will be the bid for Job K if the sequential method is used?

5. Allocate the service costs to the producing departments using the reciprocal method.
6. What will be the bid for Job K if the reciprocal method is used?

Solution

1.

	Support Departments		Producing Departments	
	A	*B*	*C*	*D*
Direct costs	$100,000	$200,000	$100,000	$ 50,000
Department A	(100,000)	—	50,000	50,000
Department B	—	(200,000)	160,000	40,000
Total	$ 0	$ 0	$310,000	$140,000

2. Department C: Overhead rate = $310,000/10,000 = $31 per machine hour. Product cost and bid price:

Prime cost	$ 67
Overhead (3 × $31)	93
Total unit cost	$160
Bid price ($160 × 1.2)	$192

3.

	Support Departments		Producing Departments	
	A	*B*	*C*	*D*
Direct costs	$100,000	$200,000	$100,000	$ 50,000
Department B	40,000	(200,000)	128,000	32,000
Department A	(140,000)	—	70,000	70,000
Total	$ 0	$ 0	$298,000	$152,000

4. Department C: Overhead rate = $298,000/10,000 = $29.80 per machine hour. Product cost and bid price:

Prime cost	$ 67.00
Overhead (3 × $29.80)	89.40
Total unit cost	$156.40
Bid price ($156.40 × 1.2)	$187.68

5. Allocation ratios:

	Proportion of Output Used by			
	A	*B*	*C*	*D*
A	—	0.1045	0.4478	0.4478
B	0.2000	—	0.6400	0.1600

$$A = \$100,000 + .2000B$$
$$B = \$200,000 + .1045A$$

$$A = \$100,000 + .2(\$200,000 + .1045A)$$
$$= \$100,000 + \$40,000 + .0209A$$
$$.9791A = \$140,000$$
$$A = \$142,988$$

$$B = \$200,000 + .1045(\$142,988)$$
$$= \$214,942$$

	Support Departments		Producing Departments	
	A	B	C	D
Direct costs	$100,000	$200,000	$100,000	$ 50,000
Department B	42,988	(214,942)	137,563	34,391
Department A	(143,002)	14,942	64,030	64,030
Total	$ (14)	$ 0	$301,593	$148,421

Note: The $14 remaining in Department A is the result of rounding error.

6. Department C: Overhead rate = $301,593/10,000 = $30.16 per machine hour. Product cost and bid price:

Prime cost	$ 67.00
Overhead (3 × $30.16)	90.48
Total unit cost	$157.48
Bid price ($157.48 × 1.2)	$188.98

KEY TERMS

Causal factors *234*

Common cost *232*

Direct method *244*

Producing department *232*

Reciprocal method *246*

Sequential (or step) method *245*

Support department *232*

QUESTIONS FOR WRITING AND DISCUSSION

1. Describe the two-stage allocation process for assigning support service costs to products in a traditional manufacturing environment.
2. Explain how allocating support service costs can be helpful in pricing decisions.
3. Why must support service costs be assigned to products for purposes of inventory valuation?
4. Explain how allocation of support service costs is useful for planning and control.

5. Assume that a company has decided not to allocate any support service costs to producing departments. Describe the likely behavior of the managers of the producing departments. Would this be good or bad? Explain why allocation would correct this type of behavior.
6. Explain how allocating support service costs will encourage service departments to operate more efficiently.

7. Why is it important to identify and use causal factors to allocate support service costs?
8. Identify some possible causal factors for the following support departments:
   a. Cafeteria
   b. Custodial services
   c. Laundry
   d. Receiving, shipping, and stores
   e. Maintenance
   f. Personnel
   g. Accounting
9. Explain why it is better to allocate budgeted support service costs rather than actual support service costs.
10. Why is it desirable to allocate variable costs and fixed costs separately?

11. Explain why either normal or peak capacity of the producing (or user) departments should be used to allocate the fixed costs of support departments.
12. Explain why variable bases should not be used to allocate fixed costs.
13. Why is the dual rate charging method better than the single rate method? In what circumstances would it not matter whether dual or single rates were used?
14. Explain the difference between the direct method and the sequential method.
15. The reciprocal method of allocation is more accurate than either the direct or sequential methods. Do you agree? Explain.

EXERCISES AND PROBLEMS

6-1
Classifying Departments as Producing or Support
LO 1

Classify each of the following departments in a factory as a producing department or a support department.

a. Assembly   P
b. Payroll   S
c. Cafeteria   S
d. General factory   S
e. Maintenance   S
f. Machining   P
g. Inspection   S
h. Blending   P

i. Finishing   P
j. Personnel   S
k. Grounds   S
l. Data processing → support (tickets, reports)
m. Packaging   P
n. Cutting   P
o. Engineering   S (separate dept)   support

6-2
Objectives of Cost Allocation
LO 2

Dr. Fred Poston, "Dermatologist to the Stars," has a practice in Southern California. The practice includes three dermatologists, three medical assistants, an office manager and a receptionist. The office space, which is rented for $5,000 per month, is large enough to accommodate four dermatologists, but Dr. Poston has not yet found the right fourth M.D. Dr. Poston developed a skin cleanser for his patients that is nongreasy and does not irritate skin still recovering from the effects of chemical peels and dermabrasion. The cleanser requires $0.50 of ingredients per 8-ounce bottle. A medical assistant mixes up several bottles at a time during lulls in her schedule. She waits until she has about fifteen minutes free and then mixes ten bottles of cleanser. She is paid $2,250 per month. Dr. Poston charges $5.00 per bottle and sells approximately 5,000 bottles annually. His accountant is considering various ways of costing the skin cleanser.

REQUIRED:

1. Give two reasons for allocating overhead cost to the cleanser. How should the cost of the office space and receptionist's salary be allocated to the cleanser? Explain.
2. Suppose that *Healthy You* magazine runs an article on Dr. Poston and his skin cleanser, which causes demand to skyrocket. Women across the country buy the cleanser via phone or mail order. Now Dr. Poston believes that he can sell about 40,000 bottles annually. He can hire someone part-time, for $1,000 per month, to mix and bottle the cleanser and to handle the financial business of the cleanser. An unused office and examining room can be dedicated to the production of the cleanser. Would your allocation choice for Requirement 1 change in this case? Explain.

6-3
Objectives of
Allocation
LO 2

Elena and Lee are taking a ski trip to Angel Fire, New Mexico, right after Christmas. They are driving Elena's car and estimate that the trip will have the following costs:

Gas (total)	$ 30
Lift tickets (each)	150
Motel (five nights)	450
Food (each)	100

They have reservations at the Snowfire Inn, which charges $75 per night for a single, $90 per night for a double, and $5 per night if a rollaway bed is added to a double room.

Elena's little sister, Jennifer, wants to go along. She doesn't ski but thinks that five days of relaxing in hot tubs and of apres ski partying would be a great way to unwind after finals. She figures that she could ride with Lee and Elena and share their room.

REQUIRED:

1. Using incremental costs only, what would it cost Jennifer to accompany Elena and Lee?
2. Using the benefits received method, what would it cost Jennifer to go on the trip?

6-4
Single and Dual
Charging Rates
LO 3

James Bodreau owns a strip mall in a suburb of Denver. Of the 12 store spaces in the mall, seven are rented by boutique owners and five are vacant. James has decided that offering more services to stores in the mall would enable him to increase occupancy. He has decided to use one of the vacant spaces to provide, at cost, a gift-wrapping service to shops in the mall. The boutiques are enthusiastic about the new service. Most of them are staffed minimally, which means that every time they have to wrap a gift, phones go unanswered and other customers in line grow impatient. James figured that the gift-wrapping service would incur the following costs. The store space would normally rent for $1,500 per month. Part-time gift wrappers could be hired for $1,000 per month. Wrapping paper and ribbon would average $0.50 per gift. The boutique owners estimated the following number of gifts to be wrapped per month.

Store	Number of Gifts Wrapped Per Month
Candles, Etc.	200
Dream Weaver Gift Shoppe	300
Back-in-the-Saddle Westernwear	100
Cuppa Java Gourmet Coffees	70
Shoe You	50
Dana's Sportswear	130
Penelope's Secret	150

After the service had been in effect for six months, James calculated the following actual average monthly number of gifts wrapped for each of the stores.

Store	Actual Number of Gifts Wrapped Per Month
Candles, Etc.	170
Dream Weaver Gift Shoppe	310
Back-in-the-Saddle Westernwear	240
Cuppa Java Gourmet Coffees	10
Shoe You	50
Dana's Sportswear	200
Penelope's Secret	450

REQUIRED:

1. Calculate a single charging rate, on a per-gift basis, to be charged to the shops. Based on the shops' actual number of gifts wrapped, how much would be charged to each shop using the single charging rate?
2. Based on the shops' actual number of gifts wrapped, how much would be charged to each shop using the dual charging rate?
3. Which shops would prefer the single charging rate? Why? Which would prefer the dual charging rate and why?
4. Several of the shop owners were angry about their bill for the gift-wrapping service. They pointed out that they were to be charged only for the cost of the service. How could you make a case for them?

6-5
Actual Versus Budgeted Costs
LO 3

Bartlett Manufacturing Company evaluates managers of producing departments on their ability to control costs. In addition to the costs directly traceable to their departments, each production manager is held responsible for a share of the costs of a support center, the maintenance department. The total costs of the maintenance department are allocated on the basis of actual maintenance hours used. The total costs of maintenance and the actual hours used by each producing department are given below.

	1997	1998
Maintenance hours used:		
Department A	2,000	2,000
Department B	3,000	2,000
Total hours	5,000	4,000
Actual maintenance cost	$100,000	$100,000
Budgeted maintenance cost	$ 90,000*	$ 80,000*

*$10 per maintenance hour plus $40,000.

REQUIRED:

1. Allocate the maintenance costs to each producing department for 1997 and 1998 using the direct method with actual maintenance hours and actual maintenance costs.
2. Discuss the following statement: "The costs of maintenance increased by 25 percent for Department A and decreased by over 16 percent for Department B. Thus, the manager of Department B must be controlling maintenance costs better than the manager of Department A."
3. Can you think of a way of allocating maintenance costs so that a more reasonable and fair assessment of cost control can be made? Explain.

6-6
Fixed and Variable Cost Allocation
LO 3

Refer to the data in **6-5**. When the capacity of the maintenance department was originally established, the normal usage expected for each department was 2,000 maintenance hours. This usage is also the amount of activity planned for the two departments in 1997 and 1998.

REQUIRED:

1. Allocate the costs of the maintenance department using the direct method and assuming that the purpose is product costing.
2. Allocate the costs of the maintenance department using the direct method and assuming that the purpose is to evaluate performance.

6-7

Direct Method and Overhead Rates

LO 4

Finlither Company manufactures men's and women's shoes, with each type of shoe produced in separate departments. Three support departments support the production departments: maintenance, building and grounds, and food services. Budgeted data on the five departments are as follows:

	Support Departments			Producing Departments	
	Maintenance	Grounds	Food	Men's Shoes	Women's Shoes
Overhead	$30,000	$70,000	$50,000	$20,000	$30,000
Number of employees	5	2	3	15	25
Square feet	2,000	—	3,000	6,750	8,250
Machine hours	—	—	—	2,000	3,000

The company does not break overhead into fixed and variable components.

REQUIRED:

1. Allocate the overhead costs to the producing departments using the direct method.
2. Using machine hours, compute departmental overhead rates.

6-8

Sequential Method

LO 4

Refer to the data in **6-7**. The company has decided to use the sequential method of allocation instead of the direct method.

REQUIRED:

1. Allocate the overhead costs to the producing departments using the sequential method.
2. Using machine hours, compute departmental overhead rates.

6-9

Reciprocal Method

LO 4

Mycles Company has two producing departments and two support centers. The following budgeted data pertain to these four departments:

	Support Departments		Producing Departments	
	Maintenance	Power	Grinding	Polishing
Overhead	$72,000	$30,000	$50,000	$ 80,000
Maintenance hours	—	3,000	6,000	6,000
Kilowatt hours	25,000	—	67,500	157,500
Direct labor hours	—	—	20,000	30,000

REQUIRED:

1. Allocate the overhead costs of the support departments to the producing departments using the reciprocal method.
2. Using direct labor hours, compute departmental overhead rates.

6-10

Direct Method

LO 4

Refer to the data in **6-9**. The company has decided to simplify its method of allocating support service costs by switching to the direct method.

REQUIRED:

1. Allocate the costs of the support departments to the producing departments using the direct method.
2. Using direct labor hours, compute departmental overhead rates. Which rate do you consider more accurate—the one using the reciprocal method or the one using the direct method? Explain.

6-11

Sequential Method

LO 4

Refer to the data in **6-9**.

REQUIRED:

1. Allocate the costs of the support departments using the sequential method.
2. Using direct labor hours, compute departmental overhead rates.

6-12

Allocation: Fixed and Variable Costs

LO 3

Thummer Temporary Employment Agency has two Texas offices, one in Dallas and one in Austin. The owner of the agency purchased a minicomputer and established a computer service center in Dallas. Arrangements were made with the phone company so that the Austin office has access to the system. The computer service center has budgeted fixed costs of $85,000 per year and a budgeted variable rate of $20 per hour of CPU time. The normal usage of the computer is 1,500 hours per year for the Dallas office and 1,200 hours per year for the Austin office. This corresponds to the expected usage for the coming year.

REQUIRED:

1. Determine the amount of computer service costs that should be assigned to each office.
2. Since the offices produce services, not tangible products, what purpose is served by allocating the budgeted costs? Should each office compute a predetermined overhead rate? If so, how would each use this rate?

6-13

Allocation: Budgeted Fixed and Variable Costs

LO 3

Refer to **6-12**. Assume that during the year, the computer service center incurred actual fixed costs of $90,000 and actual variable costs of $62,350. It delivered 3,000 hours of CPU time, 1,600 hours to Dallas and 1,400 to Austin.

REQUIRED:

1. Determine the amount of the support center's costs that should be allocated to each office. Explain the purposes of this allocation.
2. Did the costs allocated differ from the costs incurred by the support center? If so, why?

6-14

Allocation: Fixed and Variable Costs

LO 3

Walters Company is a medium-sized advertising firm on the West Coast. Walters has three departments that specialize in advertising and public relations services for different markets: Tangible Goods (headed by Sherri Donaldson); Nonprofit Organizations (headed by Mike Adams); and Public Relations (headed by Carla Wilson). Previously, Walters had subcontracted out necessary printing and graphics work. However, recent technological advances in desktop publishing led to the formation of a new in-house graphics department, which could produce brochures, booklets, posters, etc. The Tangible Goods and Public Relations departments immediately began to use the new graphics services. Nonprofit Organizations, however, was reluctant to switch from its traditional outsider supplier. Jim Walters, president and CEO of Walters Company, encouraged all departments "to get on board" with Graphics. Paul Murphy, the head of Graphics, assured Mike Adams that Graphics could serve Mike's departmental needs by spending an additional $2,000 above total 1997 costs. So during 1998, Mike Adams decided to give Graphics a try.

Data for the Graphics Department are as follows:

	1997	1998
Actual costs	$12,000	$14,000
DLH used by:		
Tangible goods	2,000	2,000
Public relations	2,000	2,000
Nonprofit organizations	—	1,000

Actual costs equaled budgeted costs in both 1997 and 1998. Graphics services are charged to using departments on the basis of actual cost per hour of graphics time used.

REQUIRED:

1. What was the graphics rate per hour charged in 1997? In 1998?
2. How much was the nonprofit department charged for graphics services in 1998? How did Mike Adams feel about it?
3. How can you reconcile the difference between the rate charged Mike Adams during 1998 and the $2,000 incremental cost cited by Paul Murphy?

6-15
Direct Method, Variable Versus Fixed; Costing and Performance Evaluation
LO 3, 4

AirBorne is a small airline operating out of Boise, Idaho. Its three flights travel to Salt Lake City, Reno, and Portland. The owner of the airline wants to assess the full cost of operating each flight. As part of this assessment, the costs of two support departments (baggage and maintenance) must be allocated to the three flights. The two support departments that support all three flights are located in Boise (any baggage or maintenance costs at the destination airports are directly traceable to the individual flights). Budgeted and actual data for 1997 are as follows for the support departments and the three flights:

	Support Centers		Flights		
	Maintenance	Baggage	Salt Lake City	Reno	Portland
Budgeted data:					
Fixed overhead	$240,000	$150,000	$20,000	$18,000	$30,000
Variable overhead	$30,000	$64,000	$5,000	$10,000	$6,000
Number of passengers*	—	—	10,000	15,000	5,000
Hours of flight time*	—	—	2,000	4,000	2,000
Actual data:					
Fixed overhead	$235,000	$156,000	$22,000	$17,000	$29,500
Variable overhead	$80,000	$33,000	$6,200	$11,000	$5,800
Number of passengers	—	—	8,000	16,000	6,000
Hours of flight time	—	—	1,800	4,200	2,500

*Normal activity levels

REQUIRED:

1. Using the direct method, allocate the support service costs to each flight, assuming that the objective is to determine the cost of operating each flight.
2. Using the direct method, allocate the support service costs to each flight, assuming that the objective is to evaluate performance. Do any costs remain in the two support departments after the allocation? If so, how much? Explain.

6-16
Comparison of Methods of Allocation
LO 4

Paulos Trucking is divided into two operating divisions: Perishable Foods and Household Goods. The company allocates Personnel and Accounting costs to each operating division. Personnel costs are allocated on the basis of number of employees and Accounting costs on the basis of the number of transactions processed. No effort is made to separate fixed and variable costs; however, only budgeted costs are allocated. Allocations for the coming year are based on the following data:

	Support Departments		Operating Divisions	
	Personnel	Accounting	Foods	Goods
Overhead costs	$100,000	$205,000	$80,000	$50,000
Number of employees	20	60	60	80
Transactions processed	2,000	200	3,000	5,000

REQUIRED:

1. Allocate the support service costs using the direct method.
2. Allocate the support service costs using the sequential method.
3. Allocate the support service costs using the reciprocal method.

6-17
Comparison of Methods of Allocation
LO 4, 5

Kare Foods Company specializes in the production of frozen dinners. The first of the two operating departments cooks the food. The second is responsible for packaging and freezing the dinners. The dinners are sold by the case, each case containing 25 dinners.

Two support departments provide support for Kare's operating units: Maintenance and Power. Budgeted data for the coming quarter are given below. The company does not separate fixed and variable costs.

	Support Departments		Producing Departments	
	Maintenance	Power	Cooking	Packaging and Freezing
Overhead costs	$340,000	$200,000	$ 75,000	$55,000
Machine hours	—	40,000	40,000	20,000
Kilowatt hours	20,000	—	100,000	80,000
Direct labor hours	—	—	5,000	30,000

The predetermined overhead rate for Cooking is computed on the basis of machine hours; direct labor hours are used for Packaging and Freezing. The prime costs for one case of standard dinners total $16. It takes 2 machine hours to produce a case of dinners in the Cooking Department and 0.5 direct labor hour to process a case of standard dinners in the Packaging and Freezing Department.

Recently, the Air Force has requested a bid on a three-year contract that would supply standard frozen dinners to Minuteman missile officers and staff on duty in the field. The locations of the missile sites were remote, and the Air Force had decided that frozen dinners were the most economical means of supplying food to personnel on duty.

The bidding policy of Kare Foods is full manufacturing cost plus 20 percent. Assume that the lowest bid of other competitors is $48.80 per case.

REQUIRED:

1. Prepare bids for Kare Foods using each of the following allocation methods:
   a. Direct method
   b. Sequential method
   c. Reciprocal method
2. Refer to Requirement 1. Did all three methods produce winning bids? If not, explain why. Which method most accurately reflects the cost of producing the cases of dinners? Why?

6-18
Predetermined Rates; Allocation for Performance Evaluation
LO 5

Morsley Company operates three vehicle rental divisions: Budget, Luxury, and Trucks. The Budget Division specializes in renting compact and subcompact cars; the Luxury Division specializes in renting large, luxury cars and vans; and the Truck Division rents pickups and small enclosed trucks for local moving.

Morsley has one support center, which is responsible for the service, maintenance, and cleanup of its fleet of vehicles. The costs of this support center are allocated to each operating unit on the basis of total miles driven. During the first quarter, the support center was expected to spend a total of $40,000. Of this total, $16,000 was viewed as being fixed. During the quarter, the support center incurred actual variable costs of $30,000 and actual fixed costs of $17,100.

The normal and actual miles logged for each rental unit during the first quarter are as follows:

	Budget	Luxury	Truck
Normal activity	120,000	100,000	80,000
Actual activity	150,000	110,000	100,000

REQUIRED:

1. Compute the predetermined support service cost per mile driven.
2. Compute the costs that would be allocated at the end of the quarter for purposes of performance evaluation.
3. Identify the costs of the support center that were not allocated to the three rental divisions. Why were these costs not allocated to the operating units?

6-19

Fixed and Variable Cost Allocation

LO 3

Sonora Sam's is a chain of restaurants serving Sonora-style Mexican food in a family-type atmosphere. The chain has grown from one restaurant in 1993 to five restaurants located in west Texas and New Mexico. In 1998, the owner of the company decided to set up an internal accounting department to centralize control of financial information. (Previously, local CPAs handled each restaurant's bookkeeping and financial reporting.) The accounting office was opened in January 1998 by renting space adjacent to corporate headquarters in Albuquerque, New Mexico. All restaurants have been supplied with PC's and modems by which to transfer information to central accounting on a weekly basis.

The Accounting Department has budgeted fixed costs of $64,000 per year. Variable costs are budgeted at $18 per hour. In 1998, actual cost for the Accounting Department was $131,500. Further information is as follows:

	Actual Revenues 1997	Actual Revenues 1998	Actual Hours of Accounting Used in 1998
El Paso	$337,500	$390,500	1,475
Albuquerque	450,000	456,000	400
Taos	360,000	375,000	938
Tucumcari	540,000	550,000	562
Amarillo	562,500	549,000	375

REQUIRED:

1. Suppose the total costs of the accounting department are allocated on the basis of 1998 sales revenue. How much will be allocated to each restaurant?
2. Suppose that Sonora Sam's views 1997 sales figures as a proxy for budgeted capacity of the restaurants. Thus, fixed accounting center costs are allocated on the basis of 1997 sales, and variable costs are allocated according to 1998 usage multiplied by the variable rate. How much accounting department cost will be allocated to each restaurant?
3. Comment on the two allocation schemes. Which restaurants would prefer Method 1? Method 2? Explain.

6-20

Fixed and Variable Rates

LO 3

Bally Company is a conglomerate with multiple divisions manufacturing unrelated products. Bally has decided to set up a corporate legal department to handle all legal matters for Bally and certain routine legal matters for the divisions (e.g., patent applications). The new corporate legal department has estimated fixed costs of $210,000 per year and variable costs of $14 per hour. Four divisions have indicated willingness to use the new legal department and have budgeted the following annual time requirements:

Great West Tissue	500
Morton Canned Meats	1,500
Pettigrew Valve and Tap	3,000
Bellini Musical Instruments	1,000

After the first year of operations, the legal department had actual fixed costs of $215,000 and variable costs of $83,145. The actual time usage of the legal department by the four divisions was:

Great West Tissue	25
Morton Canned Meats	1,400
Pettigrew Valve and Tap	3,600
Bellini Musical Instruments	1,000

REQUIRED:

1. Using the single rate method, develop a charging rate for the legal department. Using this rate and actual usage, how much was charged to the four divisions over the course of the first year?
2. Using the dual rate method, develop a charging rate for the legal department to be used for product costing. Using the dual rate, how much was charged to the four divisions over the course of the first year?
3. Using the dual rate method, evaluate the performance of the legal department for the first year. Did the department come in over or under budget and by how much?
4. Explain which charging method you think should be used.

6-21
Single Charging Rates

LO 3

House Corporation Board (HCB) of Tri-Gamma Sorority is responsible for the operation of a two-story sorority house on the State University campus. HCB has set a normal capacity of 60 women. At any given point in time, there are 100 members of the chapter, 60 living in house and 40 living elsewhere (e.g., in the freshman dorms on campus). HCB needs to set rates for the use of the house for the coming year. The following costs are budgeted: $240,000 fixed and $34,800 variable. The fixed costs are fairly insensitive to the number of women living in the house. Food is budgeted at $40,000 and is included in the fixed costs; food does not seem to vary greatly given the stated capacity. The variable expenses consist of telephone bills and some of the utilities. HCB is not responsible for Chapter dues, party fees, pledging and initiation fees, and other social expenditures. Women living in the house eat 20 meals per week there and live in a 2-person room (all in-house members' rooms, bathroom facilities, etc., are on the second floor). All members eat Monday dinner at the house and have full use of house facilities (e.g., the two TV lounges, kitchens, access to milk and cereal at any time, study facilities, and so on).

HCB has traditionally set two rates: one for in-house members and one for out-of-house members. There are 32 weeks in a school year.

REQUIRED:

1. Discuss the factors that might go into determining the charging rate for the two types of sorority members.
2. Set charging rates for the in-house and out-of-house members.

6-22
Direct Method, Reciprocal Method, Overhead Rates

LO 4, 5

Barrylou Corporation is developing departmental overhead rates based upon direct labor hours for its two production departments—Molding and Assembly. The Molding Department employs 20 people, and the Assembly Department employs 80 people. Each person in these two departments works 2,000 hours per year. The production-related overhead costs for the Molding Department are budgeted at $200,000, and the Assembly Department costs are budgeted at $320,000. Two support departments—Repair and Power—directly support the two production departments and have budgeted costs of $48,000 and $250,000, respectively. The production departments' overhead rates cannot be determined until the support departments' costs are properly allocated. The following schedule reflects the use of the Repair Department's and Power Department's output by the various departments.

	Repair	Power	Molding	Assembly
Repair hours	0	1,000	1,000	8,000
Kilowatt hours	240,000	0	840,000	120,000

REQUIRED:

1. Calculate the overhead rates per direct labor hour for the Molding Department and the Assembly Department using the direct allocation method to charge the production departments for support department cost.
2. Calculate the overhead rates per direct labor hour for the Molding Department and the Assembly Department using the reciprocal method to charge support department costs to each other and to the production departments.
3. Explain the difference between the methods, and indicate the arguments generally presented to support the reciprocal method over the direct allocation method.

(CMA adapted)

6-23
Case Using a Hospital Setting; Allocation Methods; Unit Cost Determination and Pricing Decisions

LO 3, 4

Paula Barneck, the newly appointed director of the Lambert Medical Center (LMC), a large metropolitan hospital, was reviewing the financial report for the most recent quarter. The hospital had again shown a loss. For the past several years, it had been struggling financially. The financial problems had begun with the introduction of the federal government's new diagnostic-related group (DRG) reimbursement system. Under this system, the government mandated fixed fees for specific treatments or illnesses. The fixed fees were supposed to represent what the procedures should cost and differed from the traditional cost objective of the patient day of prior years. Although no formal assessment had been made, the general feeling of hospital management was that the DRG reimbursement was hurting LMC's financial state.

The increasing popularity of health maintenance organizations (HMOs) and physician provider organizations (PPOs) was also harming the hospital's financial well-being. In HMOs, physicians, who are employed full time, are usually located in a clinic owned by the HMO, and subscribers must use these physicians. In PPOs, hospitals provide contracts with a group of physicians in private practice. These physicians usually serve non-PPO patients as well as PPO patients. The PPO patient can select any physician from the list of physicians under contract with the particular PPO. The PPO approach usually offers a greater selection of physicians and tends to preserve the patient's traditional freedom of choice. More and more of the hospital's potential patients were joining HMOs and PPOs, and, unfortunately, LMC was not capturing its fair share of the HMO and PPO business. HMOs and PPOs routinely asked for bids on hospital services and provided their business to the lowest bidder. In too many cases, LMC had not won that work.

Paula had accepted the position of hospital administrator knowing that she was expected to produce dramatic improvements in LMC's financial state. She was convinced that she needed more information about the hospital's product-costing methods. Only by having accurate cost information for the various procedures offered by the hospital could she evaluate the effects of DRG reimbursement and the hospital's bidding strategy.

Paula requested a meeting with Eric Rose, the hospital's controller. The following is their conversation:

Paula: Eric, as you know, we recently lost a bid on some laboratory tests that would be performed on a regular basis for a local HMO. In fact, I was told by the director of the HMO that we had the highest bid of the three submitted. I know the identity of the other two hospitals that submitted bids, and I have a hard time believing that their costs for these tests are any lower than ours. Describe exactly how we determine the cost of these lab procedures.

Eric: First, we classify all departments as either revenue-producing centers or service centers. Next, the costs of the service centers are allocated to the revenue-producing centers. The costs directly traceable to the revenue-producing centers are then added to the allocated costs to obtain the total cost of operating the revenue-producing center. This total cost is divided by the total revenues of the revenue-producing center to obtain a cost-to-charges ratio. Finally, the cost of a particular procedure is computed by multiplying the charge for that procedure by the cost-to-charges ratio.

Paula: Let me see if I understand. The costs of laundry, housekeeping, maintenance, and other service departments are allocated to all of the revenue-producing departments. Let's assume that the lab receives $100,000 as its share of these allocated costs. The $100,000 is then added to the direct costs—let's assume these are also $100,000—to obtain total operating costs of $200,000. If the laboratory earns revenues of $250,000, the cost-to-charges ratio is 0.80 ($200,000/$250,000). Finally, if I want to know the cost of a particular lab procedure, say a blood test for which we normally charge $20, then all I do is multiply the cost-to-charges ratio of 0.8 by $20 to obtain the cost of $16. Am I right?

Eric: Absolutely. In that bid we lost, our bid was at cost, as computed using our cost-to-charges formula. Perhaps the other hospitals are bidding below their cost to capture the business.

Paula: Eric, I don't agree. The cost-to-charges ratio is a traditional approach for costing hospital products, but I'm afraid that it is no longer useful. Given the new environment in which we're operating, we need more accurate product-costing information. We need accuracy to improve our bidding, to help us assess and deal with the new DRG reimbursement system, and to evaluate the mix of services we offer. The cost-to-charges ratio approach backs into the product cost. It is indirect and inaccurate. Some procedures require more labor, more materials, and more expensive equipment than others. The cost-to-charges approach doesn't reflect these potential differences.

Eric: Well, I'm willing to change the cost accounting system so that it meets our needs. Do you have any suggestions?

Paula: Yes. I'm in favor of a more direct computation of product costs. Allocating support service costs to the revenue-producing departments is only the first stage in product costing. We do need to allocate these support service costs to the producing departments—but we need to be certain that we are allocating them in the right way. We also need to go a step further and assign the costs accumulated in the revenue-producing departments to individual products. The costs directly traceable to each product should be identified and assigned directly to those products; indirect costs can be assigned through one or more overhead rates. The base for assigning the overhead costs should be associated with their incurrence. If at all possible, allocations should reflect the usage of support services by the revenue-producing departments; moreover, the same criterion should govern the assignment of overhead costs to the products within the department.

Eric: Sounds like an interesting challenge. With over 30,000 products, a job-order system would be too burdensome and costly. I think some system can be developed, however, that will do essentially what you want.

Paula: Good. Listen, for our next meeting, come prepared to brief me on why and how you allocate these service department costs to the revenue-producing departments. I think this is a critical step in accurate product costing. I also want to know how you propose to assign the costs accumulated in each revenue-producing department to that department's products.

As Eric mentally reviewed his meeting with Paula, he realized that the failure of bids could be attributable to inaccurate cost assignments. Because of this possibility, Eric decided to do some additional investigation to see if the cost-to-charges ratio method of costing services was responsible.

Eric pulled the current year's budgeted data from his files. He found the data presented below. The number of departments and the budget have been reduced for purposes of simplification.

	Support Departments			Revenue Departments	
	Administrative	Laundry	Janitorial	Laboratory	Nursing
Overhead	$20,000	$75,000	$50,000	$43,000	$150,000
Square feet	1,000	1,200	500	5,000	20,000
Pounds of laundry	50	200	400	1,000	4,000
Employees	1	4	7	8	20

Support department costs are allocated using the direct method.

Eric decided to compute the costs of three different lab tests using the cost-to-charges ratio and then recompute them using a more direct method, as suggested by Paula. By comparing the unit costs under each approach, he could evaluate the cost-estimating ability of the cost-to-charges ratio. The three tests selected for study were the blood count test (Test B), cholesterol test (Test C), and a chemical blood analysis (Test CB).

After careful observation of the three tests, Eric concluded that the consumption of the resources of the laboratory could be associated with the relative amount of time taken by each test. Based on the amount of time needed to perform each test, Eric developed relative value units (RVUs) and associated the consumption of materials and labor with these units. The RVUs for each test and the cost per RVU for materials and labor are given below:

Test	RVUs	Material Per RVU	Labor Per RVU
B	1	$2.00	$2.00
C	2	2.50	2.00
CB	3	1.00	2.00

Eric also concluded that the pool of overhead costs collected within the laboratory should be applied using RVUs (he was convinced that RVU was a good activity driver for overhead). The laboratory's expected RVUs for the year were 22,500. The laboratory usually performs an equal number of the three tests over a year. This year was no exception.

Eric also noted that the hospital usually priced its services so that revenues exceeded costs by a specified percentage. Based on the past total costs of the laboratory, this pricing strategy had led to the following fees for the three blood tests:

	Test B	Test C	Test CB
Fees charged	$5.00	$19.33	$22.00

REQUIRED:

1. Allocate the costs of the support departments to the two revenue-producing departments using the direct method.
2. Assuming that the three blood tests are the only tests performed in the laboratory, compute the cost-to-charges ratio (total costs of the laboratory divided by the laboratory's total revenues).
3. Using the cost-to-charges ratio computed in Requirement 2, estimate the cost per test for each blood test.
4. Compute the cost per test for each test using RVUs.
5. Which unit cost—the one using the cost-to-charges ratio or the one using RVUs—do you think is the most accurate? Explain.
6. Assume that Lambert Medical Center has been requested by an HMO to bid on Test CB. Using a 5 percent markup, prepare the bid using the cost computed in Requirement 3. Repeat, using the cost prepared in Requirement 4. Suppose that anyone who bids $20 or less will win the bid. Discuss the implications that costing accuracy have on the hospital's problems with its bidding practices.

Chapter 7
Joint Product and By-product Costing

International Flavors and Fragrances extracts flavor and scent essences from many sources. Strawberry plants yield a variety of joint products. The fruit and juice can go to canners, and strawberry essence is used in shampoos and aerosol room fresheners.

LEARNING OBJECTIVES

1. Identify the characteristics of the joint production process.
2. Allocate joint product costs according to the benefits-received approaches and the relative market value approaches.
3. Describe methods of accounting for by-products.
4. Explain why joint cost allocations may be misleading in management decision making.
5. Discuss why joint production is seldom found in service industries.

While numerous manufacturing plants produce multiple products, some are characterized by a production process in which two or more products result simultaneously from the use of one raw material. This is the case of joint production. When joint production occurs, accountants must determine how to allocate the cost of the common raw material to the jointly produced products.

GENERAL CHARACTERISTICS OF JOINT PRODUCTION

Objective 1

Identify the characteristics of the joint production process.

joint products
split-off point

Joint products are two or more products produced simultaneously by the same process up to a "split-off" point. The **split-off point** is the point at which the joint products become separate and identifiable. For example, in the meat-packing industry, packers have long boasted that they use every part of the pig but the squeal. When the raw material, a hog, is started into production, labor and overhead costs are incurred to the initial split-off point. Such costs are necessary to convert the hog into: hides, dressed meat, bones for fertilizer, hooves for gelatin, and so on. The costs of raising, slaughtering, and butchering the hogs are common to all products. Different processes can then be followed to obtain a myriad of additional products. Of course, some of the joint products may require processing beyond the split-off point. The key point, however, is that the raw material, labor, and overhead costs incurred up to the initial split-off point are joint costs that can be allocated to the final product only in some arbitrary manner. Joint products are so enmeshed that once the decision to produce has been made, management decision has little effect on the output, at least to the initial split-off point. Exhibit 7-1 depicts the joint production process. Exhibit 7-2 depicts the usual production process in which two products are manufactured independently from a common raw material. For example, a Taurus and a Mustang require steel, but the purchase of steel by Ford Motor Company does not require the manufacture of either model.

Joint products are related to each other such that an increase in the output of one increases the output of the others, although not necessarily in the same ratio.

Exhibit 7-1
Joint Production Process

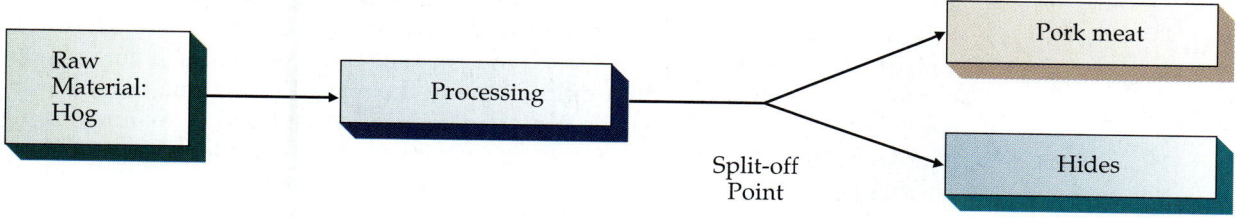

Exhibit 7-2
Independent Multiple-Product Production Using the Same Raw Material

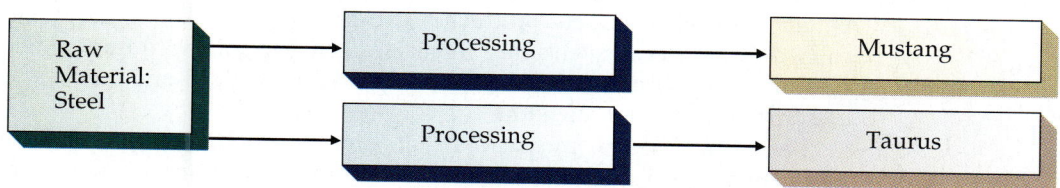

In the meat-packing industry, the relationship among some of the ultimate products is variable to a greater or lesser degree after the initial split-off point. Management can decide, beyond that point, to produce more sausage and fewer pork roasts, for example, or vary the final output in a number of other ways. Up to the initial split-off point, however, the relationship is relatively fixed and invariable.

Whether considering the raw materials and conversion costs incurred prior to the initial split-off point as depicted in Exhibit 7-1, or the costs of heat, fuel, and depreciation incurred in the type of multiple-product production depicted in Exhibit 7-2, one characteristic stands out. They are all indirect costs in the sense that allocation among the various products is necessary: that is, such costs cannot be traced directly to the ultimate products they benefit.

Cost Separability and the Need for Allocation

separable costs

Costs are either separable or not. **Separable costs** are easily traced to individual products and offer no particular problem. If not separable, they must be *allocated* to various products for various reasons. Cost allocations are arbitrary. That is, there is no well-accepted theoretical way to determine which product incurs what part of the joint cost. In reality, all joint products benefit from the entire joint cost. Our objective in joint cost allocation is to determine the most appropriate way to allocate a cost that is not really separable. Why do we allocate joint costs? The primary reason is that financial reporting (GAAP) and federal income tax law require it. As we will see later, the allocation of joint cost is not appropriate for certain types of management decisions. The basic output of the joint cost allocation process is the determination of product costs for use in income measurement and inventory valuation. In addition, these product costs are somewhat useful in calculating the cost of special lots or orders including government cost-type contracts and in justifying prices for legislative or administrative regulations.

There are two important differences between costs incurred up to the split-off point in joint product situations and those indirect costs incurred for products that are produced independently. First, certain costs such as raw materials and direct labor, which are directly traceable to products when two or more products are separately produced, become indirect and indivisible when used prior to the split-off point to produce joint products. For example, if ore contains both iron and zinc, the raw material itself is a joint product. Since neither zinc nor iron can be produced alone prior to the split-off point, the related processing costs of mining, crushing, and splitting the ore are also joint costs. Second, manufacturing overhead becomes even more indirect in joint product situations. Consider the purchase of pineapples. A pineapple, in and of itself, is not a joint product. However, when pineapples are purchased for canning, the initial processing or trimming of the fruit results in a variety of products (skin for animal feed, trimmed core for further slicing and dicing, and juice). The processing (conversion) costs to the point of split-off, as well as the cost of the original pineapples, are mutually beneficial to all products produced to that point. Both of these phenomena are caused either because the raw material itself is a joint product or because processing results in the simultaneous output of more than one product, or because of some combination of both.

Let's examine the implications of joint production for overhead in a little more detail. Suppose that there is a support department, Maintenance, which repairs and maintains production machinery throughout the factory. If pineapple juice is cooked and bottled in the Bottling Department, and pineapple chunks are canned in the Canning Department, the variable costs of the Maintenance Department can be allocated in some manner (e.g., on the basis of maintenance hours worked in each department) to the two products based on their actual need for maintenance. There is a clear cause-and-effect relationship, and allocated maintenance costs would be reliable for management control purposes both in terms of the departments and products involved. If pineapple juice and chunks are produced simultaneously in a department (say, they are cooked in the Canning Department before the juice is sent on to Bottling), the variable costs of the Maintenance Department could still be allocated between the Canning and Bottling departments with the same degree of reliability. Because of the joint product situation in the Canning Department, however, further allocation of maintenance costs between juice and chunks would have to be made on an arbitrary basis. Consequently, the allocations would be unreliable for certain management decisions, such as controlling the costs of juice and chunks. Thus, joint processing may limit the extent to which activity drivers in an activity-based costing system can effectively indicate a cause-and-effect relationship between overhead costs and joint products.

Distinction and Similarity Between Joint Products and By-products

by-product

The distinction between joint and by-products rests solely on the relative importance of their sales value. A **by-product** is a secondary product recovered in the course of manufacturing a primary product. It is a product whose total sales value is relatively minor in comparison with the sales value of the main product(s). This is not a sharp distinction, but rather one of degree. Thus, the first distinction that a manufacturer must make is whether the operation is characterized by joint production. Then any by-products must be distinguished from main or joint products. By-products can be characterized by their relationship to the main products in the following manner:

1. By-product resulting from scrap, trimmings, and so forth, of the main products in essentially nonjoint-product types of undertakings (e.g., fabric trimmings from clothing pieces).
2. Scrap and other residue from essentially joint-product types of processes (e.g., fat trimmed from beef carcasses).
3. A minor joint product situation (fruit skins and trimmings used as animal feed).

Relationships between joint products and by-products change, as do the classes of products within each of these classifications. When the relative importance of the individual products changes, the products need to be reclassified and the costing procedures changed.

As science and technology advance and new methods of production are introduced, new products are developed, some old ones are discarded, and changes are made in the status of others. Today's by-product may be tomorrow's major products, co-products, or scrap. Many by-products begin as waste materials, become economically significant (and thus become by-products), and grow still more important, finally to become full-fledged joint products. For example, sawdust and chips in sawmill operations were originally waste, but over the years, they have gained value as a major component of particle board. The various methods of accounting for by-products reflect this development. Generally, accounting for by-products began as an extension of accounting for waste material. Revenue from the sale of the by-products is recorded as separate income, when the amount of income is so small that it has little impact on either overall cost or sales. As the value of by-product revenues becomes more significant, the cost of the main product is reduced by recoveries, and finally the by-products achieve near main product status and are allocated a share of the joint cost incurred prior to split-off.

Examples of Joint Products and By-products

Significant numbers of industries are involved in joint product and by-product production, usually those in which one raw material is the source of several products. These industries are characterized as predominantly users of process cost accounting systems. Exhibit 7-3 gives examples of such basic industries.

Exhibit 7-3
Industries Involved in Joint and By-product Production

Industry	Joint Products and By-products
Agricultural and Food Industries:	
Flour milling	Patent flour, clear flour, middlings, bran, and wheatgerm
Meat packing	Meat, hides, fertilizer, gelatin, shortening, hair, and many other by-products
Cotton ginning	Cotton fiber and cottonseed
Fishing	Fresh fish, canned fish, fish meal, fish oil, and fertilizer
Cottonseed processing	Cottonseed oil, meal, hulls, and linters
Dairy products	Cream, skim and whole milk, butter, yogurt, ice cream, and other products
Canning	Various grades of fruits and vegetables (e.g., pineapples and tomatoes), juices, animal feed
Extractive Industries:	
Copper mining	Copper, gold, silver, and other metals
Sawmill operation	Several grades of lumber, slabs, and sawdust
Petroleum refining	Naphtha, gasoline, kerosene, diesel and fuel oils, paraffin, tar, and many other products
Gold mining	Gold, silver, copper, and other metals
Chemical Industries:	
Soap making	Soap and glycerine
Coke manufacture	Coke, ammonia, coal tar, gas, benzol, and other products
Manufactured gas	Gas, coke, ammonia, coal tar, and sulfur compounds
Manufacturing:	
Cement	Concrete pipe, block, aggregate
Semiconductors	Memory chips of varying quality (length of life, resistance to temperature change)

Taken from Maryanne M. Mowen, "Joint-Product and By-Product Costs," Chapter 11 of *Management Accountants' Handbook*, 4th edition, edited by D. E. Keller, J. Bulloch, and R. Shultis, John Wiley and Sons, New York, 1992, pp. 11–7 and 11–8.

Competition forces the firm to use its resources efficiently. Therefore, one of the goals of a firm is to completely utilize its raw materials to the extent that this is economically feasible. While waste and scrap are a seemingly inevitable accompaniment of the production process, world-class manufacturers seek to eliminate such waste and to obtain a 100 percent yield from the raw material. Such yield may be in the form of by-products, which make at least some contribution to income. The importance of by-product and joint product analysis is not always evident, particularly where minor products have little value and profit margins on the major product are satisfactory.

ACCOUNTING FOR JOINT PRODUCT COSTS

Objective 2

Allocate joint product costs according to the benefits-received approaches and the relative market value approaches.

The accounting for overall joint costs of production (direct materials, direct labor, and overhead) is no different from the accounting for product costs in general. It is the *allocation* of joint costs to the individual products that is the source of difficulty. Still, the allocation must be done for financial reporting purposes—to value inventory carried on the balance sheet and to determine income. Joint cost allocation is less useful for cost control and managerial decision-making purposes.

A suitable basis for joint cost allocation is necessary to obtain a value for inventory purposes. Although efforts have been made in the past to trace costs prior to split-off individually to the products produced, such an approach has no practical significance, since joint products cannot be produced independently of one another. Thus, an allocation method must be found that, though arbitrary, allocates the costs on as reasonable a basis as possible. Because judgment is involved, equally competent accountants can arrive at different costs for the same product.

Benefits-Received Approaches

Physical units expressing such things as heat content, volume, or weight are used in measuring benefits received, while relative market value approaches are used to measure the ability of individual joint products to absorb joint costs.

physical units method

Physical Units Method Under the **physical units method**, joint costs are distributed to products on the basis of some physical measure. These physical measures may be expressed in units such as pounds, tons, gallons, board feet, atomic weight, and heat units. If the joint products do not share the same physical measure (e.g., one product is measured in gallons, another in pounds), some common denominator may be used. For example, in winery accounting, the various quantities (tons, gallons, cases, and so forth) are reduced to a common denominator, the proof gallon. A proof gallon contains 50% alcohol by volume. Thus, a proof gallon is equal to one measured wine gallon at 100 proof; similarly, a spirit of 150 proof contains 75% alcohol and is equal to 1.5 proof gallons.

Computationally, the physical units method allocates to each joint product the same proportion of joint cost as the underlying proportion of units. So, if a joint process yields 300 pounds of Product A and 700 pounds of Product B, Product A receives 30 percent of the joint cost and Product B receives 70 percent. An alternative computation is to divide total joint costs by total output to find an average unit cost. The average unit cost is then multiplied by the number of units of each product. Although the method is not wholly satisfactory, it has a measure of logic behind it. Since all products are manufactured by the same process, it is impossible to say that one costs more per unit to produce than the other.

For example, suppose that a sawmill processes logs into four grades of lumber totalling 3,000,000 board feet as follows.

Grades	Board Feet
First and second	450,000
No. 1 common	1,200,000
No. 2 common	600,000
No. 3 common	750,000
Total	3,000,000

Total joint cost is $186,000. Using the physical units method, how much joint cost is allocated to each grade of lumber? First we find the proportion each grade is of the total units, then assign each grade its proportion of joint cost.

Grades	Board Feet	Percent of Units	Joint Cost Allocation
First and second	450,000	.15	$ 27,900
No. 1 common	1,200,000	.40	74,400
No. 2 common	600,000	.20	37,200
No. 3 common	750,000	.25	46,500
Totals	3,000,000		$186,000

We could also calculate the average unit cost of $.062 ($186,000/3,000,000) and multiply it by the board feet for each grade.

For example, manufacturers of forest products may add the average cost of logs entering the mill to the average conversion cost to arrive at an average finished product cost. This cost is applied to all finished products, no matter their type, grade, or market value.[1] This method serves the purpose of product costing.

The physical units method may be used in any industry that processes joint products of differing grades (e.g., flour milling, tobacco, and lumber). However, a disadvantage of the physical units method is that high profits may be reflected from the sale of the high grades, with low profits or losses reflected on the sale of lower grades, and results in incorrect managerial decisions, if not properly interpreted.

The physical units method attempts to allocate joint costs according to the benefit received from each of the end products. Thus, each unit of raw material in the final product is presumed to cost just as much to produce as any other. This is especially true where the dominant element can be traced to the product. Many feel this method often is unsatisfactory because it ignores the fact that not all costs are directly related to physical quantities. Also, the product might not have been handled at all if it had been physically separable before the split-off point from the part desired.

1.   Robert M. Simpson, "Forest-Products Industry Accounting," *The Journal of Accountancy,* Vol. 104, September 1957, p. 43.

weight factor

Weighted Average Method In an attempt to overcome the difficulties encountered under the physical unit method, weight factors are often assigned. These weight factors may include such diverse elements as amount of material used, difficulty to manufacture, time consumed, difference in type of labor used, and size of unit. These factors and their relative weights are usually combined in a single value, which we might call the **weight factor**. In the canning industry, the weight factor is given effect in the calculation of a basic case.

In some instances, the weight factor is strictly a quantitative conversion factor, while at the other extreme, the weight factor will reflect purely sales values or net sales values. If only the latter are used, the method approximates the allocation of joint costs on the basis of selling prices alone, as discussed later in this section.

An example of the use of weight factors is found in the canning industry.[2] One type of weight factor is used to convert different-size cases of peaches into a uniform size for purposes of allocating joint costs to each case. Thus, if a basic case contains 24 cans of peaches in size 2½ cans, that case is assigned a weight factor of 1.0. A case with 24 cans of size 303 (a can roughly half as large as the size 2½ can) receives a weight of 0.57, and so on. Once all types of cases have been converted into basic cases using the weight factors, joint costs can be allocated according to the physical units method. Peaches can also be assigned weight factors according to grade (e.g., fancy, choice, standard, and pie). If the standard grade is weighted at 1.00, then the better grades are weighted more heavily and the pie grade less heavily.

Let's construct an example based on grades to illustrate the weighted average method. Suppose that the peach-canning factory purchases $5,000 of peaches, grades them into fancy, choice, standard, and pie quality, then cans each grade. The following data on grade, number of cases, and weight factor apply.

Grade	Number of Cases	Weight Factor	Weighted Number of Cases	Percent	Allocated Joint Cost
Fancy	100	1.30	130	.21667	$1,083
Choice	120	1.10	132	.22000	1,100
Standard	303	1.00	303	.50500	2,525
Pie	70	0.50	35	.05833	292
			600		$5,000

By multiplying the number of cases by the weight factor, we obtain the weighted number of cases. Then the physical units method can be applied as the percentage of weighted cases for each grade is obtained and multiplied by the joint cost to yield allocated joint cost. The effect is to allocate relatively more of the joint cost to the fancy and choice grades because they represent more desirable peaches. The pie grade peaches, the good bits and pieces from bruised peaches, are relatively less desirable and are assigned a lower weight.

Frequently weight factors are predetermined and set up as part of either an estimated cost or a standard cost system. The use of carefully constructed weight factors enables the cost accountant to give more attention to several influences

---

2.   The peach-canning example is adapted from K. E. Jankowski, "Cost and Sales Control in the Canning Industry," N.A.C.A. Bulletin, Vol. 36, November 1954, p. 376.

and therefore results in more reasonable allocations. The real danger, of course, is that weights may be used that are either inappropriate in the first place or become so through the passage of time. Obviously, if arbitrary rates are used, the resulting costs of individual products will be arbitrary.

Allocation Based on Relative Market Value

Many accountants believe that joint costs should be allocated to individual products according to their ability to absorb joint costs. The advantage of this approach is that joint cost allocation will not produce consistently profitable or unprofitable items. The rationale for using ability to bear is the assumption that costs would not be incurred unless the jointly produced products together would yield enough revenue to cover all costs plus a reasonable return. The reverse also would be consistent with this theory; that is, a derived cost that the purchaser of raw materials and other joint costs is willing to incur for any individual product could be obtained by relating costs to sales values. On the other hand, fluctuations in the market value of any one or more of the end products automatically change the apportionment of the joint costs, though actually it costs no more or no less to produce than before.

The relative market value approach to joint cost allocation is better than the physical units approach if two conditions hold: (1) the physical mix of output can be altered by incurring more (less) total joint costs and (2) this alteration produces more (less) total market value.[3] Several variants of the relative market value method are found in practice.

sales-value-at-split-off method

Sales-Value-at-Split-off Method The **sales-value-at-split-off method** allocates joint cost based on each product's proportionate share of market or sales value at the split-off point. Under this method, the higher the market value, the greater the share of joint cost charged against the product. As long as the prices at split-off are stable, or the fluctuations in prices of the various products are synchronized (not necessarily in amount, but in the rate of change), their respective allocated costs remain constant.

Using the same example of lumber mill costs given in the preceding discussion of the physical units method, the joint cost of $186,000 is distributed to the various grades on the basis of their market value at split-off.

Grades	Quantity Produced (board ft.)	Price at Split-off (per 1,000 board ft.)	Sales Value at Split-off	Percent of Total Market Value	Allocated Joint Cost
First and second	450,000	$300	$135,000	.2699	$ 50,201
No. 1 common	1,200,000	200	240,000	.4799	89,261
No. 2 common	600,000	121	72,600	.1452	27,007
No. 3 common	750,000	70	52,500	.1050	19,530
Totals	3,000,000		$500,100	100.00	$185,999*

*Does not sum to $186,000 due to rounding.

3.   William L. Cats-Baril, James F. Gatti, and D. Jacque Grinnell, "Joint Product Costing in the Semiconductor Industry," *Management Accounting*, February 1986, p. 29.

Note that the joint cost is allocated in proportion to sales value at the split-off point. No. 1 common, for example, is valued at $240,000 at split-off, and that amount is 47.99 percent of the total sales value. Therefore, 47.99 percent of total joint cost is assigned to the No. 1 common grade.

The sales-value-at-split-off method can be approximated through the use of weighting factors based on price. The advantage is that the price-based weights do not change as market prices do. An example of this method is found in the glue industry. Raw material is put into process in the Cooking Department. The products from the cooking operations are the several "runs of glue." The first run is of the highest grade, has the highest market value, and costs the least. Successive runs require higher temperatures, cost more, and produce lower grades of products. Glue factories do not attempt to determine the actual cost of each skimming because the effect would be to show the lowest cost on the first grade of product and the highest cost on the lowest grade. Instead, the cost of all glue produced is determined and this total cost is spread over the various grades on the basis of their respective tests of purity. The relative degree of purity is an indicator of the quality and therefore of the market value of each run or grade produced. Hence, multiplying the yield for each run by its relative purity is equivalent to multiplying it by the market value. The amounts weighted by purity are used to allocate the joint costs to each run. Additional runs would be undertaken, of course, only as long as the incremental revenue of the additional run is equal to or exceeds the incremental costs incurred.

The weighting factor based on market value at split-off is conceptually the same as the weighting factor method under physical units. However, in this case, the weighting factor is based on sales value, while the weighting factor described in the physical units section could be based on various other considerations such as processing difficulty, size, and so on. These other considerations may or may not be related to market value.

Net Realizable Value Method When market value is used to allocate joint costs, we are talking about market value *at the split-off point*. However, on occasion, there is no ready market price for the individual products at the split-off point. In this case, the net realizable value method can be used. First, we obtain a **hypothetical sales value** for each joint product by subtracting all separable (or further) processing costs from the eventual market value. This approximates the sales value at split-off. Then, the **net realizable value method** can be used to prorate the joint costs based on each product's share of hypothetical sales value.

hypothetical sales value

net realizable value method

Suppose that a company manufactures two products, Alpha and Beta, from a joint process. One production run costs $5,750 and results in 1,000 gallons of Alpha and 3,000 gallons of Beta. Neither product is salable at split-off, but must be further processed such that the separable cost for Alpha is $1 per gallon and for Beta is $2 per gallon. The eventual market price for Alpha is $5 and for Beta $4. Joint cost allocation using the net realizable value method is as follows.

	Market Price	Further Processing Cost	Hypothetical Market Price	Number of Units	Hypothetical Market Value	Joint Cost Allocated
Alpha	$5	$1	$4	1,000	$ 4,000	$2,300
Beta	4	2	2	3,000	6,000	3,450
					$10,000	$5,750

Note that joint cost is allocated on the basis of each product's share of hypothetical market value. Thus, Alpha receives 40 percent of the joint cost ($2,300) because it accounts for 40 percent of the hypothetical market value. The net realizable value method is particularly useful when one or more products cannot be sold at the split-off point but must be processed further.

Constant Gross Margin Percentage Method The net realizable value method is easy to apply. However, it assigns all profit to the hypothetical market value. In other words, the further processing costs are assumed to have no profit value even though they are critical to selling the products. The **constant gross margin percentage method** corrects for this by recognizing that costs incurred after the split-off point are part of the cost total on which profit is expected to be earned, and it allocates joint cost such that the gross margin percentage is the same for each product.

constant gross margin percentage method

Using the data for Alpha and Beta, we can allocate the $5,750 joint cost using the constant gross margin percentage method. First, total revenues and costs are calculated to determine overall gross profit and the gross profit percentage. Then, revenues for the individual products are adjusted for gross profit, separable costs are deducted, and the resulting figure is the allocated joint cost.

		Percent
Revenue [($5 × 1,000) + ($4 × 3,000)]	$17,000	100%
Costs [$5,750 + ($1 × 1,000) + ($2 × 3,000)]	12,750	75
Gross Profit	$ 4,250	25%

	Alpha	*Beta*
Eventual market value	$5,000	$12,000
Less: Gross margin @ 25% of market value	1,250	3,000
Cost of goods sold	$3,750	$ 9,000
Less: Separable costs	1,000	6,000
Allocated joint costs	$2,750	$ 3,000

The constant gross margin percentage method allocates more joint cost to Beta than did the net realizable value method. This is due to the assumption of a relationship between cost and the cost-created value. That is, the net realizable value assumed no gross profit attributable to further processing costs, while the constant gross margin percentage method assumed not only that further processing yields profit but that it yields an identical profit percentage across products. Which assumption is correct? Two important questions are: first, whether there is a "direct relationship" between cost and value and, second, whether the relationship is necessarily the same for all products jointly produced before and after the split-off point. The practice of product-line pricing to meet competition tends to make such assumptions invalid. Although exceptions exist, many companies do not try to maintain more-or-less equal margins between prices and full costs on their various products.

Sales-to-Production Ratio The demand for joint products may vary from year to year, leaving open the possibility of holding back current-period production costs in inventory—costs representing the slower moving goods. The result is higher reported profits than what would be the case if most of the current-period production costs were assigned to products that were selling. An alternative method of allocating joint costs when economic fluctuations affect demand for a company's product has been suggested.[4] The **sales-to-production-ratio method** allocates joint costs in accordance with a weighting factor that compares percentage of sales with percentage of production. This is an ability-to-bear method in that the products that sell the most are allocated a larger share of the joint cost of current production than those products which sell less.

sales-to-production-
ratio method

Exhibit 7-4 shows the allocation of $1,000,000 of joint costs among five products based on the sales-to-production ratio. Note that under this method, less cost is assigned to slower moving goods like Product C, which accounted for 25 percent of production but only 15 percent of sales. A good like Product B, which accounted for just 15 percent of production but 20 percent of sales, receives relatively more joint cost. The end result is that relatively higher production cost is matched against current revenues, and the company claims lower net income for tax purposes.

All sales price methods are subject to an important limitation. Where cost is determined by price, price cannot be determined by cost. Therefore, all sales price methods are circular for pricing decisions as well as for many other types of decisions that have sales price as a fundamental factor. Additionally, changes in relative market prices are reflected as changes in the cost of product, even though no change may have taken place in either total costs or methods of production. This has sometimes led to undesirable shifts in sales emphasis on selling prices. Furthermore, the method could mislead management if it created the impression that all products were equally profitable because they showed the same margin per dollar of allocated cost.

ACCOUNTING FOR BY-PRODUCTS

Objective 3
Describe methods of accounting for by-products.

The main objective of by-product accounting is the same as for joint products: to determine income and inventory for financial reporting purposes. Joint cost allocations are of limited usefulness for internal decision-making purposes. The relative values of joint products and by-products do influence the amount of time

Exhibit 7-4
*Sales-to-Production-
Ratio Method*

Product	Percentage of Total Sales[a]	Percentage of Production[b]	Sales-to-Production Ratio	Percent	Costs Assigned Sales/Production
A	10	10	1.0000	19.9338	$ 199,338
B	20	15	1.3333	26.5778	265,778
C	15	25	0.6000	11.9603	119,603
D	40	30	1.3333	26.5778	265,778
E	15	20	0.7500	14.9504	149,504
	100	100	5.0166	100.001[c]	$1,000,001[c]

[a] Based on total sales of 100,000 units.
[b] Based on total production of 150,000 units.
[c] Difference from 100.000 and $1,000,000, respectively, is due to rounding.

4.   John W. Hardy, Bryce B. Orton, and Louis M. Pope, "The Sales to Production Ratio: A New Approach to Joint Cost Allocation," *Journal of Accountancy*, October 1981. Exhibit 7-5 was adapted from this article.

and effort accountants devote to measuring their costs. Joint products are material items to the firm, and allocation of costs among such products, though arbitrary, is required for income and inventory measurement. By-products are of less significance and may not require precise cost allocation.

So, how much effort should the accountant devote to by-product costing? The following factors influence by-product valuation and accounting methods: uncertainty of by-product value at the time of production; use of the by-product in other production; use of the by-product as an alternative to main products; need for separate profit calculations for sales incentives or for control.[5] These factors must be considered in determining the best way of accounting for by-products. A number of specific accounting methods have been suggested. Our purpose in this text is to understand the conceptual basis for by-product accounting. Therefore, we will discuss the subject in general terms by concentrating on two categories—noncost methods and cost methods.

Noncost Methods of Accounting for By-products

noncost methods

Methods that make no attempt to allocate joint cost to the by-product or its inventory but instead make some credit either to income or to the main product are **noncost methods**. When the credit is made to the major product, the method is generally known as the by-product method. Independent by-product inventory valuation is not necessary for these methods.

Other Income Net sales of by-products for the current period appear in the "Other income," or "Miscellaneous income," section of the income statement. When this method is used, no attempt is made to determine by-product cost. It is used by those firms where: the value of the by-product is small or indeterminable; the use of a more detailed method entails too much expense in comparison to benefits derived; or carrying by-products with the main product does not entail any appreciable difference in the cost of the main product.

There are several disadvantages associated with the noncost treatment of by-products. First, it misstates the value of inventory on the balance sheet. Because no cost is assigned to the by-product, major product inventory on the balance sheet is overstated. When this method is used, the market value of by-product inventory, if material, should be reflected in a footnote to the balance sheet. A second criticism of the noncost method is that improper matching of expenses with revenues may occur. No entry for by-products is made at the time of production, only at the time of sale. If by-product production occurs in one accounting period and sales occur in another, income will be understated in the first period and overstated in the second. A third criticism is that often no attempt is made to control the inventory of by-products, and therefore, losses due to fraud or error could be an important factor. Because this method charges all costs and expenses to the main product, the inclusion of by-product values as nonoperating income may distort operating results.

By-product Revenue Deducted from Main Product Instead of listing the revenue from the by-product as other income, it can be treated as a deduction from the

---

5.   National Association of Accountants, *Costing Joint Products*, Research Report No. 31 (New York: National Association of Accountants, 1957), pp. 13–19.

cost of the main product. Of course, reducing main product cost by by-product revenue yields a different main product cost, and a different main product inventory cost, than that of the other income methods. The basis for this treatment is that joint costs are incurred to obtain the main products, and therefore, by-product revenue should reduce the cost of the major product. Because of the close analogy to waste and scrap accounting, this method is favored by some accountants.

A criticism of this method is that it has a tendency to understate the cost of the main product. Additionally, the cost of the main product can vary from month to month because of the varying quantities of by-products sold.[6]

Revenue from the sale of by-products may be adjusted for a variety of other expenses. These adjustments can include further processing costs and selling and administrative expenses connected with handling the by-product. The net revenue is then credited to the cost of the main product. This method is fairly common in use and is better accepted than the prior methods when costs are incurred after the split-off point. This is because it matches by-product revenue with costs incurred specifically to manufacture and sell the by-product. The beef-packing industry credits the net revenue on by-products to the cost of the main product. Special interest surrounds by-product accounting in this industry because of the great variety of products resulting from operations and the complexity of the processing. The problem is one of costing one major product (dressed beef), where there are a number of by-products, such as tallow, hides, casings, and bones.

Cost Methods of Accounting for By-products

For methods that do attempt to allocate some of the costs to by-products, inventories are carried at the allocated cost. Cost methods include the following: (1) replacement cost method, (2) total costs less by-products valued at standard price method, and (3) joint cost proration.

replacement cost method

Under the **replacement cost method**, the cost of by-products utilized within the plant is valued at the opportunity cost of purchasing or replacing the products in question. For example, coke breeze is a by-product of coke production that can be used in place of natural gas as boiler fuel. Alternatively, it can be sold in the open market. Thus, a factory using the coke breeze for boiler fuel can value it in terms of the natural gas it replaces. In certain cases, an increase in the by-product is related to a decrease in the main product. When this is the case, the by-product becomes a substitute or alternative product. By-products produced under such conditions are usually assigned the value of the main product foregone.

When by-product prices are unstable, a company may choose to credit Work in Process for by-product values at a standard price. The standard may be an arbitrary figure, or it may represent the average price over a period of time. When a standard cost system includes by-product standards, a variance account is created to account for the difference between actual and standard quantities of by-products relative to the quantity of main product. The advantage of using standard prices for by-product valuation is stability. If market prices vary, so does the cost credited to main products, making it difficult to determine whether the

6.   R. Weaver Self, "Better By-product Costs for Pricing," *N.A.C.A. Bulletin*, Vol. 38, September 1956, p. 24.

resulting cost fluctuations are due to variances in the costs of the main product or of the by-products. A standard price eliminates these fluctuations and gives managers a better feel for what is happening to the main product.

Rarely, the by-product is allocated some portion of joint cost. When this occurs, each product is charged for costs incurred after the split-off point and the joint costs are apportioned among the major products and by-products on some acceptable basis. This method was described in the section on joint cost allocation. If joint cost allocations are to be made, this general method is theoretically superior. However, practical considerations may lead an accountant to decide that including by-products in the allocation of joint costs is more trouble than it is worth.

Where by-products are recorded only as sold, inventories appear as memoranda. Where market values form the basis of entries at the time of sale, the by-products on hand at closing time may be valued at current market prices, with or without a deduction for estimated distribution costs. Inventory is valued at market regardless of cost, and if costs are below market value, anticipation of profit occurs. This is particularly true of by-products that have no costs charged against them.

EFFECT OF JOINT PRODUCT COSTS ON COST CONTROL AND DECISION MAKING

Objective 4

Explain why joint cost allocations may be misleading in management decision making.

While inventory figures for balance sheet and income determination purposes may be the prime consideration in joint cost allocations, joint product costing may affect cost control and decision making. Thus, it is important to understand when the use of allocated joint product costs may be misleading. In making decisions relative to jointly produced articles, it must be remembered that the products are necessarily produced jointly. The basic problem of cost management is to establish when and how much cost is relevant to a given decision, not to develop a base for joint cost distribution. Some areas that can be affected by joint cost allocations are output decisions, further processing of joint products, and pricing jointly produced products.

Output Decisions

The usefulness of joint-cost allocations for output decisions is dependent on the ability of management to vary the ratios of joint production. Some joint products are manufactured in a fixed proportion. It is generally agreed that if the proportion of joint products is fixed, cost allocation is useless for internal management decisions, since there is no alternative but to produce the package. As a result, the total cost of the joint products has to be compared with the combined sales revenues for measuring profitability at any given point. For this reason, some companies make no attempt to determine profit or loss on individual joint products. Some companies do determine separate profit and loss figures, but cannot use them in making output decisions. Where the joint products consist of a main product and by-products, the combined profit and loss figures are generally used. Yet sometimes by-products are ignored in making output decisions for the main product.

A similar case of fixed proportions is the situation where the product mix is determined by demand. In the peach-canning example, some variation in the product mix may be possible in that the canner may choose to cut up fancy and choice peaches to make pie filling. However, products must be produced in proportions desired by customers, and the amount of fancy and choice peaches is limited by growing conditions. This is not a true case of technologically fixed proportions, but it has much the same implications for output decisions. On occasion, joint demand may be so invariable that it may be more convenient to consider it as demand for a single product; allocation, therefore, would not be useful.

Frequently joint costs are incurred for products that are alternatives to each other. Thus, increasing the output of one product will cause a reduction in the output of the other product. Here, the opportunity cost of the foregone product can be used, as in the replacement method in oil refining.

When the proportions in which the joint products emerge can be controlled, the range of control is usually greater over a long period of time than over a short period. This is true because existing manufacturing equipment limits alterations in product mix and because existing customers determine what can be sold in the short run. With additional time, a new manufacturing process can be developed, new manufacturing equipment can be acquired, and new markets can be found. The oil-refining industry is an example, as, over time, crude oil could be refined into kerosene, gasoline, naphtha, and some plastics.

In comparing alternative product mix situations when costs of individual joint products cannot be measured with certainty, it is better to measure the total cost and total sales for each alternative and to calculate the difference (profit). In this way, the overall profitability of various alternative product mixes can be determined. Where the number of variables used in evaluating alternatives is large, computations are expensive and time-consuming. In that case, either approximations are made or more precise determinations are obtained through use of computers. Output decisions for new products similarly have to take into account alternative production, not only of rival products but also of desirable or undesirable by-products.

Further Processing Decisions

Frequently managers must decide whether to sell a joint product at split-off or to process it further. Only costs and revenues incurred after the split-off point are pertinent in this decision. Costs incurred prior to the split-off point are sunk costs with respect to further processing decisions. These joint costs are incurred regardless of further processing and are therefore not relevant to the decision. When one alternative in the comparison is to use the joint product in question as material for further operations, the sales value is replaced by the cost of replacement of material from another source. Basically, this problem is a differential costing problem, not a joint cost problem, since the alternatives involve separable costs after the split-off point.

Pricing Joint Products

Costs computed for individual products by companies characterized by joint production with an inflexible output mix have little influence on pricing decisions. It is necessary to dispose of all products, and prices of individual products must be set such that the products sell in the proportions in which they are produced. The only reliable measure of profitability for an individual joint product is the contribution it makes to joint costs *after* separable costs assignable to the product are deducted from the sales value.

While the sales or market price method of joint cost allocation to joint products maintains a constant relationship of cost to market prices of the product, it cannot be used to set prices, since the selling price has to be known in order to determine cost. Even if the method is circular, it has been found useful in limited situations. The meat-packing industry, for example, is interested only in the market value of by-products, not their costs, since market value is an important determinant of the price at which the main product's cuts can be sold in order to make a profit. Such allocations also can be useful in determining prices to pay for raw materials.

Sometimes historical market differentials between products have been used to allocate joint costs. If these market differentials are fairly stable over the years, the practice can supply a guide to pricing individual products and can give figures that are comparable to those of competitors.

The sales value method has also been found worthwhile in attempts to justify prices and existing price relationships to regulatory bodies and others. However, it has been noted that joint cost allocation is not appropriate for use by the Federal Power Commission in regulating natural gas prices; joint cost allocation is to be used to determine inventory values and is "not designed to serve as a basis for determining a cost to be used in price regulation."[7]

Pricing Based on Cost of Further Production

An interesting application of joint product costing occurs in the organ transplant field. Medicare requires that costs incurred to obtain transplant organs from donors be allocated to the individual transplant patients. If only one organ is donated, no allocation problem occurs, since all costs are assigned to the individual receiving the organ. However, often a donor provides two or more organs (e.g., heart, kidneys, liver, pancreas, bone marrow, skin, corneas), which are then transplanted into several patients. The problem is to allocate the costs of obtaining the organs to the various subsequent transplant operations. The joint costs, which can range up to $30,000, include: maintaining the donor on life support systems; the provision of nursing and other medical personnel to assist in organ removal; renting jet(s) to transport the surgical team(s) to the hospital to obtain the organs; and so on.

One method that has been used to allocate the joint costs is to base them on the eventual cost of the subsequent transplant operation. For example, if a heart, two kidneys, and two corneas are donated, then joint costs of organ removal are assigned in proportion to the costs of the heart transplant, kidney transplant, and cornea transplant procedures. Since the heart transplant is the most expensive, the bulk of the joint cost would be assigned to the heart. The kidneys would be assigned relatively less joint cost, and the corneas, which are associated with the least expensive procedure, would be assigned the least joint cost. Note that this method differs from the benefits-received approaches, which entail application of average cost based on physical or weighted units. Nor is this method precisely like those based on relative market value, since the organs themselves are not sold. The efficacy and "fairness" of the method are being debated.

If joint products are of variable proportions, meaningful decisions can be made for each individual product by comparing differential cost with differential

---

7.   Horace R. Brock, "Joint-Cost Allocation—Not a Rate Basis," *N.A.A. Bulletin,* Vol. 44, February 1963, p. 26.

sales revenue. However, while costs determined for individual products may be useful guides to pricing in some situations, management should always consider the whole picture presented by a group of joint products when making pricing decisions.

JOINT PRODUCTION OF SERVICES

Objective 5
Discuss why joint production is seldom found in service industries.

We have not mentioned joint costs in connection with services because so seldom does a service yield true joint outputs. In general, a service can be directed to one effect rather than to two effects simultaneously. When the joint production process occurs with a service, it is often allied with a pricing problem. For example, an individual experiencing severe neck and shoulder pain can be treated by a massage therapist. Through a series of forty-five-minute massages, the therapist can relax and realign the muscles in the neck and upper back, thereby alleviating much of the pain. When this procedure is prescribed by a physician, it is a substitute for prescription drugs and surgery, and the massages are covered by health insurance. The problem, from the point of view of the insurance company, is that the massage does more than relieve pain, it also feels good. In fact, the same service can be used by individuals who simply want to treat themselves to a relaxing experience. In this case, the inseparability of the experiences inherent in the massage constitute a joint production situation and the insurance company may wish to allocate only a portion of the cost to the therapeutic aspect.

Similar examples abound in income tax compliance. A Certified Management Accountant is required to amass 30 hours of continuing education credit every year in order to remain certified. Suppose that Leslie O'Neill, a CMA in private practice, attends a two-day seminar on activity-based costing in a nearby state. The entire cost of the seminar is deductible as a business expense. Now suppose that the seminar is offered on a cruise ship and is spread out over a five-day period. The IRS will certainly take a closer look. Now pleasure is intermingled with business, and the cost of the seminar itself must be separated from the over-all cost of the cruise. This, too, is a joint cost allocation problem.

SUMMARY

Joint production processes result in the output of two or more products produced simultaneously. Joint or main products have relatively significant sales value. By-products have relatively less significant sales value. Joint costs must be allocated to the individual products for purposes of financial reporting. Several methods have been developed to allocate joint costs. These include the physical units method, the weighted average method, the sales-value-at-split-off method, the net realizable value method, and the constant gross margin method.

Frequently by-products are not allocated any of the joint product costs. Instead, by-product sales are listed as "Other income" on the income statement or are treated as a credit to Work in Process of the main product(s).

Joint cost allocation may interfere with management decision making. This is so because the joint costs must be incurred to produce all of the products, and thus, allocated costs are not useful for output and pricing decisions. Further processing costs, or separable costs, are used in management decision making.

The arbitrary nature of joint cost allocation has led to a dizzying array of accounting methods. These methods are meant to respond to each company's individual circumstances. A few of the methods have been covered in this chapter. To help you keep track of the bases for them, Exhibit 7-5 lists the major joint and by-product cost methods.

Exhibit 7-5
*Summary of Methods of
Accounting for Joint
Costs*

Joint Cost Allocation Methods

Physical Units Method—Joint cost is prorated to the products on the basis of each product's share of total physical units.

Weighted Average Method—Each product is assigned a weighting factor, which is multiplied by the number of units. Joint cost is prorated to the products on the basis of each product's share of total weighted units.

Sales-Value-at-Split-off Method—Joint cost is prorated to the products on the basis of each product's share of total revenue at the split-off point.

Net Realizable Value Method—Joint cost is prorated to the products on the basis of each product's share of hypothetical revenue. Hypothetical revenue is defined as eventual sales revenue minus further processing costs.

Constant Gross Margin Method—Joint cost is backed into. First, overall sales revenue minus overall costs (joint plus further processing costs) is calculated to yield gross profit and the gross profit percentage. Then, each individual product is assessed by: subtracting gross profit from individual product revenue according to the overall gross profit percentage, subtracting further processing costs, and obtaining a remainder, which represents the joint cost allocated.

Sales-to-Production-Ratio Method—Each product is assigned a weighting factor equal to its percentage of sales divided by its percentage of production. This factor is multiplied by the number of units. Joint cost is prorated to the products on the basis of each product's share of total weighted units.

By-product Accounting Treatments

Other Income—A noncost method in which any revenue from the sale of the by-product is shown on the income statement as "Other Income." Joint cost is not allocated to the by-product.

Reduction in Main Product Cost—A noncost method in which any revenue from the sale of the by-product is deducted from the costs of the main product.

Replacement Cost—A cost method used when the by-product can substitute for another resource used in production. The by-product is costed at the value of the resource replaced.

Standard Price—A cost method in which the by-product is valued at a standard price. This method is designed to avoid fluctuations in by-product value.

Joint Cost Proration—Any of the joint cost allocation methods can be used to assign a portion of joint cost to the by-product. This method is rarely used in practice.

REVIEW PROBLEM AND SOLUTION

Sanders Pharmaceutical Company purchases a raw material that is then processed to yield three chemicals: anarol, estyl, and betryl. In June, Sanders purchased 10,000 gallons of the raw material at a cost of $250,000 and incurred joint conversion costs of $70,000. June sales and production information are as follows:

	Gallons Produced	Price at Split-off	Further Processing Cost Per Gallon	Eventual Sales Price
Anarol	2,000	$55	—	—
Estyl	3,000	40	—	—
Betryl	5,000	30	$5	$60

Anarol and estyl are sold to other pharmaceutical companies at the split-off point. Betryl can be sold at the split-off point or processed further and packaged for sale as an asthma medication.

REQUIRED:

1. Allocate the joint costs to the three products using the physical units method, the sales-value-at-split-off method, and the net realizable value method.
2. Suppose that half of June's production of estyl could be purified and mixed with all of the anarol to produce a veterinary grade anesthetic. All further processing costs amount to $35,000. The selling price for the veterinary grade anarol is $112 per gallon. Should Sanders further process the anarol into 2,000 gallons of anesthetic?

Solution

1. Total joint cost to be allocated = $250,000 + $70,000 = $320,000

Physical Units Method:

	Gallons Produced	Percent of Gallons Produced	×	Joint Cost	Joint Cost Allocation
Anarol	2,000	(2,000/10,000) = .20		$320,000	$ 64,000
Estyl	3,000	(3,000/10,000) = .30		320,000	96,000
Betryl	5,000	(5,000/10,000) = .50		320,000	160,000
	10,000				$320,000

Sales-Value-at-Split-off Method:

	Gallons Produced	Price at Split-off	Revenue at Split-off	Percent of Revenue	×	Joint Cost	Joint Cost Allocation
Anarol	2,000	$55	$110,000	.28947		$320,000	$ 92,630
Estyl	3,000	40	120,000	.31579		320,000	101,053
Betryl	5,000	30	150,000	.39474		320,000	126,317
			$380,000				$320,000

Net Realizable Value Method:

Step 1: Determine hypothetical sales revenue.

	Eventual Price	−	Further Processing Cost Per Gallon	=	Hypothetical Sales Price	×	Gallons	=	Hypothetical Revenue
Anarol	$55		—		$55		2,000		$110,000
Estyl	40				40		3,000		120,000
Betryl	60		5		55		5,000		275,000
Total									$505,000

Step 2: Allocate joint cost as a proportion of hypothetical sales revenue.

	Hypothetical Sales Revenue	Percent	×	Joint Cost	=	Joint Cost Allocation
Anarol	$110,000	.21782		$320,000		$ 69,702
Estyl	120,000	.23762		320,000		76,038
Betryl	275,000	.54455		320,000		174,256
	$505,000					$319,996

2. Joint costs are irrelevant to this decision. Instead, further processing costs and the opportunity cost of lost contribution margin on the estyl diverted to anarol purification must be considered.

Added revenue ($112 − 55)(2,000)	$114,000
Less: Further processing of anarol mixture	(35,000)
Less: Lost contribution margin on estyl (1,500 × $40)	(60,000)
Increased net income	$ 19,000

KEY TERMS

By-product 271
Constant gross margin
  percentage method 278
Hypothetical sales value
  277
Joint products 269

Net realizable value
  method 277
Noncost methods 280
Physical units method
  273

Replacement cost method
  281
Sales-to-production-ratio
  method 279
Sales-value-at-split-off
  method 276

Separable costs 270
Split-off point 269
Weight factor 275

QUESTIONS FOR WRITING AND DISCUSSION

1. What is a joint cost?
2. What is the joint costing problem?
3. What is a by-product?
4. Give two purposes for which joint costs are allocated to individual products.
5. The sales-value-at-split-off method is neutral and therefore should be used to allocate joint costs to products. Do you agree or disagree with this statement? Why?
6. Explain how joint cost allocation may be misleading in managerial decision making.

7. Name three methods of allocating joint product costs.
8. How do joint costs differ from other common costs?
9. Should joint costs be considered in a sell-or-process-further decision? Explain.
10. If sales value methods are used to allocate joint product costs, then those costs cannot be used in pricing decisions. Comment.
11. What two general methods can be used to account for by-products?

EXERCISES AND PROBLEMS

7-1
Net Realizable
Value Method
LO 2

Muffet, Inc., produces two products, curds and whey, in a single process. The joint costs of this process were $11,500, and 23,000 units of curds and 8,000 units of whey were produced. Separable processing costs beyond the split-off point were: curds, $4,100; whey, $3,000. Curds sell for $0.70 per unit; whey sells for $0.75 per unit.

REQUIRED: Allocate the $11,500 joint costs using the estimated net realizable value method.

7-2
Decision to Process Further
LO 4

Refer to **7-1**. Suppose that whey could be sold at the split-off point for $0.38 per unit. Should Muffet sell whey at split-off or process it further? Show supporting computations.

7-3
Identification of Joint Products and By-products
LO 1

Sharif Company produces a number of products from a joint process that costs $10,000 per batch. Information on the output of the batch by product is as follows:

	Number of Units	Price Per Unit at Split-off
Alpha	1,000	$ 2.00
Beta	2,000	4.50
Gamma	2,500	3.75
Delta	600	8.00
Rho	3,000	.50
Chi	150	.20
Psi	1,000	.04
Omega	60	10.00

REQUIRED: Classify each product as a joint (or main) product or as a by-product. Explain your reasoning.

7-4
Units-Produced Method; By-products and Decision Making
LO 2, 3, 4

LaTonya Washington, plant manager for Ultratech, Inc., was sitting at her desk, glumly regarding the latest financial statements relating to the manufacture of silicon chips. Ultratech was purchased under a leveraged buy-out two years ago, and top management insisted on a minimum gross margin of 25% for every product—no exceptions.

The chips are manufactured in a process that requires (1) the growing of silicon cylinders, (2) slicing the cylinders into thin circular wafers and dicing these into square wafers, and (3) photolithographing the chips and baking them at high temperatures. For each batch of 2,000 raw silicon wafers started into production in Department 3, the output is:

---

375 high-density memory chips
1,125 low-density memory chips
500 defective memory chips

High-density memory chips sell for $14, and low-density memory chips sell for $8. Defective chips are thrown away. Joint costs of $8,000 are incurred through production in Department 3 and are allocated according to the units-produced method.

LaTonya's neighbor, Harmony Schultz, runs a gift shop located in the Silicon Valley. Technically oriented memorabilia and whatnots are in high demand. So, Harmony has offered to purchase the defective chips for $0.05 each to embed in key chains and related items. As Harmony points out, customers won't care if the chips work, just as long as the key chain does. At first, LaTonya was delighted with the plan. Then she saw a profit-loss statement organized by product line.

REQUIRED:

1. Calculate the gross margin and gross margin percentage by product for the high-density and low-density chips before Harmony's offer to buy defective chips was made.
2. Assume that Harmony's offer has been accepted and that Ultratech's accountant treated the defective chips as a main product. Calculate the gross margin and gross margin percentage by product. Explain why LaTonya is distressed by the results.

3. Can you suggest an alternative accounting method for the defective chips that will please LaTonya and Ultratech's management? Recalculate the gross margin and gross margin percentage by product using your method.

7-5
Special Order
LO 2, 4

The Killian Company manufactures two skin care lotions, Liquid Skin and Silken Skin, out of a joint process. The joint (common) costs incurred are $420,000 for a standard production run that generates 180,000 gallons of Liquid Skin and 120,000 gallons of Silken Skin. Additional processing costs beyond the split-off point are $1.40 per gallon for Liquid Skin and $0.90 per gallon for Silken Skin. Liquid Skin sells for $2.40 per gallon, while Silken Skin sells for $3.90 per gallon.

The Overnight Hotel Chain has asked The Killian Company to supply it with 240,000 gallons of Silken Skin at a price of $3.65 per gallon. Overnight plans to have the Silken Skin bottled in 1.5-ounce, personal-use containers, which are supplied in each of its hotel rooms as part of the complimentary personal products for guest use.

If Killian accepts the order, it will save $0.05 per gallon in packaging of Silken Skin. There is sufficient excess capacity for the order. However, the market for Liquid Skin is saturated, and any additional sales of Liquid Skin would take place at a price of $1.60 per gallon.

REQUIRED:

1. What is the profit normally earned on one production run of Liquid Skin and Silken Skin?
2. Should Killian accept the special order? Explain.

(CMA adapted)

7-6
Further Processing
LO 4

Godfrey Drug Corporation buys three chemicals that are processed to produce two popular ingredients for over-the-counter drugs. The purchased chemicals are blended for two to three hours and then heated for fifteen minutes. The results of the process are two separate chemicals, Xyrene and Yanadrene, which are sent to a drying room until their moisture content is reduced to 6 to 8 percent. For every 1,100 pounds of chemicals used, 500 pounds of each chemical are produced. After drying, Xyrene and Yanadrene are sold to companies that process them into their final form. The selling prices are $10 per pound for Xyrene and $25 per pound for Yanadrene. The costs to produce 500 pounds of each chemical are as follows:

Chemicals	$5,500
Direct labor	4,500
Overhead	3,500

The chemicals are packaged in 25-pound bags and shipped. The cost of each bag is $0.75. Shipping costs $0.10 per pound.

Godfrey could precess Xyrene further by grinding it into a fine powder and then molding the powder into tablets. The tablets can be sold directly to retail drug stores as a generic brand. If this route is taken, the revenue received per bottle of tablets would be $3.00, with five bottles produced by every pound of Xyrene. The costs of grinding and tableting total $2.50 per pound of Xyrene. Bottles cost $0.20 each. Bottles are shipped in boxes that hold 25 at a shipping cost of $1.00 per box.

REQUIRED:

1. Should Godfrey sell Xyrene at split-off or should Xyrene be processed and sold as tablets?
2. If Godfrey normally sells 180,000 pounds of Xyrene per year, what will be the difference in profits if Xyrene is processed further?

7-7

Sell or Process Further

LO 4

Triple Products produces three products from a common input: Product A, Product B, and Product C. The joint costs for a typical quarter are described below.

Direct materials	$20,000
Direct labor	30,000
Overhead	15,000

The revenues from each product are as follows: Product A, $43,000; Product B, $32,000; and Product C, $25,000.

Management is considering processing Product A beyond the split-off point, which would increase the sales value of Product A to $76,000. However, to process Product A further means that the company must rent some special equipment costing $17,500 per quarter. Additional materials and labor also needed would cost $12,650 per quarter.

REQUIRED:

1. What is the gross profit earned by the three products for one quarter?
2. Should the division process Product A further or sell Product A at split-off? What is the effect of the decision on quarterly gross profit?

7-8

Sell or Process Further; Accounting for By-products

LO 3, 4

Goodson Pharmaceutical Company manufactures three main products from a joint process: Altox, Lorex, and Hycol. Data regarding these products for the fiscal year ended May 31, 1996, are shown below.

	Altox	Lorex	Hycol
Units produced	170,000	500,000	330,000
Sales value per unit at split-off	$3.50	—	$2.00
Allocation of joint costs*	$450,000	$846,000	$504,000
Separable costs	—	$1,400,000	—
Final sales value per unit	—	$5.00	—

*Joint costs are allocated on the basis of net realizable value, and the net realizable value of any by-product is deducted from the joint costs before allocation.

The president of Goodson, Arlene Franklin, is reviewing an opportunity to change the way in which these three products are processed and sold. Proposed changes for each product are described below.

Altox is currently sold at the split-off point to a manufacturer of vitamins. Altox can also be refined for use as a medication to treat high blood pressure. However, this additional processing would cause a loss of 20,000 units of Altox. The separable costs to further process Altox are estimated to be $250,000 annually. The final product would sell for $5.50 per unit. Lorex is currently processed further after the split-off point and sold by Goodson as a cold remedy. The company has received an offer from another pharmaceutical company to purchase Lorex at the split-off point for $2.25 per unit.

Hycol is an oil produced from the joint process and is currently sold at the split-off point to a cosmetics manufacturer. Goodson's Research Department has suggested that the company process this product further and sell it as an ointment to relieve muscle pain. The additional processing would cost $75,000 annually and would result in 25 percent more units of product. The final product would be sold for $1.80 per unit.

The joint process currently used by Goodson also produces 50,000 units of Dorzine, a hazardous chemical waste product. The company must pay $.035 per unit to properly dispose of the Dorzine. Dietriech Mills Inc. is interested in using the Dorzine as a solvent; however, Goodson would have to refine the Dorzine at an annual cost of $43,000. Dietriech would purchase all the refined Dorzine produced by Goodson and is willing to pay $.75 for each unit.

REQUIRED:

1. Identify which of the three main products Goodson Pharmaceutical Company should sell at the split-off point in the future and which of the three main products the company should process further in order to maximize profits. Be sure to support your decisions with appropriate calculations.
2. Assume that the Goodson Pharmaceutical Company has decided to refine the waste product Dorzine for sale to Dietriech Mills Inc. and will treat Dorzine as a by-product of the joint process in the future.
   a. Evaluate whether or not Goodson made the correct decision regarding Dorzine, supporting your answer with appropriate calculations.
   b. Explain whether or not the decision to treat Dorzine as a by-product will affect the decision reached in Requirement 2(a) above.

(CMA adapted)

**7-9
Accounting for
By-products**
LO 3

Refer to **7-8.** Assume that Goodson negotiates a higher price and converts the Dorzine to a solvent and that the annual net revenue from the sale of Dorzine is $13,000. How could Goodson account for the by-product on its financial statements?

**7-10
Joint Production of
Services**
LO 1, 5

The Santa Luisa Museum of the Southwest is located in a lovely park-like setting on Lake Santa Luisa. The Museum houses several impressive permanent collections of early Taos art, Navajo weaving, and basket weaving and pottery from the Acoma and Santa Clara Pueblos. The museum has a restaurant and a sculpture garden. Recently several couples requested permission to rent the facilities after hours for their weddings. One couple felt the sculpture garden would provide an ideal setting for an evening wedding in June. Another couple, two potters, thought the pottery collection would be a perfect background. Each couple would need the use of the restaurant kitchen but would provide any necessary extra tables and chairs. If you were the director of the museum, what factors would you consider in determining how to treat the use of the museum for weddings and other parties?

**7-11
Joint Cost
Allocation Using
the Physical Units
and Market Value
Methods**
LO 2, 4

Vicki Thalberg owns the Sunny Trails Nursery. While the nursery sells a wide variety of flowers, houseplants, trees and shrubs, Vicki has a special interest in Chinese pistache trees. The Chinese pistache is a medium-sized ornamental tree that can have brilliant red fall foliage. Unfortunately, it can also have drab yellow-brown fall foliage. The problem to date is that it is impossible to predict which seedlings will produce the highly prized red foliage. In addition, once the seedling is one year old, its branches cannot be successfully grafted onto other rootstock (a method which would allow the production of many trees from one identified excellent producer). As a result, nurseries typically grow many seedlings and just wait until the first autumn to see what color the leaves turn. Trees with red foliage are sold for $25, and trees with brown foliage sell for $10.

In a typical year, Vicki grows 500 Chinese pistache seedlings with total joint cost (labor, fertilizer, pots, burlap, and twine) of $5,000. Based on past history, she expects roughly 30 percent of the seedlings to develop red fall foliage.

REQUIRED:

1. Allocate the joint cost to the red trees and the drab trees using the physical units method.
2. Allocate the joint cost to the red trees and the drab trees using the market value method.
3. A former classmate of Vicki's has just developed a method of determining which seedlings will yield the red foliage by scraping a few cells from the bark and comparing

their genetic structure with that of known red foliage producers. The classmate is willing to check Vicki's seedlings for $5 each.

Once the seedlings are checked, Vicki could graft twigs from the identified red seedlings onto the drab seedling rootstock. This would result in the destruction of all red seedlings and the conversion of all drab seedlings into red-foliage-producing trees. Because the genetic test results would not be known until all seedlings had been potted, fertilized, etc., all the $5,000 cost would remain. The additional grafting labor would cost about $275. Should Vicki have the seedlings checked?

7-12
Net Realizable
Value Method,
By-products
LO 2, 4

Princess Corporation grows, processes, packages, and sells three apple products—sliced apples that are used in frozen pies, applesauce, and apple juice. The outside skin of the apple, which is removed in the Cutting Department and processed as animal feed, is treated as a by-product. Princess uses the net realizable (relative sales) value method to assign costs of the joint process to its main products. The by-product is inventoried at its market value, and the net realizable value of the by-product is used to reduce the joint production cost prior to allocation to the main products. Details of Princess' production process are presented below.

A. The apples are washed, and the outside skin is removed in the Cutting Department. The apples are then cored and trimmed for slicing. The three main products and the by-product are recognizable after processing in the Cutting Department. Each product is then transferred to a separate department for final processing.
B. The trimmed apples are forwarded to the Slicing Department where they are sliced and frozen. Any juice generated during the slicing operation is frozen with the slices.
C. The pieces of apple trimmed from the fruit are processed into applesauce in the Crushing Department. Again, the juice generated during this operation is used in the applesauce.
D. The core and any surplus apple generated from the Cutting Department are pulverized into a liquid in the Juicing Department. There is a loss equal to eight percent of the weight of the *good* output produced in this department.
E. The outside skin is chopped into animal feed and packaged in the Feed Department.

A total of 270,000 pounds of apples were entered into the Cutting Department during November. The schedule presented below shows the costs incurred in each department, the proportion by weight transferred to the four final processing departments, and the selling price of each end product.

Processing Data and Costs
November 1998

Department	Costs Incurred	Proportion of Product by Weight Transferred to Departments	Selling Price/lb. of Final Product
Cutting	$60,000	none	none
Slicing	11,280	33%	$.80
Crushing	8,550	30	.55
Juicing	3,000	27	.40
Feed	700	10	.10
Total	$83,530	100%	

REQUIRED:

1. Princess Corporation uses the net realizable value method to determine inventory values for its main products and by-products. For November, calculate the:

a. Resulting output in pounds for apple slices, applesauce, apple juice, and animal feed.
b. Net realizable value at the split-off point for each of the three main products.
c. Amount of the cost of the Cutting Department assigned to each of the three main products and to the by-product in accordance with corporate policy.
d. Gross margins in dollars for each of the three main products.
2. Comment on the significance to management of the gross margin dollar information by main product for planning and control purposes, as opposed to inventory valuation.

(CMA adapted)

7-13
Comparison of Joint Costing Methods

LO 2

Janus Company manufactures two products, Coming and Going, from a joint process. One production run costs $6,000 and results in 1,000 units of Coming and 4,000 units of Going. Neither product is salable at split-off but must be further processed such that the separable cost for Coming is $3 per unit and for Going is $2 per unit. The eventual market price for Coming is $12 and for Going $14.

REQUIRED:

1. Allocate joint production costs to each product using the units-produced method.
2. Allocate joint production costs to each product using the net realizable value method.
3. Allocate joint production costs to each product using the constant gross margin method.
4. Discuss the differences among the three methods. Which do you prefer and why?

7-14
Relative Sales Value at Split-off

LO 2

Jonathan Company manufactures products N, P, and R from a joint process. The following information is available:

	Product			
	N	P	R	Total
Units produced	6,000	?	?	12,000
Sales value at split-off	?	?	$25,000	$100,000
Joint costs	$24,000	?	?	$60,000
Sales value if processed further	$55,000	$45,000	$30,000	$130,000
Additional cost if processed further	$9,000	$7,000	$5,000	$21,000

Joint product costs are allocated using the relative-sales-value-at-split-off approach.

REQUIRED:

1. What is the sales value at split-off for Product N?
2. If the company used the units-produced method to allocate joint cost, how much joint cost would be allocated to Product N?

(CPA adapted)

7-15
Methods of Accounting for Joint and By-products

LO 2, 3

Choose the best answer for each of the following multiple-choice questions.

1. A company manufactures two joint products at a joint cost of $1,000. These products can be sold at the split-off point or further processed at an additional cost and sold as higher quality items. The decision to sell at split-off or further process should be based on the:
   a. assumption that the $1,000 joint cost is irrelevant.
   b. allocation of the $1,000 joint cost using the relative sales-value approach.
   c. assumption that the $1,000 joint cost must be allocated using a physical-measure approach.
   d. allocation of the $1,000 joint cost using any equitable and rational allocation basis.

2. For purposes of allocating joint costs to joint products, the sales price at point of sale reduced by cost to complete after split-off is assumed to be equal to the:
   a. relative sales value at split-off.
   b. sales price less a normal profit margin at point of sale.
   c. joint costs.
   d. total costs.
3. Under an acceptable method of costing by-products, inventory costs of the by-product are based on the portion of the joint production cost allocated to the by-product
   a. but any subsequent processing cost is debited to the cost of the main product.
   b. but any subsequent processing cost is debited to revenue of the main product.
   c. plus any subsequent processing cost.
   d. less any subsequent processing cost.

(CPA adapted)

COST MANAGEMENT IN ACTION:
The Costs of Production

This photo essay tells the story of athletic uniform production at T.Q., Inc., in Monticello, Kentucky. T.Q., Inc. manufactures a variety of products for Hutch Sports USA, including the Little Pro's Uniform® which is a complete football uniform for children. The Little Pro's Uniform includes a helmet, shirt, pants, and shoulder pads with the name and logo of an NFL team. Let's follow the production of the shirt for the Little Pro's Uniform in this photo essay. As you look through the photographs, try to identify some of the many activities that a manufacturing firm engages in, and relate them to cost management concepts you have learned.

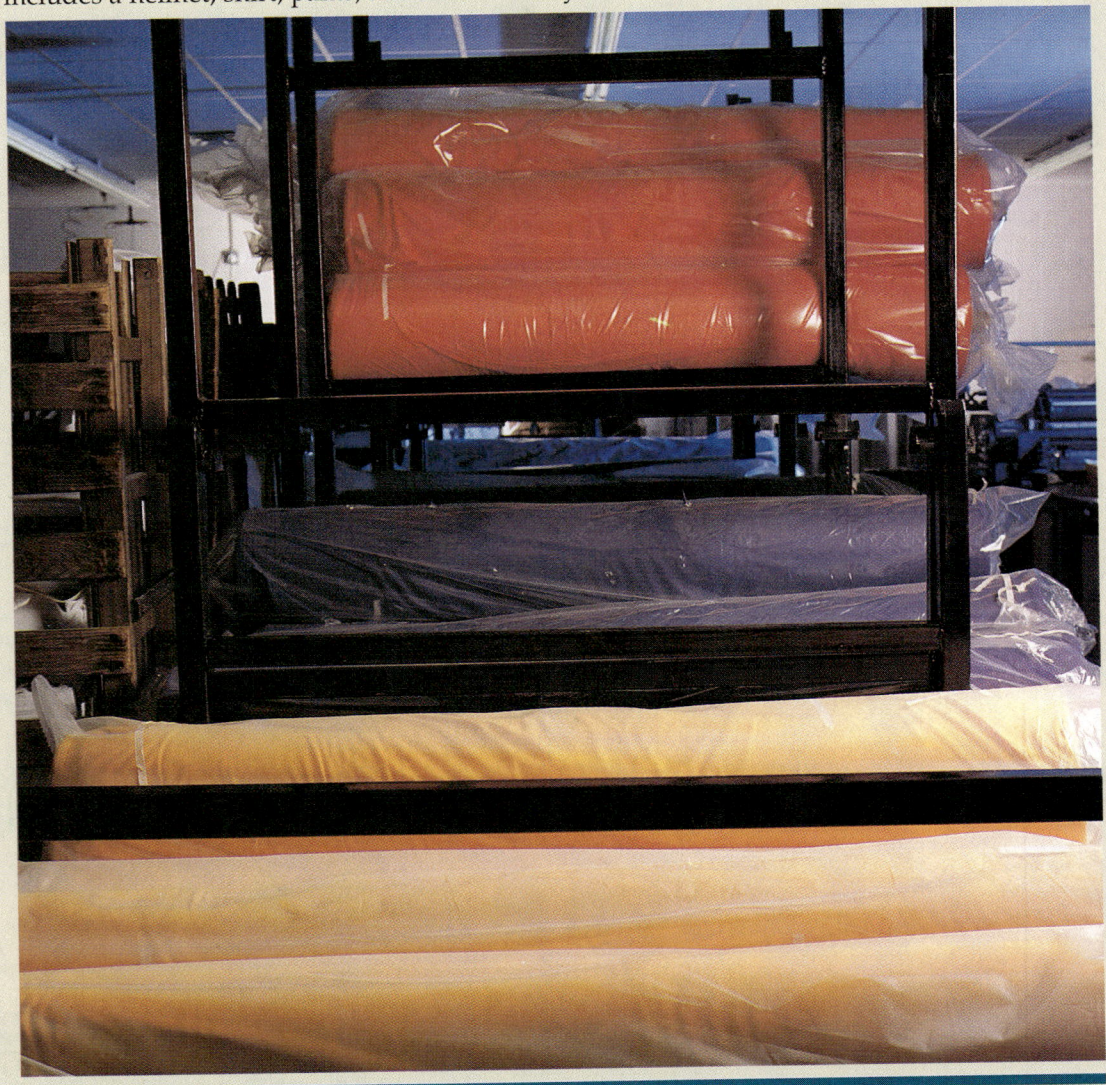

The huge bolts of fabric that you see are part of the up to 30,000 yards of fabric the company keeps on hand at any one time. The fabric inventory satisfies about two weeks of production needs. In many traditional factories, the raw materials are kept in the materials storeroom. However, T.Q., Inc. rebuilt the factory last year to make production more efficient. Now, raw materials are kept in staging areas next to the department in which they are first used. These bolts of fabric are located in the materials storage area outside the Cutting Department.

The production of shirts begins in the Cutting Department. When the Cutting Department needs fabric for a new batch of uniforms, the material is transferred from the staging area to the cutting tables. As many as 100 layers of fabric are stacked on the cutting table. Then experienced cutters lay out the pattern pieces to produce as little materials waste as possible. The pattern pieces are cut from the fabric using the mechanical cutting knife you see in the picture.

New at T.Q., Inc., is the automated silk screening machine you see in these two pictures. First, a worker positions each shirt piece on an arm of the machine and then the arm moves into position for screen printing. In the second photo you can see the machine automatically forcing ink through the screen onto a shirt piece. In this way, team names and logos are emblazoned on shirt fronts and sleeves. How would you classify the worker in this picture? The automated silk screening machine? The ink used to print the logos?

The silk screened pieces go to the dryer. When dry, they are stacked by this worker, ready to be taken to the Sewing Department. As an accountant, how would you classify the fabric pieces? What costs do they include to this point?

In the Sewing Department, the individual pieces are matched with their mates and sewn together. Can you identify direct materials, direct labor, and overhead in this department?

After the shirts are sewn, they must be turned right side out, matched with the remaining uniform components, and packaged. They become Finished Goods and are ready to be shipped to the customer. The packaging is customized to the type of order. Uniforms which are part of an order for catalog sales (e.g., through J.C. Penney's) are individually packed in plain brown boxes. Orders for retail stores (e.g., Wal-Mart or Toys R Us) are packaged individually in more colorful blue boxes. In all cases, the entire order is boxed in master cartons which you see in the next picture.

This is the warehouse. While it is physically located in the plant, the accounting system would refer to warehouse-related costs as selling expense. Note the number of master cartons awaiting customer order and/or shipping. Providing space for, caring for, insuring and moving Finished Goods inventory is a large expense.

Because inventory is a significant portion of the company's assets, inventory control is an important overhead activity. This worker keeps track of inventory using a special computer program. At T.Q., Inc., the inventory system links purchasing, receiving, and use of materials. The activities involved include entering receipt of material, monitoring inventory levels, constructing bills of material, and tracking purchases.

Chapter 8
Activity-Based Costing

The importance of efficiency, quality and timeliness are evident in this photo of The Gap's East Coast distribution center. Merchandise from this center is quickly dispatched to East Coast stores "just-in-time" for sale. Many companies find that expensive distribution activities can be made more efficient through the accurate cost identification of activity-based costing.

LEARNING OBJECTIVES

After studying this chapter, you should be able to:

1. Explain why traditional cost systems may produce distorted costs.
2. Explain how an activity-based cost system can produce more accurate product costs.
3. Provide a detailed description of how activities are identified and classified so that homogeneous cost pools can be formed.
4. Describe an activity-based relational database.
5. Describe how costs are assigned to activities.

In Chapter 2, we mentioned that cost accounting information systems can be divided into two types: traditional and contemporary. In Chapters 4 through 6, we studied traditional cost accounting information systems. These systems used traditional product cost definitions and used only unit-based activity drivers to assign overhead to products. In this chapter and the following chapter, we introduce and discuss contemporary cost accounting systems. This chapter begins by describing how activity-based costing can be used for computing traditional product costs. This enables us to compare and contrast the contemporary and traditional approaches. In Chapter 9, the discussion covers more general product cost definitions. An activity-based cost accounting system offers greater product costing accuracy but at an increased cost. The justification for a new accounting system (such as activity-based costing) must rely on the benefits of improved decisions resulting from materially different product costs. It is important to understand that a necessary condition for improved decisions is that the accounting numbers produced by a contemporary cost system must be significantly different from those produced by a traditional cost system. When will this be the case? Are there any signals that management might receive indicating that their traditional system is no longer working? Finally, assuming that an activity-based cost accounting system is called for, how does it work? What are its basic features? Detailed features? This chapter addresses these questions and other related issues.

LIMITATIONS OF TRADITIONAL COST ACCOUNTING SYSTEMS

Objective 1
Explain why traditional cost systems may produce distorted costs.

unit-based activity drivers

Traditional product costing assigns only manufacturing costs to products. Assigning the cost of direct materials and direct labor to products poses no particular challenge. These costs can be assigned to products using direct tracing or very accurate driver tracing, and most traditional cost systems are designed to ensure that this tracing takes place. Overhead costs, on the other hand, pose a different problem. The physically observable input-output relationship that exists between direct labor, direct materials, and products is simply not available for overhead. Thus, assignment of overhead must rely on driver tracing (and perhaps allocation). In a traditional cost system, only *unit-based activity drivers* are used to assign costs to products. **Unit-based activity drivers** are factors that cause changes in cost as the units produced change. The use of only unit-based drivers to assign overhead costs to products assumes that the overhead consumed by products is highly correlated with the number of units produced, measured in terms of such factors as direct labor hours, machine hours, or material costs. These unit-based activity drivers assign overhead to products through the use of either plantwide or departmental rates.

Plantwide and Departmental Rates

Exhibit 8-1 reviews the approach of traditional overhead assignment. Panel A illustrates plantwide rates, and Panel B illustrates departmental rates, using two departments. For plantwide rates, overhead costs are first accumulated in one large plantwide pool (first-stage cost assignment). Overhead costs are assigned to the pool simply by adding all the overhead costs identified in the general ledger. Since all overhead costs belong to the plant, assignment to the pool is done with complete accuracy. In this first stage, the cost object is the plant and direct tracing can be used to assign costs to the plantwide pool. In a sense, we

Exhibit 8-1
Traditional Overhead
Assignment

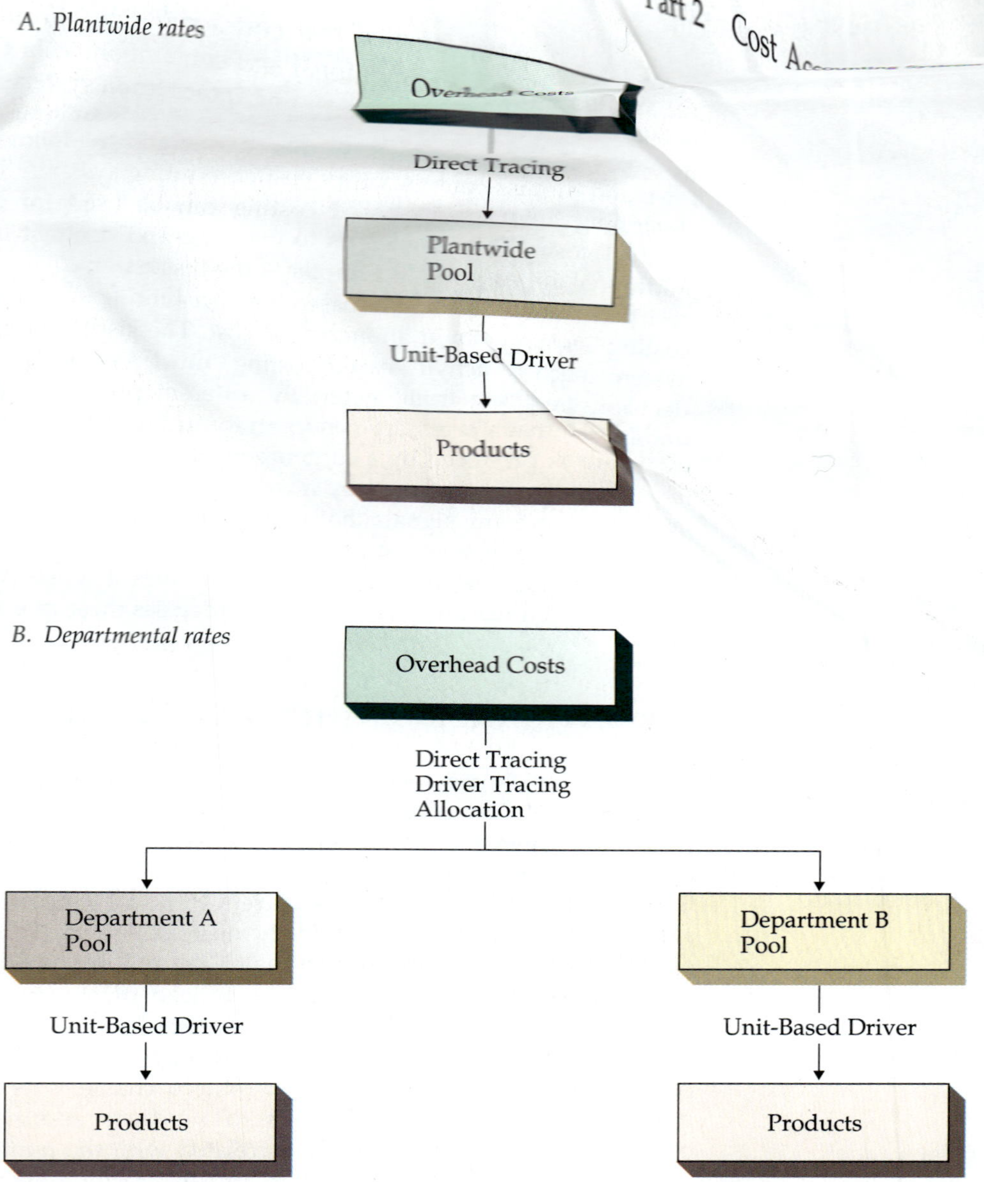

A. *Plantwide rates*

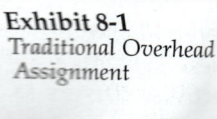

Overhead Costs

↓ Direct Tracing

Plantwide
Pool

↓ Unit-Based Driver

Products

B. *Departmental rates*

Overhead Costs

Direct Tracing
Driver Tracing
Allocation

| Department A Pool | Department B Pool |

Unit-Based Driver

Unit-Based Driver

| Products | Products |

could argue that the costs are assigned to a very broad macro activity: production. Once costs are accumulated in this pool, we then compute a plantwide rate using a single driver, which is usually direct labor hours. Products are assumed to consume overhead resources in proportion to the direct labor hours used. Thus, in the second stage, overhead costs are assigned to products multiplying the rate by the actual total direct labor hours used by each product.

For departmental rates, overhead costs are assigned to individual production departments, creating departmental overhead cost pools. In the first stage, departments are cost objects and overhead costs are assigned using direct tracing, driver tracing, and allocation. Chapter 6 discussed methods for assigning overhead costs external to individual production departments and included the direct method, the sequential method, and the reciprocal method. Although an effort is made to assign these external costs using causal factors (driver tracing), some overhead costs are assigned using assumed linkages (allocation). Once costs are assigned to individual production departments, then unit-based drivers such as direct labor hours (for labor-intensive departments) and machine hours (for machine-intensive departments) are used to compute departmental rates. Products passing through the departments are assumed to consume overhead resources in proportion to the departments' unit-based drivers (machine hours or direct labor hours used). Thus, in the second stage, overhead is assigned to products by multiplying the departmental rates by the amount of the driver used in the respective departments. The total overhead assigned to products is simply the sum of the amounts received in each department.

The Inadequacy of Plantwide and Departmental Rates

advanced manufacturing environment

Plantwide and departmental rates have been used for decades and continue to be used successfully by many organizations. In some settings, however, they do not work well and may actually cause severe product cost distortions. For companies operating in what is called the *advanced manufacturing environment*, product cost distortions can be particularly distressing. The **advanced manufacturing environment** is characterized by firms engaged in intense competition (usually on a worldwide level), continuous improvement, total quality management, total customer satisfaction, and sophisticated technology. As firms operating in this advanced environment adopt new strategies to achieve competitive excellence, their cost accounting systems often must change to keep pace. Specifically, the need for more accurate product costs has forced many companies to take a serious look at their costing procedures. Cost systems that worked reasonably well in the past may no longer be acceptable.

Often organizations experience certain symptoms indicating that their cost accounting system is outdated. For example, if costs are distorted and severe overcosting of a major, high-volume product is the outcome, then bids will be systematically lost, even when the company feels it is pursuing an aggressive bidding strategy. This can be especially puzzling when the company is confident that it is operating as efficiently as its competitors. Thus, one symptom of an outdated cost system is the inability to explain the outcome of bids. On the flip side, if competitors' prices seem unrealistically low, it should cause managers to wonder about the accuracy of their cost system. For example, if somehow an organization's cost system is systematically understating the cost of low-volume, specialty products—products that require special processes and handling—the organization may find it has a seemingly profitable niche all to itself. Yet it may find operational managers wanting to drop some of these "niche" products. These symptoms of an outdated cost system along with several others are listed in Exhibit 8-2.[1]

Organizations, such as John Deere Component Works, that have experienced the symptoms listed in Exhibit 8-2 have found that their plantwide or departmental rates are simply no longer capable of accurately assigning overhead costs to individual products. There are at least two major factors that impair the ability of the unit-based plantwide and departmental rates to assign overhead costs

1.   The list of warning signals is based on the following article: Robin Cooper, "You Need a New Cost System When....," *Harvard Business Review,* January–February, 1989, pp. 77–82.

Exhibit 8-2
Symptoms of an Out-
dated Cost System

1. The outcome of bids is difficult to explain.
2. Competitors' prices appear unrealistically low.
3. Products that are difficult to produce show high profits.
4. Operational managers want to drop products that appear profitable.
5. Profit margins are difficult to explain.
6. The company has a highly profitable niche all to itself.
7. Customers do not complain about price increases.
8. The accounting department spends a lot of time supplying cost data for special projects.
9. Some departments are using their own accounting system.
10. Product costs change because of changes in financial reporting regulations.

accurately: (1) the proportion of nonunit-related overhead costs to total overhead costs is large, and (2) the degree of product diversity is great.

Nonunit-Related Overhead Costs The use of either plantwide rates or departmental rates assumes that a product's consumption of overhead resources is related strictly to the units produced. But what if there are overhead activities that are unrelated to the number of units produced? Setup costs, for example, are incurred each time a batch of products is produced. A batch may consist of 1,000 or 10,000 units and the cost of setup is the same. Yet as more setups are done, setup costs increase. The number of setups, not the number of units produced, is the cause of setup costs. Furthermore, product engineering costs may depend on the number of different engineering work orders rather than the units produced of any given product. Both these examples illustrate the existence of *nonunit-based drivers*. **Nonunit-based activity drivers** are factors, other than the number of units produced, that measure the demands that cost objects place on activities. Thus, unit-based activity drivers cannot assign these costs accurately to products.

nonunit-based activity drivers

Using only unit-based activity drivers to assign nonunit-related overhead costs can create distorted product costs. The severity of this distortion depends on what proportion of total overhead costs these nonunit-based costs represent. For many companies, this percentage can be significant. Schrader Bellows and John Deere Component Works, for example, experienced nonunit-based overhead cost ratios of about 50 percent and 40 percent, respectively.[2] This suggests that some care should be exercised in assigning nonunit-based overhead costs. If nonunit-based overhead costs are only a small percentage of total overhead costs, the distortion of product costs would be quite small. In such a case, using only unit-based activity drivers to assign overhead costs might be acceptable.

Product Diversity The presence of significant nonunit overhead costs is a necessary but not sufficient condition for plantwide and departmental rate failure. If products consume the nonunit overhead activities in the same proportion as the unit overhead activities, then no product costing distortion will occur (with the use of traditional overhead assignment methods). The presence of *product*

2. See Robin Cooper, "Cost Classification in Unit-Based and Activity-Based Manufacturing Cost Systems," *Journal of Cost Management for the Manufacturing Industry,* Fall 1990, pp. 4–14.

product diversity

diversity is also necessary. **Product diversity** simply means that products consume overhead activities in different proportions. There are several reasons that products might consume overhead in different proportions. For example, differences in product size, product complexity, setup time, and size of batches all can cause products to consume overhead at different rates. Regardless of the nature of the product diversity, product cost will be distorted whenever the quantity of unit-based overhead that a product consumes does not vary in direct proportion to the quantity consumed of nonunit-based overhead. The proportion of each activity consumed by a product is defined as the **consumption ratio**. How nonunit overhead costs and product diversity can produce distorted product costs is best illustrated with an example.

consumption ratio

An Example Illustrating the Failure of Unit-Based Overhead Rates

To illustrate how traditional unit-based overhead rates can distort product costs, assume that Goodmark Company has a plant that produces two products: scented and regular birthday cards. Scented cards emit a pleasant fragrance when opened. There are two producing departments: Cutting and Printing. Cutting is responsible for shaping the cards, and Printing is responsible for design and wording (including the insertion of the fragrance for the scented cards). Expected product costing data are given in Exhibit 8-3. The units are boxes of one dozen cards. Because the quantity of regular cards produced is ten times greater than that of scented cards, we can label the regular cards a high-volume product and scented cards a low-volume product. The cards are produced in batches.

For simplicity, only four types of overhead activities, performed by four distinct support departments, are assumed: setting up the equipment for each batch, moving a batch, supplying electricity, and inspection. Each box of 12 cards is inspected after each department's operations. After cutting, the cards are inspected individually to ensure correct shape. After printing, the boxes of cards are also inspected individually to ensure correct wording, absence of smudges, insertion of fragrance, etc. Overhead costs are assigned to the two production departments using the direct method. Assume that the four service centers do not interact. Setup costs are assigned based on the number of production runs handled by each department. Since the number is identical, each department receives 50 percent of the total setup costs. Materials-handling costs are assigned by the number of moves used by each department (which are assumed to be the same). Power costs are assigned in proportion to the machine hours used by each department. Finally, inspection costs are assigned in proportion to the direct hours used (experience indicates almost a perfect correlation of inspection hours with direct labor hours).

Plantwide Overhead Rate The total overhead for the plant is $360,000, the sum of the overhead for each department ($108,000 + $252,000). Assume that direct labor hours are used as the unit-based activity driver. Dividing the total overhead by the total direct labor hours yields the following overhead rate:

$$\text{Plantwide rate} = \$360,000/100,000$$
$$= \$3.60 \text{ per direct labor hour}$$

Using this rate and other information from Exhibit 8-3, the unit costs for each product are calculated and shown in Exhibit 8-4.

Exhibit 8-3
Product Costing Data

	Scented Cards	Regular Cards	Total
Units produced per year	10,000	100,000	—
Prime costs	$78,000	$738,000	$816,000
Direct labor hours	10,000	90,000	100,000
Machine hours	5,000	45,000	50,000
Production runs	20	10	30
Number of moves	60	30	90

	Departmental Data		
	Cutting Dept.	Printing Dept.	Total
Direct labor hours:			
Scented cards	3,000	7,000	10,000
Regular cards	77,000	13,000	90,000
Total	80,000	20,000	100,000
Machine hours:			
Scented cards	1,000	4,000	5,000
Regular cards	9,000	36,000	45,000
Total	10,000	40,000	50,000

	Cutting Dept.	Printing Dept.	Total
Overhead costs:			
Setup	$ 60,000	$ 60,000	$120,000
Materials handling	30,000	30,000	60,000
Power	10,000	90,000	100,000
Inspection	8,000	72,000	80,000
Total	$108,000	$252,000	$360,000

Exhibit 8-4
Unit Cost Computation:
Plantwide Rate

	Scented	Regular
Prime costs	$ 78,000	$ 738,000
Overhead costs:		
$3.60 × 10,000	36,000	
$3.60 × 90,000		324,000
Total manufacturing costs	$114,000	$1,062,000
Units of production	10,000	100,000
Unit cost (Total costs/Units)	$11.40	$10.62

Departmental Rates Based on the distribution of labor hours and machine hours in Exhibit 8-3, the Cutting Department is labor-intensive and the Printing Department is machine-intensive. Moreover, the overhead costs of the Cutting Department are 40% of those of the Printing Department. Based on these observations, it could be argued that departmental overhead rates would reflect the consumption of overhead better than would a plantwide rate. If true, product costs would be more accurate. This approach would yield the following departmental rates, using direct labor hours for the Cutting Department and machine hours for the Printing Department.

Cutting Department rate = $108,000/80,000 direct labor hours
= $1.35/direct labor hour

Printing Department rate = $252,000/40,000 machine hours
= $6.30/machine hour

... and the data from Exhibit 8-3, the computation of the unit costs for each ... Exhibit 8-5.

Problems with Costing Accuracy The accuracy of the overhead cost assignment can be challenged regardless of whether the plantwide or departmental rates are used. The main problem with either procedure is the assumption that machine hours or direct labor hours drive or cause all overhead costs.

From Exhibit 8-3, we know that regular cards, the high-volume product, use nine times the direct labor hours used by the scented cards, the low-volume product (90,000 hours versus 10,000 hours). Thus, if a plantwide rate is used, the regular cards will receive nine times more overhead cost than will the scented cards. But is this reasonable? Do unit-based activity drivers explain the consumption of all overhead activities? In particular, can we reasonably assume that each product's consumption of overhead increases in direct proportion to the direct labor hours used? Let's look at the four overhead activities and see if unit-based drivers accurately reflect the demands of the regular and scented cards.

Examination of the data in Exhibit 8-3 suggests that a significant portion of overhead costs is not driven or caused by the units produced (as measured by direct labor hours). For example, each product's demands for setup and materials-handling activities are more logically related to the number of production runs and the number of moves, respectively. These nonunit activities represent 50% ($180,000/$360,000) of the total overhead costs—a significant percentage. Notice that the low-volume product, scented cards, uses twice as many runs as do the regular cards (20/10) and twice as many moves (60/30). However, use of direct labor hours, a unit-based activity driver, and a plantwide rate assigns *nine* times more setup and materials-handling costs to the regular cards than to the scented. Thus, we have product diversity and we should expect product cost distortion because the quantity of unit-based overhead that each product consumes does not vary in direct proportion to the quantity consumed of nonunit-based overhead. The consumption ratios for the two products are illustrated in Exhibit 8-6. Consumption ratios, as Exhibit 8-6 demonstrates, are simply the proportion of each activity consumed by a product. The consumption ratios suggest that a

Exhibit 8-5
Unit Cost Computation: Departmental Rate

	Scented	Regular
Prime costs	$ 78,000	$ 738,000
Overhead costs:		
[($1.35 × 3,000) + ($6.30 × 4,000)]	29,250	
[($1.35 × 77,000) + ($6.30 × 36,000)]		330,750
Total manufacturing costs	$107,250	$1,068,750
Units of production	10,000	100,000
Unit cost (Total costs/Units)	$10.73	$10.69

Exhibit 8-6
Product Diversity: Consumption Ratios

Overhead Activity	Scented Cards	Regular Cards	Activity Driver
Setups	0.67[a]	0.33[a]	Production runs
Materials handling	0.67[b]	0.33[b]	Number of moves
Power	0.10[c]	0.90[c]	Machine hours
Inspection	0.10[d]	0.90[d]	Direct labor hours

[a] 20/30 (scented) and ...
[b] 60/90 (scented) ...
[c] 5,000/... and 45,000/50,000 (regular)
[d] 10,000/100,000 (scented) and 90,000/100,000 (regular)

Note: Because direct labor hours are highly correlated with inspection hours, direct labor hours [were] used as the activity driver for the inspection activity (necessitating the fact that collection of inspection hours by product stopped when the correlation was documented) ...

plantwide rate based on direct labor hours will overcost ... [regular] cards and undercost the scented cards.

The problem is only aggravated when departmental rate[s are used]. [In the] Cutting Department, regular cards consume 25.67 times as many [machine] hours as do the scented cards (77,000/3,000). In the Printing Department, [regular] cards consume nine times as many machine hours as the scented card[s (36,000/] 4,000). Thus, the regular cards receive about 25.67 times more overhead t[han] the scented cards in the Cutting Department, and in the Printing Department they receive nine times more overhead. As Exhibit 8-5 shows, with departmental rates, the unit cost of the scented cards *decreases* to $10.73, and the unit cost of the regular cards *increases* to $10.69. This change is in the wrong direction, which emphasizes the failure of unit-based activity drivers to reflect accurately each product's demands for setup and materials-handling costs.

ACTIVITY-BASED PRODUCT COSTING: GENERAL DESCRIPTION

Objective 2
Explain how an activity-based cost system can produce more accurate product costs.

activity-based cost (ABC) system

In Exhibit 8-1, we saw that traditional overhead assignment involved two stages: first, overhead costs were assigned to an organizational unit (plant or departments), and second, overhead costs were then assigned to products. As Exhibit 8-7 illustrates, an **activity-based cost (ABC) system** is one that first *traces* costs to activities and then to products. Thus, activity-based costing is also a two-stage process, but in the first stage, it traces overhead costs to activities rather than to an organizational unit such as the plant or departments. In both traditional and activity-based costing, the second stage consists of assigning costs to the product. An ABC system, however, emphasizes direct tracing and driver tracing (exploiting cause-and-effect relationships), while a traditional cost system tends to be allocation-intensive (largely ignoring cause-and-effect relationships). Thus, the principal computational difference between the two methods concerns the nature and the number of activity drivers used. Activity-based costing uses both unit-based and nonunit-based activity drivers. These drivers must reflect a cause-and-effect relationship. In practical terms, drivers must explain a large percentage of activity cost variability. This criterion can be tested by preparing cost formulas for each activity and using the activity drivers that have high R^2s.[3] Generally, the number of drivers is greater than the number of unit-based drivers

---

3.   See Chapter 3 for a description of how activity cost formulas are estimated. Also, it should be mentioned that practical application of the R^2 criterion may require a firm to first generate data on candidate activity drivers and activity costs. For example, a traditional cost system may not have been producing data on either drivers or activity costs so that a least-squares formula can be computed. Once data are available, an organization may need to adjust its cost assignment methods based on statistical evidence.

Exhibit 8-7
Activity-Based Costing:
Two-Stage Cost
Assignment

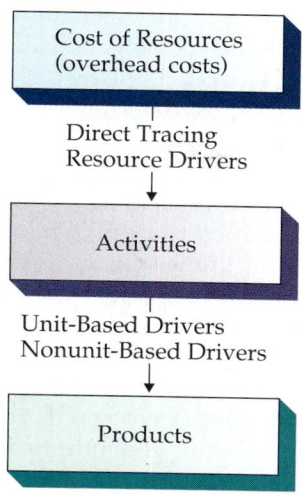

commonly used in a traditional system. As a result, the ABC method produces increased product-costing accuracy.

From a managerial perspective, however, an ABC system offers more than just more accurate product cost information. It also provides information about the cost and performance of activities and resources, and it can trace costs accurately to cost objects other than products, such as customers and channels of distribution. For example, knowing the cost of activities, their importance to the organization, and how efficiently they are performed allows managers to focus on those activities that might offer opportunities for cost savings—provided they are simplified, performed more efficiently, eliminated, and so on. For example, King Soopers automated the routing and scheduling process in one of its Denver warehouses. By getting specific information about unloading rates for various product types and information about a store's ordering habit, they are better able to tailor scheduling for the different stores. The result is that just eight of eleven trucks were needed, mileage has been reduced by 1,200 miles per week, and driver overtime has been reduced. The reduction and elimination of activities related to picking up, transporting, and unloading have resulted in savings of more than $10,000 per week.[4]

The strategic insights and process improvement capabilities of an ABC system are extremely important and are explored in Chapter 9 and Chapter 20. Furthermore, activity-based costing can significantly affect the traditional decision-making models. These effects are explored in Part 3 and are integrated into the various chapters in that section. In this chapter, however, we will focus only on ABC's product-costing dimension, beginning with a general explanation of the first-stage procedure.

First-Stage Procedure

In the first stage of activity-based costing, activities are identified, costs are associated with individual activities, and activities and their associated costs are divided into homogeneous sets. Recall that an activity is work performed within an organization. Thus, activity identification requires a listing of all the different

4.   Denise Zimmerman, "King Soopers Taps Automated Routing," *Supermarket News,* August 21, 1995, p. 13.

kinds of work, such as materials handling, inspections, process engineering, and product enhancement. A firm may have hundreds of different activities. Once an activity is defined, the cost of performing the activity is determined. At this point, the firm could determine the activity driver associated with each activity and calculate individual activity overhead rates. For the average setting, this could literally produce hundreds of overhead rates, a cumbersome method of assigning overhead to products.

To reduce the number of overhead rates required and to streamline the process, activities are grouped together in homogeneous sets based on similar characteristics: (1) they are logically related, and (2) they have the same consumption ratios for all products. Costs are associated with each of these homogeneous sets by summing the costs of the individual activities belonging to the set. The collection of overhead costs associated with each set of activities is called a **homogeneous cost pool**. Since the activities within a homogeneous cost pool have the same consumption ratio, the cost variations for this pool can be explained by a single activity driver. Once a cost pool is defined, the cost per unit of the activity driver is computed by dividing the pool costs by the activity driver's practical capacity. This is called the **pool rate**. Computation of the pool rate completes the first stage. Thus, the first stage produces five outcomes: (1) activities are identified, (2) costs are assigned to activities, (3) related activities are grouped together to form homogeneous sets, (4) the costs of grouped activities are summed to define homogeneous cost pools, and (5) pool (overhead) rates are computed.[5]

To illustrate this process, consider once again the Goodmark example. Four overhead activities have been identified: setups, materials handling, power, and inspection. The costs of the individual activities have been assigned and are described in Exhibit 8-3. Logical relationships also exist. Setup activities and materials-handling activities are performed each time a batch of products is produced. Thus, these two activities are logically related by the more general batch-level production activity. Similarly, inspection and power activities are performed each time a unit of product is produced (recall that each unit is inspected). Thus, these two activities are logically related by the more general activity of producing a unit of product. Moreover, from Exhibit 8-6 we know that the setups and materials-handling grouping and the power and inspection grouping have the same consumption ratios for both products. Thus, we are able to reduce four activities to two sets of activities. These two sets of activities can now be used to form homogeneous cost pools. Let's call the set with setups and materials handling the *batch-level pool* and the set with power and inspection the *unit-level pool*. The total cost associated with each pool is simply the sum of the related activities. Using the data from Exhibit 8-3, the pool costs are given below:

Batch-Level Pool		*Unit-Level Pool*	
Setups	$120,000	Power	$100,000
Materials handling	60,000	Inspection	80,000
	$180,000		$180,000

Now that we have identified homogeneous cost pools and determined their costs, we can assign the pool costs to each product. To do this, a pool rate must

5.   This definition of the first stage in an activity-based cost system is similar to that found in H. Thomas Johnson and Robert S. Kaplan, *Relevance Lost: The Rise and Fall of Management Accounting,* Harvard Business Press, Boston, 1987, Chapter 10.

homogeneous cost pool

pool rate

be calculated based on activity drivers. For the batch-level cost pool, the number of production runs or number of moves could be the activity driver. Since the two activity drivers have the same consumption ratios, either driver, number of setups or number of moves, will assign the same amount of overhead to both products. For the unit-level cost pool (power and inspection), machine hours or direct labor hours could be selected as the activity driver. Assume for purposes of illustration that the number of production runs and machine hours are the activity drivers chosen.[6] Using data from Exhibit 8-3, the first-stage outcomes are illustrated in Exhibit 8-8.

Second-Stage Procedure

In the second stage, the costs of each overhead pool are traced to products. This is done using the pool rates computed in the first stage and measuring of the amount of resources consumed by each product. This measure is simply the quantity of the activity driver used by each product. In our example, that would be the number of production runs and machine hours used by each type of card. Thus, the overhead assigned from each cost pool to each product is computed as follows:

$$\text{Applied overhead (to a product)} = \text{Pool rate} \times \text{Activity usage}$$

To illustrate, consider the assignment of costs from the first overhead pool to regular cards. From Exhibit 8-8, we know that the rate for this pool is $6,000 per production run. We also know from Exhibit 8-3 that the scented cards use 20 production runs and 5,000 machine hours. Thus, the overhead assigned to scented cards from the batch-level cost pool is $120,000 ($6,000 × 20 runs), and the amount assigned from the unit-level pool is $18,000 ($3.60 × 5,000 machine hours). Similar overhead cost assignments would be made for the regular cards. The total manufacturing cost for each product is obtained by adding the prime costs to the assigned overhead costs. This total is then divided by the number of

Exhibit 8-8
First-Stage Procedure: Activity-Based Costing

Batch-level pool:	
Setup costs	$120,000
Materials-handling costs	60,000
Total costs	$180,000
Production runs	30
Pool rate (cost per run)	$6,000
Unit-level pool:	
Power cost	$100,000
Direct labor fringe benefits	80,000
Total costs	$180,000
Machine hours	50,000
Pool rate (cost per machine hour)	$3.60

6. You may want to recalculate pool rates using number of moves and direct labor hours to prove that the choice of cost drivers does not affect the assignment of costs to the individual products.

units produced. The result is the manufacturing cost per unit. Exhibit 8-9 illustrates the activity-based product cost computation for each product.

Comparison of Traditional and ABC Product Costs

In Exhibit 8-10, the unit costs from activity-based costing are compared with the unit costs produced by traditional costing using either a plantwide or departmental rate. This comparison clearly illustrates the effects of using only unit-based activity drivers to assign overhead costs. The activity-based cost assignment better reflects the pattern of overhead consumption and is therefore the most accurate of the three costs shown in Exhibit 8-10. Activity-based product costing reveals that the traditional method undercosts the scented cards and overcosts the regular cards. In fact, the ABC assignment almost doubles the cost of the scented cards and decreases the cost of the regular cards by over $1.00 per box.

Using only unit-based activity drivers can lead to one product subsidizing another (as the regular cards are subsidizing the scented cards). This subsidy could create the appearance that one group of products is highly profitable and can adversely impact the pricing and competitiveness of another group of products. In a highly competitive environment, the more accurate the cost information, the better the planning and decision making.

ABC and Service Organizations

The service environment, like the manufacturing environment, is undergoing significant changes. Events such as deregulation, budget cuts, and changes in social programs are causing service organizations to reevaluate the way they conduct business. The results are surprisingly similar to manufacturing organizations.

Exhibit 8-9
Unit Costs: Activity-Based Costing

	Scented	Regular
Prime costs	$ 78,000	$738,000
Overhead costs:		
Batch-level pool:		
($6,000 × 20)	120,000	
($6,000 × 10)		60,000
Unit-level pool:		
($3.60 × 5,000)	18,000	
($3.60 × 45,000)		162,000
Total manufacturing costs	$216,000	$960,000
Units of production	10,000	100,000
Unit cost (Total costs/Units)	$21.60	$9.60

Exhibit 8-10
Comparison of Unit Costs

	Scented Cards	Regular Cards	Source
Activity-based cost	$21.60	$ 9.60	Exhibit 8-9
Traditional:			
Plantwide rate	11.40	10.62	Exhibit 8-4
Departmental rate	10.73	10.69	Exhibit 8-5

Service organizations are now emphasizing waste elimination, increased productivity, new technology, total quality management, and cost reduction. Knowing what each service costs has also become important. Providing accurate cost information about services can lead an organization to change its mix of services and help in reducing the cost of services that are going to be offered.

First Tennessee National Bank, for example, used ABC information to increase its profitability by almost seven and one-half million dollars per year.[7] They discovered, for instance, that one product, interest-bearing checking accounts, was unprofitable for a given segment of customers. ABC revealed that the cost of servicing an account was about $110 per account, regardless of the size of the balance. The interest-bearing checking account had two product features. First, interest was paid only on accounts with a balance in excess of $500. Second, the monthly service charges were eliminated for those accounts that had an average balance of $1,000 or more. The ABC analysis indicated that the bank was losing money on accounts with balances between $1,000 and $3,500. Once this was known, the loss was eliminated by changing the product features. Specifically, over a period of time the bank restored and gradually increased the monthly service charge for accounts with larger balances.

Clearly, ABC can also be useful to service organizations. All service organizations have activities and output that places demands on these activities. There are some fundamental differences, however, between service and manufacturing organizations. Activities within manufacturing organizations tend to be of the same type and performed in a similar way. The same cannot be said of service organizations. Consider, for example, how dissimilar activities are for a bank and a hospital. Another basic difference between service and manufacturing organizations is output definition. For manufacturing firms, output is easily defined (the tangible products that are manufactured), but for service organizations, output definition is more difficult.[8] Output for service organizations is less tangible. Yet output must be defined so that it can be costed.

Consider, for example, a hospital. What is the output of a hospital? The product of a hospital is commonly defined as a patient's stay and treatment. If we accept this definition, then it becomes immediately obvious that a hospital is a multiproduct firm because there are many different kinds of "stays and treatments." During the stay, a patient will consume many different services. To the extent that this consumption of services is homogeneous, product groups can be defined. For example, maternity patients without complications would all stay about the same time in the hospital and consume essentially the same services.

To illustrate the potential of activity-based costing, we will focus on one type of service provided to each patient: daily care. Daily care is made up of three activities: occupancy, feeding, and nursing. We will define output as patient days (the "stay" part of the output only). Hospitals have traditionally assigned the cost of daily care by using a daily rate (a rate per patient day). There are actually different kinds of daily care, and rates are structured to reflect these differences. For example, a higher daily rate is charged for an intensive care unit than for a maternity care unit. Within units, however, the daily rates are the same for all patients. Under the traditional approach, the daily rate is computed by dividing

---

7.   James W. May and Robert B. Sweeney "Activity-Based Costing in Banking: A Case Study," *CMA Magazine*, May 1994, pp. 19–23.
8.   For more discussion on ABC and potential applications to service organizations, see: John Antos, "Activity-Based Management for Service, Not-for-Profit, and Governmental Organizations," *Journal of Cost Management*, Summer 1992, pp. 13–23; William Rotch, "Activity-Based Costing in Service Industries," *Journal of Cost Management*, Summer 1990, pp. 4–14. The discussion in this chapter is based on these two articles.

the annual costs of occupancy, feeding, and nursing of a unit by the unit's capacity expressed in patient days. A single activity driver (patient days) is used to assign the costs of daily care to each patient.

But what if the costs of the three care activities are consumed in different proportions by patients? This would imply product diversity and a possible requirement to use more than one activity driver to assign daily care costs accurately to patients. To illustrate, assume that the demands for nursing care vary within the maternity unit, depending on the severity of a patient's case. Specifically, demand for nursing services per day increases with severity. Assume that within the maternity unit there are three levels of increasing severity: normal patients, Caesarian patients, and patients with complications. Now suppose that a hospital has provided the following activity and cost information:

Activity	Annual Cost	Activity Driver	Annual Qty
Occupancy and feeding	$1,100,000	Patient days	11,000
Nursing care	1,100,000	Hours of nursing care	55,000

The activity pool rates are $100/patient day and $20/nursing hour.

To see how activity costing can affect patient charges, assume that the three types of patients have the following annual demands:

Patient Type	Patient Days Demanded	Nursing Hours Demanded
Normal	8,000	30,000
Caesarian	2,000	13,000
Complications	1,000	12,000
Total	11,000	55,000

The traditional approach for charging daily care would produce a rate of $200/patient day ($2,200,000/11,000)—the total cost of care divided by patient days. Every maternity patient—regardless of type—would pay the daily rate of $200. Using the pool rates for each activity, however, produces a different daily rate for each patient—a rate that reflects the different demands for nursing services:

Patient	Daily Rate*
Normal	$175
Caesarian	230
Complications	340

*[($100 × 8,000) + ($20 × 30,000)]/8,000
[($100 × 2,000) + ($20 × 13,000)]/2,000
[($100 × 1,000) + ($20 × 12,000)]/1,000

This example illustrates that activity-based costing can produce significant product costing improvements in service organizations that experience product diversity. Although ABC has not yet had the reception in service organizations compared to manufacturing organizations, it has been adopted by some. Examples of service organizations that have adopted an ABC approach include Union Pacific, Amtrak, and Armistead Insurance Company.[9]

9.   William Rotch, "Activity-Based Costing in Service Industries."

ACTIVITY IDENTIFICATION AND CLASSIFICATION

Objective 3

Provide a detailed description of how activities are identified and classified so that homogeneous cost pools can be formed.

In describing activity-based product costing, the basic features have been described and illustrated with the Goodmark Company example and reinforced with an application in a hospital setting. We have learned that activity-based costing is a two-stage process. In the first stage, activities are identified, costs are assigned to activities, related activities are grouped into sets, homogeneous cost pools are formed, and pool rates are computed. In the second stage, each product's demands for the pool's resources are measured and costs are assigned to products using these demands and the respective pool rates. However, to avoid confusing the basic concepts, we avoided any detailed discussion of several steps of the first-stage procedure. We now turn to a more detailed description of the first two steps: (1) activity identification and (2) classification of activities into homogeneous sets. How costs are assigned to activities is discussed in a separate section.

Activity Identification

activity inventory

activity attributes

The focus of activity-based costing is activities. Thus, identifying activities must be the first step in designing an activity-based costing system. Activity implies action taken or work performed. Identifying activities is as simple as asking individual managers and workers the following question: "What work do you do?" Thus, activity identification entails observing and listing the work performed within an organization—work or actions taken that involve the consumption of resources. Generally, activities are what an organization does to satisfy customer needs. Activities are the building blocks for both product costing and continuous improvement. Once activities are identified, they are listed in a document called the **activity inventory**. A sample activity inventory is listed in Exhibit 8-11. Notice that each activity is described by an action verb and an object. Of course, the activity inventory for an actual organization would list more than 12 activities (200 to 300 activities are not uncommon). Once an inventory of activities exists, then *activity attributes* are used to further describe and classify the activities. **Activity attributes** are nonfinancial and financial information items that describe individual activities. What attributes are used depends on the purpose being served. If the purpose is improving performance, then quality and efficiency

Exhibit 8-11
Sample Activity Inventory

Activity Inventory

1. Developing test programs
2. Making probe cards
3. Testing products
4. Setting up lots
5. Collecting engineering data
6. Handling wafer lots
7. Inserting dies
8. Providing utilities
9. Providing space
10. Purchasing materials
11. Receiving materials
12. Paying for materials

attributes would be used. If the purpose is product costing, then attributes that reflect how products consume activities would be used. The use of activity attributes to improve performance is explored in the section on contemporary control systems and, particularly, in the chapter on contemporary responsibility accounting. Since product costing is our current concern, we now turn to the identification of activity attributes that facilitate this objective.

Classification of Activities

For product-costing purposes, activity attributes are used to group related activities into sets that form the basis for homogeneous cost pools. Grouping activities reduces the number of overhead rates needed, simplifies the task of product costing, and decreases the overall complexity of the ABC product costing model. Activities qualify for membership in the same set provided that they have three attributes in common: (1) *process attribute:* they share a common objective or purpose, (2) *activity-level attribute:* they are performed at the same general activity level, and (3) *driver attribute:* they can use the same activity driver to assign costs to a cost object.[10] The first two attributes define what logically related means, and the third attribute simply means that activities must have the same consumption ratio. These three attributes define filters that are used for grouping activities into homogeneous cost pools. Essentially, activities are combined to form homogeneous sets provided they have the *same* process classification, the *same* activity-level classification, and the *same* activity-driver classification. A homogeneous set of activities with its associated costs corresponds to what we have defined as a homogeneous cost pool. To understand this classification process, we need to understand exactly how (and why) each attribute is used to classify activities.

process

Process Classification A **process** is defined as a series of activities that are linked to perform a specific objective. In the process costing chapter, we learned that there are manufacturing processes and we explored ways of assigning costs to products passing through specific manufacturing processes. The concept of processes, however, is much broader than manufacturing. From a general systems perspective, processes receive inputs and produce outputs that are of value to internal and/or external customers. Examples of nonmanufacturing processes include product development, procurement, order fulfillment, credit issuance, and customer servicing. To illustrate a nonmanufacturing process, consider the procurement process. The common objective of the process is obtaining parts for production. Activities include purchasing, receiving, and paying suppliers. Input is usually a purchase requisition from a plant needing parts. The process customer is a production department (an internal customer), and the output is the bought-and-paid-for parts.

Although a process may correspond to a functional arrangement such as a department, activities may also be grouped by cross-functional process. For example, the procurement process used to illustrate the nonmanufacturing processes typically would involve three different organizational units: the purchasing department, the receiving department, and the accounts payable department.

---

10.   For readers who wish more information on the three classification criteria, see: Michael R. Ostrenga and Frank Probst, "Process Value Analysis: The Missing Link in Cost Management, *Journal of Cost Management,* Fall 1992, pp. 4–13; and Peter B. B. Turney and Alan J. Stratton, "Using ABC to Support Continuous Improvement," *Management Accounting,* September 1992, pp. 46–50.

The key to grouping activities is the notion of sharing a common objective or purpose (which may cut across organizational boundaries as in the procurement process example). Furthermore, from a product-costing perspective, there are two purposes for grouping by process: (1) to reduce the number of pool rates used to assign overhead and (2) to increase the accuracy of cost assignments. Understanding the first purpose is straightforward. As we have already seen, activities that are logically related may be consumed in the same proportion by products, reducing the need to have separate overhead rates for each activity. The second purpose is best illustrated with an example.

Consider two manufacturing processes: fabrication and assembly. Assume that materials handling is an activity that is performed by both the fabrication and final assembly processes. Yet fabrication and assembly are two totally different processes (their purposes differ), and the nature of materials handling can differ significantly between them. Suppose in fabrication that materials handling involves movement of batches and pallets to different locations. In this case, the number of moves is probably a good activity driver. In the assembly process, however, materials handling may be related to the number of parts or subassemblies. In this case, a good activity driver may be the number of parts.[11] Since the demands for the materials-handling activity are measured differently in each process (moves versus number of parts), classifying by process increases product-costing accuracy.

This can be illustrated numerically. Assume there are two products that are produced by the fabrication and assembly processes. Fabrication produces five parts for Product A and two parts for Product B. Assembly is responsible for putting the parts together to form the final products. The following information is provided:

	Fabrication	Assembly
Materials-handling cost	$20,000	$28,000
Number of units produced (final product)		
Product A	—	20,000
Product B	—	20,000
Number of moves		
Product A	100	20
Product B	100	20
Number of parts		
Product A	100,000	100,000
Product B	40,000	40,000

The calculation of the materials-handling cost per unit of product is shown in Exhibit 8-12. There are two calculations shown. First, process differences are ignored and the unit cost is computed using moves as the activity driver. Second, materials handling is classified by process and moves is used as the activity driver for the fabrication process and parts is used as the activity driver for the assembly process. The example illustrates that considering process differences can significantly affect product costs. Ignoring the differences causes Product A to be undercosted and Product B to be overcosted.

11.   This example is taken from the following article: Michael R. Ostrenga and Frank R. Probst, "Process Value Analysis: The Missing Link in Cost Management," *Journal of Cost Management*, Fall 1992, pp. 4–13. The benefits of process classification are demonstrated with a lengthy numerical example. Also, for a real-world description of how National Semiconductor Corporation applied these concepts, see Peter B. B. Turney and Alan J. Stratton, "Using ABC to Support Continuous Improvement."

Exhibit 8-12
Product-Costing Bene-
fits of Process
Classification

Unit cost: No process classification

1. Overhead activity rate = $48,000/240 moves = $200/move
2. Materials-handling cost per unit:
     Product A: ($200 × 120)/20,000 units = $1.20 per unit
     Product B: ($200 × 120)/20,000 units = $1.20 per unit

Unit cost: With process classification

1. Overhead activity rates:
     Fabrication: $20,000/200 moves = $100 per move
     Assembly: $28,000/140,000 parts = $0.20 per part
2. Materials-handling cost per unit:
     Product A: [($100 × 100) + ($0.20 × 100,000)]/20,000 = $1.50 per unit
     Product B: [($100 × 100) + ($0.20 × 40,000)]/20,000 = $0.90 per unit

Activity-Level Classification As a second step in building sets of related activities, process-classified activities are classified into one of the following four *general* activity categories: (1) unit-level, (2) batch-level, (3) product-level, and (4) facility-level.[12] Classifying activities into these general categories facilitates product costing because the costs of activities associated with the different levels respond to different *types* of activity drivers (cost behavior differs by level). Knowing the activity level is important because it helps management identify the activity drivers that measure how much of the activity output is being consumed by individual products. Level classification also provides insights concerning the root causes of activities and thus can help managers in their efforts to improve activity performance.

Activity Driver Classification Of the four general levels, the first three, unit-level, batch-level, and product-level, contain product-related activities. For these three levels, it is possible to measure the demands placed on the activities by individual products. Activities within these three levels can be further subdivided on the basis of consumption ratios. Activities with the same consumption ratios can use the same activity driver to assign costs. Thus, in effect, all activities *within* each of the first three levels that have the same activity driver are grouped together. This final grouping creates a homogeneous set of activities: a collection of activities that share a common objective (from the same process), are at the same level, and use the same activity driver. Exhibit 8-13 illustrates the activity classification model that creates homogeneous sets of activities. Notice that facility-level activities do not undergo the driver classification.

The fourth general category, facility-level activities, poses a problem for the ABC philosophy of tracing costs to products. Tracing activity costs to individual products depends on the ability to identify the amount of each activity consumed by a product (product demands for activities must be measured). Facility-level activities (and their costs) are common to a variety of products, and it is not pos-

12.   These categories were defined in Chapter 2.

Exhibit 8-13
Activity Classification Model

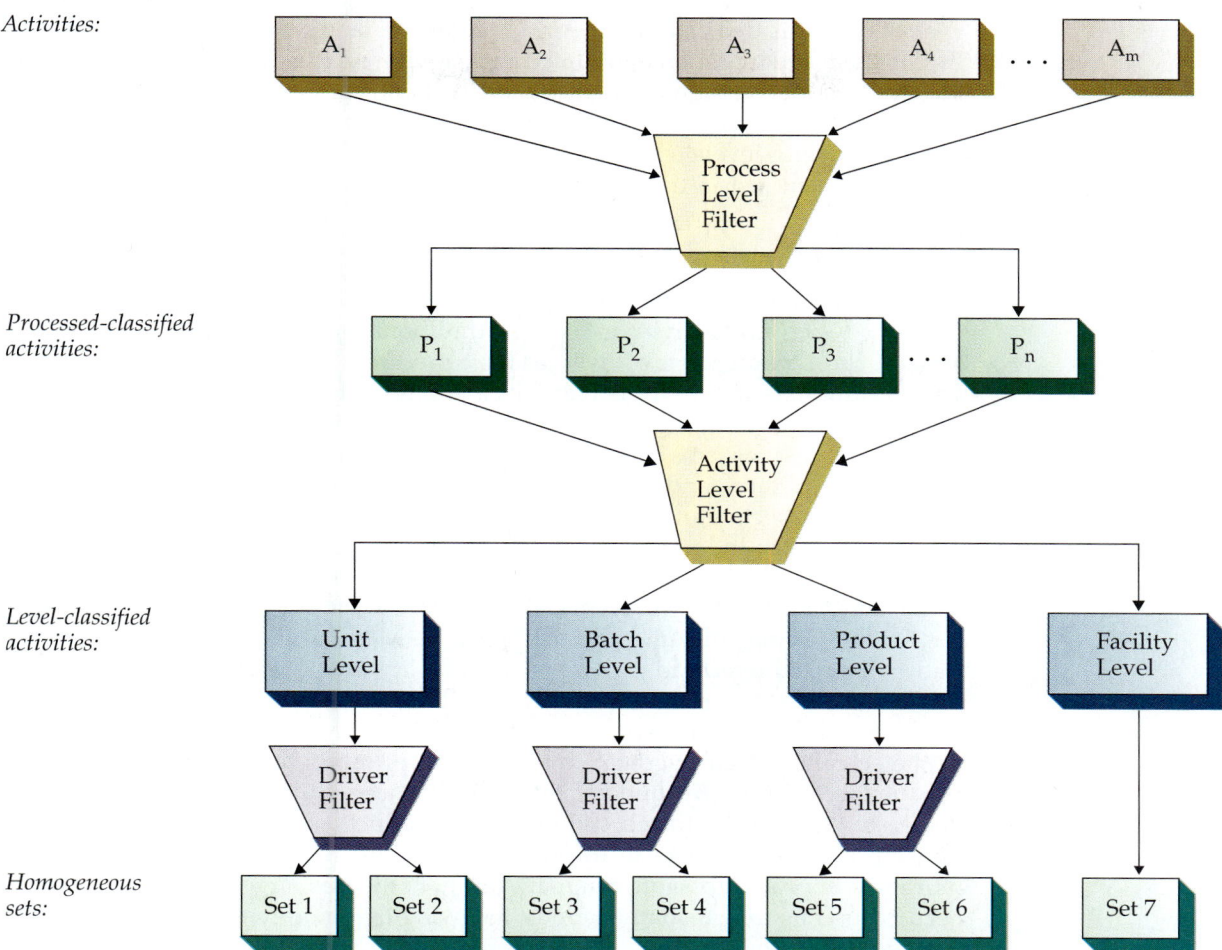

Activities:

Processed-classified activities:

Level-classified activities:

Homogeneous sets:

sible to identify how individual products consume these activities. A pure ABC system, therefore, would not assign these costs to products. They would be treated as period costs. In effect, these costs are fixed costs—costs that are not driven by any of the drivers found in any of the first three categories. In practice, companies adopting ABC systems usually implement a full-costing approach and allocate these facility-level costs to individual products.[13] Unit-level, batch-level, or product-level drivers are often used for the allocation. As a practical matter, assigning these costs may not significantly distort product costs, because they are likely to be small relative to the total costs that are appropriately traced to individual products.[14] There is, however, a possible exception to this observation

13.   A study of 31 companies and 51 cost systems revealed that all companies using an ABC system allo-cated facility-level costs to products. See Robin Cooper, "Cost Classification in Unit-Based and Activity-Based Manufacturing Systems."
14.   At least this appears to be the experience of General Motors based on its implementation of an ABC system. See Beaujon and Singhal, "Understanding the Activity Costs in an Activity-Based Cost System," pp. 51–72.

about facility-level costs and activity drivers. When a company has organized its production facilities around product lines, then it can be argued that space drivers measure the consumption of facility-level costs. This is because floor space within a plant is dedicated to the production of a single product or subassembly. In this case, square footage occupied can be viewed as a possible activity driver for facility costs. Assigning facility-level costs on the basis of space drivers can also serve to motivate managers to reduce the space needed for production, thus reducing facility-level costs over time. This outcome has been observed for firms that implement just-in-time manufacturing and is described in Chapter 9.

Comparison with Traditional Costing

The hierarchial classification of activities allows us to illustrate the fundamental differences between activity-based and traditional cost systems. In a traditional system, the consumption of overhead by products is assumed to be explained only by unit-based activity drivers. In a sophisticated traditional system, overhead costs are classified as fixed and variable with respect to unit-based drivers. Unit-based cost systems allocate fixed overhead to individual products, using fixed overhead rates, and assign variable overhead using variable overhead rates. From the perspective of activity-based costing, the variable overhead is appropriately traced to individual products (for this category, overhead consumption increases as units produced increases). However, assigning fixed overhead costs using unit-based activity drivers can be arbitrary and may not reflect the activities actually being consumed by the products. Many of the costs assigned in the traditional fixed overhead category are, in reality, batch-level, product-level, and facility-level costs that vary with drivers other than unit-level drivers. Activity-based cost systems improve product-costing accuracy by recognizing that many of the so-called fixed overhead costs vary in proportion to changes other than production volume. By understanding what causes these costs to increase or decrease, they can be traced to individual products. This cause-and-effect relationship allows managers to improve product-costing accuracy, which can significantly improve decision making. Additionally, this large pool of fixed overhead costs is no longer so mysterious. Knowing the underlying behavior of many of these costs allows managers to exert more control over the activities that cause the costs. It also allows managers to identify which of the activities add value and which do not. Value analysis is the heart of activity-based management and is the basis for continuous improvement. Activity-based management and the world of continuous improvement is explored in later chapters that deal with contemporary control systems.

An Illustrative Example

To illustrate the classification approach just described, we will build a homogeneous cost model for Marvel Components, Inc., an electronics products manufacturer.[15] In one of its plants, Marvel produces two types of wafers: Wafer A and Wafer B. A wafer is a thin slice of silicon used as a base for integrated circuits or other electronic components. The dies on each wafer represent a particular configuration—a configuration designed for use by a particular end product. Marvel produces wafers in batches, where each batch corresponds to a particular

15.   Some facts of the examples are taken from a description of National Semiconductor's wafer-sorting process. Certain elements of this model are described in Peter B. B. Turney and Alan J. Stratton, "Using ABC to Support Continuous Improvement."

type of wafer (A or B). In the wafer inserting and sorting process, dies are inserted and the wafers are tested to ensure that the dies are not defective. Assume that Marvel has the following activity inventory and costs:

Activity	Budgeted Activity Cost
1. Developing test programs	$300,000
2. Making probe cards	160,000
3. Testing products	275,000
4. Setting up batches	120,000
5. Engineering design	130,000
6. Handling wafer lots	90,000
7. Inserting dies	225,000
8. Purchasing materials	200,000
9. Receiving materials	320,000
10. Paying suppliers	180,000
11. Providing utilities (heat, lighting, etc.)	20,000
12. Providing space	50,000

Process Classification Of the twelve activities, the first seven are performed with the common objective of inserting and detecting defective dies and, therefore, are assigned to the wafer inserting and sorting process. Many of these seven activities could also be performed in other parts of the plant, but generally would be associated with other totally different processes. Because these other processes are totally different (they have different purposes), the activities are associated separately with each process. Activities 8, 9 and 10 have the common objective of procuring materials (parts) and belong to the procurement process (a non-manufacturing process). Activities 11 and 12 have the common objective of sustaining the sorting process and other processes in the plant. These two activities are classified together based on this common sustaining objective. Exhibit 8-14 illustrates process classification for Marvel Components, Inc.

Activity-Level Classification After classifying the activities by process, activity levels are identified. For the inserting and sorting process, we ask the following question: Which activities are performed each time a wafer is produced? Inserting dies and testing dies are done for each wafer and therefore are unit-level activities. Next, which activities are performed each time a batch is produced? Setting up and handling the batches are done for each batch and therefore are batch-level activities. Finally, which activities are performed to enable a product to be produced? Developing test programs, making probe cards, and engineering design are done to enable the wafers to be produced and therefore are product-level activities. The performance of these activities increases as the number of

Exhibit 8-14
Process Classification: Marvel Components, Inc.

Inserting and Sorting Process	Procurement Process	Sustaining Process
Developing test programs	Purchasing materials	Providing utilities
Making probe cards	Receiving materials	Providing space
Testing products	Paying suppliers	
Setting up batches		
Engineering design		
Handling wafer lots		
Inserting dies		

products increases. Similar questions are asked for the procurement activities. Assuming materials are ordered each time a batch is scheduled for production, purchasing can be classified as a batch-level activity. If not, then we might argue that it is a product-level activity. Paying suppliers would not correspond to either a batch-level or unit-level activity (terms and payment policies make it unlikely). Thus, it can be classified as a product-level activity. On the other hand, assuming that parts are shipped to accommodate batch production, then it can be argued that receiving is a batch activity. Finally, the activities of the sustaining process are facility-level. They are performed to enable *production* to occur. Exhibit 8-15 illustrates how the process-classified activities are grouped by level.

Activity Driver Classification Once activities have been classified by process and by level, then we must search for those activities that have the same activity driver. Activity drivers measure the demands of products for activity resources; thus, activities that have the same activity drivers are consumed in the same proportions by products. These activities can be grouped together (review Exhibit 8-6 and the associated Goodmark Company example for the specifics on how this is done). Grouping activities that have common activity drivers finishes the classification effort, and homogeneous sets of activities are formed. Driver-grouped activities with their associated costs form a homogeneous cost pool. Exhibit 8-16 illustrates activity driver classification and the formation of homogeneous cost pools. Notice that once homogeneous sets of activities are defined, then homogeneous cost pools are formed by simply adding the costs of individual activities within each homogeneous set.

Homogeneous Sets: Necessary or Not?

Once the data on activities, their costs, and their drivers are collected, it is possible to compute a rate for each activity and to use this rate to assign costs to products. Nonetheless, we have seen that process classification offers a potential increase in the accuracy of cost assignments. Furthermore, activity level classification is useful because it helps us identify the type and nature of activity drivers that can be used to assign activity costs to products. However, in both cases there is still no compelling argument *against* the calculation of individual activity rates. Process and level classifications do not preclude individual activity rates. In fact, these classifications are useful preparatory steps for the calculation of individual rates.

Exhibit 8-15
Activity-Level Classification: Marvel Components, Inc.

Inserting and Sorting Process	Procurement Process	Sustaining Process
Unit Level: Testing products, Inserting dies	*Batch level:* Purchasing materials, Receiving materials	*Facility level:* Providing utilities, Providing space
Batch level: Setting up batches, Handling wafer lots	*Product level:* Paying suppliers	
Product level: Developing test programs, Making probe cards, Engineering design		

Exhibit 8-16
Activity-Driver Classification and Homogeneous Cost Pools

Activity Level	Activity Driver	Activity Cost
	Inserting and Sorting Process:	
Unit-level activities:		
Pool 1:		
Testing products	Number of dies	$275,000
Inserting dies	Number of dies	225,000
		$500,000
Batch-level activities:		
Pool 2:		
Setting up batches	Number of batches	$120,000
Handling wafer lots	Number of batches	90,000
		$210,000
Product-level activities:		
Pool 3:		
Developing test programs	Number of products	$300,000
Making probe cards	Number of products	160,000
		$460,000
Pool 4:		
Engineering design	Number of change orders	$130,000
	Procurement Process:	
Batch-level activities:		
Pool 5:		
Purchasing materials	Number of purchase orders	$200,000
Receiving materials	Number of receiving orders	320,000
		$520,000
Product-level activities:		
Pool 6:		
Paying suppliers	Number of parts	$180,000
	Sustaining Process:	
Facility-level activities:		
Pool 7:		
Providing utilities	Direct labor hours	$20,000
Providing space	Direct labor hours	50,000
		$70,000

The principal justification for homogeneous *groups* of activities and the associated pool rates is the reduction in the number of rates needed to assign costs to products. It is the final classification—driver classification—that reduces the number of rates. Grouping activities with the same consumption ratios reduces the number of rates needed. Why is this important? In a computerized system there is no computational need to reduce the number of rates; thus, computational savings cannot be used to justify pool rates. Yet, there may be some justification for the formation of homogeneous pools when preparing reports that detail cost assignments. For example, the use of 10–20 pool rates is much more easily reported and reviewed by management than a report listing 200–300 rates. Thus, homogeneous pools make product cost reports more manageable. Even so, keep in mind that the information at the individual activity level, including activity rates, plays an important role in the contemporary control model. Detailed activity information is needed to support the objective of continuous improvement.

ABC DATA BASE

Objective 4
Describe an activity-based relational data base.

ABC data base
data set

relational structure

primary key

The data requirements of the Marvel Components example suggest a need to build an *activity-based costing (ABC) data base*. An **ABC data base** is the collected data sets that are organized and interrelated for use by an organization's activity-based costing information system. A **data set** is a grouping of logically related data. Creating an ABC data base requires three steps. First, we must define and model the entities (objects) that are involved in the operation of an activity-based costing system. The two most fundamental entities are activities and products (other entities such as customers and distribution channels could also be defined). Second, a conceptual view must be developed that portrays the entities and the logical relationships that exist among the entities. Most of the chapter has been devoted to developing a conceptual understanding of the logical relationships that exist among activities and products. Third, the attributes that should be associated with each entity must be identified. These attributes are determined by the objectives of the information system being supported and by the needs of the users. For example, the objective of building homogeneous cost pools requires the following activity attributes: process membership, activity-level membership, activity driver, and budgeted activity costs. To complete the first stage, pool rates also must be calculated. An additional activity attribute is needed for this purpose: activity capacity (measured in terms of the activity driver associated with the activity's homogeneous pool). Recall that pool rates are computed by dividing the budgeted pool costs by activity capacity.

Once the attributes and the entities are defined and identified, then a model must be selected that reflects the data structure implied by the entities and attributes. There are numerous ways of representing data structure. We will illustrate only one: *relational structure.*[16] A **relational structure** uses a table to represent the overall logical view within a data base. The table is made up of rows and columns, where the entity defines the rows and the attributes define the columns. The tables needed for a relational data base are defined by the relationships that exist among the entities. Each table should satisfy the following three properties: (1) the rows are fixed in length (each row has the same number of attributes), (2) each row is unique, and (3) the attributes for each row are directly related to a single entity.

To illustrate a relational table, consider once again the Marvel Components, Inc., example. Exhibit 8-17 presents Marvel's activity relational table. Notice that each row of the table is the same length (has the same number of attributes). Also, each row is unique, since it corresponds to a different activity. Each activity is identified by an activity number, which acts as the unique *primary key*. A **primary key** is the attribute that uniquely identifies each row of data in a table (often referred to as a *record*). The activity number is the number associated with each

16.   Much of the material in this section is based on the following source: Don R. Hansen and David Murphy, "The Design of a Relational Data Base for an Activity-Based Cost Management System," Unpublished Working Paper, Oklahoma State University, January 1994.

Exhibit 8-17
Relational Table Illustrated

		Activity Relational Table: Marvel Components, Inc.				
Activity	*Activity Name*	*Process*	*Level*	*Activity Driver*	*Capacity*	*Cost*
1	Developing test program	Sorting	Product	No. of products	2	$300,000
2	Making probe cards	Sorting	Product	No. of products	2	160,000
3	Testing products	Sorting	Unit	No. of dies	2,000,000	275,000
4	Setting up batches	Sorting	Batch	No. of batches	400	120,000
5	Engineering design	Sorting	Product	Change orders	40	130,000
6	Handling wafer lots	Sorting	Batch	No. of batches	400	90,000
7	Inserting dies	Sorting	Unit	No. of dies	2,000,000	225,000
8	Purchasing materials	Procurement	Batch	Purchase orders	800	200,000
9	Receiving materials	Procurement	Batch	Purchase orders	800	320,000
10	Paying suppliers	Procurement	Product	No. of parts	4,000,000	180,000
11	Providing utilities	Sustaining	Facility	DL hours	200,000	20,000
12	Providing space	Sustaining	Facility	DL hours	200,000	50,000

activity in the activity inventory. For this example, the activity name is unique and could also serve as the primary key. Finally, notice that all nonkey attributes are fully dependent upon the primary key.

Once a data base has been created, then data can be retrieved as needed. For example, the relational table in Exhibit 8-17 provides all the information to form homogeneous cost pools and calculate pool rates. Using the information in the relational table, you can verify the homogeneous cost pools described in Exhibit 8-16. Recall that a homogeneous set is defined as those activities that have the same process, the same activity level, and the same activity driver. Once homogeneous cost pools are defined, the pool rate is computed using the attribute, activity capacity, and the pool costs. These rates are computed and displayed in Exhibit 8-18. With the computation of the pool rates, the first stage of activity-based costing is completed.

The second stage assigns the pooled activity costs to individual products. Assigning costs to products necessitates the specification of activity demands, as measured by the drivers associated with each pool. Thus, a second relational table is needed: a product relational table. This table is centered on the "product" entity and must have attributes that identify how costs are to be assigned. A product number or name that uniquely identifies each product can be used as the primary key. The attributes for carrying out the second stage of activity-based costing are the product's demands for each pool's activity driver and the units produced of each. The product relational table for Marvel Components is shown in Exhibit 8-19. The table is structured to facilitate the addition or deletion of drivers as circumstances change. The product relational table illustrates the use

concatenated keys

of *concatenated keys*. **Concatenated keys** are two or more keys that uniquely identify a record (notice that one key, such as product name, is not sufficient). For example, in the product relational table, a row is uniquely identified by product number and driver number (or by product name and driver name). The information in this second table is vital for the second stage of ABC: assigning costs to individual products. Assigning costs to Wafer A and Wafer B is presented as a review exercise at the end of this chapter.

Exhibit 8-18
Pool Rates: Marvel Components, Inc.

Inserting and Sorting Process

Unit-level pool:
Pool 1:
Rate = $500,000/2,000,000
= $0.25 per die

Product-level pools:
Pool 3:
Rate = $460,000/2
= $230,000 per product
Pool 4:
Rate = $130,000/40
= $3,250 per engineering order

Batch-level pool:
Pool 2:
Rate = $210,000/400
= $525 per batch

Procurement Process

Batch-level pool:
Pool 5:
Rate = $520,000/800
= $650 per purchase order

Product-level pool:
Pool 6:
Rate = $180,000/4,000,000
= $0.045 per part

Sustaining Process

Pool 7:
Rate = $70,000/200,000
= $0.35 per direct labor hour

Exhibit 8-19
Product Relational Table: Marvel Components, Inc.

Product Number	Product Name	Activity Driver Number	Activity Driver Name	Activity Usage
1	Wafer A	1	Units	100,000
1	Wafer A	2	No. of dies	600,000
1	Wafer A	3	No. of batches	200
1	Wafer A	4	Change orders	10
1	Wafer A	5	No. of products	1
1	Wafer A	6	Purchase orders	400
1	Wafer A	7	No. of parts	1,000,000
1	Wafer A	8	Direct labor hours	80,000
2	Wafer B	1	Units	200,000
2	Wafer B	2	No. of dies	1,400,000
2	Wafer B	3	No. of batches	200
2	Wafer B	4	Change orders	30
2	Wafer B	5	No. of products	1
2	Wafer B	6	Purchase orders	400
2	Wafer B	7	No. of parts	3,000,000
2	Wafer B	8	Direct labor hours	120,000

ASSIGNING COSTS TO ACTIVITIES

Objective 5
Describe how costs are assigned to activities.

A vital attribute in an ABC data base is the cost of individual activities. This attribute appears in the activity relational table and is needed to compute cost pools and pool rates. As we have seen, the ultimate objective of activity classification is to build homogeneous cost pools so that the costs of activities can be assigned to products. Once homogeneous sets of activities are formed as illustrated in Exhibit 8-13, homogeneous cost pools are created by summing the costs of the individual activities within each set. Thus, an additional requirement for activity-based costing is assigning costs to individual activities. From Exhibit 8-7, we know that costs are assigned to activities using direct tracing and resource drivers. There are many costs that are physically and observably associated with individual activities. For example, the wages of maintenance workers, salary of the maintenance supervisor, and parts for repair can be assigned to the maintenance activity using direct tracing. Frequently, however, the cost of resources cannot be assigned using direct tracing. For the cost of resources that are not directly traceable, resource drivers must be used. Resource drivers are measures of the quantity of resources consumed by an activity. Resource drivers assign costs to activities based on cause-and-effect relationships. Often resource costs are assigned to activities using drivers such as effort expended or material consumed.

For example, the salary of a person working with several different activities can be assigned to each activity using the *percent of effort* as the resource driver. Thus, if a worker in the receiving department has a salary of $30,000 and spends 20% of his time on unloading goods, 5% on verifying the authenticity of the order, 25% on counting goods, 40% on inspecting, and 10% on moving the goods to the inventory storage, then the following costs would be assigned to each activity:

Activity	Cost Assigned*
Unloading goods	$ 6,000
Verifying order	1,500
Counting goods	7,500
Inspecting goods	12,000
Moving goods	3,000
Total	$30,000

*0.20 × $30,000, 0.05 × $30,000, etc.

Interviews, survey forms, questionnaires, and timekeeping systems are examples of tools that can be used to collect data on resource drivers. Notice that tracking the effort spent on different activities is similar to tracking the time laborers spend on different jobs. However, there is one critical difference. The percent of effort spent on various activities is usually fairly constant and may only need to be measured periodically (perhaps annually). The same constancy property also exists for other types of resource drivers.

The assignment of resource costs to activities requires that the resource costs described in the general ledger be unbundled and reassigned. In a traditional cost system, the general ledger reports costs by department and by spending account (based on a chart of accounts). The $30,000 salary of the receiving worker, for example, would be recorded as part of the total salaries of the receiving department. The general ledger indicates what is spent, but it does not reveal how the resources are spent. Of course, the resources are spent on the basic work (activities) performed in the department. In an activity-based cost system, costs must be reported by activity. Thus, an ABC system must restate the general ledger costs so that the new system reveals how the resources are being consumed. Exhibit 8-20 illustrates the unbundling concept for a receiving department. As the exhibit indicates, the reassignment of resource costs to individual activities contributes to the creation of an ABC data base for the organization. The assign-

Exhibit 8-20
Unbundling of General Ledger Costs

		Direct Attribution Resource Drivers	
General Ledger		→	*ABC Database*

Receiving Department

Chart-of-Accounts View		ABC View	
Salaries	$200,000	Unloading goods	$ 32,000
Supplies	20,000	Verifying order	64,000
Equipment	80,000	Counting goods	40,000
Utilities	20,000	Inspecting goods	148,000
		Delivering goods	36,000
Total	$320,000	Total	$320,000
What is spent.		*How it is spent.*	

ment of resource costs to activities creates the values needed for the activity cost attribute.

We have talked about the importance of identifying activities and assigning costs to activities. The objective has been to correctly determine the cost of activities for both product costing and for managerial decision making. However, the identification and costing of activities can also help managers "see" the activities of the business from a new perspective and even help them to act more ethically. For example, many businesses use music-on-hold to entertain telephone callers, or pipe music from the radio into offices and reception areas. This is illegal if the appropriate permissions have not been received from the songwriters. A thorough inventory of business activities will explicitly identify the "mood music" activity and accompanying costs (radio, etc.). The manager is more likely to become aware of the use of music as an activity and possibly be alerted to the need to use it legally. The payment of a yearly license fee to A.S.C.A.P. and BMI (ranging from $120 to $2,000), or the use of a company like Muzak, makes the process legal. By the way, the cost of ignoring the need for proper permission is high, up to $20,000 per pirated song.[17]

17.   R. Lee Sullivan, "Hold That Music, Please," *Fortune*, January 2, 1995, p. 17.

SUMMARY

Overhead costs have increased in significance over time and, in many firms, represent a much higher percentage of product costs than does direct labor. At the same time, many overhead activities are unrelated to the units produced. Traditional cost systems are not able to assign properly the costs of these nonunit-related overhead activities. These overhead activities are consumed by products in different proportions than are unit-based overhead activities. Because of this, assigning overhead using only unit-based drivers can distort product costs. This can be a serious matter if the nonunit-based overhead costs are a significant proportion of total overhead costs.

Overhead assignments should reflect the amount of overhead demanded (consumed) by each product. Activity-based costing recognizes that not all overhead varies with the number of units produced. By using both unit-based and nonunit-based activity drivers, overhead can be more accurately traced to individual products. This tracing is achieved by implementing the following steps: (1) identifying the major activities, (2) determining the cost of those activities, (3) identifying what causes or drives these activity costs (activity drivers), (4) grouping activities into homogeneous cost pools, (5) calculating a pool rate, (6) measuring the demands placed on activities by each product, and (7) calculating product costs.

Activities are basic units of work. Homogeneous sets of activities are collections of activities that have the same process classification, the same level classification, and the same activity driver classification. Process classification groups activities that share a common objective. Level classification places activities into one of four categories: unit level, batch level, product level, and facility level. Unit-level activities occur each time a unit of product is produced. Batch-level activities occur when batches of products are produced. Product-level activities are incurred to enable production of each different type of product. Facility-level activities sustain a facility's general manufacturing processes. Finally, level-classified activities with the same activity driver are combined to form homogeneous sets. Summing the costs associated with activities within homogeneous sets defines homogeneous cost pools. Activity drivers are then used to compute pool rates and assign costs to individual products.

Implementing an ABC system is facilitated by creating and maintaining an activity-based data base. Relational data bases offer a simple and straightforward way of collecting and organizing ABC data. At least two relational tables are needed: one for activities and one for products. Once the relational tables are created, data can be extracted so that individual product costs can be computed.

Activity cost is an essential activity attribute. Activity costs are determined by using direct tracing and resource drivers. Assigning costs to activities entails unbundling the general ledger accounts so that a clear picture emerges of how resources are spent.

REVIEW PROBLEMS AND SOLUTIONS

I.

Traditional Costing Versus Activity-Based Costing

Tyson Lamp Company is noted for a full line of quality lamps. The company operates one of its plants in Green Bay, Wisconsin. That plant produces two types of lamps: classical and modern. Jane Martinez, the president of the company, recently decided to change from a unit-based, traditional costing system to an activity-based cost system. Before making the change companywide, she wanted to assess the effect on the product costs of the Green Bay plant. This plant was chosen because it produces only two types of lamps; most other plants produce at least a dozen.

To assess the effect of the change, the following data have been gathered (for simplicity, assume one process):

Lamp	Quantity	Prime Costs	Machine Hours	Material Moves	Setups
Classical	400,000	$800,000	100,000	200,000	100
Modern	100,000	150,000	25,000	100,000	50
Dollar value	—	$950,000	$500,000*	$850,000	$650,000

*The cost of operating the production equipment

Total OH

Under the current system, the costs of operating equipment, materials handling, and setups are assigned to the lamps on the basis of machine hours. Lamps are produced and moved in batches.

REQUIRED:

1. Compute the unit cost of each lamp using the current unit-based approach.
2. Compute the unit cost of each lamp using an activity-based costing approach.

Solution

1. Total overhead is $2,000,000. The plantwide rate is $16 per machine hour ($2,000,000/125,000). Overhead is assigned as follows:

Classical lamps: $16 × 100,000 = $1,600,000
Modern lamps: $16 × 25,000 = $400,000

The unit costs for the two products are as follows:

Classical lamps: ($800,000 + $1,600,000)/400,000 = $6.00
Modern: ($150,000 + $400,000)/100,000 = $5.50

2. In the activity-based approach, the consumption ratios are the same for materials handling and setups, so a batch-level pool can be formed. The machine pool is a unit-level pool (machining is performed each time a lamp is produced). Thus, two overhead pools are formed, and rates for each of these pools are as follows:

Machining pool: $500,000/125,000 = $4.00 per machine hour	
Batch pool:	
Materials handling	$ 850,000
Setups	650,000
Total	$1,500,000
Number of setups	150
Rate (Total/Setups)	$10,000 per setup

Note: Number of moves could have been used instead of setups. This would produce a different pool rate, but the cost assignment to the two products would be the same. Whenever two or more drivers can be chosen, it makes sense to choose the one for which information is already being gathered (if possible).

Overhead is assigned as follows:

Classical lamps:	
$4 × 100,000	$ 400,000
$10,000 × 100	1,000,000
Total	$1,400,000
Modern lamps:	
$4 × 25,000	$100,000
$10,000 × 50	500,000
Total	$600,000

This produces the following unit costs:

Classical lamps:	
Prime costs	$ 800,000
Overhead costs	1,400,000
Total costs	$2,200,000
Units produced	400,000
Unit cost	$5.50

continued

Modern lamps:	
Prime costs	$150,000
Overhead costs	600,000
Total costs	$750,000
Units produced	100,000
Unit cost	$7.50

II.
Activity-Based Costing; Relational Tables; Unit Costs

The following pool rates have been computed for Marvel Components, Inc. (see Exhibit 8-18 for details):

Process	Level	Pool Number	Rate
Sorting	Unit	1	$0.25 per die
	Batch	2	$525 per batch
	Product	3	$230,000 per product
	Product	4	$3,250 per engineering order
Procurement	Batch	5	$650 per purchase order
	Product	6	$0.045 per part
Sustaining	Facility	7	$0.35 per direct labor hour

For convenience, Marvel's product relational table is reproduced below:

Product Number	Product Name	Activity Driver Number	Activity Driver Name	Activity Usage
1	Wafer A	1	Units	100,000
1	Wafer A	2	No. of dies	600,000
1	Wafer A	3	No. of batches	200
1	Wafer A	4	Change orders	10
1	Wafer A	5	No. of products	1
1	Wafer A	6	Purchase orders	400
1	Wafer A	7	No. of parts	1,000,000
1	Wafer A	8	Direct labor hours	80,000
2	Wafer B	1	Units	200,000
2	Wafer B	2	No. of dies	1,400,000
2	Wafer B	3	No. of batches	200
2	Wafer B	4	Change orders	30
2	Wafer B	5	No. of products	1
2	Wafer B	6	Purchase orders	400
2	Wafer B	7	No. of parts	3,000,000
2	Wafer B	8	Direct labor hours	120,000

REQUIRED:

1. Calculate the unit overhead costs for Wafer A and Wafer B. Arrange the costs for each product by activity level. Can you think of any advantage in reporting costs by level?
2. Suppose you decided to form a "pool" relational table (the homogeneous cost pool is the entity). Identify the attributes that would be needed so that pool rates could be computed using data from the pool relational table. Finally, using the information from Exhibit 8-18, form a pool relational table. Would this "pool table" be necessary?

Solution

1. Calculations of the unit overhead costs for Wafer A and Wafer B appear on the following page. Reporting costs by level emphasizes that costs vary with different activity drivers. Only unit-level costs vary as the number of units produced changes. The other

costs vary with other factors. It also allows managers to exclude the facility-level component, if desired. (Some argue that facility-level costs should not be assigned to products, since they cannot be traced.)

	Wafer A	Wafer B
Unit level:*		
$0.25 × 600,000/100,000	$1.50	
$0.25 × 1,400,000/200,000		$1.75
Batch-level:		
$525 × 200/100,000	1.05	
$525 × 200/200,000		0.53
$650 × 400/100,000	2.60	
$650 × 400/200,000		1.30
Product-level:		
$230,000 × 1/100,000	2.30	
$230,000 × 1/200,000		1.15
$3,250 × 10/100,000	0.33	
$3,250 × 30/200,000		0.49
$0.045 × 1,000,000/100,000	0.45	
$0.045 × 3,000,000/200,000		0.68
Facility level:		
$0.35 × 80,000/100,000	0.28	
$0.35 × 120,000/200,000		0.21
Unit overhead cost	$8.51	$6.11

*Units are obtained from the first and ninth rows of the product relational table.

2. If a pool is an entity, then the attributes needed to compute the pool rates are: pool costs, activity driver (for the pool), and the practical capacity of the pool's activity driver. The relational table would appear as follows:

Pool	Activity Driver	Activity Capacity	Cost
1	No. of dies	2,000,000	$500,000
2	No. of batches	400	210,000
3	No. of products	2	460,000
4	Engineering orders	40	130,000
5	Purchase orders	800	520,000
6	No. of parts	4,000,000	180,000
7	DL hours	200,000	70,000

The pool relational table is derived from the activity relational table and is not a necessary part of the ABC data base.

KEY TERMS

ABC data base 324
Activity attributes 315
Activity inventory 315
Activity-based cost (ABC) system 308
Advanced manufacturing environment 303

Concatenated keys 325
Consumption ratio 305
Data set 324
Homogeneous cost pool 310

Nonunit-based activity drivers 304
Pool rate 310
Primary key 324
Process 316

Product diversity 305
Relational structure 324
Unit-based activity drivers 301

QUESTIONS FOR WRITING AND DISCUSSION

1. Explain how a plantwide overhead rate, using a unit-based cost driver, can produce distorted product costs. In your answer, identify two major factors that impair the ability of plantwide rates to assign cost accurately.
2. What are nonunit-related overhead activities? Nonunit-based cost drivers? Give some examples.
3. What is an overhead consumption ratio?
4. Explain how departmental overhead rates can produce product costs that are more distorted than those computed using a plantwide rate.
5. What is meant by product diversity?
6. Overhead costs are the source of product cost distortions. Do you agree? Explain.
7. What is activity-based product costing?
8. What is a homogeneous cost pool?
9. What is the first-stage procedure in assigning overhead costs to products when using an activity-based system?
10. What is the second-stage procedure in assigning overhead costs to products when using an activity-based system?

11. What is an activity? A homogeneous set of activities?
12. What are unit-level activities? Batch-level activities? Product-level activities? Facility-level activities?
13. Explain how low-volume products can be undercosted and high-volume products overcosted if only unit-based cost drivers are used to assign overhead costs.
14. Explain how undercosting low-volume products and overcosting high-volume products can affect the competitive position of a firm.
15. Explain how homogeneous sets of activities are produced. Why are they produced?
16. What is an activity-based data base?
17. How is an activity relational table constructed? A product relational table? In providing your answer, explain how attributes are selected.
18. Explain how the cost of resources is assigned to activities. What is meant by the phrase "unbundling the general ledger accounts?"

EXERCISES AND PROBLEMS

8-1

Selection of Cost Drivers and Product Costing Accuracy

LO 1, 2

Manfield Company produces two types of wallets. Wallet A is virtually handcrafted; Wallet B is produced through a mostly automated process. Although the handcrafted wallet is labor-intensive, its production requires the use of the same equipment that Wallet B uses. Manfield Company assigns overhead using direct labor dollars. Gary Norton, sales manager, is convinced that the wallets are not being costed correctly.

To illustrate his point, he decided to focus on only the machine-related costs, which are as follows:

Depreciation	$5,000*
Operating costs	4,000

*Computed on a straight-line basis, book value at the beginning of the year was $25,000. The machine has the capability of supplying 25,000 machine hours over its remaining life.

He also collected the expected annual prime costs for each wallet, the machine hours, and the expected production (which is the normal output for the company).

	Wallet A	Wallet B
Direct labor	$9,000	$3,000
Direct materials	$3,000	$3,000
Units	3,000	3,000
Machine hours	500	4,500

REQUIRED:

1. Do you think that the direct labor costs and direct materials costs are accurately traced to each wallet? Explain.
2. The controller has suggested that overhead costs be assigned to each product using a plantwide rate based on direct labor costs. Machine costs are overhead costs. Calculate the machine cost per unit for each purse that would be assigned using this approach. Do you think that machine costs are traced accurately to each wallet? Explain.
3. Now calculate the machine cost per unit for each wallet using an overhead rate based on machine hours. Do you think machine costs are traced accurately to each wallet? Explain.
4. Suppose machine hours are used to assign *all* overhead costs of the plant to the two products. Do you think this will produce an accurate cost assignment for each wallet? Explain.

8-2
Multiple Versus
Single Overhead
Rates; Activity
Drivers
LO 1, 2

Assume that a company has two categories of overhead: machine operating costs and materials handling. The costs expected for these categories for the coming year are as follows:

Machine operating costs	$220,000
Materials handling	180,000
Total	$400,000

The plant currently applies overhead using machine hours and expected actual capacity. Expected actual capacity is 50,000 machine hours. Charlene Wells, the plant manager, has been asked to submit a bid and has assembled the following data on the proposed job:

	Potential Job
Direct materials	$4,000
Direct labor	$6,000
Overhead	$8,000
Number of machine hours	1,000
Number of material moves	5

Charlene has been told that many competitors use an activity-based approach to assign overhead to jobs. Before submitting her bid, she wants to assess the effects of this alternative approach. She estimates that 3,000 material moves will be performed plantwide next year.

REQUIRED:

1. Compute the total cost of the potential job using machine hours to assign overhead. Assuming that the bid price is full manufacturing cost plus 25 percent, what would be Charlene's bid?
2. Compute the total cost of the job using the number of material moves to assign materials-handling costs and machine hours to assign machine operating costs. Assuming a bid price of full manufacturing cost plus 25 percent, what is Charlene's bid using this approach?
3. Which approach do you think best reflects the actual cost of the job? Explain.

8-3
Multiple Versus
Single Overhead
Rates: Activity
Drivers

LO 1, 2

Swasey Company has identified the following overhead activities, costs, and activity drivers for the coming year:

Activity	Expected Cost	Activity Driver	Activity Capacity
Setup costs	$60,000	Number of setups	300
Ordering costs	45,000	Number of orders	4,500
Machine costs	90,000	Machine hours	18,000
Receiving	25,000	Number of parts	50,000

Assume for simplicity that each activity corresponds to a process. The following two jobs were completed during the year:

	Job 600	Job 700
Direct materials	$750	$850
Direct labor (50 hours per job)	$600	$600
Units completed	100	50
Number of setups	1	1
Number of orders	4	2
Machine hours	20	30
Parts used	20	40

The company's normal activity is 4,000 direct labor hours.

REQUIRED:

1. Determine the unit cost for each job using direct labor hours to apply overhead.
2. Determine the unit cost for each job using the four activity drivers.
3. Which method produces the more accurate cost assignment? Why?

8-4
Activity-Based
Costing; Activity
Classification;
Homogeneous Cost
Pools

LO 3

Riobamba Manufacturing produces specially machined parts. The parts are produced in batches in one continuous manufacturing process. Each part is custom produced and requires special engineering design activity (based on customer specifications). Once the design is completed, then the equipment can be set up for batch production. Once the batch is completed, a sample is taken and inspected to see if the parts are within the tolerances allowed. Thus, the manufacturing process has four activities: engineering, setups, machining, and inspecting. In addition, there is a sustaining process with two activities: providing utilities (plantwide) and providing space. Costs have been assigned to each activity using direct tracing and resource drivers:

Engineering	$100,000
Setups	90,000
Machining	200,000
Inspection	80,000
Providing space	25,000
Providing utilities	18,000

Activity drivers for each activity have been identified and their practical capacities listed:

Machine Hours	Setups	Engineering Hours	Inspection Hours
20,000	150	4,000	2,000

The costs of facility-level activities are assigned using machine hours.

REQUIRED:

1. Identify the activities within each process as unit-level, batch-level, product-level, or facility-level.
2. Create homogeneous cost pools. Identify the activities that belong to each pool and the activity driver that will be used for computing pool rates.
3. Identify the activity driver for each pool and compute the pool rate.

8-5
Activity Relational Table
LO 4

Refer to the data in **8-4**. Build an activity relational table that can be used to calculate pool rates.

8-6
Product Relational Table; ABC Product Costs
LO 3, 4

Golding Company recently installed an activity-based relational data base. Using the information contained in the activity relational table, the following pool rates have been computed:

$200 per purchase order
$12 per machine hour, Process R
$15 per machine hour, Process D
$40 per engineering hour
$2 per packing order
$100 per square foot

Two products are produced by Golding: a deluxe disk player and a regular disk player. Each product has an area in the plant that is dedicated to its production. The plant has two manufacturing processes, the regular process (Process R) and the deluxe process (Process D). Other processes include engineering, product handling, and procurement. The product relational table for Golding is given below:

Product Name	Activity Driver Number	Activity Driver Name	Activity Usage
Regular	1	Units	800,000
Regular	2	Purchase orders	1,000
Regular	3	Machine hours	320,000
Regular	4	Engineering hours	5,000
Regular	5	Packing orders	400,000
Regular	6	Square footage	6,000
Deluxe	1	Units	100,000
Deluxe	2	Purchase orders	500
Deluxe	3	Machine hours	40,000
Deluxe	4	Engineering hours	6,000
Deluxe	5	Packing orders	100,000
Deluxe	6	Square footage	4,000

REQUIRED:

1. Identify two different concatenated keys. What is the purpose of concatenated keys?
2. Using the pool rates and the information from the product relational table, calculate the unit overhead cost for each product.

3. Does the product relational table indicate how many activities are in each pool? Is this necessary for product costing? Explain.

8-7
Assigning Costs to Activities, Resource Drivers
LO 5

Manufacturing Engineering Department within a factory has the following activities: creating bills of materials (BOMs), studying manufacturing capabilities, improving manufacturing processes, training employees, and designing tools. The general ledger accounts reveal the following expenditures for Manufacturing Engineering:

Salaries	$500,000
Equipment	100,000
Supplies	30,000
Total	$630,000

The equipment is used for two activities: improving processes and designing tools. Forty percent of the equipment's time is used for improving processes, and sixty percent is used for designing tools. The salaries are for nine engineers, one who earns $100,000 and eight who earn $50,000 each. The $100,000 engineer spends 40% of his time training employees in new processes and 60% of his time on improving processes. One engineer spends 100% of her time on designing tools, and another engineer spends 100% of his time on improving processes. The remaining six engineers spend equal time on all activities. Supplies are consumed in the following proportions:

Creating BOMs	10%
Studying capabilities	5%
Improving processes	35%
Training employees	20%
Designing tools	30%

REQUIRED:

1. What is meant by unbundling general ledger costs? Why is it necessary?
2. What is the difference between a general ledger data base system and an activity-based data base system?
3. Using the resource drivers and direct tracing, calculate the costs of each manufacturing engineering activity. What are the resource drivers?

8-8
Cost Formulas; Regression Analysis; Unit Drivers Versus Multiple Drivers
LO 1, 2

Christina Walters, vice president of finance for Underwood Company, attended a seminar three years ago on activity-based costing. She immediately began a project to gather data on activities for three plants that produced the same products and were similar in size and organization. After the first three months, she had sufficient data to convince herself that the consumption ratios of projects differed significantly. Furthermore, the nonunit-based overhead costs represented about 47% of the total overhead costs. Based on this input, she decided to implement ABC in the three plants on a pilot basis before expanding the system to the company's remaining 47 plants. She wanted at least two years' experience with the system before committing the company's resources to a major new information system. To prepare her presentation for the rest of management, Christina decided to calculate two overhead cost formulas for the plant: one using direct labor hours as the only driver and a second using direct labor hours and other drivers for which information had been gathered over the past 18 months (in three plants). Pooling monthly data for the three plants produced 108 data points.

Computer printouts for the two equations are presented below:

Parameter	Estimate	t for H$_0$ Parameter = 0	Pr > t	Standard Error of Parameter
Intercept	80,000	2.326	0.045	34,394
Direct labor hours	1.96	9.956	0.000	0.197

R Square (R^2) 0.46
Standard Error (S$_e$) 3,000
Observations 108

Parameter	Estimate	t for H$_0$ Parameter = 0	Pr > t	Standard Error of Parameter
Intercept	22,000	1.96	.0250	11,224.490
Direct labor hours	1.90	8.67	.0001	0.219
Number of moves	100	12.50	.0001	8.000
Setup hours	50	81.96	.0001	0.610
Purchase orders	200	0.85	.2000	235.294

Multiple R Square (R^2) 0.76
Standard Error (S$_e$) 2,500
Observations 108

REQUIRED:

1. Explain how regression analysis can help Christina decide to implement ABC for the remaining plants.
2. Based on the two regression equations, evaluate the decision to use ABC for the three plants. Do the results suggest any further actions are needed?
3. After evaluating the results, Christina decided to run regressions for individual activities, including some with activity drivers that had not yet been used. Why would it be useful to know cost formulas for individual activities?

8-9
Process Classification, Regression Analysis, and Accuracy of Cost Assignments

LO 3

Larson Company, a bike manufacturer, produces two types of bikes: mountain bikes and racing bikes. The company has two manufacturing processes: frame and bar fabrication and assembly. Once the frame and bar are produced, they are transferred to assembly, where, with other purchased parts, assembly and packing are done. Both processes acquire outside materials; however, the frame and bar fabrication process requires only metal and paint, whereas the assembly process orders a variety of parts (chains, wheels, tires, gears, gear wires, pedals, etc.).

The company currently assigns the cost of the receiving activity to the different bikes using receiving orders. Having used the ABC system for several years, the company has accumulated a good data base on activities, actual and potential drivers, and activity costs. As part of the evaluation of the ABC system, the controller computed cost formulas for activities and their drivers to see if evidence existed to support the assumed relationships. Most R^2 values were respectable except for the receiving activity. Receiving orders only explained 45% of the purchase cost activity. Having read about the effect processes can have on activity cost behavior, the controller broke the receiving activity cost into process categories and computed two cost formulas: one for fabrication and one for assembly. Receiving orders were used as the driver for receiving cost in the fabrication process, and number of parts was used as the driver in the assembly process. The controller was pleasantly surprised. The R^2 for receiving cost was 0.85 in the fabrication process and 0.90 in the assembly process. Based on this outcome, the controller altered the ABC assignment, using two drivers to assign receiving costs to the two bikes: purchase orders for fabrication and number of parts for assembly. The information needed for assigning receiving costs is given below (100,000 units of each bike will be produced):

	Fabrication	Assembly
Receiving cost	$200,000	$300,000
Receiving orders:		
Mountain bikes	10,000	10,000
Racing bikes	10,000	10,000
Number of parts:		
Mountain bikes	10,000	60,000
Racing bikes	10,000	180,000

REQUIRED:

1. Explain why the controller used regression analysis to assess the effectiveness of the ABC system.
2. Explain why the process classification produced higher R^2s than did the single plant-wide activity cost formula.
3. Calculate receiving cost per unit using only purchase orders to assign costs. Repeat using purchase orders to assign costs for the fabrication process and number of parts to assign receiving costs for the assembly process. Comment on the differences.

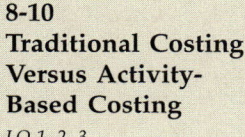

8-10
Traditional Costing Versus Activity-Based Costing
LO 1, 2, 3

White Company produces exercise equipment. One of its plants produces two versions of an exercise bike: an economy model and a custom model. The custom model has a sturdier frame, a more plush seat, and a variety of electronic gadgets to help the exerciser monitor heartbeat, calories, distance traveled, etc. At the beginning of the year, the following data were prepared for this plant:

	Economy Model	Custom Model
Expected quantity	20,000	10,000
Selling price	$90	$180
Prime costs	$40	$80
Machine hours	5,000	5,000
Direct labor hours	10,000	10,000
Engineering support (hours)	1,500	4,500
Receiving (orders processed)	250	500
Materials handling (number of moves)	2,000	4,000
Purchasing (number of requisitions)	100	200
Maintenance (hours used)	1,000	3,000
Paying suppliers (invoices processed)	250	500
Setting up batches (number of setups)	20	60

Additionally, the following overhead activity costs are reported (by process):

Technical Support:	
Maintenance	$ 84,000
Engineering support	120,000
Batch Support:	
Materials handling	120,000
Setups	96,000
Procurement:	
Purchasing	60,000
Receiving	40,000
Accounts payable	30,000
Process Sustaining:	
Providing space	20,000
	$570,000

Facility-level costs are allocated in proportion to machine hours (provided a measure-of-time facility is used by each product).

REQUIRED:

1. Calculate the cost per unit for each product using direct labor hours to assign all overhead costs.
2. Form homogeneous cost pools, and calculate pool rates. Explain why you group activities in the pools that are formed.
3. Using the pool rates computed in Requirement 2, calculate the cost per unit for each product. Compare these costs with those calculated using the traditional method. Which cost is the most accurate? Explain.

8-11
Activity-Based
Costing; Service
Industry
LO 1, 2, 3

Stillwater Medical Center operates a cardiology care unit. Currently, patients are charged the same rate per patient day for daily care services. Daily care services are broadly defined as occupancy, feeding, and nursing care. A recent study, however, revealed several interesting outcomes. First, the demands patients place on daily care services vary with the severity of the case being treated. Second, the occupancy activity is a combination of two activities: lodging and use of monitoring equipment. Since some patients require more monitoring than others, these activities should be separated. Third, the daily rate should reflect the difference in demands resulting from differences in patient type.

To compute a daily rate that reflected the difference in demands, patients were placed in three categories according to illness severity, and the following annual data were collected:

Activity	Cost of Activity	Cost Driver	Quantity
Lodging	$ 950,000	Patient days	7,500
Monitoring	700,000	No. of monitoring devices used	10,000
Feeding	150,000	Patient days	7,500
Nursing care	1,500,000	Nursing hours	75,000
	$3,300,000		

The demands associated with patient severity are also provided:

Severity	Patient Days	Monitoring Devices	Nursing Hours
High	2,500	5,000	45,000
Medium	3,750	4,000	25,000
Low	1,250	1,000	5,000

REQUIRED:

1. Suppose that the costs of daily care are assigned using only patient days as the activity driver (which is also the measure of output). Compute the daily rate using this traditional unit-based approach of cost assignment.
2. Compute pool rates using the given activity drivers.
3. Compute the charge per patient day for each patient type using the pool rates from Requirement 2 and the demands on each activity.
4. Suppose that the product is defined as "stay and treatment" where the treatment is bypass surgery. What additional information would you need to cost out this newly defined product?
5. Comment on the value of activity-based costing in service industries.

8-12
ABC Costing,
Service Firm

LO 2

Cushing First National Bank had operated for years under the assumption that profitability can be increased by increasing dollar volumes. Historically, First National's efforts had been directed towards increasing total dollars of sales and total dollars of account balances. In recent years, however, First National's profits had been eroding. Increased competition, particularly from savings and loan institutions, was the cause of the difficulties. As key managers discussed the bank's problems, it became apparent to them that they had no idea what their products were costing. Upon reflection, they realized that they had often made decisions to offer a new product which promised to increase dollar balances without any consideration of what it cost to provide the service.

After some discussion, the bank decided to hire a consultant to compute the costs of three products: checking accounts, personal loans, and the gold VISA. The consultant identified the following activities, costs, and activity drivers (annual data):

Activity	Activity Cost	Activity Driver	Activity Capacity
Providing ATM service	$ 100,000	No. of transactions	200,000
Computer processing	1,000,000	No. of transactions	2,500,000
Issuing statements	800,000	No. of statements	500,000
Customer inquiries	360,000	Telephone minutes	600,000

The following annual information on the three products was also made available.

	Checking Accounts	Personal Loans	VISA
Units of product	30,000	5,000	10,000
ATM transactions	180,000	0	20,000
Computer transactions	2,000,000	200,000	300,000
Number of statements	350,000	50,000	150,000
Telephone minutes	350,000	90,000	160,000

In light of the new cost information, Larry Roberts, the bank president, wanted to know whether a decision made two years ago to modify the bank's checking account product was sound or not. At that time the service charge was eliminated on accounts that had an average annual balance greater than $1,000. Based on increases in the total dollars in checking, Larry felt good about the new product. The checking account product is described as follows: (1) Checking account balances greater than $500 earn interest of 2% per year, and (2) A service charge of $5 per month is charged for balances less than $1,000. The bank earns 4% on checking account deposits. Fifty percent of the accounts are less than $500 and have an average balance of $400 per account. Ten percent of the accounts are between $500 and $1,000 and average $750 per account. Twenty-five percent of the accounts are between $1,000 and $2,767; the average balance is $2,000. The remaining accounts carry a balance greater than $2,767. The average balance for these accounts is $5,000. Research indicates that the $2,000 category was by far the greatest contributor to the increase in dollar volume when the checking account product was modified two years ago.

REQUIRED:

1. Calculate rates for each activity.
2. Using the rates computed in Requirement 1, calculate the cost of each product.
3. Evaluate the checking account product. Are all accounts profitable? Compute the average annual profitability per account for the four categories of accounts described in the problem. What recommendations would you make to increase the profitability of the checking account product?

**8-13
Product-Costing
Accuracy;
Corporate Strategy;
Activity-Based
Costing**

LO 1, 2, 3

Autotech Manufacturing is engaged in the production of replacement parts for automobiles. One plant specializes in the production of two parts: Part #127 and Part #234. Part #127 produced the highest volume of activity and for many years had been the only part produced by the plant. Five years ago, Part #234 had been added. Part #234 was more difficult to manufacture and required special tooling and setups. For the first three years after the addition of the new product, profits had increased. In the last two years, however, the plant had been facing intense competition, and its sales of Part #127 had dropped. In fact, the plant had shown a small loss in the most recent reporting period. Much of the competition was from foreign sources, and the plant manager was convinced that the foreign producers were guilty of selling the part below the cost of producing it. The following conversation between Patty Goodson, plant manager, and Joseph Fielding, divisional marketing manager, reflects the concerns of the division about the future of the plant and its products.

Joseph: You know, Patty, the divisional manager is real concerned about the plant's trend. He indicated that in this budgetary environment, we can't afford to carry plants that don't show a profit. We shut down one just last month because it couldn't handle the competition.

Patty: Joe, you know and I know, that Part #127 has a reputation for quality and value. It has been a mainstay for years. I don't understand what's happening.

Joseph: I just received a call from one of our major customers concerning Part #127. He said that a sales representative from another firm had offered the part at $20 per unit— $11 less than what we ask. It's hard to compete with a price like that. Perhaps the plant is simply obsolete.

Patty: No. I don't buy that. From my sources, I know we have good technology. We are efficient. And it's costing a little more than $21 to produce that part. I don't see how these companies can afford to sell it so cheaply. I'm not convinced that we should meet the price. Perhaps a better strategy is to emphasize producing and selling more of Part #234. Our margin is high on this product, and we have virtually no competition for it.

Joseph: You may be right. I think we can increase the price significantly and not lose business. I called a few customers to see how they would react to a 25 percent increase in price, and they all said that they would still purchase the same quantity as before.

Patty: It sounds promising. However, before we make a major commitment to Part #234, I think we had better explore other possible explanations. I want to know how our production costs compare to those of our competitors. Perhaps we could be more efficient and find a way to earn our normal return on Part #127. The market is so much bigger for this part. I'm not sure we can survive with Part #234. Besides, my production people hate that part. It's very difficult to produce.

After her meeting with Joseph, Patty requested an investigation of the production costs and comparative efficiency. She received approval to hire a consulting group to make an independent investigation. After a three-month assessment, the consulting group provided the following information on the plant's production activities and costs associated with the two products:

	Part #127	Part #234
Production	500,000	100,000
Selling price	$31.86	$24.00
Overhead per unit*	$12.83	$5.77
Prime cost per unit	$8.53	$6.26
Number of production runs	100	200
Receiving orders	400	1,000
Machine hours	125,000	60,000
Direct labor hours	250,000	22,500
Engineering hours	5,000	5,000
Material moves	500	400

*Calculated using a plantwide rate based on direct labor hours. This is the current way of assigning the plant's overhead to its products.

The consulting group recommended switching the overhead assignment to an activity-based approach. It maintained that activity-based cost assignment is more accurate and will provide better information for decision making. To facilitate this recommendation, it grouped the plant's activities into homogeneous sets based on common processes, activity levels, and consumption ratios. The costs of these pooled activities are presented below:

Overhead Pool*

Setup costs	$ 240,000
Machine costs	1,750,000
Receiving costs	2,100,000
Engineering costs	2,000,000
Materials-handling costs	900,000
Total	$6,990,000

*The pools are named for the major activities found within them. All overhead costs within each pool can be assigned using a single activity driver (based on the major activity after which the pool is named).

REQUIRED:

1. Verify the overhead cost per unit reported by the consulting group using direct labor hours to assign overhead. Compute the per-unit gross margin for each product.
2. After learning of activity-based costing, Patty asked the controller to compute the product cost using this approach. Recompute the unit cost of each product using activity-based costing. Compute the per-unit gross margin for each product.
3. Should the company switch its emphasis from the high-volume product to the low-volume product? Comment on the validity of the plant manager's concern that competitors are selling below the cost of making Part #127.
4. Explain the apparent lack of competition for Part #234. Comment also on the willingness of customers to accept a 25 percent increase in price for Part #234.
5. Assume that you are the manager of the plant. Describe what actions you would take based on the information provided by the activity-based unit costs.

8-14
Product Costing;
Activity-Based
Product Costs;
Activity
Classification and
Homogeneous
Pools
LO 1, 2, 3

Williamson, Inc., produces two different types of steel metal frames. There are two manufacturing processes: steel cutting and assembly. The activities, costs, and drivers associated with these processes are given below:

Process	Activity	Cost	Activity Driver	Quantity
Steel Cutting	Scheduling	$ 300,000	Work orders	500
	Machining	200,000	Machine hours	5,000
	Inspection	100,000	No. of setups	50
	Materials handling	400,000	No. of moves	8,000
	Setups	150,000	No. of setups	50
		$1,150,000		
Assembly	Changeover	$120,000	No. of batches	500
	Rework	40,000	Change orders	100
	Inspection	150,000	No. of batches	500
	Materials handling	240,000	No. of parts	40,000
	Eng. support	80,000	Change orders	100
		$630,000		

Note: In the assembly process, the materials-handling activity is a function of product characteristics rather than batch activity.

Other overhead activities, their costs, and drivers are listed below:

Activity	Cost	Activity Driver	Quantity
Purchasing	$ 90,000	Purchase requisitions	300
Receiving	180,000	Receiving orders	600
Paying suppliers	150,000	No. of invoices	600
Providing space	30,000	Machine hours	5,000
Providing utilities	40,000	Machine hours	5,000
	$490,000		

Other production information concerning the two frames is also provided:

	Frame A	Frame B
Units produced	1,000	2,000
Work orders	250	250
Batches	250	250
Machine hours	1,500	3,500
Setups	25	25
Moves	4,000	4,000
Parts	24,000	16,000
Change orders	60	40
Requisitions	200	100
Receiving orders	400	200
Invoices	400	200

REQUIRED:

1. Using a plantwide rate based on machine hours, calculate the overhead cost assigned per unit for each product.
2. Using process, activity level, and driver classification, form homogeneous pools and calculate pool rates. One of the purposes of pool formation is to reduce the total number of overhead rates needed. For this setting, how much reduction was achieved?
3. Using the pool rates from Requirement 2, compute the unit overhead cost for each product. Comment on why these costs differ from the ones computed in Requirement 1.

8-15
Activity-Based Relational Data Base
LO 4

Refer to the data given in **8-14**.

REQUIRED:

1. Prepare activity and product relational tables.
2. Comment on how the activity relational data base differs from a general ledger data base.

8-16
Activity Relational Data Base
LO 4

BKM Foundry manufactures different kinds of equipment used by the aerospace, commercial aircraft, and electronic industries. Twenty different products are created using two major manufacturing processes: molding and assembly. Two other processes in the plant are procurement and sustaining. The activity and product relational tables are given on the following page (for simplicity, only two products of the twenty produced are shown in the product relational table):

Activity Relational Table: BKM Foundry

Activity	Activity Name	Process	Level	Activity Driver	Activity Capacity	Cost
1	Designing molds	Molding	Product	No. of products	20	$600,000
2	Making molds	Molding	Product	No. of products	20	320,000
3	Inspecting molds	Molding	Batch	No. of setups	400	120,000
4	Setting up batches	Molding	Batch	No. of setups	400	120,000
5	Engineering design	Assembly	Product	Change orders	40	130,000
6	Materials handling	Assembly	Batch	No. of subassemblies	400	90,000
7	Machining	Assembly	Unit	Machine hours	200,000	225,000
8	Purchasing materials	Procurement	Batch	Purchase orders	1,000	200,000
9	Receiving materials	Procurement	Batch	Purchase orders	1,000	320,000
10	Paying suppliers	Procurement	Product	No. of molds	20,000	180,000
11	Providing utilities	Sustaining	Facility	Machine hours	20,000	20,000
12	Providing space	Sustaining	Facility	Machine hours	20,000	50,000

Product Relational Table: BKM Foundry

Product Number	Product Name	Activity Driver Number	Activity Driver Name	Activity Usage
1	Component A	1	Units	1,000
1	Component A	2	No. of molds	2,000
1	Component A	3	No. of setups	10
1	Component A	4	Change orders	4
1	Component A	5	No. of products	1
1	Component A	6	Purchase orders	50
1	Component A	7	No. of subassemblies	2
1	Component A	8	Machine hours	800
2	Component B	1	Units	2,000
2	Component B	2	No. of molds	6,000
2	Component B	3	No. of batches	20
2	Component B	4	Change orders	3
2	Component B	5	No. of products	1
2	Component B	6	Purchase orders	60
2	Component B	7	No. of subassemblies	3
2	Component B	8	Machine hours	1,000

REQUIRED:

1. Describe how activity and product relational tables are created.
2. Using the tables above, provide examples of the following:
   a. Primary key
   b. Concatenated key
   c. Record
   d. Activity attribute
   e. Product attribute
   f. An entity
3. Using the information from the relational tables, calculate pool rates for the molding process.
4. Using the pool rates computed in Requirement 3, assign molding process costs to Component A. What is the molding overhead cost per unit?

**8-17
Activity
Classification;
Activity Sets;
Homogeneous Cost
Pools**

LO 3

Sneathen Manufacturing produces two models of snow blower: small and large. Sneathen produces all parts for the blowers internally. The Framing Division produces the frames for the blowers. The Framing Division takes metal sheets and cuts them into shapes that are used to form the frame of each snow blower. Frames are produced in batches, and the metal-cutting equipment must be reconfigured as the process changes from small to large frames. (Because of customer demands, the process usually produces one batch before reconfiguration.) Other components for the snow blower are produced by other divisions of the same company and transferred to the Assembly Division. (For example, the Sneathen Small Motors Division transfers the motors for the blowers.) The frame components and parts transferred in from sister divisions are used by assembly to manufacture the final product.

The management of the Framing Division has decided to implement an activity-based costing system. A special study, conducted by a team appointed by the divisional manager, revealed the following information on activities, costs, and activity drivers for its frame production plant:

Process	Activity	Cost	Cost Driver
Batch			
	Setup	$ 400,000	No. of setups
	Materials handling	200,000	No. of moves
	Inspection	250,000	No. of setups
Conversion			
	Machine depreciation	300,000	Machine hours
	Power (machine)	100,000	Machine hours
Process sustaining			
	Scheduling	60,000	No. of products
	Maintenance	150,000	Machine hours
	Providing space	89,000	Value added*
	Plant supervision	80,000	Value added*
		$1,629,000	

*The team conducting the study recommended that facility-level costs be assigned to each product on a value-added basis (value-added is defined as the cost of direct labor plus the cost of nonfacility-level overhead).

The expected quantities of activity drivers are given below for the plant:

Activity	Cost Driver	Quantity
Setup	No. of setups	1,000
Maintenance	Machine hours	5,000
Scheduling	No. of products	2
Power (machine)	Machine hours	5,000
Depreciation	Machine hours	5,000
Inspection	No. of setups	1,000
Materials handling	No. of moves	10,000

In addition, the demands that each type of frame makes on activities are also given, at the top of the following page.

Cost Driver	Product Small Frame	Large Frame
No. of products	1	1
Machine hours	2,000	3,000
No. of setups	300	700
No. of moves	3,500	6,500

During the year, 10,000 small frames and 15,000 large frames were produced. Total direct labor cost is $230,000 ($85,000 for the small frames and the rest for the large frames).

REQUIRED:

1. Group activities into sets based on process, activity-level, and driver classification criteria.
2. Create homogeneous cost pools, and calculate pool rates.
3. Use the pool rates to compute per-unit overhead costs for the small and large frames. What do you think about assigning facility-level costs to products?

8-18
Product-Costing Accuracy; Departmental Rates; Pool Rates
LO 1, 2, 3

Springs Company produces two type of calculators: scientific and business. Both products pass through two producing departments. The business calculator is by far the most popular. The following data have been gathered for these two products:

Product-Related Data	Scientific	Business
Units produced per year	30,000	300,000
Prime costs	$100,000	$1,000,000
Direct labor hours	40,000	400,000
Machine hours	20,000	200,000
Production runs	40	60
Inspection hours	800	1,200

Department Data	Department 1	Department 2
Direct labor hours:		
Scientific calculator	30,000	10,000
Business calculator	45,000	355,000
Total	75,000	365,000
Machine hours:		
Scientific calculator	10,000	10,000
Business calculator	160,000	40,000
Total	170,000	50,000
Overhead costs:		
Setup costs	$ 90,000	$ 90,000
Inspection costs	70,000	70,000
Power	100,000	60,000
Maintenance	80,000	100,000
Total	$340,000	$320,000

660 pas

REQUIRED:

1. Compute the overhead cost per unit for each product using a plantwide, unit-based rate.
2. Compute the overhead cost per unit for each product using departmental rates. In calculating departmental rates, use machine hours for Department 1 and direct labor hours for Department 2. Repeat using direct labor hours for Department 1 and machine hours for Department 2.
3. Compute the overhead cost per unit for each product using activity-based costing (use overhead pools where possible).
4. Comment on the ability of departmental rates to improve the accuracy of product costing.

**8-19
Managerial
Decision Case:
Activity-Based
Costing;
Consideration of
Nonmanufacturing
Costs**
LO 2, 3

Sharp Paper, Inc., has three paper mills, one of which is located in Memphis, Tennessee. The Memphis mill produces 300 different types of coated and uncoated specialty printing papers. This large variety of products was the result of a full-line marketing strategy adopted by Sharp's management. Management was convinced that the value of variety more than offset the extra costs of the increased complexity.

During 1997, the Memphis mill produced 120,000 tons of coated paper and 80,000 tons of uncoated. Of the 200,000 tons produced, 180,000 were sold. Sixty products account for 80 percent of the tons sold. Thus, 240 products are classified as low-volume products.

Lightweight lime hopsack in cartons (LLHC) is one of the low-volume products. LLHC is produced in rolls, converted into sheets of paper, and then sold in cartons. In 1997, the cost to produce and sell one ton of LLHC was as follows:

Raw materials:		
Furnish (3 different pulps)	2,225 pounds	$ 450
Additives (11 different items)	200 pounds	500
Tub size	75 pounds	10
Recycled scrap paper	(296 pounds)	(20)
Total raw materials		$ 940
Direct labor		$ 450
Overhead:		
Paper machine ($100/ton × 2,500 pounds)		$ 125
Finishing machine ($120/ton × 2,500 pounds)		150
Total overhead		$ 275
Shipping and warehousing		$ 30
Total manufacturing and selling cost		$1,695

Overhead is applied using a two-stage process. First, overhead is allocated to the paper and finishing machines using the direct method of allocation with carefully selected activity drivers. Second, the overhead assigned to each machine is divided by the budgeted tons of output. These rates are then multiplied by the number of pounds required to produce one good ton.

In 1997, LLHC sold for $2,400 per ton, making it one of the most profitable products. A similar examination of some of the other low-volume products revealed that they also had very respectable profit margins. Unfortunately, the performance of the high-volume products was less impressive, with many showing losses or very low profit margins. This situation led Ryan Chesser to call a meeting with his marketing vice president, Jennifer Woodruff, and his controller, Jan Booth.

Ryan: The above-average profitability of our low-volume specialty products and the poor profit performance of our high-volume products make me believe that we should switch our marketing emphasis to the low-volume line. Perhaps we should drop some of our high-volume products, particularly those showing a loss.

Jennifer: I'm not convinced that the solution you are proposing is the right one. I know our high-volume products are of high quality, and I am convinced that we are as efficient in our production as other firms. I think that somehow our costs are not being assigned correctly. For example, the shipping and warehousing costs are assigned by dividing these costs by the total tons of paper sold. Yet . . .

Jan: Jennifer, I hate to disagree, but the $30 per ton charge for shipping and warehousing seems reasonable. I know that our method to assign these costs is identical to a number of other paper companies.

Jennifer: Well, that may be true, but do these other companies have the variety of products that we have? Our low-volume products require special handling and processing, but when we assign shipping and warehousing costs, we average these special costs across our entire product line. Every ton produced in our mill passes through our Mill Shipping Department and is either sent directly to the customer or to our distribution center and then eventually to customers. My records indicate quite clearly that virtually all the high-volume products are sent directly to customers, whereas most of the low-volume products are sent to the distribution center. Not all the products passing through the Mill Shipping Department should receive a share of the $2,000,000 annual shipping costs. I am not convinced, however, that all products should receive a share of the receiving and shipping costs of the distribution center as currently practiced.

Ryan: Jan, is this true? Does our system allocate our shipping and warehousing costs in this way?

Jan: Yes, I'm afraid it does. Jennifer may have a point. Perhaps we need to reevaluate our method to assign these costs to the product lines.

Ryan: Jennifer, do you have any suggestions concerning how the shipping and warehousing costs ought to be assigned?

Jennifer: It seems reasonable to make a distinction between products that spend time in the distribution center and those that do not. We should also distinguish between the receiving and shipping activities at the distribution center. All incoming shipments are packed on pallets and weigh one ton each (there are fourteen cartons of paper per pallet). In 1997, Receiving processed 56,000 tons of paper. Receiving employs fifteen people at an annual cost of $600,000. Other receiving costs total about $500,000. I would recommend that these costs be assigned using tons processed. Shipping, however, is different. There are two activities associated with shipping: picking the order from inventory and loading the paper. We employ thirty people for picking and ten for loading at an annual cost of $1,200,000. Other shipping costs total $1,100,000. Picking and loading are more concerned with the number of shipping items rather than tonnage. That is, a shipping item may consist of two or three cartons instead of pallets. Accordingly, the shipping costs of the distribution center should be assigned using the number of items shipped. In 1997, for example, we handled 190,000 shipping items.

Ryan: These suggestions have merit. Jan, I would like to see what effect Jennifer's suggestions have on the per-unit assignment of shipping and warehousing for LLHC. If the effect is significant, then we will expand the analysis to include all products.

Jan: I'm willing to compute the effect, but I'd like to suggest one additional feature. Currently, we have a policy to carry about twenty-five tons of LLHC in inventory. Our current cost system totally ignores the cost of carrying this inventory. Since it costs us $1,665 to produce each ton of this product, we are tying up a lot of money in inventory, money that could be invested in other productive opportunities. In fact, the return lost is about 16 percent per year. This cost should also be assigned to the units sold.

Ryan: Jan, this also sounds good to me. Go ahead and include the carrying cost in your computation.

To help in the analysis, Jan gathered the following data for LLHC for 1997:

Tons sold	10
Average cartons per shipment	2
Average shipments per ton	7

REQUIRED:

1. Identify the flaws associated with the current method to assign shipping and warehousing costs to Sharp's products.
2. Compute the shipping and warehousing cost per ton of LLHC sold using the new method suggested by Jennifer and Jan.
3. Using the new costs computed in Requirement 2, compute the profit per ton of LLHC. Compare this with the profit per ton computed using the old method. Do you think that this same effect would be realized for other low-volume products? Explain.
4. Comment on Ryan's proposal to drop some high-volume products and place more emphasis on low-volume products. Discuss the role of the accounting system in supporting this type of decision making.
5. After receiving the analysis of LLHC, Ryan decided to expand the analysis to all products. He also had Jan reevaluate the way in which mill overhead was assigned to products. After the restructuring was completed, Ryan took the following actions: (a) the prices of most low-volume products were increased, (b) the prices of several high-volume products were decreased, and (c) some low-volume products were dropped. Explain why Ryan's strategy changed so dramatically.

**8-20
Activity-Based
Product Costing
and Ethical
Behavior**
LO 2, 3

Consider the following conversation between Leonard Bryner, president and manager of a firm engaged in job manufacturing, and Chuck Davis, CMA, the firm's controller.

Leonard: Chuck, as you know, our firm has been losing market share over the past three years. We have been losing more and more bids, and I don't understand why. At first I thought other firms were undercutting simply to gain business, but after examining some of the public financial reports, I believe that they are making a reasonable rate of return. I am beginning to believe that our costs and costing methods are at fault.

Chuck: I can't agree with that. We have good control over our costs. Like most firms in our industry, we use a normal job-costing system. I really don't see any significant waste in the plant.

Leonard: After talking with some other managers at a recent industrial convention, I'm not so sure that waste by itself is the issue. They talked about activity-based management, activity-based costing, and continuous improvement. They mentioned the use of something called *activity drivers* to assign overhead. They claimed that these new procedures can help produce more efficiency in manufacturing, better control of overhead, and more accurate product costing. A big deal was made of eliminating activities that added no value. Maybe our bids are too high because these other firms have found ways to decrease their overhead costs and to increase the accuracy of their product costing.

Chuck: I doubt it. For one thing, I don't see how we can increase product costing accuracy. So many of our costs are indirect costs. Furthermore, everyone uses some measure of production activity to assign overhead costs. I imagine that what they are calling activity drivers is just some new buzz word for measures of production volume. Fads in costing come and go. I wouldn't worry about it. I'll bet that our problems with decreasing sales are temporary. You might recall that we experienced a similar problem about twelve years ago—it was two years before it straightened out.

REQUIRED:

1. Do you agree with Chuck Davis and the advice that he gave Leonard Bryner? Explain.
2. Was there anything wrong or unethical in the behavior that Chuck Davis displayed? Explain your reasoning.
3. Do you think that Chuck was well informed—that he was aware of what the accounting implications of JIT were and that he knew what was meant by activity drivers? Should he have been? Review (in Chapter 1) the first category of the standards of ethical conduct for management accountants. Do any of these apply to Chuck's case?

Chapter 9

Strategic Cost Management, Life Cycle Cost Management, and JIT

A strong understanding of strategic costing led Microsoft's management to delay introduction of the "Windows 95" operating system software by nearly a year. The extra time was spent in extensive beta testing and debugging to ensure that customers received a nearly "glitch-free" product. This reduces post-purchase costs to both the customer and the firm.

LEARNING OBJECTIVES

After studying this chapter, you should be able to:

1. Explain what strategic cost management is and how it can be used to help a firm create a competitive advantage.
2. Explain what life cycle cost management is and how it can be used to maximize profits over a product's life cycle.
3. Describe the basic features of JIT purchasing and manufacturing.
4. Describe the effect JIT has on cost traceability and product costing.

In Chapter 8, the basic concepts of activity-based costing were introduced. These concepts were illustrated using the traditional product cost definition. Activity-based product costing can significantly improve the accuracy of traditional product costs. Thus, inventory valuation is improved and managers (and other information users) have better information concerning the costs of products so that better decisions can be made. Yet the value of the traditional product cost definition is limited and may not be very useful in certain decision contexts. For example, corporations engage in decision making that affects their long-run competitive position and profitability. Strategic planning and decision making require a much broader set of cost information than that provided by the traditional product cost definition; strategic analysis also requires noncost information such as data about customers, competitors, and government regulations.

This broader set of information should satisfy two requirements. First, this set should include information about the firm's environment and the internal workings of the firm. Second, the information set also must be prospective and thus should provide insights about future periods and activities. A value-chain framework with cost data to support a value-chain analysis satisfies the first requirement. Cost information to support product life cycle analysis is needed to satisfy the second requirement. Applying value-chain analysis can produce organizational changes that fundamentally alter the nature and demand for cost information. Just-in-time (JIT) manufacturing is an example of a strategic approach that alters the nature of the cost accounting information system. In this chapter, we introduce strategic cost management, life cycle cost management, and JIT manufacturing. The JIT approach is used to illustrate the value-chain concepts. However, given the breadth of its application and its effect on cost accounting, JIT is a topic that by itself merits study. Nonetheless, JIT's linkages to strategic cost management justify this topic's inclusion in the same chapter with strategic cost management.

STRATEGIC COST MANAGEMENT

Objective 1
Explain what strategic cost management is and how it can be used to help a firm create a competitive advantage.

strategic decision making
strategic cost management
competitive advantage
customer value

Decision making that affects the long-term competitive position of a firm must explicitly consider the strategic elements of a decision. The most important strategic elements for a firm are its long-term growth and survival. Thus, **strategic decision making** involves choosing among alternative strategies with the goal of selecting a strategy, or strategies, that provides a company with reasonable assurance of long-term growth and survival. The key to achieving this goal is to gain a competitive advantage. **Strategic cost management** is the use of cost data to develop and identify superior strategies that will produce a sustainable competitive advantage.

Creating and Sustaining a Competitive Advantage

Competitive advantage is creating better customer value for the same or lower cost than that of competitors or creating equivalent value for lower cost than that of competitors. **Customer value** is the difference between what a customer receives (customer realization) and what the customer gives up (customer sacrifice). What a customer receives is more than simply the basic level of performance provided by a product.[1] What is received is called the *total product*. The

1. Keep in mind that our definition of product includes services. Services are intangible products.

total product

total product is the complete range of tangible and intangible benefits that a customer receives from a purchased product. Thus, customer realization includes basic and special product features, service, quality, instructions for use, reputation, brand name, and any other factors deemed important by customers. Customer sacrifice includes the cost of purchasing the product, the time and effort spent acquiring and learning to use the product, and **postpurchase costs**, which are the costs of using, maintaining, and disposing of the product.

postpurchase costs

There are two general strategies capable of producing a sustainable competitive advantage: (1) a low-cost strategy and (2) a strategy of differentiation. The objective of the low-cost strategy is to provide the same or better value to customers at a lower cost than do competitors. Essentially, if customer value is defined as the difference between realization and sacrifice, a low-cost strategy increases customer value by minimizing customer sacrifice. In this case, cost leadership is the goal of the organization. For example, a company might redesign a product so that fewer parts are needed, lowering production costs and the costs of maintaining the product after purchase.

A differentiation strategy, on the other hand, strives to increase customer value by increasing what the customer receives (customer realization). A competitive advantage is created by providing something to customers not provided by competitors. Thus, product characteristics must be created that set the product apart from its competitors. This differentiation can occur by adjusting the product so that it is different from the norm or by promoting some of the product's tangible or intangible attributes. Differences can be functional, aesthetic, or stylistic. For example, a retailer of computers might offer on-site repair service, a feature not offered by other rivals in the local market. Or a producer of crackers may offer animal-shaped crackers, as Nabisco did with Teddy Grahams, to differentiate its product from other brands with more conventional shapes. To be of value, however, customers must see the variations as important. Furthermore, the value added to the customer by differentiation must exceed the firm's costs of providing the differentiation. If customers see the variations as important and if the value added to the customer exceeds the cost of providing the differentiation, then a competitive advantage has been established.

Value-Chain Framework, Linkages, and Activities

Pursuing cost leadership and differentiation strategies requires managers to understand the activities that contribute to their achievement. Successful pursuit of these strategies mandates an understanding of the *industrial value chain*. The **industrial value chain** is the linked set of value-creating activities from basic raw materials to the disposal of the finished product by end-use customers. Exhibit 9-1 illustrates a possible industrial value chain for the petroleum industry. A given firm operating in the oil industry may not—and likely will not—span the entire value chain. The exhibit illustrates that different firms participate in different portions of the value chain. Most large oil firms such as Exxon, Phillips, and Mobil are involved in the value chain from exploration to service stations (like Firm A in Exhibit 9-1). Yet even these oil giants purchase oil from other producers and also supply gasoline to service station outlets that are owned by others. Furthermore, there are many oil firms that engage exclusively in smaller segments of the chain such as exploration and production or refining and distribution (like Firms B and C in Exhibit 9-1). Regardless, to create and sustain a competitive advantage, a firm must understand the entire value chain and not just the portion in which it operates.

industrial value chain

Exhibit 9-1
Value Chain for the Petroleum Industry

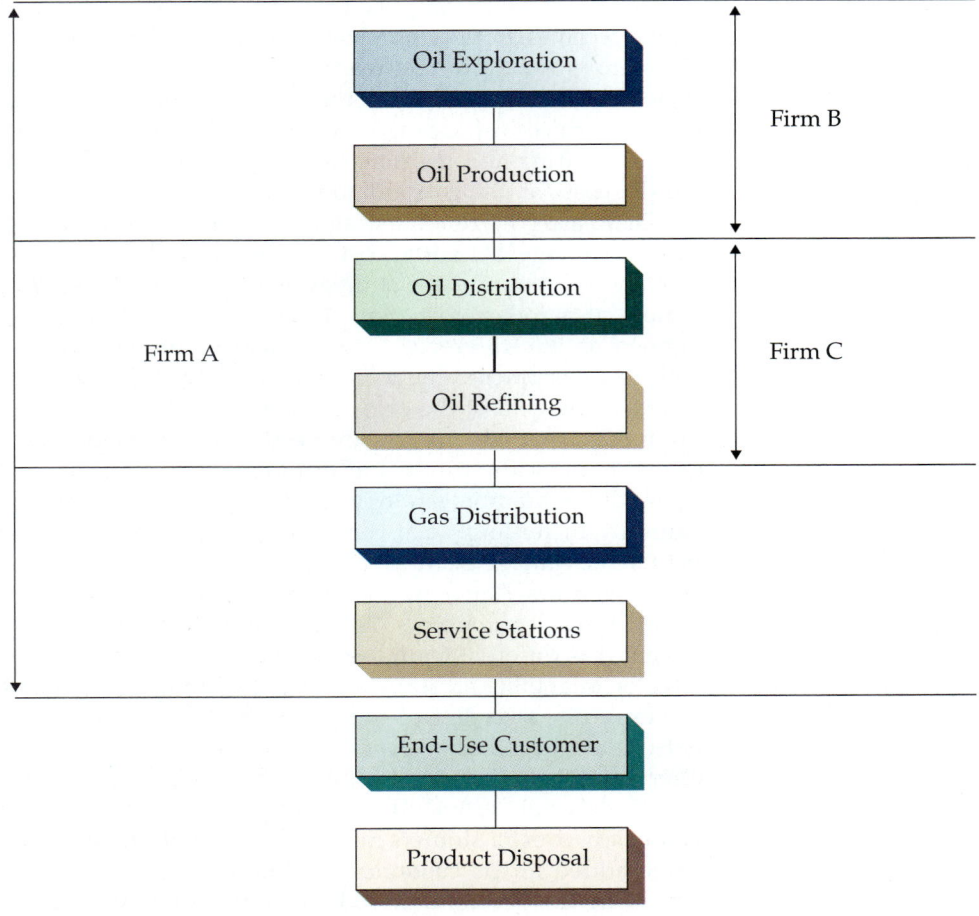

Thus, breaking down the value chain into its strategically relevant activities is basic to successful implementation of cost leadership and differentiation strategies. A value-chain framework is a compelling approach to understanding a firm's strategically important activities. Fundamental to a value-chain framework is the recognition that there exist complex linkages and interrelationships among activities both within and external to the firm. There are two types of linkages that must be analyzed and understood: *internal linkages* and *external linkages*. **Internal linkages** are relationships among activities that are performed within a firm's portion of the value chain. **External linkages**, on the other hand, describe the relationship of a firm's value-chain activities that are performed with its suppliers and customers. External linkages, therefore, are of two types: *supplier linkages* and *customer linkages*.

To exploit a firm's internal and external linkages, we must identify the firm's activities and select those that can be used to produce (or sustain) a competitive advantage. This selection process requires knowledge of the cost and value of each activity. For strategic analysis, activities are classified as *organizational activities* and *operational activities*; the costs of these activities, in turn, are determined by *organizational* and *operational cost drivers*.

internal linkages
external linkages

Organizational Activities and Drivers **Organizational activities** are activities
that determine the organization's structure and business processes. Examples
include building plants, designing plant layout, selecting and using a management structure (management structuring), selecting and using process technologies, vertically integrating, grouping employees (departments, function, teams,
etc.), providing quality, and using employees. **Organizational cost drivers** are
structural and procedural factors that determine the long-term cost structure of
an organization. Thus, organizational cost drivers play a vital role in any cost
reduction strategy. Examples of organizational cost drivers include number of
operational plants, scale, degree of centralization, plant layout type and its efficiency, management style, type of process technology, degree of vertical integration, type and number of work units, quality management approaches, and level
of employee involvement. It is also possible (and perhaps common) that a given
organizational activity can be driven by more than one driver. For example, the
cost of building plants is affected by scale, number of plants, and degree of centralization. Firms that have a commitment to a high degree of centralization may
build larger plants so that there can be more geographic concentration and
greater control. Similarly, complexity may be driven by number of different products, number of unique processes, and number of unique parts.

Organizational activities are of two types: *structural* and *procedural (or executional)*. **Structural activities** are activities that determine the underlying economic
structure of the organization. **Procedural (executional) activities** are activities
that define the processes of an organization and thus are directly related to the
ability of an organization to execute successfully. Organizational cost drivers are
described by two categories, corresponding to the two types of organizational
activities: *structural cost drivers* and *procedural* or *executional cost drivers*. Possible
structural and procedural activities with their drivers are listed by category in
Exhibit 9-2. Consider, for example, grouping employees and using employees.
How employees are organized and how many are used affects the long-term cost
structure of an organization. Furthermore, the ability to execute successfully

Exhibit 9-2
*Organizational Activi-
ties and Drivers*

Structural Activities	Structural Cost Drivers
Building plants	Number of plants, scale, degree of centralization
Management structuring	Management style and philosophy
Grouping employees	Number and type of work units
Complexity	Number of product lines, number of unique processes, number of unique parts
Vertically integrating	Buying power, selling power
Selecting and using process technologies	Types of process technologies

Procedural Activities	Procedural (Executional) Cost Drivers
Using employees	Degree of involvement
Providing quality	Quality management approach
Providing plant layout	Plant layout efficiency
Designing and producing products	Product configuration
Providing capacity	Capacity utilization

depends on how employees are used. The cost of using employees increases as the degree of involvement decreases. Employee or worker involvement refers to the culture, degree of participation, and commitment to the objective of continuous improvement.

operational activities

Operational Activities and Drivers **Operational activities** are day-to-day activities performed as a result of the structure and processes selected by the organization. Examples include receiving and inspecting incoming parts, moving materials, shipping products, testing new products, servicing products, and setting up equipment. **Operational cost drivers** (activity drivers) are those factors that drive the cost of operational activities. They include such factors as number of parts, number of moves, number of products, number of customer orders, and number of returned products. As should be evident, operational activities and drivers are the focus of activity-based costing. Possible operational activities and their drivers are listed in Exhibit 9-3.

operational cost drivers

The structural and procedural activities define the number and nature of the day-to-day activities performed within the organization. For example, if an organization decides to produce more than one product at a facility, then this structural choice produces a need for scheduling, a product-level activity. Similarly, providing a plant layout defines the nature and extent of the materials-handling activity (usually a batch-level activity). Furthermore, although organizational activities define operational activities, analysis of operational activities and drivers can be used to suggest strategic choices of organizational activities and drivers. For example, knowing that the number of moves is a measure of consumption of the materials-handling activity by individual products may suggest that resource spending can be reduced if the plant layout is redesigned to reduce the number of moves needed. Operational and organizational activities and their associated drivers are strongly interrelated. Exhibit 9-4 illustrates the circular nature of these relationships.

Exhibit 9-3
Operational Activities and Drivers

Unit-Level Activities	*Unit-Level Drivers*
Grinding parts	Grinding-machine hours
Assembling parts	Assembly labor hours
Drilling holes	Drilling-machine hours
Using materials	Pounds of material
Using power	Number of kilowatt hours
Batch-Level Activities	*Batch-Level Drivers*
Setting up equipment	Number of setups
Moving batches	Number of moves
Inspecting batches	Inspection hours
Reworking products	Number of defective units
Product-Level Activities	*Product-Level Drivers*
Redesigning products	Number of change orders
Expediting	Number of late orders
Scheduling	Number of different products
Testing products	Number of procedures

Exhibit 9-4
Organizational and
Operational Activity
Relationships

Value-Chain Analysis

value-chain analysis   **Value-chain analysis** is identifying those internal and external linkages that result in a firm achieving either a cost leadership or a differentiation strategy (whichever it determines will establish a sustainable competitive advantage). The exploitation of linkages relies on analyzing how costs and other nonfinancial factors vary as different bundles of activities are considered. For example, organizations change their structure and processes as needed to meet new challenges and take advantage of new opportunities. This may include new approaches to differentiation. Additionally, managing organizational and operational cost drivers to create long-term cost reduction outcomes is an important input in value-chain analysis when cost leadership is emphasized. The objective, of course, is to control cost drivers better than competitors can (thus creating a competitive advantage).

Exploiting Internal Linkages   Sound strategic cost management mandates the consideration of that portion of the value chain in which a firm participates (called the *internal value chain*). Exhibit 9-5 reviews the internal value-chain activities for an organization. Activities before and after production must be identified and their linkages recognized and exploited. Exploiting internal linkages means that relationships between activities are assessed and used to reduce costs and increase value. For example, product design and development activities occur before production and are linked to production activities. The way the product is designed affects the costs of production. How production costs are affected requires a knowledge of cost drivers. Thus, knowing the cost drivers of activities is crucial for understanding and exploiting linkages. If design engineers know that the number of parts is a cost driver for various production activities (mate-

Exhibit 9-5
*Value-Chain Activities
Within the Firm*

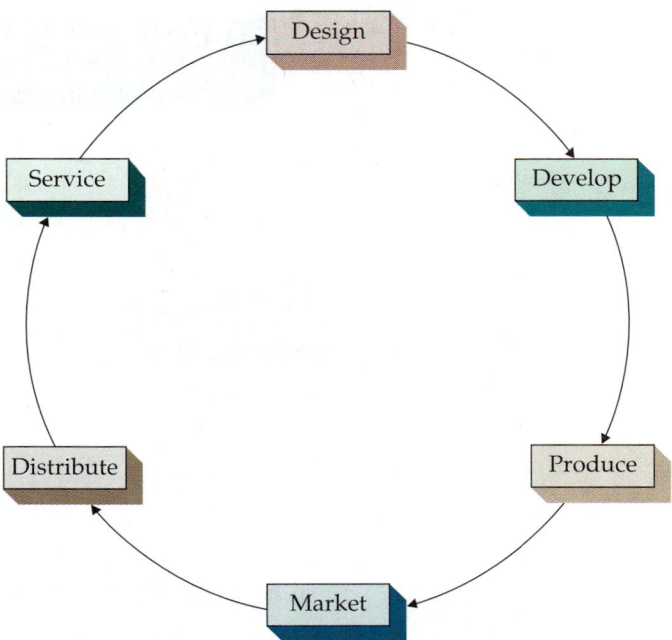

rial usage, direct labor usage, inspection, materials handling, and purchasing are examples of activities where costs could be affected by number of parts), then redesigning the product so that it has fewer parts would reduce the costs of production. Knowledge of this particular internal linkage was used by Japanese manufacturers to decrease the number of parts in VCRs by 50%. This reduction, occuring between 1977 and 1984, enabled them to reduce VCR prices from $1,300 to $298.[2]

The design activity is also linked to the service activity in the firm's value chain. By producing a product with fewer parts, there is less likelihood of product failure and, thus, less cost associated with warranty agreements (an important customer service). Furthermore, the cost of repairing products under warranty should also decrease because fewer parts usually means simpler repair procedures.

Internal Linkage Analysis: A Numerical Example To provide a more concrete foundation for the internal linkage concepts, let's consider a specific numerical example. Assume that a firm produces a variety of high-tech medical products. One of the products has twenty parts. Design engineers have been told that number of parts is a significant activity driver (operational cost driver) and that reducing the number of parts will reduce the demand for various activities downstream in the value chain. Based on this input, design engineering has produced a new configuration for the product that requires only eight parts. Management wants to know the cost reduction produced by the new design. They plan on reducing the price per unit by the per-unit savings. Currently, 10,000

2.   Michael Hergert and Deigan Morris, "Accounting Data for Value Chain Analysis," *Strategic Management Journal,* Vol. 10, pp. 175–188, 1989.

units of the product are produced. The effect of the new design on the demand for four activities is given below. Activity capacity, current activity demand (based on the 20-part configuration), and expected activity demand (based on the eight-part configuration) are provided.

Activities	Activity Driver	Capacity	Current Demand	Expected Demand
Material usage	Number of parts	200,000	200,000	80,000
Labor usage	Direct labor hours	10,000	10,000	5,000
Purchasing	Number of orders	15,000	12,500	6,500
Warranty repair	Number of defective products	1,000	800	500

Additionally, the following activity cost data are provided:

Material usage: $3 per part used; no fixed activity cost.
Labor usage: $12 per direct labor hour; no fixed activity cost.
Purchasing: three salaried clerks, each earning a $30,000 annual salary; each clerk is capable of processing 5,000 purchase orders; variable activity costs: $0.50 per purchase order processed for forms, postage, etc.
Warranty: Two repair agents, each paid a salary of $28,000 per year; each repair agent is capable of repairing 500 units per year; variable activity costs: $20 per product repaired.

Using the information in the table and the cost data, the potential savings produced by the new design are given in Exhibit 9-6. Cost behavior of individual activities is vital for assessing the impact of the new design. Knowing the cost of different design strategies is made possible by assessing the linkages of activities and the effects of changes in demand for the activities. Notice the key role that the resource usage model plays in this analysis.[3] The purchasing activity currently supplies 15,000 units of activity capacity, acquired in steps of 5,000 units. (Capacity is measured in the number of purchase orders—see Exhibit 9-7 for a graphical illustration of the activity's step cost behavior.) Unused activity for the current product configuration is 2,500 units (15,000 − 12,500). Reconfiguring the product reduces the demand from 12,500 orders to 6,500 orders. This increases the unused activity capacity to 8,500 units (15,000 − 6,500). At this

Exhibit 9-6
Cost Reduction from Exploiting Internal Linkages

Material usage	$360,000[a]
Labor usage	60,000[b]
Purchasing	33,000[c]
Warranty repair	34,000[d]
Total	$487,000
Units	10,000
Unit savings	$48.70

[a] (200,000 − 80,000)$3
[b] (10,000 − 5,000)$12
[c] [$30,000 + $0.50(12,500 − 6,500)]
[d] [$28,000 + $20(800 − 500)]

3.   The resource usage model was introduced in Chapter 3.

Exhibit 9-7
*Step Cost Behavior:
Purchasing Activity*

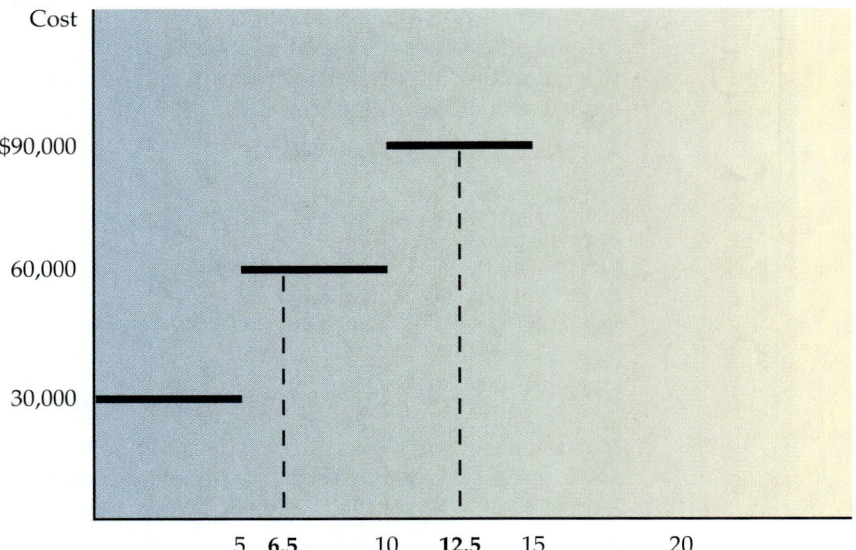

Number of Purchase Orders (in thousands)

Note: The bold numbers represent the demand before and after
product reconfiguration (12.5 before and 6.5 after).

point, management has the capability of reducing resource spending on the resources acquired in advance of usage. Since activity capacity is acquired in chunks of 5,000 units, resource spending can be reduced by $30,000 (the price of one purchasing clerk). Furthermore, since demand decreases, resource spending for the resources acquired as needed is also reduced by the variable component ($0.50 × 6,000). A similar analysis is carried out for the warranty activity. The activity-based costing model and knowledge of activity cost behavior are powerful and integral components of strategic cost management.

In the example, we implicitly assumed that resource spending on the engineering design activity would remain unchanged. Thus, there was no cost to exploiting the linkage. Suppose, however, that an increase in resource spending of $50,000 is needed to exploit the linkages between engineering design and activities downstream in the firm's value chain. Spending $50,000 to save $487,000 is certainly sound. Spending on one activity to save on the cost of other activities is a fundamental principle of strategic cost analysis.

Exploiting External Linkages Although each firm has its own value chain, as shown in Exhibit 9-1, each firm also belongs to a broader value chain—the *industrial value chain*. The value-chain system also includes value-chain activities that are performed by suppliers and buyers. A firm cannot ignore the interaction between its own value-chain activities and those of its suppliers and buyers. Linkages with activities external to the firm can also be exploited. Exploiting external linkages means managing these linkages so that both the company and the external parties receive an increase in benefits.

Suppliers provide inputs and, as a consequence, can have a significant effect on a user's cost leadership and differentiation strategies. For example, assume

total quality control

that a company adopts a *total quality control* approach to differentiate and reduce overall quality costs. **Total quality control** is an approach to managing quality that demands the production of defect-free products. Reducing defects, in turn, reduces the total costs spent on quality activities. Yet, to achieve a defect-free state, the company is strongly dependent on its suppliers' ability to provide defect-free parts. Once this linkage is understood, then a company can work closely with its suppliers so that the product being purchased meets its needs. AlliedSignal understands this linkage and incorporates it in a standard "partnering agreement" between purchaser and supplier that includes a steep initial price cut on purchased parts, a commitment from the supplier to lower costs by 6 percent per year, and a pledge to eliminate defects. AlliedSignal signed a long-term purchasing agreement with Baja Oriente of Ensenada, Mexico, to provide aluminium castings for AlliedSignal's truck components plant in nearby Mexicali. Importantly, these partnerships foster a sense of interdependence between purchaser and supplier, including a sense of trust and ethical treatment. Shortly after Baja signed the long-term contract with AlliedSignal, aluminum prices unexpectedly soared by nearly 50 percent. This price increase for raw materials coupled with fixed price for finished goods could have destroyed the small Mexican firm. It did not because AlliedSignal worked with Baja to increase orders from $500,000 to $6 million to reduce fixed cost per unit and reduce the changeovers.[4]

Similarly, customers can have a significant influence on a company's cost and differentiation position. For example, selling a medium-level quality product to low-end dealers for a special, low price because of idle capacity could threaten the main channels of distribution for the product. This is true even if the dealers apply their own private labels to the product. Why? Because selling the product to low-end dealers creates a direct competitor for its regular, medium-level dealers. Potential customers of the regular retail outlets could switch to the lower-end outlets because they can buy the same quality for a lower price. And what if the regular outlets deduce what has happened? What effect would this have on the company's medium-level differentiation strategy? The long-term damage to the company's profitability may be much greater than any short-run benefit from selling the special order.

External Linkage Analysis: A Numerical Example An example may help illustrate the importance of external linkages. Suppose that Thompson Company produces precision parts for 11 major buyers. An activity-based cost system is used to assign manufacturing costs to products. The company prices each customer's order by adding order-filling costs to manufacturing costs and then adding a 20% markup (to cover any administrative costs plus profits). Order-filling costs total $606,000 and are currently assigned in proportion to sales volume (measured by number of parts sold). Of the 11 customers, one accounts for 50% of sales, with the remaining ten accounting for the remainder of sales. The ten smaller customers purchase parts in roughly equal quantities. Orders placed by the smaller customers are also about the same size. Data concerning Thompson's customer activity are given on the following page.

4.   Shawn Tully, "Purchasing's New Muscle," *Fortune*, February 20, 1995, pp. 75–83.

	Large Customer	Ten Smaller Customers
Units purchased	500,000	500,000
Orders placed	2	200
Manufacturing cost	$3,000,000	$3,000,000
Order-filling cost allocated*	$303,000	$303,000
Order cost per unit	$0.606	$0.606

*Order-filling capacity is purchased in blocks of 45, each block costing $40,400; variable order-filling activity costs are $2,000 per order. The activity capacity is 225 orders; thus, the total order-filling cost is [(5 × $40,400) + ($2,000 × 202)] = $606,000. This total is allocated in proportion to the units purchased; thus, the large customer receives half the total cost.

Now assume that this customer complains about the price being charged and threatens to take its business elsewhere. The customer reveals a bid from a Thompson competitor that is $0.50 per part less than what Thompson charges. Confident that the ABC cost system is assigning manufacturing costs accurately, Thompson investigates the assignment of order-filling cost and discovers that the number of sales orders processed is a much better cost driver than number of parts sold. Thus, activity demand is measured by the number of sales orders, and ordering costs should be assigned to customers using an activity rate of $3,000 per order ($606,000/202 orders). Using this rate, the large customer should be charged $6,000 for order-filling costs. Thus, the large customer is being overcharged $297,000 each year, or about $0.59 per part ($297,000/500,000 parts). Actually, the overcharging is compounded by the 20% markup, producing a price that is about $0.71 too high (1.2 × $0.59). Armed with this information, Thompson's management immediately offers to reduce the price charged to its large customer by at least $0.50.

Thus, one benefit to the large customer is a price correction. This also benefits Thompson, because the price correction is needed to maintain half of its current business. Thompson, unfortunately, is also facing the difficult task of announcing a price increase for its smaller customers. However, the analysis should go much deeper than accurate cost assignment and fair pricing. Identifying the right cost driver (number of orders processed) reveals a linkage between the order-filling activity and customer behavior. Smaller, frequent orders are imposing costs on Thompson, which are then passed on to all customers through the use of the sales volume allocation. Since the total cost is marked up 20%, the price charged is even higher. Decreasing the number of orders will decrease Thompson's order-filling costs. Knowing this, Thompson can offer price discounts for larger orders. For example, doubling the size of the orders of the small customers would cut the number of orders by 50%, saving $280,800 for Thompson [(2 × $40,400) + (100 × $2,000)], almost enough to make it unnecessary to increase the selling price to the smaller customers. But there are other possible linkages as well. Larger and less frequent orders will also decrease the demand on other internal activities, such as setting up equipment and materials handling. Reduction in other activity demands could produce further cost reductions and additional price cuts, making Thompson more competitive. Thus, exploiting customer linkages can make both the seller and the buyer better off.

External Linkages and Other Strategic Insights The examples showing how management of external linkages can create significant benefits illustrate that a company must understand the entire value system and not just the portion of the chain in which it participates. An *external* focus is needed for effective strategic cost management. A company cannot ignore supplier and customer linkages and expect to establish a sustainable competitive advantage. A company needs to understand its relative position in the industrial value chain. An assessment of the economic strength and relationships of each stage in the entire value-chain system can provide a company with several significant strategic insights. For example, knowing the revenues and costs of the different stages may reveal the need to forward or backward integrate to increase overall economic performance. Alternatively, it may reveal that divestiture and a narrowing of participation in the industrial value chain is a good strategy. Finally, knowing the supplier power and buyer power can have a significant effect on how external linkages are exploited. Supplier and buyer power can be assessed for a company by comparing the percentage of profits earned in the industrial value chain with the percentages earned by suppliers and by customers. For example, suppose that the profit earned per gallon of gasoline by an independent refiner and producer is $0.15 and the profit earned by a network of service stations that buy the gasoline (not owned by the independent) is $0.05 per gallon. The percentage of profit earned in this segment of the value chain by the downstream stage is 25% ($0.05/$0.20), while the independent earns 75% of the profit. Buyer power is weak relative to the refiner and producer. If, in addition, the return on assets being earned by the service station segment is high, this may reveal that integrating forward is both desirable and possible.

LIFE CYCLE COST MANAGEMENT

Objective 2
Explain what life cycle cost management is and how it can be used to maximize profits over a product's life cycle.

Strategic cost management emphasizes the importance of an external focus and the need to recognize and exploit both internal and external linkages. Life cycle cost management is a related approach that builds a conceptual framework that facilitates management's ability to exploit internal and external linkages. To understand what is meant by life cycle cost management, we first need to understand basic product life cycle concepts.

Product Life Cycle Viewpoints

product life cycle

Product life cycle is simply the time a product exists—from conception to abandonment. Usually product life cycle refers to a product class as a whole—such as automobiles—but it can also refer to specific forms (such as station wagons) and to specific brands or models (such as Neon). Also, by replacing "conception" with "purchase," we obtain a customer-oriented definition of product life cycle. The producer-oriented definition refers to the life of classes, forms, or brands, whereas the customer-oriented definition refers to the life of a specific unit of product. These producer and customer orientations can be refined by looking at the concepts of revenue-producing life and consumable life. **Revenue-producing life** is the time a product generates revenue for a company. A product begins its revenue-producing life with the sale of the first product. **Consumable life**, on the other hand, is the length of time that a product serves the needs of a customer. Revenue-producing life is clearly of most interest to the producer, while consumable life is of most interest to the customer. Consumable life, however, is also of interest to the producer because it can be used as a competitive tool.

revenue-producing life

consumable life

Marketing Viewpoint The producer of goods or services has two viewpoints concerning product life cycle: the marketing viewpoint and the production viewpoint. The marketing viewpoint describes the general sales pattern of a product as it passes through distinct life cycle stages. Exhibit 9-8 illustrates the general

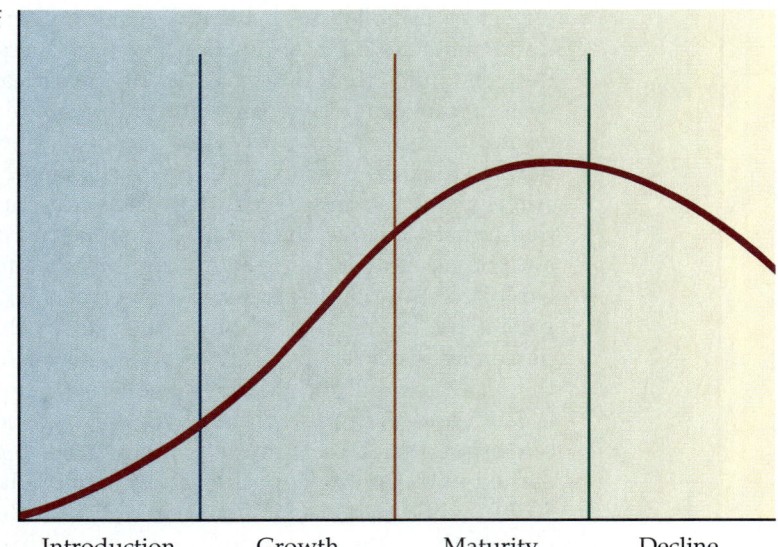

Exhibit 9-8
General Pattern of Product Life Cycle: Marketing Viewpoint

Units of Sales

Introduction   Growth   Maturity   Decline

pattern of the marketing view of product life cycle. The distinct stages identified by the exhibit are introduction, growth, maturity, and decline. The **introduction stage** is characterized by preproduction and startup activities, where the focus is obtaining a foothold in the market. As the graph indicates, there are no sales for a period of time (the preproduction period) and then slow sales growth as the product is introduced. The **growth stage** is a period of time when sales increase at an increasing rate. The **maturity stage** is a period of time when sales increase at a decreasing rate. Eventually the slope (of the sales curve) in the maturity stage becomes neutral and then turns negative in the **decline stage**. Thus, the maturity stage is when the product loses market acceptance and sales begin to decrease.

Production Viewpoint The production viewpoint of the product life cycle defines stages of the life cycle by changes in the type of activities performed: research and development activities, production activities, and logistical activities. The production viewpoint emphasizes life cycle costs, whereas the market viewpoint emphasizes sales revenue behavior. **Life cycle costs** are all costs associated with the product for its entire life cycle. These costs include research (product conception), development (planning, design, and testing), production (conversion activities), and logistics support (advertising, distribution, warranty, customer service, product servicing, and so on). The product life cycle and the associated cost commitment curve are illustrated in Exhibit 9-9. Notice that 90 percent or more of the costs associated with a product are *committed* during the development stage of the product's life cycle. Committed means that most of the costs that *will be incurred* are predetermined—set by the nature of the product design and the processes needed to produce the design.

Customer Viewpoint Like the production life cycle, the consumption life cycle's stages are related to activities. These activities define four stages: purchasing, operating, maintaining, and disposal. The consumable life cycle viewpoint emphasizes product performance for a given price. Price refers to the costs of ownership, which include the following elements: purchase cost, operating costs, maintenance costs, and disposal costs. Thus, total customer satisfaction is affected

Margin notes: introduction stage; growth stage; maturity stage; decline stage; life cycle costs

Exhibit 9-9
Product Life Cycle: Pro-
duction Viewpoint

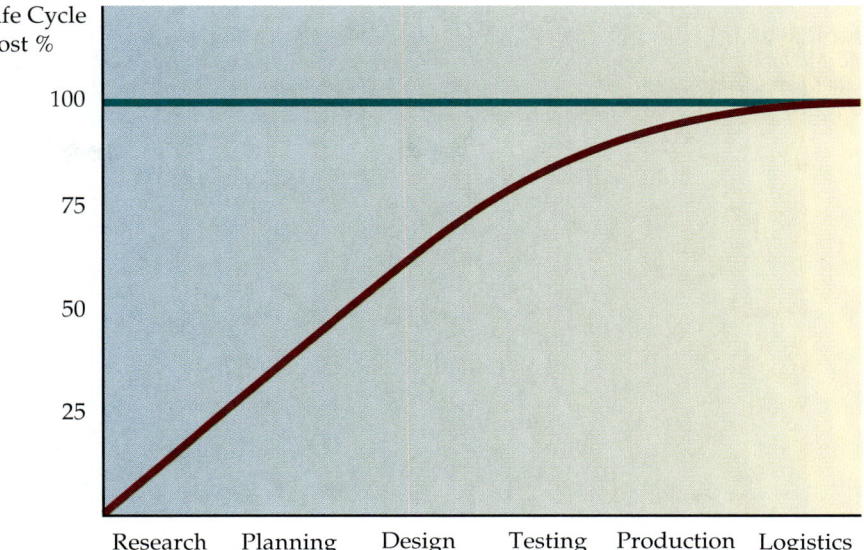

Life Cycle
Cost %

100

75

50

25

Research   Planning   Design   Testing   Production   Logistics

by both the purchase price and postpurchase costs. Because customer satisfaction is affected by postpurchase costs, producers also have a vital interest in managing the level of these costs. How producers can exploit the linkage of postpurchase activities with producer activities is a key element of product life cycle cost management.

Interactive Viewpoint

All three life cycle viewpoints offer insights that can be useful to producers of goods and services. In fact, producers cannot afford to ignore any of the three. A comprehensive life cycle cost management program must pay attention to the variety of viewpoints that exist. This observation produces an integrated, comprehensive definition of life cycle cost management. **Life cycle cost management** consists of actions taken that cause a product to be designed, developed, produced, marketed, distributed, operated, maintained, serviced, and disposed of so that life cycle profits are maximized. Maximizing life cycle profits means producers must understand and capitalize on the relationships that exist among the three life cycle viewpoints. Once these relationships are understood, then actions can be implemented that take advantage of revenue enhancement and cost reduction opportunities.

life cycle cost
management

Relationships Among Life Cycle Viewpoints The marketing viewpoint is concerned with the nature of the sales pattern over the life cycle of the product; it is a *revenue-oriented viewpoint*. The production viewpoint, however, emphasizes the internal activities needed to develop, produce, market, and service products. The production stages exist to support the sales objectives of the marketing stages. This sales support requires resource expenditure; thus, the production life cycle can be described as an *expense-oriented viewpoint*. The consumption life cycle is concerned with product performance and price (including postpurchase costs). The ability to generate revenues and the level of resource expenditure are both related to product performance and price. The producer must be concerned with what the customer receives and what the customer gives up. Thus, the consumption life cycle can be described as a *customer-value oriented viewpoint*. Exhibit 9-10 illustrates the relationships among the stages of the three viewpoints. The

Exhibit 9-10
*Typical Relationships of
Product Life Cycle
Viewpoints*

Marketing Product Life Cycles:				
Attributes	*Introduction*	*Growth*	*Maturity*	*Decline*
Sales	Low	Rapid growth	Slow growth Peak sales	Declining

Production Life Cycle:				
Attributes	*Introduction*	*Growth*	*Maturity*	*Decline*
Expenses:				
Product R&D	High	Moderate	Moderate	Low
Process R&D	Moderate	High	Moderate	Low
Plant & Equipment	Low to moderate	High	Moderate	Low
Advertising	Moderate to high	High	Moderate	Low
Service	Low	Moderate	High	Low

Consumable Life Cycle:				
Attributes	*Introduction*	*Growth*	*Maturity*	*Decline*
Customer value:				
Customer type	Innovators	Mass market	Mass market, differentiated	Laggards
Performance sensitivity	High	High	High	Moderate
Price sensitivity	Low	Moderate	High	Moderate
Competition	None	Growing	High	Low

Attributes	*Introduction*	*Growth*	*Maturity*	*Decline*
Profits	Negligible to loss	Peak levels	Moderate to high	Low

stages of marketing viewpoint are listed as columns; the other two viewpoints appear as rows. The other two viewpoints are identified by the nature of their attributes: expenses for the production life cycle and customer value for the consumable life cycle. Competition and customer type are included under customer value because they affect the producer's approach to providing customer value.

The relationships described in Exhibit 9-10 are typical but can vary depending on the nature of the product and the industry in which a producer operates. Some explanation of the relationships should reveal the potential for producers to exploit them. Relationships can be viewed vertically or horizontally. Consider, for example, the introduction stage, and examine the vertical relationships. In this stage, we would expect losses or negligible profits because of high levels of expenditure in research and development and marketing. Customers at this stage are described as innovators. These are simply the first customers to buy the product. Innovators are venturesome, willing to try something new. They are usually more concerned with the performance of the new product than with its price. This fact, coupled with the lack of competitors, may allow a high price to be charged for the new product. If the barriers to entry are high, then a high price may continue to be charged for some time. However, if competition grows as indicated by the horizontal dimension of the table, and if price sensitivity increases, then the producer will need to rely on further research and development and differentiation to maintain a competitive advantage.

Revenue Enhancement Revenue-generating approaches depend on marketing life cycle stage and on customer value effect. Pricing strategy, for example, varies with stages. In the introductory stage, higher prices can be charged because customers are less price sensitive and more interested in performance.

In the maturity stage, customers are highly sensitive to both price and performance. This suggests that adding features, increasing durability, improving maintainability, and offering customized products may all be good strategies to follow. In this stage, differentiation is important. For revenue enhancement to be viable, however, the customer must be willing to pay a premium for any improvement in product performance. Furthermore, this premium must exceed the cost the producer incurs in providing the new product attribute. In the decline stage, revenues may be enhanced by finding new uses and new customers for the product. A good example is the use of Arm & Hammer's baking soda to absorb refrigerator odors in addition to its normal role in baking goods.[5]

Cost Reduction Cost reduction, not cost control, is the emphasis of life cycle cost management. Cost reduction strategies should explicitly recognize that actions taken in the early stages of the production life cycle can lower costs for later production and consumption stages. Since 90% or more of a product's life cycle costs are determined during the development stage, it makes sense to emphasize management of activities during this phase of a product's existence. Studies have shown that every dollar spent on preproduction activities saves $8–$10 on production and postproduction activities, including customer maintenance, repair, and disposal costs.[6] Apparently, many opportunities for cost reduction occur before production begins. Managers need to invest more in preproduction assets and dedicate more resources to activities in the early phases of the product life cycle to reduce production, marketing, and postpurchase costs.

Product design and process design afford multiple opportunities for cost reduction by: (1) designing to reduce manufacturing costs, (2) designing to reduce logistical support costs, and (3) designing to reduce postpurchase costs, which includes customer time involved in maintenance, repair, and disposal. For these approaches to be successful, managers of producing companies must have a good understanding of activities, cost drivers, and how the activities interact. Manufacturing, logistical, and postpurchase activities are not independent. Some designs may reduce postpurchase costs and increase manufacturing costs. Other designs may simultaneously reduce production, logistical, and postpurchase costs. For example, today's computers are well known for the high level of consumer frustration caused by adding components (e.g., speakers, sound cards, printers, enhanced monitors). One of the goals of Microsoft product designers for the new Windows95 software was the "plug and play" feature, in which the computer itself could recognize the add-ons and adjust for them. Microsoft is well aware that consumer frustration costs both time and money now (it is estimated that every call to technical support costs $25–$50) and in the future through lost sales and slower growth.[7]

5.   Onkvisit and Shaw, "Competition and Product Management: Can the Product Life Cycle Help?" *Business Horizons*, July–August, 1986, pp. 51–62.
6.   Mark D. Shields and S. Mark Young, "Managing Product Life Cycle Costs: An Organizational Model; R. L. Engwall, "Cost Management Systems for Defense Contractors," *Cost Accounting for the 90's, Responding to Technological Change*, National Association of Accountants, Montvale, N.J., 1988.
7.   David C. Churbuck, "Help! My PC Won't Work!" *Forbes*, March 13, 1995, pp. 101–106.

Cost Reduction: An Example A traditional cost system usually will not supply the information needed to support life cycle cost management. Traditional cost systems emphasize the use of unit-based cost drivers to describe cost behavior, focus on production activities, ignore logistical and postpurchase activities, and expense research and development costs and other nonmanufacturing costs as they are incurred. Traditional cost systems never collect a complete history of a product's costs over its life cycle. Essentially, the GAAP-driven cost system does not support the demands of life cycle costing. An activity-based cost system, however, produces information about activities, including both preproduction and postproduction activities, and cost drivers.

To illustrate the importance of knowing activity information, consider Gray Company, a company that produces industrial power tools. Gray currently uses a traditional unit-based cost system, which assumes that all conversion costs are driven by direct labor hours. Because of competitive forces, management has instructed its design engineers to develop new product and process designs for existing products to reduce manufacturing costs (the products targeted for design improvements are estimated to be entering the final growth stage of their marketing life cycle). If, however, manufacturing costs are driven by factors other than direct labor hours, then design actions may produce costs much different than expected. For example, suppose that engineers are considering two new product designs for one of its power tools. Both designs reduce direct materials and direct labor content over the current model. The anticipated effects of the two designs on manufacturing, logistical, and postpurchase activities are listed below, for both the traditional cost system and an ABC system.

Cost Behavior

Unit-based system:
  Variable conversion activity rate: $40 per direct labor hour
  Material usage rate: $8 per part
ABC system:
  Labor usage: $10 per direct labor hour
  Material usage (direct materials): $8 per part
  Machining: $28 per machine hour
  Purchasing activity: $60 per purchase order
  Setup activity: $1,000 per setup hour
  Warranty activity: $200 per returned unit (usually requires extensive rework)
  Customer repair cost: $10 per repair hour

Activity and Resource Information (annual estimates)

	Design A		Design B	
Units produced	10,000		10,000	
Direct material usage	100,000	parts	60,000	parts
Labor usage	50,000	hours	80,000	hours
Machine hours	25,000		20,000	
Purchase orders	300		200	
Setup hours	200		100	
Returned units	400		75	
Repair time (customer)	800		150	

The cost analysis for each design under both the traditional unit-based and ABC cost systems is shown in Exhibit 9-11. The unit-based system computes the unit product cost using only manufacturing costs. The results of the traditional

Exhibit 9-11
Cost Analysis: Competing Product Designs

A. Traditional Cost System

	Design A	Design B
Direct materials[a]	$ 800,000	$ 480,000
Conversion cost[b]	2,000,000	3,200,000
Total manufacturing cost	$2,800,000	$3,680,000
Units produced	10,000	10,000
Unit cost	$280	$368

[a]$8 × 100,000; $8 × 60,000
[b]$40 × 50,000; $40 × 80,000

B. ABC System

	Design A	Design B
Direct materials	$ 800,000	$ 480,000
Direct labor[a]	500,000	800,000
Machining[b]	700,000	560,000
Purchasing[c]	18,000	12,000
Setups[c]	200,000	100,000
Warranty[c]	80,000	15,000
Total product costs	$2,298,000	$1,967,000
Units produced	10,000	10,000
Unit cost	$230	$197
Postpurchase costs	$8,000	$1,500

[a]$10 × 50,000; $10 × 80,000
[b]$28 × 25,000; $28 × 20,000
[c]$60 × 300; $60 × 200; etc.

analysis favor Design A. Thus, Gray would choose Design A over Design B. The ABC analysis reveals a much different picture. Relative to Design A, Design B simultaneously reduces the costs of manufacturing, logistical, and postpurchase activities. Ignoring postpurchase costs, the cost advantage is $331,000 per year for Design B. Furthermore, although the postpurchase costs seem relatively small, they could be important in a very competitive setting. Notice that the customer repair hours per unit produced for Design A are .08 (800/10,000) and are only .015 (150/10,000) for Design B. This indicates that Design B has a higher level of serviceability than does Design A and, thus, more customer value.

Role of Target Costing

target cost

Target cost is the difference between the sales price needed to capture a predetermined market share and the desired profit per unit. If the target cost is less than what is currently achievable, then management budgets cost reductions that move the actual cost toward the target cost. Progress is measured by comparing actual costs with intermediate target costs. For example, suppose that the current sales price of a product is $20 and that the market share is 24 percent. The marketing manager indicates that reducing the sales price to $17 will increase market share from 24 percent to 36 percent. The product is currently earning a profit of $4 per unit. The president of the company indicates that the profit of $4 per unit must be maintained. Thus, if the per-unit profit can be maintained and the market share is increased, then total profits will increase. Furthermore, increasing market share strengthens the long-term competitive position of the firm. A target price of $17 and a target profit of $4 per unit implies a target cost. The target cost is computed as follows:

$$\text{Target cost} = \$17 - \$4 = \$13$$

Suppose that it currently costs $15 per unit to produce the product. Thus, the cost reduction needed to achieve the target cost and desired profit is $2 ($15 − $13). To realize the target cost, management must build in cost reductions by judicious activity analysis and management. The idea is to achieve the reduction needed over time.

Since life cycle cost management emphasizes cost reduction, target costing becomes a particularly useful tool for establishing cost reduction goals. Toyota, for example, calculates the lifetime target profit for a new car model by multiplying a target profit ratio by the target sales. It then calculates the estimated profit by subtracting the estimated costs from target sales. Usually (at this point) target profit is greater than estimated profit. The cost reduction goal is defined by the difference between the target profit and the estimated profit. Toyota then searches for cost reduction opportunities through better design of the new model. Toyota's management recognizes that more opportunities exist for cost reduction during product planning than in actual development and production.[8]

Short Life Cycles

Although life cycle cost management is important for all manufacturing firms, it is particularly important for firms that have products with short life cycles. Products must recover all life cycle costs and provide an acceptable profit. If a firm's products have long life cycles, profit performance can be increased by such actions as redesigning, changing prices, cost reduction, and altering the product mix. In contrast, firms that have products with short life cycles usually do not have time to react in this way, and so their approach must be proactive. Thus, for short life cycles, good life cycle planning is critical and prices must be set properly to recover all the life cycle costs and provide a good return. Activity-based costing can be used to encourage good life cycle planning. By careful selection of cost drivers, design engineers can be motivated to choose cost-minimizing designs.

JUST-IN-TIME (JIT) MANUFACTURING AND PURCHASING

Objective 3
Describe the basic features of JIT purchasing and manufacturing.

JIT manufacturing and purchasing systems offer a prominent example of how managers can use the strategic concepts discussed earlier in the chapter to bring about significant changes within an organization. Firms that implement JIT are pursuing a cost reduction strategy by redefining the structural and procedural activities performed within an organization. Cost reduction is supportive of either a cost leadership or differentiation strategy. Cost reduction is directly related to cost leadership. Successful differentiation depends on offering greater value; yet, this value added must be less than the cost of providing it. JIT can help add value by reducing waste. Successful implementation of JIT has brought about significant improvements, such as better quality, increased productivity, reduced lead times, major reductions in inventories, reduced setup times, lower

8.   For a complete description of Toyota's approach, see Takao Tanaka, "Target Costing at Toyota," *Journal of Cost Management,* Spring 1993, pp. 4–11.

manufacturing costs, and increased production rates. For example, Oregon Cutting Systems, a manufacturer of cutting chain (for chain saws), timber-harvesting equipment, and sporting equipment, within a period of 3-5 years, reduced defects by 80%, waste by 50%, setup times from hours to minutes (one punch press had setup time reduced from 3 hours to 4.5 minutes), lead times from 21 days to three days, and manufacturing costs by 35%.[9] JIT techniques have also been implemented by the following companies:

WalMart	Chrysler	Intel
General Motors	Hewlett-Packard	Borg Warner
Toys "R" Us	Harley Davidson	Westinghouse
Ford	Motorola	John Deere
General Electric	AT&T	Mercury Marine
Black and Decker	Xerox	

Adopting a JIT manufacturing system has a significant effect on the nature of the cost management accounting system. Installing a JIT system affects the traceability of costs, enhances product-costing accuracy, diminishes the need for allocation of service-center costs, changes the behavior and relative importance of direct labor costs, impacts job-order and process costing systems, decreases the reliance on standards and variance analysis, and decreases the importance of inventory tracking systems. To understand and appreciate these effects, we need a fundamental understanding of what JIT manufacturing is and how it differs from traditional manufacturing.

JIT manufacturing

JIT manufacturing is a demand-pull system. The objective of **JIT manufacturing** is to eliminate waste by producing a product only when it is needed and only in the quantities demanded by customers. Demand pulls products through the manufacturing process. Each operation produces only what is necessary to satisfy the demand of the succeeding operation. No production takes place until a signal from a succeeding process indicates a need to produce. Parts and materials arrive just in time to be used in production. JIT assumes that all costs other than direct materials are driven by time and space drivers. JIT then focuses on eliminating waste by compressing time and space.

Inventory Effects

JIT purchasing

JIT manufacturing relies on the exploitation of a customer linkage. Specifically, production is tied to customer demand. This linkage extends back through the value chain and also affects how a manufacturer deals with suppliers. **JIT purchasing** requires suppliers to deliver parts and materials just in time to be used in production. Thus, supplier linkages are also vital. Supply of parts must be linked to production, which is linked to demand. One effect of successful exploitation of these linkages is to reduce all inventories to much lower levels. Contrast this with the traditional push-through system of manufacturing. In traditional manufacturing, materials are supplied and parts produced and transferred to the succeeding process in an effort to meet customer demand and delivery schedules. However, in a traditional, push-through environment, slow or delayed reaction time is often a problem, which in turn, creates a demand for finished goods inventories (otherwise, customers would grow old waiting for the firm to produce and deliver the needed goods). In a push-through environment, finished

9.   Jack C. Bailes and Ilene K. Kleinsorge, "Cutting Waste with JIT," *Management Accounting,* May 1992, pp. 28–32.

goods inventories are also needed to serve as a buffer when production is less than demand. Usually, the push-through system produces significantly higher levels of finished goods inventory than does a JIT system.

Traditionally, inventories of raw materials and parts are carried so that a firm can take advantage of quantity discounts and hedge against future price increases of the items purchased. The objective is to lower the cost of inventory. JIT achieves the same objective without carrying inventories. The JIT solution is to exploit supplier linkages by negotiating long-term contracts with a few chosen suppliers located as close to the production facility as possible and by establishing more extensive supplier involvement. Suppliers are not selected on the basis of price alone. Performance—the quality of the component and the ability to deliver as needed—and commitment to JIT purchasing are vital considerations. Every effort is made to establish a partners-in-profits relationship with suppliers. Suppliers need to be convinced that their well-being is intimately tied to the well-being of the buyer.

To help reduce the uncertainty in demand for the supplier and establish the mutual confidence and trust needed in such a relationship, JIT manufacturers emphasize long-term contracts. Other benefits of long-term contracts exist. They stipulate prices and acceptable quality levels. Long-term contracts also reduce dramatically the number of orders placed, which helps to drive down the ordering and receiving costs. Another effect of long-term contracting is a reduction in the cost of parts and materials—usually in the range of 5% to 20% less than what was paid in a traditional setting. Usually, the need to develop close supplier relationships drives the supplier base down dramatically. For example, Mercedes-Benz U.S. International's new factory in Vance, Alabama, saved time and money by streamlining its supplier list from 1,000 to 100 primary suppliers. In exchange for annual 5 percent price cuts, the chosen suppliers have multiyear contracts (as opposed to the yearly bidding process practiced at other Mercedes plants) and can adapt off-the-shelf parts to Mercedes' needs. The end result is lower costs for both Mercedes and suppliers.[10] Suppliers also benefit. The long-term contract ensures a reasonably stable demand for their products. A smaller supplier base typically means increased sales for the selected suppliers. Thus, both buyers and suppliers benefit, a common outcome when external linkages are recognized and exploited.

By reducing the number of suppliers and working closely with those that remain, the quality of the incoming materials can be improved significantly—a crucial outcome for the success of JIT. As the quality of incoming materials increases, some quality-related costs can be avoided or reduced. For example, the need to inspect incoming materials disappears and rework requirements decline.

Plant Layout

The type and efficiency of plant layout is another executional cost driver that is managed differently under JIT manufacturing. (See Exhibit 9-2 for a review of executional cost drivers.) In traditional job and batch manufacturing, products are moved from one group of identical machines to another. Typically, machines with identical functions are located together in an area referred to as a *department or process*. Workers who specialize in the operation of a specific machine are located in each department. Thus, the executional cost driver for a traditional

---

10.   David Woodruff and Karen Lowry Miller, "Mercedes' Maverick in Alabama," *Business Week*, September 11, 1995, pp. 64–65.

setting is departmental structure. JIT replaces this traditional plant layout with a pattern of manufacturing cells. The executional cost driver for a JIT setting is cell structure. Cell structure is chosen over departmental structure because it increases the ability of the organization to "execute" successfully. Some of the efficiencies cited earlier for Oregon Cutting Systems (OCS), such as reduced lead times and lower manufacturing costs, are a direct result of the cellular structure. The cellular manufacturing design can also affect structural activities, such as plant size and number of plants, because it typically requires less space. OCS, for example, cut its space requirement by 40%. Space savings like this can reduce the demand to build new plants and will affect the size of new plants when they are needed.

manufacturing cells   **Manufacturing cells** contain machines that are grouped in families, usually in a semicircle. The machines are arranged so that they can be used to perform a variety of operations in sequence. Each cell is set up to produce a particular product or product family. Products move from one machine to another from start to finish. Workers are assigned to cells and are trained to operate all machines within the cell. Thus, labor in a JIT environment is multiskilled, not specialized. Each manufacturing cell is essentially a minifactory; in fact, cells are often referred to as a *factory within a factory*. A comparison of the JIT's plant layout with the traditional pattern is shown in Exhibit 9-12.

Exhibit 9-12
Plant Layout Pattern: Traditional Versus JIT

Traditional Manufacturing Layout

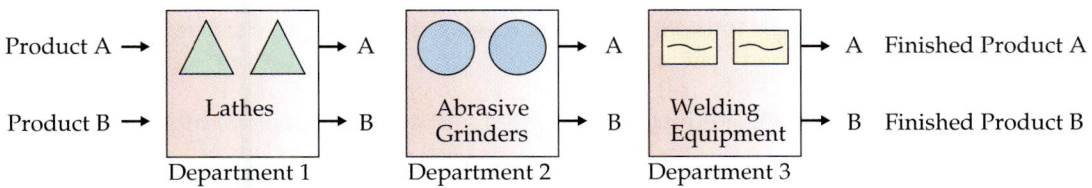

Each product passes through departments that specialize in one process. Departments process multiple products.

JIT Manufacturing Layout

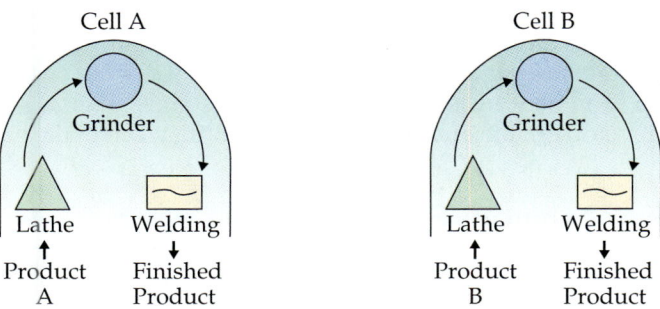

Notice that each product passes through its own cell. All machines necessary to process each product are placed within the cell. Each cell is dedicated to the production of one product or one subassembly.

Grouping of Employees

Another major structural difference between JIT and traditional organizations relates to how employees are grouped. As just indicated, each cell is viewed as a minifactory; thus, each cell requires easy and quick access to support services, which means that centralized service departments must be scaled down and their personnel reassigned to work directly with manufacturing cells. For example, with respect to raw materials, JIT calls for multiple stock points, each one near where the material will be used. There is no need for a central stores location—in fact, such an arrangement actually hinders efficient production. A purchasing agent can be assigned to each cell to handle material requirements. Similarly, other service personnel, such as manufacturing and quality engineers, can be assigned to cells.

Other support services may be relocated to the cell by training cell workers to perform the services. For example, in addition to direct production work, cell workers may perform setup duties, move partially completed goods from station to station within the cell, perform preventive maintenance and minor repairs, conduct quality inspections, and perform janitorial tasks. This multiple task capability is directly related to the pull-through production approach. Producing on demand means that production workers (formerly direct laborers) may often have "free" time. This nonproduction time can be used to perform some of the other support activities.

Employee Empowerment

A major procedural difference between traditional and JIT environments is the degree of participation allowed workers in the management of the organization. According to the JIT view, increasing the degree of participation (the executional cost driver) increases productivity and overall cost efficiency. Workers are allowed a say in how the plant operates. For example, workers are allowed to shut down production to identify and correct problems. Input is sought and used to improve production processes. Workers are often involved in interviewing and hiring other employees, sometimes even including prospective bosses. The reason? If the "chemistry is right," then the work force will be more efficient—and will work together better.

Employee empowerment, a procedural activity, also affects other structural and procedural activities. The management structure must change in response to greater employee involvement. Because workers assume greater responsibilities, fewer managers are needed and the organizational structure becomes flatter. Flatter structures speed up and increase the quality of information exchange. The style of management needed in the JIT firm also changes. Managers in the JIT environment need to act as facilitators more than as supervisors. Their role is to develop people and their skills so that they can make value-adding contributions.

Total Quality Control

JIT necessarily carries with it a much stronger emphasis on managing quality. A defective part brings production to a grinding halt. Poor quality simply cannot be tolerated in a manufacturing environment that operates without inventories. Simply put, JIT cannot be implemented without a commitment to total quality control (TQC). TQC is essentially a never-ending quest for perfect quality: the striving for a defect-free product design and manufacturing process. This approach to managing quality is diametrically opposed to the traditional doctrine, called **acceptable quality level (AQL)**. AQL permits or allows defects to occur provided they do not exceed a predetermined level.

acceptable quality
level (AQL)

The major differences between JIT manufacturing and traditional manufacturing are summarized in Exhibit 9-13. These differences will be referred to and discussed in greater detail as the implications of JIT manufacturing for cost management are examined.

JIT and Automation

Automating a complex manufacturing process is prohibitively expensive. Simplifying the product design and manufacturing process makes automation cost effective. Once a JIT system is installed, it usually reveals where automation may be of some value. Thus, it is not uncommon for a firm adopting JIT to follow it with the acquisition of advanced manufacturing technology. Firms automate to increase productive capacity, increase efficiency, improve quality and service, decrease processing time, and increase output. There are three levels of automation: the stand-alone piece of equipment, the automated cell, and the completely integrated factory.

computer-numerically
controlled (CNC)
machines

flexible
manufacturing
system (FMS)
FMS cell

computer-integrated
manufacturing
(CIM) system

The first level of automation is represented by **computer-numerically controlled (CNC) machines**, stand-alone machines controlled by a computer. The automated cell goes one step further and integrates computer-controlled machines and automated materials-handling equipment. A particular example of an automated cell is the **flexible manufacturing system (FMS)**. The **FMS cell** is a system that produces a family of products from start to finish using robots and other automated equipment under the control of a computer. The power of FMS lies in its ability to switch production from one product to another with simple programming changes. There may be several cells within a factory. The final step is a **computer-integrated manufacturing (CIM) system**. CIM integrates the computer-aided design (CAD), engineering (CAE), and manufacturing (CAM) systems. In a CIM system, all automated components are linked by a centrally controlled information system. The design changes using CAD automatically reprogram machines through a tie-in with CAE and CAM.

Exhibit 9-13
Comparison of JIT Approach with Traditional Manufacturing and Purchasing

JIT	Traditional
1. Pull-through system	1. Push-through system
2. Insignificant inventories	2. Significant inventories
3. Small supplier base	3. Large supplier base
4. Long-term supplier contracts	4. Short-term supplier contracts
5. Cellular structure	5. Departmental structure
6. Multiskilled labor	6. Specialized labor
7. Decentralized services	7. Centralized services
8. High employee involvement	8. Low employee involvement
9. Facilitating management style	9. Supervisory management style
10. Total quality control	10. Acceptable quality level
11. Buyers' market	11. Sellers' market
12. Value-chain focus	12. Value-added focus

JIT AND ITS EFFECT ON THE COST MANAGEMENT SYSTEM

Objective 5

Describe the effect JIT has on cost traceability and product costing.

The numerous changes in structural and procedural activities that we have described for a JIT system also change traditional cost management practices. Both the cost accounting and operational control systems are affected. In general, the organizational changes simplify the cost management accounting system and simultaneously increase the accuracy of the cost information being produced.

Traceability of Overhead Costs

There are three methods that cost systems use to assign costs to individual products: direct tracing, driver tracing, and allocation. Of the three methods, the most accurate is direct tracing; thus, it's preferred over the other two methods. In a JIT environment, many overhead costs assigned to products using either driver tracing or allocation are now directly attributable to products. Cellular manufacturing, multiskilled labor, and decentralized service activities are the major features of JIT responsible for this change in traceability.

In a departmental structure, many different products may be subjected to a process located in a single department (e.g., grinding). After completion of the process, the products are then transferred to other processes located in different departments (e.g., assembly, painting, and so on). Although a different set of processes is usually required for each product, most processes are applicable to more than one product. For example, thirty different products may need grinding. Because more than one product is processed in a department, the costs of that department are common to all products passing through it and therefore must be assigned to products using activity drivers or allocation. In a manufacturing-cell structure, however, all processes necessary for the production of each product or major subassembly are collected in one area called a cell. Thus, the costs of operating that cell can be assigned to the cell's product or subassembly using direct tracing. (However, if a family of products uses a cell, then we must resort to drivers and allocation to assign costs.)

Equipment formerly located in other departments, for example, is now reassigned to cells, where it may be dedicated to the production of a single product or subassembly. In this case, depreciation is now a directly attributable product cost. Multiskilled workers and decentralized services add to the effect. Workers in the cell are trained to set up the equipment in the cell, maintain it, and operate it. Additionally, cell workers may also be used to move a partially finished part from one machine to the next, to perform maintenance, setups, and materials handling. These support functions were previously done by a different set of laborers for all product lines. Additionally, people with specialized skills (e.g., industrial engineers and production schedulers) are assigned directly to manufacturing cells. Thus, because of multitask assignments and redeployment of other support personnel, many support costs can now be assigned to a product using direct tracing. Exhibit 9-14 compares the traceability of some selected costs in a traditional manufacturing environment with their traceability in the JIT environment (assuming single-product cells). Comparisons are based on the three cost assignment methods.

Product Costing

One consequence of increasing directly attributable costs is to increase the accuracy of product costing. Directly attributable costs are associated (usually by physical observation) with the product and can safely be said to belong to it.

Exhibit 9-14
*Product Cost Assign-
ment: Traditional Versus
JIT Manufacturing*

Manufacturing Cost	Traditional Environment	JIT Environment
Direct labor	Direct tracing	Direct tracing
Direct materials	Direct tracing	Direct tracing
Materials handling	Driver tracing	Direct tracing
Repairs and maintenance	Driver tracing	Direct tracing
Energy	Driver tracing	Direct tracing
Operating supplies	Driver tracing	Direct tracing
Supervision (dept.)	Allocation	Direct tracing
Insurance and taxes	Allocation	Allocation
Plant depreciation	Allocation	Allocation
Equipment depreciation	Driver tracing	Direct tracing
Custodial services	Allocation	Direct tracing
Cafeteria services	Driver tracing	Driver tracing

Other costs, however, are common to several products and must be assigned to these products using activity drivers and allocation. Because of cost and convenience, activity drivers that are less than perfectly correlated with the consumption of overhead activities may be chosen. JIT manufacturing reduces the need for this difficult assessment by converting many common costs to directly attributable costs. Note, however, that the driving force behind these changes is not the cost management system itself but the changes in the structural and procedural activities brought about by implementing a JIT system. While activity-based costing offers significant improvement in product-costing accuracy, focusing offers even more potential improvement.

Exhibit 9-14 illustrates that JIT does not convert all costs into directly attributable costs. Even with JIT in place, some overhead activities remain common to the manufacturing cells. These remaining support activities are mostly facility-level activities. In a JIT system, the batch size is one unit of product. Thus, all batch-level activities convert into unit-level activities. Additionally, many of the batch-level activities are reduced or eliminated. For example, materials handling may be significantly reduced because of reorganizing from a departmental structure to a cellular structure. Similarly, for single-product cells, there is no setup activity. Even for cells that produce a family of products, setup times would be minimal. Furthermore, it is likely that the need to use activity drivers for the cost of product-level activities is significantly diminished because of decentralizing these support activities to the cell level. Is there, then, a role for ABC in a JIT firm?

Although JIT diminishes the value of ABC for tracing manufacturing costs to individual products, an activity-based costing system has much broader application than just tracing manufacturing costs to products. For many strategic and tactical decisions, the product cost definition needs to include nonmanufacturing costs. For example, value-line and operational product costing is an invaluable tool for strategic costing analysis and for life cycle cost management. Also, including postpurchase costs as part of the product cost definition provides valuable insights. Thus, knowing and understanding general and administrative, research, development, marketing, customer service, and postpurchase activities and their cost drivers is essential for sound cost analysis. Oregon Cutting Systems, the firm whose JIT experience we described earlier, in 1990 appointed a special multidisciplinary team to explore the possibility of implementing an activity-based cost system. The team was given the charge to identify cost drivers for the organization's service areas (value-line activities other than manufacturing). The objective was to use this knowledge of activities and their drivers to achieve efficiency gains comparable to the manufacturing area. Finally, it should be mentioned that a contemporary cost management system has more objectives in mind than simply product costing. Cost drivers play a vital role in cost reduction, cost control, and performance evaluation.

JIT's Effect on Job-Order and Process Costing Systems

In implementing JIT in a job-order setting, the firm should first separate its repetitive business from its unique orders. Manufacturing cells can then be established to deal with the repetitive business. For those products where demand is insufficient to justify its own manufacturing cell, groups of dissimilar machines can be set up in a cell to make families of products or parts that require the same manufacturing sequence.

With this reorganizing of the manufacturing layout, job orders are no longer needed to accumulate product costs. Instead, costs can be accumulated at the cellular level. Additionally, because lot sizes are now too small (as a result of reducing work in process and finished goods inventories), it is impractical to have job orders for each job. Add to this the short lead time of products occurring because of the time and space compression features of JIT (virtually no setup time and cellular structures), and it becomes difficult to track each piece moving through the cell. In effect, the job environment has taken on the nature of a process costing system.

JIT simplifies process costing. A key feature of JIT is lower inventories. Assuming that JIT is successful in reducing work in process (Oregon Cutting Systems, for example, reduced work in process by 85%), then the need to compute equivalent units vanishes. Calculating product costs follows the simple pattern of collecting costs for a cell for a period of time and dividing the costs by the units produced for that period.

Backflush Costing

The JIT system also offers the opportunity to simplify the accounting for manufacturing cost flows. Given low inventories, it may not be desirable to spend resources tracking the cost flows through all the inventory accounts. In a traditional system, there was a work in process account for each department so that manufacturing costs could be traced as work proceeded through the factory. Under JIT, there are no departments and a 14-day lead time (for example) has become 4 hours, and it would be absurd to trace costs from station to station within a cell. After all, if production cycle time is in minutes or hours, and goods are shipped immediately upon completion, then all of each day's manufacturing costs flow to Cost of Goods Sold. Recognizing this outcome leads to a simplified approach of accounting for manufacturing cost flows. This simplified approach, called **backflush costing**, uses trigger points to determine when manufacturing costs are assigned to key inventory and temporary accounts. Varying the number and location of trigger points creates several variants of backflush costing. Although there are several variants of backflush costing, only two will be discussed, differentiated by the location of the trigger points. Trigger points are simply events that prompt ("trigger") the accounting recognition of certain manufacturing costs.

backflush costing

General Description Backflush costing eliminates separate materials and work in process accounts. Instead, there is a single account, Raw Materials and in Process (RIP). The RIP account is used only for the tracking of the cost of raw materials. Under both variants of backflush costing, the first trigger point is the purchase of raw materials. When materials are purchased in a JIT system, they are immediately placed into process. Thus, there is no need to record their purchase in a separate inventory account. Combining direct labor and overhead into one category is a second feature of backflush costing. As firms implement JIT and automate, the traditional direct labor cost category disappears. Multiskilled workers intermingle setup activities, machine-loading activities, maintenance, and materials handling, etc. As labor becomes multifunctional, the ability to track and report direct labor separately becomes impossible. Consequently, backflush costing usually combines direct labor costs with overhead costs in a temporary account called *Conversion Cost Control*. This account accumulates the *actual* conversion costs on the debit side and the *applied* conversion costs on the credit side. Any difference between the actual conversion costs and the applied conversion costs is closed to Cost of Goods Sold. In the first variant of backflush costing, the completion of goods triggers the recognition of the manufacturing costs used to produce the goods (the second trigger point). At this point, conversion cost application is recognized by debiting Finished Goods and crediting Conversion Cost Control; the cost of materials is recognized by debiting Finished Goods and crediting the RIP account. Thus, the costs of manufacturing are "flushed" out of the system *after* the goods are completed.

In the second variant of backflush costing, the second trigger point is defined by the point when goods are sold rather than when they are completed. For this variant, the costs of manufacturing are "flushed" out of the system *after* the goods are sold. Thus, the application of conversion cost and the transfer of materials cost are accomplished by debiting Cost of Goods Sold and crediting Conversion Cost Control and RIP, respectively.

Example: Backflushing Compared with Traditional Cost Flow Accounting To illustrate backflush costing and compare it with the traditional approach, assume that a JIT company had the following transactions during June:

1. Raw materials were purchased on account for $160,000.
2. All materials received were placed into production.
3. Actual direct labor costs, $25,000.
4. Actual overhead costs, $225,000.
5. Conversion costs applied, $235,000.
6. All work was completed for the month.
7. All completed work was sold.
8. The difference between actual and applied costs is computed.

The journal entries for the first variant of backflush costing and the traditional system are compared in Exhibit 9-15.

The second backflushing variant replaces entries 6 and 7 with the following entry:

Cost of Goods Sold	395,000	
Conversion Cost Control		235,000
Raw Materials and in Process		160,000

Exhibit 9-15
Cost Flows: Traditional Compared with JIT

Transaction	Traditional Journal Entries			Backflush Journal Entries		

1. Purchase of raw materials.	Materials
	   Accounts Payable
		160,000	160,000	Raw Materials and
				   in Process
				     Accounts Payable
					160,000	160,000

2. Materials issued to production.	Work in Process Materials	160,000	160,000	No entry		
3. Direct labor cost incurred.	Work in Process Payroll	25,000	25,000	Combined with overhead: See next entry.		

4. Overhead cost incurred.	Overhead Control
	   Accounts Payable
		225,000	225,000	Conversion Cost Control
				   Payroll
				   Accounts Payable
					250,000	25,000
						 225,000

5. Application of overhead.	Work in Process Overhead Control	210,000	210,000	No entry		

6. Completion of goods.	Finished Goods
	   Work in Process
		395,000	395,000	Finished Goods
				   Raw Materials and
				     in Process
				   Conversion Cost Control
					395,000	160,000
						 235,000

7. Goods are sold.	Cost of Goods Sold
	   Finished Goods
		395,000	395,000	Cost of Goods Sold
				   Finished Goods
					395,000	395,000

8. Variance is recognized.	Cost of Goods Sold
	   Overhead Control
		15,000	15,000	Cost of Goods Sold
				   Conversion Cost Control
					15,000	15,000

SUMMARY

Obtaining a competitive advantage so that long-term survival is ensured is the goal of strategic cost management. Different strategies create different bundles of activities. By assigning costs to activities, the costs of different strategies can be assessed. Knowledge of organization and operational activities and their associated cost drivers is fundamental to strategic cost analysis. Knowledge of the firm's value chain and the industrial value chain is also critical for strategic analysis. Value-chain analysis relies on identifying and exploiting internal and external linkages.

Life cycle cost management is related to strategic cost analysis and, in fact, could be called a type of strategic cost analysis. Life cycle cost management requires an understanding of the three types of life cycle viewpoints: the marketing viewpoint, the production viewpoint, and the consumable life viewpoint. By considering the interrelationships among the three viewpoints, insights are developed that help managers maximize life cycle profits.

JIT purchasing and manufacturing offer a totally different set of structural and procedural activities from those of the traditional organization. The differences between JIT and traditional organizational structures can be used to illustrate the types of organizational activities and cost drivers that can be managed so that a competitive advantage can be created and sustained. JIT also impacts the cost management system by changing the traceability of costs, increasing product costing accuracy, and in general, offering a simpler cost accounting system.

REVIEW PROBLEM AND SOLUTION

Assume that a firm has the following activities and associated cost behaviors:

Activities	Cost Behavior
Labor	$10 per direct labor hour
Setups	Variable: $100 per setup
	Step-fixed: $30,000 per step, step = 10 setups
Receiving	Step-fixed: $40,000 per step, step = 2,000 hours

Activities with step cost behavior are being fully utilized by existing products. Thus, any new product demands will increase resource spending on these activities.

Two designs are being considered for a new product: Design I and Design II. The following information is provided about each design (1,000 units of the product will be produced):

Cost Driver	Design I	Design II
Direct labor hours	3,000	2,000
Number of setups	10	20
Receiving hours	2,000	4,000

The company has recently developed a cost equation for manufacturing costs using direct labor hours as the driver. The equation has $R^2 = 0.60$ and is given below:

$$Y = \$150,000 + \$20X$$

REQUIRED:

1. Suppose that design engineering is told that only direct labor hours drive manufacturing costs (based on the direct labor cost equation). Compute the cost of each design. Which design would be chosen based on this unit-based cost assumption?
2. Now compute the cost of each design using all driver and activity information. Which design will now be chosen? Are there any other implications associated with the use of the more complete activity information set?
3. Consider the following statement: "Strategic cost analysis should exploit internal linkages." What does this mean? Explain, using the results of Requirements 1 and 2.
4. What other information would be useful to have concerning the two designs? Explain.

Solution

1. Design I: $20 × 3,000 = $60,000
   Design II: $20 × 2,000 = $40,000
   The unit-based analysis would lead to the selection of Design II.

2.

Design I:	
Labor ($10 × 3,000)	$ 30,000
Setups [(10 × $100) + (1 × $30,000)]	31,000
Receiving (1 × $40,000)	40,000
Total	$101,000
Design II:	
Labor ($10 × 2,000)	$ 20,000
Setups [(20 × $100) + (2 × $30,000)]	62,000
Receiving (2 × $40,000)	80,000
Total	$162,000

Design I has the lowest total cost. Notice also the difference in expected total manufacturing costs. The direct labor driver approach produces a much lower cost for both designs. This difference in cost could produce significant differences in pricing strategies.

3. Exploiting internal linkages means taking advantage of the relationships among the activities that exist within a firm's segment of the value chain. To do this, we must know what the activities are and how they are related. Activity costs and drivers are an essential part of this analysis. Using only unit-based drivers for design decisions, as in Requirement 1, ignores the effect that different designs have on nonunit-based activities. The results of Requirement 2 illustrated a significant difference between two designs—relative to the unit-based analysis. The traditional cost system simply is not rich enough to supply the information needed for a thorough analysis of linkages.

4. Linkages also extend to the rest of the firm's internal value-chain activities. Thus, it would be useful to know how design choices affect and are affected by logistical activities. Furthermore, external linkages would also help. For example, it would be interesting to know how postpurchase activities and costs are affected by the two designs.

KEY TERMS

Acceptable quality level (AQL) 377
Backflush costing 380
Competitive advantage 354
Computer-integrated manufacturing (CIM) system 377
Computer-numerically controlled (CNC) machines 377
Consumable life 365
Customer value 354

Decline stage 366
External linkages 356
Flexible manufacturing system (FMS) 377
FMS cell 377
Growth stage 366
Industrial value chain 355
Internal linkages 356
Introduction stage 366
JIT manufacturing 373
JIT purchasing 373
Life cycle costs 366

Life cycle cost management 367
Manufacturing cells 375
Maturity stage 366
Operational activities 358
Operational cost drivers 358
Organizational activities 357
Organizational cost drivers 357
Postpurchase costs 355
Procedural (executional) activities 357

Product life cycle 365
Revenue-producing life 365
Strategic cost management 354
Strategic decision making 354
Structural activities 357
Target cost 371
Total product 355
Total quality control 363
Value-chain analysis 359

QUESTIONS FOR WRITING AND DISCUSSION

1. "The most important strategic elements for a firm are its long-term growth and survival." Do you agree? Explain the role of strategic cost management in achieving long-term growth and survival.
2. What does it mean to obtain a competitive advantage? What role does the cost management system play in helping to achieve this goal?
3. What is customer value? How is customer value related to a cost leadership strategy? To a differentiation strategy?
4. Explain what internal and external linkages are.
5. What are organizational and operation activities? Organizational cost drivers? Operational cost drivers?
6. What is the difference between a structural cost driver and an executional cost driver? Provide examples of each.
7. What is value-chain analysis? What role does it play in strategic cost analysis?
8. What does it mean to exploit external and internal linkages?
9. What is an industrial value chain? Explain why a firm's strategies are tied to what happens in the rest of the value chain. Using total quality control as an example, explain how the success of this quality management approach is dependent on supplier linkages.
10. What is the difference between a producer-oriented definition of product life cycle and a customer-oriented definition?
11. What are the three viewpoints of product life cycle? How do they differ?
12. What are the four stages of the marketing life cycle?
13. What are life cycle costs? How do these costs relate to the production life cycle?
14. What are the four stages of the consumption life cycle? What are postpurchase costs? Explain why a producer may want to know postpurchase costs.
15. Explain how the life cycle viewpoints are interrelated.
16. Explain why price sensitivity increases as a product moves from the introduction to maturity stages.
17. Describe a revenue enhancement strategy during the maturity stage of a product's life cycle.
18. "Life cycle cost reduction is best achieved during the development stage of the production life cycle." Do you agree? Explain.
19. Explain why design strategies should consider production, logistical, and postpurchase activities.
20. What is target costing? What role does it have in life cycle cost management?
21. "A JIT system must exploit customer and supplier linkages to be successful." Explain.
22. Plant layout and efficiency is an important executional cost driver for JIT. Explain how this executional cost driver is chosen to increase efficiency and decrease cost.
23. Besides plant layout and efficiency, what other organizational cost drivers are used to advantage by JIT systems?
24. Explain why JIT with dedicated cellular manufacturing increases product costing accuracy.
25. In addition to product costing accuracy, what other effect(s) does JIT have on cost management systems?

EXERCISES AND PROBLEMS

9-1
Competitive Advantage: Basic Concepts

LO 1

Jason Iba has decided to purchase a personal computer. He has narrowed the choices to two: Brand A and Brand B. Both brands have the same processing speed, the same hard disk capacity, 3.5-inch disk and CD-ROM drives, and come with the same basic software support package. Both come from companies with good reputations. The selling price for each is identical. After some review, Jason discovers that the cost of operating and maintaining Brand A over a three-year period is estimated to be $200. For Brand B, the operating and maintenance cost is $600. The sales agent for Brand A emphasized the lower operating and maintenance cost. She claimed that it was lower than any other PC brand. The sales agent for Brand B, however, emphasized the service reputation of the product. He provided Jason with a copy of an article appearing in a PC magazine that rated service performance of various PC brands. Brand B was rated number one. Based on all the information, Jason decided to buy Brand B.

REQUIRED:

1. What is the total product purchased by Jason?
2. Is the Brand A company pursuing a cost leadership or differentiation strategy? The Brand B company? Explain.
3. When asked why he purchased Brand B, Jason replied, "I think Brand B offered more value than Brand A." What are the possible sources of this greater value? If Jason's reaction represents the majority opinion, what suggestions could you offer to help improve the market position of Brand A?

**9-2
Driver
Classification**

LO 1

Classify the following cost drivers as structural, executional, or operational.

a. Number of employees
b. Setup hours
c. Degree of employee involvement
d. Capacity utilization
e. Number of product lines
f. Number of distribution channels
g. Number of units sold
h. Machine hours
i. Number of vertical levels in an organization
j. Product configuration
k. Supplier linkages
l. Number of purchase orders
m. Number of defective units
n. Management style
o. Types of process technologies
p. Inspection hours
q. Type and efficiency of layout
r. Scale
s. Number of functional departments
t. Number of planning meetings

**9-3
Operational and
Organizational
Activities**

LO 1

McConkie Company has decided to pursue a cost leadership strategy. This decision is prompted, in part, by increased competition from foreign firms. McConkie's management is confident that costs can be reduced by more efficient management of the firm's operational activities. Improving operational activity efficiency, however, often requires some strategic changes in organizational activities. McConkie currently uses a very traditional manufacturing approach. Plants are organized along departmental lines. Management follows a typical pyramid structure. Labor is specialized and located in departments. Quality management follows a conventional acceptable quality level approach (batches of products are accepted if the number of defective units is below some acceptable level). Materials are purchased from a large number of suppliers, and sizable inventories of materials, work in process, and finished goods are maintained. The company produces many different products that use a lot of different parts, many of which are purchased from suppliers.

Given this brief description of the firm and its setting, for each of the following operational activities and their associated drivers, suggest some strategic changes in organizational activities (and drivers) that might reduce the cost of performing the indicated operational activity. Explain your reasoning.

Operational Activity	Operational Cost Driver
Inspecting products	Number of inspection hours
Moving materials	Distance moved
Reworking products	Number of defective units
Setting up equipment	Setup time
Purchasing parts	Number of different parts
Storing goods and materials	Days of inventory
Expediting orders	Number of late orders
Warranty work	Number of bad units sold

9-4
Internal Linkages and Strategic Decision Making
LO 1

Troy, Inc., has a traditional, unit-based cost system. The Baltimore plant of Troy produces ten different electronic products. The demand for each product is about the same. Although the products differ in complexity, each product uses about the same labor time and materials. The plant has used direct labor hours for years to assign overhead to products. To help design engineers understand the assumed cost relationships, the cost accounting department developed the following cost equation (the equation describes the relationship between total manufacturing costs and direct labor hours; the equation is supported by a coefficient of determination of 60%): ⟶ to actual

$$Y = \$5{,}000{,}000 + \$30X, \text{ where } X = \text{direct labor hours}$$

The variable rate of $30 is broken down as follows:

Direct labor	$ 9
Variable overhead	5
Direct materials	16

Because of competitive pressures, product engineering was given the charge to redesign products to reduce the total cost of manufacturing. Using the above cost relationships, product engineering adopted the strategy of redesigning to reduce direct labor content. As each design was completed, an engineering change order was cut, triggering a series of events such as design approval, vendor selection, bill of material update, redrawing of schematic, test runs, changes in setup procedures, development of new inspection procedures, and so on.

After one year of design change, the normal volume of direct labor was reduced from 250,000 hours to 200,000 hours, with the same number of products being produced. Although each product differs in its labor content, the redesign efforts reduced the labor content for all products. On average, the labor content per unit of product dropped from 1.25 hours per unit to 1 hour per unit. Fixed overhead, however, increased from $5,000,000 to $6,600,000 per year.

REQUIRED:

1. Using normal volume, compute the manufacturing cost per labor hour before the year of design changes. What is the cost per unit of an "average" product?
2. Using normal volume after the one year of design changes, compute the manufacturing cost per hour. What is the cost per unit of an "average" product?
3. What do you think is the most likely explanation for the failure of the design changes to reduce manufacturing costs? What changes would you suggest to improve Troy's efforts to reduce costs?

**9-5
External Linkages
and Strategic
Decision Making**

LO 1

BJ Manufacturing produces several types of potentiometers. The products are produced in batches according to customer order. Although there are a variety of potentiometers, they can be grouped into three product families. The number of units sold is the same for each family. The selling prices for the three families range from $0.50 to $0.80 per unit. Because the product families are used in different kinds of products, customers also can be grouped into three categories, corresponding to the product family they purchase. Historically, the costs of order entry, processing, and handling costs were expensed and not traced to individual products. These costs are not trivial and totaled $4,500,000 for the most recent year. Furthermore, these costs had been increasing over time. Recently, the company had begun to emphasize a cost reduction strategy; however, any cost reduction decisions had to contribute to the creation of a competitive advantage.

Because of the magnitude and growth of order-filling costs, management decided to explore the causes of these costs. They discovered that order-filling costs were driven by the number of customer orders processed. Further investigation revealed the following cost behavior:

Step-fixed cost component: $50,000 per step; 2,000 orders define a step*
Variable cost component: $20 per order

*BJ currently has sufficient steps to process 100,000 orders.

The expected customer orders for the year total 100,000. The expected usage of the order-filling activity and the average size of an order are given below by product family:

	Family A	Family B	Family C
Number of orders	50,000	30,000	20,000
Average order size	600	1,000	1,500

As a result of the cost behavior analysis, the marketing manager recommended the imposition of a charge per customer order. The president of the company concurred. The charge was implemented by adding the cost per order to the price of each order (computed using the projected ordering costs and expected orders). This ordering cost was then reduced as the size of the order increased and eliminated as the order size reached 2,000 units (the marketing manager indicated that any penalties imposed for orders greater than this size would lose sales from some of the smaller customers). Within a short period of communicating this new price information to customers, the average order size for all three product families increased to 2,000 units.

REQUIRED:

1. BJ traditionally has expensed order-filling costs. What is the most likely reason for this practice?
2. Consider the following claim: By expensing the order-filling costs, all products were undercosted; furthermore, products ordered in small batches are significantly undercosted. Explain, with supporting computations where possible.
3. Calculate the reduction in order-filling cost produced by the change in pricing strategy (assume that resource spending is reduced as much as possible and that the total units sold remain unchanged). Explain how exploiting customer linkages produced this cost reduction. Are there any other internal activities that might benefit from this pricing strategy?
4. One of BJ's goals is to reduce costs so that a competitive advantage might be created. Describe how the management of BJ might use this outcome to help create a competitive advantage.

9-6
Internal and External Linkages; Strategic Cost Management

LO 1

Ashton Company produces a variety of janitorial equipment, including buffers and floor sweepers. Over the past several years, competition has intensified. In order to maintain its market share and perhaps increase it, Ashton's management had decided that the overall quality of its products had to be increased. Furthermore, costs must be reduced so that the selling prices of its products could be reduced. After some investigation, Ashton concluded that many of the problems it had could be traced to the reliability of the parts that were purchased from outside suppliers. Many of these components failed to work as intended, causing performance problems. Over the years, the company had increased its inspection activity of the final products. If a problem could be detected internally, then it was usually possible to rework the buffer or floor sweeper so that the desired performance was achieved. Management also had increased its warranty coverage, and this work also had been increasing over the years.

Walter Kelly, president of Ashton Company, called a meeting with his executive committee. Bill Terry, chief engineer, Ashley Applegate, controller, and Brad Mitchell, purchasing manager, were all in attendance. How to improve the company's competitive position was the meeting's topic. The conversation of the meeting is presented below.

Walter: We need to find a way to improve the quality of our products and at the same time reduce costs. Bill, you said that you have done some research into this area. Would you share your findings.

Bill: As you know, a major source of our quality problems relates to the poor quality of the parts we acquire from the outside. We have a lot of different parts, and this adds to the complexity of the problem. What I thought would be helpful would be to redesign our products so that they can use as many interchangeable parts as possible. This will cut down the number of different parts and make it easier to inspect and cheaper to repair when it comes to warranty work. My engineering staff has already come up with some new designs that will do this for us.

Brad: I like this idea. It will simplify the purchasing activity significantly. With fewer parts, I can envision some significant savings for my area. Bill has shown me the designs, and so I know exactly the parts that would be needed. I also have a suggestion. We need to embark on a supplier evaluation program. We have too many suppliers. By reducing the number of different parts, we will need fewer suppliers. And we really don't need to use all the suppliers that produce the parts demanded by the new designs. We should pick suppliers that will work with us and provide the quality of parts that we need. I have done some preliminary work and have identified five suppliers that seem willing to work with us and give us the assurance of the quality we need. Bill may need to send some of his engineers into their plants to make sure that they can do what they are claiming.

Walter: This sounds promising. Ashley, can you look over the proposals and their estimates and give us some idea if this approach will save us any money. And if so, how much we can expect to save.

Ashley: Actually, I am ahead of the game here. Bill and Brad have both been in contact with me and have provided me some estimates on how these actions would affect different activities. I have prepared a handout that includes an activity table revealing what I think are the key activities affected. I have also assembled some tentative information about activity costs. The table gives the current demand and the expected demand after the changes are implemented. With this information, we should be able to assess the expected cost savings.

Handout

Activities	Cost Driver	Capacity	Current Demand	Expected Demand
Purchasing parts	Number of different parts	400	400	100
Inspecting products	Inspection hours	10,000	10,000	5,000
Reworking products	Number reworked	As needed	12,500	5,000
Warranty repair	Number of defective products	2,000	1,800	700

Additionally, the following activity cost data are provided:

Purchasing Parts: Variable activity cost: $30 per part number; four salaried clerks, each earning a $40,000 annual salary. Each clerk is capable of processing orders associated with 100 part numbers.

Inspecting Parts: Five inspectors each earning a salary of $35,000 per year. Each inspector is capable of 2,000 hours of inspection.

Reworking Products: Variable activity cost: $25 per unit reworked (labor and parts).

Warranty: Four repair agents, each paid a salary of $30,000 per year. Each repair agent is capable of repairing 500 units per year. Variable activity costs: $15 per product repaired.

REQUIRED:

1. Compute the total savings possible as reflected by Ashley's handout. Assume that resource spending is reduced where possible.
2. Explain how redesign and supplier evaluation are linked to the savings computed in Requirement 1. Discuss the importance of recognizing and exploiting internal and external linkages.
3. Identify the organizational and operational activities involved in the strategy being considered by Ashton Company. What is the relationship between organizational and operational activities?

9-7
External Linkages and Strategic Cost Management
LO 1

Pawnee Works makes machine parts for manufacturers of industrial equipment. Over the years, Pawnee has been a steady and reliable supplier of quality parts to medium and small machine manufacturers. Michael Murray, owner of Pawnee Works, once again was disappointed in the year-end income statement. Profits had again failed to meet expectations. The performance was particularly puzzling given that the shop was operating at 100 percent capacity and had been for two years—ever since it had landed a Fortune 500 firm as a regular customer. This firm currently supplies 40 percent of the business—a figure that had grown over the two years. Convinced that something was wrong, Michael called Brooke Harker, a partner in a large regional CPA firm. Brooke agreed to look into the matter.

A short time later, Brooke made an appointment to meet with Michael. Their conversation is recorded below.

Brooke: Michael, I think I have pinpointed your problem. I think your major difficulty is bad pricing—you're undercharging your major customer. It's getting high-precision machined parts for much less than the cost to you. And I bet that you have been losing some of your smaller customers. You may want to rethink your strategic position. You are a small player in the industrial machine industry. This Fortune 500 customer has 40% of the industrial machine market. Over the years, you have carved out a good reputation among small- and medium-size manufacturers. Right?

Michael: Well, you're right. Over the years, our customers have not been giants. But we saw this business with the Fortune 500 company as an opportunity to play in the big leagues. We thought it might mean the opportunity to expand the size of our operation. And we have expanded—at least we have added employees and some specialized engineering equipment. My engineering and programming costs have skyrocketed—resource increases we needed, though, to meet the specs of this larger customer. Profits have increased slightly, but nothing like I expected. You're also right about losing some of our smaller customers. Many have complained that the price of their jobs has increased. They have all indicated that they like the work we do and that we are conveniently located, but they argue that they simply cannot afford to keep paying the price we require. The small customers we have kept are also complaining and threatening to go elsewhere. I doubt we'll be able to hold onto their business for much longer—unless a change is made. So far, though, the business we have lost has been replaced with more orders from our large customer. I expect we could do even more business for the large customer. But how can the large buyer be getting a great deal like you've described? It has the same markup as our regular jobs—full manufacturing cost plus 25 percent.

Brooke: I have prepared a report illustrating the total overhead costs for a typical quarter. This report details your major activities and their associated costs. It also provides a comparison of a typical job for your small customers and the typical job for your large customer. Part of the problem is that your accounting system does not react to certain external events. It fails to show the effect of the large customer's activities on your activities and those that relate to your other customers. Given that you assign overhead costs using machine hours, I think you'll find it quite revealing.

Michael: I'll have my controller examine the report for me. You know, if you are right about underpricing the large customer, I have a big problem. I'm not sure that I can increase the price of the parts without losing this big guy's business. After all, it can go to a dozen machine shops like mine and get the work done. A price increase may not work. Then I'd be faced with the loss of 40% of my jobs. I suppose though that I might be able to regain most of the business with the small customers. In fact, I am positive that we could get most of that business back. I wonder if that's what I ought to do.

Report
Regional CPA Firm

I. Major Activities and Their Costs

Activity	Total Activity Costs	Cost Behavior*
Setups	$209,000	Variable
Engineering	151,200	Step fixed, step = 105 hours
NC programming	130,400	Variable
Machining	100,000	Variable
Rework	101,400	Variable
Inspection	23,000	Step fixed, step = 230 hours
Sales support	80,000	Step fixed, step = 23 orders
Total	$795,000	

*Behavior is defined with respect to individual cost drivers. The costs given are total costs for the quarter's activities. Thus, for step-fixed costs, the reported activity cost is for *all* steps being used by the activity; the cost per step is the total cost divided by the number of steps being used.

II. Job Profiles

Resources Used	Small Customer Job	Fortune 500 Job
Setup hours	3	10
Engineering hours	2	6
Programming hours	1	8
Defective units	20	10
Inspection hours	2	2
Machine hours	2,000	200
Prime costs	$14,000	$1,600
Other data:		
Job size	1,000 parts	100 parts
Quarterly jobs (orders)	15	100
Overhead rate	$14.30/machine hour	$14.30/machine hour

Note: All activities are being fully utilized each quarter (there is no unused activity capacity).

REQUIRED:

1. Without any calculation, explain why the machining company is losing money. Discuss the strategic insights provided by knowledge of activities, their costs, and customer

linkages. Comment on the observation made by Brooke that the current accounting system fails to reflect external events. What changes would be needed to correct this deficiency (if true)?

2. Compute the unit price currently being charged each customer type (using machine hours to assign overhead costs).

3. Compute the unit price that would be charged each customer assuming that overhead is assigned using an ABC approach. Was the CPA right? Is the large customer paying less than the cost of producing the unit? How is this conclusion affected if the sales support activity is traced to jobs? (Use orders—jobs—as the cost driver.)

4. Compute the quarterly profit that is currently being earned and the amount that would be earned if Pawnee Works sold only to small customers (a small customer strategy). For the second income statement, use ABC for cost assignments. For the second statement, the large customer is replaced with 10 smaller customers with the same characteristics as the 15 currently buying parts from Pawnee. Assume that any opportunities to reduce resource spending and usage will be reflected in the profit associated with a small customer strategy. Also, only the cost of activity usage is assigned to jobs. Any cost of unused activity is reported as a separate item on the income statement. Report sales support as a period expense.

5. What change in strategy would you recommend? In making this recommendation, consider the firm's value-chain framework.

9-8
Product Life Cycle

LO 2

Given below are a series of statements associated with product life cycle viewpoints. For each statement, identify whether it is associated with the marketing, production, or customer viewpoint. Where possible, identify the particular characteristic being described. If the statement fits more than one viewpoint, label it as interactive. Explain the interaction.

a. Sales are increasing at an increasing rate.
b. The cost of maintaining the product after it is purchased.
c. The product is losing market acceptance, and sales begin to decrease.
d. A design is chosen to minimize postpurchase costs.
e. Ninety percent or more of the costs are committed during the development stage.
f. The length of time that the product serves the needs of a customer.
g. All costs associated with a product for its entire life cycle.
h. The time a product generates revenue for a company.
i. Profits tend to reach peak levels during this stage.
j. Customers have the lowest price sensitivity during this stage.
k. Describes the general sales pattern of a product as it passes through distinct life cycle stages.
l. The concern is with product performance and price.
m. Actions taken so that life cycle profits are maximized.
n. Emphasizes internal activities that are needed to develop, produce, market, and service products.

9-9
Life Cycle Cost Management and Target Costing

LO 2

Kirtland Enterprises produces electronic products with short life cycles (less than two years). Development has to be rapid, and the profitability of the products is tied strongly to the ability to find designs that will keep production and logistics costs low. Recently management has also decided that postpurchase costs are important in design decisions. Last month a new product was presented to management. The total market is projected at 100,000 units (for the two-year period). The proposed selling price was $30 per unit. The manufacturing and logistics costs were estimated to be $25 per unit. At this price, market share was expected to be 20%.

Upon reviewing the projected figures, Brian Burnham called in his chief design engineer, Dennis Marshall, and his marketing manager, Katrina Lochner. The following conversation was recorded:

Brian: Dennis, although the profit of $5 per unit for this new product is reasonable, total profits need to be increased. Katrina, what suggestions do you have?

Katrina: Simple. Decrease the selling price to $27 and we expand our market share to 35%. To increase total profits, however, we need to lower costs as well.

Brian: You're right. I do not want to earn less than $5 per unit.

Dennis: Does that $5 per unit factor in preproduction costs? You know we already have spent $20,000 on developing this product. To lower costs will require more expenditure on development.

Brian: Good point. I do want a design, if possible, that will provide a $5-per-unit profit, including consideration of preproduction costs. This first design fails this criterion when we factor in preproduction costs.

Katrina: I might mention that postpurchase costs are important as well. The current design will impose about $1.00 per unit for using, maintaining, and disposing our product. That's about the same as our competitors. If we can reduce that cost to about $0.50 per unit by designing a better product, we could probably capture about 50% of the market.

REQUIRED:

1. Compute the total life cycle profit that the current design offers (including preproduction costs).

2. Suppose that the engineering department has two designs: Design A and Design B. Both designs reduce production and logistics costs to $21 per unit. Design A, however, leaves postpurchase costs at $1 per unit, while Design B reduces postpurchase costs to $0.40 per unit. Developing and testing Design A costs an additional $15,000, while Design B costs an additional $30,000. Calculate the total life cycle profits under each design. Which would you choose? Explain. What if the design you chose cost an additional $50,000? Would this have changed your decision?

3. Refer to Requirement 2. For every extra dollar spent on preproduction activities, how much benefit was generated? What does this say about the importance of knowing the linkages between preproduction activities and later activities?

9-10
Life Cycle Cost
Management
LO 2

Jolene Askew, manager of Feagan Company, has committed her company to a strategically sound cost reduction program. Emphasizing life cycle cost management is a major part of this effort. Jolene is convinced that production costs can be reduced by paying more attention to the relationships between design and manufacturing. Design engineers need to know what causes manufacturing costs. She instructed her controller to develop a manufacturing cost formula for a newly proposed product. Marketing had already projected sales of 25,000 units for the new product (the life cycle was estimated to be 18 months and the company expected to have 50% of the market and priced the product to achieve this goal). The projected selling price was $20 per unit. The following cost formula was developed:

$$Y = \$200,000 + \$10X_1$$

where X_1 = Machine hours (the product is expected to use one machine hour for every unit produced)

Upon seeing the cost formula, Jolene quickly calculated the projected gross profit, $50,000. This produced a gross profit of $2 per unit, well below the targeted gross profit of $4 per unit. Jolene then sent a memo to design engineering, instructing them to search for a new design that would lower the costs of production by at least $50,000 so that the target profit could be met.

Within two days, the Engineering Department proposed a new design that would reduce unit-variable cost from $10 per machine hour to $8 per machine hour (Design X). The chief engineer, upon reviewing the design, questioned the validity of the controller's cost formula. He suggested a more careful assessment of the proposed design's effect on activities other than machining. Based on this suggestion, the following revised cost formula was developed. This cost formula reflected the cost relationships of the most recent design (Design X).

$$Y = \$140{,}000 + \$8X_1 + \$5{,}000X_2 + \$2{,}000X_3$$
$$\text{where } X_1 = \text{Units sold}$$
$$X_2 = \text{Number of batches}$$
$$X_3 = \text{Number of engineering change orders}$$

Based on scheduling and inventory considerations, the product would be produced in batches of 1,000; thus, 25 batches would be needed over the product's life cycle. Furthermore, based on past experience, the product would likely generate about 20 engineering change orders.

This new insight into the linkage of the product with its underlying activities led to a different design (Design Y). This second design also lowered the unit-level cost by $2 per unit but decreased the number of design support requirements from 20 orders to 10 orders. Attention was also given to the setup activity, and the design engineer assigned to the product created a design that reduced setup time and lowered variable setup costs from $5,000 to $3,000 per setup. Furthermore, Design Y also creates excess activity capacity for the setup activity, and resource spending for setup activity capacity can be decreased by $40,000, reducing the fixed cost component in the equation by this amount.

Design Y was recommended and accepted. As prototypes of the design were tested, an additional benefit emerged. Based on test results, the postpurchase costs dropped from an estimated $0.70 per unit sold to $0.40 per unit sold. Using this information, the marketing department revised the projected market share upward from 50% to 60% (with no price decrease).

REQUIRED:

1. Calculate the expected gross profit per unit for Design X using the controller's original cost formula. According to this outcome, does Design X reach the targeted unit profit? Repeat using the engineer's revised cost formula. Explain why Design X failed to meet the targeted profit. What does this say about the use of traditional costing for life cycle cost management?
2. Calculate the expected profit per unit using Design Y. Comment on the value of activity information for life cycle cost management.
3. The benefit of the postpurchase cost reduction of Design Y was discovered in testing. What direct benefit did it create for Feagan Company (in dollars)? Reducing postpurchase costs was not a specific design objective. Should it have been? Are there any other design objectives that should have been considered?

9-11
JIT and
Traceability of
Costs

LO 4

Assume that a company has just recently switched to JIT manufacturing. Each manufacturing cell produces a single product or major subassembly. Cell workers have been trained to perform a variety of tasks. Additionally, many services have been decentralized. Costs are assigned to products using direct tracing, driver tracing, and allocation. For the costs listed below and on the following page, indicate the most likely product cost assignment method used *before JIT* and *after JIT*. Use three columns: Cost Item, Before JIT, and After JIT. You may assume that direct tracing is used whenever possible, followed by driver tracing, with allocation being the method of last resort.

a. Inspection costs
b. Power to heat, light, and cool plant
c. Minor repairs on production equipment
d. Salary of production supervisor (department/cell)
e. Oil to lubricate machinery
f. Salary of plant supervisor
g. Costs to set up machinery
h. Salaries of janitors

     i. Power to operate production equipment
     j. Taxes on plant and equipment
    k. Depreciation on production equipment
     l. Raw materials
    m. Salary of industrial engineer
    n. Parts for machinery
    o. Pencils and paper clips for production supervisor (department/cell)
    p. Insurance on plant and equipment
    q. Overtime wages for cell workers
     r. Plant depreciation
     s. Materials handling
     t. Preventive maintenance

9-12
JIT Features and Product-Costing Accuracy
LO 3, 4

Prior to installing a JIT system, Burrows Company used machine hours to assign maintenance costs to its three products (socket sets, pliers, and wrenches). The maintenance costs totaled $560,000 per year. The machine hours used by each product and the quantity of each product produced are as follows:

	Machine Hours	*Quantity Produced*
Socket sets	60,000	15,000
Pliers	60,000	15,000
Wrenches	80,000	20,000

After installing JIT, three manufacturing cells were created, and cell workers were trained to perform preventive maintenance and minor repairs. A full-time maintenance person was also assigned to each cell. Maintenance costs for the three cells still totaled $560,000; however, these costs are now traceable to each cell as follows:

Cell, socket sets	$152,000
Cell, pliers	168,000
Cell, wrenches	240,000

REQUIRED:

1. Compute the pre-JIT maintenance cost per product for each type.
2. Compute maintenance cost per unit for each product after installing JIT.
3. Explain why the JIT maintenance cost per unit is more accurate than the pre-JIT cost.

9-13
JIT; Traceability of Costs; Product-Costing Accuracy; JIT Effects on Cost Accounting System
LO 3, 4

Homer Manufacturing produces different models of 22-calibre rifles. The manufacturing costs assigned to its economy model rifle before and after installing JIT are given in the table on the following page. Cell workers do all maintenance and are also responsible for moving materials, cell janitorial work, and inspecting products. Janitorial work outside the cells is still handled by the janitorial department.

In both the pre- and post-JIT setting, 10,000 units of the economy model are manufactured. In the JIT setting, manufacturing cells are used to produce each product. The management of Homer Manufacturing reported a significant decrease in manufacturing costs for all of its rifles after JIT was installed. It also reported less inventory-related costs and a significant decrease in lead times. Accounting costs also decreased because Homer switched from a job costing system to a process costing system.

	Before	After
Direct materials	$ 60,000	$ 55,000
Direct labor	40,000	50,000
Maintenance	50,000	30,000
Inspection	30,000	10,000
Rework	60,000	9,000
Power	10,000	6,000
Depreciation	12,500	10,000
Material handling	8,000	2,000
Engineering	80,000	50,000*
Setups	15,000	0
Janitorial	40,000	20,000
Building and grounds	11,800	12,400
Supplies	4,000	3,000
Supervision (plant)	10,000	8,000
Cell supervision	—	35,000
Cost accounting	40,000	25,000
Departmental supervision	18,000	—
Total	$489,300	$325,400

*Salary of engineer assigned to the cell.

REQUIRED:

1. Compute the unit cost of the product before and after JIT.
2. Explain why the JIT unit cost is more accurate. Also explain what JIT features may have produced a decrease in production costs. Use as many specific cost items as possible to illustrate your explanation.
3. Explain why Homer Manufacturing switched from a job costing system to a process costing system after JIT was implemented.
4. Classify the costs in the JIT environment according to how costs are assigned to the cell: direct tracing, driver tracing, or allocation. Which cost assignment method is most common? What does this imply regarding product costing accuracy?

9-14
Backflush Costing
LO 4

Lochner Company has installed a JIT purchasing and manufacturing system and is using backflush accounting for its cost flows. It currently uses the completion of goods as the trigger point to flush the manufacturing costs out of the system. During the month of October, Lochner had the following transactions:

Raw materials purchased	$120,000
Direct labor cost	20,000
Overhead cost	100,000
Conversion cost applied	130,000*

*$20,000 labor plus $110,000 overhead.

There were no beginning or ending inventories. All goods produced were sold with a 40 percent markup. Any variance is closed to Cost of Goods Sold.

REQUIRED:

1. Prepare the journal entries that would have been made using a traditional accounting approach for cost flows.

2. Prepare the journal entries for the month using backflush costing.
3. Prepare the journal entries for the month using backflush costing, assuming that Lochner uses the sale of goods as the second trigger point instead of the completion of goods.

9-15
JIT and Product Costing
LO 3, 4

Mott Company recently implemented a JIT manufacturing system. After one year of operation, Heidi Burrows, president of the company, wanted to compare product cost under the JIT system with product cost under the old system. Mott's two products are weed eaters and lawn edgers. The unit prime costs under the old system are given below.

	Eaters	Edgers
Direct materials	$12	$45
Direct labor	4	30

Under the old manufacturing system, the company operated three service centers and two production departments. Overhead was applied using departmental overhead rates. The direct overhead costs associated with each department for the year preceding the installation of JIT are as follows:

Maintenance	$110,000
Materials handling	90,000
Building and grounds	150,000
Machining	280,000
Assembly	175,000
	$805,000

Under the old system, the overhead costs of the service departments were allocated directly to the producing departments and then to the products passing through them (both products passed through each producing department). The overhead rate for the Machining Department was based on machine hours, and the overhead rate for Assembly was based on direct labor hours. During the last year of operations for the old system, the Machining Department used 80,000 machine hours and the Assembly Department 20,000 direct labor hours. Each weed eater required 1 machine hour in Machining and 0.25 direct labor hours in Assembly. Each edger required 2 machine hours in Machining and 0.5 hours in Assembly. Bases for allocation of the service costs are given below.

	Square Feet of Space	Number of Material Moves	Machine Hours
Machining	80,000	90,000	80,000
Assembly	40,000	60,000	20,000
Total	120,000	150,000	100,000

Upon implementing JIT, a manufacturing cell for each product was created to replace the departmental structure. Each cell occupied 40,000 square feet. Maintenance and materials handling were both decentralized to the cell level. Essentially, cell workers were trained to operate the machines in each cell, assemble the components, maintain the machines, and move the partially completed units from one point to the next within the cell. During the first year of the JIT system, the company produced and sold 20,000 weed eaters and 30,000 edgers. This output was identical to that for the last year of operations under the old system. The following costs have been assigned to the manufacturing cells:

	Eater Cell	Edger Cell
Direct materials	$185,000	$1,140,000
Direct labor	66,000	660,000
Direct overhead	99,000	350,500
Allocated overhead*	75,000	75,000
Total	$425,000	$2,225,500

*Building and grounds, allocated on the basis of square footage.

REQUIRED:

1. Compute the unit cost for each product under the old manufacturing system.
2. Compute the unit cost for each product under the JIT system.
3. Which of the unit costs is the more accurate? Explain. Include in your explanation a discussion of how the computational approaches differ.
4. Calculate the decrease in overhead costs under JIT and provide some possible reasons that explain the decrease.

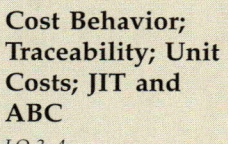

9-16
Cost Behavior;
Traceability; Unit
Costs; JIT and
ABC

LO 3, 4

Berry Company, a manufacturer of athletic shoes, has adopted JIT manufacturing. In implementing the system, three types of manufacturing cells were created, one for each type of shoe produced. The manufacturing costs for the line of basketball shoes are given below (expected production of 25,000 units). Cell labor is responsible for operating and maintaining all cell equipment, moving materials from station to station, inspecting and packing, and cell cleanup.

Cell manufacturing costs:	
Direct materials	$240,000
Cell labor	160,000
Power	25,000
Supervision	40,000
Depreciation (equipment)	20,000
Other manufacturing costs:	
Share of plant depreciation	14,000
Share of plant supervisor's salary	6,000
Engineering sustaining (50 orders)	40,000
Cost accounting (1,000 transactions)	20,000

Engineering-sustaining costs are driven by engineering orders, and cost accounting is driven by the number of transactions. These activity costs are fixed but follow a step-cost function. Engineering sustaining is acquired in units of 50. Engineering sustaining has 40 units of unused activity capacity. Cost accounting is acquired in units of 2,000. This activity has 200 units of unused activity.

REQUIRED:

1. Assume initially that all costs are strictly variable or strictly fixed with respect to units produced. Prepare a cost formula for the following costs:
   a. Direct materials
   b. Direct labor
   c. All directly attributable manufacturing costs other than labor and materials
   d. All directly attributable manufacturing costs
   e. Total manufacturing costs

2. Assuming that 25,000 pairs of basketball shoes are produced, compute the following, using the cost relationships developed in Requirement 1:
   a. Direct material costs
   b. Direct labor costs
   c. Directly attributable manufacturing costs
   d. Total manufacturing costs
   e. Unit cost
3. Using the unit-based cost formula, calculate the total manufacturing costs for 30,000 units. Also compute the unit cost. Which costs changed? Why?
4. Now classify costs as unit-level, batch-level, product-level, and facility-level. Calculate total costs for each category for 25,000 and 30,000 units. Which costs changed? Why?
5. Refer to Requirement 4. Suppose that the number of engineering orders increased from 50 to 60 and the number of transactions from 1,000 to 1,100. What happens to total costs for 25,000 units? 30,000 units? Explain.

9-17
Cost Assignment and JIT
LO 3, 4

Goldstein Company produces two types of vases (A and B). Both pass through two producing departments: Molding and Painting. It also has a Maintenance Department that services and repairs the equipment used in each producing department. Budgeted data for the three departments are given below.

	Maintenance	*Molding*	*Painting*
Overhead	$100,000	$165,000	$119,000
Maintenance hours	—	15,000	5,000
Direct labor hours	—	12,000	6,000

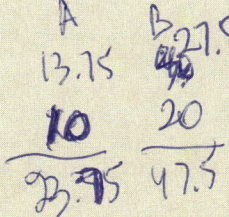

In the Molding Department, Vase A requires 1 hour of direct labor and Vase B, 2 hours. In the Painting Department, Vase A requires 0.5 hours of direct labor and Vase B, 1 hour. Expected production: Vase A, 4,000 units; Vase B, 4,000 units.

Immediately after preparing the budgeted data, a consultant suggests that two manufacturing cells be created: one for the manufacture of Vase A and the other for the manufacture of Vase B. Cell workers would be trained to perform maintenance; hence, the Maintenance Department is decentralized. The total direct overhead costs estimated for each cell are $200,000 for Cell A and $184,000 for Cell B.

REQUIRED:

1. Allocate the service costs to each department, and compute the overhead cost per unit for each vase (overhead rates use direct labor hours).
2. Compute the overhead cost per unit if manufacturing cells are created. Which unit overhead cost do you think is the more accurate—the one computed with a departmental structure or the one computed using a cell structure? Explain.
3. Note that the total overhead costs under each system are assumed to be the same. Would you expect the overhead costs to remain the same if the JIT manufacturing system is implemented? Explain. *They would probably increase*

9-18
Backflush Costing; Conversion Rate
LO 3, 4

Thayn Company has implemented a JIT-FMS system. Kit Applegate, controller of the company, has decided to reduce the accounting requirements given the expectation of lower inventories. For one thing, he has decided to treat direct labor cost as a part of overhead and to discontinue the detailed labor accounting of the past. The company has created two manufacturing cells, each capable of producing a family of products. The first cell, the Mechanical Parts Cell (the M Cell), is dedicated to producing a variety of machine parts. The second cell, the Electronic Components Cell (the E Cell), produces a variety of electrical components. The output of both cells is sold to a sister division that produces industrial machinery and to customers who use the parts and components for repair activity. Product-level and unit-level overhead costs outside the cells are assigned to each cell using appropriate drivers. Facility-level costs are allocated to each cell on the basis of square footage. The budgeted labor and overhead costs are given below.

	M Cell	E Cell
Direct labor costs	$ 40,000	$ 20,000
Direct overhead	160,000	80,000
Product sustaining	60,000	24,000
Facility level	40,000	20,000
Total conversion cost	$300,000	$144,000

The predetermined conversion cost rate is based on available production hours in each cell. The M Cell has 10,000 hours available for production, and the E Cell has 6,000 hours. Conversion costs are applied to the units produced by multiplying the conversion rate by the actual time required to produce the units. The M Cell produced 18,000 units, taking 0.5 hours to produce 1 unit of product (on average). The E Cell produced 20,000 units, taking 0.25 hours to produce one unit of product (on average).

Other actual results for the year are given below.

Materials purchased and issued	$340,000
Labor costs	60,000
Overhead	420,000

All units produced were sold. Any conversion cost variance is closed to Cost of Goods Sold.

REQUIRED:

1. Calculate the predetermined conversion cost rates for each cell.
2. Prepare journal entries using backflush accounting. Assume that completion of goods represents the second trigger point.
3. Repeat Requirement 2, assuming that the second trigger point is the sale of the goods.
4. Explain why there is no need to have a work in process account.
5. Two variants of backflush costing were presented in which each used two trigger points, with the second trigger point differing. Suppose that the only trigger point for recognizing manufacturing costs occurs when the goods are sold. What would be the entries here? When would this third variant be considered appropriate?

**9-19
Managerial
Decision Case: JIT;
Creation of
Manufacturing
Cells; Behavioral
Considerations;
Impact on Costing
Practices**

LO 3, 4

Reddy Heaters, Inc., produces insert heaters that can be used for various applications, ranging from coffeepots to submarines. Because of the wide variety of insert heaters produced, Reddy uses a job-order cost system. Product lines are differentiated by size of heater. In the early stages of the company's history, sales were strong and profits steadily increased. In recent years, however, profits have been declining and the company has been losing market share. Alarmed by the deteriorating financial position of the company, President Doug Young requested a special study to identify the problems. Sheri Butler, the head of the internal audit department, was put in charge of the study. After two months of investigation, Sheri was ready to report her findings.

Sheri: Doug, I think we have some real concerns that need to be addressed. Production is down, employee morale is low, and the number of defective units that we have to scrap is way up. In fact, over the past several years, our scrap rate has increased from 9 percent to 15 percent of total production. And scrap is expensive. We don't detect defective units until the end of the process. By that time, we lose everything. The nature of the product simply doesn't permit rework.

Doug: I have a feeling that the increased scrap rate is related to the morale problem you've encountered. Do you have any feel for why morale is low?

Sheri: I get the feeling that boredom is a factor. Many employees don't feel challenged by their work. Also, with the decline in performance, they are receiving more pressure from their supervisors, which simply aggravates the problem.

Doug: What other problems have you detected?

Sheri: Well, much of our market share has been lost to foreign competitors. The time it takes us to process an order, from time of receipt to delivery, has increased from twenty to thirty days. Some of the customers we have lost have switched to Japanese suppliers, from whom they receive heaters in less than fifteen days. Added to this delay in our delivery is an increase in the number of complaints about poorly performing heaters. Our quality has definitely taken a nosedive over the past several years.

Doug: It's amazing that it has taken us this long to spot these problems. It's incredible to me that the Japanese can deliver a part faster than we can, even in our more efficient days. I wonder what their secret is.

Sheri: I investigated that very issue. It appears that they can produce and deliver their heaters rapidly because they use a JIT purchasing and manufacturing system.

Doug: Can we use this system to increase our competitive ability?

Sheri: I think so, but we'll need to hire a consultant to tell us how to do it. Also, it might be a good idea to try it out on only one of our major product lines. I suggest the small heaters line. It is having the most problems and has been showing a loss for the past two years. If JIT can restore this line to a competitive mode, then it'll work for the other lines as well.

Within a week, Reddy Heaters hired the services of a large CPA firm. The firm sent Kim Burnham, one of its managers, to do the initial background work. After spending some time at the plant, Kim wrote up the following description of the small heater production process:

The various departments are scattered throughout the factory. Labor is specialized and trained to operate the machines in the respective departments. Additionally, the company has a centralized stores area that provides the raw materials for production, a centralized maintenance department that has responsibility for maintaining all production equipment, and a group of laborers responsible for moving the partially completed units from department to department.

Under the current method of production, small heaters pass through several departments, where each department has a collection of similar machines. The first department cuts a metal pipe into one of three lengths: three, four, or five inches long. The cut pipe is then taken to the Laser Department, where the part number is printed on the pipe. In a second department, ceramic cylinders of smaller lengths than the cut pipe are wrapped with a fine wire (using a wrapping machine). The pipe and the wrapped ceramic cylinders are then taken to the Welding Department, where the wrapped ceramic cylinders are placed inside the pipe, centered, and filled with a substance that prevents electricity from reaching the metal pipe. Finally, the ends of the pipe are welded shut with two wire leads protruding from one end. This completed heater is then transferred to the Testing Department, which uses special equipment to see if it functions properly.

The small heaters are produced in batches of 300. It takes 50 hours to cut 300 metal pipes and prepare 300 ceramic cylinders (1/6 hr. per unit, both processes occurring at the same time). After 50 hours of production time, the 300 metal pipes are transported to the Laser Department (20 minutes transport time) and the 300 ceramic cylinders are transported to the Welding Department (20 minutes transport time). In the Laser Department, it takes 50 hours to imprint the part number (1/6 hr. per pipe). The 300 metal pipes are then transported to the Welding Department. In the Welding Department, the ceramic and metal pipes are joined and welded. The welding process takes 50 hours (1/6 hr. per pipe). Finally, the 300 units are transported (20 minutes) to the Testing Department. Each unit requires 1/6 hour for testing, or a total of 50 hours for the 300 units. From start to finish, the total production time for the 300 units is as follows:

Cutting and ceramic	50 hrs.
Laser	50
Welding	50
Testing	50
Moving	1
Total time	201 hrs.

Notice that Laser must wait 50 hours before it can begin imprinting. Similarly, Welding must wait 100 hours before it can begin working on the batch, and finally, Testing must wait 150 hours before it can begin working on the batch.

Based on the information gathered, Kim estimated that the production time for 300 units could be cut from 201 hours to about 50 hours by creating a small heater manufacturing cell.

REQUIRED:

1. One of the first actions taken by Reddy Heaters was to organize a manufacturing cell for the small heater line. Describe how you would organize the manufacturing cell. How does it differ from the traditional arrangement? Will any training costs be associated with the transition to JIT? Explain.
2. Explain how, with computational support, the production time for 300 units can be reduced to about 50 hours. If this is a true reduction in production time, what implications does it have for Reddy's competitive position?
3. Describe the organizational and operational activities that must be managed to bring about the reduction in production time. What are the cost drivers associated with these activities? For operational drivers, indicate the expected effect on activity costs.
4. Initially, the employees resented the change to JIT. After a small period of time, however, morale improved significantly. Explain why the change to JIT increased employee morale.
5. Within a few months, Reddy was able to offer a lower price for its small heaters. Additionally, the number of complaints about the performance of the small heaters declined sharply. By the end of the second year, the product line was reporting profits greater than had ever been achieved. Discuss the JIT features that may have made the lower price and higher profits possible.
6. Within a year of the JIT installation, Reddy's controller remarked, "We have a much better idea than ever before of what it is costing us to produce these small insert heaters." Offer some justification for the controller's statement.
7. Discuss the impact that JIT has on other management accounting practices.

9-20
Ethical Issues

Don Homer, cost accounting manager for Tibbings, Inc., was having dinner with Spencer Gee, a friend since college days. The two had attended the same university and belonged to the same fraternity. Upon graduation, they had taken positions with two competitors whose headquarters were located in the same city. Two years ago, the top management of Tibbings had implemented a life cycle cost management program. Since then, Don had worked closely with design engineering, providing information about activities and their costs. He, in turn, became very well informed about the new product development projects. Spencer was also an accountant and had recently been promoted to assistant controller. Eventually, the conversation turned to work topics.

Spencer: How are things going at work?
Don: Very well. Our new life cycle cost management approach has made a real difference in our profitability. The latest two products have each earned significantly more than in the past.

Spencer: Interesting. How many new products are coming out this year?

Don: We have three new ones coming out—two of which should provide some significant challenges for your company.

Spencer: The last two certainly did. Our competing products earned 30% less profit—all because of yours. I don't know how you did it, but the customers seemed to like yours better.

Don: We gathered information on the cost of maintaining and using the products and then made a real effort to design the new products so that they reduced these costs. We also looked at design so that production costs were lowered. This way, we could sell the products for less and still make the same per-unit profit. It worked. Our total profits went up by about $40,000 on each product.

Spencer: What about these three new ones? Are they coming out soon? And are you planning on selling them for less than you usually do as well?

Don: As I understand it, they should all be on the market within two weeks. And yes, we will sell for less than normal. They cost less. Linking design to downstream activities has been a real benefit.

Spencer: Well, maybe we need to do something similar. Our competing products will probably come out later than yours as well. That's not good for us. Oh well. Let's talk about something more pleasant. We get enough of work during the week.

REQUIRED: Given the guidelines for ethical conduct in Chapter 1, evaluate the ethical conduct of Don and Spencer.

9-21
Research
Assignment
LO 1

Knowing how strategic cost analysis is applied in real-world settings should help you appreciate the power and utility of the methodology. Read the four articles listed below plus one source of your own, and then write a short 2–3 page paper that addresses the following issues:

1. How cost analysis is used in identifying strategic positions of different products.
2. How cost data can be used to help develop superior strategies.
3. The steps that should be followed in strategic cost analysis.
4. The role of activity-based costing and value-chain analysis in strategic cost management.
5. Your personal assessment of how strategic cost analysis differs from traditional cost analysis.

Articles to read:

John K. Shank and Vijay Govindarajan, "Strategic Cost Management: The Value Chain Perspective," *Journal of Management Accounting Research,* Fall 1992, pp. 179–197.

Michael D. Shields and S. Mark Young, "Effective Long-Term Cost Reduction: A Strategic Perspective," *Journal of Cost Management,* Spring 1992, pp. 16–30.

Vijay Govindarajan and John K. Shank, "Strategic Cost Analysis: The Crown Cork and Seal Case, *Journal of Cost Management,* Winter 1989, pp. 5–15.

John K. Shank, Vijay Govindarajan, and Eric Spiegel, "Strategic Cost Analysis: A Case Study," *Journal of Cost Management,* Fall 1988, pp. 25–33.

Chapters 4–9

Metcalf Furniture Corporation produces sofas, recliners, and lounge chairs. Metcalf is located in a medium-sized community in the Northwestern part of the United States. It is a major employer in the community. In fact, the economic well-being of the community is tied very strongly to Metcalf. Metcalf operates a sawmill, a fabric plant, and a furniture plant in the same community.

The sawmill buys logs from independent producers. The sawmill then processes the logs into four grades of lumber: first and seconds, No. 1 common, No. 2 common, and No. 3 common. All costs incurred in the mill are common to the four grades of lumber. All four grades of lumber are used by the furniture plant. The mill transfers everything it produces to the furniture plant. The grades are transferred at cost to the furniture plant. Trucks are used to move the lumber from the mill to the furniture plant. Although no outside sales exist, the mill could sell to external customers, and the selling prices of the four grades are known.

The fabric plant is responsible for producing the fabric that is used by the furniture plant. To produce three totally different fabrics (identified by fabric ID codes: FB60, FB70, and FB80, respectively), the plant has three separate production operations—one for each fabric. Thus, production of all three fabrics is occurring at the same time in different locations in the plant. Each fabric's production operation has two processes: the weaving and pattern process and the coloring and bolting process. In the weaving and pattern process, yarn is used to create yards of fabric with different designs. In the next process, the fabric is dyed, cut in 25-yard sections, and 25-yard bolts are created (the fabric is wrapped around cardboard rods). The bolts are transported by forklift to the furniture plant's receiving department. All of the output of the fabric plant is used by the furniture plant (to produce the sofas and chairs). For accounting purposes, the fabric is transferred at cost to the furniture plant.

The furniture plant produces orders for customers on a special-order basis. The customers specify the quantity, style, fabric, lumber grade, and pattern. Typically, jobs are large (involving at least 500 units). The plant has two production departments: Cutting and Assembly. In the Cutting Department, the fabric and wooden frame components are sized and cut. Other components are purchased from external suppliers and are removed from stores as needed for assembly. After the fabric and wooden components are finished for the entire job, they are moved to the Assembly Department. The Assembly Department takes the individual components and assembles the sofas (or chairs).

Metcalf Furniture has been in business for over two decades and has a good reputation. However, during the past five years, Metcalf experienced eroding profits and declining sales. Bids were being lost (even aggressive bids) on the more popular models. Yet the company was winning bids on some of the more-difficult-to-produce items. Sean Williams, the owner and manager, was frustrated. He simply couldn't understand how some of his competitors could sell for such low prices. On a common sofa job involving 500 units, Metcalf's bids were running $25 per unit or $12,500 per job more than the winning bids (on average). Yet on the more difficult items, Metcalf's bids were running about $60 per unit less than the next closest bid. Debbie Lochner, vice president of finance, had been assigned the task of doing a cost analysis of the company's product lines. Sean wanted to know if their costs were excessive. Perhaps they were being wasteful, and it was simply costing more to produce than their competitors.

Debbie prepared herself by reading recent literature on cost management and product costing and attending several conferences that explored the same issues. She then reviewed the costing procedures of the company's mill and two plants and did a preliminary assessment of their soundness. The production costs of the mill were common to all lumber grades and were assigned using the physical units method. Since the output and production costs were fairly uniform throughout the year, the mill used an actual cost system. Although Debbie had no difficulty with actual costing, she decided to explore the effects of using the sales-value-at-split-off method. Thus, cost and production data for the mill were gathered so that an analysis could be conducted. The two plants used normal cost systems. The fabric plant used process costing, and the furniture plant used job order costing. Both plants used plantwide overhead rates based on direct labor hours. Based on her initial reviews, she concluded that the costing procedures for the fabric plant were satisfactory. Essentially, there was no evidence of product diversity. A statistical analysis revealed that about 90% of the variability in the plant's overhead cost could be explained by direct labor hours. Thus, the use of a plantwide overhead rate based on direct labor hours seemed justified. Nonetheless, as part of her report to Sean, she decided to include a description of the fabric plant's costing procedures—at least for one of the fabric types. The furniture plant, however, was a more difficult matter. Product diversity was present and could be causing some distortions in product costs. Furthermore, statistical analysis revealed that only about 40% of the variability in overhead cost was explained by the direct labor hours. She decided that additional analysis was needed so that a sound product-costing method could be recommended.

With the cooperation of the cost accounting manager for the mill and each plant's controller, she gathered the following data for 1998:

Sawmill:

Joint manufacturing costs: $600,000

Grades	Quantity Produced (board ft.)	Price at Split-off (per 1,000 board ft.)
First and second	1,000,000	$300
No. 1 common	2,000,000	225
No. 2 common	1,250,000	140
No. 3 common	750,000	100
Total	5,000,000	

Fabric Plant:

Budgeted overhead: $1,200,000
Practical volume (direct labor hours): 120,000 hours
Actual overhead: $1,240,000
Actual hours worked:

	Weaving and Pattern	Coloring and Bolting	Total
Fabric FB60	20,000	16,000	36,000
Fabric FB70	28,000	14,000	42,000
Fabric FB80	26,000	18,000	44,000
	74,000	48,000	122,000

Departmental data on Fabric FB70:

	Weaving and Pattern	Coloring and Bolting
Beginning inventories:		
Units (in yards)	20,000	10,000
Costs:		
Transferred in	—	$100,000
Materials	$80,000	$8,000
Labor	$18,000	$6,600
Overhead	$22,000	$9,000
Current production:		
Units started	80,000	?
Units transferred out	80,000	80,000
Costs:		
Transferred in	$ —	$?
Materials	$320,000	$82,000
Labor	$208,000	$99,400
Overhead	$?	$?
Percentage completion:		
Beginning inventory	30	40
Ending inventory	40	50

Note: With the exception of the cardboard bolt rods, materials are added at the beginning of each process. The cost of the rods is relatively insignificant and is included in overhead.

Furniture Plant:

Activity relational table:

Activity	Activity Name	Process	Level	Activity Driver	Capacity	Cost
1	Receiving	Procurement	Product	Receiving orders	22,500	$450,000
2	Power	Process sustaining	Unit	Machine hours	75,000	$600,000
3	Maintaining equipment	Process sustaining	Product	Machine hours	75,000	$300,000
4	Setting up equipment	Cutting	Batch	Number of setups	1,000	$600,000
5	Materials handling	Cutting	Batch	Number of moves	2,500	$150,000
	Materials handling	Assembly	Product	Number of components	300,000	$150,000
6	Expediting	Assembly	Batch	Number of expediting orders	300	$225,000
7	General factory	Process sustaining	Facility	Direct labor hours	250,000	$525,000

Departmental data (budgeted):

	Service Departments				Producing Departments	
	Receiving	Power	Maint.	General Factory	Cutting	Assembly
Overhead	$450,000	$600,000	$300,000	$525,000	$750,000	$375,000
Machine hours	—	—	—	—	60,000	15,000
Receiving orders	—	—	—	—	13,500	9,000
Square feet	1,000	5,000	4,000	—	15,000	10,000
Direct labor hours	—	—	—	—	50,000	200,000

After some discussion with the furniture plant controller, Debbie decided to use machine hours to calculate the overhead rate for the cutting department and direct labor hours for the assembly department rate (the cutting department was more automated than the assembly department). As part of her report, she wanted to compare the effects of plantwide rates, departmental rates, and activity pool rates on the cost of jobs. She wanted to know if overhead costing could be the source of the pricing problems the company was experiencing.

To assess the effect of the different overhead assignment procedures, Debbie decided to examine two prospective jobs. One job, Job A500, could produce 500 sofas, using a frequently requested style and fabric FB70. Bids on this type of job were being lost more frequently to competitors. The second job, Job B75, would produce 75 specially designed recliners. This job involved a new design and was more difficult for the workers to build. It involved some special cutting requirements and an unfamiliar assembly. Recently, the company seemed to be winning more bids on jobs of this type. To compute the costs of the two jobs, Debbie assembled the following information on the two jobs:

Job A500:
    Direct materials:

Fabric FB70	4,500	yards @ $14
Lumber (No. 1 common)	20,000	board feet @ $0.12
Other components	$26,600	

    Direct labor:

Cutting Department	400	hours @ $10
Assembly Department	1,600	hours @ $8.75

    Machine time:

Cutting Department	350	machine hours
Assembly Department	50	machine hours
Material moves	5	
Setups	2	
Expediting orders	0	
Number of components	10,000	
Receiving orders	10	

Job B75:
    Direct materials:

Fabric FB70	650	yards @ $14
Lumber (firsts and seconds)	2,200	board feet @ $0.12
Other components	$3,236	

    Direct labor:

Cutting Department	70	hours @ $10
Assembly Department	240	hours @ $8.75

(continued)

Machine time:

Cutting Department	90	machine hours
Assembly Department	15	machine hours
Material moves	8	
Setups	4	
Expediting orders	1*	
Number of components	800	
Receiving orders	8	

*Finishing a job of this type on time almost never was possible. Customer pressure usually led to expediting activity.

REQUIRED:

1. Allocate the joint milling costs to each grade, and calculate the cost per board foot (for each grade): (a) using the physical units method of allocation and (b) using the sales-value-at-split-off method. Which method should the mill use? Explain. What is the effect on the cost of each proposed job if the mill switches to the sales-value-at-split-off method?
2. Calculate the plantwide overhead rate for the fabric plant.
3. Calculate the amount of under- or overapplied overhead for the fabric plant.
4. Using the weighted average method, calculate the cost per bolt for fabric FB70.
5. Discuss the effect JIT manufacturing would have on the calculation in Requirement 4. Compute the cost per yard for fabric FB70 in a JIT environment assuming that the *current* production data presented in the problem still hold.
6. Explain why activity-based costing would not be needed for the mill or fabric plant.
7. Assume that the weaving and pattern process is not a separate process for each fabric. Also assume that the yarn used for each fabric differs significantly in cost. In this case, would process costing be appropriate for the weaving and pattern process? What costing approach would you recommend? Describe your approach in detail.
8. Calculate the following overhead rates for the furniture plant: (1) plantwide rate, (2) departmental rates, and (3) activity rates. Use the direct method for assigning service costs to producing departments.
9. For each of the overhead rates computed in Requirement 8, calculate unit bid prices for Jobs A500 and B75. Assume that the company's aggressive bidding policy is unit cost plus 50%. Comment on the effect the plantwide overhead cost assignment appears to have on Metcalf's winning or losing bids. What recommendation would you make? Explain.
10. Sam Parsons, Metcalf's production engineer, has made a recommendation to convert the furniture plant to JIT manufacturing (with cellular manufacturing cells). He wants to establish separate manufacturing cells for the repetitive business (business involving production and sales of the more popular lines). Additionally, one cell would be created for the nonrepetitive business. This last cell would involve reconfiguring equipment for each new job. By taking this approach, he is convinced that the cost of production can be reduced by reducing or eliminating nonvalue-added activities. For example, setup activity would not be required for the repetitive business cells, and materials-handling costs would virtually vanish. Furthermore, by decreasing the lead time, the expediting activity would be eliminated. He also indicated that a total quality emphasis would reduce material cost (by reducing waste) by 15%. Finally, JIT purchasing arrangements with suppliers will eliminate a need for the receiving activity.
    a. Recalculate the bid prices for Job A500 assuming that the changes recommended by Parsons are made and that the predicted effects are realized. Comment on the competitive benefits that may be realized.
    b. Discuss other effects that switching to a JIT, cellular manufacturing approach would have on Metcalf's management accounting procedures (for the furniture plant only).
    c. What are the changes in the structural and executional activities that would bring about the elimination or reduction in nonvalue-added operational activities?

Part 3
Decision Making: Traditional and Contemporary Approaches

Chapter 10
Cost-Volume-Profit Analysis

Southwest Airlines advertises its irreverent "fun to fly" image. However, Southwest employees work hard and are highly productive. For example, the company has a 10-year contract with pilots that includes productivity-related bonuses and stock options during the first five years. This makes much of Southwest's personnel costs fixed and gives it one of the lowest operating cost structures of the major air carriers. As a result, the breakeven point for Southwest is below that of its competitors.

LEARNING OBJECTIVES

After studying this chapter, you should be able to:

1. Determine the number of units that must be sold to break even or to earn a targeted profit.
2. Determine the amount of revenue required to break even or to earn a targeted profit.
3. Apply cost-volume-profit analysis in a multiple product setting.
4. Prepare a profit-volume graph and a cost-volume-profit graph, and explain the meaning of each.
5. Explain the impact of risk, uncertainty, and changing variables on cost-volume-profit analysis.
6. Discuss the impact of activity-based costing on cost-volume-profit analysis.

Cost-volume-profit analysis (CVP analysis) is a powerful tool for planning and decision making. Because CVP analysis emphasizes the interrelationships of costs, quantity sold, and price, it brings together all of the financial information of the firm. CVP analysis can be a valuable tool to identify the extent and magnitude of the economic trouble a company is facing and to help pinpoint the necessary solution. For example, in 1990 GM bought a large stake in Saab and went to work trying to save the company. Over the next four years, the work force was halved, and Saab's breakeven point was reduced from 130,000 cars to 80,000.[1] CVP analysis can address many other issues as well, such as: the number of units that must be sold to break even; the impact of a given reduction in fixed costs on the break-even point; and the impact of an increase in price on profit. Additionally, CVP analysis allows managers to do sensitivity analyses by examining the impact of various price or cost levels on profit.

While this chapter deals with the mechanics and terminology of CVP analysis, your objective in studying CVP analysis is more than to learn the mechanics. You should keep in mind that CVP analysis is an integral part of financial planning and decision making. Every accountant and manager should be thoroughly conversant with its concepts.

THE BREAK-EVEN POINT IN UNITS

Objective 1
Determine the number of units that must be sold to break even or to earn a targeted profit.

break-even point

Since we are interested in how revenues, expenses, and profits behave as volume changes, it is natural to begin by finding the firm's break-even point in units sold. Two frequently used approaches to finding the break-even point in units are the operating-income approach and the contribution-margin approach. We will first discuss these two approaches to find the **break-even point** (the point of zero profit), and then see how each can be expanded to determine the number of units that must be sold to earn a targeted profit.

The firm's initial decision in implementing a units-sold approach to CVP analysis is the determination of just what a unit is. For manufacturing firms, the answer is obvious. Procter and Gamble may define a unit as a bar of Ivory soap. Service firms face a more difficult choice. Southwest Airlines may define a unit as a passenger mile or as a one-way trip. The Jacksonville Naval Supply Center, which provides naval, industrial and general supplies to U.S. Navy ships stationed in northeastern Florida and the Caribbean, defined "productive units" to measure the activities involved in delivering services. In this way, more complicated services were assigned more productive units than were less complicated services, thereby standardizing service efforts.[2]

A second decision centers on the separation of costs into fixed and variable components. CVP analysis focuses on the factors that effect a *change* in the components of profit. Because we are looking at CVP analysis in terms of units sold, we need to determine the fixed and variable components of cost and revenue with respect to units. (This assumption will be relaxed when we incorporate activity-based costing into CVP analysis.) It is important to realize that we are focusing on the firm as a whole. Therefore, the costs we are talking about are *all* costs of the company: manufacturing, marketing, and administrative. Thus, when we say variable cost, we mean all costs that increase as more units are sold,

1.   James Bennet, "Eurocars: On the Road Again," *The New York Times,* August 20, 1995, pp. F1 and F10.
2.   David J. Harr, "How Activity Accounting Works in Government," *Management Accounting,* September 1990, pp. 36–40.

including: direct materials, direct labor, variable overhead, and variable selling and administrative costs. Similarly, fixed costs include fixed overhead and fixed selling and administrative expenses.

Operating-Income Approach

The operating-income approach focuses on the income statement as a useful tool in organizing the firm's costs into fixed and variable categories. The income statement can be expressed as a narrative equation:

Operating income = Sales revenues − Variable expenses − Fixed expenses

operating income

net income

Note that we are using the term **operating income** to denote income or profit *before* income taxes. Operating income includes only revenues and expenses from the firm's normal operations. We will use the term **net income** to mean operating income minus income taxes.

Once we have a measure of units sold, we can expand the operating-income equation by expressing sales revenue and variable expenses in terms of unit dollar amounts and number of units. Specifically, sales revenue is expressed as the unit selling price times the number of units sold, and total variable costs are the unit variable costs times the number of units sold. With these expressions, the operating-income statement becomes:

Operating income = (Price × Number of units) −
(Variable costs per unit × Number of units) − Total fixed cost

Suppose you were asked how many units must be sold in order to break even, or earn a zero profit. You could answer that question by setting operating income to zero and then solving the operating-income equation for the number of units.

Let's use the following example to solve for the break-even point in units. Assume that Whittier Company manufactures a mulching lawn mower. For the coming year, the controller has prepared the following projected income statement:

Sales (1,000 units @ $400)	$400,000
Less: Variable expenses	(325,000)
Contribution margin	$ 75,000
Less: Fixed expenses	(45,000)
Operating income	$ 30,000

We see that for Whittier Company, the price is $400 per unit and the variable cost is $325 ($325,000/1,000 units). Fixed cost is $45,000. At the break-even point, then, the operating-income equation would take the following form.

$$0 = (\$400 \times \text{Units}) − (\$325 \times \text{Units}) − \$45,000$$
$$0 = (\$75 \times \text{Units}) − \$45,000$$
$$\$75 \times \text{Units} = \$45,000$$
$$\text{Units} = 600$$

Therefore, Whittier must sell 600 lawn mowers to just cover all fixed and variable expenses. A good way to check this answer is to formulate an income statement based on 600 units sold.

Sales (600 units @ $400)	$240,000
Less: Variable expenses	(195,000)
Contribution margin	$ 45,000
Less: Fixed expenses	(45,000)
Operating income	$ 0

Indeed, selling 600 units does yield a zero profit.

An important advantage of the operating-income approach is that all further CVP equations are derived from the variable-costing income statement. As a result, you can solve any CVP problem by using this approach.

Contribution-Margin Approach

contribution margin

A refinement of the operating-income approach is the contribution-margin approach. In effect, we are simply recognizing that at break-even, the total contribution margin equals the fixed expense. The **contribution margin** is sales revenue minus total variable cost. If we substitute the unit contribution margin for price minus unit variable cost in the operating-income equation and solve for the number of units, we obtain the following break-even expression.

Number of units = Fixed costs/Unit contribution margin

Using Whittier Company as an example, we can see that the contribution margin per unit can be computed in one of two ways. One way is to divide the total contribution margin by the units sold for a result of $75 per unit ($75,000/1,000). A second way is to compute price minus variable cost per unit. Doing so yields the same result, $75 per unit ($400 − $325). Now we can use the contribution-margin approach to calculate the break-even number of units.

$$\text{Number of units} = \$45,000/(\$400 - \$325)$$
$$= \$45,000/\$75 \text{ per unit}$$
$$= 600 \text{ units}$$

Of course, the answer is identical to that computed using the operating-income approach.

Profit Targets

While the break-even point is useful information, most firms would like to earn operating income greater than zero. CVP analysis gives us a way to determine how many units must be sold to earn a particular targeted income. Targeted operating income can be expressed as a dollar amount (e.g., $20,000) or as a percentage of sales revenue (e.g., 15 percent of revenue). Both the operating-income approach and the contribution-margin approach can be easily adjusted to allow for targeted income.

Targeted Income as a Dollar Amount Assume that Whittier Company wants to earn operating income of $60,000. How many mulching mowers must be sold to achieve this result? Using the operating-income approach, we form the following equation:

$$\$\ 60,000 = (\$400 \times Units) - (\$325 \times Units) - \$45,000$$
$$\$105,000 = \$75 \times Units$$
$$Units = 1,400$$

Using the contribution-margin approach, we simply *add* targeted profit of $60,000 to the fixed cost and solve for the number of units.

$$Units = (\$45,000 + \$60,000)/(\$400 - \$325)$$
$$Units = \$105,000/\$75$$
$$Units = 1,400$$

Whittier must sell 1,400 lawn mowers to earn a before-tax profit of $60,000. The following income statement verifies this outcome:

Sales (1,400 units @ $400)	$560,000
Less: Variable expenses	(455,000)
Contribution margin	$105,000
Less: Fixed expenses	(45,000)
Profit before taxes	$ 60,000

Another way to check this number of units is to use the break-even point. As was just shown, Whittier must sell 1,400 lawn mowers, or 800 more than the break-even volume of 600 units, to earn a profit of $60,000. The contribution margin per lawn mower is $75. Multiplying $75 by the 800 lawn mowers *above* break-even produces the profit of $60,000 ($75 × 800). This outcome demonstrates that contribution margin per unit for each unit above break-even is equivalent to profit per unit. Since the break-even point had already been computed, the number of lawn mowers to be sold to yield a $60,000 operating income could have been calculated by dividing the unit contribution margin into the target profit and adding the resulting amount to the break-even volume.

In general, assuming that fixed costs remain the same, the impact on a firm's profits resulting from a change in the number of units sold can be assessed by multiplying the unit contribution margin by the change in units sold. For example, if 1,500 lawn mowers instead of 1,400 are sold, how much *more* profit will be earned? The change in units sold is an increase of 100 lawn mowers, and the unit contribution margin is $75. Thus, profits will increase by $7,500 ($75 × 100).

Targeted Income as a Percent of Sales Revenue Assume that Whittier Company wants to know the number of lawn mowers that must be sold in order to earn a profit equal to 15 percent of sales revenue. Sales revenue is price multiplied by the quantity sold. Thus, the targeted operating income is 15 percent of price times quantity. Using the operating-income approach (which is simpler in this case), we have the following:

$$.15(\$400)(Units) = (\$400 \times Units) - (\$325 \times Units) - \$45,000$$
$$\$60 \times Units = (\$400 \times Units) - (\$325 \times Units) - \$45,000$$
$$\$60 \times Units = (\$75 \times Units) - \$45,000$$
$$\$15 \times Units = \$45,000$$
$$Units = 3,000$$

Does a volume of 3,000 lawn mowers achieve a profit equal to 15 percent of sales revenue? For 3,000 lawn mowers, the total revenue is $1.2 million ($400 × 3,000). The profit can be computed without preparing a formal income statement. Remember that above break-even, the contribution margin per unit is the profit per unit. The break-even volume is 600 lawn mowers. If 3,000 lawn mowers are sold, then 2,400 (3,000 − 600) lawn mowers above the break-even point are sold. The before-tax profit, therefore, is $180,000 ($75 × 2,400), which is 15 percent of sales ($180,000/$1,200,000).

After-Tax Profit Targets

When calculating the break-even point, income taxes play no role. This is because the taxes paid on zero income are zero. However, when the company needs to know how many units to sell to earn a particular net income, some additional consideration is needed. Recall that net income is operating income after income taxes and that our targeted income figure was expressed in before-tax terms. As a result, when the income target is expressed as net income, we must add back the income taxes to get operating income. Therefore, to use either approach, the after-tax profit target must first be converted to a before-tax profit target.

In general, taxes are computed as a percentage of income. The after-tax profit is computed by subtracting the tax from the operating income (or before-tax profit).

$$\text{Net income} = \text{Operating income} - \text{Taxes}$$
$$= \text{Operating income} - (\text{Tax rate} \times \text{Operating income})$$
$$= \text{Operating income}(1 - \text{Tax rate})$$

or

$$\text{Operating income} = \text{Net income}/(1 - \text{Tax rate})$$

Thus, to convert the after-tax profit to before-tax profit, simply divide the after-tax profit by (1 − Tax rate).

Suppose that Whittier Company wants to achieve net income of $48,750 and its tax rate is 35 percent. To convert the after-tax profit target into a before-tax profit target, complete the following steps:

$$\$48{,}750 = \text{Operating income} - 0.35(\text{Operating income})$$
$$\$48{,}750 = 0.65(\text{Operating income})$$
$$\$75{,}000 = \text{Operating income}$$

In other words, with a tax rate of 35 percent, Whittier Company must earn $75,000 before taxes to have $48,750 after taxes.[3] With this conversion, we can now calculate the number of units that must be sold.

$$\text{Units} = (\$45{,}000 + \$75{,}000)/\$75$$
$$\text{Units} = \$120{,}000/\$75$$
$$\text{Units} = 1{,}600$$

Let's check this answer by preparing an income statement based on sales of 1,600 lawn mowers.

---

3.   To practice the after-tax to before-tax conversion, calculate how much before-tax income Whittier would need to have $48,750 after-tax income if the tax rate were 40 percent. [Answer: $81,250]

Sales (1,600 units @ $400)	$640,000
Less: Variable expenses	(520,000)
Contribution margin	$120,000
Less: Fixed costs	(45,000)
Profit before taxes	$ 75,000
Less: Taxes (35% tax rate)	(26,250)
Profit after taxes	$ 48,750

BREAK-EVEN POINT IN SALES DOLLARS

Objective 2
Determine the amount of revenue required to break even or to earn a targeted profit.

In some cases when using CVP analysis, managers may prefer to use sales revenue as the measure of sales activity instead of units sold. A units-sold measure can be converted to a sales-revenue measure simply by multiplying the unit sales price by the units sold. For example, the break-even point for Whittier Company was computed to be 600 mulching mowers. Since the selling price for each lawn mower is $400, the break-even volume in sales revenue is $240,000 ($400 × 600). Any answer expressed in units sold can be easily converted to one expressed in sales revenue, but the answer can be computed more directly by developing a separate formula for the sales-revenue case. In this case, the important variable is sales dollars, so both the revenue and the variable costs must be expressed in dollars instead of units. Since sales revenue is always expressed in dollars, measuring that variable is no problem. Let's look more closely at variable costs and see how they can be expressed in terms of sales dollars.

To calculate the break-even point in sales dollars, variable costs are defined as a percentage of sales rather than as an amount per unit sold. Exhibit 10-1 illustrates the division of sales revenue into variable cost and contribution margin. In

Exhibit 10-1
Revenue Equal to Variable Cost Plus Contribution Margin

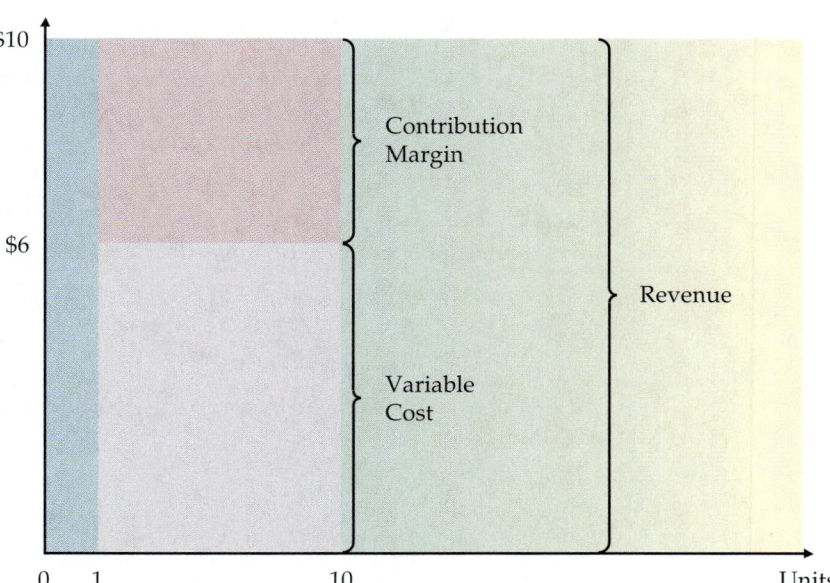

this exhibit, price is $10 and variable cost is $6. Of course, the remainder is contribution margin of $4 ($10 − $6). Focusing on ten units sold, total variable costs are $60 ($6 × 10 units sold). Alternatively, since each unit sold earns $10 of revenue, we would say that for every $10 of revenue earned, $6 of variable costs are incurred, or, equivalently, that 60 percent of each dollar of revenue earned is attributable to variable cost ($6/$10). Thus, focusing on sales revenue, we would expect total variable costs of $60 for revenues of $100 (0.60 × $100).

variable cost ratio

    In expressing variable cost in terms of sales dollars, we computed the **variable cost ratio**. It is simply the proportion of each sales dollar that must be used to cover variable costs. The variable cost ratio can be computed by using either total data or unit data. Of course, the percentage of sales dollars remaining after variable costs are covered is the contribution margin ratio. The **contribution margin ratio** is the proportion of each sales dollar available to cover fixed costs and provide for profit. In Exhibit 10-1, if the variable cost ratio is 60 percent of sales, then contribution margin must be the remaining 40 percent of sales. It makes sense that the complement of the variable cost ratio is the contribution margin ratio. After all, the proportion of the sales dollars left after variable costs are covered should be the contribution margin component.

contribution margin ratio

    Just as the variable cost ratio can be computed using total or unit figures, the contribution margin ratio (40 percent in our exhibit) can also be computed in these two ways. That is, one can divide the total contribution margin by total sales ($40/$100), or one can use unit contribution margin divided by price ($4/$10). Naturally, if the variable cost ratio is known, it can be subtracted from 1 to yield the contribution margin ratio (1 − 0.60 = 0.40).

    Where do fixed costs fit into this? Since the contribution margin is revenue remaining after variable costs are covered, it must be the revenue available to cover fixed costs and contribute to profit. Exhibit 10-2 uses the same price and variable cost data from Exhibit 10-1 to show the impact of fixed cost on profit. Panel A of Exhibit 10-2 shows the amount of fixed cost equal to contribution margin. Of course, profit is zero (the company is at break-even). Panel B of Exhibit 10-2 shows fixed cost less than contribution margin. In this case, the company earns a profit. Finally, Panel C of Exhibit 10-2 shows fixed cost greater than contribution margin. Here, the company faces an operating loss.

sales-revenue approach

    Now let's turn to a couple of examples based on Whittier Company to illustrate the **sales-revenue approach**. Restated below is Whittier Company's variable-costing income statement for 1,000 lawn mowers.

	Dollars	Percent of Sales
Sales	$400,000	100.00
Less: Variable costs	325,000	81.25
Contribution margin	$ 75,000	18.75
Less: Fixed costs	45,000	
Operating income	$ 30,000	

    Notice that sales revenue, variable costs, and contribution margin have been expressed in the form of percent of sales. The variable cost ratio is 0.8125 ($325,000/$400,000); the contribution margin ratio is 0.1875 (computed either as 1 − 0.8125 or $75,000/$400,000). Fixed costs are $45,000. Given the information

Exhibit 10-2
Impact of Fixed Cost on Profit

Panel A: Fixed Cost = Contribution Margin; Profit = 0

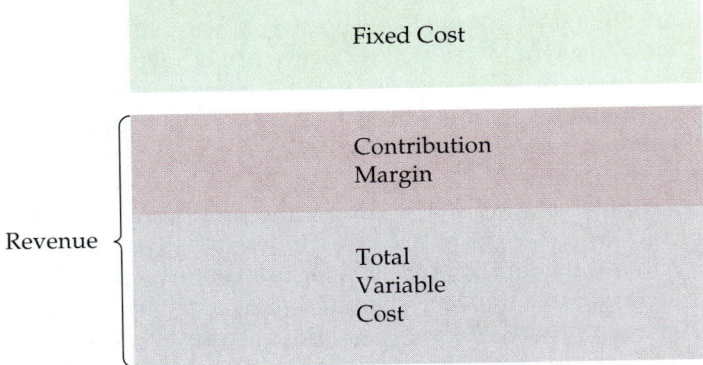

Panel B: Fixed Cost < Contribution Margin; Profit > 0

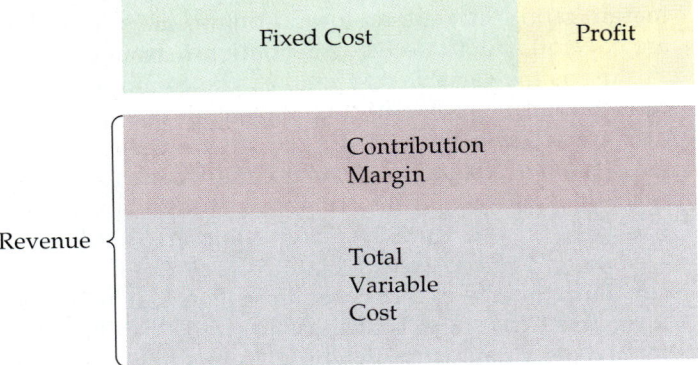

Panel C: Fixed Cost > Contribution Margin; Profit < 0

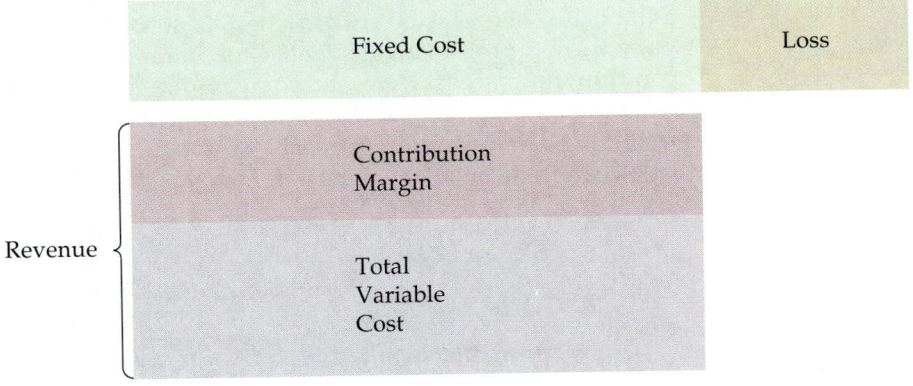

in this income statement, how much sales revenue must Whittier earn to break even?

$$
\begin{aligned}
\text{Operating income} &= \text{Sales} - \text{Variable costs} - \text{Fixed costs} \\
0 &= \text{Sales} - (\text{Variable cost ratio} \times \text{Sales}) - \text{Fixed costs} \\
0 &= \text{Sales}(1 - \text{Variable cost ratio}) - \text{Fixed costs} \\
0 &= \text{Sales}(1 - .8125) - \$45{,}000 \\
\text{Sales}(.1875) &= \$45{,}000 \\
\text{Sales} &= \$240{,}000
\end{aligned}
$$

Thus, Whittier must earn revenues totaling $240,000 in order to break even. (You might want to check this answer by preparing an income statement based on revenue of $240,000 and verifying that it yields zero profit.) Note that $1 - .8125$ is the contribution margin ratio. We can skip a couple of steps by recognizing that *Sales − (Variable cost ratio × Sales)* is equal to *Sales × Contribution margin ratio*.

What about the contribution-margin approach used in determining the break-even point in units? We can use that approach here as well. Recall that the formula for the break-even point in units is

$$
\text{Break-even units} = \text{Fixed cost}/(\text{Price} - \text{Unit variable cost})
$$

If we multiply both sides of the above equation by price, the left-hand side will equal sales revenue at break-even.

$$
\begin{aligned}
\text{Break-even units} \times \text{Price} &= \text{Price} \, [\text{Fixed cost}/(\text{Price} - \text{Unit variable cost})] \\
\text{Break-even sales} &= \text{Fixed cost} \times [\text{Price}/(\text{Price} - \text{Unit variable cost})] \\
\text{Break-even sales} &= \text{Fixed cost} \times (\text{Price}/\text{Contribution margin}) \\
\text{Break-even sales} &= \text{Fixed cost} \times \text{Contribution margin ratio}
\end{aligned}
$$

Again using Whittier Company data, the break-even sales dollars would be computed as $45,000/.1875, or $240,000. Same answer, just a slightly different approach.

Profit Targets

Consider the following question: How much sales revenue must Whittier generate to earn a before-tax profit of $60,000? (This question is similar to the one we asked earlier in terms of units, but phrases the question directly in terms of sales revenue.) To answer the question, using the contribution-margin approach, add targeted operating income of $60,000 to $45,000 fixed cost and divide by the contribution margin ratio.

$$
\begin{aligned}
\text{Sales} &= (\$45{,}000 + \$60{,}000)/0.1875 \\
&= \$105{,}000/0.1875 \\
&= \$560{,}000
\end{aligned}
$$

Whittier must earn revenues equal to $560,000 to achieve a profit target of $60,000. Since break-even is $240,000, additional sales of $320,000 ($560,000 − $240,000) must be earned above break-even. Notice that multiplying the contribution margin ratio by revenues above break-even yields the profit of $60,000 (0.1875 × $320,000). Above break-even, the contribution margin ratio is a profit ratio; therefore, it represents the proportion of each sales dollar assignable to profit. For this example, every sales dollar earned above break-even increases profits by $0.1875.

In general, assuming that fixed costs remain unchanged, the contribution margin ratio can be used to find the profit impact of a change in sales revenue. To obtain the total change in profits from a change in revenue, simply multiply the contribution margin ratio by the change in sales. For example, if sales revenue is $540,000 instead of $560,000, how will the expected profits be affected? A decrease in sales revenue of $20,000 will cause a decrease in profits of $3,750 (0.1875 × $20,000).

Comparison of the Two Approaches

For a single-product setting, converting the break-even point in units answer to a sales-revenue answer is simply a matter of multiplying the unit sales price by the units sold. Then why bother with a separate formula for the sales revenue approach? For a single-product setting, neither approach has any real advantage over the other. Both offer much the same level of conceptual and computational difficulty.

However, in a multiple-product setting, CVP analysis is more complex, and the sales-revenue approach is significantly easier. This approach maintains essentially the same computational requirements found in the single-product setting, whereas the units-sold approach becomes more difficult. Even though the conceptual complexity of CVP analysis does increase with multiple products, the operation is reasonably straightforward.

MULTIPLE-PRODUCT ANALYSIS

Objective 3
Apply cost-volume-profit analysis in a multiple product setting.

Whittier Company has decided to offer two models of lawn mowers: a mulching mower to sell for $400 and a riding mower to sell for $800. The Marketing Department is convinced that 1,200 mulching mowers and 800 riding mowers can be sold during the coming year. The controller has prepared the following projected income statement based on the sales forecast:

	Mulching Mower	Riding Mower	Total
Sales	$480,000	$640,000	$1,120,000
Less: Variable expenses	(390,000)	(480,000)	(870,000)
Contribution margin	$ 90,000	$160,000	$ 250,000
Less: Direct fixed expenses	(30,000)	(40,000)	(70,000)
Product margin	$ 60,000	$120,000	$ 180,000
Less: Common fixed expenses			(26,250)
Profit before taxes			$ 153,750

direct fixed expenses
common fixed expenses

Note that the controller has separated direct fixed expenses from common fixed expenses. The **direct fixed expenses** are those fixed costs which can be traced to each segment and would be avoided if the segment did not exist. The **common fixed expenses** are the fixed costs that are not traceable to the segments and that would remain even if one of the segments were eliminated.

Break-even Point in Units

The owner of Whittier is somewhat apprehensive about adding a new product line and wants to know how many of each model must be sold to break even.

If you were given the responsibility to answer this question, how would you respond?

One possible response is to use the equation we developed earlier in which fixed costs were divided by the contribution margin. This equation presents some immediate problems, however. It was developed for a single-product analysis. For two products, there are *two* unit contribution margins. The mulching mower has a contribution margin per unit of $75 ($400 − $325), and the riding mower has one of $200 ($800 − $600).[4]

One possible solution is to apply the analysis separately to each product line. It is possible to obtain individual break-even points when income is defined as product margin. Break-even for the mulching mower is as follows:

$$\text{Mulching mower break-even units} = \text{Fixed cost}/(\text{Price} - \text{Unit variable cost})$$
$$= (\$30,000)/\$75$$
$$= 400 \text{ units}$$

Break-even for the riding mower can be computed as well.

$$\text{Riding mower break-even units} = \text{Fixed cost}/(\text{Price} - \text{Unit variable cost})$$
$$= (\$40,000)/\$200$$
$$= 200 \text{ units}$$

Thus, 400 mulching mowers and 200 riding mowers must be sold to achieve a break-even product margin. But a break-even product margin covers only direct fixed costs; the common fixed costs remain to be covered. Selling these numbers of lawn mowers would result in a loss equal to the common fixed costs. No break-even point for the firm as a whole has yet been identified. Somehow the common fixed costs must be factored into the analysis.

Allocating the common fixed costs to each product line before computing a break-even point may resolve this difficulty. The problem with this approach is that allocation of the common fixed costs is arbitrary. Thus, no meaningful break-even volume is readily apparent.

Another possible solution is to convert the multiple-product problem into a single-product problem. If this can be done, then all of the single-product CVP methodology can be applied directly. The key to this conversion is to identify the expected sales mix, in units, of the products being marketed.

sales mix

Sales Mix **Sales mix** is the relative combination of products being sold by a firm. Sales mix can be measured in units sold or in proportion of revenue. For example, if Whittier plans on selling 1,200 mulching mowers and 800 riding mowers, then the sales mix in units is 1,200:800. Usually the sales mix is reduced to the smallest possible whole numbers. Thus, the relative mix 1,200:800 can be reduced to 12:8 and further to 3:2. That is, for every three mulching mowers sold, two riding mowers are sold.

Alternatively, the sales mix can be represented by the percent of total revenue contributed by each product. In that case, the mulching mower revenue is $480,000 ($400 × 1,200) and the riding mower revenue is $640,000 ($800 × 800). The mulching mower accounts for 42.86 percent of total revenue, and the riding mower accounts for the remaining 57.14 percent. It may seem as though the two sales mixes are different. The sales mix in units is 3:2; that is, of every five mow-

4. The variable cost per unit is derived from the income statement. For the riding mower, total variable costs are $480,000 based on sales of 800 units. This yields a per-unit variable cost of $600 ($480,000/800). A similar computation produces the per-unit variable cost for the mulching mower.

ers sold, 60 percent are mulching mowers and 40 percent are riding mowers. However, the revenue-based sales mix is 42.86 percent for the mulching mowers. There is really no difference. The sales mix in revenue takes the sales mix in units and weights it by price. Therefore, even though the underlying proportion of mowers sold remains 3:2, the lower priced mulching mowers are weighted less heavily when price is factored in. In the remaining discussion, we will use the sales mix expressed in units.

A number of different sales mixes can be used to define the break-even volume. For example, a sales mix of 2:1 will define a break-even point of 550 mulching mowers and 275 riding mowers. The total contribution margin produced by this mix is $96,250 [($75 × 550) + ($200 × 275)]. Similarly, if 350 mulching mowers and 350 riding mowers are sold (corresponding to a 1:1 sales mix), the total contribution margin is also $96,250 [($75 × 350) + ($200 × 350)]. Since total fixed costs are $96,250, both sales mixes define break-even points. Fortunately, every sales mix need not be considered. Can Whittier really expect a sales mix of 2:1 or 1:1? For every two mulching mowers sold, does Whittier expect to sell a riding mower? Or for every mulching mower, can Whittier really sell one riding mower?

According to Whittier's marketing study, a sales mix of 3:2 can be expected. That is the ratio that should be used; others can be ignored. The sales mix that is expected to prevail should be used for CVP analysis.

Sales Mix and CVP Analysis Defining a particular sales mix allows us to convert a multiple-product problem to a single-product CVP format. Since Whittier expects to sell three mulching mowers for every two riding mowers, it can define the single product it sells as a *package* containing three mulching mowers and two riding mowers. By defining the product as a package, the multiple-product problem is converted into a single-product one. To use the break-even-point-in-units approach, the package selling price and variable cost per package must be known. To compute these package values, the sales mix, the individual product prices, and the individual variable costs are needed. Given the individual product data found on the projected income statement, the package values can be computed as follows:

Product	Price	Unit Variable Cost	Unit Contribution Margin	Sales Mix	Package Unit Contribution Margin
Mulching	$400	$325	$ 75	3	$225[a]
Riding	800	600	200	2	400[b]
Package total					$625

[a] Found by multiplying the number of units in the package (3) by the unit contribution margin ($75)
[b] Found by multiplying the number of units in the package (2) by the unit contribution margin ($200)

Given the package contribution margin, the single-product CVP equation can be used to determine the number of packages that need to be sold to break even. From Whittier's projected income statement, we know that the total fixed costs for the company are $96,250. Thus, the break-even point is

Break-even packages = Fixed cost/Package contribution margin
= $96,250/$625
= 154 packages

Whittier must sell 462 mulching mowers (3 × 154) and 308 riding mowers (2 × 154) to break even. An income statement verifying this solution is presented in Exhibit 10-3.

For a given sales mix, CVP analysis can be used as if the firm were selling a single product. However, actions that change the prices of individual products can affect the sales mix because consumers may buy relatively more or less of the product. Accordingly, pricing decisions may involve a new sales mix and must reflect this possibility. Keep in mind that a new sales mix will affect the units of each product that need to be sold in order to achieve a desired profit target. If the sales mix for the coming period is uncertain, it may be necessary to look at several different mixes. In this way, a manager can gain some insight into the possible outcomes facing the firm.

The complexity of the break-even-point-in-units approach increases dramatically as the number of products increases. Imagine performing this analysis for a firm with several hundred products. This observation seems more overwhelming than it actually is. Computers can easily handle a problem with so much data. Furthermore, many firms simplify the problem by analyzing product groups rather than individual products. Another way to handle the increased complexity is to switch from the units-sold to the sales-revenue approach. This approach can accomplish a multiple-product CVP analysis using only the summary data found in an organization's income statement. The computational requirements are much simpler.

Sales Dollars Approach

To illustrate the break-even point in sales dollars, the same examples will be used. However, the only information needed is the projected income statement for Whittier Company as a whole.

Sales	$1,120,000
Less: Variable costs	(870,000)
Contribution margin	$ 250,000
Less: Fixed costs	(96,250)
Profit before taxes	$ 153,750

Exhibit 10-3
Income Statement: Break-even Solution

	Mulching Mower	Riding Mower	Total
Sales	$184,800	$246,400	$431,200
Less: Variable costs	(150,150)	(184,800)	(334,950)
Contribution margin	$ 34,650	$ 61,600	$ 96,250
Less: Direct fixed costs	(30,000)	(40,000)	(70,000)
Segment margin	$ 4,650	$ 21,600	$ 26,250
Less: Common fixed costs			(26,250)
Profit before taxes			$ 0

Notice that this income statement corresponds to the total column of the more detailed income statement examined previously. The projected income statement rests on the assumption that 1,200 mulching mowers and 800 riding mowers will be sold (a 3:2 sales mix). The break-even point in sales revenue also rests on the expected sales mix. (As with the units-sold approach, a different sales mix will produce different results.)

With the income statement, the usual CVP questions can be addressed. For example, how much sales revenue must be earned to break even? To answer this question, we divide the total fixed cost of $96,250 by the contribution margin ratio of 0.2232 ($250,000/$1,120,000).[5]

$$\text{Break-even sales} = \text{Fixed cost/Contribution margin ratio}$$
$$= \$96,250/0.2232$$
$$= \$431,228$$

The break-even point in sales dollars implicitly uses the assumed sales mix but avoids the requirement of building a package contribution margin. No knowledge of individual product data is needed. The computational effort is similar to that used in the single-product setting. Moreover, the answer is still expressed in sales revenue. Unlike the break-even point in units, the answer to CVP questions using sales dollars is still expressed in a single summary measure. The sales-revenue approach, however, does sacrifice information concerning individual product performance.

GRAPHICAL REPRESENTATION OF CVP RELATIONSHIPS

Objective 4
Prepare a profit-volume graph and a cost-volume-profit graph, and explain the meaning of each.

It may further our understanding of CVP relationships by seeing them portrayed visually. A graphical representation can help managers see the difference between variable cost and revenue. It may also help them understand quickly what impact an increase or decrease in sales will have on the break-even point. Two basic graphs, the profit-volume graph and the cost-volume-profit graph, are presented here.

The Profit-Volume Graph

profit-volume graph

A **profit-volume graph** visually portrays the relationship between profits and sales volume. The profit-volume graph is the graph of the operating income equation [Operating income = (Price × Units) − (Unit variable cost × Units) − Fixed cost]. In this graph, operating income is the dependent variable and units is the independent variable. Usually, values of the independent variable are measured along the horizontal axis and values of the dependent variable along the vertical.

To make this discussion more concrete, a simple set of data will be used. Assume that Tyson Company produces a single product with the following cost and price data:

Total fixed costs	$100
Variable costs per unit	5
Selling price per unit	10

5.   Because of rounding error in the contribution margin ratio, the sales volume is slightly overstated. The correct answer is $431,200 (obtained by multiplying the package selling price by the packages needed to break even: $2,800 × 154).

Using these data, operating income can be expressed as

$$\text{Operating income} = \$10 \times \text{units} - \$5 \times \text{units} - \$100$$
$$= \$5 \times \text{units} - \$100$$

We can graph this relationship by plotting units along the horizontal axis and operating income (or loss) along the vertical axis. Two points are needed to graph a linear equation. While any two points will do, the two points often chosen are those that correspond to zero sales volume and zero profits. When units sold are zero, Tyson experiences an operating loss of $100 (or a profit of −$100). The point corresponding to zero sales volume, therefore, is (0, −$100). In other words, when no sales take place, the company suffers a loss equal to its total fixed costs. When operating income is zero, the units sold are equal to 20. The point corresponding to zero profits (break-even) is (20, $0). These two points, plotted in Exhibit 10-4, define the profit graph shown in the same figure.

The graph in Exhibit 10-4 can be used to assess Tyson's profit (or loss) at any level of sales activity. For example, the profit associated with the sale of forty units can be read from the graph by (1) drawing a vertical line from the horizontal axis to the profit line and (2) drawing a horizontal line from the profit line to the vertical axis. As illustrated in Exhibit 10-4, the profit associated with sales of forty units is $100. The profit-volume graph, while easy to interpret, fails to

Exhibit 10-4
Profit-Volume Graph

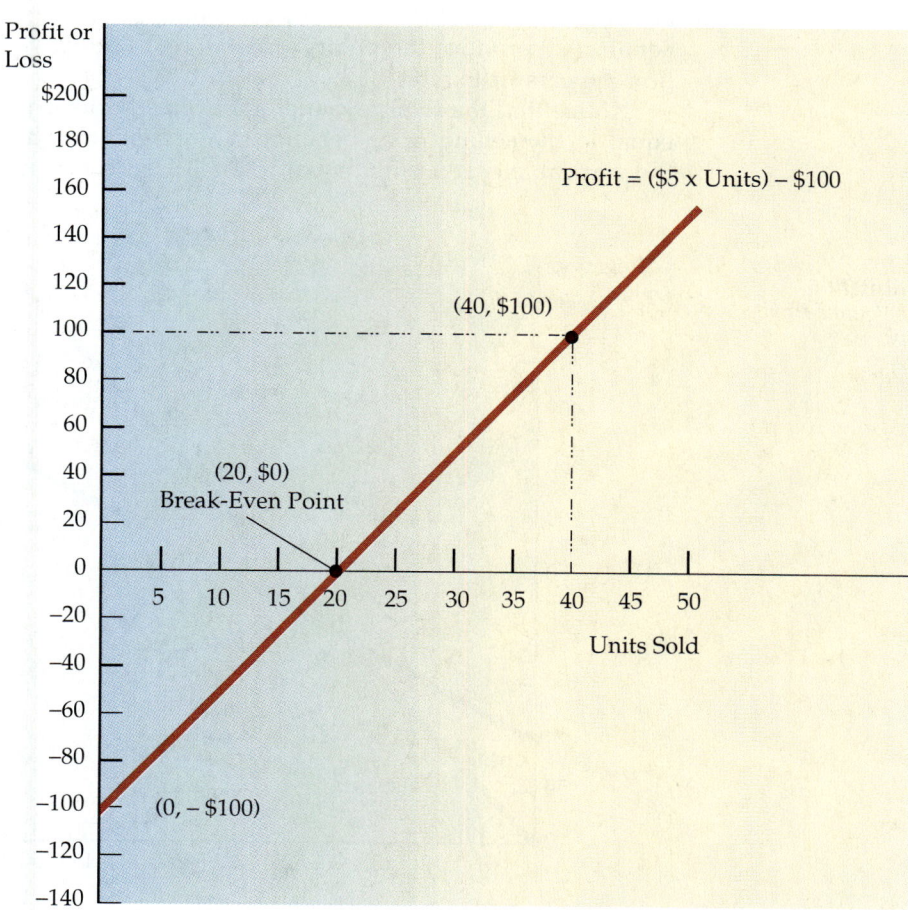

reveal how costs change as sales volume changes. An alternative approach to graphing can provide this detail.

The Cost-Volume-Profit Graph

cost-volume-profit
graph

The **cost-volume-profit graph** depicts the relationships among cost, volume, and profits. To obtain the more detailed relationships, it is necessary to graph two separate lines: the total revenue line and the total cost line. These two lines are represented, respectively, by the following two equations:

$$\text{Revenue} = \text{Price} \times \text{Units}$$
$$\text{Total cost} = (\text{Unit variable cost} \times \text{Units}) + \text{Fixed Cost}$$

Using the Tyson Company example, the revenue and cost equations are

$$\text{Revenue} = \$10 \times \text{Units}$$
$$\text{Total cost} = (\$5 \times \text{Units}) + \$100$$

To portray both equations in the same graph, the vertical axis is measured in dollars and the horizontal axis in units sold.

Two points are needed to graph each equation. We will use the same X-coordinates used for the profit-volume graph. For the revenue equation, setting number of units equal to 0 results in revenue of $0; setting number of units equal to 20 results in revenue of $200. Therefore, the two points for the revenue equation are (0, $0) and (20, $200). For the cost equation, units sold of zero and units sold equal to 20 produce the points (0, $100) and (20, $200). The graph of each equation appears in Exhibit 10-5.

Notice that the total revenue line begins at the origin and rises with a slope equal to the selling price per unit (a slope of 10). The total cost line intercepts the vertical axis at a point equal to total fixed costs and rises with a slope equal

Exhibit 10-5
*Cost-Volume-Profit
Graph*

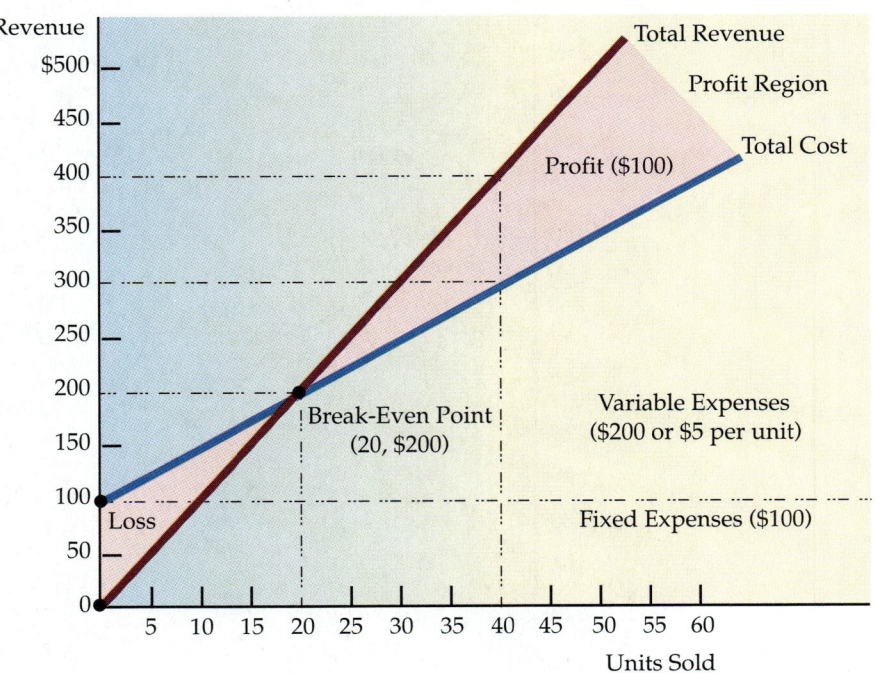

to the variable cost per unit (a slope of 5). When the total revenue line lies below the total cost line, a loss region is defined. Similarly, when the total revenue line lies above the total cost line, a profit region is defined. The point where the total revenue line and the total cost line intersect is the break-even point. To break even, Tyson Company must sell 20 units and thus receive $200 total revenues.

Now let's compare the information available from the CVP graph to that available from the profit-volume graph. To do so, consider the sale of forty units. Recall that the profit-volume graph revealed that selling forty units produced profits of $100. Examine Exhibit 10-5 again. The CVP graph also shows profits of $100, but it reveals more as well. The CVP graph discloses that total revenues of $400 and total costs of $300 are associated with the sale of forty units. Furthermore, the total costs can be broken down into fixed costs of $100 and variable costs of $200. The CVP graph provides revenue and cost information not provided by the profit-volume graph. Unlike the profit-volume graph, some computation is needed to determine the profit associated with a given sales volume. Nonetheless, because of the greater information content, managers are likely to find the CVP graph a more useful tool.

Assumptions of Cost-Volume-Profit Analysis

The profit-volume and cost-volume-profit graphs just illustrated rely on some important assumptions. Some of these assumptions are as follows.

1. The analysis assumes a linear revenue function and a linear cost function.
2. The analysis assumes that price, total fixed costs, and unit variable costs can be accurately identified and remain constant over the relevant range.
3. The analysis assumes that what is produced is sold.
4. For multiple-product analysis, the sales mix is assumed to be known.
5. The selling prices and costs are assumed to be known with certainty.

The first assumption, linear cost and revenue functions, deserves additional consideration. Let's take a look at the underlying revenue and total cost functions identified in economics. Exhibit 10-6, Panel A, portrays the curvilinear revenue and cost functions. We see that as quantity sold increases, revenue also increases, but eventually begins to rise less steeply than before. This is explained quite simply by the need to decrease price as many more units are sold. The total cost function is more complicated, rising steeply at first, then leveling off somewhat (as increasing returns to scale develop), and then rising steeply again (as decreasing returns to scale develop). How can we deal with these complicated relationships?

Relevant Range Fortunately, we do not need to consider all possible ranges of production and sales for a firm. Remember that CVP analysis is a short-run decision-making tool. (We know that it is short-run in orientation because some costs are fixed.) It is only necessary for us to determine the current operating range, or **relevant range**, for which the linear cost and revenue relationships are valid. Exhibit 10-6, Panel B, illustrates a relevant range from 5,000 to 15,000 units. Note that the cost and revenue relationships are roughly linear in this range, allowing us to use our linear CVP equations. Of course, if the relevant range changes, different fixed and variable costs and different prices must be used.

The second assumption is linked to the definition of relevant range. Once a relevant range has been identified, then the cost and price relationships are assumed to be known and constant.

relevant range

Exhibit 10-6
Cost and Revenue
Relationship

Panel A: Curvilinear CVP Relationships

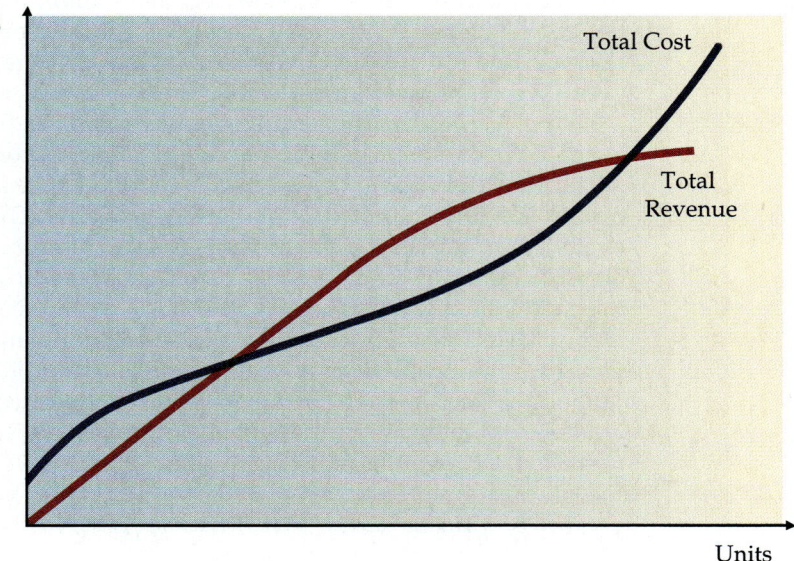

Panel B: Relevant Range and Linear CVP Relationships

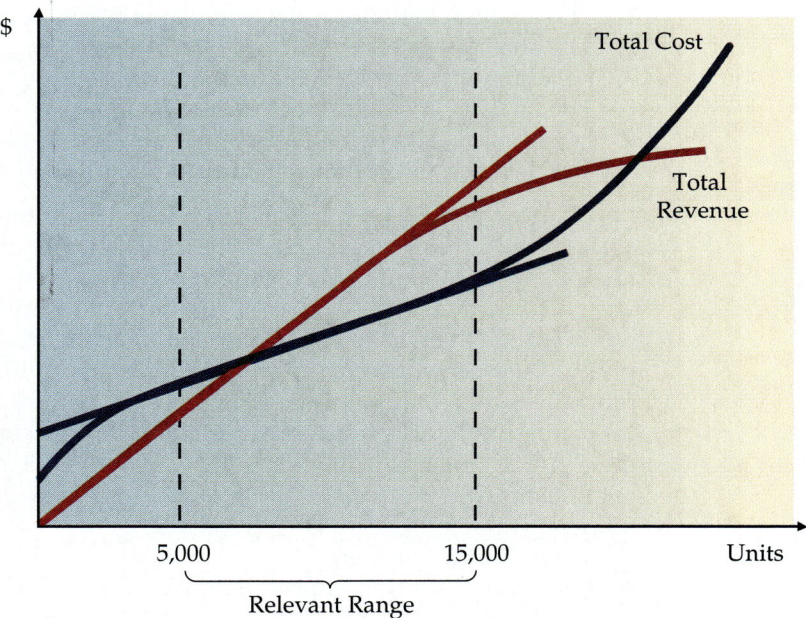

Production Equal to Sales The third assumption is that what is produced is sold. There is no change in inventory over the period. That inventory has no impact on break-even analysis makes sense. Break-even analysis is a short-run decision-making technique, so we are looking to cover all costs of a particular period of time. Inventory embodies costs of a previous period and is not considered.

Constant Sales Mix In single-product analysis, the sales mix is obviously constant—100 percent of sales is the one product. Multiple-product break-even analysis requires a constant sales mix. However, it is virtually impossible to predict with certainty the sales mix. Typically, this constraint is handled in practice through sensitivity analysis. By using the capabilities of spreadsheet analysis, the sensitivity of variables to a variety of sales mixes can be readily assessed.

Prices and Costs Known with Certainty In actuality, firms seldom know with certainty prices, variable costs, and fixed costs. A change in one variable usually affects the value of others. Often there is a probability distribution to contend with. Furthermore, there are formal ways of explicitly building uncertainty into the CVP model. Exploration of these issues is introduced in the next section.

CHANGES IN THE CVP VARIABLES

Objective 5

Explain the impact of risk, uncertainty, and changing variables on cost-volume-profit analysis.

Because firms operate in a dynamic world, they must be aware of changes in prices, variable costs, and fixed costs. They must also account for the effects of risk and uncertainty. We will take a look at the effects on the break-even point of changes in price, unit variable cost, and fixed cost. We will also look at ways managers can handle risk and uncertainty within the CVP framework.

Suppose that Whittier Company recently conducted a market study that revealed three different alternatives.

Alternative 1: If advertising expenditures increase by $8,000, sales will increase from 1,600 units to 1,725 units.

Alternative 2: A price decrease from $400 per lawn mower to $375 per lawn mower would increase sales from 1,600 units to 1,900 units.

Alternative 3: Decreasing prices to $375 and increasing advertising expenditures by $8,000 will increase sales from 1,600 units to 2,600 units.

Should Whittier maintain its current price and advertising policies, or should it select one of the three alternatives described by the marketing study?

Consider the first alternative. What is the effect on profits if advertising costs increase by $8,000 and sales increase by 125 units? This question can be answered without using the equations but by employing the contribution margin per unit. We know that the unit contribution margin is $75. Since units sold increase by 125, the incremental increase in total contribution margin is $9,375 ($75 × 125 units). However, since fixed costs increase by $8,000, the incremental increase in profits is only $1,375 ($9,375 − $8,000). Exhibit 10-7 summarizes the effects of the first alternative. Notice that we need to look only at the incremental increase in total contribution margin and fixed expenses to compute the increase in total profits.

For the second alternative, fixed expenses do not increase. Thus, it is possible to answer the question by looking only at the effect on total contribution margin. For the current price of $400, the contribution margin per unit is $75. If 1,600 units are sold, the total contribution margin is $120,000 ($75 × 1,600). If the price is dropped to $375, then the contribution margin drops to $50 per unit ($375 − $325). If 1,900 units are sold at the new price, then the new total contribution margin is $95,000 ($50 × 1,900). Dropping the price results in a profit decline of $25,000 ($120,000 − $95,000). The effects of the second alternative are summarized in Exhibit 10-8.

The third alternative calls for a decrease in the unit selling price and an increase in advertising costs. Like the first alternative, the profit impact can be assessed by looking at the incremental effects on contribution margin and fixed

Exhibit 10-7
Summary of the Effects of the First Alternative

	Before the Increased Advertising	With the Increased Advertising
Units sold	1,600	1,725
Unit contribution margin	× $75	× $75
Total contribution margin	$120,000	$129,375
Less: Fixed costs	(45,000)	(53,000)
Profit	$ 75,000	$ 76,375

	Difference in Profit
Change in sales volume	125
Unit contribution margin	× $75
Change in contribution margin	$9,375
Less: Increase in fixed expenses	(8,000)
Increase in profits	$1,375

expenses. The incremental profit change can be found by (1) computing the incremental change in total contribution margin, (2) computing the incremental change in fixed expenses, and (3) adding the two results.

As shown, the current total contribution margin (for 1,600 units sold) is $120,000. Since the new unit contribution margin is $50, the new total contribution margin is $130,000 ($50 × 2,600 units). Thus, the incremental increase in total contribution margin is $10,000 ($130,000 − $120,000). However, to achieve this incremental increase in contribution margin, an incremental increase of $8,000 in fixed costs is needed. The net effect is an incremental increase in profits of $2,000. The effects of the third alternative are summarized in Exhibit 10-9.

Of the three alternatives identified by the marketing study, the one that promises the most benefit is the third. It increases total profits by $2,000. The first alternative increases profits by only $1,375, and the second actually decreases profits by $25,000.

Exhibit 10-8
Summary of the Effects of the Second Alternative

	Before the Proposed Price Change	With the Proposed Price Decrease
Units sold	1,600	1,900
Unit contribution margin	× $75	× $50
Total contribution margin	$120,000	$95,000
Less: Fixed expenses	(45,000)	(45,000)
Profit	$ 75,000	$50,000

	Difference in Profit
Change in contribution margin ($95,000 − $120,000)	$(25,000)
Less: Change in fixed expenses	—
Decrease in profit	$(25,000)

Exhibit 10-9
*Summary of the Effects
of the Third Alternative*

	Before the Proposed Price and Advertising Change	With the Proposed Price Decrease and Advertising Increase
Units sold	1,600	2,600
Unit contribution margin	✕ $75	✕ $50
Total contribution margin	$120,000	$130,000
Less: Fixed expenses	(45,000)	(53,000)
Profit	$ 75,000	$ 77,000
		Difference in Profit
Change in contribution margin ($130,000 − $120,000)		$10,000
Less: Change in fixed expenses ($53,000 − $45,000)		(8,000)
Increase in profit		$ 2,000

These examples are all based on a units-sold approach. However, we could just as easily have applied a sales-revenue approach. The answers would be the same.

Introducing Risk and Uncertainty

An important assumption of CVP analysis is that prices and costs are known with certainty. This is seldom the case. Risk and uncertainty are a part of business decision making and must be dealt with somehow. Formally, risk differs from uncertainty in that under risk, the probability distributions of the variables are known. Under uncertainty, the probability distributions are not known. For our purposes, however, the terms will be used interchangeably.

How do managers deal with risk and uncertainty? There are a variety of methods. First, of course, is that management must realize the uncertain nature of future prices, costs, and quantities. Next, managers move from consideration of a break-even point to what might be called a break-even band. In other words, given the uncertain nature of the data, perhaps a firm might break even when 1,800 to 2,000 units are sold—instead of the point estimate of 1,900 units. Further, managers may engage in sensitivity or what-if analyses. In this, a computer spreadsheet is helpful, as managers set up the break-even (or targeted profit) relationships and then check to see the impact that varying costs and prices have on quantity sold. Two concepts useful to management are *margin of safety* and *operating leverage*. Both of these may be considered measures of risk. Each requires knowledge of fixed and variable costs.

margin of safety

Margin of Safety The **margin of safety** is the units sold or expected to be sold or the revenue earned or expected to be earned above the break-even volume. For example, if the break-even volume for a company is 200 units and the company is currently selling 500 units, the margin of safety is 300 units (500 − 200). The margin of safety can be expressed in sales revenue as well. If the break-even volume is $200,000 and current revenues are $350,000, then the margin of safety is $150,000.

The margin of safety can be viewed as a crude measure of risk. There are always events, unknown when plans are made, that can lower sales below the original expected level. If a firm's margin of safety is large given the expected sales for the coming year, the risk of suffering losses should sales take a downward turn is less than if the margin of safety were small. Managers who face a low margin of safety may wish to consider actions to increase sales or decrease costs. Southwest Airlines, for example, has lower personnel costs than the other large commercial airlines (e.g., American, United, and Delta). As a result, variable costs are lower and the margin of safety in passenger miles is higher. This cushions Southwest in the event of economic downturns or increases in other costs such as fuel.

Operating Leverage In physics, a lever is a simple machine used to multiply force. Basically, the lever multiplies the effort applied to create more work. The larger the load moved by a given amount of effort, the greater the mechanical advantage. In financial terms, operating leverage is concerned with the relative mix of fixed costs and variable costs in an organization. It is sometimes possible to trade off fixed costs for variable costs. As variable costs decrease, the unit contribution margin increases, making the contribution of each unit sold that much greater. In such a case, the effect of fluctuations in sales on profitability increases. Thus, firms that have lowered variable costs by increasing the proportion of fixed costs will benefit with greater increases in profits as sales increase than will firms with a lower proportion of fixed costs. Fixed costs are being used as leverage to increase profits. Unfortunately, it is also true that firms with a higher operating leverage will also experience greater reductions in profits as sales decrease. Therefore, **operating leverage** is the use of fixed costs to extract higher percentage changes in profits as sales activity changes.

operating leverage

The greater the degree of operating leverage, the more that changes in sales activity will affect profits. Because of this phenomenon, the mix of costs that an organization chooses can have a considerable influence on its operating risk and profit level.

degree of operating leverage

The **degree of operating leverage** can be measured for a given level of sales by taking the ratio of contribution margin to profit, as follows:

$$\text{Degree of operating leverage} = \text{Contribution margin}/\text{Profit}$$

If fixed costs are used to lower variable costs such that contribution margin increases and profit decreases, then the degree of operating leverage increases—signaling an increase in risk.

To illustrate the utility of these concepts, consider a firm that is planning to add a new product line. In adding the line, the firm can choose to rely heavily on automation or on labor. If the firm chooses to emphasize automation rather than labor, fixed costs will be higher and unit variable costs will be lower. Relevant data for a sales level of 10,000 units follow:

	Automated System	Manual System
Sales	$1,000,000	$1,000,000
Less: Variable expenses	(500,000)	(800,000)
Contribution margin	$ 500,000	$ 200,000
Less: Fixed costs	(375,000)	(100,000)
Profit before taxes	$ 125,000	$ 100,000
Unit selling price	$100	$100
Unit variable cost	50	80
Unit contribution margin	50	20

The degree of operating leverage for the automated system is 4.0 ($500,000/ $125,000). The degree of operating leverage for the manual system is 2.0 ($200,000/$100,000). What happens to profit in each system if sales increase by 40 percent? We can generate the following income statements to see.

	Automated System	Manual System
Sales	$1,400,000	$1,400,000
Less: Variable costs	(700,000)	(1,120,000)
Contribution margin	$ 700,000	$ 280,000
Less: Fixed costs	(375,000)	(100,000)
Profit before taxes	$ 325,000	$ 180,000

Profits for the automated system would increase by $200,000 ($325,000 − $125,000) for a 160 percent increase. In the manual system, profits increase by only $80,000 ($180,000 − $100,000), for an 80 percent increase. The automated system has a greater percentage increase because it has a higher degree of operating leverage.

In choosing between the two systems, the effect of operating leverage is a valuable piece of information. As the 40 percent increase in sales illustrates, this effect can bring a significant benefit to the firm. However, the effect is a two-edged sword. As sales decrease, the automated system will also show much higher percentage profit decreases. Moreover, the increased operating leverage is available under the automated system because of the presence of increased fixed costs. The break-even point for the automated system is 7,500 units ($375,000/ $50), whereas the break-even point for the manual system is 5,000 units ($100,000/$20). Thus, the automated system has greater operating risk. The increased risk, of course, provides a potentially higher profit level (as long as units sold exceed 9,167).[6]

In choosing between the automated and the manual systems, the manager must assess the likelihood that sales will exceed 9,167 units. If, after careful study, there is a strong belief that sales will easily exceed this level, the choice is obvious: the automated system. On the other hand, if sales are unlikely to exceed 9,167 units, the manual system is preferable. Exhibit 10-10 summarizes the relative difference between the manual and automated systems in terms of some of the CVP concepts.

Sensitivity Analysis and CVP

sensitivity analysis

The pervasiveness of personal computers and spreadsheets has made cost analysis within reach of most managers. An important tool is **sensitivity analysis**, a "what if" technique that examines the impact of changes in underlying assumptions on an answer. It is relatively simple to input data on prices, variable costs, fixed costs, and sales mix and set up formulas to calculate break-even points and expected profits. Then the data can be varied as desired to see what impact changes have on the expected profit.

6. This benchmark is computed by equating the profit equations of the two systems and solving for X:
$$50X − 375,000 = 20X − 100,000$$
$$X = 9,167$$

Exhibit 10-10
Differences Between Manual and Automated Systems

	Manual System	Automated System
Price	Same	Same
Variable cost	Relatively higher	Relatively lower
Fixed cost	Relatively lower	Relatively higher
Contribution margin	Relatively lower	Relatively higher
Break-even point	Relatively lower	Relatively higher
Margin of safety	Relatively higher	Relatively lower
Degree of operating leverage	Relatively lower	Relatively higher
Down-side risk	Relatively lower	Relatively higher
Up-side potential	Relatively lower	Relatively higher

In the example given above for operating leverage, a company analyzed the impact on profit of using an automated versus a manual system. The computations were essentially done by hand, and too much variation was cumbersome. Using the power of a computer, it would be an easy matter to change the sales price in $1 increments between $75 and $125, with related assumptions about quantity sold. At the same time, variable and fixed costs could be adjusted. For example, suppose that the automated system has fixed costs of $375,000, but that those costs could easily range up to twice as much in the first year, and come back down in the second and third year as bugs are worked out of the system and workers learn to use it. Again, the spreadsheet can effortlessly handle the many computations.

Finally, we must note that the spreadsheet, while wonderful for cranking out numerical answers, cannot do the most difficult job in CVP analysis. That job is the determination of the data to be entered in the first place. The accountant must be cognizant of the cost and price distributions of the firm, as well as of the impact of changing economic conditions on these variables. The fact that variables are seldom known with certainty is no excuse for ignoring the impact of uncertainty on CVP analysis. Fortunately, sensitivity analysis can also give managers a feel for the degree to which a poorly forecast variable will affect an answer. That is also an advantage.

CVP ANALYSIS AND ACTIVITY-BASED COSTING

Objective 6
Discuss the impact of activity-based costing on cost-volume-profit analysis.

Conventional CVP analysis assumes that all costs of the firm can be divided into two categories: those that vary with sales volume (variable costs) and those that do not (fixed costs). Furthermore, costs are assumed to be a linear function of sales volume.

In an activity-based costing system, costs are divided into unit- and nonunit-based categories. Activity-based costing admits that some costs vary with units produced and some costs do not. However, while activity-based costing acknowledges that nonunit-based costs are fixed with respect to production volume changes, it also argues that many nonunit-based costs vary with respect to other cost drivers.

The use of activity-based costing does not mean that CVP analysis is less useful. In fact, it becomes more useful, since it provides more accurate insights concerning cost behavior. These insights produce better decisions. CVP analysis within an activity-based framework, however, must be modified. To illustrate, assume that a company's costs can be explained by three variables: a unit-level cost driver, units sold; a batch-level cost driver, number of setups; and a product-level cost driver, engineering hours. The ABC cost equation can then be expressed as follows:

Total cost = Fixed cost + (Unit variable cost × Number of units) + (Setup cost × Number of setups) + (Engineering cost × Number of engineering hours)

Operating income, as before, is total revenue minus total cost. This is expressed as:

Operating income = Total revenue − [Fixed cost + (Unit variable cost × Number of units) + (Setup cost × Number of setups) + (Engineering cost × Number of engineering hours)]

Let's use the contribution margin approach to calculate the break-even point in units. At break-even, operating income is zero, and the number of units that must be sold to achieve break-even is as follows.

Break-even units = [Fixed Cost + (Setup cost × Number of setups) + (Engineering cost × Number of engineering hours)]/(Price − Unit variable cost)

A comparison of the ABC break-even point with the conventional break-even point reveals two significant differences. First, the fixed costs differ. Some costs previously identified as being fixed may actually vary with nonunit cost drivers, in this case setups and engineering hours. Second, the numerator of the ABC break-even equation has two nonunit-variable cost terms: one for batch-related activities and one for product-sustaining activities.

Example Comparing Conventional and ABC Analysis

To make the above discussion more concrete, a comparison of conventional cost-volume-profit analysis with activity-based costing is useful. Let's assume that a company wants to compute the units that must be sold to earn a before-tax income of $20,000. The analysis is based on the following data:

Data about variables:

Cost Driver	Unit Variable Cost	Level of Cost Driver
Units sold	$ 10	—
Setups	1,000	20
Engineering hours	30	1,000

Other data:

Total fixed costs (conventional)	$100,000
Total fixed costs (ABC)	50,000
Unit selling price	20

The units that must be sold to earn a before-tax profit of $20,000 are computed as follows:

Units = (Targeted income + Fixed cost)/(Price − Unit variable cost)
     = ($20,000 + $100,000)/($20 − $10)
     = $120,000/$10
     = 12,000 units

Using the ABC equation, the units that must be sold to earn an operating income of $20,000 are computed as follows:

$$\text{Units} = (\$20{,}000 + \$50{,}000 + \$20{,}000 + \$30{,}000)/(\$20 - \$10)$$
$$= 12{,}000 \text{ units}$$

The number of units that must be sold is identical under both approaches. The reason is simple. The total fixed cost pool under conventional costing consists of nonunit-based variable costs plus costs that are fixed regardless of the cost driver. ABC breaks out the nonunit-based variable costs. These costs are associated with certain levels of each cost driver. For the batch-level cost driver, the level is twenty setups and for the product-level variable, the level is 1,000 engineering hours. As long as the levels of activity for the nonunit-based cost drivers remain the same, then the results for the conventional and ABC computations will be the same. But these levels can change, and because of this, the information provided by the two approaches can be significantly different. The ABC equation for CVP analysis is a richer representation of the underlying cost behavior and can provide important strategic insights. To see this, let's use the same data provided above and look at a different application.

Strategic Implications: Conventional CVP Analysis Versus ABC Analysis

Suppose that after the conventional CVP analysis, marketing indicates that selling 12,000 units is not possible. In fact, only 10,000 units can be sold. The president of the company then directs the product design engineers to find a way to reduce the cost of making the product. The engineers also have been told that the conventional cost equation, with fixed costs of $100,000 and unit variable cost of $10, holds. The variable cost of $10 per unit consists of the following: direct labor, $4; direct materials, $5; and variable overhead, $1. To comply with the request to reduce the break-even point, engineering produces a new design that requires less labor. The new design reduces the direct labor cost by $2 per unit. The design would not affect materials or variable overhead. Thus, the new variable cost is $8 per unit, and the break-even point is

$$\text{Units} = \text{Fixed cost}/(\text{Price} - \text{Unit variable cost})$$
$$= \$100{,}000/(\$20 - \$8)$$
$$= 8{,}333 \text{ units}$$

And the projected income if 10,000 units are sold is

Sales ($20 × 10,000)	$200,000
Less: Variable expenses ($8 × 10,000)	(80,000)
Contribution margin	$120,000
Less: Fixed expenses	(100,000)
Income	$ 20,000

Excited, the president approves the new design. A year later, the president discovers that the expected increase in income did not materialize. In fact, a loss is realized. Why? The answer is provided by an ABC approach to CVP analysis.

The original ABC cost relationship for the example is given below:

$$\text{Total cost} = \$50,000 + (\$10 \times \text{Units}) + (\$1,000 \times \text{Setups}) + (\$30 \times \text{Engineering hours})$$

Suppose that the new design requires a more complex setup, increasing the cost per setup from \$1,000 to \$1,600. Also suppose that the new design, because of increased technical content, requires a 40 percent increase in engineering support (from 1,000 hours to 1,400 hours). The new cost equation, including the reduction in unit-level variable costs, is given below:

$$\text{Total cost} = \$50,000 + (\$8 \times \text{Units}) + (\$1,600 \times \text{Setups}) + (\$30 \times \text{Engineering hours})$$

The break-even point, setting operating income equal to zero, and using the ABC equation, is calculated as follows (assume that twenty setups are still performed):

$$\begin{aligned}\text{Units} &= [\$50,000 + (\$1,600 \times 20) + (\$30 \times 1,400)]/(\$20 - \$8) \\ &= \$124,000/\$12 \\ &= 10,333 \text{ units}\end{aligned}$$

And the income for 10,000 units is (recall that a maximum of 10,000 can be sold)

Sales (\$20 × 10,000)		\$200,000
Less: Unit-based variable expenses (\$8 × 10,000)		(80,000)
Contribution margin		\$120,000
Less: Nonunit-based variable expenses:		
Setups (\$1,600 × 20)	\$32,000	
Engineering support (\$30 × 1,400)	42,000	(74,000)
Traceable margin		\$ 46,000
Less: Fixed expenses		(50,000)
Income (Loss)		\$ (4,000)

How could the engineers have been off by so much? Didn't they know that the new design would increase setup cost and engineering support? Yes and no. They were probably aware of the increases in these two variables, but the conventional cost equation diverted attention from figuring just how much impact changes in those variables would have. The information conveyed by the conventional equation to the engineers gave the impression that any reduction in labor cost—not affecting materials or variable overhead—would reduce total costs, since changes in the level of labor activity would not affect the fixed costs. The ABC equation, however, indicates that a reduction in labor input that adversely affects setup activity or engineering support might be undesirable. By providing more insight, better design decisions can be made. Providing ABC cost information to the design engineers would probably have led them down a different path—a path that would have been more advantageous to the company.

CVP Analysis and JIT

If a firm has adopted JIT, the variable cost per unit sold is reduced and fixed costs are increased. Direct labor, for example, is now viewed as fixed instead of variable. Direct materials, on the other hand, is still a unit-based variable cost.

In fact, the emphasis on total quality and long-term purchasing makes the assumption that direct materials cost is strictly proportional to units produced even more true (because waste, scrap, and quantity discounts are eliminated). Other unit-based variable costs such as power and sales commissions also persist. Additionally, the batch-level variable is gone (in JIT, the batch is one unit). Thus, the cost equation for JIT can be expressed as follows:

$$\text{Total cost} = \text{Fixed cost} + (\text{Unit variable cost} \times \text{Units}) + (\text{Engineering cost} \times \text{Number of engineering hours})$$

Since its application is a special case of the ABC equation, no example will be given.

SUMMARY

Cost-volume-profit analysis focuses on prices, revenues, volume, costs, profits, and sales mix. It can be used to determine the sales volume or revenue necessary to break even or achieve a targeted profit. Changes in the fixed and variable cost patterns affect the profitability of a firm. The firm can use CVP analysis to see just how a particular change in price or cost would affect the break-even point.

In a single-product setting, the break-even point can be computed in units or sales dollars. Two approaches were detailed: the operating-income approach and the contribution-margin approach.

Multiple-product analysis requires that an assumption be made concerning the expected sales mix. Given a particular sales mix, a multiple-product problem can be converted into a single-product analysis. However, it should be remembered that the answers change as the sales mix changes. If the sales mix changes in a multiple-product firm, the break-even point will also change. In general, increases in the sales of high contribution margin products will decrease the break-even point, while increases in the sales of low contribution margin products will increase the break-even point.

CVP is based on several assumptions that must be considered in applying it to business problems. The analysis assumes linear revenue and cost functions, no finished goods ending inventories, and a constant sales mix. CVP analysis also assumes that selling prices and fixed and variable costs are known with certainty. These assumptions form the basis for simple graphical analysis using the profit-volume graph and the cost-volume-profit graph.

Measures of risk and uncertainty, such as the margin of safety and operating leverage, can be used to give managers more insight into CVP answers. Sensitivity analysis gives still more insight into the effect of changes in underlying variables on CVP relationships.

CVP can be used with activity-based costing, but the analysis must be modified. In effect, under ABC, a type of sensitivity analysis is used. Fixed costs are separated from a variety of costs that vary with particular activity drivers. At this stage, it is easiest to organize variable costs as: unit-level, batch-level, and product-level. Then, the impact of decisions on batches and products can be examined within the CVP framework.

The subject of cost-volume-profit analysis naturally lends itself to the use of numerous equations. Some of the more common equations used in this chapter are summarized in Exhibit 10-11.

Exhibit 10-11
Summary of Important Equations

1. Operating income = (Price × Units) − (Unit variable cost × Units) − Fixed cost

2. Break-even point in units = Fixed cost/(Price − Unit variable cost)

3. Sales revenue = Price × Units

4. Break-even point in sales dollars = Fixed cost/Contribution margin ratio
   or   = Fixed cost/(1 − Variable cost ratio)

5. Variable cost ratio = Total variable cost/Sales
   or   = Unit variable cost/Price

6. Contribution margin ratio = Contribution margin/Sales
   or   = (Price − Unit variable cost)/Price

7. Margin of safety = Sales − Break-even sales

8. Degree of operating leverage = Total contribution margin/Profit

9. Percentage change in profits = Degree of operating leverage × Percentage change in sales

10. After-tax income = Operating income − (Tax rate × Operating income)

11. Income taxes = Tax rate × Operating income

12. Before-tax income = After-tax income/(1 − Tax rate)

13. ABC total cost = Fixed cost + (Unit variable cost × Number of units) + (Batch-level cost × Batch driver) + (Product-level cost × Product driver)

14. ABC break-even units = [Fixed Cost + (Batch-level cost × Batch driver) + (Product-level cost × Product driver)]/(Price − Unit variable cost)

REVIEW PROBLEMS AND SOLUTIONS

I.

Cutlass Company's projected profit for the coming year is as follows:

	Total	Per Unit
Sales	$200,000	$20
Less: Variable costs	(120,000)	(12)
Contribution margin	$ 80,000	$ 8
Less: Fixed expenses	(64,000)	
Net income	$ 16,000	

REQUIRED:

1. Compute the break-even point in units.
2. How many units must be sold to earn a profit of $30,000?
3. Compute the contribution margin ratio. Using that ratio, compute the additional profit that Cutlass would earn if sales were $25,000 more than expected.
4. Suppose Cutlass would like to earn operating income equal to 20 percent of sales revenue. How many units must be sold for this goal to be realized? Prepare an income statement to prove your answer.
5. For the projected level of sales, compute the margin of safety.

Solution

1. The break-even point is

$$\text{Units} = \text{Fixed cost}/(\text{Price} - \text{Unit variable cost})$$
$$= \$64,000/(\$20 - \$12)$$
$$= \$64,000/\$8$$
$$= 8,000$$

2. The number of units that must be sold to earn a profit of $30,000 is

$$\text{Units} = (\$64,000 + \$30,000)/\$8$$
$$= \$94,000/\$8$$
$$= 11,750$$

3. The contribution margin ratio is $8/$20 = 0.40. With additional sales of $25,000, the additional profit would be 0.40 × $25,000, or $10,000.
4. To find the number of units sold for a profit equal to 20 percent of sales, let target income equal (0.20)(Price × Units) and solve for units.

$$\text{Operating income} = (\text{Price} \times \text{Units}) - (\text{Unit variable cost} \times \text{Units}) - \text{Fixed cost}$$
$$(.2)(\$20)\text{Units} = (\$20 \times \text{Units}) - (\$12 \times \text{Units}) - \$64,000$$
$$\$4 \times \text{Units} = \$64,000$$
$$\text{Units} = 16,000$$

The income statement is as follows:

Sales (16,000 × $20)	$320,000
Less: Variable expenses (16,000 × $12)	(192,000)
Contribution margin	$128,000
Less: Fixed expenses	(64,000)
Operating income	$ 64,000

Operating income/Sales = $64,000/$320,000 = 0.20, or 20 percent.
5. The margin of safety is 10,000 − 8,000 = 2,000 units, or $40,000 in sales revenue.

II.

Dory Manufacturing Company produces T-shirts that are screen-printed with the logos of various sports teams. Each shirt is priced at $10. Costs are as follows:

Cost Driver	Unit Variable Cost	Level of Cost Driver
Units sold	$ 5	—
Setups	450	80
Engineering hours	20	500

Other data:

Total fixed costs (conventional)	$96,000
Total fixed costs (ABC)	50,000

REQUIRED:

1. Compute the break-even point in units using conventional analysis.
2. Compute the break-even point in units using activity-based analysis.
3. Suppose that Dory could reduce the setup cost by $150 per setup and could reduce the number of engineering hours needed to 425. How many units must be sold to break even in this case?

Solution

1. Break-even units = Fixed cost/(Price − Unit variable cost)
   = $96,000/($10 − $5)
   = 19,200 units

2. Break-even units = [Fixed cost − (Setups × Setup cost) − (Engineering hours × Engineering cost)]/ (Price − Unit variable cost)
   = [$50,000 + ($450 × 80) + ($20 × 500)]/($10 − $5)
   = 19,200 units

3. Break-even units = [$50,000 + ($300 × 80) + ($20 × 425)]/($10 − $5)
   = $82,500/$5
   = 16,500 units

KEY TERMS

Break-even point *411*
Common fixed expenses *420*
Contribution margin *413*
Contribution margin ratio *417*

Cost-volume-profit graph *426*
Degree of operating leverage *432*
Direct fixed expenses *420*
Margin of safety *431*

Net income *412*
Operating income *412*
Operating leverage *432*
Profit-volume graph *424*
Relevant range *427*
Sales mix *421*

Sales-revenue approach *417*
Sensitivity analysis *433*
Variable cost ratio *417*

QUESTIONS FOR WRITING AND DISCUSSION

1. Explain how CVP analysis can be used for managerial planning.
2. Describe the difference between the units-sold approach to CVP analysis and the sales-revenue approach.
3. Define the term *break-even point*.
4. Explain why contribution margin per unit becomes profit per unit above the break-even point.
5. If the contribution margin per unit is $7 and the break-even point is 10,000 units, how much profit will a firm make if 15,000 units are sold?
6. What is the variable cost ratio? The contribution margin ratio? How are the two ratios related?
7. Suppose a firm has fixed costs of $20,000 and a contribution margin ratio equal to 0.4. How much sales revenue must the firm have in order to break even?
8. Suppose a firm with a contribution margin ratio of 0.3 increased its advertising expenses by $10,000 and found that sales increased by $30,000. Was it a good decision to increase advertising expenses?
9. Define the term *sales mix*, and give an example to support your definition.
10. Explain how CVP analysis developed for single products can be used in a multiple-product setting.
11. Assume that a firm has two products—Product A and Product B. Last year 2,000 units of A and 1,000 units of B were sold. The same sales mix is expected for the coming year. Total fixed expenses are $30,000, and the unit contribution margins are $10 for A and $5 for B. How many units of A and how many units of B must be sold to break even?
12. Wilson Company has a contribution margin ratio of 0.6. The break-even point is $100,000. During the year, Wilson earned total revenues of $200,000. What was Wilson's profit?
13. Explain how a change in sales mix can change a company's break-even point.
14. Define the term *margin of safety*. Explain how it can be used as a crude measure of operating risk.
15. Explain what is meant by the term *operating leverage*. What impact does increased leverage have on risk?
16. Why does the activity-based costing approach to CVP analysis offer more insight than the conventional approach does?
17. How does JIT affect the firm's cost equation? Affect CVP analysis?
18. How can sensitivity analysis be used in conjunction with CVP analysis?

EXERCISES AND PROBLEMS

10-1
Break-even in Units
LO 1

Ando Company manufactures automobile stereo speakers. Variable costs are $35 per pair of speakers, the price is $60, and fixed costs are $37,500.

REQUIRED:

1. What is the contribution margin for one pair of speakers?
2. How many pairs of speakers must Ando Company sell to break even?
3. If Ando Company sells 2,300 pairs of speakers, what is the operating income?

10-2
Break-even in Units
LO 1

Carroll Company publishes musical scores. Fixed costs amount to $45,000 per year. Variable expenses per score are $0.75, and the average price per score is $3.

REQUIRED:

1. How many scores must Carroll Company sell to break even?
2. If Carroll Company sells 25,000 scores in a year, what is the operating income?
3. If Carroll Company's variable expenses rise to $1 per score while the price and fixed expenses remain unchanged, what is the new break-even point?

10-3
Break-even in Units, Target Income
LO 1

Selina McDowell sells various pottery items at regional craft fairs. Her fixed expenses (depreciation on the kiln, utilities, tools, portable selling booth) are $5,000 per year. The average price for a piece of pottery is $5.50, and the average variable cost (e.g., clay, paints, glazes, price tags) is $3.50 per item.

REQUIRED:

1. How many pieces of pottery must Selina sell to just cover her expenses?
2. If Selina wants to earn $7,000 profit, how many pieces of pottery must she sell? Prepare a variable-costing income statement to verify your answer.

10-4
Break-even in Units
LO 1

Carl and Janice Bowman have started their own business, Handy Maids, which offers cleaning services for households. The Bowmans have fixed expenses of $4,000 per month for office rent, advertising, and a receptionist. Variable expenses for the maids' wages, cleaning supplies, and paper supplies are $22 per job. Handy Maids charges $42 for the average job.

REQUIRED:

1. How many jobs must Handy Maids average each month to break even?
2. What is the operating income for Handy Maids in a month with 240 jobs? With 190 jobs?
3. Suppose that Handy Maids decides to increase the price to $45 per job. What is the new break-even point in number of jobs per month?

10-5
Break-even in Units
LO 1

Alston Company has fixed costs of $125,000. At the break-even point, 100,000 units are sold. If variable costs are $2.68 per unit, what is the price?

10-6
Break-even in Units, After-Tax Target Income, CVP Assumptions
LO 1, 4, 5

Almo Company manufactures and sells adjustable canopies that attach to motor homes and trailers. The market covers both new unit purchases as well as replacement canopies. Almo developed its 1998 business plan based on the assumption that canopies would sell at a price of $400 each. The variable costs for each canopy were projected at $200, and the annual fixed costs were budgeted at $100,000. Almo's after-tax profit objective was $240,000; the company's effective tax rate is 40 percent.

While Almo's sales usually rise during the second quarter, the May financial statements reported that sales were not meeting expectations. For the first five months of the year, only 350 units had been sold at the established price, with variable costs as planned, and it was clear that the 1998 after-tax profit projection would not be reached unless some actions were taken. Almo's president assigned a management committee to analyze the situation and develop several alternative courses of action. The following mutually exclusive alternatives, labeled A, B, and C, were presented to the president.

A. Reduce the sales price by $40. The sales organization forecasts that with the significantly reduced sales price, 2,700 units can be sold during the remainder of the year. Total fixed and variable unit costs will stay as budgeted.

B. Lower the variable costs per unit by $25 through the use of less expensive raw materials and slightly modified manufacturing techniques. The sales price will also be reduced by $30, and sales of 2,200 units for the remainder of the year are forecast.

C. Cut fixed costs by $10,000, and lower the sales price by 5 percent. Variable costs per unit will be unchanged. Sales of 2,000 units are expected for the remainder of the year.

REQUIRED:

1. Determine the number of units that Almo Company must sell in order to break even assuming no changes are made to the selling price and cost structure.
2. Determine the number of units that Almo Company must sell in order to achieve its after-tax profit objective.
3. Determine which one of the alternatives Almo Company should select to achieve its annual after-tax profit objective. Be sure to support your selection with appropriate calculations.
4. The precision and reliability of CVP analysis are limited by several underlying assumptions. Identify at least four of these assumptions.

(CMA adapted)

10-7
Break-even in
Sales Dollars
LO 2, 5

JJ Motors, Inc., employs 45 sales personnel to market their line of luxury automobiles. The average car sells for $23,000, and a 6 percent commission is paid to the salesperson. JJ Motors is considering a change to the commission arrangement where the company would pay each salesperson a salary of $2,000 per month plus a commission of 2 percent of the sales made by that salesperson. What is the amount of total monthly car sales at which JJ Motors would be indifferent as to which plan to select?

(CMA adapted)

10-8
Break-even in
Sales Dollars,
Changes in
Variables
LO 2, 5

Barnes Corporation manufactures skateboards and is in the process of preparing next year's budget. The pro forma income statement for the current year is presented below.

Sales		$1,500,000
Cost of sales:		
Direct materials	$250,000	
Direct labor	150,000	
Variable overhead	75,000	
Fixed overhead	100,000	575,000
Gross profit		$ 925,000
Selling and administrative expenses:		
Variable	$200,000	
Fixed	250,000	450,000
Operating income		$ 475,000

REQUIRED:

1. What is the break-even point (rounded to the nearest dollar) for Barnes Corporation for the current year?
2. For the coming year, the management of Barnes Corporation anticipates a 10 percent increase in variable costs and a $45,000 increase in fixed expenses. What is the break-even point for next year?

(CMA adapted)

**10-9
Break-even in
Units**
LO 1

Don Masters and two of his colleagues are considering opening a law office in a large metropolitan area that would make inexpensive legal services available to those who could not otherwise afford these services. The intent is to provide easy access for their clients by having the office open 360 days per year, 16 hours each day from 7:00 a.m. to 11:00 p.m. The office would be staffed by a lawyer, paralegal, legal secretary, and clerk-receptionist for each of the two 8-hour shifts.

In order to determine the feasibility of the project, Masters hired a marketing consultant to assist with market projections. The results of this study show that if the firm spends $500,000 on advertising the first year, the number of new clients expected each day would have the following probability distribution.

Number of New Clients Per Day	Probability
20	.10
30	.30
55	.40
85	.20

Masters and his associates believe these numbers are reasonable and are prepared to spend the $500,000 on advertising. Other pertinent information about the operation of the office is given below.

The only charge to each new client would be $30 for the initial consultation. All cases that warranted further legal work would be accepted on a contingency basis with the firm earning 30 percent of any favorable settlements or judgments. Masters estimates that 20 percent of new client consultations will result in favorable settlements or judgments averaging $2,000 each. It is not expected that there will be repeat clients during the first year of operations.

The hourly wages of the staff are projected to be $25 for the lawyer, $20 for the paralegal, $15 for the legal secretary, and $10 for the clerk-receptionist. Fringe benefit expense will be 40 percent of the wages paid. A total of 400 hours of overtime is expected for the year; this will be divided equally between the legal secretary and the clerk-receptionist positions. Overtime will be paid at one and one-half times the regular wage, and the fringe benefit expense will apply to the full wage.

Masters has located 6,000 square feet of suitable office space, which rents for $28 per square foot annually. Associated expenses will be $22,000 for property insurance and $32,000 for utilities.

It will be necessary for the group to purchase malpractice insurance, which is expected to cost $180,000 annually.

The initial investment in office equipment will be $60,000; this equipment has an estimated useful life of four years.

The cost of office supplies has been estimated to be $4 per expected new client consultation.

REQUIRED:

1. Determine how many new clients must visit the law office being considered by Don Masters and his colleagues in order for the venture to break even during its first year of operations.

2. Using the information provided by the marketing consultant, determine if it is feasible for the law office to achieve break-even operations.

(CMA adapted)

10-10
After-Tax Income Target, Profit Analysis
LO 1, 5

Siberian Ski Company recently expanded its manufacturing capacity, which will allow it to produce up to 15,000 pairs of cross-country skis of the mountaineering model or the touring model. The Sales Department assures management that it can sell between 9,000 pairs and 13,000 pairs of either product this year. Because the models are very similar, Siberian Ski will produce only one of the two models.

The following information was compiled by the Accounting Department.

| | Per-Unit (Pair) Data | |
	Mountaineering	Touring
Selling price	$88.00	$80.00
Variable costs	52.80	52.80

Fixed costs will total $369,600 if the mountaineering model is produced but will be only $316,800 if the touring model is produced. Siberian Ski is subject to a 40 percent income tax rate.

REQUIRED:

1. If Siberian Ski Company desires an after-tax net income of $24,000, how many pairs of touring model skis will the company have to sell?
2. Suppose that Siberian Ski Company decided to produce only one model of ski. What is the total sales revenue at which Siberian Ski Company would make the same profit or loss regardless of the ski model it decided to produce?
3. If the Siberian Ski Company Sales Department could guarantee the annual sale of 12,000 pairs of either model, which model would the company produce and why?

(CMA adapted)

10-11
Using a Computer Spreadsheet to Solve Multiple-Product Break-even, Varying Sales Mix
LO 2

The following projected income statement for Whittier Company is repeated for your convenience. Recall that the projection is based on sales of 1,200 mulching mowers and 800 riding mowers.

	Mulching Mower	Riding Mower	Total
Sales	$480,000	$640,000	$1,120,000
Less: Variable expenses	(390,000)	(480,000)	(870,000)
Contribution margin	$ 90,000	$160,000	$ 250,000
Less: Direct fixed expenses	(30,000)	(40,000)	(70,000)
Product margin	$ 60,000	$120,000	$ 180,000
Less: Common fixed expenses			(26,250)
Operating income			$ 153,750

REQUIRED:

1. Set up the above income statement on a spreadsheet (e.g., Lotus 1-2-3® or Excel®). Then, substitute the following sales mixes, and calculate operating income. Be sure to print the results for each sales mix (a through d).

	Mulching Mower	Riding Mower
a.	1,000	1,000
b.	1,500	500
c.	500	1,500
d.	800	1,200

2. Calculate the break-even units for each product for each of the above sales mixes.

10-12
**Break-even Units
Sold; After-Tax
Profit; Margin of
Safety**
LO 1

Crunchy Morsels, Inc., manufactures and sells corn chips. Currently, Crunchy produces only one type of corn chip. The chips are packaged in 11-ounce bags and sold to retailers for $1.50 per bag. The variable costs per bag are as follows:

Corn	$0.70
Vegetable oil	0.10
Miscellaneous ingredients	0.03
Selling	0.17

Fixed manufacturing costs total $300,000 per year. Administrative costs (fixed) total $100,000.

REQUIRED:

1. Compute the number of bags of corn chips that must be sold for Crunchy to break even.
2. How many bags of corn chips must be sold for Crunchy to earn a before-tax profit of $150,000?
3. Assuming a tax rate of 60 percent, how many bags of corn chips must be sold to earn an after-tax profit of $284,000?
4. Suppose that Crunchy expects to sell 1.2 million bags of corn chips. What is the margin of safety?

10-13
**Contribution
Margin; Unit
Amounts**
LO 1

Information on four independent companies is given below. Calculate the correct amount for each question mark.

	A	B	C	D
Sales	$10,000	?	?	$9,000
Total variable cost	(8,000)	(11,700)	(9,750)	?
Contribution margin	$ 2,000	$ 3,900	$?	$?
Total fixed cost	?	(5,000)	?	(750)
Net income	$ 1,000	$?	$ 400	$2,850
Units sold	?	1,300	125	90
Price	$5	?	$130	?
Variable cost/Unit	?	$9	?	?
Contribution margin/Unit	?	$3	?	?
Contribution margin ratio	?	?	40%	?
Break-even in units	?	?	?	?

10-14
**Break-even in
Sales Dollars;
Margin of Safety**
LO 2, 5

Skyways Aviation Services had revenue of $675,000 last year, with total variable costs of $202,500 and fixed costs of $200,000.

REQUIRED:

1. What is the contribution margin ratio for Skyways based on last year's data? What is the break-even point in sales revenue?

2. What was the margin of safety for Skyways last year?
3. Skyways is considering starting a multimedia advertising campaign that is supposed to increase sales by $150,000 per year. The campaign will cost $106,000. Is the advertising campaign a good idea? Explain.

10-15
Break-even in Units

LO 1

Stevenson Company's break-even point is 1,000 units. Variable cost per unit is $150, and total fixed costs are $80,000 per year. What price does Stevenson charge?

10-16
Contribution
Margin; CVP; Net
Income; Margin of
Safety

LO 1, 5

Sweet Sue, Inc., produces a particularly rich praline fudge. Each ten-ounce box sells for $5.50. Variable unit costs are as follows:

Pecans	$ .75
Sugar	.35
Butter	1.75
Other ingredients	.24
Box, packing material	.76
Selling commission	.55

Fixed overhead cost is $24,000 per year. Fixed selling and administrative costs are $9,000 per year. Sweet Sue sold 35,000 boxes last year.

REQUIRED:

1. What is the contribution margin per unit for a box of praline fudge? What is the contribution margin ratio?
2. How many boxes must be sold to break even? What is the break-even sales revenue?
3. What was Sweet Sue's net income last year?
4. What was the margin of safety?
5. Suppose that Sweet Sue raises the price to $6.00 per box, but anticipated sales will drop to 31,500 boxes. What will be the new break-even point in units? Should Sweet Sue raise the price? Explain.

10-17
Break-even in
Sales Dollars;
Variable-Cost
Ratio;
Contribution
Margin Ratio;
Margin of Safety

LO 2, 5

Lambert produces and sells an economy line of ski parkas. The budgeted income statement for the coming year is

Sales	$600,000
Less: Variable expenses	(400,000)
Contribution margin	$200,000
Less: Fixed expenses	(120,000)
Profit before taxes	$ 80,000
Less: Taxes	(24,000)
Profit after taxes	$ 56,000

REQUIRED:

1. What is Lambert's variable cost ratio? Its contribution margin ratio?
2. Suppose Lambert's actual revenues are $60,000 greater than budgeted. By how much will before-tax profits increase? Give the answer without preparing a new income statement.
3. How much sales revenue must Lambert earn in order to break even? What is the expected margin of safety?
4. How much sales revenue must Lambert generate to earn a before-tax profit of $100,000? An after-tax profit of $84,000? Prepare a contribution income statement to verify the accuracy of your last answer.

10-18
Operating
Leverage

LO 5

Income statements for two different companies in the same industry are as follows:

	Company A	Company B
Sales	$500,000	$500,000
Less: Variable costs	(350,000)	(200,000)
Contribution margin	$150,000	$300,000
Less: Fixed costs	(50,000)	(250,000)
Operating income	$100,000	$ 50,000

REQUIRED:

1. Compute the degree of operating leverage for each company.
2. Compute the break-even point for each company. Explain why the break-even point for Company B is higher.
3. Suppose that both companies experience a 50 percent increase in revenues. Compute the percentage change in profits for each company. Explain why the percentage increase in Company B's profits is so much greater than that of Company A's.

10-19
CVP Analysis with
Multiple Products

LO 3

Thompson Company produces scientific and business calculators. For the coming year, Thompson expects to sell 200,000 scientific calculators and 100,000 business calculators. A segmented income statement for the two products is given below:

	Scientific	Business	Total
Sales	$5,000,000	$2,000,000	$7,000,000
Less: Variable costs	(2,400,000)	(900,000)	(3,300,000)
Contribution margin	$2,600,000	$1,100,000	$3,700,000
Less: Direct fixed costs	(1,200,000)	(960,000)	(2,160,000)
Segment margin	$1,400,000	$ 140,000	$1,540,000
Less: Common fixed costs			(800,000)
Operating income			$ 740,000

REQUIRED:

1. Compute the number of scientific calculators and the number of business calculators that must be sold to break even.
2. Using information only from the total column of the income statement, compute the sales revenue that must be generated for the company to break even.

10-20
Changes in Break-
even Points with
Changes in Unit
Prices

LO 5

The income statement for Sanders, Inc., is as follows:

Sales	$500,000
Less: Variable expenses	(275,000)
Contribution margin	$225,000
Less: Fixed expenses	(180,000)
Operating income	$ 45,000

Sanders produces and sells a single product. The above income statement is based on sales of 100,000 units.

REQUIRED:

1. Compute the break-even point in units and in revenue.
2. Suppose that the selling price increases by 10 percent. Will the break-even point increase or decrease? Recompute it.
3. Suppose that the variable cost per unit increases by $0.35. Will the break-even point increase or decrease? Recompute it.
4. Can you predict whether the break-even point increases or decreases if both the selling price and the unit variable cost increase? Recompute the break-even point incorporating both of the changes in Requirements 2 and 3.
5. Assume that total fixed costs increase by $50,000. (Assume no other changes from the original data.) Will the break-even point increase or decrease? Recompute it.

10-21
Break-even, After-Tax Target Income, Margin of Safety, Operating Leverage
LO 1, 2, 5

Auflager Company produces a single product. The projected income statement for the coming year is as follows:

Sales (50,000 units @ $40)	$2,000,000
Less: Variable costs	(1,100,000)
Contribution margin	$ 900,000
Less: Fixed costs	(765,000)
Operating income	$ 135,000

REQUIRED:

1. Compute the unit contribution margin and the units that must be sold to break even. Suppose that 30,000 units are sold above break-even. What is the profit?
2. Compute the contribution margin ratio and the break-even point in dollars. Suppose that revenues are $200,000 greater than expected. What would the total profit be?
3. Compute the margin of safety.
4. Compute the operating leverage. Compute the new profit level if sales are 20 percent higher than expected.
5. How many units must be sold to earn a profit equal to 10 percent of sales?
6. Assume the tax rate is 40 percent. How many units must be sold to earn an after-tax profit of $180,000?

10-22
CVP; Before- and After-Tax Targeted Net Income
LO 1

CF Company produces a line of peach chutney. Currently, CF charges a price of $3.50 per jar. Variable costs are $1.40 per jar, and fixed costs are $50,000. The tax rate is 33%. Last year, 27,300 jars were sold.

REQUIRED:

1. What is CF's net income after taxes for last year?
2. What is CF's break-even revenue?
3. Supposing CF wants to earn before-tax income of $13,000, how many units must be sold?
4. Supposing CF wants to earn after-tax income of $13,000, how many units must be sold?

10-23
Basic CVP Concepts
LO 1, 5

Topper Company produces a variety of glass products. One division makes windshields for compact automobiles. The division's projected income statement for the coming year is as follows:

Sales (150,000 units @ $50)	$7,500,000
Less: Variable expenses	(3,500,000)
Contribution margin	$4,000,000
Less: Fixed expenses	(3,200,000)
Operating income	$ 800,000

REQUIRED:

1. Compute the contribution margin per unit and calculate the break-even point in units. Repeat using the contribution margin ratio.
2. The divisional manager has decided to increase the advertising budget by $100,000 and cut the selling price to $45. These actions will increase sales revenue by $1 million. Will the division be better off?
3. Suppose sales revenue exceeds the estimated amount on the income statement by $540,000. Without preparing a new income statement, by how much are profits underestimated?
4. How many units must be sold to earn an after-tax profit of $1.254 million? Assume a tax rate of 34 percent. Repeat the analysis assuming that the after-tax profit target is 10 percent of sales revenue.
5. Compute the margin of safety based on the income statement given above.
6. Compute the operating leverage based on the income statement above. If sales revenues are 20 percent greater than expected, what is the percentage increase in profits?

10-24
CVP Equation;
Basic Concepts;
Solving for
Unknowns
LO 1, 5

Azucar Company produces a chocolate almond bar. Each bar sells for $0.40. The variable costs for each bar (sugar, chocolate, almonds, wrapper, labor, and so on) total $0.25. The total fixed costs are $60,000. During the most recent year, 1 million bars were sold. The president of Azucar, not fully satisfied with the profit performance of the chocolate bar, was considering the following options to increase the bar's profitability: (1) increase advertising; (2) increase the quality of the ingredients and, simultaneously, increase the selling price; (3) increase the selling price; (4) combinations of the three.

REQUIRED:

1. The sales manager is confident that an advertising campaign could double sales volume. If the company president's goal is to increase this year's profits by 50 percent over last year's, what is the maximum amount that can be spent on advertising?
2. Assume that the company increases the quality of its ingredients, thus increasing variable costs to $0.30. Answer the following questions:
   a. How much must the selling price be increased to maintain the same break-even point?
   b. What will the new price be if the company wants to increase the old contribution margin ratio by 50 percent?
3. The company has decided to increase its selling price to $0.50. The sales volume drops from 1 million to 800,000 bars. Was the decision to increase the price a good one? Compute the sales volume that would be needed at the new price for the company to earn the same profit as last year.
4. The sales manager is convinced that by increasing the quality of the ingredients (increasing variable costs to $0.30) and by advertising the increased quality (advertising dollars would be increased by $100,000), sales volume could be doubled. He has also indicated that a price increase would not affect the ability to double sales volume as long as the price increase is not more than 20 percent of the current selling price. Compute the selling price that would be needed to achieve the goal of increasing profits by 50 percent. Is the sales manager's plan feasible? What selling price would you choose? Why?

10-25
Basics of the Sales-Revenue Approach

LO 2, 5

Kiltop Company produces a toy dart gun. The projected income statement for the coming year follows:

Sales	$480,000
Less: Variable costs	(249,600)
Contribution margin	$230,400
Less: Fixed costs	(180,000)
Operating income	$ 50,400

REQUIRED:

1. Compute the contribution margin ratio for the toy gun.
2. How much revenue must Kiltop earn in order to break even?
3. What volume of sales must be earned if Kiltop wants to earn an after-tax income equal to 8 percent of sales? Assume that the tax rate is 34 percent.
4. What is the effect on the contribution margin ratio if the unit selling price and unit variable cost each increase by 10 percent?
5. Suppose that management has decided to give a 3 percent commission on all sales. The projected income statement does not reflect this commission. Recompute the contribution margin ratio assuming that the commission will be paid. What effect does this have on the break-even point?
6. If the commission is paid as described in Requirement 5, management expects sales revenues to increase by $80,000. Is it a sound decision to implement the commission? Support your answer with appropriate computations.
7. Refer to the original data. Compute the margin of safety and the operating leverage. Compute the percentage change in profits if sales increase by 15 percent.

10-26
CVP Analysis: Sales-Revenue Approach; Pricing; After-Tax Profit Target

LO 2, 5

Kline Consulting is a service organization that specializes in the design, installation, and servicing of mechanical, hydraulic, and pneumatic systems. For example, some manufacturing firms have machinery that cannot be turned off for servicing and therefore need some type of system to lubricate the machinery during use. To deal with this type of problem for a client, Kline designed a central lubricating system that pumps lubricants intermittently to bearings and other moving parts.

The operating results for the firm in 1997 are as follows:

Sales	$802,429
Less: Variable costs	(430,000)
Contribution margin	$372,429
Less: Fixed expenses	(154,750)
Operating income	$217,679

In 1998, Kline expects variable costs to increase by 5 percent and fixed costs by 4 percent.

REQUIRED:

1. What is the contribution margin ratio for 1997?
2. Compute Kline's break-even point for 1997 in dollars.
3. Suppose that Kline would like to see a 6 percent increase in net income in 1998. To what percent (on average) must Kline raise its bids to cover the expected cost increases and obtain the desired net income? Assume that Kline expects the same mix and volume of services in 1998 as in 1997.

4. In 1998, how much revenue must be earned for Kline to earn an after-tax profit of $175,000? Assume a tax rate of 34 percent.

10-27
Multiple Products;
Break-even
Analysis;
Operating
Leverage;
Segmented Income
Statements
LO 3, 5

Naturo Food Products produces two different types of snack bars: granola and carob. Naturo sells the bars by the case to retail outlets. Granola bars sell for $30 a case, and carob bars for $20. The projected income statement for the coming year follows:

Sales	$600,000
Less: Variable costs	(400,000)
Contribution margin	$200,000
Less: Fixed expenses	(150,000)
Operating income	$ 50,000

The owner of Naturo estimates that 60 percent of the sales revenue will be produced by granola bars, with the remaining 40 percent by carob bars. Granola bars are also responsible for 60 percent of the variable expenses. Of the fixed expenses, one-third are common to both products, and one-half are directly traceable to the granola bar product line.

REQUIRED:

1. Compute the sales revenue that must be earned for Naturo to break even.
2. Compute the number of cases of granola bars and of carob bars that must be sold for Naturo to break even.
3. Compute the degree of operating leverage for Naturo Products. Now assume that the actual revenues will be 40 percent higher than the projected revenues. By what percentage will profits increase with this change in sales volume?

10-28
Multiproduct
Break-even,
Change in Fixed
Cost
LO 3, 5

Garibaldi, Inc., manufactures two products, A and B. Fixed costs equal $146,000. Product A sells for $12 and has variable cost of $6. Product B sells for $8 and has variable costs of $5.

REQUIRED:

1. What is the contribution margin per unit and the contribution margin ratio for Product A and for Product B?
2. If Garibaldi sells 20,000 units of A and 40,000 units of B, what is the net income?
3. Assuming the sales mix given in Requirement 2, how many units of Product A and how many units of Product B must be sold for Garibaldi to break even?
4. Assume Garibaldi has the opportunity to rearrange its plant to produce only Product B. If this is done, fixed costs will decrease by $35,000, and 70,000 units of B can be produced and sold. Is this a good idea? Explain.

10-29
Break-even in
Units and Sales
Dollars, Margin of
Safety
LO 1, 2, 5

Ellis Company produces a single product. Last year's income statement is as follows:

Sales (29,000 units)	$1,218,000
Less: Variable costs	(812,000)
Contribution margin	$ 406,000
Less: Fixed costs	(300,000)
Operating income	$ 106,000

REQUIRED:

1. Compute the break-even point in units and sales dollars.
2. What was the margin of safety for Ellis Company last year?
3. Suppose that Ellis Company is considering an investment in new technology that will increase fixed costs by $250,000 per year but will lower variable costs to 45% of sales. Units sold will remain unchanged. Prepare a budgeted income statement assuming Ellis makes this investment. What is the new break-even point in units, assuming the investment is made?

10-30
Multiplant Break-even
LO 1, 5

The PTO Division of the Galva Manufacturing Company produces power take-off units for the farm equipment business. The PTO Division, headquartered in Peoria, has a newly renovated plant in Peoria and an older, less automated plant in Moline. Both plants produce the same power take-off units for farm tractors, which are sold to most domestic and foreign tractor manufacturers.

The PTO Division expects to produce and sell 192,000 power take-off units during the coming year. The division production manager has the following data available regarding the unit costs, unit prices, and production capacities for the two plants.

	Peoria		Moline	
Selling price		$150.00		$150.00
Variable manufacturing cost	$72.00		$88.00	
Fixed manufacturing cost	30.00		15.00	
Commission (5%)	7.50		7.50	
General and admin. expenses	25.50		21.00	
Total unit cost		135.00		131.50
Unit profit		$ 15.00		$ 18.50
Production rate per day	400 units		320 units	

All fixed costs are based on a normal year of 240 working days. When the number of working days exceeds 240, variable manufacturing costs increase by $3.00 per unit in Peoria and $8.00 per unit in Moline. Capacity for each plant is 300 working days.

Galva Manufacturing charges each of its plants a per-unit fee for administrative services such as payroll, general accounting, and purchasing, as Galva considers these services to be a function of the work performed at the plants. For each of the plants at Peoria and Moline, the fee is $6.50 and represents the variable portion of the general and administrative expenses.

Wishing to maximize the higher unit profit at Moline, PTO's production manager has decided to manufacture 96,000 units at each plant. This production plan results in Moline operating at capacity and Peoria operating at its normal volume. Galva's corporate controller is not happy with this plan, and he wonders if it might be better to produce relatively more at the automated plant in Peoria.

REQUIRED:

1. Determine the annual break-even units for each of PTO's plants.
2. Calculate the operating income that would result from sales of 192,000 power take-off units if 120,000 of them are produced at the Peoria plant and the remainder at the Moline plant.
3. Calculate the operating income that would result from the division production manager's plan to produce 96,000 units at each plant.

(CMA adapted)

10-31
CVP Analysis and Assumptions
LO 2, 4, 5

Marston Corporation manufactures pharmaceutical products that are sold through a network of sales agents located in the United States and Canada. The agents are currently paid an 18 percent commission on sales, and this percentage was used when Marston prepared the following Pro Forma Income Statement for the fiscal year ending June 30, 1998.

Marston Corporation		
Pro Forma Income Statement		
For the Year Ending June 30, 1998		
(in thousands)		
Sales		$26,000
Cost of goods sold:		
Variable	$11,700	
Fixed	2,870	14,570
Gross profit		$11,430
Selling and administrative costs:		
Commissions	$ 4,680	
Fixed advertising cost	750	
Fixed administrative cost	1,850	7,280
Operating income		$ 4,150
Fixed interest cost		650
Income before income taxes		$ 3,500
Income taxes (40%)		1,400
Net income		$ 2,100

Since the completion of the above statement, Marston has learned that its agents are requiring an increase in the commission rate to 23 percent for the upcoming year. As a result, Marston's president has decided to investigate the possibility of hiring its own sales staff in place of the network of sales agents and has asked Tom Ross, Marston's controller, to gather information on the costs associated with this change.

Ross estimates that Marston will have to hire eight salespeople to cover the current market area, and the annual payroll cost of each of these employees will average $80,000, including fringe benefit expense. Travel and entertainment expense is expected to total $600,000 for the year, and the annual cost of hiring a sales manager and sales secretary will be $150,000. In addition to their salary, the eight salespeople will each earn commissions at the rate of 10 percent on the first $2 million in sales and 15 percent on all sales over $2 million. For planning purposes, Ross expects that all eight salespeople will exceed the $2 million mark and that sales will be at the level previously projected. Ross believes that Marston should also increase its advertising budget by $500,000.

REQUIRED:

1. Calculate Marston Corporation's break-even point in sales dollars for the fiscal year ending June 30, 1998, if the company hires its own sales force and increases its advertising costs.
2. If Marston Corporation continues to sell through its network of sales agents and pays the higher commission rate, determine the estimated volume in sales dollars for the fiscal year ending June 30, 1998, that would be required to generate the same net income as projected in the Pro Forma Income Statement presented above.
3. Describe the general assumptions underlying break-even analysis that might limit its usefulness in this case.

(CMA adapted)

10-32
Case on a Service Organization with Multiple Products; Break-even; Pricing and Scheduling Decisions

LO 3, 5

Utah Metropolitan Ballet is located in Salt Lake City. The company is housed in the Capitol Theater, one of three buildings that make up the Bicentennial Arts Center in downtown Salt Lake City. The Ballet company features five different ballets per year. For the company season, the five ballets to be performed are *The Dream, Petrushka, The Nutcracker, Sleeping Beauty,* and *Bugaku*.

The president and general manager has tentatively scheduled the following number of performances for each ballet for the coming season:

The Dream	5
Petrushka	5
The Nutcracker	20
Sleeping Beauty	10
Bugaku	5

To produce each ballet, costs must be incurred for costumes, props, rehearsals, royalties, guest artist fees, choreography, salaries of production staff, music, and wardrobe. These costs are fixed for a particular ballet regardless of the number of performances. These direct fixed costs are given below for each ballet:

The Dream	Petrushka	The Nutcracker	Sleeping Beauty	Bugaku
$275,500	$145,500	$70,500	$345,000	$155,500

Other fixed costs are incurred as follows:

Advertising	$ 80,000
Insurance	15,000
Administrative salaries	222,000
Office rental, phone, etc.	84,000
Total	$401,000

For each performance of each ballet, the following costs are also incurred:

Utah Symphony	$3,800
Auditorium rental	700
Dancers' payroll	4,000
Total	$8,500

The auditorium where the ballet is presented has 1,854 seats, which are classified as A, B, and C. A seats have the best view, ranging to C seats for the worst. Information concerning the different types of seats is given below:

	A Seats	B Seats	C Seats
Quantity	114	756	984
Price	$35	$25	$15
Percent sold for each performance*			
The Nutcracker	100%	100%	100%
All others	100	80	75

*Based on past experience, the same proportions are expected for the coming season.

REQUIRED:

1. Compute the expected revenues from the performances that have been tentatively scheduled. Prepare a segmented income statement.
2. Calculate the number of performances of each ballet required to produce a break-even segment margin.
3. Calculate the number of performances of each ballet required for the company as a whole to break even. If you were the president and general manager, how would you alter the tentative schedule of performances?
4. Suppose that it is possible to offer a matinee of the popular *Nutcracker*. Seats would sell for $5 less than in the evening, and the rental of the auditorium will be $200 less. The president and general manager feels that five matinee performances are feasible and believes that 80 percent of each type of seat can be sold. What effect will the matinee have on the company's profitability? On the break-even point?
5. Suppose that no additional evening performances can be offered beyond those tentatively scheduled. Assume that the company will offer five matinee performances of *The Nutcracker*. Also, the company expects to receive $60,000 in government grants and contributions from supporters of the fine arts. Will the company break even? If not, what actions would you take to bring revenues in line with costs? Assume any additional performances of *The Nutcracker* are not feasible.

10-33
Case on Cost Behavior and Break-even Analysis; CVP Analysis for Evaluation and Decision Making
LO 2, 5

Reinert Moving and Storage was established in 1962 by Allen Reinert in Lincoln, Nebraska. In 1978, the company achieved million-dollar booking status. The company experienced modest growth for the next two years; however, after the deregulation of the transportation industry in 1980, the company's growth accelerated significantly for several years. Unfortunately, by the end of 1994, the company actually experienced a drop in revenues. During the next two years, the revenues earned essentially matched those of 1994. The revenues reported at the end of 1997 totaled $5.3 million. An income statement for 1997 is shown on the next page.

Upon reviewing the income statement for 1997, Allen Reinert called a meeting to discuss the financial status of the company. He invited sales manager Heidi Jackson and controller Eric Bilodeau.

Allen: Our before-tax income has dropped from a high of 12 percent of sales to about 4 percent this last year. I know that both of you are aware of our problem and have some suggestions on how we can improve the situation. I'd like to hear what you have in mind.
Heidi: Allen, competition has become quite intense in our industry. I have two suggestions to help improve sales. First, we need to increase our advertising budget. We have a good reputation, and I think we need to capitalize on it. I suggest that we emphasize our expertise in crating electronic equipment and other sensitive instruments. Our losses in this area are minuscule. We have a much better record than any of our competitors and we need to let customers—and potential customers—know about the quality of our services.
Allen: This sounds good. How much more do you need for advertising and what kind of increase in sales would you predict?
Heidi: To do it right, I would need to double our current advertising budget. I would guess that sales would increase by 20 percent. I also have another suggestion. I think we should look at the international goods and freight-moving market. Many firms ship goods internationally, and I believe that they would switch to us if we entered that market. My preliminary analysis reveals that we could pick up $500,000 of sales during the first year.
Allen: Both suggestions seem to offer some potential for improving our profitability. Eric, would you gather the data needed to estimate the effect of each of these two alternatives on our profits?
Eric: Sure. I have a suggestion also—I plan on installing a cost accounting system. At this point, we have no real idea how much each of our services is costing. I believe that there is some hope of reducing costs without affecting the quality of our services.

Allen: I'm all for reducing costs where possible. However, keep in mind that I don't want to lay off any employees yet. I like the idea of providing security to our employees. I would rather see everyone take a pay cut before we reduce our work force. So far, we have been able to keep everyone, even with the drop in sales we've had. I think it's a good policy. If these two ideas of Heidi's work out, no new hires may be necessary, and we have trained, loyal employees ready for the new business.

Revenues:		
Local	$1,433,500	
Intrastate	510,000	
Interstate	2,490,500	
Containers	333,000	
Packing	437,000	
Storage	289,000	
Total revenues		$5,493,000
Less: Expenses		
Outside vehicle repair	$ 220,000	
Fuel	352,000	
Sales commissions	102,000	
Tires, oil, lube	20,500	
Wages (driver and helper)	1,584,000	
Internal maintenance	293,000	
Advertising	88,000	
Equipment rental	422,000	
Packing materials	557,000	
Salaries	821,000	
Cargo loss claims	234,000	
Utilities	16,700	
Insurance	44,000	
Fuel taxes and tariffs	132,000	
Bad debt	193,000	
Depreciation	205,000	
Total expenses		(5,284,200)
Income before taxes		$ 208,800
Less: Taxes (state and federal: 42%)		(87,696)
Net income		$ 121,104

REQUIRED:

1. Classify all expenses in the 1997 income statement as either variable or fixed. Assume that each expense is strictly variable or strictly fixed with respect to sales revenue. Once the classification is completed, prepare a variable-costing income statement.
2. Using the information obtained in Requirement 1, compute the revenue that Reinert Moving and Storage needs to generate to break even. Now compute the revenue that is needed to earn a profit equal to 12 percent of sales revenue.
3. What is the maximum amount that Reinert can spend on additional advertising assuming profits remain unchanged for 1998 and that sales will increase by 20 percent, as predicted by Heidi? Suppose that Heidi spends the amount she requested and that sales increase by 20 percent—what is the change in profits? Should the suggestion be adopted?
4. Suppose that the directly traceable fixed expenses associated with entry into the international market are $200,000. Assume that the variable cost ratio for this segment is

the same as computed in the 1997 income statement prepared in Requirement 1. How much revenue must be generated from international shipping for this segment to break even? What is the expected margin of safety? Would you recommend entry into the international market? Why?

5. Suppose that Allen Reinert decides to both increase advertising and enter the international market. Assume that actual sales increased by 10 percent, where $340,000 of the increase came from international sales and the remainder from the increased advertising. Using data from the case in Requirements 1 and 4, answer the following questions:
   a. How much did before-tax profits change because of these two decisions?
   b. What is the profit change attributable to the advertising campaign? The international market? What is your recommendation for the coming year? Should the company continue these two strategies? Or should it do only one or neither? Explain.
   c. Suppose that the company achieved its target profit of 12 percent of sales in spite of the less than expected increase in profits from the advertising campaign and the international market. The remaining increase in profits was achieved through cutting variable costs. What is the new variable cost ratio?

10-34
Assumptions and Use of Variables

LO 1, 5

Choose the best answer for each of the following multiple-choice questions.

1. Cost-volume-profit analysis includes some inherent, simplifying assumptions. Which of the following is *not* one of these assumptions?
   a. Cost and revenues are predictable and are linear over the relevant range.
   b. Variable costs fluctuate proportionally with volume.
   c. Changes in beginning and ending inventory levels are insignificant in amount.
   d. Sales mix will change as fixed costs increase beyond the relevant range.

2. The term "relevant range" as used in cost accounting means the range
   a. over which costs may fluctuate.
   b. over which cost relationships are valid.
   c. of probable production.
   d. over which relevant costs are incurred.

3. How would the following be used in calculating the expected sales level expressed in units?

	Contribution Per Unit	Estimated Operating Loss
a.	Denominator	Numerator
b.	Numerator	Numerator
c.	Not used	Denominator
d.	Numerator	Denominator

4. Information concerning Label Corporations's Product A is as follows:

Sales	$300,000
Variable costs	240,000
Fixed costs	40,000

Assuming that Label increased sales of Product A by 20%, what should be the net income from Product A?
   a. $20,000
   b. $24,000
   c. $32,000
   d. $80,000

5. The following data apply to Freim Corporation for a given period:

Total variable cost per unit	$3.50
Contribution margin/sales	30%
Break-even sales (present volume)	$1,000,000

Freim wants to sell an additional 50,000 units at the same selling price and contribution margin. By how much can fixed costs increase to generate a gross margin equal to 10% of the sales value of the additional 50,000 units to be sold?
a. $50,000
b. $57,500
c. $67,500
d. $125,000

(CPA adapted)

10-35
CVP Analysis;
Impact of Activity-
Based Costing

LO 6

Salem Electronics currently produces two products: a programmable calculator and a tape recorder. A recent marketing study indicated that consumers would react favorably to a radio with the Salem brand name. Owner Kenneth Booth was interested in the possibility. Before any commitment was made, however, Kenneth wanted to know what the incremental fixed costs would be and how many radios must be sold to cover these costs.

In response, Betty Johnson, the marketing manager, gathered data for the current products to help in projecting overhead costs for the new product. The overhead costs follow (the high and low production volumes as measured by direct labor hours were used to assess cost behavior):

	Fixed	Variable
Setups	$ 60,000	$ —
Materials handling	—	18,000
Power	—	22,000
Engineering	100,000	—
Machine costs	30,000*	80,000
Inspection	40,000	—

*All depreciation.

The following activity data were also gathered:

	Calculators	Recorders
Units produced	20,000	20,000
Direct labor hours	10,000	20,000
Machine hours	10,000	10,000
Material moves	120	120
Kilowatt hours	1,000	1,000
Engineering hours	4,000	1,000
Hours of inspection	700	1,400
Number of setups	20	40

Betty was told that a plantwide overhead rate was used to assign overhead costs based on direct labor hours. She was also informed by engineering that if 20,000 radios were produced and sold (her projection based on her marketing study), they would have the same activity data as the recorders (use the same direct labor hours, machine hours, set-ups, and so on).

Engineering also provided the following additional estimates for the proposed product line:

Prime costs per unit	$ 18
Depreciation on new equipment	18,000

Upon receiving these estimates, Betty did some quick calculations and became quite excited. With a selling price of $26 and only $18,000 of additional fixed costs, only 4,500 units had to be sold to break even. Since Betty was confident that 20,000 units could be sold, she was prepared to recommend strongly the new product line.

REQUIRED:

1. Reproduce Betty's break-even calculation using conventional cost assignments. How much additional profit would be expected under this scenario, assuming that 20,000 radios are sold?
2. Use an activity-based costing approach and calculate the break-even point and the incremental profit that would be earned on sales of 20,000 units.
3. Explain why the CVP analysis done in Requirement 2 is more accurate than the analysis done in Requirement 1. What recommendation would you make?

10-36
ABC and CVP Analysis: Multiple Products
LO 3, 6

Good Scent, Inc., produces two colognes, Rose and Violet. Of the two, Rose is the more popular. Data concerning the two products follow:

	Rose	Violet
Expected sales (in cases)	50,000	10,000
Selling price per case	$100	$80
Direct labor hours	36,000	6,000
Machine hours	10,000	3,000
Receiving orders	50	25
Packing orders	100	50
Material cost per case	$50	$43
Direct labor cost per case	$10	$7

The company uses a conventional cost system and assigns overhead costs to products using direct labor hours. Annual overhead costs are listed below. They are classified as fixed or variable with respect to direct labor hours.

	Fixed	Variable
Direct labor benefits	$ —	$200,000
Machine costs	200,000*	262,000
Receiving department	225,000	—
Packing department	125,000	—
Total costs	$550,000	$462,000

*All depreciation

REQUIRED:

1. Using the conventional approach, compute the number of cases of Rose and the number of cases of Violet that must be sold for the company to break even.

2. Using an activity-based approach, compute the number of cases of each product that must be sold for the company to break even.

10-37
ABC and CVP Analysis, Use of Regression
LO 6

Sorrentino Company, which has been in business for one year, manufactures specialty Italian pastas. The pasta products start in the Mixing Department, where durum flour, eggs, and water are mixed to form dough. The dough is kneaded, rolled flat and cut into fettucine or lasagna noodles, then dried and packaged.

Paul Gilchrist, controller for Sorrentino Company, is concerned because the company has yet to make a profit. Sales were slow in the first quarter but really picked up by the end of the year. Over the course of the year, 726,800 boxes were sold. Paul is interested in determining how many boxes must be sold to break even. He has begun to determine relevant fixed and variable costs and has accumulated the following per-unit data.

Price	$0.90
Direct materials	0.35
Direct labor	0.25

He has had more difficulty separating overhead into fixed and variable components. In examining overhead-related activities, Paul has noticed that machine hours appear to be closely correlated with units, in that 100 boxes of pasta can be produced per machine hour. Setups are an important batch-level activity. Paul has accumulated the following information on overhead costs, number of setups, and machine hours for the past twelve months.

	Overhead	Number of Setups	Machine Hours
January	$5,700	18	595
February	4,500	6	560
March	4,890	12	575
April	5,500	15	615
May	6,200	20	650
June	5,000	10	610
July	5,532	16	630
August	5,409	12	625
September	5,300	11	650
October	5,000	12	550
November	5,350	14	593
December	5,470	14	615
Total		160	7,268

Selling and administrative expenses, all fixed, amounted to $180,000 last year.

REQUIRED:

1. Separate overhead into fixed and variable components using ordinary least-squares (regression) analysis. Run three regressions, using the following independent variables: (1) number of setups, (2) number of machine hours, and (3) a multiple regression using both number of setups and machine hours. Which regression equation is best? Why?
2. Using the results from the multiple regression equation (from Requirement 1), calculate the number of boxes of pasta that must be sold to break even.

**10-38
Multiproduct CVP
Analysis, ABC**

LO 3, 5, 6

Refer to the data in *10-37*. Sorrentino Company has decided to expand into the production of sauces to top its pastas. Sauces are also started in the Mixing Department, using the same equipment. The sauces are mixed, cooked, and packaged into plastic containers. One jar of sauce is priced at $2 and requires $0.75 of direct materials and $0.50 of direct labor. Fifty jars of sauce can be produced per machine hour. The setup is identical to the setup for pasta and should cost the same amount. The production manager believes that with careful scheduling, he can keep the total number of setups (for both pasta and sauce) to the same number as used last year. The marketing director believes Sorrentino Company can sell 2 boxes of pasta for every jar of sauce.

REQUIRED:

1. Using the data from **10-37**, and the results of the multiple regression equation, calculate the break-even number of boxes of pasta and jars of sauce.
2. Suppose that the production manager is wrong and that the number of setups doubles. Calculate the new break-even number of boxes of pasta and jars of sauce.
3. Comment on the effect of uncertainty in the sales mix and in cost estimates on risk for Sorrentino Company.

Chapter 11

Activity Resource Usage Model and Relevant Costing: Tactical Decision Making

Aveda cosmetics and aromatherapy products are made from ingredients purchased from vendors worldwide. Thus, their resource mix includes both easily altered resources and difficult to change resources. This makes tactical decision making a challenge.

LEARNING OBJECTIVES

After studying this chapter, you should be able to:

1. Describe and explain the tactical decision-making model.
2. Define and explain the concept of relevant costs and revenues.
3. Explain how the activity resource usage model is used in assessing relevancy.
4. Apply the tactical decision-making concepts in a variety of business situations.

One of the major roles of the cost management information system is supplying cost and revenue data that are useful in tactical decision making. Aveda, for example, may need to decide whether to run an in-store promotion or to advertise special gifts for a holiday such as Valentine's Day or Mother's Day. It might need cost and revenue data for various lines of scented products to determine which to keep and expand and which to drop. How cost and revenue data can be used to make tactical decisions is the focus of this chapter. To make sound decisions, the user of the cost information must be able to decide what is relevant to the decision and what is not relevant.

TACTICAL DECISION MAKING

Objective 1

Describe and explain the tactical decision-making model.

tactical decision making

Tactical decision making consists of choosing among alternatives with an immediate or limited end in view. Accepting a special order for less than the normal selling price to utilize idle capacity and increase this year's profits is an example. The immediate objective is to exploit idle productive capacity so that short-run profits can be increased. Thus, some tactical decisions tend to be *short-run* in nature; however, it should be emphasized that short-run decisions often have long-run consequences. Consider a second example. Suppose that a company is considering the possibility of producing a component instead of buying it from suppliers. The immediate objective may be to lower the cost of making the main product. Yet this tactical decision may be a small part of the overall strategy of establishing a cost leadership position for the firm. Thus, tactical decisions are often *small-scale actions* that serve a larger purpose. Recall that the overall objective of strategic decision making is to select among alternative strategies so that a long-term competitive advantage is established. Tactical decision making should support this overall objective, even if the immediate objective is short-run (accepting a one-time order to increase profits) or small-scale (making instead of buying a component). Thus, *sound* tactical decision making means that the decisions made achieve not only the limited objective but also serve a larger purpose. In fact, no tactical decision should be made that does not serve the overall strategic goals of an organization.

The Tactical Decision-Making Process

With this very important qualification, it is possible to outline the tactical decision-making process. The five steps describing the process are listed below:

1. Recognize and define the problem.
2. Identify alternatives as possible solutions to the problem, and eliminate alternatives that are not feasible.
3. Identify the predicted costs and benefits associated with each feasible alternative. Eliminate the costs and benefits that are not relevant to the decision.
4. Compare the *relevant* costs and benefits for each alternative, and relate each alternative to the overall strategic goals of the firm and other important qualitative factors.
5. Select the alternative with the greatest benefit which also supports the organization's strategic objectives.

Step 1: Defining the Problem To illustrate the steps of the process, consider an apple producer. Each year, 25% of the apples harvested are small and odd-shaped. These apples cannot be sold in the normal distribution channels and have simply been dumped in the orchards for fertilizer. This approach seems costly, and the owner is not satisfied with it. What to do with these apples is the problem facing the apple producer.

Step 2: Identifying Feasible Alternatives There are several alternatives being considered:

1. Sell the apples to pig farmers.
2. Bag the apples (five-pound bags), and sell them to local supermarkets as seconds.
3. Rent a local canning facility and convert the apples to applesauce.
4. Rent a local canning facility and convert the apples to pie filling.
5. Continue with the current dumping practice.

Of the five alternatives, alternative one was eliminated because there were not enough local pig farmers interested in the apples; alternative five represented the status quo and was eliminated at the request of the owner; alternative four was also eliminated because the local canning facility would need a major capital investment to buy fittings that would convert the equipment to pie-filling capability. The apple producer did not have the ability to raise the capital needed. However, the local facility's equipment could be used (without conversion) for producing applesauce. Thus, alternative three was a possibility. Furthermore, since local supermarkets agreed to buy five-pound bags of irregular apples and bagging could be done at the warehouse, it was also a possibility. Thus, two alternatives were deemed feasible.

Step 3: Predicting Costs and Benefits and Eliminating Irrelevant Costs Suppose that the apple producer predicts that labor and materials (bags and ties) for the bagging option would cost $0.05 per pound. The five-pound bags of apples could be sold for $1.30 per bag to the local supermarkets. Making applesauce would cost $0.40 per pound for rent, labor, apples, cans, and other materials (rent is charged on a per-pound processed basis). It takes six pounds of apples to produce five, 16-ounce cans of applesauce. Each 16-ounce can will sell for $0.78. The apple producer decides that the cost of growing and harvesting the apples is not relevant to choosing between the bagging alternative and the applesauce alternative.

Step 4: Comparing Relevant Costs and Relating to Strategic Goals The bagging alternative costs $0.25 to produce a five-pound bag, and the revenue is $1.30 per bag, or $0.26 per pound. Thus, the net benefit is $0.21 per pound ($0.26 − $0.05). For the applesauce alternative, six pounds of apples produce five 16-ounce cans of applesauce. The revenue for five cans is $3.90 (5 × $0.78), which converts to $0.65 per pound ($3.90/6). Thus, the net benefit is $0.25 per pound ($0.65 − $0.40). Of the two alternatives, the applesauce option offers $0.04 more per pound than the bagging option. The applesauce alternative, from the viewpoint of the apple producer, requires a forward integration strategy. The apple producer currently is not involved in producing any apple consumer products. Moreover, the apple producer is reluctant to move into applesauce production. The producer has absolutely no experience in this part of the industrial value chain. An outside expert would need to be hired. Also, the apple producer knows little about the channels of distribution for applesauce. Finally, the rental opportunity is a year-to-year issue. In the long term, a major capital commitment would be needed. Bagging the small apples, on the other hand, is a product differentiation strategy that allows the producer to operate within the known segment of the industrial value chain.

Step 5: Select Alternative Since the apple producer is reluctant to follow a forward integration strategy, the bagging alternative should be chosen. This alternative maintains the current position in the industrial value chain and strengthens the producer's competitive position by following a differentiation strategy for the small, poorly shaped apples.

decision model

tactical cost analysis

Summary of Decision-Making Process The five steps define a simple decision model. A **decision model** is a set of procedures that, if followed, will lead to a decision. Exhibit 11-1 summarizes and illustrates the steps for the decision model that describe the tactical decision-making process. Steps three and four define *tactical cost analysis*. **Tactical cost analysis** is the use of relevant cost data to identify the alternative that provides the greatest benefit to the organization. Thus, tactical cost analysis includes predicting costs, identifying relevant costs, and comparing relevant costs.

Tactical cost analysis, however, is only part of the overall decision process. Qualitative inputs also must be considered.

Qualitative Factors

While cost analysis plays a key role in tactical decision making, it does have its limitations. Relevant cost information is not all the information a manager should consider. Other information, often qualitative in nature, is needed to make an informed decision. For example, the relationship of the alternatives being considered to the organization's strategic objectives is essentially a qualitative assessment. Other qualitative factors are also important. For example, suppose that a firm is considering whether to buy a component or to produce it internally. Assume that the cost analysis indicates that the buy alternative is less costly than the make alternative. Cost analysis can and should be viewed as only one input for the final decision. A number of qualitative factors can significantly affect a manager's decision making. In the make-or-buy decision, the firm's manager likely would be concerned with such qualitative considerations as the quality of the components purchased externally, the reliability of supply sources, the expected stability of prices over the next several years, labor relations, community image, and so on. To illustrate the possible impact of qualitative factors on the make-or-buy decision, consider the first two factors, quality and reliability of supply.

If the quality of the component is significantly less if purchased externally than what is available internally, the quantitative advantage from purchasing may be more fictitious than real. Settling for lower-quality materials may adversely affect the quality of the final product, thus harming sales. Because of this, the firm's manager may choose to continue to produce the parts internally.

Similarly, if supply sources are not reliable, production schedules could be interrupted, and customer orders could arrive late. These factors can increase labor costs and overhead and hurt sales. Again, depending on the perceived tradeoffs, the firm's manager may decide that internal production of the parts is better than purchasing them, even if a tactical cost analysis gives the initial advantage to purchasing.

Exhibit 11-1
Decision Model: Tactical Decision-Making Process

Example

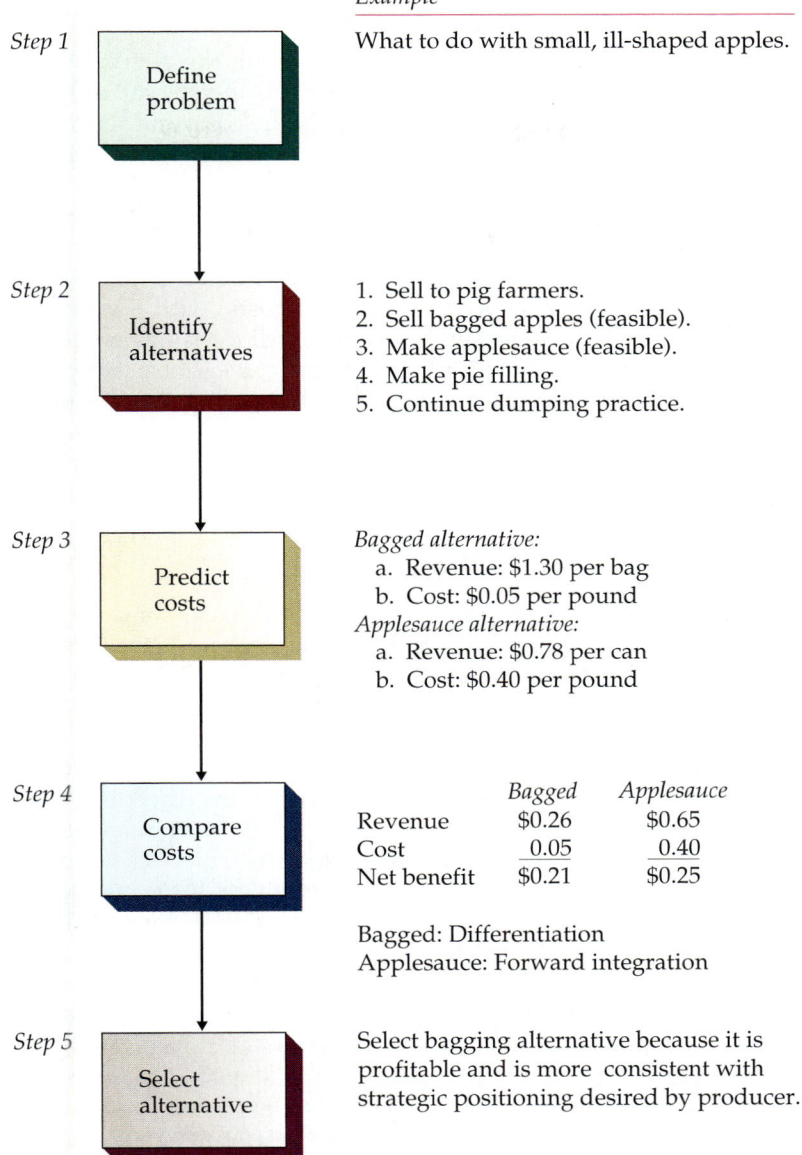

Step 1 — Define problem

What to do with small, ill-shaped apples.

Step 2 — Identify alternatives

1. Sell to pig farmers.
2. Sell bagged apples (feasible).
3. Make applesauce (feasible).
4. Make pie filling.
5. Continue dumping practice.

Step 3 — Predict costs

Bagged alternative:
  a. Revenue: $1.30 per bag
  b. Cost: $0.05 per pound
Applesauce alternative:
  a. Revenue: $0.78 per can
  b. Cost: $0.40 per pound

Step 4 — Compare costs

	Bagged	*Applesauce*
Revenue	$0.26	$0.65
Cost	0.05	0.40
Net benefit	$0.21	$0.25

Bagged: Differentiation
Applesauce: Forward integration

Step 5 — Select alternative

Select bagging alternative because it is profitable and is more consistent with strategic positioning desired by producer.

How should qualitative factors be handled in the decision-making process? First of all, they must be identified. Secondly, the decision maker should try to quantify them. Often, qualitative factors are simply more difficult to quantify, but not impossible. For example, possible unreliability of the outside supplier might be quantified as the probable number of days late multiplied by the labor cost of downtime in the plant. Finally, truly qualitative factors, such as the impact of late orders on customer relations, must be taken into consideration in the final step of the decision-making model—the selection of the alternative with the greatest overall benefit.

RELEVANT COSTS AND REVENUES

Objective 2
Define and explain
the concept of
relevant costs and
revenues.

relevant costs
　(revenues)

A significant input in choosing among the alternatives is cost. All other things being equal, the alternative with the lower cost should be chosen. In choosing between the two alternatives, only the costs and revenues relevant to the decision should be considered. Identifying and comparing relevant costs and revenues is the heart of the tactical decision model illustrated in Exhibit 11-1. Thus, it is essential to know what is meant by relevant costs and revenues. **Relevant costs (revenues)** are future costs (revenues) that differ across alternatives. The definition is the same for costs or revenues; thus, to keep things simple, our discussion will focus on relevant costs, with the understanding that the same principles also apply to revenues. All decisions relate to the future; accordingly, only future costs can be relevant to decisions. However, to be relevant, a cost must not only be a future cost, but it also must differ from one alternative to another. If a future cost is the same for more than one alternative, it has no effect on the decision. Such a cost is an *irrelevant* cost. The ability to identify relevant and irrelevant costs is an important decision-making skill.

Relevant Costs Illustrated

To illustrate the concept of relevant costs, consider Kilpack Enterprise, Inc., a company that is currently making a component (Component 67) for one of its main products. A supplier has approached the company and offered to sell the component for what appears to be an attractive price. The company is now faced with a make-or-buy decision. Assume that the cost of direct materials used to produce the components is $270,000 per year (based on normal volume). Should this cost be a factor in the decision? Is the direct materials cost a future cost that differs across the two alternatives? It is certainly a future cost. To produce the component for another year requires materials which must be purchased. But does it differ across the two alternatives? If the component is purchased from an external supplier, no internal production is needed. The need to purchase materials for producing the component can be eliminated, reducing the materials cost to zero. Thus, the cost of direct materials differs across alternatives ($270,000 for the make alternative and $0 for the buy alternative). It is therefore a relevant cost.

Implicit in this analysis is the use of a past cost to estimate a future cost. For example, assume that the most recent cost of materials to support production of the component was $260,000. Adjusting this past cost for anticipated price increases produced the projected cost of $270,000. Thus, although past costs are never relevant, they are often used as the basis for predicting what future costs will be.

Irrelevant Cost Illustrated

Kilpack uses machinery to manufacture Component 67. This machinery was purchased five years ago and is being depreciated at an annual rate of $50,000. Is this $50,000 a relevant cost? In other words, is depreciation a future cost that differs across the two alternatives?

sunk cost

Past Costs Depreciation, in this case, represents an allocation of a cost already incurred (the cost is being allocated to time periods). It is a **sunk cost**, an allocation of a past cost. Thus, regardless of which alternative is chosen, the acquisition cost of the machinery cannot be avoided. It is the same across both alternatives. Although we allocate this sunk cost to future periods and call that allocation *depreciation*, none of the original cost is avoidable. Sunk costs are past costs. They are always the same across alternatives and are therefore always irrelevant. Thus, the acquisition cost of the machinery and its associated depreciation should not be a factor in the make-or-buy decision.

Future Costs   Assume that the cost to heat and cool the plant—$40,000 per year— is allocated to different production departments, including the department that produces Component 67, which receives $4,000 of the cost. Is this $4,000 cost relevant to the make-or-buy decision facing Kilpack?

  The cost of providing plant utilities is a future cost, since it must be paid in future years. But does the cost differ across the make-and-buy alternatives? It is unlikely that the cost of heating and cooling the plant will change whether the component is produced or not. Thus, the cost is the same across both alternatives. The amount of the utility payment allocated to the remaining departments may change if production of Component 67 is stopped, but the level of the total payment is unaffected by the decision. It is therefore an irrelevant cost.

RELEVANCY, COST BEHAVIOR, AND THE ACTIVITY RESOURCE USAGE MODEL

Objective 3

Explain how the activity resource usage model is used in assessing relevancy.

Understanding cost behavior is basic in determining relevancy. When costs were primarily unit-based, a simple distinction between fixed and variable costs could be made. Now, however, the ABC model has us focusing on unit-level, batch-level, product-level, and facility-level costs. The first three are variable, but with respect to different types of activity drivers. The activity resource usage model can help us sort out the behavior of various activity costs and assess their relevance.

  The activity resource usage model has three resource categories: (1) resources acquired as used and needed, (2) resources acquired in advance of usage (single period or short term), and (3) resources acquired in advance (multiperiod service capability). These three categories and their usefulness in relevant costing are described in the following sections.

Resources Acquired as Used and Needed

Resource spending is the cost of acquiring activity capacity. What is paid for the supply of an activity is the activity cost. For resources acquired as used and needed, the activity resources demanded (used) equal the resources supplied. Thus, for this resource category, *if the demand for an activity changes across alternatives*, then resource spending will change and the cost of the activity is relevant to the decision. For example, electricity supplied internally uses fuel for the generator. Fuel is a resource acquired as used and needed. Now consider the following two alternatives: (1) accept a special, one-time order and (2) reject the special order. If accepting the order increases the demand for kilowatt hours (power's activity driver), then the cost of power will differ across alternatives by the increase in fuel consumption (assuming fuel is the only resource acquired as needed). Thus, power cost is relevant to the decision.

Resources Acquired in Advance (Short Term)

Resources acquired in advance of usage through implicit contracting are usually acquired in lumpy amounts. This category often represents resource spending associated with an organization's salaried and hourly employees. The implicit understanding is that the organization will maintain employment levels even though there may be temporary downturns in the quantity of an activity used. This means that an activity may have unused capacity available. Thus, an increase in demand for an activity across alternatives may not mean that the activity cost will increase (because all the increased demand is absorbed by the unused activity capacity). For example, assume a company has five manufacturing engineers that supply a capacity of 10,000 engineering hours (2,000 hours each). The cost of this activity capacity is $250,000, or $25 per hour. Suppose that this year the company only expects to use 9,000 engineering hours for its normal business. This means that the engineering activity has 1,000 hours of unused capacity. In deciding to reject or accept a special order that requires 500 engineering hours, the cost of engineering would be irrelevant. The order can be filled using unused engineering capacity, and the resource spending is the same for each alternative ($250,000 will be spent whether the order is accepted or not).

However, *if a change in demand across activities produces a change in resource supply*, then the activity cost will change and be relevant to the decision. A change in resource supply means a change in resource spending and consequently a change in activity cost. A change in resource spending can occur in one of two ways: (1) the demand for the resource exceeds the supply (increases resource spending) and (2) the demand for the resource drops permanently and supply exceeds demand enough so that activity capacity can be reduced (decreases resource spending).

To illustrate the first change, consider once again the engineering activity and the special order decision. Suppose that the special order requires 1,500 engineering hours. This exceeds the resource supply. To meet the demand, the organization would need to hire a sixth engineer or perhaps use a consulting engineer. Either way, resource spending increases if the order is accepted; thus, the cost of engineering is now a relevant cost.

To illustrate the second type of change, suppose that the company's manager is considering purchasing a component used for production instead of making it. Assume the same facts about engineering capacity: 10,000 hours available and 9,000 used. If the component is purchased, then the demand for engineering hours will drop from 9,000 to 7,000. This is a permanent reduction because engineering support will no longer be needed for manufacturing the component. Unused capacity is now 3,000 hours, 2,000 permanent and 1,000 temporary. Furthermore, since engineering capacity is acquired in chunks of 2,000, this means that the company can reduce activity capacity and resource spending by laying off one engineer or reassigning the engineer to another plant where the services are in demand. Either way, the resource supply is reduced to 8,000 hours. If an engineer's salary is $50,000, then engineering cost would differ by $50,000 across the make-or-buy alternatives. This cost is then relevant to the decision. However, if the demand for the engineering activity drops by less than 2,000 hours, the increase in unused capacity is not enough to reduce resource supply and resource spending; in this case, the cost of the engineering activity would not be relevant.

Resources Acquired in Advance (Multiperiod Service Capacity)

Often resources are acquired in advance for multiple periods—before the resource demands are known. Leasing or buying a building are examples. Buying multiperiod activity capacity is often done by paying cash up front. In this case, an annual expense may be recognized but no additional resource spending is needed. Up-front resource spending is a sunk cost and thus never relevant. Periodic resource spending, such as leasing, is essentially independent of resource usage. Even if a permanent reduction of activity usage is experienced, it is difficult to reduce resource spending because of formal contractual commitments.

For example, assume a company leases a plant for $100,000 per year for ten years. The plant is capable of producing 20,000 units of a product—the level expected when the plant was leased. After five years, suppose that the demand for the product drops and the plant needs to produce only 15,000 units each year. The lease payment of $100,000 still must be paid each year even though production activity has decreased. Now suppose that demand increases beyond the 20,000-unit capability. In this case, the company may consider acquiring or leasing an additional plant. Here, resource spending could change across alternatives. The decision, however, to acquire long-term activity capacity is not in the realm of tactical decision making. This is not a short-term or small-scale decision. Decisions involving multiperiod capabilities are called capital investment decisions and are covered in Chapter 12. Thus, for the multiperiod resource category, changes in activity demands across alternatives rarely affect resource spending and are therefore not usually relevant for tactical decision making. When resource spending does change, it means assessing the prospect of a multiperiod commitment, which is properly treated using capital investment decision models. Exhibit 11-2 summarizes the activity resource usage model's role in assessing relevancy.

ILLUSTRATIVE EXAMPLES OF TACTICAL DECISION MAKING

Objective 4

Apply the tactical decision-making concepts in a variety of business situations.

The activity resource usage model and the concept of relevancy are valuable tools in making tactical decisions. It is important to see how they are used to solve a variety of problems. Applications include decisions to make or buy a component, to keep or drop a segment or product line, to accept or reject a special order at less than the usual price, and to process a joint product further or sell it at the split-off point. Of course, this is not an exhaustive list. However, the same decision-making principles can be applied to other settings. Once you see how they are used, it is relatively easy to apply them in any appropriate setting. In illustrating the applications, we assume that the first two steps of the tactical decision-making model (see Exhibit 11-1) have already been done. Thus, the emphasis is on tactical cost analysis.

Make-or-Buy Decisions

make-or-buy decisions

Organizations are often faced with **make-or-buy decisions**—decisions of whether to make or to buy components or services used in making a product or providing a service. For example, a physician can buy laboratory tests from external suppliers (hospitals or for-profit laboratories) or these lab tests can be done internally. Similarly, a PC computer manufacturer can make its own disk drives or they can be bought from external suppliers. Make-or-buy decisions are not

Exhibit 11-2
Activity Resource Usage Model and Assessing Relevancy

Resource Category	Demand and Supply Relationships	Relevancy
Acquired as needed	Supply = Demand	
	a. Demand changes	a. Relevant
	b. Demand constant	b. Not relevant
Acquired in advance (short term)	Supply − Demand = Unused capacity	
	a. Demand increase < Unused capacity	a. Not relevant
	b. Demand increase > Unused capacity	b. Relevant
	c. Demand decrease (permanent)	
	1. Activity capacity reduced	1. Relevant
	2. Activity capacity unchanged	2. Not relevant
Acquired in advance (multiperiod capacity)	Supply − Demand = Unused capacity	
	a. Demand increase < Unused capacity	a. Not relevant
	b. Demand decrease (permanent)	b. Not relevant
	c. Demand increase > Unused capacity	c. Capital decision

short-run in nature, but fall into the small-scale tactical decision category. For example, the decision to make or buy may be motivated by cost leadership and/or differentiation strategies. Making instead of buying or buying instead of making may be one way of reducing the cost of producing the main product. Alternatively, choosing to make or buy may be a way of increasing the quality of the component and thus increase the overall quality of the final product (differentiating on the basis of quality).

Cost Analysis: Contemporary Cost Management System To illustrate the cost analysis for a make-or-buy problem, assume that Talmage Company produces a mechanical part used in one of its engines (Talmage produces engines for snow blowers). An outside supplier has offered to sell the part (Part 34B) for $4.75. The company normally produces 100,000 units of the part each year. The activities associated with producing the part and other useful information are listed in Exhibit 11-3. The cost formulas that use units as the activity driver refer to units of Part 34B. The remaining activity cost formulas are more general and reflect all demands made on the activity. All activity capacities are annual capacity measures. The cost of providing space includes annual plant depreciation, property taxes, and annual maintenance. This cost is allocated to the products based on the square feet of space occupied by the product's production equipment. The variable component of each activity represents the cost of resources acquired as needed. The fixed cost component represents the cost of resources acquired in advance of usage. Whenever there is a fixed component, the activity capacity refers to the capacity acquired by spending in advance of usage. Units of purchase indicate how many units of the activity (as measured by its driver) must be acquired at a time (if more than one, it is called a "lumpy" amount). For resources acquired in advance of usage, the cost of acquiring the lumpy amount is obtained by dividing the activity fixed cost by activity capacity and then multiplying this amount by the units of purchase. For example, the cost of acquiring three units of supervision is $60,000 [($300,000/15) × 3].

From the perspective of tactical cost analysis, whether or not Talmage should continue making Part 34B or buy it from an external supplier depends on how much *resource spending* can be reduced because of the ability to reduce resource

Exhibit 11-3
Activity and Cost Information

Activity	Cost Driver	Cost Formula	Activity Capacity	Expected Activity Usage	Part 34B Activity Usage	Units of Purchase
Using materials	Units	Y = $0.5X	As needed	100,000	100,000	1
Using direct labor	Units	Y = $2X	As needed	100,000	100,000	1
Providing supervision	Number of lines	Y = $300,000	15	15	3	3
Moving materials	Number of moves	Y = $250,000 + $0.60X	250,000	240,000	40,000	25,000
Providing power	Machine hours	Y = $3X	As needed	30,000	30,000	1
Inspecting products	Inspection hours	Y = $280,000 + $1.50X	16,000	14,000	2,000	2,000
Setting up equipment	Setup hours	Y = $600,000	60,000	58,000	6,000	2,000
Providing space	Square feet	Y = $1,000,000	50,000	50,000	5,000	50,000
Equipment depreciation	Units	Y = $0.50X	120,000	100,000	100,000	15,000

usage (by buying instead of making). If Talmage buys Part 34B instead of making it, *resource usage* decreases for each of the nine activities (by the amount indicated in the Part 34B Activity Usage column). Thus, for activities acquired in advance with multiperiod capacity, resource spending will not change, and so the cost of these activities is not relevant (see Exhibit 11-2). This includes the following activities: providing space and equipment depreciation. For activities with resources acquired as needed, activity demand changes and so the cost of these resources is relevant to the decision (see Exhibit 11-2). This includes using materials, using direct labor, providing power, and the variable components of moving materials and inspecting products. The change in resource spending is simply the cost per unit of driver multiplied by the variable rate in the cost formula. For example, for materials, resource spending decreases by $50,000 if Part 34B is purchased rather than made ($0.50 × 100,000). The variable cost of moving materials, on the other hand, decreases by $24,000 ($0.60 × 40,000 moves). The changes in costs for the five activities with variable components (resources acquired as needed) are listed below:

Activity	Make[a]	Buy[b]	Differential Cost[c]
Using materials	$ 50,000	$ 0	$ 50,000
Using direct labor	200,000	0	200,000
Moving materials	144,000	120,000	24,000
Providing power	90,000	0	90,000
Inspecting products	21,000	18,000	3,000

[a] Variable rate × Expected activity usage
[b] Variable rate × (Expected usage − Part 34B usage)
[c] Make activity cost − Buy activity cost

Short-term resources acquired in advance of usage is the trickiest category to analyze. There are four activities that fall in this resource category: providing supervision, moving materials, inspecting products, and setting up equipment. For the make-or-buy decision, all four activities experience a permanent decrease in activity demand. Thus, the issue is whether or not activity capacity can be reduced so that resource spending can be reduced (see Exhibit 11-2). Assume that any current unused capacity (Capacity − Expected usage) is temporary. Thus, the permanent demand decrease is measured only by the drop in Part 34B activity usage. Resource spending can be reduced if activity capacity can be decreased because of the permanent drop in resource usage. For example, providing supervision must be purchased in units of 3. The decrease in demand for this activity by dropping Part 34B is 3 units. Thus, the cost of providing supervision is relevant because resource spending on supervision can be decreased by $60,000 [($300,000/15) × 3]. The analysis for moving materials provides additional insight. If Part 34B is no longer made, the demand for this activity will decrease by 40,000 units. However, since capacity for moving materials is purchased in units of 25,000, activity capacity can only be decreased by 25,000 units. The reduction in resource spending is $25,000 [($250,000/250,000) × 25,000]. The cost is relevant, but the difference in cost between the two alternatives is less than the reduction of the cost of resource usage because of the lumpy nature of the resource. Similar analyses can be done for the inspections and setup activities. The changes in activity cost for short-term resources acquired in advance are listed below:

Activity	Make[a]	Buy[b]	Differential Cost[c]
Providing supervision	$300,000	$240,000	$60,000
Moving materials	250,000	225,000	25,000
Inspecting products	280,000	245,000	35,000
Setting up equipment	600,000	540,000	60,000

[a] Fixed activity cost
[b] (Fixed cost/Activity capacity) × Reduction in activity capacity
[c] Make activity cost − Buy activity cost

To complete the cost analysis, we only need information concerning the activity costs that are added *because* of buying rather than making. The most obvious is the acquisition cost of the part itself. For simplicity, let's assume that the procurement activities (purchasing, receiving, and paying suppliers) have sufficient unused capacity to absorb any increase in demand from acquiring Part 34B. With this assumption, the elements of the make-or-buy analysis are now complete. The cost analysis is summarized in Exhibit 11-4. The costs for each activity resource category are aggregated so that we have a total picture of the effects of making versus buying. The tactical cost analysis supports the buy alternative. This alternative provides a $72,000 benefit over the make alternative. Based on 100,000 units, buying is cheaper by $0.72 per unit ($72,000/100,000). All other things being equal, Talmage should buy Part 34B instead of making it.

Cost Analysis: Traditional Cost Management System A traditional cost management system would not supply detailed information about nonunit-level activities and costs. A traditional system would provide only unit-level activity data. Nonunit-level costs are all assumed to be fixed with respect to changes in production volume. A typical traditional analysis would identify the costs of

Exhibit 11-4
Contemporary Make-or-Buy Analysis: Talmage Company

Activity	Make	Buy	Differential Cost
Using materials	$ 50,000	$ 0	$ 50,000
Using direct labor	200,000	0	200,000
Providing supervision	300,000	240,000	60,000
Moving materials	394,000	345,000	49,000
Providing power	90,000	0	90,000
Inspecting products	301,000	263,000	38,000
Setting up equipment	600,000	540,000	60,000
Acquiring Part 34B	0	475,000	(475,000)
Totals	$1,935,000	$1,863,000	$ 72,000

materials, labor, power, and supervision of Part 34B as relevant. (Supervision of Part 34B would be viewed as a direct fixed cost and would disappear if production of Part 34B stops; therefore, it's relevant). All other costs would be classified as irrelevant because they would not change as production volume changes. A summary of the traditional make-or-buy analysis is provided in Exhibit 11-5. The traditional analysis supports the make alternative, indicating a $75,000 benefit to making over buying. This analysis is more limited because it has less access to activity information. The use of a more limited information set may lead to erroneous decisions.

Keep-or-Drop Decisions

keep-or-drop decisions

Often a manager needs to determine whether a segment, such as a product line, should be kept or dropped. **Keep-or-drop decisions** use relevant cost analysis to determine whether a segment of a business should be kept or dropped. In a traditional cost management system, segmented income statements, using unit-based fixed or variable costs, improve the ability to make keep-or-drop decisions. Similarly, by increasing traceability, segmented reporting using ABC classifications and the resource usage model offers a significant improvement in information content over the unit-based, variable-costing segmented report. JIT manufacturing offers even more capabilities. By localizing many costs that were formerly common to many products (e.g., maintenance, materials handling, and inspection) and by changing the behavior of some costs (e.g., direct labor), the number of directly attributable costs has been increased. Decisions to drop or keep a segment are facilitated by the increased number of directly attributable costs in a JIT environment.

Exhibit 11-5
Traditional Make-or-Buy Analysis: Talmage Company

Activity	Make	Buy	Differential Cost
Using materials	$ 50,000	$ 0	$ 50,000
Using direct labor	200,000	0	200,000
Providing supervision	300,000	240,000	60,000
Providing power	90,000	0	90,000
Acquiring Part 34B	0	475,000	(475,000)
Totals	$640,000	$715,000	$ (75,000)

Keep-or-Drop: Traditional Analysis The logic underlying a traditional keep-or-drop analysis is fairly straightforward. Revenues and costs that belong to a segment are identified. Directly attributable revenues, unit-based variable costs, and directly attributable fixed costs are defined as costs that belong to the segment. If the segment is dropped, then only the traceable revenues and costs should vanish; thus, the traceable revenues and costs are relevant to the decision. Furthermore, the traceable income (loss) determines whether a segment should be dropped or kept. If the segment income is positive, then the segment is kept; if negative, then the decision is to drop the segment (this assumes that the segment income is expected to persist over time). Exhibit 11-6 shows a traditional segmented income statement, where products are defined as segments. More detail is provided on the statement than usual so that the effects of moving to an activity-based statement can be illustrated more clearly. The statement indicates that both seat covers and floor mats are providing positive product margins. It is unlikely, based on the information here, that the company would drop either product line. Yet overall profitability for the company is not impressive—barely above the break-even point. An important issue—in fact, a critical issue in segmented analysis—is the ability to trace costs to individual segments. Improved traceability is offered by ABC classifications.

Keep-or-Drop: ABC Analysis Exhibit 11-7 presents an activity-based segmented statement. The same example used for traditional segmented reporting is used so that traditional and contemporary keep-or-drop decisions can be compared. For the ABC approach, machine depreciation is traced to each segment using machine hours to measure usage (units-of-production depreciation method). Two batch-level costs—inspecting products and materials handling—are assigned to

Exhibit 11-6
Traditional Segmented Income Statement

	Seat Covers	Floor Mats	Total
Sales	$950,000	$1,680,000	$2,630,000
Less: Variable costs			
Direct materials	300,000	400,000	700,000
Direct labor	210,000	210,000	420,000
Maintenance	90,000	90,000	180,000
Power	35,000	25,000	60,000
Commissions	30,000	40,000	70,000
Contribution margin	$285,000	$ 915,000	$1,200,000
Less: Direct fixed costs			
Advertising	30,000	20,000	50,000
Supervision	50,000	50,000	100,000
Product margin	$205,000	$ 845,000	$1,050,000
Less: Common fixed expenses			
Depreciation—machinery			100,000
Depreciation—plant			160,000
Inspecting products			200,000
Customer service			150,000
General administration			180,000
Materials handling			140,000
Sales administration			80,000
Income before taxes			$ 40,000

Exhibit 11-7
ABC Segmented Income Statement

	Seat Covers	Floor Mats	Total
Sales	$ 950,000	$1,680,000	$2,630,000
Less: Unit-level variable expenses			
Direct materials	300,000	400,000	700,000
Direct labor	210,000	210,000	420,000
Maintenance	90,000	90,000	180,000
Power	35,000	25,000	60,000
Commissions	30,000	40,000	70,000
Contribution margin	$ 285,000	$ 915,000	$1,200,000
Less: Traceable expenses			
Advertising, direct fixed	30,000	20,000	50,000
Supervision, direct fixed	50,000	50,000	100,000
Machine depreciation, traceable			
fixed	50,000	50,000	100,000
Inspecting products, nonunit			
variable	20,000	10,000	30,000
Inspecting products, traceable fixed	80,000	50,000	130,000
Materials handling, nonunit variable	10,000	14,000	24,000
Materials handling, traceable fixed	70,000	26,000	96,000
Customer service, traceable fixed	45,000	75,000	120,000
Sales administration, traceable fixed	50,000	30,000	80,000
Product margin	$(120,000)	$ 590,000	$ 470,000
Less: Common expenses			
Unused activity:			
Inspecting products			40,000
Materials handling			20,000
Customer service			30,000
Facility-level:			
Plant depreciation			160,000
General administration			180,000
Income before taxes			$ 40,000

products using batch-level drivers (number of batches and moves). Assume that cost analysts have determined that these two batch-level activities have both resources acquired in advance and resources acquired as needed. Resources acquired as needed are labeled as a nonunit variable expense. The cost of resources acquired in advance of usage is treated as a fixed expense and, where possible, is divided into two categories: *traceable fixed expenses*, representing the cost of fixed resource usage traced to each segment using activity drivers, and *unused activity expenses*, treated as a common fixed expense. Notice that the cost of facility-level activities is not traced to the two products. There are also two product-level costs—customer service and sales administration—assigned to products using the number of complaints and number of sales orders. Resources associated with these two activities are all acquired in advance of usage, and the resources used by each product are labeled as traceable fixed expenses. It could also be argued that advertising and supervision are product-level activities (the cost of these activities increases as the number of products increases). There is no need, however, to use an activity driver to trace advertising or supervision costs to each product line. Advertising and supervision costs are traceable to each product using direct tracing and are labeled as direct fixed costs.

The ABC segmented statement provides a much different view of product profitability than does the traditional segmented statement. First, we see that the company is paying for resources that are not being used, totaling $90,000. Second, seat covers are unprofitable—and are causing a significant drain on company resources. Thus, the ABC segmented income statement reveals three possible ways of increasing income: (1) reducing resource spending by exploiting the current unused activity capacities, (2) eliminating the unprofitable product line, and (3) a combination of (1) and (2).

Of the three ways of increasing income, the last two consider the possibility of dropping the seat cover line. Before making a decision about keeping or dropping the unprofitable line, the manager needs to know how much resource spending will change. First, all unit and nonunit variable expenses will vanish if the line is dropped, as will direct fixed expenses. Notice, however, that machine depreciation—even though unitized—is not relevant to the decision (depreciation is an allocation of a sunk cost). Dropping the unprofitable line increases the cost of unused resources from $90,000 to $335,000 (the total increases by the sum of the seat cover's traceable fixed expenses, excluding machine depreciation, since it's not relevant). If seat covers are dropped, the demand for inspecting products, customer service, materials handling, and sales administration will decrease. Thus, the key to completing the keep-or-drop analysis is assessing how much of the cost of unused capacity for these activities can be eliminated. Exhibit 11-8 provides the capacity, seat cover usage, unused capacity (before dropping), and units of purchase for each of the four activities with potentially relevant traceable fixed expenses. The unused capacity (before dropping) for inspecting and customer service is viewed as permanent—a result of a quality improvement program implemented last year. Unused capacity for the materials-handling activity is temporary.

Using the information in Exhibit 11-8, the keep-or-drop analysis can be completed. The full analysis is presented in Exhibit 11-9. Dropping the product saves the company $45,000 per year. Part of the benefit comes from adding enough to already existing unused capacity so that activity capacity can be reduced, causing a reduction in resource spending. The inspecting products activity illustrates this possibility. The activity could be done by two salaried inspectors, who can each inspect 85 batches per year. Adding 45 more batches of unused activity to the existing unused activity then makes it possible to lay off one inspector.

Special-Order Decisions

Price discrimination laws require that firms sell identical products at the same price to competing customers in the same market. These restrictions do not apply

Exhibit 11-8
Activity Information: Keep-or-Drop Analysis

Activity	Activity Driver	Activity Capacity	Unused Activity	Seat Cover Activity Usage	Units of Purchase
Inspecting products	No. of batches	170	40	45	85
Materials handling	No. of moves	2,320	400	1,400	350
Customer service	No. of complaints	300	60	90	60
Sales administration	No. of sales orders	500	0	150	500

Exhibit 11-9
Contemporary Keep-or-Drop Analysis

	Keep Alternative	Drop Alternative
Contribution margin	$285,000	$ 0
Supervision, direct fixed	(30,000)	0
Advertising, direct fixed	(50,000)	0
Inspecting products,[a] nonunit variable	(20,000)	0
Inspecting products, traceable fixed	(80,000)	0
Inspecting products, unused capacity	(40,000)	0
Materials handling,[b] nonunit variable	(10,000)	0
Materials handling, traceable fixed	(70,000)	0
Customer service,[c] traceable fixed	(45,000)	(15,000)
Total	$ (60,000)	$(15,000)

[a] Dropping seat covers will increase the unused capacity from 40 batches to 85 batches. Since activity capacity is purchased in units of 85, this allows the resource spending to be reduced by the traceable fixed expenses plus the cost of unused capacity.
[b] Dropping seat covers will increase the unused capacity from 400 moves to 1,800 moves; however, only 1,400 of the unused capacity is permanent (corresponding to the seat cover's activity usage). Since move capacity must be purchased in units of 350, capacity can be reduced by exactly 1,400 moves, saving all the traceable fixed activity expenses.
[c] Since capacity is purchased in blocks of 60, the existing unused capacity can be reduced by this amount regardless of whether the product is dropped or kept and is therefore not relevant. If the product is dropped, the effect is to create 90 more units of unused capacity. Of these 90 units, 60 units of capacity can be eliminated, reducing the cost of resource spending by $30,000 [{($45,000 + $75,000 + $30,000)/300} × 60].

special-order
decisions

to competitive bids or to noncompeting customers. Bid prices can vary to customers in the same market, and firms often have the opportunity to consider one-time special orders from potential customers in markets not ordinarily served. **Special-order decisions** focus on whether a specially priced order should be accepted or rejected. Special-order decisions are examples of tactical decisions with a short-term focus. Increasing short-term profits is the limited objective represented by these type of decisions. Special care should be taken so that acceptance of special orders does not jeopardize normal distribution channels or adversely affect other strategic elements. With this qualification, it should be noted that special orders often can be attractive, especially when the firm is operating below its maximum productive capacity and when other activities have sufficient unused capacity to absorb any incremental demands the order may make. For this situation, the company can focus its analysis on resources acquired as needed—because this will be the source of any increase in resource spending attributable to the order. Relevance is established by assessing where activity demand increases.

Suppose, for example, that Polar-Ray, Inc., an ice-cream company, is operating at 80 percent of its productive capacity. Assume a similar condition exists for nonunit-level activities. The company has a capacity of 20 million half-gallon units. The company expects to produce 8 million units each of regular and premium ice cream. The total costs associated with producing and selling 8 million units of premium ice cream are given in Exhibit 11-10.

An ice-cream distributor from a geographic region not normally served by the company has offered to buy 2 million units of premium ice cream at $1.75 per unit, provided its own label can be attached to the product. The distributor has also agreed to pay the transportation costs. Since the distributor approached the company directly, there is no sales commission. The company estimates that the special order will increase the purchase orders by 10,000, receiving orders by

Exhibit 11-10
Data for Polar-Ray, Inc.:
Premium Ice Cream

	Total[a]	Unit Cost
Unit-level variable costs:		
Dairy ingredients	$ 5,600	$0.70
Sugar	800	0.10
Flavoring	1,200	0.15
Direct labor	2,000	0.25
Packaging	1,600	0.20
Commissions	160	0.02
Distribution	240	0.03
Other	400	0.05
Total unit-level costs	$12,000	$1.50
Nonunit-level variable costs:		
Purchasing ($8 × 40,000 purchase orders)	$ 320	$0.04
Receiving ($6 × 80,000 receiving orders)	480	0.06
Setting up ($8,000 × 50 setups)	400	0.05
Total nonunit-level costs	$ 1,200	$0.15
Fixed activity costs:		
Total fixed costs[b]	$ 1,600	$0.20
Total costs	$14,800	$1.85
Wholesale selling price	$20,000	$2.50

[a] All costs expressed in thousands.
[b] The total cost of providing capacity for all activities within the firm asssigned to premium.

20,000, and setups by 13. Furthermore, although the order increases the demand for these and other activities, existing unused activity capacity is sufficient to absorb the increased demand. Should the company accept this order or reject it?

The offer of $1.75 is well below the normal selling price of $2.50; in fact, it is even below the total unit cost. Nonetheless, accepting the order may be profitable for the company. The company does have idle capacity, and the order will not displace other units being produced to sell at the normal price. Additionally, many of the costs are not relevant; spending for resources acquired in advance of usage will not change regardless of whether the order is accepted or rejected.

If the order is accepted, a benefit of $1.75 per unit will be realized that otherwise wouldn't be. However, all of the unit-level variable costs except for distribution ($0.03) and commissions ($0.02) also will be incurred, producing a cost of $1.45 per unit. Furthermore, the nonunit-level variable costs will also be incurred, producing a total incremental cost of $304,000, or $0.152 per unit (for an order of 2 million units). Therefore, the company will see a net benefit of $0.148 ($1.75 − $1.602). Thus, Polar-Ray's profits would increase by $296,000 ($0.148 × 2,000,000). The relevant cost analysis is summarized in Exhibit 11-11.

Decisions to Sell or Process Further

joint products

Joint products have common processes and costs of production up to a split-off point. At that point, they become distinguishable. For example, certain minerals such as copper and gold may both be found in a given ore. The ore must be mined, crushed, and treated before the copper and gold are separated. The point

split-off point

of separation is called the **split-off point**. The costs of mining, crushing, and treatment are common to both products.

Exhibit 11-11
Special-Order Cost Analysis: Polar-Ray, Inc.

	Accept	Reject	Differential Effect
Revenues	$3,500,000	$0	$3,500,000
Dairy ingredients	(1,400,000)	0	(1,400,000)
Sugar	(200,000)	0	(200,000)
Flavorings	(300,000)	0	(300,000)
Direct labor	(500,000)	0	(500,000)
Packaging	(400,000)	0	(400,000)
Other	(100,000)	0	(100,000)
Purchasing	(80,000)	0	(80,000)
Receiving	(120,000)	0	(120,000)
Setting up	(104,000)	0	(104,000)
Total	$ 296,000	$0	$ 296,000

Often joint products are sold at the split-off point. But sometimes it is more profitable to process a joint product further, beyond the split-off point, prior to selling it. Determining whether to **sell or process further** is an important decision that a manager must make.

sell or process further

To illustrate, consider Delrio Corporation. Delrio is an agricultural corporation that produces and sells fresh produce and canned food products. The San Juan Division of Delrio specializes in tomato products. San Juan has a large tomato farm that produces all the tomatoes used in its products. The farm is divided into manageable plots. Each plot produces approximately 1,500 pounds of tomatoes; this defines a load. Each plot must be cultivated, fertilized, sprayed, watered, and harvested. When the tomatoes are ripened, they are harvested. The tomatoes are then transported to a warehouse, where they are washed and sorted. The approximate cost of all these activities is $200 per load.

Tomatoes are sorted into two grades (A and B). Grade A tomatoes are larger and better shaped than Grade B. Grade A tomatoes are sold to large supermarkets. Grade B tomatoes are sent to the canning plant where they are processed into catsup, tomato sauce, and tomato paste. Each load produces about 1,000 pounds of Grade A tomatoes and 500 pounds of Grade B tomatoes. Recently, the manager of the canning plant requested that the Grade A tomatoes be used for a Delrio hot sauce. Studies have indicated that the Grade A tomatoes provided a better flavor and consistency for the sauce than did Grade B tomatoes. Furthermore, Grade B tomatoes are fully utilized for other products.

The hot sauce production would require using all of the Grade A output (from the San Juan farm). Grade A tomatoes are sold to large supermarkets for $0.40 per pound. In deciding whether to sell Grade A tomatoes at split-off or to process them further and sell the hot sauce, the common costs of cultivating, spraying, watering, and so on, are not relevant. Delrio must pay the $200 per load for these activities regardless of whether it sells the Grade A tomatoes at split-off or processes further. However, the revenues earned at split-off are likely to differ from the revenues that would be received if the Grade A tomatoes were sold as hot sauce. Therefore, revenues are a relevant item.

The relevance of processing costs depends on the nature of the resource demands. Clearly, the demand for resources acquired as needed will increase, and these costs are relevant (for such things as labor, peppers, water, bottles, and spices). For resources acquired in advance of usage, the increase in resource spending will depend on how much existing activity capacity must be increased. For example, the receiving activity may increase in capacity to handle the increased volume of tomatoes. The increased resource spending for receiving would be a relevant processing cost. However, it may be that the inspecting activity has sufficient permanent unused capacity to deal with the inspection requirements for the sauce. If so, then the cost of inspection would not be relevant (the cost of inspection resources is the same whether or not the hot sauce is produced).

Assume that the hot sauce sells for $1.50 per bottle. Also assume that the additional processing costs, including only resources acquired as needed and increases in activity capacity, amount to $1,000. Thus, the total revenues at split-off for Grade A tomatoes are $400 ($0.40 × 1,000). If the Grade A tomatoes are processed into hot sauce, the total revenues are $1,500 ($1.50 × 1,000 bottles). The incremental revenues from processing further are $1,100 per half ton of Grade A tomatoes ($1,500 − $400). Since revenues increase by $1,100 and processing costs by $1,000, the net benefit of processing the Grade A tomatoes is $100 per half ton. The analysis is summarized as follows:

	Sell	Process Further	Differential Amount to Process Further
Revenues	$400	$1,500	$1,100
Processing cost	—	(1,000)	(1,000)
Total	$400	$ 500	$ 100

Relevant Costing and Ethical Behavior

Relevant costs are used in making tactical decisions—decisions that have an immediate view or limited objective in mind. In making these decisions, however, decision makers should always keep the decisions within an ethical framework. Reaching objectives is important, but how you get there is perhaps more important. Unfortunately, many managers have the opposite view. Part of the reason for the problem is the extreme pressure to perform that many managers feel. Often the individual who is not a top performer may be laid off or demoted. Under such conditions, the temptation is often great to engage in questionable behavior.

For example, the price of cashmere decreased greatly in the early 1990s. The lower price of cashmere fiber meant that sweaters became much more affordable and imports from China and Hong Kong more than doubled. These sweaters represented special purchases to the U.S. department and specialty stores. Unfortunately, the quality of the sweaters was uneven. May Department Stores tested its 1994 private label sweaters from Hong Kong. The company found that the wool (not cashmere) content ranged from 10 to 30 percent, and relabeled the sweaters to show the correct fiber content. Some other stores chose to take the "low road" and continued to advertise and sell their multifabric blend sweaters as "100 percent cashmere."

There can be endless debates about what is right and what is wrong. As was pointed out in Chapter 1, ethical standards have been developed to provide guidance for individuals. Additionally, many companies are hiring full-time ethics officers. Often these officers set up hot lines so that employees can call and register complaints or ask about the propriety of certain actions. However, as pointed out in an article in *Fortune*: "The old advice is still the best: Don't do anything on the job you wouldn't want your mother to read about with her morning coffee."[1]

1.   Kenneth Labich, "The New Crisis in Business Ethics," *Fortune*, April 20, 1992, p. 172.

SUMMARY

Tactical decision making consists of choosing among alternatives with an immediate or limited end in view. Tactical decisions can be short-term or small-scale in nature but must be made so that larger strategic objectives are served. Tactical decision making follows a five-step process. The heart of the process is called tactical cost analysis. Tactical cost analysis includes identifying predicted costs and benefits associated with alternatives, eliminating those that are not relevant, and comparing the relevant costs and benefits. All other things being equal, the alternative with the greatest net benefit should be chosen.

An essential element of tactical cost analysis is identifying relevant costs and benefits. Costs and revenues are relevant provided they pertain to the future and differ across the alternatives being considered. All past costs are sunk and never relevant. The role of past costs in tactical decision making is predictive. Past costs can be used to estimate future costs.

Cost behavior is fundamental to understanding relevancy. The activity resource usage model is a useful tool for determining relevancy. Resources can be classified into three categories: those acquired as needed, those acquired in advance (short-term), and those acquired in advance of usage (multiperiod). The cost of resources for the first category is relevant provided that demand changes across alternatives. The second category is relevant provided that the demand changes across alternatives lead to a change in activity capacity. Changes in activity capacity cause resource spending to change. The third category is usually not relevant for tactical decision making.

Examples of tactical decisions include make-or-buy choices, keep-or-drop decisions, special-order decisions, and sell-or-process-further decisions. Special-order decisions are examples of tactical decisions with a short-term orientation. The other three are examples of small-scale tactical decisions.

REVIEW PROBLEM AND SOLUTION

Activity Resource Usage Model, Strategic Elements, and Relevant Costing

Perkins Company has idle capacity. Recently, Perkins received an offer to sell 2,000 units of one of its products to a new customer in a geographic region not normally serviced. The offering price is $10 per unit. The product normally sells for $14. The activity-based accounting system provides the following information:

	Cost Driver	Unused Capacity	Quantity Demanded*	Activity Rate**	
				Fixed	Variable
Direct materials	Units	0	2,000	—	$3.00
Direct labor	Direct labor hours	0	400	—	7.00
Setups	Setup hours	0	25	$50.00	8.00
Machining	Machine hours	6,000	4,000	4.00	1.00

*This only represents the amount of resources demanded by the special order being considered.
**Fixed activity rate is the price that must be paid per unit of activity capacity. The variable activity rate is the price per unit of resource for resources acquired as needed.

Although the fixed activity rate for setups is $25 per hour, any expansion of this resource must be acquired in blocks. The units of purchase for setups is 100 hours of setup servicing. Thus, any expansion of setup activity must be done 100 hours at a time. The price per hour is the fixed activity rate.

REQUIRED:

1. Compute the change in income for Perkins Company if the order is accepted. Comment on whether the order should be accepted or not (in particular, discuss the strategic issues).
2. Suppose that the setup activity had 50 hours of unused capacity. How does this affect the analysis?

Solution

1. The relevant costs are those that change if the order is accepted. These costs would consist of the variable activity costs (resources acquired as needed) plus any cost of acquiring additional activity capacity (resources acquired in advance of usage). The income will change by the following amount:

Revenues ($10 × 2,000 units)	$20,000
Less: Increase in resource spending	
Direct materials ($3.00 × 2,000 units)	(6,000)
Direct labor ($7 × 400 Direct labor hours)	(2,800)
Setups [($50 × 100 hours) + ($8 × 25 hours)]	(5,200)
Machining ($1.00 × 4,000 machine hours)	(4,000)
Income change	$ 2,000

Special orders need to be examined carefully before acceptance. This order offers an increase in income of $2,000, but it does require expansion of the setup activity capacity. If this expansion is short-run in nature, then it may be worth it. If it entails a long-term commitment, then the company would be exchanging a one-year benefit of $2,000 for an annual commitment of $5,000. In this case, the order should be rejected. Even if the commitment is short-term, other strategic factors need to be considered. Will this order affect any regular sales? Is the company looking for a permanent solution to its idle capacity or are special orders becoming a habit—a response pattern that may eventually prove disastrous? Will acceptance adversely affect the company's normal distribution channels? Acceptance of the order should be consistent with the company's strategic position.

2. If 50 hours of excess setup capacity exist, then the setup activity can absorb the special order's activity demands with no additional resource spending required for additional capacity. Thus, the profitability of the special order would be increased by $5,000 (the increase in resource spending that would have been required). Thus, total income would increase by $7,000 if the order is accepted.

KEY TERMS

QUESTIONS FOR WRITING AND DISCUSSION

1. What is tactical decision making?
2. "Tactical decisions are often small-scale decisions that serve a larger purpose." Explain what this means.
3. What is tactical cost analysis?
4. What steps in the tactical decision model correspond to tactical cost analysis?
5. What is a relevant cost? A relevant revenue?
6. Explain why depreciation on an existing asset is always irrelevant.
7. Give an example of a future cost that is not relevant.
8. Relevant costs always determine which alternative should be chosen. Do you agree? Explain.
9. Can direct materials ever be irrelevant in a make-or-buy decision? Explain.
10. Give an example of a fixed cost that is relevant.
11. When, if ever, is depreciation a relevant cost?
12. What role do past costs play in tactical cost analysis?
13. When will resources acquired as used and needed be relevant to a decision?
14. When will the cost of resources acquired in advance (through implicit contracting) be relevant to a decision?
15. Explain why resources acquired in advance with a multiperiod commitment are usually not relevant to a tactical decision.
16. What are the main differences between a traditional and contemporary make-or-buy analysis?
17. Explain why activity-based segmented reporting provides more insight concerning keep-or-drop decisions.
18. Suppose that a product can be sold at split-off for $5,000 or processed further at a cost of $1,000 and then sold for $6,400. Should the product be processed further?
19. Should joint costs be considered in a sell-or-process-further decision? Explain.
20. Why would a firm ever offer a price on a product that is below its full cost?

EXERCISES AND PROBLEMS

**11-1
Identifying
Problem and
Alternatives;
Relevant Costs**

LO 1, 2

Norton Products, Inc., manufactures potentiometers (a potentiometer is a device that adjusts electrical resistance). Currently, all parts necessary for the assembly of products are produced internally. Norton has a single plant located in Wichita, Kansas. The facilities for the manufacture of potentiometers are leased, with five years remaining on the lease. All equipment is owned by the company. Because of increases in demand, production has been expanded significantly over the five years of operation, straining the capacity of the leased facilities. Currently, the company needs more warehousing and office space, as well as more space for the production of plastic moldings. The current output of these moldings, used to make potentiometers, needs to be expanded to accommodate the increased demand for the main product.

Leo Tidwell, owner and president of Norton Products, has asked his vice president of marketing, John Tidwell, and his vice president of finance, Linda Thayn, to meet and discuss the problem of limited capacity. This is the second meeting the three have had concerning the problem. In the first meeting, Leo rejected Linda's proposal to build the company's own plant. He believed it was too risky to invest the capital necessary to build a plant at this stage of the company's development. The combination of leasing a larger facility and subleasing the current plant was also considered but was rejected; subleasing would be difficult, if not impossible. At the end of the first meeting, Leo asked John to explore the possibility of leasing another facility comparable to the current one. He also assigned Linda the task of identifying other possible solutions. As the second meeting began, Leo asked John to give a report on the leasing alternative.

"After some careful research," John responded, "I'm afraid that the idea of leasing an additional plant is not a very good one. Although we have some space problems, our current level of production doesn't justify another plant. In fact, I expect it will be at least five years before we need to be concerned about expanding into another facility like the one we have now. My market studies reveal a modest growth in sales over the next five years. All this growth can be absorbed by our current production capacity. The large increases in demand that we experienced the past five years are not likely to be repeated. Leasing another plant would be an overkill solution."

"Even modest growth will aggravate our current space problems," Leo observed. "As you both know, we are already operating three production shifts. But, John, you are right—except for plastic moldings, we could expand production, particularly during the graveyard shift. Linda, I hope that you have been successful in identifying some other possible solutions. Some fairly quick action is needed."

"Fortunately," Linda replied, "I believe that I have two feasible alternatives. One is to rent an additional building to be used for warehousing. By transferring our warehousing needs to the new building, we will free up internal space for offices and for expanding the production of plastic moldings. I have located a building within two miles of our plant that we could use. It has the capacity to handle our current needs and the modest growth that John mentioned. The second alternative may be even more attractive. We currently produce all the parts that we use to manufacture potentiometers, including shafts and bushings. In the last several months, the market has been flooded with these two parts. Prices have tumbled as a result. It might be better to buy shafts and bushings instead of making them. If we stop internal production of shafts and bushings, this would free up the space we need. Well, Leo, what do you think? Are these alternatives feasible? Or should I continue my search for additional solutions?"

"I like both alternatives," responded Leo. "In fact, they are exactly the types of solutions we are looking for. All we have to do now is choose the one best for our company."

REQUIRED:

1. Define the problem facing Norton Products.
2. Identify all the alternatives that were considered by Norton Products. Which ones were classified as not feasible? Why? Now identify the feasible alternatives.
3. For the feasible alternatives, what are some potential costs and benefits associated with each alternative? Of the costs that you have identified, which do you think are relevant to the decision?

11-2
Determining
Relevant Costs
LO 2

Kim Murphy purchased a 1992 LeBaron Convertible in 1997 for $5,000. Since purchasing the car, she has spent the following amounts on parts and labor:

Fuel pump	$ 120
Canvas top	265
Master cylinder	135
Disk brakes	150
Hoses, plugs	80
Labor	250
Total	$1,000

Kim is not totally satisfied with the LeBaron. To bring the car to a condition that she feels it should be, she anticipates the following costs of restoration:

Rebuilt engine	$ 700
New paint job	800
Tires	360
New interior	500
Miscellaneous maintenance	340
Total	$2,700

In a visit to a used car dealer, Kim found a four-year-old Mitsubishi Eclipse in mint condition for $7,000. Kim has advertised and found that she can sell the LeBaron for only $3,000. If she buys the Eclipse, Kim will pay cash, but she would need to sell the LeBaron.

REQUIRED:

1. In trying to decide whether to restore the LeBaron or buy the Eclipse, Kim is distressed because she already has spent $6,000 on the LeBaron. The investment seems too much to give up. How would you react to Kim's concern?
2. List all costs that are relevant to Kim's decision. What advice would you give Kim?

11-3
Resource Supply and Usage; Cost Behavior; Relevancy
LO 3

Brannon Manufacturing Company has three salaried clerks to process purchase orders. Each clerk is paid a salary of $30,000 and is capable of processing 5,000 purchase orders per year (if the clerk works efficiently). Each clerk uses a PC and laser printer in processing orders. Time available on each PC system is sufficient to process 5,000 orders per year. The depreciation on each PC system is $1,200 per year. In addition to the salaries, Brannon spends $9,000 for forms, postage, etc. (assuming 15,000 purchase orders are processed). During the year, 13,000 orders were processed.

REQUIRED:

1. Classify the resources associated with purchasing as (1) those acquired as used and needed, (2) those acquired in advance (short-term), and (3) those acquired in advance (multiperiod).
2. Compute the total activity availability, and break this into activity usage and unused activity.
3. Calculate the total cost of resources supplied (activity cost), and break this into the cost of activity used and the cost of unused activity.
4. (a) Suppose that a large special order will cause an additional 1,000 purchase orders. What purchasing costs are relevant? By how much will purchasing costs increase if the order is accepted? (b) Suppose that the special order causes 2,500 additional purchase orders. How will your answer to (a) change?

11-4
Special-Order Decision; Traditional Analysis; Qualitative Aspects
LO 4

Cindy Burnson, the manager of Fondike Company, was agonizing over an offer for an order requesting 7,000 boxes of birthday cards. Fondike was operating at 70 percent of its capacity and could use the extra business. Unfortunately, the order's offering price of $7.75 per box was below the cost to produce the cards. The controller was opposed to taking a loss on the deal. However, the personnel manager argued in favor of accepting the order even though a loss would be incurred; it would avoid the problem of layoffs and would help maintain the community image of the company. The full cost to produce a box of birthday cards is presented below:

Direct materials	$2.00
Direct labor	3.00
Variable overhead	1.50
Fixed overhead	2.50
Total	$9.00

The order is from a customer in a region not ordinarily serviced by the company. No variable selling or administrative expenses would be associated with the order. Nonunit-level activity costs are a small percentage of total costs and therefore not considered.

REQUIRED:

1. Assume that the company would accept the order only if it increased total profits. Should the company accept or reject the order? Provide supporting computations.

2. Consider the personnel manager's concerns. Discuss the merits of accepting the order even if it decreases total profits.

11-5
Make or Buy;
Traditional
Analysis
LO 2, 4

Switzer Company is currently manufacturing Part 67Y, producing 5,000 units annually. The part is used in the production of several products made by Switzer. The cost per unit for 67Y is as follows:

Direct materials	$3.00
Direct labor	2.00
Variable overhead	1.00
Fixed overhead	1.50
Total	$7.50

Of the total fixed overhead assigned to 67Y, $1,500 is direct fixed overhead and the remainder is common fixed overhead. An outside supplier has offered to sell the part to Switzer for $7.05. There is no alternative use for the facilities currently used to produce the part. There are no significant nonunit-based overhead costs.

REQUIRED:

1. Should Switzer Company make or buy Part 67Y?
2. What is the most Switzer would be willing to pay an outside supplier?

11-6
Make or Buy;
Traditional and
ABC Analysis
LO 3, 4

Clarkson Manufacturing, Inc., has just received an offer from a supplier to buy 6,000 units of a component used in its main product. The component is a gear that is currently produced internally. The supplier has offered to sell the gear for $44 per unit. Clarkson is currently using a conventional, unit-based cost system that assigns overhead to jobs on the basis of direct labor hours. The estimated traditional full cost of producing the gear is given below:

Direct materials	$20
Direct labor	10
Variable overhead	10
Fixed overhead	32

Prior to making a decision, the company's CEO commissioned a special study to see whether there would be any decrease in the fixed overhead costs. The results of the study revealed the following:

2 setups—$5,000 each (The setups would be avoided and total spending could be reduced by $5,000 per setup.)
One less inspector needed, $28,000.
One less materials handler needed, $20,000.
Engineering work: 500 hours, $15/hr. (Although the work decreases by 500 hours, the engineer assigned to the gear line also spends time on other products.)

REQUIRED:

1. Ignore the special study and determine whether the gear should be produced internally or purchased from the supplier.
2. Now, using the special study data, repeat the analysis.
3. Discuss the qualitative factors that would affect the decision, including strategic implications.
4. After reviewing the special study, the controller made the following remark: "This study ignores the additional activity demands that purchasing would cause. For example, although the demand for inspecting the part on the production floor decreases, will we not have a need to inspect the incoming parts in the receiving area? Will we actually save any inspection costs?" Is the controller right? Would this problem be avoided if Clarkson had an activity-based costing system in place?

11-7
Resource Usage Model; Special Order

LO 3, 4

Englewood Machining is operating at 85% of capacity. An offer to produce 4,000 units of a specially designed tool has just been received. The offering price is $20 per unit. The product normally sells for $27. The activity-based accounting system provides the following information:

	Activity Driver	Unused Capacity	Quantity Demanded**	Activity Rate* Fixed	Activity Rate* Variable
Direct materials	Units	0	3,000	—	$10
Direct labor	Direct labor hours	0	500	—	14
Setups	Setup hours	30	50	$200	16
Inspection	Inspection hours	200	100	10	3
Machining	Machine hours	6,000	4,000	20	4

*This is expected activity cost divided by activity capacity.
**This only represents the amount of resources demanded by the special order being considered.

Expansion of activity capacity for setups, inspection, and machining must be done in steps (whole units). For setups, each whole unit provides an additional 25 hours of setup activity and is priced at the fixed activity rate. For inspection, activity capacity is expanded by 2,000 hours per year and the cost is $20,000 per year (the salary for an additional inspector). Machine capacity can be leased for a year at a rate of $20 per machine hour. Machine capacity must be acquired, however, in steps of 2,500 machine hours.

REQUIRED:

1. Compute the change in income for Englewood Machining if the order is accepted. Comment on whether or not the order should be accepted (in particular, discuss the strategic issues).
2. Suppose that the setup activity has 60 hours of unused capacity. How is the analysis affected?
3. Suppose that the setup activity has 60 hours of unused capacity and that the machining activity has 3,000 hours of unused capacity. How is the analysis affected?

11-8
Keep or Drop: Traditional Versus Activity-Based

LO 3, 4

Lincoln Inc. produces two types of peanut butter: Smooth and Crunchy. Of the two, Smooth is the more popular. Data concerning the two products follow:

	Smooth	Crunchy	Unused Capacity*	Units of Purchase**
Expected sales (in cases)	50,000	10,000	—	—
Selling price per case	$100	$80	—	—
Direct labor hours	40,000	10,000	—	As needed
Machine hours	10,000	2,500	—	2,500
Receiving orders	500	250	250	500
Packing orders	1,000	500	500	250
Material cost per case	$50	$48	—	—
Direct labor cost per case	$10	$8	—	—
Advertising costs	$200,000	$60,000	—	—

*Practical capacity less expected usage (all unused capacity is permanent).
**In some cases, activity capacity must be purchased in steps (whole units). These steps are provided as necessary. The cost per step is the fixed activity rate multiplied by the step units. The fixed activity rate is the expected fixed activity costs divided by practical activity capacity.

Annual overhead costs are listed below. These costs are classified as fixed or variable with respect to the appropriate activity driver.

Activity	Fixed[a]	Variable[b]
Direct labor benefits	$ —	$200,000
Machine	200,000	250,000
Receiving	200,000	22,500
Packing	100,000	45,000
Total costs	$500,000	$517,500

[a] Costs associated with practical activity capacity. The machine fixed costs are all depreciation.
[b] These costs are for the actual levels of the cost driver.

REQUIRED:

1. Prepare traditional and activity-based segmented income statements. In the traditional system, a unit-level overhead rate is used, based on direct labor hours.
2. Using a traditional approach, determine whether the Crunchy product line should be kept or dropped.
3. Repeat the keep-or-drop analysis using an ABC approach.

11-9
Sell or Process Further; Basic Analysis
LO 2, 4

A division of Rico Products has several meat-processing plants. One plant (in Omaha) deals exclusively with chickens. The plant produces three products from a common process: packaged breasts, packaged thighs and legs, and the residual. The residual consists of backs and necks, which are sold by the pound to a local soup manufacturer. The packages are sold to supermarkets. The joint costs for a typical week are given below.

Direct materials	$30,000
Direct labor	20,000
Overhead	15,000

The revenues from each product are as follows: breasts, $43,000; legs and thighs, $32,000; and residual, $25,000.

Management of the Omaha plant is considering processing the chicken breasts beyond the split-off point, which would increase the sales value to $76,000 (the breasts would be cut into nugget-size pieces, breaded, packaged, and sold to supermarkets as chicken nuggets). However, the additional processing means that the company must rent some special equipment costing $1,250 per week. Additional materials and labor also needed would cost $12,750 per week. Resource spending would need to be expanded for other activities as well. The increase in resource spending for these activities is estimated to be $15,000 per week.

REQUIRED:

1. What is the gross profit earned by the three products for one week?
2. Should the division process chicken breasts into nuggets or continue to sell the chicken breasts at split-off? What is the effect of the decision on weekly gross profit?

**11-10
Keep or Drop;
Complementary
Effects; Traditional
Analysis**

LO 2, 4

Dutson Company manufactures running shoes and tennis shoes. The projected income statements for the two products are as follows:

	Running Shoes	Tennis Shoes
Sales	$450,000	$750,000
Less: Variable costs	270,000	300,000
Contribution margin	$180,000	$450,000
Less: Direct fixed expenses	200,000	220,000
Segment margin	$ (20,000)	$230,000
Less: Common fixed costs (allocated)	50,000	75,000
Net income (loss)	$ (70,000)	$155,000

The president of the company is considering dropping the running shoes. However, if the line is dropped, sales of tennis shoes will drop by 10 percent. There are no significant nonunit-level activity costs.

REQUIRED:

1. Should the company drop or keep the line of running shoes? Provide supporting computations.
2. Assume that increasing the advertising budget by $20,000 will increase sales of running shoes by 5 percent and tennis shoes by 3 percent. Prepare a segmented income statement that reflects the effect of increased advertising. Should advertising be increased?

**11-11
Special Order;
Traditional
Analysis**

LO 2, 4

Lancaster Company manufactures two types of hair conditioners, Creemy and Shiney, out of a joint process. The joint (common) costs incurred are $840,000 for a standard production run that generates 360,000 gallons of Creemy and 240,000 gallons of Shiney. Additional processing costs beyond the split-off point are $2.80 per gallon for Creemy and $1.80 per gallon for Shiney. Creemy sells for $4.80 per gallon, while Shiney sells for $7.80 per gallon.

Comida Buena, a supermarket chain, has asked Lancaster to supply it with 480,000 gallons of Shiney at a price of $7.30 per gallon. Comida Buena plans to have the conditioner bottled in 16-ounce bottles with its own Comida Buena label.

If Lancaster accepts the order, it will save $0.10 per gallon in packaging of Shiney. There is sufficient excess capacity for the order. However, the market for Creemy is saturated, and any additional sales of Creemy would take place at a price of $3.20 per gallon. Assume that there are no significant nonunit-level activity costs.

REQUIRED:

1. What is the profit normally earned on one production run of Creemy and Shiney?
2. Should Lancaster accept the special order? Explain.

(CMA adapted)

11-12
Resource Usage;
Special Order

LO 3, 4

Perry Medical Center (PMC) has five medical technicians who are responsible for conducting sonogram testing. Each technician is paid a salary of $36,000 and is capable of processing 1,000 tests per year. The sonogram equipment is one year old and was purchased for $150,000. It is expected to last five years. The equipment's capacity is 25,000 tests over its life. Depreciation is computed on a straight-line basis, with no salvage value expected. The reading of the sonogram technician is verified by an outside physician whose fee is $10 per test. The technician's report with the outside physician's note of verification is sent to the referring physician. In addition to the salaries and equipment, PMC spends $10,000 for forms, paper, power, and other supplies needed to operate the equipment (assuming 5,000 tests are processed). When PMC purchased the equipment, it fully expected to use 5,000 tests per year. In fact, during its first year of operation, 5,000 tests were run. However, a larger hospital has established a clinic in Perry and will siphon off some of PMC's business. During the coming years, PMC is expected to run only 4,200 sonogram tests. PMC has been charging $65 for the test—enough to cover the direct costs of the test plus an assignment of general overhead (e.g., depreciation on the hospital building, lighting and heating, and janitorial services).

At the beginning of the second year, an HMO from a neighboring community approached PMC and offered to send its clients to PMC for sonogram testing provided that the charge per test is $35. The HMO estimates that it can provide about 500 patients per year. The HMO has indicated that the arrangement is temporary—for one year only. The HMO expects to have its own testing capabilities within one year.

REQUIRED:

1. Classify the resources associated with the sonogram activity into one of the following: (1) long-term resources supplied in advance, (2) short-term resources supplied in advance, and (3) resources supplied as needed.
2. Calculate the activity rate for the sonogram testing activity. Break the activity rate into fixed and variable components. Now classify each activity resource as relevant or irrelevant with respect to the following alternatives: (1) accept the HMO offer and (2) reject the HMO offer. Explain your reasoning.
3. Assume that PMC will accept the HMO offer if it reduces the hospital's operating costs. Should the HMO offer be accepted?
4. Harry Birdwell, PMC's hospital controller, argued against accepting the HMO's offer. Instead, he argued that what the hospital ought to be doing is increasing the charge per test and not accepting business that doesn't even cover full costs. He also was concerned about local physician reaction if word got out that the HMO was receiving tests for $35. Discuss the merits of Harry's position. Include in your discussion an assessment of the price increase that would be needed if the objective is to maintain total revenues from sonogram testing experienced in the first year of operation.
5. Elaine Day, PMC's administrator, has been informed that one of the sonogram technicians is leaving for an opportunity at a larger hospital. She has met with the other technicians and they have agreed to increase their hours to pick up the slack so that PMC won't need to hire another technician. By working a couple hours extra each week, each remaining technician can perform 1,050 tests per year. They agreed to do this for an increase in salary of $2,000 per year. How does this outcome affect the analysis of the HMO offer?
6. Assuming that PMC wants to bring in the same revenues earned in the sonogram activity's first year less the reduction in resource spending attributable to using only four technicians, how much must PMC charge for a sonogram test?

11-13
Activity-Based
Resource Usage
Model; Make or
Buy
LO 3, 4

Brandy Dees recently bought Nievo Enterprises, a company that manufactures ice skates. Brandy decided to assume management responsibilities for the company and appointed herself president shortly after the purchase was completed. When she bought the company, Brandy's investigation revealed that with the exception of the blades, all parts of the skates are produced internally. The investigation also revealed that Nievo once produced the blades internally and still owned the equipment. The equipment was in good condition and was stored in a local warehouse. Nievo's former owner had decided three years earlier to purchase the blades from external suppliers.

Brandy Dees is seriously considering making the blades instead of buying them from external suppliers. The blades are purchased in sets of two and cost $8 per set. Currently, 100,000 sets of blades are purchased annually.

Skates are produced in batches, according to shoe size. Production equipment must be reconfigured for each batch. The blades could be produced using an available area within the plant. Prime costs will average $5.00 per set. There is enough equipment to set up three lines of production, each capable of producing 80,000 sets of blades. A supervisor would need to be hired for each line. Each supervisor would be paid a salary of $40,000. Additionally, it would cost $1.50 per machine hour for power, oil, and other operating expenses. Since three types of blades would be produced, there would be additional demands made on the setup activity. Other overhead activities affected include purchasing, inspection, and materials handling. The company's ABC system provides the following information about the current status of the overhead activities that would be affected. (The lumpy quantity indicates how much capacity must be purchased should any expansion of activity supply be needed—the units of purchase. The purchase cost per unit is the fixed activity rate. The variable rate is the cost per unit of resources acquired as needed for each activity.)

Activity	Cost Driver	Activity Capacity	Current Activity Usage	Lumpy Quantity	Fixed Activity Rate	Variable Activity Rate
Setups	Number of setups	1,000	800	100	$200	$500
Purchasing	Number of orders	50,000	47,000	5,000	10	0.50
Inspecting	Inspection hours	20,000	18,000	2,000	15	none
Materials handling	Number of moves	9,000	8,700	500	30	1.50

The demands that *production* of blades place on the overhead activities are given below:

Activity	Resource Demands
Machining	50,000 machine hours
Setups	250 setups
Purchasing	4,000 purchase orders (associated with raw materials)
Inspection	1,500 inspection hours
Materials handling	650 moves

If the blades are made, the purchase of the blades from outside suppliers will cease. Therefore, purchase orders will decrease by 6,500 (the number associated with their purchase). Similarly, the moves for the handling of incoming blades will decrease by 400. Any unused activity capacity is viewed as permanent.

REQUIRED:

1. Should Nievo make or buy the blades?
2. Explain how the ABC resource usage model helped in the analysis. Also, comment on how a conventional approach would have differed.

11-14
Segmented Income Statements; Keep-or-Drop Decision; Special-Order Decision; JIT and Activity-Based Costing; Strategic Considerations

LO 3, 4

Emery Company, a manufacturer of motors for washing machines, has installed a JIT purchasing and manufacturing system. After several years of operation, Emery has succeeded in reducing inventories to insignificant levels. During the coming year, Emery expects to produce 200,000 motors: 150,000 of the Regular Model and 50,000 of the Heavy Duty Model. The motors are produced in manufacturing cells. The expected output represents 80 percent of the capacity for the Regular Model cell and 100 percent of capacity for the Heavy Duty Model cell. (This capacity includes time for cell workers to perform maintenance and materials handling.) The selling price for the Regular Model is $60; that for the Heavy Duty is $70.

The relevant data for next year's expected production are as follows:

	Regular Cell	Heavy Duty Cell
Direct materials	$3,500,000	$1,000,000
Labor*	$ 900,000	$ 315,000
Power	$ 250,000	$ 100,000
Depreciation	$ 800,000	$ 300,000
Number of runs	100	100
Number of cell workers	20	5
Square footage	20,000	10,000

*Responsible for production, maintenance, and materials handling

The following overhead costs are common to each cell:

Plant depreciation	$900,000
Production scheduling	300,000
Cafeteria	100,000
Personnel	150,000

These costs are assigned to the cells using cost drivers selected from the cell activity data given above.

In addition to the overhead costs, the company expects the following nonmanufacturing costs:

Commissions (2% of sales)	$250,000
Advertising:	
Regular Model	400,000
Heavy Duty Model	200,000
Administration (all fixed)	500,000

Keith Golding, the president of Emery Company, is concerned about the profit performance of each model. He wants to know the effect on the company's profitability if the Heavy Duty Model is dropped. At the same time this request was made, the company was approached by a customer in a market not normally served by the company. This customer offered to buy 30,000 units of the Regular Model at $30 per unit. The order was requested on a direct contact basis and no commissions will be paid. Keith was inclined to reject the offer, since it was half the model's normal selling price. However, before making the decision, he wanted to know the effect of accepting the offer on the company's profits.

To help decide on the two issues, the following additional data have been made available:

Activity	Cost Driver	Supply	Usage	Lumpy Quantity*	Fixed Rate
Scheduling	Runs	250	200	25	$1,200
Cafeteria	Cell workers	45	25	15	1,800
Personnel	Cell workers	40	25	20	3,750

*Lumpy quantity is the amount of resource that would be acquired (saved) if the *capacity* of the activity is expanded (reduced); the fixed rate is the per-unit price of the resource (which, however, can only be purchased in the lumpy amounts indicated).

Of the three activities, the cafeteria activity is the only one with a variable activity rate. This rate is $760 per cell worker.

REQUIRED:

1. Prepare an ABC segmented income statement for Emery Company using products as segments. Can the unused activity be exploited to increase overall profits? Explain.
2. By how much will profits be affected if the Heavy Duty Model is dropped?
3. Prepare an analysis that shows what the effect on company profitability would have been if the special order had been accepted. Was the president correct in his feelings concerning the special order?
4. Now assume that the models are sold to companies that produce medium- to high-quality washing machines. The special-order customer will use the motors in a low-end washing machine and plans to advertise the fact that the low-end washing machine can be purchased at a lower price with the same quality as a so-called higher-quality brand. Given this information and the results of Requirement 2, should the order be accepted? Explain.

**11-15
Make or Buy;
Traditional
Analysis;
Qualitative
Considerations**

LO 2

Gray Dentistry Services is part of an HMO that operates in a large metropolitan area. Currently, Gray has its own dental laboratory to produce porcelain and gold crowns. The unit costs to produce the crowns are as follows:

	Porcelain	Gold
Raw materials	$ 60	$ 90
Direct labor	20	20
Variable overhead	5	5
Fixed overhead	22	22
Total	$107	$137

Fixed overhead is detailed as follows:

Salary (supervisor)	$30,000
Depreciation	5,000
Rent (lab facility)	20,000

Overhead is applied on the basis of direct labor hours. The rates above were computed using 5,500 direct labor hours. There are no significant nonunit-level overhead costs.

A local dental laboratory has offered to supply Gray all the crowns it needs. Its price is $100 for porcelain crowns and $132 for gold crowns; however, the offer is conditional on supplying both types of crowns—it will not supply just one type for the price indicated. If the offer is accepted, the equipment used by Gray's laboratory would be scrapped (it is old and has no market value), and the lab facility would be closed. Gray uses 1,500 porcelain crowns and 1,000 gold crowns per year.

REQUIRED:

1. Should Gray continue to make its own crowns or should they be purchased from the external supplier? What is the dollar effect of purchasing?
2. What qualitative factors should Gray consider in making this decision?
3. Suppose that the lab facility is owned rather than rented and that the $20,000 is depreciation rather than rent. What effect does this have on the analysis in Requirement 1?
4. Refer to the original data. Assume that the volume of crowns is 3,000 porcelain and 2,000 gold. Should Gray make or buy the crowns? Explain the outcome.

**11-16
Sell or Process
Further**
LO 4

Barstow Corporation buys three chemicals that are processed to produce two popular ingredients for liquid cough syrups. The three chemicals are in liquid form. The purchased chemicals are blended for two to three hours and then heated for fifteen minutes. The results of the process are two separate ingredients, Suppressant AB2 and Suppressant AB3. For every 2,200 gallons of chemicals used, 1,000 gallons of each suppressant are produced. The suppressants are sold to companies that process them into their final form. The selling prices are $10 per gallon for AB2 and $25 per gallon for AB3. The costs to produce 1,000 gallons of each chemical are as follows:

Chemicals	$11,000
Direct labor	9,000
Overhead	7,000

The suppressants are bottled in 4-gallon plastic containers and shipped. The cost of each container is $1.50. Shipping costs $0.20 per container.

Barstow Corporation could process Suppressant AB2 further by mixing it with inert powders and flavoring to form cough tablets. The tablets can be sold directly to retail drug stores as a generic brand. If this route is taken, the revenue received per case of tablets would be $6.00, with five cases produced by every gallon of Suppressant AB2. The costs of processing into tablets total $5.00 per gallon of AB2. Packaging costs $2.00 per case. Shipping costs $0.40 per case.

REQUIRED:

1. Should Barstow sell Suppressant AB2 at split-off or should AB2 be processed and sold as tablets?
2. If Barstow normally sells 360,000 gallons of AB2 per year, what will be the difference in profits if AB2 is processed further?

11-17
Plant Shutdown
or Continue
Operations;
Qualitative
Considerations;
Traditional
Analysis

LO 2, 4

GianAuto Corporation manufactures automobiles, vans, and trucks. Among the various GianAuto plants around the United States is the Denver cover plant, where vinyl covers and upholstery fabric are sewn. These are used to cover interior seating and other surfaces of GianAuto products.

Pam Vosilo is the plant manager for Denver cover. The plant was the first GianAuto plant in the region. As other area plants were opened, Vosilo, in recognition of her management ability, was given the responsibility to manage them. Vosilo functions as a regional manager, although the budget for her and her staff is charged to the Denver plant.

Vosilo has just received a report indicating that GianAuto could purchase the entire annual output of Denver cover from outside suppliers for $30 million. Vosilo was astonished at the low outside price, because the budget for Denver cover's operating costs was set at $52 million. Vosilo believes that Denver cover will have to close down operations in order to realize the $22 million in annual cost savings.

The budget (in thousands) for Denver cover's operating costs for the coming year follows:

Materials		$12,000
Labor:		
Direct	$13,000	
Supervision	3,000	
Indirect plant	4,000	20,000
Overhead:		
Depreciation—Equipment	$ 5,000	
Depreciation—Building	3,000	
Pension expense	4,000	
Plant manager and staff	2,000	
Corporate allocation	6,000	20,000
Total budgeted costs		$52,000

Additional facts regarding the plant's operations are as follows:

Due to Denver cover's commitment to use high-quality fabrics in all its products, the Purchasing Department was instructed to place blanket orders with major suppliers to ensure the receipt of sufficient materials for the coming year. If these orders are canceled as a consequence of the plant closing, termination charges would amount to 15 percent of the cost of direct materials.

Approximately 700 plant employees will lose their jobs if the plant is closed. This includes all direct laborers and supervisors as well as the plumbers, electricians, and other skilled workers classified as indirect plant workers. Some would be able to find new jobs, but many others would have difficulty. All employees would have difficulty matching Denver cover's base pay of $9.40 per hour, the highest in the area. A clause in Denver cover's contract with the union may help some employees; the company must provide employment assistance to its former employees for twelve months after a plant closing. The estimated cost to administer this service would be $1 million for the year.

Some employees would probably elect early retirement because Denver cover has an excellent pension plan. In fact, $3 million of next year's pension expense would continue whether Denver cover is open or not.

Vosilo and her staff would not be affected by the closing of Denver cover. They would still be responsible for administering three other area plants.

Denver cover considers equipment depreciation to be a variable cost and uses the units-of-production method to depreciate its equipment; Denver cover is the only GianAuto plant to use this depreciation method. However, Denver cover uses the customary straight-line method to depreciate its building.

REQUIRED:

1. Prepare a quantitative analysis to help in deciding whether or not to close the Denver cover plant. Explain how you treated the nonrecurring relevant costs.
2. Consider the analysis in Requirement 1 and add to it the qualitative factors that you believe are important to the decision. What is your decision? Would you close the plant? Explain.

(CMA adapted)

**11-18
Make or Buy;
Traditional
Analysis**

LO 1, 2, 4

Morrill Company produces two different types of gauges: a density gauge and a thickness gauge. The segmented income statement for a typical quarter is given below.

	Density Gauge	Thickness Gauge	Total
Sales	$150,000	$80,000	$230,000
Less: Variable expenses	80,000	46,000	126,000
Contribution margin	$ 70,000	$34,000	$104,000
Less: Direct fixed expenses*	20,000	38,000	58,000
Segment margin	$ 50,000	$ (4,000)	$ 46,000
Less: Common fixed expenses			30,000
Net income			$ 16,000

*Includes depreciation.

The density gauge uses a subassembly that is purchased from an external supplier for $25 per unit. Each quarter, 2,000 subassemblies are purchased. All units produced are sold, and there are no ending inventories of subassemblies. Morrill is considering making the subassembly rather than buying it. Unit-level variable manufacturing costs are as follows:

Direct materials	$2
Direct labor	3
Variable overhead	2

There are no significant nonunit-level costs.

Morrill is considering two alternatives to supply the productive capacity for the subassembly.

1. Lease the needed space and equipment at a cost of $27,000 per quarter for the space and $10,000 per quarter for a supervisor. There are no other fixed expenses.
2. Drop the thickness gauge. The equipment could be adapted with virtually no cost and the existing space utilized to produce the subassembly. The direct fixed expenses, including supervision, would be $38,000, $8,000 of which is depreciation on equipment. If the thickness gauge is dropped, there will be no effect on the sales of the density gauge.

REQUIRED:

1. Should Morrill Company make or buy the subassembly? If it makes the subassembly, which alternative should be chosen? Explain and provide supporting computations.
2. Suppose that dropping the thickness gauge will decrease sales of the density gauge by 10 percent. What effect does this have on the decision?
3. Assume that dropping the thickness gauge decreases sales of the density gauge by 10 percent and that 2,800 subassemblies are required per quarter. As before, assume that there are no ending inventories of subassemblies and that all units produced are sold.

Assume also that the per-unit sales price and variable costs are the same as in Requirement 1. Include the leasing alternative in your consideration. Now what is the correct decision?

11-19
Make or Buy:
Ethical
Considerations
LO 4

Pamela McDonald, CMA and controller for Murray Manufacturing, Inc., was having lunch with Roger Branch, manager of the company's Power Department. Over the past six months, Pamela and Roger had developed a romantic relationship and were making plans for marriage. To keep company gossip at a minimum, Pamela and Roger had kept the relationship very quiet, and no one in the company was aware of it. The topic of the luncheon conversation centered on a decision concerning the company's Power Department that Larry Johnson, president of the company, was about to make.

Pamela: Roger, in our last executive meeting, we were told that a local utility company offered to supply power and quoted a price per kilowatt hour that they said would hold for the next three years. They even offered to enter into a contractual agreement with us.
Roger: This is news to me. Is the bid price a threat to my area? Can they sell us power cheaper than we make it? And why wasn't I informed about this matter? I should have some input. This burns me. I think I should give Larry a call this afternoon and lodge a strong complaint.
Pamela: Calm down, Roger. The last thing I want you to do is call Larry. Larry made us all promise to keep this whole deal quiet until a decision had been made. He did not want you involved because he wanted to make an unbiased decision. You know that the company is struggling somewhat, and they are looking for ways to save money.
Roger: Yeah, but at my expense? And at the expense of my department's workers? At my age, I doubt that I could find a job that pays as well and has the same benefits. How much of a threat is this offer?
Pamela: Jack Lacy, my assistant controller, prepared an analysis while I was on vacation. It showed that internal production is cheaper than buying, but not by much. Larry asked me to review the findings and submit a final recommendation for next Wednesday's meeting. I've reviewed Jack's analysis and it's faulty. He overlooked the interactions of your department with other service departments. When these are considered, the analysis is overwhelmingly in favor of purchasing the power. The savings are about $300,000 per year.
Roger: If Larry hears that, my department's gone. Pam, you can't let this happen. I'm three years away from having a vested retirement. And my workers—they have home mortgages, kids in college, and families to support. No, it's not right. Pam, just tell him that your assistant's analysis is on target. He'll never know the difference.
Pamela: Roger, what you're suggesting doesn't sound right either. Would it be ethical for me to fail to disclose this information?
Roger: Ethical? Do you think it's right to lay off employees that have been loyal, faithful workers simply to fatten the pockets of the owners of this company? The Murrays already are so rich that they don't know what to do with their money. I think that it's even more unethical to penalize me and my workers. Why should we have to bear the consequences of some bad marketing decisions? Anyway, the effects of those decisions are about gone, and the company should be back to normal within a year or so.
Pamela: You may be right. Perhaps the well-being of you and your workers is more important than saving $300,000 for the Murrays.

REQUIRED:

1. Should Pamela have told Roger about the impending decision concerning the Power Department? In revealing this information, did Pamela violate any of the ethical standards described in Chapter 1?
2. Should Pamela provide Larry with the correct data concerning the Power Department? Or should she protect its workers? What would you do if you were Pamela?

Central University, a Midwestern university with approximately 13,000 students, was in the middle of a budget crisis. For the third consecutive year, state appropriations for higher education remained essentially unchanged (the university is currently in its 1997–98 academic year). Yet utilities, social security benefits, insurance, and other operating expenses have increased. Moreover, the faculty were becoming restless, and some members had begun to leave for other, higher-paying opportunities.

The president and the academic vice president had announced their intention to eliminate some academic programs and to reduce others. The savings that result would be used to cover the increase in operating expenses and for raises for the remaining faculty. Needless to say, the possible dismissal of tenured faculty aroused a great deal of concern throughout the university.

With this background, the president and academic vice president called a meeting of all department heads and deans to discuss the budget for the coming year. As the budget was presented, the academic vice president noted that Continuing Education, a separate, centralized unit, had accumulated a deficit of $504,000 over the past several years, which must be eliminated during the coming fiscal year. The vice president noted that allocating the deficit equally among the seven colleges would create a hardship on some of the colleges, wiping out all of their operating budget except for salaries.

After some discussion of alternative ways to allocate the deficit, the head of the Accounting Department suggested an alternative solution: decentralize Continuing Education, allowing each college to assume responsibility for its own continuing education programs. In this way, the overhead of a centralized continuing education could be avoided.

The academic vice president responded that the suggestion would be considered, but it was received with little enthusiasm. The vice president observed that Continuing Education was now generating more revenues than costs—and that the trend was favorable.

A week later, at a meeting of the Deans' Council, the vice president reviewed the role of Continuing Education. He pointed out that only the dean of Continuing Education held tenure. If Continuing Education were decentralized, her salary ($50,000) would continue. However, she would return to her academic department, and the university would save $20,000 of instructional wages, since fewer temporary faculty would be needed in her department. All other employees in the unit were classified as staff. Continuing Education had responsibility for all noncredit offerings. Additionally, it had nominal responsibility for credit courses offered in the evening on campus and for credit courses offered off-campus. However, all scheduling and staffing of these evening and off-campus courses were done by the heads of the academic departments. What courses were offered and who staffed them had to be approved by the head of each department. According to the vice president, one of the main contributions of the Continuing Education Department to the evening and off-campus programs is advertising. He estimated that $30,000 per year is being spent.

After reviewing this information, the vice president made available the following information pertaining to the department's performance for the past several years (the 1997–98 data were projections). He once again defended keeping a centralized department, emphasizing the favorable trend revealed by the accounting data. (All numbers are expressed in thousands.)

	1994–95	1995–96	1996–97	1997–98
Tuition revenues:				
Off-campus	$300	$ 400	$ 400	$ 410
Evening	— *	525	907	1,000
Noncredit	135	305	338	375
Total	$435	$1,230	$1,645	$1,785

(continued)

	1994–95	1995–96	1996–97	1997–98
Operating costs:				
Administration	$(132)	$ (160)	$ (112)	$ (112)
Off-campus:				
Direct**	(230)	(270)	(270)	(260)
Indirect	(350)	(410)	(525)	(440)
Evening	(—)*	(220)	(420)	(525)
Noncredit	(135)	(305)	(338)	(375)
Total	$(847)	$(1,365)	$(1,665)	$(1,712)
Income (loss)	$(412)	$ (135)	$ (20)	$ (73)

*In 1994–95, the department had no responsibility for evening courses. Beginning in 1995–96, it was given the responsibility to pay for any costs of instruction incurred when temporary or adjunct faculty were hired to teach evening courses. Tuition revenues earned by evening courses also began to be assigned to the department at the same time.
**Instructional wages.

The dean of the College of Business was unimpressed by the favorable trend identified by the academic vice president. The dean maintained that decentralization still would be in the best interests of the university. He argued that although decentralization would not fully solve the deficit, it would provide a sizable contribution each year to the operating budgets for each of the seven colleges.

The academic vice president disagreed vehemently. He was convinced that Continuing Education was now earning its own way and would continue to produce additional resources for the university.

REQUIRED: You have been asked by the president of Central University to assess which alternative, centralization or decentralization, is in the best interest of the school. The president is willing to decentralize provided that significant savings can be produced and the mission of the Continuing Education Department will still be carried out. Prepare a memo to the president that details your analysis and reasoning and recommends one of the two alternatives. Provide both qualitative and quantitative reasoning in the memo.

Chapter 12
Capital Investment Decisions

Federal Express decided early on to invest heavily in airplanes and its Memphis distribution center. Now, these huge capital outlays help FedEx to stay preeminent in the field of overnight delivery.

LEARNING OBJECTIVES

After studying this chapter, you should be able to:

1. Explain what a capital investment decision is and distinguish between independent and mutually exclusive capital investment decisions.
2. Compute the payback period and accounting rate of return for a proposed investment and explain their roles in capital investment decisions.
3. Use net present value analysis for capital investment decisions involving independent projects.
4. Use the internal rate of return to assess the acceptability of an independent project.
5. Explain why NPV is better than IRR for capital investment decisions involving mutually exclusive projects.
6. Convert gross cash flows to after-tax cash flows.
7. Describe capital investment in the contemporary manufacturing environment.

Organizations are often faced with the opportunity (or need) to invest in assets or projects that represent long-term commitments. New production systems, new plants, new equipment, and new product development are examples of assets and projects that fit this category. Usually many alternatives are available. For example, Federal Express has chosen to make a capital investment in airplanes, sorting equipment, and distribution facilities. The FedEx hub in Memphis represents a significant outlay of funds (capital outlay). Sound capital investment decision making of this type requires the estimation of a project's cash flows. How cash flows can be used to evaluate the merits of a proposed project is the focus of this chapter. We will study four financial models that are useful in capital investment analysis: the payback period, the accounting rate of return, net present value, and the internal rate of return.

TYPES OF CAPITAL INVESTMENT DECISIONS

Objective 1
Explain what a capital investment decision is and distinguish between independent and mutually exclusive capital investment decisions.

capital investment decisions

capital budgeting
independent projects

mutually exclusive projects

Capital investment decisions are concerned with the process of planning, setting goals and priorities, arranging financing, and using certain criteria to select long-term assets. Because capital investment decisions place large amounts of resources at risk for long periods of time and simultaneously affect the future development of the firm, they are among the most important decisions managers make. Every organization has limited resources, which should be used to maintain or enhance its long-run profitability. Poor capital investment decisions can be disastrous. For example, global retailing demands huge investment, and companies have erred by spending too little or too much. Parisian department store Galeries Lafayette spent $20 million before closing its New York City store. Another example of overspending, was Benetton, which overspent on U.S. expansion. Wal-Mart (along with partner Cifra) is hoping that its spending is "just right" as it adds to its $1 billion investment in 67 Sam's Clubs and discount stores in Mexico.[1] Clearly, making the right capital investment decisions is absolutely essential for long-term survival.

The process of making capital investment decisions is often referred to as **capital budgeting**. Two types of capital budgeting projects will be considered. **Independent projects** are projects that, if accepted or rejected, do not affect the cash flows of other projects. Suppose that the managers of the Marketing and the Research and Development departments jointly propose the addition of a new product line that would entail making significant outlays for working capital and equipment. GM's decision to build a new plant for the production of the Saturn line and Toyota's decision to build a new plant in Lexington, Kentucky, for the production of the Camry line are examples of independent capital investment decisions.

The second type of capital budgeting projects requires a firm to choose among competing alternatives that provide the same basic service. Acceptance of one option precludes the acceptance of another. Thus, **mutually exclusive projects** are those projects that, if accepted, preclude the acceptance of all other competing projects. For example, in 1985 Monsanto's Fiber Division decided to automate its Pensacola, Florida, plant. At some point in time, Monsanto was faced with the choice of continuing with its existing manual production operation or replacing it with an automated system. In all likelihood, part of the company's deliberation concerned different types of automated systems. If three different automated sys-

1.   Carla Rapoport and Justin Martin, "Retailers Go Global," *Fortune*, February 20, 1995, pp. 102–108.

tems were being considered, this would produce four alternatives—the current system plus the three potential new systems. Once one system is chosen, the other three are excluded; they are mutually exclusive.

Notice that one of the competing alternatives in the example is that of maintaining the status quo (the manual system). This emphasizes the fact that new investments that replace existing investments must prove to be economically superior. Of course, at times, replacement of the old system is mandatory and not discretionary if the firm wishes to remain in business (e.g., equipment in the old system may be worn out, making the old system not a viable alternative). In such a situation, going out of business could be a viable alternative, especially if none of the new investment alternatives is profitable.

Capital investment decisions often are concerned with investments in long-term capital assets. With the exception of land, these assets depreciate over their lives, and the original investment is used up as the assets are employed. In general terms, a sound capital investment will earn back its original capital outlay over its life and, at the same time, provide a reasonable return on the original investment. Thus, one task of a manager is to decide whether or not a capital investment will earn back its original outlay and provide a reasonable return. By making this assessment, a manager can decide on the acceptability of independent projects and compare competing projects on the basis of their economic merits. But what is meant by reasonable return? It is generally agreed that any new project must cover the *opportunity cost* of the funds invested. For example, if a company takes money from a money market fund that is earning six percent and invests it in a new project, then the project must provide at least a six percent return (the return that could have been earned had the money been left in the money market fund). Of course, in reality, funds for investment often come from different sources—each representing a different opportunity cost. The return that must be earned is a blend of the opportunity costs of the different sources. Thus, if a company uses two sources of funds, one with an opportunity cost of 4% and the other with an opportunity cost of 6%, then the return that must be earned is somewhere between 4% and 6%, depending on the relative amounts used from each source. Furthermore, it is usually assumed that managers should select projects that promise to maximize the wealth of the owners of the firm.

To make a capital investment decision, a manager must estimate the quantity and timing of cash flows, assess the risk of the investment, and consider the impact of the project on the firm's profits. One of the most difficult tasks is to estimate the cash flows. Projections must be made years into the future, and forecasting is far from a perfect science. Obviously, as the accuracy of cash-flow forecasts increases, the reliability of the decision improves. In making projections, managers must identify and quantify the benefits associated with the proposed project(s). For example, an automated cash deposit system can produce the following benefits (relative to a manual system): bank charge reductions, productivity gains, forms cost reduction, greater data integrity, lower training costs, and savings in time required to audit and do bank/cash reconciliations. The dollar value of these benefits must be assessed. Although forecasting future cash flows is a critical part of the capital investment process, forecasting methods will not be considered here. Consequently, cash flows are assumed to be known; the focus will be on making capital investment decisions *given* these cash flows.

Managers must set goals and priorities for capital investments. They also must identify some basic criteria for the acceptance or rejection of proposed investments. In this chapter, we will study four basic methods to guide managers in accepting or rejecting potential investments. The methods include both non-discounting and discounting decision approaches (two methods are discussed for each approach). The discounting methods are applied to investment decisions involving both independent and mutually exclusive projects.

NONDISCOUNTING MODELS

Objective 2
Compute the payback period and accounting rate of return for a proposed investment and explain their roles in capital investment decisions.

nondiscounting
models
discounting models

payback period

The basic capital investment decision models can be classified into two major categories: nondiscounting models and discounting models. **Nondiscounting models** ignore the time value of money, whereas **discounting models** explicitly consider it. Although many accounting theorists disparage the nondiscounting models because they ignore the time value of money, many firms continue to use these models in making capital investment decisions. However, the use of discounting models has increased over the years, and few firms use only one model—indeed, firms seem to use both types of models.[2] This suggests that both categories supply useful information to managers as they struggle to make capital investment decisions.

Payback Period

One type of nondiscounting model is the payback period. The **payback period** is the time required for a firm to recover its original investment. For example, assume that a dentist invests in a new set of drilling equipment costing $80,000. The cash flow (cash inflows less cash outflows) generated by the equipment is $40,000 per year. Thus, the payback period is two years ($80,000/$40,000). When the cash flows of a project are assumed to be even, the following formula can be used to compute its payback period:

Payback period = Original investment/Annual cash flow

If, however, the cash flows are uneven, the payback period is computed by adding the annual cash flows until such time as the original investment is recovered. If a fraction of a year is needed, it is assumed that cash flows occur evenly within each year. For example, suppose that a new car wash facility requires an investment of $100,000 and has a life of five years with the following expected annual cash flows: $30,000, $40,000, $50,000, $60,000, and $70,000. The payback period for the project is 2.6 years, computed as follows: $30,000 (1 year) + $40,000 (1 year) + $30,000 (0.6 year). In the third year, when only $30,000 is needed and $50,000 is available, the amount of time required to earn the $30,000 is found by dividing the amount needed by the annual cash flow ($30,000/$50,000). Exhibit 12-1 summarizes this analysis.

2.   In the mid-1950s, Robichek and McDonald reported that only 9 percent of large firms were using discounting models; by 1975, Petry reported that 66 percent of large firms were using these techniques. Also in 1975, Petty, Scott, and Bird surveyed Fortune 500 firms and found that 63.4 percent of the respondents used discounting models as their primary evaluation technique, with most of the remaining firms using them as secondary techniques. The same study also found that more than half of the firms used nondiscounting models as either a primary or a secondary evaluation technique. By 1988, Klammer, Koch, and Wilner reported that discounting models were used by over 80% of the firms as the primary evaluation technique for expansion decisions. For additional detail, see A. A. Robichek and J. G. McDonald, "Financial Planning in Transition, Long Range Planning Service," Report No. 268 (Menlo Park, Calif.: Stanford Research Institute, January 1966); G. H. Petry, "Effective Use of Capital Budgeting Tools," *Business Horizons*, Vol. 18, No. 5 (October 1975), pp. 57–65; J. W. Petty, D. F. Scott, and M. M. Bird, "The Capital Budgeting Decision Making Process of Large Corporations," *The Engineering Economist*, Vol. 20, No. 3 (Spring 1975), pp. 159–86; T. Klammer, B. Koch, and N. Wilner, "Capital Budgeting Practices—A Survey of Corporate Use," Working Paper, University of North Texas.

Exhibit 12-1
Payback Analysis:
Uneven Cash Flows

Year	Unrecovered Investment (Beginning of Year)	Annual Cash Flow
1	$100,000	$30,000
2	70,000	40,000
3	30,000*	50,000
4	—	60,000
5	—	70,000

*At the beginning of Year 3, $30,000 is needed to recover the investment. Since a net cash inflow of $50,000 is expected, only 0.6 year ($30,000/$50,000) is needed to recover the $30,000. Thus, the payback is 2.6 years (2 + 0.6).

One way to use the payback period is to set a maximum payback period for all projects and to reject any project that exceeds this level. Why would a firm use the payback period in this way? Some analysts suggest that the payback period can be used as a rough measure of risk, with the notion that the longer it takes for a project to pay for itself, the riskier it is. Also, firms with riskier cash flows could require a shorter payback period than normal. Additionally, firms with liquidity problems would be more interested in projects with quick paybacks. Another critical concern is obsolescence. In some industries, the risk of obsolescence is high; firms within these industries would be interested in recovering funds rapidly.

Another reason, less beneficial to the firm, may also be at work. Many managers in a position to make capital investment decisions may choose investments with quick payback periods out of self-interest. If a manager's performance is measured using such short-run criteria as annual net income, he or she may choose projects with quick paybacks to show improved net income as quickly as possible. Consider that division managers often are responsible for making capital investment decisions and are evaluated on divisional profit. The tenure of divisional managers, however, is typically short—three to five years would be average. Consequently, the incentive is for such managers to shy away from investments that promise healthy long-run returns but relatively meager returns in the short run. These problems can be eliminated by corporate budgeting policies and a budget review committee.

The payback period can be used to choose among competing alternatives. Under this approach, the investment with the shortest payback period is preferred over investments with longer payback periods. However, this use of the payback period is less defensible because this measure suffers from two major deficiencies: (1) it ignores the performance of the investments beyond the payback period and (2) it ignores the time value of money.

These two significant deficiencies are easily illustrated. Assume that an engineering firm is considering two different types of CAD systems—CAD-A and CAD-B. Each system requires an initial outlay of $150,000, has a five-year life, and displays the following annual cash flows:

Investment	Year 1	Year 2	Year 3	Year 4	Year 5
CAD-A	$90,000	$ 60,000	$50,000	$50,000	$50,000
CAD-B	40,000	110,000	25,000	25,000	25,000

Both investments have payback periods of two years. Thus, if a manager uses the payback period to choose among competing investments, the two investments would be equally desirable. In reality, however, the CAD-A system should be preferred over the CAD-B system for two reasons. First, the CAD-A system provides a much larger dollar return for the years beyond the payback period ($150,000 versus $75,000). Second, the CAD-A system returns $90,000 in the first year, while B returns only $40,000. The extra $50,000 that the CAD-A system provides in the first year could be put to productive use, such as investing it in another project. It is better to have a dollar now than a dollar one year from now because the dollar on hand can be invested to provide a return one year from now.

In summary, the payback period provides to managers information that can be used as follows:

1. To help control the risks associated with the uncertainty of future cash flows.
2. To help minimize the impact of an investment on a firm's liquidity problems.
3. To help control the risk of obsolescence.
4. To help control the effect of the investment on performance measures.

However, the method suffers significant deficiencies: it ignores a project's total profitability and the time value of money. While the computation of the payback period may be useful to a manager, to rely on it solely for a capital investment decision would be foolish.

Accounting Rate of Return

accounting rate of return

The accounting rate of return is the second commonly used nondiscounting model. The **accounting rate of return** measures the return on a project in terms of income, as opposed to using a project's cash flow. The accounting rate of return is computed by the following formula:

$$\text{Accounting rate of return} = \text{Average income/Original investment}$$
$$\text{or} = \text{Average income/Average investment}$$

Income is not equivalent to cash flows because of accruals and deferrals used in its computation. The average income of a project is obtained by adding the net income for each year of the project and then dividing this total by the number of years. Average net income for a project can be approximated by subtracting average depreciation from average cash flow. Assuming that all revenues earned in a period are collected and that depreciation is the only noncash expense, the approximation is exact.

Investment can be defined as the original investment or as the average investment. Letting I equal original investment, S equal salvage value, and assuming that investment is uniformly consumed, average investment is defined as follows:[3]

$$\text{Average investment} = (I + S)/2$$

To illustrate the computation of the accounting rate of return, assume that an investment requires an initial outlay of $100,000. The life of the investment is five years with the following cash flows: $30,000, $30,000, $40,000, $30,000, $50,000.

---

3.   The average investment formula is derived using the definition of the average value of a function and requires the use of calculus. The investment consumption function is $C(t) = I + [(S - I)/t^*]t$, where t is time and t^* is the life of the investment. By integrating $C(t)$ from 0 to t^* and dividing the result by t^*, the expression $(I + S)/2$ is obtained.

Assume that the asset has no salvage value after the five years and that all revenues earned within a year are collected in that year. The total cash flow for the five years is $180,000, making the average cash flow $36,000 ($180,000/5). Average depreciation is $20,000 ($100,000/5). The average net income is the difference between these two figures: $16,000 ($36,000 − $20,000). Using the average net income and original investment, the accounting rate of return is 16 percent ($16,000/$100,000). If average investment is used instead of original investment, then the accounting rate of return would be 32 percent ($16,000/$50,000).

Often debt contracts require that a firm maintain certain financial accounting ratios, which can be affected by the income reported and by the level of long-term assets. Accordingly, the accounting rate of return may be used as a screening measure to ensure that any new investment will not adversely affect these ratios. Additionally, because bonuses to managers are often based on accounting income or return on assets, they may have a personal interest in seeing that any new investment contributes significantly to net income. A manager seeking to maximize personal income will select investments that return the highest net income per dollar invested.

Unlike the payback period, the accounting rate of return does consider a project's profitability; like the payback period, it ignores the time value of money. Ignoring the time value of money is a critical deficiency in this method as well; it can lead a manager to choose investments that do not maximize profits. It is because the payback period and the accounting rate of return ignore the time value of money that they are referred to as *nondiscounting models*. Discounting models use **discounted cash flows**, which are future cash flows expressed in terms of their present value. The use of discounting models requires an understanding of the present value concepts. Present value concepts are reviewed in Appendix A. You should review these concepts and make sure that you understand them before studying capital investment discount models. Present value tables (Exhibits 12B-1 and 12B-2) are presented in Appendix B at the end of this chapter. These tables are referred to and used throughout the rest of the chapter.

discounted cash flows

DISCOUNTING MODELS: THE NET PRESENT VALUE METHOD

Objective 3
Use net present value analysis for capital investment decisions involving independent projects.

Discounting models explicitly consider the time value of money and, therefore, incorporate the concept of discounting cash inflows and outflows. Two discounting models will be considered: *net present value* (NPV) and *internal rate of return* (IRR). The net present value method will be discussed first; the internal rate of return method is discussed in the following section.

NPV Defined

net present value

Net present value is the difference in the present value of the cash inflows and outflows associated with a project:

$$\text{NPV} = [\Sigma CF_t/(1 + i)^t] - I \tag{12.1}$$
$$= [\Sigma(CF_t)(df_t)] - I$$
$$= P - I$$

where I = The present value of the project's cost (usually the initial outlay)
CF_t = The cash inflow to be received in period t, with t = 1 . . . n
i = The required rate of return
n = The useful life of the project

$$t = \text{The time period}$$
$$P = \text{The present value of the project's future cash inflows}$$
$$df_t = 1/(1 + i)^t, \text{the discount factor}$$

Net present value (NPV) measures the profitability of an investment. If the NPV is positive, it measures the increase in wealth. For a firm, this means that the size of a positive NPV measures the increase in the value of the firm resulting from an investment. To use the NPV method, a required rate of return must be defined. The **required rate of return** is the minimum acceptable rate of return. It also is referred to as the *discount rate*, the *hurdle rate*, and the *cost of capital*.

required rate of return

If the net present value is positive, it signals that (1) the initial investment has been recovered, (2) the required rate of return has been recovered, and (3) a return in excess of (1) and (2) has been received. Thus, if NPV is greater than zero, the investment is profitable and therefore is acceptable. If NPV equals zero, the decision maker will find acceptance or rejection of the investment equal. Finally, if NPV is less than zero, the investment should be rejected. In this case, it is earning less than the required rate of return.

An Example Illustrating Net Present Value

Brannon Company has developed new earphones for portable disk and tape players that it believes is superior to anything on the market. The marketing manager is excited about the new product's prospects after completing a detailed market study that revealed expected annual revenues of $300,000. The earphones have a projected product life cycle of five years. Equipment to produce the earphones would cost $320,000. After five years, that equipment can be sold for $40,000. In addition to equipment, working capital is expected to increase by $40,000 because of increases in inventories and receivables. The firm expects to recover the investment in working capital at the end of the project's life. Annual cash operating expenses are estimated at $180,000. Assuming that the required rate of return is 12 percent, should the company manufacture the new earphones?

In order to answer the question, two steps must be taken: (1) the cash flows for each year must be identified, and (2) the NPV must be computed using the cash flows from Step 1. The solution to the problem is given in Exhibit 12-2. Notice that Step 2 offers two approaches for computing NPV. Step 2A computes NPV by using discount factors from Exhibit 12B-1, p. 534. Step 2B simplifies the computation by using a single discount factor from Exhibit 12B-2, p. 535, for the even cash flows occurring in Years 1–4.

INTERNAL RATE OF RETURN

Objective 4

Use the internal rate of return to assess the acceptability of an independent project.

internal rate of return

Another discounting model is the internal rate of return (IRR) method. The **internal rate of return** is defined as the interest rate that sets the present value of a project's cash inflows equal to the present value of the project's cost. In other words, it is the interest rate that sets the project's NPV at zero. The following equation can be used to determine a project's IRR:

$$I = \Sigma CF_t/(1 + i)^t \tag{12.2}$$

where $t = 1 \ldots n$

The right-hand side of Equation 12.2 is the present value of future cash flows, and the left-hand side is the investment. I, CF_t, and t are known. Thus, the IRR

Exhibit 12-2
Cash Flows and NPV Analysis

Year	Step 1. Cash-Flow Identification Item	Cash Flow
0	Equipment	$(320,000)
	Working capital	(40,000)
	Total	$(360,000)
1–4	Revenues	$300,000
	Operating expenses	(180,000)
	Total	$120,000
5	Revenues	$300,000
	Operating expenses	(180,000)
	Salvage	40,000
	Recovery of working capital	40,000
	Total	$200,000

Year	Cash Flow[a]	Step 2A. NPV Analysis Discount Factor[b]	Present Value
0	$(360,000)	1.000	$(360,000)
1	120,000	0.893	107,160
2	120,000	0.797	95,640
3	120,000	0.712	85,440
4	120,000	0.636	76,320
5	200,000	0.567	113,400
Net present value			$ 117,960

Year	Cash Flow	Step 2B. NPV Analysis Discount Factor	Present Value
0	$(360,000)	1.000	$(360,000)
1–4	120,000	3.037	364,440
5	200,000	0.567	113,400
Net present value			$ 117,840[c]

[a] From Step 1
[b] From Exhibit 12B-1
[c] Differs from computation in Step 2A because of rounding

(the interest rate, i, in the equation) can be found using trial and error. Once the IRR for a project is computed, it is compared with the firm's required rate of return. If the IRR is greater than the required rate, the project is deemed acceptable; if the IRR is equal to the required rate of return, acceptance or rejection of the investment is equal; if the IRR is less than the required rate of return, the project is rejected.

The internal rate of return is the most widely used of the capital investment techniques. One reason for its popularity may be that it is a rate of return, a concept that managers are comfortable in using. Another possibility is that managers may believe (in most cases, incorrectly) that the IRR is the true or actual compounded rate of return being earned by the initial investment. Whatever the reasons for its popularity, a basic understanding of the IRR is necessary.

Example: Multiple-Period Setting with Uniform Cash Flows

To illustrate the computation of the IRR in a multiple-period setting, assume that a hospital has the opportunity to invest $120,000 in a new ultrasound system that will produce net cash inflows of $49,950 at the end of each year for the next three years. The IRR is the interest rate that equates the present value of the three equal receipts of $49,950 to the investment of $120,000. Since the series of cash flows is uniform, a single discount factor from Exhibit 12B-2 can be used to compute the present value of the annuity. Letting *df* be this discount factor and *CF* be the annual cash flow, Equation 12.2 assumes the following form:

$$I = CF(df)$$

Solving for *df*, we obtain:

$$df = I/CF$$
$$= \text{Investment/Annual cash flow}$$

Once the discount factor is computed, go to Exhibit 12B-2 and find the row corresponding to the life of the project, then move across that row until the computed discount factor is found. The interest rate corresponding to this discount factor is the IRR.

For example, the discount factor for the hospital's investment is 2.402 ($120,000/$49,950). Since the life of the investment is three years, we must find the third row in Exhibit 12B-2 and then move across this row until we encounter 2.402. The interest rate corresponding to 2.402 is 12 percent, which is the IRR.

Exhibit 12B-2 does not provide discount factors for every possible interest rate. To illustrate, assume that the annual cash inflows expected by the hospital are $51,000 instead of $49,950. The new discount factor is 2.353 ($120,000/$51,000). Going once again to the third row in Exhibit 12B-2, we find that the discount factor—and thus the IRR—lies between 12 and 14 percent. It is possible to approximate the IRR by interpolation; however, for our purposes, we will simply identify the range for the IRR as indicated by the table values.

Multiple-Period Setting: Uneven Cash Flows

If the cash flows are not uniform, then Equation 12.2 must be used. For a multiple-period setting, Equation 12.2 can be solved by trial and error or by using a business calculator or a software package like Lotus 1-2-3®. To illustrate solution by trial and error, assume that a $10,000 investment in a PC system produces clerical savings of $6,000 and $7,200 for each of two years. The IRR is the interest rate that sets the present value of these two cash inflows equal to $10,000:

$$P = [\$6,000/(1 + i)] + [\$7,200/(1 + i)^2]$$
$$= \$10,000$$

To solve the above equation by trial and error, start by selecting a possible value for *i*. Given this first guess, the present value of the future cash flows is computed and then compared to the initial investment. If the present value is greater than the initial investment, the interest rate is too low; if the present value is less than the initial investment, the interest rate is too high. The next guess is adjusted accordingly.

Assume the first guess to be 18 percent. Using i equal to 0.18, Exhibit 12B-1 yields the following discount factors: 0.847 and 0.718. These discount factors produce the following present value for the two cash inflows:

$$P = (0.847 \times \$6,000) + (0.718 \times \$7,200)$$
$$= \$10,252$$

Since P is greater than $10,000, the interest rate selected is too low. A higher guess is needed. If the next guess is 20 percent, we obtain the following:

$$P = (0.833 \times \$6,000) + (0.694 \times \$7,200)$$
$$= \$9,995$$

Since this value is reasonably close to $10,000, we can say that the IRR is 20 percent. (The IRR is, in fact, exactly 20 percent; the present value is slightly less than the investment because of rounding error in the discount factors found in Exhibit 12B-1.)

MUTUALLY EXCLUSIVE PROJECTS

Objective 5

Explain why NPV is better than IRR for capital investment decisions involving mutually exclusive projects.

Up to this point, we have focused on independent projects. Many capital investment decisions deal with mutually exclusive projects. How NPV analysis and IRR are used to choose among competing projects is an interesting question. An even more interesting question to consider is whether NPV and IRR differ in their ability to help managers make wealth-maximizing decisions in the presence of competing alternatives. For example, we already know that the non-discounting models can produce erroneous choices because they ignore the time value of money. Because of this deficiency, the discounting models are judged superior. Similarly, it can be shown that the NPV model is generally preferred to the IRR model when choosing among mutually exclusive alternatives.

NPV Compared with IRR

NPV and IRR both yield the same decision for independent projects. For example, if the NPV is greater than zero, then the IRR is also greater than the required rate of return; both models signal the correct decision. However, for competing projects, the two methods can produce different results. Intuitively, we believe that, for mutually exclusive projects, the project with the highest NPV or the highest IRR should be chosen. Since it is possible for the two methods to produce different rankings of mutually exclusive projects, the method that consistently reveals the wealth-maximizing project should be preferred. As will be shown, the NPV method is that model.

NPV differs from IRR in two major ways. First, NPV assumes that each cash inflow received is reinvested at the required rate of return, whereas the IRR method assumes that each cash inflow is reinvested at the computed IRR. Second, the NPV method measures profitability in absolute terms, whereas the IRR method measures it in relative terms. Since absolute measures often produce different rankings than relative measures, it shouldn't be too surprising that NPV and IRR can, on occasion, produce different signals regarding the attractiveness of projects. When a conflict does occur between the two methods, NPV produces the correct signal, as can be shown by a simple example.

Assume that a manager is faced with the prospect of choosing between two mutually exclusive investments whose cash flows, timing, NPV, and IRR are given in Exhibit 12-3 (a required rate of 8 percent is assumed for NPV computation). Both projects have the same life, require the same initial outlay, have positive NPVs, and have IRRs greater than the required rate of return. However, Project A has a higher NPV, whereas Project B has a higher IRR. The NPV and IRR give conflicting signals regarding which project should be chosen.

The preferred project can be identified by modifying the cash flows of one project so that the cash flows of both can be compared year by year. The modification, which appears in Exhibit 12-4, was achieved by carrying the Year 1 cash flow of Project B forward to Year 2. This can be done by assuming that the Year 1 cash flow of $686,342 is invested to earn the required rate of return. Under this assumption, the future value of $686,342 is equal to $741,249 (1.08 × $686,342). When $741,249 is added to the $686,342 received at the end of Year 2, the cash flow expected for Project B is $1,427,591.

As can be seen from Exhibit 12-4, Project A is preferable to Project B. It has the same outlay initially and a greater cash inflow in Year 2 (the difference is $12,409). Since the NPV approach originally chose Project A over Project B, it provided the correct signal for wealth maximization.

Some may object to this analysis, arguing that Project B should be preferred, since it does provide at the end of Year 1 a cash inflow of $686,342, which can be reinvested at a much more attractive rate than the firm's required rate of return. The response is that if such an investment does exist, the firm should still invest in Project A, then borrow $686,342 at the cost of capital and invest that money in the attractive opportunity and, at the end of Year 2, repay the money borrowed plus the interest by using the combined proceeds of Project A and the other investment. For example, assume that the other investment promises a return of 20 percent. The modified cash inflows for Projects A and B are shown in Exhibit 12-5 (assuming that the additional investment at the end of Year 1 is

Exhibit 12-3
NPV and IRR: Conflicting Signals

	Projects	
Year	A	B
0	$(1,000,000)	$(1,000,000)
1	—	686,342
2	1,440,000	686,342
IRR	20%	24%
NPV	$234,080	$223,748

Exhibit 12-4
Modified Comparison of Projects A and B

	Projects	
Year	A	Modified B
0	$(1,000,000)	$(1,000,000)
1	—	—
2	1,440,000	1,427,591*

*1.08($686,342) + $686,342

Exhibit 12-5
*Modified Cash Flows
with Additional
Opportunity*

	Projects	
Year	A	Modified B
0	$(1,000,000)	$(1,000,000)
1	—	—
2	1,522,361[a]	1,509,952[b]

[a]$1,440,000 + [(1.20 × $686,342) − (1.08 × $686,342)]. This last term is what is needed to repay the capital and its cost at the end of Year 2.
[b]$686,342 + (1.20 × $686,342)

made under either alternative). Notice that Project A is still preferable to Project B—and by the same $12,409.

NPV provides the correct signal for choosing among mutually exclusive investments. At the same time, it measures the impact competing projects have on the value of the firm. Choosing the project with the largest NPV is consistent with maximizing the wealth of shareholders. On the other hand, IRR does not consistently result in choices that maximize wealth. IRR, as a *relative* measure of profitability, has the virtue of measuring accurately the rate of return of funds that remain internally invested. However, maximizing IRR will not necessarily maximize the wealth of firm owners because it cannot, by nature, consider the absolute dollar contributions of projects. In the final analysis, what counts are the total dollars earned—the absolute profits—not the relative profits. Accordingly, NPV, not IRR, should be used for choosing among competing, mutually exclusive projects, or competing projects when capital funds are limited.

An independent project is acceptable if its NPV is positive. For mutually exclusive projects, the project with the largest NPV is chosen. There are three steps in selecting the best project from several competing projects: (1) assessing the cash-flow pattern for each project, (2) computing the NPV for each project, and (3) identifying the project with the greatest NPV. To illustrate NPV analysis for competing projects, an example is provided.

Example: Mutually Exclusive Projects

Milagro Travel Agency is setting up an office in Milwaukee and is trying to select a computer system. Two different systems are being considered: the Lavern System and the Hubert System (the systems are offered by competitors and include equipment and software). The Hubert System is more elaborate than the Lavern System and requires a larger investment and greater annual operating costs; however, it will also generate greater annual revenues. The projected annual revenues, annual costs, capital outlays, and project life for each system (in after-tax cash flows) are given below:

	Lavern System	Hubert System
Annual revenues	$240,000	$300,000
Annual operating costs	120,000	160,000
System investment	360,000	420,000
Project life	5 years	5 years

Assume that the cost of capital for the company is 12 percent.

The Lavern System requires an initial outlay of $360,000 and has a net annual cash inflow of $120,000 (revenues of $240,000 minus costs of $120,000). The Hubert System, with an initial outlay of $420,000, has a net annual cash inflow of $140,000 ($300,000 − $160,000). With this information, the cash-flow pattern for each project can be described and the NPV and IRR computed. These are shown in Exhibit 12-6. Based on NPV analysis, the Hubert System is more profitable; it has the larger NPV. Accordingly, the company should select the Hubert System.

Interestingly, both systems have identical internal rates of return. As Exhibit 12-6 illustrates, both systems have a discount factor of 3.0. From Exhibit 12B-2, it is easily seen that a discount factor of 3.0 and a life of five years yields an IRR of approximately 20 percent. Although both projects have an IRR of 20 percent, the firm should not consider the two systems equally desirable. The analysis above has just shown that the Hubert System produces a larger NPV and therefore will increase the value of the firm more than the Lavern System. The Hubert System should be chosen.

Capital Investment and Ethical Issues

Capital investment decisions often offer great temptations for misrepresentations. Divisional managers often must compete for scarce capital resources. With this competition comes the temptation to engage in deceptive behavior. Examples of such behavior are numerous. Managers have been guilty of deliberately overestimating cash inflows and underestimating cash outlays so that a pet project might have the NPV or IRR necessary to be approved. This is particularly tempting when the early cash flows are expected to be good, followed by poor cash flows. Adjusting the estimates of the poor cash flows upward may produce an approved project that has good performance in the early years and poor performance in later years. Other possibilities also exist. For example, a manager may need approval for any capital expenditure above a certain level. To obtain this approval, evidence must exist that the project will produce a positive NPV or an acceptable IRR. In one of a series of IMA ethical cases, an example is given where a local manager acquired a computerized system by purchasing it in pieces, where the cost of each piece was less than the capital expenditure approval limit. Was this right?

Managers need to realize that how objectives are reached is almost as important (maybe more so) than reaching the objectives. Furthermore, the performance evaluation systems of companies should be structured so that the reward system does not provide strong incentives for unethical behavior. As observed in a recent article, "No code of ethics and no amount of cajolery by the chief executive will have much effect if promotions go regularly to the people who pile up big numbers by cutting corners."[4] In the same article, another interesting observation was made—one that is particularly appropriate for the capital expenditure framework. A positive net present value means that the value of the firm should increase. According to the article, James Burke, CEO for Johnson & Johnson, identified a group of firms that paid a lot of attention to ethical standards. From 1950 to 1990 the market value of this group of firms grew at 11.3% annually compared to the 6.2% growth rate of the Dow Jones industrials. Perhaps ethical behavior pays off on the bottom line!

---

4.   Kenneth Labich, "The New Crisis in Business Ethics," *Fortune*, April 20, 1992, pp. 167–176.

Exhibit 12-6
Cash Flow Pattern,
NPV and IRR Analysis:
Lavern Versus Hubert

Year	Cash-Flow Pattern Lavern System	Hubert System
	Cash-Flow Pattern	
0	$(360,000)	$(420,000)
1	120,000	140,000
2	120,000	140,000
3	120,000	140,000
4	120,000	140,000
5	120,000	140,000

The Lavern System: NPV Analysis

Year	Cash Flow	Discount Factor*	Present Value
0	$(360,000)	1.000	$(360,000)
1–5	120,000	3.605	432,600
Net present value			$ 72,600
IRR			20%

IRR Analysis

Discount factor = Initial Investment/Annual cash flow
= $360,000/$120,000
= 3

The Hubert System: NPV Analysis

Year	Cash Flow	Discount Factor*	Present Value
0	$(420,000)	1.000	$(420,000)
1–5	140,000	3.605	504,700
Net present value			$ 84,700

IRR Analysis

Discount factor = Initial investment/Annual cash flow
= $420,000/140,000
= 3

From Exhibit 12B-2, df = 3 for five years implies that IRR = 20%.

*From Exhibit 12B-2.

COMPUTATION AND ADJUSTMENT OF CASH FLOWS

Objective 6
Convert gross cash
flows to after-tax cash
flows.

An important step in capital investment analysis is determining the cash-flow pattern for each project being considered. In fact, the computation of cash flows may be the most critical step in the capital investment process. Erroneous estimates may result in erroneous decisions, regardless of the sophistication of the decision models being used. Two steps are needed to compute cash flows: (1) forecasting revenues, expenses, and capital outlays and (2) adjusting these gross cash flows for inflation and tax effects. Of the two steps, the more challenging is the first. Forecasting cash flows is technically demanding, and its methodology is typically studied in management science and statistics courses. Once gross cash flows are estimated, they should be adjusted for significant inflationary effects. Finally, straightforward applications of tax law can then be used to compute the after-tax flows. At this level of study, we assume that gross cash forecasts are available and focus on adjusting forecasted cash flows to improve their accuracy and utility in capital expenditure analysis.

Adjusting Forecasts for Inflation

In the United States, inflation has been relatively modest and the need to adjust cash flows may not be as critical. For firms that operate in the international environment, however, the effect on capital investment decisions can be dramatic because inflation can be very high in certain countries. Brazil, for example, has experienced monthly double-digit inflation rates for years. Thus, it is important to know how to adjust the capital budgeting models for inflationary effects—particularly given the fact that many U.S. firms make capital investment decisions within many different national environments.

In an inflationary environment, financial markets react by increasing the cost of capital to reflect inflation. Thus, the cost of capital is composed of two elements:

1. The real rate.
2. The inflationary element (investors demand a premium to compensate for the loss in general purchasing power of the dollar or local currency).

Since the required rate of return (which should be the cost of capital) used in capital investment analysis reflects an inflationary component at the time NPV analysis is performed, inflation must also be considered in predicting the operating cash flows. If the operating cash flows are not adjusted to account for inflation, an erroneous decision may result. In adjusting predicted cash flows, specific price change indexes should be used if possible. If that is not possible, a general price index can be used.

Note, however, that the cash inflows due to the tax effects of depreciation need *not* be adjusted for inflation as long as the national tax law requires that depreciation be based on the *original* dollar investment. In this case, depreciation deductions should not be increased for inflation.

To illustrate, assume that a subsidiary of a U.S. firm operating in Mexico is considering a project that requires an investment of 5,000,000 pesos and is expected to produce annual cash inflows of 2,900,000 pesos for the coming two years. The required rate of return is 20 percent, which includes an inflationary component. The general inflation rate in Mexico is expected to average 15 percent for the next two years. Net present value analysis with and without the adjustment of predicted cash flows for inflation is given in Exhibit 12-7. (Note: All cash flows in Exhibit 12-7 are expressed in pesos.) As the analysis shows, *not* adjusting predicted cash flows for inflation leads to a decision to reject the project, whereas adjusting for inflation leads to a decision to accept it. Thus, failure to adjust the predicted cash flows for inflationary effects can lead to an incorrect conclusion.

Conversion of Gross Cash Flows to After-Tax Cash Flows

Assuming that inflation-adjusted gross cash flows are predicted with the desired degree of accuracy, the analyst must adjust these cash flows for taxes. To analyze tax effects, cash flows are usually broken into two categories: (1) the initial cash outflows needed to acquire the assets of the project and (2) the cash inflows produced over the life of the project. Cash outflows and cash inflows adjusted for tax effects are called *net* cash outflows and inflows. Net cash flows include pro-

Exhibit 12-7
The Effects of Inflation on Capital Investment

Year	Without Inflationary Adjustment Cash Flow	Discount Factor[a]	Present Value
0	$(5,000,000)	1.000	$(5,000,000)
1–2	2,900,000	1.528	4,431,200
Net present value			$ (568,800)

Year	With Inflationary Adjustment Cash Flow[b]	Discount Factor[c]	Present Value
0	$(5,000,000)	1.000	$(5,000,000)
1	3,335,000	0.833	2,778,055
2	3,835,250	0.694	2,661,664
Net present value			$ 439,719

[a] From Exhibit 12B-2.
[b] 3,335,000 pesos = 1.15 × 2,900,000 pesos (adjustment for one year of inflation).
  3,835,250 pesos = 1.15 × 1.15 × 2,900,000 pesos (adjustment for two years of inflation).
[c] From Exhibit 12B-1.

visions for revenues, operating expenses, depreciation, and relevant tax implications. They are the proper inputs for capital investment decisions.

After-Tax Cash Flows: Year 0 The net cash outflow in Year 0 (the initial out-of-pocket outlay) is simply the difference between the initial cost of the project and any cash inflows directly associated with it. The gross cost of the project includes such things as the cost of land, the cost of equipment (including transportation and installation), taxes on gains from the sale of assets, and increases in working capital. Cash inflows occurring at the time of acquisition include tax savings from the sale of assets, cash from the sale of assets, and other tax benefits such as tax credits.

Under current tax law, all costs relating to the acquisition of assets other than land must be capitalized and written off over the useful life of the assets (the write-off is achieved through depreciation). Depreciation is deducted from revenues in computing taxable income during each year of the asset's life; however, at the point of acquisition, no depreciation expense is computed. Thus, depreciation is not relevant at Year 0. The principal tax implications at the point of acquisition are related to recognition of gains and losses on the sale of existing assets and to the recognition of any investment tax credits.

Gains on the sale of assets produce additional taxes and, accordingly, reduce the cash proceeds received from the sale of old assets. Losses, on the other hand, are noncash expenses that reduce taxable income, producing tax savings. Consequently, the cash proceeds from the sale of an old asset are increased by the amount of the tax savings.

Adjusting cash inflows and outflows for tax effects requires knowledge of current corporate tax rates. Currently, most corporations face a federal tax rate of 35%. State corporate tax rates vary by state. For purposes of analysis, we will assume that 40% is the combined rate for state and federal taxes.

Let us look at an example. Currently, Champy Company uses two types of numerically controlled machines (CNC-11 and CNC-12) to produce one of its products. Recent technological advances have created a single CNC machine that can replace them. Management wants to know the net investment needed to acquire the new machine. If the new machine is acquired, the old equipment will be sold.

Disposition of Old Machines

	Book Value	Sale Price
CNC-11	$200,000	$ 260,000
CNC-12	500,000	400,000

Acquisition of New CNC

Purchase cost	$2,500,000
Freight	20,000
Installation	200,000
Additional working capital	180,000
Total	$2,900,000

The net investment can be determined by computing the net proceeds from the sale of the old machines and subtracting those proceeds from the cost of the new machine. The net proceeds are determined by computing the tax consequences of the sale and adjusting the gross receipts accordingly.

The tax consequences can be assessed by subtracting the book value from the selling price. If the difference is positive, the firm has experienced a gain and will owe taxes. Money received from the sale will be reduced by the amount of taxes owed. On the other hand, if the difference is negative, a loss is experienced—a noncash loss. However, this noncash loss does have cash implications. It can be deducted from revenues and, as a consequence, can shield revenues from being taxed; accordingly, taxes will be saved. Thus, a loss produces a cash inflow equal to the taxes saved.

To illustrate, consider the tax effects of selling CNC-11 and CNC-12 illustrated in Exhibit 12-8. By selling the two machines, the company receives the following net proceeds:

Sale price, CNC-11	$260,000
Sale price, CNC-12	400,000
Tax savings	16,000
Net proceeds	$676,000

Given these net proceeds, the net investment can be computed as follows:

Total cost of new machine	$2,900,000
Less: Net proceeds of old machines	(676,000)
Net investment (cash outflow)	$2,224,000

Exhibit 12-8
Tax Effects of the Sale of CNC-11 and CNC-12

Asset	Gain (Loss)
CNC-11[a]	$ 60,000
CNC-12[b]	(100,000)
Net gain (loss)	$ (40,000)
Tax rate	0.40
Tax savings	$ 16,000

[a]Sale price minus book value is $260,000 − $200,000.
[b]Sale price minus book value is $400,000 − $500,000.

After-Tax Cash Flows: Life of the Project In addition to determining the initial out-of-pocket outlay, managers must also estimate the annual after-tax cash flows expected over the life of the project. If the project generates revenue, the principal source of cash flows is from operations. Operating cash inflows can be assessed from the project's income statement. The annual after-tax cash flows are the sum of the project's after-tax profits and its noncash expenses. In terms of a simple formula, this computation can be represented as follows:

$$\text{After-tax cash flow} = \text{After-tax net income} + \text{Noncash expense}$$
$$CF = NI + NC$$

where

$$CF = \text{After-tax cash flow}$$
$$NI = \text{After-tax net income}$$
$$NC = \text{Noncash expenses}$$

The most prominent examples of noncash expenses are depreciation and losses. At first glance, it may seem odd that after-tax cash flows are computed using noncash expenses. Noncash expenses are not cash flows, but they do generate cash flows by reducing taxes. By shielding revenues from taxation, actual cash savings are created. The use of the income statement to determine after-tax cash flows is illustrated in the following example. The example is also used to show how noncash expenses can increase cash inflows by saving taxes.

Assume that a company plans to make a new product that requires new equipment costing $800,000. The new product is expected to increase the firm's annual revenues by $600,000. Materials, labor, and other cash operating expenses will be $250,000 per year. The equipment has a life of four years and will be depreciated on a straight-line basis. The machine will have no salvage value at the end of four years. The income statement for the project is given below.

Revenues	$600,000
Less: Cash operating expenses	(250,000)
Less: Depreciation	(200,000)
Income before taxes	$150,000
Less: Taxes (@ 40%)	(60,000)
Net income	$ 90,000

Cash flow from the income statement is computed as follows:

$$CF = NI + NC$$
$$= \$90,000 + \$200,000$$
$$= \$290,000$$

The income approach to determine operating cash flows can be decomposed to assess the after-tax, cash-flow effects of each individual category on the income statement. The decomposition approach calculates the operating cash flows by computing the after-tax cash flows for each item of the income statement:

$$CF = [(1 - \text{Tax rate}) \times \text{Revenues}] - [(1 - \text{Tax rate}) \times \text{Cash expenses}] +$$
$$(\text{Tax rate} \times \text{Noncash expenses})$$

The first term, $[(1 - \text{Tax rate}) \times \text{Revenues}]$, gives the after-tax cash inflows from cash revenues. For our example, the cash revenue is projected to be $600,000. The firm, therefore, can expect to keep $360,000 of the revenues received: $(1 - \text{Tax rate}) \times \text{Revenues} = 0.60 \times \$600,000 = \$360,000$. The after-tax revenue is the actual amount of after-tax cash available from the sales activity of the firm.

The second term, $[(1 - \text{Tax rate}) \times \text{Cash expenses}]$, is the after-tax cash outflows from cash operating expenses. Because cash expenses can be deducted from revenues to arrive at taxable income, the effect is to shield revenues from taxation. The consequence of this shielding is to save taxes and to reduce the actual cash outflow associated with a given expenditure. In our example, the firm has cash operating expenses of $250,000. The actual cash outflow is not $250,000 but $150,000 $(0.60 \times \$250,000)$. The cash outlay for operating expenses is reduced by $100,000 because of tax savings. To see this, assume that operating expense is the only expense and that the firm has revenues of $600,000. If operating expense is *not* tax deductible, then the tax owed is $240,000 $(0.40 \times \$600,000)$. If the operating expense is deductible for tax purposes, then the taxable income is $350,000 ($600,000 - $250,000), and the tax owed is $140,000 $(0.40 \times \$350,000)$. Because the deductibility of operating expense saves $100,000 in taxes, the actual outlay for that expenditure is reduced by $100,000.

The third term, $\text{Tax rate} \times \text{Noncash expenses}$, is the cash inflow from the tax savings produced by the noncash expenses. Noncash expenses, such as depreciation, also shield revenues from taxation. The depreciation *shields* $200,000 of revenues from being taxed and thus saves $80,000 $(0.40 \times \$200,000)$ in taxes.

The sum of the three items is given below.

After-tax revenues	$360,000
After-tax cash expenses	(150,000)
Depreciation tax shield	80,000
Operating cash flow	$290,000

The decomposition approach yields the same outcome as the income approach. For convenience, the three decomposition terms are summarized in Exhibit 12-9.

One feature of decomposition is the ability to compute after-tax cash flows in a spreadsheet format. This format highlights the cash-flow effects of individual items and facilitates the use of spreadsheet software packages. The spreadsheet

Exhibit 12-9
Computation of Operating Cash Flows: Decomposition Terms

After-tax cash revenues = (1 − Tax rate) × Cash revenues
After-tax cash expenses = (1 − Tax rate) × Cash expenses
Tax savings, noncash expenses = Tax rate × Noncash expenses

format is achieved by creating four columns, one for each of the three cash-flow categories and one for the total after-tax cash flow, which is the sum of the first three. This format is illustrated in Exhibit 12-10 for our example. Recall that cash revenues were $600,000 per year for three years, annual cash expenses were $250,000, and annual depreciation was $100,000.

A second feature of decomposition is the ability to compute the after-tax cash effects on an item-by-item basis. For example, suppose that a firm is considering a project and is uncertain as to which method of depreciation should be used. By computing the tax savings produced under each depreciation method, a firm can quickly assess which method is most desirable.

For tax purposes, all depreciable business assets other than real estate are referred to as *personal property*, which is classified into one of six classes. Each class specifies the life of the assets that must be used for figuring depreciation. This life must be used even if the actual expected life is different from the class life; the class lives are set for purposes of recognizing depreciation and usually will be shorter than the actual life. Most equipment, machinery, and office furniture are classified as **seven-year assets**. Light trucks, automobiles, and computer equipment are classified as **five-year assets**. Most small tools are classified as **three-year assets**. Because the majority of personal property can be put into one of these categories, we will restrict our attention to them.

The taxpayer can use either the straight-line method or the **modified accelerated cost recovery system (MACRS)** to compute annual depreciation. Current law defines MACRS as the double-declining-balance method.[5] In computing depreciation, no consideration of salvage value is required. However, under either method, a **half-year convention** applies.[6] This convention assumes that a newly acquired asset is in service for one-half of its first taxable year of service, regardless of the date that use of it actually began. When the asset reaches the

seven-year assets
five-year assets
three-year assets

modified accelerated cost recovery system (MACRS)

half-year convention

Exhibit 12-10
Illustration of the Spreadsheet Approach

Year	(1 − t)R[a]	−(1 − t)C[b]	tNC[c]	CF
1	$360,000	$(150,000)	$80,000	$290,000
2	360,000	(150,000)	80,000	290,000
3	360,000	(150,000)	80,000	290,000
4	360,000	(150,000)	80,000	290,000

[a]R = Revenues; t = tax rate; (1 − t)R = (1 − 0.40)$600,000 = $360,000
[b]C = Cash expenses; −(1 − t)C = −(1 − 0.40)$250,000 = $(150,000)
[c]NC = Noncash expenses; tNC = 0.40($200,000) = $80,000

5.   The tax law also allows the 150-percent-declining-balance method; however, we will focus on only the straight-line method and the double-declining version of MACRS.
6.   The tax law requires a mid-quarter convention if more than 40 percent of personal property is placed in service during the last three months of the year. We will not illustrate this possible scenario.

end of its life, the other half year of depreciation can be claimed in the following year. If an asset is disposed of before the end of its class life, the half-year convention allows half the depreciation for that year.

For example, assume that an automobile is purchased on March 1, 1997. The automobile costs $20,000, and the firm elects the straight-line method. Automobiles are five-year assets (for tax purposes). The annual depreciation is $4,000 for a five-year period ($20,000/5). However, using the half-year convention, the firm can deduct only $2,000 for 1997, half of the straight-line amount (0.5 × $4,000). The remaining half is deducted in the sixth year (or the year of disposal, if earlier). Deductions are shown below.

Year	Depreciation Deduction
1997	$2,000 (half-year amount)
1998	4,000
1999	4,000
2000	4,000
2001	4,000
2002	2,000 (half-year amount)

Assume that the asset is disposed of in April 1999. In this case, only $2,000 of depreciation can be claimed for 1999 (early disposal rule).

If the double-declining-balance method is selected, the amount of depreciation claimed in the first year is twice that of the straight-line method. Under this method, the amount of depreciation claimed becomes progressively smaller until eventually it is exceeded by that claimed under the straight-line method. When this happens, the straight-line method is used to finish depreciating the asset. Exhibit 12-11 provides a table of depreciation rates for the double-declining-balance method for assets belonging to the three-year, five-year, and seven-year classes. The rates shown in this table incorporate the half-year convention and therefore are the MACRS depreciation rates.

Both the straight-line method and the double-declining-balance method yield the same total amount of depreciation over the life of the asset. Both methods also produce the same total tax savings (assuming the same tax rate over the life of the asset). However, since the depreciation claimed in the early years of a project is greater using the double-declining-balance method, the tax savings are also greater during those years. Considering the time value of money, it is preferable to have the tax savings earlier than later. Thus, firms should prefer the MACRS method of depreciation over the straight-line method. This conclusion is illustrated by the following example.

Exhibit 12-11
MACRS Depreciation Rates

Year	Three-Year Assets	Five-Year Assets	Seven-Year Assets
1	33.33%	20.00%	14.29%
2	44.45	32.00	24.49
3	14.81	19.20	17.49
4	7.41	11.52	12.49
5		11.52	8.93
6		5.76	8.92
7		—	8.93
8		—	4.46

A firm is considering the purchase of computer equipment for $20,000. The tax guidelines require that the cost of the equipment be depreciated over five years. However, tax guidelines also permit the depreciation to be computed using either method. Of course, the firm should choose the double-declining-balance method because it brings the greater benefit.

From decomposition, we know that the cash inflows caused by shielding can be computed by multiplying the tax rate by the amount depreciated ($t \times NC$). The cash flows produced by each depreciation method and their present value, assuming a discount rate of 10 percent, are given in Exhibit 12-12. As can be seen, the present value of the tax savings from using MACRS is greater than that using straight-line depreciation.

CAPITAL INVESTMENT: THE CONTEMPORARY MANUFACTURING ENVIRONMENT

Objective 7

Describe capital investment in the contemporary manufacturing environment.

In the contemporary manufacturing environment, long-term investments are generally concerned with the automation of manufacturing. Before any commitment to automation is made, however, a company should first make the most efficient use of existing technology. Many benefits can be realized by redesigning and simplifying the current manufacturing process. An example often given to support this thesis is automation of materials handling. Automation of this operation can cost millions—and it is usually unnecessary because greater efficiency can be achieved by eliminating inventories and simplifying material transfers through the implementation of a JIT system.

Once the benefits from redesign and simplification are achieved, however, it becomes apparent where automation can generate additional benefits. Many companies can improve their competitive positions by adding such features as robotics, flexible manufacturing systems, and completely integrated manufacturing systems. The ultimate commitment to automation is the construction of greenfield factories. Greenfield factories are new factories designed and built from scratch; they represent a strategic decision by a company to change completely the way it manufactures.

Although discounted cash-flow analysis (using net present value and internal rate of return) remains preeminent in capital investment decisions, the new manufacturing environment demands that more attention be paid to the inputs used in discounted cash-flow models. How investment is defined, how operating cash flows are estimated, how salvage value is treated, and how the discount rate is chosen are all different in nature from the traditional approach.[7]

There is also another important dimension. Contemporary investment management involves both *financial* and *nonfinancial* criteria. It is critical that the investment management process be linked with the company's strategies. Analysis in advanced manufacturing technology should consider the contributions made to support such strategies as product enhancement, diversification, and risk reduction. For example, advanced technology may contribute to product enhancement by allowing a firm more flexibility in responding to fluctuating demands. Improving quality is also a product enhancement feature. Some of

---

7.   Much of the information on investment in the new manufacturing environment is based on the following sources: Robert A. Howell and Stephen R. Soucy, "Capital Investment in the New Manufacturing Environment," *Management Accounting*, November 1987, pp. 26–32; Callie Berliner and James A. Brimson (eds.), *Cost Management for Today's Advanced Manufacturing*, Harvard Business School Press, Boston, 1988; Thomas Klammer, "Improving Investment Decisions," *Management Accounting*, July 1993, pp. 35–43; and David Sinason, "A Dynamic Model for Present Value Analysis, *Journal of Cost Management*, Spring 1991, pp. 40–45.

Exhibit 12-12
Value of Accelerated Methods Illustrated

Year	Straight-Line Method Depreciation	Tax Rate	Tax Savings	Discount Factor	Present Value
1	$2,000	0.40	$ 800.00	0.909	$ 727.20
2	4,000	0.40	1,600.00	0.826	1,321.60
3	4,000	0.40	1,600.00	0.751	1,201.60
4	4,000	0.40	1,600.00	0.683	1,092.80
5	4,000	0.40	1,600.00	0.621	993.60
6	2,000	0.40	800.00	0.564	451.20
Net present value					$5,788.00

Year	MACRS Method Depreciation*	Tax Rate	Tax Savings	Discount Factor	Present Value
1	$4,000	0.40	$1,600.00	0.909	$1,454.40
2	6,400	0.40	2,560.00	0.826	2,114.56
3	3,840	0.40	1,536.00	0.751	1,153.54
4	2,304	0.40	921.60	0.683	629.45
5	2,304	0.40	921.60	0.621	572.31
6	1,152	0.40	460.80	0.564	259.89
Net present value					$6,184.15

*Computed by multiplying the five-year rates in Exhibit 12-11 by $20,000. For example, depreciation for Year 1 is 0.20 × $20,000.

these product enhancement features may be possible to quantify. For example, it may be possible to estimate the cost savings attributable to improved quality. Other factors may be more difficult to quantify. Assessing the cost savings or increased revenues from increased flexibility may be quite difficult. Yet the increased flexibility may be as critical for the company as improved quality. Thus, consideration of nonfinancial factors is also important to the investment management process. Nonetheless, every possible effort should be made to quantify the factors affecting the investment decision.

How Investment Differs

Investment in automated manufacturing processes is much more complex than investment in the standard manufacturing equipment of the past. For standard equipment, the direct costs of acquisition represent virtually the entire investment. For automated manufacturing, the direct costs can represent as little as 50 or 60 percent of the total investment; software, engineering, training, and implementation are a significant percentage of the total costs. Thus, great care must be exercised to assess the actual cost of an automated system. It is easy to overlook the peripheral costs, which can be substantial. U.S. bankers and insurance companies have found that their substantial investment in computer technology is only now starting to pay off. The reason is that there were very large investments to be made in training. Until the companies had experience with the technology, they were unable to adequately use its power and improve productivity.

How Estimates of Operating Cash Flows Differ

Estimates of operating cash flows from investments in standard equipment have typically relied on directly identifiable tangible benefits, such as direct savings from labor, power, and scrap. Monsanto's Fibers Division, for example, used direct labor savings as the main justification for automating its Pensacola, Florida, plant.[8] Intangible benefits and indirect savings were ignored as they often are in traditional capital investment analyses. In the new manufacturing environment, however, the intangible and indirect benefits can be material and critical to the viability of the project. Greater quality, more reliability, reduced lead time, improved customer satisfaction, and an enhanced ability to maintain market share are all important intangible benefits of an advanced manufacturing system. Reduction of labor in support areas such as production scheduling and stores are indirect benefits. More effort is needed to measure these intangible and indirect benefits in order to assess more accurately the potential value of investments. Monsanto discovered, for example, that the new automated system in its Pensacola plant produced large savings in terms of reduced waste, lower inventories, increased quality, and reduced indirect labor. Productivity increased by 50%. What if the direct labor savings had not been sufficient to justify the investment? Consider the lost returns that Monsanto would have experienced by what could have been a faulty decision. Monsanto's experience also illustrates the importance of a *postaudit*. A **postaudit** is a follow-up analysis of a capital project once it is implemented. It compares the actual benefits and costs with the estimated benefits and costs. For Monsanto, the postaudit revealed the importance of intangible and indirect benefits. In future investment decisions, these factors are more likely to be considered.

postaudit

An example can be used to illustrate the importance of considering intangible and indirect benefits. Consider a company that is evaluating a potential investment in a flexible manufacturing system (FMS). The choice facing the company is to continue producing with its traditional equipment, expected to last ten years, or to switch to the new system, which is also expected to have a useful life of ten years. The company's discount rate is 12 percent. The data pertaining to the investment are presented in Exhibit 12-13. Using these data, the net present value of the proposed system can be computed as follows:

Present value ($4,000,000 × 5.65*)	$22,600,000
Investment	(18,000,000)
Net present value	$ 4,600,000

*Discount factor for an interest rate of 12 percent and a life of ten years (see Exhibit 12B-2).

The net present value is positive and large in magnitude, and it clearly signals the acceptability of the FMS. This outcome is strongly dependent, however, on explicit recognition of both intangible and indirect benefits. If those benefits are eliminated, then the direct savings total $2.2 million, and the NPV is negative.

Present value ($2,200,000 × 5.65)	$12,430,000
Investment	(18,000,000)
Net present value	$ (5,570,000)

8.   The following article provides a good description of Monsanto's experience: Raymond C. Cole and H. Lee Hales, "How Monsanto Justified Automation," *Management Accounting,* January 1992, pp. 39–43.

Exhibit 12-13
Investment Data:
Direct, Intangible, and
Indirect Benefits

	FMS	Status Quo
Investment (current outlay):		
Direct costs	$10,000,000	$ 0
Software, engineering	8,000,000	—
Total current outlay	$18,000,000	$ 0
Net after-tax cash flow	$ 5,000,000	$1,000,000
Less: After-tax cash flow for status quo	(1,000,000)	n/a
Incremental benefit	$ 4,000,000	n/a
Incremental Benefit Explained		
Direct benefits:		
Direct labor	$ 1,500,000	
Scrap reduction	500,000	
Setups	200,000	$2,200,000
Intangible benefits: Quality savings		
Rework	$ 200,000	
Warranties	400,000	
Maintenance of competitive position	1,000,000	1,600,000
Indirect benefits:		
Production scheduling	$ 110,000	
Payroll	90,000	200,000
Total		$4,000,000

The rise of activity-based costing has made identifying indirect benefits easier with the use of activity drivers. Once they are identified, they can be included in the analysis if they are material.

Examination of Exhibit 12-13 reveals the importance of intangible benefits. One of the most important intangible benefits is maintaining or improving a firm's competitive position. A key question that needs to be asked is what will happen to the cash flows of the firm if the investment is *not* made. That is, if the company chooses to forgo an investment in technologically advanced equipment, will it be able to continue to compete with other firms on the basis of quality, delivery, and cost? (The question becomes especially relevant if competitors choose to invest in advanced equipment.) If the competitive position deteriorates, the company's current cash flows will decrease.

If cash flows will decrease if the investment is not made, this decrease should show up as an incremental benefit for the advanced technology. In Exhibit 12-13, the company estimates this competitive benefit as $1,000,000. Estimating this benefit requires some serious strategic planning and analysis, but its effect can be critical. If this benefit had been ignored or overlooked, then the net present value would have been negative, and the investment alternative rejected. This calculation is shown below.

Present value ($3,000,000 × 5.65)	$16,950,000
Investment	(18,000,000)
Net present value	$ (1,050,000)

Salvage Value

Terminal or salvage value has often been ignored in investment decisions. The usual reason offered is the difficulty to estimate it. Because of this uncertainty, the effect of salvage value has often been ignored or heavily discounted. This approach may be unwise, however, because salvage value could make the difference between investing or not investing. Given the highly competitive environment, companies cannot afford to make incorrect decisions. A much better approach to deal with uncertainty is to use sensitivity analysis. **Sensitivity analysis** changes the assumptions on which the capital investment analysis relies and assesses the effect on the cash-flow pattern. Sensitivity analysis is often referred to as **what-if analysis**. For example, this approach is used to address such questions as *what* is the effect on the decision to invest in a project *if* the cash receipts are 5 percent less than projected? 5 percent more? Although sensitivity analysis is computationally demanding if done manually, it can be done rapidly and easily using computers and software packages such as Lotus®, Excel®, and Quattro Pro®. In fact, these packages can also be used to carry out the NPV and IRR computations that have been illustrated manually throughout the chapter. They have built-in NPV and IRR functions that greatly facilitate the computational requirements.

To illustrate the potential effect of terminal value, assume that the after-tax annual operating cash flow of the project shown in Exhibit 12-13 is $3.1 million instead of $4 million. The net present value without salvage value is as follows:

sensitivity analysis

what-if analysis

Present value ($3,100,000 × 5.65)	$17,515,000
Investment	(18,000,000)
Net present value	$ (485,000)

Without the terminal value, the project would be rejected. The net present value with salvage value of $2 million, however, is a positive result, meaning that the investment should be made.

Present value ($3,100,000 × 5.65)	$17,515,000
Present value ($2,000,000 × 0.322*)	644,000
Investment	(18,000,000)
Net present value	$ 159,000

*Discount factor, 12 percent and ten years (Exhibit 12B-1).

But what if the salvage value is less than expected? Suppose that the worst possible outcome is a salvage value of $1,600,000? What is the effect on the decision? The NPV can be recomputed under this new scenario.

Present value ($3,100,000 × 5.65)	$17,515,000
Present value ($1,600,000 × 0.322)	515,200
Investment	(18,000,000)
Net present value	$ 30,200

Thus, under a pessimistic scenario, the NPV is still positive. This illustrates how sensitivity analysis can be used to deal with the uncertainty surrounding salvage value. It can also be used for other cash flow variables.

Discount Rates

Being overly conservative with discount rates can prove even more damaging. In theory, if future cash flows are known with certainty, the correct discount rate is a firm's cost of capital. In practice, future cash flows are uncertain, and managers often choose a discount rate higher than the cost of capital to deal with that uncertainty. If the rate chosen is excessively high, it will bias the selection process toward short-term investments.

To illustrate the effect of an excessive discount rate, consider the project in Exhibit 12-13 once again. Assume that the correct discount rate is 12 percent but that the firm uses 18 percent. The net present value using an 18 percent discount rate is calculated as follows:

Present value ($4,000,000 × 4.494*)	$17,976,000
Investment	(18,000,000)
Net present value	$ (24,000)

*Discount rate for 18 percent and ten years (Exhibit 12B-2).

The project would be rejected. With a higher discount rate, the discount factor decreases in magnitude much more rapidly than the discount factor for a lower rate (compare the discount factor for 12 percent, 5.65, with the factor for 18 percent, 4.494). The effect of a higher discount factor is to place more weight on earlier cash flows and less weight on later cash flows, which favors short-term over long-term investments. This outcome makes it more difficult for automated manufacturing systems to appear as viable projects, since the cash returns required to justify the investment are received over a longer period of time.

SUMMARY

Capital investment decisions are concerned with the acquisition of long-term assets and usually involve a significant outlay of funds. There are two types of capital investment projects: independent and mutually exclusive. Independent projects are projects that, if accepted or rejected, do not affect the cash flows of other projects. Mutually exclusive projects are those projects that, if accepted, preclude the acceptance of all other competing projects.

Managers make capital investment decisions by using formal models to decide whether to accept or reject proposed projects. These decision models are classified as nondiscounting and discounting, depending on whether they address the question of the time value of money. There are two nondiscounting models: the payback period and the accounting rate of return.

The payback period is the time required for a firm to recover its initial investment. For even cash flows, it is calculated by dividing the investment by the annual cash flow. For uneven cash flows, the cash flows are summed until the investment is recovered. If only a fraction of a year is needed, then it is assumed that the cash flows occur evenly within each year. The payback period ignores the time value of money and the profitability of projects because it does not consider the cash inflows available beyond the payback period. However, it does supply some useful information. The payback period is useful in assessing and controlling risk, minimizing the impact of an investment on a firm's liquidity, and controlling the risk of obsolescence.

The accounting rate of return is computed by dividing the average income expected from an investment by either the original or average investment. Unlike the payback period, it does consider the profitability of a project; however, it ignores the time value of money. The accounting rate of return may be useful to managers to screen new investments to ensure that certain accounting ratios are not adversely affected (specifically accounting ratios that may be monitored to ensure compliance with debt covenants).

NPV is the difference between the present value of future cash flows and the initial investment outlay. To use the model, a required rate of return must be identified (usually the cost of capital). The NPV method uses the required rate of return to compute the present value of a project's cash inflows and outflows. If the present value of the inflows is greater than the present value of the outflows, the net present value is greater than zero, and the project is profitable. If the NPV is less than zero, the project is not profitable and should be rejected.

The IRR is computed by finding the interest rate that equates the present value of a project's cash inflows with the present value of its cash outflows. If the IRR is greater than the required rate of return (cost of capital), the project is acceptable. If the IRR is less than the required rate of return, the project should be rejected.

In evaluating mutually exclusive or competing projects, managers have a choice of using NPV or IRR. When choosing among competing projects, the NPV model correctly identifies the best investment alternative. IRR, at times, may choose an inferior project. Thus, since NPV always provides the correct signal, it should be used.

Accurate and reliable cash-flow forecasts are absolutely critical for capital-budgeting analyses. Managers should assume responsibility for the accuracy of cash-flow projections. All cash flows in a capital-investment analysis should be after-tax cash flows. There are two different, but equivalent, ways to compute after-tax cash flows: the income method and the decomposition method. Although depreciation is not a cash flow, it does have cash-flow implications because tax laws allow depreciation to be deducted in computing taxable income. Straight-line and double-declining-balance depreciation both produce the same total depreciation deductions over the life of the depreciated asset. Because the latter method accelerates depreciation, however, it would be preferred.

Capital investment in the contemporary manufacturing environment is affected by the way in which inputs are determined. Much greater attention must be paid to the investment outlays because peripheral items can require substantial resources. Furthermore, in assessing benefits, intangible items such as quality and maintaining competitive position can be deciding factors. Choice of the required rate of return is also critical. The tendency of firms to use hurdle rates that are much greater than the cost of capital should be discontinued. Also, since the salvage value of an automated system can be considerable, it should be estimated and included in the analysis.

APPENDIX A: PRESENT VALUE CONCEPTS

An important feature of money is that it can be invested and can earn interest. A dollar today is not the same as a dollar tomorrow. This fundamental principle is the backbone of discounting methods. Discounting methods rely on the relationships between current and future dollars. Thus, to use discounting methods, we must understand these relationships.

Future Value

Suppose a bank advertises a 4 percent annual interest rate. If a customer invests $100, he or she would receive, after one year, the original $100 plus $4 interest $[\$100 + (0.04 \times \$100) = (1 + 0.04) \times \$100 = 1.04 \times \$100 = \$104]$. This result can be expressed by the following equation, where F is the future amount, P is the initial or current outlay, and i is the interest rate:

$$F = P(1 + i) \qquad (12A.1)$$

For the example, $F = \$100 \times (1 + 0.04) = \$100 \times 1.04 = \$104$.

Now suppose that the same bank offers a 5 percent rate if the customer leaves the original deposit, plus any interest, on deposit for a total of two years. How much will the customer receive at the end of two years? Again assume that a customer invests $100. Using Equation 12A.1, the customer will earn $105 at the end of Year 1 [F = $100 × (1 + 0.05) = $100 × 1.05 = $105]. If this amount is left in the account for a second year, Equation 12A.1 is used again with P now assumed to be $105. At the end of the second year, then, the total is $110.25 [F = $105 × (1 + 0.05) = $105 × 1.05 = $110.25]. In the second year, interest is earned on both the original deposit and the interest earned in the first year. The earning of interest on interest is referred to as **compounding of interest**. The value that will accumulate by the end of an investment's life, assuming a specified compound return, is the **future value**. The future value of the $100 deposit in the second example is $110.25.

compounding of interest

future value

A more direct way to compute the future value is possible. Since the first application of Equation 12A.1 can be expressed as $F = \$105 = \$100 \times 1.05$, the second application can be expressed as $F = \$105 \times 1.05 = \$100 \times 1.05 \times 1.05 = \$100(1.05)^2 = P(1 + i)^2$. This suggests the following formula for computing amounts for n periods into the future:

$$F = P(1 + i)^n \tag{12A.2}$$

Present Value

Often a manager needs to compute not the future value but the amount that must be invested *now* in order to earn some given future value. The amount that must be invested now to produce the future value is known as the **present value** of the future amount. For example, how much must be invested now in order to earn $363 two years from now, assuming that the interest rate is 10 percent? Or put another way, what is the present value of $363 to be received two years from now?

present value

In this example, the future value, the years, and the interest rate are all known; we want to know the current outlay that will produce that future amount. In Equation 12A.2, the variable representing the current outlay (the present value of F) is P. Thus, to compute the present value of a future outlay, all we need to do is solve Equation 12A.2 for P:

$$P = F/(1 + i)^n \tag{12A.3}$$

Using Equation 12A.3, we can compute the present value of $363:

$$\begin{aligned} P &= \$363/(1 + 0.1)^2 \\ &= \$363/1.21 \\ &= \$300 \end{aligned}$$

The present value, $300, is what the future amount of $363 is worth *today*. All other things being equal, having $300 today is the same as having $363 two years from now. Put another way, if a firm requires a 10 percent rate of return, the most the firm would be willing to pay today is $300 for any investment that yields $363 two years from now.

The process of computing the present value of future cash flows is often referred to as **discounting**; thus, we say that we have discounted the future value of $363 to its present value of $300. The interest rate used to discount the future cash flow is the **discount rate**. The expression $1/(1 + i)^n$ in Equation 12A.3 is the

discounting

discount rate

discount factor

discount factor. By letting the discount factor, called *df*, equal $1/(1 + i)^n$, Equation 12A.3 can be expressed as $P = F(df)$. To simplify the computation of present value, a table of discount factors is given for various combinations of i and n (see Exhibit 12B-1 in Appendix B). For example, the discount factor for $i = 10$ percent and $n = 2$ is 0.826 (simply go to the 10 percent column of the table and move down to the second row). With the discount factor, the present value of $363 is computed as follows:

$$P = F(df)$$
$$= \$363 \times 0.826$$
$$= \$300 \text{ (rounded)}$$

Present Value of an Uneven Series of Cash Flows Exhibit 12B-1 can be used to compute the present value of any future cash flow or series of future cash flows. A series of future cash flows is called an **annuity**. The present value of an annuity is found by computing the present value of each future cash flow and then summing these values. For example, suppose that an investment is expected to produce the following annual cash flows: $110, $121, and $133.10. Assuming a discount rate of 10 percent, the present value of this series of cash flows is computed in Exhibit 12A-1.

annuity

Present Value of a Uniform Series of Cash Flows If the series of cash flows is even, the computation of the annuity's present value is simplified. Assume, for example, that an investment is expected to return $100 per year for three years. Using Exhibit 12B-1 and assuming a discount rate of 10 percent, the present value of the annuity is computed in Exhibit 12A-2.

As with the uneven series of cash flows, the present value in Exhibit 12A-2 was computed by calculating the present value of each cash flow separately and then summing them. However, in the case of an annuity displaying uniform cash flows, the computations can be reduced from three to one as described in the note to the exhibit. The sum of the individual discount factors can be thought of as a discount factor for an annuity of uniform cash flows. A table of discount factors that can be used for an annuity of uniform cash flows is available in Exhibit 12B-2 in Appendix B.

Exhibit 12A-1
Present Value of an Uneven Series of Cash Flows

Yea	Cash Receipt	Discount Factor	Present Value*
1	$110.00	0.909	$100.00
2	121.00	0.826	100.00
3	133.10	0.751	100.00
			$300.00

*Rounded

Exhibit 12A-2
Present Value of Uniform Series of Cash Flows

Year	Cash Receipt	Discount Factor	Present Value
1	$100	0.909	$ 90.90
2	100	0.826	82.60
3	100	0.751	75.10
		2.486	$248.60

Note: The annual cash flow of $100 can be multiplied by the sum of the discount factors (2.486) to obtain the present value of the uniform series ($248.60).

APPENDIX B: PRESENT VALUE TABLES

Exhibit 12B-1
Present Value of $1[a]

Periods	2%	4%	6%	8%	10%	12%	14%	16%	18%	20%	22%	24%	26%	28%	30%	32%	40%
1	0.980	0.962	0.943	0.926	0.909	0.893	0.877	0.862	0.847	0.833	0.820	0.806	0.794	0.781	0.769	0.758	0.714
2	0.961	0.925	0.890	0.857	0.826	0.797	0.769	0.743	0.718	0.694	0.672	0.650	0.630	0.610	0.592	0.574	0.510
3	0.942	0.889	0.840	0.794	0.751	0.712	0.675	0.641	0.609	0.579	0.551	0.524	0.500	0.477	0.455	0.435	0.364
4	0.924	0.855	0.792	0.735	0.683	0.636	0.592	0.552	0.516	0.482	0.451	0.423	0.397	0.373	0.350	0.329	0.260
5	0.906	0.822	0.747	0.681	0.621	0.567	0.519	0.476	0.437	0.402	0.370	0.341	0.315	0.291	0.269	0.250	0.186
6	0.888	0.790	0.705	0.636	0.564	0.507	0.456	0.410	0.370	0.335	0.303	0.275	0.250	0.227	0.207	0.189	0.133
7	0.871	0.760	0.665	0.583	0.513	0.452	0.400	0.354	0.314	0.279	0.249	0.222	0.198	0.178	0.159	0.143	0.095
8	0.853	0.731	0.627	0.540	0.467	0.404	0.351	0.305	0.266	0.233	0.204	0.179	0.157	0.139	0.123	0.108	0.068
9	0.837	0.703	0.592	0.500	0.424	0.361	0.308	0.263	0.225	0.194	0.167	0.144	0.125	0.108	0.094	0.082	0.048
10	0.820	0.676	0.558	0.463	0.386	0.322	0.270	0.227	0.191	0.162	0.137	0.116	0.099	0.085	0.073	0.062	0.035
11	0.804	0.650	0.527	0.429	0.350	0.287	0.237	0.195	0.162	0.135	0.112	0.094	0.079	0.066	0.056	0.046	0.025
12	0.788	0.625	0.497	0.397	0.319	0.257	0.208	0.168	0.137	0.112	0.092	0.076	0.062	0.052	0.043	0.036	0.018
13	0.773	0.601	0.469	0.368	0.290	0.229	0.182	0.145	0.116	0.093	0.075	0.061	0.050	0.040	0.033	0.027	0.013
14	0.758	0.577	0.442	0.340	0.263	0.205	0.160	0.125	0.099	0.078	0.062	0.049	0.039	0.032	0.025	0.021	0.009
15	0.743	0.555	0.417	0.315	0.239	0.183	0.140	0.108	0.084	0.065	0.051	0.040	0.031	0.025	0.020	0.016	0.006
16	0.728	0.534	0.394	0.292	0.218	0.163	0.123	0.093	0.071	0.054	0.042	0.032	0.025	0.019	0.015	0.012	0.005
17	0.714	0.513	0.371	0.270	0.198	0.146	0.108	0.080	0.060	0.045	0.034	0.026	0.020	0.015	0.012	0.009	0.003
18	0.700	0.494	0.350	0.250	0.180	0.130	0.095	0.069	0.051	0.038	0.028	0.021	0.016	0.012	0.009	0.007	0.002
19	0.686	0.475	0.331	0.232	0.164	0.116	0.083	0.060	0.043	0.031	0.023	0.017	0.012	0.009	0.007	0.005	0.002
20	0.673	0.456	0.312	0.215	0.149	0.104	0.073	0.051	0.037	0.026	0.019	0.014	0.010	0.007	0.005	0.004	0.001
21	0.660	0.439	0.294	0.199	0.135	0.093	0.064	0.044	0.031	0.022	0.015	0.011	0.008	0.006	0.004	0.003	0.001
22	0.647	0.422	0.278	0.184	0.123	0.083	0.056	0.038	0.026	0.018	0.013	0.009	0.006	0.004	0.003	0.002	0.001
23	0.634	0.406	0.262	0.170	0.112	0.074	0.049	0.033	0.022	0.015	0.010	0.007	0.005	0.003	0.002	0.002	0.001
24	0.622	0.390	0.247	0.158	0.102	0.066	0.043	0.028	0.019	0.013	0.008	0.006	0.004	0.003	0.002	0.002	0.000
25	0.610	0.375	0.233	0.146	0.092	0.059	0.038	0.024	0.016	0.010	0.007	0.005	0.003	0.002	0.001	0.001	0.000
26	0.598	0.361	0.220	0.135	0.084	0.053	0.033	0.021	0.014	0.009	0.006	0.004	0.002	0.002	0.001	0.001	0.000
27	0.586	0.347	0.207	0.125	0.076	0.047	0.029	0.018	0.011	0.007	0.005	0.003	0.002	0.001	0.001	0.001	0.000
28	0.574	0.333	0.196	0.116	0.069	0.042	0.026	0.016	0.010	0.006	0.004	0.002	0.002	0.001	0.001	0.000	0.000
29	0.563	0.321	0.185	0.107	0.063	0.037	0.022	0.014	0.008	0.005	0.003	0.002	0.001	0.001	0.000	0.000	0.000
30	0.552	0.308	0.174	0.099	0.057	0.033	0.020	0.012	0.007	0.004	0.003	0.002	0.001	0.001	0.000	0.000	0.000

[a] $P_n = A/(1 + i)^n$

Exhibit 12B-2
Present Value of an Annuity of $1 in Arrears[a]

Periods	2%	4%	6%	8%	10%	12%	14%	16%	18%	20%	22%	24%	26%	28%	30%	32%	40%
1	0.980	0.962	0.943	0.926	0.909	0.893	0.877	0.862	0.847	0.833	0.820	0.806	0.794	0.781	0.769	0.758	0.714
2	1.942	1.866	1.833	1.783	1.736	1.690	1.647	1.605	1.566	1.528	1.492	1.457	1.424	1.392	1.361	1.331	1.224
3	2.884	2.775	2.673	2.577	2.487	2.402	2.322	2.246	2.174	2.106	2.042	1.981	1.923	1.868	1.816	1.766	1.589
4	3.808	3.630	3.465	63.312	3.170	3.037	2.914	2.798	2.690	2.589	2.494	2.404	2.320	2.241	2.166	2.096	1.849
5	4.713	4.452	4.212	3.993	3.791	3.605	3.433	3.274	3.127	2.991	2.864	2.745	2.635	2.532	2.436	2.345	2.035
6	5.601	5.242	4.917	4.623	4.355	4.111	3.889	3.685	3.498	3.326	3.167	3.020	2.885	2.759	2.643	2.534	2.168
7	6.472	6.002	5.582	5.206	4.868	4.564	4.288	4.039	3.812	3.605	3.416	3.242	3.083	2.937	2.802	2.677	2.263
8	7.325	6.733	6.210	5.747	5.335	4.968	4.639	4.344	4.078	3.837	3.619	3.421	3.241	3.076	2.925	2.786	2.331
9	8.162	7.435	6.802	6.247	5.759	5.328	4.946	4.607	4.303	4.031	3.786	3.566	3.366	3.184	3.019	2.868	2.379
10	8.983	8.111	7.360	6.710	6.145	5.650	5.216	4.833	4.494	4.192	3.923	3.682	3.465	3.269	3.092	2.930	2.414
11	9.787	8.760	7.887	7.139	6.495	5.938	5.453	5.029	4.656	4.327	4.035	3.776	3.543	3.335	3.147	2.978	2.438
12	10.575	9.385	8.384	7.536	6.814	6.194	5.660	5.197	4.793	4.439	4.127	3.851	3.606	3.387	3.190	3.013	2.456
13	11.348	9.986	8.853	7.904	7.103	6.424	5.842	5.342	4.910	4.533	4.203	3.912	3.656	3.427	3.223	3.040	2.469
14	12.106	10.563	9.295	8.244	7.367	6.628	6.002	5.468	5.008	4.611	4.265	3.962	3.695	3.459	3.249	3.061	2.478
15	12.849	11.118	9.712	8.559	7.606	6.811	6.142	5.575	5.092	4.675	4.315	4.001	3.726	3.483	3.268	3.076	2.484
16	13.578	11.652	10.106	8.851	7.824	6.974	6.265	5.668	5.162	4.730	4.357	4.033	3.751	3.503	3.283	3.088	2.489
17	14.292	12.166	10.477	9.122	8.022	7.120	6.373	5.749	5.222	4.775	4.391	4.059	3.771	3.518	3.295	3.097	2.492
18	14.992	12.659	10.828	9.372	8.201	7.250	6.467	5.818	5.273	4.812	4.419	4.080	3.786	3.529	3.304	3.104	2.494
19	15.678	13.134	11.158	9.604	8.365	7.366	6.550	5.877	5.316	4.843	4.442	4.097	3.799	3.539	3.311	3.109	2.496
20	16.351	13.590	11.470	9.818	8.514	7.469	6.623	5.929	5.353	4.870	4.460	4.110	3.808	3.546	3.316	3.113	2.497
21	17.011	14.029	11.764	10.017	8.649	7.562	6.687	5.973	5.384	4.891	4.476	4.121	3.816	3.551	3.320	3.116	2.498
22	17.658	14.451	12.042	10.201	8.772	7.645	6.743	6.011	5.410	4.909	4.488	4.130	3.822	3.556	3.323	3.118	2.498
23	18.292	14.857	12.303	10.371	8.883	7.718	6.792	6.044	5.432	4.925	4.499	4.137	3.827	3.559	3.325	3.120	2.499
24	18.914	15.247	12.550	10.529	8.985	7.784	6.835	6.073	5.451	4.937	4.507	4.143	3.831	3.562	3.327	3.121	2.499
25	19.523	15.622	12.783	10.675	9.077	7.843	6.873	6.097	5.467	4.948	4.514	4.147	3.834	3.564	3.329	3.122	2.499
26	20.121	15.983	13.003	10.810	9.161	7.896	6.906	6.118	5.480	4.956	4.520	4.151	3.837	3.566	3.330	3.123	2.500
27	20.707	16.330	13.211	10.935	9.237	7.943	6.935	6.136	5.492	4.964	4.524	4.154	3.839	3.567	3.331	3.123	2.500
28	21.281	16.663	13.406	11.051	9.307	7.984	6.961	6.152	5.502	4.970	4.528	4.157	3.840	3.568	3.331	3.124	2.500
29	21.844	16.984	13.591	11.158	9.370	8.022	6.983	6.166	5.510	4.975	4.531	4.159	3.841	3.569	3.332	3.124	2.500
30	22.396	17.292	13.765	11.258	9.427	8.055	7.003	6.177	5.517	4.979	4.534	4.160	3.842	3.569	3.332	3.124	2.500

[a]$P_n = (1/i)[1 - 1/(1 + i)^n]$

REVIEW PROBLEMS AND SOLUTIONS

I.
Basics of Capital Investment (Ignore taxes for this exercise.)

Kenn Day, manager of Day Laboratory, is investigating the possibility of acquiring some new test equipment. To acquire the equipment requires an initial outlay of $300,000. To raise the capital, Kenn will sell stock valued at $200,000 (the stock pays dividends of $24,000 per year) and borrow $100,000. The loan for $100,000 would carry an interest rate of 6 percent. Kenn figures that his weighted cost of capital is 10% [(2/3 × .12) + (1/3 × .06)]. This weighted cost of capital is the hurdle rate he will use for capital investment decisions.

Kenn estimates that the new test equipment will produce a cash inflow of $50,000 per year. Kenn expects the equipment to last for 20 years.

REQUIRED:

1. Compute the payback period.
2. Assuming that depreciation is $14,000 per year, compute the accounting rate of return (on total investment).
3. Compute the NPV of the investment.
4. Compute the IRR of the investment.
5. Should Kenn buy the equipment?

Solution

1. The payback period is $300,000/$50,000, or six years.
2. The accounting rate of return is ($50,000 − $14,000)/$300,000, or 12 percent.
3. From Exhibit 12B-2, the discount factor for an annuity with i at 10 percent and n at 20 years is 8.514. Thus, the NPV is [(8.514 × 50,000) − $300,000], or $125,700.
4. The discount factor associated with the IRR is 6.00 ($300,000/$50,000). From Exhibit 12B-2, the IRR is between 14 and 16 percent (using the row corresponding to period 20).
5. Since the NPV is positive and the IRR is greater than Kenn's cost of capital, the test equipment is a sound investment. This assumes, of course, that the cash flow projections are accurate.

II.
Capital Investment with Competing Projects (with tax effects)

Weins Postal Service (WPS) has decided to acquire a new delivery truck. The choice has been narrowed to two models. The following information has been gathered for each model:

	Custom	Deluxe
Acquisition cost	$20,000	$25,000
Annual operating costs	$ 3,500	$ 2,000
Depreciation method	MACRS	MACRS
Expected salvage value	$ 5,000	$ 8,000

WPS's cost of capital is 14 percent. The company plans to use the truck for five years and then sell it for its salvage value. Assume the combined state and federal tax rate is 40 percent.

REQUIRED:

1. Compute the after-tax operating cash flows for each model.
2. Compute the NPV for each model, and make a recommendation.

Solution

1. For light trucks, MACRS guidelines allow a five-year life. Using the rates from Exhibit 12-11, depreciation is calculated for each model.

Year	Custom	Deluxe
1	$ 4,000	$ 5,000
2	6,400	8,000
3	3,840	4,800
4	2,304	2,880
5	1,152*	1,440
Total	$17,696	$22,120

*Only half the depreciation is allowed in year of disposal.

The after-tax operating cash flows are computed using the spreadsheet format.

Custom

Year	$(1 - t)R$	$-(1 - t)C$	tNC	Other	CF
1	n/a	$(2,100)	$1,600		$ (500)
2	n/a	(2,100)	2,560		460
3	n/a	(2,100)	1,536		(564)
4	n/a	(2,100)	922		(1,178)
5	1,618[a]	(2,100)	461	$2,304[b]	2,283

[a]Salvage value ($5,000) − Book value ($20,000 − $17,696 = $2,304) = $2,696; 0.60 × $2,696 = $1,618
[b]Recovery of capital = Book value = $2,304. Capital recovered is not taxed—only the gain on sale. Footnote (a) illustrates how the gain is treated.

Deluxe

Year	$(1 - t)R$	$-(1 - t)C$	tNC	Other	CF
1	n/a	$(1,200)	$2,000		$ 800
2	n/a	(1,200)	3,200		2,000
3	n/a	(1,200)	1,920		720
4	n/a	(1,200)	1,152		(48)
5	$3,072[a]	(1,200)	576	$2,880[b]	5,328

[a]Salvage value ($8,000) − Book value ($25,000 − $22,120 = $2,880) = $5,120; 0.60 × $5,120 = $3,072
[b]Recovery of capital = Book value = $2,880. Capital recovered is not taxed—only the gain on sale of the asset. Footnote (a) illustrates how the gain is treated. The nontaxable item requires an additional column for the spreadsheet analysis.

2. NPV computation—Custom:

Year	Cash Flow	Discount Factor	Present Value
0	$(20,000)	1.000	$(20,000)
1	(500)	0.877	(439)
2	460	0.769	354
3	(564)	0.675	(381)
4	(1,178)	0.592	(697)
5	2,283	0.519	1,185
Net present value			$(19,978)

NPV computation—Deluxe:

Year	Cash Flow	Discount Factor	Present Value
0	$(25,000)	1.000	$(25,000)
1	800	0.877	702
2	2,000	0.769	1,538
3	720	0.675	486
4	(48)	0.592	(28)
5	5,328	0.519	2,765
Net present value			$(19,537)

The Deluxe model should be chosen, since it has the larger NPV, indicating that it is the least costly of the two cars. Note also that the net present values are negative and that we are choosing the least costly investment.

KEY TERMS

Accounting rate of return *507*
Annuity *532*
Capital budgeting *503*
Capital investment decisions *503*
Compounding of interest *531*
Discount factor *532*

Discount rate *531*
Discounted cash flows *508*
Discounting *531*
Discounting models *505*
Five-year assets *522*
Future value *531*
Half-year convention *522*
Independent projects *503*

Internal rate of return *509*
Modified accelerated cost recovery system (MACRS) *522*
Mutually exclusive projects *503*
Net present value *508*
Nondiscounting models *505*

Payback period *505*
Postaudit *526*
Present value *531*
Required rate of return *509*
Sensitivity analysis *528*
Seven-year assets *522*
Three-year assets *522*
What-if analysis *528*

QUESTIONS FOR WRITING AND DISCUSSION

1. Explain the difference between independent projects and mutually exclusive projects.
2. Explain why the timing and quantity of cash flows are important in capital investment decisions.
3. The time value of money is ignored by the payback period and the accounting rate of return. Explain why this is a major deficiency in these two models.
4. What is the payback period? Compute the payback period for an investment requiring an initial outlay of $80,000 with expected annual cash inflows of $30,000.
5. Name and discuss three possible reasons that the payback period is used to help make capital investment decisions.
6. What is the accounting rate of return? Compute the accounting rate of return for an investment that requires an initial outlay of $300,000 and promises an average net income of $100,000.

7. The net present value is the same as the profit of a project expressed in present dollars. Do you agree? Explain.
8. What is the cost of capital? What role does it play in capital investment decisions?
9. What is the role that the required rate of return plays for the NPV model? For the IRR model?
10. The IRR is the true or actual rate of return being earned by the project. Do you agree or disagree? Discuss.
11. Explain how the NPV is used to determine whether a project should be accepted or rejected.
12. Explain the relationship between NPV and a firm's value.
13. Explain why NPV is generally preferred over IRR when choosing among competing or mutually exclusive projects. Why would managers continue to use IRR to choose among mutually exclusive projects?

14. Suppose that a firm must choose between two mutually exclusive projects, both of which have negative NPVs. Explain how a firm can legitimately
choose among two such projects.

15. Why is it important to have accurate projections of
cash flows for potential capital investments?

16. What are the principal tax implications that should
be considered in Year 0?

17. Explain why the MACRS method of recognizing depreciation is better than the straight-line method.

18. What is the half-year convention? What is the effect
of this convention on the length of time it actually
takes to write off the cost of a depreciable asset?

19. Explain the important factors to consider for capital
investment in the contemporary manufacturing
environment.

20. Explain what a postaudit is and how it can provide useful input for future capital investment
decisions—especially those involving advanced
technology.

21. Explain what sensitivity analysis is. How can it help
in capital budgeting decisions?

EXERCISES AND PROBLEMS

12-1

Basic Concepts

LO 1, 2, 3

Each of the following parts is independent. Assume all cash flows are after-tax cash flows.

1. Harry Kingston has just invested $120,000 as a part owner of a fast-food franchise. He
expects to receive an income of $30,000 per year from the investment. What is the pay-
back period for Harry?

2. Bill Jones invested $50,000 in a car wash. The facilities have a ten-year life expectancy
with no expected salvage value. The car wash will produce a net cash flow of $15,000
per year. What is the accounting rate of return? Use original investment for the
computation.

3. Queens Manufacturing is considering the purchase of a robotics material handling system. The cash benefits will be $100,000 per year. The system costs $580,000 and will
last ten years. Compute the NPV assuming a discount rate of 12 percent. Should the
company buy the robotics system?

4. Helen Anderson has just invested $50,000 in a company. She expects to receive $8,050
per year for the next 8 years. Her cost of capital is 8 percent. Compute the internal rate
of return. Did Helen make a good decision?

12-2

**Payback;
Accounting Rate of
Return; NPV; IRR**

LO 1, 2, 3, 4

Palmroy Company is considering an investment in equipment that will be used to produce
a new type of carpet yarn. The outlay required is $500,000. The equipment is expected to
last five years and will have no salvage value. The expected after-tax cash flows associated
with the project are given below:

Year	Cash Revenues	Cash Expenses
1	$650,000	$500,000
2	650,000	500,000
3	650,000	500,000
4	650,000	500,000
5	650,000	500,000

REQUIRED:

1. Compute the project's payback period.

2. Compute the project's accounting rate of return (a) on initial investment and (b) on
average investment.

3. Compute the project's net present value, assuming a required rate of return of 10
percent.

4. Compute the project's internal rate of return.

12-3
NPV; Accounting
Rate of Return;
Payback
LO 1, 2, 3

An optometry clinic offers both vision and optical services. Because of increased business, the clinic's owners are considering adding new equipment. Both vision care and optical equipment would be needed. Each project would require an investment of $100,000. The vision and optical equipment would each last five years and have no expected salvage value. The after-tax cash inflows associated with the two independent projects are as follows:

Year	Vision Equipment	Optical Equipment
1	$50,000	$10,000
2	20,000	10,000
3	40,000	70,000
4	20,000	80,000
5	10,000	90,000

REQUIRED:

1. Assuming a discount rate of 12 percent, compute the net present value of each project.
2. Compute the payback period for each project. Assume that the manager of the company accepts only projects with a payback period of three years or less. Offer some reasons why this may be a rational strategy even though the NPV computed in Requirement 1 may indicate otherwise.
3. Compute the accounting rate of return for each project using (a) initial investment and (b) average investment.

12-4
NPV: Basic
Concepts
LO 3

Byerson Mortuary is considering an investment that requires an outlay of $100,000 and promises an after-tax cash inflow one year from now of $113,000. Byerson's cost of capital is 8 percent.

REQUIRED:

1. Break the $113,000 future cash inflow into three components: (a) the return of the original investment, (b) the cost of capital, and (c) the profit earned on the investment. Now compute the present value of the profit earned on the investment.
2. Compute the NPV of the investment. Compare this with the present value of the profit computed in Requirement 1. What does this tell you about the meaning of NPV?

12-5
Solving for
Unknowns
LO 3, 4

Solve each of the following independent cases (assume all cash flows are after-tax cash flows):

1. Hal's Stunt Company is investing $120,000 in a project that will yield a uniform series of cash inflows over the next four years. If the internal rate of return is 14 percent, how much cash inflow per year can be expected?
2. Warner Medical Clinic has decided to invest in some new blood diagnostic equipment. The equipment will have a three-year life and will produce a uniform series of cash savings. The net present value of the equipment is $1,750, using a discount rate of 8 percent. The internal rate of return is 12 percent. Determine the investment and the amount of cash savings realized each year.
3. A new lathe costing $60,096 will produce savings of $12,000 per year. How many years must the lathe last if an IRR of 18 percent is realized?
4. The NPV of a new product (a new brand of candy) is $6,075. The product has a life of four years and produces the following cash flows:

Year 1	$15,000
Year 2	20,000
Year 3	30,000
Year 4	?

The cost of the project is three times the cash flow produced in Year 4. The discount rate is 10 percent. Find the cost of the project and the cash flow for Year 4.

12-6
Advanced
Technology;
Payback; NPV;
IRR; Sensitivity
Analysis
LO 3, 4, 5, 7

Gina Ripley, president of Dearing Company, is considering the purchase of a computer-aided manufacturing system. The annual after-tax cash benefits/savings associated with the system are described below:

Decreased waste	$300,000
Increased quality	400,000
Decrease in operating costs	600,000
Increase in on-time deliveries	200,000

The system will cost $9,000,000 and will last ten years. The company's cost of capital is 12%.

REQUIRED:

1. Calculate the payback period for the system. Assume that the company has a policy of only accepting projects with a payback of five years or less. Would the system be acquired?
2. Calculate the NPV and IRR for the project. Should the system be purchased—even if it does not meet the payback criterion?
3. The project manager reviewed the projected cash flows and pointed out that two items had been missed. First, the system would have a salvage value, net of any tax effects, of $1,000,000 at the end of 10 years. Second, the increased quality and delivery performance would allow the company to increase its market share by 20%. This would produce an additional annual after-tax benefit of $300,000. Recalculate the payback period, NPV, and IRR given this new information (for the IRR computation, initially ignore salvage value). Does the decision change? Suppose that the salvage value is only half what is projected. Does this make a difference in the outcome? Does salvage value have any real bearing on the company's decision?

12-7
NPV Versus IRR
LO 5

Walton Insurance Company has decided to automate its claims process. Two PC computer systems are being considered. The systems have an expected life of two years. The after-tax cash flows associated with the two systems are shown below. The cash benefits represent the savings created by switching from a manual to an automated system.

Year	System I	System II
	$(200,000)	$(200,000)
1	—	127,714
2	271,180	127,714

The company's cost of capital is 10 percent.

REQUIRED:

1. Compute the NPV and the IRR for each investment.
2. Show that the project with the larger NPV is the correct choice for the company.

12-8
Computation of
After-Tax Cash
Flows
LO 6

The Dingle Company is considering two independent projects. One project involves a new product line and the other the acquisition of forklifts for the materials-handling department. The projected annual operating revenues and expenses are given on the following page.

Project I (investment in a new product)

Revenues	$60,000
Cash expenses	(30,000)
Depreciation	(10,000)
Income before taxes	$20,000
Taxes	(8,000)
Net income	$12,000

Project II (acquisition of two forklifts)

Cash expenses	$20,000
Depreciation	20,000

REQUIRED: Compute the after-tax cash flows of each project. The tax rate is 40 percent and includes federal and state assessments.

12-9
MACRS; NPV

LO 3, 6

Lilly Company is planning to buy a set of special tools for its grinding operation. The cost of the tools is $18,000. The tools have a three-year life and qualify for the use of the three-year MACRS. The tax rate is 40 percent; the cost of capital is 12 percent.

REQUIRED:

1. Calculate the present value of the tax depreciation shield, assuming that straight-line depreciation with a half-year life is used.
2. Calculate the present value of the tax depreciation shield, assuming that MACRS is used.
3. What is the benefit of using MACRS to the company?

12-10
Inflation

LO 3, 6

Excalibur Company is planning on introducing a new product that will have a two-year life. Producing the product requires an initial outlay of $20,000; it will generate after-tax cash inflows of $11,000 and $12,000 in the two years. The company's cost of capital is 12 percent. During the coming two years, inflation is expected to average 5 percent. The cash flows have not been adjusted for inflation. The cost of capital, however, reflects an inflationary component.

REQUIRED:

1. Compute the NPV using the unadjusted cash flows.
2. Compute the NPV using cash flows adjusted for inflationary effects.

12-11
Various Cash Flow Computations

LO 6

Solve each of the following independent cases:

1. A printing company has decided to purchase a new printing press. Its old press will be sold for $10,000 (it has a book value of $25,000). The new press will cost $50,000. Assuming that the tax rate is 40 percent, compute the net after-tax cash outflow.
2. The Maintenance Department is purchasing new diagnostic equipment costing $30,000. Additional cash expenses of $2,000 per year are required to operate the equipment. MACRS depreciation will be used (five-year property qualification). Assuming a tax rate of 40 percent, prepare a schedule of after-tax cash flows for the first four years.
3. The projected income for a project during its first year of operation is given below:

Cash revenues	$120,000
Less: Cash expenses	(50,000)
Less: Depreciation	(20,000)
Net income before taxes	$ 50,000
Less: Taxes	(20,000)
Net income	$ 30,000

REQUIRED: Compute the following:

a. After-tax cash flow.
b. After-tax cash flow from revenues.
c. After-tax cash expenses.
d. Cash inflow from the shielding effect of depreciation.

**12-12
Discount Rates;
Quality; Market
Share;
Contemporary
Manufacturing
Environment**

LO 7

Sweeney Manufacturing has a plant where the equipment is essentially worn out. The equipment must be replaced, and Sweeney is considering two competing investment alternatives. The first alternative would replace the worn-out equipment with traditional production equipment; the second alternative uses contemporary technology and has computer-aided design and manufacturing capabilities. The investment and after-tax operating cash flows are shown below for each alternative.

Year	Traditional Equipment	Contemporary Technology
0	$(1,000,000)	$(4,000,000)
1	600,000	200,000
2	400,000	400,000
3	200,000	600,000
4	200,000	800,000
5	200,000	800,000
6	200,000	800,000
7	200,000	1,000,000
8	200,000	2,000,000
9	200,000	2,000,000
10	200,000	2,000,000

The company uses a discount rate of 18 percent for all of its investments. The company's cost of capital is 14 percent.

REQUIRED:

1. Calculate the net present value for each investment using a discount rate of 18 percent.
2. Calculate the net present value for each investment using a discount rate of 14 percent.
3. Which rate should the company use to compute the net present value? Explain.
4. Now assume that if the traditional equipment is purchased, the competitive position of the firm will deteriorate because of lower quality (relative to competitors who did automate). Marketing estimates that the loss in market share will decrease the projected net cash inflows by 50 percent for Years 3 through 10. Recalculate the NPV of the traditional equipment given this outcome. What is the decision now? Discuss the importance of assessing the effect of intangible and indirect benefits.

**12-13
Payback; NPV;
Managerial
Incentives; Ethical
Behavior**

LO 1, 2, 3

Claude Jones, manager of an electronic components division, was pleased with his division's performance over the past three years. Each year, divisional profits had increased, and he had earned a sizable bonus (bonuses are a linear function of the division's reported income). He had also received considerable attention from higher management. A vice president had told him in confidence that if his performance over the next three years matched his first three, he would be promoted to higher management.

Determined to fulfill these expectations, Claude made sure that he personally reviewed every capital budget request. He wanted to be certain that any funds invested would provide good, solid returns (the division's cost of capital is 10 percent). At the moment, he is reviewing two independent requests. Proposal A involves automating a manufacturing operation that is currently labor-intensive. Proposal B centers on developing and marketing a new relay component. Proposal A requires an initial outlay of $100,000, and Proposal B requires $125,000. Both projects could be funded, given the status of the division's capital budget. Both have an expected life of six years and have the following projected after-tax cash flows:

Year	Proposal A	Proposal B
1	$60,000	$ (15,000)
2	50,000	(10,000)
3	30,000	(5,000)
4	15,000	85,000
5	10,000	110,000
6	5,000	135,000

After careful consideration of each investment, Claude approved funding of Proposal A and rejected Proposal B.

REQUIRED:

1. Compute the NPV for each proposal.
2. Compute the payback period for each proposal.
3. According to your analysis, which proposal(s) should be accepted? Explain.
4. Explain why Claude accepted only Proposal A. Considering the possible reasons for rejection, would you judge his behavior to be ethical? Explain.

12-14
Basic IRR Analysis
LO 1, 4

Timmins Company was approached by a local air conditioning company with the proposition of replacing its old cooling system with a modern, more efficient unit. The cost of the new system was quoted at $50,000, but it would produce after-tax savings of $10,000 per year in power costs. The estimated life of the new system is ten years, with no salvage value expected. Excited over the possibility of saving $10,000 per year and having a more reliable unit, the president of Timmins has asked for an analysis of the project's economic viability. All capital projects are required to earn at least the firm's cost of capital, which is 12 percent.

REQUIRED:

1. Calculate the project's internal rate of return. Should the company acquire the cooling system?
2. Suppose that power savings are less than claimed. Calculate the minimum annual cash savings that must be realized for the project to earn a rate equal to the firm's cost of capital.
3. Suppose that the life of the cooling system is overestimated by two years. Repeat Requirements 1 and 2 under this assumption.

12-15
Replacement Decision; Computing After-Tax Cash Flows; Basic NPV Analysis
LO 1, 5, 6

Morgan Manufacturing Company is considering replacing the computer that operates its CAM system with a new model manufactured by a different company. The old CAM computer was acquired three years ago, has a remaining life of five years, and will have a salvage value of $20,000. The book value is $400,000. Straight-line depreciation with a half-year convention is being used for tax purposes. The cash operating costs of the existing CAM computer, including software, personnel, and other supplies, total $200,000 per year.

The new CAM computer has an initial cost of $1,000,000 and will have cash operating costs of $100,000 per year. The new CAM computer will have a life of five years and will have a salvage value of $200,000 at the end of the fifth year. MACRS depreciation will be used for tax purposes. If the new computer is purchased, the old one will be sold for $100,000. The company needs to decide whether to keep the old CAM computer or buy the new one. The cost of capital is 12 percent. The combined federal and state tax rate is 40 percent.

REQUIRED: Compute the NPV of each alternative. Should the company keep the old CAM computer or buy the new one?

12-16
Inflation and
Capital Budgeting

LO 5, 6

Leo Thayn, manager of an electronics manufacturing division, has been pushing head-quarters to grant approval for the installation of a new computer-aided design system. Finally, in the last executive meeting, Leo was told if he could show the new system would increase the firm's value, that it would be approved. Leo has collected the following information:

Year	Old System	CAD System
Initial investment	—	$1,250,000
Annual operating costs	$300,000	$95,000
Annual depreciation	100,000	MACRS
Effective tax rate*	34%	34%
Cost of capital	12%	12%
Expected life	10 years	10 years
Salvage value	none	none

*The division is located in a state that provided a tax incentive package that lowers the tax rate from the usual average of 40% to 34%. This incentive package was granted for a fifteen-year period. Ten years of benefits remain.

With the exception of the cost of capital, the above information ignores the rate of inflation, which has been 4 percent per year and is expected to continue at this level for the next decade.

REQUIRED:

1. Compute the NPV for each system.
2. Compute the NPV for each system adjusting the future cash flows for the rate of inflation.
3. Comment on the importance of adjusting cash flows for inflationary effects.

12-17
Capital
Investment;
Discount Rates;
Intangible and
Indirect Benefits;
Time Horizon;
Contemporary
Manufacturing
Environment

LO 7

Mallette Manufacturing, Inc., produces washing machines, dryers, and dishwashers. Because of increasing competition, Mallette is considering investing in an automated man-ufacturing system. Since competition is most keen for dishwashers, the production process for this line has been selected for initial evaluation. The automated system for the dish-washer line would replace an existing system (purchased one year ago for $6 million). Although the existing system will be fully depreciated in nine years, it is expected to last another ten years. The automated system would also have a useful life of ten years.

The existing system is capable of producing 100,000 dishwashers per year. Sales and production data using the existing system are provided by the Accounting Department:

Sales per year (units)	100,000
Selling price	$300
Costs per unit:	
Direct materials	80
Direct labor	90
Volume-related overhead	20
Direct fixed overhead	40*

*All cash expenses with the exception of depreci-ation, which is $6 per unit. The existing equipment is being depreciated using straight-line with no salvage value considered.

The automated system will cost $34 million to purchase, plus an estimated $20 million in software and implementation. (Assume that all investment outlays occur at the beginning of the first year.) If the automated equipment is purchased, the old equipment can be sold for $3 million.

The automated system will require fewer parts for production and will produce with less waste. Because of this, the direct materials cost per unit will be reduced by 25 percent. Automation will also require fewer support activities, and as a consequence, volume-related overhead will be reduced by $4 per unit and direct fixed overhead (other than depreciation) by $17 per unit. Direct labor is reduced by 60 percent. Assume, for simplicity, that the new investment will be depreciated on a pure straight-line basis for tax purposes with no salvage value. Ignore the half-life convention.

The firm's cost of capital is 12 percent, but management chooses to use 20 percent as the required rate of return for evaluation of investments. The combined federal and state tax rate is 40 percent.

REQUIRED:

1. Compute the net present value for the old system and the automated system. Which system would the company choose?
2. Repeat the net present value analysis of Requirement 1 using 12 percent as the discount rate.
3. Upon seeing the projected sales for the old system, the marketing manager commented: "Sales of 100,000 units per year cannot be maintained in the current competitive environment for more than one year unless we buy the automated system. The automated system will allow us to compete on the basis of quality and lead time. If we keep the old system, our sales will drop by 10,000 units per year." Repeat the net present value analysis using this new information and a 12 percent discount rate.
4. An industrial engineer for Mallette noticed that salvage value for the automated equipment had not been included in the analysis. He estimated that the equipment could be sold for $4 million at the end of ten years. He also estimated that the equipment of the old system would have no salvage value at the end of ten years. Repeat the net present value analysis using this information, the information in Requirement 3, and a 12 percent discount rate.
5. Given the outcomes of the previous four requirements, comment on the importance of providing accurate inputs for assessing investments in automated manufacturing systems.

12-18
NPV; Make or Buy; MACRS; Basic Analysis

LO 3, 6

Jonfran Company manufactures three different models of paper shredders including the waste container, which serves as the base. While the shredder heads are different for all three models, the waste container is the same. The number of waste containers that Jonfran will need during the next five years is estimated as follows:

1997	50,000
1998	50,000
1999	52,000
2000	55,000
2001	55,000

The equipment used to manufacture the waste container must be replaced because it is broken and cannot be repaired. The new equipment would have a purchase price of $945,000 with terms of 2/10, n/30; the company's policy is to take all purchase discounts. The freight on the equipment would be $11,000, and installation costs would total $22,900. The equipment would be purchased in December 1996 and placed into service on January 1, 1997. It would have a five-year economic life and would be treated as three-year property under MACRS. This equipment is expected to have a salvage value of $12,000 at the end of its economic life in 2001. The new equipment would be more efficient than the old equipment, resulting in a 25 percent reduction in both direct material and variable overhead. The savings in direct material would result in an additional one-time decrease in working capital requirements of $2,500, resulting from a reduction in direct material inventories. This working capital reduction would be recognized at the time of equipment acquisition.

The old equipment is fully depreciated and is not included in the fixed overhead. The old equipment from the plant can be sold for a salvage amount of $1,500. Rather than replace the equipment, one of Jonfran's production managers has suggested that the waste containers be purchased. One supplier has quoted a price of $27 per container. This price is $8 less than Jonfran's current manufacturing cost, which is presented below.

Direct materials		$10
Direct labor		8
Variable overhead		6
Fixed overhead:		
Supervision	$2	
Facilities	5	
General	4	11
Total unit cost		$35

Jonfran uses a plantwide fixed overhead rate in its operations. If the waste containers are purchased outside, the salary and benefits of one supervisor, included in fixed overhead at $45,000, would be eliminated. There would be no other changes in the other cash and noncash items included in fixed overhead except depreciation on the new equipment.

Jonfran is subject to a 40 percent tax rate. Management assumes that all cash flows occur at the end of the year and uses a 12 percent after-tax discount rate.

REQUIRED:

1. Prepare a schedule of cash flows for the make alternative. Calculate the NPV of the make alternative.
2. Prepare a schedule of cash flows for the buy alternative. Calculate the NPV of the buy alternative.
3. Which should Jonfran do—make or buy the containers? What qualitative factors should be considered?
   (CMA adapted)

12-19
Capital Budgeting;
Ethical
Considerations

Peter Hennings, manager of a cosmetics division, had asked Laura Gibson, divisional controller and CMA, to meet with him regarding a recent analysis of a capital budgeting proposal. Peter was disappointed that the proposal had not met the company's minimum guidelines. Specifically, the company requires that all proposals show a positive net present value, have an IRR that exceeds the cost of capital (which is 11 percent), and have a payback period of less than five years. Funding for any new proposal had to be approved by company headquarters. Typically, proposals are approved if they meet the minimum guidelines and if the division's allocated share of the capital budget is not exhausted. The following conversation took place at their meeting:

Peter: Laura, I asked you to meet with me to discuss Proposal 678. Reviewing your analysis, I see that the NPV is negative and that the IRR is 9 percent. The payback is 5.5 years. In my opinion, the automated materials-handling system in this proposal is an absolute must for this division. I feel that the consulting firm has underestimated the cash savings.
Laura: I did some checking on my own because of your feelings about the matter. I called a friend who is an expert in the area and asked him to review the report on the system. After a careful review, he agreed with the report—in fact, he indicated that the savings were probably on the optimistic side.

Peter: Well, I don't agree. I know this business better than any of these so-called consulting experts. I think that the cash savings are significantly better than indicated.

Laura: Why don't you explain this to headquarters? Perhaps they will allow an exception this time and fund the project.

Peter: No, that's unlikely. They're pretty strict when it comes to those guidelines, especially with the report from an outside consulting firm. I have a better idea, but I need your help. So far, you're the only one besides me who has seen the outside report. I think it is flawed. I would like to modify it so that it reflects my knowledge of the potential of the new system. Then you can take the revised figures and prepare a new analysis for submission to headquarters. You need to tell me how much I need to revise the cash savings so that the project is viable. Although I am confident that the savings are significantly underestimated, I would prefer to revise them so that the minimum guidelines are slightly exceeded. Believe me, I will ensure that the project exceeds expectations once it's on line.

REQUIRED:

1. Evaluate the conduct of Peter Hennings. Is what he is suggesting unethical?
2. Suppose you were in Laura's position. What should you do?
3. Refer to the IMA code in Chapter 1. If Laura complies with Peter's request to modify the capital budgeting analysis, are any of the standards of ethical conduct for management accountants violated? Which ones, if any?
4. Suppose that Laura tells Peter that she will consider his request. She then meets with Jay Dixon, Peter's superior, and describes Peter's request. Upon hearing of the incident, Jay chuckles and says that he himself had pulled a couple of stunts like that when he was a divisional manager. He tells Laura not to worry about it—to go ahead and support Peter—and assures her that he will keep her visit confidential. Given this development, what should Laura do?

**12-20
Managerial
Decision Case:
Cash Flows; NPV;
Choice of
Discount Rate;
Contemporary
Manufacturing
Environment**

LO 3, 6, 7

Charles Bradshaw, president and owner of Wellington Metal Works, has just returned from a trip to Europe.[9] While there, he toured several plants using robotic manufacturing. Seeing the efficiency and success of these companies, Charles became convinced that robotic manufacturing is the wave of the future and that Wellington could gain a competitive advantage by adopting the new technology.

Based on this vision, Charles requested an analysis detailing the costs and benefits of robotic manufacturing for the materials handling and merchandising equipment group. This group of products consists of such items as cooler shelving, stocking carts, and bakery racks. The products are sold directly to supermarkets.

A committee, consisting of the controller, the marketing manager, and the production manager was given the responsibility to prepare the analysis. As a starting point, the controller provided the following information on expected revenues and expenses for the existing manual system:

		Percentage of Sales
Sales	$400,000	100%
Less: Variable expenses[a]	228,000	57
Contribution margin	$172,000	43
Less: Fixed expenses[b]	92,000	23
Income before taxes	$ 80,000	20

[a]Variable cost detail (as a percentage of sales):
Direct materials	16
Direct labor	20
Variable overhead	9
Variable selling	12

[b]$20,000 is depreciation; the rest are cash expenses.

9.   This case is based, in part, on the following article: David A. Greenberg, "Robotics: One Small Company's Experience," *Cost Accounting for the 90s*, National Association of Accountants, Montvale, N.J., 1986, pp. 57–63.

Given the current competitive environment, the marketing manager thought that the above level of profitability would likely not change for the next decade.

After some investigation into various robotic equipment, the committee settled on an Aide 900 system, a robot that has the capability to weld stainless steel or aluminum. It is capable of being programmed to adjust the path, angle, and speed of the torch. The production manager was excited about the robotic system because it would eliminate the need to hire welders, which was so attractive because the market for welders seemed perpetually tight. By reducing the dependence on welders, better production scheduling and fewer late deliveries would result. Moreover, the robot's production rate is four times that of a person.

It was also discovered that robotic welding is superior in quality to manual welding. As a consequence, some of the costs of poor quality could be reduced. By providing better-quality products and avoiding late deliveries, the marketing manager was convinced that the company would have such a competitive edge that it would increase sales by 50 percent for the affected product group by the end of the fourth year. The marketing manager provided the following projections for the next ten years, the useful life of the robotic equipment:

	Year 1	Year 2	Year 3	Years 4–10
Sales	$400,000	$450,000	$500,000	$600,000

Currently, the company employs four welders, who work forty hours per week and fifty weeks per year at an average wage of $10 per hour. If the robot is acquired, it will need one operator, who will be paid $10 per hour. Because of improved quality, the robotic system will also reduce the cost of direct materials by 25 percent, the cost of variable overhead by 33.33 percent, and variable selling expenses by 10 percent. All of these reductions will take place immediately after the robotic system is in place and operating. Fixed costs will be increased by the depreciation associated with the robot. The robot will be depreciated using MACRS (the manual system uses straight-line depreciation without a half-year convention and has a current book value of $200,000). If the robotic system is acquired, the old system will be sold for $40,000.

The robotic system requires the following initial investment:

Purchase price	$380,000
Installation	70,000
Training	30,000
Engineering	40,000

At the end of ten years, the robot will have a salvage value of $20,000. Assume that the company's cost of capital is 12 percent. The tax rate is 40 percent.

REQUIRED:

1. Prepare a schedule of after-tax cash flows for the manual and robotic systems.
2. Using the schedule of cash flows computed in Requirement 1, compute the NPV for each system. Should the company invest in the robotic system?
3. In practice, many financial officers tend to use a higher discount rate than is justified by what the firm's cost of capital is. For example, a firm may use a discount rate of 20 percent when its cost of capital is or could be 12 percent. Offer some reasons for this practice. Assume that the annual after-tax cash benefit of adopting the robotic system is $80,000 per year more than the manual system. The initial outlay for the robotic system is $340,000. Compute the NPV using 12 percent and 20 percent. Would the robotic system be acquired if 20 percent is used? Could this conservative approach have a negative impact on a firm's ability to stay competitive?

Chapter 13

Inventory Management: Economic Order Quantity, JIT, and the Theory of Constraints

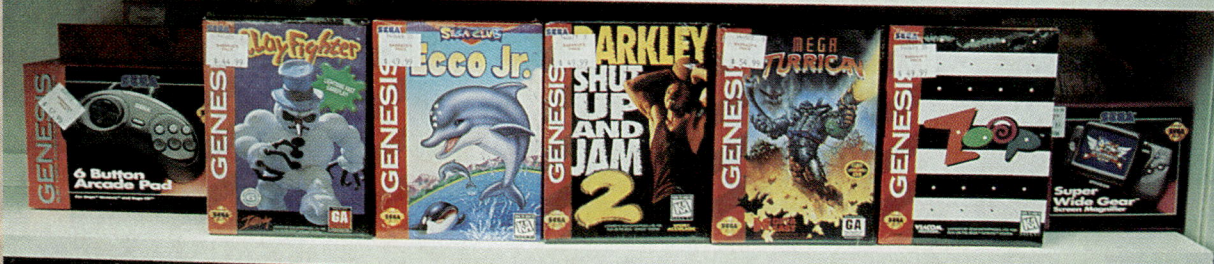

SEGA, the number 2 game maker in the U.S., has over 46 percent of the 16-bit market and is striving for dominance. Inventory management is paramount for SEGA, particularly during the all-important Christmas season—when 70 percent of video game machines are sold.

LEARNING OBJECTIVES

After studying this chapter, you should be able to:

1. Describe the traditional inventory management model.
2. Describe JIT inventory management.
3. Explain the basic concepts of constrained optimization.
4. Describe the theory of constraints, and explain how it can be used to manage inventory.

Managing the levels of inventory is fundamental to establishing a long-term competitive advantage. Quality, product engineering, prices, overtime, excess capacity, ability to respond to customers (due-date performance), lead times, and overall profitability are all affected by inventory levels. Inventory management is strongly related to the ability of firms to become strong competitors now and in the future. For example, SEGA must manage inventory appropriately to ensure that there are sufficient games ready to ship to stores in the late fall—Christmas sales are 70 percent of annual sales. Yet in the other months of the year, a leaner inventory keeps costs down.

How inventory policy can be used to aid in establishing a competitive advantage is the focus of this chapter. First, we review the traditional inventory management model—the model that has been the mainstay of American manufacturing firms for decades. Learning the basics of this model and its underlying conceptual foundation will help us understand where it can still be appropriately applied. Understanding traditional inventory management also provides the necessary background for grasping the advantages of inventory management methods that are used in the contemporary manufacturing environment. These methods include JIT and the theory of constraints. To fully appreciate the theory of constraints, a brief introduction to constrained optimization (linear programming) is also needed.

BASICS OF TRADITIONAL INVENTORY MANAGEMENT

Objective 1
Describe the traditional inventory management model.

In a world of certainty—a world in which the demand for a product or material is known with certainty for a given period of time (usually a year)—two major costs are associated with inventory. If the inventory is a material or good purchased from an outside source, then these inventory-related costs are known as *ordering costs* and *carrying costs*. If the material or good is produced internally, then the costs are called *setup costs* and *carrying costs*.

ordering costs

Ordering costs are the costs of placing and receiving an order. Examples include the costs of processing an order (clerical costs and documents), insurance for shipment, and unloading costs.

setup costs

Setup costs are the costs of preparing equipment and facilities so they can be used to produce a particular product or component. Examples are wages of idled production workers, the cost of idled production facilities (lost income), and the costs of test runs (labor, materials, and overhead).

carrying costs

Carrying costs are the costs of carrying inventory. Examples include insurance, inventory taxes, obsolescence, the opportunity cost of funds tied up in inventory, handling costs, and storage space.

Ordering costs and setup costs are similar in nature—both represent costs that must be incurred to acquire inventory. They differ only in the nature of the prerequisite activity (filling out and placing an order versus configuring equipment and facilities). Thus, in the discussion that follows, any reference to order costs can be viewed as a reference to setup costs.

stock-out costs

If demand is not known with certainty, a third category of inventory costs—called *stock-out costs*—exists. **Stock-out costs** are the costs of not having a product available when demanded by a customer. Examples are lost sales (both current and future), the costs of expediting (increased transportation charges, overtime, and so on), and the costs of interrupted production.

Traditional Reasons for Holding Inventory

Maximizing profits requires that inventory-related costs be minimized. But minimizing carrying costs favors ordering or producing in small lot sizes, whereas minimizing ordering costs favors large, infrequent orders (minimization of setup costs favors long, infrequent production runs). Thus, minimizing carrying costs encourages small or no inventories and minimizing ordering or setup costs encourages larger inventories. The need to balance these two sets of costs so that the *total* cost of carrying and ordering can be minimized is one reason organizations choose to carry inventory.

Dealing with uncertainty in demand is a second major reason for holding inventory. Even if the ordering or setup costs were negligible, organizations would still carry inventory because of stock-out costs. If the demand for materials or products is greater than expected, inventory can serve as a buffer, giving organizations the ability to meet delivery dates (thus keeping customers satisfied). Although balancing conflicting costs and dealing with uncertainty are the two most frequently cited reasons for carrying inventories, other reasons for carrying inventory also exist.

Inventories of parts and raw materials are often viewed as necessary because of supply uncertainties. That is, inventory buffers of parts and materials are needed to keep production flowing in case of late deliveries or no deliveries (strikes, bad weather, and bankruptcy are examples of uncertain events that can cause an interruption in supply). Unreliable production processes may also create a demand for producing extra inventory. For example, a company may decide to produce more units than needed to meet demand because the production process usually yields a large number of nonconforming units. Similarly, buffers of inventories may be required to continue supplying customers or processes with goods even if a process goes down because of a failed machine. Finally, organizations may acquire larger inventories than normal to take advantage of quantity discounts or to avoid anticipated price increases. Exhibit 13-1 summarizes the reasons typically offered for carrying inventory. It's important to realize that these are reasons that are given to *justify* carrying inventories. There are a host of other reasons that can be offered that *encourage* the carrying of inventories. For example, performance measures such as measures of machine and labor efficiency may promote the buildup of inventories.

Exhibit 13-1
Traditional Reasons for Carrying Inventory

1. To balance ordering or setup costs and carrying costs.
2. To satisfy customer demand (e.g., meet delivery dates).
3. To avoid shutting down manufacturing facilities because of
   a. machine failure.
   b. defective parts.
   c. unavailable parts.
   d. late delivery of parts.
4. Unreliable production processes.
5. To take advantage of discounts.
6. To hedge against future price increases.

Economic Order Quantity: The Traditional Inventory Model

In developing an inventory policy, two basic questions must be addressed.

1. How much should be ordered (or produced)?
2. When should the order be placed (or the setup done)?

The first question needs to be addressed before the second can be answered.

Order Quantity and Total Ordering and Carrying Costs Assume that demand is known. In choosing an order quantity or a lot size for production, managers need be concerned only with ordering (or setup) and carrying costs. The total ordering (or setup) and carrying cost can be described by the following equation:

$$TC = PD/Q + CQ/2 \qquad\qquad (13.1)$$
$$= \text{Ordering costs} + \text{Carrying cost}$$

$$
\begin{aligned}
\text{where } TC &= \text{The total ordering (or setup) and carrying cost} \\
P &= \text{The cost of placing and receiving an order} \\
&\quad\text{(or the cost of setting up a production run)} \\
Q &= \text{The number of units ordered each time an order} \\
&\quad\text{is placed (or the lot size for production)} \\
D &= \text{The known annual demand} \\
C &= \text{The cost of carrying one unit of stock for one year}
\end{aligned}
$$

The cost of carrying inventory can be computed for any organization that carries inventories, including retail, service, and manufacturing organizations. Of course, the inventory cost model using setup costs and lot size as inputs pertains only to those organizations that produce their own inventories (parts or finished goods). To illustrate, consider Erna Corporation, a service organization that does warranty work for a major producer of video recorders. Assume that the following values apply for a part used in the repair of the video recorders (the part is purchased from external suppliers):

$$
\begin{aligned}
D &= 25{,}000 \text{ units} \\
Q &= 500 \text{ units} \\
P &= \$40 \text{ per order} \\
C &= \$2 \text{ per unit}
\end{aligned}
$$

Dividing D by Q produces the number of orders per year, which is 50 (25,000/500). Multiplying the number of orders per year by the cost of placing and receiving an order ($D/Q \times P$) yields the total ordering cost of $2,000 (50 × $40).

The total carrying cost for the year is given by $CQ/2$; this expression is equivalent to multiplying the average inventory on hand ($Q/2$) by the carrying cost per unit (C). For an order of 500 units with a carrying cost of $2 per unit, the average inventory is 250 (500/2) and the carrying cost for the year is $500 ($2 × 250). (Assuming average inventory to be $Q/2$ is equivalent to assuming that inventory is consumed uniformly.)

Applying Equation 13.1, the total cost is $2,500 ($2,000 + $500). An order quantity of 500 with a total cost of $2,500, however, may not be the best choice. Some other order quantity may produce a lower total cost. The objective is to find the order quantity that minimizes the total cost. This order quantity is called the **economic order quantity (EOQ)**. The EOQ model is an example of a *push*

economic order
quantity (EOQ)

inventory system. In a push system, the acquisition of inventory is initiated in anticipation of future demand—not in reaction to present demand. Fundamental to the analysis is the assessment of D, the future demand.

Computing the EOQ

Since the EOQ is the quantity that minimizes Equation 13.1, a formula for computing this quantity is easily derived.[1]

$$Q = EOQ = \sqrt{(2DP/C)} \qquad (13.2)$$

Using the data from the example above, the EOQ can be computed using Equation 13.2:

$$EOQ = \sqrt{(2 \times 25,000 \times 40)/2}$$
$$= \sqrt{1,000,000}$$
$$= 1,000$$

Substituting 1,000 as the value of Q in Equation 13.1 yields a total cost of $2,000. The number of orders placed would be 25 (25,000/1,000); thus, the total ordering cost is $1,000 (25 × $40). The average inventory is 500 (1,000/2), with a total carrying cost of $1,000 (500 × $2). Notice that the carrying cost equals the ordering cost. This is always true for the simple EOQ model described by Equation 13.2. Also notice that an order quantity of 1,000 is less costly than an order quantity of 500 ($2,000 versus $2,500).

Reorder Point

reorder point

lead time

The EOQ answers the question of how much to order (or produce). Knowing when to place an order (or to set up for production) is also an essential part of any inventory policy. The **reorder point** is the point in time a new order should be placed (or setup started). It is a function of the EOQ, the lead time, and the rate at which inventory is depleted. **Lead time** is the time required to receive the economic order quantity once an order is placed or a setup is initiated.

To avoid stock-out costs and to minimize carrying costs, an order should be placed so that it arrives just as the last item in inventory is used. Knowing the rate of usage and lead time allows us to compute the reorder point that accomplishes these objectives:

$$\text{Reorder point} = \text{Rate of usage} \times \text{Lead time} \qquad (13.3)$$

To illustrate Equation 13.3, we will continue to use the video recorder example. Assume that the repair activity uses 100 parts per day and that the lead time is four days. If so, an order should be placed when the inventory level of the VCR part drops to 400 units (100 × 4). Exhibit 13-2 provides a graphical illustration. Note that the inventory is depleted just as the order arrives and that the quantity on hand jumps back up to the EOQ level.

Demand Uncertainty and the Reorder Point

If the demand for the part or product is not known with certainty, the possibility of stock-out exists. For example, if the VCR part was used at a rate of 120 parts a day instead of 100, the firm would use 400 parts after three and one-third days.

---

1. $d(TC)/dQ = C/2 - DP/Q^2 = 0$, thus $Q^2 = 2DP/C$ and $Q = \sqrt{2DP/C}$

Exhibit 13-2
The Reorder Point

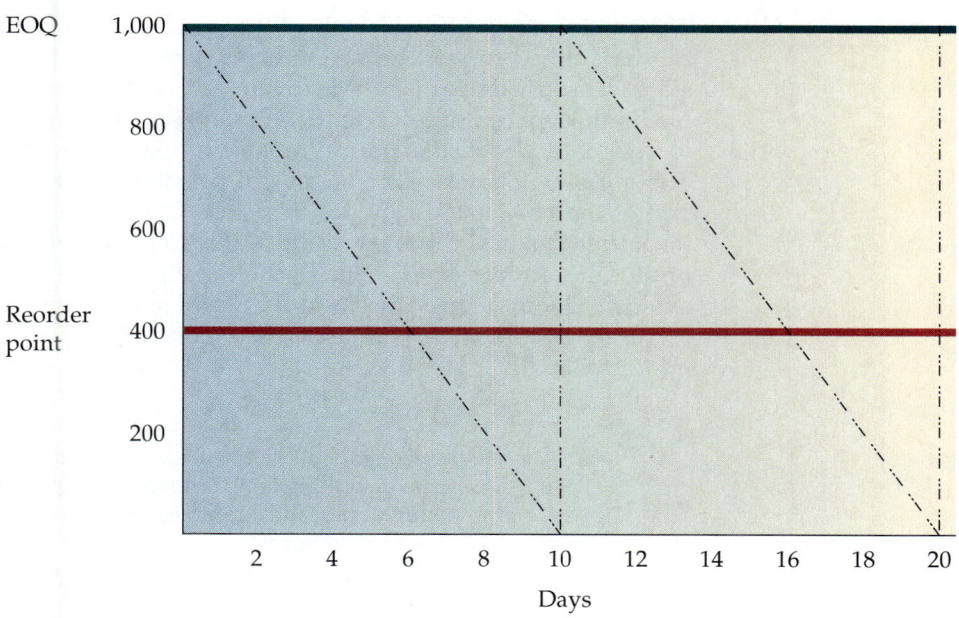

Since the new order would not arrive until the end of the fourth day, repair activity requiring this part would be idled for two-thirds of a day. To avoid this problem, organizations often choose to carry safety stock. **Safety stock** is extra inventory carried to serve as insurance against fluctuations in demand. Safety stock is computed by multiplying the lead time by the difference between the maximum rate of usage and the average rate of usage. For example, if the maximum usage of the VCR part is 120 units per day, the average usage 100 units per day, and the lead time is four days, the safety stock is computed as follows:

safety stock

Maximum usage	120
Average usage	(100)
Difference	20
Lead time	× 4
Safety stock	80

With the presence of safety stock, the reorder point is computed as follows:

Reorder point = (Average rate of usage × Lead time) + Safety stock   (13.4)

For the repair service example, the reorder point with safety stock is computed below:

$$\text{Reorder point} = (100 \times 4) + 80$$
$$= 480 \text{ units}$$

Thus, an order is automatically placed whenever the inventory level drops to 480 units.

A Manufacturing Example

The service repair setting involved the purchase of inventory. The same concepts can be applied to settings where inventory is manufactured. To illustrate, consider Benson Company, a large manufacturer of farm implements with several plants throughout the nation. Each plant produces all subassemblies necessary to assemble a particular farm implement. One large plant in the Midwest produces plows. The manager of this Midwestern plant is trying to determine the size of the production runs for the blade fabrication area. He is convinced that the current lot size is too large and wants to identify the quantity that should be produced to minimize the sum of the carrying and setup costs. He also wants to avoid stock-outs, since any stock-out would shut down the assembly department.

To help him in his decision, the controller has supplied the following information:

Average demand for blades: 320 per day
Maximum demand for blades: 340 per day
Annual demand for blades: 80,000
Unit carrying cost: $5
Setup cost: $12,500
Lead time: 20 days

Based on the above information, the economic order quantity and the reorder point are computed in Exhibit 13-3. As the computation illustrates, the blades should be produced in batches of 20,000 and a new setup should be started when the supply of blades drops to 6,800.

EOQ and Inventory Management

The traditional approach to managing inventory has been referred to as a *Just-in-Case system*.[2] In some settings, a just-in-case inventory system is entirely appropriate. For example, hospitals need inventories of medicines, drugs, and other critical supplies on hand at all times so that life-threatening situations can be handled. Using an economic order quantity coupled with safety stock would seem eminently sensible in such an environment. Relying on a critical drug to arrive just in time to save a heart attack victim is simply not practical. Furthermore, many smaller retail stores, manufacturers, and services may not have the buying power to command alternative inventory management systems such as just-in-time purchasing.

As the plow blade example illustrates (Exhibit 13-3), the EOQ model is very useful in identifying the optimal trade-off between inventory carrying costs and setup costs. It also is useful in helping to deal with uncertainty by using safety stock. The historical importance of the EOQ model in many American industries can be better appreciated by understanding the nature of the traditional manufacturing environment. This environment has been characterized by the mass production of a few standardized products that typically have a very high setup cost. The production of the plow blades fits this pattern. The high setup cost encouraged a large batch size: 20,000 units. The annual demand of 80,000 units can be satisfied using only two batches. Thus, production runs for these firms

---

2.   Eliyahu M. Goldratt and Robert E. Fox, *The Race*, North River Press, Croton-on-Hudson, New York, 1986.

Exhibit 13-3
EOQ and Reorder Point Illustrated

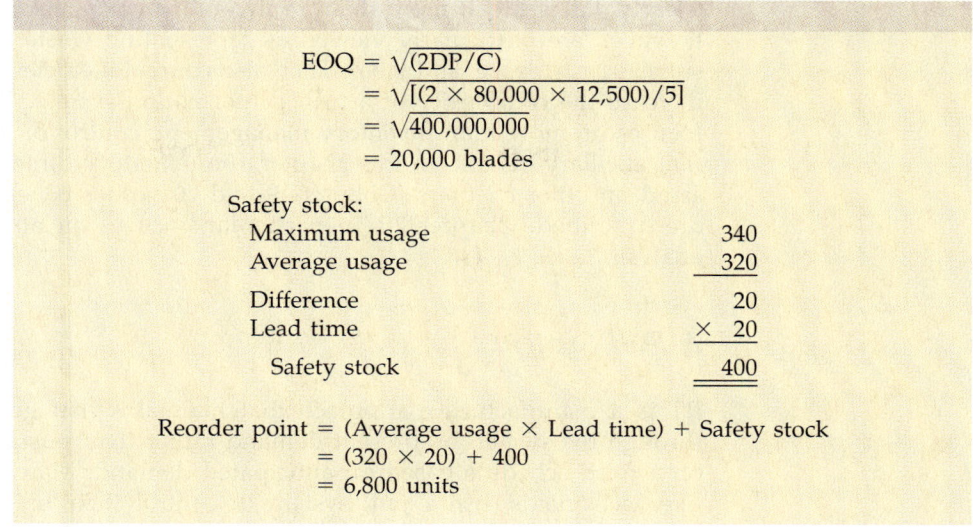

$$EOQ = \sqrt{(2DP/C)}$$
$$= \sqrt{[(2 \times 80,000 \times 12,500)/5]}$$
$$= \sqrt{400,000,000}$$
$$= 20,000 \text{ blades}$$

Safety stock:

Maximum usage	340
Average usage	320
Difference	20
Lead time	× 20
Safety stock	400

$$\text{Reorder point} = (\text{Average usage} \times \text{Lead time}) + \text{Safety stock}$$
$$= (320 \times 20) + 400$$
$$= 6,800 \text{ units}$$

tended to be quite long. Furthermore, diversity was viewed as being costly and was avoided. Producing variations of the product can be quite expensive, especially since additional, special features would usually demand even more expensive and frequent setups—the reason for the standardized products.

JIT AND INVENTORY MANAGEMENT: A DIFFERENT VIEW

Objective 2
Describe JIT inventory management.

The manufacturing environment for many of these traditional, large-batch, high-setup-cost firms has changed dramatically in the past ten to twenty years. For one thing, the competitive markets are no longer defined by national boundaries. Advances in transportation and communication have contributed significantly to the creation of global competition. Advances in technology have contributed to shorter life cycles for products, and product diversity has increased. Foreign firms offering higher-quality, lower-cost products *with specialized features* have created tremendous pressures for our domestic large-batch, high-setup-cost firms to increase both quality and product diversity while simultaneously reducing total costs. These competitive pressures have led many firms to abandon the EOQ model in favor of a JIT approach. JIT has two strategic objectives: to increase profits and to improve a firm's competitive position. These two objectives are achieved by controlling costs (enabling better price competition and increased profits), improving delivery performance, and improving quality. JIT offers increased cost efficiency and simultaneously has the flexibility to respond to customer demands for better quality and more variety. Quality, flexibility, and cost efficiency are foundation principles for world-class competition.

nonvalue-added activities

JIT manufacturing and purchasing represent the continual pursuit of productivity through the elimination of waste. *Nonvalue-added* activities are a major source of waste. **Nonvalue-added activities** are either unnecessary or necessary but inefficient and improvable. Necessary activities are essential to the business and/or are of value to customers. Eliminating nonvalue-added activities is a major thrust of JIT, but it is also a basic objective of any company following the path of continuous improvement—regardless of whether or not JIT is being used.

Clearly, JIT is much more than an inventory management system. Inventories, however, are particularly viewed as representing waste. They tie up resources such as cash, space, and labor. They also conceal inefficiencies in production and increase the complexity of a firm's information system. Thus, even though JIT focuses on more than inventory management, control of inventory is an important ancillary benefit. In this chapter, the inventory dimension of JIT is emphasized. In other chapters (Chapters 9 and 20), other benefits and features of JIT are described. Chapter 20, in particular, focuses on nonvalue-added activity analysis.

A Pull System

JIT is a manufacturing approach that maintains that goods should be pulled through the system by present demand rather than pushed through the system on a fixed schedule based on anticipated demand. Many fast food restaurants, like McDonalds, use a pull system to control their finished goods inventory. When a customer orders a hamburger, it is taken from the rack. When the number of hamburgers gets too low, then the cooks make new hamburgers. Customer demand pulls the materials through the system. This same principle is used in manufacturing settings. Each operation produces only what is necessary to satisfy the demand of the succeeding operation. The material or subassembly arrives just in time for production to occur so that demand can be met.

One effect of JIT is to reduce inventories to very low levels. The pursuit of insignificant levels of inventories is vital to the success of JIT. This idea of pursuing insignificant inventories, however, necessarily challenges the traditional reasons for holding inventories (see Exhibit 13-1). These reasons are no longer viewed as valid.

According to the traditional view, inventories solve some underlying problem related to each of the reasons listed in Exhibit 13-1. For example, the problem of resolving the conflict between ordering or setup costs and carrying costs is solved by selecting an inventory level that minimizes the sum of these costs. If demand is greater than expected or if production is reduced by breakdowns and production inefficiencies, then inventories serve as buffers, providing products to customers that otherwise might not have been available. Similarly, inventories can prevent shutdowns caused by late delivery of material, defective parts, and failures of machines used to produce subassemblies. Finally, inventories are often the solution to the problem of buying the best raw materials for the least cost through the use of quantity discounts.

JIT refuses to use inventories as the solution to these problems. In fact, the JIT approach can be seen as substituting information for inventories. Companies must track raw materials and finished goods more carefully. To do that, the logistics industry has gone high-tech. Schneider National Company, a logistics firm, uses satellite tracking to tell a customer just where a particular shipment is and when it will be delivered. In an example of partnering, Schneider engineers assist client PPG Industries by showing their Pennsylvania plant employees how to use the shipping and receiving facilities more efficiently.[3] JIT inventory management offers alternative solutions that do not require high inventories.

---

3.   Jon Bigness, "In Today's Economy There Is Big Money to Be Made in Logistics," *The Wall Street Journal*, September 6, 1995, pp. A1 and A9.

Setup and Carrying Costs: The JIT Approach

JIT takes a radically different approach to minimizing total carrying and setup costs. The traditional approach accepts the existence of setup costs and then finds the order quantity that best balances the two categories of costs. JIT, on the other hand, does not accept setup costs (or ordering costs) as a given; rather, JIT attempts to drive these costs to zero. If setup costs and ordering costs become insignificant, the only remaining cost to minimize is carrying cost, which is accomplished by reducing inventories to very low levels. This approach explains the push for zero inventories in a JIT system.

Long-Term Contracts, Continuous Replenishment, and Electronic Data Interchange Ordering costs are reduced by developing close relationships with suppliers. Negotiating long-term contracts for the supply of outside materials will obviously reduce the number of orders and the associated ordering costs. Retailers have found a way to reduce ordering costs by adopting an arrangement known as *continuous replenishment.* **Continuous replenishment** means a manufacturer assumes the inventory management function for the retailer. The manufacturer tells the retailer when and how much stock to reorder. The retailer reviews the recommendation and approves the order if it makes sense. Wal-Mart and Procter and Gamble, for example, use this arrangement.[4] The arrangement has reduced inventories for Wal-Mart and has also reduced stock-out problems. Additionally, Wal-Mart often sells Procter and Gamble's goods before it has to pay for them. Procter and Gamble, on the other hand, has become a preferred supplier, has more and better shelf space, and has also less demand uncertainty. The ability to project demand better allows Procter and Gamble to produce and deliver continuously in smaller lots—a goal of JIT manufacturing. Similar arrangements can be made between manufacturers and suppliers.

The process of continuous replenishment is facilitated by *electronic data interchange.* **Electronic data interchange (EDI)** allows suppliers access to a buyer's on-line data base. By knowing the buyer's production schedule (in the case of a manufacturer), the supplier can deliver the needed parts where they are needed just in time for their use. EDI involves no paper—no purchase orders or invoices. The supplier uses the production schedule, which is in the data base, to determine its own production and delivery schedules. When the parts are shipped, an electronic message is sent from the supplier to the buyer that a shipment is en route. When the parts arrive, a bar code is scanned with an electronic wand and this initiates payment for the goods. Clearly, EDI requires a close working arrangement between the supplier and the buyer—they almost operate as one company rather than two separate companies. General Motors' Saturn plant uses an EDI arrangement with its component suppliers. This has enabled both suppliers and Saturn to reduce overhead.[5]

Reducing Setup Times Reducing setup times requires a company to search for new, more efficient ways to accomplish setup. Fortunately, experience has indicated that dramatic reductions in setup times can be achieved. Upon adopting a JIT system, Harley-Davidson reduced setup time by more than 75 percent on the machines evaluated.[6] In some cases, Harley-Davidson was able to reduce the

continuous replenishment

electronic data interchange (EDI)

---

4.   Michael Hammer and James Champy, *Reengineering the Corporation,* Harper Business, New York, 1993.
5.   Michael Hammer and James Champy, *Reengineering the Corporation,* pp. 90–91.
6.   Gene Schwind, "Man Arrives Just in Time to Save Harley-Davidson," *Material Handling Engineering,* August 1984, pp. 28–35.

setup times from hours to minutes. Other companies have experienced similar results. Generally, setup times can be reduced by at least 75 percent.[7]

Due-Date Performance: The JIT Solution

Due-date performance is a measure of a firm's ability to respond to customer needs. In the past, finished goods inventories have been used to ensure that a firm is able to meet a requested delivery date. JIT solves the problem of due-date performance not by building inventory but by dramatically reducing lead times. Shorter lead times increase a firm's ability to meet requested delivery dates and to respond quickly to the demands of the market. Thus, the firm's competitiveness is improved. JIT cuts lead times by reducing setup times, improving quality, and using cellular manufacturing.

Manufacturing cells reduce travel distance between machines and inventory; they can also have a dramatic effect on lead time. For example, in a traditional manufacturing system, one company took two months to manufacture a valve. By grouping the lathes and drills used to make the valves into U-shaped cells, the lead time was reduced to two or three days. A chain-saw manufacturer was able to reduce travel distance from 2,620 feet to 173 feet and lead times from twenty-one days to three. Because of the reduced lead time and plans for even further reduction, the company will be filling orders directly from the factory rather than from finished goods warehouses.[8] These reductions in lead time are not unique—most companies experience at least a 90 percent reduction in lead times when they implement JIT.[9]

Manufacturers are not the only companies using a JIT approach to improve time to market. Benetton calls itself an apparel services company, not a retailer. Operating one giant distribution center in Castrette, Italy, Benetton uses robots to send the latest fashions to any of its company stores in 120 countries within 12 days.

Avoidance of Shutdown and Process Reliability: The JIT Approach

Most shutdowns occur for one of three reasons: machine failure, defective material or subassembly, and unavailability of a raw material or subassembly. Holding inventories is one solution to all three problems.

Those espousing the JIT approach claim that inventories do not solve the problems but cover up or hide them. JIT proponents use the analogy of rocks in a lake. The rocks represent the three problems, and the water represents inventories. If the lake is deep (inventories are high), then the rocks are never exposed and managers can pretend they do not exist. By reducing inventories to zero, the rocks are exposed and can no longer be ignored. JIT solves the three problems by emphasizing total preventive maintenance and total quality control and by building the right kind of relationship with suppliers.

---

7.   William J. Stoddard and Nolan W. Rhea, "Just-in-Time Manufacturing: The Relentless Pursuit of Productivity," *Material Handling Engineering*, March 1985, pp. 70–76.

8.   Richard Schonberger, "Just-in-Time Production Systems: Replacing Complexity with Simplicity in Manufacturing Management," *Industrial Engineering*, October 1984, pp. 52–63. For an excellent description of the savings realized by Oregon Cutting Systems, read the article by Jack Bailes and Ilene K. Kleinsorge, "Cutting Waste with JIT," *Management Accounting*, May 1992, pp. 28–32.

9.   See Stoddard and Rhea, "Just-in-Time Manufacturing," p. 76.

total preventive
maintenance

Total Preventive Maintenance Zero machine failures is the goal of **total preventive maintenance**. By paying more attention to preventive maintenance, most machine breakdowns can be avoided. This objective is easier to attain in a JIT environment because of the interdisciplinary labor philosophy. It is not uncommon for a cell worker to be trained in maintenance of the machines he or she operates. Because of the pull-through nature of JIT, it is also not unusual for a cell worker to have idle manufacturing time. Some of this time, then, can be used productively by having the cell workers involved in preventive maintenance.

Total Quality Control The problem of defective parts is solved by striving for zero defects. Because JIT manufacturing does not rely on inventories to replace defective parts or materials, the emphasis on quality for both internally produced and externally purchased materials increases significantly. The outcome is impressive: the number of rejected parts tends to fall by 75–90 percent.[10] Decreasing defective parts also diminishes the justification for inventories based on unreliable processes.

Kanban system

The Kanban System To ensure that parts or materials are available when needed, a system called the **Kanban system** is employed. This is an information system that controls production through the use of markers or cards. The Kanban system is responsible for ensuring that the necessary products (or parts) are produced (or acquired) in the necessary quantities at the necessary time. It is the heart of the JIT inventory management system.

A Kanban system uses cards or markers, which are plastic, cardboard, or metal plates measuring 4 inches by 8 inches. The Kanban is usually placed in a vinyl sack and attached to the part or a container holding the needed parts.

A basic Kanban system uses three cards: a *withdrawal Kanban*, a *production Kanban*, and a *vendor Kanban*. The first two control the movement of work among the manufacturing processes, while the third controls movement of parts between

withdrawal Kanban

the processes and outside suppliers. A **withdrawal Kanban** specifies the quantity that a subsequent process should withdraw from the preceding process. A

production Kanban
vendor Kanbans

production Kanban specifies the quantity that the preceding process should produce. **Vendor Kanbans** are used to notify suppliers to deliver more parts; they also specify when the parts are needed. The three Kanbans are illustrated in Exhibits 13-4, 13-5, and 13-6, respectively.

How Kanban cards are used to control the work flow can be illustrated with a simple example. Assume that two processes are needed to manufacture a product. The first process (CB Assembly) builds and tests printed circuit boards (using a U-shaped manufacturing cell). The second process (Final Assembly) puts eight circuit boards into a subassembly purchased from an outside supplier. The final product is a personal computer.

Exhibit 13-7 provides the plant layout corresponding to the manufacture of the personal computers. Refer to the exhibit as the steps involved in using Kanbans are outlined.

Consider first the movement of work between the two processing areas. Assume that eight circuit boards are placed in a container and that one such container is located in the CB stores area. Attached to this container is a production Kanban (P-Kanban). A second container with eight circuit boards is located near

10. Stoddard and Rhea, "Just-in-Time Manufacturing."

Exhibit 13-4
Withdrawal Kanban

Item No. __15670T07__	Preceding Process
Item Name __Circuit Board__	__CB Assembly__
Computer Type __TR6547 PC__	
Box Capacity __8__	Subsequent Process
Box Type __C__	__Final Assembly__

Exhibit 13-5
Production Kanban

Item No. __15670T07__	Process
Item Name __Circuit Board__	__CB Assembly__
Computer Type __TR6547 PC__	
Box Capacity __8__	
Box Type __C__	

Exhibit 13-6
Vendor Kanban

Item No. __15670T08__	Name of Receiving Company
Item Name __Computer Casing__	__Electro PC__
Box Capacity __8__	Receiving Gate
Box Type __A__	__75__
Time to Deliver __8:30 A.M., 12:30 P.M., 2:30 P.M.__	
Name of Supplier __Gerry Supply__	

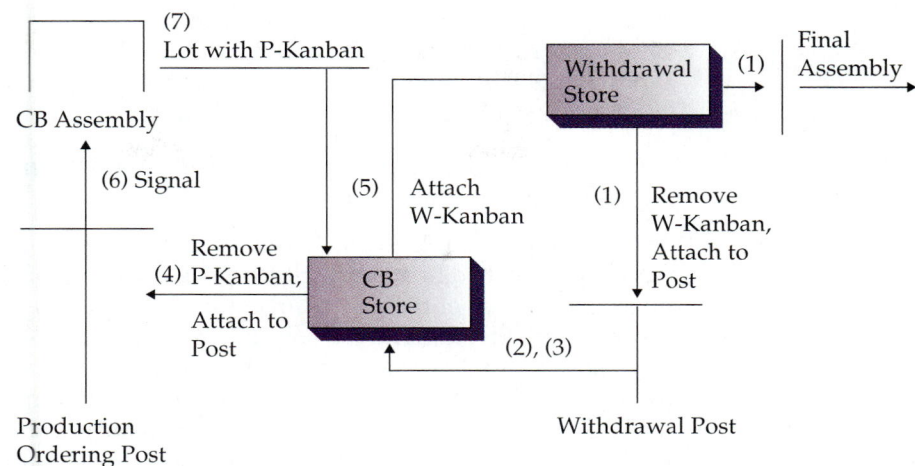

Exhibit 13-7
The Kanban Process

the Final Assembly line (the withdrawal store) with a withdrawal Kanban (W-Kanban). Now assume that the production schedule calls for the immediate assembly of a computer.

The Kanban setups can be described as follows:

1. A worker from the Final Assembly line goes to the withdrawal store, removes the eight circuit boards and places them into production. The worker also removes the withdrawal Kanban and places it on the withdrawal post.
2. The withdrawal Kanban on the post signals that the Final Assembly unit needs an additional eight circuit boards.
3. A worker from Final Assembly (or a materials handler called a *carrier*) removes the withdrawal Kanban from the post and carries it to CB stores.
4. At the CB stores area, the carrier removes the production Kanban from the container of eight circuit boards and places it on the production-ordering post.
5. The carrier next attaches the withdrawal Kanban to the container of parts and carries the container back to the Final Assembly area. Assembly of the next computer can begin.
6. The production Kanban on the production-ordering post signals the workers of the CB assembly to begin producing another lot of circuit boards. The production Kanban is removed and accompanies the units as they are produced.
7. When the lot of eight circuit boards is completed, the units are placed in a container in the CB stores area with the production Kanban attached. The cycle is then repeated.

The use of Kanbans ensures that the subsequent process (Final Assembly) withdraws the circuit boards from the preceding process (CB Assembly) in the necessary quantity at the appropriate time. The Kanban system also controls the preceding process by allowing it to produce only the quantities withdrawn by the subsequent process. In this way, inventories are kept at a minimum, and the components arrive just in time to be used.

Essentially the same steps are followed for a purchased subassembly. The only difference is the use of a vendor Kanban in place of a production Kanban. A vendor Kanban on a vendor post signals to the supplier that another order is needed. As with the circuit boards, the subassemblies must be delivered just in time for use. A JIT purchasing system requires the supplier to deliver small quantities on a frequent basis. These deliveries could be weekly, daily, or even several times a day. This calls for a close working relationship with suppliers. Long-term contractual agreements tend to ensure supply of materials.

Discounts and Price Increases: JIT Purchasing Versus Holding Inventories

Traditionally, inventories are carried so that a firm can take advantage of quantity discounts and hedge against future price increases of the items purchased. The objective is to lower the cost of inventory. JIT achieves the same objective without carrying inventories. The JIT solution is to negotiate long-term contracts with a few chosen suppliers located as close to the production facility as possible and to establish more extensive supplier involvement. Suppliers are not selected on the basis of price alone. Performance—the quality of the component and the ability to deliver as needed—and commitment to JIT purchasing are vital considerations. Other benefits of long-term contracts exist. They stipulate prices and acceptable quality levels. Long-term contracts also reduce dramatically the number of orders placed, which helps to drive down the ordering cost. Another effect of JIT purchasing is to lower the cost of purchased parts by 5 to 20 percent.[11]

JIT's Limitations

JIT is not simply an approach that can be purchased and plugged in with immediate results. Its implementation should be more of an evolutionary process than a revolutionary process. Patience is needed. JIT is often referred to as a program of simplification—yet this does not imply that it is simple or easy to implement. Time is required, for example, to build sound relationships with suppliers. Insisting on immediate changes in delivery times and quality may not be realistic and may cause difficult confrontations between a company and its suppliers. Partnership, not coercion, should be the basis of supplier relationships. To achieve the benefits that are associated with JIT purchasing, a company may be tempted to redefine unilaterally its supplier relationships. Unilaterally redefining supplier relationships by extracting concessions and dictating terms may create supplier resentment and actually may cause suppliers to retaliate. In the long run, suppliers may seek new markets, find ways to charge higher prices (than would exist with a preferred supplier arrangement), or seek regulatory relief. These actions may destroy many of the JIT benefits extracted by the impatient company.

Workers also may be affected by JIT. Studies have shown that sharp reductions in inventory buffers may cause a regimented work flow and high levels of stress among production workers.[12] Some have suggested a deliberate pace of inventory reduction to allow workers to develop a sense of autonomy and to encourage their participation in broader improvement efforts. Forced and dramatic reductions in inventories may indeed reveal problems—but it may cause more problems: lost sales and stressed workers. If the workers perceive JIT as a way of simply squeezing more out of them, then JIT efforts may be doomed. Perhaps a better strategy for JIT implementation is one where inventory reductions follow the process improvements that JIT offers. Implementing JIT is not easy, and it requires careful and thorough planning and preparation. Companies should expect some struggle and frustration.

11.   Stoddard and Rhea, "Just-in-Time Manufacturing."
12.   For a more complete discussion of supplier and worker effects of JIT, see Paul L. Zipkin, "Does Manufacturing Need a JIT Revolution?" *Harvard Business Review*, January–February 1991, pp. 40–50.

The most glaring deficiency of JIT is the absence of inventory to buffer production interruptions. Current sales are constantly being threatened by an unexpected interruption in production. In fact, if a problem occurs, JIT's approach consists of trying to find and solve the problem before any further production activity occurs. Retailers who use JIT tactics also face the possibility of shortages. JIT retailers order what they need now—not what they expect to sell—because the idea is to flow goods through the channel as late as possible, hence keeping inventories low and decreasing the need for markdowns. If demand increases well beyond the retailer's supply of inventory, the retailer may be unable to make order adjustments quickly enough to avoid irked customers and lost sales. For example, during the Christmas shopping season in 1993, many retailers such as Toys "R" Us and Target Stores, using a JIT approach, lost millions in sales because of their inability to accurately forecast demand for Mighty Morphin Power Rangers.[13] It was estimated that shipments of the power ranger action figures would be around 600,000 units (before December 25) compared to an estimated demand of 12 million units. Yet in spite of the downside, retailers seem to be strongly committed to JIT. Apparently, losing sales on surprise hits is less costly than carrying high levels of inventory.

The JIT manufacturing company is also willing to place current sales at risk to achieve assurance of future sales. This assurance comes from higher quality, quicker response time, and less operating costs. Even so, we must recognize that a sale lost today is a sale lost forever. Installing a JIT system so that it operates with very little interruption is not a short-run project. Thus, losing sales is a real cost of installing a JIT system. An alternative, and perhaps complementary approach, is the theory of constraints (TOC). In principle, TOC can be used in conjunction with JIT manufacturing. After all, JIT manufacturing environments also have constraints. Furthermore, the TOC approach has the very appealing quality of protecting current sales while also striving to increase future sales by increasing quality, lowering response time, and decreasing operating costs. However, before we introduce and discuss the theory of constraints, we need to provide a brief introduction to constrained optimization theory.

BASIC CONCEPTS OF CONSTRAINED OPTIMIZATION

Objective 3
Explain the basic concepts of constrained optimization.

Manufacturing and service organizations must choose the mix of products that they will produce and sell. Decisions about product mix can have a significant impact on an organization's profitability. Each mix represents an alternative that carries with it an associated profit level. A manager should choose the alternative that maximizes total profits. The usual approach is to assume that only unit-based variable costs are relevant to the product mix decision. Thus, assuming that nonunit-level costs are the same for different mixes of products, a manager needs to choose the mix alternative that maximizes total contribution margin.

If a firm possesses unlimited resources and the demand for each product being considered is unlimited, then the product mix decision is simple—produce an infinite number of each product. Unfortunately, every firm faces limited resources and limited demand for each product. These limitations are called **constraints**. **External constraints** are limiting factors imposed on the firm from external sources (such as market demand). **Internal constraints** are limiting factors found within the firm (such as machine time availability). Although

constraints
external constraints
internal constraints

13.   Joseph Pereira, "Tough Game: The Power Rangers Surprise," *The Wall Street Journal*, December 21, 1993, pp. A1 and A5.

resources and demands may be limited, certain mixes may not meet all the demand or use all of the resources available to be used. Constraints whose limited resources are not fully used by a product mix are **loose constraints**. If, on the other hand, a product mix uses all of the limited resources of a constraint, then the constraint is a **binding constraint**.

loose constraints

binding constraint

A manager must choose the optimal mix given the constraints faced by the firm. Assume, for example, that Confer Company produces two types of machine parts: X and Y, with unit contribution margins of $300 and $600, respectively. Assuming that Confer can sell all that is produced, some may argue that only Part Y should be produced and sold because it has the larger contribution margin. However, this solution is not necessarily the best. The selection of the optimal mix can be significantly affected by the relationships of the constrained resources to the individual products. These relationships affect the quantity of each product that can be produced and, consequently, the total contribution margin that can be earned. This point is most vividly illustrated with one binding internal resource constraint.

One Binding Internal Constraint

Assume that each part must be drilled by a special machine. The firm owns three machines that together provide 120 drilling hours per week. Part X requires one hour of drilling, and Part Y requires three hours of drilling. Assuming no other binding constraints, what is the optimal mix of parts? Since each unit of Part X requires one hour of drilling, 120 units of Part X can be produced per week (120/1). At $300 per unit, Confer can earn a total contribution margin of $36,000 per week. On the other hand, Part Y requires 3 hours of drilling per unit; therefore, 40 (120/3) parts can be produced. At $600 per unit, the total contribution margin is $24,000 per week. Producing only Part X yields a higher profit level than producing only Part Y—even though the unit contribution margin for Part Y is twice the amount of Part X.

The contribution margin per unit of each product is not the critical concern. The contribution margin per unit of *scarce resource* is the deciding factor. The product yielding the highest contribution margin per drilling hour should be selected. Part X earns $300 per machine hour ($300/1), while Part Y earns only $200 per machine hour ($600/3). Thus, the optimal mix is 120 units of Part X and none of Part Y, producing a total contribution margin of $36,000 per week.

Internal Binding Constraint and External Binding Constraint

The contribution margin per unit of scarce resource can also be used to identify the optimal product mix when a binding external constraint exists. For example, assume the same internal constraint of 120 drilling hours but also assume that Confer can sell at most 60 units of Part X and 100 units of Part Y. The internal constraint allows Confer to produce 120 units of Part X, but this is no longer a feasible choice because only 60 units of X can be sold. Thus, we now have a binding external constraint—one that affects the earlier decision to produce and sell only Part X. Since the contribution per unit of scarce resource (machine hour) is $300 for Part X and $200 for Part Y, it still makes sense to produce as much of Part X as possible before producing any of Part Y. Confer should first produce 60 units of part X, using 60 machine hours. This leaves 60 machine hours, allowing the production of 20 units of Part Y. The optimal mix is now 60 units of Part X and 20 units of Part Y, producing a total contribution margin of $30,000 per week [($300 × 60) + ($600 × 20)].

Multiple Internal Binding Constraints

It is possible for an organization to have more than one binding constraint. All organizations face multiple constraints: limitations of raw materials, limitations of labor inputs, limited machine hours, and so on. The solution of the product mix problem in the presence of multiple internal binding constraints is considerably more complicated and requires the use of a specialized mathematical technique known as *linear programming*.

linear programming

Linear Programming **Linear programming** is a method that searches among possible solutions until it finds the optimal solution. The theory of linear programming permits many solutions to be ignored. In fact, all but a finite number of solutions are eliminated by the theory, with the search then limited to the resulting finite set.

To illustrate how linear programming can be used to identify the optimal mix with multiple internally constrained resources, we will continue to use the Confer Company example. However, the example will be expanded to include a wider variety of constraints. In addition to the constraints already identified, two more internal constraints will be added. Assume that the two parts (X and Y) are produced in three sequential processes: grinding, drilling, and polishing. The grinding process uses two machines that provide a total of 80 grinding hours per week. Each part requires one hour of grinding. The polishing process is labor-intensive. This process provides 90 labor hours per week. Part X uses two hours per unit, and Part Y uses one hour per unit. Information on Confer's constraints is summarized in Exhibit 13-8. As before, the objective is to maximize Confer's total contribution margin subject to the constraints faced by Confer.

The objective of maximizing total contribution margin can be expressed mathematically. Let X be the number of units produced and sold of Part X, and let Y stand for Part Y. Since the unit contribution margins are $300 and $600 for X and Y, respectively, the total contribution margin (Z) can be expressed as

$$Z = \$300X + \$600Y \tag{13.4}$$

objective function

Equation 13.4 is called the **objective function**, the function to be optimized.

Confer also has five constraints. Using the information in Exhibit 13-8, the constraints are expressed mathematically as follows:

Internal constraints:

$$X - Y \leq 80 \tag{13.5}$$
$$X + 3Y \leq 120 \tag{13.6}$$
$$2X - Y \leq 90 \tag{13.7}$$

External constraints:

$$X \leq 60 \tag{13.8}$$
$$Y \leq 100 \tag{13.9}$$

Exhibit 13-8
Constraint Data: Confer Company

Resource Name	Resource Available	Part X Resource Usage: Per Unit	Part Y Resource Usage: Per Unit
Grinding	80 grinding hours	One hour	One hour
Drilling	120 drilling hours	One hour	Three hours
Polishing	90 labor hours	Two hours	One hour
Market demand: Part X	60 units	One unit	Zero units
Market demand: Part Y	100 units	Zero units	One unit

Confer's problem is to select the number of units of X and Y that maximize total contribution margin subject to the constraints in Equations 13.5–13.9. This problem can be expressed in the following way, which is the standard formulation for a linear programming problem (often referred to as a *linear programming model*):

$$\text{Max } Z = \$300X + \$600Y$$
subject to
$$X + Y \leq 80$$
$$X + 3Y \leq 120$$
$$2X + Y \leq 90$$
$$X \leq 60$$
$$Y \leq 100$$
$$X \geq 0$$
$$Y \geq 0$$

The last two constraints are called *nonnegativity constraints* and simply reflect the reality that negative quantities of a product cannot be produced. All constraints, taken together, are referred to as the **constraint set**.

A **feasible solution** is a solution that satisfies the constraints in the linear programming model. The collection of all feasible solutions is called the **feasible set of solutions**. For example, producing and selling one unit of Part X and one unit of Part Y would be a feasible solution and a member of the feasible set. This product mix clearly satisfies all constraints. But the mix would only earn $900 per week. There are, however, many feasible solutions that offer higher profits (for example, producing two of each part). The objective is to identify the best. The best feasible solution—the one that maximizes the total contribution margin—is called the **optimal solution**.

Graphical Solution When there are only two products, the optimal solution can be identified by graphing. Since solving the problem by graphing provides considerable insight into the way linear programming problems are solved, the Confer problem will be solved in this way. Four steps are followed in solving the problem graphically.

1. Graph each constraint.
2. Identify the feasible set of solutions.
3. Identify all corner-point values in the feasible set.
4. Select the corner point that yields the largest value for the objective function.

The graph of each constraint for the Confer example is shown in Exhibit 13-9. The nonnegativity constraints put the graph in the first quadrant. The other constraints are graphed by assuming that equality holds. Since each constraint is a linear equation, the graph is obtained by identifying two points on the line, plotting those points, and connecting them.

A feasible area for each constraint (except for the nonnegativity constraints) is determined by everything that lies below (or to the left) of the resulting line. The *feasible set* or *region* is the intersection of each constraint's feasible area. The feasible set is shown by the figure *ABCD*; it includes the boundary of the figure. Notice that only two of the five constraints qualify as candidates for binding constraints: the drilling and polishing constraints.

constraint set
feasible solution
feasible set of solutions
optimal solution

Exhibit 13-9
Graphical Solution

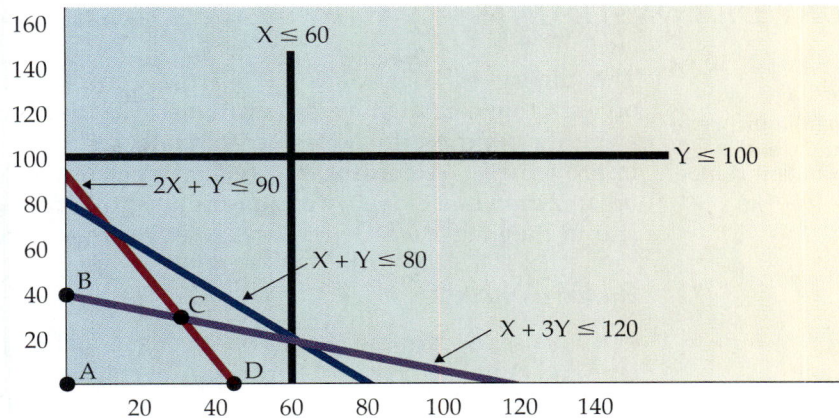

There are four corner points: *A*, *B*, *C*, and *D*. Their values, obtained directly from the graph, are (0, 0) for *A*, (0, 40) for *B*, (30, 30) for *C*, and (45, 0) for *D*. The impact of these values on the objective function is as follows (expressed in thousands):

Corner Point	X-value	Y-value	Z = $300X + $600Y
A	0	0	0
B	0	40	$24,000
C	30	30	27,000*
D	45	0	13,500

*Optimal solution

The optimal solution calls for producing and selling 30 units of Part X per week and 30 units of Part Y per week. No other feasible solution will produce a larger contribution margin. It has been shown in the literature on linear programming that the optimal solution will always be one of the corner points. Thus, once the graph is drawn and the corner points identified, finding the solution is simply a matter of computing the value of each corner point and selecting the one with the greatest value.

Graphical solutions are not practical with more than two or three products. Fortunately, an algorithm called the **simplex method** can be used to solve larger linear programming problems. This algorithm has been coded and is available for use on computers to solve these larger problems.

simplex method

The linear programming model is an important tool for making product mix decisions. Although the linear programming model produces an optimal product mix decision, its real managerial value—particularly in today's business environment—may be more related to the kinds of inputs that must be generated for the model to be used. Unit-level prices and unit-level variable costs must be assessed. Furthermore, applying the model forces management to identify internal and external constraints. Internal constraints relate to how products consume resources; thus, resource usage relationships must be identified. Once the constrained relationships are known to management, they can be used by management to identify ways of improving a firm's performance in a variety of ways, including inventory management.

THEORY OF CONSTRAINTS

The theory of constraints (TOC) recognizes that the performance of any organization is limited by its constraints. The theory of constraints then develops a specific approach to manage constraints to support the objective of continuous improvement. According to TOC, if performance is to be improved, an organization must identify its constraints, exploit the constraints in the short run, and in the longer term, find ways to overcome the constraints.

Basic Concepts

TOC focuses on three measures of organizational performance: *throughput, inventory,* and *operating expenses*. **Throughput** is the rate at which an organization generates money through sales.[14] In operational terms, throughput is the difference between sales revenue and unit-level variable costs such as materials and power. Direct labor is typically viewed as a fixed unit-level expense and is not usually included in the definition. With this understanding, throughput corresponds to contribution margin. **Inventory** is all the money the organization spends in turning raw materials into throughput. **Operating expenses** are defined as all the money the organization spends in turning inventories into throughput. Based on these three measures, the objectives of management can be expressed as increasing throughput, minimizing inventory, and decreasing operating expenses.

By increasing throughput, minimizing inventory, and decreasing operating expenses, three financial measures of performance will be affected: net income and return on investment will increase and cash flow will improve. Increasing throughput and decreasing operating expenses have always been emphasized as key elements in improving the three financial measures of performance. The role of minimizing inventory, however, in achieving these improvements has been traditionally regarded as less important than throughput and operating expenses.

The theory of constraints, like JIT, assigns inventory management a much more prominent role than does the traditional viewpoint. TOC recognizes that lowering inventory decreases carrying costs and, thus, decreases operating expenses and improves net income. TOC, however, argues that lowering inventory helps produce a competitive edge by having better products, lower prices, and faster response to customer needs.

Better Products Better products mean higher quality. It also means that the company is able to improve products and quickly provide these improved products to the market. The relationship between low inventories and quality has been described in the JIT section. Essentially, low inventories allow defects to be detected more quickly and the cause of the problem assessed.

Improving products is also a key competitive element. New or improved products need to reach the market quickly—before competitors can provide similar features. This goal is facilitated with low inventories. Low inventories allow new product changes to be introduced more quickly because the company has fewer old products (in stock or in process) that would need to be scrapped or sold before the new product is introduced.

---

14.   This follows the definition of Eli Goldratt and Robert Fox in *The Race*. Other definitions and basic concepts of the theory of constraints are also based upon the developments of Goldratt and Fox.

Lower Prices High inventories mean more productive capacity is needed and thus more investment in equipment and space. Since lead time and high work in process inventories are usually correlated, high inventories may often be the cause of overtime. Overtime, of course, increases operating expenses and lowers profitability. Lower inventories reduce carrying costs, per-unit investment costs, and other operating expenses such as overtime and special shipping charges. By lowering investment and operating costs, the unit margin of each product is increased, providing more flexibility in pricing decisions.

Responsiveness Delivering goods on time and producing goods with shorter lead times than the market dictates are important competitive tools. Delivering goods on time is related to a firm's ability to forecast the time required to produce and deliver goods. If a firm has higher inventories than its competitors, then the firm's production lead time is higher than the industry's forecast horizon. High inventories may obscure the actual time required to produce and fill an order. Lower inventories allow actual lead times to be more carefully observed and more accurate delivery dates can be provided. Shortening lead times is also crucial. Shortening lead times is equivalent to lowering work in process inventories. A company carrying ten days of work in process inventories has an average production lead time of ten days. If the company can reduce lead time from ten to five days, then the company should now be carrying only five days of work in process inventories. As lead times are reduced, it is also possible to reduce finished goods inventories. For example, if the lead time for a product is 10 days and the market requires delivery on demand, then the firms must carry, on average, 10 days of finished goods inventory (plus some safety stock to cover demand uncertainty). Suppose that the firm is able to reduce lead time to five days. In this case, finished goods inventory should also be reduced to five days. Thus, the level of inventories signals the organization's ability to respond. High levels relative to those of competitors translate into a competitive disadvantage. TOC thus emphasizes reduction of inventories by reducing lead times.

Five-Step Approach

The theory of constraints uses five steps to achieve its goal of improving organizational performance:

1. Identify an organization's constraints.
2. Exploit the binding constraints.
3. Subordinate everything else to the decisions made in Step 2.
4. Elevate the organization's binding constraints.
5. Repeat the process.

Step 1: Identify the Organization's Constraints Step 1 is identical to the process described for linear programming. Internal and external constraints are identified. The optimal product mix is identified as the mix that maximizes throughput subject to all the organization's constraints. The optimal mix reveals how much of each constrained resource is used and which of the organization's constraints are binding.

Step 2: Exploit the Binding Constraints One way to make the best use of any binding constraints is to ensure that the optimal product mix is produced. Making the best use of binding constraints, however, is more extensive than simply ensuring production of the optimal mix. This step is the heart of TOC's philosophy of short-run constraint management and is directly related to TOC's goal of reducing inventories and improving performance.

In most organizations, there are only a few binding resource constraints. The major binding constraint is defined as the *drummer*. Assume, for example, that there is only one internal binding constraint. By default, this constraint becomes the drummer. The drummer constraint's production rate sets the production rate for the entire plant. Downstream processes fed by the drummer constraint are naturally forced to follow its rate of production. Scheduling for downstream processes is easy. Once a part is finished at the drummer process, the next process begins its operation. Similarly, each subsequent operation begins when the prior operation is finished. Upstream processes that feed the drummer constraint are *scheduled* to produce at the same rate as the drummer constraint. Scheduling at the drummer rate prevents the production of excessive upstream work in process inventories.

For upstream scheduling, there are two additional features that TOC uses in managing constraints to lower inventory levels and improve organizational performance: *buffers* and *ropes*. First, an inventory buffer is established in front of the major binding constraint. The inventory buffer is referred to as the *time buffer*. A **time buffer** is the inventory needed to keep the constrained resource busy for a specified time interval. The purpose of a time buffer is to protect the throughput of the organization from any disruption that can be overcome within the specified time interval. For example, if it takes one day to overcome most interruptions that occur upstream from the drummer constraint, then a two-day buffer should be sufficient to protect throughput from any interruptions. Thus, in scheduling, the operation immediately preceding the drummer constraint should produce the parts needed by the drummer resource two days in advance of their planned usage. Any other preceding operations are scheduled backwards in time to produce so that their parts arrive just in time for subsequent operations.

Ropes are actions taken to tie the rate at which raw material is released into the plant (at the first operation) to the production rate of the constrained resource. The objective of a rope is to ensure that the work in process inventory will not exceed the level needed for the time buffer. Thus, the drummer rate is used to limit the rate of raw material release and effectively controls the rate at which the first operation produces. The rate of the first operation then controls the rates of subsequent operations. The TOC inventory system is often called the **Drum-Buffer-Rope (DBR) System**. Exhibit 13-10 illustrates the DBR structure for a general setting.

The Confer Company example used to illustrate constrained optimization also can be used to provide a specific illustration of the DBR system. Recall that there are three sequential processes: grinding, drilling, and polishing. Each of these processes has a limited amount of resources. Demand for each type of gear produced is also limited. However, from Exhibit 13-9 we know that the only binding constraints are the drilling and polishing constraints. We also know that the optimal mix consists of 30 units of Part X and 30 units of Part Y (per week). This is the most that the drilling and polishing processes can handle. Since the drilling process feeds the polishing process, we can define the drilling constraint as the drummer for the plant. Assume that the demand for each part is uniformly spread out over the week. This means that the production rate should be 6 per day of each part (for a five-day work week). A two-day time buffer would require 24 completed parts from the grinding process: 12 for Part X and 12 for Part Y.

---

time buffer

ropes

drum-buffer-rope
(DBR) system

Exhibit 13-10
*Drum-Buffer-Rope
System: General
Description*

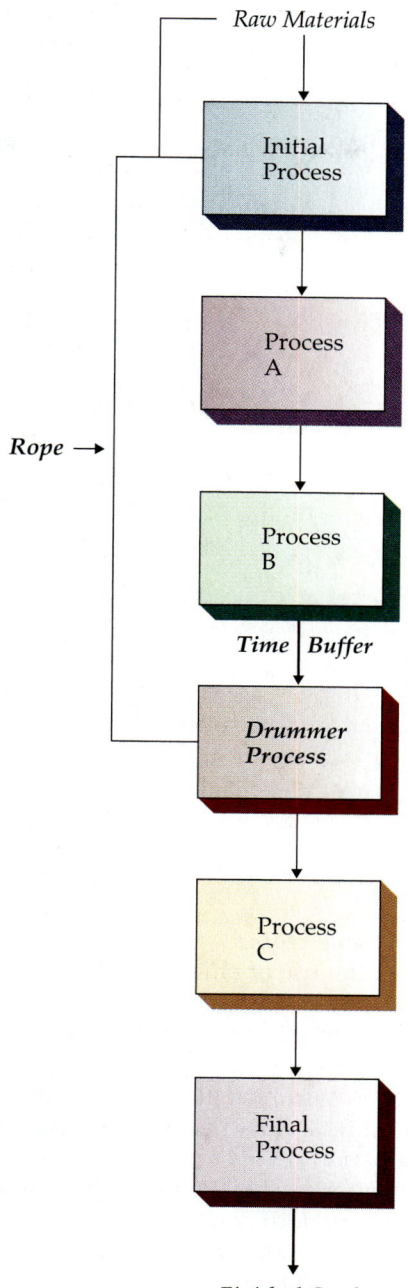

To ensure that the time buffer does not increase at a rate greater than 6 per day for each part, raw materials should be released to the grinding process such that only six of each part can be produced each day (this is the rope—tying the release of materials to the production rate of the drummer constraint). Exhibit 13-11 summarizes the specific DBR details for the Confer Company.

Step 3: Subordinate Everything Else to the Decisions Made in Step 2 The drummer constraint essentially sets the capacity for the entire plant. All remaining departments should be subordinated to the needs of the drummer constraint.

Exhibit 13-11
Drum-Buffer-Rope:
Confer Company

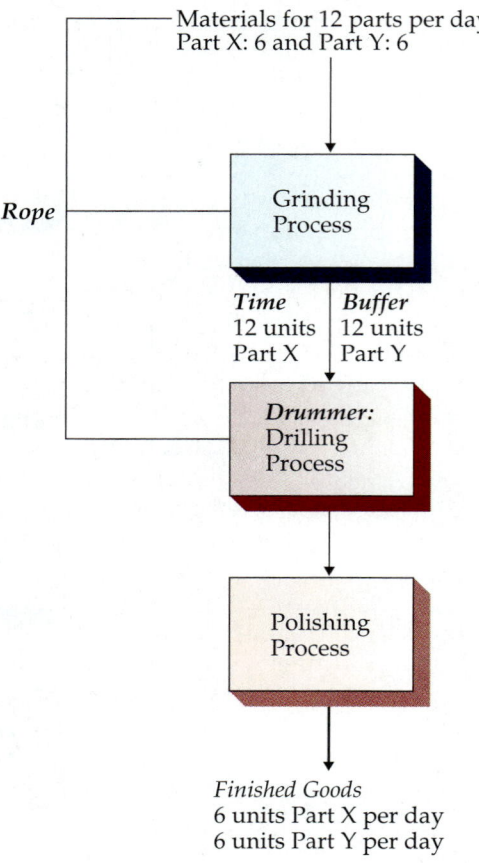

This principle requires many companies to change the way they view things. For example, the use of efficiency measures at the departmental level may no longer be appropriate. Consider the Confer Company once again. Encouraging maximum productive efficiency for the grinding department would produce excess work in process inventories. The capacity of the grinding department is 80 units per week. Assuming the two-day buffer is in place, the grinding department would add 20 units per week to the buffer in front of the drilling department. Over a period of a year, the potential exists for building very large work in process inventories (1,000 units of the two parts would be added to the buffer over a 50-week period).

Step 4: Elevate the Binding Constraint(s) Once actions have been taken to make the best possible use of the existing constraints, the next step is to embark on a program of continuous improvement by reducing the limitations that the binding constraints have on the organization's performance. However, if there is more than one binding constraint, which one should be elevated? For example, in the Confer Company setting, there are two binding constraints: the drilling constraint and the polishing constraint. In this case, the guideline is to increase the resource of the constraint that produces the greatest increase in throughput. To determine the most profitable effort, assume that one additional unit of resource is available for drilling (other resources are held constant), and then calculate the new optimal mix and throughput. Now repeat the process for the pol-

shadow prices

ishing constraint. Clearly, this approach can be tedious. Fortunately, the same information is produced as a by-product of the simplex method. The simplex method produces what are called *shadow prices*. **Shadow prices** indicate the amount by which throughput will increase for one additional unit of scarce resource. For the Confer Company example, the shadow prices for the drilling and polishing resources are $180 and $60, respectively. Thus, Confer should focus on busting the drilling constraint because it offers the most improvement.

Suppose, for example, that Confer Company adds a half shift for the drilling department, increasing the drilling hours from 120 to 180 per week. Throughput will now be $37,800, an increase of $10,800 ($180 × 60 additional hours). Furthermore, as you can check, the optimal mix is now 18 units of Part X and 54 units of Part Y. Is the half shift worth it? This question is answered by comparing the cost of adding the half shift with the increased throughput. If the cost is labor—say overtime at $50 per hour (for all employees)—then the incremental cost is $3,000, and the decision to add the half shift is a good one.

Eventually, the drilling resource constraint will be elevated to a point where the constraint is no longer binding. Suppose, for example, that the company adds a full shift for the drilling operation, increasing the resource availability to 240 hours. The new constraint set is shown in Exhibit 13-12. Notice that the drilling constraint no longer affects the optimal mix decision. The grinding and polishing resource constraints are possible candidates for the new drummer constraint. Once the drummer constraint is identified, then the TOC process is repeated (Step 5). The objective is to continually improve performance by managing constraints.

Exhibit 13-12
New Constraint Set: Confer Company

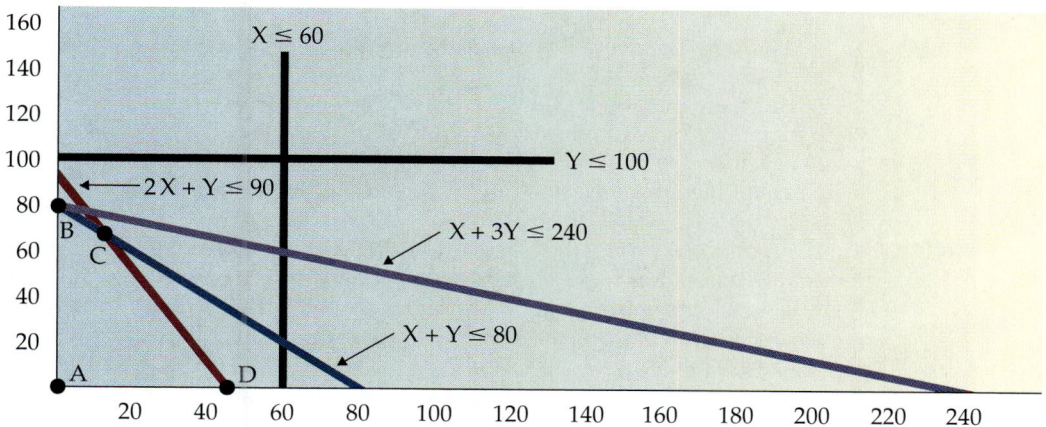

S U M M A R Y

Three approaches to managing inventory were discussed: traditional (EOQ), JIT, and theory of constraints. The traditional approach uses inventories to manage the trade-offs between ordering (setup) costs and carrying

costs. The optimal trade-off defines the economic order quantity. Other reasons for inventories are also offered: due-date performance, avoiding shutdowns (protecting throughput), hedging against future price increases, and taking advantage of discounts. JIT and TOC, on the other hand, argue that inventories are costly and are used to cover up fundamental problems that need to be corrected so that the organization can become more competitive.

JIT uses long-term contracts, continuous replenishment, and EDI to reduce (eliminate) ordering costs. Engineering efforts are made to reduce setup times drastically. Once ordering costs and setup costs are reduced to minimal levels, then it is possible to reduce carrying costs by reducing inventory levels. JIT carries small buffers in front of each operation and uses a Kanban system to regulate production. Production is tied to market demand. If an interruption occurs, throughput tends to be lost because of the small buffers. Yet future throughput tends to increase because efforts are made to improve such things as quality, productivity, and lead time.

TOC identifies an organization's constraints and exploits them so that throughput is maximized and inventories and operating costs are minimized. Identifying the optimal mix is part of this process. Linear programming is useful for this purpose. The major binding constraint is identified and is used to set the productive rate for the plant. Release of raw materials into the first process (operation) is regulated by the drummer constraint. A time buffer is located in front of critical constraints. This time buffer is sized so that it protects throughput from any interruptions. As in JIT, the interruptions are used to locate and correct the problem. However, unlike JIT, the time buffer serves to protect throughput. Furthermore, because buffers are located only in front of critical constraints, TOC may actually produce smaller inventories than JIT.

REVIEW PROBLEM AND SOLUTION

Both just-in-case and JIT inventory management systems have drummers—factors that determine the production rate of the plant. For a just-in-case system, the drummer is the excess capacity of the first operation. For JIT, the drummer is market demand.

REQUIRED:

1. Explain why the drummer of a just-in-case system is identified as excess demand of the first operation.
2. Explain how market demand drives the JIT production system.
3. Explain how a drummer constraint is used in the TOC approach to inventory management.
4. What are the advantages and disadvantages of the three types of drummers?

Solution

1. In a traditional inventory system, local efficiency measures encourage the manager of the first operation to keep the department's workers busy. Thus, raw materials are released to satisfy this objective. This practice is justified because the inventory may be needed just in case demand is greater than expected, or just in case the first operation has downtime, etc.
2. In a JIT system, when the final operation delivers its goods to a customer, a backward rippling effect triggers the release of raw materials into the factory. First, the last process removes the buffer inventory from the withdrawal store, and this leads to a P-Kanban being placed on the production post of the preceding operation. This operation then begins production, withdrawing parts it needs from its withdrawal store, leading to a P-Kanban being placed on the production post of its preceding operation. This process repeats itself—all the way back to the first operation.
3. A drummer constraint sets the production rate of the factory to match its own production rate. This is automatically true for succeeding operations. For preceding operations, the rate is controlled by tying the drummer constraint's rate of production to that of the first operation. A time buffer is also set in front of the drummer constraint to protect throughput in the event of interruptions.

4. The excess capacity drummer typically will build excess inventories. This serves to protect current throughput. However, it ties up a lot of capital and tends to cover up problems such as poor quality, bad delivery performance, and inefficient production. Because it is costly and covers up certain critical productive problems, the just-in-case approach may be a threat to future throughput by damaging a firm's competitive position. JIT reduces inventories dramatically—using only small buffers in front of each operation as a means to regulate production flow and signal when production should occur. JIT has the significant advantage of uncovering problems and eventually correcting them. However, discovering problems usually means that current throughput will be lost while problems are being corrected. Future throughput tends to be protected because the firm is taking actions to improve its operations. TOC uses time buffers in front of the critical constraints. These buffers are large enough to keep the critical constraints operating while other operations may be down. Once the problem is corrected, the other resource constraints usually have sufficient excess capacity to catch up. Thus, current throughput is protected. Furthermore, future throughput is protected because TOC uses the same approach as JIT—namely, that of uncovering and correcting problems. TOC can be viewed as an improvement on JIT methods—correcting the lost throughput problem while maintaining the other JIT features.

KEY TERMS

Binding constraint *566*
Carrying costs *551*
Constraints *565*
Constraint set *568*
Continuous replenishment *559*
Drum-buffer-rope (DBR) system *572*
Economic order quantity (EOQ) *553*
Electronic data interchange (EDI) *559*

External constraints *565*
Feasible set of solutions *568*
Feasible solution *568*
Internal constraints *565*
Inventory *570*
Kanban system *561*
Lead time *554*
Linear programming *567*
Loose constraints *566*

Nonvalue-added activities *557*
Objective function *567*
Operating expenses *570*
Optimal solution *568*
Ordering costs *551*
Production Kanban *561*
Reorder point *554*
Ropes *572*
Safety stock *555*

Setup costs *551*
Shadow prices *575*
Simplex method *569*
Stock-out costs *551*
Throughput *570*
Time buffer *572*
Total preventive maintenance *561*
Vendor Kanbans *561*
Withdrawal Kanban *561*

QUESTIONS FOR WRITING AND DISCUSSION

1. What are ordering costs? Provide examples.
2. What are setup costs? Illustrate with examples.
3. What are carrying costs? Illustrate with examples.
4. Explain why, in the traditional view of inventory, carrying costs increase as ordering costs decrease.
5. Discuss the traditional reasons for carrying inventory.
6. What are stock-out costs?
7. Explain how safety stock is used to deal with demand uncertainty.
8. Suppose that a raw material has a lead time of three days and that the average usage of the material is twelve units per day. What is the reorder point? If the maximum usage is fifteen units per day, what is the safety stock?
9. What is the economic order quantity?

10. What approach does JIT take to minimize total inventory costs?
11. One reason for inventory is to prevent shutdowns. How does the JIT approach to inventory management deal with this potential problem?
12. Explain how the Kanban system helps reduce inventories.
13. Explain how long-term contractual relationships with suppliers can reduce the acquisition cost of raw materials.
14. What is EDI and what relationship does it have to continuous replenishment?
15. What is a constraint? An internal constraint? An external constraint?
16. What are loose constraints? Binding constraints?
17. What is the purpose of linear programming?
18. What is an objective function?

19. What is a feasible solution? A feasible set of solutions?
20. Explain the procedures for graphically solving a linear programming problem. What solution method is used when the problem includes more than two or three products?
21. Define and discuss the three measures of organizational performance used by the theory of constraints.
22. Explain how lowering inventory produces better products, lower prices, and better responsiveness to customer needs.
23. What are the five steps that TOC uses to improve organizational performance?
24. What is a drum-buffer-rope system?
25. Assuming there are two or more binding constraints, how can a manager identify which one should be elevated first?

EXERCISES AND PROBLEMS

13-1
Ordering and Carrying Costs
LO 1

Eagle Company uses 12,000 brushes each year in its production of large power generators. The cost of placing an order is $125. The cost of holding one unit of inventory for one year is $3. Currently, Eagle places six orders of 2,000 brushes per year.

REQUIRED:

1. Compute the annual ordering cost.
2. Compute the annual carrying cost.
3. Compute the cost of Eagle's current inventory policy.

13-2
Economic Order Quantity
LO 1

Refer to the data in *13-1*.

REQUIRED:

1. Compute the economic order quantity.
2. Compute the ordering cost and the carrying cost for the EOQ.
3. How much money does using the EOQ policy save the company over the policy of purchasing 2,000 brushes per order?

13-3
Economic Order Quantity
LO 1

Gomer Company uses 28,125 pounds of sulphur each year. The cost of placing an order is $20, and the carrying cost for one pound of sulphur is $0.50.

REQUIRED:

1. Compute the economic order quantity for sulphur.
2. Compute the carrying cost and ordering cost for the EOQ.

13-4
Reorder Point
LO 1

Gateman Company manufactures lawn mowers. One part it orders from an outside supplier is a specialty starter unit. Information pertaining to the starter unit is as follows:

Economic order quantity	900 units
Average daily usage	30 units
Maximum daily usage	50 units
Lead time	5 days

REQUIRED:

1. What is the reorder point assuming no safety stock is carried?
2. What is the reorder point assuming that safety stock is carried?

**13-5
EOQ with Setup
Costs; Reorder
Point; Production
Scheduling**

LO 1

Cross Manufacturing produces casings for television sets: large and small. In order to produce the different casings, equipment must be set up. Each setup configuration corresponds to a particular type of casing. The setup cost per production run—for either casing—is $2,000. The cost of carrying small casings in inventory is $4 per casing per year. The cost of carrying large casings is $6 per year. The company produces 64,000 small casings and 150,000 large casings per year. The company sells an average of 196 small casings per work day and an average of 600 large casings per work day. It takes Cross two days to set up the equipment for small or large casings. Once set up, it takes seven work days to produce a batch of small casings and ten days for large casings. There are 250 work days available per year.

REQUIRED:

1. Compute the number of small casings that should be produced per setup to minimize total setup and carrying costs for this product.
2. Compute the total setup and carrying costs associated with the economic order quantity for the small casings.
3. What is the reorder point for small casings?
4. Repeat Requirements 1 through 3 for the large casings.
5. Using the economic order batch size, is it possible for Cross to produce the amount that can be sold of each casing? Does scheduling have a role here? Explain. Is this a push- or pull-system approach to inventory management? Explain.

**13-6
Safety Stock**

LO 1

Cook Manufacturing produces a component used in its production of small airplanes. The time to set up and produce a batch of the components is eight days. The average daily usage is 250 components, and the maximum daily usage is 275 components.

REQUIRED: Compute the reorder point assuming that safety stock is carried by Cook Manufacturing. How much safety stock is carried by Cook?

**13-7
EOQ; Safety Stock;
Lead Time; Batch
Size and JIT**

LO 1, 2

Bateman Company produces helmets for drivers of motorcycles. Helmets are produced in batches according to model and size. Although the setup and production time vary for each model, the smallest lead time is 6 days. The most popular model, Model HA2, takes 2 days for setup, and the production rate is 750 units per day. The expected annual demand for the model is 36,000 units. Demand for the model, however, can reach 45,000 units. The cost of carrying one HA2 helmet is $3 per unit. The setup cost is $6,000. Bateman chooses its batch size based on the economic order quantity criterion. Expected annual demand is used to compute the EOQ.

Recently, Bateman has encountered some stiff competition—especially from foreign sources. Some of the foreign competitors have been able to produce and deliver the helmets to retailers in half the time it takes Bateman to produce. For example, a large retailer recently requested a delivery of 12,000 HA2 helmets with the stipulation that the helmets be delivered within seven working days. Bateman had 3,000 units of HA2 in stock. Bateman informed the potential customer that it could deliver 3,000 units immediately and the other 9,000 units in about 14 working days—with the possibility of interim partial orders being delivered. The customer declined the offer indicating that the total order had to be delivered within seven working days so that their stores could take advantage of some special local conditions. The customer expressed regret and indicated that they would accept the order from another competitor who could satisfy the time requirements.

REQUIRED:

1. Calculate the optimal batch size for Model HA2 using the EOQ model. Was Bateman's response to the customer right? Would it take the time indicated to produce the number of units wanted by the customer? Explain with supporting computations.
2. Upon learning of the lost order, the marketing manager grumbled about Bateman's inventory policy. "We lost the order because we didn't have sufficient inventory. We need to carry more units in inventory to deal with unexpected orders like these." Do you agree? How much additional inventory would have been needed to meet customer requirements? In the future, should Bateman carry more inventory? Can you think of other solutions?
3. Fenton Gray, the head of industrial engineering, reacted differently to the lost order. "Our problem is more complex than insufficient inventory. I know that our foreign competitors carry much less inventory than we do. What we need to do is decrease the lead time. I have been studying this problem, and my staff has found a way to reduce setup time for Model HA2 from two days to 1.5 hours. Using this new procedure, setup cost can be reduced to about $94. Also, by rearranging the plant layout for this product—creating what are called manufacturing cells—we can increase the production rate from 750 units per day to about 2,000 units per day. This is done simply by eliminating a lot of move time and waiting time—both nonvalue-added activities." Assume that the engineer's estimates are on target. Compute the new optimal batch size (using the EOQ formula). What is the new lead time? Given this new information, would Bateman have been able to meet the customer's time requirements? Assume that there are eight hours available in each work day.
4. Suppose that the setup time and cost are reduced to 0.5 hour and $10, respectively. What is the batch size now? As setup time approaches zero and the setup cost becomes negligible, what does this imply? Assume for example that it takes 5 minutes to set up and costs are about $0.864 per setup.

13-8
Reasons for
Carrying Inventory
LO 1, 2, 4

The following reasons have been offered for holding inventories:

a. To balance ordering or setup costs and carrying costs.
b. To satisfy customer demand (e.g., meet delivery dates).
c. To avoid shutting down manufacturing facilities because of
   (1) machine failure.
   (2) defective parts.
   (3) unavailable parts.
d. Unreliable production processes.
e. To take advantage of discounts.
f. To hedge against future price increases.

REQUIRED:

1. Explain how the JIT approach responds to each of these reasons and, consequently, argues for insignificant levels of inventories.
2. The theory of constraints (TOC) criticizes the JIT approach to inventory management, arguing that it fails to protect throughput. Explain what this means, and describe how TOC addresses this issue.

13-9
Kanban System;
EDI
LO 2

Hales Company produces a product that requires two processes. In the first process, a subassembly is produced (subassembly A). In the second process, this subassembly and a subassembly purchased from outside (subassembly B) are assembled to produce the final product. For simplicity, assume that the assembly of one unit takes the same time as the production of subassembly A. Subassembly A is placed in a container and sent to an area called the subassembly stores (SB stores) area. A production Kanban is attached to this container. A second container, also with one subassembly, is located near the assembly line (called the withdrawal store). This container has attached to it a withdrawal Kanban.

REQUIRED:

1. Explain how withdrawal and production Kanban cards are used to control the work flow between the two processes. How does this approach minimize inventories?
2. Explain how vendor Kanban cards can be used to control the flow of the purchased subassembly. What implications does this have for supplier relationships? What role, if any, do continuous replenishment and EDI play in this process?

13-10
JIT Limitations
LO 2

Many companies have viewed JIT as a panacea—a knight in shining armor which promises rescue from sluggish profits, poor quality, and productive inefficiency. It is often lauded for its beneficial effects on employee morale and self-esteem. Yet JIT may also cause a company to struggle and may produce a good deal of frustration. In some cases, JIT appears to deliver less than its reputation seems to call for.

REQUIRED: Discuss some of the limitations and problems that companies may encounter when implementing a JIT system.

13-11
Product Mix Decision; Single Constraint
LO 3

Wilson Company makes three types of storage units for compact disks. Each of the three types of storage units requires the use of a special machine that has total operating capacity of 102,000 hours per year. Information on each of the three products is provided below:

	Basic	Standard	Deluxe
Selling price	$10.00	$15.00	$25.00
Unit variable cost	$5.00	$7.00	$12.00
Machine hours required	0.10	0.25	0.75

The marketing manager has determined that the company can sell all that it can produce of each of the three products.

REQUIRED:

1. How many of each product should be sold to maximize total contribution margin? What is the total contribution margin for this product mix?
2. Suppose that Wilson can sell no more than 50,000 units of each type at the prices indicated. What product mix would you recommend, and what would be the total contribution margin?

13-12
Product Mix Decisions; Multiple Constraints
LO 3

Cardin Company produces two types of gears: Model #12 and Model #15. Market conditions limit the number of each gear that can be sold. For Model #12, no more than 15,000 units can be sold, and for Model #15, no more than 40,000 units. Each gear must be notched by a special machine. Cardin owns eight machines that together provide 40,000 hours of machine time per year. Each unit of Model #12 requires two hours of machine time, and each unit of Model #15 requires one half hour of machine time. The unit contribution for Model #12 is $30 and for Model #15 is $15. Cardin wants to identify the product mix that will maximize total contribution margin.

REQUIRED:

1. Formulate Cardin's problem as a linear programming model.
2. Solve the linear programming model in Requirement 1.
3. Identify which constraints are binding and which are loose. Also, identify the constraints as internal or external.

13-13
Product Mix
Decision; Single
and Multiple
Constraints

LO 3

Taylor Company produces two industrial cleansers that use the same liquid chemical input: Pocolimpio and Maslimpio. Pocolimpio uses two quarts of the chemical for every unit produced, and Maslimpio uses five quarts. Currently, Taylor has 6,000 quarts of the material in inventory. All of the material is imported. For the coming year, Taylor plans to import 6,000 quarts to produce 1,000 units of Pocolimpio and 2,000 units of Maslimpio. The detail of each product's unit contribution margin is given below:

	Pocolimpio	Maslimpio
Selling price	$81	$139
Less: Variable expenses		
Direct materials	20	50
Direct labor	21	14
Variable overhead	10	15
Contribution margin	$30	$ 60

Taylor Company has received word that the source of the material has been shut down by embargo. Consequently, the company will not be able to import the 6,000 quarts it planned to use in the coming year's production. There is no other source of the material.

REQUIRED:

1. Compute the total contribution margin that the company would earn if it could import the 6,000 quarts of the material.
2. Determine the optimal usage of the company's inventory of 6,000 quarts of the material. Compute the total contribution margin for the product mix that you recommend.
3. Assume that Pocolimpio uses three direct labor hours for every unit produced and that Maslimpio uses two hours. A total of 6,000 direct labor hours are available for the coming year.
   a. Formulate the linear programming problem faced by Taylor Company. To do so, you must derive mathematical expressions for the objective function and for the material and labor constraints.
   b. Solve the linear programming problem using the graphical approach.
   c. Compute the total contribution margin produced by the optimal mix developed in Requirement 2.

13-14
Product Mix
Decision; Single
and Multiple
Constraints; Basics
of Linear
Programming

LO 3

Desayuno Products, Inc., produces corn flakes and bran flakes. The manufacturing process is highly mechanized; both products are produced by the same machinery by using different settings. For the coming period, 200,000 machine hours are available. Management is trying to decide on the quantities of each product to produce. The following data are available:

	Corn Flakes	Bran Flakes
Machine hours per unit	1.00	0.50
Unit selling price	$2.50	$3.00
Unit variable cost	$1.50	$2.25

REQUIRED:

1. Determine the units of each product that should be produced in order to maximize profits.
2. Because of market conditions, the company can sell no more than 150,000 packages of corn flakes and 300,000 boxes of bran flakes. Do the following:

a. Formulate the problem as a linear programming problem.
b. Determine the optimal mix using a graph.
c. Compute the maximum profits given the optimal mix.

13-15
Product Mix
Decisions

LO 3

Calen Company manufactures and sells three products in a factory of three departments. Both labor and machine time are applied to the products as they pass through each department. The nature of the machine processing and of the labor skills required in each department is such that neither machines nor labor can be switched from one department to another.

Calen's management is attempting to plan its production schedule for the next several months. The planning is complicated by the fact that labor shortages exist in the community and some machines will be down several months for repairs.

Following is information regarding available machine and labor time by department and the machine hours and direct labor hours required per unit of product. These data should be valid for at least the next six months.

		Department		
Monthly Capacity		*1*	*2*	*3*
Machine hours available		3,000	3,100	2,700
Labor hours available		3,700	4,500	2,750

Product	*Input Per Unit Produced*			
401	Labor hours	2	3	3
	Machine hours	1	1	2
402	Labor hours	1	2	—
	Machine hours	1	1	—
403	Labor hours	2	2	2
	Machine hours	2	2	1

Calen believes that the monthly demand for the next six months will be as follows:

Product	*Units Sold*
401	500
402	400
403	1,000

Inventory levels will not be increased or decreased during the next six months. The unit cost and price data for each product are as follows:

	Product		
	401	*402*	*403*
Unit costs:			
Direct material	$ 7	$ 13	$ 17
Direct labor	66	38	51
Variable overhead	27	20	25
Fixed overhead	15	10	32
Variable selling	3	2	4
Total unit cost	$118	$ 83	$129
Unit selling price	$196	$123	$167

REQUIRED:

1. Calculate the monthly requirement for machine hours and direct labor hours for producing Products 401, 402, and 403 to determine whether or not the factory can meet
   the monthly sales demand.
2. Determine the quantities of 401, 402, and 403 that should be produced monthly to maximize profits. Prepare a schedule that shows the contribution to profits of your product
   mix.
3. Assume that the machine hours available in Department 3 are 1,500 instead of 2,700.
   Calculate the optimal monthly product mix using the graphing approach to linear programming. Prepare a schedule that shows the contribution to profits from this optimal
   mix.

(CMA adapted)

**13-16
Drum-Buffer-Rope
System**

LO 4

Duckstein, Inc., manufactures two types of aspirin: plain and buffered. They sell all they
produce. Recently Duckstein implemented a TOC approach for its Fort Smith plant. One
binding constraint was identified, and the optimal product mix was determined. The diagram below reflects the TOC outcome.

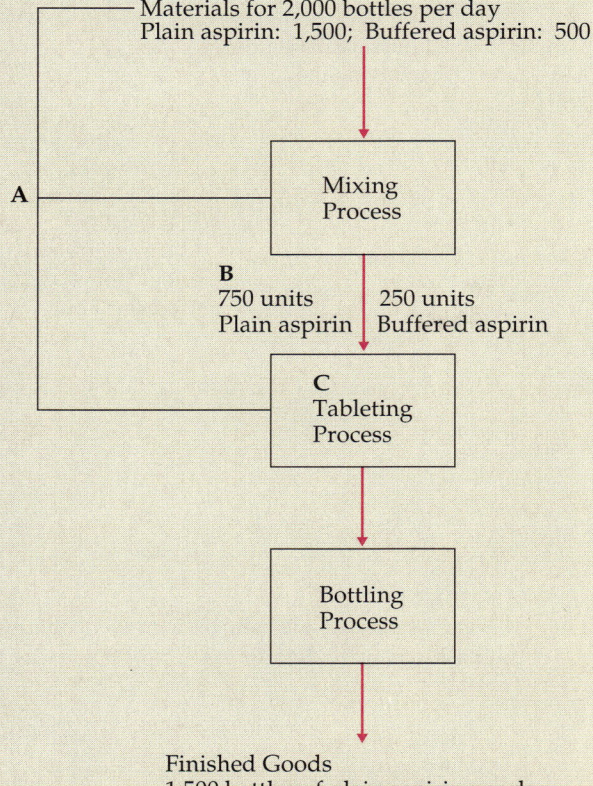

Finished Goods
1,500 bottles of plain aspirin per day
500 bottles of buffered aspirin per day

REQUIRED:

1. What is the daily production rate? Which process sets this rate?
2. How many days of buffer inventory is Duckstein carrying? How is this time buffer
   determined?
3. Explain what the letters A, B, and C represent. Discuss each of their roles in the TOC
   system.

13-17

Identifying and Exploiting Constraints; Constraint Elevation

LO 4

Berry Company produces two different metal components used in medical equipment (Component X and Component Y). The company has three processes: molding, grinding, and finishing. In molding, molds are created, and molten metal is poured into the shell. Grinding removes the gates that allowed the molten metal to flow into the mold's cavities. In finishing, rough edges caused by the grinders are removed by small, hand-held pneumatic tools. In molding, the setup time is one hour. The other two processes have no setup time required. The demand for Component X is 300 units per day and the demand for Component Y is 500 units per day. The minutes required per unit for each product are given below:

Product	Minutes Required Per Unit of Product		
	Molding	Grinding	Finishing
Component X	5	10	15
Component Y	10	15	20

The company operates one eight-hour shift. The molding process employs 12 workers (who each work eight hours). Two hours of their time, however, are used for setups (assuming both products are produced). The grinding process has sufficient equipment and workers to provide 12,000 grinding hours per shift.

The finishing department is labor-intensive and employs 35 workers, who each work eight hours per day. The only significant unit-level variable costs are materials and power. For Component X, the variable cost per unit is $40, and for Component Y, it is $50. Selling prices for X and Y are $90 and $110, respectively. Berry's policy is to use two setups per day: an initial setup to produce all that is scheduled for Component X and a second setup (changeover) to produce all that is scheduled for Component Y. The amount scheduled does not necessarily correspond to each product's daily demand.

REQUIRED:

1. Calculate the time (in minutes) needed each day to meet the daily market demand for Component X and Component Y. What is the major internal constraint facing Berry Company?
2. Describe how Berry should exploit its major binding constraint. Specifically, identify the product mix that will maximize daily throughput.
3. Assume that manufacturing engineering has found a way to reduce the molding setup time from one hour to 10 minutes. Explain how this affects the product mix and daily throughput.

13-18

Theory of Constraints; Internal Constraints

LO 4

Pratt Company produces two replacement parts for a popular line of VCRs: Part A and Part B. Part A is made up of two components, one manufactured internally and one purchased from external suppliers. Part B is made up of three components, one manufactured internally and two purchased from suppliers. The company has two processes: fabrication and assembly. In fabrication, the internally produced components are made. Each component takes twenty minutes to produce. In assembly, it takes thirty minutes to assemble the components for Part A and forty minutes to assemble the components for Part B. Pratt Company operates one shift per day. Each process employs 100 workers who each work eight hours per day.

Part A earns a unit contribution margin of $20, and Part B earns a unit contribution margin of $24 (calculated as the difference between revenue and the cost of materials and energy). Pratt can sell all that it produces of either part. There are no other constraints. Pratt can add a second shift of either process. Although a second shift would work eight hours, there is no mandate that it employ the same number of workers. The labor cost per hour for fabrication is $8, and the labor cost per hour for assembly is $7.

REQUIRED:

1. Identify the constraints facing Pratt and graph them. How many binding constraints are possible? What is Pratt's optimal product mix? What daily contribution margin is produced by this mix?
2. What is the drummer constraint? How much excess capacity does the other constraint have? Assume that a 1.5-day buffer inventory is needed to deal with any production interruptions. Describe the drum-buffer-rope concept using the Pratt data to illustrate the process.
3. Explain why the use of local labor efficiency measures will not work in Pratt's TOC environment.
4. Suppose Pratt decides to elevate the binding constraint by adding a second shift of 50 workers. Would elevation of Pratt's binding constraint improve its system performance? Explain with supporting computations.

13-19
TOC; Internal and External Constraints
LO 4

Bountiful Manufacturing produces two types of bike frames (Frame X and Frame Y). Frame X passes through four processes: Cutting, Welding, Polishing, and Painting. Frame Y uses three of the same processes: Cutting, Welding, and Painting. Each of the four processes employs ten workers who work eight hours each day. Frame X sells for $40 per unit, and Frame Y sells for $55 per unit. Raw materials is the only unit-level variable expense. The materials cost for Frame X is $20 per unit, and the materials cost for Frame Y is $25 per unit. Bountiful's accounting system has provided the following additional information about its operations and products:

Resource Name	Resource Available	Frame X Resource Usage: Per Unit	Frame Y Resource Usage: Per Unit
Cutting labor	4,800 minutes	15 minutes	10 minutes
Welding labor	4,800 minutes	15 minutes	30 minutes
Polishing labor	4,800 minutes	15 minutes	—
Painting labor	4,800 minutes	10 minutes	15 minutes
Market demand: Frame X	200 per day	One unit	—
Market demand: Frame Y	100 per day	—	One unit

Bountiful's management has determined that any production interruptions can be corrected within two days.

REQUIRED:

1. Assuming that Bountiful can meet daily market demand, compute the potential daily profit. Now compute the minutes needed for each process to meet the daily market demand. Can Bountiful meet daily market demand? If not, where is the bottleneck? Can you derive an optimal mix without using a graphical solution? If so, explain how.
2. Graph the constraints facing Bountiful. Determine the optimal mix and the maximum daily contribution margin (throughput).
3. Explain how a drum-buffer-rope system would work for Bountiful.
4. Suppose that the engineering department has proposed a process design change that will increase the polishing time for Frame X from 15 to 23 minutes per unit and decrease the welding time from 15 minutes to 10 minutes per unit (for Frame X). The cost of process redesign would be $10,000. Evaluate this proposed change. What step in the TOC process does this proposal represent?

13-20
Ethical Issues

Mac Ericson and Tammy Ferguson met at an IMA conference two months ago and began dating. Mac is the controller for Longley Enterprises, and Tammy is a marketing manager for Sharp Products. Longley is a major supplier for Piura Products, a major competitor of Sharp's. Longley has entered into a long-term agreement to supply certain materials to

Piura. Piura has been developing a JIT purchasing and manufacturing system. As part of its development, Piura and Longley have established EDI capabilities. The following conversation took place during a luncheon engagement:

Tammy: Mac, I understand that you have EDI connections with Piura. Is that right?

Mac: Sure. It's part of the partners-in-profits arrangement that we have worked so hard to get. It's working real well. Knowing Piura's production schedule helps us stabilize our own schedule. It has actually cut some of our overhead costs. It has also decreased Piura's costs. I estimate that we both have decreased production costs by about 7%–10%.

Tammy: That's interesting. You know, I have a real chance of getting promoted to VP of marketing . . .

Mac: Hey, that's great! When will you know?

Tammy: It all depends on this deal that I am trying to cut with Balboa—if I win the contract, then I think I have it. My main problem is with Piura. If I knew what their production schedule was, I could get a pretty good idea as to how long it would take them to deliver. I could then make sure that we beat their delivery offer—even if we had to work overtime and do all kinds of expediting. I know that how fast we can deliver is very important to Balboa. Our quality is as good as Piura's—but they tend to beat us on delivery time. My boss would love to lick Piura. They have beaten us too many times recently. I am wondering if you would be willing to help me out.

Mac: Tammy, you know that I would help if I could, but Piura's production schedule is confidential information. If word got out that I had leaked that kind of stuff to you, I would be history.

Tammy: Well, no one would ever know. Besides I have already had a chat with Tom Anderson, who is our CEO. Our VP of finance is retiring. He knows about you and your capabilities. I think he would be willing to hire you—especially if he knew that you helped swing this Balboa deal. You could increase your salary by 40%.

Mac: I don't know. I have my doubts about the propriety of all this. It might look kind of funny if I take over as VP of finance not long after Piura loses the Balboa deal. But a VP position and a big salary increase are tempting. It's unlikely that I'll ever have a shot at the VP position in my company.

Tammy: Think it over. If you are interested, I'll arrange a dinner with Tom Anderson. He said he'd like to meet you. He knows a little about this. I'm sure that he has the ability to keep it quiet. I don't think there is much risk.

REQUIRED:

1. Based on the above information, has Mac violated any of the IMA standards of ethical conduct? Explain.
2. Suppose that Mac decides to provide information in exchange for the VP position. What IMA standards has he violated?

Chapter 14
Pricing and Revenue Analysis

Pricing of retail products is difficult, especially for stores with the wide variety of Pottery Barn. Typically, these stores use a variant of markup pricing and then adjust prices of individual products to meet demand.

LEARNING OBJECTIVES

After studying this chapter, you should be able to:

1. Discuss basic economic pricing concepts.
2. Calculate a markup on cost and determine a cost-plus price.
3. Explain the advantages of target costing in determining price.
4. Explain how price may vary over the product life cycle.
5. Calculate the sales price variance and price volume variance and explain how they are used in controlling revenue.
6. Discuss the impact of the legal system and ethics on pricing.

One of the more difficult decisions faced by a company is pricing. Though this text is devoted to cost accounting and cost management, this chapter examines the broader arena of price setting and the role of the accountant in that setting. Just as cost has an important impact on price, price has an important impact on cost. The accountant is frequently the primary resource turned to by the firm when financial data are needed, whether that information relates to cost or to price. As a consequence, accountants must be familiar with sources of revenue data as well as the economic and marketing concepts needed to interpret those data.

BASIC ECONOMIC PRICING CONCEPTS

Objective 1
Discuss basic economic pricing concepts.

There are many factors that affect a firm's pricing decisions. Cost, customer demand, the presence of competition, time horizon, and strategy are all important. In this section, we will review some of the basic economic concepts affecting pricing. These include customer demand, the price elasticity of demand, and market structure. An understanding of economic factors, in conjunction with marketing-related concepts, can help the accountant to interpret pricing data and to assist the company in determining the amount of freedom it has to affect price.

Customer Demand

Customer demand influences all phases of business. In general, customers want high-quality goods and services at a low price. Although customer demand is studied in detail in marketing classes, accountants need to be cognizant of demand, especially as demand interacts with supply.

All else being equal, customers will buy more at lower prices, and less at higher prices. This observation is the basis for the traditional downward sloping demand curve, which illustrates the inverse relationship between price and the quantity demanded, as shown in Exhibit 14-1. Of course, the demand curve is downward sloping because at higher prices, consumers buy less, and at lower

Exhibit 14-1
Equilibrium Price Determined by Intersection of Supply and Demand Curves

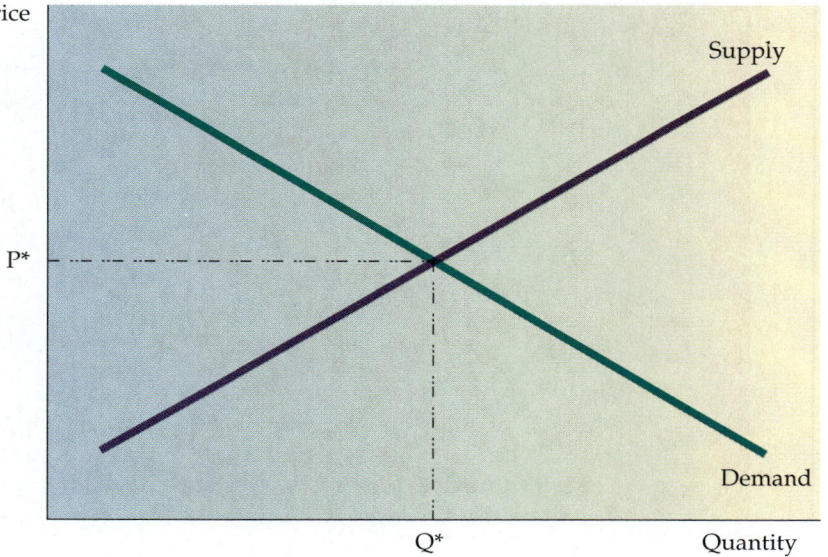

prices, consumers buy more, all else being equal. Using similar logic, the supply curve is upward sloping because at higher prices, firms are willing (and able) to supply more than they can at lower prices. The market clearing or equilibrium price, P*, is located at the intersection of the supply and demand curves. It is the price for which the amount that producers are willing to supply (Q*) just equals the amount that consumers demand (also Q*). Note that if the price is higher than P*, demand falls short of supply. In real life, producers see inventories piling up as consumers buy other goods. If the price is lower than P*, everything that is produced is bought. Shortages and backlogs occur. This is a signal to increase production and/or to raise prices.

Factors other than price that influence demand include consumer income, quality of goods offered for sale, the availability of substitutes, the demand for complementary goods, whether the good is a necessity or a luxury, and so on. However, the basic demand relationship remains, and producers know that raising prices almost inevitably results in less sold. Two factors that most influence the degree of freedom companies have to adjust price are price elasticity and market structure.

Price Elasticity of Demand

price elasticity of demand
elastic demand

inelastic demand

An important determinant of the degree to which a price change results in a quantity change is **price elasticity of demand**, or the degree to which quantity demanded changes in response to a price change. In general, **elastic demand** for a good means that a price increase of a certain percent lowers the quantity demanded by more than that percentage. Similarly, demand is elastic when a price decrease of a certain percent increases quantity demanded by more than that percent. The opposite holds for **inelastic demand**, which is when a price change of a certain percent is associated with a quantity change of less than that percent.

For example, Carter Company prints and sells art posters. Currently it sells 10,000 posters per month at $4 each. What will happen to quantity sold if price changes? Let's look at four possible cases. Case 1 is a price increase to $4.40 and quantity decrease to 9,500. Case 2 is a price decrease to $3.60 and a quantity increase to 10,500. Case 3 is a price increase to $4.40 and quantity decrease to 8,500. Case 4 is a price decrease to $3.60 and a quantity increase to 11,500. Exhibit 14-2 shows the percentage change in price and the percentage change in quantity for each case.

Exhibit 14-2
Effect of a 10 Percent Change in Price on Quantity Sold: Four Cases

	Case	Old Price	New Price	Percent Change in Price	Old Quantity	New Quantity	Percent Change in Quantity
Inelastic demand:	1	$4.00	$4.40	10%	10,000	9,500	5%
	2	$4.00	$3.60	10%	10,000	10,500	5%
Elastic demand:	3	$4.00	$4.40	10%	10,000	8,500	15%
	4	$4.00	$3.60	10%	10,000	11,500	15%

Cases 1 and 2 show inelastic demand. Price has changed by 10 percent in both cases, but quantity demanded has changed by only 5 percent. A large change in price had a relatively small impact on quantity sold. The opposite occurs in Cases 3 and 4. Here a price change of 10 percent was more than offset by quantity changes. Therefore, Cases 3 and 4 depict elastic demand. Notice that the price decrease resulted in a much greater quantity sold, and the price increase resulted in a much smaller quantity sold.

It would be helpful for firms to be able to calculate the price elasticity of demand as precisely as we have done in Exhibit 14-2. If we knew the equation for the demand curve, this would be easy to do. In practice, this equation is never known, and most companies do not want to run experiments by constantly changing the price of a product. To apply elasticity concepts, then, we must analyze the *characteristics* of goods and services, which are relatively more or less elastic. Then, managers can assess the degree to which their goods and services possess the characteristics of elasticity or inelasticity.

Characteristics of Elasticity Goods that are price elastic tend to have many substitutes, are not necessities, and take a relatively large amount of consumer income. The demand curves for movie tickets, restaurant meals, and automobiles are relatively elastic. Clearly, movies and restaurant meals are not necessities and have many substitutes. As theater owners have discovered, there are many substitutes for a night out at the movies. People can watch TV, read a book, rent a videotape, go out to dinner, attend a play or a concert, or take a walk. Demand for automobiles is also elastic because they are so expensive. A relatively small decrease in price leads to a relatively large increase in the number of people who can afford a car (or a second or third car).

Price-inelastic goods have few substitutes, are necessities, and constitute a relatively small percentage of consumer income. Prescription drugs, electricity, and telephone service are examples of price-inelastic goods. When electrical utilities raise their rates, consumption typically falls off very little. Electricity is seen as a need, and consumers continue to use roughly the same number of kilowatt hours. Additionally, it is difficult to change the demand for electricity right away. Consumers may, over time, replace electricity-hungry appliances with more energy-efficient models, but this does not happen instantaneously in response to rising rates. Toys "R" Us CEO Michael Goldstein said, "I remember talking to customers who were leaving one of our stores in Wales. When I asked what they liked about the store, every one of them said selection. No one paid attention to the pricing, which was one of our major concerns." As a result of this relatively inelastic demand, prices at Toys "R" Us in Europe are 30 to 50 percent higher than those in the United States.[1] Of course, the implication for the firm is that price increases will affect quantity demanded relatively little for inelastic goods.

It is useful to know whether the demand for a product or service is elastic or inelastic, since this gives the firm an idea of what impact a price increase or decrease will have on quantity sold and, thus, revenue. For example, Compaq Computer Corp. developed an ambitious spreadsheet-based simulation program to model trends in customer demand, pricing, dealer inventories, and competitors' potential actions. An important input was estimating demand elasticity for PCs. The software, with its critical information on demand, is now at work helping Compaq introduce and price new computers.

---

1.   Carla Rapoport with Justin Martin, "Retailers Go Global," *Fortune*, February 20, 1995, pp. 102–108.

one-price policy

Pricing Policies Companies have developed pricing policies based on the concept of elasticity. We can recognize them in contrast to the **one-price policy**, meaning that a single price is charged to all customers, which is not dependent on differing elasticities. Most retail stores in the United States adhere to a one-price policy. The price is marked on the item, and no negotiation is permitted.

This results in the same price being charged to all customers regardless of their incomes or need for the good. An advantage of the one-price policy is that relatively lower personnel costs are incurred; sales clerks need not haggle with each customer.

variable pricing policy

When a company charges different prices to different customers for the same item, it engages in a **variable pricing policy**. This practice is prevalent in the real estate and automobile industries. It is also prevalent in other countries at bazaars and markets. The typical variable-pricing seller starts with a high price, hoping to run across a customer with relatively more inelastic demand. If no such customer surfaces, then the item can be sold at a lower price—to a buyer with relatively more elastic demand (or a buyer who is simply a better negotiator).

second-market discounting

A variant of the variable pricing policy is **second-market discounting**. Based on excess capacity and differing elasticities of demand, a higher price is charged to the core market and lower prices to secondary markets. An important prerequisite for this to work is lack of arbitrage. **Arbitrage** occurs when the customers who purchase the good at the lower price are able to resell it to other customers. Clearly, if the customer with elastic demand could resell the product to a customer with inelastic demand for less than the company has set as a price for the second customer, second-market discounting would not work.

arbitrage

For example, airlines define their core market as business travelers. These travelers have inelastic demand for air travel. They need the flexibility to purchase tickets at the last minute, to change reservations, and to fly during the work week. Vacationers, on the other hand, have relatively elastic demand for air travel. A low price is the main attraction. If the airlines could fill their planes with full-fare paying business travelers, they would. However, there are not enough business travelers to completely fill the planes. In addition, the marginal cost of filling an empty seat on a plane is very low. This explains the airlines' convoluted pricing schemes. Full fares are charged for tickets purchased at the time of need and for travel during the work week. Lower prices are charged for tickets purchased 7 to 21 days in advance that include a Saturday night stay-over—a condition few business travelers can (or want to) meet. The excess capacity in air travel exists on the weekends.

Another example is the discounted price offered to new subscribers to a newspaper or magazine. This "teaser" rate is designed to "hook" the potential subscriber, whose elasticity of demand is presumed to be greater (i.e., more elastic) than that of the current subscriber. Some companies have complex pricing policies based on differing elasticities of demand in the markets they serve. Of course, elasticity of demand is just one factor that influences price. Another important determinant of price is market structure.

Market Structure and Price

Companies can tell more about the type of demand curve they face by analyzing the market structure of their industry. In general, economists classify markets into four types: perfect competition, monopolistic competition, oligopoly, and monopoly. These markets differ according to the number of buyers and sellers, the degree of uniqueness of the product, and the relative ease of entry by firms into and out of the market (i.e., barriers to entry).

perfectly competitive market

The **perfectly competitive market** is characterized by many buyers and sellers—no one of which is large enough to influence the market, a homogeneous product (one company's product is virtually identical to any other company's product), and easy entry into and exit from the industry. All firms in a perfectly competitive market are price takers.

price takers

Price takers are companies that have no ability to influence price. They cannot charge a higher price than the market price because no one would buy their product, and they will not set a lower price because they can sell all they can produce at the market price. Wheat farmers are examples of price takers. Barriers to entry are low, and there are many farmers, so no one farmer can influence the price of wheat. One grain of wheat is pretty much like any other, and good information is readily available about prices, quantities, qualities, etc.

monopoly

At the opposite extreme is monopoly. In a **monopoly**, barriers to entry are so high that there is only one firm in the market. As a result, the product is unique. This setting allows the monopolistic firm to be a price setter. However, just because the monopolist sets the price does not mean it can force consumers to buy. It does mean that a somewhat higher price (with concomitantly lower quantity sold) can be set than would be in a competitive market. Some monopolies have legally enforced barriers to entry. The United States Post Office and local cable television firms are examples. Other firms are monopolies because of patent protection or specialized knowledge or exceptionally high cost production equipment, which effectively prevents other firms from entering the market. A monopoly that does not enjoy legal protection is typically very fragile. Potential competitors see above-average profits and want to enter the market. For this reason, monopolies may price their products close to the competitive price to discourage other firms from entering the market.

monopolistic competition

Monopolistic competition has characteristics of both monopoly and perfect competition, but is much closer to the competitive situation. Basically, there are many sellers and buyers, but the products are differentiated on some basis. Restaurants are good examples of monopolistic competitors. Each restaurant serves food but attempts to differentiate itself in some way—ethnic style of food, closeness to work or schools, availability of a party room, gourmet versus casual atmosphere, and so on. The end result is to slightly raise prices above the perfectly competitive price, as customers agree to pay a little more for the unique feature that appeals to them.

oligopoly

Oligopoly is characterized by a few sellers. Typically, barriers to entry are high, and they are usually cost related. For example, the cereal industry is dominated by Kelloggs, General Mills, and Quaker Oats. The reason is not the high cost of manufacturing corn flakes. Instead, the huge selling expenditures (e.g., advertising and shelf space fees) of the big three effectively prevent smaller companies from entering the market. The oligopolist has some market power to set price, but it must be constantly aware of the actions of its competitors. Oligopoly is the "messiest" market in economic theory. Oligopolistic firms are not price takers, but they are not price setters either. Instead, the price an oligopolist sets is heavily dependent on the prices set by its competitors. Often there is a price leader, which sets a price that the others follow. The price leader may raise prices and see if the others follow suit. If they do not, the first firm, no longer a leader, typically reduces price immediately. For many years, General Motors was the price leader in the United States automotive industry. Of course, that has now changed. Part of the reason for the change is that the automobile industry is less oligopolistic. As global competition has grown, and the number of competitors has increased, this industry is becoming closer to monopolistically competitive.

The various types of market structure and their characteristics are summarized in Exhibit 14-3. Companies need to be aware of the market structure in which they operate in order to understand their pricing options. Note that these market structures also have implications for the supply or cost side. The firm in the perfectly competitive industry has lower marketing costs (advertising, positioning, discounting, coupons) than the firm in the monopolistically competitive industry, which must constantly reinforce the consumer's perception that it has a unique product. The monopolist need not incur high costs to remind consumers of its unique product. However, it typically incurs expense protecting its monopoly position, often through legal fees and lobbying (included in administrative expense).

COST-BASED PRICING

Objective 2
Calculate a markup on cost and determine a cost-plus price.

markup

Demand is one side of the pricing equation, supply is the other side. Since revenue must cover cost for the firm to make a profit, many companies start with cost to determine price. That is, they calculate product cost and add the desired profit. The mechanics of this approach are straightforward. Usually there is some cost base and a markup. The **markup** is a percentage applied to base cost; it includes desired profit and any costs not included in the base cost. Companies that bid for jobs routinely base bid price on cost.

Consider Elvin Company, owned and operated by Clare Elvin, which assembles and installs computers to customer specifications. Costs of the components and other direct materials are easy to trace. Direct labor cost is similarly easy to trace to each job. Assemblers receive, on average, $12 per hour, and the company pays benefits of approximately 25 percent of that wage. Last year, Elvin Company worked on 650 jobs which averaged 5 hours each. Overhead, consisting of utilities, small tools, building space, and so on, amounted to $80,000. Elvin Company's income statement for last year is as follows.

Exhibit 14-3
Market Structures and Characteristics

Market Structure Type	Number of Firms in Industry	Barriers to Entry	Uniqueness of Product	Expenses Related to Structure Type
Perfect competition	Many	Very low	Not unique	No special expenses
Monopolistic competition	Many	Low	Some unique features	Advertising, coupons, costs of differentiation
Oligopoly	Few	High	Fairly unique	Costs of differentiation, advertising, rebates, coupons
Monopoly	One	Very high	Very unique	Legal and lobbying expenditures

Revenues		$856,500
Cost of goods sold:		
Direct materials	$585,000	
Direct labor	48,750	
Overhead	80,000	713,750
Gross profit		$142,750
Selling & administrative expense		25,000
Operating income		$117,750

Suppose that Clare wants to earn about the same amount of profit on each job as was earned last year. She could calculate a markup on cost of goods sold by summing selling and administrative expense and operating income and dividing by cost of goods sold.

$$\text{Markup on COGS} = (\text{Selling and administrative expense} + \text{Operating income})/\text{COGS}$$
$$= (\$25,000 + \$117,750)/\$713,750$$
$$= .20$$

The markup on cost of goods sold is 20 percent. Notice that the 20 percent markup covers both profit and selling and administrative cost. The markup is not pure profit.

The markup can be calculated using a variety of bases. Clearly for Elvin Company, the cost of purchased materials is the largest component. Last year, materials were greater than all other costs and profit.

$$\text{Markup on materials} = (\text{Direct labor} + \text{Overhead} + \text{Selling and administrative expense} + \text{Operating income})/\text{Materials}$$
$$= (\$48,750 + \$80,000 + \$25,000 + \$117,750)/\$585,000$$
$$= .464$$

A markup percentage of 46.4 percent of direct materials cost would also yield the same amount of profit, assuming the level of operations and other expenses remained stable. The choice of base and markup percentage generally rests on convenience. If Clare finds that the labor varies in rough proportion to the cost of materials (e.g., more expensive components take more time to set up) and that the cost of materials is easier to track than the cost of goods sold, then materials might be the better base.

To see how the markup can be used in bidding, suppose that Clare has the opportunity to bid on a job for a local insurance company. The job requires Elvin Company to assemble 100 computers according to certain specifications. She estimates the following costs.

Direct materials (computer components, software, cables)	$100,000
Direct labor (100 × 6 hours × $15)	9,000
Overhead (@ 60 percent of direct labor cost)	5,400
Estimated cost of goods sold	$114,400
Plus 20 percent markup on COGS	22,880
Bid price	$137,280

Thus, Elvin Company's initial bid price is $137,280. Note that this is the first pass at a bid. Clare can adjust the bid based on her knowledge of competition for the job and other factors. The markup is a guideline, not an absolute rule.

If Elvin Company bids every job at cost plus 20 percent, is it guaranteed a profit? No, not at all. If very few jobs are won, the entire markup will go toward selling and administrative expense, the costs not explicitly included in the bidding calculations.

Markup pricing is often used by retail stores, and their typical markup is 100 percent of cost. Thus, if a sweater is purchased by Graham Department Store for $24, the retail price marked is $48 [$24 + (1.00)($24)]. Of course, the 100 percent markup is not pure profit; it goes toward the salaries of the clerks, payment for space and equipment (cash registers, etc.), utilities, advertising, and so on. A major advantage of markup pricing is that standard markups are easy to apply. Consider the difficulty of setting a price for every piece of merchandise in the Pottery Barn, pictured at the beginning of this chapter. The Pottery Barn stocks a wide variety of goods, from glassware and pottery to furniture and textiles. Pricing each item by assessing its supply and demand characteristics would be far too time-consuming. It is much simpler to apply a uniform markup to cost and then adjust prices as needed if less is demanded than anticipated.

TARGET COSTING AND PRICING

Objective 3
Explain the advantages of target costing in determining price.

target costing

In the previous section, we examined the way in which companies use cost to determine price. Now let's work backward and see how price can determine cost. **Target costing** is a method of determining the cost of a product or service based on the price (target price) that customers are willing to pay. This is also referred to as price-driven costing.

Most American companies, and nearly all European firms, set the price of a new product as the sum of the costs and the desired profit. The rationale is that the company must earn sufficient revenues to cover all costs and yield a profit. Peter Drucker writes, "This is true but irrelevant: Customers do not see it as their job to ensure manufacturers a profit. The only sound way to price is to start out with what the market is willing to pay."[2]

Target costing is a method of working backward from price to find cost. The marketing department determines what characteristics and price for a product are most acceptable to consumers. Then, it is the job of the company's engineers to design and develop the product such that cost and profit can be covered by that price. Japanese firms have been doing this for years; American companies are beginning to use target costing. For example, Borland International, Inc., used target pricing in developing its 1993 version of Quattro Pro® for Windows spreadsheet. Priced at $49 (compared to $495 for Lotus® and Microsoft® versions), it was designed to appeal to new spreadsheet users. "When we were developing the product, we anticipated the pricing and the people it would attract. We thought of features for that audience."[3] The features referred to included clear instructions, preformatted spreadsheets for fifty common tasks, and interactive on-screen tutorials. Soothing first-time users wasn't the only reason for Quattro Pro's inclusion of built-in help. At $49, the company could not afford numerous calls for technical advice.

2.   Peter Drucker, "The Five Deadly Business Sins," *The Wall Street Journal*, October 21, 1993, p. A22.
3.   Quotation by Joe Ammirato, group manager of the spreadsheet business unit at Borland, as reported by Lawrence M. Fisher, "Using 'Usability' to Sell Spreadsheets to the Masses," *The New York Times*, February 6, 1994, p. 12F.

Retail stores engage in a form of target costing when they look for goods which can be priced at a particular level to appeal to customers. For example, many department stores work with clothing companies to develop house labels. The house label goods are typically good quality items which cost less and are priced lower than comparable name brand items. The house label gives the store flexibility. The store is not in the business of manufacturing sweaters, for example, but can find a source which will deliver sweaters of particular quality for the cost that will allow the store to achieve a target price and profit.

Let's return to the Elvin Company example. Suppose that Clare finds that the insurance company will not consider any bid over $100,000. Her cost-plus bid was $137,280. Is she out of the running? No, not if she can tailor her bid to the customer's desired price. Recall that the original bid called for $100,000 of direct materials and $9,000 of direct labor. Clearly, adjusting the materials will yield the greatest savings. Working with the customer specifications, Clare must determine whether or not a less expensive set of components will achieve the insurance company objectives. Suppose that the insurance company has specified sufficient hard disk space on each drive to accommodate particular software and that the minimum required is 100 MB. Clare's original bid specified 300 MB hard drives. If she reduces the hard disk space to 150 MB and uses a marginally slower drive, she could save $24,000. Substituting a slightly more expensive monitor (a $20 increase) that does not require the installation of screen-saver software would result in saving $30 per computer on software and 15 minutes of direct labor time (at $15 per hour) to install it. The net reduction is $13.75 [($30 + $3.75) − $20] for each of the 100 computers. So far, Clare has developed the following costs.

Direct materials ($100,000 − $25,000)	$75,000
Direct labor (100 × 5.75 hours × $15)	8,625
Total prime cost	$83,625

Recall that Elvin Company applies overhead at the rate of 60 percent of direct labor cost. However, Clare must think carefully about this job. Perhaps somewhat less overhead will be incurred because purchasing is reduced (no need to purchase screen-saver software) and testing is reduced (the smaller hard drives require fewer hours of testing). Perhaps overhead for this job will amount to $4,313 (50 percent of direct labor). That would make the cost of the job $87,938 ($4,313 + $83,625).

Still, not all costs have been covered. There is administrative cost and desired profit. If the standard markup of 20 percent is applied, the bid would be $105,526. This is still too high. Now Clare must determine if further cuts are possible, or if she wants to decrease desired profit and administrative expense. As you can see, target costing is an iterative process. Clare will go through the cycle until she either achieves the target cost or determines that she cannot. Note, however, that given the customer's price ceiling, Clare now has a chance of winning the bid.

A further issue might cause concern. Is there anything ethically wrong with changing the components from the initial bid to the target costed bid? No, the new components meet customer specifications and are clearly described in the bid. In fact, Clare's initial bid was overspecified. If the customer wants a

Chevrolet, the bidder need not provide a Rolls-Royce, especially at Chevrolet prices. However, if in Clare's professional opinion the insurance company should upgrade its specifications, she could point that out. For example, if she knows that the insurance company's word processing program is due for an upgrade that will take more hard disk space, she could inform the company of that and encourage an increase in specified disk space.

Target costing involves much more upfront work than cost-plus pricing. However, let's not forget the additional work that must be done if the cost-plus price turns out to be higher than what customers will accept. Then, the arduous task of bringing costs into line to support a lower price, or the opportunity cost of missing the market altogether, begins. For example, the U.S. consumer electronics market is virtually nonexistent because cost-plus pricing led to higher and higher prices. Japanese (and later Korean) firms practicing target costing offered lower prices and won the market.

Target costing can be used most effectively in the design and development stage of the product life cycle. At that point, the features of the product as well as its costs are still fairly easy to adjust.

LIFE CYCLE PRICING

Objective 4
Explain how price may vary over the product life cycle.

Recall that the marketing view of the product life cycle has four stages: introduction, growth, maturity, and decline. However, for production purposes, there is a fifth stage—development. When establishing prices by considering a product's life cycle, a company takes a long-term view of pricing. Although the following strategies are based on a product's life cycle, each product is different and different firms may use different strategies, depending on market structure and price elasticities of demand.

Development Stage

This stage comes first. During it, designers and engineers design and develop the product. The development stage is critical in cost management because the majority of the product cost is "locked in" during product design. After development and during production, the materials and productive process cannot be changed easily. For example, at Digital Equipment Corporation, managers say that this stage "casts a long shadow" because about 70 percent of DEC's product costs are locked in during development.

Target costing can most easily be done during the development stage. At this point, the product exists in prototype form only. There is still time for customer testing to be sure that the appropriate features are designed. There is time to ensure that potential customers can give the company a feel for the price they would be willing to pay for the product. In other words, during this stage, the target is developed. Design and development costs are real and can be a large part of the investment in a new product. For example, automobile companies now engage in reverse engineering. That is, they purchase competitors' cars and tear them apart to see how they are made. Ford used reverse engineering in designing the Taurus. This is a customer-based approach, since the company looks for products that are already successful in the marketplace and develops the new product in accordance with proven concepts.

Introduction Stage

In the introduction stage, the product is produced and available for sale. The price set during this stage depends on the characteristics of the product and the market. A company may pursue a low-price strategy through penetration pricing or a high-price strategy through price skimming.

penetration pricing

Sometimes in the introduction stage, the company charges a very low price. **Penetration pricing** is the pricing of a new product at a low initial price, perhaps even lower than cost, to build market share quickly. This is useful when the product or service is new and customers have great uncertainty as to its value. It is important to distinguish penetration pricing from predatory pricing. The important difference is the intent. The penetration price is not meant to destroy competition. Accountants new in town, young lawyers, and other professionals often use penetration pricing to establish a customer base.

Penetration pricing may also be used for products that are basically familiar to consumers, where low price will quickly result in large market share. Promotional strategies, including discounts, coupons, and rebates, all lead to lower net prices. For example, consumer goods companies typically flood the market with free samples and discount coupons when introducing new soaps and cereals.

price skimming

Another strategy in the introductory phase is **price skimming**, in which a higher price is charged at the beginning of a product's life cycle. In essence, the company skims the cream off the market. It is used most effectively when the product is new, a small group of consumers is familiar with its value, and the company enjoys a monopolistic advantage. Companies that engage in price skimming are hoping to recoup the expenses of research and development through high initial pricing. A cost consideration is that in the start-up phase of production, economies of scale have not occurred and learning effects have not occurred. For example, in the late 1960s, Hewlett-Packard produced hand-held calculators. These were truly novel, and very expensive. They were priced at over $400 each. Only scientists and engineers, who used the calculators in their work, were convinced of the need for this product. As the market for hand-held calculators grew, and technology improved, the price dropped dramatically. By the 1980s, tiny solar calculators were given away as enticements to new subscribers to magazines.

Clearly, barriers to entry help to support price skimming. Drug companies routinely price new prescription drugs at a high price. Later, when the patent expires and generic versions are introduced, the price drops significantly.

Growth Stage

The growth stage of the product life cycle is characterized by rapid increases in sales and production. When penetration pricing has been used, the growth phase of the product life cycle supports higher prices. For manufactured products, the higher price may result from the dropping of coupons and discounts. The very fact that growth occurs indicates that competition has not caught up with the original maker or that the market is sufficiently large to accommodate all the firms in the industry. If a price skimming strategy has been used, price may fall but not by much—again due to strengthening of the market.

Maturity Stage

As the product matures, prices may decrease. This occurs for a number of reasons. On the cost side, the learning curve takes effect. The company is now a seasoned manufacturer. Bugs have been worked out of production. Again, the hand-held calculator provides a good example. Technology improved, the market expanded tremendously allowing huge economies of scale, competitors entered the market, and price dropped precipitously. Probably, the market for this product was not initially predicted. Who would have guessed in 1966 that just 15 years later many people would own several calculators?

One characteristic of the maturity stage of the product life cycle is that models proliferate. These slight changes in the underlying product help keep the product fresh and attract both old and new customers. The result is that prices are maintained at a higher rate than would be the case with just the original model. An example of model proliferation in a product in the mature stage of its life cycle is electric hair curlers. Many different types exist—varying according to number (e.g., a basic set of 20 versus the travel set of 5 or 6), type of pin used to secure the roller in one's hair, bendable or rigid construction, velour-covered rollers versus not velour-covered, with water mist or dry, and so on. The result is that women may own several sets of electric curlers.

Decline Stage

The decline phase of the product life cycle means declining revenues for the entire industry. Typically there is a shakeout and only a few firms remain. The price of the product may be high, as the few consumers who demand the product remain loyal. The remaining firms may see the lack of potential and charge high prices because the alternative—low prices—does not offer sufficient return to keep them in business. The result is that the remaining firms may enjoy high profits on the product.

PRICES AND CONTROL

Objective 5
Calculate the sales price variance and price volume variance and explain how they are used in controlling revenue.

Accountants play an important role in gathering information for price setting. They are also important in the control phase when companies evaluate the contribution that price and revenue make to profit. A traditional way in which accountants track price and revenue is through variance analysis.

Sale Price and Price Volume Variances

sales price variance

Actual revenue may differ from expected revenue because actual price differs from expected price or because quantity sold differs from expected quantity sold, or both. The **sales price variance** is the difference between actual price and expected price multiplied by the actual quantity or volume sold. In equation form, it is the following.

$$\text{Sales price variance} = (\text{Actual price} - \text{Expected price}) \times \text{Quantity sold}$$

price volume variance

The **price volume variance** is the difference between actual volume sold and expected volume sold multiplied by the expected price. It can be expressed in the following equation.

$$\text{Sales volume variance} = (\text{Actual volume} - \text{Expected volume}) \times \text{Expected price}$$

As is the case with all variances, the sales price and price volume variances are labeled favorable if the variance increases profit above the amount expected and they are labeled unfavorable if the variance decreases profit below the amount expected.

Suppose that Armour Company distributes produce. In May, Armour Company expects to sell 20,000 pounds of produce at an average price of $0.20 per pound. Actual results are 23,000 pounds sold with total revenue equal to $4,370. The sales price variance is $230 unfavorable [($0.20 × 23,000) − $4,370]. Note that the sales price variance is unfavorable because the actual price of $0.19 per pound ($4,370/23,000) is less than the expected price of $0.20. The price volume variance is $600 favorable [23,000 − 20,000) × $0.20]. The price volume variance is favorable because a higher quantity was sold than expected, acting to raise revenue.

The sum of the sales price and price volume variances is the **total (overall) sales variance**. Of course, this is simply the difference between actual and expected revenue. Breaking the overall sales variance into price and volume components gives managers a better feel for why actual revenue may differ from budgeted revenue.

Accountants routinely calculate sales variances when calculating profit-related variances, as will be discussed in Chapter 15, and cost-oriented variances, discussed in Chapter 17. It is important to note that these variances just begin to alert managers to problems in pricing and sales. As is the case with all variances, significant variances are investigated to discover the underlying reasons for the difference between expected and actual results. In the case of an unfavorable sales price variance, the reason may be the giving of unanticipated price discounts, perhaps to meet competitors' prices. The sales price and price volume variances interact. For example, an unfavorable sales price variance may be paired with a favorable price volume variance because the lower price raised quantity sold.

total (overall) sales variance (margin note)

Other Methods of Evaluating Revenue

Companies may consider sales revenue in relation to operational measures. For example, airlines often calculate revenue per passenger mile, and retail stores commonly calculate the sales per square foot. A small store in a shopping mall may find that sales revenue averaging $80 a square foot signals acceptable performance. Wal-Mart, on the other hand, has found that it generates $275 of sales per square foot in its discount stores. As a result, the company considers its Canadian stores' average of $72 a square foot as leaving lots of room for improvement.

The value of operational measures of revenue lies in the fact that they are customized to the industry using them and that they can be compared to industry averages. As a result, individual companies can determine whether their own performance is better or worse than average compared to other firms in their industry.

LEGAL SYSTEM, ETHICS, AND PRICING

Objective 6
Discuss the impact of the legal system and ethics on pricing.

Customers and costs are important economic determinants of price. The United States government also has an important impact on pricing. Over time, many laws have been passed regulating the level and way in which firms can set prices. The basic principle behind much pricing regulation is that competition is good and should be encouraged. Therefore, collusion by companies to set prices and the deliberate attempt to drive competitors out of business are prohibited.

Much federal legislation has been passed regulating business. Exhibit 14-4 gives examples of legislation affecting competition, the Federal Trade Commission, and international trade. Each group affects pricing. For example, laws encouraging competition prohibit some types of monopolistic behavior (the Sherman Act) and price discrimination (the Robinson-Patman Act). The funding of the Federal Trade Commission (FTC) put enforcement muscle behind federal legislation.

Predatory Pricing

predatory pricing

Predatory pricing is the practice of setting prices below cost for the purpose of injuring competitors and eliminating competition. It is important to note that pricing below cost is not necessarily predatory pricing. Companies frequently price an item below cost, run weekly specials in a grocery store, or practice penetration pricing, for example. State laws on predatory pricing create a patchwork of legal definitions. Twenty-two states have laws against predatory pricing, each state differing somewhat in definition and rules. Oklahoma, for example, requires retailers to sell products at a price at least 6.75% above cost, unless the store is having a sale or matching a competitor's price. A 1937 Arkansas law forbids

Exhibit 14-4
*Federal Legislation
Pertaining to Pricing*

I. Legislation that Encourages Competition

Sherman Act (1890) Prohibits combinations, contracts, or conspiracies to restrain trade or monopolize.
Clayton Act (1914) Prohibits price discrimination, exclusive dealer arrangements, and interlocking directorates that lessen competition.
Robinson-Patman Act (1936) Expands Clayton Act to prohibit sellers from offering different deals to different customers.
Celler-Kefauver Act (1950) Expands the Clayton Act to prohibit acquisition of physical assets as well as capital stock in another corporation when the effect is to injure competition.
Consumer Goods Pricing Act (1975) Repealed Fair Trade laws and prohibited price maintenance agreements among producers and resellers.

II. Legislation to Set up and Regulate the Federal Trade Commission

Federal Trade Commission Act (1914) Created the FTC and gave it investigatory powers.
Wheeler-Lea Act (1938) Expands powers of FTC to prevent injuries to competition before they occur.
Magnuson-Moss Act (1975) Grants the FTC the power to determine rules concerning warranties and provides the means for class action suits and other forms of redress.
FTC Improvement Act (1980) Provides Congress with the power to veto the FTC Industrywide Trade Regulation Rules (TRR); limits the power of the FTC.

III. Legislation Loosening Regulations on North American Trade

U.S.-Canada Trade Act (1988) Allows for free trade between the United States and Canada without tariffs and trade restrictions.
NAFTA (North American Free Trade Agreement) (1994)

companies from selling or advertising "any article or product . . . at less than the cost thereof to the vendor . . . for the purpose of injuring competitors and destroying competition."

An example of the application of state predatory pricing laws is the lawsuit filed by three Conway, Arkansas, drugstores against Wal-Mart.[4] The druggists contended that Wal-Mart engaged in predatory pricing by selling more than 100 products below cost. One difficulty is showing exactly what cost is. Wal-Mart has low overhead and phenomenal buying power. Suppliers are regularly required to shave prices to win Wal-Mart's business. Smaller concerns cannot win such price breaks. Thus, the fact that Wal-Mart prices products below competitors' costs does not necessarily mean that those products are priced below Wal-Mart's cost. (Although in this case, the CEO of Wal-Mart did concede that Wal-Mart on occasion prices products below its own cost.) More importantly, the below-cost price must be for the purpose of driving out competitors, a difficult point to prove. Wal-Mart lost a similar case in Oklahoma in 1986. A lobbying attempt to change the state's law failed, and Wal-Mart settled out of court, agreeing to raise prices in its stores throughout the state.[5] In general, states follow federal law in predatory pricing cases, and the federal law makes it difficult to prove predatory pricing, since price competition is so highly valued.

dumping

Predatory pricing on the international market is called **dumping**, which is when companies sell below cost in other countries. For years, U.S. automobile manufacturers have accused Japanese companies of dumping. Companies found guilty of dumping products in the United States are subject to trade restrictions and stiff tariffs—which act to increase the price of the good. The defense against a charge of dumping is demonstrating that the price is indeed above or equal to costs.

Price Discrimination

The federal government has a long history of pricing legislation. The Sherman Act of 1890 prohibits attempts to restrain trade or to monopolize. The FTC was formed in 1914 and given broad investigatory powers. Perhaps the most potent weapon against price discrimination is the Robinson-Patman Act.

price discrimination

The Robinson-Patman Act was passed in 1936 as a means of outlawing price discrimination.[6] **Price discrimination** refers to the charging of different prices to different customers for essentially the same product. Note that services and intangibles are *not* covered by this act. The Robinson-Patman Act states that it is unlawful "to discriminate in price between purchasers of commodities of like grade and quality . . . where the effect of such discrimination may be substantially to lessen competition to tend to create a monopoly in any line of commerce, or to injure, destroy, or prevent competition with any person who either grants or knowingly receives the benefit of such discrimination, or with customers of either of them." A key feature is that only manufacturers or suppliers are covered by the act.

Importantly, the Robinson-Patman Act does allow price discrimination under certain specified conditions: (1) if the competitive situation demands it and (2) if

---

4.   Wal-Mart lost the suit in October 1993 but won on appeal.

5.   Bob Ortega, "Suit Over Wal-Mart's Pricing Practices Goes to Trial Today in Arkansas Court," *The Wall Street Journal*, August, 23, 1993, p. A3.

6.   This section relies on two sources. William A. Rutter, *Anti Trust,* 3rd ed., Gilbert Law Summaries, Gardena, CA, 1972, pp. 57–64. William A. Baldwin, *Market Power, Competition, and Antitrust Policy,* Richard D. Irwin, Inc., Homewood, Illinois, 1987, pp. 430–435.

costs can justify the lower price. The second condition is stated more specifically as "nothing herein contained shall prevent (price) differentials which make any due allowance for differences in the cost of manufacture, sale, or delivery" of the product. Clearly, this second condition is important for the accountant, as a lower price offered to one customer must be justified by identifiable cost savings. Additionally, the amount of the discount must be at least equaled by the amount of cost saved.

What about quantity discounts—are they permissible under Robinson-Patman? Consider the quantity discounts offered by Morton Salt during the 1940s. Less-than-carload shipments were priced at $1.60 per case delivered. Carload shipments were priced at $1.50 per case, and extra discounts of 10 cents and an additional 5 cents were given for purchases of 5,000 cases and 50,000 cases, respectively, if purchased within a twelve-month period. The Supreme Court, in a 1948 decision, found that Morton Salt had violated the Robinson-Patman Act because so few buyers qualified for the quantity discount; at the time, only 5 large chain stores had purchases high enough to qualify for the lowest price of $1.35 per case. While Morton Salt argued that the discounts were available to all purchasers, the Court noted that for all practical purposes, small wholesalers and retail grocers could not qualify for the discounts. A key point here is that so few purchasers were eligible for the discount that competition was lessened. So while the act states that quantity discounts can be given, they must not appreciably lessen competition.

Freight is considered part of price for purposes of the Robinson-Patman Act. If a company requires the customer to pay freight charges, then there is no problem. However, price discrimination may occur if the price charged includes delivery. Suppose the firm charges a uniform delivered price. Then, customers located next to the firm pay the same price as customers located 1,000 miles away. Because the cost of delivering to nearby customers is much less than delivering to far-off customers, the nearby customers are paying "phantom freight."

The burden of proof for firms accused of violating the Robinson-Patman Act is on the firms. The cost justification argument must be buttressed by substantial cost data. Proving a cost justification is an absolute defense; however, the expense of preparing evidence and the FTC's restrictive interpretations of the defense have made it a seldom used choice in the past. Now, the availability of large data bases, the development of activity-based costing, and powerful computing make it a more palatable alternative. Still, problems remain. Cost allocations make such determinations particularly thorny. In justifying quantity discounts to larger companies, a company might keep track of sales calls, differences in time and labor required to make small and large deliveries, and so on.

In computing a cost differential, the company must create classes of customers based on the average costs of selling to those customers and then charge all customers in each group a cost-justifiable price.

Let's look at Cobalt, Inc., which manufactures vitamin supplements. The manufacturing costs average $163 per case (a case contains 100 bottles of vitamins). Cobalt, Inc., sold 250,000 cases last year to the following three classes of customer.

Customer	Price Per Case	Cases Sold
Large drug store chain	$200	125,000
Small local pharmacies	232	100,000
Individual health clubs	250	25,000

Clearly there is price discrimination, but is it justifiable? To answer that question, we need more information about the customer classes.

The large drug store chain requires Cobalt to put the chain's label on each bottle. This special labeling costs about $0.03 per bottle. The chain orders through electronic data interchange (EDI), which costs Cobalt about $50,000 annually in operating expense and depreciation. Cobalt pays all shipping costs, which amounted to $1.5 million last year.

The small local pharmacies order in smaller lots, which requires special picking and packing in the Cobalt factory. This special handling adds $20 to the cost of each case sold. Sales commissions to the independent jobbers who sell Cobalt products to the pharmacies average 10 percent of sales. Bad debts expense is not high and amounts to 1 percent of sales.

Individual health clubs purchase vitamins in lots even smaller than those of the local pharmacies. The special picking and packaging costs average $30 per case. There are no sales commissions for the health clubs. Instead, Cobalt advertises in health club management magazines and accepts orders by phone. In addition, Cobalt has created point-of-sale posters and displays for the clubs. These marketing costs amount to $100,000 per year. Bad debts expense is a serious problem with the health clubs, as they frequently go out of business or change ownership. Bad debts expense for this class of customer averages 10 percent.

Now it is possible to analyze the cost of each customer class. Exhibit 14-5 shows the costs associated with each customer class. It is easy to see that there are significant cost differences in serving the three classes. Cobalt realizes 10.8 percent profit on the cost of sales to the chain store [($200 − $178.40)/$200].

Exhibit 14-5
Analysis of Cobalt, Inc.,
Customer Class Costs

Chain Store	
Manufacturing cost per case	$163.00
Special labeling cost ($0.03 × 100)	3.00
EDI ($50,000/125,000 cases)	.40
Shipping ($1,500,000/125,000 cases)	12.00
Total cost per case	$178.40

Small Pharmacies	
Manufacturing cost per case	$163.00
Special handling per case	20.00
Sales commission ($232 × 0.10)	23.20
Bad debts expense ($232 × 0.01)	2.32
Total cost per case	$208.52

Health Clubs	
Manufacturing cost per case	$163.00
Special handling per case	30.00
Selling expense ($100,000/25,000 cases)	4.00
Bad debts expense ($250 × 0.1)	25.00
Total cost per case	$222.00

The pharmacies provide about 10.1 percent profit [($232 − $208.52)/$232]. The health club related profit percentage is 11.2 percent [($250 − $222)/$250)]. Even though the highest price ($250) is 25 percent above the lowest price ($200), profits vary within a narrow one percent range. The cost differences among the three classes of customer appear to explain the price differences.

Fairness and Pricing

Community standards of fairness have an important effect on prices. For example, should toy stores raise the price of sleds the morning after a heavy snowfall? They could, but generally they do not. Their customers believe that a price increase at such a time would be taking unfair advantage. Whether we characterize the store's reluctance to raise price in this situation as fairness or as an act in the long-term best interests of the company, the result is the same.

reference transaction

The notion of community standards of fairness is based on the belief that both parties in a transaction should receive benefits because of the exchange. The benefits that the parties in an exchange are entitled to can be described in terms of some reference transaction. The **reference transaction** is some other relevant transaction that guides one's expectations with respect to an appropriate price to be charged and an appropriate amount of profit to be earned. Let's return to the price of sleds after a snowstorm. The price of sleds before the storm provides a reference transaction, one which presumably afforded the toy store at least some profit. To raise the price after the storm violates notions of fairness.

Because the reference transaction includes profit, there are situations in which price increases may be acceptable to buyers. Several researchers in decision making conducted a series of surveys to determine the characteristics of acceptable and unacceptable price increases. The characteristics identified are preventing profit reduction, assigning costs to specific goods, improving efficiency, and exploiting market power.[7]

Preventing Profit Reduction Suppose that a landlord owns and rents out a single small house to a tenant who is living on a fixed income. A higher rent would mean the tenant would have to move. Other small rental houses are available. The landlord's costs have increased substantially over the past year, and the landlord raises the rent to cover the cost increases when the tenant's lease is due for renewal. Is this fair or unfair? Respondents to the survey said this rent increase was fair. It is interesting to note that fairness does not mean charity. The landlord is entitled to earn a profit. However, if the situation is changed such that there are no increases in the landlord's costs, but that the rental market has tightened considerably and rents have risen throughout the community, many people would view the rent increase as unfair.

Assigning Costs to Specific Goods Community standards of fairness allow companies to increase prices if costs have increased; however, those price increases must be tied to the goods whose costs have risen. For example, in the mid-1970s, sugar prices rose due to restriction in supply. Small grocers raised the price of sugar on their existing stock. This was a business necessity for those grocers,

---

7.   The work in the section relies heavily on "Fairness as a Constraint on Profit Seeking: Entitlements in the Market," by Daniel Kahneman, Jack L. Knetsch, and Richard Thaler, *American Economic Review,* September 1986, Vol. 76, No. 4, pp. 728–41. References to survey research in this section pertain to this article.

since they used the cash received from the sale of current stock to purchase replacement stock. The price increase was still seen by consumers as unfair, since the existing bags of sugar had been purchased at a lower cost. Large chain grocery stores with greater buying power were not forced to raise prices on existing stock, and for several weeks, customers could root through the bags of sugar for those marked with the original lower prices.[8]

Improving Efficiency   The cost-plus pricing scenarios indicate that consumers believe it is fair for sellers to pass along increased costs. But is this symmetrical— are sellers expected to pass along cost decreases or efficiencies? No, community standards of fairness simply require that customers not be made *worse* off. Therefore, if a firm is able to improve the efficiency with which it manufactures a product, it is not required to pass along the savings through a lower price.

Similarly, if the firm's materials or labor costs decrease, that need not be reflected in the price. This situation is known to consumers, and there is occasional rueful recognition of it. For example, in August 1992, when Saddam Hussain invaded Kuwait, the price of gasoline at the pumps was immediately raised. The media raised a hue and cry. This was unfair, since the gasoline currently at stations had been processed under the previously lower costs. It was pointed out at the time that should the opposite occur, i.e., if the price of crude oil were to fall, the decrease in gasoline prices could take months.

Exploiting Market Power   A basic principle of economics is that increased competition drives down prices and that monopoly power enables the producer to charge higher prices. What about the fairness of this? Respondents to Kahneman et al.'s survey considered the following scenario.

A grocery chain has stores in many communities. Most of them face competition from other groceries. In one community, the chain has no competition. Although its costs and volume of sales are the same there as elsewhere, the chain sets prices that average 5 percent higher than in other communities.

More than three-quarters of the respondents thought the grocery chain was unfair. Notice that the store without competition did not have higher costs or lower volume. In other words, there was no cost-based reason for the price increases.

Rationing is frequently referred to in economics as an important characteristic of price. However, we seldom see instances of price rationing. For example, a pediatrician becomes established in the community and is well-regarded by parents as an excellent doctor. Soon, she has more referrals than she can handle. An economist might suggest raising prices, at least for the new patients. However, it is more typical for the doctor to simply stop accepting patients. Community standards of fairness can handle the concept of "first come, first served" better than price rationing. Another example occurred during the oil embargo of Fall 1973. OPEC restricted oil supplied, and the price of crude oil and petroleum-based products shot up. Gasoline nearly doubled in price from $0.30 to $0.55 per gallon in just a couple of weeks. Those of us old enough to drive back then remember the long lines for gasoline. We remember having to plan ahead to buy gasoline, to find an open station with supplies, and to set aside the hour or so it

---

8.   This example is from an earlier time—before there were supermarket scanners. Today, the supermarket would not mark the price on the item but would instead update the price of all items in stock.

might take to wait in line at the pump. At the time, some stations tried price rationing—and this stratagem was instantly defeated. Laws were passed limiting the price of gasoline to well below the market-clearing price. Inventive gas station owners tried selling $10 car washes (with a free fill-up thrown in) and again were prevented by law. Especially for products deemed critical, price rationing is considered unfair and is not tolerated.

price gouging

Price gouging is said to occur when firms with market power price products "too high." How high is too high? Surely cost is a consideration. Any time price just covers cost, gouging does not occur. This is why so many firms go to considerable trouble to explain their cost structure and point out costs consumers may not realize exist. Pharmaceutical companies, for example, emphasize the research and development costs associated with new drugs. When a high price is clearly not supported by cost, buyers take offense. For example, after Hurricane Andrew in 1992, some companies and individuals sold ice for very high prices. Floridians faced by those prices were outraged that some suppliers would take advantage of the disaster to profiteer.

Ethics Just as a company can practice unethical behavior in applying costs, it can mislead in pricing. A good example is the practice of some airlines of providing "automatic upgrades." For example, from San Francisco to Washington, Continental Airlines had two unrestricted one-way coach prices—$409 and $703. The higher price resulted in an automatic upgrade to first class while the receipt showed "coach fare." Why would the customer want such a ticket? Easy, because the customer's company reimburses only coach fares.[9]

It is easy to see that cost as a justification for price underlies community standards of fairness. Ethics are founded on a sense of fairness. So, unethical behavior in pricing is related to taking unfair advantage of customers. Cost-related price increases are the best defense against customer rebellion.

9.   Scott McCartney, "Why Ticket Says Coach but Seat Is Up Front," *The Wall Street Journal,* September 29, 1995, p. B1.

SUMMARY

Many considerations come into the determination of price. Economic considerations include customer demand, price elasticity of demand, and market structure. In general, customers buy less at a high price than they do at a low price. Price elasticity of demand may vary from elastic to inelastic. When demand is inelastic, a price change has relatively little effect on quantity demand. The opposite holds for elastic demand. Market structure affects the firm's degree of freedom to change price.

Most American firms use cost-based pricing. First, cost is determined, and then, a desired profit is added to calculate price. This strategy does not take demand into account until late in the process, when the resulting price is considered in reference to demand and competition. The target-cost-based pricing strategy, on the other hand, begins with price, then works backward to calculate a cost which will allow the firm to achieve a desired profit. This strategy is proving to be more successful.

The product life cycle has an important impact on price. Price cannot be determined from the stage of the life cycle alone, but when used in conjunction with other influences, pricing strategies emerge.

The legal system, to an extent, supports competition. As a result, certain business practices are outlawed. Predatory pricing and certain types of price discrimination are illegal. Community standards of fairness also circumscribe pricing policies. Fairness and ethical conduct prevent the exploitation of market power in certain instances. Price gouging is considered to be unfair.

REVIEW PROBLEM AND SOLUTION

Melcher Company produces and sells small household appliances. A few years ago, it designed and developed a new hand-held mixer, named the "mixalot." The mixalot can be used to mix milkshakes, light batter, and, with the mincer attachment, can mince up to a cup of vegetables or fruits. The mixalot was very different from the standard table model Melcher mixer. Because of this, over $250,000 was spent on design and development. Another $50,000 was spent on consumer focus groups, in which prototypes of the mixalot were kitchen tested by consumers. It was in those groups that safety problems surfaced. For example, one of the testers sliced someone's hand. This necessitated adding a plastic guard around the blade. Molding and attaching the blade would add $1.50 to prime costs of the mixalot, which had originally been estimated at $3.50.

Information regarding the first five years of operations is as follows:

	Year 1	Year 2	Year 3	Year 4	Year 5
Unit sales	25,000	150,000	400,000	400,000	135,000
Price	$15	$20	$20	$18	$15
Prime costs	$125,000	$600,000	$1,640,000	$1,640,000	$526,500
Setup cost	5,000	9,600	80,000	80,000	12,000
Purchase of special equipment	65,000	—	—	—	—
Expediting	—	15,000	40,000	35,000	—
Rework	12,500	45,000	60,000	60,000	6,750
Other overhead	50,000	300,000	800,000	800,000	270,000
Warranty repair	6,250	7,500	10,000	10,000	3,375
Commissions (5%)	18,750	150,000	400,000	360,000	101,250
Advertising	250,000	150,000	100,000	100,000	25,000

During the first year, Melcher's prime costs included the safety guard. The special equipment was for molding and attaching the guard. It had a life of five years with no salvage value.

REQUIRED:

1. What is the cost of goods sold per unit for the mixalot in each of the five years?
2. What were the marketing expenses associated with the mixalot in each of the five years? Calculate them on a per-unit basis.
3. Calculate operating income for the mixalot in each of the five years. Then, compare all costs to revenues for the mixalot over the entire product life cycle. Was the mixalot profitable?
4. Discuss the pricing strategy of Melcher, Inc., for the mixalot, both initially and over the product life cycle.

Solution

1.

	Year 1	Year 2	Year 3	Year 4	Year 5
Prime cost	$125,000	$600,000	$1,640,000	$1,640,000	$526,500
Setup cost	5,000	9,600	80,000	80,000	12,000
Depreciation on special equipment	13,000	13,000	13,000	13,000	13,000
Expediting	—	15,000	40,000	35,000	—
Rework	12,500	45,000	60,000	60,000	6,750
Other overhead	50,000	300,000	800,000	800,000	270,000
Total COGS	$205,500	$982,600	$2,633,000	$2,628,000	$828,250
Divided by units	25,000	150,000	400,000	400,000	135,000
Unit COGS	$8.22	$6.55	$6.58	$6.57	$6.14

2.

	Year 1	Year 2	Year 3	Year 4	Year 5
Warranty repair	$ 6,250	$ 7,500	$ 10,000	$ 10,000	$ 3,375
Commissions (5%)	18,750	150,000	400,000	360,000	101,250
Advertising	250,000	150,000	100,000	100,000	25,000
Total marketing cost	$275,000	$307,500	$510,000	$470,000	$129,625
Divided by units	25,000	150,000	400,000	400,000	135,000
Unit marketing cost	$11.00	$2.05	$1.28	$1.18	$0.96

3.

	Year 1	Year 2	Year 3	Year 4	Year 5
Sales	$375,000	$3,000,000	$ 8,000,000	$7,200,000	$2,025,000
Less: COGS	205,500	982,600	2,633,000	2,628,000	828,250
Gross profit	$169,500	$2,017,400	$ 5,367,000	$4,572,000	$1,196,750
Less: Marketing expense	275,000	307,500	510,000	470,000	129,625
Operating income	($105,500)	$1,709,900	$ 4,857,000	$4,102,000	$1,067,125

Five-year operating income	$11,630,525
Less: Design and development expense	3,000,000
Excess of revenue over all costs	$ 8,630,525

Yes, the mixalot was profitable over the five-year cycle, even after the design and development expense was subtracted. Note that this expense does not appear on the operating income statement required for external reporting.

4. The initial price set for the mixalot was $15. This is the lowest price of those charged during the five-year period. It appears that Melcher was using a penetration pricing strategy for the mixalot. This makes sense given that the mixalot was not a radically new product, i.e., there were other appliances on the market which could do what the mixalot could do. There were blenders to mix milkshakes, knives and chopping boards to cut up vegetables, food processors to mix and chop. Melcher, Inc., needed to get the mixalot out into actual kitchens to build demand. Notice, too, the large marketing expenditures the first year to create awareness. This, too, helps to support price increases down the line. Finally, by the fifth year, the mixalot is in the declining stage of the product life cycle. Probably other companies have begun producing competing products and the number of new mixalots demanded has declined.

KEY TERMS

QUESTIONS FOR WRITING AND DISCUSSION

1. What is the demand curve? How does it relate to the firm's pricing decision?
2. Define price elasticity of demand. Give an example of a product with relatively elastic demand and an example of a product with relatively inelastic demand. (Give examples not given in the text.)
3. What are the features of a perfectly competitive market? Give two examples of competitive markets. How could a firm in such a market move to a less competitive market?
4. Many times, small startup firms are advised to find "market niches." (A market niche is a narrow segment of customers with unique needs which are currently not being served by existing companies.) Explain why this advice can be useful, given your knowledge of supply and demand.
5. Define monopoly. Why are most existing monopolies subject to government regulation? (Hint: What would happen if there were no legal regulation?)
6. How do you calculate the markup on cost of goods sold? Is the markup pure profit? Explain.
7. How does target costing differ from traditional costing? How does a target cost relate to price?
8. Define penetration pricing. Explain where it would occur in the product life cycle.
9. Define price skimming. Where would it occur in the product life cycle?
10. In the declining stage of the product life cycle, so little is demanded that the price a firm charges has to decline significantly. Do you agree or disagree with this remark?
11. What is predatory pricing? If two gas stations on opposite corners have a gas war, is that predatory pricing? Why or why not?
12. Why do gas stations in the middle of town typically charge a little less for gasoline than do gas stations located on interstate highway turnoffs?
13. What is price discrimination? Is it legal?
14. What variances do managers use in trying to understand the difference between actual and planned revenue?
15. Many colleges and universities have raised tuition over the past few years. What are some of the explanations used to justify tuition increases? Relate these to community standards of fairness.

EXERCISES AND PROBLEMS

**14-1
Elasticity of
Demand and
Market Structure**

LO 1

Janet Gordon and Phil Hopkins graduated several years ago with M.S. degrees in accounting and set up a full-service accounting firm. Janet and Phil have many small business clients and have noticed some pricing trends while compiling annual financial statements. The following data are for five of the pizza parlors which are Janet and Phil's clients.

	Quantity Sold	Average Price
Mamma Mia's	18,000	$10.00
Happy Time Pizza	21,000	7.90
Keg and Pie Pizza	22,000	8.00
Fast Freddy's Pizza	30,000	7.00
Pizza-pizza	24,000	7.50

REQUIRED:

1. Calculate the price elasticity of demand using the highest and lowest prices for your calculation. Is the demand for pizza relatively more elastic or inelastic?
2. What type of market structure characterizes the pizza industry? How do you suppose that Mamma Mia's can charge so much more per pizza than Fast Freddy does?

**14-2
Demand Curve
and Characteristics
of Market
Structure**

LO 1

Amy Chang wants to start a business supplying florists with field-grown flowers. She has located an appropriate acreage and believes she can grow daisies, asters, chrysanthemums, carnations and other assorted types during a nine-month growing period. By growing the flowers in a field as opposed to a greenhouse, Amy expects to save a considerable amount on herbicide and pesticide. She is considering passing the savings along to her customers by charging $1.25 per standard bunch versus the prevailing price of $1.50 per standard bunch.

Amy has turned to her neighbor, Bob Winters, for help. Bob is an accountant in town who is familiar with general business conditions. Bob gathered the following information for Amy.

a. There are 50 growers within a one-hour drive of Amy's acreage.
b. In general, there is little variability in price. Flowers are treated as commodities and one aster is considered to be pretty much like any other aster.
c. There are numerous florists in the city, and the amount that Amy would supply could be easily absorbed by the florists at the prevailing price.

REQUIRED:

1. What type of market structure characterizes the flower-growing industry in Amy's region? Explain.
2. Given your answer to Requirement 1, what price should Amy charge per standard bunch? Why?

**14-3
Basics of Demand,
Life Cycle Pricing**

LO 1, 4

Foster Hancock is an accountant just ready to open an accounting firm in his home town. He has heard that established accountants in town charge $65 per hour. That sounds good to Foster. In fact, he believes that he should be able to charge $75 an hour, given his high GPA and the fact that he is up to date on current accounting issues.

REQUIRED: Should Foster charge $75 per hour? What would you advise him to do?

**14-4
Markup on Cost,
Cost-Based Pricing**

LO 2

Isaac Construction Company builds commercial buildings. Each job requires a bid. ICC's bidding policy is to estimate the costs of materials, direct labor, and subcontractors' costs. These are totaled, and a markup is applied to cover overhead and profit. In the coming year, ICC believes it will be the successful bidder on 20 jobs with the following total revenues and costs.

Revenue		$22,000,000
Materials	$5,000,000	
Direct labor	7,000,000	
Subcontractors	8,000,000	20,000,000
Residual		$ 2,000,000

The residual will cover overhead and profit.

REQUIRED:

1. Given the above information, what is the markup percentage on total direct costs?
2. Suppose ICC is asked to bid on a job with estimated direct costs of $1,100,000. What is the bid? If the customer complains that the profit seems pretty high, how might ICC counter that?

**14-5
Markup on Cost**

LO 2

Many different businesses employ markup on cost to arrive at a price. For each of the following situations, explain what the markup covers and why it is the amount that it is.

1. Department stores have a markup of 100 percent of purchase cost.

2. Jewelry stores charge anywhere between 100 percent and 300 percent of cost of the jewelry. (The 300 percent markup is referred to as "keystone.")

3. Johnson Construction Company charges 12 percent on materials, direct labor, and subcontracting cost.

4. Hamilton Auto Repair charges customers for direct materials and direct labor. Customers are charged $45 per direct labor hour worked on their job; however, the employees actually cost Hamilton $15 per hour.

14-6
Target Costing and Life Cycle Pricing
LO 3, 4

Purdy Entertainment, Inc., manufactures a variety of toys and games. Jim Purdy, president and CEO, is disappointed in the sales of a new board game, which is tied to the 1998 Summer Olympics, called "Go for the Gold" (GFTG). GFTG sold only 5,000 units in 1997 when 20,000 were projected. Sales for 1998 look no better. At $35 per game, it is not a hot seller. Direct costs of the board game are $18 variable cost and $40,000 fixed. Jim is considering several options. Option One: Cut the price to $20 and perhaps sell 7,500 units. Option Two: Cut the price to $15, reduce materials costs by $3, and cut advertising by $20,000. Anticipated volume for this option is 5,000 units. Option Three: Cut the price to $25 and include a $5-mail-in rebate offer. It is anticipated that 7,500 units could be sold and only 20 percent of them would mail in the rebate coupon.

REQUIRED:

1. Which of the three options is best? Be sure to show supporting calculations.
2. Describe the product life cycle for "Go for the Gold." How could Purdy Entertainment lengthen the product life cycle for this game?

14-7
Sales Price and Price Volume Variances
LO 5

Refer to the data in *14-6*.

REQUIRED:

1. Compute the sales price and price volume variances for 1997.
2. How might the information provided by these variances be used by Jim Purdy?

14-8
Life Cycle Costing, Target Costing
LO 3, 4

Shackleford Industries has designed a new form of remote control for radios and stereo equipment—code name "Reddy Remote." The advantage of the Reddy Remote is that it will work with radios and stereo receivers that were not originally sold with a remote control. Bob Freeman, chief design engineer on the project, considers the Reddy Remote his personal baby. He is convinced he has designed a state-of-the-art masterpiece and made sure that the Reddy Remote includes top-of-the-line materials. As Bob said, "You can't skimp on materials; the extra $5 per unit really makes the difference in response time. Besides, now the Reddy Remote will last forever!" Estimated per-unit costs of the Reddy Remote are:

Direct materials	$10.50
Direct labor	8.00
Variable overhead (75% of direct labor cost)	6.00

Marketing expense is estimated at $125,000 in the first year and $25,000 in each year thereafter. To date, the design team has spent $175,000 on the project and anticipates spending $250,000 more to develop it and begin manufacturing. The marketing research department has spent $50,000 on focus groups and surveys of potential customers. They believe that one million would be sold within the first three years as long as the price did not exceed $25. At a price of $30, estimated three-year demand is 200,000 units. After three years, demand would decrease dramatically, since the Reddy Remote is most useful for old technology and people will be upgrading their radios and stereo equipment with remote-capable equipment.

REQUIRED:

1. Describe the product life cycle for the Reddy Remote with related costs.
2. Should the Reddy Remote be priced at $25 or at $30? Why?
3. At a price of $25, what steps could Shackleford Industries take to achieve a target cost of $20?

14-9
Cost-Based Pricing, Target Pricing
LO 2, 3

Julie Ford operates a catering company in Glendell, Ohio. Julie provides food and servers for parties. She also rents tables, chairs, dinnerware, glassware, and linens. The children of Bob and Eleanor Gibbs have contacted Julie about plans for their parents' fiftieth wedding anniversary. The children would like a catered affair at the Arts and Humanities Building in Glendell. They have requested an open bar, heavy hors d'oeuvres (enough to serve 75 people), a small wedding cake, ten tables with linens, dinnerware, and glassware. Julie put together the following bid.

Food (75 × $7.50)	$ 563
Wedding cake ($75)	75
Beverages (75 × $4)	300
Servers (3 × 4 hours × $10)	120
Bartender (1 × 3 hours × $12)	36
Rental of:	
Linens	20
Tables	50
Dinnerware	20
Glassware	20
Total	$1,204

REQUIRED:

1. Explain where costs for Julie's services and profit are calculated in the above bid.
2. Suppose that the Gibbs children blanch when they see the above bid. One of them suggests that they had hoped to spend no more than $750 or so on the party. How could Julie work with the Gibbs to achieve a target cost of that amount?
3. One of the brothers is appalled at the price of the wedding cake. "I can get a box of cake mix at the store for $1.99," he sputters angrily. How would you respond to this remark if you were Julie? (Hint: You want this job, and so telling him "Go bake it yourself, Cheapskate!" is *not* an option.)

14-10
Basic Economic Pricing Concepts
LO 1, 2

Fax-Menu-on-Demand is a Tulsa company which provides an automated fax system, which can be accessed 24 hours a day.[10] The system delivers menus for a variety of Tulsa restaurants to potential customers. The operator of the service, Patrick Dougal, pointed out that the menu is a restaurant's biggest marketing tool. If potential customers could easily see the type of food served and the price range, they would be more likely to dine at a given restaurant.

Potential customers call a Tulsa local number and, using a touch-tone phone, press in their fax number to receive a list of participating restaurants. The customers who have the restaurant list simply press in the code(s) for the restaurants whose menus they desire and receive by fax copies of the selected menus.

Restaurants pay a one-time setup fee of $25 and a $10-per-month service charge.

REQUIRED:

1. Don't the customers receive a service? Why aren't they charged for it?
2. Explain why Fax-Menu-on-Demand has a two-part pricing system. How do you think it corresponds to the cost of the system?

10.   This is a real company. The example was taken from "Fax Food: Service Helps Diners Choose Restaurant by Sending Menu," by Ellen Averill, *Tulsa World*, March 1, 1994, p. Business 1.

14-11
Cost-Plus Pricing

LO 2

Marcus Fibers Inc. specializes in the manufacture of synthetic fibers that the company uses in many products such as blankets, coats, and uniforms for police and firefighters. Marcus has been in business since 1975 and has been profitable every year since 1983. The company uses a standard cost system and applies overhead on the basis of direct labor hours.

Marcus has recently received a request to bid on the manufacture of 800,000 blankets scheduled for delivery to several military bases. The bid must be stated at full cost per unit plus a return on full cost of more than 9 percent after income taxes. Full cost has been defined as including all variable costs of manufacturing the product, a reasonable amount of fixed overhead, and reasonable incremental administrative costs associated with the manufacture and sale of the product. The contractor has indicated that bids in excess of $25 per blanket are not likely to be considered.

In order to prepare the bid for the 800,000 blankets, Andrea Lightner, cost accountant, has gathered the following information about the costs associated with the production of the blankets.

Raw materials	$1.50 per pound of fibers
Direct labor	$7.00 per hour
Direct machine costs*	$10.00 per blanket
Variable overhead	$3.00 per direct labor hour
Fixed overhead	$8.00 per direct labor hour
Incremental administrative costs	$2,500 per 1,000 blankets
Special fee**	$0.50 per blanket
Material usage	6 pounds per blanket
Production rate	4 blankets per direct labor hour
Effective tax rate	40 percent

*Direct machine costs consist of items such as special lubricants, replacement of needles used in stitching, and maintenance costs. These costs are not included in the normal overhead rates.
**Marcus recently developed a new blanket fiber at a cost of $750,000. In an effort to recover this cost, Marcus has instituted a policy of adding a $0.50 fee to the cost of each blanket using the new fiber. To date, the company has recovered $125,000. Lightner knows that this fee does not fit within the definition of full cost, as it is not a cost of manufacturing the product.

REQUIRED:

1. Calculate the minimum price per blanket that Marcus Fibers Inc. could bid without reducing the company's net income.
2. Using the full cost criteria and the maximum allowable return specified, calculate Marcus Fibers Inc.'s bid price per blanket.
3. Without prejudice to your answer to Requirement 2, assume that the price per blanket that Marcus Fibers Inc. calculated using the cost-plus criteria specified is greater than the maximum bid of $25 per blanket allowed. Discuss the factors that Marcus Fibers Inc. should consider before deciding whether or not to submit a bid at the maximum acceptable price of $25 per blanket.

(CMA adapted)

14-12
Life Cycle Pricing, Sales Price and Price Volume Variances

LO 4, 5

Data for Albion Company are as follows:

Budgeted price	$12
Actual price	$10
Budgeted quantity	1,200
Actual quantity sold	1,150

REQUIRED:

1. Calculate the sales price variance.
2. Calculate the price volume variance.
3. Suppose that the product is at the end of the maturity stage of the product life cycle. What information do these two variances provide to Albion's managers.

14-13
Pricing Strategy,
Sales Variances
LO 4, 5

Peterson, Inc., manufactures and sells three products: A, B, and C. In January, Peterson budgeted sales of the following.

	Budgeted Volume	Budgeted Price
Product A	120,000	$40
Product B	150,000	15
Product C	20,000	20

At the end of the year, actual sales for Product A and Product B were $4,580,000 and $2,415,000, respectively. The actual price charged for each was equal to the budgeted price. Product C, however, had revenues of $500,000. While total revenue was higher than expected, the actual price of $10 represented a last-minute revision from budget to increase consumer acceptance of the product.

REQUIRED:

1. Calculate the sales price variance and sales volume variance for each of the three products based on the original budget.
2. Suppose that Product C is a new product just introduced during the year. What pricing strategy is Peterson, Inc., following for this product?

14-14
Price Discrimina-
tion and the
Robinson-Patman
Act
LO 6

For each of the following situations, determine whether or not price discrimination has occurred and whether the Robinson-Patman Act has been violated.

1. Nobunion Shoes manufactures and sells shoes to retail outlets. A popular women's flat sells for $15 to all customers, FOB shipping from Nobunion's factory in Menomenee Falls.
2. Dr. Sidney Ferris, an orthopedic surgeon, charges $1,500 for arthroscopic knee surgery to privately insured patients. He charges a greatly reduced rate to other physicians.
3. Castle Cosmetics charges a single price for each of its products to all customers, even though Castle can document that it costs up to three times as much to sell and distribute to certain small boutiques.
4. Paxton, Inc., manufactures toothpaste and mouthwash. Paxton charges a higher price to individual drugstores than to large chains because smaller stores do not have the same purchasing power as larger chains.

14-15
Price
Discrimination
LO 6

Jared Foods manufactures and distributes frozen entrees. Annual production averages 48,000 cases. A large chain store purchases about 50 percent of Jared's production. Several thousand independent grocers purchase the other fifty percent. Jared incurs the following costs of production per case of entrees:

Direct materials	$40
Direct labor	10
Overhead	25
Total	$75

Jared has one salesperson assigned to the chain store account at a cost of $30,000 per year. Delivery is made in 1,000-case batches once a month at a delivery cost of $450 per batch. Three salespeople service the remaining accounts. They call on the stores and incur salary and mileage expenses of approximately $35,000 each. Delivery costs vary from store to store, averaging $0.65 per case. Jared charges the chain store $85 per case and the independent grocers $94 per case.

REQUIRED: Is Jared's pricing policy supported by cost differences in serving the two different classes of customer? Support your answer with relevant calculations.

14-16
Predatory Pricing
LO 6

Bellis Hardware Mart is a super store with more than twenty large hardware stores. It is a type of store called a category killer—in other words, Bellis stocks ALL hardware (just like Toys "R" Us is a category killer in toys). Bellis has significant buying power and can obtain price concessions from its suppliers, which it then passes on to customers. Recently Bellis opened a store less than a mile from Benton's Hometown Hardware Store, a small concern run for the past fifty years by the Benton family.

Bellis, to introduce itself to customers, offered many advertised specials during its grand opening, including a number of items priced below vendors' costs.

REQUIRED:

1. Is Bellis engaging in predatory pricing?
2. Suppose that Bellis maintained the sale prices over a period of months. Now is it engaging in predatory pricing?

Chapter 15
Profitability Analysis

While other baseball teams' profitability languished in the basement, the Colorado Rockies profit is "mile high." Club owner Jerry McMorris takes revenue and plows it back into the club, quadrupling the player payroll from 1993 to 1995, and spending lavishly to pamper fans at the new Coors Field.

LEARNING OBJECTIVES

After studying this chapter, you should be able to:

1. Explain why firms measure profit.
2. Calculate measures of profit using absorption and variable costing.
3. Calculate the contribution margin, sales volume, sales mix, market share, and market size variances.
4. Determine the profitability of segments.
5. Describe the impact of the short run and the long run on measuring profit.
6. Discuss the product life cycle in relation to profitability analysis.
7. Describe the impact of profits on behavior.
8. Discuss some of the limitations of profit measurement.

"A business that does not make a profit for the buyer of a commodity, as well as for the seller, is not a good business. Buyer and seller must both be wealthier in some way as a result of a transaction, else the balance is broken." Henry Ford[1]

Henry Ford's comment reminds us that the relationship between buyer and seller is an exchange relationship. Both expect to profit from it. But what is profit? How do we measure it? Generally, **profit** is the difference between revenues and costs. Therefore, we must examine both parts of the expression. Revenue, or price, is covered in more detail in the chapter on pricing. Cost, of course, is the subject of this text. In this chapter we look at the interplay of price and cost.

profit

REASONS FOR MEASURING PROFIT

Objective 1
Explain why firms measure profit.

Clearly, firms are interested in measuring profit. In fact, firms are classified according to whether or not profit is the primary objective—they are either for-profit or not-for-profit entities. There are a number of reasons for measuring profit. These include determining the viability of the firm, measuring managerial performance, determining whether or not a firm adheres to government regulations, and signaling the market about the opportunities for others to earn a profit.

Owners of a company want to know if the company is viable in both the short term and the long term. Work gives meaning to life. Staying in business is not only a means to an end but an end in itself. There is an interesting passage in *The Money Game* by Adam Smith[2] in which he puzzles through John Maynard Keynes' reference to the stock market as a game. Smith writes,

Game? Game? Why did the Master say game? He could have said business, or profession, or occupation or what have you. What is a game? It is "sport, play, frolic or fun;" "a scheme or art employed in the pursuit of an object or purpose;" "a contest, conducted according to set rules, for amusement, recreation, or winning a stake." Does that sound like Owning a Share of American Industry? Participating in the Long-Term Growth of the American Economy? No, but it sounds like the stock market.

That not only sounds like the stock market, it also sounds like many businesses. Steve Jobs started Apple Computer in a garage. Years later, a multimillionaire, he was eased out of Apple management—and immediately started Next. Sam Walton stayed involved with Wal-Mart until his death, as did John D. Rockefeller with Standard Oil. Playing the game is important, and profit is a way of keeping score. Players must maintain positive profits to stay in the game. Enough losses and you're out.

Profit can be used to measure managerial performance. In this sense, profit indicates efficiency in the use of resources, because the costs are kept below the benefits. Assessing performance is complicated, but profit, because it is measured in dollars, simplifies scorekeeping. Top management is usually evaluated on the basis of profit and/or return on investment. Both measures require benefits to exceed costs.

---

1.   Henry Ford, *Today and Tomorrow*, 1926, reprinted in 1988, Productivity Press.
2.   Actually, Adam Smith is a pseudonym for George J. W. Goodman. But you can probably find *The Money Game* (Vintage Books, New York, 1976) under Adam Smith. The book is a very readable exploration of investing and investors. The passage cited here can be found on page 16.

Regulated firms must keep profits within certain limits. The profitability of a regulated monopoly is monitored to ensure that the public is served by this structure and that prices do not escalate to the level of an unregulated monopoly. Note that price alone is not set—instead, the price must be set to ensure a "reasonable rate of return," and it is tied to the costs incurred by the regulated firm. Examples of companies subject to regulation are utilities, local telephone companies, and cablevision companies. These companies enjoy monopoly status, and they pay for the privilege through adherence to regulations.

Along the same lines, profit is of interest to those outside a company because it is a signal of the opportunities available. A highly profitable firm signals the market that others might also benefit from entry. Low profits do not entice competition. For this reason, companies may deliberately avoid high short-term profits. For example, in the 1940s, DuPont marketed nylon to manufacturers of women's hosiery and lingerie at a price that was only 60 percent of what could have been charged—despite the fact that nylon was patented and there was virtually no competition. The effect of this decision was two-fold: first, competition was delayed for five to six years, and second, the overall market for nylon expanded dramatically into unanticipated areas, such as its use in automobile tires.[3]

It should also be noted that even though a not-for-profit entity has no profit, it still is engaged in an exchange relationship and must assess its performance and long-term viability. While data on charities expands (some watchdog groups, such as the National Charities Information Bureau in New York, even have Internet websites and will take complaints on-line), the usability of the data leaves something to be desired. Corporate donors, in particular, want better measures of how well a charity fulfills its mission. The reason, of course, is that not-for-profit entities use and must account for resources. Supplies, postage, telephones, and office space all take money. Employees do not necessarily make less than a market wage. They simply have no claim to any residual. As a result, many of the concepts covered in this chapter have relevance to not-for-profit entities. The Girl Scouts of America, for example, expect to profit from cookie sales, although they may not refer to the money made above cost as profit. Not-for-profit firms are still interested in the relationship between revenues and expenses, or inflows and outflows.

MEASURES OF PROFIT

Objective 2
Calculate measures of profit using absorption and variable costing.

Profit is a measure of the difference between what a firm puts into making and selling a product or service and what it receives. It is the degree to which the firm becomes wealthier on account of engaging in transactions. The desire of firms to measure the increase in wealth has led to numerous definitions of profit. Some are used for external reporting, some for internal reporting.

Absorption Costing Approach to Measuring Profit

Absorption costing, or full costing, is required for external financial reporting. According to GAAP, profit is a long-run concept and depends on the difference between revenues and expenses. Over the long run, of course, all costs are variable. Therefore, fixed costs are treated as if they were variable by assigning some to each unit of production. **Absorption costing** assigns *all* manufacturing costs,

absorption costing

---

3.   Peter Drucker, "The Five Deadly Business Sins," *The Wall Street Journal*, October 21, 1993, p. A22.

direct materials, direct labor, variable overhead, and a share of fixed overhead, to each unit of product. In this way, each unit of product *absorbs* some of the fixed factory overhead in addition to the variable costs incurred to manufacture it. When a unit of product is finished, it takes these costs into inventory with it. When it is sold, these manufacturing costs are shown on the income statement as cost of goods sold. It is absorption costing that is used to calculate three measures of profit: gross profit, operating income, and net income.

Preparing the Absorption Costing Income Statement Lasersave, Inc., a company that recycles used toner cartridges for laser printers, began operations in August and manufactured 1,000 cartridges during the month with the following costs:

Direct materials	$ 5,000
Direct labor	15,000
Variable overhead	3,000
Fixed overhead	20,000
Total manufacturing cost	$43,000

During August, 1,000 cartridges were sold at a price of $60. Variable marketing cost was $1.25 per unit, and fixed marketing and administrative expense was $12,000. The unit product cost of each toner cartridge is $43 ($43,000/1,000 units). This amount includes direct materials ($5), direct labor ($15), variable overhead ($3), and fixed overhead ($20). Notice that the fixed overhead is treated as if it were variable. That is, the total amount is divided by production and applied to each unit. Thus, the cost of goods sold for August is $43,000 ($43 × 1,000 units sold). Exhibit 15-1 illustrates the absorption costing income statement for Lasersave for the month of August.

The income statement shown in Exhibit 15-1 is the familiar full costing income statement used for external reporting. The difference between revenue and cost of goods sold is **gross profit (or gross margin)**. This is not equal to **operating income**, because the marketing and administrative expenses remain to be covered. At one time, gross profit was a fairly useful measure of profitability. Marketing and administrative expenses were relatively stable and could be adjusted fairly easily. In today's economic environment, that is less true. Government regulations affect businesses in sometimes unforeseen ways. Environmental cleanup and modification of facilities to comply with the Americans With

gross profit (gross margin)
operating income

Exhibit 15-1
Absorption Costing Income Statement for Lasersave, Inc., for August

		Percent of Sales
Sales	$60,000	100.00
Less: Cost of goods sold	43,000	71.67
Gross profit	$17,000	28.33
Less: Variable marketing expense	1,250	2.08
Less: Fixed marketing and administrative expense	12,000	20.00
Operating income	$ 3,750	6.25

Disabilities Act are just two examples of regulations that increase nonmanufacturing expense. Additionally, research and development, also an expense subtracted from gross profit to yield operating income, is increasingly important. Now, gross profit is less useful and cannot be used as a sole measure of the long-run health of the firm.

Exhibit 15-1 also shows the "Percent of Sales" column which is often associated with the absorption costing income statement. Notice that Lasersave, Inc., earned a gross profit of just over 28 percent of sales, and that operating income was 6.25 percent of sales. Is this good or bad performance? It depends on the typical experience for the industry. If most firms in the industry earned a gross margin of 35 percent of sales, we could say that Lasersave was below average and might look for opportunities to decrease cost of goods sold or increase revenue. Kodak, for example, knows that its cost of manufacturing is as low as that of rival Fuji Photo Film of Japan. However, Kodak's marketing expenses are 26 percent of revenue as opposed to the benchmark "best of class" ratio of 22 percent. These figures help Kodak focus on areas for improvement.[4]

What about absorption costing operating income? Is it a reasonable measure of performance? Problems exist with this measure too. First, managers can remove some current period costs from the income statement by producing for inventory. Second, the absorption costing format is not useful for decision making.

Disadvantages of Absorption Costing In general, a company manufactures a product in order to sell it. In fact, that was the case for Lasersave for the month of August when every unit produced was sold. But what happens when the company produces for inventory? Suppose that in September, Lasersave produces 1,250 units but sells only 1,000. The price, variable cost per unit, and total fixed costs remain the same. Will September operating income equal August operating income? Exhibit 15-2 shows the income statement for September.

Exhibit 15-2
Absorption Costing Income Statement for Lasersave, Inc., for September

Sales	$60,000
Less: Cost of goods sold*	39,000
Gross profit	$21,000
Less: Variable marketing expense	1,250
Less: Fixed marketing and administrative expense	12,000
Operating income	$ 7,750

*Direct materials ($5 × 1,250)	$ 6,250
Direct labor ($15 × 1,250)	18,750
Variable overhead ($3 × 1,250)	3,750
Fixed overhead	20,000
Total manufacturing cost	$48,750
Add: Beginning inventory	0
Less: Ending inventory	9,750
Cost of goods sold	$39,000

4.   Peter Nulty, "Digital Imaging Had Better Boom Before Kodak Film Busts," *Fortune,* May 1, 1995, pp. 80–83.

Operating income in September is $7,750 versus operating income for August of $3,750. The same number of units was sold, at the same price, and the same costs. What happened? The culprit is treating fixed factory overhead as if it were variable. In August, 1,000 units were produced and each one absorbed $20 ($20,000/1,000) of fixed overhead. In September, however, the same total fixed factory overhead of $20,000 was spread out over 1,250 units, so each unit absorbed only $16 ($20,000/1,250). The 250 units that went into ending inventory took with them all of their variable costs of production of $5,750 ($23 × 250) plus $4,000 (250 × $16) of fixed factory overhead from September. That $4,000 of inventoried fixed factory overhead is precisely equal to the $4,000 difference in operating incomes.

Clearly, the absorption costing income statement gives the wrong message in September. It seems to say that September performance was better than August performance, when the sales performance was identical and, arguably, production was off by 250 units. (Even if the company wanted to produce for inventory, it is misleading to increase income for the period as a result.)

Of course, the whole purpose of manipulating income by producing for inventory is to increase profit above what it would have been without the extra production. Managers who are evaluated on the basis of operating income know that they can temporarily improve profitability by increasing production. They may do this to ensure year-end bonuses or promotions. As a result, the usefulness of operating or net income as a measure of profitability is weakened. Companies that use absorption costing income as a measure of profitability may institute rules regarding production. For example, a manufacturer of floor care products insists that the factory produce only the amounts called for in the master budget. While this will not erase the impact of changes in inventory on operating income, it does mean that the factory manager cannot deliberately manipulate production to increase income.

The second disadvantage of absorption costing is that it is not a useful format for decision making. Suppose that Lasersave was considering accepting a special order for 100 toner cartridges at $38. Should the company accept? If we focus on the absorption costing statement, who can tell? In August, the manufacturing cost per unit was $43. In September, it was $39. Neither figure included the marketing cost. The treatment of fixed overhead as a unit-level variable cost has made it difficult to see just what the incremental cost is.

Variable Costing Approach to Measuring Profit

variable costing

An approach to measuring profitability that avoids the problems inherent in making fixed overhead a variable cost is variable costing. **Variable costing**[5] assigns only unit-level variable manufacturing costs to the product; these costs include direct materials, direct labor, and variable overhead. Fixed overhead is treated as a period cost and is not inventoried with the other product costs. Instead, it is expensed in the period incurred.

The result of treating fixed factory overhead as a period expense is to reduce the factory costs that are inventoriable. Under variable costing, only direct materials, direct labor, and variable overhead are inventoried. (Remember that marketing and administrative expenses are never inventoried—whether variable or

---

5.   Variable costing is sometimes called direct costing. These terms are synonymous.

fixed.) Therefore, the inventoriable variable product cost for Lasersave is $23 ($5 direct materials + $15 direct labor + $3 variable overhead).

The variable costing income statement is set up a little differently from the absorption costing income statement. Exhibit 15-3 gives Lasersave's variable costing income statements for August and September. Notice that *all* unit-level variable costs (including variable manufacturing and variable marketing expense) are summed and subtracted from sales to yield contribution margin. Then, all fixed expenses for the period, whether they are incurred by the factory or by marketing and administration, are subtracted to yield operating income.

Notice that the August and September income statements for Lasersave are identical. This seems right. Each month had identical sales and costs. While September production was higher, that will show up as an increase in inventory on the balance sheet. As we can see, variable costing operating income cannot be manipulated through overproduction, since fixed factory overhead is not carried into inventory.

Let's take a closer look at each month. In August, production exactly equaled sales. In this case, none of the period's costs go into inventory and absorption costing operating income is equal to variable costing income. In September, inventory increased and absorption costing operating income is higher than variable costing operating income. The difference, $4,000 ($7,750 − $3,750), is just equal to the fixed overhead per unit multiplied by the increase in inventory ($16 × 250 units).

What happens when inventory decreases? Again, there is an effect on operating income under absorption costing, but not under variable costing. Let's take Lasersave into the month of October, when production is 1,250 units (just like September) but 1,300 units are sold. Exhibit 15-4 gives the comparative income statements for both absorption and variable costing.

In this case, when inventory decreases (or production is less than sales), variable costing operating income is greater than absorption costing operating income. The difference of $800 ($14,475 − $13,675) is equal to the 50 units that, under absorption costing, came from inventory with $16 of the previous month's fixed factory overhead attached. Exhibit 15-5 summarizes the impact of changes in inventory on operating income under absorption costing and variable costing.

Exhibit 15-3
Variable Costing Income Statements for Lasersave, Inc.

	For the Month of August	For the Month of September
Sales	$60,000	$60,000
Less: Variable expenses*	24,250	24,250
Contribution margin	$35,750	$35,750
Less: Fixed factory overhead	20,000	20,000
Less: Fixed marketing expense	12,000	12,000
Operating income	$ 3,750	$ 3,750

*Direct materials	$ 5,000
Direct labor	15,000
Variable overhead	3,000
Total variable manufacturing expenses	$23,000
Add: Variable marketing expense	1,250
Total variable expenses	$24,250

Exhibit 15-4
Comparative Income Statements for Laser-save, Inc., for October

	Absorption Costing		Variable Costing
Sales	$78,000	Sales	$78,000
Less: Cost of goods sold*	50,700	Variable expenses	31,525
Gross profit	$27,300	Contribution margin	$46,475
Less: Variable marketing expense	1,625	Less: Fixed factory overhead	20,000
Less: Fixed marketing and administrative expense	12,000	Less: Fixed marketing and administrative expense	12,000
Operating income	$13,675	Operating income	$14,475

*1,300 × $39 = $50,700

Exhibit 15-5
Changes in Inventory Under Absorption and Variable Costing

If	Then
1. Production > Sales	Absorption costing income > Variable costing income
2. Production < Sales	Absorption costing income < Variable costing income
3. Production = Sales	Absorption costing income = Variable costing income

To summarize, when inventories change from the beginning to the end of the period, the two costing approaches will give different net incomes. The reason for this is that absorption costing assigns fixed factory overhead to units produced. If those units are sold, the fixed overhead appears on the income statement under cost of goods sold. If the units are not sold, the fixed overhead goes into inventory. Under variable costing, however, all fixed overhead for the period is expensed. As a result, absorption costing allows managers to manipulate operating income by producing for inventory.

The variable costing income statement has an advantage in addition to providing better signals regarding performance. It also provides more useful information for management decision making. Look again at Exhibit 15-4. How much additional profit can be made on the sale of one more toner cartridge? The absorption costing statement indicates that $21 ($27,300/1,300) is the per-unit gross profit. However, that figure includes some fixed overhead, and fixed overhead will *not* change if another unit is produced and sold. The variable costing statement gives more useful information. Additional contribution margin of the extra unit is $35.75 ($46,475/1,300). The key insight of variable costing is that fixed expenses do not change as units produced and sold change. Therefore, while the variable costing income statement cannot be used for external reporting, it is a valuable tool for some management decisions.

The measures of profit discussed in this section all applied to the company. There are additional factors to be considered in using any income statement for internal reporting and performance evaluation. Neither operating income nor **net income** (operating income less taxes) are completely sufficient for profitability analysis. In other words, the questions that firms most want answered cannot be answered with an analysis of net income alone. One reason for the insufficiency of net income is aggregation of data. Aggregation refers to the summing of com-

net income

ponents of profit into more general categories. The fine detail necessary to determine the existence of problems and to take corrective action is missing from the income statement. For example, the income statement may indicate low revenue, but it does not indicate why. Is quantity sold down? Has price decreased? Are some products experiencing increased sales while others have experienced decreased sales? More analysis is needed to answer these questions and others.

ANALYSIS OF PROFIT-RELATED VARIANCES

Objective 3
Calculate the contribution margin, sales volume, sales mix, market share, and market size variances.

Managers frequently want to compare actual profit earned with expected profit.[6] This leads naturally to variance analysis, in which actual and budgeted amounts are compared. Profit variances center on the difference between budgeted and actual prices, volumes, and contribution margin. Profit variances can be calculated for each individual product as well as for all products taken together. The latter consideration allows us to determine the effect of sales mix on profit.

Recall that the difference between actual and expected revenue can be analyzed in terms of the sales price and price volume variances. The sales price variance is the difference between expected and actual price multiplied by actual volume sold. The price volume variance is the difference between actual and expected volume sold multiplied by the expected price. These variances give the firm valuable information regarding the sales performance of each product. However, the company may wish to analyze sales further and relate them to the contribution margin earned. In this section, we will look at the contribution margin variance, the sales volume variance, the sales mix variance, and the market share variance.

Contribution Margin Variance

contribution margin variance

The **contribution margin variance** is simply the difference between actual and budgeted contribution margin.

$$\text{Contribution margin variance} = \text{Actual contribution margin} - \text{Budgeted contribution margin}$$

This variance is favorable if the actual contribution margin earned is higher than the budgeted amount.

Consider Birdwell, Inc., which produces two types of bird feeders. The regular type is a simple plastic and wood model, which can be hung from a tree branch. The deluxe model is a larger, stand-alone model, which includes a post and a round squirrel shield to prevent squirrels from eating the bird seed. Budgeted and actual data for the two models are shown in Exhibit 15-6.

The contribution margin variance for Birdwell, Inc., is $875 favorable ($14,375 − $13,500). This variance can be broken down into a sales volume variance and a sales mix variance.

sales volume variance

Sales Volume Variance The **sales volume variance** is the difference between the actual quantity sold and the budgeted quantity sold multiplied by the budgeted average unit contribution margin. Note the difference between the sales volume variance and the price volume variance. Both look at the difference between

---

6.   Expected profit is usually found in the master budget. The master budget is discussed in detail in Chapter 16. It is not necessary for you to have read Chapter 16 to understand this chapter.

Exhibit 15-6

	Budgeted Amounts		
	Regular Model	Deluxe Model	Total
Sales:			
($10 × 1,500)	$15,000		
($50 × 500)		$25,000	$40,000
Variable expense	9,000	17,500	26,500
Contribution margin	$ 6,000	$ 7,500	$13,500

	Actual Amounts		
	Regular Model	Deluxe Model	Total
Sales:			
($10 × 1,250)	$12,500		
($50 × 625)		$31,250	$43,750
Variable expense	7,500	21,875	29,375
Contribution margin	$ 5,000	$ 9,375	$14,375

actual and budgeted volume sold. However, the price volume variance multiplies that difference by sales price, while the sales volume variance multiplies that difference by contribution margin. Therefore, the sales volume variance gives management information about gained or lost profit due to changes in the quantity of sales.

> Sales volume variance = (Actual quantity sold − Budgeted quantity sold)
> × Budgeted average unit contribution margin

The budgeted average unit contribution margin is the total budgeted contribution margin divided by the budgeted total number of units of all products to be sold.

In the Birdwell example, the total volume budgeted is 2,000 units (1,500 regular and 500 deluxe). The actual units sold amounted to 1,875 (1,250 regular and 625 deluxe). The budgeted average unit contribution margin is $6.75 ($13,500/2,000). Therefore, the sales volume variance is $843.75 unfavorable [(2,000 − 1,875)$6.75].

The unfavorable sales volume variance is clearly the result of selling fewer units, in total, than budgeted. Still, we can see that Birdwell, Inc., actually had a higher contribution margin than expected. The shift in the sales mix explains why.

Sales Mix Variance The sales mix represents the proportion of total sales yielded by each product. A company which produces only one product obviously has a sales mix of 100 percent for that product. All units sold will be that product, and there is no effect of changing sales mix on profit. Multiproduct firms, however, do experience shifting sales mix. If relatively more of the high-profit product is sold, profit will be higher than expected. If the sales mix shifts toward the low-profit product, profit will be lower than expected. We can define the **sales mix variance** as the sum of the change in units for each product multiplied by the difference between the budgeted contribution margin and the budgeted average unit contribution margin.

sales mix variance

Sales mix variance = [(Product 1 actual units − Product 1 budgeted units)
× (Product 1 budgeted unit contribution margin − Budgeted average unit
contribution margin)] + [(Product 2 actual units − Product 2 budgeted units)
× (Product 2 budgeted unit contribution margin − Budgeted average unit
contribution margin)]

The sales mix variance equation above is for two products. If three products were produced, we would simply keep adding the change in units times the change in contribution margin for every additional product.

Again consider Birdwell, Inc., data from Exhibit 15-6. The budgeted data show a sales mix of 1,500 regular models and 500 deluxe models. This reduces to a 3:1 sales ratio (1,500:500 is equivalent to 3:1). However, the actual data show that 1,250 regular models were sold and 625 deluxe models were sold. This is a ratio of 2:1.

The sales mix variance for Birdwell is computed as follows:

Birdwell sales mix variance = [(1,250 − 1,500) × ($4.00 − $6.75)]
+ [(625 − 500) × ($15 − $6.75)] = $1,718.75 Favorable

Now we can see that the favorable sales mix variance of $1,718.75, combined with the unfavorable sales volume variance of $843.75, explains the overall favorable contribution margin variance of $875.

Market Share and Size Variances

Managers want not only to look inward at contribution margin through the sales volume and sales mix variances, but also to look outward to see how their company is doing compared with the rest of their industry. **Market share** gives the proportion of industry sales accounted for by a company. **Market size** is the total revenue for the industry. Clearly, both market size and market share have an impact on a company's profits.

The **market share variance** is the difference between the actual market share percentage and the budgeted market share percentage multiplied by actual industry sales in units times budgeted average unit contribution margin. The **market size variance** is the difference between actual and budgeted industry sales in units multiplied by the budgeted market share percentage times the budgeted average unit contribution margin.

Market share variance = [(Actual market share percentage
− Budgeted market share percentage) × (Actual industry sales in units)]
× (Budgeted average unit contribution margin)

Market size variance = [(Actual industry sales in units
− Budgeted industry sales in units) × (Budgeted market share percentage)]
× (Budgeted average unit contribution margin)

Suppose that the budgeted unit sales for the bird feeder industry were 20,000 (of all model types) and actual unit sales for the industry were 23,000. Then the Birdwell budgeted market share is 10 percent (20,000/2,000). Birdwell's actual market share is 8.2 percent (1,875/23,000). The market share variance for Birdwell is $2,794.50 unfavorable [(.082 − .10) × 23,000 × $6.75]. In other words, Birdwell's reduction in market share from 10 percent to 8.2 percent cost the company $2,794.50 in contribution margin.

The impact of changing market size on Birdwell's profits can be assessed through the market size variance. It is $2,025 favorable, meaning that the company's contribution margin would have increased by this amount had the actual

market share
market size

market share variance

market size variance

market share percentage equaled the budgeted market share percentage. Unfortunately for Birdwell, the market share percentage slipped. Still, Birdwell is better off due to increasing market size, since a market share of 8.2 percent would yield even smaller profits from a smaller market.

While the contribution margin variances and the market share and market size variances yield important insights into profitability, companies may want to analyze segment profit further. The next section examines segment profitability in more detail.

PROFITABILITY OF SEGMENTS

Objective 4
Determine the profitability of segments.

Companies frequently want to know the profitability of a segment of the business. That segment could be a product, division, sales territory, or customer group. Determining the profit attributable to subdivisions of the company is harder than determining overall profit because of the need to allocate expenses. Accurate tracing of costs to each segment is difficult. Still, the importance of segmental profit to management decision making can make the exercise worthwhile.

Profit by Product Line

It is easy to understand why a firm would like to know whether or not a particular product is profitable. A product that consistently loses money and has no potential to become profitable could be dropped. This would free up resources for a product with higher potential. On the other hand, a profitable product may merit additional time and attention.

Most companies produce and sell more than one product, or more than one model of a product. Sears is the nation's number 2 retailer and sells many of its own brands, including Kenmore appliances and Craftsman tools. In an effort to bolster the "softer side of Sears," the retailer has joined forces with Lancome USA to produce and market Circle of Beauty cosmetics. Considering that cosmetics represent 10 percent of department store sales and carry gross margins of 40 percent (even more for a private label like Circle of Beauty), Sears is expanding into a new and very profitable segment.[7]

Product line profitability would be easy to compute if all costs and revenues were easily traceable to each product. This is seldom the case. Therefore, companies must first determine how profit will be computed. Three possibilities (in order of increasing accuracy) are: absorption costing, variable costing, and activity-based costing. Each allocates cost to a product line in a different way and will give a different result. The company's need for accuracy determines which is used.

Let's examine Alden Company, which manufactures two products: plain-paper fax machines and thermal-paper fax machines. Thermal paper is slick and curls when heated to make the fax. Customers find it less desirable than plain-paper faxes. The thermal-paper fax machine is low-end, uses older technology and is easier to produce. The plain-paper fax machine is the high-end machine. It uses more advanced technology and is more difficult to produce. Data on each product are on the following page.

7.   Susan Chandler, "Drill Bits, Paint Thinner, Eyeliner: Sears Lures Middle-Income Women With a Cosmetics Line," *Business Week*, September 25, 1995, pp. 83–84.

	Thermal Paper	Plain Paper
Number of units	20,000	10,000
Direct labor hours	40,000	15,000
Price	$200	$350
Prime cost per unit	$55	$95
Overhead per unit*	$30	$22.50

*Annual overhead is $825,000, and overhead is applied on the basis of direct labor hours.

Marketing expenses, all variable, amount to 10 percent of sales. Administrative expense of $2 million, all fixed, is allocated to the products in accordance with revenue. Absorption costing income by product line is shown in Exhibit 15-7.

Clearly, the plain-paper fax machine is more profitable. But what does this tell us? Can we conclude that each thermal-paper fax machine sold adds $41.65 ($833,000/20,000 units) to profit? Does each plain-paper fax machine sold add $104.20 ($1,042,000/10,000) to profit? No, Alden Company has intermingled variable and fixed costs and has allocated administrative expense on the basis of revenue, when there is no reason to believe that revenue drives administrative expense. Additionally, overhead has been assigned to the products on a per-unit basis, but we do not know just what it includes. Is $22.50 an accurate representation of the overhead resources required to produce one plain-paper fax machine? If not, a different cost system might be used.

Using Variable Costing to Measure Segment Profit Alden Company could use variable costing and segregate direct fixed and common fixed expenses as well. To apply variable costing to Alden Company, we need additional information on fixed and variable costs of overhead.

	Variable	Fixed
Overhead:		
Setups		$ 40,000
Maintenance		120,000
Supplies	$ 80,000	
Power	280,000	
Machine depreciation		250,000
Other factory costs		55,000
Total	$360,000	$465,000

Recall that overhead is applied on the basis of direct labor hours. Therefore, the variable overhead assigned to thermal-paper fax machines is $261,818 [$360,000(40,000/55,000)]. The variable overhead assigned to plain-paper fax machines is $98,182 [$360,000/(15,000/55,000)]. Now we can prepare a segmented income statement as shown in Exhibit 15-8.

While absorption-based operating income equals variable costing operating income in this case (because all units produced were sold), the variable costing income statement provides more useful information. Now we can see how much more profit is made if another fax machine is sold. An additional thermal-paper fax machine adds $111.90 ($2,238,000/20,000) to profit. An additional plain-paper fax machine adds $210.20 ($2,102,000/10,000) to profit. The key insight of vari-

Exhibit 15-7

Alden Company
Absorption Costing Income Statement
(In thousands of dollars)

	Thermal Paper	Plain Paper	Total
Sales	$4,000	$3,500	$7,500
Less: COGS	1,700	1,175	2,875
Gross profit	$2,300	$2,325	$4,625
Less: Marketing expense	400	350	750
Less: Administrative expense	1,067	933	2,000
Operating income	$ 833	$1,042	$1,875

Exhibit 15-8

Alden Company
Variable Costing Income Statement
(In thousands of dollars)

	Thermal Paper	Plain Paper	Total
Sales	$4,000	$3,500	$7,500
Less: Variable COGS	1,362	1,048	2,410
Less: Sales commission	400	350	750
Contribution margin	$2,238	$2,102	$4,340
Less: Common fixed overhead			465
Less: Administrative expense			2,000
Operating income			$1,875

able costing is that fixed expenses do not change as units produced and sold change. Therefore, while the variable costing income statement cannot be used for external reporting, it is a valuable tool for some management decisions. One problem remains with the variable costing approach. The fixed costs were not assigned to either product. Is this appropriate? If all fixed costs must be incurred despite which products are produced, the answer is yes. However, often a cost is fixed with respect to units produced but is variable according to another activity driver. In this case, activity-based costing yields more accurate cost information.

Using Activity-Based Costing to Measure Segment Profit An activity-based costing approach, with its insight into unit-level, batch-level, product-level, and facility-level costs may give management a more accurate feel for profits attributable to different product lines. Let's revisit Alden Company and look for additional information on the drivers for each overhead cost. Exhibit 15-9 contains this information along with cost driver usage by product. Note that there is no activity driver for other factory costs, since these are facility-level costs and will remain no matter which product is manufactured.

Now we can recast the product-line income statement using the activity-based costing information. This is done in Exhibit 15-10. The value of the activity-based costing income statement is that it reminds management that costs cannot be simply separated into fixed and variable components on the basis of

Exhibit 15-9
Overhead Activities and Drivers

Overhead Activities	Activity Driver	Total Cost
Setting up equipment	Number of setups	$ 40,000
Maintaining equipment	Maintenance hours	120,000
Providing supplies	Direct labor hours	80,000
Providing power	Machine hours	280,000
Machine depreciation	Machine hours	250,000
Other factory costs	(None)	55,000
		$825,000

	Activity Usage by Product (as Measured by Drivers)	
	Thermal Paper	Plain Paper
Number of setups	10	30
Maintenance hours	2,000	8,000
Direct labor hours	40,000	15,000
Machine hours	10,000	90,000

Exhibit 15-10

Alden Company
Activity-Based Costing Income Statement
(In thousands of dollars)

	Thermal Paper	Plain Paper	Total
Sales	$4,000	$3,500	$7,500
Less: Prime costs	1,100	950	2,050
Setups	10	30	40
Maintenance	24	96	120
Supplies	58	22	80
Power	28	252	280
Machine depreciation	25	225	250
Sales commission	400	350	750
Segment margin	$2,355	$1,575	$3,930
Less: Other fixed overhead			55
Less: Administrative expense			2,000
Operating income			$1,875

units alone. Alden Company can see that the plain-paper fax machines add overhead cost in the form of more setups and more usage of power and machinery. Importantly, management can now concentrate on reducing the use of drivers that directly add cost. Previously, overhead was applied on the basis of direct labor hours. This misleads management into thinking that the reduction of direct labor hours will result in decreased overhead. However, an activity-based approach shows the complexity of the manufacturing operation and reminds managers that a decrease in power costs can only be achieved with a decrease in machine usage (perhaps by the use of more efficient machinery). Similarly, a decrease in setup cost can only come about through the streamlining or elimination of setup activity. Reducing activities reduces actual costs and leads to increased profits.

It should be pointed out that a pure activity-based costing (ABC) approach is not acceptable for external financial reporting. This is because firms using a pure ABC system would treat facility-level costs as period expenses. They are certainly not attached to units produced. However, GAAP requires that units produced absorb some of this overhead. As a result, ABC is used internally for management decision making.

Once management believes the cost data are adequate and the initial profit computation is completed, they will want to ask further questions. These might relate to what the managers will do with the profitability information. A very high profit might signal that the plain-paper fax machine is overpriced—leaving the door open for competitors. A low or even negative product profit may signal the need to start looking for a replacement—one with higher potential. Declining profit, coupled with the knowledge that customers dislike curled faxes, may lead management to discontinue the thermal-paper fax machine even with the positive profit it shows. This would free up resources for production of the next generation of fax machines. Alternatively, a low-profit product may be kept if customers like dealing with a company that offers a full line of products. Management requires data on profitability to aid in sales mix decisions.

Divisional Profit

Just as companies want to know the relative profitability of different products, they may want to assess the relative profitability of different divisions of the company. Divisional profit is often used in evaluating the performance of managers. Failure to earn a profit can lead to the division's closing. For example, the Saturn subsidiary of General Motors Corp., like all other GM subsidiaries, must make a profit. After a 1992 loss of $700 million, Saturn set its sights on breaking even in 1993, then moving into the black.[8]

Divisional profit may be calculated using any of three approaches described in the preceding section. Usually, the absorption-based approach is used and a share of corporate expense is allocated to each division to remind them that all expenses of the company must be covered. Suppose that Polyglyph Inc. is a conglomerate with four divisions, Alpha, Beta, Gamma, and Delta. Corporate expenses of $10 million are allocated to each division on the basis of sales. The divisional income statements are as follows.

	Alpha	Beta	Gamma	Delta	Total
Sales	$90	$60	$30	$120	$300
Less: COGS	35	20	11	98	164
Gross profit	$55	$40	$19	$ 22	$136
Less: Division expense	20	10	15	20	65
Less: Corporate expense	3	2	1	4	10
Operating income	$32	$28	$ 3	$(2)	$ 61

---

8.   Neal Templin, "GM's Saturn Subsidiary Is Fighting for its Future," *The Wall Street Journal,* June 16, 1993, p. B4.

How might Polyglyph view these results? Clearly, Delta has an operating loss. Corporate would raise questions about Delta's continuing viability. If Delta has good potential for an improved profit picture, for example, it might be afforded additional time to turn a profit. Delta's divisional expenses are relatively high. Perhaps this is due to an ambitious research and development program. If pay-offs from this program can be anticipated, corporate management will be much less concerned than if the divisional expenses do not have potential. Corporate management will also be concerned with trends over time and the immediate and long-term prospects for each division. Even a seemingly profitable division, like Alpha, may need attention if it is in a declining industry or if it uses significantly more resources than indicated by the corporate expense allocation. Additional material on divisional profitability and responsibility accounting are covered in the chapter on decentralization and responsibility accounting.

Customer Profitability

While customers are clearly important to profit, some are more profitable than others. Companies that assess the profitability of various customer groups can more accurately target their markets and increase profits. The first step in determining customer profitability is to identify the customer. The second step is to determine which customers add value to the company.

The identification of a company's customer may seem obvious. Grocery stores and automobile repair shops can easily identify their customers, and may even know them by name. However, frequently the company is part of a complex chain of customer relationships. For example, Weldcraft Products, Inc., produces welding torches that are sold to distributors, retail stores, and, eventually, companies and individuals which use the torches to weld. Weldcraft determined that its main customer is distributors, and it used that information to examine each of the company's activities, reducing those which did not add value to distributors purchasing welding torches. For example, the time Weldcraft salespeople devote to customer contact has been reallocated so that they now spend much of their time with distributors.[9]

Originating and Keeping Customers Once customer groups have been identified, the second step is to determine which customer groups are most profitable and work to keep the existing customers in those groups and to add more of them. Sometimes the company may need to add an initially unprofitable customer group and increase efficiency to make the group profitable. The highly competitive personal computer industry is finding that out. Gateway was initially very successful selling personal computing systems to technically inclined customers. These customers know the difference between RAM and ROM; they can easily assemble their own components into a working computer. However, the company's explosive growth has meant that less technically inclined customers have become a large proportion of the customer base. This new type of customer causes Gateway to incur additional costs. The early computer-savvy customer required relatively little technical support. The new customer base knows how to operate a computer, but wants the hardware preselected and configured in a package, the software installed by the company, and one-on-one help in trouble-

---

9.   Ellen Graham, "Meat and Potatoes: Sometimes the Most Successful Courses Are the Most Basic," *The Wall Street Journal*, September 10, 1993, p. R5.

shooting problems. An important part of keeping these customers happy—so that they will continue to upgrade within the Gateway line—is good technical support. Gateway has had to greatly increase the number of technical support personnel who work with buyers on the 1-800-number.[10] Just as important in keeping the profits up in this environment is finding ways to keep the costs down, by improving quality control and simplifying the written instructions that accompany the new computer.

It is generally more costly to win a customer than to keep a customer. Originating a customer may require advertising, sales calls, the drafting of proposals, and the generation of prospective customers lists. All of these activities are costly. Keeping existing customers happy also requires effort. For example, many stores provide free gift wrapping—a service to the customer who has already made a purchase. Firms must have profitability data to understand the profit contribution of customer relationships, to match the costs of increased service with the benefits. Many companies are now taking a customer life-cycle approach, by recognizing that a loyal customer will yield significant revenue over the years. For example, the lifetime revenue stream of a pizza eater can be $8,000. For more expensive products, like a Cadillac, the amount approaches $332,000.[11]

Finally, some customers are so unprofitable that they should not be kept. Rice Lake Products, Inc., manufactures movable owl and geese decoys. The company sold to both specialty stores and to Wal-Mart. However, the Wal-Mart sales, at $19 each, infuriated the specialty stores that charged $20. Even worse from Rice Lake Products' point of view was that the profit on a Wal-Mart sale averaged just $.50 while the profit on a specialty store sale amounted to $4. The reason for the difference was that Wal-Mart required special packaging and promotion and returned product that did not sell. The company chose to concentrate on sales to specialty stores.[12]

Relational data bases and improved accounting systems can greatly assist the effort to track customer profitability. Profitability analysis of various customer classes requires information on product and marketing and administrative activities used to serve each class. Let's analyze Barton, Inc., a manufacturer of highly realistic model horses that are sold to three classes of customer: large discount chains, small independent toy stores, and hobbyists. Each model is made of high-density plastic, from a detailed mold. A team of designers ensures that the design is accurate for the breed depicted. Color pigments are deep and rich. While Barton produces many designs, they all incur roughly the same manufacturing costs. Exhibit 15-11 provides manufacturing and marketing data.

Each class of customer places different demands on Barton. The large toy chains purchase 63 percent of the output. They receive price discounts averaging $1.25 per unit and are linked to Barton through electronic data interchange. As a result, when supplies at the chains run low, an order is transmitted electronically to Barton's factory and another shipment of models dispatched. No commissions are paid on chain store sales. However, Barton must pay each chain store outlet $1,500 per year for shelf space (this ensures premium shelf position within the stores). There are 75 outlets. Barton pays shipping costs. The chain stores are not particular about which models are shipped; therefore, Barton typ-

10.   Lois Therrien, "Why Gateway Is Racing to Answer on the First Ring," *Business Week,* September 13, 1993, pp. 92–94.

11.   James L. Heskett, Thomas O. Jones, Gary W. Loveman, W. Early Sasser, Jr., and Leonard A. Schlesinger, "Putting the Service-Profit Chain to Work," *Harvard Business Review,* March/April 1994, pp. 164–174.

12.   Christie Brown, "A Great Way to Retire," *Forbes,* October 9, 1995, pp. 96–97.

Exhibit 15-11

Information for Barton, Inc.

Units produced	500,000
Average price per model	$15
Manufacturing expenses:	
Direct materials per unit	$5
Direct labor per unit	3
Overhead per unit	1
Marketing expenses:	
Commissions (per model sold)	$.75
Special packaging per unit	.20
EDI costs per year	$100,000
Fair expense	75,000
Shipping	157,500
Shelf space charges	112,500

ically sends whatever is in stock at the time. There is no special packaging involved.

The independent toy stores are smaller and typically stock upscale toys with a heavily educational flavor. About 35 percent of Barton's production is sold to them. No price discounts are given to these stores, and no shelf space is paid. However, a sales commission of $0.75 per unit sold is paid to independent whole-sale jobbers who sell to the stores. The stores pay any shipping cost from Barton's factory. The independent toy stores prefer models with a story attached. For example, a series of models of Indian war horses with accompanying explanatory booklets and special packaging were quite popular. Therefore, Barton attempts to ship all models with special packaging to the independents.

The final 2 percent of Barton's sales take place at the summer fairs. Each summer Barton stages five Model Fairs around the United States. Fun and colorful, the fairs are designed to display the Barton models, to provide a meeting opportunity for model horse hobbyists, and to generate interest in the Barton product. Barton reserves meeting rooms at a hotel for two days, invites local area hobbyists to put on shows and demonstrations, and sets up a series of trading booths for model horse fanciers. Several of Barton's staff (designers, the president, the vice president of marketing) attend to chat with customers, answer questions, and display (and sell) the latest models. To generate additional interest in the fairs, a special model available only at that summer's fair is designed and produced. The special model requires 150 hours of design time (at $14 per hour) and one setup (costing $1,000).

Given this information, we can analyze profitability by customer class. Exhibit 15-12 provides profit statements for each class of customer. The chain stores yield the most revenue, but it must be adjusted for discounts. Expenses directly attributable to the chain store outlets include shelf space payments, shipping charges, and the cost of the electronic data interchange equipment and personnel. The independent toy stores receive no price discount, but do require the payment of commissions and special packaging. The fairs have the lowest revenue, and expenses consist of fair expense, special design, and setup.

Clearly, the chain stores are the most profitable, followed by the independent toy stores. The fairs are unprofitable. An activity-based analysis can give Barton's management a better idea of which activities to emphasize and where cost cutting might occur. For example, the fairs are money losers on the basis of sales. Perhaps management might consider them promotional activity and not a cus-

Exhibit 15-12

Profit from Chain Stores

Sales	$4,725,000
Less: Discounts	(393,750)
Net sales	$4,331,250
Less: COGS	2,835,000
Gross profit	$1,496,250
Less: Shelf space	(112,500)
Shipping	(157,500)
EDI	(100,000)
Profit	$1,126,250

Profit from Independent Toy Stores

Sales	$2,625,000
Less: COGS	1,575,000
Gross profit	$1,050,000
Less: Commissions	(131,250)
Special packaging	(35,000)
Profit	$ 883,750

Profit from Fairs

Sales	$150,000
Less: COGS	90,000
Gross profit	$ 60,000
Less: Fair expense	(75,000)
Design time	(2,100)
Setup	(1,000)
Loss	$ (18,100)

tomer class at all. In fact, the major objective of the fairs is to stimulate interest in the entire Barton line, not merely to sell 10,000 models. Thus, the entire cost of the fairs could be added to overall marketing expense.

These activity-based data can also give management a good idea of the cost of expanding into one area and away from another. For example, should Barton sell to one more chain outlet if it is at capacity? Each chain outlet averages sales of 4,200 models (315,000/75 outlets). These 4,200 models would not be sold to the independent toy stores. The analysis is as follows:

Revenue from additional outlet	$63,000
Less: Discount	5,250
Net additional revenue	$57,750
Less: COGS	37,800
Shipping	2,100
Shelf space	1,500
Profit from added outlet	$16,350

The profit from selling 4,200 models to independent toy stores would be:

Revenue	$63,000
Less: COGS	37,800
Special packaging	840
Commission	3,150
Profit from independent toy stores	$21,210

Barton should continue to sell to the independent toy stores, as the outlet chains are less profitable.

Activity-based accounting can provide data on these marketing activities, which are important in customer profitability analysis. However, it is important to remember that activities alone do not cause costs. Other factors such as time, business volumes, and earlier decisions may lead to efficiencies or inefficiencies.

Example of Customer Profitability Analysis in a Service Company BZW Securities, the investment arm of Barclays Bank in the United Kingdom, developed an ABC model of service profitability.[13] BZW executes trades for clients and also trades on its own account. Thus, it has two sources of profit: net commissions on customer trades and gains (or losses) on its own trades. Like many securities firms, BZW had difficulty tracing revenues and costs to particular trades. As a result, managers could not determine whether or not certain customers were profitable. For example, customers of BZW can call brokers at the firm to obtain market research, trading advice, trading services, and so on. The cost to BZW of providing each service differs. However, clients are not charged on the basis of which services they use, or even how much of the service they use. Clients are charged only commissions on stocks bought and sold. In general, a commission of 0.20 percent is charged on the price of each trade, so if a customer buys £50,000 of stock, the commission is £100 (£50,000 × .002). It is easy to see that a customer who requires significant market advice yet trades only £10,000 may be less profitable than a customer who requires the same amount of market advice but trades £100,000. To remedy this problem, BZW created an activity-based model to track revenues and costs to each trading transaction.

After all the data on customer trades, costs, and revenues were collected, BZW segmented customers into four classes. The first class consists of customers with adequate profit levels and the potential for increased trading volume. Customers in this class are targeted for additional contact by BZW's senior people. The second class is composed of customers who are profitable at their current mix of services but unlikely to respond to attempts to upgrade. The current mix of services is maintained for these clients. The third class of customers includes those customers whose revenues do not fully cover costs but whose marginal revenue does contribute to fixed overhead and who do have the potential for upgrade. Discussions with these clients may lead to upgraded volume or to a reduction in the services least valued by the clients. In other words, BZW attempts to increase the profitability of this class through frank discussion and

13.   Information in this section was taken from Nicolas Stuchfield and Bruce W. Weber, "Modeling the Profitability of Customer Relationships: Development and Impact of Barclays de Zoete Wedd's BEATRICE," *Journal of Management Information Systems,* Fall 1992, Vol. 9, No. 2, pp. 53–76.

decision making. For example, less profitable clients are encouraged to use electronic order entry, an alternative that requires less telephone time with BZW's staff. A further alternative for BZW is to change the mix of services provided to a client by altering the seniority of its staff.

The fourth class is definitely unprofitable and has little potential to improve. BZW has a number of alternatives regarding unprofitable customers. It can try to increase trading volume with that customer, offer fewer services, or increase the commission charged.

Prior to the development of the activity-based costing model, BZW could calculate only the total revenue (commissions) associated with each customer. Individual customer profitability was impossible to calculate, since costs could not be traced to each customer. BZW's management could not assess the effectiveness of its expenditures and service efforts. Now it can assess not only the profitability of each client but also the reasons why.

Overall Profit

The computation of segmental profit is clearly useful in many management decisions. However, the allocation problems inherent in computing profit on divisions, segments, and product lines, may mean that overall profit is most useful in some contexts. It is certainly easiest to compute, and it does have meaning. If the overall profit is consistently positive, the company remains in business, even if one or more segments is losing money. For example, High Flight is a company that engages in three activities: pilot training, short-haul flight services (basically a courier service for regional banks), and airplane leasing. High Flight had real difficulty determining the profitability of each service. The same planes were used for each, so the allocation of airplane depreciation to the three services would seem reasonable. But the owner of High Flight realized that such an allocation would divert attention from the underlying question: Should all three services be offered? Some costs were easily traceable to each segment, e.g., fuel costs and pilot services. Other costs were difficult to allocate; plane depreciation and hangar rent are examples. Ultimately, High Flight performed a modified profitability analysis of each service and determined that flight training was probably a money loser. What did management decide? They kept all three because they realized that pilots preferred to rent planes from the place where they received flight training. Thus, the linkage between flight training and airplane rental meant that the company had to retain both or neither.

TIME AND PROFIT

Objective 5

Describe the impact of the short run and the long run on measuring profit.

short run

long run

The usefulness of profitability analysis depends on the type of decision being made. Time plays an important role. Decisions with only a short-run impact require different information from those having a long-run impact. Of course, the **short run** is the period of time for which at least one cost is fixed. The short run may range from an hour to several years, depending on which costs we are talking about. A factory that purchases more material than is needed for immediate production has a fixed cost for the amount of time (maybe a week) it would take to use up the material. The factory building may be difficult to alter or sell in less than a year. The short run is longer for the building cost. The **long run** is the period of time in which no costs are fixed but are all variable. What does this have to do with profit? Managers and owners are interested in both short-run and long-run profitability.

Short-Run Profitability

A consideration of short-run profitability suggests two possibilities. One is that certain costs and/or revenues will only occur for a period of time and then will change. For example, public accounting firms are thought to charge less on an initial audit of a company in anticipation of a long-run relationship that will lead to greater revenues in future years. This "low-ball" approach to pricing is not applied to all audit jobs. We will look at this situation in more detail in a later section of this chapter on life cycle production. The second possibility is a true one-time situation like the special order of differential costing. The decision to accept a one-time special order means that the price is lower than usual and that certain costs are ignored. Those costs are the fixed costs which will not change if the order is accepted. However, over the long run and for the company as a whole, all costs must be covered. A company cannot exist on special orders alone.

contribution margin

A useful concept for analyzing short-run profits is the **contribution margin**, or the difference between sales and all variable costs. The variable expenses include manufacturing and marketing and administrative expense. Contribution margin is the amount left from sales to cover all fixed expenses and contribute to profit. It is a short-run measure, because only in the short run do fixed costs exist. Contribution margin is important for examining the break-even point and the short-run viability of the firm. While some would argue that the division of costs into fixed and variable parts does not go far enough in describing cost behavior, many firms would find this division at least a start.

cash flow

A short-run measure that is helpful in assessing a firm's immediate future viability is cash flow. **Cash flow** is simply cash inflows minus cash outflows. Financial accounting conventions leading to revenue and expense recognition are ignored. Positive cash flow is necessary to stay in business one more month. It is possible to have negative cash flow and positive net income. In that case, a firm's creditors may force it out of business before the net income turns into cash. As a result, firms consider cash flow critical.

Long-Run Profitability

In the long run, all costs are variable. Net income is a long-run measure, because costs that are fixed in the short run are unitized (through cost of goods sold) and applied to units sold. This approach treats fixed costs of production as variable costs. It reminds the manager that sales must eventually cover all costs. One might think that the long run is just a series of short runs. This has a certain arithmetic appeal but is not true. Basically, actions that are good for the short run may not be good for the long run. For example, a special order, priced just above variable cost, may make sense to the company. However, if other customers learn of the lower price charged on the special order, they may believe that the lower price is the one that should be charged. Similarly, the purchase of substandard materials may improve cash flow this month, while eroding the reputation of the company for quality and increasing future warranty costs. It is important to balance the needs of the short run against the needs of the long run. Consideration of the product life cycle helps us to understand the rhythm of changing time perspectives.

THE PRODUCT LIFE CYCLE

Many products have a predictable profit or product life cycle. Using the marketing viewpoint, the **product life cycle** describes the profit history of the product according to four stages: introduction, growth, maturity, and decline. In the introductory phase, profits are low for two reasons. First, revenues are low as the product gains market acceptance. Second, investment and learning may be high, leading to higher expenses. The growth stage is characterized by increasing market acceptance and sales, as well as economies of scale, which bring down expenses. The product breaks even and profit rises. In the maturity phase, profits stabilize. The product has found its market, and revenues are relatively stable. Investment is down, and all learning effects in production are realized, leading to stable costs. Finally, in the decline phase, the product reaches the end of its cycle, and revenues, and profits, decline. Costs may still be low, but not enough to slip in below sales. Exhibit 15-13 illustrates the interaction of profit and the product life cycle with its four stages of introduction, growth, maturity, and decline.

The product life cycle helps marketers to understand the different competitive pressures on a product in each stage. Thus, it is important for planning purposes. The regularities in manufacturing, costs, and profit make the product life cycle just as important in cost management. Each stage of the product life cycle demonstrates a fairly predictable impact on various types of costs. Exhibit 15-14 summarizes these effects.

How long is the product life cycle? That depends on the product and the environment that the product faces. Television took years to reach maturity, partially due to its introduction during World War II, when necessary technical assets were diverted to the war effort. Video games typically reach maturity very quickly—in a matter of months. Fad products, such as Sourballs, may zip through the product life cycle in a matter of weeks.

Knowledge of the product life cycle is important for cost management. We can easily see the impact of the four stages on marketing and the growth and

Exhibit 15-13
Product Life Cycle

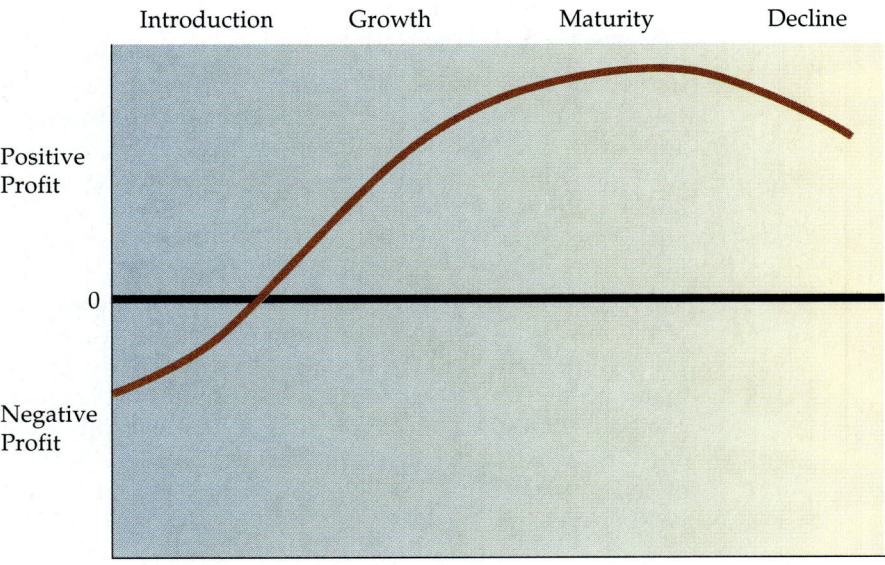

Exhibit 15-14

Impact of the Product Life Cycle on Cost Management

	Introduction	*Growth*	*Maturity*	*Decline*
Product	Basic design, few models	Some improvements, expanding product line	Proliferation of product lines, extensive differentiation	Minimal changes, reduced number of product lines
Learning effects	High costs, much learning, but little payoff	Still strong, learning begins to reduce costs	Stable production, little to no learning	No learning, labor as efficient as it can be
Setups	Few, but new and unfamiliar	More, as new models are introduced	Many, as product differentiation occurs	Fewer, as only best selling lines are produced
Purchasing	May be high as new materials and suppliers are sought	Lower, reliable suppliers found, few materials changes	May be high depending on line changes	Fewer suppliers and orders as existing inventories are liquidated
Marketing expense	Low selling and distribution cost to small number of target markets	Increased advertising and distribution	Supportive advertising, increased trade discounts, high distribution cost	Minimal advertising, distribution, and promotion

decline of sales. Less obvious is the impact on the cost side. Manufacturing must be aware of the impact of newness on costs. Any time a new product is introduced, there are learning effects. In other words, as you make more of the product, you become better at it. Purchasing locates and becomes familiar with suppliers of the needed raw materials. Manufacturing learns to set up more quickly and efficiently the equipment for a new batch. The industrial engineers are able to "work the bugs out" of the process. The whole production process smoothes out and becomes faster and more efficient—and less expensive. However, that is not the whole story. As we can see in Exhibit 15-14, the maturity phase is marked by extensive product differentiation as line extensions proliferate. Mattel's Barbie is a venerable 36 years of age—but we're not just talking basic Barbie and Ken anymore. Barbie's changed. Her arms and legs are bendable, and her hair is any number of lengths and colors. She has a dizzying array of outfits. Each version requires different materials and setups. In addition, Barbie and Ken have *lots* of friends—each with different production requirements. With each decade's new cohort of little girls, Barbie and Ken may be in the maturity phase for quite some time to come.

The product life cycle has implications for activity-based costing. Recall that ABC categories are unit level, batch level, product level, and facility level. Unit-level costs are highest in the introduction phase, as new materials are sought in small order quantities. In addition, direct labor is higher per unit as labor learns how to manufacture the new item. Unit-level costs begin to fall in the growth phase as learning takes effect and quantity discounts on materials may occur.

Similarly, the maturity phase should lead to stable unit-level costs. The decline phase, with fewer units produced, does not enjoy quantity discounts, but unit costs may remain low due to the liquidation of existing inventories and the avoidance of increasing prices.

Batch-level costs follow a similar pattern. Purchasing, receiving, setups, and inspection are high in the introductory phase due to unfamiliarity. In the growth phase, batch-level costs should decrease as the positive impact of learning occurs. Workers are better able to execute setups, for example. In the maturity phase, batch-level costs may increase as product differentiation occurs. Setup number and complexity increase, purchasing orders rise, and inspection costs may increase. Finally, in the decline stage, batch-level costs again fall as product lines are streamlined to just a few best-selling lines and batches decrease in number and complexity.

Product-level costs are highest in the introductory phase and generally fall throughout the rest of the life cycle—with possible spikes upward for new models in the maturity phase. An example is engineering change orders, which occur most frequently when the product is started into production. Facility-level costs may or may not be affected unless the product calls for a new facility or equipment—then, they are highest in the introductory phase. Exhibit 15-15 depicts the general direction of costs in the ABC categories throughout the product life cycle.

THE IMPACT OF PROFIT ON BEHAVIOR

Objective 7
Describe the impact of profits on behavior.

The existence of profit has a strong impact on people's behavior. Predictably, individuals prefer profit to loss. Their jobs, promotions, and bonuses may depend on the annual profit, and this dependence can affect their behavior in expected and unexpected ways. As accountants, it is important to realize that profit measurement can lead to different incentives for individuals to work harder and to act ethically.

Behavioral Decision Theory

Recent work by researchers in behavioral decision theory can give us some idea of the way people feel about profits and losses.[14] A knowledge of these feelings can give us insight into the incentives that earning a profit or loss provides, and to their impact on people's behavior.

Recall that in economics, expected utility theory is used to describe the amount of utility, or value, people place on goods. Let's review some of the basics

Exhibit 15-15
Product Life Cycle Costs in the ABC Categories

	Product Life Cycle Phase			
ABC Category	*Introduction*	*Growth*	*Maturity*	*Decline*
Unit-level costs	High	Lower	Low to stable	Low
Batch-level costs	High	Lower	Higher	Low
Product-level costs	High	Lower	Low to stable	Low
Facility-level costs	High	Low	Low	Low

14.   This section is not meant to be a technical or complete explanation of behavioral decision theory or of prospect theory, which is the underlying theory discussed. Instead, we present only an introduction. Those who wish additional information may want to read "Prospect Theory: An Analysis of Decision Under Risk," by D. Kahneman and A. Tversky in *Econometrica*, Vol. 47, 1979, pp. 263–291.

of expected utility theory. Put simply, economists believe that more is better than less. They also believe that people experience decreasing marginal utility as they receive more and more of a good. For example, your first slice of pizza is wonderful, the second slice good, the third OK, and so on. Each slice has utility, or value, but the value per slice decreases as more and more slices are received. Finally, in expected utility theory, the utility of something is measured at the margin. So, if you receive $10 in the mail (perhaps a gift from your grandmother), you value it in comparison to everything you already own. If your assets equal $1,000, the gift has a certain amount of utility. But if your assets equal $10,000, the gift has somewhat less utility.

prospect theory

Prospect theory is an extension of expected utility theory. In prospect theory, more is still better than less and goods are subject to decreasing marginal utility. However, two key differences between prospect theory and expected utility theory are important. First, the value of goods can be measured in relation to a reference point other than total assets. Going back to your grandmother's gift, that $10 can be valued according to some other reference point (like the amount you currently have in your wallet), instead of your overall asset level. This focus on a reference point is important because it encourages us to look at gains and losses apart from total asset position.

The second feature of prospect theory is that people feel losses more deeply than gains. For example, if you lose $10 (maybe it's a windy day and you open your wallet to extract some money and a $10 bill blows away), you typically experience greater unhappiness than the happiness you experienced from receiving the $10 gift. How does this apply to profit? People hate losses and will therefore try to avoid them. Income of $1,000 means more if it can reduce a $1,000 loss to break even than the same $1,000 would mean if it raised net income from $8,000 to $9,000. This helps to explain why companies try to avoid a loss to the extent possible. It also explains management accounting's emphasis on finding the break-even point.

Finally, given that people feel losses more deeply than gains, but that diminishing marginal utility applies to both losses and gains, and that individual profits and losses can be unbundled and experienced separately, prospect theory explains why people like to bunch losses and unbundle gains. Individually profitable products will be spotlighted separately in a firm's annual report while individual losses will be totaled to the extent possible. In this way, the utility associated with each individual gain can be maximized. For example, suppose that you go to the horse races and place a $2 bet on each of ten races. You lose all bets except two; on the fifth race your bet pays $6, and on the tenth race your bet pays $11. How would you describe the afternoon's experience? Would you say that you lost $3 (10 races × $2 less the $17 won)? Not likely. You might mention the $2 bets on the races, but emphasize the $6 and the $11 won—and you probably wouldn't even adjust the winnings for the original $2 bet. Here, you are separating your wins from your losses, since the utility of $6 and the utility of $11 is greater than the utility of $17.

Sometimes firms deliberately take losses. Consider the "big bath" phenomenon. If a firm is already going to take a loss, it will sometimes bunch as many losses as possible into that year. Why? Diminishing marginal utility again provides insight. Gains aren't the only thing subject to diminishing marginal returns, so are losses. Thus, a loss of $1 million is bad, but a loss of $2 million is not that much worse. Why not get it over with? Thus we frequently see new CEOs of troubled firms taking sharp write-offs in the first year. Take the bath, clean up the financial statements, and prepare the way for future profits. Many firms will have to take a charge to profits for retiree health benefits. This could lead to enormous net losses for a number of firms. We can expect to see these firms write off other charges as well, perhaps for increased bad debts reserves, inventory write-offs, and so on. Those smaller write-offs, which might have led to lower net income or even small net losses in prior years (and thus were avoided), will hardly be noticed in the year of massive health benefit charges.

Ethics

People's desire to avoid losses and the taking of a short-run perspective can affect the potential for unethical conduct. Unethical actions can take any number of forms, but basically it comes down to lying. Companies may try to pass off inferior work or materials as high-quality work—worthy of a higher price. Companies may keep two sets of books—for the purpose of cheating on income and inventory taxes. They may overstate the value of inventory in order to understate the cost of goods sold and thereby overstate net income. Leslie Fay, Inc., saw its stock price (and the value of the company) plummet in 1993 when it became known that the company grossly overvalued inventories and net income. It will take years for the company to regain its good reputation.

Companies that value numerical profit above all else should not be surprised if employees act accordingly and do what is in their power to increase the numbers. Not only does this overreliance on numerical profit lead to unethical behavior, it also provides incentives to ignore the less measurable outcomes which might benefit the company. Workers basically look for companies to "put their money where their mouth is." If raises, promotions, and bonuses are awarded only on the basis of profit, employees will work to increase profits. Even if the company says other factors are important (e.g., good corporate citizenship, innovation, and high-quality products), this will be seen as mere lip service.

The ever-present salience of monthly, quarterly, and annual profit and loss statements may cause companies to emphasize short-run results. Too much emphasis on short-run optimization can lead to ethical problems. A solution is to focus on the long run. Companies that take a long-run orientation know that you cannot cheat customers and expect to retain their business. Eventually, shoddy materials and workmanship will be realized by the customer. The customer will go elsewhere, and regaining trust, once lost, is an agonizingly slow process. As a result, ethical people and companies often emphasize the long run as the basis for behavior.

Honesty in sharing profit information (if the information is to be shared) is also important. Hugh Aaron, in a *Wall Street Journal* article wrote:

Before our closely held company opened its books to our employees, everyone thought we were making a killing. When they saw that we had losses as well as profits, they understood how hard it was to consistently stay in the black. Revealing our profits and losses meant that when profits were good, we'd have to, in all conscience, share them. When they were bad, however, we found mutual understanding. No one made demands again. Morale improved, efficiency increased, and profits overall kept climbing."[15]

Many larger companies could take note. For example, management in larger companies may try to understate profits in negotiations with labor unions. This

15.   Hugh Aaron, "Do the Right Thing in Business," *The Wall Street Journal*, June 21, 1993, p. A10.

is not a long-run winning strategy. As Hugh Aaron found out, sharing the unpleasant information about lower profits can lead to increases in profits.

LIMITATIONS OF PROFIT MEASUREMENT

Objective 7

Discuss some of the limitations of profit measurement.

Profit measurement is subject to numerous limitations. Different measures are appropriate for different purposes. Data may be hard to get. In particular, accounting data collected for certain time periods may not be useful in some instances. While many firms want to measure profit on a segment or product line basis, allocations are always a problem. The time frame of a decision may also present difficulties.

Another limitation to profitability analysis is the unpredictability of the economic environment. Consistent profitability, brought about by great management, productive employees, and a high-quality product, does not guarantee success when economic conditions change. At that point, shifts in strategy may prove crucial. For example, Marriott, the hotel and service industry company, grew at a 20 percent annual rate in the 1980s until it was hit by a collapsing real estate market, an oversupply of hotel rooms, and a recession. Marriott changed course and now it is moving into franchising. It plans to move from almost 27% franchised in 1993 to 50% by 1997. Other strategies taken to strengthen its business presence include developing a loyal customer base through Marriott Miles program, consistent marketing, and developing a product in every price category (J W Marriott for the high end, Marriott for business travelers, Courtyard by Marriott for moderate, and Fairfield Inns for the budget traveler).[16] The point is that companies must remain flexible and aware of changing business conditions. Profit measurement tends to focus on past performance, not future performance.

The savvy cost manager is aware of economic and environmental trends outside the company. These can determine the success of management plans. They also help provide a reference point for management in determining whether or not profits are good or bad. A small increase in profit during a recession may signal outstanding performance. The same increase during economic expansion raises doubts about management's ability.

A final limitation is profit's emphasis on quantifiable measures. Henry Ford said that both buyer and seller must be wealthier in some form as a result of a transaction. But must wealth always be measured in money? Some aspects of profit are, no doubt, qualitative. Start-up companies may be thrilled to have made it past the one-year mark. The confidence that comes with being able to successfully start and continue a business is part of their wealth. Many companies give back to their communities; this too is a form of wealth. Let's take another look at the Colorado Rockies. The club is one of the few in major league baseball that earned a profit in 1995. The stadium is full and ticket demand is strong. Why? The Rockies put the fans first. While some tickets sell for five to ten times face value, the team also sells the cheapest seats in the league—in the 2,300-seat section behind center field called the "Rockpile," where a family of four can watch a game for $4. In addition, owner Jerry McMorris plows much of the revenue back into player salaries. As a result, the Rockies reached post-season play faster than any expansion team in baseball history (in three years versus the previous record of eight years). So far, everyone is profiting in Denver baseball.

16.   Faye Rice, "Know When to Change the Game," *Fortune,* June 28, 1994, pp. 101–2.

SUMMARY

An analysis of profitability helps a firm to determine its short- and long-run viability. Profit aids performance evaluation. It signals others regarding opportunities in a particular market. Various measures of profit have been suggested. Absorption costing income measurement is required for external financial reporting. Variable costing and ABC give better signals regarding performance and incremental costs.

Profitability analysis can be accomplished for individual segments. These segments include divisions, product lines, and customer groups. Each analysis adds to management understanding.

The time frame affects profit. Short-run profits differ from long-run profits in that some costs are irrelevant in the short run. As a result, some decisions may be acceptable in the short run (such as the acceptance of a one-time special order). The product life cycle forces management to explicitly consider time and profitability. The four stages of the product life cycle are introduction, growth, maturity, and decline. Each has different implications for costs and revenues.

Profit measurement has a strong impact on behavior. In general, people strive to avoid losses. Ethical behavior may be compromised by overemphasis on profits and short-run optimization.

REVIEW PROBLEM AND SOLUTION

Absorption and Variable Costing; Segmented Income Statements

Acme Novelty Company produces coin purses and key chains. Selected data for the past year are presented below.

	Coin Purses	Key Chains
Production (units)	100,000	200,000
Sales (units)	90,000	210,000
Selling price	$5.50	$4.50
Direct labor hours	50,000	80,000
Manufacturing costs:		
Direct materials	$ 75,000	$100,000
Direct labor	250,000	400,000
Variable overhead	20,000	24,000
Fixed overhead:		
Direct	50,000	40,000
Common[a]	20,000	20,000
Nonmanufacturing costs:		
Variable selling	$ 30,000	$ 60,000
Direct fixed selling	35,000	40,000
Common fixed selling[b]	25,000	25,000

[a] Common overhead totals $40,000 and is divided equally between the two products.
[b] Common fixed selling cost totals $50,000 and is divided equally between the two products.

Budgeted fixed overhead for the year, $130,000, equaled the actual fixed overhead. Fixed overhead is assigned to products using a plantwide rate based on expected direct labor hours, which were 130,000. The company had 10,000 key chains in inventory at the beginning of the year. These key chains had the same unit cost as the key chains produced during the year.

REQUIRED:

1. Compute the unit cost for the coin purses and key chains using the variable costing method. Compute the unit cost using absorption costing.
2. Prepare an income statement using absorption costing.
3. Prepare an income statement using variable costing.
4. Explain the reason for any difference between absorption and variable costing operating incomes.
5. Prepare a segmented income statement using products as segments.

Solution

1. Unit cost for the coin purse is as follows:

Direct materials ($75,000/100,000)	$0.75
Direct labor ($250,000/100,000)	2.50
Variable overhead ($20,000/100,000)	0.20
Variable cost per unit	$3.45
Fixed overhead [(50,000 × $1.00)/100,000]	0.50
Absorption cost per unit	$3.95

The unit cost for the key chain is as follows:

Direct materials ($100,000/200,000)	$0.50
Direct labor ($400,000/200,000)	2.00
Variable overhead ($24,000/200,000)	0.12
Variable cost per unit	$2.62
Fixed overhead [(80,000 × $1.00)/200,000]	0.40
Absorption cost per unit	$3.02

Notice that the only difference between the two unit costs is the assignment of the fixed overhead cost. Notice also that the fixed overhead unit cost is assigned using the predetermined fixed overhead rate ($130,000/130,000 hours = $1 per hour). For example, the coin purses used 50,000 direct labor hours and so receive $1 × 50,000, or $50,000, of fixed overhead. This total, when divided by the units produced, gives the $0.50 per-unit fixed overhead cost. Finally, observe that variable nonmanufacturing costs are not part of the unit cost under variable costing. For both approaches, only manufacturing costs are used to compute the unit costs.

2. The income statement under absorption costing is as follows:

Sales [($5.50 × 90,000) + ($4.50 × 210,000)]	$1,440,000
Less: Cost of goods sold [($3.95 × 90,000) + ($3.02 × 210,000)]	989,700
Gross margin	$ 450,300
Less: Selling expenses*	215,000
Net income	$ 235,300

*The sum of selling expenses for both products.

3. The income statement under variable costing is as follows (on next page):

Sales [($5.50 × 90,000) + ($4.50 × 210,000)]	$1,440,000
Less: Variable expenses:	
Variable cost of goods sold	
[($3.45 × 90,000) + ($2.62 × 210,000)]	860,700
Variable selling expenses	90,000
Contribution margin	$ 489,300
Less: Fixed expenses:	
Fixed overhead	130,000
Fixed selling	125,000
Net income	$ 234,300

4. Variable costing income is $1,000 less ($235,300 − $234,300) than absorption costing income. This difference can be explained by the net change of fixed overhead found in inventory under absorption costing.

Coin purses:	
Units produced	100,000
Units sold	90,000
Increase in inventory	10,000
Unit fixed overhead	× $0.50
Increase in fixed overhead	$5,000
Key chains:	
Units produced	200,000
Units sold	210,000
Decrease in inventory	(10,000)
Unit fixed overhead	× $0.40
Decrease in fixed overhead	$ (4,000)

The net change is a $1,000 ($5,000 − $4,000) increase in fixed overhead in inventories. Thus, under absorption costing, there is a net flow of $1,000 of the current period's fixed overhead into inventory. Since variable costing recognized all of the current period's fixed overhead as an expense, variable costing income should be $1,000 lower than absorption costing, as it is.

5. Segmented income statement:

	Coin Purses	Key Chains	Total
Sales	$495,000	$945,000	$1,440,000
Less: Variable expenses:			
Variable cost of goods sold	310,500	550,200	860,700
Variable selling expenses	30,000	60,000	90,000
Contribution margin	$154,500	$334,800	$ 489,300
Less: Direct fixed expenses:			
Direct fixed overhead	50,000	40,000	90,000
Direct selling expenses	35,000	40,000	75,000
Product margin	$ 69,500	$254,800	$ 324,300
Less: Common fixed expenses:			
Common fixed overhead			40,000
Common selling expenses			50,000
Net income			$ 234,300

KEY TERMS

Absorption costing *621*	Gross profit (gross	Market share variance	Profit *620*
Cash flow *641*	margin) *622*	*629*	Prospect theory *645*
Contribution margin *641*	Long run *640*	Market size variance *629*	Sales mix variance *628*
Contribution margin	Market share *629*	Net income *626*	Sales volume variance
variance *627*	Market size *629*	Operating income *622*	*627*
		Product life cycle *642*	Short run *640*
			Variable costing *624*

QUESTIONS FOR WRITING AND DISCUSSION

1. Why do firms measure profit?
2. Why do regulated firms care about the level of profit?
3. Why would a company avoid earning the highest possible profit in the short run?
4. What is a segment, and why would a company want to measure profits of segments?
5. Suppose that Alpha Company has four product lines, three of which are profitable and one (let's call it "Loser") which generally incurs a loss. Give several reasons why Alpha Company may choose not to drop the "Loser" product line.
6. How does absorption costing differ from variable costing? When will absorption costing operating income exceed variable costing operating income?
7. Is ABC appropriate for external financial reporting? Explain your reasoning.
8. What are some advantages and disadvantages of using net income as a measure of profitability?
9. Describe the product life cycle.
10. How do unit-level costs behave in relation to the product life cycle? Batch-level costs? Product-level costs? Facility-level costs?
11. Why do some firms measure customer profitability? In what situation(s) would a firm not want to measure customer profitability?
12. What are the three major implications of prospect theory for profitability analysis?
13. What is the "big bath," and why would firms want to take one?
14. Carol Jackson is the public relations coordinator for Selmore, Inc., a nationwide chain of retail drug stores. During the past month, Selmore has experienced the following: the construction of two new stores in inner city neighborhoods; theft of restricted drugs by employees; uninsured fire damage in one store; an employee training program, which promises to increase productivity and customer satisfaction; the filing of a suit against Selmore for injuries incurred by a customer who was hit by a car in the parking lot of one store; and operating profits which were twice as high as anticipated in one-third of the stores. How should Carol handle the publicity for these items?
15. There is no point in measuring profit, since numbers cannot tell the whole story. Discuss this statement. Do you agree or disagree with it and why?

EXERCISES AND PROBLEMS

15-1
Reasons for Measuring Profit

LO 1

Janet Evans, Phil Bostian, and Donna Jerrell are graduating seniors at State University. Each has a 3.40 overall GPA. Janet's average for each of her years in college were as follows: freshman year, 2.60; sophomore year, 3.30; junior year, 3.80; senior year, 3.90. Phil's average has been consistently 3.40 since his freshman year. Donna's average started out high in her freshman year (4.00) and then declined to 3.60 in her sophomore year, 3.40 in her junior year, and 2.60 in her senior year.

REQUIRED: As a recruiter, with access only to the above information, would you view Janet, Phil, and Donna as identical? Why or why not? How might you view GPA as akin to profit?

**15-2
Unit Costs;
Inventory
Valuation; Variable
and Absorption
Costing**

LO 2

Jasper Company produced 70,000 units during its first year of operations and sold 65,000 at $8 per unit. The company chose practical activity—at 70,000 units—to compute its pre-determined overhead rate. Manufacturing costs are as follows:

Expected and actual fixed overhead	$140,000
Expected and actual variable overhead	35,000
Direct labor	280,000
Direct materials	105,000

REQUIRED:

1. Calculate the unit cost and the cost of finished goods inventory under absorption costing.
2. Calculate the unit cost and the cost of finished goods inventory under variable costing.
3. What is the dollar amount that would be used to report the cost of finished goods inventory to external parties. Why?

**15-3
Income
Statements;
Variable and
Absorption
Costing**

LO 2

The following information pertains to Elvis, Inc., for last year:

Beginning inventory, units	—
Units produced	10,000
Units sold	8,000
Ending inventory, units	2,000
Variable costs per unit:	
Direct materials	$5.00
Direct labor	3.00
Variable overhead	2.50
Variable selling expenses	3.50
Fixed costs per year:	
Fixed overhead	$20,000
Fixed selling and administrative	25,000

There are no work in process inventories. Normal activity is 10,000 units. Expected and actual overhead costs are the same.

REQUIRED:

1. Without preparing an income statement, indicate what the difference will be between variable-costing income and absorption-costing income.
2. Assume the selling price per unit is $25. Prepare an income statement (a) using variable costing and (b) using absorption costing.

**15-4
Income Statements
and Firm
Performance:
Variable and
Absorption
Costing**

LO 2

Tan Company had the following operating data for its first two years of operations:

Variable costs per unit:	
Direct materials	$4
Direct labor	5
Variable overhead	3
Fixed costs per year:	
Overhead	$120,000
Selling and administrative	20,000

Tan produced 20,000 units in the first year and sold 15,000. In the second year, it produced 15,000 units and sold 20,000 units. The selling price per unit each year was $21. Tan uses an actual cost system for product costing.

REQUIRED:

1. Prepare income statements for both years using absorption costing. Has firm performance, as measured by income, improved or declined from Year 1 to Year 2?
2. Prepare income statements for both years using variable costing. Has firm performance, as measured by income, improved or declined from Year 1 to Year 2?
3. Which method do you think more accurately measures firm performance? Why?

15-5
Absorption and Variable Costing Income Statements
LO 2

Portland Optics Inc. specializes in manufacturing lenses for large telescopes and cameras used in space exploration. Because the specifications for the lenses are determined by the customer and vary considerably, the company uses a job order cost system. Factory overhead is applied to jobs on the basis of direct labor hours, utilizing the absorption (full) costing method. Portland's predetermined overhead rates for 1997 and 1998 were based on the following estimates.

	1997	1998
Direct labor hours	32,500	44,000
Direct labor cost	$325,000	$462,000
Fixed factory overhead	130,000	176,000
Variable factory overhead	162,500	198,000

Jim Bradford, Portland's controller, would like to use variable (direct) costing for internal reporting purposes as he believes statements prepared using variable costing are more appropriate for making product decisions. In order to explain the benefits of variable costing to the other members of Portland's management team, Bradford plans to convert the company's income statement from absorption costing to variable costing. He has gathered the following information for this purpose, along with a copy of Portland's 1997–1998 comparative income statement.

Portland Optics Inc.
Comparative Income Statement
For the Years Ended December 31, 1997 and 1998

	1997	1998
Net sales	$1,140,000	$1,520,000
Cost of goods sold:		
Finished goods at Jan. 1	$ 16,000	$ 25,000
Cost of goods manufactured	720,000	976,000
Total available	$ 736,000	$1,001,000
Finished goods at Dec. 31	25,000	14,000
Unadjusted cost of goods sold	$ 711,000	$ 987,000
Overhead adjustment	12,000	7,000
Cost of goods sold	$ 723,000	$ 994,000
Gross profit	$ 417,000	$ 526,000
Selling expense	150,000	190,000
Administrative expense	160,000	187,000
Operating income	$ 107,000	$ 149,000

Portland's actual manufacturing data for the two years are presented below.

	1997	1998
Direct labor hours	30,000	42,000
Direct labor cost	$300,000	$435,000
Raw materials used	$140,000	$210,000
Fixed factory overhead	$132,000	$175,000

The company's actual inventory balances were:

	12/31/96	12/31/97	12/31/98
Raw materials	$32,000	$36,000	$18,000
Work in process			
Costs	$44,000	$34,000	$60,000
Direct labor hours	1,800	1,400	2,500
Finished goods			
Costs	$16,000	$25,000	$14,000
Direct labor hours	700	1,080	550

For both years, all administrative costs were fixed, while a portion of the selling expense resulting from an eight percent commission on net sales was variable. Portland reports any over- or underapplied overhead as an adjustment to the cost of goods sold.

REQUIRED:

1. For the year ended December 31, 1998, prepare the revised income statement for Portland Optics Inc. utilizing the variable costing method. Be sure to include the contribution margin on the revised income statement
2. Describe two advantages of using variable costing rather than absorption costing.

(CMA adapted)

15-6
Contribution Margin Variance, Sales Volume Variance, Sales Mix Variance

LO 3

Melwin Inc. manufactures coin purses and key chains. Actual results from last year are as follows.

	Coin Purses	Key Chains
Sales (units)	90,000	210,000
Selling price	$5.50	$4.50
Variable expenses	3.70	3.00

Melwin had budgeted the following amounts.

	Coin Purses	Key Chains
Sales (units)	100,000	200,000
Selling price	$5.00	$4.75
Variable expenses	4.00	3.00

REQUIRED:

1. Calculate the contribution margin variance.
2. Calculate the sales volume variance.
3. Calculate the sales mix variance.

15-7
Contribution Margin Variance, Sales Volume Variance, Market Share Variance, Market Size Variance
LO 3

Folsom Fashions sells a line of women's dresses. Folsom's performance report for November follows.

	Actual	Budget
Dresses sold	5,000	6,000
Sales	$235,000	$300,000
Variable costs	145,000	180,000
Contribution margin	$ 90,000	$120,000
Market size (in units)	500,000	550,000

REQUIRED:

1. Calculate the contribution margin variance.
2. Calculate the market share variance and the market size variance.

(CMA adapted)

15-8
Segmented Income Statements; Analysis of Proposals to Improve Profits
LO 2, 4

Shannon, Inc., has two divisions. One produces and sells paper party supplies (napkins, paper plates, invitations); the other produces and sells cookware. A segmented income statement for the most recent quarter is given below.

	Party Supplies Division	Cookware Division	Total
Sales	$500,000	$750,000	$1,250,000
Less: Variable expenses	425,000	460,000	885,000
Contribution margin	$ 75,000	$290,000	$ 365,000
Less: Direct fixed expenses	85,000	110,000	195,000
Segment margin	$ (10,000)	$180,000	$ 170,000
Less: Common fixed expenses			130,000
Net income			$ 40,000

On seeing the quarterly statement, Madge Shannon, president of Shannon, Inc., was distressed. "The party supplies division is killing us," she complained. "It's not even covering its own fixed costs. I'm beginning to believe that we should shut down that division. This is the seventh consecutive quarter it has failed to provide a positive segment margin. I was certain that Paula Kelly could turn it around. But this is her third quarter, and she hasn't done much better than the previous divisional manager."

"Well, before you get too excited about the situation, perhaps you should evaluate Paula's most recent proposals," remarked Bob Ferguson, the company's vice president of finance. "She wants to spend $10,000 per quarter for the right to use familiar cartoon figures on a new series of invitations, plates, and napkins and at the same time increase the advertising budget by $25,000 per quarter to let the public know about them. According to her marketing staff, sales should increase by 10 percent if the right advertising is done—and done quickly. In addition, Paula wants to lease some new production machinery that will increase the rate of production, lower labor costs, and result in less waste of materials. Paula claims that variable costs will be reduced by 30 percent. The cost of the lease is $95,000 per quarter."

Upon hearing this news, Madge calmed considerably and, in fact, was somewhat pleased. After all, she was the one who had selected Paula and had a great deal of confidence in Paula's judgment and abilities.

REQUIRED:

1. Assuming that Paula's proposals are sound, should Madge Shannon be pleased with the prospects for the party supplies division? Prepare a segmented income statement for the next quarter that reflects the implementation of Paula's proposals. Assume that the cookware division's sales increase by 5 percent for the next quarter and that the same cost relationships hold.
2. Suppose that everything materializes as Paula projected except for the 10 percent increase in sales—no change in sales revenues took place. Are the proposals still sound? What if the variable costs are reduced by 40 percent instead of 30 percent with no change in sales?

**15-9
Impact of
Inventory Changes
on Absorption
Costing Income,
Divisional
Profitability**

LO 2, 4

Dana Bard was manager of a new medical supplies division. She had just finished her second year and had been visiting with the company's vice president of operations. In the first year, the net income for the division had shown a substantial increase over the prior year. Her second year saw an even greater increase. The vice president was extremely pleased and promised Dana a $5,000 bonus if the division showed a similar increase in profits for the upcoming year. Dana was elated. She was completely confident that the goal could be met. Sales contracts were already well ahead of last year's performance, and she knew that there would be no increases in costs.

At the end of the third year, Dana received the following data regarding operations for the first three years:

	Year 1	Year 2	Year 3
Production	10,000	11,000	9,000
Sales (in units)	8,000	10,000	12,000
Unit selling price	$10.00	$10.00	$10.00
Unit costs:			
Fixed overhead*	$2.90	$3.00	$3.00
Variable overhead	1.00	1.00	1.00
Direct materials	1.90	2.00	2.00
Direct labor	1.00	1.00	1.00
Variable selling	0.40	0.50	0.50
Actual fixed overhead	$29,000	$30,000	$30,000
Other fixed costs	$ 9,000	$10,000	$10,000

*The predetermined fixed overhead rate is based on expected actual units of production and expected fixed overhead. Expected production each year was 10,000 units. Any under- or overapplied fixed overhead is closed to Cost of Goods Sold.

	Yearly Income Statements		
	Year 1	Year 2	Year 3
Sales revenue	$80,000	$100,000	$120,000
Less: Cost of goods sold*	54,400	67,000	86,600
Gross margin	$25,600	$ 33,000	$ 33,400
Less: Selling and administrative	12,200	15,000	16,000
Net income	$13,400	$ 18,000	$ 17,400

*Assumes a LIFO inventory flow.

Upon examining the operating data, Dana was pleased. Sales had increased by 20 percent over the previous year, and costs had been kept stable. However, when she saw the yearly income statements, she was dismayed and perplexed. Instead of seeing a significant increase in income for the third year, she saw a small decrease. Surely the Accounting Department had made an error.

REQUIRED:

1. Explain to Dana why she lost her $5,000 bonus.
2. Prepare variable costing income statements for each of the three years. Reconcile the differences between the absorption costing and variable costing incomes.
3. If you were the vice president of Dana's company, which income statement (variable costing or absorption costing) would you prefer to use for evaluating Dana's performance? Why?

**15-10
Ethical Issues;
Absorption
Costing;
Performance
Measurement**
LO 2, 7

Bill Fremont, division controller and CMA, was upset by a recent memo he received from the divisional manager, Steve Preston. Bill was scheduled to present the division's financial performance at headquarters in one week. In the memo, Steve had given Bill some instructions for this upcoming report. In particular, he had been told to emphasize the significant improvement in the division's profits over last year. Bill didn't believe, however, that there was any real underlying improvement in the division's performance and was reluctant to say otherwise. He knew that the increase in profits was because of Steve's conscious decision to produce for inventory.

In an earlier meeting, Steve had convinced his plant managers to produce more than they knew they could sell. He argued that by deferring some of this period's fixed costs, reported profits would jump. He pointed out two significant benefits. First, by increasing profits, the division could exceed the minimum level needed so that all the managers would qualify for the annual bonus. Second, by meeting the budgeted profit level, the division would be better able to compete for much-needed capital. Bill had objected but had been overruled. The most persuasive counterargument was that the increase in inventory could be liquidated in the coming year as the economy improved. Bill, however, considered this event unlikely. From past experience, he knew that it would take at least two years of improved market demand before the productive capacity of the division was exceeded.

REQUIRED:

1. Discuss the behavior of Steve Preston, the divisional manager. Was the decision to produce for inventory an ethical one?
2. What should Bill Fremont do? Should he comply with the directive to emphasize the increase in profits? If not, what options does he have?
3. In Chapter 1, ethical standards for management accountants were listed. Identify any standards that apply in this situation.

**15-11
Segmented Income
Statements;
Adding and
Dropping Product
Lines**
LO 2, 4

Louise Bordner has just been appointed manager of Palmroy's glass products division. She has two years to make the division profitable. If the division is still showing a loss after two years, it will be eliminated, and Louise will be reassigned as an assistant divisional manager in another division. The divisional income statement for the most recent year is given below.

Sales	$5,350,000
Less: Variable expenses	4,750,000
Contribution margin	$ 600,000
Less: Direct fixed expenses	750,000
Divisional margin	$ (150,000)
Less: Common fixed expenses (allocated)	200,000
Divisional profit (loss)	$ (350,000)

Upon arriving at the division, Louise requested the following data on the division's three products:

	Product A	Product B	Product C
Sales (units)	10,000	20,000	15,000
Unit selling price	$150	$140	$70
Unit variable cost	$100	$110	$103.33
Direct fixed costs	$100,000	$500,000	$150,000

She also gathered data on a proposed new product (Product D). If this product is added, it would displace one of the current products. The quantity that could be produced and sold would equal the quantity sold of the product it displaces, although demand limits the maximum quantity that could be sold to 20,000 units. Because of specialized production equipment, it is not possible for the new product to displace part of the production of still another product. The information on Product D is as follows:

Unit selling price	$	70
Unit variable cost		30
Direct fixed costs	640,000	

REQUIRED:

1. Prepare segmented income statements for Products A, B, and C.
2. Determine the products that Louise should produce for the coming year. Prepare segmented income statements that prove your combination is the best for the division. By how much will profits improve given the combination that you selected? (Hint: Your combination may include one, two, or three products.)

15-12
Net Income for
Segments
LO 2, 4

Dorman, Inc., manufactures and sells water heaters through three divisions: Southwest, Midwest, and Northeast. Each division is evaluated as a profit center. Data for each division for last year are as follows:

	(in thousands of dollars)		
	Southwest	*Midwest*	*Northeast*
Sales	$1,800	$940	$1,235
COGS	1,080	710	740
Selling and administrative expense	200	180	340

Dorman, Inc., had corporate administrative expenses equal to $150,000; these were not allocated to the divisions.

REQUIRED:

1. Prepare a segmented income statement for Dorman, Inc., for last year.
2. Comment on the performance of each of the divisions.

15-13
Time Perspective;
Not-for-Profit
Considerations
LO 5, 8

In October, Tom and Jeanette Hines opened their own real estate agency in Little Creek, a small town in the Pacific Northwest. Due to heavy start-up expenses (e.g., renting and refurbishing the office and running advertisements for listed properties) and low revenues (the real estate agency receives no fee until a property is sold), Tom and Jeanette must watch every penny. In November, Susan Scott, a senior at Little Creek High School, approached Jeanette about purchasing an ad in the high school yearbook. Jeanette said no. As she explained to Tom later, "We just can't afford any unnecessary expenditures. Besides, no high school kid is going to buy real estate." Tom reacted with surprise, "I didn't know you'd already turned her down. When Susan asked me, I said 'sure' and bought a quarter-page ad."

REQUIRED:

1. Was Jeanette taking a short-run or long-run view of profitability? Explain your reasoning.
2. Explain why Tom decided to purchase the ad. Was his view short-run or long-run? Why?
3. Discuss any relevant considerations other than profit that might apply to the Hines's decision regarding the ad.

**15-14
Product
Profitability**

LO 4

Porter Insurance Company has three lines of insurance: automobile, property, and life. The life insurance segment has been losing money for the past five quarters, and Leah Harper, Porter's controller, has done an analysis of that segment. She has discovered that the commission paid to the agent for the first year the policy is in place is 55 percent of the first-year premium. The second-year commission is 20 percent, and in all succeeding years, a commission equal to 5 percent of premiums is paid. No salaries are paid to agents, however, Porter does advertising on television and in magazines. Last year the advertising expense was $500,000. The loss rate (payout on claims) averages 50 percent. Administrative expenses equal $450,000 per year. Revenue last year was $10,000,000 (premiums). The percentage of policies of various lengths is as follows:

First year in force	65 percent
Second year in force	25 percent
More than two years in force	10 percent

Experience has shown that if a policy remains in effect for more than two years, it is rarely canceled.

Leah is considering two alternative plans to turn this segment around. Plan 1 requires spending $250,000 on improved customer service in hopes that the percentage of policies in effect will take on the following distribution:

First year in force	50 percent
Second year in force	15 percent
More than two years in force	35 percent

Total premiums would remain constant at $10,000,000, and there are no other changes in fixed or variable cost behavior.

Plan 2 involves dropping the independent agent and commission system and having potential policyholders phone in requests for coverage. Leah estimates that revenue would drop to $7,000,000. Commissions would be zero, but administrative expenses would rise by $1,200,000, and advertising (including direct mail solicitation) would increase by $1,000,000.

REQUIRED:

1. Prepare a variable costing income statement for last year for the life insurance segment of Porter Insurance Company.
2. What impact would Plan 1 have on income?
3. What impact would Plan 2 have on income?

**15-15
Customer
Profitability, Life
Cycle Revenue**

LO 3, 5

Refer to the original data in *15-14.* Fred Morton has just purchased a life insurance policy from Porter with premiums equal to $1,500 per year.

REQUIRED:

1. Assuming Fred holds the policy for one year and then drops it, what is his contribution to Porter's operating income?

2. Assuming Fred holds the policy for three years, what is his contribution to Porter's operating income in the second and third years? Over a three-year period? What implications does this hold for Porter's efforts to retain policyholders?

**15-16
Customer
Profitability**
LO 4

Olin Company manufactures and distributes carpentry tools. Production of the tools is in the mature portion of the product life cycle. Olin has a sales force of 20. Salespeople are paid a commission of 7 percent of sales plus expenses of $35 per day for days spent on the road away from home plus $0.30 per mile. They deliver product in addition to making the sales, and each salesperson is required to own a truck suitable for making deliveries.

For the coming quarter, Olin estimates the following:

Sales	$1,300,000
Cost of goods sold	450,000

On average, a salesperson travels 6,000 miles per quarter and spends 38 days on the road. The fixed marketing and administrative expenses total $400,000 per quarter.

REQUIRED:

1. Prepare an income statement for Olin Company for the next quarter.
2. Suppose that a large hardware chain, MegaHardware, Inc., wants Olin Company to produce its new SuperTool line. This would require Olin Company to sell 80 percent of total output to the chain. The tools will be imprinted with the SuperTool brand, requiring Olin to purchase new equipment, to use somewhat different materials, and to reconfigure the production line. Olin's industrial engineers estimate that cost of goods sold for the SuperTool line would increase by 15 percent. No sales commission would be incurred, and MegaHardware would link Olin to its EDI system. This would require annual cost of $100,000 on the part of Olin. MegaHardware would pay shipping. As a result, the sales force would shrink by 80 percent. Should Olin accept MegaHardware's offer? Support your answer with appropriate calculations.

**15-17
Life Cycle
Profitability**
LO 6

Shangri-La Videos is marketing a new line of wellness-oriented videotapes. These videotapes emphasize proper nutrition, low-impact exercise, and stress reduction techniques. Shangri-La's marketing director (and president), Sherry Benson, believes that a comprehensive marketing campaign to introduce the videotapes will be necessary. Sherry has estimated the following marketing costs:

Commission	3 percent of undiscounted price
Market testing	$7,000 per city
Rebates:	
Fixed cost to print the certificates	$625
Variable cost to redeem each certificate	$7.50
Advertising:	
Quarter 1	$25,000
Quarter 2	$50,000
Quarters 3 through 7	$20,000 per quarter
Quarter 8	none

The market testing will occur during the first quarter. Sherry believes that conducting tests in three cities will be sufficient to gather feedback regarding the video.

Sherry estimates that the total cost of writing the script and producing the master for the videotape will come to $55,000. The cost of copying a new videotape from the master and packaging and shrink-wrapping it will be $3 per tape. The videotape market is fickle and competitive. Sherry believes that the wellness tape can be sold for at most 8 quarters.

Her estimates of unit sales for each quarter are as follows:

Quarter	Unit Sales
1	5,000
2	15,000
3	27,000
4	30,000
5	30,000
6	30,000
7	15,000
8	2,000

In Quarters 1 through 7, the videotape will be priced at $20. In Quarter 8, the price will decrease to $10 and no commission will be paid. In Quarter 1, the rebate certificate will be attached. Customers who buy the videotape and mail in the certificate (with original cash register receipt) will receive $5 by return mail. Past experience indicates that only 25 percent of the customers eligible for the rebate will take advantage of it. (The remaining 75 percent who do not claim the rebate are referred to as "slippage." The company counts on a hefty amount of slippage when offering a generous rebate program.)

REQUIRED:

1. Tell which phase of the product life cycle for the wellness videotape applies to each quarter.
2. Prepare income statements for each quarter for the eight quarters. (You may round all amounts to the nearest $1,000.) Is the videotape profitable in each quarter? Overall?

15-18
Time Perspective,
Life Cycle
Profitability

LO 5, 6

Cherokee County National Bank (CCNB) is a small, well-regarded bank in the Midwest. The focus of a number of articles on innovative banking practices, CCNB's president, Reggie Thurman, often points out that the bank must grow and change in order to survive in a dynamic world.

A decade ago, CCNB decided to move into electronic banking. Customers were offered the opportunity to call the bank to authorize payments to their creditors. The bank would then cut the checks and mail them to the creditors. To avail themselves of this service (called telecheck), customers filled out a form listing all of their creditors with appropriate account numbers and addresses. A sample form is shown below for Barbara and Bill Randall, who have a checking account with CCNB.

Customer Name	Barbara and/or William Randall
Address	208 E. Fordham Drive, Cherokee City, ST 12345
Checking Account Number	443-816

1. VISA   Acct. No. 112-4458730596
   P. O. Box 123
   Big City, TX 00000
2. Cherokee County Public Utility   Acct. No. 23415
   1714 W. 8th Street
   Cherokee City, ST 12344
3. Midwest Bell Telephone   Acct. No. 504-555-1212
   P. O. 4412
   Houston, TX 09045
4. Cherokee Cablevision   Acct. No. 83-6672
   12 Main St.
   Cherokee City, ST 12344

Continued

5. Madeline's Clothing   Acct. No. none
   101 Second Avenue
   Cherokee City, ST 12344

When Barbara wanted to pay bills during the month, she simply called the telecheck number, read in her account number, the creditor number, and the dollar amount of the check. She could bundle all the bills into one call, or space them throughout the month. CCNB guaranteed that checks would be mailed to her creditors within three working days. The fee for this service was $1 per month.

REQUIRED:

1. Assess the profitability of the telecheck service from the bank's point of view. From Barbara and Bill's point of view.
2. Why do you suppose that the bank offered the telecheck service at such a low price? Relate this price to the product life cycle.

**15-19
Profits and
Behavior**

LO 7

Howard Davis was recently named manager of Loristar, Inc.'s largest division. The division has had a lackluster performance record but Howard believes that it has real potential for improvement. Loristar's president has given Howard three years to turn the division around and offered him the chance to earn a hefty annual bonus based on improvements in operating income. If Howard can improve divisional performance during the three-year period, he is virtually guaranteed the post for many years. This type of job could groom him for succession to president or CEO.

Howard was delighted, until the end of his first week on the job. The division was in worse shape than he thought. Inventory was obsolete, and machinery was old and required significant repair and maintenance (expenditures the previous division head had postponed). Sales were below average, and the sales force seemed to lack enthusiasm.

REQUIRED: Discuss the approach Howard might take to improving divisional performance. Should his approach be short-run or long-run oriented? How will the structure of his bonus affect his behavior?

**15-20
Case on Variable
Costing,
Absorption
Costing,
Segmented
Reporting**

LO 2, 4

The Clock Division of Thurmond Company produces both wall clocks and table clocks. The clocks are sold in two regions, the West and the Southwest. The table below gives the sales of the Clock Division during 1997 (in units).

	West	Southwest	Total
Wall clocks	100,000	250,000	350,000
Table clocks	250,000	520,000	770,000

Production data for 1997 are as follows (there were no beginning or ending work in process inventories):

	Wall Clocks	Table Clocks
Production	300,000	800,000
Direct labor hours	30,000	40,000
Manufacturing costs:		
Direct materials	$450,000	$720,000
Direct labor	210,000	200,000
Variable overhead	60,000	90,000
Fixed overhead*	360,000	540,000

*Common fixed overhead of $280,000 has been allocated to the two products on the basis of actual direct labor hours and is included in each total.

The selling prices are $4.50 for wall clocks and $3 for table clocks. Variable nonmanufacturing costs are 20 percent of the selling price for wall clocks and 30 percent of the selling price for table clocks. Total fixed nonmanufacturing costs are $300,000: one-third common to both products and one-third directly traceable to each product. Of the fixed costs (both manufacturing and nonmanufacturing), 20 percent are common to both sales regions, 40 percent are directly traceable to the West, and 40 percent are directly traceable to the Southwest.

Overhead is applied on the basis of direct labor hours. Normal volume is 75,000 hours (300,000 wall clocks, 900,000 table clocks), and the preceding actual overhead figures correspond to the budgeted figures used to compute the predetermined overhead rate. Any under- or overapplied overhead is closed to Cost of Goods Sold. Assume that any beginning finished goods inventory has the same unit costs as current production. The company uses LIFO to value inventories.

REQUIRED:

1. Compute the unit costs for each product using (a) absorption costing and (b) variable costing.
2. Prepare absorption costing and variable costing income statements for 1997. Reconcile the difference between the two income figures.
3. Prepare a segmented income statement on a variable costing basis where segments are defined as products.
4. Prepare a segmented income statement on a variable costing basis where segments are defined as sales regions.

15-21
Case on
Segmented
Reporting and
Variances
LO 3, 4, 7

Pittsburgh-Walsh Company (PWC) is a manufacturing company whose product line consists of lighting fixtures and electronic timing devices. The Lighting Fixtures Division assembles units for the upscale and mid-range markets. The Electronic Timing Devices Division manufactures instrument panels that allow electronic systems to be activated and deactivated at scheduled times for both efficiency and safety purposes. Both divisions operate out of the same manufacturing facilities and share production equipment.

PWC's budget for the year ending December 31, 1998, is shown below and was prepared on a business segment basis under the following guidelines.

a. Variable expenses are directly assigned to the incurring division.
b. Fixed overhead expenses are directly assigned to the incurring division.
c. The production plan is for 8,000 upscale fixtures, 22,000 mid-range fixtures, and 20,000 electronic timing devices. Production equals sales.

PWC Budget
For the Year Ending December 31, 1998
(in thousands)

| | Lighting Fixtures | | Electronic | |
	Upscale	Mid-range	Timing Devices	Total
Sales	$1,440	$770	$800	$3,010
Variable expenses:				
Cost of goods sold	720	439	320	1,479
Selling and administrative	170	60	60	290
Contribution margin	$ 550	$271	$420	$1,241
Fixed overhead expenses	140	80	80	300
Segment margin	$ 410	$191	$340	$ 941

PWC established a bonus plan for division management that required meeting the budget's planned net income by product line, with a bonus increment if the division exceeds the planned product line net income by ten percent or more.

Shortly before the year began, the CEO, Jack Parkow, suffered a heart attack and retired. After reviewing the 1998 budget, the new CEO, Joe Kelly, decided to close the lighting fixtures mid-range product line by the end of the first quarter and use the available production capacity to grow the remaining two product lines. The marketing staff advised that electronic timing devices could grow by 40 percent with increased direct sales support. Increases above that level and increasing sales of upscale lighting fixtures would require expanded advertising expenditures to increase consumer awareness of PWC as an electronics and upscale lighting fixtures company. Kelly approved the increased sales support and advertising expenditures to achieve the revised plan. Kelly advised the divisions that for bonus purposes the original product line net income objectives must be met, but he did allow the Lighting Fixtures Division to combine the net income objectives for both product lines for bonus purposes.

Prior to the close of the fiscal year, the division controllers were furnished with preliminary actual data for review and adjustment, as appropriate. These preliminary year-end data reflect the revised units of production amounting to 12,000 upscale fixtures, 4,000 mid-range fixtures, and 30,000 electronic timing devices and are presented below.

PWC Preliminary Actuals
For the Year Ending December 31, 1998
(in thousands)

| | Lighting Fixtures | | Electronic | |
	Upscale	Mid-range	Timing Devices	Total
Sales	$2,160	$140	$1,200	$3,500
Variable expenses				
Cost of goods sold	1,080	80	480	1,640
Selling and administrative	260	11	96	367
Contribution margin	$ 820	$ 49	$ 624	$1,493
Fixed overhead expenses	140	14	80	234
Segment margin	$ 680	$ 35	$ 544	$1,259

The controller of the Lighting Fixtures Division, anticipating a similar bonus plan for 1999, is contemplating deferring some revenues to the next year on the pretext that the sales are not yet final, and accruing in the current year expenditures that will be applicable to the first quarter of 1999. The corporation would meet its annual plan, and the division would exceed the ten percent incremental bonus plateau in the year 1998 despite the deferred revenues and accrued expenses contemplated.

REQUIRED:

1. Outline the benefits that an organization realizes from segment reporting. Evaluate segment reporting on a variable cost basis versus an absorption cost basis.
2. Calculate the contribution margin, sales volume, and sales mix variances.
3. Explain why the variances occurred.

(CMA adapted)

Chapters 10–15

Dalcogene, Inc., is a small biotechnology company which was founded in 1986 by Ed Corey and Brianna Dalhart. Dalcogene uses genetic engineering to develop and manufacture pharmaceuticals that attack specific diseases. Ed and Brianna are excited to learn that the company has just received FDA approval to market a new drug, sucratase, which halts the progress of Dexter's disease. Dexter's disease is a rare disorder that results from a sudden inability of the body to break down and utilize complex sugars from food. The result is a painful buildup of sugars, which eventually (in three to five years) leads to death. Sucratase provides the missing enzyme enabling the body to metabolize the sugars and allows victims of Dexter's disease to lead a normal life.

Sucratase is the fifth drug to be developed by Dalcogene. The first four drugs are variations of existing hormones and chemotherapy. An income statement for last year is as follows.

Income Statement	
Dalcogene, Inc.	
For the Year Ending December 31	
(in thousands)	
Sales	$368,000
Less: Sales discounts	18,000
Net sales	$350,000
Cost of goods sold	192,500
Gross profit	$157,500
Marketing expense	35,000
Administrative expense	5,000
Research and development	30,000
Operating income	$ 87,500
Income taxes	31,500
Net income	$ 56,000

Shortly after learning of the FDA approval, Ed and Brianna met to discuss the production and marketing of sucratase.

Ed: It sure is good to have the approval on sucratase! We've got to swing into production right away and get the drug to the Dexter's disease patients. I've gotten six phone messages already this morning from doctors who need to start their patients on sucratase.

Brianna: You're right, Ed. What a relief that the research phase is behind us. I've talked with Mike in production. He started amassing the raw material in anticipation of approval. He tells me we can begin processing in a couple of days and should be up to full speed in three months.

Ed: OK, now let's determine the amount of production needed, the relevant costs, and the price.

Brianna: I'm way ahead of you, Ed. I asked Marylou in Accounting to project the cost figures and Paul in Marketing to get me projected demand. Here's Marylou's memo on costs.

MEMORANDUM

TO: Brianna Dalhart
FROM: Marylou Anderson
RE: Projected Costs for Sucratase

After talking with Mike in Production, I've put together a listing of the manufacturing costs that we normally include in the unit cost of each drug. As you know, sucratase is an unusually expensive drug to manufacture. The extraction of the protein needed to generate the enzyme requires large amounts of the cambium, or inner bark, of the southern catalpa tree. We have located sources of the tree in Central and South America. Logging companies must cut the trees and have them debarked and the cambium layer split out, chipped, and bathed in preservative within 24 hours of cutting. Drums of the preserved chips are sent to our facilities. Then we process the cambium chips, remove the protein, and develop sucratase. Considering the current number of patients with Dexter's disease, 1,100, and the fact that each one will need to take a dose of sucratase intravenously every two weeks, I have projected the following annual manufacturing costs.

Materials	$42,185,000
Labor cost	4,661,800
Allocated overhead and R&D	1,773,200
Manufacturing cost	$48,620,000

These are the manufacturing costs we normally assign to each drug, so it is easy to calculate a per-dose cost of $1,700. I might add that the only truly variable costs are for materials; labor, overhead, and R&D are fixed.

These costs do not included marketing. I was less comfortable with projecting those costs on a per dose basis. A major problem here is that some of the selling costs depend on the sales price. Commissions for the drug retailers, for example, usually run about 5 percent of sales. I suggest you talk with Paul first, to see what price range we're talking about.

Finally, let's not forget about return on investment. I know Ed wants the company to sell more stock to finance a new manufacturing facility. Right now, our return on investment is pretty average for a biotechnology company. Last year we earned 15 percent ROI on assets of $373 million. I think we need to consider a healthy profit on sucratase in order to shore up our rate of return and make the stock offering attractive. Call me if you need any more information.

Ed: Wow! Seeing the costs in black and white sure makes a difference. Do you realize that if each dose costs $1,700, and the average patient needs one every two weeks, then the cost per patient per year is $44,200—and that's just manufacturing cost—it doesn't even include administrative and selling expense!

Brianna: I know! Thank goodness for health insurance. I talked with Paul as soon as I got Marylou's memo. He says she's right about the number of Dexter's disease patients. He's been surveying doctors in anticipation of today's news and tells me that of the 1,100, 75 percent are privately insured and their insurance companies will have to cover sucratase. There is no other treatment for Dexter's disease; sucratase stops it, and the drug is not experimental. Another 15 percent are covered by Medicaid. We'll have to negotiate with the states on reimbursement. Based on past experience, I'd anticipate a Medicaid discount of roughly 12 percent. Still, we'll be able to sell the drug—again, it's not experimental. Finally, the remaining 10 percent don't have health insurance and aren't on Medicaid.

There's no way they can afford this drug; we'll have to do something about them. We can't withhold a lifesaving drug just because people can't afford it.

Ed: You're right. I think we can handle the bottom 10 percent through our free drug program. We've faced this problem before, and Paul can figure out how to check eligibility and get sucratase to the appropriate people.

Now, about pricing. Don't we normally triple manufacturing cost to take care of the corporate and selling expenses? If we do that here, the price will be $5,100 per dose. Boy, that's high! Get Paul—and Marylou. We need to talk about this.

A little later, Paul Jenkins (Vice President of Marketing) and Marylou Anderson (Corporate Controller) joined Ed and Brianna.

Paul: I never really thought the price would be over $5,000 per dose—that's $132,600 per year for just one patient. I'll get heat from the insurance companies on this—not to mention senators and representatives in Washington! Marylou, are you sure about those figures?

Marylou: I'm sure. I've been over and over them. The problem is the processing cost. There's no way to whittle that down. It's an expensive drug. In addition, I think the marketing and distribution expenses will be higher than normal. With a drug this costly and used by so few people, we'll have to spend extra time educating doctors on the availability and use of sucratase. We'll also have to spend lots of extra time with insurance companies. Then there's the free drug program. Paul, how had you planned to manage that?

Paul: You've got a point, Marylou. With prices this high, I may need to hire a full-time social worker to manage the free drug program—to advise doctors, coordinate the patient paperwork, and approve the drug donation. Salary and ancillary costs of the program could run $75,000 per year, and that's not including the value of the drug itself. As far as normal marketing costs go, we usually pay drug retailers a commission of 5 percent of the undiscounted price. With the price as high as this will be, they should be happy with that. About the only other marketing cost associated with sucratase would be additional marketing and distribution expense of $400,000 a year.

Marylou: Does that distribution expense vary with the amount of drug shipped or is it pretty much a fixed cost?

Paul: It's fixed. I'll have to hire additional marketing staff for sucratase, publish and distribute explanatory booklets and educational materials, and advertise in medical journals.

Brianna: Given the high price of the drug, Paul, could we lower the sales commission—say to 3 percent?

Paul: No way, Brianna. While the commission is high in absolute dollars per dose, so few patients are involved that there will be relatively little sold. In addition, this drug has no potential to be used for any other disease. Besides, you've told me that after a year on sucratase, patients can cut back the dosage by half, so sales will decrease the second year. In fact, if the drug reverses the disease, third year usage could decline, too. Mel, in the lab, thinks that could happen. I think a conservative estimate would be that use of sucratase would decline by half again in the third year, then stabilize. No, I don't think a reduction in commission will be acceptable to the sales force. They are independents and can simply refuse to handle our work.

Ed: Okay, Paul, you're right on the decrease in use. So we've agreed that marketing expense will be higher than average for sucratase. Any other considerations? Marylou, review the basis for tripling the manufacturing cost to get a price.

Marylou: Sure, Ed. Basically, drug revenue has to cover all costs involved in research and development, manufacturing, selling and distribution, administration and, finally, make a contribution to profit. Tripling the manufacturing costs seems high, but remember that we don't get the entire price from some patients. There are Medicare and Medicaid rebates and free drugs. Of course, the remaining revenue needs to cover that. Also, we have high research and development expenses. The general research we do each year runs in the millions of dollars. Of course, much of that will not result in an approved drug. In fact, when you look at the development of sucratase, we've spent over $50 million to date. Next year's budgeted R&D is $42.5 million, $12.5 million allocable to sucratase.

There are corporate and marketing costs to be allocated, too. Last year, fixed marketing and administrative costs were about $22.5 million. If they remain at that level this year, sucratase ought to cover its fair share. We could allocate those costs based on revenue, but we don't have a price for sucratase yet. So maybe a rough estimate would be that 20 percent of the total could be allocated to sucratase in addition to the $400,000 Paul already mentioned.

Another factor to consider is our return on investment. Last year's 15 percent isn't that great. Now Ed says he'd like to sell another issue of stock. Frankly, Ed, I think you'll have problems with ROI at 15 percent. Many investors are uncomfortable with biotechnology companies returning less than 25 percent. They think the risk is just too great.

Ed: You're right about the new stock issue. Not only is the processing of catalpa cambium outrageously expensive, if we keep up our demand for this tree, we'll run into deforestation problems. If we could build a state-of-the-art biogenetic manufacturing facility, we would manufacture sucratase much more cheaply. We could genetically alter sugar cane cells to generate the enzyme glucosucratase and get totally away from the need to obtain catalpa wood. The use of the cells would not require destroying a whole tree. Well, that's in the future. Let's settle on the price of sucratase and then meet again in a week or so to talk about the new plant.

Brianna: I'm all in favor of meeting again on the plant. Let's set the price of sucratase initially at $5,100 per dose and then adjust it as needed. If we can generate some profit on sucratase, we can justify the new plant and reduce costs and price.

One month later, Ed, Brianna, Marylou, and Mike Elcar (Production Manager) met in Ed's office to discuss the proposed new manufacturing facility.

Ed: Brianna, you've met with our attorneys and investment bankers. Could you fill us in on that meeting?

Brianna: Sure, Ed. Basically, that meeting confirmed what Marylou told us last month. She said we'd need a higher ROI to interest investors, and our investment bankers concur. They suggest an ROI of at least 25 percent. Frankly, I think that's higher than it should be, but investors are convinced that this business is particularly risky. We definitely need thorough documentation on the costs and benefits of the new plant.

Mike: I think that new plant is a sure thing. The architects and contractor estimate cost of $50 million. The exciting part, though, is what the new facility can do to manufacturing costs. Once we get it on line, the processing costs of sucratase will decrease dramatically.

Brianna: That's right, Mike. The new facility will enable us to move to a more truly biogenetically engineered product. We won't need discarded catalpa trees any more. We can insert genes designed to produced glucosucratase, the enzyme of sucratase, into sugar cane cells and those cells will produce the sucratase. It's wonderful—no more contracting with logging companies and worrying about freight problems! No more huge drums of chips swimming in preservative! In addition, quality control is tighter and the chance of viral infection will be zero.

Marylou: I checked the cost savings and they are as dramatic as Mike indicated. We should be able to reduce the materials and labor cost I originally estimated for sucratase production by 85 percent—that's actual cash savings. Of course, overhead will be higher at first, as we add the new plant's depreciation. Assuming a useful life of 5 years, and in bioengineering a state-of-the-art plant won't stay state-of-the-art much longer than that, annual overhead should amount to $26 million. Still, I think that any analysis of the project from a capital budgeting standpoint will be very favorable. I'm preparing a net present value analysis for the bankers using a discount rate of 25 percent, which reflects the higher risk investors place on our type of company.

Ed: Sounds good. Let's get the analyses prepared, meet with the investment bankers and start this project.

REQUIRED:

1. Using the markup-on-cost-of-goods-sold approach to pricing, what percent markup on manufacturing cost is usually used by Dalcogene, Inc., in its initial pricing of new drugs? What costs are included in the markup? Why do you suppose that Dalcogene uses a general markup on cost to price drugs?

2. Discuss the pricing of sucratase. What are the determinants of demand? Do you suppose the price elasticity of demand is relatively more elastic or inelastic and why? Are there any ethical problems with setting the price of sucratase at $5,100 per dose?

3. Generate a life-cycle income statement for sucratase. Include the development phase and the first five years of sales.

4. Prepare a variable costing income statement for last year, assuming that the variable cost of goods sold is 20 percent of total cost of goods sold, and that the only other variable expense is sales commissions at 5 percent of sales. Calculate the break-even point in revenue for Dalcogene for last year. What was Dalcogene's margin of safety for last year?

5. Prepare a variable costing income statement for Dalcogene for this year assuming that data for the original four drugs remain the same and that Dalcogene markets sucratase according to plan. Calculate the break-even point in revenue for Dalcogene for this year (including sucratase). What is the anticipated margin of safety this year? Why doesn't it make any sense to calculate the break-even point for sucratase alone?

6. How did Marylou come up with the 15 percent ROI for last year? What is Dalcogene's budgeted ROI for this year, including sales of sucratase and the other four drugs?

7. For the new manufacturing facility that Dalcogene is considering building, calculate the payback period, net present value (use a discount rate of 26 percent), and internal rate of return. Is Dalcogene's enthusiasm about the new facility supported by your results? Supposing that the new plant cost $65 million, would it be a good investment? How does a high discount rate work against the acceptance of new high-technology projects?

COST MANAGEMENT IN ACTION:
The New Manufacturing Environment

*I*n this section, ten photos are presented that provide some glimpses of the new manufacturing environment. The photos illustrate the production processes of Cincinnati Milacron, a manufacturer of plastics machinery. Cincinnati Milacron builds injection molding machines. These injection machines have flexible manufacturing capabilities and are used to produce a variety of plastic products. In making their products, Cincinnati Milacron uses automated production cells, JIT manufacturing practices, total quality control, and emphasizes continuous improvement. The first photo illustrates the product produced by Cincinnati Milacron and the second photo illustrates the kind of plastic products that can be produced by injection molding machines. The next eight photos show the manufacturing cells used to produce the injection machines. Many of the cells are used to produce major subassemblies for the injection machines. As you examine the photos, try to envision the cost management issues that would exist in this environment.

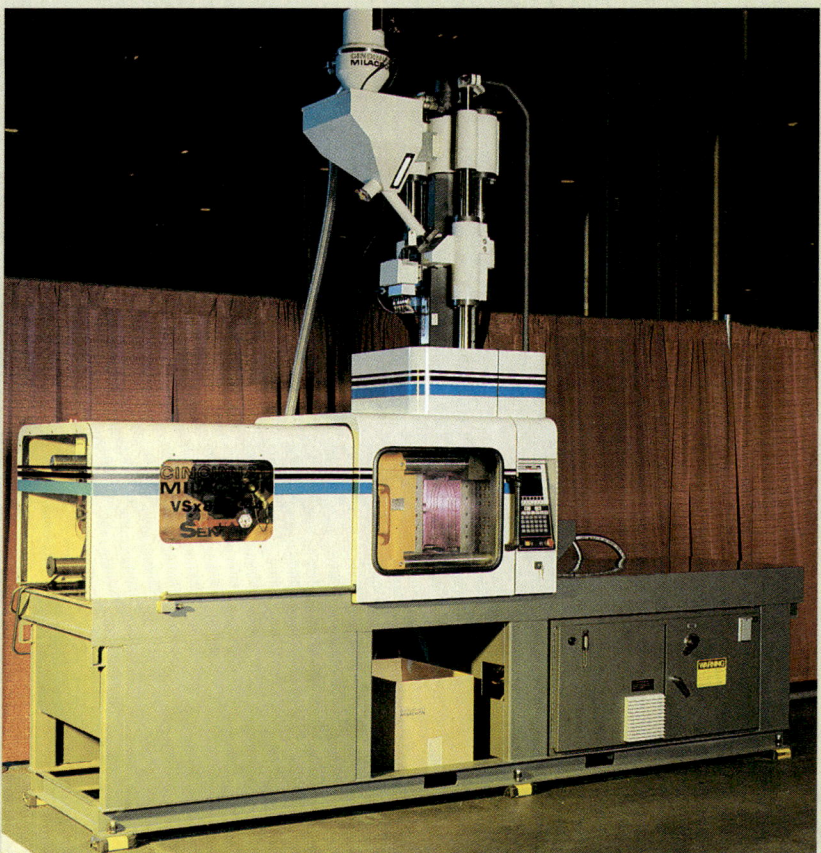

There are a variety of plastic products that can be produced by the injection machines. This photo illustrates finished plastics products ranging from ice trays to tooth brushes. How would you assign the costs of the machine to individual products?

This photo shows a small injection molding machine. Milacron produces a wide variety of injection unit sizes. Notice the control panel on this machine. This panel provides a variety of menus that allow the user to change setup configurations for up to 40 molds. All production functions can be controlled from the panel, including an automatic quality monitoring system. Alarm limits can be set to flag excessive variation. Consider how this automated system has solved the setup time and quality problems that are faced by many plastic products manufacturers using more traditional production methods.

Raw materials used in the production of the injection machine are shown here. As you might imagine, raw materials would be a significant percentage of the total cost of the injection machines. Since Cincinnati Milacron uses automated production cells, the direct labor content would be a much smaller percentage. But what about overhead costs? These costs would be a much higher percentage of total product cost. Consider what the overhead costs would be as you examine the photos illustrating the manufacturing cells.

Each injection machine rests on a base. In this base cell, the bases for all sizes of injection machines are produced. Thus, more than one type of base is produced in this cell. In many cell configurations, only one type of product of subassembly is produced. In this case, the cell produces more than one subassembly. How does this affect product costing? How would you assign costs to each type of base?

The injection unit inserts the raw plastic into the system. This unit controls the injection rates and pressures that are used to produce the plastic products. How would you use a JIT manufacturing system to control the rate of production for injector units?

671

This cell produces the hydraulic module for the injection machines. Cincinnati Milacron emphasizes the compact, simple design of the system. It also emphasizes its energy efficiency and the lack of noise and vibration. What do these features have to do with postpurchase costs? Can they provide a competitive advantage for Cincinnati Milacron?

The motor that runs the hydraulic system is produced in this cell. The motor is advertised as having long-term, reliable, and highly efficient operation. Performance quality is emphasized. Obviously, Milacron considers quality as an important competitive dimension. Can you think of ways that Cincinnati Milacron can measure and report quality to determine if its claims concerning the motor are valid?

This photo illustrates the construction of the power panel. This microprocessor panel is the brain of the flexible injection machine system. The microprocessor has the following features: 40 mold internal data storage, integral machine/control diagnostics, process monitoring and alarms, and an alarm/data log. From this panel, the user controls setups and production functions. Think about how this manufacturing flexibility affects cost accounting and cost control. How long must a manager wait, for example, to receive information about variability in product specifications?

The clamp module is the machine component that allows for mold changes. Cincinnati Milacron emphasizes an innovative clamp design that increases part-to-part consistency and cycle time. Notice how quality and time-based competition are accepted as being important and form a key part of the advertising for the injection machines. Suppose that the Milacron machines do provide faster cycle time and more part consistency. As a customer of Milacron, how would you know this? Should the accounting information system play a role in this analysis?

Clamp, injection, and base assemblies come together for final assembly and testing. Here, machines, after being assembled, are tested with customers' molds and resins before being shipped to customers' plants for installation. Is this testing activity a value-added or non-value-added activity?

673

Part 4
Cost Planning and Control Systems

Chapter 16
Budgeting for Planning and Control

Budgeting at Birkenstock must start with anticipated sales around the world and extend through production, marketing, and administrative planning.

LEARNING OBJECTIVES

After studying this chapter, you should be able to:

1. Define budgeting and discuss its role in planning, controlling, and decision making.
2. Prepare the operating budget, identify its major components, and explain the interrelationships of the various components.
3. Identify the components of the financial budget and prepare a cash budget.
4. Identify and discuss the key features that a budgetary system should have to encourage managers to engage in goal-congruent behavior.
5. Describe budgets for merchandising and service firms and zero-base budgeting.

Failure to plan, either formally or informally, can lead to financial disaster. Managers of businesses, whether small or large, must know their resource capabilities and have a plan that details the use of these resources. Careful planning is vital to the health of any organization.

THE ROLE OF BUDGETING IN PLANNING AND CONTROL

Objective 1
Define budgeting and discuss its role in planning, controlling, and decision making.

budgets
control

Budgeting plays a crucial role in planning and control. Plans identify objectives and the actions needed to achieve them. **Budgets** are the quantitative expressions of these plans, stated in either physical or financial terms or both. When used for planning, a budget is a method for translating the goals and strategies of an organization into operational terms. Budgets can also be used in control. **Control** is the process of setting standards, receiving feedback on actual performance, and taking corrective action whenever actual performance deviates significantly from planned performance. Thus, budgets can be used to compare actual outcomes with planned outcomes, and they can steer operations back on course, if necessary.

Exhibit 16-1 illustrates the relationship of budgets to planning, operating, and control. Budgets evolve from the long-run objectives of the firm; they form the basis for operations. Actual results are compared with budgeted amounts through control. This comparison provides feedback both for operations and for future budgets.

Purposes of Budgeting

Budgets are usually prepared for areas within an organization (departments, plants, divisions, and so on) and for activities (sales, production, research, and so on). This system of budgets serves as the comprehensive financial plan for the organization as a whole and gives an organization several advantages.

1. It forces managers to plan.
2. It provides resource information that can be used to improve decision making.
3. It aids in the use of resources and employees by setting a benchmark that can be used for the subsequent evaluation of performance.
4. It improves communication and coordination.

Budgeting forces management to plan for the future—to develop an overall direction for the organization, foresee problems, and develop future policies. When managers spend time planning, they grow to understand the capabilities of their businesses and where the resources of the business should be used. All businesses and not-for-profit entities should budget. All large businesses do budget. In fact, the budgeting activity of a company such as Conoco or IBM consumes significant amounts of time and involves many managers at a variety of levels. Some small businesses do not budget, and many of those go out of business in short order.

Budgets convey significant information about the resource capabilities of an organization, making better decisions possible. For example, a cash budget points out potential excesses and deficiencies of cash. If the company has extra cash, managers can invest it in short-term investments, rather than leaving it idle. A cash deficiency, on the other hand, may suggest the importance of improved accounts receivable collection.

Exhibit 16-1
The Master Budget and Its Interrelationships

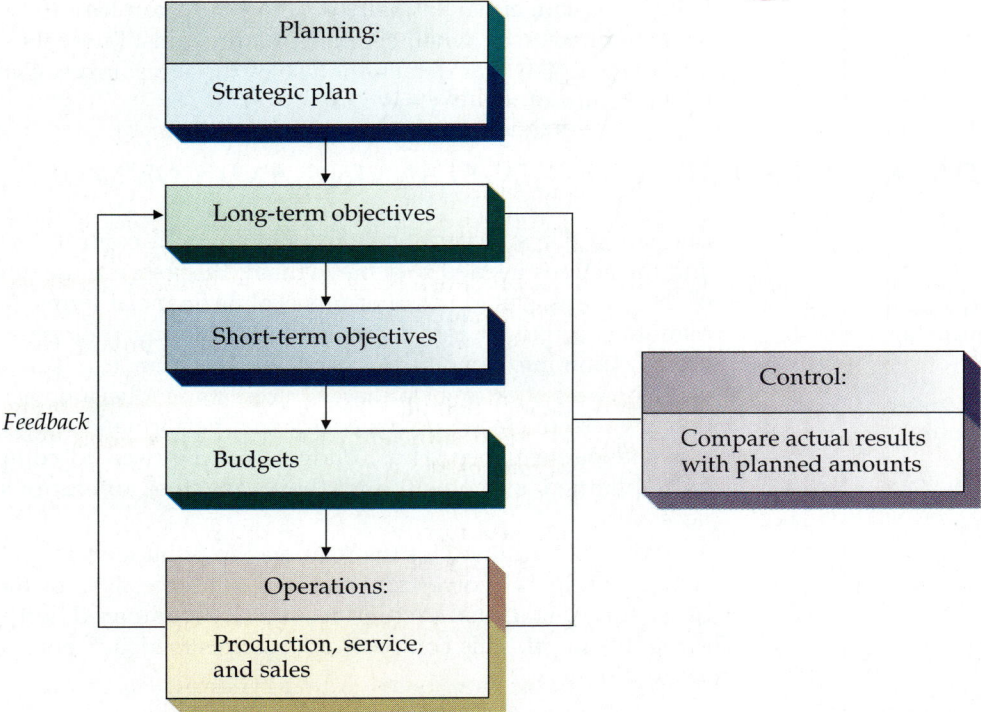

Budgets also set standards that can control the use of a company's resources and control and motivate employees. Fundamental to the overall success of a budgetary system, control ensures that steps are being taken to achieve the objectives outlined in an organization's master plan.

Budgets also serve to communicate the plans of the organization to each employee and to coordinate their efforts. Accordingly, all employees can be aware of their role in achieving those objectives. This is why explicitly linking the budget to the long-run plans of the organization is so important. The budget is not a series of vague, rosy scenarios, but a set of specific plans to achieve those objectives. Budgets encourage coordination because the various areas and activities of the organization must all work together to achieve the stated objectives. The role of communication and coordination becomes more important as an organization increases in size. Birkenstock, for example, sells its shoes both in Europe and the United States. Careful planning in production, distribution, and marketing is critical to the success of an international firm.

The Budgeting Process

The budgeting process can range from the fairly informal process undergone by a small firm, to an elaborately detailed, several-month procedure employed by large firms. Key features of the process include directing and coordinating the compilation of the budget.

budget director

budget committee

Directing and Coordinating Every organization must have someone responsible for directing and coordinating the overall budgeting process. This **budget director** is usually the controller or someone who reports to the controller. The budget director works under the direction of the budget committee. The **budget committee** has the responsibility to review the budget, provide policy guidelines and budgetary goals, resolve differences that may arise as the budget is prepared, approve the final budget, and monitor the actual performance of the organization as the year unfolds. The budget committee also has the responsibility to ensure that the budget is linked to the strategic plan of the organization. The president of the organization appoints the members of the committee, who are usually the president, vice presidents, and the controller.

Large companies with multiple divisions must have budgets for each division. Within a division, a budget is prepared for each subdivision. For example, Patton, Inc., owns three companies which are operated as profit centers. Each company must prepare a budget for the coming year. These budgets are then sent to corporate headquarters where they are consolidated with the overall corporate budget. Patton, Inc., went through a leveraged buyout two years ago, and so cash flow and certain financial ratios are critically important to ensure that the corporation does not default on its bonds. If the initial budgets for the three companies do not yield sufficient cash flow to pay bond interest on time, corporate headquarters returns the budgets with directions to improve them, e.g., by cutting costs, increasing sales, and so on. This process may be repeated until the budgets meet corporate satisfaction. At that point, the final budget becomes the plan for the coming year.

Types of Budgets When we refer to the company's budget for the year, we are talking about the master budget. The **master budget** is a comprehensive financial plan made up of various individual departmental and activity budgets. A master budget can be divided into *operating* and *financial* budgets. **Operating budgets** are concerned with the income-generating activities of a firm: sales, production, and finished goods inventories. The ultimate outcome of the operating budgets is a pro forma or budgeted income statement. Note that "pro forma" is synonymous with "budgeted" and "estimated." In effect, the pro forma income statement is done "according to form" but with estimated, not historical, data. **Financial budgets** are concerned with the inflows and outflows of cash and with financial position. Planned cash inflows and outflows are detailed in a cash budget, and expected financial position at the end of the budget period is shown in a budgeted, or pro forma, balance sheet. Exhibit 16-2 illustrates the components of the master budget.

The master budget is usually prepared for a one-year period corresponding to the company's fiscal year. The yearly budgets are broken down into quarterly and monthly budgets. The use of shorter time periods allows managers to compare actual data with budgeted data as the year unfolds and to make timely corrections. Because progress can be checked more frequently with monthly budgets, problems are less likely to become too serious.

Most organizations prepare the budget for the coming year during the last four or five months of the current year. However, some organizations have developed a continuous budgeting philosophy. A **continuous (or rolling) budget** is a moving twelve-month budget. As a month expires in the budget, an additional month in the future is added so that the company always has a twelve-month plan on hand. Proponents of continuous budgeting maintain that it forces managers to plan ahead constantly.

Similar to a continuous budget is a continuously updated budget. The objective of this budget is not to have twelve months of budgeted information at all times, but instead to update the master budget each month as new information becomes available. An example of a type of continuously updated budget is the one prepared by Chandler Engineering, Inc., for its parent company. Each

master budget

operating budgets

financial budgets

continuous (or rolling) budget

Exhibit 16-2
Components of the Master Budget

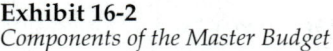

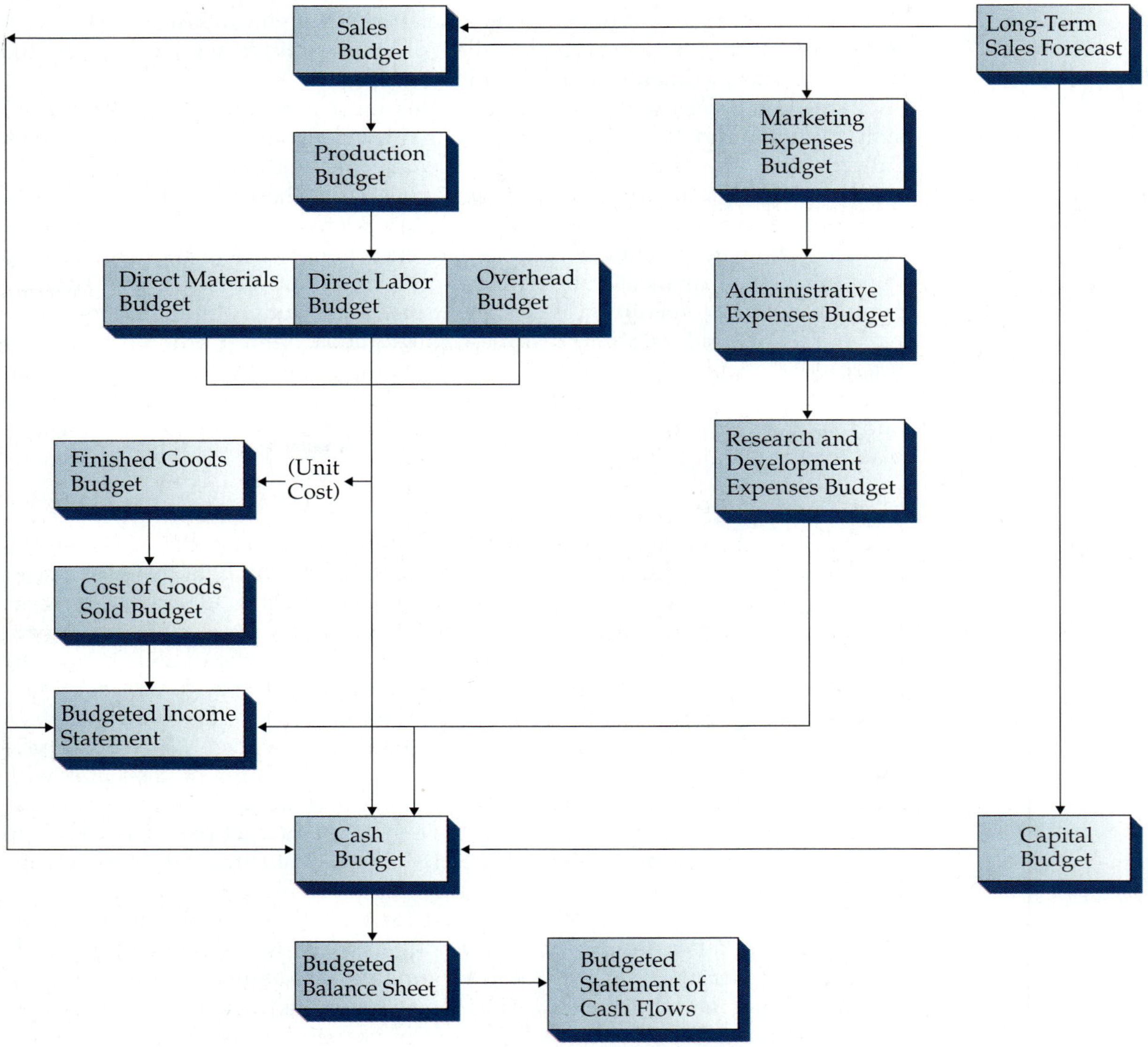

autumn, Chandler Engineering prepares a budget for the coming year. In January of the new year, the budget is transformed into a rolling forecast. That is, at the end of each month, Chandler shows year-to-date results and the forecast for the remainder of the year. In essence, the budget is continually updated throughout the year.

Gathering Information for Budgeting

At the beginning of the master budgeting process, the budget director alerts all segments of the company to the need for gathering budget information. The data used to create the budget come from many sources. Historical data are one possibility. For example, last year's direct materials costs may give the production manager a good feel for potential materials costs for next year. Still, historical data alone cannot tell a company what to expect in the future.

Sales Forecast The sales forecast is the basis for the sales budget, which, in turn, is the basis for all of the other operating budgets and most of the financial budgets. Accordingly, the accuracy of the sales forecast strongly affects the soundness of the entire master budget.

Creating the sales forecast is usually the responsibility of the marketing department. One approach is for the chief sales executive to have individual salespeople submit sales predictions, which are aggregated to form a total sales forecast. The accuracy of this sales forecast may be improved by considering other factors such as the general economic climate, competition, advertising, pricing policies, and so on. Some companies supplement the marketing department forecast with more formal approaches, such as time-series analysis, correlation analysis, and econometric modeling, and industry analysis.

To illustrate an actual sales forecasting approach, consider the practices of a company that manufactures oil field equipment on a job order basis. Each month, the finance and sales department heads meet to construct a sales forecast based on bookings. A booking is a probable sales order submitted by sales personnel in the field; it is meant to alert engineering and manufacturing to a potential job. Past experience has shown that bookings are generally followed by sales/shipments within 30 to 45 days. Exhibit 16-3 shows the short-term bookings forecast for the company. Notice that the dollar amount of each booking is multiplied by its probability of occurrence to obtain a weighted dollar amount. The sum of weighted amounts is the forecast for sales for the month. The probability estimate requires additional explanation. The probability is determined jointly by the salesperson and the controller. Each probability is initially set at 50 percent. Then, it is adjusted upward or downward based on any additional information about the sale. The probability is really a prediction of a compound event, the prediction of both getting the order and determining the month in which it will happen. The sales department tends toward overconfidence—both in terms of getting the order and in landing it sooner rather than later. As a result, the controller takes a more pessimistic view and modifies the forecast. The end result is the form shown in the exhibit.

The sales forecast often relies on information and events external to the firm. For example, Campbell Soup Company monitors weather forecasts to predict short-term demand for its product. Bad weather in the northeastern United States translates into robust sales of soup. Heinz's Weight Watchers Food Company knows that 65 percent of its sales take place during 40 percent of the calendar year: after the holidays, just before summer bathing suit season, and the fall.[1]

Once the sales forecast has been constructed, it is presented to the budget committee for consideration. The budget committee may decide that the forecast is too pessimistic or too optimistic and revise it appropriately. For example, if the budget committee decides that the forecast is too low, it may recommend specific actions to increase sales beyond the forecast level, such as increasing promotional activities and hiring additional salespeople.

Forecasting Other Variables Of course, sales are not the only concern in budgeting. Costs and cash-related items are critical. Many of the same factors considered in sales forecasting apply to cost forecasting. Here, historical amounts can be of real value. Managers can adjust past figures based on their knowledge of

---

1.   Eben Shapiro, "Food Firms Seek a Plan for All Seasons," *The Wall Street Journal,* July 29, 1993, B1.

Exhibit 16-3
Short-Term Bookings Forecast for Oil Field Equipment Company

Quote #	Region/ Country	Customer	Product	$ Amount	Prob.	Weighted Month Total
March 1997						
1194-17	Spain	Valencia	repair 3224	$ 37,500	100%	$ 37,500
1294-03	Bulgaria	Luecim	1256, 7188	74,145	80%	59,316
0195-55	USA	Exxon	4498	25,000	95%	23,750
0295-19	USA	BP/TX	6766, 1267	150,442	100%	150,442
0295-23	China	China Res	7541, 8875	55,900	75%	41,925
0295-45	China	China Res	8879, 0944	34,500	80%	27,600
0395-36	Abu Dhabi	ADES	7400, 6751, 5669 & spares	30,000	50%	15,000
March total						$355,533
April 1997						
1294-14	China	Jiang Han	6524, 5523, 0412, 4578, 3340	$234,000	80%	$187,200
0295-43	Russia	Geoserv	3356	76,800	60%	46,080
0295-10	Venezuela	Petrolina	4450, 6713, 7122	112,500	90%	101,250
0395-37	Indonesia	Chevron	8890, 0933	98,000	65%	63,700
0395-71	Italy	CV Internat'l	7815	16,000	70%	11,200
April total						$409,430
May 1997						
0295-21	Mexico	Instituto Mexicana	8900 & spares	$ 34,000	40%	$ 13,600
0395-29	Venezuela	Petrolina	8416, 8832	165,000	50%	82,500
0495-11	USA	Branchwater, Inc.	9043, 8891	335,000	60%	201,000
0495-68	Saudi Arabia	Aramco	0453	3,500	50%	1,750
May total						$298,850

coming events. For example, a three-year union contract takes much of the uncertainty out of wage prediction. (Of course, if the contract is expiring, the uncertainty is back.) Alert purchasing agents will have an idea of changing raw materials prices. In fact, large companies such as Nestle and Coca Cola have whole departments devoted to the forecasting of commodity prices and supplies. They invest in commodity futures to smooth out price fluctuations, an action that facilitates budgeting. Overhead is broken down into its component costs; these can be predicted using past data and relevant inflation figures.

For example, United Airlines had its ups and downs in forecasting 1995 operating costs.[2] Some cost increases were far more than expected, such as the added $124 million for United's new Denver International Airport hub. Others were somewhat lower. United expected fuel costs to rise by 9 percent in 1995 while other analysts expected only a 3.5 percent rise. Finally, some costs increased as a result of management decision making—such as the increased advertising of United's new California-based shuttle service.

2.   Susan Chandler, "United: So Many Cuts, So Little Relief," *Business Week,* December 5, 1994, page 42.

The cash budget is a critically important part of the master budget, and certain of its components, especially payment of accounts receivable, also require forecasting. This is discussed in more detail in the section on cash budgeting.

PREPARING THE OPERATING BUDGET

Objective 2

Prepare the operating budget, identify its major components, and explain the interrelationships of the various components.

The first section of the master budget is the operating budget. It consists of a series of schedules for all phases of operations, culminating in a budgeted income statement. The following are the components of the operating budget.

1. Sales budget
2. Production budget
3. Direct material purchases budget
4. Direct labor budget
5. Overhead budget
6. Ending finished goods inventory budget
7. Cost of goods sold budget
8. Marketing expense budget
9. Research and development budget
10. Administrative expense budget
11. Budgeted income statement

You may want to refer back to Exhibit 16-2 to see how these components of the operating budget fit into the master budget.

The example used to illustrate the components of the operating budget is based on ABT, Inc., a manufacturer of concrete block and pipe for the construction industry. For simplicity, we will prepare the operating budget for ABT's concrete block line. (The budget for the pipe product line is prepared in the same way and merged into the overall company budget.)

sales budget

Sales Budget The **sales budget** is the projection approved by the budget committee that describes expected sales for each product in units and dollars.

Schedule 1 illustrates the sales budget for ABT's concrete block line. (For a multiple-product firm, the sales budget reflects sales for each product in units and sales dollars.) Notice that the sales budget reveals that ABT's sales fluctuate seasonally. Most sales (75 percent) take place in the spring and summer. Also note that ABT expects price to increase from $0.70 to $0.80 in the summer quarter. Because of the price change within the year, an average price must be used for the column that describes the total year's activities ($0.75 = $12,000/16,000 units).

**Schedule 1
(in thousands)**

Sales Budget
For the Year Ended December 31, 1998

| | Quarter | | | | |
	1	2	3	4	Year
Units	2,000	6,000	6,000	2,000	16,000
Unit selling price	× $0.70	× $0.70	× $0.80	× $0.80	× $0.75
Sales	$ 1,400	$4,200	$ 4,800	$ 1,600	$12,000

Production Budget The **production budget** describes how many units must be produced in order to meet sales needs and satisfy ending inventory requirements. From Schedule 1, we know how many concrete blocks are needed to satisfy sales demand for each quarter and for the year. If there were no inventories, the concrete blocks to be produced would just equal the units to be sold. In the JIT firm, for example, units sold equal units produced, since a customer order triggers production.

Usually, however, the production budget must consider the existence of beginning and ending inventories. Assume that ABT company policy sets desired ending inventory of concrete blocks for each quarter as follows.

Quarter	Ending Inventory
1	500,000
2	500,000
3	100,000
4	100,000

To compute the units to be produced, we must know both unit sales and units in desired finished goods inventory.

> Units to be produced = Units, ending inventory
> + Unit sales − Units, beginning inventory

The formula is the basis for the production budget in Schedule 2. Notice that the production budget is expressed in terms of units; we do not yet know how much they will cost.

Direct Materials Budget After the production schedule is completed, we can prepare budgets for direct materials, direct labor, and overhead. The **direct materials budget** is similar in format to the production budget; it is based on the amount of materials needed for production and the inventories of direct materials.

Expected direct materials usage is determined by the input-output relationship (the technical relationship existing between direct materials and output). This relationship is often determined by the engineering department or the industrial designer. For example, one lightweight concrete block requires approximately 26 pounds of raw materials (cement, sand, gravel, shale, pumice, and

**Schedule 2
(in thousands)**

Production Budget
For the Year Ended December 31, 1998

	Quarter				
	1	*2*	*3*	*4*	*Year*
Sales (Schedule 1)	2,000	6,000	6,000	2,000	16,000
Desired ending inventory	500	500	100	100	100
Total needs	2,500	6,500	6,100	2,100	16,100
Less: Beginning inventory	(100)	(500)	(500)	(100)	(100)
Units to be produced	2,400	6,000	5,600	2,000	16,000

water). The relative mix of these ingredients is fixed for a specific kind of concrete block. Thus, it is fairly easy to determine expected usage for each raw material from the production budget by multiplying the amount of raw material needed per unit of output times the number of units of output.

Once expected usage is computed, the purchases (in units) can be computed as follows:

Purchases = Desired ending inventory of direct materials + Expected usage − Beginning inventory of direct materials

The quantity of direct materials in inventory is determined by the firm's inventory policy. ABT's policy is to have 2,500 tons of raw materials (5 million pounds) in ending inventory for the third and fourth quarters and 4,000 tons of raw materials (8 million pounds) in ending inventory for the first and second quarters. The direct materials budget for ABT is presented in Schedule 3. For simplicity, all raw materials are treated jointly (as if there were only one raw material input). In reality, a separate schedule would be needed for each kind of raw material.

direct labor budget

Direct Labor Budget The **direct labor budget** shows the total direct labor hours needed and the associated cost for the number of units in the production budget. As with direct materials, the usage of direct labor is determined by the technological relationship between labor and output. For example, if a batch of 100 concrete blocks requires 1.5 direct labor hours, then the direct labor time per block is 0.015 hour. Assuming that the labor is used efficiently, this rate is fixed for the existing technology. The relationship will change only if a new approach to manufacturing is introduced.

**Schedule 3
(in thousands)**

Direct Materials Budget
For the Year Ended December 31, 1998

			Quarter		
	1	2	3	4	Year
Units to be produced (Schedule 2)	2,400	6,000	5,600	2,000	16,000
Direct materials per unit (lbs.)	× 26	× 26	× 26	× 26	× 26
Production needs (lbs.)	62,400	156,000	145,600	52,000	416,000
Desired ending inventory (lbs.)	8,000	8,000	5,000	5,000	5,000
Total needs	70,400	164,000	150,600	57,000	421,000
Less: Beginning inventory*	(5,000)	(8,000)	(8,000)	(5,000)	(5,000)
Direct materials to be purchased (lbs.)	65,400	156,000	142,600	52,000	416,000
Cost per pound	× $0.01	× $0.01	× $0.01	× $0.01	× $0.01
Total purchase cost	$ 654	$ 1,560	$ 1,426	$ 520	$ 4,160

*Follows the inventory policy of having 8 million pounds of raw materials on hand at the end of the first and second quarters and 5 million pounds on hand at the end of the third and fourth quarters.

**Schedule 4
(in thousands)**

Direct Labor Budget
For the Year Ended December 31, 1998

	Quarter				
	1	2	3	4	Year
Units to be produced (Schedule 2)	2,400	6,000	5,600	2,000	16,000
Direct labor time per unit (hrs.)	× 0.015	× 0.015	× 0.015	× 0.015	× 0.015
Total hours needed	36	90	84	30	240
Wage per hour	× $8	× $8	× $8	× $8	× $8
Total direct labor cost	$ 288	$ 720	$ 672	$ 240	$ 1,920

Given the direct labor used per unit of output and the units to be produced from the production budget, the direct labor budget is computed as shown in Schedule 4. In the direct labor budget, the wage rate used ($8 per hour in this example) is the *average* wage paid the direct laborers associated with the production of the concrete blocks. Since it is an average, it allows for the possibility of differing wage rates paid to individual laborers.

overhead budget

Overhead Budget The **overhead budget** shows the expected cost of all indirect manufacturing items. Unlike direct materials and direct labor, there is no readily identifiable input-output relationship for overhead items. Recall, however, that overhead consists of two types of costs: variable and fixed. Past experience can be used as a guide to determine how overhead varies with activity level. Items that vary with activity level are identified (e.g., supplies and utilities), and the amount that is expected to be spent for each item per unit of activity is estimated. Individual rates are then totaled to obtain a variable overhead rate. For ABT, assume that the variable overhead rate is $8 per direct labor hour.

Since fixed overhead does not vary with the activity level, total fixed overhead is simply the sum of all amounts budgeted. Assume that fixed overhead is budgeted at $1.28 million ($320,000 per quarter). Using this information and the budgeted direct labor hours from the direct labor budget, the overhead budget in Schedule 5 is prepared.

**Schedule 5
(in thousands)**

Overhead Budget
For the Year Ended December 31, 1998

	Quarter				
	1	2	3	4	Year
Budgeted direct labor hours (Schedule 4)	36	90	84	30	240
Variable overhead rate	× $8	× $8	× $8	× $8	× $8
Budgeted variable overhead	$288	$ 720	$672	$240	$1,920
Budgeted fixed overhead*	320	320	320	320	1,280
Total overhead	$608	$1,040	$992	$560	$3,200

*Includes $200,000 of depreciation in each quarter.

Schedule 6
(in thousands)

Ending Finished Goods Inventory Budget
For the Year Ended December 31, 1998

Unit cost computation:

:---	---:	
Direct materials (26 lbs. @ $0.01)[a]	$0.26	
Direct labor (0.015 hr. @ $8)[b]	0.12	
Overhead:		
Variable (0.015 hr. @ $8)[c]	0.12	
Fixed (0.015 hr. @ $5.33)[d]	0.08	
Total unit cost	$0.58	

	Units	Unit Cost	Total
Finished goods: Concrete blocks	100	$0.58	$58

[a] Amounts taken from Schedule 3.
[b] Amounts taken from Schedule 4.
[c] Amounts taken from Schedule 5.
[d] Budgeted fixed overhead (Schedule 5)/Budgeted direct labor hours (Schedule 4) = $1,280/240 = $5.33

ending finished goods
inventory budget

Ending Finished Goods Inventory Budget The **ending finished goods inventory budget** supplies information needed for the balance sheet and also serves as an important input for the preparation of the cost of goods sold budget. To prepare this budget, the unit cost of producing each concrete block must be calculated using information from Schedules 3, 4, and 5. The unit cost of a concrete block and the cost of the planned ending inventory are shown in Schedule 6.

Budgeted Cost of Goods Sold Assuming that the beginning finished goods inventory is valued at $55,000, the budgeted cost of goods sold schedule can be prepared using Schedules 3, 4, 5, and 6. The cost of goods sold schedule (Schedule 7) will be used as an input for the budgeted income statement.

marketing expense
budget

Marketing Expense Budget The next budget to be prepared—the **marketing expense budget**—outlines planned expenditures for selling and distribution activities. As with overhead, marketing expenses can be broken into fixed and

Schedule 7
(in thousands)

Cost of Goods Sold Budget
For the Year Ended December 31, 1998

Direct materials used (Schedule 3)*	$4,160
Direct labor used (Schedule 4)	1,920
Overhead (Schedule 5)	3,200
Budgeted manufacturing costs	$9,280
Beginning finished goods	55
Goods available for sale	$9,335
Less: Ending finished goods (Schedule 6)	(58)
Budgeted cost of goods sold	$9,277

*Production needs × $0.01 = 416,000 × $0.01

Marketing Expense Budget
For the Year Ended December 31, 1998

	Quarter				
	1	2	3	4	Year
Planned sales in units (Schedule 1)	2,000	6,000	6,000	2,000	16,000
Variable marketing expense per unit	× $0.05	× $0.05	× $0.05	× $0.05	× $0.05
Total variable expenses	$ 100	$ 300	$ 300	$ 100	$ 800
Fixed marketing expense:					
Salaries	$ 10	$ 10	$ 10	$ 10	$ 40
Advertising	10	10	10	10	40
Depreciation	5	5	5	5	20
Travel	3	3	3	3	12
Total fixed expenses	$ 28	$ 28	$ 28	$ 28	$ 112
Total marketing expenses	$ 128	$ 328	$ 328	$ 128	$ 912

variable components. Such items as sales commissions, freight, and supplies vary with sales activity. Salaries of the marketing staff, depreciation on office equipment, and advertising are fixed expenses. The marketing expense budget is illustrated in Schedule 8.

Research and Development Expense Budget ABT, Inc., has a small research and development group that works on product line extensions, for example, brick and paving tile. The expenditures by this group are estimated for the coming year and presented in the **research and development expense budget**. This budget is illustrated, by quarter, in Schedule 9.

research and development expense budget

Administrative Expense Budget The final budget to be developed for operations is the administrative expense budget. Like the research and development or marketing expense budgets, the **administrative expense budget** consists of estimated expenditures for the overall organization and operation of the company. Most administrative expenses are fixed with respect to sales. They include salaries,

administrative expense budget

Research and Development Expense Budget
For the Year Ended December 31, 1998

	Quarter				
	1	2	3	4	Year
Salaries	$18	$18	$18	$18	$ 72
Prototype design and development	10	10	10	10	40
Total R&D expenses	$28	$28	$28	$28	$112

**Schedule 10
(in thousands)**

	Administrative Expense Budget For the Year Ended December 31, 1998				
	Quarter				
	1	2	3	4	Year
Salaries	$25	$25	$25	$25	$100
Insurance	—	—	15	—	15
Depreciation	10	10	10	10	40
Travel	2	2	2	2	8
Total administrative expenses	$37	$37	$52	$37	$163

depreciation on the headquarters building and equipment, legal and auditing fees, and so on. The administrative expense budget is shown in Schedule 10.

Budgeted Income Statement With the completion of the administrative expense schedule, ABT has all the operating budgets needed to prepare an estimate of operating income. This budgeted income statement is shown in Schedule 11. The ten schedules already prepared, along with the budgeted operating income statement, define the operating budget for ABT.

Operating income is *not* equivalent to the net income of a firm. To yield net income, interest expenses and taxes must be subtracted from operating income. The interest expense deduction is taken from the cash budget shown in Schedule 12. The taxes owed depend on the current tax laws.

PREPARING THE FINANCIAL BUDGET

Objective 3
Identify the components of the financial budget and prepare a cash budget.

capital expenditures budget

The remaining budgets found in the master budget are the financial budgets. The usual financial budgets prepared are the cash budget, the budgeted balance sheet, the budgeted statement of cash flows, and the budget for capital expenditures.

While the master budget is a plan for one year, the **capital expenditures budget** is a financial plan outlining the expected acquisition of long-term assets and typically covers a number of years. Decision making in regard to capital expen-

**Schedule 11
(in thousands)**

Budgeted Income Statement For the Year Ended December 31, 1998	
Sales (Schedule 1)	$12,000
Less: Cost of goods sold (Schedule 7)	9,277
Gross margin	$ 2,723
Less: Marketing expenses (Schedule 8)	912
Research and development expenses (Schedule 9)	112
Administrative expenses (Schedule 10)	163
Operating income	$ 1,536
Less: Interest expense (Schedule 12)	42
Income before taxes	$ 1,494
Less: Income taxes	600
Net income	$ 894

Schedule 12 (in thousands)

Cash Budget
For the Year Ended December 31, 1998

	Quarter				Year	Source[a]
	1	2	3	4		
Beginning cash balance	$ 120	$ 113	$ 152	$1,334	$ 120	a
Collections:						
Cash sales	700	2,100	2,400	800	6,000	c, 1
Credit sales:						
Current quarter	490	1,470	1,680	560	4,200	c, 1
Prior quarter	300	210	630	720	1,860	c, 1
Total cash available	$1,610	$3,893	$4,862	$3,414	$12,180	
Less: Disbursements						
Raw materials:						
Current quarter	$ 523	$1,248	$1,141	$ 416	$ 3,328	d, 3
Prior quarter	100	131	312	285	828	d, 3
Direct labor	288	720	672	240	1,920	4
Overhead	408	840	792	360	2,400	e, 5
Marketing expense	123	323	323	123	892	8
R&D expense	28	28	28	28	112	9
Administrative	27	27	42	27	123	10
Income taxes	—	—	—	600	600	g, 11
Equipment	600	—	—	—	600	f
Total disbursements	$2,097	$3,317	$3,310	$2,079	$10,803	
Minimum cash balance	100	100	100	100	100	a
Total cash needs	$2,197	$3,417	$3,410	$2,179	$10,903	
Excess (deficiency) of cash available over needs	$ (587)	$ 476	$1,452	$1,235	$ 1,277	
Financing:						
Borrowings	600	—	—	—	600	
Repayments (outflows)	—	400	200	—	600	b
Interest[b] (outflows)	—	24	18	—	42	b
Total financing	600	424	218	—	42	
Plus: Minimum cash balance	100	100	100	100	100	
Ending cash balance[c]	$ 113	$ 152	$1,334	$1,335	$ 1,335	

[a] Letters refer to the information on page 692. Numbers refer to schedules already developed.
[b] Interest payments are 6/12 × 0.12 × $400 and 9/12 × 0.12 × $200, respectively. Since borrowings occur at the beginning of the quarter and repayments at the end of the quarter, the first principal repayment takes place after six months, and the second principal repayment takes place after nine months.
[c] Total cash available minus total disbursements plus (or minus) total financing.

ditures is considered in the chapter on capital investment analysis. Details on the budgeted statement of cash flows is appropriately reserved for another course. Accordingly, only the cash budget and the budgeted balance sheet will be illustrated here.

The Cash Budget

Knowledge of cash flows is critical to managing a business. Often a business is successful in producing and selling a product but fails because of timing problems associated with cash inflows and outflows. By knowing when cash deficiencies and surpluses are likely to occur, a manager can plan to borrow cash when needed and to repay the loans during periods of excess cash. Bank loan officers use a company's cash budget to document the need for cash, as well as the ability to repay. Because cash flow is the lifeblood of an organization, the cash budget is one of the most important budgets in the master budget.

cash budget

Components of the Cash Budget The **cash budget** is the detailed plan that shows all expected sources and uses of cash. The cash budget, illustrated in Exhibit 16-4, has the following five main sections:

1. Total cash available
2. Cash disbursements
3. Cash excess or deficiency
4. Financing
5. Cash balance

The cash available section consists of the beginning cash balance and the expected cash receipts. Expected cash receipts include all sources of cash for the period being considered. The principal source of cash is from sales. Because a significant proportion of sales is usually on account, a major task of an organization is to determine the pattern of collection for its accounts receivable.

If a company has been in business for a while, it can use past experience in creating an accounts receivable aging schedule. In other words, the company can determine, on average, what percentages of its accounts receivable are paid in the months following the sales.

The cash disbursements section lists all planned cash outlays for the period except for interest payments on short-term loans (these payments appear in the financing section). All expenses not resulting in a cash outlay are excluded from the list (depreciation, for example, is never included in the disbursements section).

The cash excess or deficiency section compares the cash available with the cash needed. Cash needed is the total cash disbursements plus the minimum cash balance required by company policy. The minimum cash balance is simply the lowest amount of cash on hand that the firm finds acceptable. Consider your own checking account. Probably you try to keep at least some cash in the account,

Exhibit 16-4
The Cash Budget

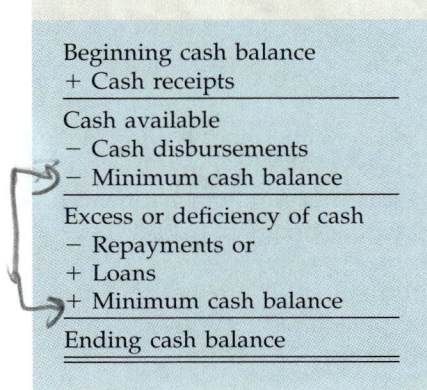

```
  Beginning cash balance
+ Cash receipts
  ─────────────────────────
  Cash available
− Cash disbursements
− Minimum cash balance
  ─────────────────────────
  Excess or deficiency of cash
− Repayments or
+ Loans
+ Minimum cash balance
  ─────────────────────────
  Ending cash balance
  ═════════════════════════
```

perhaps because a minimum balance avoids service charges or because a minimum balance allows you to make an unplanned purchase. Similarly, companies also require minimum cash balances. The amount varies from firm to firm and is determined by each company's particular needs and policies. If the total cash available is less than the cash needs, a deficiency exists. In such a case, a short-term loan will be needed. On the other hand, with a cash excess (cash available is greater than the firm's cash needs), the firm has the ability to repay loans and perhaps make some temporary investments.

The financing section of the cash budget consists of borrowings and repayments. If there is a deficiency, the financing section shows the necessary amount to be borrowed. When excess cash is available, the financing section shows planned repayments, including interest.

The final section of the cash budget is the planned ending cash balance. Remember that the minimum cash balance was subtracted to find the cash excess or deficiency. However, the minimum cash balance is not a disbursement, so it must be added back to yield the planned ending balance.

Cash Budgeting Example To illustrate the cash budget, let's extend the ABT example by assuming the following.

a. ABT requires a $100,000 minimum cash balance for the end of each quarter. On Dec. 31, 1997, the cash balance was $120,000.

b. Money can be borrowed and repaid in multiples of $100,000. Interest is 12 percent per year. Interest payments are made only for the amount of the principal being repaid. All borrowing takes place at the beginning of a quarter, and all repayment takes place at the end of a quarter.

c. Half of all sales are for cash; half are on credit. Of the credit sales, 70 percent are collected in the quarter of sale, and the remaining 30 percent are collected in the following quarter. The sales for the fourth quarter of 1997 were $2 million.

d. Purchases of raw materials are made on account; 80 percent of purchases are paid for in the quarter of purchase. The remaining 20 percent are paid in the following quarter. The purchases for the fourth quarter of 1997 were $500,000.

e. Budgeted depreciation is $200,000 per quarter for overhead.

f. The capital budget for 1998 revealed plans to purchase additional equipment to handle increased demand at a small plant in Nevada. The cash outlay for the equipment, $600,000, will take place in the first quarter. The company plans to finance the acquisition of the equipment with operating cash, supplementing it with short-term loans as necessary.

g. Corporate income taxes are approximately $600,000 and will be paid at the end of the fourth quarter (Schedule 11).

Given the above information, the cash budget for ABT is shown in Schedule 12 (all figures are rounded to the nearest thousand).

Much of the information needed to prepare the cash budget comes from the operating budgets. In fact, Schedules 1, 3, 4, 5, 8, 9, and 10 all supply essential input. However, these schedules by themselves do not supply all of the needed information. The collection pattern for revenues and the payment pattern for materials must be known before the cash flow for sales and purchases on credit can be found.

Exhibit 16-5 displays the pattern of cash inflows from both cash and credit sales. Of course, the credit sales must be adjusted to show how much will be paid in cash during a particular quarter. Let's look at the cash receipts for the first quarter of 1998. Cash sales during the quarter are budgeted for $700,000 (0.5 × $1,400,000). Collections on account for the first quarter relate to credit sales made during the last quarter of the previous year and the first quarter of 1998. Quarter 4, 1997, credit sales equaled $1,000,000 (0.5 × $2,000,000), and $300,000 of those sales (0.3 × $1,000,000) remain to be collected in Quarter 1, 1998. Quarter 1, 1998, credit sales are budgeted at $700,000, and 70 percent will be collected in that quarter. Therefore, $490,000 will be collected on account for credit sales made in that quarter. Similar computations are made for the remaining quarters.

Cash is disbursed for purchases of materials, payment of wages, and payment of other expenses. This information comes from Schedules 3, 4, 5, 8, 9, and 10. However, all noncash expenses, such as depreciation, need to be removed from the total amounts reported in the expense budgets. Thus, the budgeted expenses in Schedules 5, 8, and 10 were reduced by the budgeted depreciation for each quarter. Overhead expenses in Schedule 5 were reduced by depreciation of $200,000 per quarter. Marketing expenses and administrative expenses were reduced by $5,000 per quarter and $10,000 per quarter, respectively. The net amounts are what appear in the cash budget.

The cash budget shown in Schedule 12 underscores the importance of breaking down the annual budget into smaller time periods. The cash budget for the year gives the impression that sufficient operating cash will be available to finance the acquisition of the new equipment. Quarterly information, however, shows the need for short-term borrowing because of both the acquisition of the new equipment and the timing of the firm's cash flows. Breaking down the annual cash budget into quarterly time periods conveys more information. Even smaller time periods often prove to be useful. Most firms prepare monthly cash budgets, and some even prepare weekly and daily budgets.

Another significant piece of information emerges from ABT's cash budget. By the end of the third quarter, the firm holds a considerable amount of cash ($1,334,000). A similar amount is also held by the end of the year. It is certainly not wise to allow this much cash to sit idly in a bank account. The management of ABT should consider paying dividends and making long-term investments. At the very least, the excess cash should be invested in short-term marketable securities. Once plans are finalized for use of the excess cash, the cash budget should be revised to reflect those plans. Budgeting is a dynamic process. As the

Exhibit 16-5
Pattern of Cash Receipts for ABT, Inc.

Source	Quarter 1	Quarter 2	Quarter 3	Quarter 4
Cash sales	$ 700,000	$2,100,000	$2,400,000	$ 800,000
Received on account from sales in:				
Quarter 4, 1997	300,000			
Quarter 1, 1998	490,000	210,000	630,000	720,000
Quarter 2, 1998		1,470,000		
Quarter 3, 1998			1,680,000	
Quarter 4, 1998				560,000
Total cash receipts	$1,490,000	$3,780,000	$4,710,000	$2,080,000

budget is developed, new information becomes available and better plans can be formulated.

Budgeted Balance Sheet The budgeted balance sheet depends on information contained in the current balance sheet and in the other budgets in the master budget. The balance sheet for the beginning of the year is given in Exhibit 16-6. The budgeted balance sheet for December 31, 1998, is given in Schedule 13. Explanations for the budgeted figures follow the schedule.

As we have described the individual budgets that make up the master budget, the interdependencies of the component budgets have become apparent. You may want to refer back to Exhibit 16-2 to review these interrelationships.

USING BUDGETS FOR CONTROL

Objective 4

Identify and discuss the key features that a budgetary system should have to encourage managers to engage in goal-congruent behavior.

Budgets are useful control measures. To be used in performance evaluation, however, two major considerations must be addressed. The first is to determine how budgeted amounts should be compared with actual results. The second consideration involves the impact of budgets on human behavior.

Static Budgets Versus Flexible Budgets

Master budget amounts, while vital for planning, are less useful for control. The reason for this is that the anticipated level of activity rarely equals the actual level

Exhibit 16-6

ABT, Inc.
Balance Sheet
December 31, 1997
(in thousands)

Assets

Current assets:		
Cash	$ 120	
Accounts receivable	300	
Raw materials inventory	50	
Finished goods	55	
Total current assets		$ 525
Property, plant, and equipment (PP&E):		
Land	$2,500	
Building and equipment	9,000	
Accumulated depreciation	(4,500)	
Total PP&E		7,000
Total assets		$7,525

Liabilities and Stockholders' Equity

Current liabilities:		
Accounts payable		$ 100
Stockholders' equity:		
Common stock, no par	$ 600	
Retained earnings	6,825	
Total stockholders' equity		7,425
Total liabilities and stockholders' equity		$7,525

**Schedule 13
(in thousands)**

ABT, Inc.
Budgeted Balance Sheet
December 31, 1998

Assets

Current assets:		
Cash	$1,335[a]	
Accounts receivable	240[b]	
Raw materials	50[c]	
Finished goods	58[d]	
Total current assets		$1,683
Property, plant, and equipment:		
Land	$2,500[e]	
Building and equipment	9,600[f]	
Accumulated depreciation	(5,360)[g]	
Total property, plant, and equipment		6,740
Total assets		$8,423

Liabilities and Stockholders' Equity

Current liabilities:		
Accounts payable		$ 104[h]
Stockholders' equity:		
Common stock	$ 600[i]	
Retained earnings	7,719[j]	
Total stockholders' equity		8,319
Total liabilities and stockholders' equity		$8,423

[a] Ending balance from Schedule 12.
[b] 30 percent of fourth-quarter credit sales (0.30 × $800,000)—see Schedules 1 and 12.
[c] From Schedule 3.
[d] From Schedule 6.
[e] From the December 31, 1997, balance sheet.
[f] December 31, 1997, balance ($9,000,000) plus new equipment acquisition of $600,000 (see the 1997 ending balance sheet and Schedule 12).
[g] From the December 31, 1997, balance sheet, Schedules 5, 8, and 10 ($4,500,000 + $800,000 + $20,000 + $40,000).
[h] 20 percent of fourth-quarter purchases (0.20 × $520,000)—see Schedules 3 and 12.
[i] From the December 31, 1997, balance sheet.
[j] $6,825,000 + $894,000 (December 31, 1997, balance plus net income from Schedule 11).

of activity. Therefore, the costs and revenues associated with the anticipated level of activity cannot be readily compared with actual costs and revenues for a different level of activity.

static budget

Static Budgets A **static budget** is a budget for a particular level of activity. Master budgets are static budgets. Because the revenues and costs prepared for static budgets depend on a level of activity that rarely equals actual activity, they are not very useful when it comes to preparing performance reports.

To illustrate, suppose that ABT provides quarterly performance reports. Further suppose that sales activity was greater than expected in the first quarter; 2.6 million concrete blocks were sold instead of the 2 million budgeted in Schedule 1. Because of increased sales activity, production was increased over the planned level. Instead of producing 2.4 million units (Schedule 2), ABT produced

3 million units. A performance report comparing the actual production costs for the first quarter with the original planned production costs is given in Exhibit 16-7. In contrast to Schedule 5, budgeted amounts for individual overhead items are provided. Thus, the individual budgeted amounts for each overhead item are new information (except for depreciation). Usually this information would be detailed in an overhead budget.

According to the report, unfavorable variances occur for direct materials, direct labor, all variable overhead items, and supervision. However, there is something fundamentally wrong with the report. Actual costs for production of 3 million concrete blocks are being compared with planned costs for production of 2.4 million. Because direct materials, direct labor, and variable overhead are variable costs, we would expect them to be greater at a higher activity level. Thus, even if cost control were perfect for the production of 3 million units, unfavorable variances would be produced for all variable costs.

To create a meaningful performance report, actual costs and expected costs must be compared at the *same* level of activity. Since actual output often differs from planned output, some method is needed to compute what the costs should have been for the actual output level.

Flexible Budgets The budget that provides expected costs for a range of activity is called a **flexible budget**. Flexible budgeting can be used in planning by showing what costs will be at various levels of activity. When used this way, managers can deal with uncertainty by examining the expected financial results for a number of plausible scenarios. Spreadsheets are particularly useful in developing this type of flexible budget.

The flexible budget can be used after the fact, for control, to compute what costs should have been for the actual level of activity. Once expected costs are known for the actual level of activity, a performance report that compares those expected costs to actual costs can be prepared. When used for control, flexible budgets help managers compare "apples to apples" in assessing performance.

flexible budget (margin term)

Exhibit 16-7
Performance Report: Quarterly Production Costs (in thousands)

	Actual	Budgeted	Variance	
Units produced	3,000	2,400	600	F[a]
Direct materials cost	$ 927.3	$ 624.0[b]	$303.3	U[c]
Direct labor cost	360.0	288.0[d]	72.0	U
Overhead:[e]				
Variable:				
Supplies	80.0	72.0	8.0	U
Indirect labor	220.0	168.0	52.0	U
Power	40.0	48.0	(8.0)	F
Fixed:				
Supervision	90.0	100.0	(10.0)	F
Depreciation	200.0	200.0	0.0	
Rent	30.0	20.0	10.0	U
Total	$1,947.3	$1,520.0	$427.3	U

[a] F means the variance is favorable.
[b] From Schedule 3 (62,400 lbs. × $0.01).
[c] U means the variance is unfavorable.
[d] From Schedule 4.
[e] Schedule 5 provides the aggregate amount of budgeted overhead (e.g., the aggregate variable overhead is $0.015 × 2,400,000 × $8 = $288,000, and the total budgeted fixed overhead is $320,000).

To illustrate the power of flexible budgeting, let's prepare one for ABT for three different activity levels (the number of concrete blocks produced). Since the flexible budget gives the expected cost at various levels of activity, we must know the cost behavior patterns of each budget item. Recall that the cost behavior pattern can be expressed as the sum of fixed cost and a variable rate multiplied by activity level. From Schedule 6, we know the variable rates for direct materials ($0.26 per unit), direct labor ($0.12 per unit), and variable overhead ($0.12 per unit). To increase the detail of the flexible budget, let us assume the variable rates per unit for supplies ($0.03), indirect labor ($0.07), and power ($0.02). These three individual rates sum to $0.12. From Schedule 5, we also know that fixed overhead is budgeted at $320,000 per quarter. Exhibit 16-8 displays a flexible budget for production costs when 2,400, 3,000, and 3,600 concrete blocks are produced.

Notice in Exhibit 16-8 that total budgeted production costs increase as the activity level increases. Budgeted costs change because of variable costs. Because of this, flexible budgets are sometimes referred to as **variable budgets**.

Exhibit 16-8 reveals what the costs should have been for the actual level of activity (3 million blocks). A revised performance report that compares actual and budgeted costs for the actual level of activity is given in Exhibit 16-9.

The revised performance report in Exhibit 16-9 paints a much different picture than the one in Exhibit 16-7. By comparing budgeted costs for the actual level of activity with actual costs for the same level, **flexible budget variances** are generated. Managers can locate possible problem areas by examining these variances. According to the ABT flexible budget variances, expenditures for direct materials are excessive. (The other unfavorable variances seem relatively small.) With this knowledge, management can search for the causes of the excess expenditures and prevent the same problems from occurring in the future.

The flexible budget provides an assessment of the efficiency of a manager. In addition to measuring the efficiency of a manager, it is often desirable to measure whether a manager accomplishes the company's output goals. The static budget represented these output goals. A manager is *effective* if the goals described by

variable budgets

flexible budget variances

Exhibit 16-8
Flexible Production Budget (in thousands of dollars)

	Variable Cost Per Unit	Range of Production (units)		
		2,400	3,000	3,600
Production Costs:				
Variable:				
Direct materials	$0.26	$ 624	$ 780	$ 936
Direct labor	0.12	288	360	432
Variable overhead:				
Supplies	0.03	72	90	108
Indirect labor	0.07	168	210	252
Power	0.02	48	60	72
Total variable costs	$0.50	$1,200	$1,500	$1,800
Fixed overhead:				
Supervision		$ 100	$ 100	$ 100
Depreciation		200	200	200
Rent		20	20	20
Total fixed costs		$ 320	$ 320	$ 320
Total production costs		$1,520	$1,820	$2,120

Exhibit 16-9
*Actual Versus Flexible
Performance Report:
Quarterly Production
Costs (in thousands)*

	Actual	Budgeted*	Variance	
Units produced	3,000	3,000	—	
Production costs:				
Direct materials	$ 927.3	$ 780.0	$147.3	U
Direct labor	360.0	360.0	0.0	
Variable overhead:				
Supplies	80.0	90.0	(10.0)	F
Indirect labor	220.0	210.0	10.0	U
Power	40.0	60.0	(20.0)	F
Total variable costs	$1,627.3	$1,500.00	$127.3	U
Fixed overhead:				
Supervision	$ 90.0	$ 100.0	$ (10.0)	F
Depreciation	200.0	200.0	0.0	
Rent	30.0	20.0	10.0	U
Total fixed costs	$ 320.0	$ 320.0	$ 0.0	
Total costs	$1,947.3	$ 1,820.0	$127.3	U

*From Exhibit 16-8.

the static budget are achieved or exceeded. Any differences between the flexible budget and the static budget are attributable to differences in volume. They are called *volume variances*. A five-column performance report that reveals both the flexible budget variances and the volume variances can be used. Exhibit 16-10 provides an example of this report using the ABT data.

As the report in Exhibit 16-10 reveals, production volume was 600,000 units greater than the original budgeted amount. Thus, the manager exceeded the output goal. This volume variance is labeled *favorable* because it exceeds the original production goal. (Recall that the *reason* for the extra production was because the demand for the product was greater than expected. Thus, the increase in production over the original amount was truly favorable.) On the other hand, the budgeted variable costs are greater than expected because of the increased production. This difference is labeled unfavorable because the costs are greater than expected; however, the increase in costs is because of an increase in production. Thus, it is totally reasonable. For this particular example, the effectiveness of the manager is not in question; thus, the main issue is how well the manager controlled costs as revealed by the flexible-budget variances.

The Behavioral Dimension of Budgeting

Budgets are often used to judge the actual performance of managers. Bonuses, salary increases, and promotions are all affected by a manager's ability to achieve or beat budgeted goals. Since a manager's financial status and career can be affected, budgets can have a significant behavioral effect. Whether that effect is positive or negative depends to a large extent on how budgets are used.

Positive behavior occurs when the goals of individual managers are aligned with the goals of the organization and the manager has the drive to achieve them. The alignment of managerial and organizational goals is often referred to as **goal congruence**. In addition to goal congruence, however, a manager must also exert effort to achieve the goals of the organization.

goal congruence

Exhibit 16-10
Managerial Performance Report: Quarterly Production (in thousands)

	Actual Results (1)	Flexible Budget (2)	Flexible Budget Variances (3) = (1) − (2)	Static Budget (4)	Volume Variances (5) = (2) − (4)
Units produced	3,000	3,000	—	2,400	600 F
Production costs:					
Direct materials	$ 927.3	$ 780.0	$147.3 U	$ 624.0	$156.0 U
Direct labor	360.0	360.0	0.0	288.0	72.0 U
Supplies	80.0	90.0	(10.0) F	72.0	18.0 U
Indirect labor	220.0	210.0	10.0 U	168.0	42.0 U
Power	40.0	60.0	(20.0) F	48.0	12.0 U
Supervision	90.0	100.0	(10.0) F	100.0	0.0
Depreciation	200.0	200.0	0.0	200.0	0.0
Rent	30.0	20.0	10.0 U	20.0	0.0
Total costs	$1,947.3	$1,820.0	$127.3 U	$1,520.0	$300.0 U

dysfunctional behavior

If the budget is improperly administered, the reaction of subordinate managers may be negative. This negative behavior can be manifested in numerous ways, but the overall effect is subversion of the organization's goals. **Dysfunctional behavior** is individual behavior that is in basic conflict with the goals of the organization.

A theme underlying the behavioral dimension of budgeting is ethics. The importance of budgets in performance evaluation and managers' pay raises and promotions leads to the possibility of unethical action. All of the dysfunctional actions that can be taken regarding budgets can have an unethical aspect. For example, a manager who deliberately underestimates sales and overestimates costs for the purpose of making the budget easier to achieve is engaging in unethical behavior. It is the responsibility of the company to create budgetary incentives that do not encourage unethical behavior. It is the responsibility of the manager not to engage in such behavior.

An ideal budgetary system is one that achieves complete goal congruence, and simultaneously creates a drive in managers to achieve the organization's goals in an ethical manner. While an ideal budgetary system probably does not exist, research and practice have identified some key features that promote a reasonable degree of positive behavior. These features include frequent feedback on performance, monetary and nonmonetary incentives, participation, realistic standards, controllability of costs, and multiple measures of performance.

Frequent Feedback on Performance Managers need to know how they are doing as the year unfolds. Providing them with frequent, timely performance reports allows them to know how successful their efforts have been, to take corrective actions, and to change plans as necessary. Frequent performance reports can reinforce positive behavior and give managers the time and opportunity to adapt to changing conditions.

The use of flexible budgets allows management to see if actual costs and revenues are in accord with budgeted amounts. Selective investigation of significant variances allows managers to focus only on areas that need attention. This process is called *management by exception.*

incentives

Monetary and Nonmonetary Incentives

A sound budgetary system encourages goal-congruent behavior. The means an organization uses to influence a manager to exert effort to achieve an organization's goal are called **incentives**. Incentives can be either negative or positive. Negative incentives use fear of punishment to motivate; positive incentives use the expectation of reward. What incentives should be tied to an organization's budgetary system?

Traditional organization theory assumes that individuals are primarily motivated by monetary rewards, resist work, and are inefficient and wasteful.[3] Companies accepting this view impose budgets from above and hold managers strictly accountable for each line in the budget. In this way, top management can control a subordinate manager's tendency to shirk and waste resources. Since managers are believed to be primarily motivated by **monetary incentives**, this control is achieved by relating budgetary performance to salary increases, bonuses, and promotions. The threat of dismissal is the ultimate economic sanction for poor performance.

monetary incentives

The above view of human behavior is too simplistic. Individuals are motivated by more than just external rewards. In addition to the economic factors, individuals are motivated by a complex set of intrinsic psychological and social factors. These factors include the satisfaction of a job well done, recognition, responsibility, self-esteem, and the nature of the work itself. A successful budgetary control system does not ignore the complex forces motivating individuals. Monetary rewards alone are not enough to achieve the desired level of motivation in managers. **Nonmonetary incentives**, including job enrichment, increased responsibility and autonomy, nonmonetary recognition programs, and so on, can be used to enhance a budgetary control system.

nonmonetary
incentives

participative
budgeting

Participative Budgeting

Rather than imposing budgets on subordinate managers, **participative budgeting** allows subordinate managers considerable say in how the budgets are established. Typically, overall objectives are communicated to the manager, who helps develop a budget that will accomplish these objectives. In participative budgeting, the emphasis is on the accomplishment of the broad objectives, not on individual budget items.

The budget process described earlier for ABT uses participative budgeting. The company provides the sales forecast to its profit centers and requests a budget that shows planned expenditures and expected profits given that level of sales. The managers of the profit centers are fully responsible for preparing the budgets by which they will later be evaluated. Although the budgets must be approved by the president, disapproval is not common; the budgets are usually in line with the sales forecast and last year's operating results adjusted for expected changes in revenues and costs.

Participative budgeting communicates a sense of responsibility to subordinate managers and fosters creativity. Since the subordinate manager creates the budget, it is more likely that the budget's goals will become the manager's personal goals, resulting in greater goal congruence. Advocates of participative budgeting claim that the increased responsibility and challenge inherent in the process provide nonmonetary incentives that lead to a higher level of performance. They argue that individuals involved in setting their own standards will work harder

---

3.   An excellent discussion of traditional and modern views of organization theory and their implications for managerial accounting is given by Edwin H. Caplan, *Management Accounting and Behavioral Science*, Addison-Wesley, Reading, Mass., 1971.

to achieve them. In addition to the behavioral benefits, participative budgeting has the advantage of involving individuals whose knowledge of local conditions may enhance the entire planning process.

Participative budgeting has three potential problems that should be mentioned.

1. Setting standards that are either too high or too low.
2. Building slack into the budget (often referred to as *padding the budget*).
3. Pseudoparticipation.

Some managers may tend to set the budget either too loose or too tight. Since budgeted goals tend to become the manager's goals when participation is allowed, making this mistake in setting the budget can result in decreased performance levels. If goals are too easily achieved, a manager may lose interest, and performance may actually drop. Challenge is important to aggressive and creative individuals. Similarly, setting the budget too tight ensures failure to achieve the standards and frustrates the manager. This frustration, too, can lead to poor performance. The trick is to get managers in a participative setting to set high but achievable goals.

budgetary slack

The second problem with participative budgeting is the opportunity for managers to build slack into the budget. **Budgetary slack** (or *padding the budget*) exists when a manager deliberately underestimates revenues or overestimates costs. Either approach increases the likelihood that the manager will achieve the budget and consequently reduces the risk that the manager faces. Padding the budget also unnecessarily ties up resources that might be used more productively elsewhere.

Slack in budgets can be virtually eliminated by having top management dictate lower expense budgets. However, the benefits to be gained from participation may far exceed the costs associated with padding the budget. Even so, top management should carefully review budgets proposed by subordinate managers and provide input, where needed, in order to decrease the effects of building slack into the budget.

pseudoparticipation

The third problem with participation occurs when top management assumes total control of the budgeting process, seeking only superficial participation from lower-level managers. This practice is termed **pseudoparticipation**. Top management is simply obtaining formal acceptance of the budget from subordinate managers, not seeking real input. Accordingly, none of the behavioral benefits of participation will be realized.

Realistic Standards Budgeted objectives are used to gauge performance; accordingly, they should be based on realistic conditions and expectations. Budgets should reflect operating realities such as actual levels of activity, seasonal variations, efficiencies, and general economic trends. Flexible budgets, for example, are used to ensure that the budgeted costs provide standards that are compatible with the actual activity level. Another factor that should be considered is that of seasonality. Some businesses receive revenues and incur costs uniformly throughout the year; thus, spreading the annual revenues and costs evenly over quarters and months is reasonable for interim performance reports. However, for businesses with seasonal variations, this practice would result in distorted performance reports.

Such factors as efficiency and general economic conditions are also important. Occasionally, top management makes arbitrary cuts in prior-year budgets with the belief that the cuts will reduce fat or inefficiencies that allegedly exist. In reality, some units may be operating efficiently and others inefficiently. An across-the-board cut without any formal evaluation may impair the ability of some units to carry out their missions. General economic conditions also need to be considered. Budgeting for a significant increase in sales when a recession is projected is not only foolish but potentially harmful. For example, for years Kodak confidently predicted that their film business would grow by 8 percent when the industry was growing by only 4 percent.[4] The predicted growth did not occur. This type of unfounded optimism did nothing to improve sales and only hurt stock analysts' perception of the company.

controllable costs

Controllability of Costs Conventional thought maintains that managers should be held accountable only for costs over which they have control. **Controllable costs** are costs whose level a manager can influence. In this view, a manager who has no responsibility for a cost should not be held accountable for it. For example, divisional managers have no power to authorize such corporate-level costs as research and development and salaries of top managers. Therefore, they should not be held accountable for the incurrence of those costs.

Many firms, however, do put noncontrollable costs in the budgets of subordinate managers. Making managers aware of the need to cover all costs is one rationale for this practice. If noncontrollable costs are included in a budget, they should be separated from controllable costs and labeled as *noncontrollable*.

myopic behavior

Multiple Measures of Performance Often organizations make the mistake of using budgets as their only measure of managerial performance. Overemphasis on this measure can lead to a form of dysfunctional behavior called *milking the firm* or *myopia*. **Myopic behavior** occurs when a manager takes actions that improve budgetary performance in the short run but bring long-run harm to the firm.

There are numerous examples of myopic behavior. To meet budgeted cost objectives or profits, managers can reduce expenditures for preventive maintenance, for advertising, and for new product development. Managers can also fail to promote promotable employees to keep the cost of labor low and choose to use lower-quality materials to reduce the cost of raw materials. In the short run, these actions will lead to improved budgetary performance, but in the long run, productivity will fall, market share will decline, and capable employees will leave for more attractive opportunities.

Managers who engage in this kind of behavior often have a short tenure. In these cases, managers spend three to five years before being promoted or moving to a new area of responsibility. Their successors are the ones who pay the price for their myopic behavior. The best way to prevent myopic behavior is to measure the performance of managers on several dimensions, including some long-run attributes. Productivity, quality, and personnel development are examples of other areas of performance that could be evaluated. Financial measures of performance are important, but overemphasis on them can be counterproductive.

---

4.   Peter Nulty, "Digital Imaging Had Better Boom Before Kodak Film Busts," Fortune, May 1, 1995, pp. 80–83.

OTHER TYPES OF BUDGETS

Objective 5

Describe budgets for merchandising and service firms and zero-base budgeting.

While the master and flexible budgets described above are widely used for planning and control in manufacturing firms, the special needs of service and merchandising firms deserve mention. Additionally, a different approach to budgeting, called zero-base budgeting, can be used for long-term planning.

Operating Budgets for Merchandising and Service Firms

In a merchandising firm, the production budget is replaced with a merchandise purchases budget. This budget identifies the quantity of each item that must be purchased for resale, the unit cost of the item, and the total purchase cost. The format is identical to that of the direct materials budget in a manufacturing firm. The only other difference between the operating budgets of manufacturing and merchandising firms is the absence of direct materials and direct labor budgets in a merchandising firm.

In a for-profit service firm, the sales budget is also the production budget. The sales budget identifies each service and the quantity of it that will be sold. Since finished goods inventories are nonexistent, the services produced will be identical to the services sold. For example, the Colorado Rockies baseball team budgets the number of seats it expects to fill at each game and the price per ticket. Other revenues (such as television royalties and concession sales) are also budgeted.

In a not-for-profit service firm, the sales budget is replaced by a budget that identifies the levels of the various services that will be offered for the coming year and the associated funds that will be assigned to the services. The source of the funds may be tax revenues, contributions, payments by users of the services, or some combination. For example, the board of directors for a local United Way budgets the campaign target (dollars of contributions) for the coming year and then distributes the total among the qualifying agencies according to three levels—pessimistic, expected, and optimistic.

Both for-profit and not-for-profit service organizations lack finished goods inventory budgets. However, all the remaining operating budgets found in a manufacturing organization have counterparts in service organizations. For a not-for-profit service organization, the income statement is replaced by a statement of sources and uses of funds.

Zero-Base Budgeting

incremental (or baseline) budgeting

The traditional approach to budgeting is the incremental approach. **Incremental (or baseline) budgeting** starts with last year's budget and adds or subtracts from that budget to reflect changing assumptions for the coming year. For example, if last year's budgeted expenditures for an agency or department were $1.2 million, the agency or department may request a 5 percent increase ($60,000) to provide the same level of service for the coming year. The typical justification for increased expenditures is the increased cost of inputs (labor, materials, and so on). The incremental approach may not entail a careful evaluation of the level of services being offered or of whether they are being offered efficiently.

Under the incremental approach, heads of budgeting units often strive to spend all of the year's budget so that no surplus exists at the end of the year. (This is particularly true for government agencies.) This action is taken to maintain the current level of the budget and enable the head of the unit to request additional funds. For example, at an Air Force base, a bomber wing was faced with the possibility of a surplus at the end of the fiscal year. The base commander, however, found ways to spend the extra money before the year ended. Missile officers, who normally drove to the missile command site, were flown to the sites in helicopters; several bags of lawn fertilizer were given away to all personnel with houses on base; and new furniture was acquired for the bachelor officer quarters. The waste and inefficiency portrayed in this example is often perpetuated and encouraged by incremental budgeting.

zero-base budgeting   **Zero-base budgeting** is an alternative approach.[5] Unlike incremental budgeting, the prior year's budgeted level is not taken for granted. Existing operations are analyzed, and continuance of the activity or operation must be justified on the basis of its need or usefulness to the organization. The burden of proof is on each manager to justify why any money should be spent at all. In effect, each subunit of a company starts from ground zero and prepares a series of budgets—one for every decision package being considered.

decision package   A **decision package** is a description of services, with associated costs, that a decision unit can or would like to offer. Along with a budget, each package should contain a statement of the unit's goals, programs to achieve these goals, the benefits expected, and the consequences of not approving the package. The best of the alternative packages is chosen, and the others are discarded. This process forces managers to take a fresh look at their operations and consider the best way to carry out their objectives.

Zero-base budgeting requires extensive, in-depth analysis. Although this approach has been used successfully in industry and government (e.g., Texas Instruments and the state of Georgia), it is time-consuming and costly. Advocates of the incremental approach argue that incremental budgeting also uses extensive, in-depth reviews but not as frequently because they are not justified on a cost-benefit basis. A reasonable compromise may be to use zero-base budgeting every three to five years in order to weed out waste and inefficiency. Especially in a period of intense competition and reengineering, zero-base budgeting can force managers to "break set" and see their units in a different perspective.

5.   Zero-based budgeting was developed by Peter Pyhrr of Texas Instruments. For a detailed discussion of the approach, see Peter Pyhrr, *Zero-Base Budgeting*, Wiley, New York, 1973.

SUMMARY

Budgeting is the creation of a plan of action expressed in financial terms. Budgeting plays a key role in planning, controlling, and decision making. Budgets also serve to improve communication and coordination, a role that becomes increasingly important as organizations grow in size.

The master budget, the comprehensive financial plan of an organization, is made up of the operating and financial budgets. The operating budget is the budgeted income statement and all supporting schedules. These schedules include the sales budget, the production budget, the direct materials purchases budget, the direct labor budget, the overhead budget, the marketing expense budget, the administrative expense budget, the research and development expense budget, the finished goods ending inventory budget, and the budgeted cost of goods sold. The budgeted income statement outlines the net income to be realized if budgeted plans come to fruition.

The financial budget includes the cash budget, the capital expenditures budget, and the budgeted balance sheet. The cash budget is simply the beginning balance in the cash account, plus anticipated receipts, minus anticipated disbursements, plus or minus any necessary borrowing. The budgeted (or pro forma) balance sheet gives the anticipated ending balances of the asset, liability, and equity accounts if budgeted plans hold.

The success of a budgetary system depends on how seriously human factors are considered. To discourage dysfunctional behavior, organizations should avoid overemphasizing budgets as a control mechanism. Other areas of performance should be evaluated in addition to budgets. Budgets can be improved as performance measures by the use of participative budgeting and other nonmonetary incentives, by providing fre-

quent feedback on performance, by the use of flexible budgeting, by ensuring that the budgetary objectives reflect reality, and by holding managers accountable for only controllable costs.

Zero-base budgeting does not take the prior year's budgeted levels for granted. Existing operations are analyzed, and continuance of the activity must be justified on the basis of its usefulness to the organization.

REVIEW PROBLEM AND SOLUTION

Young Products produces coat racks. The projected sales for the first quarter of the coming year and the beginning and ending inventory data are as follows:

Sales	100,000 units
Unit price	$15
Beginning inventory	8,000 units
Targeted ending inventory	12,000 units

derived →

The coat racks are molded and then painted. Each rack requires (four) pounds of metal, which costs $2.50 per pound. The beginning inventory of raw materials is 4,000 pounds. Young Products wants to have 6,000 pounds of metal in inventory at the end of the quarter. Each rack produced requires thirty minutes of direct labor time, which is billed at $9 per hour.

ERM 0.5

REQUIRED:

1. Prepare a sales budget for the first quarter.
2. Prepare a production budget for the first quarter.
3. Prepare a direct materials purchases budget for the first quarter.
4. Prepare a direct labor budget for the first quarter.

Solution

1.

Young Products
Sales Budget
For the First Quarter

Units	100,000
Unit price	× $15
Sales	$1,500,000

2.

Young Products
Production Budget
For the First Quarter

Sales (in units)	100,000
Desired ending inventory	12,000
Total needs	112,000
Less: Beginning inventory	8,000
Units to be produced	104,000

3.

	Young Products
	Direct Materials
	For the First Quarter

Units to be produced	104,000
Direct materials per unit (lbs.)	× 4
Production needs (lbs.)	416,000
Desired ending inventory (lbs.)	6,000
Total needs (lbs.)	422,000
Less: Beginning inventory (lbs.)	(4,000)
Materials to be purchased (lbs.)	418,000
Cost per pound	× $2.50
Total purchase cost	$1,045,000

4.

	Young Products
	Direct Labor Budget
	For the First Quarter

Units to be produced	104,000
Labor: Time per unit	× 0.5
Total hours needed	52,000
Cost per hour	× $9
Total direct labor cost	$468,000

KEY TERMS

Administrative expense
  budget 688
Budgets 677
Budget committee 678
Budget director 678
Budgetary slack 701
Capital expenditures
  budget 689
Cash budget 691
Continuous (or rolling)
  budget 679
Control 677
Controllable costs 702

Decision package 704
Direct labor budget 685
Direct materials budget
  684
Dysfunctional behavior
  699
Ending finished goods
  inventory budget 687
Financial budgets 679
Flexible budget 696
Flexible budget variances
  697
Goal congruence 698

Incentives 700
Incremental (or baseline)
  budgeting 703
Marketing expense
  budget 687
Master budget 679
Monetary incentives 700
Myopic behavior 702
Nonmonetary incentives
  700
Operating budgets 679
Overhead budget 686

Participative budgeting
  700
Production budget 684
Pseudoparticipation 701
Research and
  development expense
  budget 688
Sales budget 683
Static budget 695
Variable budget 697
Zero-base budgeting 704

QUESTIONS FOR WRITING AND DISCUSSION

1. Define the term *budget*. How are budgets used in planning?
2. Define *control*. How are budgets used to control?
3. Discuss some of the reasons for budgeting.
4. What is the master budget? An operating budget? A financial budget?
5. Explain the role of a sales forecast in budgeting. What is the difference between a sales forecast and a sales budget?
6. All budgets depend on the sales budget. Is this true? Explain.
7. How do the master budgets differ among manufacturing, merchandising, and service organizations?
8. Why is goal congruence important?
9. Discuss the roles of monetary and nonmonetary incentives. Do you believe that nonmonetary incentives are needed? Why?
10. What is participative budgeting? Discuss some of its advantages.
11. A budget too easily achieved will lead to diminished performance. Do you agree? Explain.
12. What is the role of top management in participative budgeting?
13. Explain why a manager has an incentive to build slack into the budget.
14. Discuss the differences between static and flexible budgets. Why are flexible budgets superior to static budgets for performance reporting?
15. Why is it important for a manager to receive frequent feedback on his or her performance?
16. Explain how a manager can milk the firm to improve budgetary performance.
17. Identify performance measures other than budgets that can be used to discourage myopic behavior. Discuss how you would use these measures.
18. How important are the behavioral aspects of a budgetary control system? Explain.
19. Explain the difference between incremental budgeting and zero-base budgeting.
20. Advocates of zero-base budgeting maintain that padding the budget is easier under an incremental system than under a zero-base system. Explain why padding is less likely for a zero-base budgeting system.

EXERCISES AND PROBLEMS

16-1

Sales Budget

LO 1, 2

Milan Cereal Company produces wheat flakes and corn flakes. Both products are sold in 12-ounce boxes. Wheat flakes sell for $1.50 per box, and corn flakes sell for $1.30 per box. Projected sales (in boxes) for the coming four quarters are given below.

	Wheat Flakes	Corn Flakes
First quarter	500,000	600,000
Second quarter	600,000	600,000
Third quarter	700,000	700,000
Fourth quarter	750,000	800,000

The president of the company believes that the projected sales are realistic and can be achieved by the company.

REQUIRED:

1. Prepare a sales budget for each quarter and for the year in total. Show sales by product and in total for each time period.
2. What factors might Milan Cereal Company have considered in preparing the sales budget?

16-2
Production Budget
LO 2

Whiskers Products, Inc., produces a variety of products for cats. Among them is a 16-ounce can of cat food. The sales budget for the first four months of the year is presented below.

	Unit Sales	Dollar Sales
January	100,000	$50,000
February	120,000	60,000
March	110,000	55,000
April	100,000	50,000

Company policy requires that ending inventories for each month be 20 percent of next month's sales. At the beginning of January, the inventory of cat food is 20,000 cans.

REQUIRED: Prepare a production budget for the first quarter of the year. Show the number of units that should be produced each month as well as for the quarter in total.

16-3
Direct Materials Purchases Budget, Direct Labor Budget
LO 2

Dulce Company produces a 6-ounce chocolate candy bar. Each 6-ounce bar contains three ounces of sugar, which costs $0.025 per ounce. Dulce has budgeted production of the chocolate bar for the next four months as follows:

	Units
October	400,000
November	800,000
December	500,000
January	600,000

Inventory policy requires that sufficient sugar be in ending monthly inventory to satisfy 15 percent of the following month's production needs. Inventory of sugar at the beginning of October equals exactly the amount needed to satisfy the inventory policy.
  Each chocolate bar produced requires (on average) 0.01 direct labor hours. The average cost of direct labor is $9 per hour.

REQUIRED:

1. Prepare a direct materials purchases budget for the last quarter of the year showing purchases in units and in dollars for each month and for the quarter in total.
2. Prepare a direct labor budget for the last quarter of the year showing the hours needed and the direct labor cost for each month and for the quarter in total.

16-4
Sales Forecast and Budget
LO 1, 2

Allen, Inc., manufactures six models of molded plastic waste containers. It is now early 1998, and Allen's budgeting team is finalizing the sales budget for 1998. Sales in units and dollars for 1997 were as follow:

Model	Number Sold	Price	Revenue
W-1	14,000	$ 9	$126,000
W-2	15,000	15	225,000
W-3	21,000	13	273,000
W-4	13,500	10	135,000
W-5	2,000	22	44,000
W-6	1,000	26	26,000
			$829,000

In looking over the 1997 sales figures, Allen's sales budgeting team recalled the following:

a. Model W-1 costs were rising faster than the price could rise. Preparatory to phasing out this model, Allen, Inc., planned to slash advertising for this model and raise its price by 50 percent. The number of units of Model W-1 to be sold were forecast to be 20 percent of 1997 units.

b. Models W-5 and W-6 were introduced on November 1, 1997. They are brightly colored, heavy-duty wheeled garbage containers designed for household use. Allen estimates that demand for both models will continue at the 1997 rate.

c. A competitor has announced plans to introduce an improved version of Model W-3. Allen believes that the Model W-3 price must be cut 20 percent to maintain unit sales at the 1997 level.

d. It was assumed that unit sales of all other models would increase by 10 percent, prices remaining constant.

REQUIRED: Prepare a sales forecast by product and in total for Allen, Inc., for 1998.

16-5
Purchases Budget
LO 2

Al's Auto Supply ("Everything you need for your car") carries a variety of auto parts including oil filters. The sales budget for oil filters for the first six months of the year is presented below.

	Unit Sales	Dollar Sales
January	200	$ 900
February	180	810
March	220	990
April	250	1,125
May	300	1,350
June	260	1,170

Al believes that ending inventories should be sufficient to cover 30 percent of the next month's projected sales. On January 1, 84 oil filters were in inventory.

REQUIRED:

1. Prepare a purchases budget in units of oil filters for as many months as you can.
2. If oil filters are priced at 50 percent above cost, what is the dollar cost of purchases for each month of your purchases budget?

16-6
Cash Receipts Budget
LO 3

CeCe's Gift Shop in Sedona, Arizona, sells a variety of t-shirts (screen printed with desert themes) and objets d'art. CeCe accepts cash, checks, and VISA, MasterCard, and American Express charges. These methods of payment have the following characteristics:

Cash	Payment is immediate; no fee is charged.
Check	Payment is immediate; the bank charges $0.25 per check; 1 percent of check revenue is from "bad" checks that CeCe cannot collect.
VISA/MasterCard	CeCe accumulates these credit card receipts throughout the month and submits them in one bundle for payment on the last day of the month. The money is credited to CeCe's account by the fifth day of the following month. A fee of 1.5 percent is charged by the credit card company.
American Express	CeCe accumulates these receipts throughout the month and mails them to American Express for payment on the last day of the month. American Express credits CeCe's account by the 6th day

of the following month. A fee of 3.5 percent is charged by American Express.

During a typical month, CeCe has sales of $20,000, broken down as follows:

American Express	20%
VISA/MasterCard	50%
Check	5% (checks average $37.50 each)
Cash	25%

REQUIRED: If CeCe estimates sales of $20,000 in April and $30,000 in May, what are her planned net cash receipts for May?

16-7
Overhead Budget;
Flexible Budgeting
LO 2, 4

Toolson Manufacturing, Inc., has developed the following flexible budget for overhead for the coming year. Activity level is measured in direct labor hours.

	Variable Cost Formula	Activity Level (hours)		
		10,000	15,000	20,000
Variable costs:				
Maintenance	$1.50	$15,000	$22,500	$ 30,000
Supplies	0.50	5,000	7,500	10,000
Power	0.10	1,000	1,500	2,000
Total variable costs	$2.10	$21,000	$31,500	$ 42,000
Fixed costs:				
Depreciation		$ 6,000	$ 6,000	$ 6,000
Salaries		60,000	60,000	60,000
Total fixed costs		$66,000	$66,000	$ 66,000
Total overhead costs		$87,000	$97,500	$108,000

Toolson produces two different hammers. The production budget for April is 12,000 units for Hammer A and 15,000 units for Hammer B. Hammer A requires three minutes of direct labor time, and Hammer B requires two minutes. Fixed overhead costs are incurred uniformly throughout the year.

REQUIRED: Prepare an overhead budget for April.

16-8
Cash Budget
LO 3

The owner of a small mining supply company has requested a cash budget for June. After examining the records of the company, you find the following:

a. Cash balance on June 1 is $1,000.
b. Actual sales for April and May are as follows:

	April	May
Cash sales	$10,000	$15,000
Credit sales	25,000	35,000
Total sales	$35,000	$50,000

c. Credit sales are collected over a three-month period: 50 percent in the month of sale, 30 percent in the second month, and 15 percent in the third month. The remaining sales are uncollectible.

d. Inventory purchases average 60 percent of a month's total sales. Of those purchases, 40 percent are paid for in the month of purchase. The remaining 60 percent are paid for in the following month.

e. Salaries and wages total $8,000 a month, including a $4,500 salary paid to the owner.

f. Rent is $1,000 per month.

g. Taxes to be paid in June are $5,000.

The owner also tells you that he expects cash sales of $20,000 and credit sales of $40,000 for June. There is no minimum cash balance required. The owner of the company does not have access to short-term loans.

REQUIRED:

1. Prepare a cash budget for June. Include supporting schedules for cash collections and cash payments.
2. Did the business show a negative cash balance for June? Assuming that the owner has no hope of establishing a line of credit for the business, what recommendations would you give the owner for dealing with a negative cash balance?

16-9
Flexible Budget
LO 4

Penny Johnson, controller for Lansing Company, has been instructed to develop a flexible budget for overhead costs. The company produces two fertilizers called *Ferone* and *Fertwo* that use common raw materials in different proportions. The company expects to produce 100,000 50-pound bags of each product during the coming year. Ferone requires 0.25 direct labor hour per bag, and Fertwo requires 0.30. Penny has developed the following cost formulas for each of the four overhead items (X is measured in direct labor hours):

	Cost Formula
Maintenance	$10,000 + 0.3X
Power	0.5X
Indirect labor	$24,500 + 1.5X
Rent	$18,000

At the end of the year, Lansing actually produced 120,000 bags of Ferone and 100,000 of Fertwo. The actual overhead costs incurred were:

Maintenance	$ 26,700
Power	34,000
Indirect labor	108,000
Rent	18,000

REQUIRED:

1. Prepare an overhead budget for the expected activity level for the coming year.
2. Prepare an overhead budget that reflects production that is 10 percent higher than expected (for both products) and one for production that is 20 percent lower than expected.
3. Prepare a performance report for the period.

4. Based on the report, would you judge any of the variances to be significant? Can you think of some possible reasons for the variances?

16-10
Budgeted Cash Collections; Budgeted Cash Payments
LO 3

Information pertaining to Noskey Corporation's sales revenue is presented below.

	November 1997 (Actual)	December 1997 (Budget)	January 1998 (Budget)
Cash sales	$ 80,000	$100,000	$ 60,000
Credit sales	240,000	360,000	180,000
Total sales	$320,000	$460,000	$240,000

Management estimates that 5 percent of credit sales are uncollectible. Of the credit sales that are collectible, 60 percent are collected in the month of sale and the remainder in the month following the sale. Purchases of inventory each month are 70 percent of the next month's projected total sales. All purchases of inventory are on account; 25 percent are paid in the month of purchase, and the remainder are paid in the month following the purchase.

REQUIRED:

1. What are Noskey's budgeted cash collections in December 1997 from November 1997 credit sales?
2. What are total budgeted cash receipts in January 1998?
3. What is Noskey budgeting for total cash payments in December 1997 for inventory purchases?

(CMA adapted)

16-11
Participative Versus Imposed Budgeting
LO 4

An effective budget converts the goals and objectives of an organization into data. The budget serves as a blueprint for management's plans. The budget is also the basis for control. Management performance can be evaluated by comparing actual results with the budget.

Thus, creating the budget is essential for the successful operation of an organization. Finding the resources to implement the budget—that is, getting from a starting point to the ultimate goal—requires the extensive use of human resources. How managers perceive their roles in the process of budgeting is important to the successful use of the budget as an effective tool for planning, communicating, and controlling.

REQUIRED:

1. Discuss the behavioral implications of planning and control when a company's management employs:
   a. An imposed budgetary approach.
   b. A participative budgetary approach.
2. Communications plays an important role in the budgetary process whether a participative or imposed budgetary approach is used.
   a. Discuss the differences between communication flows in these two budgetary approaches.
   b. Discuss the behavioral implications associated with the communication process for each of the budgetary approaches.

(CMA adapted)

16-12
Flexible Budgeting
LO 4

Budgeted overhead costs for two different levels of activity are given below.

	Direct Labor Hours	
	1,000	2,000
Maintenance	$10,000	$15,000
Depreciation	5,000	5,000
Supervision	15,000	15,000
Supplies	1,300	2,600
Power	600	1,200
Other	8,100	8,200

REQUIRED: Prepare a flexible budget for an activity level of 1,500 direct labor hours.

16-13
Cash Receipts Budget
LO 3

Hillerman's Department Store has found from past experience that 20 percent of its sales are for cash. The remaining 80 percent are on credit. An aging schedule for accounts receivable reveals the following pattern:

10% of credit sales are paid in the month of sale.
70% of credit sales are paid in the month following sale.
17% of credit sales are paid in the second month following sale.
3% of credit sales are never collected.

Credit sales that have not been paid until the second month following sale are considered overdue and are subject to a 2 percent late charge.

Hillerman's Department Store has developed the following sales forecast:

May	$ 76,000
June	85,000
July	68,000
August	80,000
September	100,000

REQUIRED: Prepare a schedule of cash receipts for August and September.

16-14
Cash Disbursements Schedule
LO 3

Hillerman's Department Store purchases a wide variety of merchandise. Purchases are made evenly throughout the month and all are on account. On the first of every month, Hillerman's accounts payable clerk pays for all of the previous month's purchases. Terms are 2/10, n/30 (i.e., a 2 percent discount can be taken if the bill is paid within ten days; otherwise the entire amount is due within thirty days).

The forecast purchases for the months of May through September are as follows:

May	$40,000
June	50,000
July	30,000
August	60,000
September	64,000

REQUIRED:

1. Prepare a cash disbursements schedule for the months of August and September.
2. Now suppose that the store manager wants to see what difference it would make to have the accounts payable clerk pay for any purchases that have been made three times per month, on the 1st, the 11th, and the 21st. Prepare a cash disbursements schedule for the months of July and August assuming this new payment schedule.
3. Suppose that Hillerman's accounts payable clerk does not have time to make payments on two extra days per month and that a temporary employee is hired on the 11th and 21st at $22 per hour, for four hours each of those two days. Is this a good decision? Explain.

16-15
Operating Budget;
Comprehensive
Analysis

LO 2, 3

The Stadler Division of Jones Manufacturing produces a handle assembly used in the production of bows. The assembly is sold to various bow manufacturers throughout the United States. Projected sales for the coming four months are given below.

January	20,000
February	25,000
March	30,000
April	30,000

The following data pertain to production policies and manufacturing specifications followed by the Stadler Division:

a. Finished goods inventory on January 1 is 16,000 units. The desired ending inventory for each month is 80 percent of the next month's sales.
b. The data on materials used are as follows:

Direct Material	Per-Unit Usage	Unit Cost
Number 325	5	$8
Number 326	3	2

Inventory policy dictates that sufficient materials be on hand at the beginning of the month to produce 50 percent of that month's estimated sales. This is exactly the amount of material on hand on January 1.

c. The direct labor used per unit of output is two hours. The average direct labor cost per hour is $9.25.
d. Overhead each month is estimated using a flexible budget formula. (Activity is measured in direct labor hours.)

	Fixed Cost Component	Variable Cost Component
Supplies	$ —	$1.00
Power	—	0.50
Maintenance	15,000	0.40
Supervision	8,000	—
Depreciation	100,000	—
Taxes	6,000	—
Other	40,000	1.50

e. Monthly selling and administrative expenses are also estimated using a flexible budgeting formula. (Activity is measured in units sold.)

	Fixed Costs	Variable Costs
Salaries	$25,000	$ —
Commissions	—	1.00
Depreciation	20,000	—
Shipping	—	0.50
Other	10,000	0.30

f. The unit selling price of the handle assembly is $90.

g. All sales and purchases are for cash. The cash balance on January 1 equals $200,000. If the firm develops a cash shortage by the end of the month, sufficient cash is borrowed to cover the shortage. Any cash borrowed is repaid one month later, as is the interest due. The interest rate is 12 percent per annum.

REQUIRED: Prepare a monthly operating budget for the first quarter with the following schedules:

1. Sales budget
2. Production budget
3. Direct materials purchases budget
4. Direct labor budget
5. Overhead budget
6. Selling and administrative expense budget
7. Ending finished goods budget
8. Cost of goods sold budget
9. Budgeted income statement
10. Cash budget

**16-16
Cash Budget; Pro
Forma Balance
Sheet**
LO 3

Richard Raleigh, controller for Opple Retailers, has assembled the following data to assist in the preparation of a cash budget for the third quarter of 1998:

a. Sales

May (actual)	$100,000
June (actual)	120,000
July (estimated)	90,000
August (estimated)	100,000
September (estimated)	135,000
October (estimated)	110,000

b. Each month, 30 percent of sales are for cash and 70 percent are on credit. The collection pattern for credit sales is 20 percent in the month of sale, 50 percent in the following month, and 30 percent in the second month following sale.

c. Each month, the ending inventory exactly equals 50 percent of the cost of next month's sales. The markup on goods is 33.33 percent of cost.

d. Inventory purchases are paid for in the month following purchase.

e. Recurring monthly expenses are as follows:

Salaries and wages	$10,000
Depreciation on plant and equipment	4,000
Utilities	1,000
Other	1,700

f. Property taxes of $15,000 are due and payable on July 15, 1998.
g. Advertising fees of $6,000 must be paid on August 20, 1998.
h. A lease on a new storage facility is scheduled to begin on September 2. Monthly payments are $5,000.
i. The company has a policy to maintain a minimum cash balance of $10,000. If necessary, it will borrow to meet its short-term needs. All borrowing is done at the beginning of the month. All payments on principal and interest are made at the end of a month. The annual interest rate is 9 percent. The company must borrow in multiples of $1,000.
j. A partially completed balance sheet as of June 30, 1998, is given below. (Accounts payable is for inventory purchases only.)

Cash	$?	
Accounts receivable	?	
Inventory	?	
Plant and equipment	425,000	
Accounts payable		$?
Common stock		210,000
Retained earnings		268,750
Total	$?	$?

REQUIRED:

1. Complete the balance sheet given in Part (j).
2. Prepare a cash budget for each month in the third quarter and for the quarter in total (the third quarter begins on July 1). Provide a supporting schedule of cash collections.
3. Prepare a pro forma balance sheet as of September 30, 1998.

16-17
Participative Budgeting; Not-for-Profit Setting

LO 4, 5

Scott Weidner, the controller in the division of social services for the state, recognizes the importance of the budgetary process for planning, control, and motivation. He believes that a properly implemented process of participative budgeting and management by exception will motivate his subordinates to improve productivity within their particular departments. Based upon this philosophy, Scott has implemented the following budgetary procedures:

1. An appropriation target figure is given to each department manager. This amount represents the maximum funding that each department can expect to receive in the next fiscal year.
2. Department managers develop their individual budgets within the following spending constraints as directed by the controller's staff:
    a. Requests for spending cannot exceed the appropriated target.
    b. All fixed expenditures should be included in the budget. Fixed expenditures include such items as contracts and salaries at current levels.
    c. All government projects directed by higher authority should be included in the budget in their entirety.
3. The controller's staff consolidates the requests from the various departments into one budget for the entire division.
4. Upon final budget approval by the legislature, the controller's staff allocates the appropriation to the various departments on instructions from the division manager. However, a specified percentage of each department's appropriation is held back in anticipation of potential budget cuts and special funding needs. The amount and use of this contingency fund is left to the discretion of the division manager.
5. Each department is allowed to adjust its budget when necessary to operate within the reduced appropriation level. However, as stated in the original directive, specific projects authorized by higher authority must remain intact.

6. The final budget is used as the basis of control for a management-by-exception form of reporting. Excessive expenditures by account for each department are highlighted on a monthly basis. Department managers are expected to account for all expenditures over budget. Fiscal responsibility is an important factor in the overall performance evaluation of department managers. Scott believes his policy of allowing the department managers to participate in the budget process and then holding them accountable for the final budget is essential, especially in times of limited resources. He further believes that the department managers will be motivated to increase the efficiency and effectiveness of their departments because they have provided input into the initial budgetary process and are required to justify any unfavorable performances.

REQUIRED:

1. Discuss the advantages and limitations of participative budgeting.
2. Identify deficiencies in Scott Weidner's outline for a budgetary process. Recommend how each deficiency identified can be corrected.

(CMA adapted)

16-18
Cash Budgeting

LO 3

The controller of Gardner Company is gathering data to prepare the cash budget for April. He plans to develop the budget from the following information:

a. Of all sales, 30 percent are cash sales.
b. Of credit sales, 60 percent are collected within the month of sale. Half of the credit sales collected within the month receive a 2 percent cash discount (for accounts paid within ten days). Twenty percent of credit sales are collected in the following month; remaining credit sales are collected the month thereafter. There are virtually no bad debts.
c. Sales for the first six months of the year are given below. (The first three months are actual sales, and the last three months are estimated sales.)

	Sales
January	$230,000
February	300,000
March	500,000
April	565,000
May	600,000
June	567,000

d. The company sells all that it produces each month. The cost of raw materials equals 20 percent of each sales dollar. The company requires a monthly ending inventory equal to the coming month's production requirements. Of raw materials purchases, 50 percent are paid for in the month of purchase. The remaining 50 percent are paid for in the following month.
e. Wages total $50,000 each month and are paid in the month of incurrence.
f. Budgeted monthly operating expenses total $168,000, of which $22,000 is depreciation and $3,000 is expiration of prepaid insurance (the annual premium of $36,000 is paid on January 1).
g. Dividends of $65,000, declared on March 31, will be paid on April 15.
h. Old equipment will be sold for $13,000 on April 3.
i. On April 10, new equipment will be purchased for $80,000.
j. The company maintains a minimum cash balance of $10,000.
k. The cash balance on April 1 is $12,500.

REQUIRED: Prepare a cash budget for April. Give a supporting schedule that details the cash collections from sales.

16-19
Revision of
Operating Budget;
Pro Forma
Statements for
Income and Cost
of Goods Sold
LO 2

Mary Dalid founded Molid Company three years ago. The company produces a modem for use with minicomputers and microcomputers. Business has expanded rapidly since the company's inception. Bob Wells, the company's general accountant, prepared a budget for the fiscal year ending August 31, 1998. The budget was based on the prior year's sales and production activity because Mary believed that the sales growth experienced during the prior year would not continue at the same pace. The pro forma statements of income and cost of goods sold that were prepared as part of the budgetary process are presented below:

	Molid Company	
	Pro Forma Statement of Income	
	For the Year Ending August 31, 1998	
	(in thousands)	
Net sales		$31,248
Less: Cost of goods sold		(20,765)
Gross profit		$10,483
Less: Operating expenses		(5,400)
Net income before taxes		$ 5,083

	Molid Company		
	Pro Forma Statement of Goods Sold		
	For the Year Ending August 31, 1998		
	(in thousands)		
Direct materials:			
Materials inventory, September 1, 1997		$ 1,360	
Materials purchased		14,476	
Available for use		$15,836	
Less: Materials inventory, August 31, 1998		(1,628)	
Direct materials used			$14,208
Direct labor			1,134
Overhead:			
Indirect materials		$ 1,421	
General		3,240	4,661
Cost of goods manufactured			$20,003
Finished goods, September 1, 1997			1,169
Total goods available			$21,172
Less: Finished goods, August 31, 1998			(407)
Cost of goods sold			$20,765

On December 10, 1997, Mary and Bob met to discuss the first quarter operating results. Bob believed that several changes should be made to the budget assumptions that had been used to prepare the pro forma statements. He prepared the following notes that summarized the changes, which had not become known until the first quarter results were compiled. He submitted the following data to Mary.

a. Actual first-quarter production was 35,000 units. The estimated production for the fiscal year should be increased from 162,000 to 170,000, with the balance of production being scheduled in equal segments over the last nine months of the fiscal year.
b. The planned ending inventory for finished goods of 3,300 units at the end of the fiscal year remains unchanged. The finished goods inventory of 9,300 units as of September

1, 1995, had dropped to 9,000 units by November 30, 1997. The finished goods inventory at the end of the fiscal year will be valued at the average manufacturing costs for the year.

c. Direct materials sufficient to produce 16,000 units were on hand at the beginning of the fiscal year. The plan to have the equivalent of 18,500 units of production in direct materials inventory at the end of the fiscal year remains unchanged. Direct materials inventory is valued on a LIFO basis. Direct materials equivalent to 37,500 units of output were purchased for $3.3 million during the first quarter of the fiscal year. Molid's suppliers have informed the company that direct material prices will increase 5 percent on March 1, 1998. Direct materials needed for the rest of the fiscal year will be purchased evenly throughout the last nine months.

d. On the basis of historical data, indirect material cost is projected at 10 percent of the cost of direct materials consumed.

e. One-half of general factory overhead and all marketing and general and administrative expenses are considered fixed.

REQUIRED: Based on the revised data presented by Bob Wells, prepare new pro forma statements for income and cost of goods sold for the year ending August 31, 1998.

(CMA adapted)

**16-20
Performance
Reporting;
Behavioral
Considerations**

LO 4

Berwin, Inc., is a manufacturer of small industrial tools with annual sales of approximately $3.5 million. Sales growth has been steady during the year, and there is no evidence of cyclical demand. Production has increased gradually during the year and has been evenly distributed throughout each month. The company has a sequential processing system. The four manufacturing departments—Casting, Machining, Finishing, and Packaging—are all located in the same building. Fixed overhead is assigned using a plantwide rate.

Berwin has always been able to compete with other manufacturers of small tools. However, its market has expanded only in response to product innovation. Thus, research and development is very important and has helped Berwin to expand as well as maintain demand.

Carla Viller, controller, has designed and implemented a new budget system in response to concerns voiced by George Berwin, president. Carla prepared an annual budget that has been divided into twelve equal segments; this budget can be used to assist in the timely evaluation of monthly performance. George was visibly upset upon receiving the May performance report for the Machining Department. George exclaimed, "How can they be efficient enough to produce nine extra units every working day and still miss the budget by $300 per day?" Gene Jordan, supervisor of the Machining Department, could not understand "all the red ink" when he knew that the department had operated more efficiently in May than it had in months. Gene stated, "I was expecting a pat on the back, and instead, the boss tore me apart. What's more, I don't even know why!"

Berwin, Inc.
Machining Department Performance Report
For the Month Ended May 31, 1998

	Actual	*Budgeted*	*Variance*
Volume in units	3,185	3,000	185 F
Variable manufacturing costs:			
Direct materials	$ 24,843	$24,000	$ 843 U
Direct labor	29,302	27,750	1,552 U
Variable overhead	35,035	33,300	1,735 U
Total variable costs	$ 89,180	$85,050	$4,130 U

continued

	Actual	Budgeted	Variance
Fixed manufacturing costs:			
Indirect labor	$ 3,334	$ 3,300	$ 34 U
Depreciation	1,500	1,500	—
Taxes	300	300	—
Insurance	240	240	—
Other	1,027	930	97 U
Total fixed costs	$ 6,401	$ 6,270	$ 131 U
Corporate costs:			
Research and development	$ 3,728	$ 2,400	$1,328 U
Selling and administrative	4,075	3,600	475 U
Total corporate costs	$ 7,803	$ 6,000	$1,803 U
Total costs	$103,384	$97,320	$6,064 U

REQUIRED:

1. Review the May performance report. Based on the information given in the report and elsewhere
   a. Discuss the strengths and weaknesses of the new budgetary system.
   b. Identify the weaknesses of the performance report and explain how it should be revised to eliminate each weakness.
2. Prepare a revised report for the Machining Department using the May data.
3. What other changes would you make to improve Berwin's budgetary system?

(CMA adapted)

**16-21
Master Budget;
Comprehensive
Review**
LO 2, 3

Electra Company is a high-technology organization that produces a mass-storage system. The design of Electra's system is unique and represents a breakthrough in the industry. The units Electra produces combine positive features of both floppy and hard disks. The company is completing its fifth year of operations and is preparing to build its master budget for the coming year (1998). The budget will detail each quarter's activity and the activity for the year in total. The master budget will be based on the following information:

a. Fourth quarter sales for 1997 are 55,000 units.
b. Unit sales by quarter (for 1998) are projected as follows:

First quarter	60,000
Second quarter	65,000
Third quarter	75,000
Fourth quarter	90,000

The selling price is $400 per unit. All sales are credit sales. Electra collects 85 percent of all sales within the quarter in which they are realized; the other 15 percent are collected in the following quarter. There are no bad debts.

c. There is no beginning inventory of finished goods. Electra is planning the following ending finished goods inventories for each quarter:

First quarter	13,000 units
Second quarter	15,000 units
Third quarter	20,000 units
Fourth quarter	10,000 units

d. Each mass-storage unit uses five hours of direct labor and three units of direct materials. Laborers are paid $10 per hour, and one unit of materials costs $80.

e. There are 65,700 units of direct materials in beginning inventory as of January 1, 1998. At the end of each quarter, Electra plans to have 30 percent of the raw materials needed for next quarter's unit sales. Electra will end the year with the same level of raw materials found in this year's beginning inventory.

f. Electra buys raw materials on account. One-half of the purchases is paid for in the quarter of acquisition, and the remaining half is paid for in the following quarter. Wages and salaries are paid on the fifteenth and thirtieth of each month.

g. Fixed overhead totals $1 million each quarter. Of this total, $350,000 represents depreciation. All other fixed expenses are paid for in cash in the quarter incurred. The fixed overhead rate is computed by dividing the year's total fixed overhead by the year's expected actual units produced.

h. Variable overhead is budgeted at $6 per direct labor hour. All variable overhead expenses are paid for in the quarter incurred.

i. Fixed selling and administrative expenses total $250,000 per quarter, including $50,000 depreciation.

j. Variable selling and administrative expenses are budgeted at $10 per unit sold. All selling and administrative expenses are paid for in the quarter incurred.

k. The balance sheet as of December 31, 1997, is as follows:

Assets

Cash	$ 250,000
Inventory	5,256,000
Accounts receivable	3,300,000
Plant and equipment	33,500,000
Total assets	$42,306,000

Liabilities and Equity

Accounts payable	$ 7,248,000*
Capital stock	27,000,000
Retained earnings	8,058,000
Total liabilities and equity	$42,306,000

*For purchase of materials only.

Electra will pay quarterly dividends of $300,000. At the end of the fourth quarter, $2 million of equipment will be purchased.

REQUIRED: Prepare a master budget for Electra Company for each quarter of 1998 and for the year in total. The following component budgets must be included:

a. Sales budget
b. Production budget
c. Direct materials purchases budget
d. Direct labor budget
e. Overhead budget
f. Selling and administrative expense budget
g. Ending finished goods inventory budget
h. Cost of goods sold budget
i. Cash budget
j. Pro forma income statement (using absorption costing)
k. Pro forma balance sheet

Denny Daniels is production manager of the Alumalloy Division of WRT, Inc. Alumalloy has limited contact with outside customers and no sales staff. Most of its customers are handled by other corporate divisions. Therefore, Alumalloy is treated as a cost center rather than a profit center.

Denny perceives the Accounting Department as the unit that generates historical numbers but provides little useful information. The Accounting Department creates the budgets at the beginning of the year and then gathers the actual costs incurred by production. Denny wonders whether the accountants even understand the nature of the production process itself. It seems all they are concerned with are numbers—whether they mean anything or not. In his opinion, the whole accounting process is a negative motivational device that does not reflect how hard or efficiently he has worked as a production manager. Denny tried to discuss these perceptions and concerns with John Scott, the controller for Alumalloy. Denny told John, "I know I've had better production over a number of operating periods, but the cost report still says I have excessive costs. Look, I'm not an accountant, I'm a production manager. I know how to get a good quality product out. Over a number of years, I've even cut the raw materials used to do it. But the cost report doesn't show any of this. It's always negative no matter what I do. There is no way you can win with accounting or those people at corporate who use those reports."

John gave Denny little consolation. John stated that the accounting system and the cost reports generated by headquarters are just part of the corporate game and almost impossible for an individual to change. "Although these reports are the basis for evaluating the efficiency of your division and the means for corporate to determine whether you have done the job it wants, you shouldn't worry too much. You haven't been fired yet! Besides, these cost reports have been used by WRT for the last twenty-five years."

From talking to the production manager of the zinc division, Denny perceived that most of what John said was true. However, some minor cost reporting changes for zinc had been agreed to by corporate headquarters. He also knew from the trade grapevine that the turnover of production managers was considered high at WRT, even though relatively few managers were fired. Most seemed to end up quitting, usually in disgust, out of the belief that they were not being evaluated fairly.

A recent copy of the cost report prepared by corporate headquarters for Alumalloy is shown below. Because of an unexpected increase in demand for the final product, Alumalloy produced 10,000 units more than the 40,000 originally budgeted. Denny does not like this report because he believes that it fails to reflect the division's operations properly, thereby resulting in an unfair evaluation of performance.

Alumalloy Division
Cost Report
For the Month of April 1998
(in thousands)

	Actual Cost	*Master Budget*	*Variance*
Aluminum	$ 477	$ 400	$ 77 U
Labor	675	560	115 U
Overhead	110	100	10 U
Total	$1,262	$1,060	$202 U

REQUIRED:

1. Comment on Denny's perception of
   a. John Scott, the controller.
   b. Corporate headquarters.
   c. The cost report.
   d. Himself as a production manager.

e. Discuss how his perception of these items affects his performance as a production manager of WRT.

2. List the deficiencies of WRT's budgetary system. Prepare a list of recommendations to improve the system so that the process and the reports produced are more useful and less threatening to the production managers.

(CMA adapted)

16-23

Cash Budget, Importance of Cash Budget

LO 1, 3

CrossMan Corporation, a rapidly expanding crossbow distributor to retail outlets, is in the process of formulating plans for 1998. Joan Caldwell, director of marketing, has completed her 1997 forecast and is confident that sales estimates will be met or exceeded. The following sales figures show the growth expected and will provide the planning basis for other corporate departments.

Month	Forecasted Sales
January	$1,800,000
February	2,000,000
March	1,800,000
April	2,200,000
May	2,500,000
June	2,800,000
July	3,000,000
August	3,000,000
September	3,200,000
October	3,200,000
November	3,000,000
December	3,400,000

George Brownell, assistant controller, has been given the responsibility for formulating the cash flow projection, a critical element during a period of rapid expansion. The following information will be used in preparing the cash analysis.

CrossMan has experienced an excellent record in accounts receivable collection and expects this trend to continue. Sixty percent of billings are collected in the month after the sale and 40 percent in the second month after the sale. Uncollectible accounts are nominal and will not be considered in the analysis.

The purchase of the crossbows is CrossMan's largest expenditure; the cost of these items equals 50 percent of sales. Sixty percent of the crossbows are received one month prior to sale, and 40 percent are received during the month of sale.

Prior experience shows that 80 percent of accounts payable are paid by CrossMan one month after receipt of the purchased crossbows, and the remaining 20 percent are paid the second month after receipt.

Hourly wages, including fringe benefits, are a factor of sales volume and are equal to 20 percent of the current month's sales. These wages are paid in the month incurred.

General and administrative expenses are projected to be $2,640,000 for 1998. The composition of the expenses is given below. All of these expenses are incurred uniformly throughout the year except the property taxes. Property taxes are paid in four equal installments in the last month of each quarter.

Salaries	$ 480,000
Promotion	660,000
Property taxes	240,000
Insurance	360,000
Utilities	300,000
Depreciation	600,000
Total	$2,640,000

Income tax payments are made by CrossMan in the first month of each quarter based on the income for the prior quarter. CrossMan's income tax rate is 40 percent. CrossMan's net income for the first quarter of 1998 is projected to be $612,000.

CrossMan has a corporate policy of maintaining an end-of-month cash balance of $100,000. Cash is invested or borrowed monthly, as necessary, to maintain this balance.

CrossMan uses a calendar-year reporting period.

REQUIRED:

1. Prepare a Pro Forma Schedule of Cash Receipts and Disbursements for CrossMan Corporation, by month, for the second quarter of 1998. Be sure that all receipts, disbursements, and borrowing/investing amounts are presented on a monthly basis. Ignore the interest expense and/or interest income associated with the borrowing/investing activities.
2. Discuss why cash budgeting is particularly important for a rapidly expanding company such as CrossMan Corporation.

(CMA adapted)

16-24
Budgeting Process and Participatory Budgeting
LO 1, 4

Five years ago, Jack Cadence and two colleagues left their positions with a large industrial firm to start up Advanced Technologies Co. (ATC), a software design company. Cadence, the major owner, obtained venture capital, and ATC commenced work on the design of a unique software package to make the use and integration of PCs easier. Since the completion of this package, there has been good market acceptance, and Cadence has been able to raise the additional capital necessary to operate during the initial marketing stages. Cadence has concentrated on managing the company, while the other two minority owners focused on design and development activities. ATC has now started on the development of new software to permit the ready usage of the underapplied power of the advanced microprocessors that have entered the marketplace.

With the continued sales growth of the initial software and the ongoing development of new programming products, Cadence has hired several seasoned marketing, sales, and production managers, as well as Jeff Cross, a senior accountant with a budgeting background.

ATC currently employs 70 people in the Design & Development, Marketing, Sales, Accounting, and Legal Departments. Recently, Cadence decided that, with the expansion of ATC, a formalized planning and control process should be established. Cadence asked Cross to work with him in developing the initial budget for ATC.

As several of the senior managers were new to the company, Cadence forecasted the sales revenue based on his projections for both the market growth for the initial software and the successful completion of new product developments. Cadence further prepared production and expense projections. Cross used this information to construct departmental budgets and the overall company budget. Cadence and Cross reviewed and revised these budgets on several occasions.

When Cadence and Cross were satisfied, the various budgets were distributed with a cover letter advising that ATC was adopting a formalized planning procedure. The letter further requested everyone's assistance in working together to achieve the budget objectives in order to continue the company's successful and growing operations.

Several of the department managers, particularly the newly hired seasoned personnel, were displeased with how the planning process was undertaken. In discussing the situation among themselves, they felt that some of the budget projections were overly optimistic and not realistically attainable.

REQUIRED:

1. The planning process that Jack Cadence and Jeff Cross utilized is referred to as a top-down budgeting process.
   a. Explain why this is a top-down budgeting process, and compare it to a participatory budgeting process.
   b. Describe the advantages associated with a top-down budgeting process.

2. a. Describe the personal behavioral issues faced by Jack Cadence, as the founder of ATC, in initiating a formalized budgeting process.
   b. Describe the behavioral problems for the remainder of the employees at ATC that may result from a top-down budgeting process.
3. a. Outline specific recommendations that Cadence and Cross could have employed to initiate a participatory budgeting process.
   b. Describe the advantages associated with a participatory budgeting process.

(CMA adapted)

16-25
Information for
Budgeting; Ethics
LO 1, 4

Norton Company, a manufacturer of infant furniture and carriages, is in the initial stages of preparing the annual budget for 1998. Scott Ford recently joined Norton's accounting staff and is eager to learn as much as possible about the company's budgeting process. During a recent lunch with Marge Atkins, sales manager, and Pete Granger, production manager, Scott initiated the following conversation.

Scott: Since I'm new around here and am going to be involved with the preparation of the annual budget, I'd be interested to learn how the two of you estimate sales and production numbers.

Marge: We start out very methodically by looking at recent history, discussing what we know about current accounts, potential customers, and the general state of consumer spending. Then, we add that dose of intuition to come up with the best forecast we can.

Pete: I usually take the sales projections as the basis for my projections. Of course, we have to make an estimate of what this year's closing inventories will be, which is sometimes difficult.

Scott: Why does that present a problem? There must have been an estimate of closing inventories in the budget for the current year.

Pete: Those numbers aren't always reliable, since Marge makes some adjustments to the sales numbers before passing them on to me.

Scott: What kind of adjustments?

Marge: Well, we don't want to fall short of the sales projections, so we generally give ourselves a little breathing room by lowering the initial sales projection from 5-10 percent.

Pete: So you can see why this year's budget is not a very reliable starting point. We always have to adjust the projected production rates as the year progresses, and of course, this changes the ending inventory estimates. By the way, we make similar adjustments to expenses by adding at least 10 percent to the estimates; I think everyone around here does the same thing.

REQUIRED:

1. Marge Atkins and Pete Granger have described the use of budgetary slack.
   a. Explain why Marge and Pete behave in this manner, and describe the benefits they expect to realize from the use of budgetary slack.
   b. Explain how the use of budgetary slack can adversely affect Marge and Pete.
2. As a management accountant, Scott Ford believes that the behavior described by Marge Atkins and Pete Granger may be unethical and that he may have an obligation not to support this behavior. By citing the specific standards of competence, confidentiality, integrity, and/or objectivity from the "Standards of Ethical Conduct for Management Accountants" (in Chapter 1), explain why the use of budgetary slack may be unethical.

(CMA adapted)

16-26
Flexible Budget,
Behavioral
Considerations
LO 4

Greenleaf Inc. manufactures power mowers that are sold throughout the United States and Canada. The company used a comprehensive budgeting process and compares actual results to budgeted amounts on a monthly basis. Each month, Greenleaf's accounting department prepares a variance analysis and distributes the report to all responsible parties. Al Richmond, production manager, is upset about the results for May that are shown below. Richmond, who is responsible for the cost of goods manufactured, has implemented several cost-cutting measures in the manufacturing area and is discouraged by the unfavorable variance in variable costs.

	Actual	Master Budget	Variance	
		Operating Results For the Month of May		
Units sold	4,800	5,000	200	U
Revenue	$1,152,000	$1,200,000	$48,000	U
Variable costs	780,000	760,000	20,000	U
Contribution margin	$ 372,000	$ 440,000	$68,000	U
Fixed overhead	180,000	180,000	—	
Fixed G&A	115,000	120,000	5,000	F
Operating income	$ 77,000	$ 140,000	$63,000	U

When the master budget was prepared, Greenleaf's cost accountant, Joan Ballard, supplied the following unit costs: direct materials, $60; direct labor, $44; variable overhead, $36; and variable selling, $12.

The total variable costs of $780,000 for May are comprised of $320,000 direct materials, $192,000 direct labor, $176,000 variable overhead, and $92,000 variable selling expenses. Ballard believes that Greenleaf's monthly reports would be more meaningful to everyone if the company adopted flexible budgeting and prepared more detailed analyses.

REQUIRED:

1. Using the data given above:
   a. prepare a flexible budget for Greenleaf Inc. for the month of May that includes separate variable cost budgets.
   b. determine the flexible budget variances.
2. Discuss how the revised budget and variance data are likely to impact the behavior of Al Richmond, production manager.

(CMA adapted)

Chapter 17
Standard Costing: A Traditional Control Approach

Snapple's carefully developed standards for ingredients ensure that each bottle of Mango Madness Cocktail contains exactly the right amounts of both mango and madness (well, maybe just mango). The result is that consumers know just what to expect with each purchase.

LEARNING OBJECTIVES

After studying this chapter, you should be able to:

1. Explain how unit standards are set and why standard cost systems are adopted.
2. Explain the purpose of a standard cost sheet.
3. Describe the basic concepts underlying variance analysis and explain when variances should be investigated.
4. Compute and journalize the materials and labor variances and explain how they are used for control.
5. Compute overhead variances three different ways and explain overhead accounting.
6. Calculate mix and yield variances for materials and labor.

Budgets set standards that are used to control and evaluate managerial performance. However, budgets are *aggregate* measures of performance; they identify the revenues and costs in total that an organization should experience if plans are executed as expected. By comparing the actual costs and actual revenues with the corresponding budgeted amounts at the same level of activity, a measure of managerial efficiency emerges.

Although the budgetary process just described provides significant information for control, control can be enhanced by developing standards for *unit* amounts as well as for total amounts. In fact, the groundwork for unit standards already exists within the framework of flexible budgeting. For flexible budgeting to work, the budgeted variable cost per unit of input for each unit of output must be known for every item in the budget. The budgeted variable input cost per unit of output is a unit standard. Unit standards are the basis or foundation on which a flexible budget is built. Unit standards are also the building elements for a standard cost system.

UNIT STANDARDS

Objective 1
Explain how unit standards are set and why standard cost systems are adopted.

quantity standards
price standards

To determine the unit standard cost for a particular input, two decisions must be made: (1) how much of the input should be used per unit of output (the *quantity decision*) and (2) how much should be paid for the quantity of the input to be used (the *pricing decision*). The quantity decision produces **quantity standards**, and the pricing decision produces **price standards**. The unit standard cost for a particular input can be computed by multiplying these two standards (Standard price × Standard quantity).

For example, an ice cream company may decide that 25 ounces of yogurt should be used for every quart of frozen yogurt produced (the quantity standard) and that the price of the yogurt should be $0.02 per ounce (the price standard). The standard cost of the yogurt per quart of frozen yogurt is then $0.50 ($0.02 × 25). The standard cost of yogurt per quart can be used to predict what the total cost of yogurt should be as the activity level varies; it thus becomes a flexible budget formula. Thus, if 20,000 quarts of frozen yogurt are produced, the total expected cost of yogurt is $10,000 ($0.50 × 20,000); if 30,000 quarts are produced, the total expected cost of yogurt is $15,000 ($0.50 × 30,000).

How Standards Are Developed

Historical experience, engineering studies, and input from operating personnel are three potential sources of quantitative standards. Although historical experience may provide an initial guideline for setting standards, it should not be used without caution. Often processes are operating inefficiently; adopting input-output relationships from the past thus perpetuates these inefficiencies. Engineering studies can determine the most efficient way to operate and can provide very rigorous guidelines; however, engineered standards are often too rigorous. They may not be achievable by operating personnel. Since operating personnel are accountable for meeting the standards, they should have significant input in setting standards. The same principles pertaining to participative budgeting pertain to setting unit standards.

Price standards are the joint responsibility of operations, purchasing, personnel, and accounting. Operations determines the quality of the inputs required; personnel and purchasing have the responsibility to acquire the input quality requested at the lowest price. Market forces, trade unions, and other external forces limit the range of choices for price standards. In setting price standards, purchasing must consider discounts, freight, and quality; personnel, on the other hand, must consider payroll taxes, fringe benefits, and qualifications. Accounting is responsible for recording the price standards and for preparing reports that compare actual performance to the standard.

Types of Standards

ideal standards

currently attainable standards

Standards are traditionally classified as either *ideal* or *currently attainable*. **Ideal standards** are standards that demand maximum efficiency and can be achieved only if everything operates perfectly. No machine breakdowns, slack, or lack of skill (even momentarily) are allowed. **Currently attainable standards** can be achieved under efficient operating conditions. Allowance is made for normal breakdowns, interruptions, less than perfect skill, and so on. These standards are demanding but achievable.

Of the two types, currently attainable standards offer the most behavioral benefits. If standards are too tight and never achievable, workers become frustrated and performance levels decline. However, challenging but achievable standards can lead to higher performance levels—particularly when the individuals subject to the standards have participated in their creation.

Why Standard Cost Systems Are Adopted

Two reasons for adopting a standard cost system are frequently mentioned: to improve planning and control and to facilitate product costing.

Planning and Control Standard costing systems enhance planning and control and improve performance measurement. Unit standards are a fundamental requirement for a flexible budgeting system, which is a key feature of a meaningful planning and control system. Budgetary control systems compare actual costs with budgeted costs by computing variances, the difference between the actual and planned costs for the actual level of activity. By developing unit price and quantity standards, an overall variance can be decomposed into a *price variance* and a *usage or efficiency variance*.

By performing this decomposition, a manager has more information. If the variance is unfavorable, a manager can tell whether it is attributable to discrepancies between planned prices and actual prices, to discrepancies between planned usage and actual usage, or to both. Since managers have more control over the usage of inputs than over their prices, efficiency variances provide specific signals regarding the need for corrective action and where that action should be focused. Thus, in principle, the use of efficiency variances enhances operational control. Additionally, by breaking out the price variance, over which managers have little control, the system provides an improved measure of managerial efficiency.

The benefits of operational control, however, may not extend to the contemporary manufacturing environment. The use of a standard cost system for operational control in a contemporary manufacturing environment can produce dysfunctional behavior. For example, materials price variance reporting may encourage the purchasing department to buy in large quantities, to take advantage of discounts. Yet this may lead to holding significant inventories, something not desired by JIT firms. Thus, the detailed computation of variances—at least at the operational level—is discouraged in this new environment. Nonetheless, standards in the contemporary manufacturing environment are still useful for planning, for example, in the creation of bids. Also, variances may still be computed and presented in reports to higher-level managers so that the financial dimension can be monitored.

Finally, it should be mentioned that there are many firms that are operating with traditional manufacturing systems. Standard cost systems are widely used. In a recent survey, 87 percent of the firms responding used a standard cost system.[1] Furthermore, the survey revealed that significant numbers of the respondents were calculating variances at the operational level. For example, about 40 percent of the firms using a standard costing system reported labor variances for small work crews or individual workers.

Product Costing In a standard cost system, costs are assigned to products using quantity and price standards for all three manufacturing costs: direct materials, direct labor, and overhead. In contrast, a normal cost system predetermines overhead costs for the purpose of product costing but assigns direct materials and direct labor to products by using actual costs. Overhead is assigned using a budgeted rate and actual activity. At the other end of the cost assignment spectrum, an actual cost system assigns the actual costs of all three manufacturing inputs to products. Exhibit 17-1 summarizes these three cost assignment approaches.

Standard product costing has several advantages over normal costing and actual costing. One, of course, is the greater capacity for control. Standard cost systems also provide readily available unit cost information that can be used for pricing decisions. This is particularly helpful for companies that do a significant amount of bidding and for those paid on a cost-plus basis.

Other simplifications are also possible. For example, if a process costing system uses standard costing to assign product costs, there is no need to compute a unit cost for each equivalent unit-cost category. A standard unit cost would exist for materials, transferred-in, and conversion cost categories.[2] Additionally, there is no need to distinguish between the FIFO and weighted average methods of accounting for beginning inventory costs. Usually, a standard process costing system will follow the equivalent-unit calculation of the FIFO approach. That is, *current* equivalent units of work are calculated. By calculating current equivalent work, current actual production costs can be compared with standard costs (costs allowed for current production) for control purposes.

STANDARD PRODUCT COSTS

Objective 2

Explain the purpose of a standard cost sheet.

The most common application of standard costing is found within manufacturing organizations. Standard costs also can be used in service organizations. The IRS, for example, could set standard processing times for different categories of returns. If the standard processing time is 3 minutes for a 1040EZ, and the stan-

---

1.   Bruce R. Gaumnitz and Felix P. Kollaritsch, "Manufacturing Variances: Current Practice and Trends," *Journal of Cost Management* (Spring 1991), pp. 58–64.
2.   If you have not read the chapter on process costing, the example illustrating the simplifications made possible by standard costing will not be as meaningful. However, the point being made is still relevant: Standard costing can bring useful computational savings.

Exhibit 17-1
Cost Assignment Approaches

	Manufacturing Costs		
	Direct Materials	*Direct Labor*	*Overhead*
Actual cost system	Actual	Actual	Actual
Normal cost system	Actual	Actual	Budgeted
Standard cost system	Standard	Standard	Standard

dard price of labor is $9 per hour, then the standard cost of processing a 1040EZ is $0.45 ($9 × 3/60). Other examples exist. The federal government is using a standard costing system for purposes of reimbursement of Medicare costs. Based on several studies, illnesses have been classified into diagnostic related groups (DRGs) and the hospital costs that should be incurred for an average case identified. (The costs include patient days, food, medicine, supplies, use of equipment, and so on.) The government pays the hospital the standard cost for the DRG. If the cost of the patient's treatment is greater than the DRG allows, the hospital suffers a loss. If the cost of the patient's treatment is less than the DRG reimbursement, the hospital gains. On average, the hospital supposedly breaks even.

standard cost per unit
standard cost sheet

Standard costs are developed for materials, labor, and overhead used in producing a product or service. Using these costs, the **standard cost per unit** is computed. The **standard cost sheet** provides the detail underlying the standard unit cost. To illustrate, let us develop a standard cost sheet for a quart of deluxe strawberry frozen yogurt, produced by Helado Company (Helado sells its frozen yogurt only at specialty shops). The production of the frozen strawberry yogurt begins by creating two different mixtures. The first mixture consists of milk and gelatin. These two ingredients are mixed, heated, and then cooled. The second mixture consists of yogurt, whipped cream, and crushed strawberries. The two mixtures are blended and mixed well. This final mixture is then poured into a one-quart container and frozen. The process is automated. Labor is used to operate the equipment and inspect the product for consistency and flavor. The standard cost sheet is given in Exhibit 17-2.

Five materials are used to produce the strawberry: yogurt, strawberries, milk, cream, and gelatin. The container in which the yogurt is placed is also classified as a direct material. Direct labor consists of machine operators (who also inspect). Variable overhead is made up of three costs: gas (used in cooking), electricity (used to operate the equipment), and water (used for cleaning); it is applied using direct labor hours. Fixed overhead is also applied using direct labor hours and consists of salaries, depreciation, taxes, and insurance. Notice that 37 ounces of liquids (yogurt, milk, and cream) are used to produce a quart of frozen yogurt. This extra input is needed for two reasons. First, some liquid is lost through evaporation. Second, Helado wants slightly more than 32 ounces of frozen yogurt placed in each container to ensure customer satisfaction.

Exhibit 17-2 also reveals other important insights. The standard usage for variable and fixed overhead is tied to the direct labor standards. For variable overhead, the rate is $6.00 per direct labor hour. Since one quart of frozen yogurt uses 0.01 direct labor hour, the variable overhead cost assigned to a quart is $0.06

Exhibit 17-2
Standard Cost Sheet for Deluxe Frozen Straw-berry Yogurt

Description	Standard Price		Standard Usage		Standard Cost	Subtotal
Direct materials:						
Yogurt	$0.020	×	25 oz.	=	$0.50	
Strawberries	0.010	×	10 oz.	=	0.10	
Milk	0.015	×	8 oz.	=	0.12	
Cream	0.025	×	4 oz.	=	0.10	
Gelatin	0.010	×	1 oz.	=	0.01	
Container	0.030	×	1	=	0.03	
Total direct materials						$0.86
Direct labor:						
Machine operators	8.00	×	.01 hr.	=	$0.08	
Total direct labor						0.08
Overhead:						
Variable overhead	6.00	×	.01 hr.	=	$0.06	
Fixed overhead	20.00	×	.01 hr.	=	0.20	
Total overhead						0.26
Total standard unit cost						$1.20

($6.00 × 0.01). For fixed overhead, the rate is $20 per direct labor hour, making the fixed overhead cost per quart $0.20 ($20 × 0.01). Using direct labor hours as the only driver to assign overhead reveals that Helado uses a traditional cost accounting system.

The standard cost sheet also reveals the quantity of each input that should be used to produce one unit of output. The unit quantity standards can be used to compute the total amount of inputs allowed for the actual output. This computation is an essential component in computing efficiency variances. A manager should be able to compute the **standard quantity of materials allowed** *(SQ)* and the **standard hours allowed** *(SH)* for the actual output. This computation must be done for every class of direct material and for every class of direct labor. Assume, for example, that 20,000 quarts of frozen strawberry yogurt are produced during the first week of March. How much yogurt should have been used for the actual output of 20,000 quarts? The unit quantity standard is 25 ounces of yogurt per quart (see Exhibit 17-2). For 20,000 quarts, the standard quantity of yogurt allowed is computed as follows:

standard quantity of materials allowed

standard hours allowed

$$SQ = \text{Unit quantity standard} \times \text{Actual output}$$
$$= 25 \times 20,000$$
$$= 500,000 \text{ ounces}$$

The computation of standard direct labor hours allowed can also be illustrated. From Exhibit 17-2, we see that the unit quantity standard is 0.01 hour per quart produced. Thus, if 20,000 quarts are produced, the standard hours allowed is as follows:

$$SH = \text{Unit quantity standard} \times \text{Actual output}$$
$$= 0.01 \times 20,000$$
$$= 200 \text{ direct labor hours}$$

VARIANCE ANALYSIS: GENERAL DESCRIPTION

Objective 3
Describe the basic concepts underlying variance analysis and explain when variances should be investigated.

A flexible budget can be used to identify the costs that should have been incurred for the actual level of activity. This figure is obtained by multiplying the amount of input allowed for the actual output by the standard unit price. Letting *SP* be the standard unit price of an input and *SQ* the standard quantity of inputs allowed for the actual output, the planned or budgeted input cost is $SP \times SQ$. The actual input cost is $AP \times AQ$, where *AP* is the actual price per unit of the input and *AQ* is the actual quantity of input used.

Price and Efficiency Variances

total budget variance

The **total budget variance**, expressed in financial terms, is simply the difference between the actual cost of the input and its planned cost. For simplicity, we will refer to the total budget variance as the *total variance*.

$$\text{Total variance} = (AP \times AQ) - (SP \times SQ)$$

price (rate) variance
usage (efficiency) variance

In a standard cost system, the total variance is broken down into price and usage variances. **Price (rate) variance** is the difference between the actual and standard unit price of an input multiplied by the number of inputs used. **Usage (efficiency) variance** is the difference between the actual and standard quantity of inputs multiplied by the standard unit price of the input. As mentioned earlier, by breaking the total budget variance down into these two components, managers can better analyze and control the total variance. They are able to identify the origin of cost increases and take appropriate corrective action. Usually, the total variance is divided into price and efficiency components for direct materials and direct labor. The treatment of overhead is discussed later in the chapter.

Dividing the total variance into price and efficiency components is accomplished by subtracting and adding $SP \times AQ$ to the right-hand side of the total variance equation:

$$\begin{aligned}
\text{Total variance} &= [(AP \times AQ) - (SP \times AQ)] + [(SP \times AQ) - (SP \times SQ)] \\
&= (AP - SP)AQ + (AQ - SQ)SP \\
&= \text{Price variance} + \text{Usage variance}
\end{aligned}$$

Exhibit 17-3 presents a three-pronged diagram that describes this process.

unfavorable (U) variances
favorable (F) variances

Unfavorable (U) variances occur whenever actual prices or usage of inputs are greater than standard prices or usage. When the opposite occurs, **favorable (F) variances** are obtained. Since the price and usage formulas are set up so that actual less standard is computed (e.g., AP − SP), a *positive* number indicates an unfavorable variance and a *negative* number indicates a favorable variance. The same is true of the three-pronged diagram. Favorable and unfavorable variances are not equivalent to good and bad variances. The terms merely indicate the relationship of the actual prices or quantities to the standard prices and quantities. Whether or not the variances are good or bad depends on *why* they occurred. Determining why requires managers to do some investigation.

The Decision to Investigate

Rarely will actual performance exactly meet the established standards, nor does management expect it to. Random variations around the standard are expected. Because of this, management should have in mind an acceptable range of per-

Exhibit 17-3
Variance Analysis: General Description

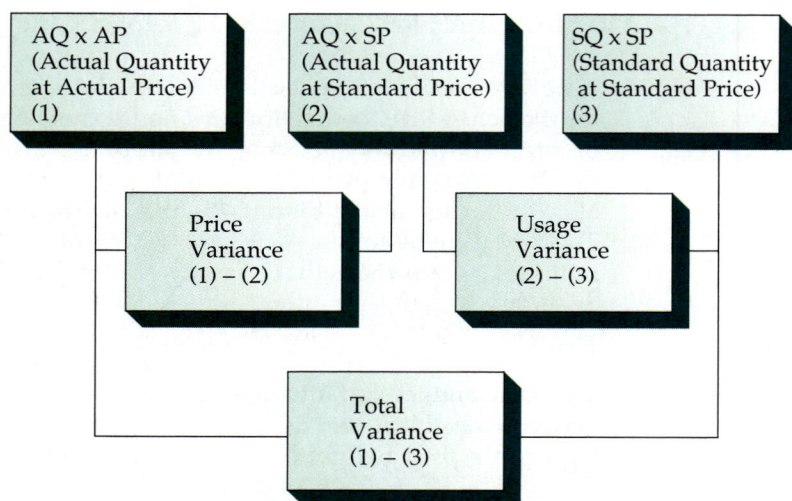

Note: An unfavorable (favorable) variance occurs whenever the left prong − right prong is positive (negative). Thus, if (1) − (2) > 0, then we have an unfavorable price variance; if (2) − (3) > 0, then we have an unfavorable usage variance. Similarly, if (1) − (2) < 0, then we have a favorable price variance; if (2) − (3) < 0, then we have a favorable usage variance.

formance. When variances are within this range, they are assumed to be caused by random factors. When a variance falls outside this range, the deviation is likely to be caused by nonrandom factors, either factors that managers can control or factors they cannot control. In the noncontrollable case, managers need to revise the standard.

Whether or not to investigate variances is a critical issue. Investigating the cause of variances and taking corrective action, like all activities, have a cost associated with them. As a general principle, an investigation should be undertaken only if the anticipated benefits are greater than the expected costs. Assessing the costs and benefits of a variance investigation is not an easy task, however. A manager must consider whether a variance will recur. If so, the process may be permanently out of control, meaning that periodic savings may be achieved if corrective action is taken. But how can we tell if the variance is going to recur unless an investigation is conducted? And how do we know the cost of corrective action unless the cause of the variance is known?

Because it is difficult to assess the costs and benefits of variance analysis on a case-by-case basis, many firms adopt the general guideline of investigating variances only if they fall outside an acceptable range. They are not investigated unless they are large enough to be of concern. They must be large enough to be caused by something other than random factors and large enough (on average) to justify the costs of investigating and taking corrective action.

How do managers determine whether variances are significant? How is the acceptable range established? The acceptable range is the standard plus or minus an allowable deviation. The top and bottom measures of the allowable range are called the **control limits**. The *upper control limit* is the standard plus the allowable deviation, and the *lower control limit* is the standard minus the allowable deviation. Current practice sets the control limits subjectively: based on past experi-

control limits

ence, intuition, and judgment, management determines the allowable deviation from standard.[3]

The control limits are usually expressed both as a percentage of the standard and as an absolute dollar amount. For example, the allowable deviation may be expressed as the lesser of 10 percent of the standard amount or $10,000. In other words, management will not accept a deviation of more than $10,000 even if that deviation is less than 10 percent of the standard. Alternatively, even if the dollar amount is less than $10,000, an investigation is required if the deviation is more than 10 percent of the standard amount.

Formal statistical procedures can also be used to set the control limits. In this way, less subjectivity is involved and a manager can assess the likelihood of the variance being caused by random factors. At this time, the use of such formal procedures has gained little acceptance.[4]

VARIANCE ANALYSIS AND ACCOUNTING: MATERIALS AND LABOR

Objective 4

Compute and journalize the materials and labor variances and explain how they are used for control.

The total variance measures the difference between the actual cost of materials and labor and their budgeted costs for the actual level of activity. To illustrate, consider these selected data for Helado Company for the first week of May. To keep the example simple, only one material (yogurt) is used. A complete analysis for the company would include all categories of materials.

Actual production: 30,000 quarts
Actual yogurt usage: 780,000 ounces (no beginning or ending yogurt inventory)
Actual price paid per ounce of yogurt: $0.025
Actual direct labor hours: 325 hours
Actual wage rate: $8.20 per hour

Using the above actual data and the unit standards from Exhibit 17-2, a performance report for the first week of May is developed and illustrated in Exhibit 17-4. As has been mentioned, the total variance can be divided into price and usage variances, providing more control information to the manager.

Direct Materials Price and Usage Variances

The three-pronged approach illustrated in Exhibit 17-3 can be used to calculate the materials price and usage variances. This calculation for the Helado Company example is illustrated in Exhibit 17-5. Only the price and usage variances for yogurt are shown. Many find this graphical approach to be easier than the use of variance formulas.

materials price variance

Materials Price Variance: Formula Approach The materials price variance can be calculated separately. The **materials price variance** (*MPV*) measures the differ-

---

3.   Gaumnitz and Kollaritsch, "Manufacturing Variances: Current Practice and Trends," report that about 45–47 percent of the firms use dollar or percentage control limits. Most of the remaining use judgment rather than any formal identification of limits.
4.   According to Gaumnitz and Kollaritsch, "Manufacturing Variances: Current Practice and Trends," only about 1 percent of the responding firms used formal statistical procedures.

Exhibit 17-4
Performance Report:
Total Variances

	Actual Costs	Budgeted Costs*	Total Variance
Yogurt	$19,500	$15,000	$4,500 U
Direct labor	2,665	2,400	265 U

*The standard quantities for materials and labor are computed as follows, using unit quantity standards from Exhibit 17-2: Yogurt: $25 \times 30,000 = 750,000$ ounces; Labor: $0.01 \times 30,000 = 300$ hours. Multiplying these standard quantities by the unit standard prices given in Exhibit 17-2 produces the budgeted amounts appearing in this column.

ence between what should have been paid for raw materials and what was actually paid. A simple formula for computing this variance is

$$MPV = (AP \times AQ) - (SP \times AQ)$$

or, factoring, we have

$$MPV = (AP - SP)AQ$$

where

$$AP = \text{The actual price per unit}$$
$$SP = \text{The standard price per unit}$$
$$AQ = \text{The actual quantity of material used}$$

Computation of the Materials Price Variance Helado Company purchased and used 780,000 ounces of yogurt for the first week of May. The purchase price was $0.025 per ounce. Thus, *AP* is $0.025, *AQ* is 780,000 ounces, and *SP* (from Exhibit 17-2) is $0.02. Using this information, the materials price variance is computed as follows (see Exhibit 17-5 to compare the three-pronged approach with the formula approach):

$$
\begin{aligned}
MPV &= (AP - SP)AQ \\
&= (\$0.025 - \$0.020)780,000 \\
&= \$0.005 \times 780,000 \\
&= \$3,900 \text{ U}
\end{aligned}
$$

Responsibility for the Materials Price Variance The responsibility for controlling the materials price variance is usually the purchasing agent's. Admittedly, the price of materials is largely beyond his or her control; however, the price variance can be influenced by such factors as quality, quantity discounts, distance of the source from the plant, and so on. These factors are often under the control of the agent.

Using the price variance to evaluate the performance of purchasing has some limitations. Emphasis on meeting or beating standard can produce some undesirable outcomes. For example, if the purchasing agent feels pressured to produce favorable variances, materials of lower quality than desired may be purchased or too much inventory may be acquired to take advantage of quantity discounts.

Analysis of the Materials Price Variance The first step in variance analysis is deciding whether the variance is significant or not. If it is judged to be insignificant, no further steps are needed. Assume that an unfavorable materials price variance of $3,900 is judged to be significant. The next step is to find out why it occurred.

Exhibit 17-5
Price and Usage Variances: Direct Materials

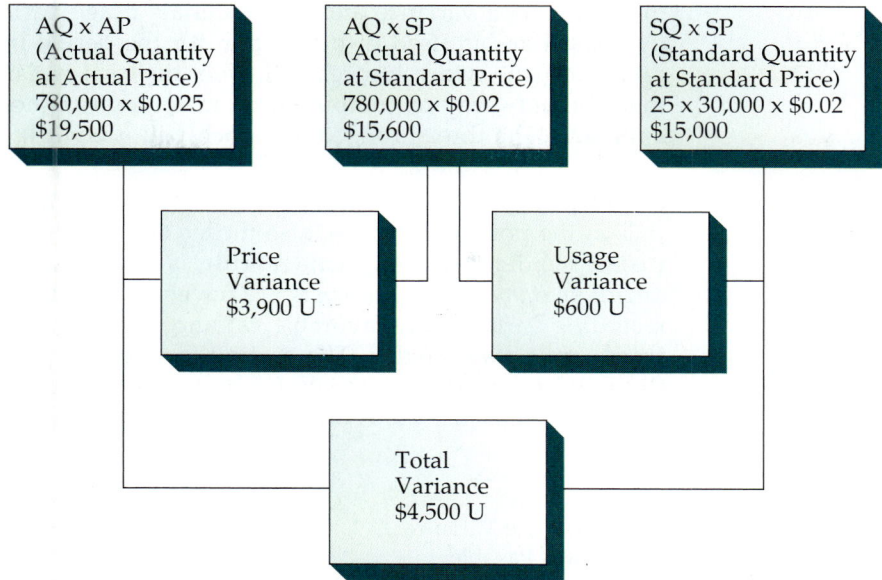

| AQ x AP (Actual Quantity at Actual Price) 780,000 x $0.025 $19,500 | AQ x SP (Actual Quantity at Standard Price) 780,000 x $0.02 $15,600 | SQ x SP (Standard Quantity at Standard Price) 25 x 30,000 x $0.02 $15,000 |

Price Variance $3,900 U

Usage Variance $600 U

Total Variance $4,500 U

Notice that the right side of the three-pronged diagram is simply the amount of materials allowed per unit × the units produced × the standard price.

For the Helado Company example, the investigation revealed that a higher-quality yogurt was purchased because of a shortage of the usual grade in the market. Once the reason is known, corrective action can be taken if necessary—and possible. In this case, no corrective action is needed. The firm has no control over the supply shortage; it will simply have to wait until market conditions improve.

Timing of the Price Variance Computation The materials price variance can be computed at one of two points: (1) when the raw materials are issued for use in production or (2) when they are purchased. Computing the price variance at the point of purchase is preferable. It is better to have information on variances earlier than later. The more timely the information, the more likely proper managerial action can be taken. Old information is often useless information.

Materials may sit in inventory for weeks or months before they are needed in production. By the time the materials price variance is computed, signaling a problem, it may be too late to take corrective action. Or, even if corrective action is still possible, the delay may cost the company thousands of dollars. For example, suppose a new purchasing agent is unaware of the availability of a quantity discount on a raw material. If the materials price variance that ignores the discount is computed when a new purchase is made, the resulting unfavorable signal would lead to quick corrective action. (In this case, the action would be to use the discount for future purchases.) If the materials price variance is not computed until the material is issued to production, it may be several weeks or even months before the problem is discovered.

If the materials price variance is computed at the point of purchase, then *AQ* needs to be redefined as the actual quantity of materials *purchased*, rather than actual materials used. Since the materials purchased may differ from the materials used, the overall materials budget variance is not necessarily the sum of the materials price variance and the materials usage variance. When the materials purchased are all used in production for the period in which the variances are calculated, the two variances will equal the total variance. If this is not the case, then the only way to compute each materials variance is by using the formula approach. The three-pronged approach will not work.

Accounting for Materials Price Variance Recognizing the price variance for materials at the point of purchase also means that the raw materials inventory is carried at standard cost. As a general rule, *in a standard cost system, all inventories are carried at standard*. Actual costs are never entered into an inventory account. In recording variances, unfavorable variances are always debits and favorable variances are always credits. The general form of the journal entry associated with the purchase of raw materials for a standard cost system is given below. The entry assumes an unfavorable MPV and that AQ is defined as materials purchased.

Materials	$SP \times AQ$	
Materials Price Variance	$(AP - SP)AQ$	
Accounts Payable		$AP \times AQ$

For the Helado company example, the entry pertaining to the acquisition of yogurt would be:

Materials	15,600	
Materials Price Variance	3,900	
Accounts Payable		19,500

materials usage variance

Direct Materials Usage Variance: Formula Approach The **materials usage variance** (*MUV*) measures the difference between the direct materials actually used and the direct materials that should have been used for the actual output. The formula for computing this variance is

$$MUV = (SP \times AQ) - (SP \times SQ)$$

or, factoring,

$$MUV = (AQ - SQ)SP$$

where
AQ = The actual quantity of materials used
SQ = The standard quantity of materials allowed for the actual output
SP = The standard price per unit

Computation of the Materials Usage Variance Helado Company used 780,000 ounces of yogurt to produce 30,000 quarts of yogurt. Therefore, *AQ* is 780,000. From Exhibit 17-2, we see that *SP* is $0.02 per ounce of yogurt. Although standard materials allowed (*SQ*) has already been computed in Exhibit 17-4, the details underlying the computation need to be reviewed. Recall that *SQ* is the product of the unit quantity standard and the actual units produced. From Exhibit 17-2, the unit standard is 25 ounces of yogurt for every quart of yogurt. Thus, *SQ* is 25 × 30,000, or 750,000 ounces. The materials usage variance is computed as follows (see Exhibit 17-5 to compare the formula approach with the three-pronged approach):

$$MUV = (AQ - SQ)SP$$
$$= (780,000 - 750,000)\$0.02$$
$$= \$600 \text{ U}$$

Responsibility for the Materials Usage Variance The production manager is generally responsible for materials usage. Minimizing scrap, waste, and rework are all ways in which the manager can ensure that the standard is met. However, at times, the cause of the variance is attributable to others outside the production area. For example, the purchase of lower-quality materials may produce bad output. In this case, responsibility would be assigned to purchasing rather than production.

As with the price variance, using the usage variance to evaluate performance can lead to undesirable behavior. For example, a production manager feeling pressure to produce a favorable variance might allow a defective unit to be transferred to finished goods. While this avoids the problem of wasted materials, it may create customer-relations problems (some customer gets stuck with the bad product).

Analysis of the Variance Investigation revealed that the unfavorable materials usage variance was the result of rejecting a 1,200-quart batch because of poor consistency and flavor. Some settings in the mixing process had been mistakenly altered, resulting in a faulty mix of ingredients. The setting was corrected and no further problems were noticed.

Timing of the Computation of the Materials Usage Variance The materials usage variance should be computed as materials are issued for production. To facilitate this process, many companies use three forms: a standard bill of materials, color-coded excessive usage forms, and color-coded returned-materials forms. The **standard bill of materials** identifies the quantity of materials that should be used to produce a predetermined quantity of output. A standard bill of materials for Helado Company is illustrated in Exhibit 17-6.

The standard bill of materials acts as a materials requisition form. The production manager presents this form to the stores area and receives the standard quantity allowed for the indicated output. If the production manager has to return to requisition more materials, the excessive usage form is used. This form, different in color from the standard bill of materials, provides immediate feedback to the production manager that excess raw materials are being used. If, on

standard bill of materials

Exhibit 17-6
Standard Bill of Materials

Product: quarts of frozen strawberry yogurt	Output: 30,000 quarts	
Raw Material	*Unit Standard*	*Total Requirements*
Yogurt	25 oz.	750,000 oz.
Strawberries	10 oz.	300,000 oz.
Milk	8 oz.	240,000 oz.
Cream	4 oz.	120,000 oz.
Gelatine	1 oz.	30,000 oz.
Containers	1 container	30,000 containers

the other hand, fewer materials are used than the standard requires, the production manager can return the leftover materials, along with the returned-materials form. This form also provides immediate feedback.

Accounting for Materials Usage Variances The materials usage variance is recognized when materials are issued. The standard cost of the materials issued is assigned to Work in Process. The general form for the entry to record the issuance and usage of materials, assuming an unfavorable MUV, is as follows:

Work in Process	SQ × SP	
Materials Usage Variance	(AQ − SQ)SP	
Materials		AQ × SP

The entry to record Helado's usage of yogurt during the first week of May is given below:

Work in Process	15,000	
Materials Usage Variance	600	
Materials		15,600

Direct Labor Variances

The rate (price) and efficiency (usage) variances for labor can be calculated using either the three-pronged approach, as in Exhibit 17-3, or a formula approach. The three-pronged calculation is illustrated in Exhibit 17-7 for direct labor at the Helado Company plant. The calculation using formulas is discussed next.

Exhibit 17-7
Rate and Efficiency Variances: Direct Labor

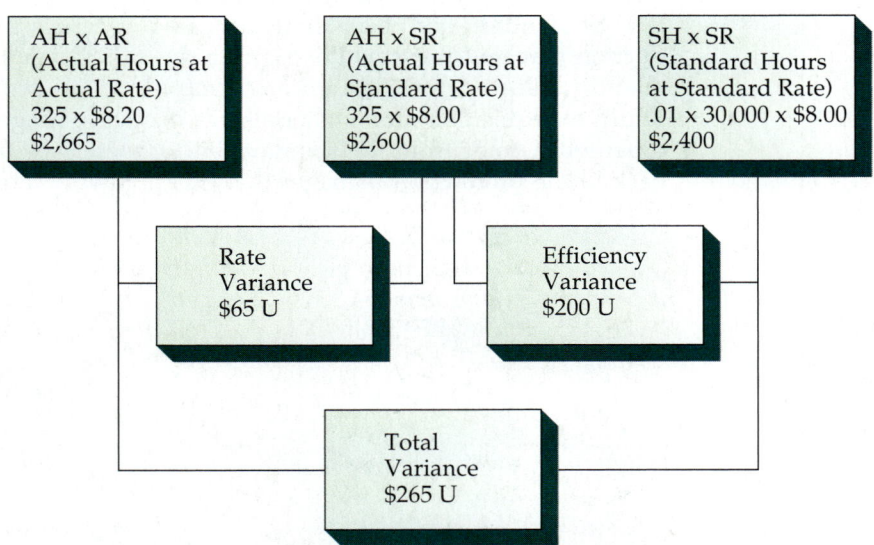

Note: As shown in the third prong, the standard hours allowed are computed by multiplying the unit standard by the units produced.

labor rate variance

Labor Rate (Price) Variance: Formula Approach The **labor rate variance** *(LRV)* computes the difference between what was paid to direct laborers and what should have been paid:

$$LRV = (AR \times AH) - (SR \times AH)$$

or, factoring,

$$LRV = (AR - SR)AH$$

where

$$
\begin{aligned}
AR &= \text{The actual hourly wage rate} \\
SR &= \text{The standard hourly wage rate} \\
AH &= \text{The actual direct labor hours used}
\end{aligned}
$$

Computation of the Labor Rate Variance Direct labor activity for Helado Company's machine operators will be used to illustrate the computation of the labor rate variance. We know that 325 hours were used during the first week in May. The actual hourly wage paid for machine operation was $8.20. From Exhibit 17-2, the standard wage rate is $8.00. Thus, *AH* is 325, *AR* is $8.20, and *SR* is $8.00. The labor rate variance is computed as follows:

$$
\begin{aligned}
LRV &= (AR - SR)AH \\
&= (\$8.20 - \$8.00)325 \\
&= \$0.20 \times 325 \\
&= \$65\ \text{U}
\end{aligned}
$$

Responsibility for the Labor Rate Variance Labor rates are largely determined by such external forces as labor markets and union contracts. When labor rate variances occur, they often do so because an average wage rate is used for the rate standard or because more skilled and more highly paid laborers are used for less skilled tasks.

   Wage rates for a particular labor activity often differ among workers because of differing levels of seniority. Rather than selecting labor rate standards reflecting those different levels, an average wage rate is often chosen. As the seniority mix changes, the average rate changes. This will give rise to a labor rate variance; it also calls for a new standard to reflect the new seniority mix. Controllability is not assignable for this cause of a labor rate variance.

   However, the *use* of labor is controllable by the production manager. The use of more skilled workers to perform less skilled tasks (or vice versa) is a decision that a production manager consciously makes. For this reason, responsibility for the labor rate variance is generally assigned to the individuals who decide how labor will be used.

Analysis of the Labor Rate Variance If the $65 unfavorable labor rate variance is judged significant, an investigation may be warranted. Assume that an investigation is conducted and that the cause is found to be the use of overtime. Overtime occurred because a batch of 1,200 quarts was rejected because of poor flavor and consistency and had to be redone. Machine settings were adjusted to correct for the flavor and consistency problem, which caused the excessive labor rate.

labor efficiency
variance

Labor Efficiency Variance The **labor efficiency variance** *(LEV)* measures the difference between the labor hours that were actually used and the labor hours that should have been used:

$$LEV = (AH \times SR) - (SH \times SR)$$

or, factoring,

$$LEV = (AH - SH)SR$$

where

AH = The actual direct labor hours used
SH = The standard direct labor hours that should have been used
SR = The standard hourly wage rate

Computation of the Labor Efficiency Variance Helado Company used 325 direct labor hours while producing 30,000 quarts of yogurt. From Exhibit 17-2, 0.01 hour per quart at a cost of $8 per hour should have been used. The standard hours allowed are 300 (0.01 × 30,000). Thus, *AH* is 325, *SH* is 300, and *SR* is $8. The labor efficiency variance is computed as follows:

$$
\begin{aligned}
LEV &= (AH - SH)SR \\
&= (325 - 300)\$8 \\
&= 25 \times \$8 \\
&= \$200 \text{ U}
\end{aligned}
$$

Responsibility for the Labor Efficiency Variance Generally speaking, production managers are responsible for the productive use of direct labor. However, as is true of all variances, once the cause is discovered, responsibility may be assigned elsewhere. For example, frequent breakdowns of machinery may cause interruptions and nonproductive use of labor. But the responsibility for these breakdowns may be faulty maintenance. If so, the maintenance manager should be charged with the unfavorable labor efficiency variance.

Production managers may be tempted to engage in dysfunctional behavior if too much emphasis is placed on the labor efficiency variance. For example, to avoid losing hours and to avoid using additional hours because of possible rework, a production manager could deliberately transfer defective units to finished goods.

Analysis of the Labor Efficiency Variance The $200 unfavorable variance was judged to be significant, and its cause was investigated. The investigation revealed that more hours were used because of the bad batch of frozen yogurt that was produced. Also, some fault was assigned to lack of experience and training. Two new operators had been hired, and they took more time to perform their duties because of their lack of experience. Adjusting machine settings to avoid future flavor and consistency problems and additional training were the actions taken to correct the excess labor usage.

Accounting for the Labor Rate and Efficiency Variances The journal entry to record the labor rate and efficiency variance is made simultaneously. The general form of this journal entry is given below (it assumes a favorable labor rate variance and an unfavorable efficiency variance):

Work in Process	SH × SR	
Labor Efficiency Variance	(AH − SH)SR	
Labor Rate Variance		(AR − SR)AH
Payroll		AH × AR

Notice that only standard hours and standard rates are used to assign labor costs to Work in Process. Actual prices and quantities are not used. This emphasizes the principle that all inventories are carried at standard.

The journal entry for Helado's use of direct labor during the first week of May is given below. Since both variances are unfavorable, the variance accounts are debited:

Work in Process	2,400	
Labor Rate Variance	65	
Labor Efficiency Variance	200	
Payroll		2,665

Disposition of Materials and Labor Variances

Most companies dispose of the variances at the end of the year by either closing them to Cost of Goods Sold or prorating them among Work in Process, Cost of Goods Sold, and Finished Goods. If the variances are immaterial, then the most expedient way of disposition is simply to assign them to Cost of Goods Sold. To illustrate, assume that the variances we have computed for the first week in May are the year-end variances. Assuming the variances are immaterial, the following entry would be made to dispose of them:

Cost of Goods Sold	4,765	
Materials Price Variance		3,900
Materials Usage Variance		600
Labor Rate Variance		65
Labor Efficiency Variance		200

If the variances are judged to be material, then the proration option is usually exercised. This option is driven by GAAP requirements that inventories and cost of goods sold be reported at actual costs. Yet if variances are measures of inefficiency, it seems difficult to justify carrying costs of inefficiency as assets. It seems more logical to write off the costs of inefficiency as a cost of the period. With this conceptual qualification, we will illustrate one method of proration, using Helado's May variances as year-end variances. We will assume that the materials and labor are added uniformly throughout the process; thus, the material and labor variances can be assigned in proportion to the total prime costs in each of the three inventory accounts. Assume that the standard prime costs (before allocation of the materials and labor variances) are as follows (these are assumed values):

	Prime Costs	Percentage of Total
Work in Process	$ 0	0%
Finished Goods	3,480	20
Cost of Goods Sold	13,920	80
Total	$17,400	100%

Using these percentages, the materials and labor variances would be assigned as follows:

Finished Goods: 0.2 × \$4,765 = \$953
Cost of Goods Sold: 0.8 × \$4,765 = \$3,812

The journal entry to close out the variance accounts is given below:

Finished Goods	953	
Cost of Goods Sold	3,812	
Materials Price Variance		3,900
Materials Usage Variance		600
Labor Rate Variance		65
Labor Efficiency Variance		200

Other proration variations are possible. For example, materials variances could be assigned in proportion to the total materials cost in each account and the labor variances could be assigned in proportion to the total labor costs. Some even argue that finer assignments of the variances may be needed. The materials price variance, for example, could be assigned to the MUV account, the materials inventory account, work in process, finished goods, and the cost of goods sold account (with the other variances assigned only to the usual three inventory accounts).

VARIANCE ANALYSIS: OVERHEAD COSTS

Objective 5
Compute overhead variances three different ways and explain overhead accounting.

For direct materials and direct labor, total variances are broken down into price and efficiency variances. The total overhead variance—the difference between applied and actual overhead—is also broken down into component variances. How many component variances are computed depends on the method of variance analysis used. We will emphasize the four-variance method: two variances for variable overhead and two variances for fixed overhead. We first divide overhead into categories: variable and fixed. Next, we look at component variances for each category. The total variable overhead variance is divided into two components: the variable overhead spending variance and the variable overhead efficiency variance. Similarly, the total fixed overhead variance is divided into two components: the fixed overhead spending variance and the fixed overhead volume variance. Although the four-variance method provides the most detail, it also requires a company to identify the actual variable and fixed costs as well as budgeted rates and costs. For companies that wish to avoid the need to track actual variable and fixed costs, the two-variance and three-variance methods can be used. These methods also will be briefly reviewed.

In analyzing overhead variances, a traditional approach is assumed. Standard overhead rates are computed in basically the same way that was described in Chapter 4. Traditional overhead rate computations rely on unit-level drivers such as direct labor hours and machine hours. The overhead analysis in this chapter assumes that direct labor hours is the only driver used to assign overhead costs to products. Thus, when we speak of variable and fixed overhead, we are assuming that it is fixed or variable with respect to direct labor hours, a unit-level driver. In Chapter 20, variance analysis is extended to a more general setting where both unit and nonunit-level drivers are allowed.

Four-Variance Method: Variable Overhead Variances

To illustrate the variable overhead variances, we will examine activity for Helado Company during the month of May. The following data were gathered for this time period:

Variable overhead rate (standard)	$6.00 per direct labor hour[a]
Actual variable overhead costs	$7,540
Actual hours worked	1,300
Quarts of strawberry yogurt produced	120,000
Hours allowed for production	1,200[b]
Applied variable overhead	$7,200[c]

[a] Budgeted variable overhead/standard hours allowed for practical volume.
[b] .01 × 120,000 (see Exhibit 17-2, for unit standards and prices).
[c] $6.00 × 1,200 (overhead is applied using standard hours allowed).

Total Variable Overhead Variance The total variable overhead variance is the difference between the actual and the applied variable overhead. For our example, the total variable overhead variance is computed as follows:

$$\text{Total variance} = \$7,540 - \$7,200$$
$$= \$340 \text{ U}$$

This total variance can be divided into spending and efficiency variances. This computation is illustrated using a three-pronged approach in Exhibit 17-8.

variable overhead spending variance

Variable Overhead Spending Variance The **variable overhead spending variance** measures the aggregate effect of differences in the actual variable overhead rate (*AVOR*) and the standard variable overhead rate (*SVOR*). The actual variable overhead rate is simply actual variable overhead divided by actual hours. For

Exhibit 17-8
Variance Overhead Variance Analysis

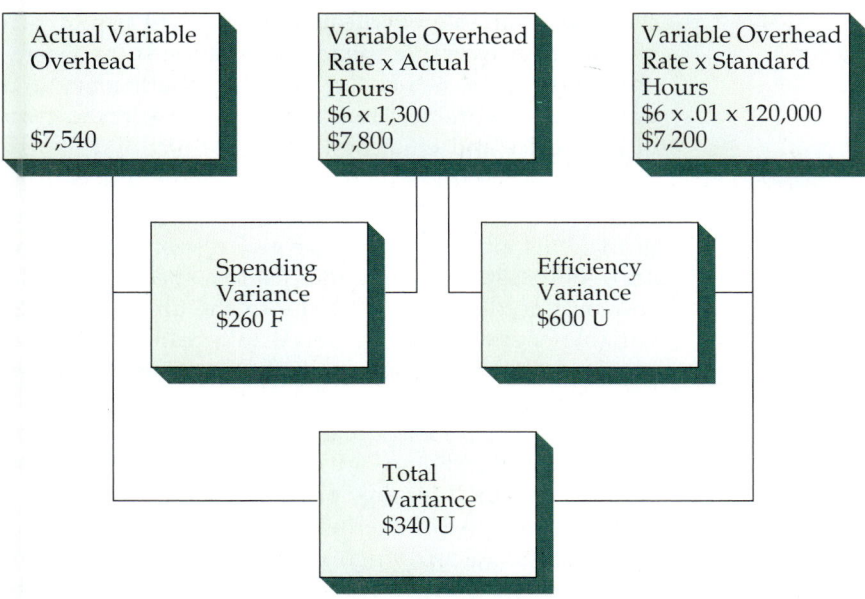

our example, this rate is $5.80 ($7,540/1,300 hrs.). The formula for computing the variable overhead spending variance is given below:

$$\text{Variable overhead spending variance} = (\text{AVOR} \times \text{AH}) - (\text{SVOR} \times \text{AH})$$
$$= (\text{AVOR} - \text{SVOR})\text{AH}$$
$$= (\$5.80 - \$6.00)1,300$$
$$= \$260 \text{ F}$$

Comparison to the Price Variances of Materials and Labor The variable overhead spending variance is similar but not identical to the price variances of materials and labor, though there are some conceptual differences. Variable overhead is not a homogeneous input—it is made up of a large number of individual items such as indirect materials, indirect labor, electricity, maintenance, and so on. The standard variable overhead rate represents the weighted cost per direct labor hour that should be incurred for all variable overhead items. The difference between what should have been spent per hour and what actually was spent per hour is a type of price variance.

A variable overhead spending variance can arise because prices for individual variable overhead items have increased or decreased. Assume, for the moment, that the price changes of individual overhead items are the only cause of the spending variance. If the spending variance is unfavorable, then price increases for individual variable overhead items are the cause; if the spending variance is favorable, then price decreases are dominating.

If the only source of the variable overhead spending variance were price changes, then it would be completely analogous to the price variances of materials and labor. Unfortunately, the spending variance also is affected by how efficiently overhead is used. Waste or inefficiency in the use of variable overhead increases the actual variable overhead cost. This increased cost, in turn, is reflected in an increased actual variable overhead rate. Thus, even if the actual prices of the individual overhead items were equal to the budgeted or standard prices, an unfavorable variable overhead spending variance could still take place. Similarly, efficiency can decrease the actual variable overhead cost and decrease the actual variable overhead rate. Efficient use of variable overhead items contributes to a favorable spending variance. If the waste effect dominates, then the net contribution will be unfavorable; if efficiency dominates, then the net contribution is favorable. Thus, the variable overhead spending variance is the result of both price and efficiency.

Responsibility for the Variable Overhead Spending Variance Many variable overhead items are affected by several responsibility centers. For example, utilities are a joint cost. Assigning the cost to a specific area of responsibility requires that cost be traced—not allocated—to the area. To the extent that consumption of variable overhead can be traced to a responsibility center, responsibility can be assigned. Consumption of indirect materials is an example of a traceable variable overhead cost.

Controllability is a prerequisite for assigning responsibility. Price changes of variable overhead items are essentially beyond the control of supervisors. If price changes are small (as they often are), the spending variance is primarily a matter of the efficient use of overhead in production, which is controllable by production supervisors. Accordingly, responsibility for the variable overhead spending variance is generally assigned to production departments.

Analysis of the Variable Overhead Spending Variance The $260 favorable variance simply reveals that, in the aggregate, Helado Company spent less on variable overhead than expected. Even if the variance were insignificant, it reveals nothing about how well costs of individual variable overhead items were controlled. Control of variable overhead requires line-by-line analysis for each individual item. Exhibit 17-9 presents a performance report that supplies the line-by-line information essential for proper control of variable overhead. Assuming that Helado investigates any item that deviates more than 10% from budget, the cost of gas would be the only item that would be investigated. The investigation reveals that the utility company lowered the price of natural gas, as a result of a state regulatory hearing. The reduction is expected to be permanent. In this case, the cause of the favorable variance is beyond the control of the company. The correct response is to revise the budget formula to reflect the decreased cost of natural gas.

Variable Overhead Efficiency Variance Variable overhead is assumed to vary as the production volume changes. Thus, variable overhead changes in proportion to changes in the direct labor hours used. The **variable overhead efficiency variance** measures the change in variable overhead consumption that occurs because of efficient (or inefficient) use of direct labor. The efficiency variance is computed using the following formula:

variable overhead
efficiency variance

$$\text{Variable overhead efficiency variance} = (AH - SH)SVOR$$
$$= (1,300 - 1,200)\$6$$
$$= \$600 \text{ U}$$

Responsibility for the Variable Overhead Efficiency Variance The variable overhead efficiency variance is directly related to the direct labor efficiency or usage variance. If variable overhead is truly driven by direct labor hours, then like the labor usage variance, the variable overhead efficiency variance is caused by efficient or inefficient use of direct labor. If more (or fewer) direct labor hours are used than the standard calls for, then the total variable overhead cost will increase (or decrease). The validity of the measure depends on the validity of the relationship between variable overhead costs and direct labor hours. In other

Exhibit 17-9

Helado Company, Inc.
Performance Report
For the Month Ended May 31, 1998

	Cost Formula[a]	Actual Costs	Spending Budget[b]	Variance
Natural gas	$3.80	$4,400	$4,940	$540 F
Electricity	2.00	2,840	2,600	240 U
Water	0.20	300	260	40 U
Total cost	$6.00	$7,540	$7,800	$260 F

[a] Per direct labor hour.
[b] The budget allowance is computed using the cost formula and an activity level of 1,300 actual direct labor hours.

words, do variable overhead costs *really* change in proportion to changes in direct labor hours? If so, responsibility for the variable overhead efficiency variance should be assigned to the individual who has responsibility for the use of direct labor: the production manager.

Analysis of the Variable Overhead Efficiency Variance The reasons for the unfavorable variable overhead efficiency variance are generally the same as those offered for the unfavorable labor usage variance. For example, some of the variance can be explained by the fact that overtime hours were used during the first week to make up for a bad batch of yogurt. The remaining deficiency was caused by the use of new employees who took longer to carry out tasks because of lack of experience.

More information concerning the effect of labor usage on variable overhead is available in a line-by-line analysis of individual variable overhead items. This can be accomplished by comparing the budget allowance for the actual hours used with the budget allowance for the standard hours allowed for each item. A performance report that makes this comparison for all variable overhead costs is shown in Exhibit 17-10. From Exhibit 17-10, we can see that the cost of gas is affected most by inefficient use of labor. For example, the extra time required to make up for a bad batch would increase gas consumption. Similarly, inexperienced laborers may heat the mix of gelatin and milk longer than is really needed, thus using more gas.

The column labeled *Budget for Standard Hours* gives the amount that should have been spent on variable overhead for the actual output. The total of all items in this column is the applied variable overhead, the amount assigned to production in a standard cost system. Note that in a standard cost system, variable overhead is applied using the hours allowed for the actual output *(SH)*, while in normal costing, variable overhead is applied using actual hours.

Although not shown in Exhibit 17-10, the difference between actual costs and this column is the total variable overhead variance (underapplied by $340). Thus, the underapplied variable overhead variance is the sum of the spending and efficiency variances.

Exhibit 17-10

Helado Company, Inc.
Performance Report
For the Month Ended May 31, 1998

Cost	Cost Formula[a]	Actual Costs	Budget for Actual Hours	Spending Variance[b]	Budget for Standard Hours	Efficiency Variance[c]
Natural gas	$3.80	$4,400	$4,940	$540 F	$4,560	$380 U
Electricity	2.00	2,840	2,600	240 U	2,400	200 U
Water	0.20	300	260	40 U	240	20 U
	$6.00	$7,540	$7,800	$260 F	$7,200	$600 U

[a] Per direct labor hour.
[b] Spending variance = Actual costs − Budget for actual hours.
[c] Efficiency variance = Budget for actual hours − Budget for standard hours.

Four-Variance Analysis: Fixed Overhead Variances

We will again use the Helado Company example to illustrate the computation of the fixed overhead variances. The data needed for the example are given below:

Budgeted/Planned Items (May)

Budgeted fixed overhead	$20,000
Expected activity	1,000 direct labor hours[a]
Standard fixed overhead rate	$20[b]

[a] Hours allowed to produce 100,000 quarts of frozen yogurt (.01 × 100,000).
[b] $20,000/1,000.

Actual Results

Actual production	120,000 quarts
Actual fixed overhead cost	$20,500
Standard hours allowed for actual production	1,200[a]

[a] 0.01 × 120,000.

Total Fixed Overhead Variance

The total fixed overhead variance is the difference between actual fixed overhead and applied fixed overhead, when applied fixed overhead is obtained by multiplying the standard fixed overhead rate by the standard hours allowed for the actual output. Thus, the applied fixed overhead is

$$\text{Applied fixed overhead} = \text{Standard fixed overhead rate} \times \text{Standard hours}$$
$$= \$20 \times 1{,}200$$
$$= \$24{,}000$$

The total fixed overhead variance is the difference between the actual fixed overhead and the applied fixed overhead:

$$\text{Total fixed overhead variance} = \$20{,}500 - \$24{,}000$$
$$= \$3{,}500 \text{ Overapplied}$$

To help managers understand why fixed overhead was overapplied by $3,500, the total variance can be broken down into two variances: the fixed overhead spending variance and the fixed overhead volume variance. The calculations of the two variances are illustrated in Exhibit 17-11.

fixed overhead spending variance

The Fixed Overhead Spending Variance The **fixed overhead spending variance** is defined as the difference between the actual fixed overhead and the budgeted fixed overhead. The spending variance is favorable because less was spent on fixed overhead items than was budgeted. The formula for computing the fixed overhead variance is given below (AFOH = actual fixed overhead, and BFOH = budgeted fixed overhead):

$$\text{Fixed overhead spending variance} = \text{AFOH} - \text{BFOH}$$
$$= \$20{,}500 - \$20{,}000$$
$$= \$500 \text{ U}$$

Responsibility for the Spending Variance Fixed overhead is made up of a number of individual items such as salaries, depreciation, taxes, and insurance. Many

Exhibit 17-11
Fixed Overhead Variances

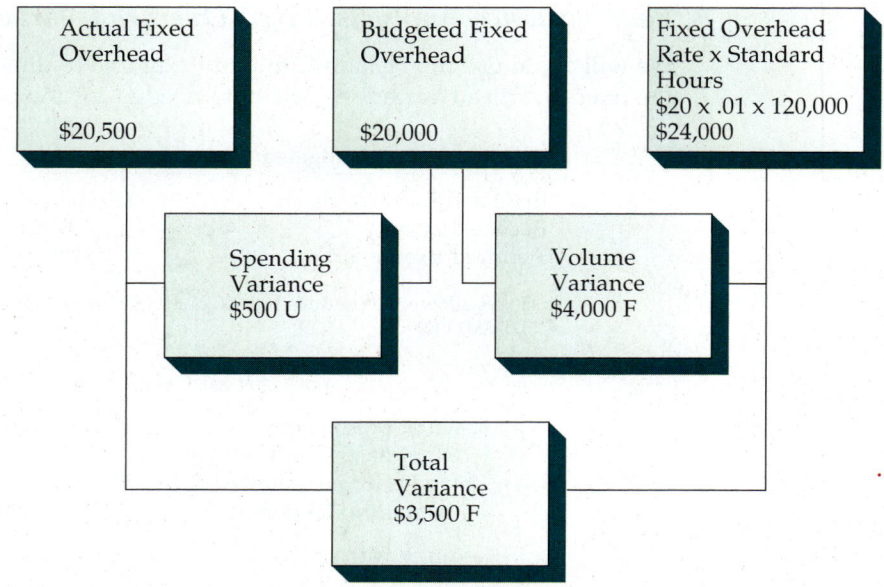

fixed overhead items—long-run investments, for instance—are not subject to change in the short run; consequently, fixed overhead costs are often beyond the immediate control of management. Since many fixed overhead costs are affected primarily by long-run decisions, not by changes in production levels, the budget variance is usually small. For example, depreciation, salaries, taxes, and insurance costs are not likely to be much different than planned.

Analysis of the Spending Variance Because fixed overhead is made up of many individual items, a line-by-line comparison of budgeted costs with actual costs provides more information concerning the causes of the spending variance. Exhibit 17-12 provides such a report. The report reveals that the fixed overhead spending variance is essentially in line with expectations. The fixed overhead spending variances, both on a line-item basis and in the aggregate, are relatively small (all less than 10% of the budgeted costs).

fixed overhead
volume variance

Fixed Overhead Volume Variance The **fixed overhead volume variance** is the difference between budgeted fixed overhead and applied fixed overhead. The volume variance measures the effect of the actual output departing from the output used at the beginning of the period to compute the predetermined standard fixed overhead rate. To see this, let *SH(D)* represent the standard hours allowed for the denominator volume (the volume used at the beginning of the period to compute the predetermined fixed overhead rate). The standard fixed overhead rate is computed in the following way:

Standard fixed overhead rate = Budgeted fixed overhead/SH(D)

From this equation, we know that the budgeted fixed overhead can be computed by multiplying the standard fixed overhead rate by the denominator hours

Budgeted fixed overhead = Standard fixed overhead rate × *SH(D)*

Exhibit 17-12

Helado Company, Inc.
Performance Report
For the Month Ended May 31, 1998

Fixed Overhead Items	Actual Cost	Budgeted Cost	Variance
Depreciation	$ 5,000	$ 5,000	$ —
Salaries	13,400	13,000	400 U
Taxes	1,100	1,050	50 U
Insurance	1,000	950	50 U
Total fixed	$20,500	$20,000	$500 U

From Exhibit 17-11, we know that the volume variance can be computed as follows:

$$
\begin{aligned}
\text{Volume variance} &= \text{Budgeted fixed overhead} - \text{Applied fixed overhead} \\
&= [\text{Standard fixed overhead rate} \times SH(D)] - (\text{Standard} \\
&\quad \text{fixed overhead rate} \times SH) \\
&= \text{Standard fixed overhead rate} \times [SH(D) - SH] \\
&= \$20(1,000 - 1,200) \\
&= \$4,000 \text{ F}
\end{aligned}
$$

Thus, for a volume variance to occur, the denominator hours, $SH(D)$, must differ from the standard hours allowed for the actual volume, SH. For example, at the beginning of May, Helado expected to produce 100,000 quarts of frozen yogurt, using 1,000 direct labor hours. The actual outcome was 120,000 quarts produced, using 1,200 standard hours. Thus, more was produced than expected and a favorable volume variance arises.

But what is the meaning of this variance? The variance occurs because the actual output differs from predicted output volume. At the beginning of the month, if management had expected 120,000 quarts with 1,200 standard hours as the denominator volume, the volume variance would not have existed. In this view, the volume variance is seen as prediction error—a measure of the inability of management to select the correct volume over which to spread fixed overhead.

If, however, the denominator volume represented the amount that management believed *could* be produced and sold, the volume variance conveys more significant information. If the actual volume is more than the denominator volume, the volume variance signals management that a gain has occurred (relative to expectations). That gain is not equivalent, however, to the dollar value of the volume variance. The gain is equal to the increase in contribution margin on the extra units that were produced and sold. However, the volume variance is positively correlated with the gain. For example, suppose that the contribution margin per standard direct labor hour is $50. By producing 120,000 quarts of frozen yogurt instead of 100,000 quarts, the company gained sales of 20,000 quarts. This is equivalent to 200 hours (0.01 × 20,000). At $50 per hour, the gain is $10,000 ($50 × 200). The favorable volume variance of $4,000 signals this gain but understates it. In this sense, the volume variance is a measure of utilization of capacity.

Responsibility for the Volume Variance Assuming that volume variance measures capacity utilization implies that the general responsibility for this variance should be assigned to the Production Department. At times, however, investigation into the reasons for a significant volume variance may reveal the cause to be factors beyond the control of production. In this instance, specific responsibility may be assigned elsewhere. For example, if Purchasing acquires a raw material of lower quality than usual, significant rework time may result, causing lower production and an unfavorable volume variance. In this case, responsibility for the variance rests with Purchasing, not Production.

Graphical Representation of Fixed Overhead Variances Exhibit 17-13 provides a graph that illustrates the fixed overhead variances. The graph is structured so that the actual fixed overhead is greater than the budgeted fixed overhead. Notice that applying fixed overhead by multiplying the fixed overhead rate by the standard hours allowed for production has the effect of converting fixed overhead into a unit-level variable cost (SFOR × SH is represented by a line coming out of the origin, with slope SFOR). Converting a fixed cost into a variable cost contributes significantly to the creation of the volume variance (as well as to the total fixed overhead variance). Notice also that the volume variance has a lot to do with how well we estimate SH (the hours allowed for actual production). If SH = SH(D), there is no volume variance (this is where the applied line intersects with the BFOH line). Notice also how the total variance breaks down into the spending and volume variances.

Accounting for Overhead Variances Overhead is applied to production by debiting Work in Process and crediting variable and fixed overhead control accounts. The amount assigned is simply the respective overhead rates multiplied by the standard hours allowed for actual production. The actual overhead is accumulated on the debit side of the overhead control accounts. Periodically (e.g.,

Exhibit 17-13
Graph of Fixed Overhead Variances

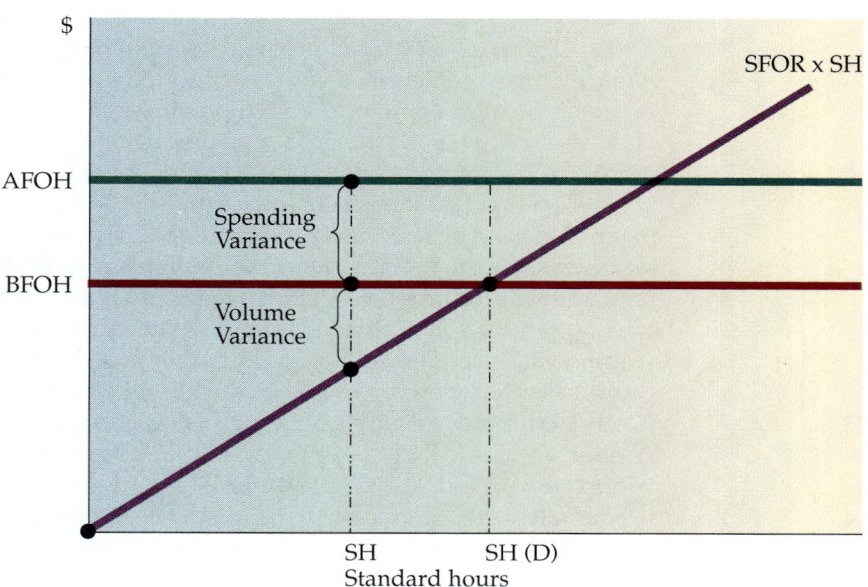

monthly), overhead variance reports are prepared. At the end of the year, the applied variable and fixed overhead costs and the actual fixed overhead costs are closed out and the variances isolated. The overhead variances are then disposed of by closing then to Cost of Goods Sold if they are not material or by prorating them among Work in Process, Finished Goods, and Cost of Goods Sold if they are material. We will use the May transactions for Helado Company to illustrate the process that would occur at the end of the year. Essentially we are assuming that the May transactions reflect an entire year for illustrative purposes.

To assign overhead to production, we have the following entry:

Work in Process	31,200	
Variable Overhead Control		7,200
Fixed Overhead Control		24,000

To recognize the incurrence of actual overhead:

Variable Overhead Control	7,540	
Fixed Overhead Control	20,500	
Miscellaneous Accounts		28,040

To recognize the variances:

Fixed Overhead Control	3,500	
Variable Overhead Efficiency Variance	600	
Fixed Overhead Spending Variance	500	
Variable Overhead Control		340
Variable Overhead Spending Variance		260
Fixed Overhead Volume Variance		4,000

Finally, to close out the variances to Cost of Goods Sold, we would have the following entries (assumes that variances are immaterial):

Fixed Overhead Volume Variance	4,000	
Variable Overhead Spending Variance	260	
Cost of Goods Sold		4,260

Cost of Goods Sold	1,100	
Variable Overhead Efficiency Variance		600
Fixed Overhead Spending Variance		500

Two- and Three-Variance Analyses

Two- and three-variance analyses do not require knowledge of actual variable and actual fixed overhead. The methods provide less detail and, thus, less information. We will simply present the method of computation for the two methods. The four-variance method is recommended over these two approaches. The May data for Helado Company will be used to illustrate the two methods with the assumption that only the total actual overhead is known: $28,040.

Two-Variance Analysis The two-variance analysis is shown in Exhibit 17-14. There are several points that should be made relative to the four-variance analysis appearing in Exhibits 17-8 and 17-11. First, the total variance is the sum of the total fixed and variable overhead variances. Second, the volume variance is the same as that of the four-variance method. Notice that in the computation of the volume variance, the applied variable overhead term, SVOR × SH, is common to the middle and right prongs of the diagram. Thus, when the right number

Exhibit 17-14
Two-Variance Analysis:
Helado Company

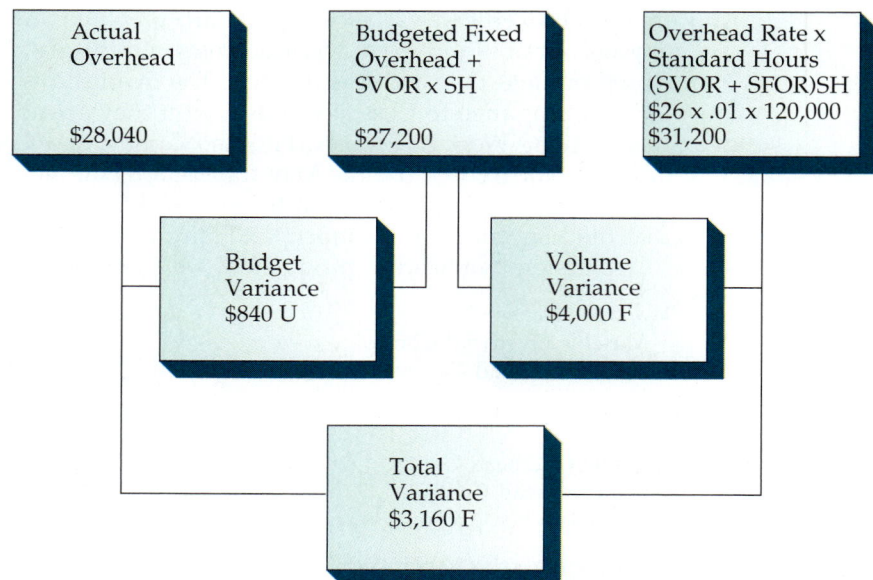

Note: SFOR = standard fixed overhead rate.

is subtracted from the left number, we are left with BFOH − SFOR × SH term, which is the fixed overhead volume variance. Third, the budget variance is the sum of the spending and efficiency variances of the four-variance method ($260 F + $500 U + $600 U = $840 U). As indicated, the two-variance method sacrifices a lot of information.

Three-Variance Method The three variance method is shown in Exhibit 17-15. Again, some observations can be made about the method relative to the four-variance method. First, the total variance is again the sum of the total variable and fixed overhead variances. Second, the spending variance is the sum of the variable and fixed overhead spending variances. The variable overhead efficiency and the fixed overhead volume variances are the same. The three-variance method also illustrates that the budget variance of the two-variance method breaks down into spending and efficiency variances.

MIX AND YIELD VARIANCES: MATERIALS AND LABOR

Objective 6

Calculate mix and yield variances for materials and labor.

For some production processes, it may be possible to substitute one material input for another or one type of labor for another. Usually a standard mix specification identifies the proportion of each material and the proportion of each type of labor that should be used for producing the product. For example, in producing an orange-pineapple fruit drink, the standard materials mix may call for 30% pineapple and 70% orange and the standard labor mix may call for 33% of fruit preparation labor and 67% of fruit processing labor. Clearly, within reason, it is possible to make input substitutions. Substituting materials or labor,

Exhibit 17-15
Three-Variance Analysis: Helado Company

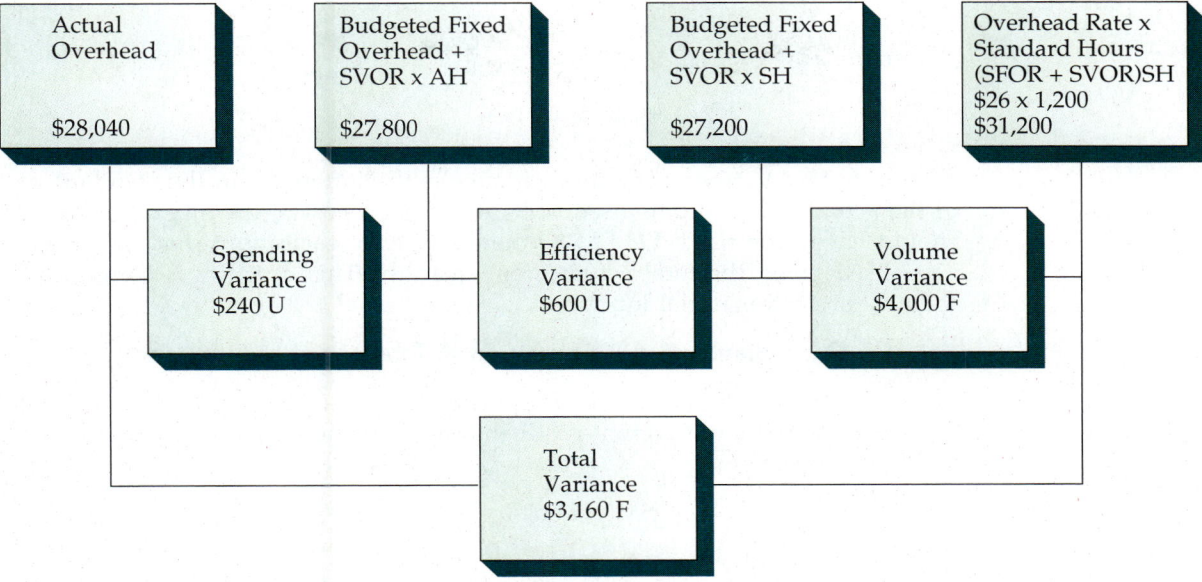

Actual Overhead	Budgeted Fixed Overhead + SVOR x AH	Budgeted Fixed Overhead + SVOR x SH	Overhead Rate x Standard Hours (SFOR + SVOR)SH $26 x 1,200
$28,040	$27,800	$27,200	$31,200

Spending Variance $240 U	Efficiency Variance $600 U	Volume Variance $4,000 F

Total Variance $3,160 F

mix variance
yield variance

however, may produce *mix* and *yield* variances. A **mix variance** is created whenever the actual mix of inputs differs from the standard mix. A **yield variance** occurs whenever the actual yield (output) differs from the standard yield. For materials, the sum of the mix and yield variances equals the materials usage variance; for labor, the sum is the labor efficiency variance.

Materials Mix and Yield Variances

To illustrate materials mix and yield variances, let us look at Malcom Nut Company. Malcom produces a variety of mixed nuts. One type of mixed nuts uses peanuts and almonds. Malcom developed the following standard mix for producing 120 pounds of mixed nuts (almonds and peanuts are purchased in the shell and processed):

Standard Mix Information: Materials

Material	Mix	Mix Proportion	SP	Standard Cost
Peanuts	128 lbs.	0.80	$0.50	$64
Almonds	32 lbs.	0.20	1.00	32
Total	160 lbs.			$96
Yield	120 lbs.			

Yield ratio: 0.75(120/160)
Standard cost of yield (SP_y): $0.80 per pound ($96/120 pounds of yield)

Now suppose that Malcom processes a batch of 1,600 pounds and produces the following actual results:

Material	Actual Mix	Percentages*
Peanuts	1,120 lbs.	70%
Almonds	480 lbs.	30
Total	1,600 lbs.	100%
Yield	1,300 lbs.	81.3%

*Uses 1,600 lbs. as the base.

Materials Mix Variance The mix variance is the difference in the standard cost of the actual mix of inputs used and the standard cost of the mix of inputs that should have been used. Let SM be the quantity of each input that should have been used given the total actual input quantity. This quantity is computed as follows for each material input:

SM = Standard mix proportion × Total actual input quantity

For example, the standard mix proportion for peanuts is 0.80. Thus, if 1,600 pounds of actual input were used, then the mix standard calls for the following amount of peanuts:[5]

$$SM(peanuts) = 0.80 \times 1,600$$
$$= 1,280 \text{ pounds}$$

A similar computation produces SM = 320 pounds for almonds (0.20 × 1,600). Given SM, the mix variance is computed as follows:

$$\text{Mix Variance} = \Sigma(AQ_i - SM_i)SP_i \tag{17.1}$$

The formula can be applied most easily using the following approach:

Material	AQ	SM	AQ − SM	SP	(AQ − SM)SP
Peanuts	1,120	1,280	(160)	$0.50	$ (80)
Almonds	480	320	160	1.00	160
Mix variance					$ 80 U

Notice that the mix variance is unfavorable. This occurs because more almonds are used than the standard mix calls for and almonds are a more expensive input.

Materials Yield Variance Using the standard mix information and the actual results, the yield variance is computed by the following formula:

$$\text{Yield variance} = (\text{Standard yield} - \text{Actual yield})SP_y \tag{17.2}$$

where

$$\text{Standard yield} = \text{Yield ratio} \times \text{Total actual inputs}$$

5.   The standard mix amounts are not the standard quantities allowed for actual output. The total standard quantity allowed is computed by dividing the actual yield by the standard yield ratio. The total standard input allowed is then multiplied by the standard mix ratios to compute the quantity of each material input that should have been used for the actual output. Alternatively, the unit material standards can be developed by dividing the standard input mix quantity by the standard yield. Multiplying the unit standards by the actual yield will also produce SQ for each input.

Thus, for the actual input of 1,600 pounds, the standard yield is 1,200 pounds (0.75 × 1,600). The yield variance is computed as follows:

$$\text{Yield variance} = (1,200 - 1,300)\$0.80$$
$$= \$80 \text{ F}$$

The yield variance is favorable because the actual yield is greater than the standard yield.

Labor Mix and Yield Variances

The labor mix and yield variances are computed in the same way as the materials mix and yield variances. Specifically, Equations 17.1 and 17.2 apply to labor in the same way with the notation defined appropriately for labor. For example, AQ, in Equation 17.1, is interpreted as AH, the actual hours used, and SP as the standard price of labor. With this understanding, the computation of mix and yield variances will be illustrated using the Malcom Company example. Suppose that Malcom has two types of labor, shelling labor and mixing labor. Malcom has developed the following standard mix for labor (yield, of course, is measured in lbs. of output and corresponds to the same batch size used for the materials standards):

Standard Mix Information

Labor Type	Mix	Mix Proportion	SP	Standard Cost
Shelling	3 hrs.	0.60	$ 8.00	$24
Mixing	2 hrs.	0.40	15.00	30
Total	5 hrs.			$54

Yield   120 lbs.
Yield ratio: 24 = (120/5), or 2,400%
Standard cost of yield (SP_y): $0.45 per pound ($54/120 pounds of yield)

As earlier, suppose that Malcom processes 1,600 pounds of nuts and produces the following actual results:

Labor Type	Actual Mix	Percentages*
Shelling	20 hrs.	40%
Mixing	30 hrs.	60
Total	50 hrs.	100%
Yield	1,300 lbs.	2,600%

*Uses 50 hours as the base.

Labor Mix Variance   The standard mix proportion for shelling labor is 0.60. Thus, if 50 hours of actual input were used, then the mix standard calls for the following amount of shelling labor:

$$\text{SM(shelling)} = 0.60 \times 50$$
$$= 30 \text{ hours}$$

A similar computation produces SM = 20 hours for mixing labor (0.40 × 50).

Given SM, the labor mix variance is computed as follows (using Equation 17.1):

Labor Type	AH	SM	AH − SM	SP	(AH − SM)SP
Shelling	20	30	(10)	$ 8.00	$ (80)
Mixing	30	20	10	15.00	150
Labor mix variance					$ 70 U

Notice that the mix variance is unfavorable. This occurs because more mixing labor was used than the standard mix called for and mixing labor is more expensive than shelling labor.

Yield Variance Using the standard mix information and the actual results, the yield variance is computed as follows:

$$\text{Yield variance} = (\text{Standard yield} - \text{Actual yield})SP_y$$
$$\text{Yield variance} = [(24 \times 50) - 1{,}300]\$0.45$$
$$= (1{,}200 - 1{,}300)\$0.45$$
$$= \$45 \text{ F}$$

The yield variance is favorable because the actual yield is greater than the standard yield.

SUMMARY

A standard cost system budgets quantities and costs on a unit basis. These unit budgets are for labor, material, and overhead. Standard costs, therefore, are the amount that should be expended to produce a product or service. Standards are set using historical experience, engineering studies, and input from operating personnel, marketing, and accounting. Currently attainable standards are those that can be achieved under efficient operating conditions. Ideal standards are those achievable under maximum efficiency—under ideal operating conditions. Standard cost systems are adopted to improve planning and control and to facilitate product costing. By comparing actual outcomes with standards and breaking the variance into price and quantity components, detailed feedback is provided to managers. This

information allows managers to exercise a greater degree of cost control than that found in a normal or actual cost system. Decisions such as bidding are also made easier when a standard cost system is in place.

The standard cost sheet provides the detail for the computation of the standard cost per unit. It shows the standard costs for materials, labor, variable overhead, and fixed overhead. It also reveals the quantity of each input that should be used to produce one unit of output. Using these unit quantity standards, the standard quantity of materials allowed and the standard hours allowed can be computed for the actual output. These computations play an important role in variance analysis.

REVIEW PROBLEM AND SOLUTION

Wangsgard Manufacturing has the following standard cost sheet for one of its products:

Direct materials (2 feet @ $5)	$10
Direct labor (0.5 hr. @ $10)	5
Fixed overhead (0.5 hr. @ $2*)	1
Variable overhead (0.5 hr. @ $4*)	2
Standard unit cost	$18

*Rate based on expected activity of 2,500 hours.

During the most recent year, the following actual results were recorded:

Production	6,000 units
Fixed overhead	$ 6,000
Variable overhead	10,500
Direct materials (11,750 ft. purchased and used)	61,100
Direct labor (2,900 hrs.)	29,580

REQUIRED: Compute the following variances:

1. Materials price and usage variances.
2. Labor rate and efficiency variances.
3. Variable overhead spending and efficiency variances.
4. Fixed overhead spending and volume variances.

Solution

1. Materials variances:

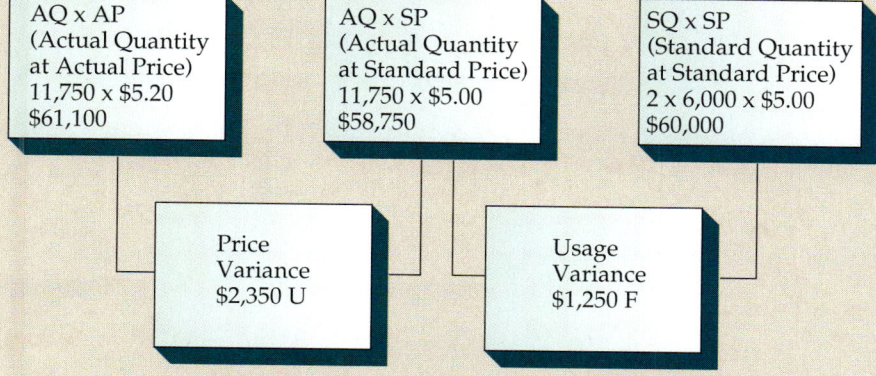

Or, using formulas

$$MPV = (AP - SP)AQ$$
$$= (\$5.20 - \$5.00)11{,}750$$
$$= \$2{,}350 \text{ U}$$
$$MUV = (AQ - SQ)SP$$
$$= (11{,}750 - 12{,}000)\$5.00$$
$$= \$1{,}250 \text{ F}$$

2. Labor variances:

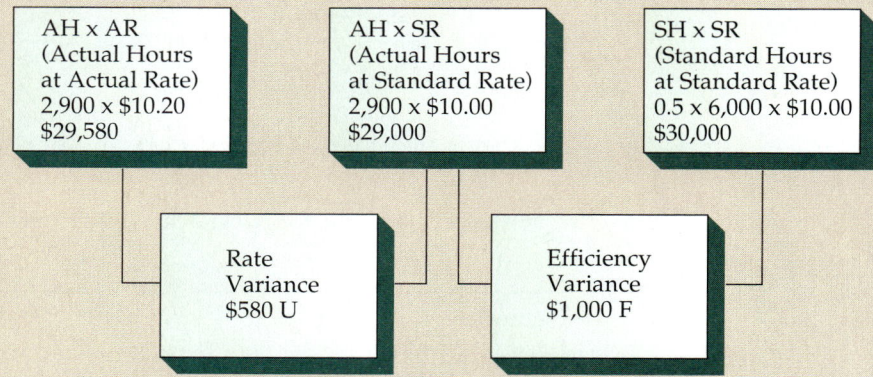

Or, using formulas:

$$LRV = (AR - SR)AH$$
$$= (\$10.20 - \$10.00)2{,}900$$
$$= \$580 \text{ U}$$
$$LEV = (AH - SH)SR$$
$$= (2{,}900 - 3{,}000)\$10.00$$
$$= \$1{,}000 \text{ F}$$

3. Variable overhead variances:

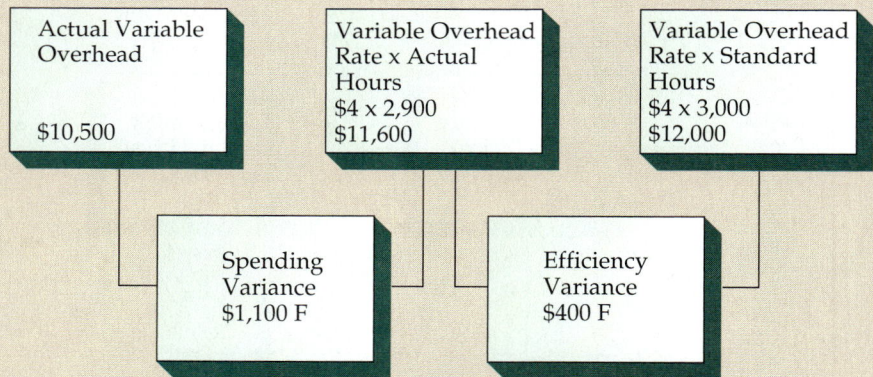

4. Fixed overhead variances:

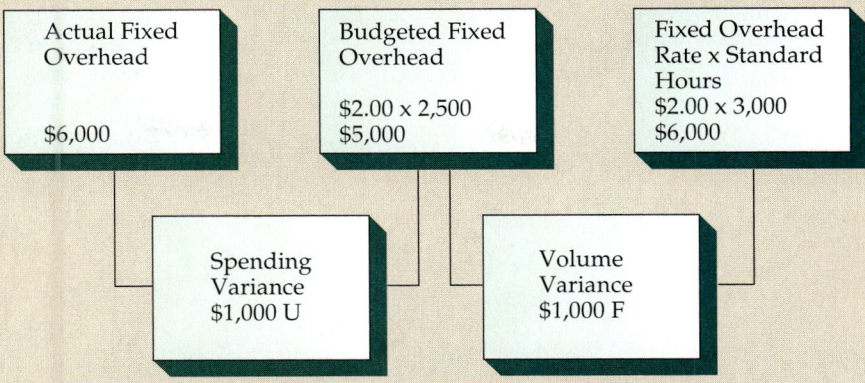

KEY TERMS

QUESTIONS FOR WRITING AND DISCUSSION

1. Discuss the difference between budgets and standard costs.
2. Describe the relationship that unit standards have with flexible budgeting.
3. What is the quantity decision? The pricing decision?
4. Why is historical experience often a poor basis for establishing standards?
5. Should standards be set by engineering studies? Why or why not?
6. What are ideal standards? Currently attainable standards? Of the two, which is usually adopted? Why?
7. How does standard costing improve the control function?
8. Discuss the differences between actual costing, normal costing, and standard costing.
9. What is the purpose of a standard cost sheet?

10. The budget variance for variable production costs is broken down into quantity and price variances. Explain why the quantity variance is more useful for control purposes than the price variance.
11. Explain why the materials price variance is often computed at the point of purchase rather than at the point of issuance.
12. The materials usage variance is always the responsibility of the production supervisor. Do you agree or disagree? Why?
13. The labor rate variance is never controllable. Do you agree or disagree? Why?
14. Suggest some possible causes of an unfavorable labor efficiency variance.
15. Explain why the variable overhead spending variance is not a pure price variance.

16. The variable overhead efficiency variance has nothing to do with efficient use of variable overhead. Do you agree or disagree? Why?
17. Explain why the fixed overhead spending variance is usually very small.
18. What is the cause of an unfavorable volume variance? Does the volume variance convey any meaningful information to managers?
19. When should a standard cost variance be investigated?

20. What are control limits and how are they set?
21. Which do you think is more important for control of fixed overhead costs: the spending variance or the volume variance? Explain.
22. Explain why standard cost systems are adopted.
23. Explain how the two-variance, three-variance, and four-variance overhead analyses are related.
24. Explain what mix and yield variances are.

E X E R C I S E S   A N D   P R O B L E M S

17-1
Setting Standards;
Ethical Behavior

LO 1, 2

Quincy Farms is a producer of items made from farm products that are distributed to supermarkets. For many years, Quincy's products have had strong regional sales on the basis of brand recognition. However, other companies have been marketing similar products in the area and price competition has become increasingly important. Doug Gilbert, the company's controller, is planning to implement a standard cost system for Quincy and has gathered considerable information from his coworkers on production and material requirements for Quincy's products. Gilbert believes that the use of standard costing will allow Quincy to improve cost control and make better operating decisions.

Quincy's most popular product is strawberry jam. The jam is produced in ten-gallon batches, and each batch requires six quarts of good strawberries. The fresh strawberries are sorted by hand before entering the production process. Because of imperfections in the strawberries and spoilage, one quart of strawberries is discarded for every four quarts of acceptable berries. Three minutes is the standard direct labor time for sorting that is required to obtain one quart of strawberries. The acceptable strawberries are then processed with the other ingredients: processing requires 12 minutes of direct labor time per batch. After processing, the jam is packaged in quart containers. Gilbert has gathered the following information from Joe Adams, Quincy's cost accountant, relative to processing the strawberry jam.

a. Quincy purchases strawberries at a cost of $0.80 per quart. All other ingredients cost a total of $0.45 per gallon.
b. Direct labor is paid at the rate of $9.00 per hour.
c. The total cost of material and labor required to package the jam is $0.38 per quart.

Adams has a friend who owns a strawberry farm that has been losing money in recent years. Because of good crops, there has been an oversupply of strawberries; and prices have dropped to $0.50 per quart. Adams has arranged for Quincy to purchase strawberries from his friend's farm in hopes that the $0.80 per quart will put this friend's farm in the black.

REQUIRED:

1. Discuss who the coworkers probably were that Doug consulted to set standards. What factors should Doug consider in establishing the standards for materials and labor?
2. Develop the standard cost sheet for the prime costs of a ten-gallon batch of strawberry jam.
3. Citing the specific standards of the IMA code of ethics described in Chapter 1, explain why Joe Adams' behavior regarding the cost information provided to Doug Gilbert is unethical.

(CMA adapted)

17-2
Computation of Inputs Allowed; Materials and Labor
LO 2

During the year, Randle Company produced 45,800 units of a machine tool. Randle's material and labor standards are

Direct materials (5 lbs. @ 0.80)	$4.00
Direct labor (0.2 hr. @ $10.50)	2.10

REQUIRED:

1. Compute the standard hours allowed for the production of 45,800 units.
2. Compute the standard pounds of materials allowed for the production of 45,800 units.

17-3
Materials and Labor Variances
LO 4

Sabrosa Company produces a popular frozen dessert, which is sold in quarts. Recently the company adopted the following standards for one quart of the frozen dessert:

Direct materials (35 oz. @ $0.008)	$0.28
Direct labor (0.1 hr. @ $8.60)	0.86
Standard prime cost	$1.14

During the first week of operation, the company experienced the following actual results:

a. Quarts produced: 5,000.
b. Ounces of materials purchased: 185,000 ounces at $0.0085.
c. There are no beginning or ending inventories of raw materials.
d. Direct labor: 490 hours at $8.60.

REQUIRED:

1. Compute price and usage variances for direct materials.
2. Compute the rate variance and the efficiency variance for direct labor.
3. Prepare the journal entries associated with materials and labor.

17-4
Overhead Variances; Four-Way Analysis
LO 5

Benson Products uses a standard cost system and develops its overhead rates from the current annual budget. The budget is based on an expected annual output of 50,000 units requiring 250,000 direct labor hours. Annual budgeted overhead costs total $875,000, of which $375,000 is fixed overhead. A total of 52,000 units using 270,000 direct labor hours was produced during the year. Actual variable overhead costs for the year were $520,000, and actual fixed overhead costs were $400,000.

REQUIRED:

1. Compute the fixed overhead spending and volume variances.
2. Compute the variable overhead spending and efficiency variances.

17-5
Overhead Variances; Two- and Three-Way Analyses
LO 5

Refer to the data in **17-4**.

REQUIRED:

1. Compute overhead variances using a two-way analysis.
2. Compute overhead variances using a three-way analysis.
3. Illustrate how the two- and three-way analyses are related to the four-way analysis.

17-6
Materials Usage
Variance; Materials
Mix and Yield
Variances

LO 4, 6

Oblad Company produces chemical compounds that are sold to other manufacturers that use them for making household products. Two liquid chemicals, GH-2 and HK-3, are mixed and heated to produce a liquid compound that is sold to companies that produce mouthwashes. After the liquid is produced by mixing and heating, it is bottled in one-gallon plastic jugs and moved to a warehouse. The compound is produced in batches and has the following standards:

Material	Standard Mix	Standard Unit Price	Standard Cost
GH-2	7,000 gallons	$1.00 per gallon	$ 7,000
HK-3	3,000 gallons	3.00 per gallon	9,000
	10,000 gallons		$16,000
Yield	8,000 gallons		

During May, the following actual production information was provided:

Material	Actual Mix
GH-2	60,000 gallons
HK-3	40,000 gallons
Total	100,000 gallons
Yield	72,000 gallons

REQUIRED:

1. Compute the materials mix and yield variances.
2. Compute the total materials usage variance for GH-2 and HK-3. Show that the total materials usage variance is equal to the sum of the materials mix and yield variances.

17-7
Labor Efficiency
Variance; Labor
Mix and Yield
Variances

LO 4, 6

Refer to the data in **17-6**. Oblad Company also uses two different types of labor in producing the mouthwash compound: mixing and bottling labor. For each batch of 10,000 gallons of material input, the following standards have been developed for labor:

Labor Type	Mix	SP	Standard Cost
Mixing	1,000 hrs.	$10	$10,000
Bottling	500 hrs.	5	2,500
Total	1,500 hrs.		$12,500
Yield	8,000 gallons		

The actual labor hours used for the output produced in May is also provided:

Labor Type	Mix
Mixing	9,000 hrs.
Bottling	6,000 hrs.
Total	15,000 hrs.
Yield	72,000 gallons

REQUIRED:

1. Compute the labor mix and yield variances.
2. Compute the total labor efficiency variance. Show that the total labor efficiency variance is equal to the sum of the labor mix and yield variances.

17-8
Investigation of Variances
LO 3

Franklin Company uses the following rule to determine whether labor efficiency variances ought to be investigated. A labor efficiency variance will be investigated anytime the amount exceeds the lesser of $16,000 or 10 percent of the standard labor cost. Reports for the past five weeks provided the following information:

Week	LEV	Standard Labor Cost
1	$14,000 F	$160,000
2	15,600 U	150,000
3	12,000 F	160,000
4	18,000 U	170,000
5	14,000 U	138,000

REQUIRED:

1. Using the rule provided, identify the cases that will be investigated.
2. Suppose that investigation reveals that the cause of an unfavorable labor efficiency variance is the use of lower-quality materials than are usually used. Who is responsible? What corrective action would likely be taken?
3. Suppose that investigation reveals that the cause of a significant favorable labor efficiency variance is attributable to a new approach to manufacturing that takes less labor time but causes more material waste. Upon examining the materials usage variance, it is discovered that it is unfavorable and is larger than the favorable labor efficiency variance. Who is responsible? What action should be taken? How would your answer change if the unfavorable variance were smaller than the favorable?

17-9
Standard Costs; Decomposition of Budget Variances; Materials and Labor
LO 2, 4

Zapato Corporation produces leather boots. The company uses a standard cost system and has set the following standards for materials and labor (for one pair of boots):

Leather (3 strips @ $10)	$30
Direct labor (2 hrs. @ $12)	24
Total prime cost	$54

During the year, Zapato produced 2,000 pairs of leather boots. The actual leather purchased was 6,200 strips at $9.96 per strip. There were no beginning or ending inventories of leather. Actual direct labor was 4,200 hours @ $12.50.

REQUIRED:

1. Compute the costs of leather and direct labor that should have been incurred for the production of 2,000 pairs of boots.
2. Compute the total budget variances for materials and labor.
3. Break down the total variance for materials into a price variance and a usage variance. Prepare the journal entries associated with these variances.
4. Break down the total variance for labor into a rate variance and an efficiency variance. Prepare the journal entries associated with these variances.

**17-10
Overhead
Application;
Overhead
Variances; Journal
Entries**

LO 5

Iverson Company produces microwave ovens. Iverson's plant in Buffalo uses a standard cost system. The standard cost system relies on direct labor hours to assign overhead costs to production. The direct labor standard indicates that four direct labor hours should be used for every microwave unit produced (the Buffalo plant only produces one model). The normal production volume is 120,000 units of this product. The budgeted overhead for the coming year is given below.

Fixed overhead	$1,286,400
Variable overhead	888,000*

*At normal volume.

Iverson applies overhead on the basis of direct labor hours.

During the year, Iverson produced 119,000 units, worked 487,900 direct labor hours, and incurred actual fixed overhead costs of $1.3 million and actual variable overhead costs of $927,010.

REQUIRED:

1. Calculate the standard fixed overhead rate and the standard variable overhead rate.
2. Compute the applied fixed overhead and the applied variable overhead. What is the total fixed overhead variance? Total variable overhead variance?
3. Break down the total fixed overhead variance into a spending variance and a volume variance. Discuss the significance of each.
4. Compute the variable overhead spending and efficiency variances. Discuss the significance of each.
5. Now assume that Iverson's cost accounting system only reveals the total actual overhead. In this case, a three-way analysis can be performed. Using the relationships between a three-way and four-way analysis, indicate the values for the three overhead variances.
6. Prepare the journal entries that would be related to fixed and variable overhead during the year and at the end of the year. Assume variances are closed to Cost of Goods Sold.

**17-11
Materials, Labor,
and Overhead
Variances**

LO 4, 5

The Henryetta plant of Middlemist Company produces a pesticide. At the beginning of the year, the Henryetta plant had the following standard cost sheet:

Direct materials (5 lbs. @ 1.60)	$ 8.00
Direct labor (1.5 hrs. @ $9.00)	13.50
Fixed overhead (1.5 hrs. @ $2.00)	3.00
Variable overhead (1.5 hrs. @ $1.50)	2.25
Standard cost per unit	$26.75

The Henryetta plant computes its overhead rates using practical volume, which is 72,000 units. The actual results for the year are:

a. Units produced: 70,000.
b. Materials purchased: 372,000 pounds at $1.50.
c. Materials used: 368,000 pounds.
d. Direct labor: 112,000 hours at $8.95.
e. Fixed overhead: $214,000.
f. Variable overhead: $175,400.

REQUIRED:

1. Compute price and usage variances for materials.
2. Compute the labor rate and labor efficiency variances.
3. Compute the fixed overhead spending and volume variances.
4. Compute the variable overhead spending and efficiency variances.
5. Prepare journal entries for the following:
   a. The purchase of raw materials.
   b. The issuance of raw materials to production (Work in Process).
   c. The addition of labor to Work in Process.
   d. The addition of overhead to Work in Process.
   e. The incurrence of actual overhead costs.
   f. Closing out of variances to Cost of Goods Sold.

17-12
Incomplete Data
LO 2, 4, 5

Riogrande Company uses a standard cost system. During the past quarter, the following variances were computed:

Variable overhead efficiency variance	$20,000 U
Labor efficiency variance	80,000 U
Labor rate variance	50,000 U

Riogrande applies variable overhead using a standard rate of $2 per direct labor hour allowed. Four direct labor hours are allowed per unit produced (only one type of product is manufactured). During the quarter, Riogrande used 20 percent more direct labor hours than should have been used.

REQUIRED:

1. What were the actual direct labor hours worked? The total hours allowed?
2. What is the standard hourly rate for direct labor? The actual hourly rate?
3. How many actual units were produced?

17-13
Basic Variance
Analysis; Revision
of Standards;
Journal Entries
LO 1, 2, 4, 5

The Emerson Division of Golding Company produces small kitchen appliances. The company uses a standard cost system for production costing and control. The standard cost sheet for its most popular product, a toaster, is given below.

Direct materials (2.5 lbs. @ $4.00)	$10.00
Direct labor (0.7 hr. @ $10.50)	7.35
Variable overhead (0.7 hr. @ $6.00)	4.20
Fixed overhead (0.7 hr. @ $3.00)	2.10
Standard unit cost	$23.65

During the year, Emerson experienced the following activity relative to the production of toasters:

a. Production of toasters totaled 50,000 units.
b. A total of 130,000 pounds of raw materials was purchased at $3.70 per pound.
c. There were 10,000 pounds of raw materials in beginning inventory (carried at $4 per pound). There was no ending inventory.
d. The company used 36,500 direct labor hours at a total cost of $392,375.
e. Actual fixed overhead totaled $95,000.
f. Actual variable overhead totaled $210,000.

Emerson produces all of its toasters in a single plant. Normal activity is 45,000 units per year. Standard overhead rates are computed based on normal activity measured in standard direct labor hours.

REQUIRED:

1. Compute the materials price and usage variances.
2. Compute the labor rate and efficiency variances.
3. Compute overhead variances using a two-way analysis.
4. Compute overhead variances using a four-way analysis.
5. Assume that the purchasing agent for the toaster plant purchased a lower-quality raw material from a new supplier. Would you recommend that the company continue to use this cheaper raw material? If so, what standards would likely need revision to reflect this decision? Assume that the end product's quality is not significantly affected.
6. Prepare all possible journal entries (assuming a four-way analysis of overhead variances).

**17-14
Unit Costs;
Multiple Products;
Variance Analysis;
Journal Entries**

LO 1, 2, 4, 5

Business Specialty, Inc., manufactures two staplers, small and regular. The standard quantities of labor and materials per unit for the year are

	Small	Regular
Direct materials (oz.)	6.0	10.00
Direct labor (hrs.)	0.1	0.15

The standard price paid per pound of direct materials is $1.60. The standard rate for labor is $8. Overhead is applied on the basis of direct labor hours. A plantwide rate is used. Budgeted overhead for the year is given below.

Budgeted fixed overhead	$360,000
Budgeted variable overhead	480,000

The company expects to work 12,000 direct labor hours during the year; standard overhead rates are computed using this activity level. For every small stapler produced, the company produces two regular staplers.

Actual operating data for the year are

a. Units produced: small staplers, 35,000; regular staplers, 70,000.
b. Direct materials purchased and used: 56,000 pounds at $1.55: 13,000 for the small stapler and 43,000 for the regular stapler. There were no beginning or ending raw materials inventories.
c. Direct labor: 14,800 hours: 3,600 hours for the small stapler, and 11,200 hours for the regular. Total cost of labor: $114,700.
d. Variable overhead: $607,500.
e. Fixed overhead: $350,000.

REQUIRED:

1. Prepare a standard cost sheet showing the unit cost for each product.
2. Compute the materials price and usage variances for each product. Prepare journal entries to record materials activity.
3. Compute the labor rate and efficiency variances. Prepare journal entries to record labor activity.
4. Compute the variances for fixed and variable overhead. Prepare journal entries to record overhead activity. All variances are closed to Cost of Goods Sold.

5. Assume that you know only the total direct materials used for both products and the total direct labor hours used for both products. Can you compute the total materials and labor usage variances? Explain.

17-15

Materials Usage Variances; Materials Mix and Yield Variances

LO 4, 6

Energy Products Company produces a gasoline additive, Gas Gain. This product increases engine efficiency and improves gasoline mileage by creating a more complete burn in the combustion process.

Careful controls are required during the production process to ensure that the proper mix of input chemicals is achieved and that evaporation is controlled. If the controls are not effective, there can be loss of output and efficiency.

The standard cost of producing a 500-liter batch of Gas Gain is $135. The standard materials mix and related standard cost of each chemical used in a 500-liter batch are as follows:

Chemical	Mix	SP	Standard Cost
Echol	200 liters	$0.200	$ 40.00
Protex	100 liters	0.425	42.50
Benz	250 liters	0.150	37.50
CT-40	50 liters	0.300	15.00
Total	600 liters		$135.00

The quantities of chemicals purchased and used during the current production period are shown in the schedule below. A total of 140 batches of Gas Gain were manufactured during the current production period. Energy Products determines its cost and chemical usage variations at the end of each production period.

Chemical	Quantity Used
Echol	26,600 liters
Protex	12,880 liters
Benz	37,800 liters
CT-40	7,140 liters
Total	84,420 liters

REQUIRED: Compute the total materials usage variance and then break down this variance into its mix and yield components.

(CMA adapted)

17-16

Incomplete Data; Overhead Analysis

LO 2, 4, 5

Roth Company produces a single product. Roth employs a standard cost system and uses a flexible budget to predict overhead costs at various levels of activity. For the most recent year, Roth used a standard overhead rate equal to $8.50 per direct labor hour. The rate was computed using normal activity. Budgeted overhead costs are $100,000 for 10,000 direct labor hours and $160,000 for 20,000 direct labor hours. During the past year, Roth generated the following data:

a. Actual production: 1,400 units.
b. Fixed overhead volume variance: $5,000 U.
c. Variable overhead efficiency variance: $3,000 F.
d. Actual fixed overhead costs: $42,670.
e. Actual variable overhead costs: $82,000.

REQUIRED:

1. Determine the fixed overhead spending variance.
2. Determine the variable overhead spending variance.
3. Determine the standard hours allowed per unit of product.
4. Assuming the standard labor rate is $9.25 per hour, compute the labor efficiency variance.

17-17
Flexible Budget;
Standard Cost
Variances;
T-Accounts
LO 1, 4, 5

Correr Company manufactures a line of running shoes. At the beginning of the period, the following plans for production and costs were revealed:

Units to be produced and sold	25,000
Standard cost per unit:	
Direct materials	$10
Direct labor	8
Variable overhead	4
Fixed overhead	3
Total unit cost	$25

During the year, 30,000 units were produced and sold. The following actual costs were incurred:

Direct materials	$320,000
Direct labor	220,000
Variable overhead	125,000
Fixed overhead	89,000

There were no beginning or ending inventories of raw materials. The materials price variance was $5,000 unfavorable. In producing the 30,000 units, 39,000 hours were worked, 4 percent more hours than the standard allowed for the actual output. Overhead costs are applied to production using direct labor hours.

REQUIRED:

1. Prepare a flexible budget showing the total expected costs for the actual production. Also prepare a performance report comparing expected costs to actual costs.
2. Determine the following:
   a. Materials usage variance.
   b. Labor rate variance.
   c. Labor usage variance.
   d. Fixed overhead spending and volume variances.
   e. Variable overhead spending and efficiency variances.
3. Use T-accounts to show the flow of costs through the system. In showing the flow, you do not need to show detailed overhead variances. Show only the over- and under-applied variances for fixed and variable overhead.

17-18
Standard Costing:
Planned Variances
LO 2, 4

As part of its cost control program, Tracer Company uses a standard cost system for all manufactured items. The standard cost for each item is established at the beginning of the fiscal year, and the standards are not revised until the beginning of the next fiscal year. Changes in costs, caused during the year by changes in material or labor inputs or by changes in the manufacturing process, are recognized as they occur by the inclusion of planned variances in Tracer's monthly operating budgets.

Presented below is the labor standard that was established for one of Tracer's products effective June 1, 1998, the beginning of the fiscal year:

Assembler A labor (5 hours @ $10)	$ 50
Assembler B labor (3 hours @ $11)	33
Machinist labor (2 hours @ $15)	30
Standard cost per 100 units	$113

The standard was based on the labor being performed by a team consisting of five persons with Assembler A skills, three persons with Assembler B skills, and two persons with machinist skills; this team represents the most efficient use of the company's skilled employees. The standard also assumed that the quality of materials that had been used in prior years would be available for the coming year.

For the first seven months of the fiscal year, actual manufacturing costs at Tracer have been within the standards established. However, the company has received a significant increase in orders, and there is an insufficient number of skilled workers to meet the increased production. Therefore, beginning in January, the production teams will consist of eight persons with Assembler A skills, one person with Assembler B skills, and one person with machinist skills. The reorganized teams will work more slowly than the normal teams, and as a result, only 80 units will be produced in the same time period in which 100 units would normally be produced. Faulty work has never been a cause for units to be rejected in the final inspection process, and it is not expected to be a cause for rejection with the reorganized teams.

Furthermore, Tracer has been notified by its materials supplier that lower-quality materials will be supplied beginning January 1. Normally, one unit of raw materials is required for each good unit produced, and no units are lost due to defective material. Tracer estimates that 6 percent of the units manufactured after January 1 will be rejected in the final inspection process due to defective material.

REQUIRED:

1. Determine the number of units of lower-quality material that Tracer Company must enter into production in order to produce 47,000 good finished units.
2. How many hours of each class of labor must be used to manufacture 47,000 good finished units?
3. Determine the amount that should be included in Tracer's January operating budget for the planned labor variance caused by the reorganization of the labor teams and the lower-quality material.
(CMA adapted)

17-19
Decision Case:
Establishment of
Standards;
Variance Analysis

LO 1, 2, 4

Crunchy Chips, a potato chip manufacturer, was established in 1938 by Paula Golding. In 1980, Paula Golding died, and her son, Edward, took control of the business. By 1998, the company was facing stiff competition from national snack-food companies. Edward was advised that the company's plants needed to gain better control over production costs. To assist in achieving this objective, he hired a consultant to install a standard cost system. To help the consultant in establishing the necessary standards, Edward sent her the following memo:

To: Diana Craig, CMA
From: Edward Golding, President, Crunchy Chips
Subject: Description and Data Relating to the Production of Our Plain Potato Chips
Date: September 28, 1998

The manufacturing process for potato chips begins when the potatoes are placed into a large vat in which they are automatically washed. After washing, the potatoes flow directly to an automatic peeler. The peeled potatoes then pass by inspectors who manually cut out deep eyes or other blemishes. After inspection, the potatoes are automatically sliced and dropped into the cooking oil. The frying process is closely monitored by an employee. After they are cooked, the chips pass under a salting device and then pass by more inspectors, who sort out the unacceptable finished chips (those that are discolored or too small). The chips then continue on the conveyor belt to a bagging machine that bags them in one-pound bags. After bagging, the bags are placed in a box and shipped. The box holds fifteen bags.

The raw potato pieces (eyes and blemishes), peelings, and rejected finished chips are sold to animal feed producers for $0.16 per pound. The company uses this revenue to reduce the cost of potatoes; we would like this reflected in the price standard relating to potatoes.

Crunchy Chips purchases high-quality potatoes at a cost of $0.245 per pound. Each potato averages 4.25 ounces. Under efficient operating conditions, it takes four potatoes to produce one 16-ounce bag of plain chips. Although we label bags as containing 16 ounces, we actually place 16.3 ounces in each bag. We plan to continue this policy to ensure customer satisfaction. In addition to potatoes, other raw materials are the cooking oil, salt, bags, and boxes. Cooking oil costs $0.04 per ounce, and we use 3.3 ounces of oil per bag of chips. The cost of salt is so small that we add it to overhead. Bags cost $0.11 each, and boxes $0.52.

Our plant produces 8.8 million bags of chips per year. A recent engineering study revealed that we would need the following direct labor hours to produce this quantity if our plant operates at peak efficiency:

Raw potato inspection	3,200
Finished chip inspection	12,000
Frying monitor	6,300
Boxing	16,600
Machine operators	6,300

I'm not sure that we can achieve the level of efficiency advocated by the study. In my opinion, the plant is operating efficiently for the level of output indicated if the hours allowed are about 10 percent higher.

The hourly labor rates agreed upon with the union are:

Raw potato inspectors	$7.60
Finished chip inspectors	5.15
Frying monitor	7.00
Boxing	5.50
Machine operators	6.50

Overhead is applied on the basis of direct labor dollars. We have found that variable overhead averages about 116 percent of our direct labor cost. Our fixed overhead is budgeted at $1,135,216 for the coming year.

REQUIRED:

1. Discuss the benefits of a standard cost system for Crunchy Chips.
2. Discuss the president's concern about using the result of the engineering study to set the labor standards. What standard would you recommend?
3. Develop a standard cost sheet for Crunchy Chips' plain potato chips.
4. Suppose that the level of production was 8.8 million bags of potato chips for the year as planned. Assuming that 9.5 million pounds of potatoes were used, compute the materials usage variance for potatoes.

**17-20
Standard Costs
and Ethical
Behavior**

Pat James, the purchasing agent for a local plant of the Oakden Electronics Division, was considering the possible purchase of a component from a new supplier. The component's purchase price, $0.90, compared favorably with the standard price of $1.10. Given the quantity that would be purchased, Pat knew that the favorable price variance would help offset an unfavorable variance for another component. By offsetting the unfavorable variance, his overall performance report would be impressive and good enough to help him qualify for the annual bonus. More importantly, a good performance rating would help him secure a position at divisional headquarters at a significant salary increase.

Purchase of the part, however, presented Pat with a dilemma. Consistent with his past behavior, Pat made inquiries regarding the reliability of the new supplier and the part's quality. Reports were basically negative. The supplier had a reputation for making the first two or three deliveries on schedule but being unreliable from then on. Worse, the part itself was of questionable quality. The number of defective units was only slightly higher than that for other suppliers, but the life of the component was 25 percent less than what normal sources provided.

If the part were purchased, no problems with deliveries would surface for several months. The problem of shorter life would cause eventual customer dissatisfaction and perhaps some loss of sales, but the part would last at least eighteen months after the final product began to be used. If all went well, Pat expected to be at headquarters within six months. He saw very little personal risk associated with a decision to purchase the part from the new supplier. By the time any problems surfaced, they would belong to his successor. With this rationalization, Pat decided to purchase the component.

REQUIRED:

1. Do you agree with Pat's decision? Why or why not? How important do you think Pat's assessment of his personal risk was in the decision? Should it be a factor?
2. Do you think that the use of standards and the practice of holding individuals accountable for their achievement played major roles in Pat's decision?
3. Review the ethical standards for management accountants in Ch. 1. Though Pat is not a management accountant, identify the standards that might apply to his situation.
4. Should every company adopt a set of ethical standards to apply to employees, regardless of their specialty? Identify some possible company benefits from such a code.

Chapter 18

Decentralization: Responsibility Accounting, Performance Evaluation, and Transfer Pricing

Decentralization at Wal-Mart pushes some of the responsibility and decision-making authority down to the store level.

LEARNING OBJECTIVES

After studying this chapter, you should be able to:

1. Define responsibility accounting and describe the four types of responsibility centers.
2. Explain why firms choose to decentralize.
3. Compute and explain return on investment (ROI), residual income (RI), and economic value added (EVA).
4. Discuss methods of evaluating and rewarding managerial performance.
5. Explain the role of transfer pricing in a decentralized firm.
6. Discuss the methods of setting transfer prices.

As a firm becomes larger, duties are divided and spheres of responsibility are created, eventually becoming centers of responsibility. Closely allied to the subject of responsibility is decision-making authority. Most companies tend to be decentralized in decision-making authority. Issues related to decentralization include: performance evaluation, management compensation, and transfer pricing.

RESPONSIBILITY ACCOUNTING

Objective 1
Define responsibility accounting and describe the four types of responsibility centers.

In general, a company is organized along the lines of responsibility. The traditional organizational chart, with its pyramid shape, illustrates the lines of responsibility flowing from the CEO through the vice presidents to middle- and lower-level managers. As organizations increase in size, these lines of responsibility become longer and more numerous. There is a strong link between the structure of an organization and its responsibility accounting system. Ideally, the responsibility accounting system mirrors and supports the structure of an organization.

Types of Responsibility Centers

As the firm grows, top management typically creates areas of responsibility, which are known as responsibility centers, and assigns subordinate managers to those areas. A **responsibility center** is a segment of the business whose manager is accountable for specified sets of activities. **Responsibility accounting** is a system that measures the results of each responsibility center and compares those results with some measure of expected or budgeted outcome. There are four major types of responsibility centers.

responsibility center
responsibility accounting

1. **Cost center:** A responsibility center in which a manager is responsible only for costs.

cost center

2. **Revenue center:** A responsibility center in which a manager is responsible only for sales.

revenue center

3. **Profit center:** A responsibility center in which a manager is responsible for both revenues and costs.

profit center

4. **Investment center:** A responsibility center in which a manager is responsible for revenues, costs, and investments.

investment center

A production department within the factory, such as assembly or finishing, is an example of a cost center. The supervisor of a production department does not set price or make marketing decisions, but can control manufacturing costs. Therefore, the producing department supervisor is evaluated on the basis of how well costs are controlled.

The marketing department manager sets price and projected sales. Therefore, the marketing department may be evaluated as a revenue center. Direct costs of the marketing department and overall sales are the responsibility of the sales manager.

In some companies, plant managers are given the responsibility to price and market products they manufacture. These plant managers control both costs and revenues, putting them in control of a profit center. Operating income would be an important performance measure for profit center managers.

Finally, divisions are often cited as examples of investment centers. In addition to having control over cost and pricing decisions, divisional managers have the power to make investment decisions, such as plant closings and openings, and decisions to keep or drop a product line. As a result, both operating income and some type of return on investment are important performance measures for investment center managers.

It is important to realize that while the responsibility center manager has responsibility for only the activities of that center, decisions made by that manager can affect other responsibility centers. For example, the sales force at a floor care products firm routinely offers customers price discounts at the end of the month. Sales increase dramatically, and the factory is forced to institute overtime shifts to keep up with demand.

The Role of Information and Accountability

Information is the key to appropriately holding managers responsible for outcomes. For example, a production department manager is held responsible for departmental costs but not for sales. This is because the production department manager not only controls some of these costs but also is best informed regarding them. Any deviation between actual and expected costs can best be explained at this level. Sales are the responsibility of the sales manager, again because this manager can best explain what is happening regarding price and quantity sold.

Responsibility also entails accountability. Accountability implies performance measurement, which means that actual outcomes are compared with expected or budgeted outcomes. This system of responsibility, accountability, and performance evaluation is often referred to as *responsibility accounting* because of the key role that accounting measures and reports play in the process.

DECENTRALIZATION

Objective 2
Explain why firms choose to decentralize.

centralized decision making
decentralized decision making
decentralization

Firms with multiple responsibility centers usually choose one of two approaches to manage their diverse and complex activities: centralized decision making or decentralized decision making. In **centralized decision making**, decisions are made at the very top level and lower-level managers are charged with implementing these decisions. On the other hand, **decentralized decision making** allows managers at lower levels to make and implement key decisions pertaining to their areas of responsibility. **Decentralization** is the practice of delegating or decentralizing decision-making authority to the lower levels.

Organizations range from highly centralized to strongly decentralized. Although some firms lie at either end of the continuum, most fall somewhere between the two extremes, with the majority of these tending toward decentralized.

Reasons for Decentralization

Seven reasons why firms may prefer the decentralized approach to management include: better access to local information; cognitive limitations; more timely response; focusing of central management; training and evaluation of segment managers; motivation of segment managers; and the exposure of segments to market forces. These reasons for delegating decision-making authority to lower levels of management are discussed in more detail in the following sections.

Better Access to Local Information The quality of decisions is affected by the quality of information available. Lower-level managers who are in contact with immediate operating conditions (e.g., the strength and nature of local competition, the nature of the local labor force, and so on) have better access to local information. As a result, local managers are often in a position to make better decisions. This advantage of decentralization is particularly applicable to multinational corporations, where far-flung divisions may be operating in a number of different countries, subject to various legal systems and customs. International issues in management accounting are discussed in a later chapter.

Cognitive Limitations Even if local information somehow were made available to central management, those managers would face another problem. In a large, complex organization that operates in diverse markets with hundreds or thousands of different products, no one person has all of the expertise and training needed to process and use the information. Cognitive limitations means that individuals with specialized skills would still be needed. Rather than having different individuals at headquarters for every specialized area, why not let these individuals have direct responsibility in the field? In this way, the firm can avoid the cost and bother of collecting and transmitting local information to headquarters. The structure of American business is changing. No longer are middle managers individuals with "people skills" and organizing skills only. They must have specific fields of expertise in addition to managerial talent. For example, a middle manager in a bank may refer to herself as a financial specialist even though she manages twenty people. The capability to add skilled expertise is seen as crucial in today's downsized environment.

More Timely Response In a centralized setting, time is needed to transmit the local information to headquarters and to transmit the decision back to the local unit. These two transmissions cause delay and increase the potential for miscommunication, decreasing the effectiveness of the response. In a decentralized organization, where the local manager both makes and implements the decision, this problem does not arise.

Focusing of Central Management The nature of the hierarchical pyramid is that higher-level managers have broader responsibilities and powers. By decentralizing the operating decisions, central management is free to focus on strategic planning and decision making. The long-run survival of the organization should be of more importance to central management than day-to-day operations.

Training and Evaluation An organization always has a need for well-trained managers to replace higher-level managers who retire or move to take advantage of other opportunities. By decentralizing, lower-level managers are given the opportunity to make decisions as well as to implement them. What better way to prepare a future generation of higher-level managers than by providing them the opportunity to make significant decisions? These opportunities also enable top managers to evaluate the local manager's capabilities. Those who make the best decisions are the ones who can be selected for promotion to central management.

Motivation By giving local managers freedom to make decisions, some of their higher-level needs (self-esteem and self-actualization) are being met. Greater responsibility can produce more job satisfaction and motivate the local manager to exert greater effort. More initiative and more creativity can be expected. Of course, the extent to which the motivational benefits can be realized depends to a large degree on how managers are evaluated and rewarded for their performance.

Enhanced Competition In a highly centralized company, large overall profit margins can mask inefficiencies within the various subdivisions. A decentralized approach allows the company to determine each division's contribution to profit and to expose each division to market forces.

The Units of Decentralization

Decentralization is usually achieved by segmenting the company into *divisions*. One way in which divisions are differentiated is by the types of goods or services produced. For example, divisions of PepsiCo include Snack Ventures Europe division (a joint venture with General Mills), Frito-Lay, Inc., and Pizza Hut, as well as its flagship soft drink division. These divisions are organized on the basis of product lines. Notice that some divisions depend on other divisions. At Pizza Hut, for example, the cola you purchase will be Pepsi—not Coke. In a decentralized setting, some interdependencies usually exist; otherwise, a company would merely be a collection of totally separate entities. The presence of these interdependencies creates the need for transfer pricing, which is discussed later in this chapter.

In a similar vein, companies create divisions according to the type of customer served. Wal-Mart has four divisions. The Wal-Mart stores division targets discount store customers. Sam's Club focuses on buyers for small business. McLane Company is a distribution and food manufacturing operation that supplies convenience stores. Finally, the international division concentrates on global opportunities.

Divisions may also be created along geographic lines. For example, Northwest Airlines, Inc., has three regional divisions: the Pacific division, the Atlantic division, and the domestic division. The presence of divisions spanning one or more regions creates the need for performance evaluation that can take into account differences in divisional environments.

Organizing divisions as responsibility centers not only differentiates them on the degree of decentralization but also creates the opportunity for control of the divisions through the use of responsibility accounting. Control of cost centers is achieved by evaluating the efficiency and the effectiveness of divisional managers. Performance reports are the typical instruments used in this evaluation. Profit centers are evaluated by assessing the unit's profit contribution, measured on income statements. Since performance reports and contribution income statements have been discussed previously, this chapter will focus on the evaluation of managers of investment centers.

MEASURING THE PERFORMANCE OF INVESTMENT CENTERS

Objective 3
Compute and explain return on investment (ROI), residual income (RI), and economic value added (EVA).

When companies decentralize decision making, they maintain control by organizing responsibility centers, developing performance measures for each, and basing rewards on an individual's performance at controlling the responsibility center.

Performance measures are developed to provide some direction for managers of decentralized units and to evaluate their performance. The development of performance measures and the specification of a reward structure are major issues for a decentralized organization. Because performance measures can affect the behavior of managers, the measures chosen should encourage a high degree of goal congruence. In other words, they should influence managers to pursue the company's objectives. Three performance evaluation measures for investment centers are return on investment, residual income, and economic value added.

Return on Investment

Because each division of a company has an income statement, couldn't we simply rank the divisions on the basis of net income? Unfortunately, the use of income statements may provide misleading information regarding segment performance. For example, suppose that two divisions report profits of $100,000 and $200,000, respectively. Can we say that the second division is performing better than the first? What if the first division used an investment of $500,000 to produce the contribution of $100,000, while the second used an investment of $2 million to produce the $200,000 contribution? Does your response change? Clearly, relating the reported operating profits to the assets used to produce them is a more meaningful measure of performance.

One way to relate operating profits to assets employed is to compute the profit earned per dollar of investment. For example, the first division earned $0.20 per dollar invested ($100,000/$500,000); the second division earned only $0.10 per dollar invested ($200,000/$2,000,000). In percentage terms, the first division is providing a 20 percent rate of return and the second division 10 percent. This method of computing the relative profitability of investments is known as the return on investment.

return on investment (ROI)

Return on investment (ROI) is the most common measure of performance for an investment center. It can be defined in the following three ways:

$$\text{ROI} = \text{Operating income/Average operating assets}$$
$$= (\text{Operating income/Sales}) \times (\text{Sales/Average operating assets})$$
$$= \text{Operating income margin} \times \text{Operating asset turnover}$$

operating income

operating assets

Of course, **operating income** refers to earnings before interest and taxes. Operating income is typically used for divisions, and net income is used in the calculation of ROI for the company as a whole. **Operating assets** are all assets acquired to generate operating income. They usually include cash, receivables, inventories, land, buildings, and equipment. The figure for average operating assets is computed as follows:

$$\text{Average operating assets} = (\text{Beginning net book value} + \text{Ending net book value})/2$$

Opinions vary regarding how long-term assets (plant and equipment) should be valued (e.g., gross book value versus net book value or historical cost versus current cost). Most firms use historical cost net book value.[1]

margin

turnover

Margin and Turnover The initial ROI formula is decomposed into two component ratios: *margin* and *turnover*. **Margin** is the ratio of operating income to sales. It expresses the portion of sales that is available for interest, taxes, and profit. **Turnover** is a different measure; it is found by dividing sales by average operating assets. The result shows how productively assets are being used to generate sales.

---

1.   For a discussion of the relative merits of gross book value, see James S. Reese and William R. Cool, "Measuring Investment Center Performance," *Harvard Business Review* (May–June 1978), pp. 28–46, 174–176.

Both measures can affect ROI. For example, Amoco aims to be the most profitable of the big oil companies, but is currently behind Exxon. The strategy is to leverage Amoco's strong margins on gasoline by concentrating on turnover. One possibility being explored is to add to its base of 9,600 gas stations by sharing sites with fast food outlets such as Burger King and McDonald's.[2] If successful, the strategy will lead to greater sales of gasoline, increasing turnover, and increasing ROI.

Let's examine the relationship of margin, turnover, and ROI more closely by considering the data presented in Exhibit 18-1. The Snack Foods Division improved its ROI from 18 percent to 20 percent from 1996 to 1997. The Appliance Division's ROI, however, dropped from 18 percent to 15 percent. A better picture of what caused the change in rates is revealed by computing the margin and turnover ratios for each division. These ratios are also presented in Exhibit 18-1.

Notice that the margins for both divisions dropped from 1996 to 1997. In fact, the divisions experienced the *same* percentage of decline (16.67 percent). A declining margin could be explained by increasing expenses, by competitive pressures (forcing a decrease in selling prices), or both.

In spite of the declining margin, the Snack Foods Division was able to increase its rate of return. This increase resulted from an increase in the turnover rate that more than compensated for the decline in margin. The increase in turnover could be explained by a deliberate policy to reduce inventories. (Notice that the average assets employed remained the same for the Snack Foods Division even though sales increased by $10 million.)

The Appliance Division, on the other hand, faced decreasing ROI because margin declined and the turnover rate remained unchanged. Although more

Exhibit 18-1

Comparison of Divisional Performance

Comparison of ROI

	Snack Foods Division	Appliance Division
1996:		
Sales	$30,000,000	$117,000,000
Operating income	1,800,000	3,510,000
Average operating assets	10,000,000	19,500,000
ROI[a]	18%	18%
1997:		
Sales	$40,000,000	$117,000,000
Operating income	2,000,000	2,925,000
Average operating assets	10,000,000	19,500,000
ROI[a]	20%	15%

Margin and Turnover Comparisons

	Snack Foods Division		Appliance Division	
	1996	*1997*	*1996*	*1997*
Margin[b]	6.0%	5.0%	3.0%	2.5%
Turnover[c]	× 3.0	× 4.0	× 6.0	× 6.0
ROI	18.0%	20.0%	18.0%	15.0%

[a] Operating income divided by average operating assets.
[b] Operating income divided by sales.
[c] Sales divided by average operating assets.

2.   Toni Mack, "Catching Up to Exxon," *Forbes*, March 13, 1995, pp. 64–66.

information is needed before any definitive conclusion is reached, the different responses to similar difficulties may say something about the relative skills of the two managers.

Advantages of the ROI Measure   When ROI is used to evaluate division performance, division managers naturally try to increase it. This can be accomplished by increasing sales, decreasing costs, and decreasing investment. Three advantages of the use of ROI are:

1. It encourages managers to pay careful attention to the relationships among sales, expenses, and investment, as should be the case for a manager of an investment center.
2. It encourages cost efficiency.
3. It discourages excessive investment in operating assets.

Each of these three advantages is discussed in turn.

The first advantage is that ROI encourages managers to consider the interrelationship of income and investment. Suppose that a division manager is faced with the suggestion from her marketing vice president that the advertising budget be increased by $100,000. The marketing vice president is confident that this increase will boost sales by $200,000 and raise the contribution margin by $110,000. If the division were evaluated on the basis of operating income, this information might be enough. However, if the division is evaluated on the basis of ROI, the manager will want to know how much additional investment, if any, is required to support the anticipated increase in production and sales. Suppose that an additional $50,000 of operating assets will be needed. Currently, the division has sales of $2 million, net operating income of $150,000, and operating assets of $1 million.

If advertising increased by $100,000 and the contribution margin by $110,000, operating income would increase by $10,000 ($110,000 − $100,000). Investment in operating assets must also increase by $50,000. The ROI without the additional advertising is 15 percent ($150,000/$1,000,000). With the additional advertising, the ROI is 15.24 percent ($160,000/$1,050,000). Since the ROI is increased by the proposal, the divisional manager should increase advertising.

The second advantage is that ROI encourages cost efficiency. The manager of an investment center always has control over costs. Therefore, increasing efficiency through judicious cost reduction is a common method of increasing ROI. For example, Tenneco, Inc. is focusing on cost reduction in its plants by reducing nonvalue-added activities. Materials-handling costs are very high at some plants. Improving the layout of the plants to reduce the time and distance materials must travel is a way of reducing handling costs. Notice that encouraging cost efficiency means that nonvalue-added costs must be reduced or productivity must be improved. There are ways to decrease costs in the short run that have a harmful effect on the business. This possibility is discussed in the section on disadvantages of ROI.

The third advantage is that ROI encourages efficient investment. Divisions that have cut costs to the extent possible must focus on investment reduction. For example, operating assets can be trimmed through the reduction of raw materials and work in process inventory, perhaps by installing just-in-time purchasing and manufacturing systems. New, more productive machinery can be installed, inefficient plants can be closed, and so on. Companies are taking a hard look at the level of investment and acting to reduce it. This is a positive result of ROI-based evaluation.

Disadvantages of the ROI Measure The use of ROI to evaluate performance also has disadvantages. Two negative aspects associated with ROI are frequently mentioned.

1. It discourages managers from investing in projects that would decrease the divisional ROI but would increase the profitability of the company as a whole (generally, projects with an ROI less than a division's current ROI would be rejected).
2. It can encourage myopic behavior, in that managers may focus on the short run at the expense of the long run.

The first disadvantage can be illustrated by an example. Consider a cleaning products division that has the opportunity to invest in two projects for the coming year. The outlay required for each investment, the dollar returns, and the ROI are as follows:

	Project I	*Project II*
Investment	$10,000,000	$4,000,000
Operating income	1,300,000	640,000
ROI	13%	16%

The division is currently earning an ROI of 15 percent, using operating assets of $50 million to generate operating income of $7.5 million. The division has approval to request up to $15 million in new investment capital. Corporate headquarters requires that all investments earn at least 10 percent (this rate represents how much the corporation must earn to cover the cost of acquiring the capital). Any capital not used by a division is invested by headquarters so that it earns exactly 10 percent.

The divisional manager has four alternatives: (A) invest in Project I, (B) invest in Project II, (C) invest in both Projects I and II, and (D) invest in neither project. The divisional ROI was computed for each alternative.

	Alternatives			
	A	*B*	*C*	*D*
Operating income	$ 8,800,000	$ 8,140,000	$ 9,440,000	$ 7,500,000
Operating assets	60,000,000	54,000,000	64,000,000	50,000,000
ROI	14.67%	15.07%	14.75%	15.00%

The divisional manager chose to invest only in Project II (alternative B), since it would have a favorable effect on the division's ROI (15.07 percent is greater than 15.00 percent).

Assuming that any capital not used by the division is invested at 10 percent, the manager's choice produced a lower profit for the company than could have been realized. If Project I had been selected, the company would have earned $1.3 million. By not selecting Project I, the $10 million in capital is invested at 10 percent, earning only $1 million (0.10 × $10,000,000). By maximizing the division's ROI, then, the divisional manager cost the company $300,000 in profits ($1,300,000 − $1,000,000).

The second disadvantage of evaluating performance using ROI is that it can encourage myopic behavior. We saw earlier that one of the advantages of ROI is that it encourages cost reduction. However, while cost reduction can result in more efficiency, it can also result in lower efficiency in the long run. The emphasis

myopic behavior

on short-run results at the expense of the long run is **myopic behavior**. Managers engaging in myopic behavior usually try to cut operating expenses by attacking discretionary costs. Examples are laying off more highly paid employees, cutting the advertising budget, delaying promotions and employee training, reducing preventive maintenance, and using cheaper raw materials.

Each of these steps reduces expenses, increases income, and raises ROI. While these actions increase the profits and ROI in the short run, they have some long-run negative consequences. Laying off more highly paid salespeople may adversely affect the division's future sales. For example, it has been estimated that the average monthly cost of replacing a sales representative with five to eight years' experience with a representative with less than one year of experience was $36,000 of lost sales. Low employee turnover has been linked to high customer satisfaction.[3] Future sales could also be harmed by cutting back on advertising and using cheaper raw materials. By delaying promotions, employee morale would be affected, which could, in turn, lower productivity and future sales. Finally, reducing preventive maintenance will likely cut into the productive capability of the division by increasing downtime and decreasing the life of the productive equipment. While these actions raise current ROI, they lead to lower future ROI.

Residual Income

residual income

In an effort to overcome the tendency to use ROI to turn down investments that are profitable for the company but that lower a division's ROI, some companies have adopted an alternative performance measure known as *residual income*. **Residual income** is the difference between operating income and the minimum dollar return required on a company's operating assets:

$$\text{Residual income} = \text{Operating income} - (\text{Minimum rate of return} \times \text{Operating assets})$$

Advantages of Residual Income   To illustrate the use of residual income, consider the cleaning products division example again. Recall that the division manager rejected Project I because it would have reduced divisional ROI, which cost the company $300,000 in profits. The use of residual income as the performance measure would have prevented this loss. The residual income for each project is computed below.

Project I

Residual income = Operating income − (Minimum rate of return × Operating assets)
   = $1,300,000 − (0.10 × $10,000,000)
   = $1,300,000 − $1,000,000
   = $300,000

Project II

Residual income = $640,000 − (0.10 × $4,000,000)
   = $640,000 − $400,000
   = $240,000

3.   James L. Heskett, Thomas O. Jones, Gary W. Loveman, W. Earl Sasser, Jr., and Leonard A. Schlesinger, "Putting the Service-Profit Chain to Work," *Harvard Business Review*, March/April 1994, Vol. 74, No. 2, pp. 164–174.

Notice that both projects increase residual income; in fact, Project I increases divisional residual income more than does Project II. Thus, both would be selected by the divisional manager. For comparative purposes, the divisional residual income for each of the four alternatives identified earlier follows:

	Alternatives			
	A	B	C	D
Operating assets	$60,000,000	$54,000,000	$64,000,000	$50,000,000
Operating income	$ 8,800,000	$ 8,140,000	$ 9,440,000	$ 7,500,000
Minimum return*	6,000,000	5,400,000	6,400,000	5,000,000
Residual income	$ 2,800,000	$ 2,740,000	$ 3,040,000	$ 2,500,000

*0.10 × Operating assets.

As indicated, selecting both projects produces the greatest increase in residual income. Alternative C is now the preferred alternative. With this new measure employed, managers are encouraged to accept any project that earns above the minimum rate.

Disadvantages of Residual Income Two disadvantages of residual income are that it is an absolute measure of return and that it does not discourage myopic behavior. Absolute measures of return make it difficult to directly compare the performance of divisions. For example, consider the residual income computations for Division A and Division B, where the minimum required rate of return is 8 percent.

	Division A	*Division B*
Average operating assets	$15,000,000	$2,500,000
Operating income	$ 1,500,000	$ 300,000
Minimum return[a]	(1,200,000)	(200,000)
Residual income	$ 300,000	$ 100,000
Residual return[b]	2%	4%

[a]0.08 × Operating assets.
[b]Residual income divided by operating assets.

At first glance, it is tempting to claim that Division A is outperforming Division B, since its residual income is three times higher. Notice, however, that Division A used six times as many assets to produce this difference. If anything, Division B is more efficient.

One possible way to correct this disadvantage is to compute a residual return on investment by dividing residual income by average operating assets. This measure indicates that Division B earned 4 percent while Division A earned only 2 percent. Another possibility is to compute both return on investment and residual income and use both measures for performance evaluation. ROI could then be used for interdivisional comparisons.[4]

---

4.   In their study, Reese and Cool found that only 2 percent of the companies surveyed used residual income by itself, whereas 28 percent used both residual income and return on investment. See Reese and Cool, "Measuring Investment Center Performance."

The second disadvantage of residual income is that it, like ROI, can encourage a short-run orientation. Just as a manager can choose to cut maintenance, training, and sales force expenses when being evaluated under ROI, the manager being evaluated on the basis of residual income can take the same actions. The problem of myopic behavior is not solved by switching to this measure. A method of reducing the myopic behavior problem of residual income is economic value added.

Economic Value Added

economic value added (EVA)

Another measure of profitability for performance evaluation of investment centers is economic value added (EVA). **Economic value added (EVA)** is after-tax operating profit minus the total annual cost of capital. If EVA is positive, the company is creating wealth. If it is negative, then the company is destroying capital. Over the long term, only those companies creating capital, or wealth, can survive.

EVA is a dollar figure, not a percentage rate of return. However, it does bear a resemblance to rates of return such as ROI because it links net income (return) to capital employed. The key feature of EVA is its emphasis on *after-tax* operating profit and the *actual* cost of capital. Other return measures may use accounting book value numbers which may or may not represent the true cost of capital. Residual income, for example, typically uses a minimum expected rate of return. Investors like EVA because it relates profit to the amount of resources needed to achieve it.

Calculating EVA EVA is after-tax operating income minus the dollar cost of capital employed. The equation for EVA is expressed as follows.

$$\text{EVA} = \text{After-tax operating income} - (\text{Weighted average cost of capital} \times \text{Total capital employed})$$

The difficulty faced by most companies is computing the cost of capital employed. There are two steps involved: (1) determine the weighted average cost of capital (a percentage figure), and (2) determine the total dollar amount of capital employed.

To calculate the weighted average cost of capital, the company must identify all sources of invested funds. Typical sources are borrowing and equity (stock issued). Any borrowed money usually has an interest rate attached, and that rate can be adjusted for its tax deductibility. For example, if a company has issued 10-year bonds at an annual interest rate of 8 percent, and the tax rate is 40%, then the after-tax cost of the bonds is 4.8 percent [.08 − (.4 × .08)]. Equity is handled differently. The cost of equity financing is the opportunity cost to investors. Over time, stockholders have received an average return that is six percentage points higher than the return on long-term government bonds. If these bond rates are about 6 percent, then the average cost of equity is 12 percent. Riskier stocks command a higher return; more stable and less risky stocks a somewhat lower return. Finally, the proportionate share of each method of financing is multiplied by its percentage cost and summed to yield a weighted average cost of capital.

Suppose that a company has two sources of financing: $2 million of long-term bonds paying 9 percent interest and $6 million of common stock, which is considered to be of average risk. If the company's tax rate is 40 percent, and the rate of interest on long-term government bonds is 6 percent, the company's weighted average cost of capital is computed as follows.

	Amount	*Percent*	×	*After-Tax Cost*	=	*Weighted Cost*
Bonds	$2,000,000	.25		.09(1 − .4) = .054		.0135
Equity	6,000,000	.75		.06 + .06 = .120		.0900
Total	$8,000,000					.1035

Thus, the company's weighted average cost of capital is 10.35 percent.

The second datum necessary to calculate the dollar cost of capital employed is the amount of capital employed. Clearly, the amount paid for buildings, land, and machinery must be included. However, other expenditures meant to have a long-term payoff, such as research and development, employee training, and so on, should also be included. Despite the fact that these latter are classified by GAAP as expenses, EVA is an internal management accounting measure, and therefore, they can be thought of as the investments that they truly are.

EVA Example Suppose that Furman, Inc., had after-tax operating income last year of $1,583,000. Three sources of financing were used by the company: $2 million of mortgage bonds paying 8 percent interest, $3 million of unsecured bonds paying 10 percent interest, and $10 million in common stock, which was considered to be no more or less risky than other stocks. Furman, Inc., pays a marginal tax rate of 40 percent. The after-tax cost of the mortgage bonds is .048 [1 − (.4 × .08)]. The after-tax cost of the unsecured bonds is .06 [1 − (.4 × .10)]. There are no tax adjustments for equity, so the cost of the common stock is 12 percent (6 percent return on long-term treasury bonds plus the 6 percent average premium). The **weighted average cost of capital** is computed by taking the proportion of capital from each source of financing and multiplying it by its cost. The weighted average cost of capital for Furman, Inc., is computed as follows.

weighted average cost of capital

	Dollar Amount	*Percent*	×	*After-Tax Cost*	=	*Weighted Cost*
Common stock	$10,000,000	.667		.120		.080
Mortgage bonds	2,000,000	.133		.048		.006
Unsecured bonds	3,000,000	.200		.060		.012
Total	$15,000,000					.098

When the weighted average cost of capital is multiplied by total capital employed, the dollar cost of capital is known. For Furman, Inc., the amount of capital employed is $15 million, so the cost of capital is $1,470,000 (.098 × $15,000,000).

Furman, Inc.'s EVA is calculated as follows:

After-tax profit	$1,583,000
Less: Weighted average cost of capital	(1,470,000)
EVA	$ 113,000

The positive EVA means that Furman, Inc., earned operating profit over and above the cost of the capital used. It is creating wealth.

Companies such as AT&T and Coca Cola have found a strong correlation between EVA and stock prices. In fact, stock prices follow EVA better than other accounting measures of return such as earnings per share or return on equity.[5]

---

5.   Shawn Tully, "The Real Key to Creating Wealth," *Fortune,* September 20, 1993, pp. 38–50.

Behavioral Aspects of EVA A number of companies have discovered that EVA helps to encourage the right kind of behavior from their divisions in a way that emphasis on operating income alone cannot. The underlying reason is EVA's reliance on the true cost of capital. In many companies, the responsibility for investment decisions rests with corporate management. As a result, the cost of capital is considered a corporate expense. If a division builds inventories and investment, the cost of financing that investment is passed along to the overall income statement. It does not show up as a reduction from the division's operating income; investment seems free to the divisions, and of course, they want more. As a result, EVA should be measured for subsets of the company. For example, Briggs and Stratton, manufacturer of engines, divided up the company into areas according to types of engine and critical function (e.g., manufacturing, distribution). It then calculates EVA for each area. The result is to make the performance of different areas of the company clearer.[6]

Suppose that Supertech Inc. has two divisions, the Hardware Division and the Software Division. Operating income statements for the divisions are shown below.

	Hardware	*Software*
Sales	$5,000,000	$2,000,000
Cost of goods sold	2,000,000	1,100,000
Gross profit	$3,000,000	$ 900,000
Divisional selling, administrative and taxes	2,000,000	400,000
Net income	$1,000,000	$ 500,000

It looks like the Hardware Division is doing a good job, and so is Software. Now let's consider each division's use of capital. Suppose that Supertech's weighted average cost of capital is 11 percent. Hardware, through a buildup of inventories of components and finished goods, use of warehouses, and so on, uses capital amounting to $10 million, so its dollar cost of capital is $1,100,000 (.11 × $10,000,000). Software does not need large raw materials inventories, but does invest heavily in research and development and training. Its capital usage is $2 million, and its dollar cost of capital is $220,000 (.11 × $2,000,000). The EVA for each division can be calculated as follows.

	Hardware Division	*Software Division*
Operating income	$1,000,000	$500,000
Less: Cost of capital	1,100,000	220,000
EVA	$ (100,000)	$280,000

Now it is clear that the Hardware Division is actually losing money by using too much capital. The Software Division, on the other hand, has created wealth for Supertech. By using EVA, the Hardware Division's manager will no longer consider inventories and warehouses to be "free" goods. Instead, the manager will strive to reduce capital usage and increase EVA. A reduction of capital usage to

6. G. Bennett Stewart III, "EVA Works—But Not If You Make These Common Mistakes," *Fortune*, May 1, 1995, pp. 117–118.

$8 million, for example, would boost EVA to $120,000 [$1,000,000 − (.11 × $8,000,000)].

Quaker Oats faced a similar situation. Prior to 1991, Quaker Oats evaluated its business segments on the basis of quarterly profits. In order to keep quarterly earnings on an upward march, segment managers offered sharp discounts on products at the end of each quarter. This resulted in huge orders from retailers and sharp surges in production at Quaker's plants at the end of each three-month period. This practice is called trade loading because it "loads up the trade" (retail stores) with product. It is not inexpensive, however, because trade loading requires massive amounts of capital—e.g., working capital, inventories, and warehouses to store the quarterly spikes in output. Quaker's plant in Danville, Illinois, produces snack foods and breakfast cereals. Before EVA, the Danville plant ran well below capacity throughout the early part of the quarter. Purchasing, however, bought huge quantities of boxes, plastic wrappers, granola, and chocolate chips. The raw materials purchases buildup was in anticipation of the production surge of the last six weeks of the quarter. As the products were finished, Quaker packed 15 warehouses with finished goods. All costs associated with inventories were absorbed by corporate headquarters. As a result, they appeared to be free to the plant managers, who were encouraged to build ever higher inventories. The advent of EVA and the cancelation of trade loading led to a smoothing of production throughout the quarter, higher overall production (and sales), and lower inventories. Quaker's Danville plant reduced inventories from $15 million to $9 million. Quaker has closed one-third of its fifteen warehouses, saving $6 million annually in salaries and capital costs.[7]

Multiple Measures of Performance

ROI, residual income, and EVA are important measures of managerial performance. However, they are financial measures. As such, the temptation exists for managers to focus only on dollar figures. This focus may not tell the whole story for the company. In addition, lower-level managers and employees may feel helpless to affect net income or investment. As a result, nonfinancial operating measures have been developed. For example, top management could look at such factors as market share, customer complaints, personnel turnover ratios, and personnel development. By letting lower-level managers know that attention to long-run factors is also vital, the tendency to overemphasize financial measures is reduced.

Managers in a contemporary manufacturing environment are especially likely to use multiple measures of performance and to include nonfinancial as well as financial measures. For example, the Saturn plant measures absenteeism (it averages 2.5 percent versus the 10 to 14 percent experienced by other GM plants).[8] Hewlett-Packard has found that product profitability is higher the sooner a new product reaches the market. Thus, in the design phase of a new product, strict conformance to schedule is one of HP's key performance measures.[9]

---

7.   Ibid.
8.   David Woodruff, "Where Employees Are Management," *Business Week,* Reinventing America 1992, p. 66.
9.   Robert D. Hof, "From Dinosaur to Gazelle," *Business Week,* Reinventing America 1992, p. 65.

MEASURING AND REWARDING THE PERFORMANCE OF MANAGERS

Objective 4

Discuss methods of evaluating and rewarding managerial performance.

While some companies consider the performance of the division to be equivalent to the performance of the manager, there is a compelling reason to separate the two. Often, the performance of the division is subject to factors beyond the manager's control. It is particularly important, then, to take a responsibility accounting approach. That is, managers should be evaluated on the basis of factors under their control. A serious concern is the creation of a compensation plan that is closely tied to the performance of the division. This is important in the determination of managerial compensation.

Incentive Pay for Managers—Encouraging Goal Congruence

The subjects of managerial evaluation and incentive pay would be of little concern if all managers were equally likely to perform up to the best of their abilities, and if those abilities were known in advance. In the case of a small company, owned and managed by the same person, there is no problem. The owner puts in as much effort as she wishes and receives all of the income from the firm as a reward for her performance. However, in most companies, the owner hires managers to operate the company on a day-to-day basis and delegates decision-making authority to them. For example, the stockholders of a company hire the CEO through the board of directors. Similarly, division managers are hired by the CEO to operate their divisions on behalf of the owners. Then, the owners must ensure that the managers are providing good service.

Why would managers not provide good service? There are three reasons: (1) they may have low ability, (2) they may prefer not to work hard, and (3) they may prefer to spend company resources on perquisites. The first reason requires owners to discover information about the manager before hiring him. Think back to the reasons for decentralization—one was that it provided training for future managers. This is true, and it also provides signals to higher management about the managerial ability of division managers. The second and third reasons require the owner to monitor the manager or to arrange an incentive scheme that will more closely ally the manager's goals with those of the owner. Some managers may not want to do hard or routine work. In addition, some may be risk-averse and not take actions which expose them, and the company, to risky situations. Thus, it is necessary to compensate them for undertaking risk and hard work. Closely related to the desire of some managers to shirk is the tendency of managers to overuse perquisites. **Perquisites** are a type of fringe benefit received over and above salary. Some examples are a nice office, use of a company car or jet, expense accounts, and company-paid country club memberships. While some perquisites are legitimate uses of company resources, they can be abused. A well-structured incentive pay plan can help to encourage goal congruence between managers and owners.

perquisites

Managerial Rewards

Managerial rewards frequently include incentives tied to performance. The objective is to encourage goal congruence, so that managers will act in the best interests of the firm. Arranging managerial compensation to encourage managers to adopt the same goals as the overall firm is an important issue. Managerial rewards include salary increases, bonuses based on reported income, stock options, and noncash compensation.

Cash Compensation Cash compensation includes salaries and bonuses. One way a company may reward good managerial performance is by granting periodic raises. However, once the raise takes effect, it is usually permanent. Bonuses give a company more flexibility. Many companies use a combination of salary and bonus to reward performance by keeping salaries fairly level and allowing bonuses to fluctuate with reported income. Managers may find their bonuses tied to divisional net income or to targeted increases in net income. For example, a division manager may receive an annual salary of $75,000 and a yearly bonus of five percent of the increase in reported net income. If net income does not rise, the manager's bonus is zero. This incentive pay scheme makes increasing net income, an objective of the owner, important to the manager as well.

Of course, income-based compensation can encourage dysfunctional behavior. The manager may engage in unethical practices, such as postponing needed maintenance. If the bonus is capped at a certain amount (say the bonus is equal to one percent of net income but cannot exceed $50,000), managers may postpone revenue recognition from the end of year in which the maximum bonus has already been achieved to the next year. Those who structure the reward systems need to understand both the positive incentives built into the system as well as the potential for negative behavior.

Profit-sharing plans make employees partial owners in the sense that they receive a share of the profits. They are not owners in the sense of decision making or downside risk sharing. This is a form of risk sharing, in particular, sharing of upside risk. Typically, employees are paid a flat rate, and then, any profits to be shared are over and above wages. The objective is to provide an incentive for employees to work harder and smarter.

Stock-Based Compensation Stock is a share in the company, and theoretically, it should increase in value as the company does well and decrease in value as the company does poorly. Thus, the issue of stock to managers makes them part owners of the company and should encourage goal congruence. Many companies encourage employees to purchase shares of stock, or they grant shares as a bonus. A disadvantage of stock as compensation is that share price can fall for reasons beyond the control of managers. For example, Wal-Mart stock rose and fell in value in the early 1990s. When stock price fell, managers worried about employee morale. To keep morale high, the company created a cash bonus pool to be distributed for meeting sales and income targets.

stock option

Companies frequently offer stock options to managers. A **stock option** is the right to buy a certain number of shares of the company's stock, at a particular price and after a set length of time. The objective of awarding stock options is to encourage managers to focus on the longer term. The price of the option shares is usually set approximately at market price at the time of issue. Then, if the stock price rises in the future, the manager may exercise the option, thus purchasing stock at a below-market price and realizing an immediate gain.

For example, Lois Canfield, head of the toiletries division of Palgate, Inc., was granted an option to purchase 100,000 shares of Palgate stock at the current market price of $20 per share. The option was granted in August 1995 and could be exercised after two years. If, by August 1997, Palgate stock has risen to $23 per share, Lois can purchase all 100,000 shares for $2,000,000 (100,000 × $20 option price) and immediately sell them for $2,300,000 (100,000 × $23). She will realize a profit of $300,000. Of course, if Palgate drops below $20, Lois will not exercise the option. Typically, however, stock prices rise along with the market and Lois can safely bet on a future profit as long as Palgate does not perform worse than the market.

Companies are becoming more aware of the opportunity for windfall profits based on the sale of stock purchased with low cost options, which are profits that appear to be more closely related to the overall rise in the stock market and less related to outstanding performance by top management. As a result, many companies are starting to grant premium options. Premium options are options to purchase stock at a price well above the price at the time of the grants. In early 1994, Time-Warner, Inc., granted its CEO premium options priced $8 to $16 above the stock price at the time.[10] Of course, the options are worthless if the stock price does not exceed the premium price.

Typically there are constraints on the exercise of the options. For example, the stock purchased with options may not be sold for a certain period of time. A disadvantage of stock options is that the price of the stock is based on many factors and is not completely within the manager's control.

Issues to Consider in Structuring Income-Based Compensation   The underlying objective of a company that uses income-based compensation is goal congruence between owner and manager. To the extent that the owners of the company want net income to rise and stock price to rise, basing management compensation on such increases helps to encourage managerial efforts in that direction. However, single measures of performance, which are often the basis of bonuses, are often subject to gaming behavior. That is, managers may increase short-term measures at the expense of long-term measures. For example, a manager may keep net income up by refusing to invest in more modern and efficient equipment. Depreciation expense remains low, but so do productivity and quality. Clearly, the manager has an incentive to understand the computation of the accounting numbers used in performance evaluation. An accounting change from FIFO to LIFO or in the method of depreciation, for example, will change net income even though sales and costs remain unchanged. Frequently we see that a new CEO of a troubled corporation will take a number of losses (e.g., inventory write-downs) all at once. This is referred to as the "big bath" and usually results in very low (or negative) net income in that year. Then, the books are cleared for a good increase in net income, and a correspondingly large bonus, for the next year.

Both cash bonuses and stock options can encourage a short-term orientation. To encourage a longer-term orientation, some companies are requiring top executives to purchase and hold a certain amount of company stock to retain employment. Eastman-Kodak, Xerox, CSX Corporation, Gerber Products, Union Carbide, and Hershey Foods are all companies that have stock ownership guidelines for their top management. A survey of companies in which top executives own relatively large amounts of company stock shows that they tend to perform better in terms of share price than low-ownership companies.[11]

Another issue to be considered in structuring management compensation plans is that frequently owners and managers are affected differently by risk. When managers have so much of their own capital—both financial and human

10.   Joann S. Lublin, "Looking Good," *The Wall Street Journal,* April 13, 1994, pp. R1–R2.
11.   Joann S. Lublin, "Buy or Bye," *The Wall Street Journal,* April 21, 1993, p. R9.

—invested in the company, they may be less apt to take risks. Owners, because of their ability to diversify away some of the risk, may prefer a more risk-taking attitude. As a result, managers must be somewhat insulated from catastrophic downside risk in order to encourage them to make entrepreneurial decisions.

Noncash Compensation Noncash compensation is an important part of the management reward structure. Autonomy in the conduct of their daily business is an important type of noncash compensation. At Hewlett-Packard, cross-functional teams "own" their business and have the authority to reinvest earnings to react quickly to changing markets.

Perquisites are also important. We often see managers who trade off increased salary for improvements in title, office location and trappings, use of expense accounts, and so on. Perquisites can be well used to make the manager more efficient. For example, a busy manager may be able to effectively employ several assistants and may find that use of a corporate jet allows him to more efficiently schedule travel in overseeing far-flung divisions. However, perquisites may be abused as well. For instance, one wonders how the shareholders of RJR Nabisco benefited from previous CEO F. Ross Johnson's use of corporate jets to fly friends around the country.[12]

TRANSFER PRICING

Objective 5
Explain the role of transfer pricing in a decentralized firm.

transfer prices

Often the output of one division can be used as input for another division. For example, integrated circuits produced by one division can be used by a second division to make video recorders. **Transfer prices** are the prices charged for goods produced by one division and transferred to another. The price charged affects the revenues of the transferring division and the costs of the receiving division. As a result, the profitability, return on investment, and managerial performance evaluation of both divisions are affected.

The Impact of Transfer Pricing on Income

Exhibit 18-2 illustrates the effect of the transfer price on two divisions of ABC, Inc. Division A produces a component and sells it to another division of the same company, Division C. The $30 transfer price is revenue to Division A and increases division income; clearly, Division A wants the price to be as high as possible. Conversely, the $30 transfer price is cost to Division C and decreases division income, just like the cost of any raw materials. Division C prefers a lower transfer price. For the company as a whole, A's revenue minus C's cost equals zero.

While the actual transfer price nets out for the company as a whole, transfer pricing can affect the level of profits earned by the company as a whole if it affects divisional behavior. Divisions, acting independently, may set transfer prices that maximize divisional profits but adversely affect firmwide profits. For

---

12.   Bryan Burrough and John Helyar, *Barbarians at the Gate: The Fall of RJR Nabisco,* Harper and Row Publishers, New York, 1990, p. 95.

Exhibit 18-2
Impact of Transfer Price on Transferring Divisions and the Company as a Whole

ABC, Inc.	
A Division	**C Division**
Produces component and transfers it to C for transfer price of $30 per unit.	Purchases component from A at transfer price of $30 per unit and uses it in production of final product.
Transfer price = $30 per unit	Transfer price = $30 per unit
Revenue to A	Cost to C
Increases net income	Decreases net income
Increases ROI	Decreases ROI

Transfer price revenue = Transfer price cost
Zero impact on ABC, Inc.

example, suppose that Division A in Exhibit 18-2 sets a transfer price of $30 for a component that costs $24 to produce. If Division C can obtain the component from an outside supplier for $28, it will refuse to buy from Division A. Division C will realize a savings of $2 per component ($30 internal transfer price − $28 external price). However, assuming that Division A cannot replace the internal sales with external sales, the company as a whole will be worse off by $4 per component ($28 external cost − $24 internal cost). This outcome would increase the total cost to the firm as a whole. Thus, how transfer prices are set can be critical for profits of the business as a whole.

The Transfer Pricing Problem

A transfer pricing system should satisfy three objectives: accurate performance evaluation, goal congruence, and preservation of divisional autonomy.[13] Accurate performance evaluation means that no one divisional manager should benefit at the expense of another (in the sense that one division is made better off while the other is made worse off). Goal congruence means that divisional managers select actions that maximize firmwide profits. Autonomy means that central management should not interfere with the decision-making freedom of divisional managers. The **transfer pricing problem** concerns finding a system that simultaneously satisfies all three objectives.

transfer pricing problem

We can evaluate the degree to which a transfer price satisfies the objectives of a transfer pricing system by considering the opportunity cost of the goods transferred. The *opportunity cost approach* can be used to describe a wide variety of transfer pricing practices. Under certain conditions, this approach is compatible with the objectives of performance evaluation, goal congruence, and autonomy.

opportunity cost approach

The **opportunity cost approach** identifies the minimum price that a selling division would be willing to accept and the maximum price that the buying division would be willing to pay. These minimum and maximum prices correspond

---

13.   Joshua Ronen and George McKinney, "Transfer Pricing for Divisional Autonomy," *Journal of Accounting Research,* Spring 1970, pp. 100–101.

to the opportunity costs of transferring internally. They are defined for each division as follows:

minimum transfer price

maximum transfer price

1. The **minimum transfer price** is the transfer price that would leave the selling division no worse off if the good is sold to an internal division.
2. The **maximum transfer price** is the transfer price that would leave the buying division no worse off if an input is purchased from an internal division.

The opportunity cost rule signals when it is possible to increase firmwide profits through internal transfers. Specifically, a good should be transferred internally whenever the opportunity cost (minimum price) of the selling division is less than the opportunity cost (maximum price) of the buying division. By its very definition, this approach ensures that the divisional manager of either division is no worse off by transferring internally. This means that total divisional profits are not decreased by the internal transfer.

SETTING TRANSFER PRICES

Objective 6

Discuss the methods of setting transfer prices.

Rarely does central management set specific transfer prices. Instead, most companies develop some general policies that divisions must follow. Three commonly used policies are market-based transfer pricing, negotiated transfer pricing, and cost-based transfer pricing. Each of these can be evaluated according to the opportunity cost approach.

Market Price

If there is an outside market for the intermediate product (the good to be transferred) and that outside market is perfectly competitive, the correct transfer price is the market price.[14] In such a case, divisional managers' actions will simultaneously optimize divisional profits and firmwide profits. Furthermore, no division can benefit at the expense of another division. In this setting, central management will not be tempted to intervene.

The opportunity cost approach also signals that the correct transfer price is the market price. Since the selling division can sell all that it produces at the market price, transferring internally at a lower price would make that division worse off. Similarly, the buying division can always acquire the intermediate good at the market price, so it would be unwilling to pay more for an internally transferred good. Since the minimum transfer price for the selling division is the market price and since the maximum price for the buying division is also the market price, the only possible transfer price is the market price.

In fact, moving away from the market price will decrease the overall profitability of the firm. This principle can be used to resolve divisional conflicts that may occur, as the following example illustrates.

Yarrow Manufacturers is a large, privately held corporation that produces small appliances. The company has adopted a decentralized organizational structure. The Parts Division, which is at capacity, produces parts that are used by the

---

14.   A perfectly competitive market for the intermediate product requires four conditions: (1) the division producing the intermediate product is small relative to the market as a whole and cannot influence the price of the product; (2) the intermediate product is indistinguishable from the same product of other sellers; (3) firms can easily enter and exit the market; and (4) consumers, producers, and resource owners have perfect knowledge of the market.

Motor Division. The parts can also be sold to other manufacturers and to whole-salers at a market price of $8. For all practical purposes, the market for the parts is perfectly competitive.

Suppose that the Motor Division, operating at 70 percent capacity, receives a special order for 100,000 motors at a price of $30. Full manufacturing cost of the motors is $31, broken down as follows.

Direct materials	$10
Transferred-in part	8
Direct labor	2
Variable overhead	1
Fixed overhead	10
Total cost	$31

Notice that the motor includes a part transferred in from the Parts Division at a market-based transfer price of $8. Should the Parts Division lower the transfer price to allow the Motor Division to accept the special order? We can use the opportunity cost approach to answer this question.

Since the Parts Division can sell all that it produces, the minimum transfer price is the market price of $8. Any lower price would make the Parts Division worse off. For the Motor Division, identifying the maximum transfer price that can be paid so that it is no worse off is a bit more complex.

Since the Motor Division is under capacity, the fixed overhead portion of the motor's cost is not relevant. The relevant costs are those additional costs that will be incurred if the order is accepted. These costs, excluding for the moment the cost of the transferred-in component, equal $13 ($10 + $2 + $1). Thus, the con-tribution to profits before considering the cost of the transferred-in component is $17 ($30 − $13). The division could pay as much as $17 for the component and still break even on the special order. However, since the component can always be purchased from an outside supplier for $8, the maximum price that the divi-sion should pay internally is $8. As a result, the market price is the best transfer price.

Negotiated Transfer Prices

Perfectly competitive markets rarely exist. In most cases, producers *can* influence price (e.g., by being large enough to influence demand by dropping the price of the product or by selling closely related but differentiated products). When imperfections exist in the market for the intermediate product, market price may no longer be suitable. In this case, negotiated transfer prices may be a practical alternative. Opportunity costs can be used to define the boundaries of the nego-tiation set.

Negotiated outcomes should be guided by the opportunity costs facing each division. A negotiated price should be agreed to only if the opportunity cost of the selling division is less than the opportunity cost of the buying division.

Example 1: Avoidable Distribution Costs To illustrate, assume that a division produces a circuit board that can be sold in the outside market for $22. The divi-sion can sell all that it produces at $22; however, the division incurs a distribution cost of $2 per unit. Currently, the division sells 1,000 units per day, with a variable manufacturing cost of $12 per unit. Alternatively, the board can be sold internally to the company's Electronic Games Division. The distribution cost is avoidable if the board is sold internally.

The Electronic Games Division is also at capacity, producing and selling 350 games per day. These games sell for $45 per unit and have a variable manufacturing cost of $32 per unit. Variable selling expenses of $3 per unit are also incurred. Sales and production data for each division are summarized in Exhibit 18-3.

Since the Electronic Games Division was acquired very recently, no transfers between the two divisions have yet taken place. Susan Swift, the manager of the circuit board division, requested a meeting with Randy Schrude, manager of the games division, to discuss the possibility of internal transfers. The following is their conversation:

Susan: Randy, I'm excited about the possibility of supplying your division with circuit boards. What is your current demand for the type of board we produce? And how much are you paying for the boards?

Randy: We would use one in each of our video games, and our production is about 350 games per day. We pay $22 for each board.

Susan: We can supply that amount simply by displacing external sales. Furthermore, we would be willing to sell them at the same price—that's the price we charge outside customers. We can at least meet your price—that way you are no worse off.

Randy: Actually, I was hoping for a better price than $22. The circuit board is by far our most expensive input. By transferring internally, you can avoid some selling, transportation, and collection expenses. I called corporate headquarters, which estimated these costs at approximately $2 per unit. I'd be willing to pay $20 each for your units. You'd be no worse off, and with a less expensive component, I can make about $700 per day more profit. This deal would make the company $182,000 more during the coming year.

Susan: Your information about avoiding $2 per unit is accurate. I also understand how the cheaper component can allow you to increase your profits. However, if you were to purchase the board at $22, I could increase my division's profits, and the corporation's for that matter, by $700 per day—just by selling you the 350 units and saving the $2 per unit I must spend to sell externally. You would be no worse off, and my division and the corporation would be better off

Exhibit 18-3
Summary of Sales and Production Data

	Board Division	Games Division
Units sold:		
Per day	1,000	350
Per year*	260,000	91,000
Unit data:		
Selling price	$22	$45
Variable costs:		
Manufacturing	$12	$32
Selling	$2	$3
Annual fixed costs	$1,480,000	$610,000

*There are 260 selling days in a year.

by the $182,000 per year that you mentioned. It seems to me that most of the benefits to the corporation come from avoiding the distribution costs incurred when we sell externally. Nonetheless, I'll sweeten the deal. Since we're both members of the same family, I'll let you have the 350 boards for $21.50 each. That price allows you to increase your profits by $175 per day and reflects the fact that most of the savings are generated by my division.

Randy: I don't agree that most of the savings are generated by your division. You can't achieve those savings unless I buy from you. I'm willing to buy internally, but only if there is a fair sharing of the joint benefits. I think a reasonable arrangement is to split the benefits equally; however, I will grant a small concession. I'll buy 350 units at $21.10 each—that will increase your divisional profits by $385 per day and mine by $315 per day. Deal?

Susan: Sounds reasonable. Let's have a contract drawn up.

This dialogue illustrates how the minimum transfer price ($20) and the maximum transfer price ($22) set the limits of the negotiation set. The example also demonstrates how negotiation can lead to improved profitability for each division and for the firm as a whole. Exhibit 18-4 provides income statements for each division before and after the agreement. Notice how total profits of the firm increase by $182,000 as claimed; notice, too, how that profit increase is split between the two divisions.

Example 2: Excess Capacity In perfectly competitive markets, the selling division can sell all that it wishes at the prevailing market price. In a less ideal setting, a

Exhibit 18-4
Comparative Income Statements

Before Negotiation: All Sales External			
	Board Division	*Games Division*	*Total*
Sales	$5,720,000	$4,095,000	$9,815,000
Less: Variable expenses			
Cost of goods sold	3,120,000	2,912,000	6,032,000
Variable selling	520,000	273,000	793,000
Contribution margin	$2,080,000	$ 910,000	$2,990,000
Less: Fixed expenses	1,480,000	610,000	2,090,000
Net income	$ 600,000	$ 300,000	$ 900,000

After Negotiation: Internal Transfers @ $21.10			
	Board Division	*Games Division*	*Total*
Sales	$5,638,100	$4,095,000	$9,733,100
Less: Variable expenses			
Cost of goods sold	3,120,000	2,830,100	5,950,100
Variable selling	338,000	273,000	611,000
Contribution margin	$2,180,100	$ 991,900	$3,172,000
Less: Fixed expenses	1,480,000	610,000	2,090,000
Net income	$ 700,100	$ 381,900	$1,082,000
Change in net income	$ 100,100	$ 81,900	$ 182,000

selling division may be unable to sell all that it produces; accordingly, the division may reduce its output and, as a consequence, have excess capacity.[15]

To illustrate the role of transfer pricing and negotiation in this setting, consider the dialogue between Sharon Bunker, manager of a plastics division, and Carlos Rivera, manager of a pharmaceutical division:

Carlos: Sharon, my division has shown a loss for the past three years. When I took over the division at the beginning of the year, I set a goal with headquarters to break even. At this point, projections show a loss of $5,000—but I think I have a way to reach my goal, if I can get your cooperation.

Sharon: If I can help, I certainly will. What do you have in mind?

Carlos: I need a special deal on your plastic bottle Model 3. I have the opportunity to place our aspirins with a large retail chain on the West Coast—a totally new market for our product. But we have to give it a real break on price. The chain has offered to pay $0.85 per bottle for an order of 250,000 bottles. My variable cost per unit is $0.60, not including the cost of the plastic bottle. I normally pay $0.40 for your bottle, but if I do that, the order will lose me $37,500. I cannot afford that kind of loss. I know that you have excess capacity. I'll place an order for 250,000 bottles, and I'll pay your variable cost per unit, provided it is no more than $0.25. Are you interested? Do you have sufficient excess capacity to handle a special order of 250,000 bottles?

Sharon: I have enough excess capacity to handle the order easily. The variable cost per bottle is $0.15. Transferring at that price would make me no worse off; my fixed costs will be there whether I make the bottles or not. However, I would like to have some contribution from an order like this. I'll tell you what I'll do. I'll let you have the order for $0.20. That way we both make $0.05 contribution per bottle, for a total contribution of $12,500. That'll put you in the black and help me get closer to my budgeted profit goal.

Carlos: Great. This is better than I expected. If this West Coast chain provides more orders in the future—as I expect it will—and at better prices, I'll make sure you get our business.

Notice again the role that opportunity costs play in the negotiation. In this case, the minimum transfer price is the plastic division's variable cost ($0.15), representing the incremental outlay if the order is accepted. Since the division has excess capacity, only variable costs are relevant to the decision. By covering the variable costs, the order does not affect the division's total profits. For the buying division, the maximum transfer price is the purchase price that would allow the division to cover its incremental costs on the special order ($0.25). Adding the $0.25 to the other costs of processing ($0.60), the total incremental costs incurred are $0.85 per unit. Since the selling price is also $0.85 per unit, the division is made no worse off. Both divisions, however, can be better off if the transfer price is between the minimum price of $0.15 and the maximum price of $0.25.

Comparative statements showing the contribution margin earned by each division and the firm as a whole are shown in Exhibit 18-5 for each of the four transfer prices discussed. These statements show that the firm earns the same profit for all four transfer prices; however, different prices do affect the individual divisions' profits differently. Because of the autonomy of each division, there is

---

15. Output can be increased by decreasing selling price. Of course, decreasing selling price to increase sales volume may not increase profits—in fact, profits could easily decline. We assume in this example that the divisional manager has chosen the most advantageous selling price and that the division is still left with excess capacity.

Exhibit 18-5
Comparative Statements

	Transfer Price of $0.40		
	Pharmaceuticals	*Plastics*	*Total*
Sales	$212,500	$100,000	$312,500
Less: Variable expenses	250,000	37,500	287,500
Contribution margin	$(37,500)	$ 62,500	$ 25,000

	Transfer Price of $0.25		
Sales	$212,500	$ 62,500	$275,000
Less: Variable expenses	212,500	37,500	250,000
Contribution margin	$ 0	$ 25,000	$ 25,000

	Transfer Price of $0.20		
Sales	$212,500	$ 50,000	$262,500
Less: Variable expenses	200,000	37,500	237,500
Contribution margin	$ 12,500	$ 12,500	$ 25,000

	Transfer Price of $0.15		
Sales	$212,500	$ 37,500	$250,000
Less: Variable expenses	187,500	37,500	225,000
Contribution margin	$ 25,000	$ 0	$ 25,000

no guarantee that the firm will earn the maximum profit. For example, if Sharon had insisted on maintaining the price of $0.40, no transfer would have taken place and the $25,000 increase in profits would have been lost.

Disadvantages of Negotiated Transfer Prices Negotiated transfer prices have three disadvantages that are commonly mentioned.

1. One divisional manager, possessing private information, may take advantage of another divisional manager.
2. Performance measures may be distorted by the negotiating skills of managers.
3. Negotiation can consume considerable time and resources.

It is interesting to observe that Carlos, the manager of the pharmaceutical division, did not know the variable cost of producing the plastic bottle. Yet that cost was a key to the negotiation. This lack of knowledge gave Sharon, the other divisional manager, the opportunity to exploit the situation. For example, she could have claimed that the variable cost was $0.27 and offered to sell for $0.25 per unit as a favor to Carlos, saying that she would be willing to absorb a $5,000 loss in exchange for a promise of future business. In this case, she would capture the full $25,000 benefit of the transfer. Alternatively, she could have misrepresented the figure and used it to turn down the request, thus preventing Carlos from achieving his budgetary goal; after all, she may be competing with Carlos for promotions, bonuses, salary increases, and so on.

Fortunately, Sharon displayed sound judgment and acted with integrity. For negotiation to work, managers must be willing to share relevant information. How can this requirement be satisfied? The answer lies in the use of good internal control procedures.

Perhaps the best course of action is to hire managers with integrity, managers who have a commitment to ethical behavior. Additionally, top management can take other actions to discourage the use of private information for exploitive purposes. For example, corporate headquarters could base some part of the management reward structure on overall profitability to encourage actions that are in the best interests of the company as a whole.

The second disadvantage of negotiated transfer prices is that the practice distorts the measurement of managerial performance. According to this view, divisional profitability may be affected too strongly by the negotiating skills of managers, masking the actual management of resources entrusted to each manager. Although this argument may have some merit, it ignores the fact that negotiating skill is also a desirable managerial skill. Perhaps divisional profitability *should* reflect differences in negotiating skills.

The third criticism of this technique is that negotiating can be very time-consuming. The time spent in negotiation by divisional managers could be spent managing other activities, which may have a bearing on the success of the division. Sometimes, negotiations may reach an impasse, forcing top management to spend time mediating the process.[16] Although the use of managerial time may be costly, a mutually satisfactory negotiated outcome can produce increased profits for the firm that easily exceed the cost of the managerial time involved. Furthermore, negotiation does not have to be repeated each time for similar transactions.

Advantages of Negotiated Transfer Prices Although time-consuming, negotiated transfer prices offer some hope of complying with the three criteria of goal congruence, autonomy, and accurate performance evaluation. As previously mentioned, decentralization offers important advantages for many firms. Just as important, however, is the process of making sure that actions of the different divisions mesh together so that the company's overall goals are attained. Negotiated transfer prices have been identified as an important integrating mechanism, a means by which goal congruence can be achieved.[17] If negotiation helps ensure goal congruence, the temptation for central management to intervene is diminished considerably. There is, quite simply, no need to intervene. Finally, if negotiating skills of divisional managers are comparable or if the firm views these skills as an important managerial skill, concerns about motivation and accurate performance measures are avoided.

---

16.   The involvement of top management may be very cursory, however. In the case of a very large oil company that negotiates virtually all transfer prices, two divisional managers could not come to an agreement after several weeks of effort and appealed to their superior. His response: "Either come to an agreement within twenty-four hours, or you are both fired." Needless to say, an agreement was reached within the allotted time.

17.   For an excellent discussion of the role of negotiated transfer prices in a decentralized organization, see David Watson and John Baumler, "Transfer Pricing: A Behavioral Context," *The Accounting Review,* July 1975, pp. 466–474.

Cost-Based Transfer Prices

Three forms of cost-based transfer pricing will be considered: full cost, full cost plus markup, and variable cost plus fixed fee. In all three cases, to avoid passing on the inefficiencies of one division to another, standard costs should be used to determine the transfer price. For example, the Micro Products Division of Tandem Computers, Inc., uses a corporate materials overhead rate, rather than the division-specific rate, to facilitate cost-based transfers between divisions.[18] A more important issue, however, is the propriety of cost-based transfer prices. Should they be used? If so, under what circumstances?

Full-Cost Transfer Pricing Perhaps the least desirable type of transfer-pricing approach is that of full cost. Its only real virtue is simplicity. Its disadvantages are considerable. Full-cost transfer pricing can provide perverse incentives and distort performance measures. As we have seen, the opportunity costs of both the buying and selling division are essential for determining the propriety of internal transfers. At the same time, they provide useful reference points for determining a mutually satisfactory transfer price. Only rarely will full cost provide accurate information about opportunity costs.

A full-cost transfer price would have shut down the negotiated prices described earlier. In the first example, the manager would never have considered transferring internally if the price had to be full cost. Yet by transferring at selling price less some distribution expenses, both divisions—and the firm as a whole—were better off. In the second example, the manager of the pharmaceutical division could never have accepted the special order with the West Coast chain. Both divisions and the company would have been worse off, both in the short run and in the long run.

Full Cost Plus Markup Full cost plus markup suffers from virtually the same problems as full cost. It is somewhat less perverse, however, if the markup can be negotiated. For example, a full-cost-plus-markup formula could have been used to represent the negotiated transfer price of the first example. In some cases, a full-cost-plus-markup formula may be the outcome of negotiation; if so, it is simply another example of negotiated transfer pricing. In these cases, the use of this method is fully justified. Using full cost plus markup to represent all negotiated prices, however, is not possible (e.g., it could not be used to represent the negotiated price of the second example). The superior approach is negotiation, since more cases can be represented and full consideration of opportunity costs is possible.

Variable Cost Plus Fixed Fee Like full cost plus markup, variable cost plus fixed fee can be a useful transfer pricing approach provided that the fixed fee is negotiable. This method has one advantage over full cost plus markup: if the selling division is operating below capacity, variable cost is its opportunity cost. Assuming that the fixed fee is negotiable, the variable cost approach can be equivalent to negotiated transfer pricing. Negotiation with full consideration of opportunity costs is preferred.

18.   Earl D. Bennett, Sarah A. Reed, and Ted Simmonds, "Learning from a CIM Experience," *Management Accounting*, July 1991, pp. 28–33.

Propriety of Use In spite of the disadvantages of cost-based transfer prices, companies actively use these methods, especially full cost and full cost plus markup.[19] There must be some compelling reasons for their use—reasons that outweigh the benefits associated with negotiated transfer prices and the disadvantages of these methods. The methods do have the virtue of being simple and objective. These qualities, by themselves, cannot justify their use, however. Some possible explanations for the use of these methods can be given. In many cases, transfers between divisions have a small impact on the profitability of either division. For this situation, it may be cost beneficial to use an easy-to-identify cost-based formula rather than spending valuable time and resources on negotiation.

In other cases, the use of full cost plus markup may simply be the formula agreed upon in negotiations. That is, the full-cost-plus-markup formula is the outcome of negotiation, but the transfer pricing method being used is reported as full cost plus markup. Once established, this formula could be used until the original conditions change to the point where renegotiation is necessary. In this way, the time and resources of negotiation can be minimized. For example, the goods transferred may be custom-made, and the managers may have little ability to identify an outside market price. In this case, reimbursement of full costs plus a reasonable rate of return may be a good surrogate for the transferring division's opportunity costs.

19.   In a survey of profit centers, Umapathy found that 42 percent used full cost and full cost plus markup. Over 50 percent used either market price or negotiated prices. See Srinivasan Umapathy, "Transfers Between Profit Centers," in Richard F. Vancil (ed.), *Decentralization: Managerial Ambiguity by Design*, Dow Jones-Irwin, Homewood, Ill., 1978.

SUMMARY

Responsibility accounting is closely allied to the structure and decision-making authority of the firm. In order to increase overall efficiency, many companies choose to decentralize. The essence of decentralization is decision-making freedom. In a decentralized organization, lower-level managers make and implement decisions, whereas in a centralized organization, lower-level managers are responsible only for implementing decisions.

Reasons for decentralization are numerous. Companies decentralize because local managers can make better decisions using local information. Local managers can also provide a more timely response to changing conditions. Additionally, decentralization for large, diversified companies is necessary because of cognitive limitations—it is impossible for any one central manager to be fully knowledgeable of all products and markets. Other reasons include training and motivating local managers and freeing top management from day-to-day operating conditions so that they can spend time on longer-range activities, such as strategic planning.

Three measures of divisional performance are return on investment (ROI), residual income, and economic value added (EVA). All three relate income to the operating assets used to achieve the income.

Decentralized firms may encourage goal congruence by constructing management compensation programs that reward managers for taking actions which benefit the firm. Possible reward systems include cash compensation, stock options, and noncash benefits.

When one division of a company produces a product that can be used in production by another division, transfer pricing exists. The transfer pricing problem involves finding a mutually satisfactory transfer price that is compatible with the company's goals of accurate performance evaluation, divisional autonomy, and goal congruence. There are three commonly used methods of setting transfer prices. They are market-based, cost-based, and negotiated. In general, the market price is best, followed by negotiated, and then cost-based transfer prices.

REVIEW PROBLEMS AND SOLUTIONS

I.

The Components Division produces a part that is used by the Goods Division. The cost of manufacturing the part is given below:

Direct materials	$10
Direct labor	2
Variable overhead	3
Fixed overhead*	5
Total cost	$20

*Based on a practical volume of 200,000 parts.

Other costs incurred by the Components Division are as follows:

Fixed selling and administrative	$500,000
Variable selling	$1 per unit

The part usually sells for between $28 and $30 in the external market. Currently, the Components Division is selling it to external customers for $29. The division is capable of producing 200,000 units of the part per year; however, because of a weak economy, only 150,000 parts are expected to be sold during the coming year. The variable selling expenses are avoidable if the part is sold internally.

The Goods Division has been buying the same part from an external supplier for $28. It expects to use 50,000 units of the part during the coming year. The manager of the Goods Division has offered to buy 50,000 units from the Components Division for $18 per unit.

REQUIRED:

1. Determine the minimum transfer price that the Components Division would accept.
2. Determine the maximum transfer price that the manager of the Goods Division would pay.
3. Should an internal transfer take place? Why? If you were the manager of the Components Division, would you sell the 50,000 components for $18 each? Explain.
4. Suppose that the average operating assets of the Components Division total $10 million. Compute the ROI for the coming year, assuming that the 50,000 units are transferred to the Goods Division for $21 each.

Solution

1. The minimum transfer price is $15. The Components Division has idle capacity and so must cover only its incremental costs, which are the variable manufacturing costs. (Fixed costs are the same whether or not the internal transfer occurs; the variable selling expenses are avoidable.)
2. The maximum transfer price is $28. The Goods Division would not pay more for the part than what it has to pay an external supplier.

3. Yes, an internal transfer ought to occur. The opportunity cost of the selling division is less than the opportunity cost of the buying division. The Components Division would earn an additional $150,000 profit ($3 × 50,000). The total joint benefit, however, is $650,000 ($13 × 50,000). The manager of the Components Division should attempt to negotiate a more favorable outcome for that division.

4. Income statement:

Sales ([$29 × 150,000] + [$21 × 50,000])	$5,400,000
Less: Variable cost of goods sold ($15 × 200,000)	3,000,000
Less: Variable selling expenses ($1 × 150,000)	150,000
Contribution margin	$2,250,000
Less: Fixed overhead ($5 × 200,000)	1,000,000
Less: Fixed selling and administrative expenses	500,000
Operating income	$ 750,000

$$\text{ROI} = \text{Operating income/Average operating assets}$$
$$= \$750,000/\$10,000,000$$
$$= 0.075$$

II.

Surfit Company, which manufactures surfboards, has been in business for six years. Sam Foster, owner of Surfit, is pleased with the firm's profit picture and is considering taking the company public (i.e., selling stock in Surfit on the NASDAQ exchange). Data for the past year are as follows:

Net income	$ 250,000
Total capital employed	1,060,000
Long-term debt (interest at 9%)	100,000
Owner's equity	900,000

Surfit Company pays taxes at the rate of 35 percent.

REQUIRED:

1. Calculate the weighted average cost of capital, assuming that owner's equity is valued at the average cost of common stock of 12 percent. Calculate the total cost of capital for Surfit Company last year.

2. Calculate EVA for Surfit Company.

Solution

1.
Long-term debt	$ 100,000	.10	.0585	.0059
Owner's equity	900,000	.90	.1200	.1080
Total	$1,000,000			.1139

The weighted average cost of capital is .1139.
The cost of capital last year = .1139 × $1,060,000 = 120,734
2. EVA = $250,000 − $120,734 = $129,266

KEY TERMS

Centralized decision making 776

Cost center 775

Decentralization 776

Decentralized decision making 776

Economic value added (EVA) 785

Investment center 775

Margin 779

Maximum transfer price 794

Minimum transfer price 794

Myopic behavior 783

Operating assets 779

Operating income 779

Opportunity cost approach 793

Perquisites 789

Profit center 775

Residual income 783

Responsibility accounting 775

Responsibility center 775

Return on investment (ROI) 779

Revenue center 775

Stock options 790

Transfer prices 792

Transfer pricing problem 793

Turnover 779

Weighted average cost of capital 786

QUESTIONS FOR WRITING AND DISCUSSION

1. What is decentralization? Discuss the differences between centralized and decentralized decision making.
2. Explain why firms choose to decentralize.
3. Explain how access to local information can improve decision making.
4. One division had operating profits of $500,000, and a second division had operating profits of $3 million. Which divisional manager did the best job? Explain.
5. What are margin and turnover? Explain how these concepts can improve the evaluation of an investment center.
6. What are the three benefits of ROI? Explain how each can lead to improved profitability.
7. What are two disadvantages of ROI? Explain how each can lead to decreased profitability.
8. What is residual income? Explain how residual income overcomes one of ROI's disadvantages.
9. What disadvantage is shared by ROI and residual income? What can be done to overcome this problem?
10. What is EVA? How does it differ from ROI and residual income?
11. What problems do owners face in encouraging goal congruence of managers?

12. What is a stock option? How can it encourage goal congruence?
13. What is a transfer price?
14. Explain how transfer prices can impact performance measures, firmwide profits, and the decision to decentralize decision making.
15. What is the transfer pricing problem?
16. Explain the opportunity cost approach to transfer pricing.
17. If the minimum transfer price of the selling division is less than the maximum transfer price of the buying division, the intermediate product should be transferred internally. Do you agree? Why?
18. If an outside, perfectly competitive market exists for the intermediate product, what should the transfer price be? Why?
19. Discuss the advantages and disadvantages of negotiated transfer prices.
20. Identify three cost-based transfer prices. What are the disadvantages of cost-based transfer prices? When might it be appropriate to use cost-based transfer prices?

EXERCISES AND PROBLEMS

18-1
ROI; Margin; Turnover

LO 3

The following data have been collected for the past two years for one of the larger divisions of Foley Company:

	1998	1999
Sales	$40,000,000	$50,000,000
Net operating income	3,000,000	3,200,000
Average operating assets	20,000,000	20,000,000

REQUIRED:

1. Compute the ROI for each year.
2. Compute the margin and turnover ratios for each year.
3. Explain why the division experienced decreased ROI from 1998 to 1999.

**18-2
ROI; Margin;
Turnover**

LO 3

Data are provided below for a second division of Foley Company (see **18-1**).

	1998	1999
Sales	$25,000,000	$25,000,000
Net operating income	1,500,000	1,400,000
Average operating assets	10,000,000	10,000,000

REQUIRED:

1. Compute the ROI for the second division for each year.
2. Compute the margin and turnover ratios for each year.
3. How does the performance of the manager of the second division compare with the performance of the manager of the first division (refer to **18-1**)?

**18-3
ROI and
Investment
Decisions**

LO 3

The manager of a division that produces sleeping bags, tents, and other camping gear is faced with the opportunity to invest in two independent projects. The first will provide the capability to produce a new type of camp stove. The second will provide the opportunity to produce a backpack, a product the division does not currently offer. Without the investments, the division will have average assets for the coming year of $15 million and expected operating income of $2.4 million. The outlay required for each investment and the expected operating incomes are as follows:

	Camp Stove	Backpack
Outlay	$1,000,000	$500,000
Operating income	140,000	67,000

Corporate headquarters has made available $2 million of capital for the camping goods division. Any funds not invested by the division will be retained by headquarters and invested to earn the company's minimum required rate, 12 percent.

REQUIRED:

1. Compute the ROI for each investment.
2. Compute the divisional ROI for each of the following four alternatives:
   a. No investment is made.
   b. The camp stove investment is made.
   c. The backpack investment is made.
   d. Both investments are made.
      Assuming that divisional managers are evaluated and rewarded on the basis of ROI performance, which alternative do you think the divisional manager will choose?
3. Compute the profit gained or lost for the company as a whole, based on your answer given for Requirement 2. Was the correct decision made?

18-4
Residual Income and Investment Decisions
LO 3

Refer to the data given in **18-3**.

REQUIRED:

1. Compute the residual income for each of the opportunities.
2. Compute the divisional residual income for each of the following four alternatives:
    a. No investment is made.
    b. The camp stove investment is made.
    c. The backpack investment is made.
    d. Both investments are made.

    Assuming that divisional managers are evaluated and rewarded on the basis of residual income, which alternative do you think the divisional manager will choose?
3. Based on your answer in Requirement 2, compute the gain or loss from the divisional manager's investment decision. Was the correct decision made?

18-5
Calculating EVA
LO 3

Borgia Company manufactures pesticides. Last year Borgia earned an operating profit of $350,000 after taxes. Capital employed equaled $2 million. Borgia is 50 percent equity and 50 percent ten-year bonds paying 6 percent interest. Borgia's marginal tax rate is 35 percent. Borgia is considered a fairly risky investment and probably commands a 9 point premium above the 6 percent rate on long-term treasury bonds.

REQUIRED:

1. Calculate EVA.
2. Borgia is considering expanding but needs additional capital. The company could borrow money, but it is considering selling more common stock, which would increase equity to 80 percent of total financing. Total capital employed would be $3,000,000. The new after-tax operating income would be $450,000. Assuming all the other data remain unchanged, recalculate EVA. Comment on Borgia's plan.

18-6
Net Income for Segments
LO 3

Dorman, Inc., manufactures and sells water heaters through three divisions: Southwest, Midwest, and Northeast. Each division is evaluated as a profit center. Data for each division for last year are as follows.

| | *(in thousands of dollars)* | | |
	Southwest	*Midwest*	*Northeast*
Sales	$1,800	$940	$1,235
Cost of goods sold	1,080	710	740
Selling and administrative expense	200	180	340

The income tax rate for Dorman, Inc., is 40 percent.

Dorman, Inc., has two sources of financing: bonds paying 8 percent interest, which account for 30 percent of total investment, and equity accounting for the remaining 70 percent of total investment. Dorman, Inc., has been in business for over 40 years and is considered a relatively stable stock, despite its link to the cyclical construction industry. As a result, Dorman stock has an opportunity cost of 5 percent over the 6 percent long-term government bond rate. Dorman's total capital employed is $3 million ($2,100,000 for the Southwest Division, $500,000 for the Midwest Division, and the remainder for the Northeast Division).

REQUIRED:

1. Prepare a segmented income statement for Dorman, Inc., for last year.
2. Calculate Dorman's weighted average cost of capital.
3. Calculate EVA for each division and for Dorman, Inc.
4. Comment on the performance of each of the divisions.

18-7
Transfer Pricing;
Idle Capacity

LO 5, 6

The Box Division of Belding, Inc., produces boxes that can be sold externally or internally to Belding's candy division. Sales and cost data on the most popular box are given below:

Unit selling price	$0.95
Unit variable cost	0.60
Unit product fixed cost*	0.15
Practical capacity	500,000 units

*$75,000/500,000

During the coming year, the Box Division expects to sell 350,000 units of this box. The Candy Division currently plans to buy 150,000 units of the box on the outside market for $0.95 each. Nell Harper, manager of the Box Division, has approached Martha Padgett, manager of the Candy Division, and offered to sell the 150,000 boxes for $0.94 each. Nell explained to Martha that she can avoid selling costs of $0.02 per box and that she would split the savings by offering a $0.01 discount on the usual price.

REQUIRED:

1. What is the minimum transfer price that the Box Division would be willing to accept? What is the maximum transfer price that the Candy Division would be willing to pay? Should an internal transfer take place? What would be the benefit (or loss) to the firm as a whole if the internal transfer takes place?
2. Suppose Martha knows that the Box Division has idle capacity. Do you think that she would agree to the transfer price of $0.94? Suppose she counters with an offer to pay $0.85. If you were Nell, would you be interested in this price? Explain with supporting computations.
3. Suppose that Belding, Inc., policy is that all internal transfers take place at full manufacturing cost. What would the transfer price be? Would the transfer take place?

18-8
ROI and Residual
Income

LO 3

Consider the following data for two divisions of the same company:

	Paper Products	Plastic Products
Sales	$3,000,000	$10,000,000
Average operating assets	1,000,000	3,000,000
Net operating income	120,000	330,000
Minimum required return	8%	8%

REQUIRED:

1. Compute residual income for each division. By comparing residual income, is it possible to make a useful comparison of divisional performance? Explain.
2. Compute the residual rate of return by dividing the residual income by the average operating assets. Is it possible now to say that one division outperformed the other? Explain.
3. Compute the return on investment for each division. Can we make meaningful comparisons of divisional performance? Explain.
4. Add the residual rate of return computed in Requirement 2 to the required rate of return. Compare these rates with the ROI computed in Requirement 3. Will this relationship always be the same?

18-9

Margin; Turnover; ROI

LO 3

Calculate the missing data for each of the four independent companies below.

	A	B	C	D
Revenue	$10,000	$30,000	$192,000	—
Expenses	8,000	—	180,000	—
Net income	2,000	12,000	—	—
Assets	20,000	—	96,000	9,600
Margin	—%	40%	—%	6.25%
Turnover	—	0.3125	—	2.00
ROI	—	—	—	—

18-10

Residual Income

LO 3

Refer to **18-9**. Assume that the cost of capital is 12 percent for each of the four firms.

REQUIRED: Compute the residual income for each of the four firms.

18-11

Transfer Pricing

LO 5, 6

Adler Industries is a vertically integrated firm with several divisions that operate as decentralized profit centers. Adler's Systems Division manufactures scientific instruments and uses the products of two of Adler's other divisions. The Board Division manufactures printed circuit boards (PCBs). One PCB model is made exclusively for the Systems Division using proprietary designs, while less complex models are sold in outside markets. The products of the Transistor Division are sold in a well-developed competitive market; however, one transistor model is also used by the Systems Division. The costs per unit of the products used by the Systems Division are presented below:

	PCB	Transistor
Direct materials	$2.50	$0.80
Direct labor	4.50	1.00
Variable overhead	2.00	0.50
Fixed overhead	0.80	0.75
Total cost	$9.80	$3.05

The Board Division sells its commercial product at full cost plus a 25 percent markup and believes the proprietary board made for the Systems Division would sell for $12.25 per unit on the open market. The market price of the transistor used by the Systems Division is $3.70 per unit.

REQUIRED:

1. What is the minimum transfer price for the Transistor Division? What is the maximum transfer price of the transistor for the Systems Division?
2. Assume the Systems Division is able to purchase a large quantity of transistors from an outside source at $2.90 per unit. Further assume that the Transistor Division has excess capacity. Can the Transistor Division meet this price?
3. The Board and Systems Divisions have negotiated a transfer price of $11 per printed circuit board. Discuss the impact this transfer price will have on each division.

(CMA adapted)

18-12

ROI, Residual Income

LO 1, 3, 4

Raddington Industries produces tool and die machinery for manufacturers. The company expanded vertically in 1984 by acquiring one of its suppliers of alloy steel plates, Reigis Steel Company. To manage the two separate businesses, the operations of Reigis are reported separately as an investment center.

Raddington monitors its divisions on the basis of both unit contribution and return on average investment (ROI), with investment defined as average operating assets employed. Management bonuses are determined on ROI. All investments in operating assets are expected to earn a minimum return of 11 percent before income taxes.

Reigis's cost of goods sold is considered to be entirely variable, while the division's administrative expenses are not dependent on volume. Selling expenses are a mixed cost with 40 percent attributed to sales volume. Reigis contemplated a capital acquisition with an estimated ROI of 11.5 percent; however, division management decided against the investment because it believed that the investment would decrease Reigis's overall ROI.

The 1999 operating statement for Reigis is presented below. The division's operating assets employed were $15,750,000 at November 30, 1999, a 5 percent increase over the 1998 year-end balance.

Reigis Steel Division
Operating Statement
For the Year Ended November 30, 1999
($000 omitted)

Sales revenue		$25,000
Less: Expenses		
Cost of goods sold	$16,500	
Administrative expenses	3,955	
Selling expenses	2,700	23,155
Income from operations before income taxes		$ 1,845

REQUIRED:

1. Calculate the unit contribution for Reigis Steel Division if 1,484,000 units were produced and sold during the year ended November 30, 1999.
2. Calculate the following performance measures for 1999 for the Reigis Steel Division:
   a. Pretax return on average investment in operating assets employed (ROI).
   b. Residual income calculated on the basis of average operating assets employed.
3. Explain why the management of the Reigis Steel Division would have been more likely to accept the contemplated capital acquisition if residual income rather than ROI were used as a performance measure.
4. The Reigis Steel Division is a separate investment center within Raddington Industries. Identify several items that Reigis should control if it is to be evaluated fairly by either the ROI or residual income performance measures.

(CMA adapted)

18-13
Stock Options
LO 4

Draper, Inc., has acquired two new companies, one in consumer products and the other in financial services. Draper top management believes that the executives of the two newly acquired companies can be most quickly assimilated into the parent company if they own shares of Draper stock. Accordingly, on February 1, Draper approved a stock option plan whereby the top four executives of each company could purchase up to 10,000 shares of Draper stock at $45 per share. The option will expire in five years.

REQUIRED:

1. If Draper stock rises to $67 per share by December 1, what is the value of the option to each executive?
2. Discuss some of the advantages and disadvantages of the Draper stock option plan.

18-14
ROI, Residual
Income

LO 3

The following selected data pertain to Beck Company's Beam Division for 1999:

Sales	$1,000,000
Variable costs	600,000
Traceable fixed costs	100,000
Average invested capital	200,000
Imputed interest rate	15%

REQUIRED:

1. How much is the residual income?
2. How much is the return on investment?

(CPA adapted)

18-15
Bonuses and Stock
Options

LO 4

Jill Fredericks graduated from State U with a major in accounting five years ago. She obtained a position with a well-known public accounting firm upon graduation and has become one of their outstanding performers. In the course of her work, she has developed numerous contacts with business firms in the area. One of them, Posner, Inc., recently offered her a position as head of their financial services division. The offer includes a salary of $40,000 per year, annual bonuses of one percent of divisional net income, and a stock option for 5,000 shares of Posner stock to be exercised at $10 per share in two years. Last year the financial services division earned $1,110,000. This year it is budgeted to earn $1,600,000. Posner stock has increased in value at the rate of twenty percent per year over the past five years. Jill currently earns $55,000.

REQUIRED: Advise Jill on the relative merits of the Posner offer.

18-16
Setting Transfer
Prices—Market
Price Versus Full
Cost

LO 5, 6

Sandia, Inc., manufactures radios, televisions, and VCRs in its four divisions: Radio, TV, VCR, and Components. The Components Division produces electronic components that can be used by the other three. All the components this division produces can be sold to outside customers; however, from the beginning, about 70 percent of its output has been used internally. The current policy requires that all internal transfers of components be transferred at full cost.

Recently, Jasper Ferguson, the new chief executive officer of Sandia, decided to investigate the transfer pricing policy. He was concerned that the current method of pricing internal transfers might force decisions by divisional managers that would be suboptimal for the firm. As part of his inquiry, he gathered some information concerning Component 12F, used by the Radio Division in its production of a clock radio, Model 357K.

The Radio Division sells 100,000 units of Model 357K each year at a unit price of $21. Given current market conditions, this is the maximum price that the division can charge for Model 357K. The cost of manufacturing the radio is:

Component 12F	$ 7
Direct materials	6
Direct labor	3
Variable overhead	1
Fixed overhead	2
Total unit cost	$19

The radio is produced efficiently, and no further reduction in manufacturing costs is possible.

The manager of the Components Division indicated that she could sell 100,000 units (the division's capacity for this part) of Component 12F to outside buyers at $12 per unit. The Radio Division could also buy the part for $12 from external suppliers. She supplied the following details on the manufacturing cost of the component:

Direct materials	$3.00
Direct labor	0.50
Variable overhead	1.50
Fixed overhead	2.00
Total unit cost	$7.00

REQUIRED:

1. Compute the firmwide contribution margin associated with Component 12F and Model 357K. Also, compute the contribution margin earned by each division.
2. Suppose that Jasper Ferguson abolishes the current transfer pricing policy and gives divisions autonomy in setting transfer prices. Can you predict what transfer price the manager of the Components Division will set? What should be the minimum transfer price for this part? The maximum?
3. Given the new transfer pricing policy, predict how this will affect the production decision for Model 357K of the manager of the Radio Division. How many units of Component 12F will the manager of the Radio Division purchase, either internally or externally?
4. Given the new transfer price set by the Components Division and your answer to Requirement 3, how many units of 12F will be sold externally?
5. Given your answers to Requirements 3 and 4, compute the firmwide contribution margin. What has happened? Was Jasper's decision to grant additional decentralization good or bad?

**18-17
Transfer Pricing
with Idle Capacity**
LO 3, 5, 6

Dormeer Company produces mattresses, chairs, and couches in its two divisions: the Mattress Division and the Couch Division. The Couch Division produces a hideaway bed. All of the components for the bed are produced internally with the exception of the mattress, which is purchased from the Mattress Division. Company policy, however, permits each manager freedom to decide whether or not to buy or sell internally. Each divisional manager is evaluated on the basis of return on investment and residual income.

Recently an outside supplier has offered to sell the mattress to the Couch Division for $68. Since the current price paid to the Mattress Division is $70, Angela Fuller, the manager of the Couch Division, was interested in the offer. However, before making the decision to switch to the outside supplier, Angela decided to approach Enrique Delorio, manager of the Mattress Division, to see if he wanted to offer an even better price. If not, then Angela would buy from the outside supplier.

Upon receiving the information from Angela about the outside offer, Enrique gathered the following information about the mattress:

Direct materials	$20
Direct labor	10
Variable overhead	10
Fixed overhead*	10
Total unit cost	$50
Selling price	$70
Production capacity	20,000
Internal sales	10,000

*Fixed overhead is based on $200,000/ 20,000 units.

REQUIRED:

1. Suppose that the Mattress Division is producing at capacity and can sell all that it produces to outside customers. How should Enrique respond to Angela's request for a lower transfer price? What will be the effect on firmwide profits? Compute the effect of this response on each division's profits.
2. Now assume that the Mattress Division is currently selling 18,000 units. If no units are sold internally, the total sales of the hideaway mattress will drop to 16,000 units. Suppose that Enrique refuses to lower the transfer price from $70. Compute the effect on firmwide profits and on each division's profits.
3. Refer to Requirement 2. What are the minimum and maximum transfer prices? Suppose that the transfer price is the maximum price less $1. Compute the effect on the firm's profits and on each division's profits. Who has benefitted from the outside bid?
4. Refer to Requirement 2. Suppose that the Mattress Division has operating assets of $2,000,000. What is divisional ROI based on the current situation? Now refer to Requirement 3. What will divisional ROI be if the transfer price of the maximum price less $1 is implemented? How will the change in ROI affect Enrique? What information has he gained as a result of the transfer pricing negotiations?

18-18
Transfer Pricing: Various Computations
LO 5, 6

Robinson Company has a decentralized organization with a divisional structure. Each divisional manager is evaluated on the basis of ROI.

The Plastics Division produces a plastic container that the Chemical Division can use. Plastics can produce up to 100,000 of these containers per year. The variable costs of manufacturing the plastic containers are $4. The Chemical Division labels the plastic containers and uses them to store an important industrial chemical, which is sold to outside customers for $50 per container. The division's capacity is 20,000 units. The variable costs of processing the chemical (in addition to the cost of the container itself) are $26.

REQUIRED: Assume each part is independent, unless otherwise indicated.

1. Assume that all of the plastic containers produced can be sold to external customers for $10 each. The Chemical Division wants to buy 20,000 containers per year. What should be the transfer price?
2. Refer to Requirement 1. Assume $1 of avoidable distribution costs. Identify the maximum and minimum transfer prices. Identify the actual transfer price, assuming that negotiation splits the difference.
3. Assume that the Plastics Division is operating at 75 percent capacity. The Chemical Division is currently buying 20,000 containers from an outside supplier for $7.50 each. Assume that any joint benefit will be split evenly between the two divisions. What is

the expected transfer price? How much will the profits of the firm increase under this arrangement? How much will the profits of the Plastics Division increase, assuming that it sells the extra 20,000 containers internally?

4. Assume that both divisions have excess capacity. Currently, 15,000 containers are being transferred between divisions at a price of $8. The Chemical Division has an opportunity to take a special order for 5,000 containers of chemical at a price of $33.75 per container. The manager of the Chemical Division approached the manager of the Plastics Division and offered to buy an additional 5,000 plastic containers for $5 each. Assuming that the Plastics Division has excess capacity totaling at least 5,000 units, should the manager take the offer? What is the minimum transfer price? The maximum? Assume that the manager of the Plastics Division counters with a price of $5.50. Would the manager of the Chemical Division be interested?

18-19
Managerial
Performance
Evaluation
LO 1, 2, 3

Greg Peterson has recently been appointed vice president of operations for Webster Corporation. Peterson has a manufacturing background and previously served as operations manager of Webster's Tractor Division. The business segments of Webster include the manufacture of heavy equipment, food processing, and financial services.

In a recent conversation with Carol Andrews, Webster's chief financial officer, Peterson suggested that segment managers be evaluated on the basis of the segment data appearing in Webster's annual financial report. This report presents revenues, earnings, identifiable assets, and depreciation for each segment for a five-year period. Peterson believes that evaluating segment managers by criteria similar to that used in evaluating the company's top management would be appropriate. Andrews has expressed her reservations about using segment information from the annual financial report for this purpose and has suggested that Peterson consider other ways to evaluate the performance of segment managers.

REQUIRED:

1. Explain why the segment information prepared for public reporting purposes may not be appropriate for the evaluation of segment management performance.
2. Describe the possible behavioral impact of Webster Corporation's segment managers if their performance is evaluated on the basis of the information in the annual financial report.
3. Identify and describe several types of financial information that would be more appropriate for Greg Peterson to review when evaluating the performance of segment managers.

(CMA adapted)

18-20
Management
Compensation
LO 4

Renslen Inc., a truck manufacturing conglomerate, has recently purchased two divisions: Meyers Service Company and Wellington Products Inc. Meyers provides maintenance service on large truck cabs for 18-wheeler trucks, and Wellington produces air brakes for the 18-wheeler trucks.

The employees at Meyers take pride in their work, as Meyers is proclaimed to offer the best maintenance service in the trucking industry. The management of Meyers, as a group, has received additional compensation from a ten percent bonus pool based on income before taxes and bonus. Renslen plans to continue to compensate the Meyers management team on this basis as it is the same incentive plan used for all other Renslen divisions.

Wellington offers a high-quality product to the trucking industry and is the premium choice even when compared to foreign competition. The management team at Wellington strives for zero defects and minimal scrap costs; current scrap levels are at two percent. The incentive compensation plan for Wellington management has been a one percent bonus based on gross profit margin. Renslen plans to continue to compensate the Wellington management team on this basis.

Below are the condensed income statements for both divisions for the fiscal year ended May 31, 1998.

Renslen, Inc.
Divisional Income Statements
For the Year Ended May 31, 1998

	Meyers Service Company	Wellington Products Inc.
Revenues	$4,000,000	$10,000,000
Cost of product	$ 75,000	$ 4,950,000
Salaries*	2,200,000	2,150,000
Fixed selling expenses	1,000,000	2,500,000
Interest expense	30,000	65,000
Other operating expense	278,000	134,000
Total expenses	$3,583,000	$ 9,799,000
Income before taxes and bonus	$ 417,000	$ 201,000

*Each division has $1,000,000 of management salary expense that is eligible for the bonus pool.

Renslen has invited the management teams of all its divisions to an off-site management workshop in July where the bonus checks will be presented. Renslen is concerned that the different bonus plans at the two divisions may cause some heated discussion.

REQUIRED:

1. Determine the 1998 bonus pool available for the management team at
   a. Meyers Service Company.
   b. Wellington Products Inc.
2. Identify at least two advantages and at least two disadvantages to Renslen Inc. of the bonus pool incentive plan at
   a. Meyers Service Company.
   b. Wellington Products Inc.
3. Having two different types of incentive plans for two operating divisions of the same corporation can create problems.
   a. Discuss the behavioral problems that could arise within management for Meyers Service Company and Wellington Products Inc. by having different types of incentive plans.
   b. Present arguments that Renslen Inc. can give to the management teams of both Meyers and Wellington to justify having two different incentive plans.

18-21
ROI, Residual Income, Behavioral Issues
LO 3

Jump Start Company (JSC), a subsidiary of Mason Industries, manufactures go-carts and other recreational vehicles. Family recreational centers that feature not only go-cart tracks but miniature golf, batting cages, and arcade games as well have increased in popularity. As a result, JSC has been receiving some pressure from the Mason management to diversify into some of these other recreational areas. Recreational Leasing, Inc. (RLI), one of the largest firms leasing arcade games to these family recreational centers, is looking for a friendly buyer. Mason's top management believes that RLI's assets could be acquired for an investment of $3.2 million and has strongly urged Bill Grieco, division manager of JSC, to consider acquiring RLI.

Grieco has reviewed RLI's financial statements with his controller, Marie Donnelly, and they believe that the acquisition may not be in the best interest of JSC. "If we decide not to do this, the Mason people are not going to be happy," said Grieco. "If we could convince them to base our bonuses on something other than return on investment, maybe this acquisition would look more attractive. How would we do if the bonuses were based on residual income using the company's 15 percent cost of capital?"

Mason has traditionally evaluated all of its divisions on the basis of return on investment, which is defined as the ratio of operating income to total assets. The desired rate of return for each division is 20 percent. The management team of any division reporting an annual increase in the return on investment is automatically eligible for a bonus. The management of divisions reporting a decline in the return on investment must provide convincing explanations for the decline to be eligible for a bonus, and this bonus is limited to 50 percent of the bonus paid to divisions reporting an increase.

Presented below are condensed financial statements for both JSC and RLI for the fiscal year ended May 31, 1998.

	JSC	RLI
Sales revenue	$10,500,000	
Leasing revenue		$2,800,000
Variable expenses	7,000,000	1,000,000
Fixed expenses	1,500,000	1,200,000
Operating income	$ 2,000,000	$ 600,000
Current assets	$ 2,300,000	$1,900,000
Long-term assets	5,700,000	1,100,000
Total assets	$ 8,000,000	$3,000,000
Current liabilities	$ 1,400,000	$ 850,000
Long-term liabilities	3,800,000	1,200,000
Shareholders' equity	2,800,000	950,000
Total liabilities and shareholders' equity	$ 8,000,000	$3,000,000

REQUIRED:

1. If Mason Industries continues to use return on investment as the sole measure of division performance, explain why JSC would be reluctant to acquire RLI. Be sure to support your answer with appropriate calculations.
2. If Mason Industries could be persuaded to use residual income to measure the performance of JSC, explain why JSC would be more willing to acquire RLI. Be sure to support your answer with appropriate calculations.
3. Discuss how the behavior of division managers is likely to be affected by the use of
   a. return on investment as a performance measure.
   b. residual income as a performance measure.

(CMA adapted)

**18-22
Case on ROI and
Residual Income;
Ethical
Considerations**

LO 3

Grate Care Company specializes in producing products for personal grooming. The company operates six divisions, including the Hair Products Division. Each division is treated as an investment center. Managers are evaluated and rewarded on the basis of ROI performance. Only those managers who produce the best ROIs are selected to receive bonuses and to fill higher-level managerial positions. Fred Olsen, manager of the Hair Products Division, has always been one of the top performers. For the past two years, Fred's division has produced the largest ROI; last year, the division earned a net operating income of $2.56 million and employed average operating assets valued at $16 million. Fred is pleased with his division's performance and has been told that if the division does well this year, he would be in line for a headquarters position.

For the coming year, Fred's division has been promised new capital totaling $1.5 million dollars. Any of the capital not invested by the division will be invested to earn the company's required rate of return (9 percent). After some careful investigation, the marketing and engineering staff recommended that the division invest in equipment that could be used to produce a crimping and waving iron, a product currently not produced by the division. The cost of the equipment was estimated at $1.2 million. The division's marketing manager estimated operating earnings from the new line to be $156,000 per year.

After receiving the proposal and reviewing the potential effects, Fred turned it down. He then wrote a memo to corporate headquarters, indicating that his division would not be able to employ the capital in any new projects within the next eight to ten months. He did note, however, that he was confident that his marketing and engineering staff would have a project ready by the end of the year. At that time, he would like to have access to the capital.

REQUIRED:

1. Explain why Fred Olsen turned down the proposal to add the capability of producing a crimping and waving iron. Provide computations to support your reasoning.
2. Compute the effect that the new product line would have on the profitability of the firm as a whole. Should the division have produced the crimping and waving iron?
3. Suppose that the firm used residual income as a measure of divisional performance. Do you think Fred's decision might have been different? Why?
4. Explain why a firm like Grate Care might decide to use both residual income and return on investment as measures of performance.
5. Did Fred display ethical behavior when he turned down the investment? In discussing this issue, consider why he refused to allow the investment.

18-23
Case on Transfer Pricing; Behavioral Considerations

LO 5, 6

Lynsar Corporation started as a single plant that produced the major components assembled into electric motors—the company's main product. Lynsar later expanded by developing outside markets for some of the components used in its motors. Eventually, Lynsar reorganized into four manufacturing divisions: Bearing, Casing, Switch, and Motor. Each of the four manufacturing divisions operates as an autonomous unit, and divisional performance is the basis for year-end bonuses.

Lynsar's transfer pricing policy permits the manufacturing divisions to sell externally to outside customers as well as internally to the other divisions. The price for goods transferred between divisions is to be negotiated between the buying and selling divisions without any interference from top management.

Lynsar's profits have dropped for the current year even though sales have increased, and the drop in profits can be traced almost entirely to the Motor Division. Jere Feldon, Lynsar's chief financial officer, has determined that the Motor Division has purchased switches for its motors from an outside supplier during the current year rather than buying them from the Switch Division. The Switch Division is at capacity and has refused to sell the switches to the Motor Division because it can sell them to outside customers at a price higher than the actual full (absorption) manufacturing cost that has always been negotiated in the past with the Motor Division. When the Motor Division refused to meet the price the Switch Division was receiving from its outside buyer, the Motor Division had to purchase the switches from an outside supplier at an even higher price.

Feldon is reviewing Lynsar's transfer pricing policy because he believes that suboptimization has occurred. While the Switch Division made the correct decision to maximize its divisional profit by not transferring the switches at actual full manufacturing cost, this decision was not necessarily in the best interest of Lynsar. The Motor Division paid more for the switches than the selling price the Switch Division charged its outside customer. The Motor Division has always been Lynsar's largest division and has tended to dominate the smaller divisions. Feldon has learned that the Casing and Bearing Divisions are also resisting the Motor Division's desires to continue using actual full manufacturing cost as the negotiated price.

Feldon has requested that the corporate accounting department study alternative transfer pricing methods that would promote overall goal congruence, motivate divisional management performance, and optimize overall company performance. Three of the transfer pricing methods being considered are listed below. If one of these methods should be selected, it would be applied uniformly across all divisions.

A. Standard full manufacturing costs plus markup.
B. Market selling price of the products being transferred.
C. Outlay (out-of-pocket) costs incurred to the point of transfer plus opportunity cost per unit.

REQUIRED:

1. a. Discuss both the positive and negative behavioral implications that can arise from employing a negotiated transfer price system for goods that are exchanged between divisions.
   b. Explain the behavioral problems that can arise from using actual full (absorption) manufacturing costs as a transfer price.
2. Discuss the behavioral problems that could arise if Lynsar Corporation decides to change from its current policy covering the transfer of goods between divisions to a revised transfer pricing policy that would apply uniformly to all divisions.
3. Discuss the likely behavior of both "buying" and "selling" divisional managers for each of the following transfer pricing methods being considered by Lynsar Corporation.
   a. Standard full manufacturing costs plus markup.
   b. Market selling price of the products being transferred.
   c. Outlay (out-of-pocket) costs incurred to the point of transfer plus opportunity cost per unit.

                                                                                    (CMA adapted)

Chapter 19
International Issues in Cost Management

Across the street or around the world, U.S. firms establish manufacturing and service presence. KFC's Chinese stores must balance the fried chicken that made the company famous with the need to appeal to local tastes.

LEARNING OBJECTIVES

After studying this chapter, you should be able to:

1. Explain the role of the accountant in the international environment.
2. Discuss the varying levels of involvement that firms can take in international trade.
3. Explain the ways accountants can manage foreign currency risk.
4. Explain why multinational firms choose to decentralize.
5. Explain how environmental factors can affect performance evaluation in the multinational firm.
6. Discuss the role of transfer pricing in the multinational firm.
7. Discuss ethical issues that affect firms operating in the international environment.

MANAGEMENT ACCOUNTING IN THE INTERNATIONAL ENVIRONMENT

Objective 1
Explain the role of the accountant in the international environment.

Doing business in a global environment requires management to shift perspective. While many aspects of business dealings remain the same, other aspects are quite different. The company doing business in both its home country and other countries may find that practices that work well in the home country work imperfectly or not at all in another country. Much of the difference can be related to the business environment—that is, the cultural, legal, political, and economic environment of the various countries. Just as a fish supposedly is not aware of water, we in the United States take our business environment for granted. We have grown accustomed to a market economy and to the concept of private property. We are accustomed to a legal system that enforces contracts. Our sense of ethics grew in tandem with the underlying environment. When the environment changes, ethical problems may arise. Different divisions of the same company may well face different ethical problems; therefore, evaluating the ethical content of divisional decisions is common.

Where does the accountant fit into the global business environment? Business looks to the accountant for financial and business expertise. The accountant's job is not cut and dried. Knowledge, creativity, and flexibility are needed to help managers make decisions. We might take a cue from the IMA Standards of Ethical Conduct (given in Chapter 1) and consider competence. Good training, education, and staying up to date with one's field are important to any accountant. However, the job of the accountant in the international firm is made more challenging by the ambiguous and ever-changing nature of global business. Since much of the accountant's job is to provide relevant information to management, staying up to date requires one to read books and articles in a variety of business areas including information systems, marketing, management, politics, and economics. In addition, the accountant must be familiar with the financial accounting rules of the countries in which the firm operates.

The remainder of this chapter will touch on various issues facing the multinational firm. Our focus is on the internal accountant and the interaction of cost and revenue management with those issues.

LEVELS OF INVOLVEMENT IN INTERNATIONAL TRADE

Objective 2
Discuss the varying levels of involvement that firms can take in international trade.

multinational
corporation (MNC)

A **multinational corporation (MNC)** is one that "does business in more than one country in such a volume that its well-being and growth rest in more than one country."[1] From this definition, we can see that the involvement of the MNC in international trade may take many forms. On a fairly simple level, the MNC may import raw materials and/or export finished products. On a more complex level, the MNC may be a large firm consisting of a parent company and a number of divisions in various countries.

In the international environment, the choice of company structure goes beyond the issue of centralized versus decentralized firm structure described in an earlier chapter. While multinational companies are very often decentralized, with subsidiaries that are wholly owned by the parent firm, the many business environments in which the firm may operate have led to various company struc-

---

1.   Yair Aharoni, "On the Definition of a Multinational Corporation," in A. Kapoor and Phillip D. Grub (eds.), *The Multinational Enterprise in Transition*, Darwin Press, Princeton, N.J., 1972, p. 4.

tures. Some of the choices are importing and exporting, wholly owned subsidiaries, and joint ventures.

Importing and Exporting

A relatively simple form of multinational involvement is importing and exporting. A company may import parts for production. Similarly, a company may export finished product to foreign countries. Even such simple transactions as importing and exporting can present new risks and opportunities for companies.

Importing   A company may import raw materials for use in production. While this transaction may look identical to the purchase of materials from domestic suppliers, U.S. tariffs add complexity and cost. Recall that freight-in is a materials cost. An imported part may have tariff (or duty) in addition to freight-in. A **tariff** is a tax on imports levied by the federal government. This tax is also a cost of materials. Companies search for ways to reduce tariffs. They may restrict the amount of imported materials, alter the materials by adding U.S. resources (to increase the domestic content and gain more favorable tariff status), or utilize foreign trade zones.

Foreign Trade Zones   The United States government has set up **foreign trade zones**, areas that are physically on U.S. soil but considered to be outside U.S. commerce. Because foreign trade zones must be located near a customs port of entry, they are often located near seaports or airports. San Antonio, New Orleans, and the Port of Catoosa, Oklahoma, are examples of cities with foreign trade zones. Goods imported into a foreign trade zone are duty-free until they leave the zone. This has important implications for manufacturing firms that import raw materials. Some U.S. companies set up manufacturing plants within the foreign trade zones. Since tariffs are not paid until the imported materials leave the zone, as part of a finished product, the company can postpone payment of duty and the associated loss of working capital. Additionally, the company does not pay duty on defective materials or inventory that has not yet been included in finished products.

An example may help to illustrate the cost advantages of operating a plant in a foreign trade zone. Suppose that Roadrunner, Inc., operates a petrochemical plant located in a foreign trade zone. The plant imports volatile materials (i.e., chemicals that experience substantial evaporation loss during processing) for use in production. Wilycoyote, Inc., operates an identical plant just outside the foreign trade zone. Consider the impact on duty and related expenditures for the two plants for the purchase of $400,000 of crude oil imported from Venezuela. Both Roadrunner and Wilycoyote use the oil in chemical production. Each purchases the oil about three months before use in production, and the finished chemicals remain in inventory about five months before sale and shipment to the customer. About 30 percent of the oil is lost through evaporation during production. Duty is assessed at 6 percent of cost. Each company faces 12 percent carrying cost.

Wilycoyote pays duty, at the point of purchase, of $24,000 (0.06 × $400,000). In addition, Wilycoyote has carrying cost associated with the duty payment of 12 percent per year times the portion of the year that the oil is in raw materials or finished goods inventory. In this case, the months in inventory equal 8 (3 + 5). Total duty-related carrying cost is $1,920 (0.12 × 8/12 × $24,000). Total duty

tariff (margin note)

foreign trade zones (margin note)

and duty-related carrying cost is $25,920. Roadrunner, on the other hand, pays duty at the time of sale because it is in a foreign trade zone, and imported goods do not incur duty until (unless) they are moved out of the zone. Since 70 percent of the original imported oil remains in the final product, duty equals $16,800 (0.7 × $400,000 × 0.06). There is no carrying cost associated with the duty. The duty-related costs for the two companies are summarized below.

	Roadrunner	Wilycoyote
Duty paid at purchase	$ 0	$24,000
Carrying cost of duty	0	1,920
Duty paid at sale	16,800	0
Total duty and related cost	$16,800	$25,920

Clearly, Roadrunner has saved $9,120 ($25,920 − $16,800) on just one purchase of imported raw materials by locating in the foreign trade zone.

Foreign trade zones provide additional advantages. For example, goods that do not meet U.S. health, safety, and pollution control regulations are subject to fine. Noncomplying foreign goods can be imported into foreign trade zones and modified to comply with the law without being subject to the fine. Another example of the efficient use of foreign trade zones is the assembly of high-tariff component parts into a lower-tariff finished product. In this case, the addition of domestic labor raises the domestic content of the finished product and makes the embedded foreign parts eligible for more favorable tariff treatment.[2]

The number of foreign trade zones has grown substantially. In the decade from 1980 to 1990, the number of general-purpose foreign trade zones increased from 59 to 158 and the number of subzones increased from 9 to 168. While the paperwork involved in establishing a foreign trade zone is extensive—and very expensive—reallocating the space of an existing foreign trade zone is relatively easy. The owners of foreign trade zones (typically city or county authorities) can then work with companies to maximize the advantages of the zone.

For example, suppose that Worldwide Enterprises, an export-import company, is considering expansion and wants to build a distribution center in the southwest part of the United States. The distribution center must be convenient to the interstate highway system and to rail transportation. Additionally, because Worldwide imports a significant amount of inventory, it wants to establish the center in a foreign trade zone. Further suppose that a city in which the center might be located has an already established foreign trade zone on 200 acres near its airport. The city has offered Worldwide the chance to purchase land in the zone on which to build the center. However, the land does not meet the company's criteria for rail and highway access. Worldwide has located a ten-acre parcel of land in the city that meets its transportation criteria but is not in the foreign trade zone. Now what? The city is anxious to win Worldwide's center, as it will mean nearly 500 new jobs and a healthy increase in the city economy. Fortunately, the flexibility of foreign trade zones makes it possible for the city to name Worldwide's preferred parcel of land a foreign trade subzone (and to reduce the airport foreign trade zone area by 10 acres).

A final factor should be mentioned in connection with foreign trade zones, the possibility of political ramifications. By their nature, plants located in foreign

---

2.   These examples are taken from James E. Groff and John P. McCray, "Foreign-Trade Zones: Opportunity for Strategic Development in the Southwest," *Journal of Business Strategies*, Spring 1992, 14–26.

trade zones are engaged in international trade. On occasion, political priorities may supersede business priorities. For example, Japanese car plants in Illinois, Indiana, Kentucky, Ohio, and Tennessee are located in foreign trade zones. Nissan Motor Company (producer of a popular compact pickup truck) and Mitsubishi (maker of the Eclipse) can import Asian components at half the usual duty for final assembly in the U.S. In April, 1995, the U.S. government considered the option of curtailing these special foreign trade zones as a weapon in the fight to get Japan to purchase more U.S. auto parts. The message for cost and management accountants is that they must be aware of much more than narrow business interests in evaluating the advantages and disadvantages of international trade.

Exporting Exporting is the sale of a company's products in foreign countries. It is not necessary to have a production facility in the foreign country: finished product can simply be transported to the buyer. However, exporting is usually more complex than the sale of finished goods within the home country. Foreign countries have a variety of import and tariff regulations. The job of complying with the foreign rules and regulations often falls to the controller's office, just as compliance with U.S. tax regulations is an accounting function. Alternatively, a U.S. company may choose to work with an experienced distributor, familiar with the legal complexities of the other countries. In some cases, the distributor is wholly owned; in other cases, the distributor is a separate company.

Wholly Owned Subsidiaries

A company may choose to purchase an existing foreign company, making the purchased company a wholly owned subsidiary of the parent. This strategy has the virtue of simplicity. The foreign company has established an outlet for the product and has the production and distribution facilities already set up. For example, in 1989, Whirlpool expanded into the European market by purchasing the appliance business of Philips N.V., Europe's third largest appliance manufacturer. This purchase gave Whirlpool immediate access to production and distribution facilities, as well as an established brand name. Even so, the approach is not inexpensive. The first three years were spent blending company cultures, before the European operation could be streamlined to cut costs. Finally, more investment was necessary in marketing, to replace the Philips name with Whirlpool's, and to develop a marketing plan for all of Europe as opposed to the more fragmented country-by-country approach used previously.[3]

If the laws of the country permit, an MNC can simply set up a wholly owned subsidiary or branch office in the country. In Ireland, for example, U.S. insurance and software companies have set up branch offices. Quarterdeck Office Systems, a California-based software company, routes customer calls to its second phone-answering operation in Dublin. Scores of multilingual workers take calls from all over Europe—and from the United States. When it is 5:00 a.m. in California, Irish workers are well into their working day and can answer calls from customers in the U.S. Eastern Time Zone. The Irish Development Authority provides generous tax and other incentives worth about a year's pay for each job created.[4]

Outsourcing of technical and professional jobs is becoming an important issue for resource-conscious U.S. firms. **Outsourcing** is the payment by a company for a business function that was formerly done in-house. For example, some domes-

outsourcing

---

3. Barry Rehfeld, "Where Whirlpool Flies, and Maytag Sputters," *The New York Times,* January 3, 1993, p. 5.
4. "Your New Global Work Force," *Fortune,* December 14, 1992, pp. 52–66.

tic companies outsource their legal needs to outside law firms rather than hiring corporate attorneys. In the context of the MNC, outsourcing refers to the move of a business function to another country. For example, Texas Instruments set up an engineering facility in Bangalore, India. The availability of underemployed college graduates in India meant the combination of low wage rates and high productivity. However, the underdeveloped Indian infrastructure required considerable capital investment. TI installed its own electrical generators and satellite dishes, some hauled in by oxcart, to operate efficiently. Now the company's engineers in Dallas and in Miho, Japan, design parts of a memory chip and forward their work via computers and satellite to engineers at Bangalore for completion. The chip is then fabricated in Texas and returned to Bangalore for debugging.

Money is not the only resource saved when MNCs locate operations in foreign countries. Time is a valuable resource, and many companies have found that a global presence leads to time and quality enhancement. TI's global network of R&D facilities work simultaneously and around the clock on some projects. In one instance, a customer asked TI for a quote on a hand-held bidding device for stock exchange traders. TI's Dallas, Texas, design group began working on the problem, and then, at the end of the day, transferred their work electronically to designers in Tokyo. The Tokyo group continued developing the design, and at quitting time, transferred the design to the Nice, France, design group. By the next day, the Dallas group had a completed design, quote, and preliminary picture of the device.[5]

PepsiCo Inc. has also found that wholly owned subsidiaries can increase quality. Pepsi Foods International is the overseas snack foods division. It found that potato chips are the most popular snack, with a world-wide market of $4 billion, and plans to capitalize on that to increase demand even more. Quality is PepsiCo's secret weapon. It had grown internationally by buying foreign competitors or entering into joint ventures. However, the chips were of uneven quality. Now, the division emphasizes uniform quality standards. New equipment handles potatoes more gently and slices them more evenly. Chips are "redesigned" to meet the local market's tastes. For example, the Chinese do not like cheese on their Cheetos, so Chinese Cheetos are cheeseless. The company is also developing a seafood-flavored Cheeto for this market.

Outsourcing is done by foreign firms, as well. Swissair transferred its accounting operations to Bombay. British Airways sold its division in South Wales that had done major engine overhauls and contracted out the work to General Electric. Increased efficiency should save BA about $262 million.[6] The accountant must be aware of numerous costs and benefits of outsourcing outside the United States. The varying tax structures and incentives of local authorities, as well as the overall educational level of the country, and the infrastructure all play a role in the accountant's assessment of costs and benefits.

Joint Ventures

joint venture   On occasion, the companies with expertise needed by MNCs do not exist or are not for sale. A joint venture may work. A **joint venture** is a type of partnership in which investors co-own the enterprise. General Electric Company (GE) owns 50 percent of a medical systems venture with Wipro Ltd. of India. Wipro GE produces CT scanners, applications software, and ultrasound devices, including a

5.   Myron Magnet, "Who's Winning the Information Revolution," *Fortune,* November 30, 1992, pp. 110–117.
6.   Rahul Jacob, "Thriving in a Lame Economy," *Fortune,* October 5, 1992, pp. 44–54.

20-pound ultrasound unit that fits into the back of a car, enabling Indian doctors to take the technology to remote villages. The technology for the new equipment was obtained from GE's joint venture with Yokogawa Medical Systems Ltd. in Japan. Now, Indian engineers work side by side with Japanese and American designers and engineers to create less expensive medical technology to sell in both Asian and U.S. markets.[7] Similarly, Kia, the second-largest Korean automaker, has developed manufacturing alliances with Ford Motor Company and Mazda to build cars and to accumulate technological knowledge. For example, Kia's Sephia is powered by a fuel-injected Mazda engine, and Kia uses Ford's plants to assemble cars in Taiwan and Venezuela. More joint ventures include: Hewlett-Packard and Hitachi, Boeing and Mitsubishi, Apple Computer and Sharp Electronics.

Sometimes a joint venture is required because of restrictive laws. In China, for example, MNCs are not allowed to purchase companies or set up their own subsidiaries. Joint ventures with Chinese firms are required. Similarly, India and Thailand demand local ownership. Loctite Corporation, maker of Super Glue, runs joint ventures in both India and Thailand for that reason.

maquiladoras

A special case of joint venture cooperation is the maquiladora. **Maquiladoras** are manufacturing plants located in Mexico that process imported materials and reexport them to the United States. Originally designed to encourage U.S. firms to invest in Mexico, the program has now expanded to include other foreign firms, such as Nissan and Sony. Basically, the maquiladora enjoys special status in both Mexico, which grants operators an exemption from Mexican laws governing foreign ownership, and the United States, which grants exemptions from or reductions in custom duties levied on reexported goods. Most maquiladoras are located in cities bordering the United States to take advantage of ready access to U.S. transportation and communication facilities. The Mexican advantage is low-cost, high-quality labor. The structure of the maquiladora is flexible. Mexico permits different levels of involvement. The minimal level combines low risk with low cost savings. In this case, the U.S. firm transfers materials to an existing Mexican firm and imports them back in finished form. All hiring and operating of the Mexican plant is accomplished by the Mexican owners. The highest level of involvement offers both high risk and high cost savings. At this level, the U.S. firm owns the Mexican subsidiary and oversees all the operations.[8]

Maquiladoras are an example of a government program to increase production that has worked well. Foreign investment has moved well beyond the border cities to a broad band of northern Mexico. Improvements in Mexican infrastructure (e.g., roads and communications) have enticed companies further into the interior, lowering nonlabor costs. While U.S. companies were originally drawn to the maquiladoras for the cheap labor (wage rates of approximately $1.50 per hour versus $17.50 per hour for U.S. assemblers), other reasons keep them. For example, Ford's plant in Chihuahua was built to satisfy export requirements for doing business in Mexico. Now, it supports Ford's sales to Mexico, establishing a marketing reason for the plant's presence.

No matter which structure the MNC takes, it faces issues of foreign trade. An important issue is foreign currency exchange. This is addressed in the next section.

---

7.   Tim Smart, Pete Engardio, and Geri Smith, "GE's Brave New World," *Business Week,* November 8, 1993, pp. 64–70.
8.   James E. Groff and John P. McCray, "Maquiladoras: The Mexico Option Can Reduce Your Manufacturing Cost," *Management Accounting,* January 1991, pp. 43–46.

FOREIGN CURRENCY EXCHANGE

Objective 3
Explain the ways accountants can manage foreign currency risk.

exchange rates

currency risk management

transaction risk

economic risk

translation (or accounting) risk

When a company operates only in its home country, only one currency is used, and exchange issues never arise. However, when a company begins to operate in the international arena, it must use foreign currencies. These foreign currencies can be exchanged for the domestic currency using **exchange rates**. If the exchange rates never changed, problems would not occur. Exchange rates do change, however, often on a daily basis. Thus, a dollar that could be traded for 350 yen one day may be worth only 325 yen on another day. Currency rate fluctuations add considerably to the uncertainty of operating in the international arena.

The accountant plays an important role in managing the company's exposure to currency risk. **Currency risk management** refers to the company's management of its transaction, economic, and translation exposure due to exchange rate fluctuations. **Transaction risk** refers to the possibility that future cash transactions will be affected by changing exchange rates. **Economic risk** refers to the possibility that a firm's present value of future cash flows will be affected by exchange fluctuations. **Translation (or accounting) risk** is the degree to which a firm's financial statements are exposed to exchange rate fluctuation. Let's look more closely at these three components of currency risk and ways in which the accountant can manage the company's exposure to them.

Managing Transaction Risk

spot rate

Today's MNC deals in many different currencies. These currencies may be traded for one another depending on the exchange rate in effect at the time of the trade. The **spot rate** is the exchange rate of one currency for another for immediate delivery (i.e., today). Exhibit 19-1 lists a number of widely used currencies and their spot rates as of December 19, 1995. While the spot rates are surely different now, as you read this book, you can gain an idea of relative values. Changes in the spot rates can affect the value of a company's future cash transactions, posing transaction risk. Let's first get a feel for currency appreciation and depreciation, before we go on to exchange gains and losses and hedging.

currency appreciation

currency depreciation

Currency Appreciation and Depreciation When one country's currency strengthens relative to another country's currency, **currency appreciation** occurs, and one unit of the first country's currency can buy more units of the second country's currency. Conversely, **currency depreciation** means that one country's currency has become relatively weaker and buys fewer units of another currency. For example, in mid-1985, the U.S. dollar was worth 240 yen. (Yen is the unit of Japanese currency and is symbolized by ¥.) By mid-1986, the dollar had weakened to only 156 yen. This had an impact on trade between the two countries. Fujinon Optical Company sold rubber-coated marine binoculars for ¥93,600. In mid-1985, this meant a price of $390 (93,600/240) to U.S. importers. In mid-1986, however, the same binoculars, priced at the same ¥93,600, would cost U.S. importers $600 (93,600/156). Of course, while the dollar weakened, the yen strengthened.

Exchange Gains and Losses Let's examine the impact of changes in exchange rates on the sale of goods to other countries. Suppose that SuperTubs, Inc., based in Oklahoma, sells its line of whirlpool tubs at home and to foreign distributors. On January 15, Bonbain, a French distributor of luxury plumbing fixtures, orders 100 tubs at a price of $1,000 per tub, to be delivered immediately, and to be paid in French francs on March 15. Has SuperTubs just made a sale of $100,000

Exhibit 19-1
Currencies and Spot Rates

Country	Currency Name	Exchange Rate for $1 on 12/19/95
Australia	Australian Dollar	1.3485
Canada	Canadian Dollar	1.3744
China	Renminbi	8.3176
France	Franc	4.9565
Germany	Deutsch Mark	1.4410
Great Britain	Pound	.6484
Hong Kong	Hong Kong Dollar	7.7344
India	Rupee	34.9700
Indonesia	Rupiah	2,287.0000
Israel	Shekel	3.1332
Italy	Lira	1,594.7500
Japan	Yen	102.0000
Mexico	Peso	7.6750
Netherlands	Guilder	1.6140
Peru	New Sol	2.3155
Russia	Ruble	4,639.0000
Saudi Arabia	Riyal	3.7504
Singapore	Singapore Dollar	1.4146
South Korea	Won	771.4500
Sweden	Krona	6.6395
Switzerland	Swiss Franc	1.1565
Taiwan	Taiwan Dollar	27.3310
Thailand	Baht	25.1600
Venezuela	Bolivar	289.6200

$(100 \times \$1,000)$? The payment is to be in francs, not dollars, so we must look at the exchange rate for francs. If the exchange rate on January 15 is 5 francs per dollar, then Bonbain is really promising to pay 500,000 francs ($5 \times \$100,000$) on March 15. If the exchange rate remains at 5 francs per dollar on March 15, SuperTubs would receive 500,000 francs convertible to $100,000. But suppose that the exchange rate on March 15 is 5.1 francs per dollar. Bonbain still pays 500,000 francs, but SuperTubs can convert that amount into only $98,039 (500,000/5.1), not the $100,000 it anticipated back in January when the sale was made. The difference between the two amounts, $1,961, is the loss on currency exchange. The impact of transaction risk on this example can be summarized as follows.

Receivable in dollars on 1/15	$100,000
Received in dollars on 3/15	98,039
Exchange loss	$ 1,961

exchange loss

An **exchange loss**, then, is a loss on the exchange of one currency for another due to depreciation of the home currency.

exchange gain

Of course, if the franc had strengthened against the dollar, say an exchange rate of 4.9 francs per dollar, an exchange gain would occur. An **exchange gain** is the gain on the exchange of one currency for another due to appreciation of the home currency. In our example, Bonbain again pays 500,000 francs, which SuperTubs is able to convert into $102,041 (500,000/4.9). In that case, the impact of transaction risk would result in a gain.

Receivable in dollars on 1/15	$100,000
Received in dollars on 3/15	102,041
Exchange gain	$ 2,041

Transaction risk also affects the purchase of commodities from foreign companies. Suppose that on February 20, Video Services, Inc. (based in Los Angeles) purchases computers from NEC for $50,000, payable in yen on May 20. Assume the spot rate for yen is 130 per dollar on February 20. It is easy to see that Video Services' true payable is for ¥6,500,000 (50,000 × 130). If the spot rate for yen is 135 on May 20, it will only cost Video Services $48,148 (6,500,000/135) to get enough yen to pay NEC.

Liability in dollars, 2/20	$50,000
Liability in dollars, 5/20	48,148
Exchange gain	$ 1,852

As we can see, the more favorable May 20 spot rate has resulted in an exchange gain. Clearly, transaction risk caused by the movement of foreign currency against the dollar must be taken into account by managers as it affects the prices paid and received for goods. Suppose management does not want to be involved in gambling on exchange rates? The following section on hedging explains how the accountant can manage a company's exposure to exchange gains and losses.

Hedging One way of ensuring against gains and losses on foreign currency exchanges is **hedging**. Typically, a forward exchange contract is used as a hedge. The **forward contract** requires the buyer to exchange a specified amount of a currency at a specified rate (the forward rate) on a specified future date.

hedging
forward contract

Let's return to our example of SuperTubs' sale of $100,000 to the French company. The spot rate on January 15 was 5 francs per dollar. SuperTubs' problem is that it does not know what the exchange rate will be on March 15. If it is more than 5 francs per dollar, SuperTubs will receive less than the $100,000 anticipated in accounts receivable. Of course, if the rate is less, SuperTubs will receive more. But the difficulty is in predicting short-term exchange rate movements. Super-Tubs may well decide it is in the business of manufacturing and selling tubs, not in the business of betting on exchange rate fluctuations. Therefore, it may forego the opportunity for exchange rate gains by hedging against exchange rate losses. Here is how it might work using forward contracts.

On January 15, SuperTubs purchases a contract to convert 500,000 francs into dollars on March 15 at a forward rate of 5.02 francs. SuperTubs has agreed to sell francs for dollars. At this point, SuperTubs has locked in the exchange rate. The .02 difference between the spot rate of 5 and the forward rate of 5.02 is the premium SuperTubs pays the exchange dealer on the transaction. Think of it as an insurance premium.

On March 15, the following transactions will occur. Bonbain pays SuperTubs 500,000 francs, SuperTubs pays the exchange dealer 500,000 francs, and the exchange dealer pays SuperTubs $99,602 (500,000/5.02). The difference between the $100,000 original account receivable and $99,602 cash paid is charged to an exchange premium expense account. Remember that in our original example, the exchange rate on March 15 is 5.1 francs per dollar. Had SuperTubs not hedged, it would have received only $98,039. Therefore, the exchange premium expense of $398 saved SuperTubs a loss of $1,961.

Receivable in dollars on 1/15	$100,000
Received in dollars on 3/15	99,602
Premium expense	$ 398

Of course, the hedging can also be done by agreeing to exchange dollars for a foreign currency at a future date. Recall the previous example of Video Services' purchase of ¥6,500,000 worth of computer equipment. At a spot rate of 130, Video Services expects to pay $50,000 to satisfy its liability. Video Services may fear that the rate will decline, say to ¥125 per dollar. If it did, Video Services would have to pay $52,000 (6,500,000/125) for the same ¥6,500,000. A hedging transaction would resolve Video Services' uncertainty. Perhaps the forward rate is ¥128.7 per dollar. Then Video Services would purchase a forward contract to purchase ¥6,500,000 on May 20 for $50,505 (6,500,000/128.7).

Liability in dollars, Feb. 20	$50,000
Payment in dollars, May 20	(50,505)
Premium expense	$ 505

Hedging transactions can become much more complex than the foregoing example. Companies with significant transaction exposure may choose to hedge all or part of their exposure. Hedging may also be used as a tool to manage economic risk. That use will be addressed in the following section.

Managing Economic Risk

Dealing in different currencies can introduce an economic dimension into currency exchange transactions. Recall that economic risk was defined as the impact of exchange rate fluctuations on the present value of a firm's future cash flows. The risk can affect the relative competitiveness of the firm, even if it never participates directly in international trade. Take a simple example based on the market for heavy equipment between 1981 and 1985.

Suppose that U.S. consumers can choose to purchase heavy equipment from either Caterpillar (based in the U.S.) or from Komatsu (based in Japan). Assume the price of one type of equipment is $80,000 from both makers. However, while Caterpillar truly means $80,000, Komatsu really is interested in 10,400,000 yen, its own currency. At an exchange rate of $1 equals 130 yen, the price of $80,000 is set. Now suppose that the value of the dollar strengthens against the yen and the exchange rate becomes $1 equals 140 yen. To get the same 10,400,000 yen, Komatsu requires a price of only $74,286. The cost structures of the two firms have not changed, neither has customer demand, but because of currency fluctuations, the Japanese firm has become more "competitive." Of course, as the dollar weakens, the position is reversed and U.S. exports become relatively cheaper to foreign customers.

How does the accountant manage the company's exposure to economic risk? Most important is awareness of the risk, by understanding the position of the firm in the global economy. As we can see in the Caterpiller-Komatsu example, the two firms were competitors and were linked through their customers' participation in the global marketplace. The accountant provides financial structure and communication for the firm. In preparing the master budget, for example, budgeted sales must take into account potential strengthening or weakening of the currencies of competitors' countries. Often the controller's office is responsible for forecasting foreign exchange movements.

Hedging can provide another means of managing economic risk. For example, the Toronto Blue Jays baseball team receives its revenues in Canadian dollars but pays most of its expenses in U.S. dollars (due to the team traveling within the U.S.). In 1985 the team anticipated a loss due to unfavorable exchange rate fluctuations. To prevent this, in 1984 the team purchased forward contracts of U.S. dollars at $0.75 per Canadian dollar. The exchange rate at the end of 1984 was $0.7568 per Canadian dollar. The exchange rate dropped steadily throughout 1985, to $0.7156 by the end of the fourth quarter of 1985. The depreciation of Canada's currency, carefully hedged against through the purchase of forward contracts, resulted in a profit to the team.[9]

Managing Translation Risk

Often the parent company restates all subsidiaries' income into the home currency. This restatement can result in gain and loss opportunities on the revaluation of foreign currencies and can impact a subsidiary's financial statements and the related ROI and residual income computations.

Suppose you are a division manager based in Mexico. Your division earned 320,000 pesos this year, up from 200,000 pesos the year before, a hefty 60 percent increase. Now suppose that your income is translated into dollars. If the exchange rate last year was 1.5 pesos per dollar and the exchange rate this year is 3 pesos per dollar, your net income figures translate into $133,333 net income last year and $106,667 net income this year. Suddenly, there is a 20 percent decrease in net income. Similar unpleasant surprises await ROI and net worth computations. The potential for gain or loss on currency revaluation is particularly relevant for countries whose currencies are volatile—and depreciating relative to the home company's currency.

Foreign currency fluctuations also cause difficulties in evaluating the local manager's adherence to company policy. Monsanto faced this problem in the early 1980s. The company noticed declining sales in some of its foreign markets. The local managers were instructed to increase promotional expenditures. However, dollar-denominated reports showed no increases. Top management continued to press local managers to carry out instructions. Local managers were frustrated by their inability to convince higher management that they had increased expenditures, since the reports showed fewer dollars being spent. Eventually, local currency statements were placed alongside dollar-denominated reports. These comparative statements clearly showed that increased expenditures had taken place.

A simple numerical example based on Monsanto's experience, but not using their figures, may illustrate the problem. Assume that Multinational, Inc., has made a strategic decision to emphasize the production of technologically advanced, high-quality products. As a result, Multinational's top management has instructed its foreign division, FD, to increase expenditures on research and development. FD managers do increase R&D expenditures over the following four quarters as follows.

9.   Paul V. Mannino and Ken Milani, "Budgeting for an International Business," *Management Accounting,* February 1992, pp. 36–41.

Quarter	Expenditures in Local Currency
1	LC 100,000
2	LC 110,000
3	LC 121,000
4	LC 133,100

As we can see, R&D expenditures have grown by ten percent in each quarter. However, Multinational managers do not see the above table. Instead, they see dollar-denominated reports. In order to translate local currency figures into dollars, we need the exchange rates for each quarter. Suppose the dollar has strengthened against the local currency and the quarterly exchange rates of $1 for units of local currency are 1.00, 1.20, 1.35, and 1.50. Then FD's R&D expenditures in dollars would be as follows.

Quarter	Expenditures in Dollars
1	$100,000
2	91,670
3	89,630
4	88,730

What a difference! Not only have local managers not increased expenditures, it looks like they have actually decreased expenditures. Only by comparing the dollar-denominated figures with those denominated in local currency can Multinational see the two effects of an increase in R&D expenditures and the strengthening of the dollar. In this case, FD's increase was hidden in currency translation.

The objective of dollar-denominated internal reports is to measure all figures on the same basis. While this strategy may work at any one point in time, it may mislead managers when comparisons are made over time. The accountant must be aware of this source of translation risk.

DECENTRALIZATION

Objective 4
Explain why multinational firms choose to decentralize.

Frequently, firms that are decentralized in the home country may exercise tighter control over foreign divisions, at least until they gain more experience with their overseas operations. Just as decentralization offers advantages for home country divisions, it also offers advantages for foreign divisions. Let's review some of those advantages.

Advantages of Decentralization in the MNC

The quality of information is better at the local level, and that can improve the quality of decisions. This is particularly true in MNCs, where far-flung divisions may be operating in a number of different countries, subject to various legal systems and customs. As a result, local managers are often in a position to make better decisions. Decentralization allows an organization to take advantage of this specialized knowledge. For example, Loctite Corporation has local managers run their own divisions. In particular, marketing and pricing are under local control. Language is not a problem as local managers are in control. Similarly, local managers are conversant with their own laws and customs.

Local managers in the MNC are capable of a more timely response in decision making. They are able to respond quickly to customer discount demands, local government demands, and changes in the political climate.

In Chapter 18, we discussed the need for centralized managers to transmit instructions and the chance that the manager responsible for implementing the decision might misinterpret the instructions. The different languages native to managers of divisions in the MNC make this an even greater problem. MNCs address this problem in two ways. First, a decentralized structure pushes decision making down to the local manager level, eliminating the need to interpret instructions from above. Second, MNCs are learning to incorporate technology that overrides the language barrier and eases cross-border data transfer. Technology is of great help in smoothing communication difficulties between parent and subsidiary and between one subsidiary and another. Loctite's plant in Ireland uses computerized labeling on adhesives bound for Britain or Israel. Bar code technology "reads" the labels, eliminating the need for foreign language translation.

Just as decentralization gives the lower-level managers in the home country a chance to develop managerial skills, foreign subsidiary managers also gain valuable experience. Just as important, home country managers gain broader experience by interacting with managers of foreign divisions. The chance for learning from each other is much greater in a decentralized MNC. Off and on throughout the latter half of the twentieth century, a tour of duty at a foreign subsidiary has been a part of the manager's climb to the top. Now, foreign subsidiary managers may expect to spend some time at headquarters in the home office, as well. At GE, for example, senior executives are sent on four-week tours of foreign markets and return to brief top management. Other senior executives are posted to Asian and Indian divisions. Similarly, foreign executives receive GE management training.

Creation of Divisions

The MNC has great flexibility in creating types of divisions. Divisions are often created along geographic lines. IBM, for example, has divisional boundaries that organize production and sales for Asia and the Far East (AFE), North America, Latin and South America, and Europe and Africa.

Product lines may afford a rationale for the creation of divisions. Many MNCs are diversified, manufacturing and selling a number of different products. The MNC may decide that the major difference is the type of product sold, not the country in which it is sold. An oil company, for example, may have an exploration division, a refining division, and a chemicals division. Each of these divisions may include plants or operations in a number of different countries.

Divisions may follow functional management lines. In the early 1970s, Avon created three regional marketing and planning centers, in New York, London, and Australia. These worked reasonably well for a while and achieved the objective of sharing expertise and training divisional managers. However, national needs and differences caused conflict. So by the late 1980s, Avon disbanded the regional centers and decentralized to the individual country level.[10]

---

10.   Louis V. Consiglio, "Global Competitive Advantage: Lessons from Avon," Working Paper No. 1, July 1992, Center for Applied Research, Lubin School of Business, Pace University.

The presence of divisions in more than one country creates the need for performance evaluation that can take into account differences in divisional environments. The next section examines performance evaluation in the MNC.

MEASURING PERFORMANCE IN THE MULTINATIONAL FIRM

Objective 5

Explain how environmental factors can affect performance evaluation in the multinational firm.

It is important for the MNC to separate the evaluation of the *manager* of a division from the evaluation of the *division*. The manager's evaluation should not include factors over which he exercises no control, such as currency fluctuations, taxes, and so on. Instead, managers should be evaluated on the basis of revenues and costs incurred. It is particularly difficult to compare the performance of a manager of a division (or subsidiary) in one country with the performance of a manager of a division in another country. Even divisions that appear to be similar in terms of production may face very different economic, social, or political forces. The manager should be evaluated on the basis of the performance she can control. Once a manager is evaluated, then the subsidiary financial statements can be restated to the home currency and uncontrollable costs can be allocated.[11]

International environmental conditions may be very different from, and more complex than, domestic conditions.[12] Environmental variables facing local managers of divisions include economic, legal, political, social, and educational factors. Some important economic variables are inflation, foreign exchange rates, taxes, and transfer prices. Legal and political actions also have differing impacts. For example, a country may not allow cash outflows, forcing the corporation to find ways to trade for the host country's output.[13] Educational variables vary from country to country as does the sophistication of the accounting system. Sociological and cultural variables affect how the multinational firm is treated by the subsidiary's country.

The existence of differing environmental factors makes interdivisional comparison of ROI potentially misleading. Suppose a U.S.-based MNC has three divisions, located in Canada, Brazil, and Spain, with the following information given in millions of dollars:

	Assets	Revenues	Net Income	Margin	Turnover	ROI*
Brazil	$10	$ 6	$ 3	0.50	0.60	0.30
Canada	18	13	10	0.77	0.72	0.55
Spain	15	10	6	0.60	0.67	0.40

*Rounded to two decimal places.

On the basis of ROI, it appears that the manager of the Canadian subsidiary did the best job, while the manager of the Brazilian subsidiary did the worst job. But is this a fair comparison? Spain and Canada face very different legal, polit-

---

11.   Gerhard G. Mueller, Helen Gernon, and Gary Meek, *Accounting: An International Perspective*, Richard D. Irwin, Homewood, Ill., 1987.

12.   Wagdy M. Abdallah, "Change the Environment or Change the System," *Management Accounting*, October 1986, pp. 33–36.

13.   One MNC faced with Philippine prohibitions on taking cash out of the country decided to hold its annual meeting in Manila. All corporate costs of the meeting (e.g., hotel, meals) could then be paid in pesos earned by the MNC's Philippine subsidiary. Example taken from Jeff Madura, *International Financial Management*, 2nd ed., West Publishing Company, St. Paul, Minn., 1989, p. 382.

ical, educational, and economic conditions. Inflation has been very high in South America compared to North America. Many South American firms have responded by adjusting reported financial amounts for inflation. Suppose in our example that the Canadian firm reports its assets at historical cost and that the Brazilian firm adjusts its assets for inflation. If inflation during the period the assets have been held has averaged 100 percent (not an unreasonable assumption in a country that has faced monthly double-digit inflation rates for years), then the historical cost of the Brazilian assets would be $5 million. The calculation is as follows:

$$X + 100\%X = \$10$$
$$X + 1.00X = \$10$$
$$2X = \$10$$
$$X = \$5$$

If we restate the Brazilian subsidiary's assets to historical cost, then the ROI would be 60 percent (3/5 = 0.6). If this computation is used, the Brazilian subsidiary appears to be the most successful, not the least. It should be noted that accounting for inflationary effects on income and assets is very complicated and that the simple restatement shown above is not a comprehensive approach. Additionally, top management is typically aware of the existence of differential inflation rates. Still, the lack of consistency in internal reporting may obscure interdivisional comparison, and the accountant must be aware of this problem.

Other environmental factors can differ between countries. A minimum wage law in one country will restrict the manager's ability to affect labor costs. Another country may prevent the export of cash. Still others may have a well-educated work force but poor infrastructure (transportation and communication facilities). Therefore, the corporation must be aware of and control these differing environmental factors when assessing managerial performance. Exhibit 19-2 lists some environmental factors that may make interdivisional comparisons misleading.

Political and Legal Factors Affecting Performance Evaluation

On June 3, 1989, the Chinese military opened fire on students in Beijing's Tiannenman Square. The world was stunned, glued to CNN and other media for news of the uprising. Would the Chinese government fall? Would an already repressive regime clamp down even more tightly? Half a world away, the controller of a manufacturer of custom oil field equipment weighed the Chinese events in a business decision. Should he accept a Chinese letter of credit? His company's product was loaded on a ship in Houston, set to sail for China within the week. The sale was booked, and it was an important one, $3 million (the company's total annual sales revenue was $15 million). But was the letter of credit still good? Ordinarily, the Foreign Credit Insurance Association (underwriting insurance through the World Bank) guarantees letters of credit drawn on banks in approved countries. After the Tiannenman Square massacre, China was suspended from the approved countries list. If the Bank of China refused to pay, there would be no insurance, leaving the controller's company holding $3 million of worthless paper. The controller waited three days, evaluating the constantly changing situation, before cancelling the shipment.[14]

---

14.   Several months later, when China had been reinstated on the approved countries list, the company did make the sale.

Exhibit 19-2
Environmental Factors Affecting Performance Evaluation in the Multinational Firm*

Economic Factors

Organization of central banking system
Economic stability
Existence of capital markets
Currency restrictions

Political and Legal Factors

Quality, efficiency, and effectiveness of legal structure
Effect of defense policy
Impact of foreign policy
Level of political unrest
Degree of governmental control of business

Educational Factors

Literacy rate
Extent and degree of formal education and training systems
Extent and degree of technical training
Extent and quality of management development programs

Sociological Factors

Social attitude toward industry and business
Cultural attitude toward authority and persons in subordinate positions
Cultural attitude toward productivity and achievement (work ethic)
Social attitude toward material gain
Cultural and racial diversity

*Adapted from Wagdy M. Abdallah, "Change the Environment or Change the System," *Management Accounting*, October 1986, pp. 33–36. Used with the permission of the Institute of Accountants.

The accountant in the MNC must be aware of more than business and finance. Political and legal systems have important implications for the company. Sometimes the political system changes quickly, throwing the company into crisis mode, as it did for the controller in the Chinese letter of credit dilemma. Other times, the situation evolves more slowly. The shift in Spain's political system, from Franco's dictatorship to a democracy, is a case in point.

Management accounting has gained increased importance in Spain since the early 1980s. Part of the increased importance is due to the increase in competitive pressures. The profitability of many Spanish firms has eroded, and firms see the need for more formal mechanisms of control, such as budgeting and standard costing. A second reason is the shift from a sheltered economy and political dictatorship to a democratic society. The previous dictatorship favored external methods of control, reinforcing a coercive political and social structure. The system was isolated from the rest of Europe, with a highly regulated economy. The shift to a more democratic society and a loosening of the regulatory environment has allowed Spanish firms more freedom of action in business and has led to the need for management accounting control.[15]

15. Joan M. Amat Salas, "Management Accounting Systems in Spanish Firms," in the proceedings of the Second European Management Control Symposium, Volume 1, 1992.

On occasion, the political structure may mean that standard U.S.-based methods of control may not "work" in foreign countries. For example, under the communist regime in the USSR, manufacturers received a budget, actual results were compared with the budget, and variances were computed. However, variance analysis did not have the same meaning that it has in the United States. If a company faced a variance, the solution was to send the plant's senior political operative to Central Planning Headquarters with a case of champagne or cognac. The hoped-for result was a change in the plan such that it matched actual results and the variance disappeared. The business objective was not efficiency or effectiveness, but to comply with the central plan. While the Central Planning Headquarters no longer exists, what does exist is the culture of matching the plan to actual by after-the-fact altering the plan.

Multiple Measures of Performance

Rigid evaluation of the performance of foreign divisions of the MNC ignores the overarching strategic importance of developing a global presence. The interconnectedness of the global company weakens the independence or stand-alone nature of any one segment. As a result, residual income and ROI are less important measures of managerial performance for divisions of the MNC. MNCs must use additional measures of performance that relate more closely to the long-run health of the company. In addition to ROI and residual income, top management looks at such factors as market potential and market share. For example, Gillette has begun to sell Oral-B toothbrushes in China at $0.90 each (versus the U.S. price of $0.19). The size of the Chinese market means that even if Gillette gets only 10 percent of the market, it will sell more toothbrushes in China than in the United States. Procter & Gamble, Bausche & Lomb, and Citicorp are expanding into Indian and Asian markets for the same reason.

Additionally, the use of ROI and RI in the evaluation of managerial performance in divisions of a MNC is subject to problems beyond those faced by a decentralized company that operates in only one country. It is particularly important, then, to take a responsibility accounting approach and evaluate managers on the basis of factors under their control. For example, the manager of the Moscow McDonald's cannot simply purchase food; it is not available locally, and imports from Denmark and Finland are very expensive. As a result, some food is grown locally. Similar difficulties are faced by companies in Eastern Europe. Multiple measures of performance, keyed to local operating conditions, can spotlight managers' response to different and difficult operating conditions.

TRANSFER PRICING AND THE MULTINATIONAL FIRM

Objective 6
Discuss the role of transfer pricing in the multinational firm.

For the multinational firm, transfer pricing must accomplish two objectives, performance evaluation and optimal determination of income taxes.

Performance Evaluation

Divisions are frequently evaluated on the basis of net income and return on investment.[16] As is the case for any transfer price, the selling division wants a high transfer price that will raise its net income, and the buying division wants

---

16. A study of 70 multinationals revealed that 80 percent used these measures. See Helen Gernon Morsicato, *Currency Translation and Performance Evaluation in Multinationals*, UMI Research Press, Ann Arbor, 1982.

a low transfer price that will raise its net income. A problem arises in that transfer prices in MNCs are frequently set by the parent company. Therefore, the use of mandated transfer prices makes the use of ROI and net income suspect. That is, they are not under the control of division managers and no longer serve as indicators of management performance.

Income Taxes and Transfer Pricing

If all countries had the same tax structure, then transfer prices would be set independently of taxes. However, there are high-tax countries (like the United States) and low-tax countries (such as the Cayman Islands). As a result, MNCs may use transfer pricing to shift costs to high-tax countries and shift revenues to low-tax countries. Exhibit 19-3 illustrates this concept, as two transfer prices are set. The first transfer price is $100 as title for the goods passes from the Belgian subsidiary to the reinvoicing center in Puerto Rico. Because the first transfer price is equal to full cost, profit is zero, and taxes on zero profit also equal zero. The second transfer price is set at $200 by the reinvoicing center in Puerto Rico. The transfer from Puerto Rico to the United States does result in profit, but this profit does not result in any tax because Puerto Rico has no corporate income taxes. Finally, the U.S. subsidiary sells the product to an external party at the $200 transfer price. Again, price equals cost, so there is no profit on which to pay income taxes. Consider what would have happened without the reinvoicing center. The goods would have gone directly from Belgium to the United States. If the transfer price was set at $200, the profit in Belgium would have been $100, subject to the 42 percent tax rate. Alternatively, if the transfer price set was $100, no Belgian tax would have been paid, but the U.S. subsidiary would have realized a profit of $100, and that would have been subject to the U.S. corporate income tax rate of 35 percent.

U.S.-based multinationals are subject to Internal Revenue Code Section 482 on the pricing of intercompany transactions. This section gives the IRS the authority to reallocate income and deductions among divisions if it believes that such reallocation will reduce potential tax evasion. Basically, Section 482 requires that sales be made at "arm's length." That is, the transfer price set should match

Exhibit 19-3
Use of Transfer Pricing to Affect Taxes Paid

Action	Tax Impact
Belgian subsidiary of Parent Company produces a component at a cost of $100 per unit. Title to the component is transferred to a Reinvoicing Center* in Puerto Rico at a transfer price of $100/unit.	42% tax rate $100 revenue − $100 cost = $0 Taxes paid = $0
Reinvoicing Center in Puerto Rico, also a subsidiary of Parent Company, transfers title of component to U.S. subsidiary of Parent Company at a transfer price of $200/unit.	0% tax rate $200 revenue − $100 cost = $100 Taxes paid = $0
U.S. subsidiary sells component to external company at $200 each.	35% tax rate $200 revenue − $200 cost = $0 Taxes paid = $0

*A reinvoicing center takes title to the goods but does not physically receive them. The primary objective of a reinvoicing center is to shift profits to divisions in low-tax countries.

the price that would be set if the transfer were being made by unrelated parties, adjusted for differences that have a measurable effect on the price. Differences include landing costs and marketing costs. Landing costs (freight, insurance, customs duties, and special taxes) can increase the allowable transfer price. Marketing costs are usually avoided for internal transfers and reduce the transfer price. The IRS allows three pricing methods that approximate arm's-length pricing. In order of preference, these are the comparable uncontrolled price method, the resale price method, and the cost-plus method. The **comparable uncontrolled price method** is essentially market price. The **resale price method** is equal to the sales price received by the reseller less an appropriate markup. That is, the subsidiary purchasing a good for resale sets a transfer price equal to the resale price less a gross profit percentage. The **cost-plus method** is simply the cost-based transfer price.

comparable uncontrolled price method
resale price method

cost-plus method

The determination of an arm's-length price is a difficult one. Many times, the transfer pricing situation facing a company does not "fit" any of the three preferred methods outlined above. Then the IRS will permit a fourth method—a transfer price negotiated between the company and the IRS. The IRS, taxpayers, and the Tax Court have struggled with negotiated transfer prices for years. However, this type of negotiation occurs after the fact—after income tax returns have been submitted and the company is being audited. Recently, the IRS has authorized the issuance of **advance pricing agreements (APAs)** to assist tax-paying firms to determine whether or not a proposed transfer price is acceptable to the IRS in advance of tax filing. "An APA is an agreement between the IRS and a taxpayer on the pricing method to be applied in an international transaction. It can cover transfers of intangibles (such as royalties on licenses), sales of property, provision of services, and other items. An APA is binding on both the IRS and the taxpayer for the years specified in the APA and is not made public."[17] Since the APA procedure is so new, neither the IRS nor the firms are sure of the informational requirements. Currently, the IRS may limit its advance rulings on transactions between U.S.-based companies and divisions in treaty countries, such as Australia, Canada, Japan, and the U.K. For example, Apple Computer obtained an advance pricing agreement from the IRS on transfers of Apple products to its Australian subsidiary.[18]

advance pricing agreements (APAs)

Transfer-pricing abuses are illegal—if they can be proved to be abuses. Many examples exist of both foreign and U.S. firms charging unusual transfer prices. The IRS successfully showed that Toyota had been overcharging its U.S. subsidiary for cars, trucks, and parts sold in the United States. The effect was to lower Toyota's reported income substantially in the United States and increase income reported in Japan. The settlement reportedly approached $1 billion.[19]

The super royalty provision of Section 482 was added in 1986 to require companies to value their intangibles more fairly. The IRS suspected that U.S. companies were transferring their intangibles (patents, copyrights, customer lists, etc.) to foreign subsidiaries at less than fair market value. For example, a U.S. pharmaceutical firm would develop a new drug and license its Puerto Rican subsidiary to produce it. The drug would then be purchased by the parent company

---

17. "New Intercompany Pricing Rulings Create and Eliminate Tax Uncertainty," *Deloitte & Touche Review*, March 25, 1991, p. 6.
18. Roger Y.W. Tang, "Transfer Pricing in the 1990s" *Management Accounting*, February 1992, pp. 22–26.
19. "The Corporate Shell Game," *Newsweek*, April 15, 1991, pp. 48–49.

for sale in the United States, and a royalty would be charged to the Puerto Rican subsidiary. The royalty rate, taxable income to the parent, was low but was similar to other third-party transactions. Thus, the IRS could not challenge it. The super royalty provision changed this situation by linking the transfer price of the intangible to the income attributable to the intangible. "A Study on Intercompany Pricing" issued in 1990 requires much stricter documentation for the pricing of intangibles.[20]

The IRS also regulates the transfer pricing of foreign companies with U.S. subsidiaries. A U.S. company that is at least 25% foreign owned must keep extensive documentation of arm's-length transfer pricing.

Of course, MNCs are also subject to taxation by other countries as well as the United States. Since income taxes are virtually universal, consideration of income tax effects pervades management decision making. Canada, Japan, the European Community, and South Korea have all issued transfer pricing regulations within the past ten years.[21] This increased emphasis on transfer price justification may account for the increased use of market prices as the transfer price by MNCs. A survey of transfer pricing methods used by Fortune 500 companies in 1977 and 1990 shows that MNCs have reduced their reliance on cost-based transfer prices in favor of market-based transfer prices over the thirteen-year period.[22] Additionally, the most important environmental variable considered by MNCs in setting a transfer pricing policy is overall profit to the company—with overall profit including the income tax impact of intracompany transfers.

The Secretaria de Hacienda y Credito Publico (Hacienda), the tax authority of Mexico, now requires maquiladoras to comply with both Mexican and U.S. transfer pricing rules. Because the United States sees maquiladoras as service providers, an appropriate transfer pricing approach is a markup on operating expenses. The amount of markup depends on the particular circumstances of each maquiladora. Hacienda has an additional enforcement tool, the 1.8% Mexican asset tax. Maquiladoras out of compliance with transfer pricing rules must pay the asset tax on all noninventory assets in Mexico. The tax implications for U.S. companies operating in Mexico include not only income taxes, but also the customs valuation of goods imported into Mexico and mechandise assembled by the maquiladora and returned to the United States, as well as the NAFTA Certificant of Origin computations. This is a case where the APA may be especially valuable.[23]

Managers may legally avoid taxes; they may not evade them. The distinction is important. Unfortunately, the difference between avoidance and evasion is less a line than a blurry gray area. While the situation depicted in Exhibit 19-3 is clearly abusive, other tax-motivated actions are not. For example, an MNC may decide to establish a needed research and development center within an existing subsidiary in a high-tax country, since the costs are deductible. MNCs may have tax-planning information systems that attempt to accomplish global tax minimization. This is not an easy task.

20.   Alfred M. King, "The IRS's New Neutron Bomb," *Management Accounting,* December 1992, pp. 35–38.
21.   Tang, op. cit.
22.   Tang, op. cit.
23.   "Maquiladoras: Transfer Pricing and Customs Planning," *Deloitte & Touche Review,* February 6, 1995, pp. 5 and 6. and "Mexico Sets Tight Deadline on Maquiladora Transfer Pricing," *Deloitte & Touche Review,* April 17, 1995, pp. 5 and 6.

ETHICS IN THE INTERNATIONAL ENVIRONMENT

Objective 7

Discuss ethical issues that affect firms operating in the international environment.

Business ethics pose difficulties in a single-country context. But ethics pose far more problems in a global context. Richard J. Mahoney, CEO of Monsanto Company, wrote, "As Monsanto becomes a global enterprise, we continually face the problem of different cultures and different cultural expectations. A service fee in one country is a bribe in another. Environmental laws can be extraordinarily strict in a country but not be enforced—and your industrial neighbors laugh at you for obeying the laws."[24] Given these difficulties, how does the modern corporation conduct business in an ethical manner? Is each country different? Is there a baseline? Some research indicates that human societies do share an ethical basis. However, there are some prerequisites for the establishment of an ethical business environment. These include: basic societal stability; legitimacy and accountability of government; legitimacy of private ownership and personal wealth; confidence in one's own and society's future; confidence in the ability to provide for one's family; and knowledge of how the system works and how to participate.[25]

For example, the Russian equivalent of insider trading or conflict of interest is *blat*. Blat is "an informal system of acquiring goods and services based on influence and back-door favors between acquaintances."[26] Blat is a natural extension of culture which emphasized personal relationships over impersonal monetary transactions. Legal contracts are still in a rudimentary phase because enforcement is weak. As a result, personal relationships, which characterize blat, are a stronger basis for business dealings.

A strong underlying system is important for enforcing contracts, and it provides the basis for confidence in ethical dealings. For some countries (e.g., the United States and Western European countries), that system is legal with deviations punishable by law. For others (e.g., Japan and countries in the Middle East), it is cultural, and deviations are punished at least as severely by loss of honor. The importance of a strong underlying social code of conduct is clearly evident in illegal business dealings. For obvious reasons, you would be loathe to contact the police or district attorney about your purchase of low-quality marijuana. Similarly in India, where foreign currency exchange is tightly controlled, the black market in currency exchange is rife with unethical conduct. If you would like to exchange dollars for rupees, you can get a significantly better rate from the black market. However, the method of exchange requires you to first hand the black marketeer your rupees and then wait a minute or two while he goes to a back room to get the dollars. Sometimes he returns with the requisite number of dollars, sometimes not. As an Indian friend of ours said, "Then what? You can hardly go to the police!" Indians do not face this risky situation in a bank.

Other ethical problems with bribes and differing business laws exist. For example, Russian tax law changes quickly and without warning. Even worse, the taxes are frequently retroactive. For example, in early 1995, Russian tax authorities scrapped a tax exemption on imported construction materials used at a new

---

24. Richard J. Mahoney, "Ethics: Doing the Right Thing at Monsanto," *Management Accounting*, June 1991, p. 24.
25. Cynthia Scharf, "The Wild, Wild East: Everyone's a Capitalist in Russia Today, and Nobody Knows the Rules," *Business Ethics*, November/December 1992, p. 23.
26. Ibid., p. 22.

Coca-Cola plant. Coca-Cola's tax bill increased immediately by $1.4 million. A month or so later, Coke faced a brand new "excess wage" tax on nearly all of its Russian employees—retroactive to January 1, 1994. While all businesses operating in Russia are subject to the same tax rules, many local companies are adept at bribing tax officials. As a result, it is the foreign companies, accustomed to obeying the law, that are hit hardest. Some, like Huntsman Chemical Corporation of Salt Lake City, are forced to drop out of the Russian market.[27]

Another serious ethical problem arises with enforcement of local labor laws. Central American children can begin work at age 11. Youngsters in Thailand may begin work even earlier. Our own history includes immigrant children of ten and twelve at work in the steel mills of Bethlehem, Pennsylvania. Currently, many department and discount stores are grappling with the issue of child labor. Levi Strauss hires its own inspectors. J.C. Penney relies on local control to enforce its code. Still, it is clear that many underage (less than 14 years old in Guatamala) workers produce clothing for U.S. markets. Should companies enforce local labor laws more stringently? A Leslie Fay official points out that the company codes may be having some effect, since there are 12 and 13 year olds at work but no 8 or 9 year olds, as is the case in other countries. Also, the strict enforcement of rules can have a negative effect on local income. Wal-Mart cancelled its order at a Guatamalan factory found to hire underage workers. As a result, the factory fired 300 workers.[28] An ethical solution is not clear-cut.

Finally, what about bribes to government officials? The stories of rampant bribery of Middle Eastern officials are legendary. In some countries, these bribes are considered a necessary part of doing business. Similarly, insider trading is not illegal in Europe, but it is definitely illegal in the United States.

To go back to our original question, what is a company to do when faced with conflicting sets of ethics? What if an action is legally permissible? Early in Monsanto's history, it faced the possibility of bankruptcy. John Queeny, the company's founder, was advised to "close down the plant, lay off all the workers, and then open up with new people at lower wages. 'Since when,' Mr. Queeny asked, 'do we lie to our employees?'" As a result, Monsanto holds that doing the right thing is nonnegotiable.[29] Perhaps the answer is to ask, is the action right legally? And then, is the action right morally?

27.   Peter Galuszka and Sandra Dallas, "And You Think You've Got Tax Problems," *Business Week*, May 29, 1995, p. 50.
28.   Bob Ortega, "Conduct Codes Garner Goodwill for Retailers, But Violations Go On," *The Wall Street Journal*, July 3, 1995, pp. A1 and A4.
29.   Mahoney, op. cit., p. 24.

SUMMARY

The accountant provides financial and business expertise. The job of the accountant in the international firm is made more challenging by the ambiguous and ever-changing nature of global business. He or she must stay up to date in a variety of business areas ranging from information systems to marketing to management to politics and economics. In addition, the accountant must be familiar with the financial accounting rules of the countries in which his/her firm operates.

Companies involved in international business may structure their activities in three major ways. They may engage in import/export activities. They may purchase wholly owned subsidiaries. They may participate in joint ventures. Accountants must be aware of the potential exposure of their firms to transaction risk, economic risk, and translation risk. They may hedge to limit exposure to these risks.

MNCs choose to decentralize for much the same reasons domestic companies choose to decentralize. Reasons for decentralization are numerous. Companies decentralize because local managers can make better decisions using local information. Local managers can also provide a more timely response to changing conditions. Additionally, decentralization for large, diversified companies is necessary because of cognitive limitations—it is impossible for any one central manager to be fully knowledgeable of all products and markets. Other reasons include training and motivating local managers and freeing up top management from day-to-day operating conditions so that they can spend time on more long-range activities, such as strategic planning.

Environmental factors are those social, economic, political, legal, and cultural factors that differ from country to country and that managers cannot affect. These factors, however, do affect profits and ROI. Therefore, evaluation of the divisional manager should be separated from evaluation of the subsidiary.

When one division of a company produces a product that can be used in production by another division, transfer pricing exists. The transfer price is revenue to the selling division and cost to the buying division. As is the case with domestic companies, MNCs may use transfer prices in performance evaluation. MNCs with subsidiaries in both high-tax and low-tax countries may use transfer pricing to shift costs to the high-tax countries (where their deductibility will lower tax payments) and to shift revenues to low-tax countries.

MNCs face ethical issues different from those of domestic companies. Other countries have business customs and laws that differ from those of the home country. The firm must determine whether a particular custom is merely a different way of doing business or a violation of its own code of ethics.

REVIEW PROBLEM AND SOLUTION

Golo, Inc. has two manufacturing plants, one in Singapore and the other in San Antonio. The San Antonio plant is located in a foreign trade zone. On March 1, Golo received a large order from a Japanese customer. The order is for ¥10,000,000 to be paid on receipt of the goods, scheduled for June 1. Golo assigned this order to the San Antonio plant; however, one necessary component for the order is to be manufactured by the Singapore plant. The component will be transferred to San Antonio on April 1 using a cost-plus transfer price of $10,000 (U.S. dollars). Typically, 2 percent of the Singapore parts are defective. U.S. tariff on the component parts is 30 percent. Carrying cost for Golo is 15 percent per year.

The following spot rates for $1 U.S. are as follows.

	Exchange Rates of $1 for	
	Yen	Singapore Dollars
March 1	107.00	1.60
April 1	107.50	1.55
June 1	107.60	1.50

REQUIRED:

1. What is the total cost of the imported parts from Singapore to the San Antonio plant in U.S. dollars?
2. Supposing the San Antonio plant were not located in a foreign trade zone, what would be the total cost of the imported parts from Singapore?
3. How much does Golo expect to receive from the Japanese customer in U.S. dollars using the spot rate at the time of the order?
4. How much does Golo expect to receive from the Japanese customer in U.S. dollars using the spot rate at the time of payment?
5. Suppose that on March 1, the forward rate for June 1 delivery of $1 for ¥ is 107.20. If Golo's policy is to hedge foreign currency transactions, what is the amount Golo expects to receive on June 1 in dollars?

Solution   1.

Transfer price	$10,000
Tariff ($9,800 × 0.3)	2,940
Total cost	$12,940

The transfer price was set in U.S. dollars, so there is no currency exchange involved for the San Antonio plant.

The San Antonio plant is in a foreign trade zone, so the 30 percent tariff is paid only the good parts costing $9,800 ($10,000 × 0.98).

2. If the San Antonio plant were located outside the foreign trade zone, the cost of the imported parts would be as follows.

Transfer price	$10,000
Tariff ($10,000 × 0.3)	3,000
Carrying cost of tariff*	75
Total cost	$13,075

*$3,000 × 2/12 × 0.15 = $75

3. On March 1, Golo expects to receive $93,458 (¥10,000,000/107).
4. On June 1, Golo expects to receive $92,937 (¥10,000,000/107.60).
5. If Golo hedges, the forward rate is used, and the amount to be received on June 1 is $93,284 (¥10,000,000/107.20).

KEY TERMS

Advance pricing agreements (APAs) *838*
Comparable uncontrolled price method *838*
Cost-plus method *838*
Currency appreciation *826*

Currency depreciation *826*
Currency risk management *826*
Economic risk *826*
Exchange gain *827*
Exchange loss *827*
Exchange rate *826*

Foreign trade zones *821*
Forward contract *828*
Hedging *828*
Joint venture *824*
Maquiladoras *825*
Multinational corporation (MNC) *820*

Outsourcing *823*
Resale price method *838*
Spot rate *826*
Tariff *821*
Transaction risk *826*
Translation (or accounting) risk *826*

QUESTIONS FOR WRITING AND DISCUSSION

1. How do international issues affect the role of the accountant?
2. What is a foreign trade zone, and what advantages does it offer U.S. companies?
3. Define outsourcing, and discuss why companies may outsource various functions.
4. What are joint ventures, and why do companies engage in them?
5. What are maquiladoras? Why have so many U.S. firms joined forces with maquiladoras?

6. What is an exchange rate for currency? What is the difference between a spot rate and future rate?
7. Define currency appreciation. What impact does currency appreciation have on a company's ability to import goods?
8. What impact does currency appreciation have on a company's ability to export its goods?
9. Mexico is considering devaluing the peso versus the dollar. You are the controller for a company considering production in Mexico through the maquiladora

program. How does this news affect the decision? Now suppose you are a local labor union leader, how do you take the news?

10. What is transaction risk? Economic risk? Translation risk?

11. What is hedging? If a company imports raw materials, payable in full in 90 days in the foreign currency, why might the company want to hedge?

12. The performance of the subsidiary manager is equivalent to the performance of a subsidiary. Do you agree? Explain.

13. What environmental factors may affect divisional performance in a multinational firm?

14. What is the purpose of Internal Revenue Code Section 482? What four methods of transfer pricing are acceptable under this section?

EXERCISES AND PROBLEMS

19-1

Preparation for Becoming an Accountant in an MNC

LO 1

A close friend of yours is majoring in accounting and would like to work for a multinational corporation upon graduation. Your friend is unsure just what courses would help prepare for that goal and wants your advice.

REQUIRED: Advise your friend on the kind of courses that might prepare him/her for this goal.

19-2

Foreign Trade Zones

LO 2

North Pole Novelties, Inc., is considering opening a new warehouse to serve the Pacific Northwest region. Dave Shaut, controller for North Pole Novelties, has been reading about the advantages of foreign trade zones. He wonders if locating in one would be of benefit to his company, which imports about 90 percent of its merchandise (e.g., nutcrackers from the Black Forest region of Germany, spun-glass ornaments from Mexico). Dave estimates that the new warehouse will store imported merchandise costing about $700,000 per year. Inventory shrinkage at the warehouse (due to breakage and mishandling) is about 5 percent of the total. Average tariff rate on these imports is 15 percent.

REQUIRED: Will locating the warehouse in a foreign trade zone save North Pole Novelties money? How much?

19-3

Currency Exchange

LO 3

Allen Distributors, Inc., based in Fort Lauderdale, Florida, is an export-import firm. On June 1, Allen purchased goods from a British company costing £20,000. Payment is due in pounds on September 1. The spot rate on June 1 was 1.70 dollars per pound, and on September 1, it was 1.79 dollars per pound.

REQUIRED:

1. Did the dollar strengthen or weaken against the pound during the three-month period?
2. How much would Allen have to pay for the purchase (in dollars) if it paid on June 1? How much would Allen have to pay for the purchase (in dollars) if it paid on September 1?

19-4

Exchange Gains and Losses

LO 3

Refer to **19-3**. If Allen paid for the purchase using the September 1 spot rate, what was the exchange gain or loss?

19-5

Hedging

LO 3

Corvallis Company engages in many foreign currency transactions. Company policy is to hedge exposure to exchange gains and losses using forward contracts. On July 1, Corvallis sold merchandise to a German company for 50,000 Deutsche Marks (DM), payable on September 30. Exchange rates of $1 for DM were as follows:

Spot rate, July 1	.59
Forward rate, September 30	.58
Spot rate, September 30	.57

REQUIRED:

1. Did Corvallis Company buy or sell marks for future delivery?
2. According to company policy, how many dollars did Corvallis receive for this sale?

19-6
Currency Exchange Rates
LO 3

Suppose you are in the market for a BMW and are considering going to Germany to purchase it, drive it around Europe for a couple of weeks, and then ship it home. The car of your choice costs DM 70,000. When you first looked into the possibility of buying a car in Germany, the rate of exchange was DM 1.4 to $1. Now, the exchange rate is DM 1.6 to $1.

REQUIRED: Has the dollar appreciated or depreciated against the German mark? Would this news about the exchange rate change please or displease you? Why?

19-7
Divisional Performance Evaluation in the MNC
LO 5

Bianca Phillips, vice president for Electronics for Consolidated, Inc., was reviewing the latest results for two divisions. The first, located in Baja California, Mexico, had posted net income of $150,000 on assets of $1,500,000. The second, in Punt-on-Thames, England, showed net income of $230,000 on assets of $2,000,000.

REQUIRED:

1. Calculate the ROI for each division.
2. Can a meaningful comparison be made of the British division's ROI to the Mexican division's ROI? Explain.

19-8
Transfer Pricing in the MNC
LO 6

Carnover, Inc., manufactures a broad line of industrial and consumer products. One of its plants is located in Madrid, Spain, and another in Singapore. The Madrid plant is operating at 85 percent capacity. Softness in the market for its main product, electric motors, has led to predictions of further softening of the market, leading perhaps to production at 65 percent capacity. If that happens, workers will have to be laid off and one wing of the factory closed. The Singapore plant manufactures heavy-duty industrial mixers that use the motors manufactured by the Madrid plant as an integral component. Demand for the mixers is strong. Price and cost information for the mixers is as follows:

Price	$2,200
Direct materials	630
Direct labor	125
Variable overhead	250
Fixed overhead	100

Fixed overhead is based on an annual budgeted amount of $3,500,000 and budgeted production of 35,000 mixers. The direct materials cost includes the cost of the motor at $200 (market price).

The Madrid plant capacity is 20,000 motors per year. Cost data are as follows:

Direct materials	$ 75
Direct labor	60
Variable overhead	60
Fixed overhead	100

Fixed overhead is based on budgeted fixed overhead of $2,000,000.

REQUIRED:

1. What is the maximum transfer price the Singapore plant would accept?
2. What is the minimum transfer price the Madrid plant would accept?
3. Consider the following environmental factors.

Madrid Plant	Singapore Plant
Full employment is very important. Local government prohibits layoffs without permission (which is rarely granted). Accounting is legalistic and conservative, designed to ensure compliance with government objectives.	Cheap labor is plentiful. Accounting is based on British-American model, oriented toward decision-making needs of creditors and investors.

How might these environmental factors impact on the transfer pricing decision?

19-9
Transfer Pricing
LO 6

Thomas Company has a division in the United States that produces wheels for automobiles. These wheels are transferred to an automobile division in Sweden. The wheels can be (and are) sold externally in the United States for $45 each. It costs $2 per wheel for shipping and $6 per wheel for import duties. When the wheels are sold externally, Thomas spends $1 per wheel for commissions and an average of $0.50 per wheel for advertising.

REQUIRED:

1. Which Section 482 method should be used to calculate the allowable transfer price?
2. Using the appropriate Section 482 method, calculate the transfer price.

19-10
Decentralization in the MNC
LO 4

Latest Styles Inc. (LSI) supplies a limited range of garments to several boutiques in New York. LSI produces these garments in a small factory owned and operated in Nuevo Laredo, Mexico. LSI has been more responsive to the boutiques' needs for delivery of changing styles than has the Asian garment producers, where shipments take 30 days. As a result, several other boutiques have approached LSI as a potential supplier. Victoria Johnson, president of LSI, has decided that expansion will be required to meet the needs of these additional boutiques.

After discussing the situation with her colleagues, Frank Corrigan, controller, and Tom Conway, production and shipping manager, it was agreed that the expansion should be undertaken. Since Johnson makes most of the decisions that involve day-to-day operations and does the majority of the designing, Corrigan and Conway are concerned about her managing the expansion at the same time. Corrigan and Conway expressed this concern in a meeting with Johnson, who agreed that the additional workload resulting from the planned expansion would be too great for her to handle. Accordingly, Johnson has decided to delegate some of these increased functions to Corrigan and Conway.

During these discussions, Johnson stated that, in view of the Mexican-American negotiations to establish a North American free-trade zone, she is considering even further expansion to increase the range of garments produced and also to supply boutiques in Philadelphia and Boston. As a consequence, she is considering further decentralization of the business as expanded operations in Mexico, increased product lines, and supplying two new geographical areas will require hands-on, operational management at these locations to keep up with inventory needs and differing local fashion trends. Both Corrigan and Conway are capable of handling these operational duties, although they will need to hire new managers to assist them in the expansion and decentralization.

REQUIRED:

1. Decentralization is the extent to which power and authority are systematically delegated throughout an organization.
   a. Discuss the factors that generally determine the degree of decentralization in an organization.
   b. Describe several benefits to an organization that can generally be derived from decentralization.
   c. Discuss several disadvantages to an organization from decentralization.
2. How does the NAFTA affect Victoria Johnson's decision?

(CMA adapted)

19-11
Decentralization, Performance Evaluation, and Transfer Pricing Issues
LO 4, 5, 6

Scott Gray has recently been promoted to vice president of U.S. operations for Yashima Corporation. Yashima Corporation is headquartered in Japan and has several divisions located in the United States. Yashima has followed a policy of only hiring natives to operate the divisions of the host countries. In the last two years, there have been some complaints from American managers about the way they have been evaluated and rewarded. They have also complained about the attitude of their Japanese counterparts. American managers feel that they have outperformed the Japanese divisions but have not received the credit associated with this relative performance. Furthermore, some Japanese divisional managers are unhappy with the transfer pricing policies that are in place. The higher management of Yashima is frustrated and hasn't been able to resolve the differences between the two groups. Fundamentally, they are not convinced that the complaints of either group have any legitimacy. Nonetheless, in an effort to resolve the conflict, they have assigned Scott Gray and Yoki Mizukawa (his Japanese counterpart) to investigate the issues. The following is a record of a recent meeting between the two vice presidents.

Scott: I've had some rather extensive talks with American managers. They have a hard time understanding how most of the American divisions have been ranked below their Japanese counterpart when they have consistently earned an ROI that ranges from two to four percentage points higher than those of Japanese managers. I've compiled a typical statement showing the average differences between the two groups (expressed as a percentage of sales and based on U.S. dollars):

Sales	100.0%	100.0%
Cost of goods sold	70.2%	75.3%
Selling and administrative expenses	19.8%	14.7%
Income taxes	3.4%	5.5%
Assets	100.0%	125.0%

Yoki: The Japanese managers argue that the differences between the two countries explain the ROI differences. For example, we calculate the ROI using after-tax net income. Yet the corporate income tax rate is much higher than that of the U.S.
Scott: Well, that's a good point. Perhaps we can recommend using before-tax income.
Yoki: That's not all. In Japan, there is no difference between the income reported for taxes and the financial income. As a result, Japanese firms always use accelerated depreciation. The U.S. divisions tend to use straight-line depreciation for financial reporting and accelerated depreciation for tax reporting. Have you made any adjustments for this difference?
Scott: No. No adjustments for any differences in financial reporting procedures were made. However, I also know that our divisions use LIFO for financial reporting and yours use weighted average. LIFO is rarely used in Japan. Also, your division uses the cost method for marketable securities and ours uses the lower-of-cost-or-market method.
Yoki: True. I guess another recommendation would be to adjust for differences in accounting principles.

Scott: Well, I think this is a good idea. But even with this, I wonder if we can come to a meaningful basis for comparison. In talking with some of your divisional managers, I sense some fundamental differences between the two environments. Your managers, for example, take a great deal of pride in market share and seem much less concerned with profitability ratios. I also see much lower accounts receivable turnover ratios and much higher inventory turnover ratios.

Yoki: There are cultural, political, and economic differences that must be accounted for. Somehow we must do this if we want to maintain a decentralized format. I also might mention some related complaints of the Japanese divisional managers. They argue that the corporation is hurting their profitability by requiring them to find ways to price their goods as low as possible for transfer to the U.S. Yet for goods transferred to Japanese divisions, the policy is exactly the opposite—goods are transferred at what they view as inflated prices. If profitability ratios are going to be important measures of performance, then it seems we may need to grant more autonomy in transfer pricing decisions.

REQUIRED:

1. Calculate the typical ROI before and after taxes for the U.S. and Japanese divisions (using the "typical" data provided). Does this solve the ROI problem? Now calculate the margin and turnover ratios for each divisional type—before and after taxes. Discuss the additional insight provided by these calculations.
2. Assume that adjustments are made for the accounting differences mentioned in the problem. For each accounting difference, describe the effect the adjustment would likely have on ROI. For simplicity, assume the assets used to calculate ROI remain the same.
3. Assume that the adjustments made in Requirement 2 narrow the difference between the Japanese and U.S. ROI by only a fourth of a percentage point. What additional factors might help explain the remaining difference? What recommendations would you make concerning the use of ROI for this firm?
4. Offer an explanation for the centrally dictated transfer pricing policy. Do you agree with Yoki that the transfer pricing decision ought to be decentralized? Explain.
5. Can you think of any reasons that might explain the lower receivables turnover ratio and the higher inventory turnover ratio? What implications might this have when dealing with differences in performance measures between the two countries?

**19-12
Exporting,
Maquiladoras,
Foreign Trade
Zones**

LO 2

Paladin Company manufactures plain-paper fax machines in a small factory in Minnesota. Sales have increased by fifty percent in each of the past three years, as Paladin has expanded its market from the United States to Canada and Mexico. As a result, the Minnesota factory is at capacity. Beryl Adams, president of Paladin, has examined the situation and developed the following alternatives.

1. Add a permanent second shift at the plant. However, the semiskilled workers who assemble the fax machines are in short supply, and the wage rate of $15 per hour would probably have to be increased across the board to $18 per hour in order to attract sufficient workers from out of town. The total wage increase (including fringe benefits) would amount to $125,000. The heavier use of plant facilities would lead to increased plant maintenance and small tool cost.
2. Open a new plant and locate it in Mexico. Wages (including fringe benefits) would average $3.50 per hour. Investment in plant and equipment would amount to $300,000.
3. Open a new plant and locate it in a foreign trade zone, possibly in Dallas. Wages would be somewhat lower than in Minnesota, but higher than in Mexico. The advantages of postponing tariff payments on imported parts could amount to $50,000 per year.

REQUIRED: Advise Beryl of the advantages and disadvantages of each of her alternatives.

19-13
Foreign Currency Exchange, Hedging
LO 3

Kalman Shutters, Inc., manufactures custom window shutters on a job-order basis. Kalman has invested heavily in precision woodworking equipment. As a result, the company has a reputation for producing excellent quality interior shutters. Sales are made in all fifty states. On July 1, Kalman received orders from interior designers in France and Japan. Rick Kalgano, president and co-owner of Kalman Shutters, was delighted. The French order is for shutters priced at $50,000. The order is due in Marseilles on September 1, with payment due in full on October 1. The Japanese order for shutters is $65,000. It is due in Tokyo on August 1, with payment due in full on October 1. Both orders are to be paid in the customer's currency. The French customer has a reputation in the industry for late payment, and it could take as long as six months. Rick has never received payment in foreign currency before. He had his accountant prepare the following table of exchange rates.

	Exchange Rate for $1	
	French Franc	Yen
Spot Rate	5.4235	107.60
30 Day Forward	5.4456	107.61
90 Day Forward	5.4825	107.60
180 Day Forward	5.5300	107.55

REQUIRED:

1. If the price of the shutters is set using the spot rate as of July 1, how many francs does Rick expect to be paid on October 1? How many yen does he expect on October 1?
2. Using the number of francs and yen calculated in Requirement 1, how many dollars does Rick expect to receive on October 1? Will he receive that much? What is the value of hedging in this situation?

19-14
Transfer Pricing
LO 6

The U.S. division of MegaBig, Inc., has excess capacity. MegaBig's European division, located in Lisbon, has offered to buy a component that would increase the U.S. division's utilization of capacity from 70 to 80 percent. The component has an outside market in the United States with a unit selling price of $12. The variable costs of production for the component are $6. Landing costs total $2 per unit, and an internal transfer avoids $1.25 per unit of variable marketing costs. The European and U.S. divisions agree on a transfer price of $9. The European division can purchase the component locally for $12.

REQUIRED: Suppose you have scheduled a meeting with an IRS representative. What arguments would you make for an advance pricing agreement that would permit the use of the $9 price?

19-15
Transfer Pricing
LO 6

Diamond Company manufactures riding lawn mowers at plants in Arkansas, Delaware, and Wyoming. It also has distribution centers in Brussels, Belgium, and Montreal, Canada. The market price of the Model 413 riding mower is $350. The unit costs are as follows.

Variable product costs	$125
Fixed factory overhead	60
Landing costs (Canada)	20
Landing costs (Belgium)	25
Avoidable marketing costs	45

Diamond has set a transfer price of $350 to both the Canadian and Belgian division.

REQUIRED:

1. Calculate the transfer price under the comparable uncontrolled price method for both the Canadian and Belgian transfers.
2. Will the IRS be concerned about the transfer price actually set by Diamond?

19-16
Involvement in
International Trade
LO 2

Makenzie Gibson is the owner of Healthblend Nutritional Supplements. Makenzie feels that the time is ripe for expansion, and she would like to begin selling in Europe, Canada, and Mexico. Her major problem right now is to determine how best to do that.

REQUIRED: Advise Makenzie of the ways in which she could become involved in international trade.

19-17
Transfer Pricing
and Ethical Issues
LO 7

Paterson Company is a U.S.-based company that manufactures and sells electronic components worldwide.[30] Virtually all of the manufacturing takes place in the United States. The company has marketing divisions located throughout Europe, including one in France. Debbie Kishimoto is manager of this division; she was hired away from a competitor three years ago. Debbie, recently informed of a price increase in one of the major product lines, had requested a meeting with Jeff Phillips, the marketing vice president.

"Jeff, I simply don't understand why the price of our main product has increased from $5 to $5.50 per unit. We negotiated an agreement earlier in the year with our manufacturing division in Philadelphia for a price of $5 for the entire year. I called the manager of that division, and he indicated that the original price was still acceptable—he said that the increase was a directive from headquarters. That's why I requested a meeting with you. I need some explanations. When I was hired, I was told that pricing decisions were made at the divisional level—that divisions were given a lot of decision-making latitude. This directive not only interferes with this decentralized philosophy but also will lower my division's profits. Given current market conditions, there is no way that we can pass on the cost increase. Profits for my division will drop at least $600,000 if this price is maintained. I think a mid-year increase of this magnitude is unfair to my division."

"Debbie, under normal operating conditions, headquarters will *not* interfere with divisional decisions. As a company, however, we are having some problems. What you just told me is exactly why the price of your product has been increased. We want the profits of all of our European marketing divisions to drop."

"Wait a minute. What do you mean that you want the profits to drop? That doesn't make any sense. Aren't we in business to make money?"

"Debbie, what you lack is corporate perspective. We *are* in business to make money, and that's why we want European profits to decrease. Let me explain. Our divisions in the United States are not doing well this year. Projections show significant losses. At the same time, projections for European operations show good profitability. By increasing the cost of key products transferred to Europe—to your division, for example—we increase revenues and profits in the United States. By decreasing your profits, we avoid paying taxes in France. With losses on other U.S. operations to offset the corresponding increase in domestic profits, we avoid paying taxes in the United States as well. The net effect is a much-needed increase in our cash flow. Besides, you know how difficult it is in some of these European countries to transfer out capital. This is a clean way of doing it."

"I'm not so sure that it's clean. It doesn't seem right to me. I can't imagine the tax laws permitting this type of scheme. There is another problem as well. You know that the company's bonus plans are tied to a division's profitability. This plan could cost all the European managers a lot of money."

"Debbie, you have no reason to worry about the effect on your bonus—or on our evaluation of your performance, for that matter. Corporate management has already taken

---

30. This case is based on the experiences of an actual firm. Names have been changed to preserve confidentiality.

steps to ensure no loss of compensation. The plan is to compute what income would have been if the old price had prevailed and base bonuses on that figure. I plan to meet with the other divisional managers and explain the situation to them as well."

"The bonus adjustment seems fair, although I wonder if the reasons for the drop in profits will be remembered in a couple of years when I'm being considered for promotion. Anyway, I still have some strong concerns about the propriety of all this. How does this scheme relate to the tax laws?"

"We will be in technical compliance with the tax laws. In the United States, Section 482 of the Internal Revenue Code governs this type of transaction. The key to this law, as well as most European laws, is evidence of an arm's-length price. Since you're a distributor, we can use the resale price method to determine such a price. Essentially, the arm's-length price for the transferred good is backed into by starting with the price at which you sell the product and then adjusting that price for the markup and other legitimate differences, such as tariffs and transportation."

"If I were a French tax auditor, I would wonder why the markup dropped from last year to this year. I also wonder if we are being good citizens and meeting the fiscal responsibilities imposed on us by each country in which we operate."

"Well, a French tax auditor might wonder about the drop in markup. The markup, however, is still within reason, and we can make a good argument for increased costs. In fact, we have already instructed the managers of our manufacturing divisions to find as many costs as they can that can be legitimately reassigned to the European product lines affected by this increase. So far, they have been very successful. I think our records will support the increase that you are receiving. Debbie, you really do not need to be concerned with the tax authorities. Our tax department assures me that this has been carefully researched and planned—it's unlikely that a tax audit will create any difficulties. It'll all be legal and above board. We've done this several times in the past with total success. We have some good people in that department."

REQUIRED:

1. Do you think that the tax minimization scheme described to Debbie Kishimoto is in harmony with the ethical behavior that should be displayed by top corporate executives? Why or why not? What would you do if you were Debbie?
2. Apparently, the Tax Department of Paterson Company has been strongly involved in developing the tax-minimization scheme. Assume that the accountants responsible for the decision are CMAs and members of the IMA, subject to the IMA standards of ethical conduct. Review the IMA standards for ethical conduct in Chapter 1. Are any of these standards being violated by the accountants in Paterson's Tax Department? If so, identify them. What should these tax accountants do if requested to develop a questionable tax-minimization scheme?

19-18
Transfer Pricing;
International
Setting; Tax
Implications
LO 6

Valley Electronics Corporation is a large multinational firm involved in the manufacture and marketing of various electronic components. Recently, Rhonda Cooper, president of Valley Electronics, received some complaints from divisional managers about the company's international transfer pricing practices. Essentially, the managers believed that they had less control over how prices were set than they wished. After reviewing some of the practices, Rhonda found that three different methods were being used: (1) the comparable uncontrolled price method, (2) the resale price method, and (3) the cost-plus method. Unable to determine why there were three methods and exactly how each worked, Rhonda had requested a meeting with Wayne Sill, vice president of finance.

Rhonda: Wayne, I need to respond to our divisional managers' concerns about the transfer pricing policies that we apply to goods shipped internationally. It appears that three methods are being used and that they differ across divisions.

Wayne: The three methods used are the ones allowed by Section 482 of the Internal Revenue Code. Which method is applicable depends on the operating circumstances surrounding the transfer of a particular component.

Rhonda: So the way we price these internal transfers is driven to some degree, at least, by tax laws. Interesting. Perhaps you can describe for me how each method works and what conditions dictate that we use that method.

Wayne: The basic concept underlying any transfer price we use is the notion of an arm's-length price. Ideally, an arm's-length price is the price that an unrelated party would pay for the good being transferred. The IRS allows four methods to determine the arm's-length price. We use three of those methods. The comparable uncontrolled method is based on market price. If the good being transferred has an external market, then the transfer price should be the price paid by an unrelated party, adjusted for differences that have a measurable effect on the price.

Rhonda: What kind of differences? Give me some examples.

Wayne: Well, the market price can be adjusted for differences such as landing costs (freight, insurance, customs duties, and special taxes) and marketing costs (commissions and advertising can be avoided with internal transfers). Adding landing costs and subtracting avoidable marketing costs are allowable adjustments to the market price.

Rhonda: I see. What happens if we sell the product to a related buyer who then resells it without any further processing? Or if the transferred good has no outside market at all?

Wayne: For the resale scenario, we use the resale price method. We take the resale price realized by our marketing divisions and adjust that price for the markup percentage and any differences like the ones we mentioned for the comparable uncontrolled method. We work back from the third-party selling price to obtain an allowable transfer price.

Rhonda: How is the markup determined?

Wayne: It corresponds to the percentage of gross profit earned by the reseller or the gross profit percentage earned by other parties who buy and resell similar products.

Rhonda: I'm beginning to understand why we have three different methods. We have divisions that fit both of the first two types. We also have some transfers that have no outside market, nor do they have any potential for resale. These goods are simply used as components of other products that are sold. Is this where cost-plus pricing is used?

Wayne: Absolutely. In this case, the transfer price is defined as the costs of production plus an appropriate gross profit percentage, with adjustments for differences such as landing costs.

Rhonda: How do we define the appropriate gross profit percentage?

Wayne: Well, it could be the gross profit percentage earned by the seller on the sale of the final product. Or if we can obtain the information, it could be the gross profit percentage earned by another party on a similar product.

Rhonda: Seems to me that the cost-plus method could be used for all three settings. Why don't we do that so that we have some uniformity in the way we compute transfer prices?

Wayne: There is a problem. If the requirements are met for any one of the methods, then it must be used—unless we can show that another method is more appropriate. The burden of proof is on us. I doubt that uniformity would be an acceptable justification. If the IRS audits us and determines that the transfer price does not fairly reflect profits recognized in the United States, it can reallocate corporate income for purposes of taxation.

REQUIRED:

1. Assume that Valley Electronics transfers a component from a U.S. division to a German division for $11.70. The landing costs are $2.50 per unit, and the avoidable commissions and advertising total $0.50 per unit. The component has a market price within the United States of $10. Is the company complying with the comparable uncontrolled price method? Would the IRS be concerned if the transfer price is greater than the market price after adjustments? Why or why not?

2. Assume that a manufacturing division in the United States transfers a component to a marketing division for resale. The resale price is $8, the gross profit percentage (gross profit divided by sales) is 25 percent, and landing costs total $1.20 per unit. Suppose that the actual transfer price (excluding landing costs) is $4.50. Should the company continue transferring at $4.50?

3. Suppose that a U.S. division has excess capacity. A European division has offered to buy a component that would increase the U.S. division's utilization of its capacity. The component has an outside market in the United States with a unit selling price of $12. The variable costs of production for the component are $6. Landing costs total $2 per unit, and an internal transfer avoids $1.25 per unit of marketing costs. The European division can purchase the component locally for $12. Ignoring income taxes, what is the minimum price that the European division should pay for the component (including landing costs)? The maximum price? Assuming that the joint benefit is split equally, what is the transfer price? Now discuss the impact of the Section 482 regulations on this decision. (*Hint*: Consider Wayne's closing statement.)

(CMA adapted)

19-19
Research
Assignment

Use the library to research the development of the North American Free Trade Agreement (NAFTA). What are the implications of its passage for companies located in the United States? In Mexico? In Canada?

Chapter 20
Contemporary Responsibility Accounting

Ben & Jerry's Ice Cream makers emphasize concern for the employee and the establishment of multiple measures of performance—in tune with contemporary responsibility accounting.

LEARNING OBJECTIVES

After reading this chapter, you should be able to:

1. Compare and contrast traditional responsibility accounting with contemporary responsibility accounting.
2. Describe process value analysis and explain its role in the contemporary responsibility accounting model.
3. Describe activity-based flexible budgeting.
4. Describe life cycle cost budgeting.
5. Discuss how control at the operational level in a contemporary environment differs from that in a conventional environment.

The type of environment in which a firm operates can have a significant effect on the type of control system chosen and implemented. Consider, for example, a firm that produces concrete pipes and blocks. The products and production processes are well-defined and relatively stable. Competition tends to be local or regional as opposed to national or international. A successful firm operating in this type of environment would tend to emphasize maintaining the status quo: preservation of market share, stable growth, and continuation of efficient production. A firm like Hewlett Packard, on the other hand, involved in producing computers and computer-related products, operates in an environment where change is rapid—where products and processes are constantly being redesigned and improved and stiff national and international competition are always present. Organizations operating in a dynamic, rapidly changing environment are finding that adaptation and change are essential to survival. Hewlett Packard and other firms in a similar kind of environment are forced to re-evaluate how they do things—to find ways to improve performance. Improving performance translates into constantly searching for ways to eliminate waste—a process known as *continuous improvement*. Waste reduction, the theme of continuous improvement, is made possible through the use of various waste reduction tools such as JIT purchasing and manufacturing, reengineering, total quality management, employee empowerment, and computer-aided manufacturing. These tools or methods attempt to eliminate waste that appears in the form of such things as inventories, unnecessary activities, defective products, rework, setup time, and underutilization of employee talents and skills.

What is measured, monitored, and rewarded can have an important effect on an organization's efforts to achieve its objectives. The adages, "You get what you measure and reward," and "if you don't measure it, it won't improve, and if you don't monitor it, it will get worse," are both relevant issues when designing and selecting a control system. Consider, for example, the unemployment agency that wanted to increase the number of applicants placed in the work place. To encourage achievement of this objective, management selected "number of persons interviewed" as the performance measure and rewarded their employees based on this measure. What the agency got was an increase in the number of interviews and less placement. When they changed the measure to number of applicants placed instead of number interviewed, behavior and results changed. This anecdotal example suggests that the control system for firms operating in a stable environment ought to be different from those operating in a dynamic environment. After all, maintaining status quo is a very different objective than that of continuous improvement. In other words, the control system selected is contingent upon the environment in which the firm operates.

RESPONSIBILITY ACCOUNTING

Objective 1

Compare and contrast traditional responsibility accounting with contemporary responsibility accounting.

The accounting system plays a key role in measuring actions and outcomes and in defining the rewards to be received by individuals. This role is referred to as responsibility accounting and is a fundamental tool of managerial control. The responsibility control model is defined by four essential elements: (1) assigning responsibility, (2) establishing performance measures or benchmarks, (3) evaluating performance, and (4) assigning rewards.

Traditional vs. Contemporary Responsibility Accounting

The responsibility accounting system for a stable environment is referred to as *traditional responsibility accounting*. The traditional system was developed when most firms were operating in relatively stable environments. *Contemporary responsibility* accounting, on the other hand, is the responsibility accounting system that is emerging for those firms operating in dynamic environments. Exhibits 20-1 and 20-2 illustrate the four responsibility elements for each of the two approaches. An element by element comparison of these two approaches provides some key insights about the differences between the two environments.

Assigning Responsibility Exhibit 20-1 reveals that traditional responsibility accounting focuses on organizational units and individuals. First, a responsibility center is identified. This center is typically an organizational unit such as a department or production line, or a work team. Whatever the unit is, responsibility is assigned to the individual in charge. Responsibility is defined in financial terms (e.g., costs). Exhibit 20-2 reveals that in a contemporary responsibility system, the control point changes from units and individuals to processes and teams. The reasons for the change of focus are simple. In a dynamic environment, continuous improvement is the governing principle. Constant change and constant learning are needed for continuous improvement to work. Processes are chosen because they are the units of change. Processes are activities linked by a common objective and describe the way things are done in an organization. Processes have inputs and create an output that is of value to a customer. The customer can be internal or external to the organization. Procurement, product development, customer acquisition, and customer service are examples of processes.

Since processes are the way things are done, changing the way things are done means changing processes. There are two methods of changing the way

Process improvement

Process innovation (business reengineering)

things are done: *process improvement* and *process innovation*. **Process improvement** refers to incremental and constant increases in the efficiency of an existing process. **Process innovation (business reengineering)** refers to the performance of a process in a radically new way with the objective of achieving dramatic improvements in response time, quality, and efficiency. IBM Credit, for example, radically redesigned its credit approval process and reduced its time for preparing a quote for leasing or buying a computer from seven days to one; similarly,

Exhibit 20-1
Elements of a Traditional Responsibility Accounting System

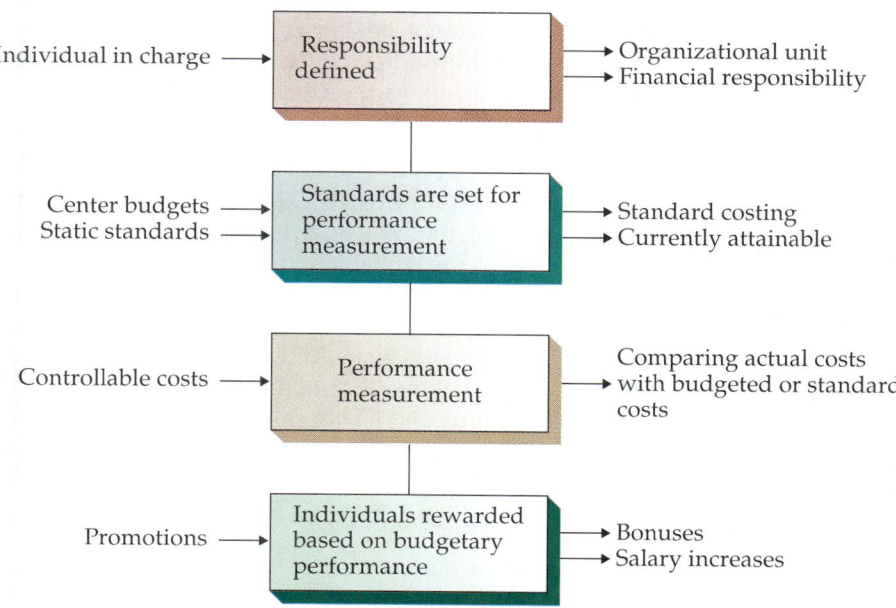

Exhibit 20-2
Elements of a Contemporary Responsibility Accounting System

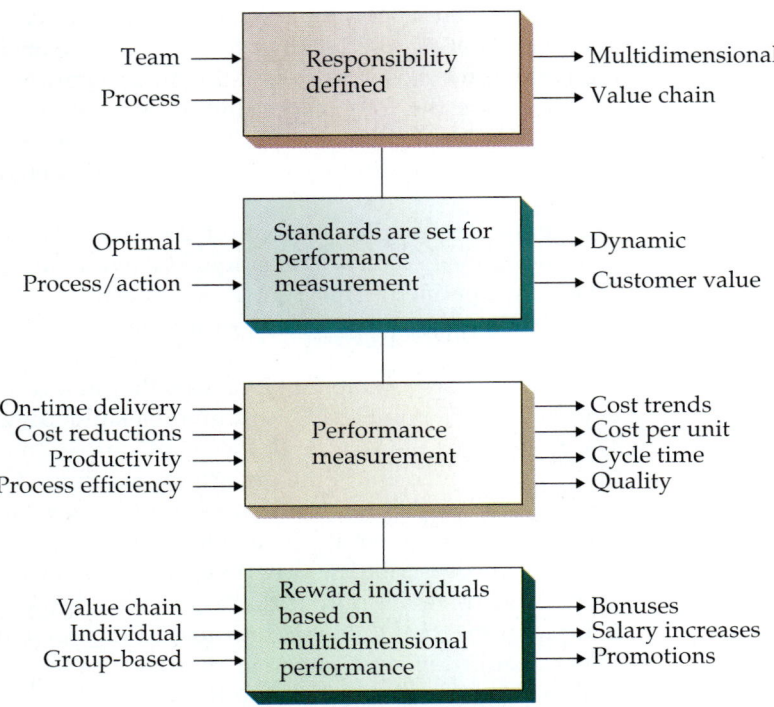

Federal Mogul, a parts manufacturer, used process innovation to reduce development time for part prototypes from twenty weeks to twenty days.[1]

Many processes cut across functional boundaries. This facilitates an integrated approach that emphasizes the firm's value-chain activities. It also means that cross-functional skills are needed for effective process management. Teams are the natural outcome of this process management requirement. Teams also improve the quality of work life by fostering friendships and a sense of belonging. Process improvement and innovation require significant group activity (and support) and cannot be carried out effectively by individuals. General Electric, Xerox, Martin Marietta, and Aetna Life Insurance are some companies that have begun to use teams as their basic work unit.[2]

Selection of Standards Standards are set to serve as benchmarks for performance measurement. According to Exhibit 20-1, budgeting and standard costing are the cornerstones of the benchmark activity for a traditional framework. Standards tend to remain fairly stable over time. Furthermore, they tend to support a currently attainable norm. Exhibit 20-2 shows some striking differences for firms operating in a dynamic environment. First, standards are process-oriented. They relate to process efficiency and process output. Standards also are structured to support change. Thus, optimal or ideal standards are set and effort exerted to reach the ideal levels. Furthermore, standards are dynamic in nature. They need to change to reflect new conditions and new goals and to help maintain any progress that has been realized. For example, standards can be set that reflect some

1.   Thomas H. Davenport, *Process Innovation*, (Boston: Harvard Business School Press, 1993), p. 2.
2.   Thomas H. Davenport, *Process Innovation*, p. 97.

desired level of improvement for a process. Once the desired level is achieved, the standard is changed to encourage an additional increment of improvement. In an environment where constant improvement is sought, standards cannot be static. Standards also should support the objective of increasing customer value.

Performance Measurement In a traditional framework (see Exhibit 20-1), performance is measured by comparing actual outcomes with budgeted outcomes. In principle, individuals are held accountable only for those items over which they have control. Cost performance is strongly emphasized. In the contemporary framework, time, quality, and efficiency are all critical dimensions of performance (see Exhibit 20-2). Decreasing the time a process takes to deliver its output to customers is viewed as basic. Thus, measures such as cycle time and on-time deliveries become important. Performance measures relating to quality and efficiency are also vital. Productivity measures are emphasized for assessing changes in efficiency. Cost measures are also important measures of efficiency. Improving a process should translate into better financial results. Thus, measures of cost reductions achieved, trends in cost, and cost per unit of output are all useful indicators of whether a process has improved. Progress towards achieving optimal standards and interim standards need to be measured. One approach is to measure the trends of actual costs (or other actual operational measures) against optimal standards. The objective is to provide low cost, high quality products, delivered on a timely basis. Thus, performance measures are a blend of operational and financial factors, all of which relate to process performance.

Reward In both systems individuals are rewarded or penalized according to the policies and discretion of higher management. Of course, as Exhibit 20-1 reveals, the traditional reward system is designed to encourage individuals to manage costs—to achieve or beat budgetary standards. For the contemporary system illustrated in Exhibit 20-2, rewarding individuals is more complicated than in the traditional setting. Individuals simultaneously have accountability for team and individual performance. Since the emphasis is on process improvement, and improvement is mostly achieved through team efforts, group-based rewards are more suitable than individual rewards. In one company (a producer of electronic components), for example, optimal standards have been set for unit costs, on-time delivery, quality, inventory turns, scrap, and cycle time.[3] Bonuses are awarded to the team whenever performance is maintained on all measures and improves on at least one measure. Notice the multidimensional nature of this measurement and reward system.

The differences between the two approaches are significant. Yet, a logical question to ask is why the traditional responsibility system is not suitable for a firm operating in a dynamic environment. The emphasis of the traditional responsibility accounting system is on managing costs, maintaining the status quo, and organizational stability. In light of this, the usefulness of the traditional control system for a dynamic, intensively competitive environment is questionable. In this type of environment, firms are competing on the basis of time, quality, and efficiency. Why? These competitive dimensions are in response to customer demands. Customers are demanding that the products they want are delivered on time, are defect free, have short lead times, have low prices and low

---

3.   C. J. McNair, "Responsibility Accounting and Controllability Networks, *Handbook of Cost Management*, (Boston: Warren Gorham Lamont, 1993), pp. E4–1—E4–33.

postpurchase costs. Customers want greater value: more realization and less sacrifice. To provide this greater value, firms must do more with less. Doing more with less means that firms must find ways of being more productive. Firms that advocate continuous improvement usually alter the role of standard costing and budgeting as managerial control tools. The reason is simple. Traditional performance measures provide incentives that actually may serve as impediments to continuous improvement. Traditional performance measures are limited in their ability to support the objective of continuous improvement and the use of its associated tools such as just-in-time, total quality management, and advanced technology. To fully understand this reasoning, some specific limitations need to be listed and described.

Limitations of Traditional Responsibility Accounting

Traditional responsibility accounting places too much emphasis on standards and variance computations (for a dynamic environment). Standards tend to be static in nature and are sometimes out-of-date and may not reflect the changes that are taking place within the organization (or environment). They encourage the status quo and organizational stability. Standards also typically allow for given levels of inefficiency, accepting some downtime, some waste, some lack of skill, and so on. Furthermore, the variances computed are the *result* of management action and organizational performance and not the *cause* of it. Understanding what causes performance is fundamental to improving performance. One manager is quoted as saying the following: "Using financial measures to improve performance is like concentrating on the scoreboard in a football game. While the scoreboard tells you whether you are winning or losing, it doesn't provide much guidance about the plays that should be called."[4] For a dynamic environment, a number of specific limitations can be listed and described—limitations that clearly suggest the need for the type of responsibility accounting model described in Exhibit 20-2.

Internal Focus Standards, budgets, and variances tend to be internally focused. Standards are usually based on internal expectations. Variances, then, are comparisons of internal expectations with actual outcomes. Yet, as one executive remarked: "A revenue increase of 15% over last year and 5% ahead of budget is not such good news when the market grew 30% and our leading competitor increased its sales by 40%."[5] An external focus is also needed.

Overemphasis on Labor In the traditional setting many companies emphasize control of labor costs over the cost of any other input. For companies that have automated, the direct labor content in products is greatly decreased. Furthermore, for companies that have implemented JIT, the distinction between direct and indirect labor is largely artificial. Cell workers do much more than work on products. According to one source, labor content in some manufacturing is less than 2%, making labor standards much less meaningful.[6] Hewlett Packard, for

---

4.   Robert G. Eccle and Phillip J. Pyburn, "Creating a Comprehensive System to Measure Performance," *Management Accounting* (October 1992), pp. 41–44.
5.   Ibid., pp. 41–42.
6.   F. B. Green, Felix Amenkhienan, and George F. Johnson, "Performance Measures and JIT," *Management Accounting* (February 1991), pp. 50–53.

example, no longer tracks labor separately but includes it as a component of overhead. In the advanced manufacturing environment, there is more emphasis on *process efficiency* than on labor efficiency. A manager of a plant using a JIT approach made the following observation: "The system converts materials into product, not people at workstations. Therefore, process efficiency is more important than labor efficiency. As well, the process may be improved by using direct labor to perform indirect tasks. . . ."[7]

Ignores Nonvalue-Added Costs The traditional responsibility accounting system does not classify and report costs that are targeted for elimination. In a continuous improvement environment, certain costs called *nonvalue-added costs* are identified and isolated so they can eventually be eliminated. As we shall see in more detail later on, these costs are targeted for elimination because they are unnecessary and provide no value to the customer or organization. This identification and isolation of nonvalue-added costs is basic to a continuous improvement program. Nonvalue-added costs must be tracked and reported, otherwise there is no promise of change: "Costs not reported are invisible and are all but ignored in the management process."[8]

Perverse Incentives Standard costing encourages those responsible for the achievement of standards to produce favorable variances. But the pressure to meet standards may create dysfunctional behavior. For example, purchasing agents may acquire materials of low quality or in large lots in order to produce a favorable materials price variance. As a consequence, scrap, the number of defective units, and the amount of rework activity may increase, or raw materials inventories may be excessive. These outcomes run contrary to the advanced environment's objectives of total quality control and zero inventories.

As indicated, in the advanced manufacturing environment, labor efficiency reporting receives considerably less emphasis—but this decrease in emphasis is attributable to incentive problems as well as the reduction in labor content (some firms may still have significant labor content). Labor efficiency variances computed at the cell level may encourage workers to produce more than needed to achieve targeted efficiency levels or to avoid an unfavorable volume variance. For example, including setup labor as part of the labor standard (as is often done) encourages large production runs and, thus, excess production; by using fewer setup hours, the actual hours reported move closer to standard. But producing more product than needed is diametrically opposed to the goal of zero inventories. In a JIT environment, idle workers (in the short run) are not necessarily viewed as bad—keeping workers active by overproducing can be much more costly than the labor services lost.

The computation of materials usage variances can also pose problems for the advanced manufacturing environment. Workers may pass on poor quality components to avoid an unfavorable materials usage variance. Unfortunately, defective parts disrupt production in a JIT environment. Because there are no inventories to serve as a buffer for interruptions in production, incentives that encourage defective components are not desirable. Thus, the traditional approach

7.   C. J. McNair, "Responsibility Accounting and Controllability Networks," *Handbook of Cost Management* (Boston: Warren Gorham Lamont, 1994), p. E4–17.
8.   C. J. McNair, "Responsibility Accounting and Controllability Networks," p. E4–7.

to control operations through efficiency reporting and variance analysis is not compatible with the advanced manufacturing environment.

Emphasis on individual overhead variances can also be detrimental. Avoiding preventive maintenance to ensure a favorable budget variance may result in equipment being unavailable for production. This behavior, however, runs counter to the JIT objective of total preventive maintenance and creates an incentive for buffer inventories.

The concept of currently attainable standards is also opposed to the objective of continuous improvement. Currently attainable standards allow for a certain level of inefficiency. All too often, in a standard costing system, those who achieve the standard believe that they have arrived and that no further efforts are needed to improve efficiency. Of course, this is possible because the standard allows for inefficiency and is viewed as somewhat static in nature. Yet JIT and this new business process demand that efforts be continually exerted to improve quality, to improve efficiency, and to find better ways to do the same task. Innovation and simplicity are encouraged and rewarded. A dynamic view of efficiency, not a static one, is needed for an environment in which continuous improvement is stressed.

Overemphasis of Financial Measures Traditional responsibility accounting emphasizes financial control. Yet many of the gains made are nonfinancial in nature. Response time, for example, is not measured in dollars, yet this has emerged as one of the key competitive dimensions. This suggests that a contemporary responsibility accounting system must incorporate both financial and nonfinancial measures of performance. Exhibit 20-3 summarizes the limitations of a traditional responsibility accounting system.

Activity-Based Management

Identifying the limitations helps us understand why the contemporary responsibility accounting model shown in Exhibit 20-2 is needed. Although Exhibit 20-2 offers a general overview of a contemporary responsibility accounting system, it does not offer operational details. The emergence of activity accounting is the key to operationalizing the concepts presented in Exhibit 20-2. Processes

Exhibit 20-3
Limitations of Traditional Responsibility Accounting

1. Overreliance on standards and variances.
2. Standards tend to be static.
3. Standards support the status quo and organizational stability.
4. Standards allow for given levels of inefficiency.
5. Variances are lagged indicators: they reveal results, not the cause.
6. Focus is internal, not external.
7. Overemphasis on direct labor.
8. Ignores nonvalue-added costs.
9. Traditional variances and performance reports provide perverse incentives (inappropriate measures of performance):
   a. Encourage overproduction and unneeded inventories.
   b. Work against zero defects and total quality control.
   c. May work against machine availability (especially bad for bottlenecks).
10. Overemphasis on financial measures.

are the focus of responsibility and control. Processes are made up of activities that are linked to perform a specific objective. Improving processes means improving the way activities are performed. Thus, management of activities—not costs—is the key to successful control for firms operating in dynamic environments. The realization that activities are crucial to both improved product costing and effective control has led to a new view of business processes called *activity-based management*.

activity-based
management (ABM)

Activity-based management (ABM) is a system-wide, integrated approach that focuses management's attention on activities with the objective of improving customer value and the profit achieved by providing this value. Activity-based management encompasses both product costing and process value analysis. Thus, the activity-based management model has two dimensions: a *cost dimension* and a *process dimension*. This two-dimensional model was first introduced in Chapter 2 and for convenience is shown again in Exhibit 20-4. The cost dimension provides cost information about resources, activities, products, and customers (and other cost objects that may be of interest). As the model suggests, the cost of resources is traced to activities, and then the cost of activities is assigned to products and customers. This activity-based costing dimension is useful for product costing, strategic cost management, and tactical analysis. The second dimension—the process dimension—provides information about what activities are performed, why activities are performed, and how well they are done. It is this dimension that provides the ability to engage in and measure continuous improvement. To understand how the process view connects with the world of continuous improvement, we need to have a more explicit understanding of process value analysis.

Exhibit 20-4
*The Two-Dimensional
ABM Model*

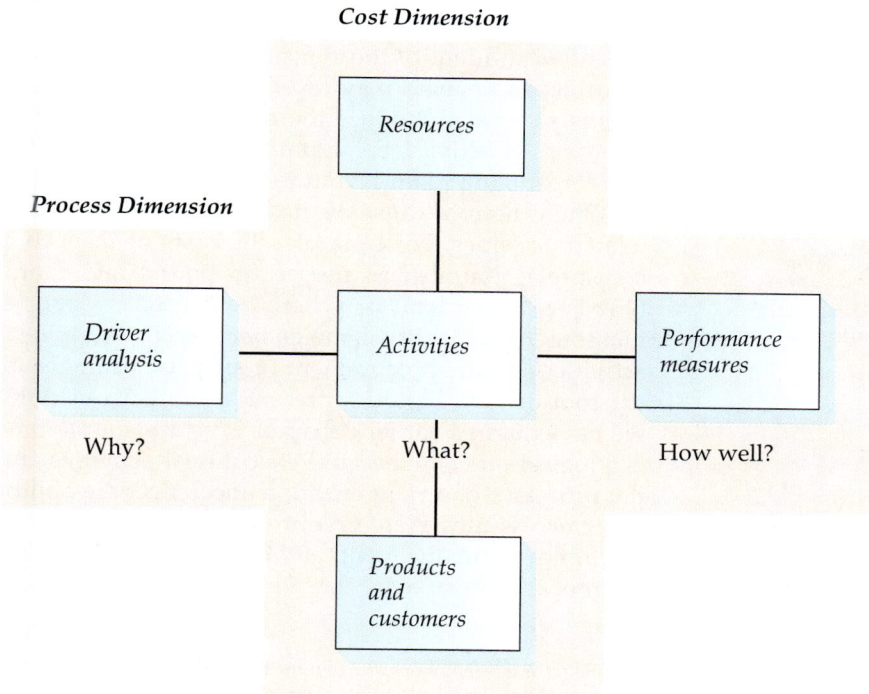

PROCESS VALUE ANALYSIS

Objective 2
Describe process value analysis and explain its role in the contemporary responsibility accounting model.

process value analysis

Process value analysis defines activity-based responsibility accounting, focuses on accountability for activities rather than costs, and emphasizes the maximization of systemwide performance instead of individual performance. Process value analysis allows the concepts of contemporary responsibility accounting to become operational. As the model in Exhibit 20-4 illustrates, process value analysis is concerned with *driver analysis*, *activity analysis*, and *performance measurement*.

Driver Analysis: The Search for Root Causes

activity inputs
activity output

Managing activities requires an understanding of what causes activity costs. To understand what is meant by driver analysis, some additional activity terminology is helpful.[9] Every activity has inputs and outputs. **Activity inputs** are the resources consumed by the activity in producing its output. **Activity output** is the result or product of an activity. For example, if the activity is moving materials, the inputs would be such things as labor, fuel, and a forklift. The output would be material movement. An **activity output measure** is the number of times the activity is performed. It is the quantifiable measure of the output. For example, the number of moves is a possible output measure for moving materials.

activity output measure

The output measure effectively is a measure of the demands placed on an activity and is what we have been calling an activity driver. As the demands for an activity change, the cost of the activity can change. For example, as the number of moves increases, the activity of moving material may need to consume more inputs (labor, fuel, etc.). However, output measures, such as the number of moves, may not and usually do not correspond to the *root causes* of activity costs; rather, they are the consequences of the activity being performed. The purpose of *driver analysis* is to reveal the root causes. Thus, **driver analysis** is the effort expended to identify those factors that are the root causes of activity costs. For example, an analysis may reveal that the root cause of the cost of moving materials is plant layout. Once the root cause is known, then action can be taken to improve the activity. For example, the cost of moving materials can be reduced by reorganizing plant layout.

driver analysis

Often the root cause of the cost of an activity is also the root cause of other related activities. For example, the costs of inspecting purchased parts (Output measure = Number of inspection hours) and reordering (Output measure = Number of reorders) may both be caused by poor supplier quality. By implementing total quality management and a supplier evaluation program, both activities and the procurement process itself may be improved. In both examples, the root drivers should represent a familiar outcome. The root causes are what we have defined earlier (Chapter 9) as *executional (procedural) activity drivers*. This is a logical outcome because executional activities are those activities that define the processes of an organization and reflect the ability of an organization to execute successfully. Plant layout efficiency, quality management approach, degree of employee involvement, and other executional drivers are all good candidates for root drivers of activities within an organization.

9.   Some of the definitions are from the following source: James A. Brimson and Michael J. Burtha, "Activity Accounting," *Handbook of Cost Management*, Warren Gorham Lamont, Boston, 1993, pp. C1–1—C1–38.

Activity Analysis

activity analysis

The heart of process value analysis is *activity analysis*. **Activity analysis** is the process of identifying, describing, and evaluating the activities an organization performs. Activity analysis should produce four outcomes: (1) what activities are done, (2) how many people perform the activities, (3) the time and resources required to perform the activities, (4) an assessment of the value of the activities to the organization, including a recommendation to select and keep only those that add value. Step 4, determining the value-added content of activities, may be the most important step in activity analysis. Activities can be classified as *value-added* or *nonvalue-added*. **Value-added activities** are necessary activities—activities that are necessary to remain in business. **Value-added costs** are the costs caused by value-added activities that are performed with perfect efficiency. **Nonvalue-added activities** are unnecessary—all activities other than those that are absolutely essential to remain in business. **Nonvalue-added costs** are costs that are caused either by nonvalue-added activities or the inefficient performance of valued-added activities. Because of increased competition, many firms are attempting to eliminate nonvalue-added activities because they add unnecessary cost and impede performance; firms are also striving to optimize value-added activities. Thus, activity analysis attempts to identify and eventually eliminate all unnecessary activities and simultaneously increase the efficiency of necessary activities.

value-added activities
value-added costs
nonvalue-added
  activities
nonvalue-added costs

The theme of activity analysis is waste elimination. As waste is eliminated, costs are reduced. The cost reduction *follows* the elimination of waste. Note the value of managing the *causes* of the costs rather than the costs themselves. Managing costs may increase the efficiency of an activity—but if the activity is unnecessary, what does it matter if it's performed efficiently? An unnecessary activity is wasteful and should be eliminated. For example, moving raw materials and partially finished goods is often cited as a nonvalue-added activity. Installing an automated materials-handling system may increase the efficiency of this activity, but changing to cellular manufacturing with on-site, just-in-time delivery of raw materials could virtually eliminate the activity. It's easy to see which is preferable.

Examples of Nonvalue-Added Activities Reordering parts, expediting production, and rework because of defective parts are examples of nonvalue-added activities. Other examples include warranty work, handling customer complaints, and reporting defects. Nonvalue-added activities can exist anywhere in the organization. In the manufacturing operation, five major activities are often cited as wasteful and unnecessary. These activities are listed and defined below.

1. Scheduling: An activity that uses time and resources to determine when different products have access to processes (or when and how many setups must be done) and how much will be produced.
2. Moving: An activity that uses time and resources to move raw materials, work in process, and finished goods from one department to another.
3. Waiting: An activity in which raw materials or work in process use time and resources by waiting on the next process.
4. Inspecting: An activity in which time and resources are spent ensuring that the product meets specifications.
5. Storing: An activity that uses time and resources while a good or raw material is held in inventory.

None of these activities adds any value for the customer. They are not necessary to remain in business. Thus, the challenge of activity analysis is to find ways to produce the good without using any of these activities.

Cost Reduction Continuous improvement carries with it the objective of cost reduction. Competitive conditions dictate that companies must deliver products the customers want, on time, and at the lowest possible cost. This means that an organization must continually strive for cost improvement. Activity analysis is the key to achieving cost reduction objectives. Activity analysis can reduce costs in four ways:[10]

1. Activity elimination
2. Activity selection
3. Activity reduction
4. Activity sharing

activity elimination

Activity elimination focuses on nonvalue-added activities. Once activities that fail to add value are identified, measures must be taken to rid the organization of these activities. For example, the activity of inspecting incoming parts seems necessary to ensure that the product using the parts functions according to specifications. Use of a bad part can produce a bad final product. Yet this activity is necessary only because of the poor quality performance of the supplying firms. Selecting suppliers who are able to supply high-quality parts or who are willing to improve their quality performance to achieve this objective eventually will allow the elimination of incoming inspection. Cost reduction then follows.

activity selection

Activity selection involves choosing among different sets of activities that are caused by competing strategies. Different strategies cause different activities. Different product design strategies, for example, can require significantly different activities. Activities, in turn, cause costs. Each product design strategy has its own set of activities and associated costs. All other things being equal, the lowest-cost design strategy should be chosen. Thus, activity selection can have a significant effect on cost reduction.

activity reduction

Activity reduction decreases the time and resources required by an activity. This approach to cost reduction should be primarily aimed at improving the efficiency of necessary activities or a short-term strategy for improving nonvalue-added activities until they can be eliminated. Setup activity, for example, is a necessary activity that is often cited as an example for which less time and fewer resources need to be used.

activity sharing

Activity sharing increases the efficiency of necessary activities by using economies of scale. Specifically, the quantity of the activity output is increased without increasing the total cost of the activity itself. This lowers the per-unit cost of the activity output and the amount of cost that is traceable to the products that consume the activity. For example, a new product can be designed to use components already being used by other products. By using existing components, the activities associated with these components already exist and the company avoids the creation of a whole new set of activities.

Performance Measurement

Activities are also the foundation of a contemporary performance measurement system. Activity performance measures deal with quality, time, cost, and flexi-

10.   This classification and its discussion are based on Peter B. B. Turney, "How Activity-Based Costing Helps Reduce Cost," *Journal of Cost Management*, Winter 1991, pp. 29–35.

bility and are both financial and nonfinancial in nature. These measures are designed to assess how well an activity was performed and the results achieved. They are also designed to reveal if constant improvement is being realized. Improving activity performance means eliminating nonvalue-added activities and optimizing value-added activities. Thus, a firm should identify and report the value-added and nonvalue-added costs of each activity. Progress can then be assessed by preparing trend and cost reduction reports.

Value- and Nonvalue-Added Cost Reporting A company's accounting system should distinguish between value-added costs and nonvalue-added costs. The distinction is necessary so that management can focus on reducing and eventually eliminating nonvalue-added costs. Highlighting nonvalue-added costs also reveals the magnitude of the waste the company is currently experiencing. Reporting nonvalue-added costs separately encourages managers to place more emphasis on controlling nonvalue-added activities. Furthermore, tracking these costs over time permits managers to assess the effectiveness of their activity-management programs. Cost reduction should follow, and knowing the amount of costs saved is important for strategic purposes. For example, if an activity is eliminated, then the costs saved should be traceable to individual products. These savings can produce price reductions for customers and make the firm more competitive. Changing the pricing strategy, however, requires knowledge of the cost reductions created by activity analysis. A cost reporting system, therefore, is an important ingredient in an activity-based responsibility accounting system. The activity-based cost report should include both value-added and nonvalue-added costs.

Value-added costs are the only costs that an organization should incur. The value-added standard calls for the complete elimination of nonvalue-added activities; for these activities, the optimal output is zero with zero cost. The value-added standard also calls for the complete elimination of the inefficiency of activities that are necessary but inefficiently carried out. Thus, value-added activities also have an optimal output level. A **value-added standard**, therefore, identifies the optimal activity output. Identifying the optimal activity output requires activity output measurement.

value-added standard

Setting value-added standards does not mean that they will be (or should be) achieved immediately. The idea of continuous improvement is to move toward the ideal, not to achieve it immediately. Workers (teams) can be rewarded for improvement. Moreover, operational performance measures, nonfinancial in nature, can be used to supplement and support the goal of eliminating nonvalue-added costs (these are discussed later in the chapter). Finally, measuring the efficiency of individual workers and supervisors is not the way to eliminate nonvalue-added activities. Remember, activities cut across departmental boundaries and are part of processes. Focusing on activities and providing incentives to improve processes is a more productive approach. Improving the process should lead to improved results.

By comparing actual activity costs with value-added activity costs, management can assess the level of nonproductive activity and become informed concerning the potential for improvement. Fundamental to identifying and calculating value- and nonvalue-added costs is the identification of output measures for each activity. Once output measures are identified, then value-added standard quantities for each activity can be defined. Value-added costs can be computed by multiplying the value-added standard quantities by the price standard. Nonvalue-added costs can be calculated as the difference between the actual level of the activity's output and the value-added level, multiplied by the unit standard cost. These formulas are presented in Exhibit 20-5. Some further explanation is needed. For resources acquired as needed, AQ is the actual quantity of activity used. For resources acquired in advance of usage, AQ represents the actual quantity of activity capacity acquired, as measured by the activity's practical capacity. This definition of AQ allows the computation of nonvalue-added costs for both variable and fixed activity costs. For fixed activity costs, SP is the budgeted activity costs divided by AQ, where AQ is practical activity capacity.

To illustrate the power of the above concepts, let's focus on the following four activities for a product manufactured in a JIT environment: material usage, rework of defective products, setups, and incoming inspections. Of the four activities, two are viewed as necessary: material usage and setups; inspection and rework are unnecessary (in an ideal sense, there should be no defective parts or products). Furthermore, assume that the first three activities acquire resources as needed, whereas incoming inspecting capacity is acquired in advance of usage (salaries are budgeted at $60,000 for two inspectors). The following data pertain to the four activities:

	Activity Driver	SQ	AQ	SP
Material usage	Pounds	40,000	44,000	$40.00
Rework	Labor hours	0	10,000	9.00
Setups	Setup time	0	6,000	60.00
Inspection	Inspection hours	0	4,000	15.00

Notice that the value-added standards for rework and inspection call for their elimination; the value-added standard for setups calls for a zero setup time. As pointed out earlier, ideally, there should be no defective products and parts; by improving quality, changing production processes, and so on, inspection can eventually be eliminated. Setups are necessary, but in a JIT environment, efforts are made to drive setup times to zero.

Exhibit 20-6 classifies the costs for the four activities as value-added or non-value-added. For simplicity, and to show the relationship to actual costs, the actual price per unit of the activity driver is assumed to be equal to the standard price. In this case, the value-added cost plus the nonvalue-added cost equals actual cost. Normally, it might be necessary to add a price variance column. This possibility is illustrated later in the chapter when flexible budgeting is discussed.

The cost report in Exhibit 20-6 allows managers to see the nonvalue-added costs; as a consequence, it emphasizes the opportunity for improvement. By decreasing scrap and waste, management can reduce its material cost. By training

Exhibit 20-5

Computational Formulas for Value- and Non-value-Added Costs

$$\text{Value-added costs} = SQ \times SP$$
$$\text{Nonvalue-added costs} = (AQ - SQ)SP$$

where SQ = The value-added output level for an activity

AQ = The actual quantity of activity output used (if resources are supplied as needed)

or AQ = The actual quantity of activity capacity acquired (if resources are supplied in advance of usage)

Exhibit 20-6
*Value- and Nonvalue-
Added Cost Report*

| | Value- and Nonvalue-Added Cost Report | | |
| | For the Year Ending December 31, 1998 | | |
Activity	*Value-Added*	*Nonvalue-Added*	*Actual*
Material usage	$1,600,000	$160,000	$1,760,000
Setups	0	360,000	360,000
Rework	0	90,000	90,000
Inspection	0	60,000	60,000
Total	$1,600,000	$670,000	$2,270,000

cell workers, and improving labor skill, management can reduce rework. Reducing setup time and implementing a supplier evaluation program are actions that can be taken to improve performance for the setup and inspection activities.

Thus, reporting value- and nonvalue-added costs at a point in time may trigger actions to manage activities more effectively. Seeing the amount of waste may induce managers to search for ways to reduce, select, share, and eliminate activities to bring about cost reductions. Reporting these costs may also help managers improve planning, budgeting, and pricing decisions. For example, lowering the selling price to meet a competitor's price may be seen as possible if a manager can see the potential for reducing nonvalue-added costs to absorb the effect of the price reduction.

Trend Reporting As managers take actions to reduce, eliminate, select, and share activities, do the cost reductions follow as expected? One way to answer this question is to compare the costs for each activity over time. The goal is activity improvement, as measured by cost reduction, and so we should see a decline in nonvalue-added costs from one period to the next—provided activity analysis is effective. Assume, for example, that at the beginning of 1998, the following actions are taken to manage the four activities in Exhibit 20-6:

1. Material usage activity: Statistical process control is implemented. Scrap and waste are expected to decrease.
2. Setups: The product is redesigned, creating a requirement for a simpler configuration. The simpler configuration should reduce setup time.
3. Rework: A training program for a new assembly process is expected to reduce the number of defective products; a positive effect is also expected from using statistical process control.
4. Incoming Inspection: A supplier evaluation program is being started. Only those suppliers that will be willing to supply parts that are free from defects will be kept (time for conforming to the requirement will be given; however, some of the worse offenders will be dropped with some short-term improvement expected).

Four major activity-management decisions were made: the use of statistical process control, product redesign, labor training program for a new assembly process, and a supplier evaluation program. How effective were these decisions? Did a cost reduction occur as expected? Exhibit 20-7 provides a cost report that compares the nonvalue-added costs of 1999 with those that occurred in 1998 (after implementing the changes described above). The 1999 costs are assumed

Activity	1998	1999	Change
Material usage	$160,000	$100,000	$ 60,000 F
Setups	360,000	160,000	200,000 F
Rework	90,000	50,000	40,000 F
Inspection*	60,000	30,000	30,000 F
Totals	$670,000	$340,000	$330,000 F

*During the year, the supplier evaluation program decreased the number of defective parts to the point where one inspector was reassigned to an open position in the assembly department.

but would be computed the same way as shown for 1998. We assume that SQ is the same for both years. Comparing 1999 nonvalue-added costs directly with 1998 value-added costs requires SQ to be the same for both years. If SQ changes, prior-year nonvalue-added costs are adjusted by simply assuming the same percentage deviation from standard in the current year as was realized in the prior year.

The trend report reveals that cost reductions followed, as expected. Nearly half of the nonvalue-added costs have been eliminated. There is still ample room for improvement, but activity improvement so far has been successful. As a note of interest, comparison of the actual costs of the two periods would have revealed the same reduction. Reporting nonvalue-added costs, however, not only reveals the reduction but also provides managers with information on how much potential for cost reduction remains. There is an important qualification, however. Value-added standards, like other standards, are not cast in stone. New technology, new designs, and other innovations can change the nature of activities performed. Value-added activities can be converted to nonvalue-added activities, and value-added levels can change as well. Thus, as new ways for improvement surface, value-added standards can change. Managers should not become content but should continually seek higher levels of efficiency.

The Role of Interim (Currently Attainable) Standards

If a company is emphasizing the reduction of nonvalue-added costs, interim standards can be set which identify the amount of improvement expected for the coming year. These standards can be thought of, in a sense, as currently attainable standards. They reflect the increased efficiency expected for the year. Comparing actual costs with the currently attainable standards would then provide a measure of how well the current year's goals for improvement have been met. However, this brand of currently attainable standards differs from the conventional type. They are dynamic—changing each year to reflect that year's improvement targets.

This use of currently attainable standards is equivalent to emphasizing actual costs and trends in actual costs. Cost reduction targets are set; evaluations concern how well managers meet these targets. Of course, comparison of actual costs with cost reduction targets is equivalent to comparing them to a currently attainable standard, provided that the currently attainable standard is defined as last year's actual costs less the targeted reduction.

For example, assume that a medical products division inspects every unit produced of a particular surgical instrument. The unit-level value-added standard for this product calls for 0 inspection hours per unit and a value-added inspection cost of $0 per unit. Assume that in the prior year, the company used 15 minutes to inspect each instrument at a cost of $15 per inspection hour. Thus, the actual inspection cost per unit is $3.75 ($15 × 1/4 hr.). This is also the non-value-added cost. For the coming year, the company is installing a new production process that is expected to increase the precision with which the instrument is produced. These changes are expected to reduce the inspection time from 15 minutes to 10 minutes. Thus, the cost reduction goal is $1.25 per unit. The interim or currently attainable standard is defined as 10 minutes per unit. The currently attainable standard cost of inspection per unit is $2.50, the actual prior year cost less the targeted reduction ($3.75 − $1.25). For the following year, additional improvements would be sought and a new currently attainable standard defined. For example, the company is planning on installing a statistical process control system that will increase the reliability of the process even more so that inspection time can be further reduced. This will then produce a different standard than the one for the current year.

Benchmarking

Benchmarking

Another approach to standard setting that is used to help identify opportunities for activity improvement is called *benchmarking*. **Benchmarking** uses best practices as the standard for evaluating activity performance. Benchmarking has been used to obtain significant improvement by such companies as Alcoa, DuPont, Hewlett Packard, Johnson & Johnson, Kodak, and Motorola.[11] There are three types of benchmarking approaches: internal, competitive, and generic. Internal benchmarking focuses on the best-performing units within an organization. Within an organization, different units (e.g., different plant sites) that perform the same activities are compared. The unit with the best performance for a given activity sets the standard. Other units then have a target to meet or exceed. Furthermore, the best practices unit can share information with other units on how they have achieved their superior results. For this process to work, it is necessary to ensure that activity definitions and activity output measures are consistent across units. Such things as activity rates, the cost per unit of activity output, or the amount of activity output per unit of *process* output can be used to rank activity performance and identify the best performer.

For example, assume the output of the purchasing activity is measured by the number of purchase orders. Suppose further that the cost of the purchasing activity for one plant is $90,000, and activity output is 4,500 purchase orders. Dividing the cost of the purchasing activity by the number of purchase orders prepared gives a unit cost of $20 per order. Now if the best unit cost is $15 per purchase order, then the plant with the $20 per unit cost knows it has the ability to improve activity efficiency by at least $5 per unit. By studying the purchasing practices of the best plant, activity efficiency should increase.

The objective of benchmarking is to become the best at performing activities and processes. Ideally, benchmarking should involve comparisons with competitors. This is called *competitive benchmarking*. Competitive benchmarking identifies best practices of competitors and the factors that led to those best practices. A related approach is comparing similar functions within the same industry. Often, a third party is used so that sensitive competitive information is not disclosed. However, it is often difficult to obtain the necessary data for competitive

11.   American Productivity and Quality Center, *The Benchmarking Management Guide,* Productivity Press, Portland, 1993.

benchmarking to work. Finally, it may be possible to study best practices of non-competitors. There are certain activities and processes that are common to all organizations. *Generic benchmarking* studies the best practices of these common activities and uses them as standards to motivate internal improvements—but only if the external best practice is superior to any internal unit's achievement.

Drivers and Behavioral Effects

Activity output measures are needed to compute and track nonvalue-added costs. Reducing nonvalue-added activity should produce a reduction in the demand for the activity and, therefore, a reduction in the activity output measures. If a team's performance is affected by its ability to reduce nonvalue-added costs, then the selection of drivers (as output measures) and how they are used can affect behavior. For example, if the output measure for setup costs is chosen as setup time, an incentive is created for workers to reduce setup time. Since the value-added standard for setup costs calls for their complete elimination, then the incentive to drive setup time to zero is compatible with the company's objectives, and the induced behavior is beneficial.

Suppose, however, that the objective is to reduce the number of unique parts a company processes, thus simplifying activities such as incoming inspection, preparation of bills of materials, and vendor selection.[12] If the costs of these activities are assigned to products based on the number of parts, the incentive created is to reduce the number of parts in a product. While this behavior may be desirable to a point, it can also have negative consequences. Design teams may actually reduce the marketability of the product by reducing the number of parts too greatly and adversely affecting its functionality.

This type of behavior can be discouraged by the proper use of standard costing. First, if the number of parts truly drives the costs of incoming inspection, preparation of bills of materials, and vendor selection, then a budgeted cost per unit of activity driver can be computed (i.e., a standard price per unit). Next, the value-added standard number of parts for each product should be identified (the standard quantity). The value-added costs are then simply the product of the standard price and standard quantity $(SP \times SQ)$. As before, nonvalue-added costs are the difference between the actual parts used and the standard parts allowed, multiplied by the standard price $[(AQ - SQ)SP]$.

For example, assume that a company produces two machines: lathes and drills. The company has determined that activities driven by parts should cost $400 per part (SP). The value-added quantity and actual parts for each product are given below.

	Lathes	*Drills*
Value-added number *(SQ)*	5	10
Actual number *(AQ)*	10	15

The value-added and nonvalue-added costs for each product are presented below.

	Lathes	*Drills*
Value-added costs	$2,000	$4,000
Nonvalue-added costs	2,000	2,000

---

12. This example is based on the discussion concerning behavioral effects of cost drivers found in Robin Cooper, "The Rise of Activity-Based Costing—Part Three: How Many Cost Drivers Do You Need, and How Do You Select Them?" *Journal of Cost Management for the Manufacturing Industry*, Winter 1989, pp. 34–46.

Designers should be encouraged to reduce the nonvalue-added costs by reaching the value-added standard, but indiscriminate use of activity drivers can produce dysfunctional behavior. This example illustrates the importance of setting standards. The absence of any standard can lead designers to reduce parts in order to reduce costs, without any sense of direction or purpose. However, by identifying, before the fact, the number of parts each product *should* have, using the number of parts as an activity driver can encourage reduction of only nonvalue-added costs. The standard has provided a concrete objective and defined the kind of behavior that the incentive allows.

ACTIVITY FLEXIBLE BUDGETING

Objective 3

Describe activity-based flexible budgeting.

activity flexible budgeting

The ability to identify changes in activity costs as the activity output measure changes allows managers to more carefully plan and monitor activity improvements. **Activity flexible budgeting** allows the prediction of what activity costs will be as activity (output) usage changes. Variance analysis within this activity framework allows managers to break activity costs into value-added and nonvalue-added components, distinguish between price effects and volume effects, and report on the cost of used and unused activity capacity. Also, the ability to compute costs for different activity usage levels makes it possible to compute the expected cost for interim activity standards. Finally, traditional budgetary performance reporting can be markedly improved through the use of activity flexible budgets.

In a traditional setting, budgeted costs for the actual level of activity are obtained by assuming that all costs are driven by a single unit-based driver (usually direct labor hours). A cost formula is developed for each cost item as a function of direct labor hours. This formula is then used to predict what the costs ought to be for any level of activity. Exhibit 20-8 illustrates a traditional flexible budget. If, however, costs vary with respect to more than one driver and the drivers are not highly correlated with direct labor hours, then prediction of activity costs can be misleading.

The solution, of course, is to build flexible budget formulas for more than one driver. To simplify the presentation of a multiple-driver flexible budget, homogeneous activities are grouped together and budgets are developed for each

Exhibit 20-8
Traditional Flexible Budget

| | Formula | | Direct Labor Hours | |
	Fixed	Variable	10,000	20,000
Direct materials	$ —	$10	$100,000	$200,000
Direct labor	—	8	80,000	160,000
Supplies	—	2	20,000	40,000
Maintenance	20,000	3	50,000	80,000
Power	15,000	1	25,000	35,000
Inspections	120,000	—	120,000	120,000
Setups	16,000	—	16,000	16,000
Receiving	22,000	—	22,000	22,000
Total	$193,000	$24	$433,000	$673,000

homogeneous set using a single driver. Cost estimation procedures (e.g., high-low method and the method of least squares) can be used to estimate the cost formulas for each activity. In principle, the variable cost component for each activity should correspond to resources acquired as needed and the fixed cost component should correspond to resources acquired in advance of usage. This multiple-formula approach allows managers to predict more accurately what costs ought to be for different levels of activity usage, as measured by the activity output measure. These costs can then be compared with the actual costs for purposes of assessing budgetary performance. Exhibit 20-9 illustrates an activity flexible budget. Notice that the budgeted amounts for materials, labor, and supplies are the same as those reported in Exhibit 20-8; they use the same activity output measure. The budgeted amounts for the other items differ significantly from the traditional amounts because the activity output measures differ.

Assume that the first level of drivers for Exhibit 20-9 corresponds to the actual activity usage levels. Exhibit 20-10 compares the budgeted costs for the actual activity usage levels with the actual costs. One item is on target, and the other seven items are mixed. The net outcome is a favorable variance of $18,000.

Exhibit 20-9
Activity Flexible Budget

	Driver: Direct Labor Hours			
	Formula		**Level of Activity**	
	Fixed	*Variable*	*10,000*	*20,000*
Direct materials	$ —	$10	$100,000	$200,000
Direct labor	—	8	80,000	160,000
Supplies	—	2	20,000	40,000
Subtotal	$ 0	$20	$200,000	$400,000

	Driver: Machine Hours			
	Formula		**Level of Activity**	
	Fixed	*Variable*	*8,000*	*16,000*
Maintenance	$20,000	$5.50	$ 64,000	$108,000
Power	15,000	2.00	31,000	47,000
Subtotal	$35,000	$7.50	$ 95,000	$155,000

	Driver: Number of Setups			
	Formula		**Level of Activity**	
	Fixed	*Variable*	*25*	*30*
Setups	$ —	$ 800	$ 20,000	$ 24,000
Inspections	80,000	2,100	132,500	143,000
Subtotal	$80,000	$2,900	$152,500	$167,000

	Driver: Number of Orders			
	Formula		**Level of Activity**	
	Fixed	*Variable*	*120*	*150*
Receiving	$6,000	$200	$ 30,000	$ 36,000
Total			$477,500	$758,000

The performance report in Exhibit 20-10 compares total budgeted costs for the *actual* level of activity with the total actual costs for each activity. It is also possible to compare the actual fixed activity costs with the budgeted fixed activity costs and the actual variable activity costs with the budgeted variable costs. For example, assume that the actual fixed inspection costs are $82,000 (due to a mid-year salary adjustment, reflecting a less favorable union agreement than anticipated) and that the actual variable inspection costs are $43,500. The variable and fixed budget variances for the inspection activity are computed as follows:

Activity	Actual Cost	Budgeted Cost	Variance
Inspection			
Fixed	$ 82,000	$ 80,000	$2,000 U
Variable	43,500	52,500	9,000 F
Total	$125,500	$132,500	$7,000 F

Breaking each variance into fixed and variable components provides more insight concerning the source of the variation in planned and actual expenditures.

These total variances, however, do not tell the whole story. Managers need to know where money is being wasted and where opportunities for improvement exist. Comparing budgeted activity costs for the actual level of activity with actual activity costs may have some value, but it does not reveal opportunities for improvement.[13] Nor does it reveal what improvement has occurred. If activity flexible budgeting is to be a useful tool in the contemporary manufacturing environment, then there must be a connection to the objective of continuous improvement. The connection is made by classifying activities within the budget as value-added and nonvalue-added and by identifying the standard quantities of activity driver associated with each activity. Given this information, more

Exhibit 20-10
*Activity-Based Performance Report**

	Actual Costs	Budgeted Costs	Budget Variance
Direct materials	$101,000	$100,000	$ 1,000 U
Direct labor	80,000	80,000	—
Supplies	23,500	20,000	3,500 U
Maintenance	55,000	64,000	9,000 F
Power	29,000	31,000	2,000 F
Inspections	125,500	132,500	7,000 F
Setups	21,500	20,000	1,500 U
Receiving	24,000	30,000	6,000 F
Total	$459,500	$477,500	$18,000 F

*Actual levels of cost drivers: 10,000 direct labor hours, 8,000 machine hours, 25 setups, and 120 receiving orders.

13.   Much of the material in this section is based on the following two pages: (1) Y. T. Mak and Melvin L. Roush, "Flexible Budgeting and Variance Analysis in an ABC Environment," *Accounting Horizons*, June 1994, pp.93–103. This paper argues that the basic flexible budgeting and variance analysis frameworks remain useful for cost control and performance evaluation in an ABC setting; (2) Robin C. Cooper and Robert Kaplan, "Activity-Based Systems: Measuring the Costs of Resource Usage," *Accounting Horizons*, September 1992, pp. 1–13. This paper argues that flexible budgeting in an ABC setting for nonunit-level activities is unnecessary. Our approach basically agrees with the Mak and Roush position; however, we must also confess that our fixed activity cost variance analysis reflects the insights provided by the Cooper and Kaplan paper. These insights mesh very well with the activity-based flexible budgeting framework.

detailed analyses can be made that provide managers with valuable information for planning and control.

Fixed Activity Variances: Detailed Analysis

To illustrate how fixed activity variance analysis can be expanded, we will continue to focus on inspection cost. Similar analyses would be carried out for the fixed costs of the other activities in the budget. Assume the $80,000 of budgeted fixed inspection costs represents the salaries of two inspectors, where each is paid $40,000. Thus, the $80,000 is the expected cost of resources *acquired in advance of usage* for the inspection activity. Suppose that each inspector is capable of efficiently carrying out inspections of 20 batches. The *practical activity capacity* is 40 batches, and the *fixed activity rate (SP)* is $2,000 per batch ($80,000/40).[14]

Spending and Volume Variances Exhibit 20-11, Part A, illustrates how the total flexible fixed budget variance is broken down using two levels of activity: the actual activity level acquired (practical capacity, AQ) and the value-added standard quantity of activity that should be used (SQ). We assume that inspection is a nonvalue-added activity that can be eliminated eventually; thus, SQ = 0 is the value-added standard. The volume variance in this framework has a useful economic interpretation: it is the *nonvalue-added cost* of the inspection activity. The spending variance is a *price* variance.

Unused Capacity Variance The volume variance measures the amount of improvement that is possible through analysis and management of activities. However, since the supply of the activity in question (inspections) must be acquired in blocks (one inspector at a time), it is also important to measure the demand for the activity (actual usage). When supply exceeds demand by a large enough quantity, management can take action to reduce the quantity of the activity performed. Thus, the *unused capacity variance*, the difference between activity availability and activity usage, is important information that should be provided to management. The calculation of this variance is illustrated in Exhibit 20-11, Part B. Notice that the unused capacity is 15 batches valued at $30,000. Assume that this unused capacity exists because management has been engaged in a quality improvement program which has reduced the need to inspect certain batches of products. This difference between the supply of the inspection resources and their usage should impact future spending plans (reduction of a nonvalue-added activity is labeled as favorable).

For example, we know that the supply of inspection resources is greater than its usage. Furthermore, because of the quality improvement program, we can expect this difference to persist and even become greater (with the ultimate goal of reducing the cost of inspection activity to zero). Management now must be willing to exploit the unused capacity they have created. Essentially, activity availability can be reduced and, thus, the spending on inspection can be decreased. There are several options that a manager can use to achieve this outcome. When inspection demand is reduced by five more batches, the company will need only one full-time inspector. The extra inspector could be permanently reassigned to an activity where resources are in short supply. (Even now, 75% of the inspector's time could be reassigned to other activities that are short in resources.) If reassignment is not feasible, the company should lay off the extra inspector.

---

14.   We assume that each batch requires a setup; therefore, the number of setups equals the number of batches.

Exhibit 20-11
Variance Analysis of
Fixed Activity Costs

Part A: Spending and Volume Variances

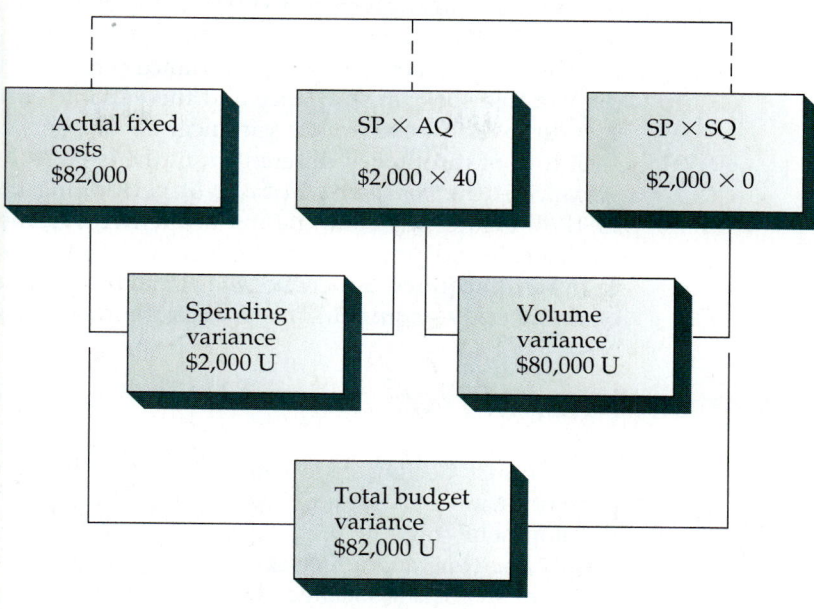

Part B: Unused Capacity Variances

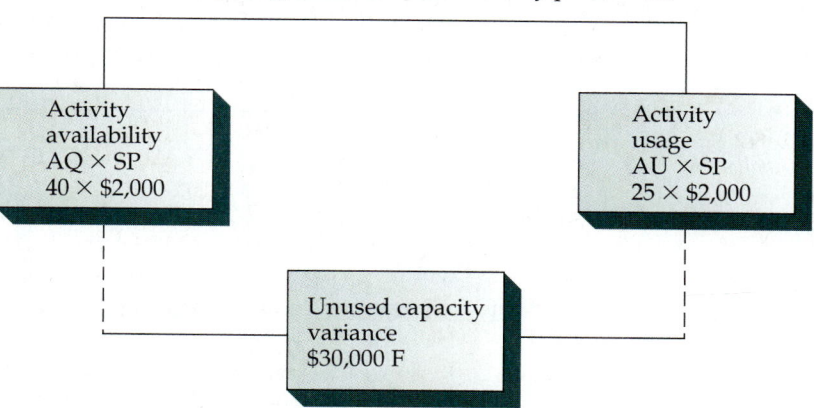

This example illustrates an important feature of activity improvement. Activity improvement can create unused capacity, but managers must be willing and able to make the tough decisions to reduce resource spending on the redundant activities to gain the potential profit increase. Profits can be increased by reducing resource spending or by transferring the resources to other activities that will generate more revenues.

Variable Activity Variances: Detailed Analysis

The analysis of variable activity variances will also be illustrated using the inspection activity. Assume that the budgeted $52,500 represents the cost of a chemical that must be used in the inspection process. This resource is acquired as needed and is therefore a variable activity cost. The budget of $52,500 is for

25 actual setups; thus, the *variable activity rate* is $52,500/25 setups = $2,100/ setup (rate is also given in Exhibit 20-9). The actual rate (AP) is the actual cost divided by the number of setups: $43,500/25 setups = $1,740 per setup.

The variable activity budget variance can be decomposed into two variances: the variable spending variance and the variable efficiency variance. The variable spending variance is a *price* variance—it can only occur if the amount paid for each unit of resource is different from the expected price. The variable efficiency variance is the *nonvalue-added cost* of performing the inspection activity. Exhibit 20-12 illustrates the computation of the two variances.

There is no unused capacity variance for variable activity cost. Since the resource is acquired as needed, the actual usage always equals the actual amount of the activity acquired. This makes the analysis simpler for variable activity costs.

LIFE CYCLE COST BUDGETING

Objective 4
Describe life cycle cost budgeting.

product life cycle

whole-life cost

The product design stage can have a significant impact on costs. In fact, 90 percent or more of the costs associated with a product are *committed* during the development stage of the product's life cycle. Recall that **product life cycle** is simply the time a product exists—from conception to abandonment. Life cycle costs are all costs associated with the product for its entire life cycle. These costs include development (planning, design, and testing), production (conversion activities), and logistics support (advertising, distribution, warranty, and so on). Because total customer satisfaction has become a vital issue in the new business setting, *whole-life cost* has emerged as the central focus of life cycle cost budgeting. **Whole-life cost** is the life cycle cost of a product plus postpurchase costs that consumers incur, including operation, support, maintenance, and disposal.[15]

Exhibit 20-12
Variance Analysis for Variable Activity Costs

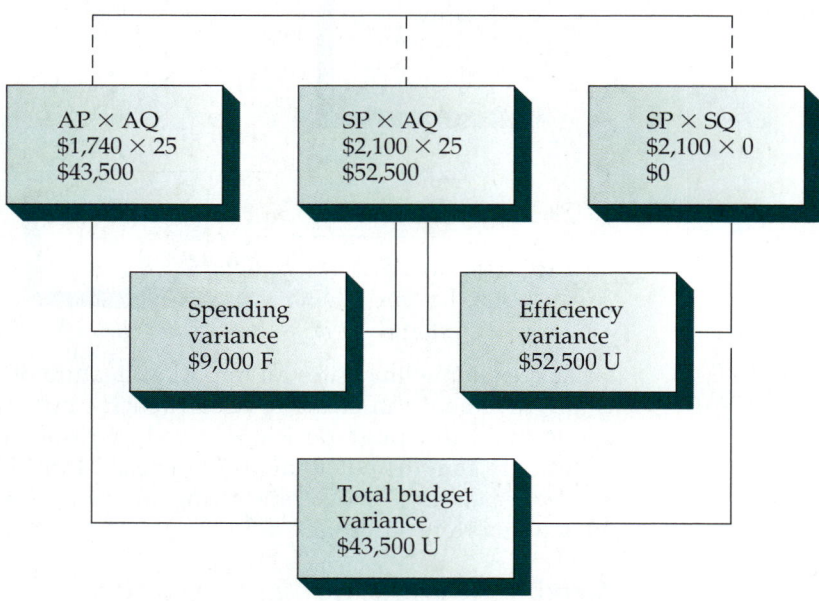

15.   It can be argued that whole life cost is an alternative definition of life cycle cost—one that includes the customer's perspective as well as the production point of view. For an excellent treatment of life cycle costing, see Michael D. Shields and S. Mark Young, "Managing Product Life Cycle Costs: An Organizational Model," *Journal of Cost Management*, Fall 1991, pp. 39–52. Many of the concepts presented in this section are based on this article.

Since the costs a purchaser incurs *after* buying a product can be a significant percentage of whole-life costs and thus an important consideration in the purchase decision, managing activities so that whole-life costs are reduced can provide an important competitive advantage.

Whole-Life Product Cost

From a whole-life point of view, product cost is made up of four major elements: (1) nonrecurring costs (planning, designing, and testing), (2) manufacturing costs, (3) logistic costs, and (4) the customer's postpurchase costs. Measuring, accumulating, and reporting all of a product's whole-life costs allows managers to better assess the effectiveness of life cycle planning and to build more effective and sophisticated marketing strategies. This assessment is accomplished by comparing actual whole-life costs with budgeted whole-life costs. Life cycle budgeting and performance reporting also increase management's ability to make good pricing decisions and to improve the assessment of product profitability. Life cycle budgeting and performance reporting are particularly important for products with short life cycles. Good planning is critical, since there is very little opportunity to make mid-cycle adjustments.

Budgeting Life Cycle Costs: An Example

Murphy Company produces electronic products that typically have about a 27-month life cycle. At the beginning of the last quarter of 1997, a new component was proposed. Design engineering believed that the product would be ready to produce by the beginning of 1998. To produce this and other similar products, resistors had to be inserted into a circuit board. Management had decided that the cost of the circuit board was driven by the number of resistor insertions. Knowing this, design engineering produced the new component using fewer insertions of resistors than the products in the past had employed.

The budgeted costs and profits for the product over its 27-month life cycle are illustrated in Exhibit 20-13. Notice that the life cycle unit cost is $10 per unit, compared with the traditional definition of $6 (which includes only the production costs) and the whole-life cost of $12. To be viable, of course, the product must cover all of its life cycle costs and produce an acceptable profit. The $15 price was set with this objective in mind. Focusing only on the $6 cost could have led to a suboptimal pricing decision. Changing the focus requires managers to move away from the traditional, financially driven definition of product cost. Traditional cost systems do not directly identify development costs with the product being developed. The whole-life cost provides even more information—information that could prove vital for the company's life cycle strategy. For example, if competitors sell a similar product for the same price but with postpurchase costs of only $1 per unit, the company could be at a competitive disadvantage. Given this information, actions can be considered that can eliminate the disadvantage (e.g., redesign of the product to lower the postpurchase costs).

Feedback on the effectiveness of life cycle planning is also helpful. This information can help future new product planning as well as be useful for assessing how design decisions affect operational and support costs. Comparing actual life cycle costs with the budgeted costs can provide useful insights. Exhibit 20-14 illustrates a simple life cycle cost performance report. As can be seen, production costs were greater than expected. Investigation revealed that costs are driven by total number of insertions, not just insertions of resistors. Further analysis also

Exhibit 20-13
Life Cycle Costing: Bud-geted Costs and Income

Unit Cost and Price Information

Unit production cost	$ 6
Unit life cycle cost	10
Unit whole-life cost	12
Budgeted unit selling price	15

Budgeted Costs

Item	1997	1998	1999	Item Total
Development costs	$200,000	$ —	$ —	$ 200,000
Production costs	—	240,000	360,000	600,000
Logistics costs	—	80,000	120,000	200,000
Annual subtotal	$200,000	$320,000	$480,000	$1,000,000
Postpurchase costs	—	80,000	120,000	200,000
Annual total	$200,000	$400,000	$600,000	$1,200,000
Units produced		40,000	60,000	

Budgeted Product Income Statements

Year	Revenues	Costs	Annual Income	Cumulative Income
1997	$ —	$(200,000)	$(200,000)	$(200,000)
1998	600,000	(320,000)	280,000	80,000
1999	900,000	(480,000)	420,000	500,000

Note: The postpurchase costs are costs incurred by the customer and so would not be included in the budgeted income statements.

revealed that by reducing the total number of insertions, postpurchase costs could be reduced. Thus, future design work on similar products can benefit by the assessment.

CONTROL AT THE OPERATING LEVEL

Objective 5
Discuss how control at the operational level in a contemporary environment differs from that in a conventional environment.

Nonfinancial measures of performance play a key role in a contemporary responsibility accounting system. In the advanced environment, operational control becomes more before the fact than after the fact. In a traditional environment, actual results are periodically compared with standards. While the comparison may be made as often as weekly or monthly, there is often a delay from the time actual performance is achieved to when it is reported to managers. Control in a contemporary environment tends to be much more timely. To achieve this change in orientation, worker involvement in the control process increases. Up front, workers are encouraged to reduce scrap, minimize the number of units reworked, and, in general, to find ways to improve the productive process and the overall quality of the goods being manufactured. In effect, operating results are reported on a real-time basis—as they happen—rather than on a delayed basis. Immediate feedback allows a quicker reaction time and increases in efficiency.

Exhibit 20-14
Performance Report:
Life Cycle Costs

Year	Item	Actual Costs	Budgeted Costs	Variance
1997	Development	$190,000	$200,000	$10,000 F
1998	Production	300,000	240,000	60,000 U
	Logistics	75,000	80,000	5,000 F
1999	Production	435,000	360,000	75,000 U
	Logistics	110,000	120,000	10,000 F

Analysis: Production costs were higher than expected because insertions of diodes and integrated circuits also drive costs (both production and postpurchase costs).
Conclusion: The design of future products should try to minimize total insertions.

Since workers relate to operational measures more readily than financial measures, such things as scrap and rework are reported on an operating as well as a financial basis. Thus, management accountants should now be involved in measuring and reporting many physical and nontraditional gauges of operational performance. Lack of involvement will likely diminish the influence of the management accountant. Involvement, on the other hand, expands the role of the management accountant. Management accountants who involve themselves in the operational process are seen as more than just providers of control information. They are also viewed as facilitators and experts on the control and measurement process.[16]

operational measures   **Operational measures** concern physical measures of input and output. For example, pounds of scrap divided by pounds of materials issued provides an operational manager and workers an idea of the amount of waste being produced. Operational measures should relate to the factors considered essential to successful competition. The measures should also motivate and support the overall objective of continuous improvement. Furthermore, the use of the measures should translate into improved financial results. Five major areas of operating control have been identified: quality, inventory, materials cost, delivery performance, and machine performance.[17] To these five, productivity probably should be added. A key success factor for a firm is customer satisfaction. Delivery performance and quality are both important measures that relate to customer satisfaction. Also important to success is manufacturing excellence. Materials cost, machine performance, inventory, and productivity all are part of manufacturing excellence.

Quality

Control of quality costs is discussed extensively in Chapter 21. The importance of control of quality cannot be overemphasized. Significant savings are available to firms if they increase the quality of their products. Operational measures of quality include defects per unit, number of defective units/total units produced, percentage of external failures, pounds of scrap per total pounds of material

---

16.   The role of controllers in developing and implementing nonfinancial performance measures is discussed in the following article: Joseph Fisher, "The Use of Nonfinancial Measures," *Journal of Cost Management,* Spring 1992, pp. 31–38. In this study, interviews with department heads and employees of five high-technology plants revealed both the diminishing role of controllers who were not involved as well as the expanded role of those who were involved. This article also serves as a source for other material presented in this section on operational measures.
17.   Robert A. Howell and Stephen R. Soucy, "Operating Controls in the New Manufacturing Environment," *Management Accounting,* October 1987, pp. 25–31.

issued, and so on. The overall objective of total quality control is zero defects. Thus, the objective of operational measures is to assess the firm's progress and to motivate workers to continue looking for ways to improve. Tracking these operational measures over time is particularly useful. Some firms display graphical reports posted on bulletin boards in operational areas. These operational measures, as well as the costs of quality, are reported and used for control purposes.

Inventory

Control of work in process and finished goods inventories also presents a firm with exceptional opportunities for savings. These savings and how they can be achieved were discussed in Chapter 13. The key to controlling these inventories is the use of JIT manufacturing and the Kanban information network. Operational measures such as inventory turnover rates, days of inventory, and number of inventoried items can be used to assess how successfully the firm is reducing inventories to reasonable levels. For example, trends in days of inventory can be assessed; if the number of days of inventory is decreasing, the trend is favorable.

Materials Cost

Materials cost presents another example of before-the-fact control. Rather than emphasizing materials price variance, the JIT firm emphasizes *quality* and *availability*. Price reductions are achieved by negotiating long-term contracts with suppliers. By becoming a regular and reliable purchaser, the JIT firm can extract price concessions and, at the same time, choose suppliers that are most reliable and willing (as well as able) to supply quality raw materials. Developing close relationships with suppliers is a key requisite for this form of control.

Productivity

Productivity concerns how efficiently inputs are used in producing output. This topic is covered thoroughly in Chapter 22. Both operational and financial measures of productivity are developed and presented. In particular, the operational measures of productivity are linked with financial measures. Nonetheless, a brief overview of operational productivity measures is offered here. Operational measures of productivity include output/materials, output/labor hours, output/kilowatt hours, and output/persons employed. Output can be units of product or it can be activity output. Using activity output measures changes in activity and process productivity. The objective is to improve productivity. This can be achieved, for example, by using less inputs to produce the same output or to produce more output with the same inputs.

Delivery Performance

As competition has increased, delivery performance has become more important. For example, Tellabs, a telecom manufacturer and customer of Motorola, wanted Motorola to improve its delivery time to 100%. Motorola responded by setting up two stores on Tellabs premises. This cut delivery time from 50 days to less than 24 hours. The improved delivery time also allowed Tellabs to quote lead times that were often half that of its competitors. Furthermore, Motorola's sales to Tellabs increased from $1.7 million in 1993 to $4.5 million in 1994.[18]

18.   Managing, "Corporate Reputations," *Fortune*, March 6, 1995, pp. 57–58.

There are two dimensions to delivery performance: *reliability* and *responsiveness*. Reliability concerns the ability to meet promised delivery dates. Responsiveness, on the other hand, concerns the lead time required to fill an order. Both are important to successful competition.

Reliability   One measure of delivery performance is *on-time delivery*. To measure on-time delivery, a firm sets delivery dates and then finds on-time delivery performance by dividing the orders delivered on time by the total number of orders delivered. The goal, of course, is to achieve a ratio of 100 percent. Some have found, however, that this measure used by itself may produce undesirable behavioral consequences.[19] Specifically, plant managers were giving priority of filling orders *not yet late* over orders that were already late. The performance measure was encouraging managers to have one very late shipment rather than several moderately late shipments! A chart measuring the age of late deliveries may help mitigate this problem.

Cycle Time and Velocity: Measures of Responsiveness   Delivering on time is an important measure of delivery performance but perhaps not the most important. The length of time required to fill a customer's order may be even more critical. Cycle time and velocity are even more essential measures because they assess the ability of a company to respond to a customer's requests. **Cycle time** is the length of time it takes to manufacture a product (time divided by units produced). **Velocity** is the number of units that can be produced in a given period of time. Both velocity and cycle time are used to measure the time it takes a product to move through a cell.

cycle time

velocity

Velocity and cycle time have become important operational measures of performance because of the increased emphasis on time-based capabilities. In fact, time-based capabilities may be one of the more critical competitive dimensions for firms in the 1990s. If this is true, then these time-based measures and others may receive increased attention.

Incentives can be used to encourage operational managers to reduce cycle time or increase velocity and thus improve delivery performance. A natural way to accomplish this objective is to tie product costs to cycle time and reward operational managers for reducing product costs. For example, cell conversion costs can be assigned to products on the basis of the time that it takes a product to move through the cell. Using the theoretical productive time available for a period (in minutes), a value-added standard cost per minute can be computed.

$$\text{Standard cost per minute} = \text{Cell conversion costs/Minutes available}$$

To obtain the conversion cost per unit, this standard cost per minute is multiplied by the actual cycle time used to produce the units during the period. By comparing the unit cost computed using the actual cycle time with the unit cost possible using the theoretical or optimal cycle time, a manager can assess the potential for improvement. Note that the more time it takes a product to move through the cell, the greater the unit product cost. With incentives to reduce product cost, this approach to product costing encourages operational managers and cell workers to find ways to decrease cycle time or increase velocity.

An example can be used to illustrate the concepts. Assume that a company has the following data for one of its manufacturing cells:

19.   See Joseph Fisher, "Nonfinancial Performance Measures," pp. 34–35.

Theoretical velocity: 12 units per hour
Productive minutes available (per year): 400,000
Annual conversion costs: $1,600,000
Actual velocity: 10 units per hour

The actual and theoretical conversion costs per unit are shown in Exhibit 20-15. Notice from Exhibit 20-15 that the per-unit conversion cost can be reduced from $24 to $20 by decreasing cycle time from six minutes per unit to five minutes per unit (or increasing velocity from ten units per hour to twelve units per hour). At the same time, the objective of improving delivery performance is achieved.

Manufacturing Cycle Efficiency Another time-based operational measure calculates manufacturing cycle efficiency (MCE) as follows:

$$MCE = \text{Processing time}/(\text{Processing time} + \text{Move time} + \text{Inspection time} + \text{Waiting time})$$

where processing time is the time it takes to convert raw materials into a finished good. The other activities have been defined earlier in the chapter and were identified as nonvalue-added activities. Processing, on the other hand, is a value-added activity. Thus, the ideal is to eliminate the nonvalue-added activities by reducing to zero the time spent on them. If this is accomplished, the value of MCE would be 1.0. As MCE improves (moves toward 1.0), cycle time decreases. Furthermore, since the only way MCE can improve is by decreasing the nonvalue-added activities, cost reduction must also follow.[20]

To illustrate MCE, let's use the data from Exhibit 20-15. The actual cycle time is 6.0 minutes, and the theoretical cycle time is 5.0 minutes. Thus, the time attributable to nonvalue-added activities is 1.0 minute (6.0 − 5.0), and MCE is computed as shown at the top of the following page.

Exhibit 20-15
Conversion Cost Computations

Actual Conversion Cost per Unit

$$\text{Standard cost per minute} = \$1,600,000/400,000$$
$$= \$4 \text{ per minute}$$
$$\text{Actual cycle time} = 60 \text{ minutes}/10 \text{ units}$$
$$= 6 \text{ minutes per unit}$$
$$\text{Actual conversion cost} = \$4 \times 6$$
$$= \$24 \text{ per unit}$$

Theoretical (Ideal) Conversion Cost per Unit

$$\text{Theoretical cycle time} = 60 \text{ minutes}/12 \text{ units}$$
$$= 5 \text{ minutes per unit}$$
$$\text{Ideal conversion cost} = \$4 \times 5$$
$$= \$20 \text{ per unit}$$

20. The source for this measure is Berliner and Brimson, *Cost Management for Today's Advanced Manufacturing*.

$$MCE = 5.0/6.0$$
$$= 0.83$$

Actually, this is a fairly efficient process, as measured by MCE. Many manufacturing companies have MCEs less than 0.10.[21]

Machine Performance

In a JIT environment, machine performance receives increased attention. Equipment can be placed into one of two categories: *nonbottleneck equipment* and *bottleneck equipment*. Bottleneck equipment is critical for production, and the demand for its services is the greatest (often more than it can handle, thus the label *bottleneck*). When equipment in this category is down, it usually means an interruption in production. For a JIT firm, this downtime can be costly, since there are no inventories to buffer interruptions in production. Thus, great efforts are made to ensure that machinery in this category is available and utilized. When available, one would expect bottleneck equipment to be utilized 100 percent of the time.

For nonbottleneck equipment, machine availability is the relevant performance measure, not machine utilization. This equipment is not needed all the time and thus should not be used constantly. Using machine utilization as the measure encourages unnecessary production and, thus, the buildup of inventories. However, when needed, the equipment should be available; thus, availability is important for all equipment.

Machine utilization and machine availability are both operational, nonfinancial measures. In addition to these measures, detailed maintenance records can help managers monitor the care that equipment is receiving.

Operational Measures: A Qualification

Operational measures can be of tremendous value. They can be produced quickly and can be expressed in terms that operational personnel can readily understand. These measures, if used in isolation, can be detrimental to the firm's overall objectives. Operational measures may actually conflict—for instance, increasing material productivity may cause a decline in labor productivity. Yet encouraging this outcome may be much better than increasing both operational measures. It depends on the value of the tradeoffs. For operational measures to work, there must be a tight linkage between the operational control system and the overall objectives of the business.[22] Since the overall success of the firm is defined in financial terms, there must be a linkage between operational performance and financial performance. The profit-linked productivity measure is described in Chapter 22 and is an example of how these linkages ought to exist. By knowing the linkages, operational measures can be used to foster the achievement of the firm's strategic objectives.

For convenience, the operational measures are summarized in Exhibit 20-16. You should realize that this listing is simply a sample of possible measures and is not exhaustive by any means.

---

21.   Berliner and Brimson, *Cost Management for Today's Advanced Manufacturing*, p. 4.
22.   Kelvin Cross and Richard Lynch, "Accounting for Competitive Performance," *Journal of Cost Management*, Spring 1989, pp. 20–28.

Exhibit 20-16
Summary of Operational Measures

Quality:

Defects/Units
Number of defective units/Total units
Percentage of external failures
Pounds of scrap/Pounds of materials issued

Inventory:

Inventory turnover
Days of inventory
Number of inventoried items
Trends in days of inventory

Time-based:

Cycle time
Velocity
MCE

Productivity:

Output/Pounds of material
Output/Hours of labor
Output/Kilowatt hours
Output/Person employed

Machine performance:

Machine availability
Machine utilization

SUMMARY

The control procedures used in traditional manufacturing environments are not directly transferable to a contemporary environment. Detailed variance analysis, based on currently attainable standards, can provide incentives that are not compatible with the operating objectives found in a contemporary environment. Using materials price variances as a measure, for example, can encourage the purchase of larger lots than desirable in order to take advantage of quantity discounts or lesser quality. This behavior encourages inventories of raw materials and low-quality materials, both of which are in opposition to the objectives of zero inventories and total quality control.

Contemporary responsibility accounting focuses on managing activities rather than the costs. It recognizes that activities cause costs and that management of activities will produce more efficient outcomes. There are two dimensions that define activity-based management: the cost dimension and the process view dimension. The cost dimension is concerned with accurate assignment of activity costs to cost objects—particularly products. The second dimension—process value analysis—provides information about why work is done and how well it is done. It is concerned with activity driver analysis,

activity analysis, and performance measurement. It is this dimension that offers the connection to the concept of continuous improvement. A key element of activity-based control is activity analysis. Activity analysis is the process of identifying and describing a firm's activities, assessing their value to the organization, and selecting only those that are of value. Cost reduction is realized by decreasing, eliminating, selecting, and sharing activities. Emphasis is placed on identifying nonvalue-added costs and eliminating them. These costs are the result of unnecessary activities and inefficiencies found in necessary activities.

Activity flexible budgeting calculates costs for different levels of activities, using multiple drivers. The outcome is more accurate budgeting. Furthermore, by specifying value-added standards for the activity drivers, the budget variance can be decomposed into a variance that reflects nonvalue-added costs and price variances. For fixed activity costs, it is also possible to assess the cost of unused capacity and use this information to make resource allocation decisions.

Operational measures are increasing in importance in the contemporary manufacturing environment. At this level, there is an increased emphasis on real-time feedback and the use of operational measures. More worker involvement in the day-to-day control process is being encouraged. This involvement impacts quality, inventories, materials cost, delivery performance, productivity, and machine performance. Firms are increasing their ability to compete by decreasing the time it takes to produce and deliver a product. Time-based operational measures such as cycle time and MCE provide barometers of a firm's time-based capabilities.

REVIEW PROBLEMS AND SOLUTIONS

1.

Traditional Responsibility Versus Contemporary Responsibility

The labor standard for a company is 2.0 hours per unit produced, which includes setup time. At the beginning of the last quarter, 20,000 units had been produced and 44,000 hours used. The production manager was concerned about the prospect of reporting an unfavorable labor efficiency variance at the end of the year. Any unfavorable variance over 9 to 10 percent of the standard usually meant a negative performance rating. Bonuses were adversely affected by negative ratings. Accordingly, for the last quarter, the production manager had decided to reduce the number of setups and use longer production runs. He knew that his production workers usually were within 5 percent of standard. The real problem was with setup times. By reducing the setups, the actual hours used would be within 7 to 8 percent of the standard hours allowed.

REQUIRED:

1. Explain why the behavior of the production manager is unacceptable for a contemporary manufacturing environment.
2. Explain how a contemporary responsibility accounting approach would discourage the kind of behavior described.

Solution

1. In a contemporary manufacturing environment, efforts are made to reduce inventories and eliminate nonvalue-added costs. The production manager is focusing on meeting the labor usage standard and is ignoring the impact on inventories that longer production runs may have.
2. Contemporary responsibility focuses on activities and activity performance. For the setup activity, the value-added standard would be zero setup time and zero setup costs. Thus, avoiding setups would not save labor time and it would not affect the labor variance. Of course, labor variances themselves would not be computed—at least not at the operational level.

2.

Value-Added and Nonvalue-Added Cost Reports; Currently Attainable (Interim) Standards

Pollard Manufacturing has developed value-added standards for material usage, purchasing, and inspecting. The value-added output levels for each of the activities, their actual levels achieved, and the standard prices are as follows:

	Activity Driver	SQ	AQ	SP
Material usage	Board feet	24,000	30,000	$10
Purchasing	Purchase orders	800	1,000	50
Inspection	Inspection hours	0	4,000	12

Assume that material usage and purchasing represent resources acquired as needed and that inspection is acquired in blocks or steps of 2,000 hours. The actual prices paid for the inputs equal the standard prices.

REQUIRED:

1. Prepare a cost report that details value- and nonvalue-added costs.
2. Suppose that the company wants to reduce nonvalue-added costs by 30 percent in the coming year. Prepare interim standards that can be used to evaluate the company's progress towards this goal. How much will this save in resource spending?

Solution

1.

	Value-Added Costs	Nonvalue-Added Costs	Total
Material usage	$240,000	$ 60,000	$300,000
Purchasing	40,000	10,000	50,000
Inspection	0	48,000	48,000
Totals	$280,000	$118,000	$398,000

2.

	Interim Standards	
	Quantity	Cost
Material usage	28,200	$282,000
Purchasing	940	47,000
Inspection	2,800	33,600

If the standards are met, then the savings are as follows:

Material usage: $10 × 1,800 =	$18,000
Purchasing: $50 × 60 =	3,000
Total	$21,000

There is no reduction in resource spending for inspections because it must be purchased in steps of 2,000 and only 1,200 hours were saved—another 800 hours must be reduced before any reduction of resource spending is possible.

KEY TERMS

Activity analysis 865
Activity elimination 866
Activity flexible
   budgeting 873
Activity inputs 864
Activity output 864
Activity output measure
   864

Activity reduction 866
Activity selection 866
Activity sharing 866
Activity-based
   management (ABM) 863
Benchmarking 871
Business reengineering
   857

Cycle time 883
Driver analysis 864
Nonvalue-added activities
   865
Nonvalue-added costs
   865
Operational measures 881
Process improvement 857

Process innovation 857
Process value analysis 864
Product life cycle 878
Value-added activities 865
Value-added costs 865
Value-added standard 867
Velocity 883
Whole-life cost 878

QUESTIONS FOR WRITING AND DISCUSSION

1. Describe a traditional responsibility accounting system.
2. Describe a contemporary responsibility accounting system. How does it differ from traditional responsibility accounting?
3. Explain how materials price variances can work against the JIT objectives of zero inventories and total quality control.
4. Explain how materials usage variances can impede JIT manufacturing.
5. Traditional currently attainable standards are not compatible with the objective of continuous improvement. Do you agree? Explain your reasoning.
6. What are the two dimensions of the activity-based management model? How do they differ?
7. What is driver analysis? What role does it play in process value analysis?
8. What is meant by activity inputs? Activity output? Activity output measurement?
9. What is activity analysis? Why is this approach compatible with the goal of continuous improvement?
10. Identify and define four different ways to manage activities so that costs can be reduced.
11. What are nonvalue-added activities? Nonvalue-added costs? Give an example of each.
12. What are value-added costs?
13. Explain how value-added standards are used to identify value-added and nonvalue-added costs.
14. What is the standard cost allowed for nonvalue-added activities that are unnecessary? Explain why.
15. Explain how trend reports of nonvalue-added cost can be used.
16. Explain how benchmarking can be used to improve activity performance.
17. In controlling nonvalue-added costs, explain how activity output measures (activity drivers) can induce behavior that is either beneficial or harmful. How can value-added standards be used to reduce the possibility of dysfunctional behavior?
18. Describe the benefits of life cycle cost budgeting.
19. Explain how the use of multiple activity drivers can improve performance reports that compare actual costs with budgeted costs.
20. What is the meaning of the fixed activity volume variance? Explain how the unused capacity variance is useful to managers.
21. Why are nonfinancial measures of performance used more at the operating level?
22. In a non-JIT company, price reductions for raw materials are often obtained through the use of quantity discounts. In a JIT company, how are price reductions obtained?
23. Identify and define two operational measures of delivery performance.
24. What is cycle time? Velocity?
25. What is manufacturing cycle efficiency?
26. Explain why time-based performance measures are becoming more important.
27. Identify two operational measures of machine performance.
28. Machine performance is more important in a JIT environment than in a non-JIT environment. Do you agree? Explain.

EXERCISES AND PROBLEMS

20-1

Labor Efficiency Variance; Ethical Issues; Incentives

LO 1

Ron Booth, plant manager, was given the charge to produce 200,000 bolts used in the manufacture of jet airliners. He had two weeks to produce the units. He had received a directive from his divisional manager to give the bolt production priority over other jobs. Meeting the delivery date was crucial for renewal of a major contract with a large airplane manufacturer. Each bolt requires 15 minutes of direct labor and four ounces of metal. After producing a batch of bolts, each bolt in the batch is subjected to a stress test. Those bolts passing the stress test are placed in a carton, and the carton is stamped "inspected by inspector no. XX," where the number inserted corresponds to the ID # of the person doing the inspecting. Defective units are discarded and have no salvage value. Because of the nature of the process, rework is not possible.

At the end of the first week, the plant had produced 100,000 units and used 27,000 direct labor hours, 2,000 hours more than the standard allowed. Furthermore, 106,000 bolts had been produced and 6,000 had been rejected, creating an unfavorable materials usage variance of 24,000 ounces. Ron knew that a performance report would be prepared when the 200,000 bolts were completed. This report would compare the labor and materials used with the labor and materials allowed. Any variance in excess of 5 percent of standard would be investigated. Ron expected the same or worse performance for the coming week and was worried about a poor performance rating for him. Accordingly, at the beginning of the second week, Ron moved his inspectors to the production line (all inspectors had production experience). However, for reporting purposes, the production hours provided by inspectors would not be counted as part of direct labor. They would still appear as a separate budget item on the performance report. Additionally, Ron instructed the inspectors to pack the completed bolts in the cartons and stamp them as inspected. One inspector objected, and Ron reassigned the inspector temporarily to materials handling and gave an inspection stamp with a fabricated ID # to a line worker who was willing to stamp the cartons of bolts as inspected.

REQUIRED:

1. Explain why Ron stopped inspections on the bolts and reassigned inspectors to production and materials handling. Discuss the ethical ramifications of this decision.
2. What features in the traditional responsibility accounting system provided the incentive(s) for Ron to take the actions described?
3. What likely effect would Ron's actions have on the quality of the bolts? Was the decision justified by the need to obtain renewal of the contract—particularly if the plant returns to a normal inspection routine after the rush order is completed? Do you have any suggestions about the quality approach taken by this company?

**20-2
Traditional Control Measures**

LO 1

For each action below, describe the following: (1) what feature(s) of a traditional responsibility accounting system motivated the action and (2) the weaknesses or limitations of the control feature (include a brief discussion of the consequences of the action).

1. Cheaper, lower-quality parts were acquired by the purchasing department.
2. A large lot of raw materials is purchased to take advantage of a quantity discount.
3. To reduce the amount of rework, inspection labor was temporarily transferred to materials handling.
4. Production is increased so that idle time for direct laborers is minimized.
5. The maintenance supervisor refuses to buy a critical piece of diagnostic equipment in order to meet budget. As a result, maintenance workers are forced to focus more on repair and less on preventive care.
6. The plant manager refuses to acknowledge concerns expressed by manufacturing engineers about the efficiency of the current manufacturing procedures. After all, the plant has produced favorable labor and materials efficiency variances for the past three years. Why upset the apple cart?

**20-3
Traditional Versus Contemporary Responsibility Accounting**

LO 1

Consider the following three quotes taken from within the chapter:

"A revenue increase of 15% over last year and 5% ahead of budget is not such good news when the market grew 30% and our leading competitor increased its sales by 40%."

"The system converts materials into product, not people at workstations. Therefore, process efficiency is more important than labor efficiency. . . ."

"Costs not reported are invisible and are all but ignored in the management process."

REQUIRED: Discuss how these comments can be viewed as criticisms of traditional responsibility accounting, and then describe the features of a contemporary responsibility accounting system that address the criticisms.

20-4
Contemporary
Versus Traditional
Responsibility
Accounting
LO 1

For each of the following situations, identify which characteristic (A or B) is descriptive of contemporary responsibility accounting and which is descriptive of traditional responsibility accounting. Provide a brief commentary on the differences between the two systems for each situation, addressing the advantages of the contemporary view over the traditional view.

Situation 1:
A: Control point focuses on processes and teams.
B: Control point focuses on organizational units and individuals.

Situation 2:
A: Rewards are group-based and are based on multidimensional performance.
B: Individuals are rewarded based on budgetary performance.

Situation 3:
A: Assumes that activities can be collected into independent subgroups.
B: Assumes that activities are linked.

Situation 4:
A: The focus is the organization.
B: The focus is individuals.

Situation 5:
A: Performance is measured by comparing actual financial outcomes with budgeted financial outcomes.
B: Performance is measured by a blend of financial and nonfinancial factors, all of which relate to process performance characteristics such as time, quality, cost, and efficiency.

Situation 6:
A: The control emphasis is costs.
B: The control emphasis is activities.

Situation 7:
A: Standards are engineered and tend to be static.
B: Standards are optimal, dynamic, and process-oriented.

Situation 8:
A: The focus is both internal and external.
B: The focus is mostly internal.

20-5
Driver Analysis;
Activity Analysis
LO 2

For each of the following situations, provide the following information:

a. An estimate of the nonvalue-added cost caused by each activity.
b. The root causes of the activity cost.
c. The cost reduction measures: activity elimination, activity reduction, activity sharing, or activity selection.

Situation 1. It takes 30 minutes and five pounds of material to produce a product using a traditional manufacturing process. A process reengineering study provided a new manufacturing process design (using existing technology) that would take 15 minutes and four pounds of material. The cost per labor hour is $12, and the cost per pound of materials is $8.

Situation 2. With its original design, a product requires five hours of setup time. Redesigning the product could reduce the setup time to an absolute minimum of 30 minutes. The cost per hour of setup time is $500.

Situation 3. A product currently requires eight moves. By redesigning the manufacturing layout, the number of moves can be reduced from eight to zero. The cost per move is $10.

Situation 4. Expediting time for a plant is 8,000 hours per year. The cost of expediting consists of a 50% overtime labor premium for each expediting hour plus the salary of one person (an expeditor) who works in scheduling. The wage rate is $10 per hour, and the salary is $27,000. A JIT purchasing and manufacturing system with cellular manufacturing eliminated the need for expediting.

Situation 5. Each unit of a product requires five components. The average number of components is 5.3, due to component failure, requiring rework, and extra components. By developing relations with the right suppliers and increasing the quality of the purchased component, the average number of components can be reduced to five components per unit. The cost per component is $600.

Situation 6. A plant produces 100 different electronic products. Each product requires an average of eight components that are purchased externally. The components are different for each part. By redesigning the products, it is possible to produce the 100 products so that they all have four components in common. This will reduce the demand for purchasing, receiving, and paying bills. Estimated savings from the reduced demand are $900,000 per year.

20-6
Calculation of Value-Added and Nonvalue-Added Costs; Unused Capacity
LO 2, 3

Truman Water Products produces a variety of products for water sports. The company uses a conventional, departmental structure. After a careful study, the company decided that the number of shipping orders was a good activity driver for shipping costs. During the last year, the company incurred fixed shipping costs of $192,000 (salaries of eight employees) and also spent an average of $8 per order for variable shipping costs. Management decided that the value-added standard number of shipping orders is 16,000. The number of orders is a function of the size of the order. Truman has a minimum order size policy, and this policy, in combination with Truman's market share goal, was a vital input for determining the value-added quantity. Much of the nonvalue-added cost occurs because Truman does not enforce its minimum order size policy. The fixed costs provide a capacity of processing 32,000 orders (4,000 per employee at practical capacity). Assume that the actual shipping orders processed were 28,000. Also assume that the cost formula above is a good predictor of shipping costs.

REQUIRED:

1. Calculate the cost of unused capacity for shipping.
2. Calculate the value-added and nonvalue-added costs for shipping.
3. Prepare a report that presents value-added, nonvalue-added, and actual costs. Explain why highlighting the nonvalue-added costs is important.

20-7
Cost Report; Value-Added and Nonvalue-Added Costs
LO 2

Chesser Company has developed value-added standards for four activities: performing setups, administering parts, running machines, and assembling components. The activities, the activity driver, the value-added and actual quantities, and the price standards are given below for 1997.

Activities	Activity Driver	SQ	AQ	SP
Performing setups	Setups	750	1,050	$450
Administering parts	Parts	12,000	12,750	15
Running machines	Machine hours	90,000	99,000	9
Assembling components	Labor hours	30,000	37,500	10

The actual prices paid per unit of each activity driver were equal to the standard prices.

REQUIRED:

1. Prepare a cost report that lists the value-added costs, nonvalue-added costs, and actual costs for each activity.
2. Which of the four activities are nonvalue-added? Explain how it is possible to have nonvalue-added costs for value-added activities.

20-8
Trend Report:
Nonvalue-Added
Costs
LO 2

Refer to **20-7**. Suppose that Chesser Company used an activity analysis program during 1998 in an effort to reduce nonvalue-added costs. The value-added standards, actual quantities, and prices for 1998 are given below.

Activities	Activity Driver	SQ	AQ	SP
Performing setups	Setups	750	900	$450
Administering parts	Parts	12,000	11,700	15
Running machines	Machine hours	90,000	93,000	9
Assembling components	Labor hours	30,000	39,000	10

REQUIRED:

1. Prepare a report that compares the nonvalue-added costs for 1998 with those of 1997.
2. Comment on the value of a trend report.

20-9
Activity Analysis,
Activity Drivers,
Driver Analysis,
and Behavioral
Effects
LO 2

Kenzie Vest, controller of Riqueza Company, has been helping an outside consulting group install a contemporary cost management system. This new accounting system is being designed to support the company's efforts of becoming more competitive (by creating a competitive advantage). For the past two weeks, Kenzie has been identifying activities, associating workers with activities, and assessing the time and resources consumed by individual activities. Now she and the consulting group have entered into the fourth phase of activity analysis: assessing value content. At this stage, Kenzie and the consultants also plan to identify drivers for assigning costs to cost objects. Furthermore, as a preliminary step to improving activity efficiency, they decided to identify potential root causes of activity costs. Kenzie's assignment for today is to assess the value content of five activities, choose a suitable activity driver, and identify the possible root causes of the activities. Listed below are the five activities she is investigating along with possible activity drivers.

Activity	Possible Activity Drivers
Setting up equipment	Setup time, number of setups
Creating scrap	Pounds of scrap, number of defective units
Running machines	Machine hours, labor hours
Materials handling	Number of moves, distance moved
Incoming inspection	Hours of inspection, number of defective parts

Kenzie ran a regression analysis for each potential activity driver, using the method of least squares to estimate the variable and fixed cost components. In all five cases, costs were highly correlated with the potential drivers. Thus, all drivers appeared to be good candidates for assigning costs to products. The company plans to reward production managers for reducing product costs.

REQUIRED:

1. For each activity, assess the value content and classify each activity as value-added or nonvalue-added. Identify some possible root causes of each activity and describe how

this knowledge can be used to improve activity management. For purposes of discussion, assume that the value-added activities are not performed with perfect efficiency.

2. Describe the behavior that each activity driver will encourage, and evaluate the suitability of that behavior for the company's objective of creating a sustainable competitive advantage.

20-10
Value-Added and
Interim Standards;
Nonvalue-Added
Costs; Volume
Variance; Unused
Capacity
LO 2, 3

Clement Mallett, vice president of Suegros Company (a producer of a variety of plastic products), has been supervising the implementation of a contemporary cost management system. One of Clement's objectives is to improve process efficiency by improving the activities that define the processes. To illustrate the potential of the new system to the president, Clement has decided to focus on two processes: production and customer service. Within each process, one activity will be selected for improvement: material usage for production and sustaining engineering for customer service (sustaining engineers are responsible for redesigning products based on customer needs and feedback). Value-added standards are identified for each activity. For material usage, the value-added standard calls for 6 pounds per unit of output. (Although the plastic products differ in shape and function, their size, as measured by weight, is uniform.) The value-added standard is based on the elimination of all waste due to defective molds. The standard price of materials is $5 per pound. For sustaining engineering, the standard is 50% of current practical activity capacity. This standard is based on the fact that about half of the complaints have to do with design features that could have been avoided or anticipated by the company. Current practical capacity (at the end of 1997) is defined by the following requirements: 3,000 engineering hours for each product group that has been on the market or in development for five years or less and 1,200 hours per product group of more than five years. Four product groups have fewer than five years' experience, and ten product groups have more. There are twelve engineers, each paid a salary of $50,000. Each engineer can provide 2,000 hours of service per year. There are no other significant costs for the engineering activity.

Actual material usage for 1997 was 20 percent above the level called for by the value-added standard; engineering usage was 23,000 hours. There were 40,000 units of output produced. Clement and the operational managers have selected some improvement measures that promise to reduce nonvalue-added activity usage by 30 percent in 1998. Selected actual results achieved for 1998 are as follows:

Units produced	40,000
Materials used	292,400
Engineering hours	17,700

The actual prices paid for materials and engineering hours are identical to the standard or budgeted prices.

REQUIRED:

1. For 1997, calculate the nonvalue-added usage and costs for material usage and sustaining engineering. Also calculate the cost of unused capacity for the engineering activity.

2. Using the targeted reduction, establish interim standards for materials and engineering (for 1998).

3. Using the interim standards prepared in Requirement 2, compute the 1998 usage variances, expressed in both physical and financial measures, for materials and engineering. (For engineering, compare actual resource usage with the interim (current) standard and explain why you do this.) Comment on the company's ability to achieve its

targeted reductions. In particular, discuss what measures the company must take to capture any realized reductions in resource usage.

20-11

Benchmarking and Nonvalue-Added Costs

LO 2

Medco Products has two plants that manufacture a line of wheelchairs. One plant is located in Sioux City, and the second plant is located in St. Louis. Each plant is set up as a profit center. During the past year, both plants sold the regular model for $340. Sales volume averages 10,000 units per year in each plant. Recently, the Sioux City plant reduced the price of the regular model to $300. Discussion with the Sioux City manager revealed that the price reduction was possible because the plant had reduced its manufacturing and selling costs by reducing what were called nonvalue-added costs. The Sioux City plant manufacturing and selling costs for the regular chair were $260 per unit. The Sioux City manager offered to loan the St. Louis plant his cost accounting manager to help the St. Louis plant achieve similar results. The St. Louis plant manager readily agreed, knowing that his plant must keep pace—not only with the Sioux City plant but also with competitors. A local competitor had also reduced its price on a similar model, and St. Louis's marketing manager indicated that the price must be matched or sales will drop dramatically. In fact, the marketing manager suggested that if the price is dropped to $290 by the end of the year, then the plant could expand its share of the market by 20%. The plant manager agreed but insisted that the current profit per unit must be maintained and wants to know if the plant can at least match the $260-per-unit cost of the Sioux City plant. He also wants to know if the plant can achieve the cost reduction using the approach of the Sioux City plant. The plant controller and the Sioux City cost accounting manager have assembled the following data for the most recent year. The actual cost of inputs, their value-added (ideal) quantity levels, and the actual quantity levels are provided (for production of 10,000 units). Assume there is no difference between actual prices of activity units and standard prices.

	SQ	AQ	Actual Cost
Materials (lbs.)	237,500	250,000	$1,500,000
Labor (hrs.)	57,000	60,000	750,000
Setups (hrs.)	—	4,000	150,000
Materials handling (moves)	—	10,000	100,000
Warranties (number repaired)	—	10,000	500,000
Total			$3,000,000

REQUIRED:

1. Calculate the target cost for expanding the St. Louis plant's market share by 20%, assuming that the per-unit profitability is maintained as requested by the plant manager.
2. Calculate the nonvalue-added cost per unit. Assuming that nonvalue-added costs can be reduced to zero, can the St. Louis plant match the Sioux City plant's per-unit cost? Can the target cost for expanding market share be achieved? What actions would you take if you were the plant manager?
3. Describe the role benchmarking played in the effort of the St. Louis plant to protect and improve its competitive position.

20-12

Flexible Budgeting with Multiple Drivers

LO 3

The following activities and drivers have been identified:

Activity	Output Measure (Driver)
Using materials	Units produced
Handling materials	Number of moves
Training employees	Number of persons

Using the method of least squares, the following cost formulas have been developed:

$$\text{Materials cost} = \$10X$$
$$\text{Materials-handling cost} = \$100Y$$
$$\text{Training cost} = \$50,000 + \$200Z$$

The variables in each equation correspond to the value chosen for the appropriate activity output measure.

For the coming month, the company has estimated three possible levels of activity.

	Level 1	Level 2	Level 3
Units produced	40,000	60,000	80,000
Number of moves	100	120	150
Number of persons	30	40	45

REQUIRED: Prepare a flexible budget for the three levels of activity using the cost formulas.

20-13
Life Cycle
Budgeting
LO 4

Bill Austin, president of Electron Components, Inc., just completed examining a projected profit summary for two components that would be used in stereo units. Both units were still in a very preliminary planning stage, and a decision had to be made regarding their continued viability. The components would be developed, produced, and sold at the same time. Each product's life cycle is thirty months. The projected profit performance of the two items promised a return on sales of 8 percent—less than the 14 percent rate set by company standards. From the statements below, it appeared to Bill that the culprit was Component S11—its gross profit percentage was much lower than that of Component S10. Component S11 simply did not contribute enough to help cover the period costs.

	Component S10	Component S11	Total
Sales	$1,000,000	$1,000,000	$2,000,000
Cost of goods sold	(500,000)	(700,000)	(1,200,000)
Gross profit	$ 500,000	$ 300,000	$ 800,000
Research and development expenses			(500,000)
Selling expenses			(140,000)
Profit before taxes			$ 160,000

REQUIRED:

1. Explain why Bill may be wrong in his assessment of the relative performances of the two products. What change in the company's life cycle budgeting approach would you suggest?
2. Suppose that the 80 percent of the R&D and selling expenses are traceable to Component S10. Prepare budgeted life cycle income statements for each product, and calculate the return on sales. What does this tell you about the importance of accurate life cycle budgeting? Managerial product costing?
3. Explain why whole-life cost may be a better measure of managerial product cost than life cycle cost. Explain why life cycle cost budgeting should encompass the firm's value chain.

20-14
Cycle Time and Velocity; Conversion Cost Per Unit; MCE
LO 5

A manufacturing cell has the theoretical capability to produce 60,000 space heaters per quarter. The conversion cost per quarter is $300,000. There are 20,000 production hours available within the cell per quarter.

REQUIRED:

1. Compute the theoretical velocity (per hour) and the theoretical cycle time (minutes per unit produced).
2. Compute the ideal amount of conversion cost that will be assigned per heater.
3. Suppose the actual time required to produce a heater is thirty minutes. Compute the amount of conversion cost actually assigned to each speaker. Discuss how this approach to assigning conversion cost can improve delivery time.
4. Calculate MCE. How much nonvalue-added time is being used? How much is it costing per heater?
5. Cycle time, velocity, MCE, conversion cost per unit (Theoretical conversion rate × Actual conversion time), and nonvalue-added costs are all measures of performance for the cell process. Discuss the incentives provided by these measures.

20-15
Manufacturing Cycle Efficiency
LO 2, 5

A company makes a product that experiences the following activities and times:

Scheduling	2 hours
Processing (two departments)	15 hours
Moving (three moves)	4 hours
Inspecting	1 hour
Waiting (for the second process)	13 hours
Storage (before delivery to customer)	15 hours

REQUIRED:

1. Compute the MCE for this product.
2. Discuss how process value analysis can help improve this efficiency measure.

20-16
Traditional Versus Contemporary Responsibility Accounting
LO 1

Continuous improvement is the governing principle of a contemporary responsibility accounting system. Listed below are several performance measures. Some of these measures would be associated with a traditional responsibility accounting system, and some would be associated with a contemporary system.

a. Materials price variances
b. Cycle time
c. Comparison of actual product costs with target costs
d. Materials quantity or efficiency variances
e. Comparison of actual product costs over time (trend reports)
f. Comparison of actual overhead costs, item by item, with the corresponding budgeted costs
g. Comparison of product costs with competitors' product costs
h. Percentage of on-time deliveries
i. Quality reports
j. Reports of value-added and nonvalue-added costs
k. Labor efficiency variances
l. Machine utilization rates
m. Days of inventory
n. Downtime
o. Manufacturing cycle efficiency (MCE)
p. Unused activity capacity variance

q. Labor rate variance
r. Using a sister plant's best practices as a performance standard

REQUIRED:

1. Classify each measure as traditional or contemporary. If traditional, discuss the measure's limitations for a contemporary environment. If contemporary, describe how the measure supports the objectives of a contemporary environment.
2. Classify the measures into operational and financial categories. Explain why operational measures are better for control at the shop level (production floor) than financial measures. Should any financial measures be used at the operational level?

**20-17
Activity Analysis;
Nonvalue-Added
Costs; Target Costs**
LO 3

George Metcalf, president of Thayn Business Products, was concerned about the end-of-year marketing report that he had just received from Carol Atwood, marketing manager. Carol's report called for a price decrease for the coming year on the company's business calculators. According to Carol, the price decrease was needed to maintain the company's annual sales volume. A price decrease would simply add to the declining profitability of this once very profitable product. The current selling price of $27 per unit was producing a $3-per-unit profit—sixty percent of the customary $5-per-unit profit. Foreign competitors kept reducing their prices, forcing Thayn to follow suit. To match the latest prices offered by competitors would reduce the price from $27 to $22. This would create a loss of $2 per unit for every unit sold. George was baffled by the ability of his competitors to offer such low prices.

Having read some recent articles in business magazines about process improvement and activity management, George decided to hire a consulting firm to find out if there were problems with the company's operations. Perhaps some changes were called for. The consulting firm limited its evaluation to two processes: manufacturing and customer support. These processes and their costs were the inputs that defined the company's product costs. After two weeks, the consultant had identified the following activities and costs associated with each process:

Manufacturing process activities:	
Setting up equipment	$ 187,500
Handling materials	270,000
Inspecting product	183,000
Using materials	750,000
Using power	72,000
Using assembly labor[a]	375,000
Using other direct labor	225,000
Process total	$2,062,500
Customer support process:	
Providing engineering support	$ 180,000
Servicing customer complaints	150,000
Filling warranties	255,000
Storing goods	120,000
Expediting goods	112,500
Process total	$ 817,500
Total costs	$2,880,000[b]

[a] The integrated circuit board is inserted manually into the calculator casing.
[b] This total cost produces a unit cost of $24 for last year's sales volume.

The partner in charge of the consulting engagement indicated that a preliminary analysis showed that per-unit costs can be reduced by at least $10. Given that the marketing report indicated that the market share (sales volume) for the boards could be increased by 50 percent if the price could be reduced to $20, George became quite excited. In a phone conversation with the consulting firm, the partner in charge of the engagement assured George that significant savings were possible but only if the firm committed itself to an activity management approach with a strong effort to implement findings that would come from an extensive process value analysis. The partner also suggested that process innovation rather than process improvement might be the way to go—particularly if the firm wanted the kind of dramatic cost reductions that had been mentioned in the initial report.

REQUIRED:

1. What is activity-based management? What phases of process value analysis were provided by the consulting firm? What else remains to be done?
2. Explain the difference between process innovation and process improvement. Do you agree with the consulting partner? Should Thayn Business Products emphasize process innovation? Is there a role for process improvement if innovation is emphasized? Explain.
3. Assess the value content for each process, identifying as many nonvalue-added costs as possible. Compute the cost savings per unit that would be realized if these activities were reduced or eliminated. Was the consultant correct in his preliminary cost reduction assessment? Discuss actions that the company can take to reduce/eliminate the nonvalue-added activities. What part of process value analysis is critical for assessing these actions? Explain.
4. Compute the target cost required to maintain current market share, while earning a profit of $6 per unit. Now compute the target cost required to expand sales by 50 percent. How much cost reduction would be required to achieve each target?
5. Assume that further analysis revealed the following: switching to automated assembly would save $90,000 of engineering support and $285,000 of direct labor. Now what is the total potential cost reduction per unit available from activity analysis? With these additional reductions, can Wagner achieve the target cost to maintain current sales? To increase it by 50 percent? What form of activity analysis is this: reduction, sharing, elimination, or selection?

20-18
Life Cycle Cost Budgeting
LO 4

Gordon Toys, Inc., manufactures toys with life cycles that average three years. The first year of the three years involves product development, and the remaining two years concern production and sales. A budgeted life cycle income statement has been developed for two proposed products and is presented below. Each product will sell 400,000 units. The price has been set to yield a 50 percent gross margin ratio.

	BigJeep	3-Wheeler	Total
Sales	$8,000,000	$10,000,000	$18,000,000
Cost of goods sold	(4,000,000)	(5,000,000)	(9,000,000)
Gross margin	$4,000,000	$ 5,000,000	$ 9,000,000
Period expenses:			
Research and development			(4,000,000)
Marketing			(2,300,000)
Life cycle income			$ 2,700,000

Upon seeing the budget, Ann Turvey, president of Gordon Toys, called in Jared Smith, marketing manager, and Jim Oblad, design engineer.

Ann: These two products are earning only a 15 percent return on sales. We need 20 percent to earn an acceptable return on our investment. Can't we raise prices?

Jared: I doubt the market would bear any increase in prices. However, I will do some additional research and see what's possible. The gross profit ratio is already high. The problem appears to be with R&D. Those expenses seem higher than normal.

Jim: These products are more complex than usual and we need to have the extra resources—at least if you want to have these toys function as we are claiming they will. Also, we are charting some new waters with the features these products are offering. Specifically, our design is intended to reduce the postpurchase costs that consumers incur, including operation, support, maintenance, and disposal. Jared, if you recall, you mentioned to us a year ago that our competitors were providing products that had lower postpurchase costs. This new design was intended to make us market leaders in this area. At any rate, in the future, we can probably get by on less—after we gain some experience. But it wouldn't be much less—perhaps $50,000.

Ann: That would still allow us to earn only about 15.6 percent—even after you get more proficient. Maybe we ought to stay with our more standard features.

Jared: Before we abandon these two new toys, perhaps we ought to look at each product individually. Maybe one could be retained. These new features will give us an edge in the market. Also, I'll bet Jim could redesign the product so that production costs could be lowered—if he knew what was driving those costs. I'm concerned that our competitors will exploit their postpurchase cost advantage. We really need to be leaders in this postpurchase area—our reputation is at stake. If we're not careful, we could begin losing market share.

REQUIRED:

1. What specific improvements would you suggest to Ann to improve Gordon's life cycle cost budgeting?
2. Assume that the "period" expenses are traceable to each product. BigJeep is responsible for 60 percent of R&D costs and 50% of marketing costs. Prepare a revised income statement for each product. Based on this analysis, should either product be produced?
3. Based on the revised income statements (from Requirement 2), how much must production costs be reduced to make each product acceptable? Discuss how process value analysis can help achieve this outcome. Explain why this should occur now, not after the products are in production.
4. According to Jim, the motivation for the new design was to reduce the postpurchase costs of the new products. Explain why whole-life cost should be the focus of life cycle cost budgeting.

20-19
Cost Report;
Value-Added and
Nonvalue-Added
Costs; Target Costs;
Activity-Based
Management

LO 3

For 1998, Barnes Company is expecting to produce and sell 200,000 video players: 180,000 units of its budget model and 20,000 units of its luxury model. This expected output is identical to the output of the year just completed. The actual quantities of activities used and actual costs associated with the production of the budget and luxury models in 1997 are as follows:

	Actual Usage		
Activity	Luxury	Budget	Actual Cost
Plastic components	112,000	728,000	$ 6,720,000
Electronic components	114,000	726,000	8,400,000
Labor (hours)	60,000	540,000	6,000,000
Power (kilowatt hours)	20,000	180,000	600,000
Receiving (orders)	10,000	36,000	1,500,000
Setups (setup time)	4,000	8,000	480,000
Materials handling (moves)	8,000	32,000	960,000
Maintenance (maintenance hours)	12,000	60,000	1,512,000
Warranty (number of defects)	1,000	11,200	1,098,000
Total			$27,270,000

Of the nine activities, five have strictly variable activity costs (representing only resources acquired as needed): plastic components, electronic components, labor, power, and warranty. Receiving, setups, materials handling, and maintenance use only resources acquired in advance of usage (representing fixed short-run costs). The available capacity (actual capacity acquired for the year) of these four activities is listed below with each activity's resource block size:

	Practical Capacity	Block Size*
Receiving	50,000 orders	1,000
Setups	16,000 setup hours	2,000
Materials handling	48,000 moves	1,200
Maintenance	75,600 hours	1,800

*Block size is defined as the number of units of the activity that must be purchased at a time. For example, for receiving, one employee can process 1,000 orders per year; thus, receiving capability must be acquired in units of 1,000.

The actual price paid per unit of input in 1997 is equal to the standard price for that year. The value-added quantities of each activity that should have been used in producing the budget and luxury models are also known.

	Value-Added Quantities		
	Luxury Model	Budget Model	Total
Plastic components	100,000	720,000	820,000
Electronic components	100,000	720,000	820,000
Labor (hours)	54,000	506,000	560,000
Power (kilowatt hours)	18,000	162,000	180,000
Receiving (orders)	2,000	8,000	10,000
Setups (setup time)	0	0	0
Materials handling (moves)	1,000	3,800	4,800
Maintenance (maintenance hours)	10,800	54,000	64,800
Warranty (defectives)	0	0	0

The selling price per unit of the luxury model is $216. The largest competitor sells a comparable unit for $190. Annette Swasey, the marketing manager for Barnes, has estimated that the company could increase its current sales from 20,000 to 30,000 units (increasing its share of the market by 50 percent) by dropping its price to $180. Rod Clark, president of Barnes, is willing to drop the price immediately if the company can increase the total profits it currently is earning on the luxury model by 10 percent. Rod is willing to implement the price reduction, however, only if the target profit can be reached by the end of 1998.

REQUIRED:

1. Prepare a cost report that details the total value- and nonvalue-added costs for 1997.
2. Compute the actual cost of producing one unit of the luxury model in 1997, excluding the unused activity capacity costs. Should unused activity capacity costs be excluded from calculating unit product cost? Explain.
3. Compute the value-added cost per unit for the luxury model.
4. What is the unit target cost for the luxury model assuming the price is lowered to $180 and the 10% increase in profits is required?
5. Refer to Requirement 4. Suppose that all cost reductions will come by eliminating nonvalue-added costs. Is it possible for the company to reach the targeted cost? To answer

this question, compute the value-added unit cost for 1998, assuming an output of 30,000 units. Explain how activity-based management would be helpful in achieving this target.

20-20
Nonvalue-Added
Costs; Unused
Capacity
LO 3

Refer to the data in **20-19**. Assume that in 1998 the sales volume for the budget model remains the same. Also assume that the price reduction for the luxury model is necessary to *maintain* current sales volume. The president agrees to implement the price change at the beginning of 1998. The company then begins an aggressive program to reduce nonvalue-added costs.

REQUIRED: Suppose that in 1998 the *usage* of nonvalue-added activity quantities is reduced by 50%. Calculate the potential savings that can be captured by all unused nonvalue-added activity quantities. Will the savings automatically be realized by reducing the nonvalue-added quantities? If not, what additional actions must management take to capture the savings?

20-21
Flexible
Budgeting;
Multiple Activity
Drivers; Variance
Analysis
LO 3

Billy Adams, controller for Westcott, Inc., prepared the following budget for manufacturing costs at two different levels of activity for 1998:

Direct Labor Hours		
	Level of Activity	
	50,000	*100,000*
Direct materials	$ 300,000	$ 600,000
Direct labor	200,000	400,000
Depreciation	100,000	100,000
Subtotal	$ 600,000	$1,100,000

Machine Hours		
	Level of Activity	
	200,000	*300,000*
Maintenance	$ 360,000	$ 510,000
Power	112,000	162,000
Subtotal	$ 472,000	$ 672,000

Material Moves		
	Level of Activity	
	20,000	*40,000*
Handling materials	$ 120,000	$ 120,000

Number of Batches Inspected		
	Level of Activity	
	100	*200*
Inspections	$ 125,000	$ 225,000
Total	$1,317,000	$2,117,000

During 1998, Westcott worked a total of 80,000 direct labor hours, used 250,000 machine hours, used 32,000 moves, and performed 120 batch inspections. The following actual costs were incurred:

Direct materials	$440,000
Direct labor	355,000
Depreciation	100,000
Maintenance	425,000
Power	142,000
Handling materials	132,500
Inspections	160,000

Westcott applies overhead using pool rates based on direct labor hours, machine hours, number of moves, and number of batches. The second level of activity (the right column in the table on the preceding page) is the practical level of activity (the available activity for resources acquired in advance of usage) and is used to compute predetermined overhead pool rates.

REQUIRED:

1. Prepare a performance report for Westcott's manufacturing costs in 1998.
2. Assume that one of the products produced by Westcott used 10,000 direct labor hours, 15,000 machine hours, and 500 moves and was produced in 5 batches. A total of 10,000 units were produced during the year. Calculate the unit manufacturing cost.
3. Assume that the value-added quantity for materials handling is zero (SQ = 0). Also assume that the materials-handling activity must be purchased in blocks (whole units) of 2,000 moves. Calculate spending, volume, and unused capacity variances, and discuss their meaning.
4. Assume that SQ = 0 is the value-added quantity of batch inspections. Calculate the variable spending and efficiency variances for inspections, and explain their meaning. Assume that actual variable inspections costs are $135,000.

20-22
Cycle Time;
Velocity; Product
Costing
LO 5

Silverman Company has a JIT system in place. Each manufacturing cell is dedicated to the production of a single product or major subassembly. One cell, dedicated to the production of guns, has four operations: machining, finishing, assembly, and qualifying (testing). The machining process is automated, using computers. In this process, the gun's frame, slide, and barrel are constructed. In finishing, sandblasting, buffing, and bluing are done. In assembly, the three parts of the gun are assembled along with the grip, the sight, the label, the magazine, and the clip. Finally, each firearm is tested using twenty rounds of ammunition.

For the coming year, the firearm cell has the following budgeted costs and cell time (both at theoretical capacity):

Budgeted conversion costs	$2,500,000
Budgeted raw materials	$3,000,000
Cell time	4,000 hours
Theoretical output	30,000 guns

During the year, the following actual results were obtained:

Actual conversion costs	$2,500,000
Actual materials	$2,600,000
Actual cell time	4,000 hours
Actual output	25,000 guns

REQUIRED:

1. Compute the velocity (number of guns per hour) that the cell can theoretically achieve. Now compute the theoretical cycle time (number of hours or minutes per gun) that it takes to produce one gun.
2. Compute the actual velocity and the actual cycle time.
3. Compute MCE. Comment on the efficiency of the operation.
4. Compute the budgeted conversion cost per minute. Using this rate, compute the conversion cost per gun if theoretical output is achieved. Using this measure, compute the conversion cost per gun for actual output. Does this product-costing approach provide an incentive for the cell manager to reduce cycle time? Explain.

20-23
Ethical
Considerations

Tim Ireland, controller of Roberts Electronics Division, was having lunch with Jimmy Jones, chief design engineer. Tim and Jimmy were good friends, having belonged to the same fraternity during their college days. The luncheon, however, was more business than pleasure.

Jimmy: Well, Tim, you indicated this morning that you have something important to tell me. I hope this isn't too serious. I don't want my weekend ruined.
Tim: Well, the matter is important. You know that at the beginning of this year, I was given the charge to estimate postpurchase costs for new products. This is not an easy task.
Jimmy: Yeah. I know. That's why I had our department supply you engineering specs on the new products—stuff like expected component life.
Tim: This new product you've been developing has a problem. According to your reports, there are two components that will wear out within about 14 months. According to your test runs, the product starts producing subpar performance during the 13th month.
Jimmy: Long enough to get us past the 12-month warranty. So why worry? There are no warranty costs for us to deal with.
Tim: Yes—but the customer then must incur substantial repair costs. And the product will have to be repaired once again before its useful life is ended. The estimated repair costs, when added to the normal life cycle costs, puts the whole-life cost above the target cost. According to the new guidelines, we are going to have to scrap this new product—at least using its current design. Perhaps you can find a new design that avoids the use of these two components—or find ways that they won't be so stressed so that they last much longer.
Jimmy: Listen, Tim. I don't have the time or the budget to redesign this product. I have to come under budget, and I have to meet the targeted production date or I'll have the divisional manager down my throat. Besides, you know that I'm up for the engineering management position at headquarters. If this project goes well, then it'll give me what I need to edge out Thompson Division's chief engineer. If I do the redesign, my opportunity for the job is gone. Help me out on this. You know how much this opportunity means to me.
Tim: I don't know what I can do. I have to file the whole-life cost report and I'm required to supply supporting documentation from marketing and engineering.
Jimmy: Well, that's easy to solve. Linda, the engineer who ran the tests on this product owes me a favor. I'll get her to redo the tests so that the data produce a 24-month reliability period for the components. That should cut your estimated repair costs in half. Would that be enough to meet the targeted whole-life costs?
Tim: Yes, but. . . .
Jimmy: Hey, don't worry. If I tell Linda that I'll push her for chief divisional engineer, she'll cooperate. No sweat. This is a one-time thing. How about it? Are you a player?

REQUIRED:

1. Assume you are Tim. What pressures does he have to comply with Jimmy's request? Do you think he should comply? Would you, if you were Tim? If not, how would you handle the situation?

2. Assume that Tim cooperates with Jimmy and covers up the design deficiency. What standards of ethical conduct for management accountants were violated? (See the IMA code described in Chapter 1.)

3. Suppose that Tim refuses to cooperate. Jimmy then gets Linda to rerun the tests anyway, with the new, more optimistic results. He then approaches you with the tests and indicates that he is sending a copy of the latest results to the divisional manager. Jimmy then indicates that he will challenge any redesign recommendations that Tim recommends. What should Tim do?

Chapter 21
Quality Costing: Measurement and Control

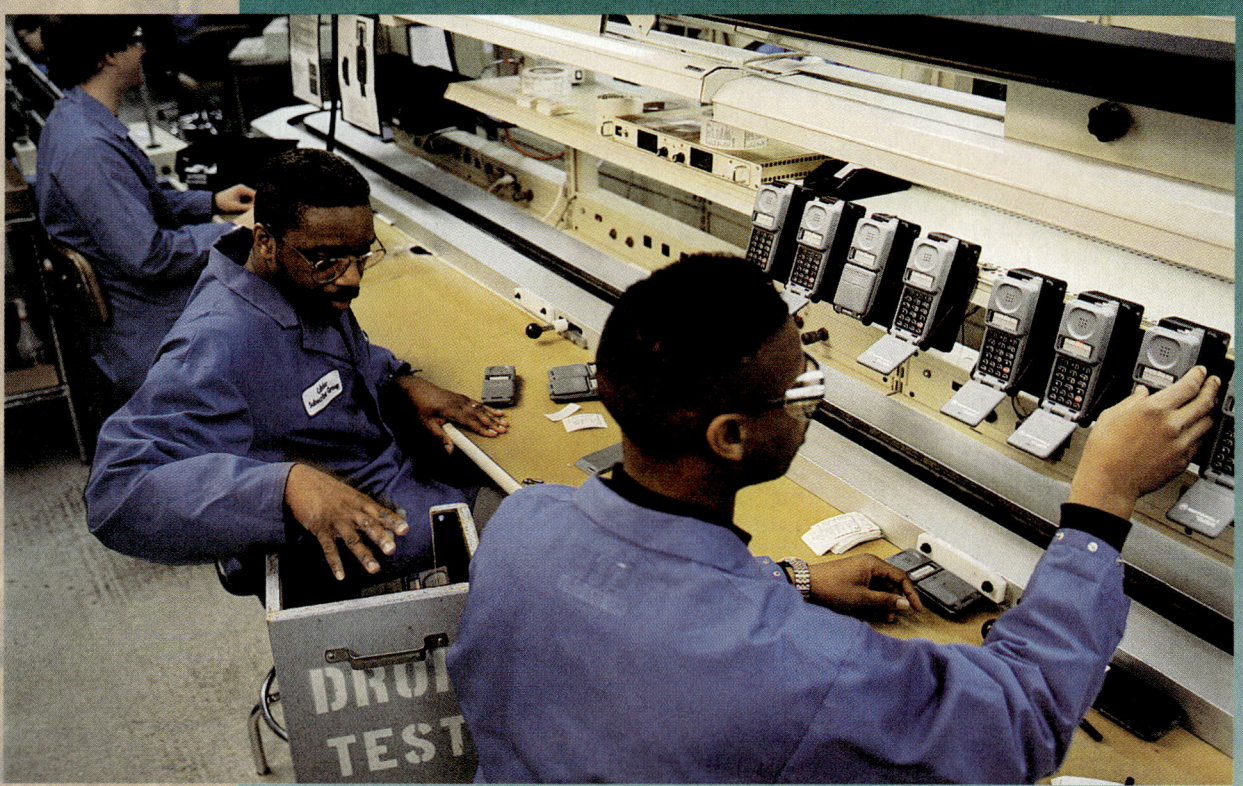

Malcolm Baldridge Award winner Motorola is a leader in total quality management. Motorola's "Six Sigma" program aims to decrease product defects to less than 4 per million.

LEARNING OBJECTIVES

After studying this chapter, you should be able to:

1. Define quality, discuss the different approaches to quality, and describe the four types of quality costs.
2. Prepare a quality cost report and explain the difference between the conventional view of acceptable quality level and the view espoused by total quality control.
3. Explain why quality cost information is needed and how it is used.
4. Describe and prepare three different types of quality performance reports.

In the last two decades, U.S. firms have faced increasing competition from foreign firms in both world and domestic markets. Often foreign firms have sold higher-quality products at lower prices, gaining market share from U.S. firms. In an effort to combat this stiff competition, U.S. firms have begun to pay increasing attention to quality. This increased attention to quality is a result of not only increased competition but also increased demands by customers for higher-quality products and services. Improving quality may actually be the key to survival for many firms. Many believe that improving quality can improve a firm's financial and competitive position. IBM, for example, is claiming that improving quality may actually be the solution to the competitive difficulties that it has been experiencing.[1]

The U.S. government has recognized the importance of quality in today's economy. One indication of the national importance of quality is the creation in 1987 of the Malcolm Baldridge National Quality Award.[2] The Baldridge award was created to recognize U.S. companies that excel in quality management and quality achievement. First given in 1988, the award categories have expanded to include: manufacturing, small business, service, educational, and health entities. Since no more than two awards are given in each category, they are difficult to achieve, and highly sought after. Past winners include: Motorola, Inc., Federal Express, Cadillac Motor Car Company, Zytec Corporation, Globe Metallurgical, Inc., Texas Instruments, Inc., and the Ritz-Carlton Hotel Company.

An emphasis on quality increases profitability in two ways: (1) by increasing customer demand and (2) by decreasing the costs of providing goods and services. Quality is important to both manufacturing and service firms. In this chapter, we will examine the costs of quality and methods of measuring and reporting these costs.

MEASURING THE COSTS OF QUALITY

Objective 1

Define quality, discuss the different approaches to quality, and describe the four types of quality costs.

The costs of quality can be substantial and a source of significant savings. Studies indicate that costs of quality for American companies are typically 20–30% of sales.[3] Yet quality experts maintain that the optimal quality level should be about two to four percent of sales. The difference between 20–30% of sales and 2–4% of sales represents a veritable gold mine of opportunity. Improving quality can produce significant improvements in profitability. Xerox Corporation, for example, over a four year period saved over $200 million by improving quality.[4]

In the last two decades, quality has become an important competitive dimension for both service and manufacturing organizations. Quality is an integrating theme for all organizations. Often foreign firms have been selling higher-quality products at lower prices. Consequently, many U.S. firms have lost market share. In an effort to combat this stiff competition, U.S. firms have begun to pay increasing attention to quality and productivity, especially because of the potential to reduce costs and improve product quality simultaneously. The senior manage-

---

1. Lawrence Carr and Thomas Tyson, "Planning Quality Cost Expenditures," *Management Accounting,* October 1992, pp. 52–56.
2. The Malcolm Baldridge National Quality Award was created by Public Law 100-107 in 1987. The first awards were given in 1988.
3. Michael R. Ostrenga, "Return on Investment Through the Cost of Quality," *Journal of Cost Management,* Summer 1991, pp. 37–44.
4. Lawrence P. Carr, "How Xerox Sustains the Cost of Quality," *Management Accounting,* August 1995, pp. 26–32.

ment of IBM Corporation, for example, has identified poor quality as the root cause of its recent problems. In an effort to solve some of these problems the company has implemented a quality program called "Market Driven Quality." The Chairman of IBM, John Akers, indicated very simply that quality improvement was a survival issue.[5] Other American companies are following suit and are striving to meet consumer quality expectations. Some are even calling this push for increased quality a "second industrial revolution."[6]

As companies like IBM implement quality improvement programs, a need arises to monitor and report on the progress of these programs. Managers need to know what quality costs are and how they are changing over time. Reporting and measuring quality performance is absolutely essential to the success of an ongoing quality improvement program. A fundamental prerequisite for this reporting is measuring the costs of quality. But to measure those costs, an operational definition of quality itself is needed.

Quality Defined

The typical dictionary definition of *quality* is the degree or grade of excellence; in this sense, quality is a relative measure of goodness. Defining quality as goodness is so general that it offers no operational content. How do we build an operational definition? The answer is by adopting a customer focus. Operationally, a **quality product or service** is one that meets or exceeds customer expectations. In effect, quality is customer satisfaction. But what is meant by customer expectations? Operationally, expectations can be described by quality attributes or what are often referred to as dimensions of quality.[7] Thus, a quality product or service is one which meets or exceeds customer expectations on the following eight dimensions:

quality product or service

1. Performance
2. Aesthetics
3. Serviceability
4. Features
5. Reliability
6. Durability
7. Conformance
8. Fitness for use

The first four dimensions describe important quality attributes, but are difficult to measure. **Performance** refers to how consistently and well a product functions. For services, the inseparability principle means that the service is performed in the presence of the customer. Thus, the performance dimension for services can be further defined by the attributes of responsiveness, assurance, and empathy. Responsiveness is simply the willingness to help customers and provide prompt, consistent service. Assurance refers to the knowledge and courtesy of employees and their ability to convey trust and confidence. Empathy means the provision of caring, individualized attention to customers. **Aesthetics** is con-

performance

aesthetics

5.   See Lawrence Carr and Thomas Tyson, "Planning Quality Cost Expenditures," p. 55.
6.   James B. Simpson and David L. Muthler, "Quality Costs: Facilitating the Quality Initiative," *Journal of Cost Management*, Spring 1987, pp. 25–34.
7.   These dimensions are based on the following two sources: Edwin S. Schecter, *Managing For World Class Quality*, ASQC Quality Press, Milwaukee, 1992 and Leonard L. Berry and A. Parasurman, *Marketing Services: Competing Through Quality*, The Free Press, Macmillan, Inc., New York, 1991, p. 16.

cerned with the appearance of tangible products (for example, style and beauty) as well as the appearance of the facilties, equipment, personnel, and communication materials associated with services. **Serviceability** has to do with the ease of maintaining and/or repairing the product. **Features (quality of design)** refer to characteristics of a product that differentiate functionally similar products. For example, the function of automobiles is to provide transportation. Yet one auto may have a four-cylinder engine, a manual transmission, vinyl seats, room to seat four passengers comfortably, and front disk brakes; another may have a six-cylinder engine, an automatic transmission, leather seats, room to seat six passengers comfortably, and anti-lock brakes. Similarly, first-class air travel and economy air travel reflect different design qualities. First-class air travel, for example, offers more leg room, better meals, and more luxurious seats. Obviously, in both cases the product features are different. Higher design quality is usually reflected in higher manufacturing costs and in higher selling prices. Quality of design helps a company determine its market. There is a market for both the four-cylinder and the six-cylinder cars as well as economy air travel and first-class air travel.

    Reliability is the probability that the product or service will perform its intended function for a specified length of time. **Durability** is defined as the length of time a product functions. **Quality of conformance** is a measure of how a product meets its specifications. For example, the specifications for a machined part may be a drilled hole that is three inches in diameter plus or minus one-eighth of an inch. Parts falling within this range are defined as conforming parts. **Fitness for use** is the suitablity of the product for carrying out its advertised functions. If there is a fundamental design flaw, the product may fail in the field even if it conforms to its specifications. Product recalls are frequently the result of fitness-for-use failures.

    Improving quality, then, means improving one or more of the eight quality dimensions while maintaining performance on the remaining dimensions. Providing a higher quality product than a competitor means outperforming the competitor on at least one dimension while matching performance on the remaining dimensions. Although all eight dimensions are important and can affect customer satisfaction, the quality attributes that are measurable tend to receive more emphasis. Conformance, in particular, is strongly emphasized. In fact, many quality experts believe that "quality is conformance" is the best operational definition. There is some logic to this position. Product specifications should explicitly consider such things as reliability, durability, fitness for use, and performance. Implicitly, a conforming product is reliable, durable, fit for use, and performs well. The product should be produced as the design specifies it; specifications should be met. Conformance, at least, is the basis for defining what is meant by a defective product.

    A **defective product** is one that does not conform to specifications. **Zero defects** means that all products conform to specifications. But what is meant by conforming to specifications? The *traditional view* of conformance assumes that there is an acceptable range of values for each specification or quality characteristic. A target value is defined, and upper and lower limits are set which describe acceptable product variation for a given quality characteristic. Any unit that falls within the limits is deemed nondefective. For example, losing or gaining zero minutes per month may be the target value for a watch, and any watch that keeps time correctly within plus or minus two minutes per month is judged acceptable. On the other hand, the *robust quality view* of conformance emphasizes fitness for use. Robustness means hitting the target value every time. There is no range in which variation is acceptable. A nondefective watch in the robust setting would be one that does not gain or lose any minutes during the month. Since evidence exists that product variation can be costly, the robust quality definition of conformance is superior to the traditional definition.

An example of the difference between the zero-defects approach and the robust quality approach can be found in two plants of the Sony Corporation. Both the Tokyo and the San Diego plants produce color television sets. One important feature of a color television set is color density. Sony sets a target value for color density as well as an upper specification limit and a lower specification limit. Any set with color density falling outside the specification limits is considered defective. Does that mean any set falling within the specification limits is acceptable? The viewpoint differs between the two plants. The San Diego plant emphasized zero defects in the traditional sense. In evaluating the quality of the color density of television sets, any television falling within the specification limits was deemed acceptable and shipped to customers. Sony of Tokyo, working with a robust quality viewpoint, strove to hit the target value for color density. Exhibit 21-1 illustrates the distribution of color density of television sets shipped from the two plants.

When Sony evaluated customer satisfaction, it found that customers preferred the reduced variation of televisions produced at the Tokyo plant. These customers reported greater satisfaction and filed fewer warranty claims.[8]

Costs of Quality Defined

costs of quality

Quality-linked activities are those activities performed because poor quality may or does exist. The costs of performing these activities are referred to as costs of quality. Thus, the **costs of quality** are the costs that exist because poor quality

Exhibit 21-1
Distribution of Color Density of Sony Television Sets

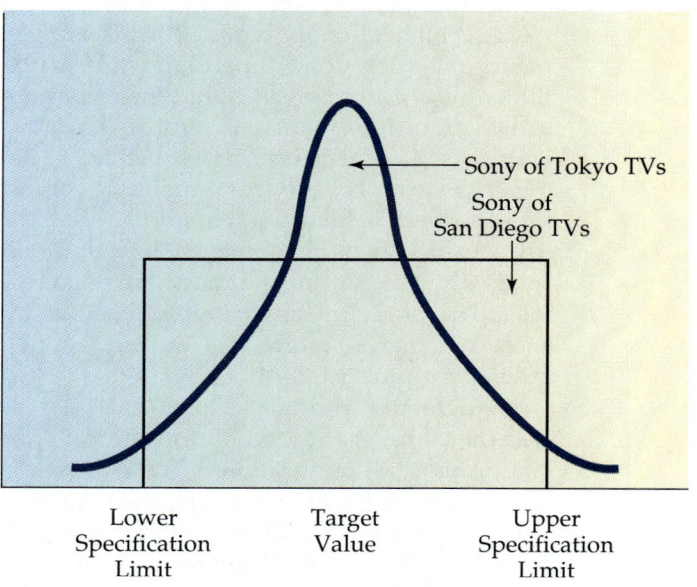

8.   For additional information, see Harold P. Roth and Thomas L. Albright, "What Are the Costs of Variability?" *Management Accounting*, June 1994, pp. 51–55; and Genichi Taguchi and Don Clausing, "Robust Quality," *Harvard Business Review*, January–February 1990, pp. 65–75.

control activities

control costs
failure activities

failure costs

prevention costs

appraisal costs

internal failure costs

external failure costs

may or does exist.[9] This definition implies that quality costs are associated with two subcategories of quality-related activities: *control activities* and *failure activities*. **Control activities** are the activities performed by an organization to prevent or detect poor quality (because poor quality *may* exist). Thus, control activities are made up of prevention and appraisal activities. **Control costs** are the costs of performing control activities. **Failure activities** are the activities performed by an organization or its customers in response to poor quality (poor quality *does* exist). If the response to poor quality occurs before delivery of a bad (nonconforming, unreliable, not durable, etc.) product to a customer, the activities are classified as internal failure activities; otherwise, they are classified as external failure activities. **Failure costs** are the costs incurred by an organization because failure activities are performed. Notice that the definition of failure activities and failure costs implies that customer response to poor quality can impose costs on an organization. The definitions of quality-related activities also imply four categories of quality costs: prevention costs, appraisal costs, internal failure costs, and external failure costs.

Prevention costs are incurred to prevent poor quality in the products or services being produced. As prevention costs increase, we would expect the costs of failure to decrease. Examples of prevention costs are quality engineering, quality training programs, quality planning, quality reporting, supplier evaluation and selection, quality audits, quality circles, field trials, and design reviews.

Appraisal costs are incurred to determine whether products and services are conforming to their requirements or customer needs. Examples include inspecting and testing raw materials, packaging, inspection, supervising appraisal activities, product acceptance, process acceptance, measurement (inspection and test) equipment, and outside endorsements. Two of these terms require further explanation.

Product acceptance involves sampling from batches of finished goods to determine whether they meet an acceptable quality level; if so, the goods are accepted. *Process acceptance* involves sampling goods while in process to see if the process is in control and producing nondefective goods; if not, the process is shut down until corrective action can be taken. The main objective of the appraisal function is to prevent nonconforming goods from being shipped to customers.

Internal failure costs are incurred because products and services do not conform to specifications or customer needs. This nonconformance is detected prior to being shipped or delivered to outside parties. These are the failures detected by appraisal activities. Examples of internal failure costs are scrap, rework, downtime (due to defects), reinspection, retesting, and design changes. These costs disappear if no defects exist.

External failure costs are incurred because products and services fail to conform to requirements or satisfy customer needs after being delivered to customers. Of all the costs of quality, this category can be the most devastating. Costs of recalls, for example, can run into the hundreds of millions of dollars. Other examples include lost sales because of poor product performance, returns and allowances because of poor quality, warranties, repair, product liability, customer dissatisfaction, lost market share, and complaint adjustment. External failure costs, like internal failure costs, disappear if no defects exist.

Exhibit 21-2 summarizes the four quality cost categories and lists specific examples of costs within each category.

9. This is the definition in Morse, Roth, and Poston, *Measuring, Planning, and Controlling*, p. 19.

Exhibit 21-2
Examples of Quality Costs by Category

Prevention Costs	Appraisal (Detection) Costs
Engineering	Inspection of raw materials
Training	Packaging inspection
Recruiting	Product acceptance
Quality audits	Process acceptance
Design reviews	Field testing
Quality circles	Continuing supplier verification
Marketing research	Prototype inspection
Vendor certification	

Internal Failure Costs	External Failure Costs
Scrap	Lost sales (performance-related)
Rework	Returns/allowances
Downtime (defect-related)	Warranties
Reinspection	Discounts due to defects
Retesting	Product liability
Design changes	Complaint adjustment
Repairs	Recalls
	Ill will

Measuring Quality Costs

observable quality costs

hidden quality costs

Quality costs can also be classified as *observable* or *hidden*. **Observable quality costs** are those that are available from an organization's accounting records. **Hidden quality costs** are opportunity costs resulting from poor quality (opportunity costs are not usually recognized in accounting records). Consider, for example, all the examples of quality costs listed in the prior section. With the exceptions of lost sales, customer dissatisfaction, and lost market share, all the quality costs are observable and should be available from the accounting records. Note also that the hidden costs are all in the external failure category. These hidden quality costs can be significant and should be estimated. Although estimating hidden quality costs is not easy, three methods have been suggested: (1) the multiplier method, (2) the market research method, and (3) the Taguchi quality loss function.

The Multiplier Method The multiplier method assumes that total failure costs is simply some multiple of measured failure costs:

Total External Failure Cost = k(Measured External Failure Costs)

The value of k, the multiplier effect, is based on experience. For example, Westinghouse Electric reports a value of k between 3 and 4.[10] Thus, if the measured external failure costs are $2,000,000, the actual external failure costs are between $6,000,000 and $8,000,000. Including hidden costs in assessing the amount of external failure costs allows management to more accurately determine the level of resource spending for prevention and appraisal activities. Specifically, with an

---

10.   T. L. Albright and P. R. Roth, "The Measurement of Quality Costs: An Alternative Paradigm," *Accounting Horizons*, June 1992, pp. 15–27. This article also describes the three approaches to measuring hidden quality costs.

increase in failure costs, we would expect management to increase its investment in control costs.

Market Research Method Formal market research methods are used to assess the effect of poor quality on sales and market share. Customer surveys and interviews with members of a company's sales force can provide significant insights into the magnitude of a company's hidden costs. Market research results can be used to project future profit losses attributable to poor quality.

Taguchi Quality Loss Function The traditional zero defects definition assumes that hidden quality costs exist only for units that fall outside the upper and lower specification limits. The **Taguchi loss function** assumes any variation from the target value of a quality characteristic causes hidden quality costs. Furthermore, the hidden quality costs increase quadratically as the actual value deviates from the target value. The Taguchi quality loss function is illustrated in Exhibit 21-3 and can be described by the following equation:

Taguchi loss function

$$L(y) = k(y - T)^2 \tag{21.1}$$

where

k = a porportionality constant dependent upon the organization's external failure cost structure
y = actual value of quality characteristic
T = target value of quality characteristic

Exhibit 21-3 reveals that the quality cost is zero at the target value and increases symmetrically, at an increasing rate, as the actual value varies from the target value. Assume, for example, that $k = \$400$ and $T = 10$ inches in diameter. Exhibit 21-4 illustrates the computation of the quality loss for four units. Notice that the cost quadruples when the deviation from target doubles (units 2 and 3). Notice

Exhibit 21-3
The Taguchi Quality Loss Function

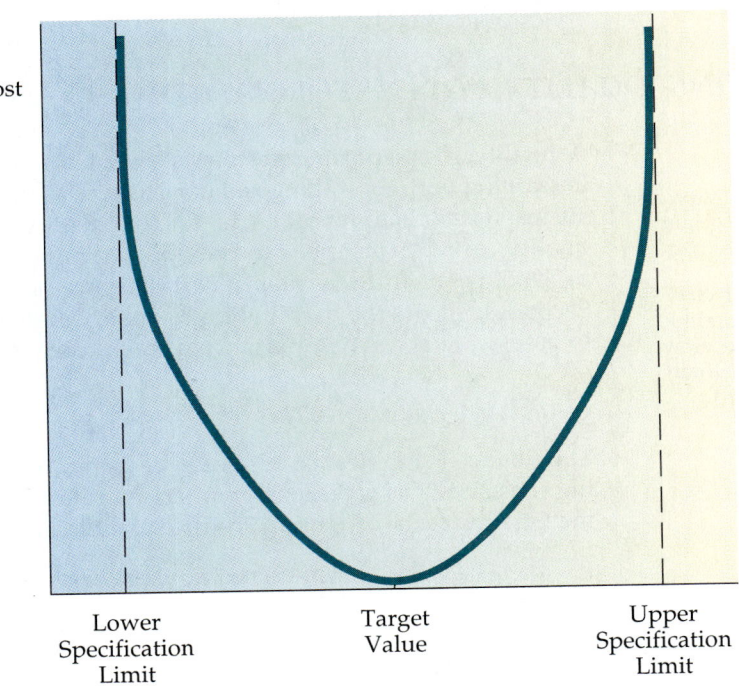

$ Cost

Lower Specification Limit

Target Value

Upper Specification Limit

Exhibit 21-4
Quality Loss Computa-tion Illustrated

Unit No.	Actual diameter (y)	y − T	(y − T)₂	k(y − T)²
1	9.9	−0.10	0.010	$ 4.00
2	10.1	0.10	0.010	4.00
3	10.2	0.20	0.040	16.00
4	9.8	−0.20	0.040	16.00
			0.100	$40.00
Average			0.025	$10.00

also that the average deviation squared and the average loss per unit can be com-puted. These averages can be used to compute the *total* expected hidden quality costs for a product. If, for example, the total units produced are 2,000 and the average squared deviation is 0.025, then the expected cost per unit is $10 (0.025 × $400) and the total expected loss for the 2,000 units would be $20,000 ($10 × 2,000).

To apply the Taguchi loss function, k must be estimated. The value for k is computed by dividing the estimated cost at one of the specification limits by the squared deviation of the limit from the target value:

$$k = c/d^2$$

where

c = loss at the lower or upper specification limit
d = distance of limit from target value

This means that we still must estimate the loss for a given deviation from the target value. The first two methods, the multiplier method or the market research method, may be used to help in this estimation (a one-time assessment need). Once k is known, the hidden quality costs can be estimated for any level of vari-ation from the target value.

REPORTING QUALITY COST INFORMATION

Objective 2
Prepare a quality cost report and explain the difference between the conventional view of acceptable quality level and the view espoused by total quality control.

A quality cost reporting system is essential if an organization is serious about improving and controlling quality costs. The first and simplest step in creating such a system is to report current actual quality costs. A detailed listing of actual quality costs by category can provide two important insights. First, it shows how much is spent in each quality cost category and its financial impact on profits. Second, it shows the distribution of quality costs by category, allowing managers to assess the relative importance of each category.

Quality Cost Reports

The financial significance of quality costs can be assessed more easily by express-ing these costs as a percentage of actual sales. Exhibit 21-5, for example, reports the quality costs of Jensen Products for fiscal 1998.[11] According to the report,

11.   The quality cost report given in Exhibit 21-5 parallels the format used by ITT except for several minor differences. First, the ITT report combines the internal and external categories into one failure category. Sec-ond, the ITT report has a third column allowing the reporting unit to express quality costs as a percentage of a measure other than sales. For more detail, see Morse, Roth, and Poston, *Measuring, Planning, and Con-trolling Quality Costs*, pp. 78–81.

Exhibit 21-5

	Jensen Products Quality Cost Report For the Year Ended March 31, 1998		
		Quality Costs	Percentage of Sales[a]
Prevention costs:			
Quality training	$35,000		
Reliability engineering	80,000	$115,000	4.11%
Appraisal costs:			
Materials inspection	$20,000		
Product acceptance	10,000		
Process acceptance	38,000	68,000	2.43
Internal failure costs:			
Scrap	$50,000		
Rework	35,000	85,000	3.04
External failure costs:			
Customer complaints	$25,000		
Warranty	25,000		
Repair	15,000	65,000	2.32
Total quality costs		$333,000	11.90%[b]

[a] Actual sales of $2,800,000.
[b] $333,000/$2,800,000 = 11.89 percent. Difference is rounding error.

quality costs represent almost 12 percent of sales. Given the rule of thumb that quality costs should be no more than about 2.5 percent, Jensen Products has ample opportunity to improve profits by decreasing quality costs. Understand, however, that reduction in costs should come through improvement of quality. Reduction of quality costs without any effort to improve quality could prove to be a disastrous strategy.

A pie chart visually depicts the relative distribution of quality costs. Exhibit 21-6 provides a pie chart based on the quality costs reported in Exhibit 21-5. Man-

Exhibit 21-6
Pie Chart: Quality Costs

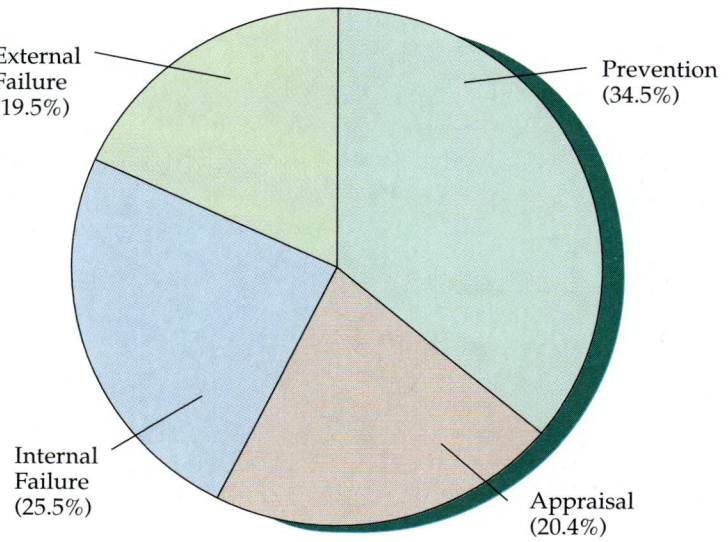

External Failure (19.5%)

Prevention (34.5%)

Internal Failure (25.5%)

Appraisal (20.4%)

agers, of course, are responsible for determining both the optimal level of quality and the relative amount that should be spent in each category. There are two views concerning optimal quality costs: the traditional view, calling for an *acceptable quality level*, and the view being adopted by contemporary firms referred to as *total quality control*. Each view offers managers insights about how quality costs ought to be managed.

Optimal Distribution of Quality Costs: Traditional View

The traditional view of quality is that there is a trade-off between control costs (prevention and appraisal) and failure costs (internal and external failure). As prevention and appraisal costs increase, failure costs should decrease. As long as the decrease in failure costs is greater than the corresponding increase in control costs, a company should continue to expand its efforts to prevent or detect non-conforming units. Eventually a point is reached at which any additional increase in this effort costs more than the corresponding reduction in failure costs. Without any change in technology, this point represents the minimum level of total quality costs. It is the optimal balance between control costs and failure costs and is illustrated in Exhibit 21-7.

In Exhibit 21-7, two cost functions are assumed: one for control costs and one for failure costs. Notice that the control cost function is downward sloping, indicating that the percentage of defective units increases as the amount spent on prevention and appraisal activities decreases. The failure cost function, on the other hand, is upward sloping, indicating that failure costs increase as the number of defective units increases. From the total quality cost function, we see that total quality costs decrease as quality improves up to a point. After that, no further improvement is possible. An optimal level of defective units is identified, and the company works to achieve this level. This level of allowable defective units is defined as the **acceptable quality level (AQL)**.

acceptable quality
level (AQL)

Exhibit 21-7
*Traditional Quality Cost
Graph*

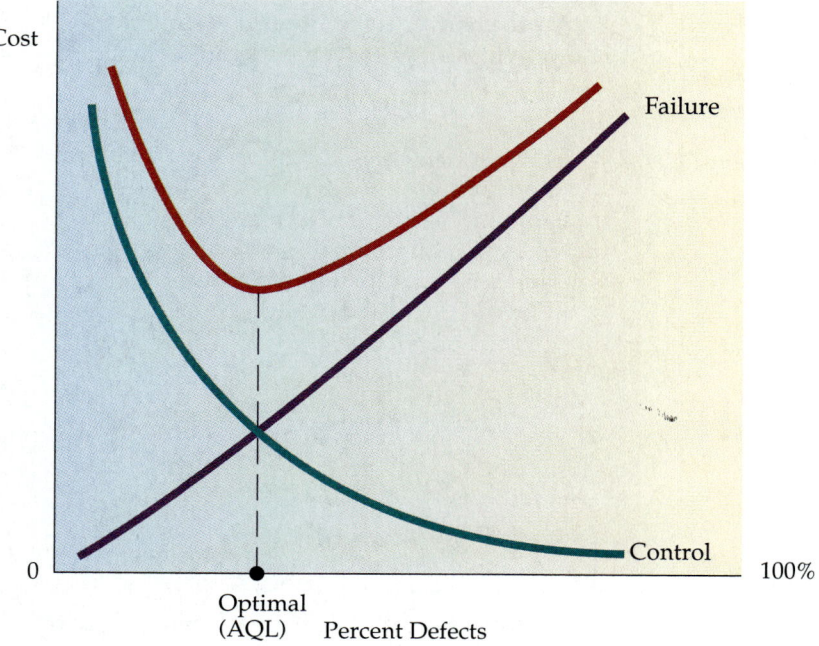

Quality Cost Function: Contemporary View

The AQL viewpoint is based on a traditional defective product definition. In the classic sense, a product is defective if it falls outside the tolerance limits for a quality characteristic. Under this view, failure costs are incurred only if the product fails to conform to specifications and an optimal tradeoff exists between failure and control costs. The AQL view permitted and, in fact, encouraged the production of a given number of defective units. This model prevailed in the quality control world until the late 1970s. In the late 1970s, the AQL model was challenged by the zero-defects model. Essentially, the zero-defects model made the claim that it was cost-beneficial to reduce nonconforming units to zero. Firms producing less and less nonconforming units became more competitive relative to firms that continued the traditional AQL model. In the mid 1980s, the zero-defects model was taken one step further by the robust quality model. The robust quality model challenged the definition of a defective unit. According to the robust view, a loss is experienced from producing products that vary from a target value and the greater the distance from the target value, the greater the loss. Furthermore, the loss is incurred even if the deviation is within the specification limits. In other words, variation from the ideal is costly, and specification limits serve no useful purpose and, in fact, may be deceptive. The zero-defects model understates the quality costs and thus the potential for savings from even greater efforts to improve quality (remember the multiplication factor of Westinghouse). Thus, the robust quality model tightened the definition of a defective unit, refined our view of quality costs, and intensified the quality race.

For firms operating in an intensely competitive environment, quality can offer an important competitive advantage. If the robust quality view is correct, then firms can capitalize on it by decreasing the number of defective units (robustly defined) while simultaneously decreasing their total quality costs. This is what appears to be happening for those firms that are striving to achieve a robust zero-defect state for their products (a robust zero-defect state is one with zero tolerance). The optimal level for quality costs is where products are produced that meet their target values. The quest to find ways to achieve the target value creates a dynamic quality world as opposed to the static quality world of AQL.

Dynamic Nature of Quality Costs   The discovery that tradeoffs among quality cost categories can be managed differently from what is implied by the relationships portrayed in Exhibit 21-7 is analogous to the discovery that inventory cost tradeoffs can be managed differently from what the traditional inventory model (EOQ) implied. Essentially, what happens is that as firms increase their prevention and appraisal costs and reduce their failure costs, they discover that they can then cut back on the prevention and appraisal costs. What initially appears to be a tradeoff turns out to be a permanent reduction in costs for all quality cost categories. Exhibit 21-8 displays the changes in quality cost relationships. A total quality cost function consistent with the quality cost relationships described is shown in Exhibit 21-8. There are some key differences. First, control costs do not increase without limit as a robust zero-defect state is approached. Second, control costs may increase and then decrease as the robust state is approached. Third, failure costs can be driven to zero.

Suppose, for example, that a firm has decided to improve the quality of its raw material inputs through the implementation of a supplier selection program. The objective is to identify and use suppliers who are willing to meet certain

Exhibit 21-8
*Contemporary Quality
Cost Graph*

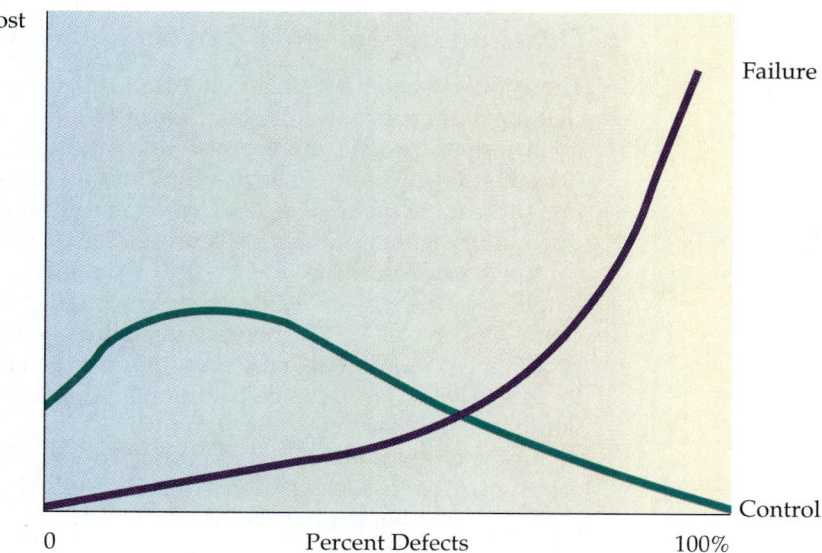

quality standards. As the firm works to implement this program, additional costs may be incurred (e.g., review of suppliers, communication with suppliers, contract negotiations, and so on). And, initially, other prevention and appraisal costs may continue at their current levels. However, once the program is fully implemented and evidence is surfacing that the failure costs are being reduced (for example, less rework, fewer customer complaints, and fewer repairs), then the company may decide to cut back on inspections of incoming raw materials, reduce the level of product acceptance activities, and so on. The net effect is a reduction in *all* quality cost categories. And quality has increased!

The example just given is consistent with the strategy to reduce quality costs as recommended by the American Society for Quality Control:[12]

The strategy for using quality costs is quite simple: (1) take direct attack on failure costs in an attempt to drive them to zero; (2) invest in the "right" prevention activities to bring about improvement; (3) reduce appraisal costs according to results achieved; and, (4) continuously evaluate and redirect prevention efforts to gain further improvement. This strategy is based on the premise that:
- *For each failure there is a* root cause.
- *Causes are* preventable.
- *Prevention is always* cheaper.

This ability to reduce total quality costs dramatically in all categories is borne out by real-world experiences. For example, Tennant Company, a manufacturer of industrial floor care products, reduced its costs of quality from 17% of sales in 1980 to 2.5% of sales in 1988 and, at the same time, significantly altered the relative distribution of the quality cost categories. In 1980, failure costs accounted for 50% of the total costs of quality (8.5% of sales) and control costs 50% (8.5% of sales). In 1988, failure costs accounted for only 15% of the total costs of quality (.375% of sales) and control costs had increased to 85% of the total (2.125% of

12.   Jack Campanella (editor), *Principles of Quality Costs,* ASQC Quality Press, Milwaukee, 1990, p. 12.

sales). Tennant increased quality, reduced quality costs in every category and in total, and shifted the distribution of quality costs to the control categories, with the greatest emphasis on prevention. This outcome argues strongly against the traditional quality cost model portrayed in Exhibit 21-7. Further support for the total quality control model is provided by Westinghouse Electric Company, which found that profits continued to improve until control costs accounted for about 70% to 80% of total quality costs.[13] Based on these two companies' experiences, we know that it is possible to reduce total quality costs significantly—in all categories—and that the process radically alters the relative distribution of the quality cost categories.

Activity-Based Management and Optimal Quality Costs   Activity-based management classifies activities as value-added and nonvalue-added and keeps only those that add value. This principle dovetails nicely with total quality management, as customers want and will pay for value-added activities but do not want (and will not pay for) nonvalue-added activities. Notice that quality costs are classified into four areas, and activities associated with each area are identified. Then, it is easy to take the next step in classifying those activities as value-added or nonvalue-added.

Internal and external failure activities and their associated costs are nonvalue-added and should be eliminated eventually. We say eventually because of the dynamic nature of total quality management. Initially, some defective units are produced and the firm must continue to perform failure-related activities such as rework and warranty work. Prevention activities—performed efficiently—can be classified as value-added and should be retained. Initially, however, prevention activities may not be performed efficiently, and activity reduction and activity selection (and perhaps even activity sharing) can be used to achieve the desired value-added state. Appraisal activities are more difficult to assess. The initial reaction may be to classify all appraisal activities as nonvalue-added. However, in reality, some level of these activities may be needed to prevent backsliding. Quality audits, for example, may serve a value-added objective. Similarly, it seems unrealistic to totally eliminate supplier verification. Conditions change, and without any monitoring, suppliers may also backslide.[14]

Once the activities are identified for each category, resource drivers can be used to improve cost assignments to the individual activities. Root or executional drivers can also be identified and used to help managers understand what is causing the costs of the activities. This information can then be used to select ways of reducing quality costs to the level revealed by Exhibit 21-8. In effect, activity-based management supports both the zero-defect and robust quality views of quality costs. There is no optimal trade-off between control and failure costs. Failure costs are nonvalue-added costs and should be reduced to zero. Inefficiently performed control activities also cause costs that should be reduced to lower levels.

---

13.   These factual observations are based on those reported by Lawrence P. Carr and Thomas Tyson, "Planning Quality Cost Expenditures."
14.   In Michael Ostrega, "Return on Investment Through the Cost of Quality," it is suggested that activity-based costing can be used to help managers understand the nature of quality costs. In this article, failure and appraisal activities are labeled as nonvalue-added. Only prevention activities were classified as value-added.

The Interface Between Cost Management and Total Quality

The important role played by accountants in generating quality cost information makes it critically important that they understand the impact of that information on the operations of the company. An example may help explain.[15]

In 1987, Analog Devices, Inc. (ADI), a manufacturer of integrated circuits, began a total quality management program. Within three years, dramatic quality improvements were achieved. Semiconductor yield nearly doubled, manufacturing cycle time had decreased by fifty percent, defects had been reduced by a factor of ten. One might expect that ADI's financial performance had similarly improved. However, this was not the case. Share price and return on equity had fallen, and ADI was forced into its first lay-off. How did this happen?

An analysis of ADI's quality program showed that it was well-implemented. The financial difficulties were caused by unanticipated side effects. We must remember that a shift to total quality entails change and that change seldom occurs smoothly. For example, ADI saw manufacturing yields double, but in the short run, these improvements led to excess inventory and problems with production scheduling, as organizational norms which had worked well in the past no longer applied. Another example occurred in pricing. Formerly, ADI based price on manufacturing costs. The quality program led to rapid improvement in operations and decreases in direct costs. Unfortunately, indirect costs of R&D, sales, and administration did not fall as quickly. As a result, price dropped too rapidly and operating margins eroded.

The point of this cautionary tale is that the accountant must be alert for the way in which functions and activities of the company interact. A shift in cost in one activity can have unintended effects on other activities or functions. For this reason, cooperation between the quality program and the cost management program is essential.

USING QUALITY COST INFORMATION

Objective 3

Explain why quality cost information is needed and how it is used.

Quality costs are reported to improve managerial planning, control, and decision making. For example, if a company wants to implement a supplier selection program to improve the quality of raw materials purchases, it will need to assess: current quality costs by item and by category; the additional costs associated with the program; and the projected savings by item and by category. *When* the costs and savings will occur must also be projected. Then a capital budgeting analysis can be done to determine the merits of the proposed program. If the outcome is favorable and the program is initiated, then it becomes important to monitor the program through performance reporting.

Using quality cost information to implement and monitor the effectiveness of quality programs is only one use of a quality cost system. Other important uses can also be identified. Quality cost information is an important input to management decision making. It is also important to outside parties as they assess the quality of the company, through programs such as ISO 9000.

---

15.   This example is taken from Fred Kofman, Nelson Repenning, and John Sterman, "Unanticipated Side Effects of Successful Quality Programs: Exploring a Paradox of Organizational Improvement," Working Paper, MIT Sloan School of Management, Cambridge, MA, March 1994.

Using Quality Cost Information for Decision Making

Managers need quality cost information in a number of decision-making contexts. Two of these contexts are strategic pricing and cost-volume-profit analysis.

Strategic Pricing Consider AMD, Inc., which produces electronic measurement devices. Market share for the company's low-level electronic measurement instruments had been steadily dropping. Linda Werther, marketing manager, identified price as the major problem. She knew that Japanese firms produced and sold the low-level instruments for less than AMD could. If AMD reduced its price to that of the competition, the new price would be below cost. Yet if something were not done, the Japanese firms would continue to expand their market share. One possibility was simply to drop the low-level line and concentrate on instruments in the medium and high-level categories. Linda knew, however, that this was a short-term solution, since soon the same Japanese firms would be competing at the higher levels. A brief income statement for the low-level instruments is given below.

Revenues (1,000,000 @ $20)	$20,000,000
Cost of goods sold	(15,000,000)
Operating expenses	(3,000,000)
Product-line income	$ 2,000,000

Linda strongly believed that a 15 percent price decrease would restore the instrument line's market share and profitability to their former levels. One possibility was the implementation of total quality management. Her first action was to request information on the quality costs for the lower-level instruments. AMD's controller, Eugene Sadler, admitted that the costs were not tracked separately. For example, the cost of scrap was buried in the work in process account. He did promise, however, to estimate some of the costs. Data from his report for the low-level instruments are given below.

Quality costs (estimated):	
Inspection of raw materials	$ 200,000
Scrap	800,000
Rejects	500,000
Rework	400,000
Product inspection	300,000
Warranty work	1,000,000
Total estimate	$3,200,000

Upon receiving the report, Linda, Eugene, and Art Smith, manager of the Quality Control Department, met to determine possible ways of reducing quality costs for the low-level line. Art was confident that the quality costs could be reduced by 50 percent within eighteen months. He had already begun planning the implementation of a new quality program. Linda calculated that a 50 percent reduction in the quality costs associated with the low-level instruments would reduce costs by about $1.60 per unit ($1,600,000/1,000,000)—which would make up slightly more than half of the $3 reduction in selling price that would be needed (the reduction is 15 percent of $20). Based on this outcome, Linda decided to implement the price reduction in three phases: a $1 reduction immediately, a $1 reduction in six months, and the final reduction of $1 in twelve months. This phased reduction would likely prevent any further erosion of market share and would start increasing it sometime into the second phase. By phasing in the price reductions, it would give the quality department time to reduce costs so that any big losses could be avoided.

The AMD, Inc., example illustrates that both quality cost information and the implementation of a total quality control program contributed to a significant strategic decision. It also illustrates that improving quality was not a panacea. The reductions were not as large as needed to bear the full price reduction. Other productivity gains will be needed to ensure the long-range viability of the product line. Implementing JIT manufacturing, for example, might reduce inventories and decrease costs of materials handling and maintenance.

Cost-Volume-Profit Analysis Traditionally, cost-volume-profit analysis relies on the analysis of fixed and variable costs in conjunction with cost. Terry Foster, the marketing manager, and Sharon Fox, the design engineer, discovered shortcomings in the traditional analysis when they proposed a new product. They had been certain that a proposal for the new product was going to be approved. Instead, they received the following report from the controller's office.

Report: New Product Analysis, Project #675

Projected sales potential: 44,000 units
Production capacity: 45,000 units
Unit selling price: $60
Unit variable costs: $40
Fixed costs:

Product development	$ 500,000
Manufacturing	200,000
Selling	300,000
Total	$1,000,000

Projected break-even: 50,000 units
Decision: Reject
Reason(s): The break-even point is greater than the production capacity as well as the projected sales volume.

In an effort to discover just why the cost figures came out so badly for a project both felt strongly was profitable, the two met with Bob Brown, the assistant controller. The following conversation took place.

Sharon: Bob, I would like to know why there is a $3-per-unit scrap cost. Can you explain it?
Bob: Sure. It's based on the scrap cost that we track for existing, similar products.
Sharon: Well, I think you have overlooked the new design features of this new product. Its design virtually eliminates any waste—especially when you consider that the product will be made on a numerically controlled machine.

Terry: Also, this $2-per-unit charge for repair work should be eliminated. The new design that Sharon is proposing solves the failure problems we have had with related products. It also means that the $100,000 of fixed costs associated with the repair center can be eliminated.

Bob: Sharon, how certain are you that this new design will eliminate some of these quality problems?

Sharon: I'm absolutely positive. The early prototypes did exactly as we expected. The results of those tests are included in the proposal.

Bob: Right. Reducing the variable cost by $5 per unit and the fixed costs by $100,000 produces a break-even point of 36,000 units. These changes alone make the project viable. I'll change the report to reflect a positive recommendation.

The above scenario illustrates the importance of further classifying quality costs by behavior. Although only unit-based behavior is assumed, activity-based classification is also possible and could enhance the decision usefulness of quality costs. The scenario also reinforces the importance of identifying and reporting quality costs separately. The new product was designed to reduce its quality costs, and only by knowing the quality costs assigned could Sharon and Terry have discovered the error in the break-even analysis.

Certifying Quality Through ISO 9000

Just as a company assesses the quality of its suppliers, that same company may supply other companies that require vendor certification of quality. A relatively new program called ISO 9000 has evolved in response to the need for a standardized set of procedures for supplier quality verification.

ISO (pronounced ICE-OH) 9000 is a standard of quality measurement. Developed by the International Organization for Standardization in Geneva, Switzerland, it is a series of five international quality standards. These standards center around the concept of documentation and control of nonconformance and change. ISO 9000 has been a success in Europe, and U.S. companies that do business in Europe were the first to board the ISO 9000 bandwagon, simply because it is a requirement of doing business. Companies that attain ISO 9000 certification have been audited by an independent test company that certifies that the company meets certain quality standards. These standards do not apply to the production of a particular product or service. Instead, they apply to the way in which a company ensures quality by, for example, testing products, training employees, keeping records, and fixing defects. "To become registered, a business must prove it is following its own procedures for inspecting production processes, updating engineering drawings, maintaining machinery, calibrating equipment, training workers, and dealing with customer complaints."[16]

It is important to note that ISO 9000 does not certify either the quality of the product itself or the commitment of the company to continuous improvement. In fact, ISO 9000 is a vocabulary and a set of five standards. These are given in Exhibit 21-9.[17] As a result, companies that require ISO 9000 certification (like Motorola or GE) do not stop auditing their suppliers. Requiring ISO 9000 certification is just a first step.

---

16.   Ronald Henkoff, "The Hot New Seal of Quality," *Fortune,* June 28, 1993, pp. 116–120.

17.   These steps are listed in A. Faye Borthick and Harold P. Roth, "Will Europeans Buy Your Company's Products?" *Management Accounting,* July 1992, pp. 28–32. This article is an excellent introduction to ISO 9000 certification and includes a useful listing of quality definitions.

Exhibit 21-9
ISO 9000 Standards

ISO 8402: Quality—Vocabulary.

ISO 9000: Quality management and quality assurance standards—Guidelines for selection and use.

ISO 9001: Quality systems—Model for quality assurance in design/development, production, installation, and servicing.

ISO 9002: Quality systems—Model for quality assurance in production and installation.

ISO 9003: Quality systems—Model for quality assurance in final inspection and test.

ISO 9004: Quality management and quality system elements—Guidelines.

On the plus side, many companies have found that the process of applying for ISO 9000 certification, while lengthy and expensive (it can take many months and cost up to $200,000), yields important benefits in terms of self-knowledge. For example, Haworth, Inc., a maker of office furniture, posts placards with words and pictures at work stations throughout its five factories to show employees exactly what should be done. These placards help to ensure that all workers are following company policies consistently, a hallmark of quality of conformance. Similarly, Allen-Bradley's Twinsburg plant has improved quality and productivity significantly by replacing a system of paper manuals with an electronic mail system. Now, when engineering changes are made, the system purges the old instructions and inserts the new ones. Workers no longer tape personal directions to their work stations, directions which were quickly out of date.

ISO 9000 is not a quality system. It is a first step in supplier certification. However, companies are finding it hard to resist paying for an independent audit of their quality processes. By mid-1993, nearly 1,400 U.S. firms had won certification. In Britain, over 17,000 certificates have been issued. ISO 9000 standards have been adopted by 60 countries. Many large companies, including DuPont, GE, Eastman Kodak, and British Telecom, are urging their suppliers to obtain certificates.

U.S. companies are using ISO 9000 certification as a competitive tool, as well. For example, PPG Industries, Inc., a manufacturer of glass and chemical products, has encouraged its divisions to achieve certification. PPG Specialty Chemicals found out that many of its competitors had achieved ISO 9002 certification and believed that achieving an even broader certification would differentiate PPG from the competition. ISO certification would also bring the manufacturing plants into closer cooperation with the research and development facilities.[18] The process of applying for certification required extensive quality audits. PPG Specialty Chemicals discovered good aspects of its quality program and aspects in need of improvement. For example, the audits uncovered areas in need of documentation. The documentation developed outlines the relevant procedures to be followed and just how to do them.

---

18.   John D. Flister and Joseph J. Jozaitis, "PPG's Journey to ISO 9000," *Management Accounting,* July 1992, pp. 33–38.

Reporting quality costs so that they can be used for decision making is only one objective of a good quality costing system. Another objective is controlling quality costs—a factor critical in helping expected outcomes of decisions come to fruition. The AMD, Inc. pricing decision considered earlier, for example, depended on the plan to reduce quality costs.

CONTROLLING QUALITY COSTS

Objective 4

Describe and prepare three different types of quality perfor-mance reports.

Quality costs must be reported and controlled. Control enables managers to compare actual outcomes with standard outcomes to gauge performance and take any necessary corrective actions. Quality cost performance reports have two essential elements: actual outcomes and standard or expected outcomes. Deviations of actual outcomes from the expected outcomes are used to evaluate managerial performance and provide signals concerning possible problems.

Performance reports are essential to quality improvement programs. A report like the one shown in Exhibit 21-5 forces managers to identify the various costs that should appear in a performance report, to identify the current quality per-formance level of the organization, and to begin thinking about the level of qual-ity performance that should be achieved. Identifying the quality standard is a key element in a quality performance report.

Choosing the Quality Standard

The Traditional Approach In the traditional approach, the appropriate quality standard is an acceptable quality level (AQL). An AQL is simply an admission that a certain number of defective products will be produced and sold. For exam-ple, the AQL may be set at 3 percent. In this case, any lot of products (or pro-duction run) that has no more than 3 percent defective units will be shipped to customers. Typically, the AQL reflects the current operating status, not what is possible if a firm has an excellent quality program. As the basis for a quality standard, AQL has the same problems as historical experience does for materials and labor usage standards: it may perpetuate past operating mistakes.

Unfortunately, AQL has additional problems. Setting a 3 percent AQL is a commitment to deliver defective products to customers. Out of every 1 million units sold, 30,000 will yield dissatisfied customers. Why plan to make a certain number of defective units? Why not plan instead to make the product according to its specifications? Is there not a matter of integrity involved here? How many customers would accept a product if they knew that it was defective? How many people would consult a surgeon if they knew that the surgeon planned to botch three of every one hundred operations?

The Total Quality Approach These questions reflect a new attitude towards qual-ity. A more sensible standard is to produce products as they were intended to be. This standard will be referred to as the robust *zero-defects standard*. It reflects a philosophy of total quality control and calls for products and services to be produced and delivered that meet the targeted value. Thus, when we say zero defects, we are referring to defective units in the robust sense. Recall that the need for total quality control is inherent in a JIT manufacturing approach. Thus, the movement towards total quality control is being sustained by the firms adopt-ing JIT. JIT, however, is not a prerequisite for moving towards total quality con-trol. This approach can stand by itself.

Admittedly, the total quality standard is one that may not be completely attainable; however, evidence exists that it can be closely approximated. Defects are caused either by lack of knowledge or by lack of attention. Lack of knowledge can be corrected by proper training; lack of attention by effective leadership. Note also that total quality control implies the ultimate elimination of failure costs. Those believing that no defects should be permitted will continue to search for new ways to improve quality costs.

Some may wonder whether adherence to the ideal is a realistic standard. Consider the following anecdote. An American firm placed an order for a particular component with a Japanese firm. In the order, the American firm specified that 1,000 components should be delivered with an AQL of 5 percent defects. When the order arrived, it came in two boxes—one large and one small. A note explained that the large box contained 950 good components and the small one fifty defective components; the note also asked why the firm wanted fifty defective parts (implying the capability of delivering no defective parts).

Consider another case. A firm engaged in a significant volume of business through mailings. On average, 15 percent of the mailings were sent to the wrong address. Returned merchandise, late payments, and lost sales all resulted from this error rate. In one case, a tax payment was sent to the wrong address. By the time the payment arrived, it was late, causing a penalty of $300,000. Why not spend the resources (surely less than $300,000) to get the mailing list right and have no errors? Is a mailing list that is 100 percent accurate really impossible to achieve? Why not do it right the first time?

Quantifying the Quality Standard Quality can be measured by its costs; as the costs of quality decrease, higher quality results—at least up to a point. Even if the standard of zero defects is achieved, a company must still have prevention and appraisal costs. A company with a well-run quality management program can get by with quality costs of about 2.5 percent of sales. (If zero defects are achieved, this cost is for prevention and appraisal.) This 2.5 percent standard is accepted by many quality control experts and many firms that are adopting aggressive quality improvement programs.

The 2.5 percent standard is for total costs of quality. Costs of individual quality factors, such as quality training or materials inspection, will be less. Each organization must determine the appropriate standard for each individual factor. Budgets can be used to set spending for each standard so that the total budgeted cost meets the 2.5 percent goal.

Physical Standards For line managers and operating personnel, physical measures of quality—such as number of defects per unit, the percentage of external failures, billing errors, contract errors, and other physical measures—may be more meaningful. For physical measures, the quality standard is zero defects or errors. The objective is to get everyone to do it right the first time.

Use of Interim Standards For most firms, the standard of zero defects is a long-range goal. The ability to achieve this standard is strongly tied to supplier quality. For most companies, materials and services purchased from outside parties make up a significant part of the cost of the product. For example, more than 65 percent of the product cost for Tennant Company was from materials and parts purchased from more than 500 different suppliers. To achieve the desired quality level, Tennant had to launch a major campaign to involve its suppliers in similar quality improvement programs. Developing the relationships and securing the needed cooperation from suppliers takes time—in fact, it takes years. Similarly, getting people within the company itself to understand the need for quality improvement and to have confidence in the program can take several years.

Because improving quality to the zero-defects level can take years, yearly quality improvement standards should be developed so that managers can use performance reports to assess the progress made on an interim basis. These **interim quality standards** express quality goals for the year. Progress should be reported to managers and employees in order to gain the confidence needed to achieve the ultimate standard of zero defects. Even though reaching the zero-defects level is a long-range project, management should expect significant progress on a yearly basis. For example, Tennant cut its quality costs from 17 percent of sales in 1980 to 8 percent of sales in 1986—an average reduction of more than 1 percent per year. Furthermore, once the 2.5 percent goal is reached, efforts must be expended continuously to maintain it. Performance reports, at this stage, assume a strict control role.

interim quality standards

Types of Quality Performance Reports

Quality performance reports measure the progress realized by an organization's quality improvement program. Three types of progress can be measured and reported:

1. Progress with respect to a current-period standard or goal (an interim standard report).
2. The progress trend since the inception of the quality improvement program (a multiple-period trend report).
3. Progress with respect to the long-range standard or goal (a long-range report).

Interim Standard Report The organization must establish an interim quality standard each year and make plans to achieve this targeted level. Since quality costs are a measure of quality, the targeted level can be expressed in dollars budgeted for each category of quality costs and for each cost item within the category. At the end of the period, the **interim quality performance report** compares the actual quality costs for the period against the budgeted costs. This report measures the progress achieved within the period relative to the planned level of progress for that period. Exhibit 21-10 illustrates such a report.

interim quality performance report

The interim report reveals the within-period quality improvement relative to specific objectives as reflected by the budgeted figures. For Jensen Products, the overall performance is close to what was planned: total actual quality costs differ by only $2,000 from total budgeted quality costs and the actual costs, a mere 0.07 percent as a percentage of sales.

Multiple-Period Trend The report in Exhibit 21-10 provides management with information concerning the within-period progress measured relative to specific goals. Also useful is a picture of how the quality improvement program has been doing since its inception. Is the multiple-period trend—the overall change in quality costs—in the right direction? Are significant quality gains being made each period? Answers to these questions can be given by providing a chart or graph that tracks the change in quality from the beginning of the program to the present. Such a graph is called a **multiple-period quality trend report**. By plotting quality costs as a percentage of sales against time, the overall trend in the quality program can be assessed. The first year plotted is the year prior to the implementation of the quality improvement program. Assume that Jensen Products has experienced the following:

multiple-period quality trend report

Exhibit 21-10

Jensen Products
Interim Standard Performance Report: Quality Costs
For the Year Ended March 31, 1998

	Actual Costs	Budgeted Costs	Variance
Prevention costs:			
Quality training	$ 35,000	$ 30,000	$ 5,000 U
Reliability engineering	80,000	80,000	0
Total prevention costs	$115,000	$110,000	$ 5,000 U
Appraisal costs:			
Materials inspection	$ 20,000	$ 28,000	$ 8,000 F
Product acceptance	10,000	15,000	5,000 F
Process acceptance	38,000	35,000	3,000 U
Total appraisal costs	$ 68,000	$ 78,000	$10,000 F
Internal failure costs:			
Scrap	$ 50,000	$ 44,000	$ 6,000 U
Rework	35,000	36,500	1,500 F
Total internal failure costs	$ 85,000	$ 80,500	$ 4,500 U
External failure costs:			
Customer complaints	$ 25,000	$ 25,000	$ 0
Warranty	25,000	20,000	5,000 U
Repair	15,000	17,500	2,500 F
Total external failure costs	$ 65,000	$ 62,500	$ 2,500 U
Total quality costs	$333,000	$331,000	$ 2,000 U
Percentage of actual sales*	11.89%	11.82%	0.07% U

*Actual sales of $2,800,000.

	Quality Costs	Actual Sales	Costs as a Percentage of Sales
1994	$440,000	$2,200,000	20.0
1995	423,000	2,350,000	18.0
1996	412,500	2,750,000	15.0
1997	406,000	2,800,000	14.5
1998	280,000	2,800,000	10.0

Letting 1994 be Year 0, 1995 be Year 1, and so on, the trend graph is shown in Exhibit 21-11. Periods of time are plotted on the horizontal axis and percentages on the vertical. The ultimate quality cost objective of 2.5 percent, the target percentage, is represented as a horizontal line on the graph.

The graph reveals that there has been a steady downward trend in quality costs expressed as a percentage of sales. The graph also reveals that there is still ample room for improvement towards the long-run target percentage.

Additional insight can be provided by plotting the trend for each individual quality category. Assume that each category is expressed as a percentage of sales for the same period of time.

Exhibit 21-11
Multiple-Period Trend Graph: Total Quality Costs

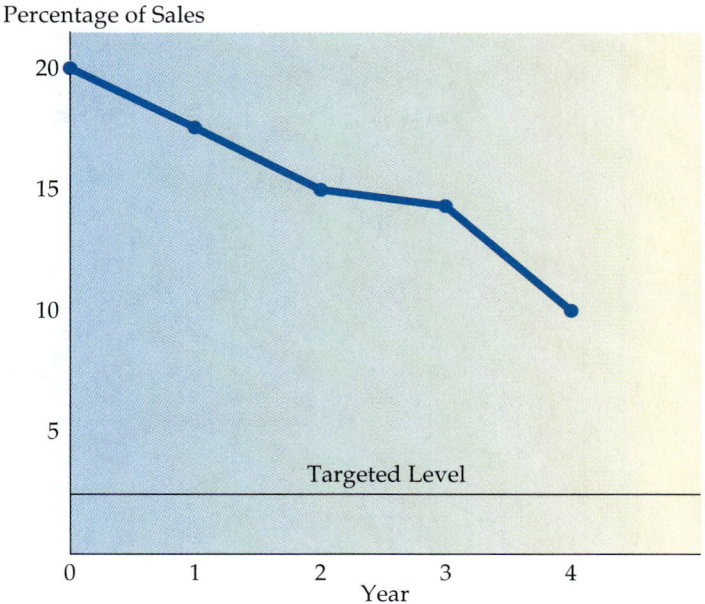

Percentage of Sales

Targeted Level

Year

	Prevention	Appraisal	Internal Failure	External Failure
1994	2.0%	2.0%	6.0%	10.0%
1995	3.0	2.4	4.0	8.6
1996	3.0	3.0	3.0	6.0
1997	4.0	3.0	2.5	4.5
1998	4.1	2.4	2.0	1.5

The graph showing the trend for each category is displayed in Exhibit 21-12. From Exhibit 21-12, we can see that the company has had dramatic success in reducing external and internal failures. More money is being spent on prevention (the amount has doubled as a percentage). Appraisal costs have increased and then decreased. Note also that the relative distribution of costs has changed. In 1994, failure costs were 80% of the total quality costs (16%/20%). In 1998, they are 35% of the total (3.5%/10%). The potential to reduce quality costs also affects the way decisions are made. The usefulness of quality cost information for decision making and planning should not be underestimated.

Long-Range Standard At the end of each period, a report that compares the period's actual quality costs with the costs that the firm eventually hopes to achieve should be prepared. This report forces management to keep the ultimate quality goal in mind, reveals the room left for improvement, and facilitates planning for the coming period. Under a zero-defects philosophy, the costs of failure should be virtually nonexistent (they are nonvalue-added costs). Reducing the costs of failure increases a firm's competitive ability. Tennant Company, for example, is now able to offer warranties that last two to four times longer than those of its competitors because of improved quality resulting in lower external failure rates.

Exhibit 21-12
Multiple-Period Trend Graph: Individual Quality Cost Categories

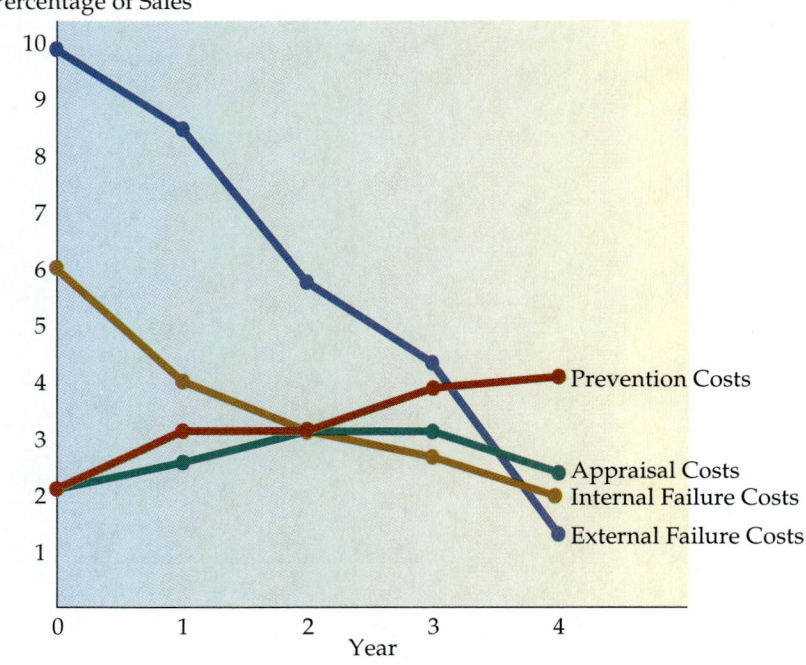

Thus, not only have quality costs been reduced by almost 50 percent, but because of improved quality, sales performance has increased.

Remember that achieving higher quality will not totally eliminate prevention and appraisal costs. (In fact, increased emphasis on zero defects may actually increase the cost of prevention, depending on the type and level of prevention activities initially present.) Generally, we would expect appraisal costs to decrease. Product acceptance, for example, may be phased out entirely as product quality increases; however, increased emphasis on process acceptance is likely. The firm must have assurance that the process is operating in a zero-defects mode. Exhibit 21-13 illustrates a **long-range quality performance report**. It compares the current period's actual costs with the costs that would be allowed if the zero-defects standard were being met (assuming a sales level equal to that of the current period). The target costs are, if chosen properly, value-added costs. The variances are nonvalue-added costs. Thus, the long-range performance report is simply a variation of the value- and nonvalue-added cost report.

long-range quality
performance report

The report emphasizes the fact that the company is still spending too much money on quality—too much money for not doing things right the first time. As quality improves, savings can be realized by having fewer workers to correct the mistakes made initially. Rework costs, for example, will disappear when there is no more rework, warranty costs will stop when there are no failures in the field, and so on.

By spending less money on defects, a company can use the money to expand and to employ additional people to support this expansion. Increased quality may naturally cause expansion by increasing the competitive position of a firm. By having fewer problems with existing products, a firm can focus more attention on growth. Thus, although improved quality may mean fewer jobs in some areas, it also means that additional jobs will be created through expanded business activity. In fact, more jobs will probably be added than are lost.

Exhibit 21-13

Jensen Products
Long-Range Performance Report
For the Year Ended March 31, 1998

	Actual Costs	*Target Costs**	*Variance*
Prevention costs:			
Fixed:			
Quality training	$ 35,000	$15,000	$ 20,000 U
Reliability engineering	80,000	40,000	40,000 U
Total prevention costs	$115,000	$55,000	$ 60,000 U
Appraisal costs:			
Variable:			
Materials inspection	$ 20,000	$ 5,000	$ 15,000 U
Product acceptance	10,000	—	10,000 U
Process acceptance	38,000	10,000	28,000 U
Total appraisal costs	$ 68,000	$15,000	$ 53,000 U
Internal failure costs:			
Variable:			
Scrap	$ 50,000	$ —	$ 50,000 U
Rework	35,000	—	35,000 U
Total internal failure costs	$ 85,000	$ —	$ 85,000 U
External failure costs:			
Fixed:			
Customer complaints	$ 25,000	$ —	$ 25,000 U
Variable:			
Warranty	25,000	—	25,000 U
Repair	15,000	—	15,000 U
Total external failure costs	$ 65,000	$ 0	$ 65,000 U
Total quality costs	$333,000	$70,000	$263,000 U
Percentage of actual sales	11.89%	2.5%	9.39% U

*Based on actual current sales of $2,800,000. These costs are value-added costs.

Incentives for Quality Improvement Most organizations provide both monetary and nonmonetary recognition for significant contributions to quality improvement. Of the two types of incentives, most quality experts believe that the nonmonetary are more useful.

error cause identification

As with budgets, participation helps employees internalize quality improvement goals as their own. One approach used by many companies in their efforts to involve employees is the use of error cause identification forms. **Error cause identification** is a program in which employees describe problems that interfere with their ability to do the job right the first time. The error-cause-removal approach is one of the fourteen steps in Philip Crosby's quality improvement program.[19] To ensure the success of the program, each employee submitting an

19. Crosby, former quality manager for ITT, is the author of *Quality is Free,* New American Library, New York, 1980. While he served as quality manager for ITT, ITT reduced the manufacturing cost of quality by 5 percent of sales. The savings in 1976 alone were estimated as $530 million. His book provides an excellent account of the fourteen-step quality program he developed and Tennant Company followed.

entry should receive a note of appreciation from management. Additional recognition should be given to those who submit particularly beneficial information. Tennant Company, for example, gives 20 percent of the first year's savings from submissions that are adopted to the employees who made them.

Other nonfinancial awards can also be given to recognize employees for their efforts. One restaurant, for example, gives monthly awards to food servers who have made no errors when punching diners' orders into the kitchen printout computer. Servers who make the most errors see their names posted on an error list (no punishment, just names). The error rate has plummeted, saving the restaurant thousands of dollars a month in wasted food.[20] The important thing is not the award itself but the public recognition of outstanding achievement. By publicly recognizing significant quality contributions, management underscores its commitment to quality improvement. Also, the individuals and groups so recognized feel the benefits of that recognition, which include pride, job satisfaction, and a further commitment to quality.

Using Quality Reports for Control

The various types of quality reports and variances lead to the question—how are they used? Just like traditional variances, quality variances are not answers but suggestions of questions to ask. Quality reports are aids to root cause analysis, the analysis of the real reason(s) for quality problems. When a company sees that prevention costs are rising over the years but failure costs are not falling, it is necessary to determine why. Why are prevention costs not leading to decreased failure? Is training inadequate? Are the wrong people being trained (e.g., middle managers rather than operating personnel)? Are incorrect systems still in place? When the root cause has been identified, then steps can be taken to correct it and get quality on track. For example, GE has greatly improved the quality of its locomotives over the past few years. One improvement was the result of a suggestion by a customer, CSX. CSX noticed that its maintenance people sometimes inserted the wrong brush into an electric traction motor. Two brush types were possible and were lookalikes. GE redesigned the brush holders to accept only the correct brush. Failures were reduced to zero.[21]

Quality control is a process and permeates all phases of business. Increases in quality also positively affect productivity, which is the topic of the next chapter.

---

20. Example taken from Berry and Parasuraman, *Marketing Services, Competing Through Quality.*
21. William M. Carley, "GE Locomotive Unit, Long and Also-Ran, Overtakes Rival GM," *The Wall Street Journal,* September 3, 1993, pp. A1 and A4.

SUMMARY

To understand quality costs, it is first necessary to understand what is meant by quality. There are two types of quality: quality of design and quality of conformance. Quality of design concerns quality differences that arise for products with the same function but different specifications. Quality of conformance, on the other hand, concerns meeting the specifications required by the product.

Two philosophical approaches to quality were described. The zero-defects approach allows variation from a target within certain specification limits. The robust quality approach stresses reduction of variation, noting that any variation entails hidden quality costs. The Taguchi quality loss function illustrates the hidden quality costs associated with the robustness philosophy.

Quality costs are those costs that are incurred because products may or actually fail to meet design specifications (and are therefore associated with quality of conformance). There are four categories of quality costs: prevention, appraisal, internal failure, and external failure. Prevention costs are those incurred to prevent poor quality. Appraisal costs are those incurred to detect poor quality. Internal failure costs are those incurred because products fail to conform to requirements and this lack of conformity is discovered before an external sale. External failure costs are those incurred because products fail to conform to requirements after an external sale is made.

A quality cost report is prepared by listing costs for each item within each of the four major quality cost categories. See Exhibit 21-2. There are two views concerning the optimal distribution of quality costs: the conventional view and the world-class view. The conventional view holds that there is a trade-off between costs of failure and prevention and appraisal costs. This trade-off produces an optimal level of performance called the *acceptable quality level*. AQL is the level at which the number of defects allowed minimizes total quality costs. The world-class view, on the other hand, espouses total quality control. Total quality control maintains that the conflict between failure and appraisal and prevention costs is more conjecture than real. The actual optimal level of defects is the zero-defects level; companies should be striving to achieve this level of quality. Although quality costs do not vanish at this level, they are much lower than the optimal envisioned by the conventional view.

Quality cost information is needed to help managers control quality performance and to serve as input for decision making. It can be used to evaluate the overall performance of quality improvement programs. It can also be used to help improve a variety of managerial decisions, for example, strategic pricing and cost-volume-profit analysis. Perhaps the most important observation is that quality cost information is fundamental in a company's pursuit of continual improvement. Quality is one of the major competitive dimensions for world-class competitors. Many companies now have their dedication to quality certified by an external reporting firm under, for example, ISO 9000 specifications.

Four reports are mentioned in the chapter: (1) the interim report, (2) the one-period trend report, (3) the multiple-period trend report, and (4) the long-range report. The interim report is used to evaluate the firm's ability to meet its budgeted quality costs. Managers use the report to compare the actual quality costs with those that were targeted for the period. The one-period trend report is used to compare the actual quality costs with those of the prior period, adjusting for differences in activity (a flexible-budget adjustment). This report allows managers to evaluate the progress made relative to the previous year. The multiple-period trend report is a trend graph for several years. The graph allows managers to assess the direction and magnitude of change since the inception of a total quality program. Finally, the long-range report compares actual costs with the ideal level.

REVIEW PROBLEM AND SOLUTION

At the beginning of the year, Kare Company initiated a quality improvement program. Considerable effort was expended to reduce the number of defective units produced. By the end of the year, reports from the production manager revealed that scrap and rework had both decreased. The president of the company was pleased to hear of the success but wanted some assessment of the financial impact of the improvements. To make this assessment, the following financial data were collected for the current and preceding year:

	Preceding Year (1997)	Current Year (1998)
Sales	$10,000,000	$10,000,000
Scrap	400,000	300,000
Rework	600,000	400,000
Product inspection	100,000	125,000
Product warranty	800,000	600,000
Quality training	40,000	80,000
Materials inspection	60,000	40,000

REQUIRED:

1. Classify the costs as prevention, appraisal, internal failure, or external failure.
2. Compute quality cost as a percentage of sales for each of the two years. By how much has profit increased because of quality improvements? Assuming that quality costs can be reduced to 2.5 percent of sales, how much additional profit is available through quality improvements (assume that sales revenues will remain the same)?

Solution

1. Prevention costs: quality training
   Appraisal costs: product inspection and materials inspection
   Internal failure costs: scrap and rework
   External failure costs: warranty
2. *Preceding year*—Total quality costs: $2,000,000; percentage of sales: 20 percent ($2,000,000/$10,000,000). *Current year*—Total quality costs: $1,545,000; percentage of sales: 15.45 percent ($1,545,000/$10,000,000). Profit has increased by $455,000. If quality costs drop to 2.5 percent of sales, another $1,295,000 of profit improvement is possible ($1,545,000 − $250,000).

KEY TERMS

QUESTIONS FOR WRITING AND DISCUSSION

1. What is the difference between quality of design and quality of conformance?
2. Why are quality costs the costs of doing things wrong?
3. What is the difference between the zero-defects philosophy and the robust quality philosophy?
4. Describe the Taguchi quality loss function and relate it to robust quality.
5. Identify and discuss the four kinds of quality costs.
6. Explain why external failure costs can be more devastating to a firm than internal failure costs.
7. What is the difference between an AQL standard and a zero-defects standard?
8. Explain why activity-based management supports a zero-defects standard over an AQL standard.
9. Many quality experts maintain that quality is free. Do you agree? Why or why not?
10. What is the purpose of interim quality standards?
11. Describe the three types of quality performance reporting. How can managers use each report to help evaluate their quality improvement programs?
12. Discuss the different kinds of incentives that can be used to motivate employees to become involved in quality improvement programs.
13. If a firm's annual sales are $200 million, what percentage of sales should be spent on quality costs? Suppose that the firm is spending 18 percent of sales on quality costs. What is the potential savings from quality improvement?
14. Explain why it is important for a manager to assess the relative distribution of quality costs among the four categories.
15. Discuss the benefits of quality cost reports that simply list the quality costs for each category.
16. Explain why the accounting department should be responsible for producing quality cost reports.
17. What is ISO 9000? Why do so many companies want this certification?

EXERCISES AND PROBLEMS

21-1
Quality Definition and Quality Costs

LO 1

Goldy Lawks, president of a company that manufactures electronic components, has a number of questions concerning quality and quality costs. She has heard a few things about quality and has asked you to respond to the following:

1. What is meant by a quality product? Describe for me the dimensions that define quality.
2. What is the difference, if any, between a quality product and a quality service?
3. I have heard that quality costs are those costs incurred because poor quality may or does exist. Explain how these quality costs exist for each of the quality attributes or dimensions that you described for me earlier.
4. Are there other dimensions of quality that exist besides those you listed? What about quality perception? Is this a dimension of quality? After all, it does cause costs. I recently ordered a significant advertising campaign to overcome some incorrect perceptions about the quality of our products.
5. Yesterday, my quality manager told me that we need to redefine what we meant by a defective product. He said that conforming to specifications ignores the cost of product variability and that further reduction of product variability is a veritable gold mine— just waiting to be mined. What did he mean?

21-2
Taguchi Loss Function

LO 1

Edmun Company has decided to estimate its hidden external failure costs using the Taguchi loss function. After some study, it was determined that $k = \$400$ and $T = 30$ inches in diameter. A sample of four units produced the following values:

Unit No.	Actual Diameter (y)
1	29.8
2	30.2
3	30.4
4	29.6

REQUIRED:

1. Calculate the average loss per unit.
2. Assuming that 10,000 units were produced, what is the total hidden cost?
3. Assume that the multiplier for Edmun is four. What are the measured external costs? Explain the difference between measured costs and hidden costs.

21-3
Quality Cost Classification
LO 1

Classify the following quality costs as prevention costs, appraisal costs, internal failure costs, or external failure costs:

1. Scrap
2. Inspection labor
3. Extra raw materials for rework
4. Warranty work
5. Goods returned because they failed to meet customer specifications
6. Goods returned because they were damaged in transit
7. Training program for new personnel
8. Work stoppage to correct process malfunction (discovered using statistical process control procedures)
9. Settlement of a product liability suit
10. Extra overhead and labor for rework
11. Lost sales because of incorrect product labeling
12. Internal audit
13. Engineering design changes
14. Purchase order changes
15. Replacement of defective product
16. Test labor
17. Field service personnel
18. Software correction
19. Supplier evaluations
20. Packaging inspection
21. Consumer complaint department
22. Prototype inspection and testing
23. Retest work

21-4
Quality Improvement and Profitability
LO 2, 3

Reading Company reported the following sales and quality costs for the past four years. Assume that all quality costs are variable and that all changes in the quality cost ratios are due to a quality improvement program.

Year	Sales Revenues	Quality Costs as Percent of Revenues
1	$10,000,000	0.21
2	11,000,000	0.18
3	11,000,000	0.14
4	12,000,000	0.10

REQUIRED:

1. Compute the quality costs for all four years. By how much did net income increase from Year 1 to Year 2 because of quality improvements? From Year 2 to Year 3? From Year 3 to Year 4?
2. The management of Reading Company believes it is possible to reduce quality costs to 2.5% of sales. Assuming sales will continue at the Year 4 level, calculate the additional profit potential facing Reading. Is the expectation of improving quality and reducing costs to 2.5% of sales realistic? Explain.

3. Assume that Reading produces one type of product, which is sold on a bid basis. In Years 1 and 2, the average bid was $200. In Year 1, total variable costs were $125 per unit. In Year 3, competition forced the bid to drop to $190. Compute the total contribution margin in Year 3 assuming the same quality costs as in Year 1. Now compute the total contribution margin in Year 3 using the actual quality costs for Year 3. What is the increase in profitability resulting from the quality improvements made from Year 1 to Year 3?

21-5
Quality Costs:
Profit
Improvement and
Distribution
Across Categories

LO 2, 3

Vladimir Company had sales of $10,000,000 in 1991. In 1998, sales had increased to $12,500,000. A quality improvement program was implemented in 1991. Overall conformance quality was targeted for improvement. The quality costs for 1991 and 1998 are shown below. Assume any changes in quality costs are attributable to improvements in quality.

	1991	1998
Internal failure costs	$ 750,000	$ 37,500
External failure costs	1,000,000	25,000
Appraisal costs	450,000	93,750
Prevention costs	300,000	156,250
Total quality costs	$2,500,000	$312,500

REQUIRED:

1. Compute the quality cost-to-sales ratio for each year. Is this type of improvement possible?
2. Calculate the relative distribution of costs by category for 1991. What do you think of the way costs are distributed? How do you think they will be distributed as the company approaches a zero-defects state?
3. Calculate the relative distribution of costs by category for 1998. What do you think of the level and distribution of quality costs? Do you think further reductions are possible?
4. The quality manager for Vladimir indicated that the external failure costs reported are only the measured costs. He argued that the 1998 external costs were much higher than those reported and that additional investment ought to be made in control costs. Discuss the validity of his viewpoint.

21-6
Trade-offs Among
Quality Cost
Categories; Total
Quality Control

LO 2

Annenberg Company has sales of $1 million and quality costs of $200,000. The company is embarking on a major quality improvement program. During the next three years, Annenberg intends to increase its appraisal and prevention costs in order to reduce failure costs. The increase in control costs will result from adding five specific activities: sorting, process control, quality training, supplier evaluation, and engineering redesign of two major products. Current quality costs and the costs of these five activities are given in the following table. Each activity is added sequentially so that its effect on the cost categories can be assessed. For example, after sorting is added, the control costs increase to $40,000 and the failure costs drop to $130,000. Even though the activities are presented sequentially, they are totally independent of each other.

	Control Costs	Failure Costs
Current quality costs	$ 20,000	$180,000
Sorting	40,000	130,000
Process control	65,000	90,000
Quality training	75,000	82,000
Supplier evaluation	90,000	25,000
Engineering redesign	120,000	15,000

Upon seeing the effect of the quality improvement program, the president of Annen-berg was pleased—especially with the fact that total failure costs would be reduced to only $15,000 after all five activities are implemented. Even so, the president was concerned about whether all five activities should be implemented or some subset of the five. He wanted to be sure that the most profitable outcome was achieved.

REQUIRED:

1. Identify the control activities that should be implemented, and calculate the total qual-ity costs associated with this selection.
2. Given the activities selected in Requirement 1, calculate the following: (a) the reduction in total quality costs and (b) the percentage distribution for control and failure costs.
3. What do the outcomes of Requirements 1 and 2 suggest about the relationship between the two failure categories and appraisal and prevention? Do you think that quality costs can be reduced more? Discuss the role of activity management in this process.

21-7
Trend; Long-Range Performance Report

LO 4

In 1997, Tru-Delite Frozen Desserts, Inc., instituted a quality improvement program. At the end of 1998, the management of the corporation requested a report to show the amount saved by the measures taken during the year. The actual sales and actual quality costs for 1997 and 1998 are as follows:

	1997	1998
Sales	$600,000	$600,000
Scrap	15,000	15,000
Rework	20,000	10,000
Training program	5,000	6,000
Consumer complaints	10,000	5,000
Lost sales, incorrect labeling	8,000	—
Test labor	12,000	8,000
Inspection labor	25,000	24,000
Supplier evaluation	15,000	13,000

Tru-Delite's management believes that quality costs can be reduced to 2.5 percent of sales within the next five years. At the end of Year 5, Tru-Delite's sales are projected to have grown to $750,000. The relative distribution of quality costs at the end of Year 5 is as follows:

Scrap	15%
Training	20
Supplier evaluation	25
Test labor	25
Inspection	15
Total quality costs	100%

REQUIRED:

1. By how much did profits increase because of quality improvements made in 1998?
2. Prepare a long-range performance report that compares the quality costs incurred at the end of 1998 with the quality-cost structure expected at the end of 2003.
3. Are the targeted costs in the year 2003 all value-added costs? How would you interpret the variances *if* the targeted costs are value-added costs?
4. What would be the increase in profits in 2003 if the 2.5 percent performance standard is met in that year?

21-8
Multiple-Year
Trend Reports

LO 4

The controller of Gordon Company has computed quality costs as a percentage of sales for the past five years (1995 was the first year the company implemented a quality improvement program). This information is presented below:

	Prevention	Appraisal	Internal	External	Total
1994	2%	3%	8%	12%	25%
1995	3	4	8	10	25
1996	4	4	5	7	20
1997	5	3	3	5	16
1998	6	4	1	2	13

REQUIRED:

1. Prepare a trend graph for total quality costs. Comment on what the graph has to say about the success of the quality improvement program.
2. Prepare a graph that shows the trend for each quality cost category. What does the graph have to say about the success of the quality improvement program? Does this graph supply more insight than does the total cost trend graph? What does the graph have to say about the distribution of quality costs in 1994?

21-9
Quality Cost
Report; Taguchi
Loss Function

LO 1, 2

Barry Norton, president of Emery Products, was concerned with the trend in sales and profitability. The company had been losing customers at an alarming rate. Furthermore, the company was barely breaking even. Investigation revealed that poor quality was at the root of the problem. At the end of 1998, Barry decided to begin a quality improvement program. As a first step, they identified the following costs in their accounting records as quality related:

	1998
Sales (100,000 units @ $40)	$4,000,000
Scrap (internally rejected products)	120,000
Rework	160,000
Training program	48,000
Consumer complaints	80,000
Warranty	160,000
Test labor	120,000
Inspection labor	100,000
Supplier evaluation	12,000

REQUIRED:

1. Prepare a quality cost report by quality cost category.
2. Calculate the relative distribution percentages for each quality cost category. Comment on the distribution.
3. Using the Taguchi loss function, an average loss per unit is computed to be $6 per unit. What are the hidden costs of external failure? How does this affect the relative distribution?
4. Emery's quality manager decided not to bother with the hidden costs. His reasoning? Any efforts to reduce measured external failure costs will also reduce the hidden costs. Do you agree? Explain.

21-10
Taguchi Loss
Function
LO 2

Weil Company manufactures a component for portable computers. The weight of the component is of prime concern for the computer manufacturers. The component has a target value of 1,000 grams. Specification limits are 1,000 grams plus or minus 50 grams. Products produced at the lower specification limit of 950 grams lose $100. A sample of five units produced the following measures:

Unit No.	Measured Weight
1	1,010
2	1,025
3	1,050
4	925
5	950

During the first quarter, 40,000 units were produced.

REQUIRED:

1. Calculate the loss for each unit. Calculate the average loss for the sample of five.
2. Using the average loss, calculate the hidden quality costs for the first quarter.

21-11
Quality Costs;
Pricing Decisions;
Market Share
LO 3

Gaston Company manufactures furniture. One of its product lines is an economy-line kitchen table. During the last year, Gaston produced and sold 100,000 units for $100 per unit. Sales of the table are on a bid basis, but Gaston has always been able to win sufficient bids using the $100 price. This year, however, Gaston was losing more than its share of bids. Concerned, Larry Franklin, owner and president of the company, called a meeting of his executive committee (Megan Johnson, marketing manager; Fred Davis, quality manager; Kevin Jones, production manager; and Helen Jackson, controller).

Larry: I don't understand why we're losing bids. Megan, do you have an explanation?
Megan: Yes, as a matter of fact. Two competitors have lowered their price to $92 per unit. That's too big a difference for most of our buyers to ignore. If we want to keep selling our 100,000 units per year, we will need to lower our price to $92. Otherwise, our sales will drop to about 20,000 to 25,000 per year.
Helen: The unit contribution margin on the table is $10. Lowering the price to $92 will cost us $8 per unit. Based on a sales volume of 100,000, we'd make $200,000 in contribution margin. If we keep the price at $100, our contribution margin would be $200,000 to $250,000. If we have to lose, let's just take the lower market share. It's better than lowering our prices.
Megan: Perhaps. But the same thing could happen to some of our other product lines. My sources tell me that these two companies are on the tail-end of a major quality improvement program—one that allows them significant savings. We need to rethink our whole competitive strategy—at least if we want to stay in business. Ideally, we should match the price reduction and work to reduce the costs to recapture the lost contribution margin.
Fred: I think I have something to offer. We are about to embark on a new quality improvement program of our own. I have brought the following estimates of the current quality costs for this economy line. As you can see on the overhead, these costs run about 16 percent of current sales. That's excessive, and we believe that they can be reduced to about 4 percent of sales over time.

Scrap	$ 700,000
Rework	300,000
Rejects (sold as seconds to discount houses)	250,000
Returns (due to poor workmanship)	350,000
	$1,600,000

Larry: This sounds good. Fred, how long will it take you to achieve this reduction?

Fred: All these costs vary with sales level, so I'll express their reduction rate in those terms. Our best guess is that we can reduce these costs by about 1 percent of sales per quarter. So it should take about twelve quarters, or three years, to achieve the full benefit. Keep in mind that this is with an improvement in quality.

Megan: This offers us some hope. If we meet the price immediately, we can maintain our market share. Furthermore, if we can ever reach the point of reducing the price beyond the $92 level, then we can increase our market share. I estimate that we can increase sales by about 10,000 units for every $1 of price reduction beyond the $92 level. Kevin, how much extra capacity for this line do we have?

Kevin: We can handle an extra 30,000 or 40,000 tables per year.

REQUIRED:

1. Assume that Gaston immediately reduces the bid price to $92. How long will it be before the unit contribution margin is restored to $10, assuming that quality costs are reduced as expected and that sales are maintained at 100,000 units per year (25,000 per quarter)?

2. Assume that Gaston holds the price at $92 until the 4 percent target is achieved. At this new level of quality costs, should the price be reduced? If so, by how much should price be reduced and what is the increase in contribution margin? Assume that price can be reduced only in $1 increments.

3. Assume that Gaston immediately reduces the price to $92 and begins the quality improvement program. Now suppose that Gaston does not wait until the end of the three-year period before reducing prices. Instead, prices will be reduced when profitable to do so. Assume that prices can be reduced only by $1 increments. Identify when the first future price change should occur (if any).

4. Discuss the differences in viewpoints concerning the decision to decrease prices and the short-run contribution margin analysis done by Helen, the controller. Did quality cost information play an important role in the strategic decision making illustrated by the problem?

21-12
Classification of
Quality Costs

LO 1

Classify the following quality costs as prevention, appraisal, internal failure, or external failure. Also, label each cost as variable or fixed with respect to sales volume.

1. Quality engineering
2. Scrap
3. Product recalls
4. Returns and allowances because of quality problems
5. Data reentered because of keypunching errors
6. Supervision of in-process inspection
7. Quality circles
8. Component inspection and testing
9. Quality training
10. Reinspection of reworked product
11. Product liability
12. Internal audit assessing the effectiveness of quality system
13. Disposal of defective product
14. Downtime attributable to quality problems
15. Quality reporting
16. Proofreading
17. Correction of typing errors
18. In-process inspection
19. Process controls
20. Pilot studies

21-13
Quality Cost
Summary

LO 2

Barbara Buehler, the president of Wayne Company, recently returned from a conference on quality and productivity. At the conference, she was told that many American firms have quality costs totaling 20% to 30% of sales. She, however, was skeptical about this statistic. But even if the quality gurus were right, she was sure that her company's quality costs were much lower—probably less than 5%. On the other hand, if she was wrong, she would be passing up an opportunity to improve profits significantly and simultaneously strengthen her competitive position. The possibility was at least worth exploring. She knew that her company produced most of the information needed for quality cost reporting—but there never was a need to bother with any formal quality data gathering and analysis.

This conference, however, had convinced her that a firm's profitability can increase significantly by improving quality—provided the potential for improvement exists. Thus, before committing the company to a quality improvement program, Barbara requested a preliminary estimate of the total quality costs currently being incurred. She also indicated that the costs should be classified into four categories: prevention, appraisal, internal failure, and external failure costs. She has asked you to prepare a summary of quality costs and to compare the total costs to sales and profits. To assist you in this task, the following information has been prepared from the past year, 1998:

a. Sales revenue, $5,000,000; net income, $500,000.
b. During the year, customers returned 30,000 units needing repair. Repair cost averages $1 per unit.
c. Four inspectors are employed, each earning an annual salary of $20,000. These four inspectors are involved only with final inspection (product acceptance).
d. Total scrap is 50,000 units. Of this total, 60 percent is quality-related. The cost of scrap is about $5 per unit.
e. Each year, approximately 150,000 units are rejected in final inspection. Of these units, 80 percent can be recovered through rework. The cost of rework is $0.75 per unit.
f. A customer canceled an order that would have increased profits by $50,000. The customer's reason for cancellation was poor product performance.
g. The company employs three full-time employees in its complaint department. Each earns $13,500 a year.
h. The company gave sales allowances totaling $15,000 due to substandard products being sent to the customer.
i. The company requires all new employees to take its three-hour quality training program. The estimated annual cost of the program is $10,000.

REQUIRED:

1. Prepare a simple quality cost report classifying costs by category.
2. Compute the quality cost-sales ratio. Also, compare the total quality costs with total profits. Should Barbara be concerned with the level of quality costs?
3. Prepare a pie chart for the quality costs. Discuss the distribution of quality costs among the four categories. Are they properly distributed? Explain.
4. Discuss how the company can improve its overall quality and at the same time reduce total quality costs.
5. By how much will profits increase if quality costs are reduced to 2.5 percent of sales?

21-14
Quality Costs;
Profitability
Analysis

LO 2, 3

At the end of 1995, Powell, Inc., a large electronics firm, hired Pat Haley to manage one of its troubled divisions. Pat had the reputation of turning around businesses that were having difficulty. In 1996, the division had sales of $25,000,000, a variable cost ratio of 0.8, and total fixed costs of $6,000,000. The division produced only one product and sales were all to external customers. Seeking to solve the division's problems, Pat asked for a report on quality costs for 1996 and received the following report:

	Fixed	Variable
Prevention costs	$ 200,000	$ —
Appraisal costs	300,000	1,000,000
Internal failure costs	500,000	2,000,000
External failure costs	1,000,000	5,000,000
Total costs	$2,000,000	$8,000,000

Pat was astounded at the level of expenditure on quality costs. Although he had heard of companies with quality costs that had reached as high as 60% of sales, he had never personally seen any greater than 20% to 30% of sales. This division's level of 40% was clearly excessive. He immediately implemented a program to improve conformance quality. By the end of 1997, the following quality costs were reported:

	Fixed	Variable
Prevention costs	$1,000,000	$ —
Appraisal costs	1,000,000	1,000,000
Internal failure costs	500,000	1,000,000
External failure costs	1,000,000	3,500,000
Total costs	$3,500,000	$5,500,000

Revenues and other costs were unchanged for 1997.

Pat projects that by 2001 the defective rate will be 0.1 percent, compared to the AQL rate of 2 percent of 1996. He also projects that quality costs will be reduced to $500,000, distributed as follows:

	Fixed	Variable
Prevention costs	$200,000	$ —
Appraisal costs	200,000	—
Internal failure costs	—	20,000
External failure costs	—	80,000
Total costs	$400,000	$100,000

REQUIRED:

1. Calculate the break-even point in revenues for 1996. How much was the division losing?
2. Calculate the break-even point in 1997. Explain the change.
3. Calculate the break-even point in 2001, assuming that revenues and other costs have remained the same. Is it possible to reduce quality costs as dramatically as portrayed?
4. Assume that from 1996 to 2001, the division was forced to cut selling prices so that total revenues dropped to $15,000,000. Calculate the income (loss) that would be reported under a 1996 cost structure. Now calculate the income (loss) that would be reported under the 2001 quality-cost structure (assuming all other costs remain unchanged). Discuss the strategic significance of quality cost management.

21-15
Quality Cost Report; Interim Performance Report
LO 1, 2, 4

Recently, Ulrich Company received a report from an external consulting group on its quality costs. The consultants reported that the company's quality costs total about 21 percent of its sales revenues. Somewhat shocked by the magnitude of the costs, Rob Rustin, president of Ulrich Company, decided to launch a major quality improvement program. For the coming year, it was decided to reduce quality costs to 17 percent of sales revenues. Although the amount of reduction was ambitious, most company officials believed that the goal could be realized. To improve the monitoring of the quality improvement program, Rob directed Pamela Golding, the controller, to prepare quarterly performance reports comparing budgeted and actual quality costs. Budgeted costs and sales for the first two months of the year are as follows:

	January	February
Sales	$500,000	$600,000
Quality costs:		
Warranty	$ 15,000	$ 18,000
Scrap	10,000	12,000
Incoming materials inspection	2,500	2,500
Product acceptance	13,000	15,000
Quality planning	2,000	2,000
Field inspection	12,000	14,000
Retesting	6,000	7,200
Allowances	7,500	9,000
New product review	500	500
Rework	9,000	10,800
Complaint adjustment	2,500	2,500
Downtime (defective parts)	5,000	6,000
Quality training	1,000	1,000
Total budgeted costs	$ 86,000	$100,500
Quality costs-sales ratio	17.2%	16.75%

Actual sales and actual quality costs were reported for January:

Sales	$500,000
Quality costs:	
Warranty	17,500
Scrap	12,500
Incoming materials inspection	2,500
Product acceptance	14,000
Quality planning	2,500
Field inspection	14,000
Retesting	7,000
Allowances	8,500
New product review	700
Rework	11,000
Complaint adjustment	2,500
Downtime	5,500
Quality training	1,000

REQUIRED:

1. Reorganize the quarterly budgets so that quality costs are grouped in one of four categories: appraisal, prevention, internal failure, and external failure (essentially, prepare a budgeted cost of quality report). Also, identify each cost as variable or fixed. (Assume that none are mixed costs.)

2. Prepare a performance report for January that compares actual costs with budgeted costs. Comment on the company's progress in improving quality and reducing its quality costs.

**21-16
Quality Cost
Performance
Reporting: One-
Year Trend; Long-
Range Analysis**
LO 4

In 1997, Danvers Company initiated a full-scale quality improvement program. At the end of the year, the president noted with some satisfaction that the defects per unit of product had dropped significantly compared to the prior year. She was also pleased that relationships with suppliers had improved and defective raw materials had declined. The new quality training program was also well-accepted by employees. Of most interest to the president, however, was the impact of the quality improvements on profitability. To help assess the dollar impact of the quality improvements, the actual sales and the actual quality costs for 1997 and 1998 are given below by quality category:

	1997	1998
Sales	$20,000,000	$25,000,000
Appraisal costs:		
Product inspection	800,000	750,000
Raw material inspection	100,000	70,000
Prevention costs:		
Quality training	10,000	100,000
Quality reporting	5,000	50,000
Quality improvement projects	5,000	250,000
Internal failure costs:		
Scrap	700,000	600,000
Rework	900,000	800,000
Yield losses	400,000	250,000
Retesting	500,000	400,000
External failure costs:		
Returned materials	400,000	400,000
Allowances	300,000	350,000
Warranty	1,000,000	1,100,000

All prevention costs are fixed (by discretion). Assume all other quality costs are unit-level variable.

REQUIRED:

1. Compute the relative distribution of quality costs for each year. Do you believe that the company is moving in the right direction in terms of the balance among the quality-cost categories? Explain.
2. Prepare a one-year trend performance report for 1998. How much have profits increased because of the quality improvements made by Danvers Company?
3. Estimate the additional improvement in profits if Danvers Company ultimately reduces its quality costs to 2.5 percent of sales revenues (assume sales of $25 million).

**21-17
Distribution of
Quality Costs**
LO 2

Paper Products Division produces paper diapers, napkins, and paper towels. The divisional manager has decided that quality costs can be minimized by distributing quality costs evenly among the four quality categories and reducing them to no more than 5 percent of sales. He has just received the following quality cost report:

Paper Products Division
Quality Cost Report
For the Year Ending December 31, 1998

	Diapers	Napkins	Towels	Total
Prevention costs:				
Quality training	$ 3,000	$ 2,500	$ 2,000	$ 7,500
Quality engineering	3,500	1,000	2,500	7,000
Quality audits	—	500	1,000	1,500
Quality reporting	2,500	2,000	1,000	5,500
Total prevention costs	$ 9,000	$ 6,000	$ 6,500	$ 21,500
Appraisal costs:				
Inspection, materials	$ 2,000	$ 3,000	$ 3,000	$ 8,000
Process acceptance	4,000	2,800	1,200	8,000
Product acceptance	2,000	1,200	2,300	5,500
Total appraisal costs	$ 8,000	$ 7,000	$ 6,500	$ 21,500
Internal failure costs:				
Scrap	$10,000	$ 3,000	$ 2,500	$ 15,500
Disposal costs	7,000	2,000	1,500	10,500
Downtime	1,000	1,500	2,500	5,000
Total internal failure costs	$18,000	$ 6,500	$ 6,500	$ 31,000
External failure costs:				
Allowances	$10,000	$ 3,000	$ 2,750	$ 15,750
Customer complaints	4,000	1,500	3,750	9,250
Product liability	1,000	—	—	1,000
Total external failure costs	$15,000	$ 4,500	$ 6,500	$ 26,000
Total quality costs	$50,000	$24,000	$26,000	$100,000

Assume that all prevention costs are fixed and that the remaining quality costs are variable (unit-level).

REQUIRED:

1. Assume that the sales revenue for the year totaled $2 million, with sales for each product as follows: diapers, $1 million; napkins, $600,000; towels, $400,000. Evaluate the distribution of costs for the division as a whole and for each product line. What recommendations do you have for the divisional manager?
2. Now assume that total sales of $1 million have this breakdown: diapers, $500,000; napkins, $300,000; towels, $200,000. Evaluate the distribution of costs for the division as a whole and for each product line in this case. Do you think it is possible to reduce the quality costs to 5 percent of sales for each product line and for the division as a whole and, simultaneously, achieve an equal distribution of the quality costs? What recommendations do you have?
3. Assume total sales of $1 million with this breakdown: diapers, $500,000; napkins, $180,000; towels, $320,000. Evaluate the distribution of quality costs. What recommendations for the divisional manager do you have?
4. Discuss the value of having quality costs reported by segment.

21-18
Trend Analysis;
Quality Costs
LO 4

In 1994, Jim Thane, president of Cawdor Electronics, received a report indicating that quality costs were 23 percent of sales. Faced with increasing pressures from imported goods, Jim resolved to take measures to improve the overall quality of the company's products. After hiring a consultant, the company began in 1995 an aggressive program of total quality control. At the end of 1998, Jim requested an analysis of the progress the company had made in reducing and controlling quality costs. The Accounting Department assembled the following data:

	Sales	Prevention	Appraisal	Internal Failure	External Failure
1994	$500,000	$ 5,000	$10,000	$40,000	$50,000
1995	600,000	20,000	20,000	50,000	60,000
1996	700,000	30,000	25,000	30,000	40,000
1997	600,000	35,000	35,000	20,000	25,000
1998	500,000	35,000	15,000	8,000	12,000

REQUIRED:

1. Compute the quality costs as a percentage of sales by category and in total for each year.
2. Explain why quality costs increased in total and as a percentage of sales in 1995, the first year of the quality improvement program.
3. Prepare a multiple-year trend graph for quality costs, both by total costs and by category. Using the graph, assess the progress made in reducing and controlling quality costs. Does the graph provide evidence that quality has improved? Explain.
4. Using the 1994 quality cost relationships (assume all costs are variable), calculate the quality costs that would have prevailed in 1997. By how much did profits increase in 1997 because of the quality improvement program? Repeat for 1998.

21-19
Case on Quality
Cost Performance
Reports
LO 4

Iona Company, a large printing company, is in its fourth year of a five-year quality improvement program. The program began in 1994 with an internal study that revealed the quality costs being incurred. In that year, a five-year plan was developed to lower quality costs to 10 percent of sales by the end of 1998. Sales and quality costs for each year are as follows:

	Sales Revenues	Quality Costs
1994	$10,000,000	$2,000,000
1995	10,000,000	1,800,000
1996	11,000,000	1,815,000
1997	12,000,000	1,680,000
1998*	12,000,000	1,320,000

*Budgeted figures

Quality costs by category are expressed as a percentage of sales as follows:

	Prevention	Appraisal	Internal Failure	External Failure
1994	1.0%	3.0%	7.0%	9.0%
1995	2.0	4.0	6.0	6.0
1996	2.5	4.0	5.0	5.0
1997	3.0	3.5	4.5	3.0
1998	3.5	3.5	2.0	2.0

The detail of the 1998 budget for quality costs is also provided.

Prevention costs:	
Quality planning	$ 150,000
Quality training	20,000
Quality improvement (special project)	80,000
Quality reporting	10,000
Appraisal costs:	
Proofreading	$ 500,000
Other inspection	50,000
Failure costs:	
Correction of typos	$ 150,000
Rework (because of customer complaints)	75,000
Plate revisions	55,000
Press downtime	100,000
Waste (because of poor work)	130,000
Total quality costs	$1,320,000

All prevention costs are fixed; all other quality costs are variable.

During 1998, the company had $12 million in sales. Actual quality costs for 1997 and 1998 are as follows:

	1998	1997
Quality planning	$150,000	$140,000
Quality training	20,000	20,000
Special project	100,000	120,000
Quality reporting	12,000	12,000
Proofreading	520,000	580,000
Other inspection	60,000	80,000
Correction of typos	165,000	200,000
Rework	76,000	131,000
Plate revisions	58,000	83,000
Press downtime	102,000	123,000
Waste	136,000	191,000

REQUIRED:

1. Prepare an interim quality cost performance report for 1998. Comment on the firm's ability to achieve its quality goals for the year.
2. Prepare a graph that shows the trend in total quality costs as a percentage of sales since the inception of the quality improvement program.
3. Prepare a graph that shows the trend for all four quality-cost categories for 1994 through 1998. How does this graph help management know that the reduction in total quality costs is attributable to quality improvements?
4. Assume that the company is preparing a second five-year plan to reduce quality costs to 2.5 percent of sales. Prepare a long-range quality cost performance report assuming sales of $15 million at the end of five years. Assume that the final planned relative distribution of quality costs is as follows: proofreading, 50 percent; other inspection, 13 percent; quality training, 30 percent; and quality reporting, 7 percent.

**21-20
Quality
Performance and
Ethical Behavior**

Lindell Manufacturing embarked on an ambitious quality program that is centered around continual improvement. This improvement is operationalized by declining quality costs from year to year. Lindell rewards plant managers, production supervisors, and workers with bonuses ranging from $100 to $1,000 if their factory meets its annual quality cost goals.

Len Smith, the manager of Lindell's Boise plant, felt obligated to do everything he could to provide this increase to his employees. Accordingly, he has decided to take the following actions during the last quarter of the year to meet the plant's budgeted quality cost targets:

a. Decrease inspections of the process and final product by 50 percent and transfer inspectors temporarily to quality training programs. Len believes this move will increase the inspectors' awareness of the importance of quality; also, decreasing inspection will produce significantly less downtime and less rework. By increasing the output and decreasing the costs of internal failure, the plant can meet the budgeted reductions for internal failure costs. Also, by showing an increase in the costs of quality training, the budgeted level for prevention costs can be met.

b. Delay replacing and repairing defective products until the beginning of the following year. While this may increase customer dissatisfaction somewhat, Len believes that most customers expect some inconvenience. Besides, the policy of promptly dealing with dissatisfied customers could be reinstated in three months. In the meantime, the action would significantly reduce the costs of external failure, allowing the plant to meet its budgeted target.

c. Cancel scheduled worker visits to customers' plants. This program, which has been very well-received by customers, enables Lindell workers to see just how the machinery they make is used by the customer and also gives them first-hand information on any remaining problems with the machinery. Workers who have gone on previous customer site visits came back enthusiastic and committed to Lindell's quality program. Lindell quality program staff believe that these visits will reduce defects during the following year.

REQUIRED:

1. Evaluate Len's ethical behavior. In this evaluation, consider his concern for his employees. Was he justified in taking the actions described in the problem? If not, what should he have done?

2. Assume that the company views Len's behavior as undesirable. What can it do to discourage it?

3. Assume that Len is a CMA and a member of the IMA. Refer to the ethical code for management accountants in Chapter 1. Are any of these ethical standards violated?

Chapter 22
Productivity: Measurement and Control

Virtual supermarket Peapod, Inc., sells time, not groceries. Customers order grocery items through a computer modem and receive their order at home during a 90-minute customer-specified delivery window. To maintain low prices, Peapod emphasizes productivity by modularizing its processes of ordering, shopping, holding, and delivery.

LEARNING OBJECTIVES

After studying this chapter, you should be able to:

1. Explain what productive efficiency means and describe the difference between technical and input tradeoff efficiency.
2. Explain what partial productivity measurement is and describe its advantages and disadvantages.
3. Explain what total productivity measurement is and describe its advantages.
4. Describe the role of productivity measurement in assessing activity improvement.

951

Continuous improvement implies that efficiency is increasing over time. In fact, to be competitive, organizations must increase efficiency. An organization must be as good or better than its competitors at taking materials, labor, machines, power, and other inputs and turning out high-quality goods and services. A company can create a competitive advantage by using fewer inputs to produce a given output or by producing more output for a given set of inputs. Management needs to assess the potential and actual effectiveness of decisions that are geared to improve efficiency. Management also needs to monitor and control efficiency changes. Efficiency measures satisfy these performance and control objectives. In previous chapters, various approaches to measuring efficiency have been presented. For example, we have presented and discussed such measurement approaches as value-added and nonvalue-added cost reports, trends in cost, and activity flexible budgeting. In this chapter, we will explore efficiency measures that are concerned with the relationship of inputs and outputs, referred to as *productivity measures.*

PRODUCTIVE EFFICIENCY

Objective 1

Explain what productive efficiency means and describe the difference between technical and input tradeoff efficiency.

productivity
total productive
  efficiency
technical efficiency
input tradeoff
  efficiency

Productivity is concerned with producing output efficiently and specifically addresses the relationship of output and the inputs used to produce the output. Usually, different combinations or mixes of inputs can be used to produce a given level of output. **Total productive efficiency** is the point at which two conditions are satisfied: (1) for any mix of inputs that will produce a given output, no more of any one input is used than necessary to produce the output and (2) given the mixes that satisfy the first condition, the least costly mix is chosen. The first condition is driven by technical relationships and, therefore, is referred to as **technical efficiency**. Viewing activities as inputs, the first condition requires the elimination of all nonvalue-added activities and that value-added activities be performed with the minimal quantities needed to produce the given output. The second condition is driven by relative input price relationships and, therefore, is referred to as **input tradeoff efficiency**. Input prices determine the *relative proportions* that should be used of each input. Deviation from these fixed proportions creates input tradeoff inefficiency.

Productivity improvement programs involve moving towards a state of total productive efficiency. Technical improvements in productivity can be achieved by using fewer inputs to produce the same output or by producing more output using the same inputs or more output with relatively fewer inputs. For example, in 1987, Birmingham Steel Corporation produced 167,000 tons of steel with 184 workers—an average of 908 tons of steel per worker.[1] By 1992, the output had increased to 276,000 tons of steel using 207 workers—an average of 1,333 tons per worker. By 1987 productivity standards, about 303 workers would have been needed to produce 276,000 tons. Thus, output increased and fewer workers were needed. Exhibit 22-1 illustrates the three ways to achieve an improvement in technical efficiency. The output is tons of steel, and the inputs are labor (number of workers) and capital (dollars invested in automated equipment). Notice that the relative proportions of the inputs are held constant so that all productivity improvement is attributable to improving technical efficiency. Productivity

1.   Steven Rattner, "If Productivity's Rising, Why Are Jobs Paying Less?" *New York Times Magazine,* September 19, 1993, pp. 54, 96–97.

Exhibit 22-1
Improving Technical Efficiency

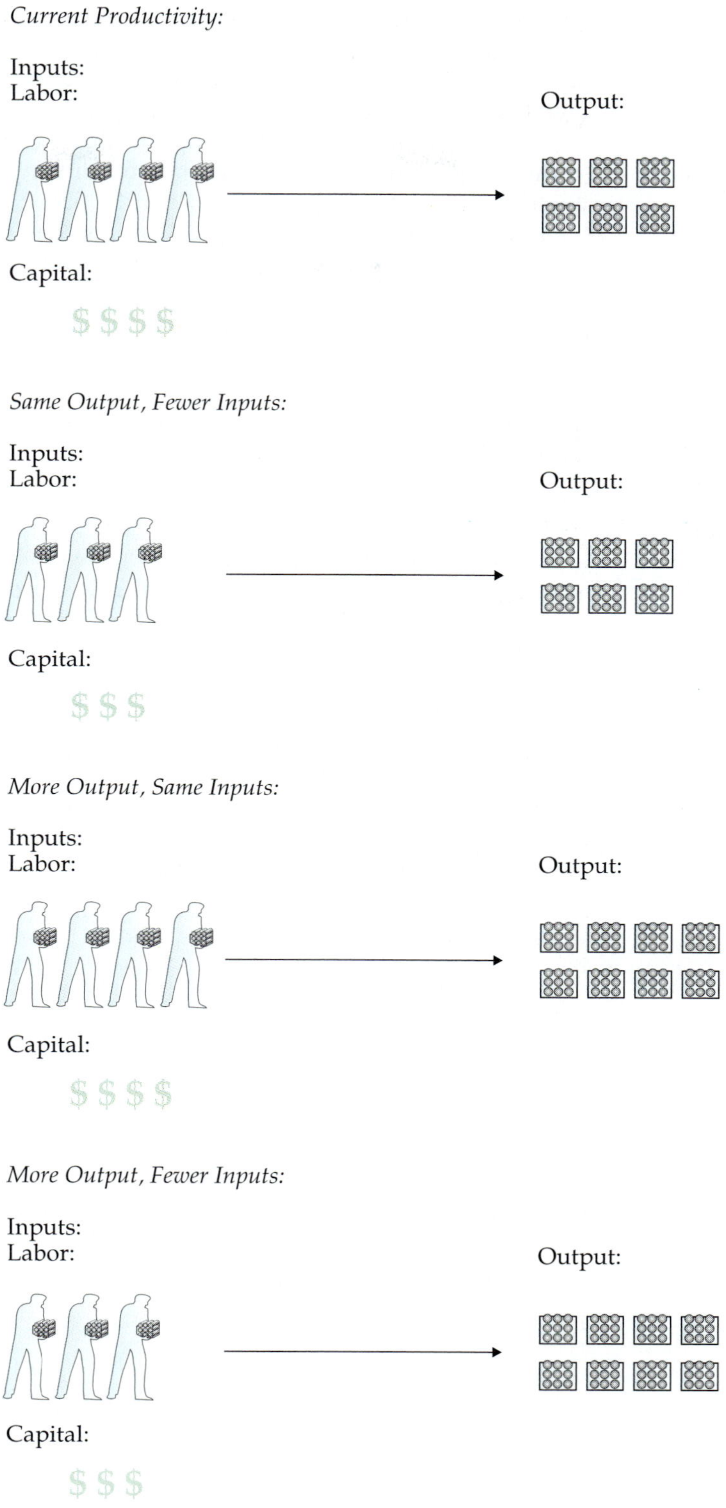

Current Productivity:

Inputs:
Labor: Output:

Capital:

$ $ $ $

Same Output, Fewer Inputs:

Inputs:
Labor: Output:

Capital:

$ $ $

More Output, Same Inputs:

Inputs:
Labor: Output:

Capital:

$ $ $ $

More Output, Fewer Inputs:

Inputs:
Labor: Output:

Capital:

$ $ $

improvement can also be achieved by trading off more costly inputs for less costly inputs. Exhibit 22-2 illustrates the possibility of improving productivity by increasing input tradeoff efficiency. Although improving technical efficiency is what most think of when improving productivity is mentioned, input tradeoff efficiency can offer significant opportunities for increasing overall economic efficiency. Choosing the right combination of inputs can be as critical as choosing the right quantity of inputs. Notice in Exhibit 22-2 that input Combination I produces the same output as input Combination II but that the cost is $5,000,000 less. Total measures of productivity are usually a combination of changes in technical and input tradeoff efficiency.

PARTIAL PRODUCTIVITY MEASUREMENT

Objective 2
Explain what partial productivity measurement is and describe its advantages and disadvantages.

productivity measurement
partial productivity measurement

Productivity measurement is simply a quantitative assessment of productivity changes. The objective is to assess whether productive efficiency has increased or decreased. Productivity measurement can be actual or prospective. Actual productivity measurement allows managers to assess, monitor, and control changes. Prospective measurement is forward-looking, and it serves as input for strategic decision making. Specifically, prospective measurement allows managers to compare relative benefits of different input combinations, choosing the inputs and input mix that provide the greatest benefit. Productivity measures can be developed for each input separately or for all inputs jointly. Measuring productivity for one input at a time is called **partial productivity measurement**.

Exhibit 22-2
Input Tradeoff Efficiency

Technically Efficient Combination I:
Total cost of inputs = $20,000,000

Labor:

Capital:

$ $ $

Output:

Technically Efficient Combination II:
Total cost of inputs = $25,000,000

Labor:

Capital:

$ $ $ $

Output:

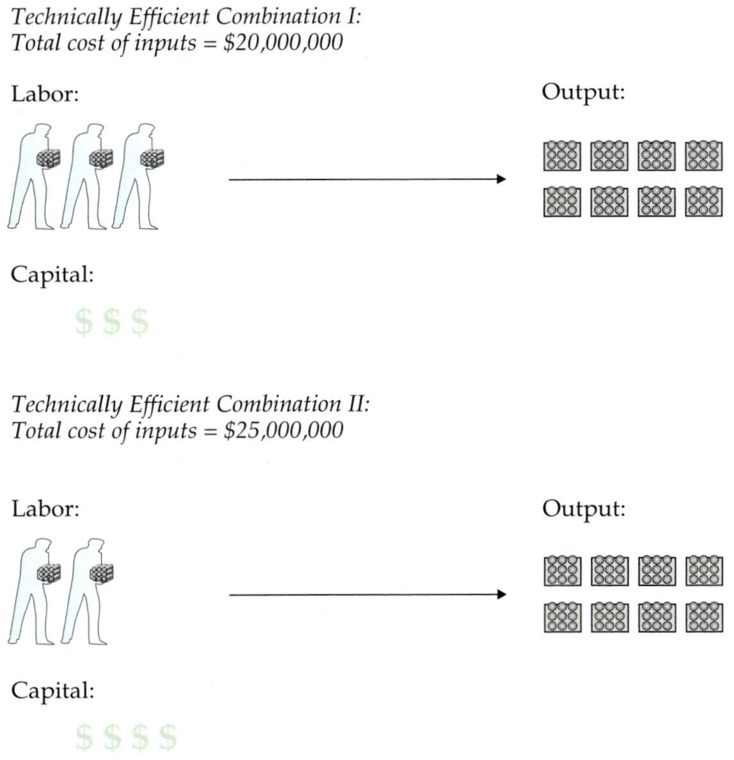

Partial Productivity Measurement Defined

Productivity of a single input is typically measured by calculating the ratio of the output to the input:

$$\text{Productivity ratio} = \text{Output/Input}$$

operational
productivity
measure

financial productivity
measure

Because the productivity of only one input is being measured, the measure is called a *partial productivity measure*. If both output and input are measured in physical quantities, then we have an **operational productivity measure**. If output or input is expressed in dollars, then we have a **financial productivity measure**.

Assume, for example, that in 1997, Kankul Company produced 120,000 motors for small window air conditioning units and used 40,000 hours of labor. The labor productivity ratio is three motors per hour (120,000/40,000). This is an operational measure, since the units are expressed in physical terms. If the selling price of each motor is $50 and the cost of labor is $12 per hour, then output and input can be expressed in dollars. The labor productivity ratio, expressed in financial terms, is $12.50 of revenue per dollar of labor cost ($6,000,000/$480,000).

Partial Measures and Measuring Changes in Productive Efficiency

The labor productivity ratio of three motors per hour measures the 1997 productivity experience of Kankul. By itself, the ratio conveys little information about productive efficiency or whether the company has improving or declining productivity. It is possible, however, to make a statement about increasing or decreasing productivity efficiency by measuring *changes* in productivity. To do so, the actual current productivity measure is compared with the productivity measure of a prior period. This prior period is referred to as the **base period** and serves to set the benchmark or standard for measuring changes in productive efficiency. The prior period can be any period desired. It could, for example, be the preceding year, the preceding week, or even the period during which the last batch of products was produced. For strategic evaluations, the base period is usually chosen as an earlier year. For operational control, the base period tends to be close to the current period—such as the preceding batch of products or the preceding week.

base period

To illustrate, assume that 1997 is the base period and that the labor productivity standard, therefore, is three motors per hour. Further assume that late in 1997, Kankul decided to try a new procedure for producing and assembling the motors with the expectation that the new procedure would use less labor. In 1998, 150,000 motors were produced, using 37,500 hours of labor. The labor productivity ratio for 1998 is four motors per hour (150,000/37,500). The *change* in productivity is a one-unit-per-hour *increase* in productivity (from three units per hour in 1997 to four units per hour in 1998). The change is a significant improvement in labor productivity and provides evidence supporting the efficacy of the new process.

Advantages of Partial Measures

Partial measures allow managers to focus on the use of a particular input. Operating partial measures have the advantage of being easily interpreted by all within the organization. Consequently, partial operational measures are easy to use for assessing productivity performance of operating personnel. Laborers, for instance, can relate to units produced per hour or units produced per pound of material. Thus, partial operational measures provide feedback that operating personnel can relate to and understand—measures that deal with the specific inputs over which they have control. The ability to understand and relate to the measures increases the likelihood that they will be accepted by operating personnel. Furthermore, for operational control, the standards for performance are often very short-run in nature. For example, standards can be the productivity ratios of prior batches of goods. Using this standard, productivity trends within the year itself can be tracked.

Disadvantages of Partial Measures

Partial measures, used in isolation, can be misleading. A decline in the productivity of one input may be necessary to increase the productivity of another. Such a tradeoff is desirable if overall costs decline, but the effect would be missed by using either partial measure. For example, changing a process so that direct laborers take less time to assemble a product may increase scrap and waste while leaving total output unchanged. Labor productivity has increased, but productive use of materials has declined. If the increase in the cost of waste and scrap outweighs the savings of the decreased labor, overall productivity has declined.

Two important conclusions can be drawn from this example. First, the possible existence of tradeoffs mandates a total measure of productivity for assessing the merits of productivity decisions. Only by looking at the total productivity effect of all inputs can managers accurately draw any conclusions about overall productivity performance. Second, because of the possibility of tradeoffs, a total measure of productivity must assess the aggregate financial consequences and, therefore, should be a financial measure.

TOTAL PRODUCTIVITY MEASUREMENT

Objective 3
Explain what total productivity measurement is and describe its advantages.

total productivity measurement

Measuring productivity for all inputs at once is called **total productivity measurement**. In practice, it may not be necessary to measure the effect of all inputs. Many firms measure the productivity of only those factors that are thought to be relevant indicators of organizational performance and success. Thus, in practical terms, total productivity measurement can be defined as focusing on a limited number of inputs, which, in total, indicates organizational success. In either case, total productivity measurement requires the development of a multifactor measurement approach. A common multifactor approach suggested in the productivity literature (but found rarely in practice) is the use of aggregate productivity indices. Aggregate indices are complex and difficult to interpret and have not been generally accepted. Two approaches that have gained some acceptance are *profile measurement* and *profit-linked productivity measurement*.

Profile Productivity Measurement

profile measurement

Producing a product involves numerous critical inputs such as labor, materials, capital, and energy. **Profile measurement** provides a series or vector of separate and distinct partial operational measures. Profiles can be compared over time to provide information about productivity changes. To illustrate the profile approach, we will use only two inputs: labor and materials. Let's return to the Kankul Company example. As before, Kankul implements a new production and assembly process in 1998. Only now let's assume that the new process affects both labor and materials. Initially, let's look at the case for which the productivity of both inputs moves in the same direction. The following data for 1997 and 1998 are available:

	1997	1998
Number of motors produced	120,000	150,000
Labor hours used	40,000	37,500
Materials used (lbs.)	1,200,000	1,428,571

Exhibit 22-3 provides productivity ratio profiles for each year. The 1997 profile is (3, 0.100), and the 1998 profile is (4, 0.105). Comparing profiles for the two years, we can see that productivity increased for both labor and materials (from 3 to 4 for labor and from 0.100 to 0.105 for materials). The profile comparison provides enough information for a manager to conclude that the new assembly process has definitely improved overall productivity. The *value* of this improvement, however, is not revealed by the ratios.

As just shown, profile analysis can provide managers with useful insights about changes in productivity. However, comparing productivity profiles will not always reveal the nature of the overall change in productive efficiency. In some cases, profile analysis will not provide any clear indication of whether a productivity change is good or bad. To illustrate this, let's revise the Kankul data to allow for tradeoffs among the two inputs. Assume that all the data are the same except for materials used in 1998. Let the materials used in 1998 be 1,700,000 pounds. Using this revised number, the productivity profiles for 1997 and 1998 are presented in Exhibit 22-4. The productivity profile for 1997 is still (3, 0.100), but the profile for 1998 has changed to (4, 0.088). Comparing productivity profiles now provides a mixed signal. Productivity for labor has increased from 3 to 4, but productivity for materials has decreased from 0.100 to 0.088. The new process has caused a tradeoff in the productivity in the two measures. Furthermore, while a profile analysis reveals that the tradeoff exists, it does not reveal whether the tradeoff is good or bad. If the economic effect of the productivity changes is positive, then the tradeoff is good; otherwise, it must be viewed as bad.

Exhibit 22-3
Productivity Measurement: Profile Analysis, No Tradeoffs

Partial Operational Productivity Ratios	1997 Profile[a]	1998 Profile[b]
Labor productivity ratio	3.000	4.000
Material productivity ratio	0.100	0.105

[a] Labor: 120,000/40,000; Materials: 120,000/1,200,000
[b] Labor: 150,000/37,500; Materials: 150,000/1,428,571

Exhibit 22-4
Productivity Measurement: Profile Analysis with Tradeoffs

Partial Operational Productivity Ratios	1997 Profile[a]	1998 Profile[b]
Labor productivity ratio	3.000	4.000
Material productivity ratio	0.100	0.088

[a] Labor: 120,000/40,000; Materials: 120,000/1,200,000
[b] Labor: 150,000/37,500; Materials: 150,000/1,700,000

Valuing the tradeoffs would allow us to assess the economic effect of the decision to change the assembly process. Furthermore, by valuing the productivity change, we obtain a total measure of productivity.

Profit-Linked Productivity Measurement

Assessing the effects of productivity changes on current profits is one way to value productivity changes. Profits change from the base period to the current period. Some of that profit change is attributable to productivity changes. Measuring the amount of profit change attributable to productivity change is defined as **profit-linked productivity measurement**.[2]

profit-linked
productivity
measurement

Assessing the effect of productivity changes on current-period profits will help managers understand the economic importance of productivity changes. Linking productivity changes to profits is described by the following rule:

Profit-Linkage Rule. For the current period, calculate the cost of the inputs that would have been used in the absence of any productivity change and compare this cost with the cost of the inputs actually used. The difference in costs is the amount by which profits changed because of productivity changes.

To apply the linkage rule, the inputs that would have been used for the current period in the absence of a productivity change must be calculated. Let *PQ* represent this productivity-neutral quantity of input. To determine the productivity-neutral quantity for a particular input, divide the current-period output by the input's base-period productivity ratio:

$$PQ = \text{Current output/Base-period productivity ratio}$$

To illustrate the application of the profit-linked rule, let's return to the Kankul example with input tradeoffs. To the data, we must add some cost information. The expanded Kankul data set is given below:

	1997	1998
Number of motors produced	120,000	150,000
Labor hours used	40,000	37,500
Materials used (lbs.)	1,200,000	1,700,000
Unit selling price (motors)	$50	$48
Wages per labor hour	$11	$12
Cost per pound of material	$2	$3

Current output (1998) is 150,000 motors. From Exhibit 22-4, we know that the base-period productivity ratios are 3 and 0.10 for labor and materials, respec-

2.   Several profit-linked productivity measures have been developed and used by firms. The American Productivity Center has developed a profit-linked measure described in J. G. Belcher Jr., *The Productivity Management Process*, The American Productivity Center, Houston, 1984. D. M. Miller developed and used a profit-linked measure while working for Ethyl Corporation. It is described in D. M. Miller, "Profitability = Productivity + Price Recovery," *Harvard Business Review*, May–June 1984, pp. 145–153. A third profit-linked measure is described in R. D. Banker, S. M. Datar, and R. S. Kaplan, "Productivity Measurement and Management Accounting," *Journal of Accounting, Auditing, and Finance*, 1989. The profit-linked measure described in this text is essentially a modification of the three measures above. The modification increases the accuracy of profit-linked measurement and allows a connection to the operational and partial measures of productivity. It also establishes an equivalency among the three measures. See Don R. Hansen, Maryanne Mowen, and Lawrence Hammer, "Profit-Linked Productivity Measurement," *Journal of Management Accounting Research*, Fall 1992, pp. 79–98.

tively. Using this information, the productivity-neutral quantity for each input is computed as follows:

$$PQ \text{ (labor)} = 150,000/3 = 50,000 \text{ hrs.}$$
$$PQ \text{ (materials)} = 150,000/0.10 = 1,500,000 \text{ lbs.}$$

For our example, PQ gives labor and material inputs that *would have been used* in 1998, assuming no productivity change. What the cost would have been for these productivity-neutral quantities in 1998 is computed by multiplying each individual input quantity *(PQ)* by its current price *(P)* and adding:[3]

Cost of labor: $PQ \times P = 50,000 \times \$12 =$	$ 600,000
Cost of materials: $PQ \times P = 1,500,000 \times \$3 =$	4,500,000
Total *PQ* cost	$5,100,000

The actual cost of inputs is obtained by multiplying the actual quantity *(AQ)* by current input price *(P)* for each input and adding:

Cost of labor: $AQ \times P = 37,500 \times \$12 =$	$ 450,000
Cost of materials: $AQ \times P = 1,700,000 \times \$3 =$	5,100,000
Total current cost	$5,550,000

Finally, the productivity effect on profits is computed by subtracting the total current cost from the total PQ cost.

$$
\begin{aligned}
\text{Profit-linked effect} &= \text{Total PQ cost} - \text{Total current cost} \\
&= \$5,100,000 - \$5,550,000 \\
&= \$450,000 \text{ decrease in profits}
\end{aligned}
$$

The calculation of the profit-linked effect is summarized in Exhibit 22-5.

The summary in Exhibit 22-5 reveals that the net effect of the process change was unfavorable. Profits declined by $450,000 because of the productivity changes. Notice also that profit-linked productivity effects can be assigned to individual inputs. The increase in labor productivity creates a $150,000 increase in profits; however, the drop in materials productivity caused a $600,000 decrease in profits. Most of the profit decrease came from an increase in materials usage— apparently waste, scrap, and spoiled units are much greater with the new process. Thus, the profit-linked measure provides partial measurement effects as well as a total measurement effect. The total profit-linked productivity measure is the sum of the individual partial measures. This property makes the profit-linked measure ideal for assessing tradeoffs. A much clearer picture of the effects of the changes in productivity emerges. Unless waste and scrap can be brought under better control, the company ought to return to the old assembly process. Of course, it is possible that the learning effects of the new process are not yet fully captured and further improvements in labor productivity might be observed. As

3.   Base-period input prices are frequently used to value productivity changes. It has been shown, however, that current input prices should be used for accurate profit-linked productivity measurement. See Hansen, Mowen, and Hammer, "Profit-Linked Productivity Measurement."

Exhibit 22-5

*Profit-Linked Productiv-
ity Measurement*

Input	(1) PQ*	(2) PQ × P	(3) AQ	(4) AQ × P	(2) − (4) (PQ × P) − (AQ × P)
Labor	50,000	$ 600,000	37,500	$ 450,000	$ 150,000
Materials	1,500,000	4,500,000	1,700,000	5,100,000	(600,000)
		$5,100,000		$5,550,000	$(450,000)

*Labor: 150,000/3; Materials: 150,000/0.10

labor becomes more proficient at the new process, it is possible that the material usage could also decrease.

Price-Recovery Component

The profit-linked measure computes the amount of profit change from the base period to the current period attributable to productivity changes. This generally will not be equal to the total profit change between the two periods. The difference between the total profit change and the profit-linked productivity change is called the **price-recovery component**. This component is the change in revenue less a change in the cost of inputs, *assuming no productivity changes*. It therefore measures the ability of revenue changes to cover changes in the cost of inputs, assuming no productivity change.

price-recovery
component

To calculate the price recovery component, we first need to compute the change in profits for each period. This computation is shown below:

	1998	1997	Difference
Revenues	$7,200,000	$6,000,000	$ 1,200,000
Cost of inputs	5,550,000	2,840,000	2,710,000
Profit	$1,650,000	$3,160,000	$(1,510,000)

$$\text{Price recovery} = \text{Profit change} - \text{Profit-linked productivity change}$$
$$= \$(1,510,000) - \$(450,000)$$
$$= \$(1,060,000)$$

The increase in revenues would not have been sufficient to recover the increase in the cost of the inputs. The decrease in productivity simply aggravated the price recovery problem. Note, however, that increases in productivity can be used to offset price recovery losses.

MEASURING CHANGES IN ACTIVITY EFFICIENCY

Objective 4
Describe the role of productivity measurement in assessing activity improvement.

A contemporary responsibility accounting system focuses on activities and seeks to improve the efficiency with which activities are performed. Measuring changes in activity efficiency can be an important part of an activity-based management system. As we have seen, productivity measurement deals with the relationship of inputs and outputs. Two approaches for activity productivity analysis will be discussed: (1) activity productivity analysis and (2) process productivity

activity productivity
analysis

process productivity
analysis

analysis. **Activity productivity analysis** is an approach that directly measures changes in activity productivity. In this case, an activity is viewed as an entity that uses inputs to produce an output. **Process productivity analysis** measures activity productivity by treating activities as inputs to a process that produces an output. In this instance, activity output is treated as a process input and partial productivity measures are used to evaluate activity efficiency. Both approaches provide useful insights, although the process approach provides a richer analysis because it considers the linkages among activities.

Activity Productivity Analysis

An activity can be viewed as an entity that transforms inputs into an output. The inputs are the resources consumed by an activity. Recall that resources are the economic elements that allow an activity to be performed. Thus, in effect, resources are the inputs or factors of production that are used by an activity to create its output. These inputs or resources are identical in concept to the factors used to produce a product: materials, labor, capital, energy, etc. Accordingly, the key to activity productivity analysis is defining activity output and an appropriate activity output measure. Once the output measure is identified, then both profile and profit-linked productivity analyses are possible. Exhibit 22-6 illustrates the activity model that provides the conceptual foundation for activity productivity analysis.

An Illustrative Example To illustrate activity productivity analysis, we will focus on a single activity. Suppose that the activity is purchasing. The output of purchasing is a purchase order, and the number of purchase orders is a possible output measure. For simplicity, assume that labor and materials (forms, postage stamps, and envelopes) are the only resources consumed by the activity. At the end of 1997, the purchasing activity had been streamlined by redesigning the purchase order, reducing the number of suppliers, and reducing the number of

Exhibit 22-6
*Activity Productivity
Model*

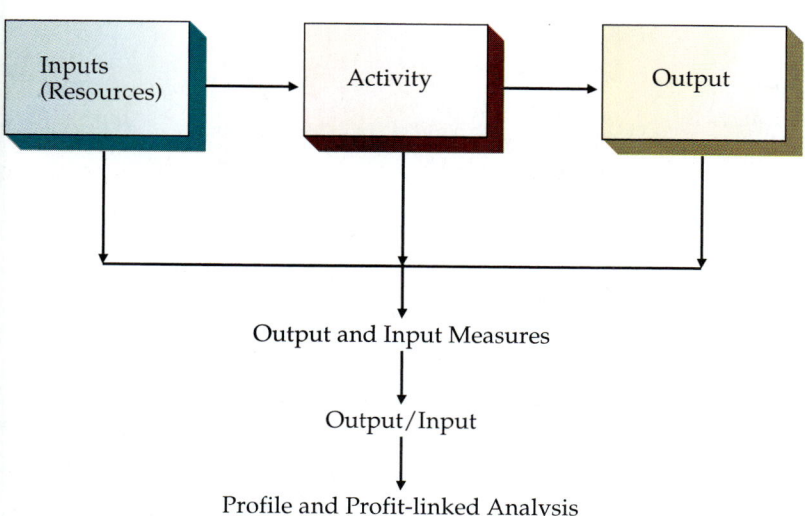

distinct parts that needed to be ordered. Activity data for purchasing is given below for 1997 and 1998. The 1998 data reflect the effect of the activity improvements.

	1997	1998
Number of purchase orders	200,000	240,000
Materials used (lbs.)	50,000	50,000
Labor used (number of workers)	40	30
Cost per pound of material	$1	$0.80
Cost (salary) per worker	$30,000	$33,000

Exhibit 22-7 presents the profile and profit-linked analyses for the purchasing activity. Profile analysis reveals that productivity improved for both partial input measures. The value of these productivity improvements is $602,000—with the majority of the value being created by an increase in purchasing labor productivity. Thus, changes in activity productivity can be assessed or predicted using the same methodology available for assessing manufacturing productivity.

Limitations of Activity Productivity Analysis Activities within an organization can be classified as value-added and nonvalue-added. Value-added activities that are performed inefficiently cause nonvalue-added costs and can be improved. Thus, activity productivity analysis can be a useful tool for predicting and monitoring efficiency improvements for the value-added category of activities. Nonvalue-added activities are unnecessary activities, and firms should strive to eliminate these activities. Increasing the efficiency of an unnecessary activity does not make a lot of sense. In fact, it is possible that productivity ratios taken over time might signal a decrease in nonvalue-added activity productivity, and yet the underlying change may very well be consistent with the objective of reducing and eliminating the nonvalue-added activity. For example, suppose that the output of materials handling is measured by number of moves and that labor is the only significant activity input. Suppose that efforts are made to reduce the user demands for materials handling. In 1997, 50,000 moves were made using 10

Exhibit 22-7
Activity Productivity Analysis Illustrated

Profile Analysis:

	1997	1998
Materials	4	4.8
Labor	5,000	8,000

Profit-Linked Productivity Measurement:

Input	(1) PQ*	(2) PQ × P	(3) AQ	(4) AQ × P	(2) − (4) (PQ × P) − (AQ × P)
Labor	60,000	$ 48,000	50,000	$ 40,000	$ 8,000
Materials	48	1,584,000	30	990,000	594,000
		$1,632,000		$1,030,000	$602,000

*240,000/4; 240,000/5,000

workers, producing a productivity ratio of 5,000 moves per worker. In 1998, the demand for materials movement decreased to 22,000 moves and 5 workers because of the improvement efforts, producing a productivity ratio of 4,400 moves per worker. Comparing ratios indicates that activity productivity has decreased. Yet the actions taken have produced results that are fully consistent with reducing and eliminating the materials-handling activity. Thus, it seems reasonable to restrict activity productivity analysis to value-added activities.

Process Productivity Analysis

Process productivity analysis treats activities as inputs and evaluates activity productivity by relating activities to the output produced by the process. A partial measure of productivity is computed for each activity that belongs to the process. These partial measures are used for profile and profit-linked analyses. This approach has the advantage of allowing both value-added and nonvalue-added activities to be considered simultaneously. Maintaining or increasing process output while reducing and eliminating nonvalue-added activities should show up as a productivity improvement (the same or greater output with fewer inputs is a technical efficiency improvement). Similarly, improving value-added activities should be reflected as a productivity improvement. Also, it is possible to evaluate the effect on process productivity resulting from tradeoffs among activities that make up the process. Process improvement or innovation means finding new ways—often radically new ways—of producing the process's output. This is accomplished by using activity selection, activity reduction, activity elimination, and activity sharing. The effect is to change the mix and quantity of activities that define the process. Process productivity analysis offers a way to measure the proposed and actual *economic* effects of process improvement or innovation.

Process Productivity Model Exhibit 22-8 summarizes and illustrates the process productivity model. Defining the input measure for each activity is a key element of the model. Since the output of each activity is consumed by the output of the process, the input measure is simply the activity output measure. The cost per

Exhibit 22-8
Process Productivity Model

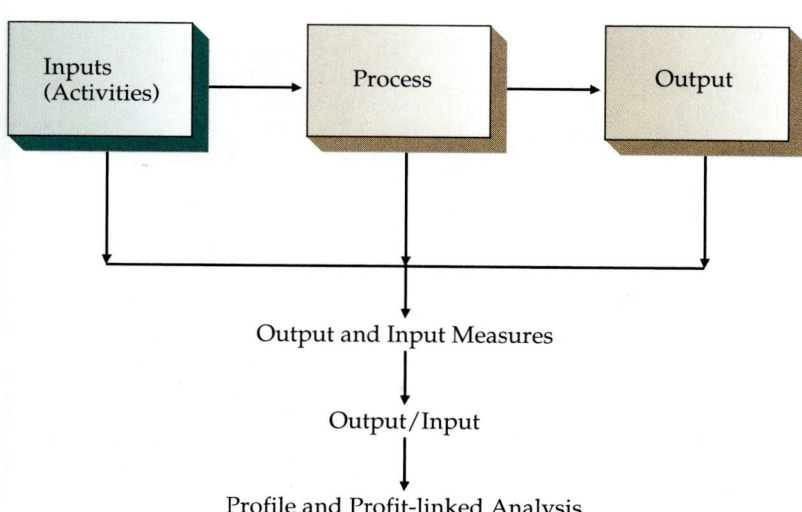

unit of activity input is the *activity rate*. Process output must also be defined and measured. Each organization has a variety of processes such as product development, procurement, manufacturing, sales, order fulfillment, and customer service. Each process has one or more outputs. Manufacturing, for example, may produce two or more products. In this case, products are the output of manufacturing. Where a process has multiple output measures, productivity analysis is carried out for each type of output. Inputs are measured by computing the demands that each product (output) makes on each activity. For profit-linked analysis, an aggregate process productivity measure is obtained by summing the profit-linked measures for each output.

An Illustrative Example Carthage Company produces two different types of hunting rifles in the same plant: Model A and Model B. Assume that the manufacturing process is defined by the following activities: machining, assembly, inspection, and rework. Of the four activities, machining and assembly are value-added and inspection and rework are nonvalue-added. At the end of 1997, Carthage initiated some process changes that were designed to improve quality and production methods. The changes in methods were expected to increase the precision of machining and decrease required machine time; however, the resulting parts would be slightly more difficult to assemble and were expected to take more assembly time. If the increase in quality occurred as expected, then the process would need less inspection activity and would have less rework to do. Information relating to the process and its two products is presented in Exhibit 22-9. Exhibit 22-10 provides the process productivity analysis based on the data provided in Exhibit 22-9.

The productivity results in Exhibit 22-10 show that activity productivity increased for all activities except for assembly (based on the profile analysis for both models). Notice that output increased and nonvalued-added inputs decreased significantly, producing dramatic increases in productivity ratios for the two nonvalue-added activities. Thus, the changes in activity productivity

Exhibit 22-9
Productivity Data:
Carthage Company
Example

	1997	1998
Model A:		
Units produced	20,000	25,000
Machine hours used	20,000	20,000
Assembly hours used	5,000	6,500
Inspection hours used	10,000	5,000
Units reworked	1,000	500
Model B:		
Units produced	10,000	12,000
Machine hours used	5,000	4,000
Assembly hours used	2,000	2,600
Inspection hours used	4,000	2,200
Units reworked	400	200
Activity rates:		
Machining (per machine hour)	$39	$40
Assembly (per assembly hour)	9	10
Inspection (per inspection hour)	10	12
Rework (per unit reworked)	20	20

Exhibit 22-10
*Process Productivity
Analysis Illustrated:
Carthage Example*

Model A
Profile Analysis:

	1997	1998
Machining	1	1.25
Assembly	4	3.8
Inspection	2	5.0
Rework	20	50.0

Profit-Linked Productivity Measurement:

Input	(1) PQ*	(2) PQ × P	(3) AQ	(4) AQ × P	(2) − (4) (PQ × P) − (AQ × P)
Machining	25,000	$1,000,000	20,000	$800,000	$200,000
Assembly	6,250	62,500	6,500	65,000	(2,500)
Inspection	12,500	150,000	5,000	60,000	90,000
Rework	1,250	25,000	500	10,000	15,000
		$1,237,500		$935,000	$302,500

*25,000/1; 25,000/4; 25,000/2; 25,000/20

Model B
Profile Analysis:

	1997	1998
Machining	2.0	3.0
Assembly	5.0	4.6
Inspection	2.5	5.5
Rework	25.0	60.0

Profit-Linked Productivity Measurement:

Input	(1) PQ*	(2) PQ × P	(3) AQ	(4) AQ × P	(2) − (4) (PQ × P) − (AQ × P)
Machining	6,000	$240,000	4,000	$160,000	$ 80,000
Assembly	2,400	24,000	2,600	26,000	(2,000)
Inspection	4,800	57,600	2,200	26,400	31,200
Rework	480	9,600	200	4,000	5,600
		$331,200		$216,400	$114,800

*12,000/2; 12,000/5; 12,000/2.5; 12,000/25

Aggregate Process Productivity:
Profit-Linked Measure

Model A	$302,500
Model B	114,800
Total	$417,300

occurred as expected. Furthermore, the value of the productivity changes is positive, indicating a favorable tradeoff—the fact that assembly productivity decreased is not a bad outcome given the gains made with the other activities. Finally, the aggregate measure tells us that total process productivity improved by $417,300. This success was achieved by reducing the levels of nonvalue-added activities and by improving the machining activity.

Service Productivity The process productivity model is easily adapted to service organizations. All organizations have processes. These processes can be identified, activities and output can be defined, and productivity measurement can occur. IBM Credit, for example is a service organization, offering financing for the computers, software, and services that IBM Corporation sells.[4] Within IBM Credit, one of the major processes is its quote preparation process. The quote preparation process is defined by the following activities: logging the request, assessing creditworthiness, modifying loan covenants, pricing, and preparing and delivering a quote letter. Since the activities were located in separate departments, the process also included a movement activity—an activity that required the transfer of each activity's output from one location to another. Essentially, the customer's credit application was transferred from department to department, a transfer occurring only after a particular department had finished its activity (e.g., the credit department transfers the application to the business practices department after it has assessed creditworthiness). The process's output can be defined as financing approval and can be measured by the number of quotes. Before any effort at process improvement, it took about six days to prepare a quote. IBM Credit redesigned the process by eliminating the nonvalue-added movement activity. It accomplished this by having one person process the entire application from beginning to end. This had two outcomes. First, the time required to process an application was reduced from six days to a few hours. Second, the labor productivity ratio was dramatically improved. The number of workers remained about the same, and yet the number of quotes being processed increased 100 times. This means, for example, that if the partial labor productivity ratio was 10 before the improvement, it is now 1,000!

Limitations and Cautions of Process Productivity Measurement Since activity output is process input, reducing nonvalue-added activities should normally show up as a process productivity improvement. Why? Reducing nonvalue-added activities means finding ways to produce the same or higher process output with less nonvalue-added activity output, and, thus, the output/input ratios will show an increase. The objective is to produce process output without any nonvalue-added activity input. Reducing and eliminating nonvalue-added activities means improving the technical efficiency of processes. Thus, it is important to identify all nonvalue-added activity inputs for a process. This means that we must exercise caution in identifying and defining the activities that are used by the process being evaluated.

Consider, for example, the procurement process. This process is made up of three major (macro) activities: purchasing, receiving, and paying bills. These

4.   A more complete discussion of the IBM Credit example can be found in the following two sources: Michael Hammer and James Champy, *Reengineering the Corporation,* HarperBusiness, New York, 1993, pp. 36–39; Thomas H. Davenport, *Process Innovation,* Harvard Business School Press, Boston, 1993, pp. 2, 32–33, and 158.

activities would generally be classified as value-added. In reality, however, these activities may be subprocesses and are made up of other, finer activities. Some of these finer activities that define these subprocesses may themselves be non-value-added. For example, paying bills may be defined by activities such as comparing and matching source documents, resolving discrepancies, and issuing checks. Of the three finer activities, resolving discrepancies is clearly a nonvalue-added activity and reducing and eliminating this activity should improve overall process productivity. Yet, if this activity is buried in the paying bills activity and process productivity is measured relative to this more macro activity, then the improvement may not be detected. Specifically, eliminating the nonvalue-added activity of resolving discrepancies may not affect the activity output measure, number of bills paid, or the process output measure, number of bought and paid for parts. Thus, the productivity measure would remain unchanged in spite of a process productivity improvement. The solution is to define the process inputs at the finer level (resolving discrepancies should be a process input, measured by number of discrepancies resolved).

Value-added activities also pose a similar problem. Improving the efficiency of a value-added activity within a process may not show up as a process productivity improvement. For example, less inputs may be used to produce the same value-added activity output, which in turn, is used to produce the same process output. Thus, separate activity productivity analyses for value-added activities is needed. The sum of the individual profit-linked measures for all value-added activities within the process could be used to measure the effect on process productivity of individual activity improvements. Of course, there are process productivity improvements for value-added activities that will be picked up by process level productivity analysis—specifically those improvements (or innovations) that directly affect the quantity and type of activity output used by a process. Both measures should be used to provide managers with sound performance information.

Quality and Productivity

Improving quality may improve productivity and vice versa. For example, consider rework, an internal failure activity. If rework is reduced by producing fewer defective units, then less labor and fewer materials are used to produce the same output. Reducing the number of defective units improves quality; reducing the amount of inputs used improves productivity.

Since most quality improvements reduce the amount of resources used to produce and sell an organization's output, most quality improvements will improve productivity. Thus, quality improvements generally will be reflected in productivity measures. However, there are other ways to improve productivity other than through quality improvement. A firm may produce a good with little or no defects but still have an inefficient process.

For example, consider a good that passes through two 5-minute processes. (Assume the good is produced free of defects.) One unit, then, requires ten minutes to pass through both processes. Currently, units are produced in batches of 1,200. Process 1 produces 1,200 units. Then, the batch is conveyed by forklift to another location, where the units pass through Process 2. Thus, for each process, a total of 6,000 minutes, or 100 hours, are needed to produce a batch. The 1,200 finished units, then, require a total of 200 hours (100 hours for each process) plus conveyance time (assume that to be 15 minutes).

By redesigning the manufacturing process, efficiency can be improved. Suppose that the second process is located close enough to the first process so that as soon as a unit is completed by the first process, it is passed to the second process. In this way, the first and second processes can be working at the same time. The second process no longer has to wait for the production of 1,200 units plus conveyance time before it can begin operation. The total time to produce 1,200 units now is 6,000 minutes plus the waiting time for the first unit (five minutes). Thus, production of 1,200 units has been reduced from 200 hours, 15 minutes to 100 hours, 5 minutes. More output can be produced with fewer inputs. The moving and waiting activities are nonvalued-added inputs that have been virtually eliminated, thereby improving process productivity.

SUMMARY

Productivity concerns how efficiently inputs are used to produce the output. Partial measures of productivity evaluate the efficient use of single inputs. Total measures of productivity assess efficiency for all inputs. Profit-linked productivity effects are calculated by using the linkage rule. Essentially, the profit effect is computed by taking the difference between the cost of the inputs that would have been used without any productivity change and the cost of the actual inputs used. Because of the possibility of input tradeoffs, it is essential to value productivity changes. Only in this way can the effect of pro-

ductivity changes be properly assessed. Productivity analysis can be used to assess activity performance. There are two approaches that can be used to assess activity efficiency: activity productivity analysis and process productivity analysis. Activity productivity analysis is primarily used for assessing changes in the efficiency of value-added activities. Process productivity analysis can be used to assess productivity of processes and of both value- and nonvalue-added activities that define the process.

REVIEW PROBLEM AND SOLUTION

Productivity

At the end of 1997, Homer Company implemented a new labor process and redesigned its product with the expectation that input usage efficiency would increase. Now, at the end of 1998, the president of the company wants an assessment of the changes on the company's productivity. The data needed for the assessment are given below.

	1997	1998
Output	10,000	12,000
Output prices	$20	$20
Materials (lbs.)	8,000	8,400
Materials unit price	$6	$8
Labor (hrs.)	5,000	4,800
Labor rate per hour	$10	$10
Power (kwh)	2,000	3,000
Price per kwh	$2	$3

REQUIRED:

1. Compute the partial operational measures for each input for both 1997 and 1998. What can be said about productivity improvement?
2. Prepare an income statement for each year and calculate the total change in profits.

3. Calculate the profit-linked productivity measure for 1998. What can be said about the productivity program?
4. Calculate the price-recovery component. What does this tell you?

Solution

1. Partial measures:

	1997	1998
Material	10,000/8,000 = 1.25	12,000/8,400 = 1.43
Labor	10,000/5,000 = 2.00	12,000/4,800 = 2.50
Power	10,000/2,000 = 5.00	12,000/3,000 = 4.00

Profile analysis indicates that productive efficiency has increased for materials and labor and decreased for power. The outcome is mixed, and no statement about overall productivity improvement can be made without valuing the tradeoff.

2. Income statements:

	1997	1998
Sales	$200,000	$240,000
Cost of inputs	102,000	124,200
Income	$ 98,000	$115,800

Total change in profits: $115,800 − $98,000 = $17,800 increase

3. Profit-linked measurement:

Input	(1) PQ^*	(2) $PQ \times P$	(3) AQ	(4) $AQ \times P$	(2) − (4) $(PQ \times P) - (AQ \times P)$
Materials	9,600	$ 76,800	8,400	$ 67,200	$ 9,600
Labor	6,000	60,000	4,800	48,000	12,000
Power	2,400	7,200	3,000	9,000	(1,800)
		$144,000		$124,200	$19,800

*Materials: 12,000/1.25; Labor: 12,000/2; Power: 12,000/5

The value of the increases in efficiency for materials and labor more than offsets the increased usage of power. Thus, the productivity improvement program should be labeled successful.

4. Price recovery:

Price recovery component = Total profit change − Profit-linked productivity change

$$\text{Price recovery component} = \$17,800 - \$19,800$$
$$= \$(2,000)$$

This says that without the productivity improvement, profits would have declined by $2,000. The $40,000 increase in revenues would not have offset the increase in the cost of inputs. From the solution to Requirement 3, the cost of inputs without a productivity increase would have been $144,000 (column 2). The increase in the input cost without productivity would have been $144,000 − $102,000 = $42,000. This is $2,000 more than the increase in revenues. Only because of the productivity increase did the firm show an increase in profitability.

KEY TERMS

Activity productivity analysis *961*
Base period *955*
Financial productivity measure *955*
Input tradeoff efficiency *952*

Operational productivity measure *955*
Partial productivity measurement *954*
Price-recovery component *960*

Process productivity analysis *961*
Productivity *952*
Productivity measurement *954*
Profile measurement *956*

Profit-linked productivity measurement *958*
Technical efficiency *952*
Total productive efficiency *952*
Total productivity measurement *956*

QUESTIONS FOR WRITING AND DISCUSSION

1. Define *total productive efficiency*.
2. Explain the difference between technical and input tradeoff efficiency.
3. What is productivity measurement?
4. Explain the difference between partial and total measures of productivity.
5. What is an operational productivity measure? A financial measure?
6. Discuss the advantages and disadvantages of partial measures of productivity.
7. What is the purpose of a base period?
8. What is profile measurement and analysis? What are the limitations of this approach?
9. What is profit-linked productivity measurement and analysis?
10. Explain why profit-linked productivity measurement is important.
11. What is the price-recovery component?
12. What is activity productivity analysis, and what are its limitations?
13. What is process productivity analysis?
14. Can productivity improvements be achieved without improving quality? Explain.
15. Why is it important for managers to be concerned with both productivity and quality?
16. Discuss the role accounting has in productivity measurement.
17. What are the differences between quality and productivity? The similarities?

EXERCISES AND PROBLEMS

22-1
Technical and Price Efficiency

LO 1

Listed below are several possible input combinations for producing 1,000 units of a men's watch. Two of the input combinations are technically efficient.

	Materials	Labor	Energy
Unit input prices	$8	$10	$2
Input combinations:			
A	100	200	500
B	110	220	550
C	95	190	760
D	90	180	720

REQUIRED:

1. Identify the technically efficient input combinations. Explain your choices.
2. Which of the two technically efficient input combinations should be used? Explain.

**22-2
Productivity
Measurement;
Technical and
Input Tradeoff
Efficiency; Partial
Measures**

LO 1, 2

Arequipa Sweaters Company produces alpaca sweaters that use two inputs, materials and labor. During the past quarter, 2,000 sweaters were produced, requiring 8,000 pounds of material and 4,000 hours of labor. An engineering efficiency study commissioned by the local university revealed that Arequipa can produce the same output of 2,000 sweaters using either of the following two combinations of inputs:

	Materials	Labor
Combination A	7,000	3,500
Combination B	8,000	3,000

The cost of materials is $5 per pound; the cost of labor is $10 per hour.

REQUIRED:

1. Compute the output-input ratio for each input of Combination A. Does this represent a productivity improvement over the current use of inputs? What is the total dollar value of the improvement? Classify this as a technical or input tradeoff efficiency improvement.
2. Calculate output-input ratios for each input of Combination B. Does this represent a productivity improvement over the current use of inputs? Now compare these ratios to those of Combination A. What has happened?
3. Compute the cost of producing 2,000 units of output using Combination B. Compare this cost to the cost using Combination A. Does moving from Combination A to Combination B represent a productivity improvement? Explain.

**22-3
Interperiod
Measurement of
Productivity;
Profiles; Profit-
linked Measures;
Price Recovery**

LO 2, 3

Harrison Company has begun a program of continuous improvement for its operations. One of its plants reported the following results for the base period and its most recent year of operations:

	1997	1998
Output	32,000	40,000
Power (quantity used)	4,000	2,000
Materials (quantity used)	8,000	9,000
Unit price (Power)	$1.00	$2.00
Unit price (Materials)	$8.00	$10.00
Unit selling price	$3.00	$4.00

REQUIRED:

1. Compute the productivity profiles for each year. Did productivity improve? Explain.
2. Compute the profit-linked productivity measure. By how much did profits increase due to productivity?
3. Calculate the price-recovery component for 1998. Explain its meaning.

**22-4
Productivity
Measurement:
Tradeoffs; Profile
and Profit-Linked
Analyses**

LO 2, 3

Bradshaw Company has recently installed a computer-aided manufacturing system. The decision to automate was made so that material waste could be reduced. Better quality and a reduction of labor inputs were also expected. After one year of operation, management wants to see if the expected productivity improvements have materialized. The president is particularly interested in knowing whether the tradeoff between capital, labor, and materials was favorable. Data concerning output, labor, materials, and capital are provided for the year before implementation and the year after.

	Year Before	Year After
Output	100,000	120,000
Input quantities:		
Material (lbs.)	25,000	20,000
Labor (hours)	5,000	2,000
Capital (dollars)	10,000	300,000
Input prices:		
Materials	$5	$5
Labor	$10	$10
Capital	10%	10%

REQUIRED:

1. Prepare a productivity profile for each year. Evaluate the productivity changes.
2. Calculate the change in profits attributable to the change in productivity of the three inputs. Assuming that these are the only three inputs, evaluate the decision to automate.

22-5
Prospective
Productivity
Measurement;
Technical and
Input Tradeoff
Efficiency; Profile
and Profit-Linked
Analyses
LO 1, 2, 3

The manager of Blakely Company was reviewing two competing projects for the Molding Department. The projects represented different methods of preparing the molds for one of the company's more popular product lines. One project changed the way molds were poured and promised a savings in materials usage. The second project redesigned the process so that labor was used more efficiently. The fiscal year was coming to a close, and the manager wanted to make a decision concerning the proposed process changes so that they could be used, if beneficial, during the coming year. The process changes would affect the department's input usage. For the year just ending, the Accounting Department provided the following information about the inputs used to produce 100,000 units of output:

	Quantity	Unit Prices
Materials	200,000 lbs.	$ 8
Labor	80,000 hrs.	10
Energy	40,000 kwh	2

Each project offers a different process design from the one currently used. And neither project would cost anything to implement. Expected input usage for producing 120,000 units (the expected output for the coming year) for each project is given below:

	Project I	Project II
Materials	200,000 lbs.	220,000 lbs.
Labor	80,000 hrs.	60,000 hrs.
Energy	40,000 kwh	40,000 kwh

Input prices are expected to remain the same for the coming year.

REQUIRED:

1. Prepare a productivity profile analysis for the most recently completed year and each project. Does either proposal improve technical efficiency? Explain. Can you make a recommendation about either project using only the physical measures?
2. Calculate the profit-linked productivity measure for each proposal. Which proposal offers the best outcome for the company? How does this relate to the concept of price efficiency? Explain.

22-6
Basics of
Productivity
Measurement

LO 1, 2, 3

Menendez Company gathered the following data for the past two years:

	Base Year	Current Year
Output	300,000	360,000
Output prices	$30	$30
Input quantities:		
Materials (lbs.)	400,000	360,000
Labor (hrs.)	100,000	180,000
Input prices:		
Materials	$10	$12
Labor	$16	$16

REQUIRED:

1. Prepare a productivity profile for each year.
2. Prepare income statements for each year. Calculate the total change in income.
3. Calculate the change in profits attributable to productivity changes.
4. Calculate the price recovery component. Explain its meaning.

22-7
Activity
Productivity

LO 3, 4

In an effort to become more competitive, Hardy Company has embarked on a program to reduce and eliminate its nonvalue-added activities and to improve the efficiency of its value-added activities. The activity of paying bills has been classified as value-added and in need of improvement. The major inputs for the activity are clerks, personal computers (PCs), and supplies. Activity output is defined as "paid bills" and is measured by the number of checks issued. The materials-handling activity, on the other hand, is classified as a nonvalue-added activity and is targeted for reduction and possible elimination (at least as a significant activity). The major inputs for material movement (the output) are labor, forklifts, and supplies. Over a two-year period, Hardy has made some changes in the way each activity is performed. For example, Hardy has redesigned its plant layout to reduce the demand for material movement. Process innovation also dramatically changed the way that bills were paid. Data are provided for the two activities for a base year and the most recent year completed. The year just completed was the second year of Hardy's improvement program.

Activity	Base Year	Year Just Completed
Paying bills:		
Output	300,000	320,000
Inputs:		
Clerks (no.)	15	5
PCs (no.)	15	5
Supplies (lbs.)	150,000	40,000
Moving materials:		
Output	20,000	5,000
Inputs:		
Labor (hrs.)	10,000	3,000
Forklifts (no.)	5	2
Supplies (lbs.)	4,000	2,000

REQUIRED:

1. Prepare productivity profiles for both activities. Comment on the usefulness of these profiles for assessing improvement in activity performance.

2. Given the following most recent year's input prices for the paying bills activity, calculate the activity's profit-linked measure:

Clerks: $25,000 per person
PCs: $5,000 per system
Supplies: $1 per pound

**22-8
Process and
Activity
Productivity**

LO 3, 4

In 1994, Gutten Auto's motor division hired a consulting firm to help identify and define the processes used within the division. Wilson Dorr, the divisional manager, also asked the consulting firm to make recommendations concerning the reengineering of the processes to improve overall efficiency. Six major processes were defined. The consulting firm prepared six documents—one for each process. The following memo from Sally Field, the consulting partner in charge, summarizes the major points for the procurement process (the procurement process is one of the six major processes).

MEMO

To: Wilson Dorr, Divisional Manager
From: Sally Field, Partner, Jackson Consulting
Subject: Procurement Process
Date: March 15, 1996

The procurement process consists of three major activities: purchasing, receiving, and paying bills. Currently, the procurement process begins with the purchasing department sending a purchase order to a supplier. When the order is received from the supplier, the receiving department fills out a receiving document and sends it to accounts payable. Accounts payable also receives an invoice from the supplier (through the mail). Clerks in accounts payable compare the three documents and issue a check if all three match. At times, there are discrepancies and accounts payable clerks are responsible for resolving these discrepancies before payment is made. Resolution of discrepancies may take weeks and often consumes considerable clerical resources. This resolution activity is nonvalue-added, and a process redesign can eliminate it and save significant resources. We estimate that about 80% of clerical time is spent dealing with these discrepancies.

We recommend that payment authorization be changed from accounts payable to receiving. This change requires the acquisition of several terminals that will be used to access purchase information in the company's database. It also requires new software that will permit the following: (1) When the goods arrive from a supplier, the receiving clerk will check to see if the shipment is supported with an outstanding purchase order; (2) If there is a corresponding purchase order indicating the type and quantity of goods received, then the clerk can signal acceptance using the keyboard and the computer will issue a check at the appropriate time for payment; (3) If there is no supporting documentation or if the type and quantity of goods received differ from the purchase order, then the goods are simply shipped back to the supplier.

After reviewing the memo, Wilson Dorr set in motion the necessary actions to implement the consultant's recommendations. The terminals were purchased and the required supporting software was developed. Since suppliers often shipped partial orders, the software was modified to allow for this possibility. Now, two years later, Wilson wants an analysis of the productivity gains or losses that have resulted from the process changes that have been implemented. Output for the procurement process is defined as the number of units purchased and paid for (of all types). Data for 1996 and 1998 are provided below for the procurement process:

	1996	1998
Units purchased and paid for	3,000,000	3,600,000
Purchase orders	100,000	120,000
Receiving orders	150,000	180,000
Bills paid	150,000	180,000
Activity rates:		
Purchasing (per purchase order)	$6.00	$6.25
Receiving (per receiving order)	$8.33	$12.50
Paying bills (per bill paid)	$16.67	$1.40

REQUIRED:

1. Compute the productivity profiles for 1996 and 1998. Is there any indication of improvement in process productivity? Do you believe this outcome? Explain and discuss the limitations of profile analysis.
2. Compute the profit-linked measure of productivity for the procurement process. Explain the outcome.
3. Suppose that you had the following information on inputs for the three procurement process activities:

	Purchasing	Receiving	Paying Bills
1996:			
Supplies (lbs.)	50,000	40,000	75,000
Clerks (no.)	24	50	100
Capital (dollars)	$100,000	$200,000	$50,000
1998:			
Supplies (lbs.)	60,000	30,000	5,000
Clerks (no.)	25	50	10
Capital (dollars)	$120,000	$300,000	$100,000

Prepare productivity profiles for each activity, and explain the results.
4. The redesign of the procurement process eliminated the nonvalue-added activity of resolving discrepancies. The number of discrepancies dropped from 8,000 in 1996 to 0 in 1998. How would this kind of information affect the analysis in Requirements 1 and 2? Does it suggest an important modification to the process productivity analysis approach originally taken? Explain.

**22-9
Productivity and
Quality;
Prospective
Analysis**

LO 2, 3

Berry Company is considering the acquisition of a computerized manufacturing system. The new system has a built-in quality function that increases the control over product specifications. An alarm sounds whenever the product falls outside the programmed specifications. An operator can then make some adjustments on the spot to restore the desired product quality. The system is expected to decrease the number of units scrapped because of poor quality. The system is also expected to decrease the amount of labor inputs needed. The production manager is pushing for the acquisition because he believes that productivity will be greatly enhanced—particularly when it comes to labor and material inputs. Output and input data are given below. The data for the computerized system are projections.

	Current System	Computerized System
Output (units)	50,000	50,000
Output selling price	$40	$40
Input quantities:		
Materials	200,000	175,000
Labor	100,000	75,000
Capital (dollars)	100,000	500,000
Energy	50,000	125,000
Input prices:		
Materials	$4.00	$4.00
Labor	$9.00	$9.00
Capital (percent)	10.00%	10.00%
Energy	$2.00	$2.50

REQUIRED:

1. Compute the partial operational ratios for labor and materials under each alternative. Is the production manager right in thinking that labor and materials productivity increase with the automated system?
2. Compute the productivity profiles for each system. Does the computerized system improve productivity?
3. Determine the amount by which profits will change if the computerized system is adopted. Are the tradeoffs among the inputs favorable? Comment on the system's ability to improve productivity.

**22-10
Productivity
Measurement;
Basics**
LO 3

Fowler Company produces handcrafted leather purses. Virtually all the manufacturing cost consists of labor and materials. Over the past several years, profits have been declining because the cost of the two major inputs has been increasing. Wilma Fowler, the president of the company, has indicated that the price of the purses cannot be increased; thus, the only way to improve or at least stabilize profits is to increase overall productivity. At the beginning of 1998, Wilma implemented a new cutting and assembly process that promised less material waste and a faster production time. At the end of 1998, Wilma wants to know how much profits have changed from the prior year because of the new process. In order to provide this information to Wilma, the controller of the company gathered the following data:

	1997	1998
Unit selling price	$16	$16
Purses produced and sold	18,000	24,000
Materials used	36,000	40,000
Labor used	9,000	10,000
Unit price of materials	$4	$4.50
Unit price of labor	$9	$10.00

REQUIRED:

1. Compute the productivity profile for each year. Comment on the effectiveness of the new production process.
2. Compute the increase in profits attributable to increased productivity.
3. Calculate the price-recovery component, and comment on its meaning.

22-11
Productivity
Measurement;
Technical and Price
Efficiency
LO 1, 3

In 1997, Melrose Company used the following input combination to produce 10,000 units of output:

Materials	6,000 lbs.
Labor	12,000 hrs.

In 1998, Melrose again planned to produce 10,000 units and was considering two different changes in process, both of which would be able to produce the desired output. The following input combinations are associated with each process change:

	Change I	*Change II*
Materials	7,000 lbs.	5,000 lbs.
Labor	8,000 hrs.	10,000 hrs.

The following combination is optimal for an output of 10,000 units. However, this optimal input combination is unknown to Melrose.

Materials	4,000 lbs.
Labor	8,000 hrs.

The cost of materials is $60 per pound, and the cost of labor is $15 per hour. These input prices hold for 1997 and 1998.

REQUIRED:

1. Compute the productivity profiles for each of the following:
   a. The actual inputs used in 1997
   b. The inputs for each proposed 1998 process change
   c. The optimal input combination
   Will productivity increase in 1998 regardless of which change is used? Which process change would you recommend based on the prospective productivity profiles?
2. Compute the cost of 1997's productive inefficiency relative to the optimal input combination. Repeat for 1998 proposed input changes. Will productivity improve from 1997 to 1998 for each process change? By how much? Explain. Include in your explanation a discussion of changes in technical and input tradeoff efficiency.
3. Since the optimal input combination is not known by Melrose, suggest a way to measure productivity improvement. Use this method to measure the productivity improvement achieved from 1997 to 1998. How does this measure compare with the productivity improvement measure computed using the optimal input combination?

22-12
Process
Productivity
Measurement
LO 3, 4

Wright Manufacturing has recently studied its order-filling process and initiated some changes that were expected to improve its efficiency. The changes involved such things as redesign of the plant layout, redesign of documents, keyboard training, and improvement in automated system controls. The changes were expected to improve process productivity over a period of several years. The order-filling process is defined by the following three activities: handling goods, entering data, and detecting errors. The output measure for the process is the number of orders filled. The handling activity's output (movement of goods) is measured by yards traveled; the entering data activity's output is measured by data entry time; and the output of detecting errors is measured by the number of documents inspected (compares document data with input record). Data for the year prior to the changes and for two years following the changes are given below:

	1996	1997	1998
Output measures:			
Number of orders filled	150,000	165,000	200,000
Yards traveled	1,500,000	825,000	400,000
Data entry time (hrs.)	50,000	41,250	40,000
Documents inspected	150,000	82,500	50,000
Activity rates:			
Handling goods (per yard)	$1	$1	$1.25
Entering data (per hour)	$7	$7	$8.00
Detecting errors (per document)	$2	$2	$2.00

REQUIRED:

1. Calculate the productivity profiles for all three years. What can you say about productivity improvement? Comment on the value of multiyear comparisons of productivity profiles.
2. Calculate the profit-linked measures for 1997 and 1998, using 1996 as the base year for 1997 and using 1997 as the base year for 1998. Is there any value to changing base years? Explain.

22-13
Productivity
Measurement;
Price Recovery
LO 2, 3

The small motors division of Polson Company has recently engaged in a vigorous effort to reduce manufacturing costs by increasing productivity (through process innovation). Over the past several years, price competition has become very intense, and recent events called for another significant price decrease. Without the price decrease, the marketing manager estimates that the division's market share would drop by 30 percent. The marketing manager estimates that a price decrease of $5.00 per unit is needed in 1998 to maintain market share. (Since the market is expanding, maintaining the market share means an increase in units sold.) The small motors sold for $70 each in 1997. However, the divisional manager indicated that the revenues lost by the price decrease must be offset by increased cost efficiency. Any further deterioration in profits could threaten the division's continued existence. Thus, in 1998, processes were reengineered in an effort to improve productivity. At the end of 1998, the divisional manager wanted an assessment of the effects of the process changes. To assess the changes in productive efficiency, the following data were gathered:

	1997	1998
Output	50,000	60,000
Input quantities:		
Materials	50,000	40,000
Labor	200,000	100,000
Capital	$2,000,000	$5,000,000
Energy	50,000	150,000
Input prices:		
Materials	$8.00	$10.00
Labor	$10.00	$12.00
Capital	$0.15	$0.10
Energy	$2.00	$2.00

REQUIRED:

1. Calculate the productivity profile for each year. Can you say that productivity has improved? Explain.
2. Calculate the total profit change from 1997 to 1998. How much of this change is attributable to productivity? To price recovery?
3. Calculate the cost per unit for 1997 and 1998. Was the division able to decrease its per-unit cost by at least $5.00? Comment on the relationship of competitive advantage and productive efficiency.

22-14
Quality and Productivity; Interaction; Use of Operational Measures
LO 3

Andy Confer, production-line manager, had arranged a visit with Will Keating, plant manager. He had some questions about the new operational measures that were being used.

Andy: Will, my questions are more to satisfy my curiosity than anything else. At the beginning of the year, we began some new procedures that require us to work towards increasing our output per pound of material and decreasing our output per labor hour. As instructed, I've been tracking these operational measures for each batch we've produced so far this year. Here's a copy of a trend report for the first five batches of the year. Each batch had 10,000 units in it.

Batches	Material Usage	Ratio	Labor Usage	Ratio
1	4,000 lbs.	2.50	2,000 hrs.	5.00
2	3,900 lbs.	2.56	2,020 hrs.	4.95
3	3,750 lbs.	2.67	2,150 hrs.	4.65
4	3,700 lbs.	2.70	2,200 hrs.	4.55
5	3,600 lbs.	2.78	2,250 hrs.	4.44

Will: Andy, this report is very encouraging. The trend is exactly what we hoped for. I'll bet we meet our goal of getting the batch productivity measures. Let's see, those goals were 3.00 units per pound for materials and 4.00 units per hour for labor. Last year's figures were 5.00 for labor and 2.50 for materials. Things are looking good. I guess tying bonuses and raises to improving these productivity stats was a good idea.

Andy: Maybe so—but I don't understand why you want to make these tradeoffs between labor and materials. Labor costs $10 per hour and the materials cost only $5 per pound. It seems like you're simply increasing the cost of making this product.

Will: Actually, it may seem that way, but it's not so. There are other factors to consider. You know we've been talking quality improvement. Well, the new procedures you are implementing are producing products that conform to the product's specification. More labor time is needed to achieve this, and as we take more time, we do waste fewer materials. But the real benefit is the reduction in our external failure costs. Every defect in a batch of 10,000 units costs us $1,000—warranty work, lost sales, a customer service department, and so on. If we can reach the labor and material productivity goals, our defects will drop from 20 per batch to 5 per batch.

REQUIRED:

1. Discuss the advantages of using only operational measures of productivity for controlling shop-level activities.
2. Assume that the batch productivity statistics are met by the end of the year. Calculate the change in a batch's profits from the beginning of the year to the end that is attributable to changes in labor and materials productivity.
3. Now assume that three inputs are to be evaluated: materials, labor, and quality. Quality is measured by the number of defects per batch. Calculate the change in a batch's profits from the beginning of the year to the end that is attributable to changes in productivity of all three inputs. Do you agree that quality is an input? Explain.

**22-15
Productivity;
Tradeoffs; Price
Recovery**

LO 5

Kathy Shorts, president of Carbon Industrial Cleaners, had just concluded a meeting with two of her plant managers. She had told each of them that one of their high-volume industrial cleaners was going to have a 50 percent increase in demand—next year—over this year's output (which is expected to be 50,000 barrels). A major foreign source of the raw material had been shut down because of a trade embargo. It would be years before the source would be available again. The result was two-fold. First, the price of the raw material was expected to quadruple. Second, many of the less efficient competitors would leave the business, creating more demand and higher output prices—in fact, output prices would double.

In discussing the situation with her plant managers, she reminded them that the automated process now allowed them to increase the productivity of the raw material. By using more machine hours, evaporation could be decreased significantly (this was a recent development and would be operational by the beginning of the new fiscal year). There were, however, only two other feasible settings beyond the current setting. The current usage of inputs for the 50,000-barrel output (current setting) and the input usage for the other two settings are given below. The input usage for the remaining two settings is for an output of 75,000 barrels. Inputs are measured in barrels for the material and in machine hours for the equipment.

	Current	Setting A	Setting B
Input quantities:			
Material	125,000	75,000	150,000
Equipment	30,000	75,000	37,500

The current prices for this year's inputs are $3 per barrel for materials and $12 per machine hour for the equipment. The materials price will change for next year as explained, but the $12 rate for machine hours will remain the same. The chemical is currently selling for $20 per barrel. Based on separate productivity analyses, one plant manager chose setting A and the other chose setting B.

The manager who chose setting B justified his decision by noting that it was the only setting that clearly signaled an increase in both partial measures of productivity. The other manager agreed that setting B was an improvement but that setting A was even better.

REQUIRED:

1. Prepare productivity profiles for the current year and for the two settings. Which of the two settings signals an increase in productivity for both inputs?
2. Calculate the profits that will be realized under each setting for the coming year. Which setting provides the greatest profit increase?
3. Calculate the profit change for each setting attributable to productivity changes. Which setting offers the greatest productivity improvement? By how much? Explain why this happened.

**22-16
Ethical
Considerations:
Research
Assignment**

Go to the library and find two examples of ethical lapses (for an industrial setting) that have been described in the press or journals during the past three years. Write a short paper that addresses the following:

1. A brief summary of the facts that describe the ethical lapse.
2. A description of what behavior was viewed as unethical.
3. An analysis of what motivated the unethical behavior.
4. A description of which standards of ethical conduct were violated. (Use the IMA code of ethics in Chapter 1 as the point of reference.)
5. An assessment of the importance and effectiveness of formal standards of ethical conduct.

Chapters 16–22

Computador Company produces computers of various sizes and capabilities. It has three divisions, two that are located in the United States and one that is located in Singapore. The disk division is located in Colorado Springs. The other two divisions are computer fabrication and assembly divisions. The U.S. fabrication and assembly division is located in Denver. The disk division produces both hard and floppy disk drives. The disk drives are sold both internally and externally. The fabrication and assembly divisions manufacture the motherboard, case, and all other components except for disk drives. They buy the hard and floppy drives from either the disk division or outside suppliers. All three divisions are treated as investment centers.

Computador uses a standard costing system in all three of its divisions. The following standard cost sheet is provided for the 170 megabyte hard drive produced by the disk division:

Materials (3 lbs. @ $16.00)	$48.00
Labor (2 hrs. @ $9.00)	18.00
Fixed overhead (2 hrs. @ $5.00)*	10.00
Variable overhead (2 hrs. @ $3.00)*	6.00
Standard unit cost	$82.00

*Overhead rates are based on a practical capacity of 1,600,000 direct labor hours for all products.

The disk division has the capacity of producing and selling 400,000 units of the 170 MB drives, but demand for the drives has softened due to intense competition, and the division plans on selling 320,000 units for the coming year. A similar drop in demand is also being experienced for the other drives produced by the division. A recent market analysis indicated that foreign competitors were selling disk drives for a lower price with higher performance quality. The market share for the drives was eroding in both the U.S. and Singapore. The other two divisions were also facing intense competitive pressures.

Because of the challenges facing Computador, a consulting firm was hired to evaluate the efficiency of the disk division. The consulting firm had developed a reputation for process innovation. If significant improvements were possible, the consulting engagement would be expanded to include the other two divisions. After a two-month analysis by two partners, several observations and recommendations were made in a formal report. According to the report, it was imperative that the disk division decrease its prices to match (or even beat) those of the foreign competitors. Lowering prices, however, was not sufficient. Costs had to be reduced also, so that reasonable profits could be earned. In addition, quality performance had to be improved. In fact, according to the consultants, improving quality would also reduce costs. They also indicated that further cost reductions could be realized by improving productivity. By eliminating nonvalue-added activities, less inputs would be needed. According to the consultants' report, adopting a process view was fundamental to achieving these results. Focusing on the work done within the organization rather than the organization's structure offers the most opportunity for improvement. The two partners identified six major business processes within the disk division: executive, support, gaining new business, product and service design, operations, and after-sales support. They noted that these major business processes can be broken down into subprocesses and that the subprocesses, in turn, can be broken down into activities. Driver analysis, activity analysis, and monitoring activity performance were essential for continuous improvement.

To help management understand the potential of activity-based cost management, information was gathered on activities within the operations process. The operations process was defined as all activities associated with producing quality products. The activity information, including budgeted supply (practical capacity), budgeted costs, and budgeted demands placed on the activities by the division's products, is presented below.

Activity Drivers	Activity Availability	Budgeted Activity Usage
Quality related:		
Inspection hours	168,000	128,000
Quality training hours	16,000	16,000
Pounds of scrap	800,000	800,000
Rework hours	50,000	50,000
Warranty hours	400,000	320,000
Hours of field testing	8,000	8,000
Nonquality related:		
Machine hours	3,200,000	3,200,000
Setup hours	240,000	240,000
Receiving orders	80,000	56,000
Direct labor hours	1,600,000	1,600,000

Activities[a]	Budgeted Costs[b]
Inspection (final product)	$3,280,000
Quality training	320,000
Scrap creation	1,200,000
Rework	400,000
Warranty work	3,200,000
Field testing	400,000
Machining	4,400,000[c]
Setup	2,400,000
Receiving	800,000

[a] For calculation of the direct labor hour overhead rates (fixed and variable), the scrap, rework, and machining costs (less depreciation) are treated as variable costs. From an activity-based perspective, inspection, quality training, and receiving all are strictly fixed activity costs (resources acquired in advance of usage only); scrap and rework are strictly variable activity costs (resources acquired as needed); 20% of warranty, field testing, and setup costs represent resources acquired as needed, with the residual representing resources acquired in advance of usage; machine depreciation is a resource acquired in advance of usage with the remaining machine costs representing resources acquired as needed.

[b] Budgeted costs are computed using activity-based cost formulas.

[c] $1,200,000 is machine depreciation (straight-line, ten years of depreciation remaining with no salvage value anticipated).

REQUIRED:

1. Suppose that the disk division has 96,000 units of the 170 MB hard drive in beginning finished goods inventory. The division sells this drive for $100 per unit. Because of the consultants' report, the division plans on modifying the operations process by implementing a JIT manufacturing system. As part of this plan, inventories will be reduced. For the coming year, the division hopes to have finished goods inventories of the 170 MB drive reduced to 16,000 units. The beginning raw materials inventory supporting the production of the 170 MB drives has 200,000 lbs. Because of supplier JIT delivery agreements, the division expects to reduce this budget to 20,000 lbs. Using this information, the standard cost sheet for the 170 MB drive, and any other information needed, prepare the following budgets for the 170 MB drive:
   a. Production budget
   b. Sales budget
   c. Raw materials purchases budget
   d. Direct labor budget
   e. Variable overhead budget
   f. Cost of goods sold budget
   Discuss how standard costing helped in the preparation of the budget. Does this role disappear in the contemporary manufacturing environment? Explain.
2. Suppose that the units of the 170 MB drive actually produced are equal to budgeted production (Requirement 1). Also assume that the following actual results were obtained relative to inputs used by the 170 MB drive: purchases, 580,000 lbs. @ $16.10 per pound; material usage, 760,000 lbs.; labor, 475,000 hours @ $8.90. Compute the following variances:
   a. Materials price variance
   b. Materials usage variance
   c. Labor rate variance
   d. Labor efficiency variance
   Discuss the role, if any, that these variances would have in the contemporary manufacturing environment.
3. Suppose that the disk division had the following plantwide results:

Actual fixed overhead	$8,200,000
Actual variable overhead	5,000,000
Total actual direct labor hours	1,700,000
Hours allowed for actual production	1,650,000

   Compute the following overhead variances:
   a. Variable overhead spending variance
   b. Variable overhead efficiency variance
   c. Fixed overhead spending variance
   d. Fixed overhead volume variance
4. Prepare a quality cost report for the disk division. Discuss the current distribution of quality costs. Can you estimate the potential savings from quality improvements, assuming that the disk division has total sales of $64,000,000?
5. Prepare a budgeted value-added and nonvalue-added cost report. Assume the following: (a) the actual prices of resources equal standard prices; (b) sales total $64,000,000, and value-added quality costs are 2.5% of sales, equally divided among value-added quality activities; (c) value-added machine costs (excluding depreciation) are 80% of the total budgeted amount; (d) the division expects to operate a JIT purchasing and manufacturing system.
6. The following activities are acquired in blocks (whole units) as indicated:

Activity	Block
Inspection	2,100 hours
Quality training	2,000 hours
Field testing	1,000 hours
Warranty work	2,500 hours

Compute the unused capacity and volume variance for each activity. Explain the difference in meaning for each variance. How can each be used by management? Assume total sales of $64,000,000 for the division.

7. The consultants' report urged the management of the disk division to adopt a process view. Describe the essential elements of a process view, and indicate how this approach differs from the traditional approach to accounting control.

8. Suppose that the total investment of the disk division is $120,000,000. Calculate the increase in ROI if all nonvalue-added costs are eliminated. How much of this increase would be attributable to achieving a zero-defects state?

9. Assume that management is considering a new manufacturing process for the 170 MB drive. The new process would increase the labor content but would reduce scrap so that the total materials usage drops. The projected effects of the process compared with last year's inputs are provided below (output for last year was 320,000 units; usage is projected based on an expected output of 400,000 units):

	Last Year Usage	Projected Usage
Labor hours	640,000	840,000
Pounds of materials	1,000,000	1,200,000

Calculate the productivity profiles for each year and the effect on profits if the process is implemented (use standard input prices for the computation of the profit-linked productivity measure). Should the new process be implemented? Discuss the value of profit-linked productivity measurement.

10. The Singapore division has idle capacity and has just received a request for a special order of 64,000 computers using 170 MB drives, at $700 per computer (which can be accommodated using idle capacity). Normally, the Singapore division pays the Colorado Springs division $100 for the 170 MB drive, adjusted for import duties ($5 per unit—paid for by the Singapore division) and avoidable marketing costs ($3). The Singapore division's variable manufacturing and selling costs, excluding the 170 MB drive's costs, are $610. The Singapore division can buy the drive from an Asian supplier for $80 plus import duties of $5 per unit. Using the traditional standard cost system of the Colorado Springs disk division, calculate the minimum and maximum transfer prices for the 64,000 drives. Assuming any joint benefit is split evenly, what is the negotiated transfer price? By how much will the profits of each division increase if this price is used? What arguments would you use to obtain an advance pricing agreement with the IRS so that the negotiated transfer price is acceptable? Would the Singapore tax authorities likely have any objection to this arrangement? Explain.

Glossary

A

ABC data base the collected data sets that are organized and interrelated for use by an organization's activity-based costing information system. (p. 324)

absorption costing a costing method that assigns *all* manufacturing costs, direct materials, direct labor, variable overhead, and a share of fixed overhead to each unit of product. (p. 651)

absorption-costing (full-costing) income income computed by following a functional classification. (p. 46)

acceptable quality level (AQL) a predetermined level of defective products that a company permits to be sold. (pp. 377, 916)

accounting information system a system consisting of interrelated manual and computer parts that uses processes such as collecting, recording, summarizing, analyzing (using decision models), and managing data to provide output information to users. (p. 32)

accounting rate of return the rate of return obtained by dividing the average accounting net income by the original investment (or by average investment). (p. 507)

activity a basic unit of work performed within an organization. It also can be defined as an aggregation of actions within an organization useful to managers for purposes of planning, controlling, and decision making. (p. 38)

activity analysis the process of identifying, describing, and evaluating the activities an organization performs. (p. 865)

activity attributes nonfinancial and financial information items that provide descriptive labels for individual activities. (p. 315)

activity capacity the ability to perform activities. (p. 82)

activity drivers factors that measure the demands placed on activities by cost objects and use these measures to assign the cost of activities to cost objects. (p. 40)

activity elimination the process of eliminating non-value-added activities. (p. 866)

activity flexible budgeting the prediction of what activity costs will be as activity usage changes. (p. 873)

activity inputs resources consumed by an activity in producing its output. (They are the factors that enable the activity to be performed.) (pp. 48, 864)

activity inventory a listing of the activities performed within an organization. (p. 315)

activity output (usage) the result or product of an activity. (pp. 49, 84, 864)

activity output measure assesses the number of times the activity is performed. It is the quantifiable measure of the output. (pp. 49, 864)

activity productivity analysis an approach that directly measures changes in activity productivity. (p. 961)

activity rate the average unit cost, obtained by dividing the resource expenditure by the activity's practical capacity. (p. 86)

activity reduction decreasing the time and resources required by an activity. (p. 866)

activity selection the process of choosing among sets of activities caused by competing strategies. (p. 866)

activity sharing increasing the efficiency of necessary activities by using economies of scale. (p. 866)

activity-based cost (ABC) system a cost accounting system that uses both unit and nonunit-based cost drivers to assign costs to cost objects by first tracing costs to activities and then tracing costs from activities to products. (pp. 57, 308)

activity-based costing assigns costs to cost objects by first tracing costs to activities and then tracing costs to cost objects. (p. 40)

activity-based management (ABM) an advanced control system that focuses management's attention on activities with the objective of improving the value received by the customer and the profit received by providing this value. It includes driver analysis, activity analysis, and performance evaluation and draws on activity-based costing as a major source of information. (p. 57)

actual cost system a cost measurement system in which actual manufacturing costs are assigned to products. (p. 133)

adjusted cost of goods sold normal cost of goods sold adjusted to include overhead variance. (p. 153)

administrative costs all costs associated with the general administration of the organization that cannot be reasonably assigned to either marketing or production. (p. 45)

administrative expense budget a budget consisting of estimated expenditures for the overall organization and operation of the company. (p. 688)

advance pricing agreement an agreement between the internal revenue service and a taxpayer on the acceptability of a transfer price. The agreement is private and is binding on both parties for a specified period of time. (p. 838)

advanced manufacturing environment an environment characterized by intense competition (usually worldwide), sophisticated technology, total quality control, and continuous improvement. (p. 303)

aesthetics a quality attribute that is concerned with the appearance of tangible products (for example, style and beauty) as well as the appearance of the facilities, equipment, personnel, and communication materials associated with services. (p. 908)

allocation assignment of indirect costs to cost objects. (p. 41)

annuity a series of future cash flows. (p. 532)

applied overhead the overhead assigned to production using a predetermined overhead rate. (p. 139)

appraisal costs costs incurred to determine whether or not products and services are conforming to requirements. (p. 911)

arbitrage situation when customers who purchase a good at a lower price are able to resell it to other customers. (p. 593)

assets unexpired costs. (p. 37)

B

backflush costing a simplified approach for cost flow accounting that uses trigger points to determine when manufacturing costs are assigned to key inventory and temporary accounts. (p. 380)

base period a prior period used to set the benchmark for measuring productivity changes. (p. 955)

batch production processes a process that produces batches of different products that are identical in many ways but differ in others. (p. 203)

batch-level activities those activities performed each time a batch is produced. (p. 49)

batch-level drivers output measures for batch-level activities. (p. 50)

benchmarking uses best practices as the standard for evaluating activity performance. (p. 871)

best-fitting line the line that fits a set of data points the best in the sense that the sum of the squared deviations of the data points from the line is the smallest. (p. 95)

binding constraint constraints whose limited resources are fully used by a product mix. (p. 566)

break-even point the point where total sales revenue equals total costs, i.e., the point of zero profits. (p. 411)

budget a plan of action expressed in financial terms. (p. 677)

budget committee a committee responsible for setting budgetary policies and goals, reviewing and approving the budget, and resolving any differences that may arise in the budgetary process. (p. 678)

budget director the individual responsible for coordinating and directing the overall budgeting process. (p. 678)

budgetary slack the process of padding the budget by overestimating costs and underestimating revenues. (p. 701)

business reengineering *see* **process innovation.** (p. 857)

by-product a secondary product recovered in the course of manufacturing a primary product during a joint process. (p. 271)

C

capital budgeting the process of making capital investment decisions. (p. 503)

capital expenditures budget a financial plan outlining the acquisition of long-term assets. (p. 689)

capital investment the process of planning, setting goals and priorities, arranging financing, and identifying criteria for making long-term investments. (p. 503)

capital investment decisions decisions concerned with the process of planning, setting goals and priorities, arranging financing, and using certain criteria to select long-term assets. (p. 503)

carrying costs the costs of holding inventory. (p. 551)

cash budget a detailed plan that outlines all sources and uses of cash. (p. 691)

cash flow cash inflows minus cash outflows. (p. 651)

causal factors activities or variables that invoke service costs. Generally, it is desirable to use causal factors as the basis for allocating service costs. (p. 234)

centralized decision making a system in which decisions are made at the top level of an organization and local managers are given the charge to implement them. (p. 776)

Certified Internal Auditor (CIA) an accountant certified to possess the professional qualifications of an internal auditor. (p. 21)

Certified Management Accountant (CMA) an accountant who has satisfied the requirements to hold a certificate in management accounting. (p. 20)

Certified Public Accountant (CPA) an accountant certified to possess the professional qualifications of an external auditor. (p. 20)

coefficient of correlation the square root of the coefficient of determination, which is used to express not only the degree of correlation between two variables but also the direction of the relationship. (p. 98)

coefficient of determination the percentage of total variability in a dependent variable (e.g., cost) that is explained by an independent variable (e.g., activity level). It assumes a value of between 0 and 1. (p. 98)

committed fixed expenses costs incurred for the acquisition of long-term activity capacity, usually as the result of strategic planning. (p. 83)

common cost the cost of a resource used in the output of two or more services or products. (p. 232)

common fixed expenses fixed costs that are not traceable to the segments and that would remain even if one of the segments were eliminated. (p. 420)

comparable uncontrolled price method the transfer price most preferred by the Internal Revenue Service under Section 482. The comparable uncontrolled price is essentially equal to the market price. (p. 837)

competitive advantage creating better customer value for the same or lower cost than can competitors or equivalent value for lower cost than can competitors. (p. 354)

compounding of interest paying interest on interest. (p. 531)

computer-integrated manufacturing (CIM) system a system integrating the computer-aided design, engineering, and manufacturing systems. (p. 377)

computer-numerically controlled (CNC) machines stand-alone machines controlled by a computer. (p. 377)

concatenated keys two or more keys that uniquely identify a record. (p. 326)

confidence interval prediction interval that provides a range of values for the actual cost with a prespecified degree of confidence. (p. 97)

constant gross margin percentage method a joint cost allocation method that maintains the same gross margin percentage for each product. (p. 278)

constraint a mathematical expression that expresses a resource limitation. (p. 565)

constraint set the collection of all constraints that pertain to a particular optimization problem. (p. 568)

consumable life the length of time that a product serves the needs of a customer. (p. 365)

consumption ratio the proportion of an overhead activity consumed by a product. (p. 305)

contemporary cost accounting system a system emphasizing tracing over allocation, whereby the role of tracing is significantly expanded by identifying drivers unrelated to the volume of product produced. (p. 57)

contemporary responsibility accounting a control system defined by centering responsibility on processes and teams where activity performance is measured in terms of time, quality, and efficiency. (p. 857)

continuous (or rolling) budget a moving twelve-month budget with a future month added as the current month expires. (p. 679)

continuous replenishment when a manufacturer assumes the inventory management function for the retailer. (p. 559)

contribution margin the difference between revenue and all variable expenses. (pp. 413, 641)

contribution margin ratio contribution margin divided by sales revenue. It is the proportion of each sales dollar available to cover fixed costs and provide for profit. (p. 417)

contribution margin variance the difference between actual and budgeted contribution margin. (p. 627)

control the process of setting standards, receiving feedback on actual performance, and taking corrective action whenever actual performance deviates significantly from planned performance. (p. 677)

control activities activities performed by an organization to prevent or detect poor quality (because poor quality *may* exist). (p. 911)

control costs costs incurred from performing control activities. (p. 911)

control limits the maximum allowable deviation from a standard. (p. 734)

controllable costs costs that managers have the power to influence. (p. 702)

controller the chief accountant of an organization. (p. 14)

controlling the monitoring of a plan through the use of feedback to ensure that the plan is being implemented as expected. (p. 15)

conversion cost the sum of direct labor cost and overhead cost. (p. 45)

cost the cash or cash equivalent value sacrificed for goods and services that are expected to bring a current or future benefit to the organization. (p. 37)

cost accounting a hybrid of the financial and management accounting systems. It provides information on a company's costs and may be used for both internal and external purposes. (p. 2)

cost accounting information system a cost management subsystem designed to assign costs to individual products and services and other objects as specified by management. (p. 36)

cost accumulation the recognition and recording of costs. (p. 131)

cost assignment the process of associating manufacturing costs with the units produced. (p. 131)

cost behavior the way in which a cost changes in relation to changes in activity usage. (pp. 49, 81)

cost center a responsibility center in which a manager is responsible for cost. (p. 775)

cost drivers factors that cause changes in cost. (p. 39)

cost formula a linear function, $Y = F + VX$, where Y = total mixed cost, F = fixed cost, V = variable cost per unit of activity, and X = activity level. (p. 92)

cost management the use of long- and short-run costs of activities, processes, goods and services for planning, controlling, and decision making. (p. 3)

cost management information system an accounting information subsystem that is primarily concerned with producing outputs for internal users using inputs and processes needed to satisfy management objectives. (p. 33)

cost measurement the process of assigning dollar values to cost items. (p. 131)

cost object any item such as products, departments, projects, activities, and so on, for which costs are measured and assigned. (p. 37)

cost of capital the cost of investment funds, usually viewed as a weighted average of the costs of funds from all sources. (p. 509)

cost of goods manufactured the total cost of goods completed during the current period. (p. 45)

cost of goods sold the cost of direct materials, direct labor, and overhead attached to the units sold. (p. 46)

cost of resource usage the activity rate multiplied by the actual activity usage. (p. 86)

cost of unused activity the activity rate multiplied by the unused activity. (p. 86)

cost reconciliation determining whether the costs assigned to units transferred out and to units in ending work in process are equal to the costs in beginning work in process plus the manufacturing costs incurred in the current period. (p. 139)

cost-plus method a transfer price acceptable to the Internal Revenue Service under Section 482. The cost-plus method is simply a cost-based transfer price. (p. 837)

cost-volume-profit graph a graph that depicts the relationships among costs, volume, and profits. It consists of a total revenue line and a total cost line. (p. 426)

costs of quality costs incurred because poor quality may exist or because poor quality does exist. (p. 910)

currency appreciation the state of a country's currency becoming stronger and being able to purchase more units of another country's currency. (p. 826)

currency depreciation the state of a country's currency becoming weaker and being able to purchase fewer units of another country's currency. (p. 826)

currency risk management a company's management of its transaction, economic, and translation exposure due to exchange rate fluctuations. (p. 825)

currently attainable standard a standard that reflects an efficient operating state; it is rigorous but achievable. (p. 729)

customer value the difference between what a customer receives (customer realization) and what the customer gives up (customer sacrifice). (p. 354)

cycle time the length of time required to produce one unit of a product. (p. 883)

D

data set a grouping of logically related data. (p. 324)

decentralization the granting of decision-making freedom to lower operating levels. (p. 776)

decentralized decision making a system in which decisions are made and implemented by lower-level managers. (p. 776)

decision making the process of choosing among competing alternatives. (p. 16)

decision model a set of procedures that, if followed, will lead to a decision. (p. 456)

decision package a description of services, with associated costs, that a decision unit can or would like to offer. (p. 704)

decline stage the stage in a product's life cycle when the product loses market acceptance and sales begin to decrease. (p. 366)

defective product a product or service that does not conform to specifications. (p. 909)

degree of operating leverage (DOL) a measure of the sensitivity of profit changes to changes in sales volume. It measures the percentage change in profits resulting from a percentage change in sales. (p. 432)

dependent variable a variable whose value depends on the value of another variable. For example, Y in the cost formula Y = F + VX depends on the value of X. (p. 89)

deviation the difference between the cost predicted by a cost formula and the actual cost. It measures the distance of a data point from the cost line. (p. 94)

direct costs costs that can be easily and accurately traced to a cost object. (p. 38)

direct fixed expenses fixed costs that can be traced to each segment and would be avoided if the segment did not exist. (p. 420)

direct labor labor that is traceable to the goods or services being produced. (p. 44)

direct labor budget a budget showing the total direct labor hours needed and the associated cost for the number of units in the production budget. (p. 685)

direct materials those materials that are traceable to the good or service being produced. (p. 44)

direct materials budget a budget that outlines the expected usage of materials production and purchases of the direct materials required. (p. 684)

direct method a method that allocates service costs directly to producing departments. This method ignores any interactions that may exist among service departments. (p. 244)

direct tracing the process of identifying costs that are specifically or physically associated with a cost object. (p. 39)

discount factor the factor used to convert a future cash flow to its present value. (p. 532)

discount rate the rate of return used to compute the present value of future cash flows. (p. 531)

discounted cash flows future cash flows expressed in present value terms. (p. 508)

discounting the act of finding the present value of future cash flows. (p. 531)

discounting model any capital investment model that explicitly considers the time value of money in identifying criteria for accepting or rejecting proposed projects. (p. 505)

discretionary fixed expenses costs incurred for the acquisition of short-term capacity or services, usually as the result of yearly planning. (p. 83)

driver analysis the effort expended to identify those factors that are the root causes of activity costs. (p. 864)

driver tracing the use of *drivers* to assign costs to cost objects. (p. 39)

drivers factors that *cause* changes in resource usage, activity usage, costs, and revenues. (p. 39)

drum-buffer-rope system the TOC inventory management system that relies on the drum beat of the major constrained resource, time buffers, and ropes to determine inventory levels. (p. 572)

dumping predatory pricing on the international market. (p. 604)

durability the length of time a product functions in its intended manner. (p. 909)

dysfunctional behavior individual behavior that conflicts with the goals of the organization. (p. 699)

E

economic order quantity (EOQ) the amount that should be ordered (or produced) to minimize the total ordering (or setup) and carrying costs. (p. 553)

economic risk the possibility that a firm's present value of future cash flows can be affected by exchange fluctuations. (p. 825)

economic value added (EVA) the after-tax operating profit minus the total annual cost of capital. (p. 785)

efficiency variance see **usage variance**. (p. 733)

elastic demand when a price increase (decrease) of a certain percent lowers (raises) the quantity demanded by more than that percentage. (p. 591)

electronic data interchange (EDI) an inventory management method that allows suppliers access to a buyer's on-line data base. (p. 559)

ending finished goods inventory budget a budget that describes planned ending inventory of finished goods in units and dollars. (p. 687)

equivalent units of output the whole units that could have been produced in a period given the amount of manufacturing inputs used. (p. 188)

error cause identification a program in which employees describe problems that prevent them from doing their jobs right the first time. (p. 931)

error costs the costs associated with making poor decisions based on inaccurate product costs (or bad cost information). (p. 58)

ethical behavior behavior that results in choices/actions that are right, proper, and just. (p. 16)

exchange gain a gain on the exchange of one currency for another due to appreciation in the home currency. (p. 827)

exchange loss a loss on the exchange of one currency for another due to depreciation in the home currency. (p. 827)

exchange rate the rate at which a foreign currency can be exchanged for the domestic currency. (p. 825)

expected activity level the level of production activity expected for the coming period. (p. 138)

expenses expired costs. (p. 37)

external constraints limiting factors imposed on the firm from external sources. (p. 565)

external failure costs costs incurred because products fail to conform to requirements after being sold to outside parties. (p. 911)

external linkages the relationship of a firm's activities within its segment of the value chain with those activities of its suppliers and customers. (p. 356)

F

facility-level activities those activities that sustain a facility's general manufacturing process. (p. 50)

failure activities activities performed by an organization or its customers in response to poor quality (poor quality *does* exist). (p. 911)

failure costs the costs incurred by an organization because failure activities are performed. (p. 911)

favorable variance a variance produced whenever the actual amounts are less than the budgeted or standard allowances. (p. 733)

feasible set of solutions the collection of all feasible solutions. (p. 568)

feasible solution a product mix that satisfies all constraints. (p. 568)

features (quality of design) characteristics of a product that differentiate functionally similar products. (p. 909)

feedback information that can be used to evaluate or correct steps being taken to implement a plan. (p. 15)

FIFO costing method a unit-costing method that excludes prior-period work and costs in computing current-period unit work and costs. (p. 191)

financial accounting the branch of the accounting system that is concerned with the preparation of financial reports for users external to the organization. (p. 2)

financial accounting information system an accounting information subsystem that is primarily concerned with producing outputs for external users and uses well-specified economic events as inputs and processes that meet certain rules and conventions. (p. 32)

financial budget that portion of the master budget that includes the cash budget, the budgeted balance sheet, the budgeted statement of cash flows, and the capital budget. (p. 679)

financial productivity measure a productivity measure in which inputs and outputs are expressed in dollars. (p. 955)

fitness for use the suitability of the product for carrying out its advertised functions. (p. 909)

five-year assets assets with an expected life for depreciation purposes of five years; light trucks, automobiles, and computer equipment fall into this category. (p. 522)

fixed costs costs that *in total* are constant within the relevant range as the level of the cost driver varies. (p. 50)

fixed overhead spending variance the difference between actual fixed overhead and applied fixed overhead. (p. 749)

fixed overhead volume variance the difference between budgeted fixed overhead and applied fixed overhead; it is a measure of capacity utilization. (p. 750)

flexible budget a budget that can specify costs for a range of activity. (p. 696)

flexible budget variance the difference between actual costs and expected costs given by a flexible budget. (p. 697)

flexible manufacturing system (FMS) cell a system that produces a family of products from start to finish using robots and other automated equipment under the control of a computer. (p. 377)

foreign trade zones areas physically on U.S. soil but considered to be outside U.S. commerce. Goods imported into a foreign trade zone are duty-free until they leave the zone. (p. 821)

forward contract an agreement that requires the buyer to exchange a specified amount of a currency at a specified rate (the forward rate) on a specified future date. (p. 828)

future value the value that will accumulate by the end of an investment's life if the investment earns a specified compounded return. (p. 531)

G

goal congruence the alignment of a manager's personal goals with those of the organization. (p. 698)

goodness of fit the degree of association between Y and X (cost and activity). It is measured by how much of the total variability in Y is explained by X. (p. 97)

gross profit (gross margin) the difference between revenue and cost of goods sold. (p. 622)

growth stage the stage in a product's life cycle when sales increase at an increasing rate. (p. 366)

H

half-year convention a convention that assumes a newly acquired asset is in service for one-half of its first taxable year of service, regardless of the date that use of it actually began. (p. 522)

hedging one way of ensuring against gains and losses on foreign currency exchange. (p. 828)

heterogeneity refers to the greater chances for variation in the performance of services than in the production of products. (p. 127)

hidden quality costs opportunity costs resulting from poor quality. (p. 911)

high-low method a method for fitting a line to a set of data points using the high and low points in the data set. For a cost formula, the high and low points represent the high and low activity levels. It is used to break out the fixed and variable components of a mixed cost. (p. 89)

homogeneous cost pool a collection of overhead costs associated with activities that have the same process, have the same level, and can use the same activity driver to assign costs to products. (p. 310)

hurdle rate *see* **required rate of return.** (p. 509)

hypothesis test of cost parameters a statistical assessment of a cost formula's reliability that indicates whether the parameters are different from zero. (p. 97)

hypothetical sales value an approximation of the sales value of a joint product at split-off. It is found by subtracting all separable (or further) processing costs from the eventual market value. (p. 277)

I

ideal standards standards that reflect perfect operating conditions. (p. 729)

incentives the positive or negative measures taken by an organization to induce a manager to exert effort toward achieving the organization's goals. (p. 700)

incremental (or baseline) budgeting the practice of taking the prior year's budget and adjusting it upward or downward to determine next year's budget. (p. 703)

independent projects projects that, if accepted or rejected, will not affect the cash flows of another project. (p. 503)

independent variable a variable whose value does not depend on the value of another variable. For example, in the cost formula Y = F + VX, the variable X is an independent variable. (p. 89)

indirect costs costs that cannot be traced to a cost object. (p. 38)

industrial value chain the linked set of value-creating activities from basic raw materials to end-use customers. (p. 355)

inelastic demand when a price increase (decrease) of a certain percent is associated with a quantity decrease (increase) of less than that percent. (p. 591)

input tradeoff efficiency the least-cost, technically efficient mix of inputs. (p. 952)

inseparability an attribute of services that means that production and consumption are inseparable. (p. 127)

intangibility refers to the nonphysical nature of services as opposed to products. (p. 127)

intercept parameter the fixed cost, representing the point where the cost formula intercepts the vertical axis. In the cost formula Y = F + VX, F is the intercept parameter. (p. 89)

interim quality performance report a comparison of current actual quality costs with short-term budgeted quality targets. (p. 927)

interim quality standard a standard based on short-run quality goals. (p. 927)

internal constraints limiting factors found within the firm. (p. 565)

internal failure costs costs incurred because products and services fail to conform to requirements where lack of conformity is discovered prior to external sale. (p. 911)

internal linkages relationships among activities within a firm's value chain. (p. 356)

internal rate of return the rate of return that equates the present value of a project's cash inflows with the present value of its cash outflows (i.e., it sets the NPV equal to zero). Also, the rate of return being earned on funds that remain internally invested in a project. (p. 509)

introduction stage a product life cycle stage characterized by preproduction and startup activities, where the focus is on obtaining a foothold in the market. (p. 366)

inventory the money an organization spends in turning raw materials into throughput. (p. 570)

investment center a responsibility center in which a manager is responsible for revenues, costs, and investments. (p. 775)

J

job-order cost sheet a document or record used to accumulate manufacturing costs for a job. (p. 144)

job-order costing system a cost accumulation method that accumulates manufacturing costs by job. (p. 143)

joint products two or more products, each having relatively substantial value, that are produced simultaneously by the same process up to a "split-off" point. (pp. 269, 470)

joint venture a type of partnership in which investors co-own the enterprise. (p. 824)

just-in-time (JIT) manufacturing a demand-pull system that strives to produce a product only when it is needed and only in the quantities demanded by customers. (pp. 9, 373)

just-in-time (JIT) purchasing a system that requires suppliers to deliver parts and materials just in time to be used in production. (p. 373)

K

kanban system an information system that controls production on a demand-pull basis through the use of cards or markers. (p. 561)

keep-or-drop decision a relevant costing analysis that focuses on keeping or dropping a segment of a business. (p. 465)

L

labor efficiency variance the difference between the actual direct labor hours used and the standard direct labor hours allowed multiplied by the standard hourly wage rate. (p. 742)

labor rate variance the difference between the actual hourly rate paid and the standard hourly rate multiplied by the actual hours worked. (p. 741)

lead time for purchasing, the time to receive an order after it is placed. For manufacturing, the time to produce a product from start to finish. (p. 554)

life cycle cost management actions taken that cause a product to be designed, developed, produced, marketed, distributed, operated, maintained, serviced, and disposed of so that life cycle profits are maximized. (p. 367)

life cycle costs all costs associated with the product for its entire life cycle. (p. 366)

line position a position in an organization filled by an individual who is directly responsible for carrying out the organization's basic objectives. (p. 14)

linear programming a method that searches among possible solutions until it finds the optimal solution. (p. 567)

long run period of time for which all costs are variable, i.e., there are no fixed costs. (pp. 81, 640)

long-range quality performance report a performance report that compares current actual quality costs with long-range targeted quality costs (usually in the 2%–3% range). (p. 930)

loose constraints constraints whose limited resources are not fully used by a product mix. (p. 566)

loss a cost that expires without producing any revenue benefit; a negative profit. (p. 37)

M

make-or-buy decision a decision that focuses on whether a component (service) should be made (provided) internally or purchased externally. (p. 461)

management accounting the branch of the accounting system that is concerned with providing information for users internal to the organization. (p. 2)

manufacturing cells a plant layout containing machines grouped in families, usually in a semicircle. (p. 375)

maquiladoras manufacturing plants located in Mexico that process imported materials and reexport them to the United States. (p. 824)

margin the ratio of net operating income to sales. (p. 779)

margin of safety the units sold or expected to be sold or sales revenue earned or expected to be earned above the break-even volume. (p. 431)

market share the proportion of industry sales accounted for by a company. (p. 629)

market share variance the difference between the actual market share percentage and the budgeted market share percentage multiplied by actual industry sales in units times budgeted average unit contribution margin. (p. 629)

market size the total revenue for the industry. (p. 629)

market size variance the difference between actual and budgeted industry sales in units multiplied by the budgeted market share percentage times the budgeted average unit contribution margin. (p. 629)

marketing expense budget a budget that outlines planned expenditures for selling and distribution activities. (p. 687)

marketing or selling costs those costs necessary to market and distribute a product or service. (p. 45)

markup a percentage applied to base cost for the purpose of calculating price; the markup includes desired profit and any costs not included in the base. (p. 595)

master budget the collection of all area and activity budgets representing a firm's comprehensive plan of action. (p. 679)

materials price variance the difference between the actual price paid per unit of materials and the standard price allowed per unit multiplied by the actual quantity of materials purchased. (p. 735)

materials requisition form a document used to identify the cost of raw materials assigned to each job. (p. 144)

materials usage variance the difference between the direct materials actually used and the direct materials allowed for the actual output multiplied by the standard price. (p. 738)

maturity stage the stage in a product's life cycle when sales increase at a decreasing rate. (p. 366)

maximum transfer price the transfer price that will make the buying division no worse off if an input is acquired internally. (p. 794)

measurement costs the costs associated with the measurements required by a cost management system. (p. 58)

method of least squares a statistical method to find a line that best fits a set of data. It is used to break out the fixed and variable components of a mixed cost. (p. 96)

minimum transfer price the transfer price that will make the selling division no worse off if the intermediate product is sold internally. (p. 794)

mix variance the difference in the standard cost of the mix of actual material inputs and the standard cost of the material input mix that should have been used. (p. 755)

mixed costs costs that have both a fixed and a variable component. (p. 54)

modified accelerated cost recovery system (MACRS) a method of computing annual depreciation; defined as double-declining-balance method. (p. 522)

monetary incentives the use of economic rewards to motivate managers. (p. 700)

monopolistic competition a market that is close to the competitive market. There are many sellers and buyers, low barriers to entry, but the products are differentiated on some basis. (p. 594)

monopoly a market in which barriers to entry are so high that there is only one firm selling a unique product. (p. 594)

multinational corporation (MNC) a corporation for which a significant amount of business is done in more than one country. (p. 820)

multiple regression the use of least-squares analysis to determine the parameters in a linear equation involving two or more explanatory variables. (p. 102)

multiple-period quality trend report a graph that plots quality costs (as a percentage of sales) against time. (p. 927)

mutually exclusive projects projects that, if accepted, preclude the acceptance of competing projects. (p. 503)

myopic behavior managerial actions that improve budgetary performance in the short run at the expense of the long-run welfare of the organization. (pp. 702, 782)

N

net income operating income less taxes, interest expense, and research and development expense. (pp. 412, 626)

net present value the difference between the present value of a project's cash inflows and the present value of its cash outflows. (p. 508)

net realizable value method a method of allocating joint production costs to the joint products based on their proportionate share of eventual revenue less further processing costs. (p. 277)

noncost methods methods that make no attempt to cost the by-product or its inventory, but instead make some credit either to income or to main product. (p. 280)

nondiscounting model capital investment models that identify criteria for accepting or rejecting projects without considering the time value of money. (p. 505)

noninventoriable (period) costs costs expensed in the period in which they are incurred. (p. 45)

nonmonetary incentives the use of psychological and social rewards to motivate managers. (p. 700)

nonproduction costs those costs associated with the functions of selling and administration. (p. 43)

nonunit-based activity cost drivers factors, other than the number of units produced, that measure the demands that cost objects place on activities. (p. 304)

nonvalue-added activities activities either unnecessary or necessary but inefficient and improvable. (pp. 557, 865)

nonvalue-added costs costs that are caused either by nonvalue-added activities or the inefficient performance of valued-added activities. (p. 865)

normal activity level the average activity level that a firm experiences over more than one fiscal period. (p. 139)

normal cost of goods sold the cost of goods sold figure obtained when the per-unit normal cost is used. (p. 153)

normal costing system a cost measurement system in which the actual costs of direct materials and direct labor are assigned to production and a predetermined rate is used to assign overhead costs to production. (p. 134)

O

objective function the function to be optimized, usually a profit function; thus, optimization usually means maximizing profits. (p. 567)

observable quality costs those quality costs that are available from an organization's accounting records. (p. 911)

oligopoly a market structure characterized by a few sellers and high barriers to entry. (p. 594)

one-price policy a single price is charged to all customers. (p. 593)

operating assets those assets used to generate operating income, consisting usually of cash, inventories, receivables, property, plant, and equipment. (p. 779)

operating budgets budgets associated with the income-producing activities of an organization. (p. 679)

operating expenses the money an organization spends in turning inventories into throughput. (p. 570)

operating income revenues minus expenses from the firm's normal operations. Income taxes are excluded. (pp. 412, 622, 779)

operating leverage the use of fixed costs to extract higher percentage changes in profits as sales activity changes. Leverage is achieved by increasing fixed costs while lowering variable costs. (p. 432)

operation costing a costing system that uses job-order costing to assign materials costs and process costing to assign conversion costs. (p. 204)

operational activities day-to-day activities performed as a result of the structure and processes selected by an organization. (p. 358)

operational control information system a cost management subsystem designed to provide accurate and timely feedback concerning the performance of managers and others relative to their planning and control of activities. (p. 36)

operational cost drivers those factors that drive the cost of operational activities. (p. 358)

operational measures physical or nonfinancial measures of performance. (p. 881)

operational productivity measures measures that are expressed in physical terms. (p. 955)

opportunity cost approach a transfer pricing system that identifies the minimum price that a selling division would be willing to accept and the maximum price that a buying division would be willing to pay. (p. 793)

optimal cost management system the system that minimizes the sum of measurement costs and error costs. (p. 58)

optimal solution the feasible solution that produces the best value for the objective function (the largest value if seeking to maximize the objective function; the minimum otherwise). (p. 568)

ordering costs the costs of placing and receiving an order. (p. 551)

organizational activities activities that determine the structure and procedures of an organization. (p. 357)

organizational cost drivers structural and procedural factors that determine the long-term cost structure of an organization. (p. 357)

outsourcing the payment by a company for a business function that was formerly done in-house. (p. 823)

overapplied overhead the overhead variance resulting when applied overhead is greater than the actual overhead cost incurred. (p. 141)

overhead all production costs other than direct materials and direct labor. (p. 44)

overhead budget a budget that reveals the planned expenditures for all indirect manufacturing items. (p. 686)

overhead variance the difference between the actual overhead and the applied overhead. (p. 141)

P

partial productivity measurement a ratio that measures productive efficiency for one input. (p. 954)

participative budgeting an approach to budgeting that allows managers who will be held accountable for budgetary performance to participate in the budget's development. (p. 700)

payback period the time required for a project to return its investment. (p. 505)

penetration pricing the pricing of a new product at a low initial price, perhaps even lower than cost, to build market share quickly. (p. 600)

perfectly competitive market a market (or industry) characterized by many buyers and sellers—no one of which is large enough to influence the market—a homogeneous product, and easy entry into and exit from the industry. (p. 594)

performance refers to how consistently and well a product functions. (p. 908)

performance reports accounting reports that provide feedback to managers by comparing planned outcomes with actual outcomes. (p. 15)

perishability an attribute of services that means that they cannot be inventoried but must be consumed when performed. (p. 127)

perquisites a type of fringe benefit over and above salary which is received by managers. (p. 789)

physical flow schedule a schedule that accounts for all units flowing through a department during a period. (p. 192)

physical units method a method of allocating joint production costs based on each product's share of total units. (p. 273)

planning setting objectives and identifying methods to achieve those objectives. (p. 15)

pool rate the overhead costs for a homogeneous cost pool divided by the practical capacity of the activity driver associated with the pool. (p. 310)

postaudit a follow-up analysis of an investment decision. (p. 526)

postpurchase costs the costs of using, maintaining, and disposing of a product. (p. 355)

practical activity level the output a firm can achieve if it is operating efficiently. (p. 139)

practical capacity the efficent level of activity performance. (p. 82)

predatory pricing the practice of setting prices below cost for the purpose of injuring competitors and eliminating competition. (p. 603)

predetermined overhead rate estimated overhead divided by the estimated level of production activity. It is used to assign overhead to production. (p. 136)

present value the current value of a future cash flow. It represents the amount that must be invested now if the future cash flow is to be received assuming compounding at a given rate of interest. (p. 531)

prevention costs costs incurred to prevent defects in products or services being produced. (p. 911)

price discrimination charging different prices to different customers for essentially the same commodity. (p. 604)

price elasticity of demand the degree to which quantity demanded changes in response to a price change. (p. 591)

price gouging when firms with market power (i.e., little or no competition) price products "too high." (p. 609)

price skimming a pricing strategy in which a higher price is charged at the beginning of a product's life cycle, then lowered at later phases of the life cycle. (p. 600)

price standard the price that should be paid per unit of input. (p. 728)

price takers companies that, individually, have no ability to influence price. (p. 594)

price variance the difference between standard price and actual price multiplied by the actual quantity of inputs used. (p. 733)

price volume variance the difference between actual volume sold and expected volume sold multiplied by the expected price. (p. 601)

price-recovery component the difference between the total profit change and the profit-linked productivity change. (p. 960)

primary key the attribute that uniquely identifies each row of data in a table. (p. 324)

prime cost the sum of direct materials cost and direct labor cost. (p. 45)

procedural (executional) activities activities that define the processes of an organization. (p. 357)

process a series of activities (operations) that are linked to perform a specific objective. (pp. 181, 316)

process costing principle the period's unit cost is computed by dividing the costs of the period by the output of the period. (p. 186)

process costing system a cost accumulation method that accumulates costs by process or department. (p. 181)

process improvement incremental and constant increases in the efficiency of an existing process. (p. 857)

process innovation the performance of a process in a radically new way with the objective of achieving dramatic improvements in response time, cost, quality, and other important competitive factors. (p. 857)

process productivity analysis an approach that measures activity productivity by treating activities as inputs to a process and relating the input to the process's output. (p. 961)

process value analysis an analysis that defines activity-based responsibility accounting, focuses on accountability for activities rather than costs, and emphasizes the maximization of systemwide performance instead of individual performance. (p. 864)

producing department a unit within an organization responsible for producing the products or services that are sold to customers. (p. 232)

product cost a cost assignment method that satisfies a well-specified managerial objective. (p. 42)

product diversity the situation present when products consume overhead in different proportions. (p. 305)

product life cycle the time a product exists—from conception to abandonment; the profit history of the product according to four stages: introduction, growth, maturity, and decline. (pp. 365, 642, 878)

product-level drivers output measures for product-level activities. (p. 50)

product-level (sustaining) activities those activities performed to enable the production of each different type of product. (p. 50)

production budget a budget that shows how many units must be produced to meet sales needs and satisfy ending inventory requirements. (p. 684)

production costs those costs associated with the manufacture of goods or the provision of services. (p. 43)

Production Kanban a card or marker that specifies the quantity the preceding process should produce. (p. 561)

production report a report that summarizes the manufacturing activity for a department during a period and discloses physical flow, equivalent units, total costs to account for, unit cost computation, and costs assigned to goods transferred out and to units in ending work in process. (p. 184)

productivity producing output efficiently, using the least quantity of inputs possible. (p. 952)

productivity measurement assessment of productivity changes. (p. 954)

profile measurement a series or vector of separate and distinct partial operational measures. (p. 956)

profit the difference between the revenues and expenses of a business. (p. 620)

profit center a responsibility center in which a manager is responsible for both revenues and costs. (p. 775)

profit-linked productivity measurement an assessment of the amount of profit change—from the base period to the current period—attributable to productivity changes. (p. 958)

profit-volume graph a graphical portrayal of the relationship between profits and sales activity. (p. 424)

prospect theory an extension of expected utility that is characterized by asymmetry in the valuation of gains and losses (i.e., losses are felt more deeply than gains) and by valuing amounts relative to some reference point. (p. 645)

pseudoparticipation a budgetary system in which top management solicits inputs from lower-level managers and then ignores those inputs. Thus, in reality, budgets are dictated from above. (p. 701)

Q

quality of conformance conforming to the design requirements of the product. (p. 909)

quality of design quality differences that arise for products with the same function but different specifications. (p. 909)

quality product (service) a product which meets or exceeds customer expectations. (p. 908)

quantity standard the quantity of input allowed per unit of output. (p. 728)

R

rate variance *see* **price variance**. (p. 733)

reciprocal method a method that simultaneously allocates service costs to all user departments. It gives full consideration to interactions among service departments. (p. 246)

reference transaction a relevant precedent that is characterized by a reference price and by a positive reference profit to the firm. (p. 607)

relational structure a data structure that uses a table to represent the overall logical view within a database. (p. 324)

relevant costs future costs that differ across alternatives. (p. 458)

relevant range the range over which an assumed cost relationship is valid for the normal operations of a firm. (pp. 51, 427)

relevant revenues future revenues that differ across alternatives. (p. 458)

reliability the probability that the product or service will perform its intended function for a specified length of time. (p. 909)

reorder point the point in time at which a new order (or setup) should be initiated. (p. 554)

replacement cost method the cost of by-products utilized within the plant are valued at the opportunity cost of purchasing or replacing the products in question. (p. 281)

required rate of return the minimum rate of return that a project must earn in order to be acceptable. Usually corresponds to the cost of capital. (p. 509)

resale price method a transfer price acceptable to the Internal Revenue Service under Section 482. The resale price method computes a transfer price equal to the sales price received by the reseller less an appropriate markup. (p. 837)

research and development expense budget a budget that outlines planned expenditures for research and development. (p. 706)

residual income the difference between operating income and the minimum required dollar return on a company's operating assets. (p. 783)

resource drivers factors that measure the demands placed on resources by activities and are used to assign the cost of resources to activities. (p. 39)

resource spending the cost of acquiring capacity to perform an activity. (p. 82)

resource usage the amount of activity capacity used in producing an organization's output. (p. 82)

resources economic elements that are consumed in performing activities. (p. 82)

resources supplied as used and needed resources acquired from outside sources, where the terms of acquisition do not require any long-term commitment for any given amount of the resource. (p. 82)

resources supplied in advance of usage resources acquired by the use of either an explicit or implicit contract to obtain a given quantity of resource, regardless of whether or not the quantity of the resource available is fully used. (p. 82)

responsibility accounting a system that measures the results of each responsibility center and compares those results with some measure of expected or budgeted outcome. (p. 775)

responsibility center a segment of the business whose manager is accountable for specified sets of activities. (p. 775)

return on investment (ROI) the ratio of operating income to average operating assets. (p. 779)

revenue center a responsibility center in which a manager is responsible only for sales. (p. 775)

revenue-producing life the time a product generates revenue for a company. (p. 365)

ropes actions taken to tie the rate at which raw material is released into the plant (at the first operation) to the production rate of the constrained resource. (p. 572)

S

safety stock extra inventory carried to serve as insurance against fluctuations in demand. (p. 555)

sales budget a budget that describes expected sales in units and dollars for the coming period. (p. 683)

sales mix the relative combination of products (or services) being sold by an organization. (p. 421)

sales mix variance the sum of the change in units for each product multiplied by the difference between the budgeted contribution margin and the budgeted average unit contribution margin. (p. 628)

sales price variance the difference between actual price and expected price multiplied by the actual quantity or volume sold. (p. 601)

sales volume variance the difference between the actual quantity sold and the budgeted quantity sold multiplied by the budgeted average unit contribution margin. (p. 627)

sales-revenue approach an approach to CVP analysis that uses sales revenue to measure sales activity. Variable costs and contribution margin are expressed as percentages of sales revenue. (p. 417)

sales-to-production-ratio method allocates joint costs in accordance with a weighting factor that compares percentage of sales with percentage of production. (p. 279)

sales-value-at-split-off method a method of allocating joint production costs based on each product's share of revenue realized at the split-off point. (p. 276)

scattergraph a plot of (X, Y) data points. For cost analysis, X is activity usage and Y is the associated cost at that activity level. (p. 91)

scatterplot method a method to fit a line to a set of data using two points that are selected by judgment. It is used to break out the fixed and variable components of a mixed cost. (p. 90)

second-market discounting when a company has excess capacity and customers with differing elasticities of demand and a higher price is charged to the core market (with inelastic demand) and lower prices to secondary markets (with elastic demand). (p. 593)

sell or process further relevant costing analysis that focuses on whether or not a product should be processed beyond the split-off point. (p. 471)

sensitivity analysis a "what if" technique that examines altering certain key variables to assess the effect on the original outcome. (pp. 433, 528)

separable costs costs that are easily traced to individual products. (p. 270)

sequential (or step) method a method that allocates service costs to user departments in a sequential manner. It gives partial consideration to interactions among service departments. (p. 245)

service a task or activity performed for a customer or an activity performed by a customer using an organization's products or facilities. (p. 42)

serviceability the ease of maintaining and/or repairing a product. (p. 909)

setup costs the costs of preparing equipment and facilities so that they can be used for production. (p. 551)

seven-year assets assets with an expected life for depreciation purposes of seven years; equipment, machinery, and office furniture fall into this category. (p. 522)

shadow price the amount by which throughput will increase for one additional unit of scarce resource. (p. 575)

short run period of time in which at least one cost is fixed. (pp. 81, 640)

simplex method an algorithm that identifies the optimal solution for a linear programming problem. (p. 569)

slope parameter the variable cost per unit of activity usage, represented by V in the cost formula $Y = F + VX$. (p. 89)

source document a document that describes a transaction and is used to keep track of costs as they occur. (p. 131)

special-order decisions decisions that focus on whether a specially priced order should be accepted or rejected. (p. 479)

split-off point the point at which the joint products become separate and identifiable. (pp. 269, 470)

spot rate the exchange rate of one currency for another for immediate delivery. (p. 826)

staff position a position in an organization filled by an individual who provides support for the line function; thus, a staff person is only indirectly involved with the basic objectives of an organization. (p. 14)

standard bill of materials a listing of the type and quantity of materials allowed for a given level of output. (p. 739)

standard cost per unit the per-unit cost that should be achieved given materials, labor, and overhead standards. (p. 731)

standard cost sheet a listing of the standard costs and standard quantities of direct materials, direct labor, and overhead that should apply to a single product. (p. 731)

standard hours allowed the direct labor hours that should have been used to produce the actual output (Unit labor standard × Actual output). (p. 732)

standard quantity of materials allowed the quantity of materials that should have been used to produce the actual output (Unit materials standard × Actual output). (p. 732)

static budget a budget for a particular level of activity. (p. 695)

step-cost function a cost function in which cost is defined for ranges of activity usage rather than point values. The function has the property of displaying constant cost over a range of activity usage and then changing to a different cost level as a new range of activity usage is encountered. (p. 84)

step-fixed cost a step-cost function in which cost remains constant over wide ranges of activity usage. (p. 85)

step-variable cost a step-cost function in which cost remains constant over relatively narrow ranges of activity. (p. 85)

stock options the right to purchase a certain amount of stock at a fixed price. (p. 790)

stock-out costs the costs of insufficient inventory. (p. 551)

strategic cost management the use of cost data to develop and identify superior strategies that will produce a sustainable competitive advantage. (p. 354)

strategic decision making choosing among alternative strategies with the goal of selecting a strategy or strategies that provide a company with reasonable assurance of long-term growth and survival. (p. 354)

structural activities activities that determine the underlying economic structure of the organization. (p. 357)

sunk cost a past cost—a cost already incurred. (p. 458)

supplies materials necessary for production but that do not become part of the finished product or are not used in providing a service. (p. 44)

support department a unit within an organization that provides essential support services for producing departments. (p. 232)

system a set of interrelated parts that performs one or more processes to accomplish specific objectives. (p. 31)

T

tactical cost analysis the use of relevant cost data to identify the alternative that provides the greatest benefit to the organization. (p. 456)

tactical decision making choosing among alternatives with only an immediate or limited end in view. (p. 454)

Taguchi loss function a function that assumes any variation from the target value of a quality characteristic causes hidden quality costs. (p. 912)

tangible products goods produced by converting raw materials through the use of labor and capital inputs such as plant, land, and machinery. (p. 42)

target cost the difference between the sales price needed to achieve a projected market share and the desired per-unit profit. (p. 371)

target costing a method of determining the cost of a product or service based on the price that custom-

ers are willing to pay. Also referred to as price-driven costing. (p. 597)

tariff the tax on imports levied by the federal government. (p. 821)

technical efficiency point at which for any mix of inputs that will produce a given output, no more of any one input is used than is absolutely necessary. (p. 952)

theoretical activity level the maximum output possible for a firm under perfect operating conditions. (p. 139)

three-year assets assets with an expected life for depreciation purposes of three years; most small tools fall into this category. (p. 522)

throughput the rate at which an organization generates money through sales. (p. 570)

time buffer the inventory needed to keep the constrained resource busy for a specified time interval. (p. 572)

time ticket a document used to identify the cost of direct labor for a job. (p. 146)

total budget variance the difference between the actual cost of an input and its planned cost. (p. 733)

total (overall) sales variance the sum of the sales price and sales volume variances. (p. 602)

total preventive maintenance a program of preventive maintenance that has zero machine failures as its standard. (p. 561)

total product the complete range of tangible and intangible benefits a customer receives from a product. (p. 355)

total productive efficiency the point at which technical and price efficiency are achieved. (p. 952)

total productivity measurement an assessment of productive efficiency for all inputs combined. (p. 956)

total quality control an approach to managing quality that demands the production of defect-free products. (p. 363)

total quality management a philosophy that requires managers to strive to create an environment that will enable workers to manufacture perfect (zero-defects) products. (p. 7)

traceability the ability to assign a cost directly to a cost object in an economically feasible way using a causal relationship. (p. 39)

tracing assigning costs to a cost object using an observable measure of the cost object's resource consumption. (p. 39)

traditional cost system a cost accounting system that uses only unit-based activity drivers to assign costs to cost objects. (p. 56)

traditional operation control system a system that assigns costs to organizational units and then holds the organizational unit manager responsible for controlling the assigned costs. (p. 56)

traditional responsibility accounting a control system defined by centering responsibility on organizational units and individuals with traditional budgets and standard costing used to evaluate and monitor performance. (p. 856)

transaction risk the possibility that future cash transactions will be affected by changing exchange rates. (p. 825)

transfer price the price charged for goods transferred from one division to another. (p. 792)

transfer pricing problem the problem of finding a transfer pricing system that simultaneously satisfies the three objectives of accurate performance evaluation, goal congruence, and autonomy. (p. 793)

transferred-in cost the cost of goods transferred in from a prior process. (p. 182)

translation (or accounting) risk the degree to which a firm's financial statements are exposed to exchange rate fluctuation. (p. 825)

treasurer the financial officer responsible for the management of cash and investment capital. (p. 14)

turnover the ratio of sales to average operating assets. (p. 780)

U

underapplied overhead the overhead variance resulting when the actual overhead cost incurred is greater than the applied overhead. (p. 141)

unfavorable variance a variance produced whenever the actual input amounts are greater than the budgeted or standard allowances. (p. 733)

unit-based activity drivers factors that cause changes in cost as the units produced change. (p. 301)

unit-level activities activities that are performed each time a unit is produced. (p. 49)

unit-level drivers output measures for unit-level activities. (p. 49)

unused capacity the difference between the acquired activity capacity and the actual activity usage. (p. 82)

usage variance the difference between standard quantities and actual quantities multiplied by standard price. (p. 733)

V

value chain the set of activities required to design, develop, produce, market, distribute, and service a product (the product can be a service). (pp. 6, 34)

value-added activities activities that are necessary to achieve corporate objectives and remain in business. (p. 865)

value-added costs costs caused by value-added activities. (p. 865)

value-added standard the optimal output level for an activity. (p. 867)

value-chain analysis exploiting internal and external linkages by following cost leadership and differentiation strategies to establish a sustainable competitive advantage. (p. 359)

variable budget *see* **flexible budget.** (p. 697)

variable cost ratio variable costs divided by sales revenue. It is the proportion of each sales dollar needed to cover variable costs. (p. 417)

variable costing a costing method that assigns only variable manufacturing costs to the product; these costs include direct materials, direct labor, and variable overhead. Fixed overhead is treated as a period cost and is expensed in the period incurred (p. 624).

variable costs costs that in total vary in direct proportion to changes in a cost driver. (p. 52)

variable overhead efficiency variance the difference between the actual direct labor hours used and the standard hours allowed multiplied by the standard variable overhead rate. (p. 747)

variable overhead spending variance the difference between the actual variable overhead and the budgeted variable overhead based on actual hours used to produce the actual output. (p. 745)

variable pricing policy a pricing strategy in which a company charges different prices to different customers for the same item. (p. 593)

velocity the number of units that can be produced in a given period of time (e.g., output per hour). (p. 883)

Vendor Kanban a card or marker that signals to a supplier the quantity of materials that need to be delivered and the time of delivery. (p. 561)

W

weight factor a value used to assign weights to various joint products in accordance with their relative size, difficulty to produce, etc. (p. 275)

weighted average cost of capital the proportionate share of each method of financing is multiplied by its percentage cost and summed. (p. 786)

weighted average method a unit-costing method that merges prior-period work and costs with current-period work and costs. (p. 196)

what-if analysis *see* **sensitivity analysis.** (p. 528)

whole-life cost the life cycle cost of a product plus costs that consumers incur, including operation, support, maintenance, and disposal. (p. 878)

Withdrawal Kanban a marker or card that specifies the quantity that a subsequent process should withdraw from a preceding process. (p. 561)

work in process consists of all partially completed units found in production at a given point in time. (p. 47)

work orders used to collect production costs for product batches and to initiate production. (p. 205)

work-in-process file a collection of open job-order cost sheets or job-order cost records. (p. 144)

Y

yield variance the difference in the standard material cost of the standard yield and the standard material cost of the actual yield. (p. 755)

Z

zero-base budgeting a method of budgeting in which the prior year's budgeted level is not taken for granted. Existing operations are analyzed, and continuance of the activity or operation must be justified on the basis of its need or usefulness to the organization. (p. 704)

zero defects a quality performance standard that requires all products and services to be produced and delivered according to specifications. (p. 909)

Company Index

Subject Index

Check Figures

2-5	1. Cost of Goods Manufactured = $216,450
2-6	Income Before Taxes = $175,000
2-7	1. Total Current Manufacturing Costs = $26,470
2-8	2. Prime Costs = $175,050
2-9	5. Unit Cost = $2.50
2-17	3. Gross Margin = $356,050
2-18	Beginning Work in Process = $30,000
2-19	3. Income Before Taxes = $400,000
2-20	2. Goods Available for Sale = $370,000
2-21	4. Per Unit Cost: VCR = $42; TV = $64
2-22	2. Gross Margin = $381,360
3-2	2. Activity Rate = $18.35 per test
3-5	2. F = $1,393.60
3-6	2. Y = 3,150
3-7	3. R2 = .84
3-8	2. Power: Y = $19,500
	3. Y = $183,400
3-9	2. Y = $130,500
3-10	2. Y = $6,500
3-12	2. Resource spending decrease = $45,000
	3. Cost of unused activity: Inspection = 3.750
3-13	3. Total cost: Unit Variable Cost = $68
3-14	4. V = $15.15 per order
	5. Deviation Squared = $37,879,950
3-15	3. Unit Cost = $222
3-16	3. V = $1.21
	4. Least Squares: Y = $34,707.5
3-17	3. Fixed Activity Rate = $0.60 per order
3-18	1. V = $51.67
3-19	2. Budgeted setup costs for 80 setups = $9,226.94
3-20	2. Y = $34,851
3-21	2. 1996 = $2,150,000
4-2	2. Total cost = $489
4-3	1. Applied overhead = $100,650
	2. Overapplied OH = $2,650
4-4	2. April unit cost = $210
	3. Unit cost = $215
4-5	2. $570,000

4-6	2. Applied OH = $681,300
4-7	1. $27 per machine hour
4-8	2. Alpha overapplied OH = $23,000
4-9	2. b. $26,665
4-10	1. $50 per machine hour
4-11	3. WIP ending balance = $39,500
4-12	1. Underapplied OH = $10,500
	2. COGM = $524,750
4-13	3. Job #22 OH (plantwide rate) = $280
	Job #22 OH (dept. rates) = $305
4-14	1. $33.95
4-15	3. $230,000
	5. Direct materials = $5,000
4-16	4. Unit cost Job 689 = $139.73
4-17	1. Job #18 total cost = $19,793
	3. WIP ending balance = $21,300
4-18	2. WIP ending balance = $38,000
	4. COGS increases by $5,550
4-19	3. Underapplied OH = $20,850
4-20	1. $7 per direct labor hour
	2. $17 per direct labor hour
4-21	2. Job 416 total cost = $115.25
4-22	2. Hoboken job total cost = $14,440
4-24	1. $35,813
	4. Selling price = $66,329
4-25	2. Job 97-28 unit bid price = $14.67
4-27	1. Gross profit = $19
	2. Gross profit for 3 surface filling = $20.67
4-28	1. Unit cost = $7.16
	3. Actual unit cost = $7.54
4-29	2. Dept. 2 Overapplied OH = $1,000
	4. Job 689 total cost = $7,658
4-30	1. $50
4-31	2. Total cost = $25.05
5-1	1. Finished Goods = $270,000
5-4	3. Total Unit Cost = $1.25
5-5	Unit materials cost = $1.00;
	Unit conversion cost = $5.00
5-6	3. Equivalent units of output: materials = 10,000
5-7	1. Total ending work in process = $27,000
5-8	Completed D = 52,000
5-9	BWIP = 20,250
5-10	2. Cost of ending work in process = $56,250
5-11	2. Unit cost = $5.20 per completed unit
5-12	2. Unit cost = $6.65
5-13	2. Unit cost = $6.46
5-14	2. WIP − assembly ending inventory = $1,100
5-15	3. Total unit cost = $0.39
5-16	4. Cost of EWIP = $198.55
5-18	2. Unit cost: Regular Strength = $2.17
5-19	Cost per equivalent unit = $4.00
5-20	Current costs to finish units = $10,800
5-21	3. Goods transferred out = $200,864
5-22	2. d. Ending work in process = $11,000

5-23	1. Cost per equivalent unit: materials = $3.60753
	2. Cost per equivalent unit: conversion = $4.13372
5-24	Goods transferred out = $191,033
5-25	Total costs accounted for: EWIP = $2,042
5-26	Total costs to account for: materials = $1,668
5-27	1c. Unit cost = $5.6857
	3c. Unit cost = $11.0082
5-28	1c. Unit cost = $5.70
	3c. Unit cost = $11.0133
5-29	1. Encapsulating Dept. unit conversion cost = $0.0245
5-30	Picking Department Goods started and completed: transferred-out = $14,697
5-31	1. Unit cost = $70.71
	2. Unit cost = $48.75
5-32	1. Total costs added = $497,776
5-34	3. Goods transferred out = $1,155,000
5-35	3. Goods transferred out = $1,095,600
6-2	2. Unit Cost = $1.18
6-3	2. Cost allocated = $268.33
6-4	1. Single charging rate = $3/gift
	2. Total charge to Cuppa Java = $180
6-5	1. 1995 Dept. A allocation = $40,000
6-6	1. 1995 Dept. B total cost = $40,000
	2. 1995 Dept. B total cost = $50,000
6-7	1. Total cost assigned to Women = $117,750
6-8	1. Total cost assigned to Men = $81,278
6-9	2. Grinding OH rate = $4.64 per DLH
6-10	1. Total cost for Polishing = $137,000
	2. Grinding OH rate = $4.75 per DLH
6-11	1. Total cost for Grinding = $92,120
6-12	1. Dallas = $77,226
6-13	1. b. Dallas = $79,226
6-14	1. 1998 graphics rate = $2.80 per hour
6-15	1. Reno total cost = $242,000
	2. Portland total cost = $107,175
6-16	1. Total cost of Foods = $199,775
	2. Total cost of Foods = $201,989
	3. Total cost of Foods = $200,000
6-17	1. a. Bid price = $49.12
	1. b. Cooking OH rate = $9.94 per machine hour
	1. c. Bid price = $48.60
6-18	1. $0.1333 per mile
6-19	1. Amarillo = $31,111
	2. El Paso total cost = $36,150
6-20	1. Bellini Musical Instruments = $49,000
	2. Great West Tissue total cost = $17,849
6-21	2. In-House Member rate = $3,893
6-22	1. Assembly overhead rate = $2.4620 per DLH
	2. Assembly overhead rate = $2.6625 per DLH
6-23	1. Nursing total costs = $264,280
	2. Cost-to-charge ratio = .90
	3. Cost of Test B = $4.50
	4. Cost of Test B = $7.28

7-1	Whey cost allocation = $2,300
7-2	Incremental value of further processing = $3,000
7-3	Gamma revenue at split-off = $9,375
7-4	1. Low-density gross profit = $3,000
	2. Low-density gross profit = $4,500
7-5	1. Silken Skin contribution margin = $360,000
	2. Loss on special order = $96,000
7-6	2. Additional income per pound = $1.43
7-7	1. Gross profit = $35,000
7-8	1. Altox gross profit if processed further = $575,000
	2. Loss on sale of Dorzine = $3,750
7-11	1. Red trees joint cost = $1,500
	2. Red trees joint cost = $2,586
7-12	1. b. Net realizable value of Juice = $24,000
7-13	1. Going joint cost = $4,800
	2. Going joint cost = $5,053
7-14	1. Product N sales value at split-off = $40,000
8-1	3. Overhead rate = $1.80 per machine hour
8-2	2. Bid = $18,375
8-3	1. Unit cost job 600 = $41
8-4	2. Total cost pool 2 = $270,000
8-5	1. Inspecting = $80,000
8-6	2. Unit overhead cost − regular = $7.05
8-7	3. Designing tooling = 179,000
8-9	3. Activity rate for fabrication process = $10 per order
8-10	2. Pool 4 rate = $173.33
8-11	3. High severity daily rate = $646.67
8-12	2. $55.33 per checking account
8-13	2. Unit gross profit job 127 = $16.60; job 234 = $(18.54)
8-14	2. Pool 6 rate = $700 per receiving order
8-15	1. Machining = $200,000
8-16	3. Pool 1 rate = $46,000 per product
8-17	3. Unit overhead cost for small frame = $57.50
8-18	2. Overhead cost per unit for scientific = $0.96
8-19	3. Revised profit per ton = $(35.41)
9-4	2. Cost per unit of average product = $63
9-5	2. Activity rate = $45 per order
9-6	1. Total savings = $463,000
9-7	3. ABC price for small customer = $26.25; large customer = $96.25
9-9	2. Life cycle income = $175,000
9-10	1. Unit loss for engineer's formula = ($0.20)
9-12	1. Maintenance cost per machine hour = $2.80
9-15	1. Overhead assignment to eaters = $10.07; to edgers = $20.14
9-16	2. Unit cost = $22.60
9-17	2. Vase A = $50 per unit
9-18	2. Dr. Finished Goods 730,000;
	Cr. Materials in Process 340,000
	Cr. Conversion Cost Control 390,000
10-1	2. Breakeven units = 1,500 pairs
10-2	1. Breakeven units = 20,000
10-3	1. Breakeven units = 2,500
10-4	2. At 190 jobs, monthly loss = $200
10-5	Price = $3.93

10-6	2. Units = 2,500
	3. Alternative B after-tax profit = $239,400
10-7	Monthly revenue = $2,250,000
10-8	1. Breakeven revenue = $636,364
	2. Breakeven revenue = $782,178
10-9	1. Clients = 10,220
	2. Annual clients = 18,000
10-10	1. Touring model skis = 13,118 pairs
	2. Revenue = $880,000
10-11	1. a. Operating income = $178,750
	1. d. Operating income = $203,750
	2. a. Breakeven riding mowers = 350
	2. c. Breakeven riding mowers = 428
10-12	2. 1,100,000 bags
	4. 400,000 bags
10-13	C fixed costs = $6,100
10-14	2. Margin of safety = $389,286
10-15	Price = $230
10-16	2. Breakeven revenue = $165,000
	5. New net income = $17,400
10-17	2. $20,000
10-18	2. Company B = $416,667
10-19	2. Revenue = $5,600,000
10-20	1. Breakeven units = 80,000
	4. Revenue = $412,500
10-21	3. Margin of safety = $300,000
10-22	2. Breakeven revenue = $83,333
10-23	1. Breakeven units = 119,985
	6. Operating leverage = 5
10-24	2. New price = $.45
10-25	2. $375,000
	5. Breakeven revenue = $400,000
10-26	2. Revenue = $333,513
	3. Increase in bid prices = 11.6 percent
10-27	2. Breakeven cases of granola = 9,000
10-28	2. Operating income = $94,000
10-29	2. Margin of safety = $318,000
10-30	1. Breakeven unit Peoria = 73,500
	2. Operating income = $4,094,400
10-31	1. Breakeven revenue = $18,025
10-32	1. B seats for Bugaku = 3,024;
	Nutcracker revenue = $753,000
	2. Breakeven performances of Petroushka = 7
	5. Loss = $135,980
10-33	2. Variable cost ratio = .67
	4. Breakeven revenue = $606,061
10-35	1. Additional profit = $62,000
	2. Breakeven units = 20,920
10-36	1. Breakeven cases of Rose = 14,960
10-37	2. Total fixed costs = $209,475
10-38	1. Breakeven jars of sauce = 180,582
	2. Breakeven jars of sauce = 192,916
11-3	3. Cost of unused activity = $12,160
	4. (a) $600
11-4	1. Increase in income: $8,750

11-5	2. Maximum price = $6.30
11-6	1. Relevant cost of making = $240,000
11-7	1. Income increases by $20,900
	2. Income increases by $25,900
	3. Income decreases by $24,100
11-8	1. Traditional, Crunchy margin = $90,000; ABC, Crunchy margin = $(7,500)
	3. Dropping Crunchy saves $32,500
11-9	1. $35,000
	2. Processing increases profits by $4,000
11-10	1. Dropping decreases profits by $25,000
	2. Advertise as income increases by $2,500
11-11	1. $240,000
	2. No. Loss = $192,000
11-12	2. Fixed rate = $42 per test
	4. Charge per test = $77.38
	6. $70.71
11-13	1. Making saves $50,875
11-14	2. Decrease of $1,316,200
11-15	1. Purchasing saves $10,500
	4. Making has a $29,000 advantage
11-16	2. $1,233,000 increase
11-17	1. $3 million in favor of buying (without nonrecurring costs)
11-18	1. Drop and make saves $3,000 over lease and make and $2,000 over the buy alternative.
12-1	3. $(15,000)
	4. 6%
12-2	3. $68,500
	4. 14%−16%
12-3	1. Vision, $7,460 (NPV)
12-4	2. NPV = $4,638
12-5	1. CF = $41,180.50
	2. I = $24,020
	3. 14 years
	4. Cost = $60,350
12-6	3. NPV = $1,492,000
12-7	1. System I, NPV = $23,995; IRR = 16.5%
12-9	1. NPV = $5,457
	2. NPV = $5,792
12-10	2. NPV = $858
12-11	3. (a) $50,000, (d) $8,000
12-12	2. NPV, advanced = $399,600
	4. NPV = $190,900 (conventional)
12-13	1. NPV, A = $37,645
12-14	2. $8,850
	3. $10,064
12-15	NPV, new = $(631,624)
12-16	2. NPV, CAD = $(1,387,259)
12-17	2. NPV, new = $20,133,000
	3. NPV = $13,680,000
12-18	2. NPV = $(3,039,662)
12-20	2. NPV, Robotics = $708,254
13-1	3. $3,750
13-2	3. $750

13-3	2. Carrying cost = $375
13-4	2. ROP = 250 units
13-5	2. Total cost = $28,000
	4. Total cost = $60,000
13-7	1. Time needed = 14 days
	3. EOQ = 1,502; lead time = 7.5 hours
13-11	1. Basic unit, 100,000 with CM = $500,000
	2. Total CM = $410,000
13-12	2. Total CM = $900
13-13	3. Optimal CM = $81,840
13-14	1. 400,000 units of bran flakes
	2. X = 50,000 Y = 300,000
13-15	3. Optimal CM = $113,250
13-17	3. CM increases by $7,200 per day
13-18	4. Net improvement = $11,200
13-19	1. Daily contribution = $5,800
	4. Daily contribution increases by $990
14-1	1. Price elasticity = 1.56
14-4	2. $1,210,000
14-6	1. Option 1 loss = $25,000
14-7	1. Price Volume Variance = $525,000 U
14-8	2. 3-year loss @ $25 price = $150,000
14-11	2. Bid price = $29.90
14-12	1. $2,300 U
14-13	1. C's Price Volume Variance = $600,000 F
14-15	Chain store cost per case = $1.70
15-2	1. Unit cost = $8
15-3	2. a. Operating income = $43,000
15-4	1. Year 2 COGS = $390,000
	2. Year 1 COGS = $180,000
15-5	1. Operating income = $146,720
15-6	1. Contribution margin variance = $27,000 F
	3. Sales mix variance = $7,500 F
15-7	2. Market size variance = $11,000 U
15-8	1. Total income = $72,250
15-9	2. Year 3 income = $26,200
15-11	1. Net loss = $350,000
15-12	1. Midwest division profit = $50,000
15-14	1. Operating loss = $75,000
	3. Operating income = $350,000
15-15	1. First year profit = $675
	2. Third year profit = $1,425
15-16	2. Operating income = $265,280
15-17	2. Quarter 6 profit = $472,000
15-20	1. a. Wall clock unit cost = $3.60
	2. Net loss (absorption costing) = $177,500
	3. Net loss = $135,500
15-21	2. Sales Mix Variance = $362,520 F
16-1	1. Quarter 4 total sales = $2,165,000
16-2	March production = 108,000
16-3	1. December purchases = 1,545,000 ounces
	2. Total direct labor cost = $153,000
16-4	W-6 total sales = $156,000

16-5	1. April unit purchases = 265
16-6	May cash receipts = $22,685
16-7	Activity level = 1,100 direct labor hours
16-8	1. Total cash available = $55,250
16-9	1. Total overhead cost = $179,000
	2. 20% lower total overhead = $153,700
16-10	3. $283,500
16-12	Total overhead cost = $43,500
16-13	September cash receipts = $82,233
16-14	1. August cash payments = $29,800
	2. July cash payments = $35,933
16-15	1. March sales = $2,700,000
	3. March purchases of No. 326 = $180,000
	6. January total = $91,000
	8. Budgeted COGS = $5,805,620
	10. March ending cash balance = $354,621
16-16	1. July purchases = $71,250
	2. August ending cash balance = $17,420
16-18	Total cash available = $541,927
16-19	Net sales for year = $32,736,000
	COGS for year = $22,049,000
16-20	2. May total budgeted costs = $96,565
16-21	G. Unit cost of finished goods = $333.33
	H. COGS = $96,666,700
	I. Quarter 3 ending cash balance = $4,868,000
16-23	1. May total disbursements = $1,806,000
16-26	1. Operating income = $122,400
	2. Operating income variance = $45,400 U
17-1	2. Total standard prime cost = $27.95
17-3	1. MUV = $80 U
	2. LRV = $0
17-4	1. Volume variance = $15,000 F
	2. VOH Spending = $20,000 F
17-5	1. Budget variance = $25,000 U
	2. Spending variance = $5,000 U
17-6	1. Mix variance = $20,000 U
	2. MUV = $36,000 U
17-7	1. Yield variance = $12,500 U
	2. LEV = $7,500 U
17-9	3. MUV = $3,000 U
17-10	3. Volume variance = $10,720 U
	4. VOH efficiency = $22,015
17-11	1. MPV = $37,200 F
	2. LRV = $5,600 F
	4. VOH efficiency = $10,500 U
17-12	1. AH = 60,000
	3. 12,500 units
17-13	1. MUV = $60,000 U
	2. LEV = $15,750 U
	3. Volume variance = $10,500 F
17-14	2. MUV (small) = $200 F
	3. LEV (reg) = $5,600 U
17-15	Mix variance = $388.50 F

17-16	2. VOH spending = \$1,000 U
	4. LEV = \$4,625 F
17-17	2. (a) MUV = \$15,000 U
	(e) VOH efficiency = \$4,800 U
17-18	1. 50,000 units
	3. Total planned labor variance = \$13,140 U
17-19	3. Cost per bag = \$0.7294
18-1	1. 1999 ROI = 16%
18-2	2. 1998 turnover = 2.5
18-3	1. Backpack ROI = 13.4%
18-4	2. c. Residual Income = \$607,000
18-5	1. EVA = \$161,000
18-6	2. Weighted average cost of capital = 9.18%
18-7	1. Minimum price = \$.58
18-8	2. Plastic = 3%
18-9	B's ROI = 12.5%; D's revenue = \$19,200
18-10	C's residual income = \$480
18-12	1. Unit contribution margin = \$5
	2. b. residual income = \$153,750
18-13	1. Value of option = \$220,000
18-14	2. ROI = 150%
18-15	Gain = \$22,000
18-16	1. Company contribution margin = \$600,000
18-17	3. minimum transfer price = \$64
18-18	3. Addition to Plastics' profit = \$35,000
18-20	1. b. Bonus pool = \$50,500
18-21	2. RLI residual income = \$120,000
18-22	2. Residual income = \$48,000
19-4	2. Exchange loss = \$1,800
19-6	At new exchange rate, \$40,625 needed
19-7	1. British division ROI = 11.5%
19-9	2. Transfer price = \$51.50
19-13	1. French order = 271,175 francs
19-14	Comparable controlled transfer price = \$12.75
19-15	1. Belgian transfer price = \$330
19-18	2. Allowable transfer price = \$7.20
20-6	1. \$24,000 U
	2. Nonvalue added = \$192,000
20-7	1. Nonvalue added (total) = \$302,250
20-8	1. Total change = \$113,250 F
20-10	1. Unused capacity variance (eng) = \$25,000 F
	2. SQ (materials) = 273,600 lbs
20-11	1. Target cost = \$250
	2. Unit nonvalue-added cost = \$86.25
20-13	2. Return on sales (S11) = 17.2%
20-14	2. Cost per unit = \$5
	3. \$15; MCE = 0.67
20-15	1. 0.30
20-17	3. Potential unit cost reduction = \$10.65
	5. Unit savings = \$13.78
20-18	2. Return on sales (BigJeep) = 5.6%